THE BLACK WORKER

VOL. 8

THE BLACK WORKER SINCE THE

AFL-CIO MERGER, 1955-1980

Other volumes in this series:

I   The Black Worker to 1869

II   The Era of the National Labor Union

III   The Era of the Knights of Labor

IV   The Era of the American Federation of Labor
and the Railroad Brotherhoods

V   The Black Worker from 1900 to 1919

VI   The Era of Post-War Prosperity and the
Great Depression, 1920-1936

VII   The Black Worker from the Founding of the
CIO to the AFL-CIO Merger, 1936-1955

The Black Worker
A Documentary History from Colonial
Times to the Present

Volume **VIII**

The Black Worker since the AFL-CIO Merger, 1955–1980

Edited by
Philip S. Foner, Ronald L. Lewis,
and Robert Cvornyek

Temple University Press, Philadelphia

Temple University Press, Philadelphia, 19122
© by Temple University. All rights reserved
Published 1984
Printed in the United States of America

Library of Congress Cataloging in Publication Data
(Revised for volume 8)
Main entry under title: 331,6396
                              B627
The Black worker.   v.8

    Vol. 8 also edited by Robert Cvornyek.
    Includes bibliographical references and indexes.
    Contents: v. 1. The Black worker to 1869.--v. 2. The
Black worker during the era of the National Labor Union.
--(etc.)--v. 8. The Black worker since the AFL-CIO
merger, 1955-1980.
    1. Afro-Americans--Employment. 2. Afro-Americans--
Economic conditions. 3. Trade-unions--United States--
Afro-American membership. 4. United States--Race
relations. I. Foner, Philip Sheldon, 1910-   .
II. Lewis, Ronald L., 1940-   . III. Cvornyek, Robert
HD8081.A44B56   331.6'3'96073   78-7825
ISBN 0-87722-136-7 (v. 1)
ISBN 0-87722-198-7 (v. 8)

TABLE OF CONTENTS

PART I

THE CHALLENGE OF EQUAL ECONOMIC OPPORTUNITY

Introduction   2

CONDITION OF THE BLACK WORKER   3

   1. Economic Status of Nonwhite Workers, 1955-62,
         by Matthew A. Kessler   3
   2. Statement of Whitney M. Young, Jr.   13
   3. 35% Black Jobless Rate Says Top Economist   16
   4. Displaced Farm Workers Lose Industrial Jobs in Rural South,
         by Roy Reed   17
   5. Black Workers: Progress Derailed, by Barbara Becnel   18
   6. Last Hired, and Usually the First Let Go, by Charlayne Hunter 25
   7. Black Manpower Priorities: Planning New Directions, by
         Walter W. Stafford and Lewis J. Carter, III   27
   8. Black Workers Expose Kaiser Racism, by Mike Giocondo   31
   9. Weber Case Hits Unions, Minorities   32
  10. High Court Decision Backs Affirmative Action on Jobs,
         by David L. Perlman   34
  11. A Kind of 'Tolerance', by Tom Wicker   36
  12. Court Oversteps Bounds, by George F. Will   37
  13. Voluntary Affirmative Action Meets Goals of Civil Rights Act 38
  14. The Weber Decision, by James Johnson   39
  15. Appeal of Black Conservatives Rings Hollow to Workers, Poor,
         by Norman Hill   40
  16. Administration Policies Fail to Address Needs of Blacks,
         by Norman Hill   42
  17. Progress of Black Americans Reversed Under GOP Policies,
         by Gus Tyler   43
  18. Where Reaganomics Hits Hardest: Minorities & Women   44

PART II

THE AFL-CIO AND THE CIVIL RIGHTS ISSUE

Introduction   48

THE AFL-CIO AND THE CIVIL RIGHTS STRUGGLE   49

   1. AFL-CIO Merger Agreement   49
   2. Correspondence to the Merger Convention   50
   3. Report of the Resolutions Committee on Civil Rights, 1955   51
   4. What Goes on Here?   56
   5. New Day Dawns for Negro Labor in AFL-CIO Merger Here,
         by Ethel L. Payne   57
   6. About Randolph and Townsend   58
   7. Solidarity Forever   59
   8. AFL-CIO Resolution on Civil Rights, 1957   59
   9. AFL-CIO Resolution on Civil Rights, 1961   63
  10. AFL-CIO Resolution on Civil Rights, 1963   78
  11. AFL-CIO Resolution on Civil Rights, 1965   100
  12. Statement by the AFL-CIO Executive Council on Civil
         Rights Act of 1966   102
  13. Black Power and Labor   102
  14. AFL-CIO Executive Council Report on Civil Rights, 1967   105
  15. AFL-CIO Resolution on Civil Rights, 1969   110

16. The Fight for Civil Rights Is Alive and Well 113
17. AFL-CIO Executive Council Report on Civil Rights, 1975 115
18. Real Exercise of Civil Rights Linked to Full Employment 118
19. Meany Hails Solidarity of Civil Rights Alliance 119
20. Labor's Civil Rights Goals Linked to Demand for Full Employment 120
21. A Coalition for People 120
22. Lack of Opportunity Thwarts Strides Toward Racial Justice 121

A. PHILIP RANDOLPH: "GENTLEMAN OF ELEGANT IMPATIENCE" 123

23. AFL-CIO Seats Two Negroes 123
24. Randolph Says Negro Not Free 124
25. AFL-CIO Report on Civil Rights, 1961 124
26. Council Rejects Randolph Charges, Backs AFL-CIO Rights Record 131
27. Along the N.A.A.C.P. Battlefront 133
28. "Take What's Yours--And Keep It!"--Randolph 134
29. AFL-CIO Resolution on Negro Civil Rights--Labor Alliance, 1965 135
30. A "Freedom Budget" For All Americans 139
31. Minutes, A. Philip Randolph Institute 151
32. $100 Billion Freedom Fund 153
33. Comments on a "Freedom Budget" For All Americans 157
34. Phil Randolph, The Best of Men, Touched and Changed All of Us 159
35. Randolph's Vision Recalled to Nation 160
36. A. Philip Randolph Memorial 161
37. House Votes Gold Medal Honoring Phil Randolph 161

THE NAACP AND THE AFL-CIO 162

38. The NAACP Hails the AFL-CIO Merger 162
39. Racism Within Organized Labor: A Report of Five Years of the AFL-CIO, 1955-1960 162
40. The NAACP vs. Labor 169
41. Reflections on the Negro and Labor, by Daniel Bell 171
42. AFL-CIO Saves NAACP 175
43. Benjamin Hooks, Executive Director, NAACP, to the AFL-CIO Convention, 1979 175
44. NAACP to Join Labor's Solidarity Day Protest 179
45. Roy Wilkins Provided Strength During Critical Civil Rights Era, by Bayard Rustin 180
46. Delegates Hit Reagan on Civil Rights Retreat 181

BLACK CIVIL RIGHTS LEADERS SPEAK BEFORE AFL-CIO CONVENTIONS 182

47. Thurgood Marshall 182
48. Martin Luther King, Jr. 184
49. Roy Wilkins 189
50. Mary Moultrie 193
51. Benjamin Hooks 195
52. Vernon Jordan, Jr. 201

PART III

RADICAL BLACK WORKERS

Introduction 206

THE BLACK WORKERS CONGRESS 207

	1.	The Black Liberation Struggle, the Black Workers	
		Congress and Proletarian Revolution	207
	2.	Excerpts from the Black Workers Congress Manifesto	227
	3.	Organize the Revolution, Disorganize the State!	228
	4.	Conditions Facing Black and Third World Workers	229
	5.	Black Workers Delegation in Vietnam	233

AUTO   234

	6.	Black Workers in Revolt	234
	7.	Wildcat! by Detroit NOC	246
	8.	Confront the Racist UAW Leadership	254
	9.	Black Workers Protest UAW Racism	256
	10.	League of Revolutionary Black Workers General Policy	
		Statement, Labor History, and the League's Labor	
		Program	259
	11.	DRUM Beats Will Be Heard	263
	12.	Black Worker Raps	265
	13.	National Workers Program	267
	14.	Black Workers--Dual Unions	268
	15.	Auto Mongers Plot Against Workers	269
	16.	Black Worker Shoots Foremen: Resolve Problem	
		with Management	270
	17.	MARUM Newsletter	273

THE PROGRESSIVE LABOR PARTY   275

| | 18. | Black Workers: Key Revolutionary Force | 275 |
| | 19. | Black Workers Must Lead | 281 |

MORE BLACK LABOR RADICALISM   284

	20.	Racism and the Workers' Movement	284
	21.	United Community Construction Workers, 1971	298
	22.	Black Workers Fight Imperialism: Polaroid Corporation	299
	23.	Boycott Polaroid	300
	24.	Polaroid Blacks Ask Worldwide Boycott	301

PART IV

THE NEGRO-LABOR ALLIANCE

Introduction   304

NEGRO LABOR ASSEMBLY   305

| | 1. | Minutes of the Negro Labor Assembly, October 14, 1959 | 305 |
| | 2. | Minutes, Negro Labor Assembly, September 30, 1965 | 308 |

NEGRO AMERICAN LABOR COUNCIL   311

	3.	Keynote Address to the Second Annual Convention of the	
		Negro American Labor Council, November 10, 1961	311
	4.	Unless Something Special Happens, by Whitney M. Young, Jr.	314
	5.	Randolph Fears Crisis on Rights, by Raymond H. Anderson	317
	6.	Negro Jobs for a Strong Labor Movement	317
	7.	Frustration in the Ghettos: A National Crisis	320
	8.	NALC Head Asks Labor Aid March of Poor	322
	9.	Something New in the House of Labor	324
	10.	NALC Delegates Warn Against Redbaiters	330
	11.	NALC Convention Urges Political Action	330

COALITION OF BLACK TRADE UNIONISTS   332

    12. Conference Proceedings, Coalition of Black
           Trade Unionists   332
    13. Black Unionists Form Coalition   364
    14. A Giant Step Toward Unity   366
    15. Newest Black Power: Black Leaders Building Massive
           Labor Coalition Inside Unions   368
    16. Black Caucus in the Unions   370

BAYARD RUSTIN   373

    17. Morals Concerning Minorities: Mental Health and
           Identity, by Bayard Rustin   373
    18. Address to the 1969 Convention of the AFL-CIO, Bayard Rustin 377
    19. The Blacks and the Unions, by Bayard Rustin   381
    20. Labor's Highest Award Honors Bayard Rustin, by
           James M. Shevis   386

UNITED STEELWORKERS OF AMERICA   387

    21. Steelworkers Fight Discrimination, by David J. McDonald   387
    22. USWA's Civil Rights Program Wins Praise   391
    23. Address by Vernon E. Jordan, Jr.   392
    24. History of the United Steelworkers of America: Steel
           Union Buttresses Racism, by Staughton Lynd   396
    25. National Ad Hoc Committee of Concerned Steelworkers
           Annual Meeting, 1972   398
    26. Black Steelworkers' Parley Spurs Representation Fight   400
    27. The Fight Against Racism in the USWA   401

MUNICIPAL WORKERS   403

    28. Union Battle Won in Memphis   403
    29. Memphis: King's Biggest Gamble   404
    30. Economic Boycott in Memphis to Continue   405
    31. The Struggle in Memphis   406
    32. In Memphis: More Than a Garbage Strike, by
           J. Edwin Stanfield   407

UNITED AUTO WORKERS   422

    33. Address of Walter P. Reuther Before the Annual
           Convention of the NAACP, June 26, 1957   422
    34. There's No Half-Way House on the Road to Freedom   429
    35. Watts: Where They Manufacture Hope   430
    36. A Black Caucus Formed in Auto Union   433
    37. Out of Struggle--Solidarity, by Cornelius Cobbs   434
    38. Bannon Urges More Opportunity for Minorities to
           Enter Trades   439
    39. Black Caucus Builds Black-White Solidarity at
           Chrysler Plant, by Johnny Woods   439
    40. Black-White Caucuses Win UAW Offices, by Ted Pearson   442
    41. Stepp Named First Black UAW Head At Big 3 Plant,
           by William Allan   444
    42. Labor, Blacks Meet, Map Political Push   444

BUILDING TRADES   445

    43. NAACP Battle Front   445
    44. NY Building Trades Unions Face Discrimination Hearings   446
    45. Building Trades Take Solid Stand Against Discrimination   447
    46. Building Unions Boiling Over Gov't. Hiring Ruling   449
    47. Opposition to Philadelphia Plan   451

48. Revised Philadelphia Plan   451
49. Black Claims Bias in Union Training Plan, by
       Martin J. Herman   452
50. LEAP   454
51. Coalition Demands Hiring of Minority Workers   456
52. The Bricks and Mortar of Racism, by Paul Good   458
53. Civil Rights and Church Leaders Warn of Attacks
       on Black People   467

PART V

1199 AND THE BLACK WORKER

Introduction   470

OVERVIEW   471

1. Twenty Years in the Hospitals: A Short
      History of 1199   471
2. Local 1199 Makes Realistic Gains for its
      Newly-Organized Members, by Moe Foner   482
3. Local 1199 Sparks National Union for Hospital,
      Nursing Home Workers   486

HOSPITAL WORKERS ORGANIZE   488

4. Hospital Strike is Settled; $40 Minimum, Other
      Gains Won   488
5. One Big Union Established for All Hospital Workers:
      Local 1199 Hospital Division, AFL-CIO   489
6. More Hospitals Organizing into Local 1199   490
7. Strike Settlement Sets Stage for Organizing Drive
      to Build Strong 1199 in Hospitals   490
8. The Challenge of Bronxville: 1199 Takes It Up With
      All-Out Drive to Win Lawrence Hospital Strike   492
9. The Bronxville Strike   493
10. Truce in Bronxville   494
11. Ballad of the Bronxville Hospital Strike   494
12. For Sam Smith, Hospital Orderly: A Battle Whose
      Time Has Come, by John M. McClintock   496
13. The Plight of Hospital Workers   498
14. Hospital Woes   498
15. Pittsburgh: Hospital Workers Fight for Union Rights   499
16. Battle in Pittsburgh, by Dan North   501

THE STRUGGLE IN CHARLESTON   502

17. Hugh A. Brimm, Office of Civil Rights, To Dr. William
      M. McCord, President of Medical College of South
      Carolina, September 19, 1968   502
18. Carolina Strike Unites Rights, Labor Groups,
      by Murray Seeger   508
19. Mrs. King's Crusade   511
20. National Organizing Committee Hospital and
      Nursing Home Employees   512
21. A Gathering Storm in Charleston, S.C.   512
22. Text of Speech by Mrs. Coretta Scott King at
      Dinner Honoring A. Philip Randolph   513
23. The Charleston Coalition   515
24. Charleston's Rights Battleground, by Ronald Sarro   516

25. Text of Address by Mrs. Coretta Scott King to Rally
     at Charleston's Stoney Field Stadium   520
26. Charleston: Our Strike for Union and Human Rights   523
27. 113-Day Hospital Strike in Charleston   526
28. Letters from Charleston Strikers   528

BREAD AND ROSES   537

29. Is This Any Way to Run a Union?   537
30. Bread and Roses, by Moe Foner   540
31. Bread and Roses Union Brings Cultural Events
     to Members, by Kay Bartlett   544
32. Images of Labor (Gallery 1199), by Cynthia Nadelman   546
33. Strong 'Images of Labor', by Benjamin Forgey   547
34. "Take Care, Take Care"   549
35. United We Laugh, by Barbara Garson   549
36. Union Musical to Premiere at Boro Hospital   551
37. Hospital Revue Hits 'Home' for Employees   551
38. A Revue That's Good Medicine, by Lucinda Fleeson   553

                    NOTES AND INDEX   555

NOTES   557

INDEX   575

PREFACE

This is the eighth volume of THE BLACK WORKER: A DOCUMENTARY HISTORY
FROM COLONIAL TIMES TO THE PRESENT, the first compilation of original
materials to encompass the entire history of Black American labor. As with
the preceding volumes, documents are placed in historical context by
introductions and notes. Original spellings have been retained except where
they obscure the intended meaning.

Volume VIII begins with an overview of the economic status of the black
worker during the era since the AFL-CIO merger. Extensive documentation is
presented on the battle waged within the house of labor to purge it of racial
discrimination, and the corresponding relations which existed between the
labor movement and Negro civil rights groups. The difficulty inherent in this
purging process led some young black nationalists to espouse radical,
separatist solutions to the race problem confronting black workers.
Nevertheless, most Afro-Americans sought to strengthen the traditional
alliance of blacks and the more progressive forces in the labor movement, and
formed black caucuses in order to reform, rather than destroy, the established
unions. The period from the merger to the present, therefore, is
characterized by an increasing realization by organized labor that the civil
rights of blacks, and social justice for all workers, make them natural
allies. Current indications suggest that this realization will deepen with
the rise of neo-conservatism in the 1980s.

The editors wish to express their appreciation to those who have
assisted in the compilation of these documents. In particular, we thank the
staffs of the following institutions: Lincoln University Library (Pa.);
University of Delaware Library; U.S. Department of Labor Library; Columbia
University Library; Schomburg Collection of the New York Public Library; A.
Philip Randolph Institute, New York; The Tamiment Institute, New York; and
Local 1199 Archives, New York. We are also grateful to the National
Association for the Advancement of Colored People for permission to use items
from THE CRISIS, and to the AFL-CIO for materials from convention PROCEEDINGS
and the AFL-CIO NEWS. We also thank Vernon E. Jordan, Jr. for permission to
reprint a speech he delivered before a convention of the United Steelworkers
of America convention, and Moe Foner of Local 1199 for his assistance in
acquiring the materials for Part V.

It is fortunate that Volume VIII is the last in the series for we have
drained the well of apt phrases for thanking those who have assisted us in the
preparation of these volumes. This book was typed by Gail Brittingham who has
devoted so much beyond what one might gracefully expect from an assistant that
we are humbled in offering our appreciation. The same must be said for Susan
E. Lewis, who copy edited all of the volumes in this series, including this
one. Only through their good natured assistance could this non-funded project
ever have been completed. Finally, we gratefully acknowledge the material
assistance of the Black American Studies Program, and the College of Arts and
Science at the University of Delaware.

Philip S. Foner
Philadelphia, PA

Ronald L. Lewis
Newark, DE

Robert Cvornyek
North Arlington, NJ

PART I
THE CHALLENGE OF EQUAL ECONOMIC OPPORTUNITY

THE CHALLENGE OF EQUAL ECONOMIC OPPORTUNITY

American historians have characterized the decade following the landmark
Brown v. Board of Education Supreme Court decision in 1954 as one of such
dramatic improvement for blacks as to constitute a "Second Reconstruction."
Paradoxically, alongside this remarkable social and political progress came a
relative, and in some ways an absolute, decline in the economic status of Afro-
Americans. In 1960, 50 to 84 per cent of all black wage-earners fell into
menial and unskilled job categories; 23 per cent of Negro families in Los
Angeles lived below the government's "poverty line" of $3,000 annual income, 24
in Newark, 27 in Chicago and New York, 30 in Philadelphia, 32 in Baltimore, and
36 in Pittsburgh. Unemployment figures were also revealing. In Detroit, where
blacks were comparatively well off, 16.8 per cent of the black labor force were
out of work in 1940 and 17.4 per cent in 1960. Unemployment figures were also
revealing. In Detroit, where blacks were comparatively well off, 16.8 per cent
of the black labor force were out of work in 1940 and 17.4 per cent in 1960.
The rate rose in the inner cities after 1960 as the flight of blacks from the
South to the northern ghettoes intensified. These migrants arrived at a time
when the spread of automation was robbing blacks already resident in the
northern ghettoes of their traditional unskilled places in industry.

Blacks did make important gains in the labor movement. The days were gone
when entire industries were "lily-white" and when unions excluded blacks from
membership. By 1970 there were more than 2.5 million black unionists in the
U.S., and at 15 per cent their membership in unions was higher than their
percentage of the total population. Nevertheless, in 1970 the black unemployment rate was still a little over twice that of whites, median annual income
for black families was only 61 per cent that for their white counterparts, and
blacks remained grossly over represented in lower paying, lower skilled jobs.
Part of the explanation lay in the technological revolution as unskilled jobs
increasingly were eliminated by automation. Also, there was the continuing
drift of jobs to the suburbs as new plants and new jobs were established outside
of the cities where blacks did not live. Moreover, serious economic recessions
gripped the nation during the seventies, and black unemployment reached a
depression level by the end of the decade, making a mockery of affirmative action
programs mandated by federal law. A major reason for this was the seniority
rule, the determinant for order in lay-offs and prospects for advancement on the
job. While seniority is crucial to the economic interests of the factory worker,
it does discriminate against blacks who most frequently are the last hired.

The primary issue underlying the contemporary battle against on-the-job
discrimination is how to reconcile equal employment opportunity with seniority
rights and, in numerous legal suits during the 1970s and early 1980s, black
workers have challenged the rule. The general thrust of the court decisions in
these cases has been to establish the principle that seniority plans must
intentionally discriminate against the workers it covers in order to be illegal.
One of the most important of these cases was that of Brian Weber, a white
employee of Kaiser Aluminum, and a member of the United Steelworkers of America.
A lab technician, Weber had applied for a craft training position, but was
rejected because over thirty whites had more seniority. He had more seniority
than two of the five blacks selected from a separate minority list, however, and
Weber sued charging "reverse discrimination." The lower courts ruled in his
favor, but in June 1979 the U.S. Supreme Court ruled that Congress had "left
employers and unions in the private sector free to take . . . . race conscious
steps to eliminate manifest racial imbalance in traditionally white job
categories." The decision left many questions unanswered, however, and the
issue remains in flux.

THE CHALLENGE OF EQUAL ECONOMIC OPPORTUNITY

CONDITION OF THE BLACK WORKER

1. ECONOMIC STATUS OF NONWHITE WORKERS,
1955-62

By Matthew A. Kessler

The gradual movement of nonwhite workers (over 90 percent of whom are Negroes) into higher skilled and better paying jobs has continued since the mid-1950's. However, despite these recent gains, large gaps continue to exist between white and nonwhite workers, as measured by most indicators of social and economic well-being.

Nonwhites continue to be concentrated in less-skilled jobs and are subject to more unemployment than whites. The jobless rates of nonwhites are still at least one and one-half times higher than for whites in every age-sex grouping, and for some age groupings are three times as high. Unemployment bears disproportionately on the nonwhite worker whatever his industry or occupation. Not only is he subject to more frequent spells of unemployment; once out of a job, he has tended to remain jobless for a longer period of time.

After achieving relatively substantial gains in money income during the early postwar period, nonwhite families have failed to keep pace with the rise in average income of white families since the mid-1950's, despite the continued shift of nonwhite workers into higher paying jobs.

During the past two decades, nonwhites have narrowed the educational gap that had historically existed between themselves and white persons, a development which has helped to foster their steady ladder. Since the mid-1950's, however, differences in the level of educational attainment between whites and nonwhites have remained essentially unchanged.

Industry and Occupation Changes

Throughout the postwar period, there has been a dramatic shift of nonwhites out of agriculture. In 1962, 12 out of every 100 employed nonwhite workers were employed in agriculture, compared with 16 out of 100 in 1955 and 21 out of 100 in 1948 (See Table 1). The precipitous fall in this proportion throughout the postwar period is a result of the exodus of nonwhites from sharecropping and marginal farms, particularly in the South, as well as the growth of alternative employment opportunities in other sectors of the economy.

In this quest for a higher money income, however, many nonwhites who shifted to nonfarm employment paid the price of greater job insecurity. As they often lack education and vocational training and are limited by discriminatory hiring and layoff practices, their employment opportunities are restricted to relatively unskilled and semi-skilled occupations. These are the very lines of work that are particularly sensitive to the business cycle and are vulnerable to large-scale reductions through automation. Although professional and clerical occupations have provided a major source of both white and nonwhite employment growth since the mid-1950's, nonwhites continue to be overrepresented in such occupations as domestic servants, laborers, and semiskilled operatives.

White-Collar Occupations. Between 1955 and 1962, an increasing number and proportion of nonwhite workers entered the higher skilled and better paying white-collar occupations. In 1962, however, only 17 percent of all employed nonwhites were in white-collar occupations, compared with 47 percent

TABLE 1

EMPLOYED PERSONS, BY INDUSTRY AND COLOR,
1948, 1955, AND 1962

(Percent Distribution)

INDUSTRY	WHITE			NONWHITE		
	1962	1955	1948	1962	1955	1948
Total employed:						
Number (thousands)......	60,749	56,698	53,434	7,098	6,496	5,944
Percent................	100.0	100.0	100.0	100.0	100.0	100.0
Goods-producing indus-						
tries...................	41.4	46.2	48.6	36.2	41.5	47.5
Agriculture............	7.2	10.1	12.6	11.7	15.7	21.1
Mining, forestry, and						
fisheries.............	1.1	1.4	1.5	.4	.7	3.0
Construction...........	6.4	6.5	6.0	5.7	5.3	4.4
Manufacturing..........	26.8	28.2	28.5	18.4	19.7	18.9
Service-producing indus-						
tries...................	58.6	53.8	51.4	63.8	58.5	52.5
Transportation and						
public utilities.......	7.0	7.4	8.3	5.4	6.0	6.4
Trade..................	19.8	20.2	20.1	13.8	13.5	11.5
Service and finance.....	26.8	21.5	18.5	39.1	34.7	31.4
Private households......	2.6	2.2	1.7	15.8	16.3	16.1
Educational services....	5.5	4.0	2.8	4.4	3.0	2.1
Professional services,						
except education.......	6.9	5.3	3.9	7.4	4.9	3.3
Business and repair						
services..............	2.8	2.5	2.4	2.2	1.4	1.0
Other services, includ-						
ing entertainment......	4.3	3.5	4.2	7.2	7.2	7.4
Finance, insurance,						
and real estate........	4.7	4.0	3.5	2.1	1.9	1.5
Public administration...	5.1	4.6	4.6	5.4	4.2	3.3

of white workers (Table 2). White workers in this group outnumbered nonwhites
28 to 1, in marked contrast to their comparative representation in the
civilian labor force (9 white for each nonwhite worker). The number of nonwhites in white-collar jobs has risen by 50 percent since 1955, about the
same rate of increase as noted during the early postwar period and two and
one-half times the increase for whites. However, unless there is a substantial acceleration of these trends, the percentage of nonwhite workers in
white-collar employment will still be substantially below that of white
workers for many years.

Nonwhite workers have been entering the professional, technical, and
clerical fields faster than other white-collar occupations. These occupations
have risen by 60 percent since the mid-1950's, reflecting expanded job
opportunities, particularly in public administration. The largest concentration of nonwhite workers in the white-collar group (almost 1 out of 2) is
employed in such clerical occupations as office machine operators, bookkeepers, typists, secretaries, stenographers, and filing and recording clerks.

The largest relative gains posted by nonwhites during 1955-62 were in
professional services (such as hospital, medical, and other health services,
welfare and religious institutions) and business and repair services--all of
which grew nearly 70 percent in the 7-year span. This approximated advances
noted in the earlier postwar period and compared with about a 35-percent
increase for whites since 1955. Nonwhites also recorded relatively sharp
gains in the growing field of educational services--up by 60 percent compared

with a 50-percent rise among whites. Governmental policies assuring non-
discriminatory employment practices may account for the continued gains
registered by nonwhites in the public administration since the mid-1950's--
up 40 percent compared with an 18-percent rise among whites.

Nonwhite employment in the professional and technical fields has
increased at a somewhat faster rate than for whites since the mid-1950's.
Yet in 1962, only about 5 percent of all employed nonwhites were engaged in
these occupations compared with 12½ percent of all white workers. While
teaching provides a major source of professional employment for both whites
and nonwhites, a higher proportion of nonwhite than white professional
workers (mainly women) were employed as elementary and secondary school
teachers in 1962--nearly two-fifths and one-fifth, respectively. Indicating
of nonwhites' recent progress in the professional field is the fivefold
increase in their employment in the growing engineering occupations during
the 1950's compared with a two-thirds rise for the occupational group as a
whole. Nevertheless, nonwhites accounted for only 1½ percent of all professional engineers by 1960.

TABLE 2

EMPLOYED PERSONS BY OCCUPATION GROUP AND COLORS,
1948, 1955, AND 1962

(Percent Distribution)

MAJOR OCCUPATION GROUP	WHITE			NONWHITE		
	1962	1955	1948	1962	1955	1948
Total employed:						
Number (thousands).....	60,749	56,698	53,434	7,098	6,496	5,944
Percent................	100.0	100.0	100.0	100.0	100.0	100.0
White-collar workers.....	47.3	42.1	39.1	16.7	12.0	9.0
Professional and tech-						
nical workers.........	12.6	9.8	7.2	5.3	3.5	2.4
Managers, officials,						
and proprietors,						
except farm..........	11.9	11.1	11.6	2.6	2.3	2.3
Clerical workers.......	15.8	14.2	13.6	7.2	4.9	3.3
Sales workers.........	7.0	6.9	6.7	1.6	1.3	1.1
Blue-collar workers......	35.4	39.0	40.5	39.5	41.8	39.7
Craftsmen and foremen..	13.6	14.1	14.6	6.0	5.2	5.3
Operatives.............	17.5	20.2	21.0	19.9	20.9	20.1
Laborers, except farm						
and mine.............	4.3	4.7	4.9	13.6	15.8	14.3
Service workers.........	10.6	9.0	7.9	32.8	31.6	30.3
Private household						
workers..............	2.1	1.8	1.5	14.7	14.8	15.6
Other service workers..	8.5	7.2	6.4	18.1	16.8	14.7
Farm workers............	6.8	9.9	12.4	11.0	14.5	21.0
Farmers and managers...	4.0	6.0	7.8	2.7	5.0	8.5
Laborers and foremen...	2.8	3.9	4.6	8.3	9.5	12.5

Only 4 of every 100 nonwhites were employed as managers, officials, and
proprietors and as sales workers in 1962, a somewhat higher proportion than
in 1955 and 1948. The proportion of white workers in these occupations in
1962 was much higher (19 percent).

Blue-Collar Occupations. After registering small gains in the early
postwar period, the proportion of nonwhites employed in blue-collar occupations fell slightly between 1955 and 1962, returning to levels prevailing in

1948. Blue-collar jobs have accounted for two-fifths of total nonwhite
employment throughout most of the postwar period. During the more recent
7-year period, the proportion of white workers in these occupational
categories also declined moderately.

More than 8 out of every 10 nonwhite workers in blue-collar jobs
(compared with 6 out of 10 white workers) continued to be in either the
semiskilled or unskilled occupations. These jobs tend to be concentrated in
those goods-producing and related industries (such as transportation) which
are quite sensitive to the business cycle. Moreover, the demand for this
type of labor has diminished steadily during the postwar period as a result
of automation and other technological developments.

Service Occupations. Nonwhites are still seven times as likely as white
workers to be employed as private household workers (including maids, baby-
sitters, housekeepers, chauffeurs, laundresses). During the earlier postwar
period, the number of nonwhite private household workers remained virtually
unchanged, while nonwhite employment in other service occupations, such as
hospital attendant, barber, and cook, rose significantly (25 percent).
During the 1955-62 period, this trend appears to have continued, with little
change in nonwhite private household employment and a substantial gain (18
percent) in the number of nonwhites entering other service jobs. Among white
workers also there was a steady rise in the proportion of service workers
outside of private households throughout the postwar period--up between 20
and 25 percent in each of the two periods. In 1962, as in the earlier postwar period, proportionately twice as many nonwhite as white workers were in
these rapidly expanding but still relatively low-paying and low-to-moderately
skilled service occupations.

TABLE 3

UNEMPLOYMENT RATES, BY COLOR, 1947-62

YEAR	WHITE	NON-WHITE	NON-WHITE AS PERCENT OF WHITE	YEAR	WHITE	NON-WHITE	NON-WHITE AS PERCENT OF WHITE
1962	4.9	11.0	224	1954	4.5	8.9	198
1961	6.0	12.5	208	1953	2.3	4.1	178
1960	5.0	10.2	204	1952	2.4	4.6	192
1959	4.9	10.7	218	1951	2.8	4.8	171
1958	6.1	12.6	207	1950	4.6	8.5	185
1957	3.9	8.0	205	1949	5.2	8.2	158
1956	3.3	7.5	227	1948	3.2	5.2	163
1955	3.6	7.9	219	1947	3.3	5.4	164

Manpower Utilization

Unemployment. Throughout the postwar period, unemployment has consistently fallen most heavily on the nonwhite worker. Comprising only a tenth
of a civilian labor force in 1962, nonwhites accounted for two-tenths of the
jobless total. This disparity was evident among both men and women.

The unemployment rate for nonwhites, at 11.0 percent in 1962, stood at
its third highest level in the postwar period (Table 3) and was only slightly
lower than rates recorded in the recession affected years of 1958 and 1961.
Their 1962 unemployment rate was double the jobless rate of white workers.
This relationship has persisted throughout the postwar period, and in fact
tended to increase in the latter part of the postwar period. In the years
1947-49, the nonwhite unemployment rate averaged about 60 percent higher than
for white workers, whereas in each year from 1954 through 1962, it was consistently twice as high.

Nonwhite boys and girls 14 to 19 years of age continued to have one of
the highest jobless rates of any age-color group (See Table 4). In 1962, the
unemployment rate of nonwhite teenagers remained near 25 percent, compared

with about 12 percent for white youth of the same ages. Since 1955, the jobless rate of nonwhite teenagers has increased faster than for white youngsters--up about 60 percent among nonwhites compared with a 30-percent rise for white youth.

TABLE 4

UNEMPLOYMENT RATES, BY COLOR, AGE, AND SEX,
1948, 1955, AND 1962

AGE AND SEX	WHITE			NONWHITE		
	1962	1955	1948	1962	1955	1948
Males, 14 years and over.................	4.6	3.4	3.1	11.0	8.2	5.1
14 to 19 years...........	12.3	9.6	8.3	20.7	13.2	7.6
20 to 24 years...........	8.0	6.3	5.8	14.6	11.2	10.6
25 to 34 years...........	3.8	2.5	2.4	10.5	8.0	4.2
35 to 44 years...........	3.1	2.4	1.9	8.6	7.4	4.5
45 to 54 years...........	3.5	2.8	2.2	8.3	5.8	3.1
55 years and over........	4.1	3.7	2.8	10.1	7.8	3.5
Females, 14 years and over.................	5.5	3.9	3.4	11.1	7.5	5.2
14 to 19 years...........	11.5	8.2	6.9	28.2	16.2	10.4
20 to 24 years...........	7.7	4.5	3.6	18.2	11.4	8.9
25 to 34 years...........	5.4	3.8	3.2	11.5	9.1	6.1
35 to 44 years...........	4.5	3.4	2.3	8.9	4.9	3.3
45 to 54 years...........	3.7	2.9	2.5	7.1	4.6	2.4
55 years and over........	3.5	2.8	2.6	3.6	4.4	2.2

In 1962, nonwhite men in both the 25-34 and 35-44 age brackets (primarily family breadwinners) recorded unemployment rates about three times as high as for white men (about 9 and 3 percent, respectively). A differential of similar proportions was recorded in 1955.

Even within the same major occupation group large differences in unemployment rates persisted, with rates for nonwhites generally substantially exceeding those of white persons. Among both white and nonwhite workers at the lower end of the occupational hierarchy, both nonfarm laborers and operatives usually have relatively high unemployment rates; however, differences are not (and have not been) as great as in most other occupation groups (Table 5). This may reflect a high proportion of such workers in highly unionized mass-production industries, some of which provide for non-discrimination clauses in their collective bargaining agreements.

Differences in overall unemployment rates by color are partially explained by the higher concentration of nonwhites at the lower rungs of the occupational skill ladder. Even assuming there were no differences in the occupational distribution of both groups, however, nonwhites still would have had a greater unemployment rate than whites in 1962. But assuming that the experienced nonwhite civilian labor force had the same occupational distribution as the experienced white civilian labor force, and applying actual jobless rates of nonwhites to this adjusted occupational distribution, the difference in the overall jobless rate between whites and nonwhites in 1962 would have been cut in half. Under these assumptions, the unemployment rate for nonwhites would have been 8.1 rather than 11.0 percent of their number in the labor force, compared with an actual rate of 4.9 percent for whites.

Nonwhite workers not only have higher rates; they are also subject to more frequent spells of unemployment. For persons experiencing any unemployment throughout the year, the chances are much greater that nonwhites rather

TABLE 5

UNEMPLOYMENT RATES OF EXPERIENCED WORKERS, BY COLOR AND
MAJOR OCCUPATION GROUP, 1955 AND 1962

MAJOR OCCUPATION GROUP	WHITE		NONWHITE		NONWHITE AS PERCENT OF WHITE	
	1962	1955	1962	1955	1962	1955
All occupation groups..	4.9	3.5	11.0	7.7	224	208
Clerical and sales workers	3.8	3.2	7.7	7.0	203	219
Craftsmen and foremen.....	4.8	3.9	9.7	8.8	202	226
Operatives...............	6.9	5.5	12.0	8.4	174	153
Private household workers.	3.1	3.0	7.1	5.6	229	187
Other service workers.....	5.3	5.2	10.8	8.8	204	169
Farm laborers and foremen.	3.9	3.0	5.8	6.3	149	210
Laborers, except farm and mine....................	11.0	9.8	15.8	12.1	144	123

than whites in 1962. But assuming that the experienced nonwhite civilian
labor force had the same occupational distribution as the experienced white
civilian labor force, and applying actual jobless rates of nonwhites to this
adjusted occupational distribution, the difference in the overall jobless
rate between whites and nonwhites in 1962 would have been cut in half. Under
these assumptions, the unemployment rate for nonwhites would have been 8.1
rather than 11.0 percent of their number in the labor force, compared with
an actual rate of 4.9 percent for whites.

Nonwhite workers not only have higher rates; they are also subject to
more frequent spells of unemployment. For persons experiencing any unemployment throughout the year, the chances are much greater that nonwhites rather
than whites will have repeated spells of unemployment during the year. About
3 of every 10 nonwhite men who had been unemployed sometime during the year
were subject to 3 spells or more of unemployment in 1961, compared with 2 of
every 10 white men who had some unemployment. Moreover, nonwhite workers
spend considerably longer periods of time on layoff or looking for work
between jobs. Since 1954 (earliest year for which these data are available),
nonwhites have consistently accounted for 20 to 30 percent of both long-term
unemployment of 15 weeks or more and very long-term unemployment of 27 weeks
or more, as the following tabulation shows:

Year	Nonwhites as a percent of total unemployed for--	
	15 weeks or more	27 weeks or more
1962	25.9	28.4
1961	22.5	23.6
1960	24.9	26.0
1959	24.3	26.2
1958	22.0	23.0
1957	22.4	23.8
1956	21.8	21.6
1955	20.0	21.5
1954	20.4	24.0

TABLE 6

EMPLOYED PERSONS IN NONAGRICULTURAL INDUSTRIES, BY FULL- OR PART-TIME
STATUS AND COLOR, 1956 AND 1962

(Percent distribution)

FULL- OR PART-TIME STATUS	WHITE		NONWHITE	
	1962	1956	1962	1956
All employed persons:				
Number (thousands)......................	56,388	52,661	6,267	5,733
Percent................................	100.0	100.0	100.0	100.0
At work--				
On full-time schedules..................	85.7	88.4	78.6	79.5
On part time for economic reasons.......	3.2	3.0	10.3	9.0
Usually work full time................	1.6	1.8	2.8	3.3
Usually work part time................	1.6	1.2	7.5	5.7
On part time for other reasons;				
usually work part time................	11.1	8.6	11.0	11.5

Since the peak of the 1957 cycle (on a seasonally adjusted basis), non-whites have consistently had a higher proportion of their total unemployment concentrated in the group of work 15 weeks or more than have the white unemployed.

In the 1957-59 cycle, after seasonal adjustment, unemployment among both whites and nonwhites rose about 70 percent between the third quarter of 1957 (prerecession peak) and the second quarter of 1958 (recession trough). During the downturn phase of the most recent cycle (1960-62), the number of jobless white and nonwhite workers both increased by similar proportions from prerecession peak to the recession trough--up 30 and 25 percent, respectively. In the upturn of the 1957-59 cycle (four quarters after the trough had been reached), differences in the rate of decline in unemployment among whites and nonwhites were not significant. There was, however, a relatively sharper drop in the rates for whites in the 1961-62 recovery period. During this later period, whites recorded a 25-percent decline in joblessness, compared with only a 10-percent dip among nonwhites. By the subsequent quarter, however, the improvement from the trough was about the same for both groups.

Part-Time Employment. In every year since 1956, a higher proportion of nonwhite than white persons were working at part-time jobs. In 1962, 21 percent of all employed nonwhites, compared with 14 percent of all white workers, were working less than 35 hours a week; however, the rate of "economic part time" continued to be three times as high for nonwhites as for white workers--10 percent of total nonwhite employment (Table 6). In 1962, as in previous years, nonwhites accounted for about one-fourth of all nonfarm workers on part time for economic reasons while constituting only 10 percent of nonagricultural employment.

Nonwhite workers in 1962 accounted for 16 percent of those on reduced workweeks because of economic reasons (such as slack work and material shortages), while comprising 35 percent of those in part time because they were unable to find full-time jobs. This latter category is likely to have a high proportion of young workers and adult women, many of whom are employed in private household and other service occupations.

The proportion of nonwhite workers on part time for economic reasons has risen significantly over the past 6 years, while that of white workers has remained about the same. On the other hand, the entire rise in voluntary part-time employment was among white workers.

The difference in the proportion of white and nonwhite workers who work at year-round full-time jobs is appreciable. Only one-half of nonwhite men compared with two-thirds of white men with work experience were reported to have worked steadily at full-time jobs in 1961. This difference has persisted since the late 1940's when such data first became available. During the postwar period, nonwhite women made sizable gains in full-time year-round jobholding, while the proportion of white women in this category remained relatively stable. This improvement among nonwhite women has resulted in part from their shift away from farm occupations--jobs where work schedules tend to be unstable. In 1961, there were proportionately almost as many nonwhite as white women in full-time year-round jobs (32 and 38 percent, respectively).

Labor Force Participation. A salient development in labor force activity of nonwhite workers in recent years has been the sharp decline in labor force participation rates of teenage boys and older men (Table 7). In 1962, rates for nonwhites in these groups were below those of white men in the same ages. The especially sharp decline for nonwhites continued a secular trend, including the long-term decline in agriculture, increased years of schooling, and liberalized retirement programs--developments which have also affected whites greatly in recent years.

TABLE 7

CIVILIAN LABOR FORCE PARTICIPATION RATES, BY AGE, COLOR, AND SEX,
1948, 1955, AND 1962

AGE AND SEX	WHITE			NONWHITE		
	1962	1955	1948	1962	1955	1948
Both sexes...............	56.1	57.1	56.7	60.0	61.9	63.5
Male..................	78.6	82.8	84.2	76.4	81.8	84.8
14 to 19 years...........	40.8	45.6	50.7	38.4	48.8	58.4
20 to 24 years...........	86.5	86.5	84.4	89.3	89.7	85.6
25 to 34 years...........	97.4	97.8	96.0	95.3	95.8	95.3
35 to 44 years...........	97.9	98.3	98.0	94.5	96.2	97.2
45 to 54 years...........	96.0	96.7	95.9	92.2	94.2	94.6
55 to 64 years...........	86.7	88.4	89.6	81.5	83.1	88.4
65 years and over........	30.6	39.5	46.4	27.2	40.0	50.3
Female...............	35.6	33.7	30.6	45.6	44.4	44.4
14 to 19 years...........	29.7	30.5	32.8	24.0	25.3	30.4
20 to 24 years...........	47.1	45.8	45.1	48.6	46.7	47.1
25 to 34 years...........	34.1	32.8	31.3	52.0	51.3	50.6
35 to 44 years...........	42.2	39.9	35.1	59.7	56.0	53.2
45 to 54 years...........	48.9	42.7	33.3	60.5	54.8	51.1
55 to 64 years...........	38.0	31.8	23.3	46.1	40.7	37.6
65 years and over........	9.8	10.5	8.6	12.2	12.1	17.3

During the 1950's, at least 70 percent of the net migration from farms consisted of young people under 20 or who reached 20 during the decade. In general, farm youth, whether in or out of school, tend to be an integral part of the farm labor force. Their rates of labor force participation are usually higher than those of nonfarm youngsters of the same ages. In view of the continuing decline in the proportion of nonwhites employed in agriculture between 1955 and 1962, it is reasonable to assume that many of these young farm leavers were nonwhite. A sharp rise in the number of youngsters enrolled in school, as well as unusually high jobless rates which have prevailed in recent years among nonwhite teenagers, may have contributed to their drop in participation.

Participation rates of both white and nonwhite older men (65 and over) dropped very significantly between 1955 and 1962--down about 9 and 13 percentage points, respectively. Probably because of the trend toward earlier retirement, participation has also been declining (although to a much smaller extent) among men 55 to 64 years of age, with the nonwhites again showing sharper declines.

Among men in the central age group 25 to 64 years, where participation rates tend to be the highest, nonwhite men continued to have somewhat lower rates than whites. This may be due to a higher incidence of disabling illness and injury among nonwhite men, associated with their concentration in manual, more hazardous occupations.

Nonwhite women historically have participated in the labor force in greater proportions than white women. The postwar rise in labor force participation rates of adult women has occurred both among white and nonwhite women. Despite these changes, only about two-fifths of all white women 25 to 64 were in the labor force in 1962, compared with nearly three-fifths of nonwhite women of the same ages.

TABLE 8

MEDIAN FAMILY INCOME, BY COLOR, 1948-61

YEAR	WHITE	NON-WHITE	NONWHITE AS PERCENT OF WHITE	YEAR	WHITE	NON-WHITE	NONWHITE AS PERCENT OF WHITE
1948	$3,310	$1,768	53.4	1955	$4,605	$2,549	55.4
1949	3,232	1,650	51.1	1956	3,993	2,628	52.6
1950	3,445	1,869	54.3	1957	5,166	2,764	53.5
1951	3,859	2,032	52.7	1958	5,300	2,711	51.2
1952	4,114	2,338	56.8	1959	5,643	2,917	51.7
1953	4,392	2,461	56.0	1960	5,835	3,233	55.4
1954	4,339	2,410	55.5	1961	5,981	3,191	53.4

Income and Education

Income. Nonwhites tend to have a somewhat larger number of wage earners per family unit and higher rates of labor force participation than whites, which tend to reduce white-nonwhite income differentials. Partially offsetting this is the relatively high concentration of nonwhites in agriculture, where income received in kind is excluded. Family income is nevertheless a useful criterion of socioeconomic wellbeing since many expenditure patterns relate to the family unit as a separate entity.

The average (median) income of both white and nonwhite families has increased quite substantially in dollar amounts during the past two decades. Very notable income advances by nonwhites were made particularly during World War II and the early postwar period as a result of wartime induced shortages of unskilled workers and governmental action designed to raise the income level of lower paid workers. The family income of nonwhites climbed from less than 40 percent of white family income in 1939 to nearly 60 percent in the early 1950's. Although since then nonwhites have continued to raise their money income, they have failed to bring about a further narrowing of income differentials between the two groups. In fact, on a relative basis, nonwhite family income as a percent of white family income has shown little change since 1952-1953 (Table 8). This phenomenon seems to be due to the fact that during the past decade, professional, technical, and managerial workers (where nonwhites are still very underrepresented) showed much larger relative income gains (up nearly 70 percent) than workers at the lower rung of the occupational skill ladder (where nonwhites are still disproportionately concentrated). The incomes of laborers and service workers rose by only 40 percent during this same period, compared with an increase of about 180 percent during the forties.

In 1948, nearly 8 of every 10 nonwhite families had money incomes of less than $3,000 (See Table 9). This proportion had dropped by 6 out of 10 by 1955 and 5 out of 10 by 1961, but it was about 2½ times the proportion of white families in this relatively low income category. Since 1955, the

proportion of nonwhite families in the $5,000 to $10,000 category had
increased by approximately one-half (to 23 percent), but was still well below
the comparable proportion of white families in that category (45 percent).
At the upper end of the income scale--$10,000 or more--6 percent of nonwhite
families were in this group in 1961, in sharp contrast to their negligible
proportion in 1948 and 1955 (about 0.5 percent in both years). Despite
recent employment gains made by nonwhites, which is reflected by their movement into higher money income groups, a substantial gap continues to exist,
with proportionately three times as many white families in the $10,000 or
more bracket.

TABLE 9

TOTAL MONEY INCOME OF FAMILIES, BY COLOR,
1948, 1955, AND 1961

FAMILY INCOME	1961		1955		1948	
	WHITE	NON-WHITE	WHITE	NON-WHITE	WHITE	NON-WHITE
All income classes	100.0	100.0	100.0	100.0	100.0	100.0
Under $3,000	18.6	47.5	25.7	57.3	42.6	78.1
$3,000 to $4,999	19.4	24.4	30.3	28.3	35.2	16.3
$5,000 to $9,999	44.7	22.8	36.6	13.7	19.1	5.3
$10,000 and over	17.1	5.6	6.5	.6	3.1	.4
Median income	$5,981	$3,191	$4,605	$2,549	$3,310	$1,768

TABLE 10

MEDIAN INCOME OF FAMILIES IN 1961, BY COLOR AND
EDUCATIONAL ATTAINMENT BY FAMILY HEAD

YEARS OF SCHOOL COMPLETED	TOTAL	WHITE	NONWHITE	NONWHITE AS PERCENT OF WHITE
Elementary..............	$4,074	$4,378	$2,539	58.0
Less than 8 years.........	3,279	3,656	2,294	62.7
8 years...................	4,772	4,911	3,338	68.0
High School.............	6,032	6,186	3,863	62.4
1 to 3 years..............	5,644	5,882	3,449	58.6
4 years...................	6,302	6,390	4,559	71.3
College................	8,210	8,288	6,444	77.8
1 to 3 years.............	7,250	7,344	5,525	75.2
4 years or more...........	9,264	9,315	7,875	84.5

Educational Attainment. Very large strides have been made during the
past two decades in reducing the persistent educational gap between nonwhite
and white persons. By 1962, the average white person 25 to 29 years of age
had completed 12.5 years of schooling, compared with 11.2 years of schooling
completed by the average nonwhite person in the same age bracket. For non-
white men, this represented a gain of some 4½ years of school since 1940; for
whites, the average gain was 2 years. This narrowing of the educational gap

during the postwar period can be largely attributed to the rising proportion
of nonwhite youngsters who have been enrolled in school. At the elementary
school level, the differential has been markedly reduced. But at the high
school level, despite some narrowing differentials during this period, the
percentage of nonwhites attending school falls appreciably below that of
whites.

Since the mid-1950's, however, the gap has essentially remained the same,
with both groups showing a rise of about 1 full year in median school years
completed, which departs from previous longrun trends. Recent income data
by color and educational attainment of the head of the family also support
conclusions found in other studies that the income gap between whites and
nonwhites is not completely closed even when educational levels of both
groups increase (Table 10). However, the differential is substantially
reduced at the college level, with the family income of nonwhite college
graduates in 1961 about 85 percent of that of white college graduates.

Monthly Labor Review, 86 (July, 1963):780-88.

2.
STATEMENT OF
WHITNEY M. YOUNG, JR.
EXECUTIVE DIRECTOR
NATIONAL URBAN LEAGUE TO THE
SENATE LABOR AND PUBLIC WELFARE SUBCOMMITTEE
ON EMPLOYMENT, MANPOWER, AND POVERTY
CONCERNING S. 1308
TO PROMOTE EQUAL EMPLOYMENT OPPORTUNITIES
MAY 4, 1967

Mr. Chairman and Members of the Subcommittee:

My name is Whitney M. Young, Jr., and I am Executive Director of the
National Urban League. We appreciate your invitation and the opportunity it
provides the Urban League to support this vitally needed legislation. To be
effective, the Equal Employment Opportunity Commission needed enforcement
power from its inception.[1]

We also wish to take this opportunity to commend Senators Clark and
Javits, who are responsible for introducing this important piece of legislation.[2]

The legislation to which we address ourselves would make an indispensable
contribution toward the protection of the equal employment rights of
individuals. The major division is that which grants EEOC the power to issue
cease and desist orders.

We believe that President Johnson, in his message to Congress, emphasized
the need for cease and desist order power when he stated:

> Unlike most Federal regulatory agencies, the Equal
> Employment Opportunity Commission was not given
> enforcement powers. If efforts to conciliate or
> persuade are unsuccessful, the Commission, itself,
> is powerless. For the individual discriminated
> against, there remains only a time consuming and
> expensive lawsuit.[3]

It is increasingly apparent, from EEOC's brief operation, that more effective
machinery for enforcement authority must be given to the Commission to bring
about conciliation.

We note that of thirty-five States with FEPC laws, twenty-eight provide
for enforcement procedures. Of the remaining seven that had initially relied
upon voluntary compliance, four have amended their laws to provide for
enforcement procedures.

Federal enforcement toward Equal Employment Opportunity continues to be
a major issue with minority citizens. While the employment status of Negro
workers has improved considerably during the past two decades, there remain

significant differentials between white and Negro workers. In spite of the
Nation's improved economic status, the employment opportunities of Negroes
continues to lag behind their white counterparts.

Nation-wide studies document that they are still confined largely to the
unskilled and semi-skilled jobs, when employed. They are employed fewer hours
per week and their unemployment rates are twice as high as those of whites.
Negro men continue to earn sixty per cent as much as white men, while Negro
women earn a little more than half as much as white women. The lower earning
power of Negro men makes it necessary for more Negro women to work than white
women.

Even more striking data is available on employment and unemployment from
a recent study, conducted by the Department of Labor, entitled "A Sharper Look
at Unemployment in U.S. Cities and Slums." Gathered from the twenty largest
U.S. metropolitan areas, it reveals an unemployment rate that varies greatly
from two point seven per cent in Washington, D.C. to five point two per cent
in San Francisco and six per cent in Los Angeles. In ten of these areas, the
rate is significantly above the national average of about three to four per
cent. In five, it is about the same; in five others, it is significantly
lower.

The non-white unemployment rate is about three times higher than the
white unemployment rate in eight of these areas, two times higher in six more
and fifty per cent higher in two others. This study partially corrects, for
the first time, a fault which had been discovered in the 1960 Census - i.e.
the missing completely of a large number of Negroes: one out of every six
Negro men between the ages of twenty and thirty. This means that past non-
white unemployment figures have understated the situation substantially.

The highest unemployment rates in the twelve larger areas, covered by the
study of fourteen to nineteen year-old non-whites, range from eighteen point
four per cent in Washington, D.C. to thirty-six per cent in Philadelphia.
The rate is above thirty per cent in seven of these areas.

Many of the differentials in the employment status of Negroes are due to
their inability to obtain jobs commensurate with their training. Likewise,
discriminatory hiring practices adversely affect both the Negro individually
and the total economy. They account for the disproportionate representation
on the public welfare rolls. Discrimination in employment has a greater
direct and indirect impact on the AFDC Program than any other single socio-
economic factor. It causes desertion, divorce and unwed parenthood with all
of their concomitant personal, social and economic costs. It also has similar
significant causal relationships to unemployment.

Title VII of the Civil Rights Act of 1964, under which the Equal Employment Opportunity Commission was established, engendered great hope that this
mechanism would deal meaningfully with the problems surrounding discrimination
in employment. The actual agency experience, which has demonstrated that the
Commission cannot enforce compliance, has given rise to disillusionment and
lack of confidence. These conditions have led the American Negro to suspect
that legislation, supposedly guaranteed to provide equality of opportunity,
is full of loopholes and political terminology. He is rapidly losing faith
in the democratic process to achieve his goal of equality of opportunity.[4]

Within the next few months, the Federal Government will sponsor a Concentrated Employment Program in nineteen of our major cities throughout the
country. The Government will spend from two and one-half to eight million
dollars in each selected city. The ultimate objective of this program is to
make it possible for the unemployed slum residents to obtain and hold regular
jobs, primarily in the private sector of the economy. The immediate short
range goal is to provide twenty-five thousand to forty thousand new jobs for
previously unemployed slum residents. Many of the people participating in
this crash effort will be Negroes, who, because of prior deprivation and
discrimination, need all of the legislative tangibles to assist them in
becoming productive and useful citizens. They cannot become discouraged, in
their desires to attain full equality of opportunity, by additional "token
legislation" to appease the wishes of a few, while ignoring the crying needs
of the disadvantaged poor.

The Urban League's fifty-seven years of existence have been dedicated to
the cause of equality of opportunity. Through our Job Development Program,
Skills Bank Program, and more recently, our On the Job Training Program, we

have worked with thousands of business and industry personnel. In these
efforts, we have been and are still being thwarted by subtle *and* overt
discriminatory practices, that are perpetuated by biased employers who hide
behind the legislative jargon, to deny compliance. At present, we have no
leverage which requires violators to terminate their unlawful policies and
practices.

We feel that the proposed legislation improves tremendously upon the
present Act. Therefore, we are in general agreement with most of its provisions. However, we would like to submit some suggestions regarding the
provisions listed below.

It seems appropriate that there should be a provision for the Commission
to effect its own litigation. This should also include employers who hold
government contracts and are under Executive Order 11246. This would serve
as a dual control to insure maximum compliance under the law.[5]

We strongly recommend that greater consideration be given to the
"charging party" involved. Under the proposed legislation, the charging
party has little involvement with conciliation and agreements can be worked
out between government representatives and management.

We also strongly feel that an aggrieved person should be able to institute a civil action against the respondent named in the charge in the
appropriate United States district court, without regard to the amount in
controversy, or in any state or local court of competent jurisdiction. This
protects the rights of all citizens, regardless of the nature and size of the
act.

The National Urban League's experience demonstrates the need for the
pending legislation.

I wish to thank you for inviting me to present this testimony, in behalf
of the National Urban League. The problems we face in the coming months and
years may well rest in your hands.

In addition to the moral implications, there is a dollar-and-cents logic
to equal employment opportunity. There are some costs which taxpayers are
shelling out, because of Jim Crow, that could easily be eliminated. There
are the billions spent on public welfare; there is the cost of public housing,
much of which would be unnecessary if more Negroes could buy their own homes;
there is the cost of sending thousands of building inspectors into the field
every day to ferret out violations of slum landlords; there is the cost of
arresting, jailing, trying, and paroling teen-age colored boys for purse
snatching because they can't find work.

These items in America's Bigotry Budget cost taxpayers more than twenty
billion dollars a year. This twenty billion dollars, which we are virtually
throwing away, is equivalent to all U.S. exports abroad with all the one
hundred-thirty nations of the world.

In the opinion of W. W. Heller, former chairman of the President's
Council of Economic Advisors, lifting the income of Negroes to that of whites
would *double* their current rate of economic growth. If the non-white labor
force earned as much as their white counterparts, Negroes would spend an
additional three point six billion dollars on food; one point seven billion
dollars on clothing; one point five billion dollars on housing; one point
three billion on household operation; one point two billion dollars on cars
and transportation; one point two billion dollars on recreation and amusement;
five hundred million dollars more on utilities; and eight million dollars more
on personal care and miscellaneous items.

You have an obligation, I believe, to give a ray of hope to the deprived
- those who have been deprived, by circumstances, in the past. You must make
sure that disadvantaged persons will have the full equality of opportunity,
that our economy demands.

Thank you!

Testimony of Whitney Young before the U.S. Senate Committee on Labor and
Public Welfare, May 4, 1967, Whitney Young Papers, Columbia University.

3.   35% BLACK JOBLESS SAYS TOP ECONOMIST

ATLANTA--Thirty-five percent of the nation's Black work force between
the ages of 16 to 64 is out of work in ghettos across the country and existing
national manpower policy is inadequate to help them, Dr. Vivian Henderson, Black economist and President of Clark College declared here recently.
Dr. Henderson's remarks came during a session of the National Urban
League's 4th Annual Labor Education Advancement Program (LEAP) Conference.
Henderson explained that Federal unemployment statistics of 11 percent
Black unemployment include only those who are actively seeking jobs and can't
find them, but this 35 percent figure also included one million Black male
heads of households who are forced to take seasonal or part-time work that is
not enough to sustain them, and in addition, "discouraged workers" - a
category that is regularly separated out of unemployment data by the government.
Henderson said the latter group --estimated at one to every four "unemployed" workers by the government -- are "the people who never get counted,
who have given up hope, who drift onto welfare rolls or are teenagers with no
previous work experience, and who will never join the labor force under such
circumstances."

Dismal, Sad

Henderson termed the total picture "dismal and sad," and said, "I do not
see the situation getting any better becuase of the employment policy of our
national leadership. On the other hand, I see it getting worse."
Henderson's assessment of the economy and the Black worker came as over
300 national, regional and local LEAP staff from 42 cities, and the Executive
Directors of local Urban Leagues from which they operate, joined civil rights
and labor leaders and Department of Labor representatives in a three-day
Conference on LEAP and the effect of national economic policies on the
minority community.
Earlier at the Conference, National Urban League Executive Director
Vernon E. Jordan, Jr., had praised LEAP's efforts, which have placed 5000
minorities in the construction trades since 1967 and made LEAP the nation's
largest contractor involved in such placements. [6]
But Jordan commented:
"However willing the unions might be; however supportive of their efforts
the government and business might be; however imaginative and industrious
agencies like the Urban League may be, without an expanding, healthy economy,
we will all fail."
Jordan said the issue for Blacks now is "survival," and criticized the
government's "trickle down" theory of economics, calling instead for a
"percolate up" theory which would create jobs, raise minimum wage "to a
realistic level," and increase the purchasing power of the average family to
get the economy going again.
Other major speakers during public sessions March 22nd included Secretary
of Labor James D. Hodgson; Atlanta Vice Mayor Maynard Jackson; Rev. Andrew
Young, Chairman, Atlanta Community Relations Commission; Walter Davis,
Director, Education Department, AFL-CIO; John Lewis, Director, Voter Education
Project, Atlanta; Emma Darnell, Intergovernment Programs Coordinator, Atlanta;
and Lemond Godwin, Assistant Professor, Labor and Industrial Relations,
Rutgers University, New Brunswick, N.J. [7]

Special Award

A special award for outstanding performance was presented to the LEAP
program by Hugh Murphy, Director of the Bureau of Apprenticeship Training,
U.S. Department of Labor. Adolph Holmes, National Urban League Deputy Director
for Programs and Field Operation also received an award from League Labor
Affairs Director Napoleon Johnson, II, "for the support which has made the
LEAP program first in the nation."
James C. Gildea, Executive Assistant to the President, AFL-CIO, addressed
the Annual Conference Dinner Thursday evening, at which time awards for outstanding service to LEAP were also presented to Alex Fuller, Director of
Civil Rights, United Steelworkers of America; and Robert Powell, Vice President, International Laborers Union of North America.

Denver Urban League LEAP Director Hubert L. Jones received LEAP's award
for outstanding local project performance, and Phoenix Urban League LEAP
Director George Floore received LEAP's award this year for the most innova-
tive project.

New York Amsterdam News, June 10, 1972.

4. DISPLACED FARM WORKERS LOSE INDUSTRIAL
JOBS IN RURAL SOUTH

By Roy Reed

MADISON, Ark., Jan. 18--Even though he is 49 years old and hardened in
the body, B. B. Williams's eyes are bright with innocence. Maybe that
explains why he is not so much disillusioned as simply puzzled.

"I didn't get a chance to go to no school," he said as he began to trace
the story: born to a black family on a white man's farm, his earliest memory is
learning to plow behind a mule, living out his boyhood and most of his manhood working on white men's farms in this rich delta land, and finally when
the big farmers replaced him with machines and he at the same time having
tired of toiling 10 hours a day for $4, taking for the first time a steady
job in town at one of the new factories and thereby earning more money than
he had ever imagined.

Six weeks ago he took the latest in his series of jobs, this one running
a grinding instrument in a machine shop 30 miles away in West Memphis. One
week ago he and several others were laid off. He did not know exactly why.

"They said business was kind of gettin' slow," he said. The timing was
unfortunate for Mr. and Mrs. Williams and the seven of their children still
at home. "My wife, she was working at the old folks' hospital at Forrest
City but she got laid off week before last."

The old people in the textile country of the Carolinas have known it a
long time. But it is just now, with their first bad recession, that the
recent converts in other parts of the South are learning that the salvation
offered by the new God industry, is a sometime thing.

It was the last great industrial push of the nineteen-sixties that
finally brought factories to the rural Southern areas like St. Francis County.
The plants were mainly light industrial -- electronics assembly, small motors,
watches and clocks, garment sewing rooms -- and they were brought in for the
express purpose of providing for thousands of farm workers like B. B. Williams
who had been displaced by the mechanical cotton picker and its technological
cousins.

Now those new plants are being hit as hard as industry everywhere by the
downturn. The Bureau of Labor Statistics office in Atlanta said this week
that 168,000 manufacturing jobs were lost in eight Southeastern states from
November, 1973 through November, 1974. The next reports are expected to be
worse.

The unemployment rate in Arkansas, one of the last states to begin industrializing, was only 4 per cent in the fall of 1973. The latest figure
showed it had increased to 6.3 per cent last November.

Thus the leaders of towns like Forrest City, the county seat five miles
down the road, who scratched, hustled and sometimes sold their souls to lure
industry during the last several years, are now facing the same awkwardness
and pain that the older industrial towns have known from the beginning. The
emergency public service jobs bill signed by President Ford earlier this
month is no help. It will provide two new jobs in this entire county.

The largest plant here, Warwick Electronics, which makes television sets
for the Sears, Roebuck Co., shut down production and laid off 1,100 workers
just before Christmas to let sales catch up with inventory. The plant plans
to reopen Feb. 3, with only 550 workers called back.

Half-a-dozen other plants have been built in St. Francis County since
1960. They make hoists, farm equipment, garments and small motors for automobiles. Most have stopped hiring and some, like the auto parts plant, are
laying off.

The severest impact of the faltering of the new industrialization can be seen in a town like Madison, a Forrest City suburb seven miles from the nearest of the new plants.

The 1,427 Madison residents are almost entirely farm people who moved here as adults or as children with their parents when mechanization and their own yearning for wider horizons moved them off the land. Willard Whitaker, the town's first black Mayor, says 65 per cent of the population is black.

Official unemployment figures are not available for a town this size, but Mayor Whitaker estimates that half of the Madison people who normally have jobs are out of work.

The town itself has little industry--two sawmills and an embalming fluid plant that altogether employ 25 persons. About 100 others work in Forrest City. Another 25 or 30 work in other towns, at least five of them in jobs as far away as Memphis, 40 miles east.

The Agriculture Department and the University of Arkansas sent a team of scholars to spend a summer studying Madison in 1971. Their study, reported a few weeks ago, did not find here the hopelessness and fatalism, or "culture of the poverty," often attributed to poor people.

"As a group," the report said, "blacks were more willing to work, to move, or to commute to find employment--and they held better images of work-- than their white counterparts." Mayor Whitaker says the town has "a lot of pride."

Massive layoffs, rising costs--the Agriculture Department just yesterday announced an increase in the price of food stamps, which about 65 per cent of Madison's residents use--and the old problem of transportation are beginning to test the spirit of the community.

And now a new problem is building up. People who moved to the big cities to work years ago are losing their jobs and many are coming home to Madison and St. Francis County.

The homeowners are finding special disappointment. They learn first that jobs are as hard to find here as in Detroit and Chicago. Then they discover that they can no longer go back to the land, the sustaining black soil and the life-giving creeks, bayous and woods, because the land has passed from them.

New York Times, January 22, 1975.

5.   BLACK WORKERS: PROGRESS DERAILED

By Barbara Becnel

The economic progress of black Americans is determined by many factors, and as a result, the progress has been very uneven. What works for one sector of the black population doesn't always work for another.

Blacks made tremendous economic strides between 1960 and 1969, but the income levels and living standards have been varied. Education, sex, age, family status, geographic location, union affiliation and numerous other characteristics have affected that progress.

Thus sharp income differentials prevail not only between black and white workers, but also among sectors of the black labor force.

Further, a sector of the black population remains outside the mainstream economy--the hardcore impoverished who never benefited from the advances of the 1960s.

Many blacks were able to benefit from the 1960s--a time of advancing national economy, a rising level of social awareness and such vital pieces of legislation as the 1964 Civil Rights Act and manpower and economic opportunity programs.

Unfortunately, the economic and social advances of the 1960s did not last long. The economic policies of a new administration began to slow down --in some instances halt or even reverse--the social and economic progress that had been occurring in America. In 1969-70, a recession took hold and Americans in general, but blacks in particular, were forced to tighten their

belts. And even worse off was that sizable group of blacks who had never
benefited from the economic gains of the 1960s.
      The evidence is widespread that blacks have been sorely pressed by the
economic climate since 1969:

● Unemployment rates for all Americans rose to 7.7 percent in 1976, but
for blacks it rose to 13.8 percent.

● Unemployment rates for black teenagers have reached catastrophic
levels. In 1976 they averaged 39.2 percent, and in July 1977 they reached
an all-time recorded high of 45.5 percent.

● The median income of black families, as a percent of the median
income of white families, fell back to 59.5 percent or $9,242 in 1976. In
1969 this figure had been 61 percent of the white median.

● During 1974-75, the number of persons living below the government-
defined poverty level rose by 2.5 million--the largest single-year increase
observed since poverty data was first kept in 1959. As in previous years,
blacks continued to be disproportionately represented, a little more than 31
percent of all low-income persons.

● From 1975 to 1976 the median income for black families, after correction for inflation declined in all regions except the South. In the Northeast it declined by as much as 8 percent. This is in sharp contrast to the
31.4 percent growth in the median income of black families experienced during
the period 1965 to 1970.

      All of this contrasts with the 1960s, when Americans witnessed a steady
decline in unemployment. The decade began with overall unemployment at 5.5
percent and black unemployment at 10.2 percent. Yet by 1969, expansionary
economic policies reduced unemployment drastically--3.5 percent for all
persons and 6.4 percent for blacks. It was in this period that blacks made
their major advances in median income. In 1964, the median income of black
families was $3,724, or 54 percent of the white median. By 1969, it had
grown to the high point of 61 percent of the white median, or $5,999.

      Moreover, by 1970, approximately 25 percent of all black families
residing in the North and West were earning incomes of $15,000 or more
annually. In contrast, the 1965 figure had been only 14 percent.

      Increased educational opportunities, occupational upgrading, and voca-
tional training played a key role in the economic advancement made by blacks
during the 1960s. In fact, the gains in educational attainment were startling.
Blacks age 20 to 24 completing four years of high school or more rose to 65
percent in 1970--up from 42 percent in 1960. The percentage of blacks
completing four or more years of college also increased, from 4.1 percent to
6.1 percent over the 10-year period, 1960 to 1970.

      Staying in school longer enabled blacks to begin improving the quality
of jobs they held. While in 1964 the proportion of non-white males employed
as white-collar workers was only 16 percent, by 1970 it was up to 22 percent.
And for black women the increase was even more dramatic--from 22 percent to
36 percent of their ranks in white-collar jobs.

      The evidence shows many blacks were able to secure major economic and
educational gains during the 1960s--but not all blacks benefited. Millions
of black Americans remained impoverished, and for those blacks left behind
in the earlier progress, the economic upheavals of this decade have been
particularly devastating.

      The nation's economy was not given time to recuperate from the 1969-70
recession when in 1973 an alarming rate of inflation set in. And by December
1974, the preceding 28-month period saw a drop in workers' real purchasing
power, after taxes, of more than 10 percent. The economy continued into a
precipitous decline and by 1975 approximately one-third of the nation's
industrial plant and equipment was left idle, with unemployment reaching
levels not seen since before World War II. Thus, the nation was left to
recover two serious back-to-back recessions--in 1969-70 and again in 1973-75.

      Unemployment declined during 1976, but the levels were still very high,
averaging 7.7 percent for all Americans and 13.8 percent for blacks. The
duration of unemployment also increased, averaging 15.7 weeks for all unemployed
person and 16.7 weeks for non-whites in 1976, up from 14.1 and 14.8 weeks,
respectively, in 1975.

      During the first half of 1977 the overall unemployment rate dropped to
a still very high 7.2 percent. Nearly all of the decrease in unemployment,

however, was among white workers. Black adult males witnessed some improvement but black teenagers continued to experience the highest joblessness.

All Americans have been dealt a severe blow by the contracting economy of this decade. But for blacks the economic upheaval has wreaked havoc with many of the gains made during the 1960s—in fact, some gains have begun to vanish.

In this dismal economic climate it is not surprising there has been a decrease in labor force participation—the proportion of the civilian non-institutional officially counted as part of the labor force. For non-white adult males, participation rates have dropped in almost all age categories.

Between 1954 and 1966 the labor force participation rate for adult white males stayed almost the same, dropping only two-tenths of 1 percent for that entire 12-year period. Since 1966, however, their rate has declined more sharply—dropping 2.4 percentage points by 1976, from 97.3 down to 94.9. But for black men of prime working age, the decline has been continuous since 1958, dropping by 7.5 percentage points, from 96 to 88.5. For white men most of the decline in rates took place among those age 45 to 54. However, black men have shown significant drops in the 35 to 44 years age group, and since 1964, among those age 25 to 34.

Proportionally, black men are twice as likely to be outside of the labor force as are white men, even though the age distributions of black non-participants and the black population are essentially the same as for whites. Yet in 1976, blacks accounted for 22.2 percentage of all non-participant men of prime working age, although they made up only 11 percent of the population.

However, the reverse proved true among non-white adult women. In nearly all age categories, non-white participation in the labor force was higher than that of their white counterparts. This points up a fact now widely recognized about women in the workplace: they work for the same reasons men do, because they have to; and black women have to work more often. Consequently, overall labor force participation rates for black women 16 years and older has changed only slightly over the past 12 years, registering 50.5 percent in 1976.

During the 1960s black adult men made tremendous strides in the number of jobholders, recording employment rates that rose to twice the rate of the total labor force growth. During the same period white adult males, while experiencing comparable growth in the number of people eligible for the labor force, did not experience the same growth in employment. However, from 1970 to 1974, employment increased at about the same rate for both races, approximately 8 percent.

But during 1974, the employment of blacks did not grow at all, and by the end of 1974 and the beginning of 1975, the number of employed blacks declined substantially. In contrast, white employment grew moderately throughout most of 1974. Nonetheless, as the year drew to a close, whites too began experiencing a rapid decline in employment.

Employment growth resumed in 1975, accelerated at the onset of 1976, but slowed down considerably by the end of the year. The average annual gain in 1976—2.7 million—was primarily a result of the increases occurring during the first six months. The employment patterns of white and non-white workers were roughly the same during 1976, marked by gains that were strong at the beginning of the year, while tapering off in the final two quarters.

Total employment increased rapidly during the first half of 1977. However, almost half of the rise occurred among adult women. Both white and black workers shared in the growth, but job gains among whites were proportionately greater. And for black teenagers, employment did not rise at all.

The lackluster performance of the economy during the bicentennial decade has brought frustration and despair to many American workers. Thousands have been out of work and unable to support their families for weeks, months, or even years. In fact, about 64 percent of men in the prime working age who were not in the labor force reported in 1976 that they had been unemployed for more than a year. And more than 25 percent of this group had worked at some point during the previous year.

For blacks, however, the problem is even more acute. Non-participation is of longer duration for non-white men age 25 to 34 years than for their white counterparts. In 1976, 20.4 percent of the non-white men not in the labor force reported that they had been outside the labor force for more than five years. That same age category of non-white men reported that 17.9

percent of them had in fact never worked. The corresponding white figures
are 15.6 percent and 14.7 percent, respectively. Also, a substantially
smaller proportion of the younger blacks than whites had worked within the
preceding year.

Many workers have given up the search for a job. Older blacks and black
teenagers have faced an impossible situation in securing employment. Thus,
many blacks have joined the ranks of "discouraged workers"--workers who after
trying for many months and sometimes years to obtain employment, finally give
up because they know no jobs are available.

The downturn in the economy has also brought an increase in the number
of "involuntary" part-time workers--those who want full-time employment, but
because of workweek cutbacks and the inability to locate full-time work in a
declining economy, have been forced to accept part-time work. Involuntary
part-time work can be found disproportionately among the less educated,
unskilled and the young--thus making the problem particularly serious for
blacks.

The Bureau of Labor Statistics does not count discouraged and involuntary
part-time workers in the jobless rates, and thus it seriously understates the
nation's real unemployment rate.

For the first 11 months of 1977, an average of 1.4 million non-white
workers were without jobs, or 14 percent of the 9.7 million non-whites in the
civilian labor force. Adding to the average 303,000 non-white discouraged
workers and one-half of the 610,000 non-whites working part-time involuntarily
--and one-half of them should be counted as unemployed--brings the non-white
jobless total in the first 11 months of 1977 to 1.8 million, or 19.7 percent
of the adjusted non-white civilian labor force of 10 million. That is
decidedly more than the "official" non-white unemployment rate of 14 percent.

To a degree, blacks have been able to hold onto the higher occupational
status obtained during the 1960s. In 1964, 48 percent of non-white men were
employed in low-income, unskilled occupations like non-farm laborer, service
worker and farm worker, as compared to 19 percent of white men. This proportion had dropped dramatically by 1970, to 37 percent of all non-white men,
whereas the white male proportion remained about the same. The proportion of
non-white men holding more skilled jobs as craftsmen increased slightly in
the same period, from 12 percent to 14 percent. Again, the comparable percentage among whites barely changed, remaining at approximately 20 percent.

Black women made remarkable progress on the occupational ladder during
the period 1964 to 1970. A large number of black women moved out of low-
income unskilled jobs in private households and farm work into higher paying
jobs as clerical workers and professional and technical workers. In 1964,
62 percent of all non-white women were employed as private household employees,
other types of service workers and farm workers.

By 1970, the proportion of non-white women employed in these occupations
had dropped to 45 percent. At the other end of the occupational scale, the
proportion of non-white women employed as white-collar workers moved up from
22 percent to 36 percent over the same period. However, at least half of
the women employed as white-collar workers are in clerical occupations--the
lower paying end of the white-collar occupations. Thus the move into "white
collar" is not as distinctive for them as it is for black men, who are more
concentrated in the professional, technical, managerial, and administrative
(except farm) positions. In fact, at least two-thirds of all male white-
collar workers are in the higher paying white-collar occupations.

Since 1969 the favorable change in the occupational status of black
workers has slowed down considerably. By 1976, the proportion of non-white
men employed as white-collar workers had risen to only 25.4 percent, up from
22 percent in 1970, and registering an actual decrease since the 1975 figure
of 26 percent. There was a dramatic improvement in the proportion of non-
white males who make up the nation's non-farm laborers, service workers and
farm workers between 1964 and 1970, decreasing from 48 to 37 percent. But
between 1970 and 1976, the improvement was only marginal--from 37 percent to
34.7 percent. And in between, there was a period between 1974 and 1966 when
the figures went the other way, moving from 34 percent to 34.7 percent.

For black women the occupational gains continued, but were not nearly as
great as in the preceding period. Thus despite major improvements during the
1960s, blacks are still over-represented in the low-paying, unskilled jobs

and under-represented in the higher-paying professional, technical, and managerial jobs.

Black teenagers, black women, and the black elderly are the three major groups for whom much remains to be done in improving job prospects and economic status. The position of black teenagers in the U.S. economy has worsened during the past 15 years, and has been relatively unaffected by both the progress of black people in general and by conditions among other young people. In spite of an increase in the number of years spent in school, unemployment rates for young blacks are still at castastrophic levels.

By 1960, the jobless rate for young non-whites was approximately 45 percent. In 1970, it was down to 29.1 percent, but by 1976 the unemployment rate for black teenagers had jumped back to 39.2 percent and in July 1977 it registered 45.5 percent--an all-time recorded high. The black teenage unemployment problem has become so chronic as to prompt a commonly accepted rule of thumb measure: the black teenage unemployment rate will be generally twice the white teenage rate and a little more than four times the unemployment rate of the total civilian labor force.

These high rates of unemployment have been coupled with a downward trend in the labor force participation rate of black youth. An increasing number of black teenagers are giving up and dropping out of the labor force. By 1976, their participation rates had reached the point where only two of every five even made an effort to obtain a job. Even though some of this lack of participation can be attributed to school attendance, black teenagers still consistently maintain lower participation rates than their white counterparts.

Traditionally, young blacks have held jobs that were in urban centers and were related to the service and retail trade industries. In recent years, however, those employers have been migrating toward the suburbs, leaving black youths behind--unemployed and isolated in the central cities. The impact has been devastating.

To the extent that a job can keep young people in high school and college, high unemployment rates seriously affect black schooling and education.

To the extent that a job can keep young people off the streets, earning an income while learning job skills and good work habits, high unemployment and low labor force participation rates can lead to high crime rates--increased incidents of burglary, drug addiction and rape.

Across the country, inner city youths are between 10 and 20 times more likely than other young people to be arrested for violent criminal offenses--inevitable by-products of long periods of idleness coupled with feelings of little self-worth. Discouragement and despair, resulting from one job turn-down after another, can cause a permanent undermining of self-confidence of black youths.

A study commissioned by the congressional Joint Economic Committee shows that all Americans pay social costs when national economic policy permits high levels of unemployment to persist for long periods of time. For example, a sustained 1 percent rise in unemployment will be followed by an increase in the homicide rate over that year and the subsequent five years. Thus the effect is cumulative. Moreover, the increase in homicide is comparable to 5.7 percent of the homicides which occur in the fifth year following the sustained rise in unemployment. This conclusion is based on 34-year data from 1940 to 1973.

That same 1 percent rise in unemployment was also found to be followed by state prison admissions. That increase was comparable to 4 percent of all state prison admissions occurring in the fifth year following the rise in unemployment. The analogous rate for suicides was 4.1 percent.

This study reveals the potent impact that unemployment has on society. Since black youth have consistently maintained higher levels of unemployment and longer periods of unemployment than most of the nation, the results of this study underscore the urgency of the need to provide jobs for all Americans in general, and black teenagers in particular.

For black women, the expanding economy of the 1960s coupled with a changing social attitude in favor of career-oriented women, combined to encourage them to seek employment and establish careers. In large part, however, women came to the job market generally unskilled and lacking experience. Consequently, they have a disproportionate share of low-level, low paying occupations, and a high susceptibility to layoffs and involuntary part-time employment.

The economic status of black women is an important factor in the overall progress attained by blacks. In the past, proportionally more black wives than white wives worked to maintain family income. Recent figures show that this trend has not changed. In 1975, 60 percent of black wives with pre-school children and 70 percent of those whose youngest child was 6 or older worked at some time during the year. The respective proportions of whites were 46 and 59 percent. Moreover, 46 percent of black mothers who worked at some time in 1975 held full-time jobs all year, compared with 32 percent of the whites.

Additionally, black wives contribute a greater proportion to family income than white wives do. In 1975, black wives' earnings averaged 32 percent of family income--42 percent if they worked year-round, fulltime--compared with 26 percent for white wives. The difference is explained in part by the greater likelihood of black wives working year-round, full time. Also black husbands had much lower earnings than white husbands--a median income of $7,800 for black husbands vs. $11,600 for whites.

Families headed by women with no husband present represent a growing proportion of all American families, increasing by one-third since 1970--black female heads increased by 45 percent and white female heads increased by 29 percent. The proportion of black female-headed families has grown from 28 percent of all black families in 1967, to 36 percent in 1976. During that period, however, the comparable white female proportion was only 9 percent in 1967 and 11 percent in 1976.

What is more, the percentage of low-income, female-headed black families is on the increase. In 1967, 46 percent of all poor black families were female-headed, compared to 26 percent of all poor white families.

Yet by 1976 the proportion of low-income, female-headed black families had increased to 69.4 percent, while the comparable white figure had increased to 38.7 percent.

Black families with a female-head had a median income of $5,069 in 1976--$7,804 below that of male-headed black families. This represents an increasing gap since in 1974 the median income of female-headed black families was only $5,900 below the black male counterpart. Among whites, female-headed families also trail badly. Their median income was $8,226 in 1976, or $8,192 below that of male-headed white families. Still, white female-headed families maintained a median income that was $3,157 greater than that of their black-female headed counterparts. Furthermore, from 1975 to 1976, after correction for inflation, the median income of black female-headed families registered a decrease of 2.2 percent while the corresponding white figure increased by 1.7 percent.

Since 1970, a downward trend has developed with respect to the number of black families with both husband and wife present as a percent of all black families. Although the percentage of white husband-wife families barely changed between 1970 and 1976, black husband-wife families have registered a considerable decrease, dropping from 68.1 to 60 percent. And since husband-wife families commonly have a higher median income than most other types of families--because more frequently both husband and wife are employed--the percentage decrease in black husband-wife families could have a downward effect on black family income.

Thus the importance of the role played by black women in the overall advancement of the black population cannot be overstated. The data prove that how black women fare in the labor force has a major influence on how black families fare.

The South--where the majority of blacks reside--is still the primary location of black poverty. Approximately 53.7 percent of all blacks maintained residence in the South by 1976, as compared to 17.1 percent residing in the Northeast and 8.7 percent residing the West. Although the 1976 figure of 53.7 percent is well below the 60 percent of the black population that lived in the South in 1960, it represents an increase over the 1974 figure of 53 percent.

During the 1960s, 1.4 million blacks migrated to the North. However, from March 1970 to March 1974, according to the Bureau of the Census, only 184,000 blacks migrated to the North while 276,000 blacks migrated to the South. And by the end of this period, the South was left with a net increase in black population of 35,000, while the North had a net decrease of 158,000.

One explanation for the reverse migration is that many of the traditional types of employment found in the northern industrial centers were eliminated during the 1960s by technological change, and by the move of factories from urban centers to the suburbs. Since many of the blacks migrating from the southern farmlands were unskilled, their occupational mobility was severely limited, and they were left abandoned in the central cities. Yet, 57.1 percent of all blacks existing on incomes below the poverty-line still resided in the South in 1976, vs. 35.7 percent residing in the Northeast and North Central part of the United States. However, there appears to be a change occurring in the location of black poverty. The percent of poor blacks residing in the South has declined from the 1974 figure of 60.5 percent; and the percent of poor blacks residing in the Northeast and North Central part of the United States has increased from the 1974 figure of 33.3 percent.

The median income of black families residing in the South is lower than that of black families residing in the Northeast, but is growing at a much faster rate than that of northern black families. Over the period 1970 to 1974, the median income of southern black families increased by 28.8 percent, in contrast to only a 13 percent increase in the Northeast. And from 1975 to 1976, the median income of black families, after correction for inflation, declined in all regions except the South. In fact, black families residing in the South saw a growth in median income over that period of 4.7 percent, while declines were 8 percent in the Northeast and 4.3 percent in the West.

Still, in 1970, the median income of southern black families was $5,226, or 57 percent of southern white median income. But in the Northeast, the median black family income was $7,774, or 71 percent of the comparable white figure. However, the declining economy of recent years has resulted, for some regions, in a dramatic decrease in the ratio of black to white median incomes, and by 1976, black families residing in the Northeast recorded a median income of $9,727, only 61.5 percent of white median income.

The South, however, has been able not only to hold on to its gain, but what is more, the ratio of black to white median income actually increased slightly--moving to 59.2 percent of white median income, or $8,526, in 1976 vs. 57 percent, or $5,226 in 1970.

Increased educational attainment has played a major role in the economic advances obtained by young black families, and is perhaps the most impressive black gain of the 1960s. In 1966, the median years of school completed by blacks was 10.5 years, as compared to 12.3 years for whites. By 1976, however, that gap had almost closed--with 12.3 years of school completed by blacks vs. 12.6 years for whites.

Blacks have also made tremendous progress in college enrollment. Indeed, college enrollment has increased more rapidly for blacks than for whites. Between 1970 and 1976, black college enrollment increased 27.9 percent. By 1976, blacks accounted for 11 percent of all college enrollment, up from 7 percent in 1970.

College completion has also continued to increase among blacks, but the gap in the proportion of young blacks completing college and young whites completing college was larger in 1976 than in 1960. An approximate eight-point gap in 1960 had expanded to a 12.2 point gap in 1976. The percentage of blacks between the ages of 25 and 34 who completed 4 years of college or more was 4.1 percent in 1960, 6.1 percent in 1970, and 11.3 in 1976--far behind the white proportions of 11.9, 16.6 percent and 23.5 percent. Still, a great deal of the gain in young black family income can be attributed to the educational advances made by blacks.

Older blacks, however, have not been able to avail themselves of the educational opportunities made available to younger blacks. By 1969, 30.5 percent of all non-whites 65 years old and over were still illiterate. This represented more than twice the proportion of illiterate whites of the same age.

Thus, not surprisingly, many older blacks had extremely low incomes. In 1975, 35.5 percent of blacks age 55 to 64 years old had incomes below $2,500. This was true of 18.9 percent among whites the same age. The median income of blacks age 55 to 64 was $3,800, or 52.3 percent of the comparable white income. With blacks age 65 years old and over, 56.7 percent received incomes of less than $2,500. Their median income was $2,359, or 64.6 percent of whites with the same characteristics.

In 1976, nearly 35 percent of all blacks age 65 years and over were existing below the poverty threshold. Thus, whatever the gains of other age groups, poverty is rampant in the older black community.

Black union members fare considerably better than non-union blacks. Not only are their incomes much higher, but within the ranks of union members, the income gap between black and white is less than among non-union workers. Additionally, a research paper prepared for the Industrial Relations Research Association shows that blacks in the unionized, middle-aged blue-collar category are less likely to experience unemployment than their non-union counterparts.

In May 1974, the median earnings for all full-time black union workers were $169 a week, 82 percent of the median for full-time white union workers. For non-union black workers, the median weekly earnings were $124, or 76.5 percent of the comparable white income. Among black women union members, the gap was even smaller, with their median weekly earnings of $141 representing 96.6 percent of white female union income. And their median weekly earnings were 28.2 percent higher than the $110 median for non-union black females.

Black men are part of a similar phenomenon. Black males who were full-time workers and union members had median weekly earnings of $183, or 83.6 percent of the comparable white figure. Non-union black male workers had a median of $141, or 70.2 percent of the median of their non-union white counterparts. For black male union members, their earnings were 29.8 percent greater than their non-union counterparts.

During the 1960s, progress was made toward eliminating overt job discrimination, but the rights alone could not take care of the entire task. A black person gains little in the right to a job if jobs do not exist. Further, the right to a job also needs to be backed up with the training and skills to perform the duties.

An expanding and healthy economy that was providing jobs, training and educational opportunities gave meaning to the social legislation of the 1960s. The Manpower Development and Training Act of 1962 and the Economic Opportunity Act of 1964 provide examples of the types of programs that were initiated during the 1960s.

Only full employment can make it possible for blacks to attain work--experience and seniority in better jobs, and thus begin to participate fully in the mainstream of the American economy.

Since blacks have suffered the most from the mismanagement and social neglect that has characterized the nation's economic policies since 1969, they also have the biggest stake in programs that will transform the present weak and ailing economy into a healthy, full employment economy. Only then will blacks be afforded the opportunity of achieving their full potential.

AFL-CIO American Federationist (January, 1978):1-8.

6. LAST HIRED, AND USUALLY THE FIRST LET GO

By Charlayne Hunter

Charlotte Brown, a 24-year old black woman, was hired last January by Twentieth Century-Fox to be trained in publicity and advertising.

Seven months later, before she ever got to the advertising side, she was told that the company was cutting back the publicity department for fiscal reasons, and that she would be "terminated" in a month.

"I was hired because of the pressure on companies to hire blacks," Miss Brown said recently. "But they couldn't keep me, the shop steward said, because that would start a fight with the unions."

A company official agreed that Miss Brown was hired as a result of company policy that had developed within the last three years to increase the hiring of minorities. He cited the declining economy as a factor in the discharge, but said that the major reason had been the elimination of the publicity department altogether.

Last Hired-First Fired

Whatever the reasons, Miss Brown is one of a growing number of people hit hardest by the economic downturn: the last hired-first fired.

Calling it "an exceedingly critical issue that needs to be approached," the president of the National Urban Coalition, M. Carl Holman said that he and a national task force were in the process of setting up an affirmative action conference in Washington in February.

But, he said, although early responses indicate that some of those invited from both the public and private sectors of the economy welcome a chance to work in the problem--W. Willard Wirtz, a former Secretary of Labor, has agreed to chair the conference--others are 'leery' because they see the problem as a very prickly one.[8]

"It's so potentially extremely explosive that they feel you have to approach it the way you approach a live hand grenade," Mr. Holman said.

"What makes it tough," he said, "are the conflicting claims--both of which have merit. You don't want to erode all that has been done in the last five years and after a great deal of pressure."

"But the claims of seniority of service are serious claims and have to be taken into account."

'Logic of the Courts'

Despite the confusion that reigns, however, many lawyers argue that "the consistent logic of the courts," according to one employment law specialist, "is that people are not to be adversely affected as a result of race or sex."

New York City Human Rights Commissioner Eleanor Holmes Norton has issued stern warnings to city agencies, as well as to trade associations, about the legal liability of placing the burden of reductions, layoffs and reduced opportunities unequally on minority and female workers. In proposing alternatives, she has also urged employers not to suspend affirmative action efforts.[9]

"The economic risk to employers of large monetary awards to such laid-off employes is substantial, and the complications and practical difficulties arising from remedial orders have a tremendous potential for creating dislocation and discord," she stated in a widely circulated memorandum.

The memorandum goes on, however, to suggest that employers consider cost savings "by other cuts and economies, such as reduced work weeks, shift changes, payless work days, payless holidays and cuts in various areas, departments, and in different job categories and levels to spread the burden."

In the event of unavoidable layoffs, Mrs. Norton advised employers to "take measures to lessen the impact on terminated employes, such as transfers to other areas of the company not experiencing retrenchment, offering counseling on unemployment benefits and job seeking."

She also suggested that they "establish and explain employe-recall rights, so that employes who are terminated will be called back before outside hiring is begun."

Mrs. Norton and others have expressed concern, however, over maintaining the gains for minorities while not exacerbating racial hostilities.

'Polarization' Issue

"The polarization effect cannot be underestimated," she said in an interview. "And this is the hardest issue we've come up against."

Concurring, another civil rights lawyer said of polarization: "The prospect is deepening. It has not ripened yet because not enough people are hurting. The whole notion of sharing the burden is new because there've always been blacks to lay off."

In anticipation of such a problem, Mrs. Norton said that she had been meeting with whites, blacks and women "asking for ideas."

"We have an obligation when there is a clash of rights to search for remedies that are as equitable as possible," she said.

The New York Times, January 29, 1975.

7. BLACK MANPOWER PRIORITIES:
PLANNING NEW DIRECTIONS

By Walter W. Stafford and Lewis J. Carter, III

As the nation approaches the 1980s, there is a growing awareness of the
need to establish long-range policies to reduce persistent social and
economic inequities. Basic to the process of establishing these policies and
priorities is the recognition that the American labor force is expected to be
continually faced with technological advancements, shifts in the location of
employment centers, and changes in the demands for occupations. The composition of the labor force will also change. Women are expected to continue
their increase in the work force; age will remain a major policy consideration;
and migration will influence the pattern of service demands.

There is a general concensus among socially sensitive analysts and
leaders, that these structural changes should be guided by a coherent and
flexible manpower policy. For blacks and labor leaders the shaping of such
a policy is an immediate priority. A growing number of groups and analysts
are concerned with the incremental development of national manpower policy
and the failure of programs to adjust to rapid economic changes. Long-range
policy must be grounded in the goals of full employment, and programs and
priorities developed toward that end. An important element in devising this
process is the shaping of policies and programs to meet the current and projected manpower needs of the black labor force.

Three factors must be continually recognized in relating manpower policy
to the needs of blacks. These are an awareness of discriminatory patterns,
the priorities of training programs, and the projected needs and demands of
the economy. Policy cannot be divorced from overall economic changes.
Employment opportunities for blacks have prospered and declined in tandem
with structural changes, and this relationship is expected to continue.

A basic factor affecting black employment has been and will continue to
be the shifts of job opportunities to major employment sectors. From 1950-77,
the fastest growing job opportunities in the private sector have been concentrated in lower paying employment sectors. Overall, the number of jobs in the
labor force has increased, but the income benefits have been mixed. The
higher employment sectors (mining, construction, manufacturing, transportation,
utilities and wholesales) have declined from 55.3 percent of all employment
in 1950 to 40 percent in 1976. By contrast, the lower paying jobs in services
and retail trades have expanded from 27 percent of employment in 1950 to 35
percent in 1977.

These changes in job patterns by employment sectors have been critical
in meeting the needs of blacks. Of essential importance have been the high
unemployment rates for blacks in the higher paying sectors, and the reduced
opportunities for entry by younger black workers. The percentage of black
workers 20-24 in the higher paying employment sectors declined from 49 percent
of that age group in 1968 to 39 percent in 1976. For blacks 25-34, the
percentage within this interval declined from 44 percent to 42 percent. These
age groups are important because of changes in the structure of the black labor
force. In 1968, the age group 20-35 comprised 36 percent of the black labor
force. By 1977, blacks within these age intervals were 46.6 percent of the
black population 16 and above.

The problems of black entry into the higher paying employment sectors
are increasing. As younger blacks entered or attempted to retain jobs in the
higher paying private sector, they were confronted with shrinking employment
opportunities. Employment projections by the Bureau of Labor Statistics are
only slightly encouraging. Construction employment, manufacturing, transportation, utilities and wholesale employment will increase, but they are expected
to constitute only 35.5 percent of total employment by 1985. Additionally,
several of the employment sectors with substantial percentages of blacks are
projected to decline. Among these are primary metals, tobacco manufacturing,
leather products, food and kindred products, and water and rail transportation.
Blacks are faced with dual problems as the 1980s progress: maintenance of
jobs in declining employment areas; and entry into jobs in slower growing
sectors. These problems require a specific manpower policy devised for the
higher paying employment sectors.

In the lower paying employment sectors, blacks are confronted with a different set of problems. First, many of the jobs in the lower paying sectors do not require extensive training, and they have historically been subjected to high unemployment. Second, in the areas which do require skills and pay higher earnings (finance, securities, etc.), the percent of blacks is low, and outlets for training are few. Third, a large number of younger blacks are disproportionately concentrated in lower paying service employment and retail trades requiring few skills.

The third point deserves increased attention because those persons employed in retail trades and services are expected to represent 44 percent of total employment in 1985. Retail trades, services, and finances represent different problems for blacks. The percent of blacks in the retail trades has remained around 7.7 percent of that employment in 1968. Within the black labor force, however, employment in retail accounted for approximately 14 percent of employment in 1976. Blacks in service employment have declined as a percent of those jobs since 1968. Still, service employment accounted for one third of black employment in 1975. The percentage of blacks in finance, insurance and real estate has increased since 1968, but most of that was due to lower paying jobs in banks and real estate organizations.

The data only briefly describe the problems of blacks in these lower paying employment sectors. Overall demand for services is increasing, as is employment. However, there are not enough training programs geared for the higher skilled and higher paying jobs in the service-producing employment sectors. This is a critical factor. Data analyzed from unpublished Bureau of Labor Statistics sources show that as the higher paying employment sectors have declined as a point of entry for black workers, the lower paying employment sectors have remained a source of the low wage jobs. In 1968, 44 percent of employed blacks 25-34 were located in services, finance, and retail trades. By 1976, approximately half of this age group was employed in these sectors. Equally, or more important, these employment sectors have become a dominant area for blacks in the age interval 20-24. Over half (52 percent) of the employed blacks in that age interval in 1975 had jobs in the three sectors.

The major changes in manpower policy for blacks in the service-producing sector should emphasize upgrading of skills and redistribution of opportunities outside of the lowest paying employment sectors. Policies targeted to the employment sectors projected to increase in demand are a basic avenue to shift the emphasis of manpower programs. Three of the basic areas are health, environment and data services. Training linked to demand is the key. In a service society in which 87.4 percent of the labor force 20-40 years of age is expected to have completed at least four years of high school by the 1980s, and almost a quarter of those 25-34 four years of college, technical skills are a prerequisite for job competition. Traditional educational institutions will not provide the necessary programs for blacks. For black youth, there is an immediate need to address programs for areas of employment demand. Black adults need training programs, which recognize the changes expected in the 1980s.

Historically, blacks have placed a heavy reliance on the public sector for good jobs. In the economy as a whole, jobs developed in the public sector have been much better paying than those developed in the private sector, and for blacks, this factor was particularly important. As employment in state and local government increased by over 50 percent between 1950-77, blacks have been able to increase their opportunities for numerous higher paying jobs. In 1974, black employers on government payrolls earned about 14 percent more than their counterparts in the private sector in 1974.

Partially because of the heavy reliance on these sectors, a large number of younger blacks continually seek public service employment. In 1976, blacks comprised approximately 14 percent of governmental employees, and because of the projected growth in public employment, this remains an important sector. State and local government employment is projected to grow by 3.3 percent, but Federal jobs by less than 1 percent.

The reliance on the public sector has many limitations. The first, of course, is the sensitivity of these employment sectors to economic crises. The second is the strain this reliance has placed on local governments, and the third is the political limitation it places on the black community. From the perspective of manpower policy, the first two points are important in devising strategies which will upgrade the skills of black workers in these areas. The most important factor, however, is the need for policies which will permit expansion of employment in the public sector as broader urban policies are developed. Temporary policies are untenable. The continued growth of the public sector necessitates a flexible long-term policy.

The structural changes in the private and public employment sectors have greatly influenced the type and variations of occupational growth since 1950. These changes have been particularly important in evaluating black mobility and upgrading. During the past decades, blacks have often benefited from the growth of professional occupations, but they have also remained in lower paying and lower skilled occupations.

For analytical discussion, occupational changes in the black labor force have to be separated by sex. The discussion of males should concentrate on earnings, skills, and age. Occupationally, the high concentration of black males as laborers and service workers continually limits their earnings, as is shown by median earnings of $10,000 for black males in 1976. Indeed, black males represent the true paradox of the American labor force. At the professional level, the black male had the highest level of education of any sex by race in 1976, yet, irrespective of training, his earnings remained lower than that of his white counterpart.

The complexities of devising manpower policies for the black male represent the most difficult challenge for the future. Age is a key consideration. In the professional-technical fields, 41 percent of the black male employees in 1976 were new entrants, ages 25-34. The older black male with limited skills had few options if he was not employed in one of the better paying public and private sectors. The progress of younger black males, however, disguised other realities. In 1976, 23 percent of the black males 25-34 were laborers or in service occupations, as were almost one third of those 20-24. Overall, black males comprised 10 percent of the unemployed male labor force, but 20 percent of the male laborers. By contrast, black males in 1976 constituted only 6 percent of employed professionals and technicians.

The continued concentration of black males as laborers, service workers and operatives represents a serious problem for the nation. These occupations, aside from being low-paying, offer few transferable skills. Indeed, one of the clearest failures of manpower programs is the fact that 34 percent of employed black laborers were 20-35 in 1976, a percent almost equal to what this age group comprised of these occupations in the early 1970s. The clearest challenge for manpower training for black males is to bring them into the mainstream of the growing occupations. At a time when over half of the labor force is in white collar occupations, only 26 percent of employed black males in 1976 had entered these occupations.

The situation for black females is somewhat different. Fifty-six percent of the new entrants in 1975 were concentrated in service and clerical occupations. The younger black female, 25-34, accounted for 39.7 percent of all professional and technical occupations in 1975, a percentage similar to that of males. However, these are essential differences. The black female labor force is essentially white collar. In 1976, 44 percent of employed women were in white collar occupations. The critical avenue for females is raising their skill levels and incomes. The median income level for black females in 1975 was $7,486, and for marginally educated service employees $5,214.

The combined sexes represent a major challenge for manpower policy. Their concentration as service workers, laborers, and clerical employees reflects the absence of workable manpower programs. Indeed, in 1975, 32 percent of black full-time wage and salary workers in service occupations earned less than $5,000. The major reality of the occupational policies is that after decades of assuming occupational changes, the percent of blacks entering occupations is beginning to resemble that of retiring blacks who were confined to lower level occupations by discrimination and lack of skills. Simply stated, entering occupational areas for blacks are often no better than they were for their parents.

The downward occupational trends can only be reversed through an aggressive manpower policy linked to projected occupational and employment changes. The approach is critical because dislocations of black workers will probably occur as the lower-paying private sectors continually introduce new technologies. Based on 1974-75 projections, declines are expected in nine occupational areas associated with industrial and service shifts which have been critical to black employment concentrations. Blacks compromise at least 10 percent of these occupations. They include: stenographers, clothing press operators, keypunch operators, taxi drivers, spinners, sanders, plasterers, seamstresses, and telephone operators.

By contrast, there are numerous occupations projected to increase which are associated with the service and financial sectors in which blacks can be upgraded through training or trained for new occupations. Based on current black concentrations, it is clear that many blacks in service and professions can be retrained to meet the demand for health care, welfare, and environment planning. These occupations include: practical nurses, teacher aides, health workers, welfare aides, health aides, lab technicians, drafters, analysts, plumbers, and environmental specialists. The third area should emphasize new emerging occupations which have few blacks and require new training approaches. A large number of these occupations are in health and energy-related areas. These include: hygienists, insulators, computer programmers, roofers and slaters, air-conditioning repair technicians, electricians, chemical technicians and data clerks. The basic apprenticeship programs for blacks should be concentrated in those occupations expected to grow, or where upgrading is feasible.

As the above assessments indicate, our interpretations of the changes in the economy and occupations have led us to emphasize areas of growth which are part of the larger needs of the nation. These areas involve resource planning, health, data interpretation, and related scientific concerns. History is the guide. It is all too evident that previous programs failed to help a large segment of the black community, notably males, adjust to the 1980s. In order to achieve these new directions, organized labor must have a major responsibility in the planning and shaping of manpower policy. Labor must be a catalyst. It has already become apparent that geographical shifts in industry require a new labor and black coalition. This is readily apparent in the projected decline in textile workers, and the tobacco industries where blacks may be dislocated. In fact, the shift in employment activities to the South may have been a temporary use of black labor until more inexpensive technical approaches could be developed.

Blacks and labor organizations also need to shape the context of apprentice programs to address the future. Several of the key growth areas of occupations are not classified as apprenticeable. This omission should be corrected since a large number of these occupations are linked to resource planning, health, and related scientific areas and thereby provide an excellent opportunity for black training requirements. We are specifically concerned with increasing occupational mobility out of low-wage employment sectors and developing skills for geographical mobility. A cornerstone of our framework is the problems of economically depressed cities and regions where blacks are trapped in low-wage service industries. All available evidence documents that lower income blacks do not readily migrate to faster growing areas. The development of skills related to the demands of the new employment centers offers a mechanism for mobility. These apprentice skills are also basic for income gains in redeveloping areas. The journeyman's card is a key to a mobile labor force.

Finally, mobility and training are integral to the problems of black teenage employment. One major problem for this age group is directing them away from long-term employment in the low-wage service sectors. As temporary jobs, these sectors can reduce their job search; however, over the long term, there is considerable evidence that black youth are falling into a low-wage spiral. As the entrance into the higher paying industrial sectors has been reduced, black youth are being presented with a narrow view of their economic future. The spiral is particularly critical for black males. More than any group in the nation, their training has to be linked to occupational and employment projections. An essential step for all black males is to create a place for them in the service society, through well-structured training programs.

This analysis has repeatedly illustrated the impending changes in the labor force, and the probable effects on blacks. It is incumbent upon minorities to become involved and provide planning bodies a greater voice in shaping manpower policy for the future. It is a threatening sign that after years of demanding that governmental bodies make their planning priorities clear, there are few blacks involved in shaping the directions. It cannot continue.

The Crisis, 85 (December, 1978).

8. BLACK WORKERS EXPOSE KAISER RACISM

By Mike Giocondo

NEW YORK, June 1--Testimony now before the Supreme Court reveals that a "plantation mentality" was perpetuated by the Kaiser Company at its Gramercy, La., plant where the Weber "reverse discrimination" case originated.

The Weber case is soon to be decided by the Supreme Court. Thousands of protesters of the Weber case are expected to rally in Washington tomorrow.

The Weber case stems from charges filed by a white worker, Brian Weber, at the Gramercy plant, who falsely claims he was a victim of "reverse discrimination" when denied a position in the company's initial affirmative action program in 1974.

If the Supreme Court rules in Weber's favor, it will wipe out affirmative action programs across the country that are designed to open job opportunities for minority workers.

Definite Discrimination

Pam Bayer, an attorney in New Orleans, who filed a Supreme Court motion to intervene in the Weber case on behalf of five Black workers at the Kaiser plant, said the motion exposes past discrimination at the plant and a "plantation mentality."

She said that the effect of the overt discrimination was to keep Blacks in menial jobs and under threat of firing.

It is interesting that in 1973 Weber was elected to the post of chairman of the grievance committee at the plant, a position he held until this year.

The motion filed two weeks ago asks the Supreme Court not to rule in the Weber case and to send it back to the lower courts. It states that the lower court erred in never questioning Kaiser on the crucial issue of past discrimination and did not open testimony from the very people affected by discrimination--Black workers.

First Of Its Kind

The motion, the first of its kind in a Supreme Court case, came after the court heard arguments in the case in late April. "The motion is unprecedented," Bayer told the *Daily World* in a phone interview, "but so then is the Weber case."

She said Kaiser attorneys want the motion and the testimony on discrimination thrown out. "They claim that the motion is too late in the proceedings," she said.

Whatever the legal outcome of the motion, the important fact is that Black workers at Kaiser have taken a public stand on the issue of past discrimination.

Gerald Horne, director of the Affirmative Action Coordinating Center in New York, said the affidavits filed in the motion show that "Black workers are telling the corporate world that from now on they are going to expose discrimination and will intervene to protect their rights."

Intimidated Workers

In the motion are sworn statements that show Black workers were constant victims of discriminatory discipline and firing. According to Edward Miller, one of the workers, the discrimination "created an atmosphere of intimidation that chills any action to try to change the situation."

Miller was fired on charges of some activity that took place off the job. After six months he was rehired. He said that no white worker was ever fired for similar off-the-job activity.

Another worker, Clinton Wiltz, said he was fired on charges of insubordination. "I never heard of any white worker who was fired on that charge, even though they refused to obey a Black foreman," he said.

"Harassments and firings prevented Blacks from getting seniority and advancement," Wiltz affirmed.

The Kaiser Company has denied there was any past discrimination at their Gramercy plant, despite the fact that the total workforce in the community is 40 percent Black and only 15 percent of the workers in the plant are Black and less than two percent are employed in skilled jobs.

Prior to 1974, Kaiser was under pressure by the Equal Employment Opportunity Commission to initiate an affirmative action program. With the United Steelworkers Union, they worked out a program that called for 13 workers, six whites and seven Blacks and women, to be upgraded in on-the-job training.

The selection for the program was based on seniority. Weber applied and was not selected because of his low seniority rating.

Kaiser said that the program was a voluntary effort and was not designed to correct past discrimination. By not admitting to past discrimination, the company seeks to avoid suits by Black and minority workers seeking remedy.

Upgrading Workers

Voluntary affirmative action programs are seen as important means to help upgrade workers. But in the Weber case and the charge of "reverse discrimination," the issue of past discrimination and the record of hiring and firing becomes crucial in deciding the case.

In his legal case Weber is being supported by a number of rightwing and reactionary groups. Legal foundations with funding from big business, like the Pacific Legal Foundation, which receives major funding from Arco oil and Dupont Corporation, filed briefs supporting Weber.

A decision in the case is expected sometime this month.

Daily World, June 2, 1979.

9.   WEBER CASE HITS UNIONS, MINORITIES

GRAMERCY, La.--This community is a part of the most industrialized area of the "New South." About 30 miles up river from the port of New Orleans (second only to New York City in this country), is part of the complex of grain and oil docking facilities, light industry, and commerce that abutt the Mississippi River.

This is the area chosen to launch the "Weber Case," a major attack against the labor and civil rights movements. It is the site of a Kaiser Aluminum Company plant where Brian Weber, a white worker, filed the "reverse discrimination" case which has now reached the Supreme Court. If Weber wins affirmative action in industry will be set back by about 30 years.

The Weber-Kaiser case began back in 1974 when an apprentice training program was negotiated between the company and the United Steel Workers of America. Prior to that time Kaiser refused to upgrade its employees, Black or white, but hired skilled workers at the gate.

When the new training program was instituted it followed the example of the Basic Steel Consent Decree in that it set up procedures to guarantee that minority workers would at last have a chance to enter the skilled trades on a one-to-one ratio to make up for past exclusion.

Program Stopped

Weber filed suit when he was passed over in the first selections (he would have been next in line and would now have finished his training). As a result of his suit the apprenticeship program was halted and Kaiser went back to the old system of hiring outsiders.

"This case is holding back a whole lot of people, both Black and white," says Charles Pittman, a leader of rank and file workers in the plant. "We can lose all the gains we have won over the years since I started working here."

Lionel Turner expressed surprise that Weber had sued the union as well as the company. "It isn't right to be an officer of the union and then sue it like that," he felt.

Kernell Goudia, a Black worker in a skilled job who credits the affirmative action program with getting him a better deal, defended the union program. "A lot of people saw the need to have minorities in the crafts. None of us had experience, so how could we get into the training program otherwise? It would have been 10 to 15 years before we got in. We didn't have the damn seniority."

Women were part of the agreement too, but it didn't last long enough to get to them.

The Brian Weber case has become a rallying point for the anti-labor and racist forces throughout the country. A batch of "friend of the court" briefs have been entered by right-wing foundations. The traditional enemies of the labor and civil rights movements - the press and radio, big industry, and of course, the right wing organizations - have either distorted or buried the stories about it.

But the labor movement is becoming more and more aware of the inherent dangers of the Weber position. The AFL-CIO recently filed an amicus brief with the Supreme Court and other unions are in the process of doing so. Rank and file groups, including National Steelworkers Rank and File Committee, plan to do so.

Our own union, USWA, has had a mixed reaction to the suit. As a defendant along with Kaiser the union opposed Weber. But it did not bring in testimony necessary to the case - that there had been prior discrimination at Kaiser, fearing that it would throw itself open to suit. It thereby let Weber win.

It is astonishing to note that up to this point no Black worker or organization has had any testimony in this case!

Lynch Lending Fight

Since the acceptance of the case by the Supreme Court USWA has taken a better stance. Vice President Leon Lynch has been going around the country (where he can be invited by the district directors) rallying the members of the union to express opposition to the appeals court decision in favor of Weber. He was the featured speaker at a civil rights conference called by District 31.

The rank and file must continue to press for more support of the USWA fight. We need more district meetings. We need resolutions and motions in the local unions. We need invitations extended to Brother Lynch. We need to create a climate of rejection of "reverse discrimination."

Labor Today, the rank and file paper, is sponsoring a conference in March to rally support (write Labor Today Associates, 343 S. Dearborn, Room 600, Chicago, IL 60604 for more information).

This is an important fight against the attack on the right of all unions to bargain collectively.

The resolution below was adopted unanimously by USWA Local 65, an 8,000 member local at U.S. Steel in Chicago. Similar resolutions have been passed by other major locals; such as 1010 (18,000 members), 1014 (14,000 members) and 1104 (7,500 members).

We strongly urge that you help such a resolution adopted in your local. Let us know if you do so we can help get the word out.

WHEREAS; The recent 19th Constitutional Convention of the USWA adopted a Civil Rights Resolution which states: "Employer sponsored right-wing 'Legal Foundations' and others have challenged our Union's right to negotiate fair and even handed affirmative action programs such as The Steel Industry Consent Decree and comparable programs in other industries, and our Union has vigorously resisted these challenges;" And

WHEREAS; The court suit of Brian Weber in challenging the Affirmative Action Program of our Union at the Kaiser Aluminum Plant in Gramercy, La., strikes at the heart of our unity of our Union as well as undermining all agreements reached between the USWA and the steel companies; And

WHEREAS; Affirmative action programs such as the one at Kaiser are a small step towards correcting the many years of discriminatory hiring and promotional practices of the steel industry;

THEREFORE BE IT RESOLVED; That Local ___ reaffirms its support of Affirmative Action Programs with quotas to Guarantee Job Equality for minorities and women;

AND BE IT FURTHER RESOLVED; That we support our International Union in its action to alert our Union Membership and the Labor Movement to the threat to all working people posed by the Weber case now before the U.S. Supreme Court;

AND BE IT FURTHER RESOLVED; That copies of this resolution be sent to the press, the U.S. Supreme Court, and to our International Officers in Pittsburgh.

(Willie Hill, Recording Secretary & John Chico, President of Local 65).

National Steelworkers Rank and File Committee *Report* (1979?). Mimeograph flier in possession of editors.

10.   HIGH COURT DECISION BACKS AFFIRMATIVE ACTION ON JOBS

By David L. Perlman

Labor Hails Ruling As 'Total Victory'

The Supreme Court upheld a voluntary affirmative action agreement negotiated by the Steelworkers and agreed with the AFL-CIO that a union and an employer can set up a plan to overcome racial imbalance even if neither party has been guilty of past discrimination.

"We are delighted with the decision," AFL-CIO President George Meany said. It allows unions and employers to use the collective bargaining process to speed up "elimination of the vestiges of centuries of racial injustice."

The 5-2 decision, rejecting a "reverse discrimination" charge brought by a white worker at a Kaiser Aluminum plant in Louisiana, was hailed as "a total victory" by the Steelworkers.

It validates similar affirmative action training agreements with other aluminum producers and the major steel and container companies, the union said, and will encourage voluntary action elsewhere.

The national agreement with Kaiser that was tested in the Supreme Court sought to remedy a virtual absence of blacks in skilled craft jobs at a number of plants. The imbalance reflected the lack of opportunities for minorities in the communities and not illegal discrimination at the hiring gate, which could have been corrected by a court order.

At the bargaining table, the union and the company agreed to set up in-plant training programs that would give both black and white production workers an opportunity to acquire higher-paid skills.

The agreement set aside 50 percent of the training slots for under-represented minority workers until their ratio in skilled jobs matched their proportion in the community.

Once in the program, all trainees had to meet the same rigorous standards that require an average of three years of on-the-job training, supplemented by classroom instruction and home study.

A divided federal appellate court agreed with the reverse discrimination charge of a white worker, Brian F. Weber, who didn't have the seniority for one of the training slots open to white workers but had longer service than several black workers accepted for the program.

The Steelworkers and the AFL-CIO contended in a joint brief to the Supreme Court and in oral argument that the imbalance in skilled jobs was undesirable and voluntary efforts to remedy it should not be blocked by a narrow reading of the Civil Rights Act that distorts the law's intent.

While the path it took may not have been required by law, the union said, it was certainly not prohibited by law. And the fact remains that the affirmative action program "created opportunities for both black and white USWA members which neither would have enjoyed otherwise."

Justice William Brennan, writing for the Supreme Court majority, found as the AFL-CIO had urged that Congress had "left employers and unions in the private sector free to take . . . race-conscious steps to eliminate manifest racial imbalance in traditionally segregated job categories."[10]

Since the agreement does not involve state action and was adopted voluntarily, he said, the only issue before the court was whether Title VII of the Civil Rights Act—the fair employment provision—forbids such a plan.

It does not, the court majority concluded, and "it would be ironic indeed if a law triggered by a nation's concern over centuries of racial injustice" were used to prevent voluntary, private measures to overcome inequities.

Brennan cautioned against an assumption that all affirmative action plans would be upheld by the court, and his decision declined to "define in detail the line of demarcation between permissible and impermissible affirmative action plans."

But he did give a strong indication of the criteria the Supreme Court would apply by noting that the purpose of the Kaiser plan "mirrors" the intent of the Civil Rights Act, "to break down old patterns of racial segregation and hierarchy."

Furthermore, the program "does not unnecessarily trammel the interests of the white employees" and "does not require the discharge of white workers and their replacement with new black hires."

It provides an opportunity for whites as well as blacks, and its racial quota is a temporary measure to be dropped after the racial imbalance has been eliminated.

Dissenting from the opinion were Chief Justice Warren E. Burger and Justice William H. Rehnquist, who contended that the court majority was sub-stituting its own views of desirable social conduct for the specific language of the law. Justices Lewis F. Powell, Jr., who has been ill, and John Paul Stevens did not participate in the case.[11]

Meany said the reasoning of the Supreme Court majority exactly paralleled the AFL-CIO understanding of Title VII of the Civil Rights Act.[12]

He found the decision "a victory for all who, like the AFL-CIO, believe in racial justice and who are committed to private voluntary action to end discrimination."

Leon Lynch, Steelworkers vice president for human affairs, expressed appreciation to all of the organizations that backed the union's position in the case and said the decision will enable unions and employers to adopt similar programs "without having to worry about reverse discrimination suits."

The Supreme Court decision makes a clear distinction between the Weber case, involving a voluntary affirmative action agreement in the private sector, and the earlier Bakke case in which the court overturned a governmental quota system involving admission to a state medical school.[13]

While the AFL-CIO did not take a position on the Bakke case, an Executive Council statement following the Supreme Court decision stressed the federation's continuing commitment to affirmative action.

That council statement, which set the stage for the AFL-CIO to join the Steelworkers in defending the negotiated job training program, urged "aggressive, positive efforts to integrate, instead of mere passive agreement not to discriminate."

AFL-CIO News, June 30, 1979.

11.   A KIND OF 'TOLERANCE'

By Tom Wicker

NEW YORK -- Congress has prohibited racial discrimination in public accommodations. If blacks happen some night to book most of the rooms in a formerly whites-only hotel, are whites who are unable to get a reservation there the victims of racial discrimination?

Few would argue that they are. But Congress has prohibited racial discrimination in employment, too. If blacks, therefore, are now getting training and some jobs that only whites used to receive, are the displaced whites victims of racial discrimination?

They are apt to think so, and understandably, if they have reason to feel that the black's color had something to do with his getting the job or the training. Shouldn't an end to racial discrimination mean that employment practices must be entirely "color-blind" (a phrase rarely heard in the days when blacks lost jobs because of their color).

But the Supreme Court has just ruled that in eradicating racial discrimination in employment, some consideration of color may be permitted because it is necessary to achieve the desired result. A good many white Americans are nevertheless likely to agree with Bryan Weber, who lost his suit against Kaiser Aluminum, that he was a victim of the racial discrimination that the Civil Rights Act of 1964 was enacted to prohibit.

This view -- that black workers in Kaiser's plant in Gramercy, La., received preferential training because they are black, and that this discriminated against Weber because he is white -- "is not without force," as Justice Brennan noted in the majority opinion. In fact, two lower courts have sustained that argument, and Justice Rehnquist observed in a biting dissent that the Supreme Court majority had rejected it only "by a tour de force reminiscent not of jurists such as Hale, Holmes and Hughes, but of escape artists such as Houdini."

But it also requires the agility of a Houdini to escape the larger purpose of the act in question "to put an end to the kind of racial discrimination against blacks that since the emancipation proclamation has been pervasive in American life. No one in 1964, either in Congress or out, was in doubt about that, and no reading of the legislative record can dispute it.

The Weber argument that Justice Rehnquist found conclusive rests on the assumption that the remedy Congress intended for racial discrimination and employment was color-blind employment practices. But that is not a remedy for the victims of an existing evil: It is a prescription for the elimination of the evil itself. And it cannot reasonably be supposed that Congress sought to eliminate a conceded, undeniable evil, but refused to permit a remedy for those who had already suffered its effects.

Two workers, one white, one black, of equal physical and mental ability, enter the employment of a company. After 10 years, because of racial discrimination, the white worker has a high supervisory position and twice the salary of the black, who remains at a low level job. At this point, Congress orders color-blind employment practices. The kind of discrimination of which the black was a victim must thereafter cease; but he remains at his low level job and his low salary, while the white retains all his ill gained advantages.

That would be no remedy for the victim. Nor would it be much of a remedy if the only redress available to the black was to hire a lawyer and bring a suit, a difficult, costly process not readily available to the unskilled poor -- particularly since the Burger court has limited the use of class action suits. Moreover, had Congress intended that nothing could or should

be done to provide a practical remedy for victims conceded to exist, it could
have said so.

It did not; it said only that employers like Kaiser could not be required
to give preferential treatment to blacks or any other group, except after
having been found guilty of discrimination against them. Congress did not
say that Kaiser could not voluntarily seek to diversify its work force or
make planning and advancement opportunities more readily available to all its
workers, blacks as well as whites. It did not say that levels and avenues
of employment traditionally closed to blacks might not be open to them by the
voluntary acts of employers and unions.

Rehnquist complained that the ruling rested on "a tolerance for the very
evil that the law was intended to eradicate" and offered no "clue as to what
the limits on that tolerance may be."

But to adopt his and Bryan Weber's narrow construction of the Civil
Rights Act would mean that the admitted effects of the evil could not be
eradicated for years, if ever. And the Kaiser affirmative action plan, the
only one specifically approved by the court, states its own limit on the kind
of "tolerance" necessary for eradication. It is to remain in force only until
the number of blacks in skilled jobs reaches the proportion of blacks in the
labor force from which Kaiser plants recruit.

New York Times, July 2, 1979.

12. COURT OVERSTEPS BOUNDS

By George F. Will

WASHINGTON -- The Supreme Court's 5-2 decision in the Weber case completes
the process of turning the civil rights impulse inside out, and standing the
1964 Civil Rights Act on its head. The decision affirms, resoundingly, the
right to discriminate racially.

Under federal pressure, Brian F. Weber's union and Kaiser Aluminum and
Chemical Corp. designed a reverse discrimination plan to eliminate "racial
imbalances" in Kaiser's craft work force. The plan reserved for blacks 50
percent of the places in certain training programs. Blacks with less
seniority received preference over Weber, who charged that this violated
Title VII of the 1964 Act, which says:

"It shall be an unlawful employment practice for an
employer . . . to discriminate against any individual . . .
because of such individual's race . . . to limit or classify
his employees . . . in any way which would . . . adversely
affect (any individual) . . . because of . . . race. . . ."

Having won in two lower courts, Weber lost in the Supreme Court, where
the majority argued, incredibly, that a literal reading of Title VII must be
inappropriate because it conflicts with what the majority insists is the
"spirit" of the Act. And because Title VII says it shall not be construed to
"require" reverse discrimination, the majority says, against an ocean of
contrary evidence, that Congress must have meant to "permit" such discrimination.

Justice Rehnquist's dissent, with Chief Justice Burger concurring,
relentlessly demonstrates that the majority does violence to the Court's
previous construction of, and the unambiguous legislative history of, Title
VII.

In 1971, in its first construction, the Court held that "discriminatory
preference, for any group, minority or majority, is precisely and only what
Congress has proscribed." In 1978, in its most recent construction, the
Court said: "It is clear beyond cavil that the obligation imposed by Title
VII is to provide an equal opportunity for each applicant regardless of race,
without regard to whether members of the applicant's race are already proportionately represented in the work force."

Rehnquist demonstrates that what the Court previously called Title VII's "uncontradicted legislative history" is unambiguous, and contradicts the majority's bizarre contention that Congress intended to "permit" reverse discrimination.

Rep. Emanuel Celler, D-N.Y., who introduced the 1964 Act in the House, said it would "prevent . . . employers from discriminating against or in favor of workers because of race." In 83 days of Senate debate, supporters of the Act took pains to refute all other interpretations.[14]

Sen. Hubert Humphrey, D-Minn., the prime mover, said Title VII forbids action "based on race." It "provides that race shall not be a basis for making personnel decisions." It "would prohibit preferential treatment for any particular group."[15]

Sen. Thomas H. Kuchel, R-Calif., said: "Employers and labor organizations could not discriminate in favor of or against a person because of his race . . . The bill . . . is color-blind."[16]

Sen. Leverett Saltonstall, R-Mass.: Title VII "provides no preferential treatment for any group of citizens. In fact, it specifically prohibits such treatment." And so on.[17]

Reverse discrimination may be the most direct way of building a black middle class. A black middle class is devoutly to be desired. Nevertheless, it should be promoted lawfully.

Perhaps the Court majority has expressed what Congress should have intended in the 1964 Act; or what Congress somehow "really" intended but for some reason gave no evidence of intending; or what Congress would intend were it to pass the 1964 Act in 1979. But Rehnquist's dissent is unanswerable on what is, or should be, the central point: What does the language of the Act and the record of the debate show that Congress actually intended?

Neither the words of the statute, nor words said about it, sustain the majority's social preferences. So the majority baldly asserts that the "spirit" of the Act permits what the letter of the Act forbids.

The majority opinion is reasoned, but there is precious little judicial reasoning about social justice and how best to achieve it; there is the reasoning of well-intentioned legislators. But the reasoning is not discernibly grounded in a judicial responsibility.

The Weber decision suggests that the pertinent question is not whether this is a "conservative" or "liberal" Court, but whether this is, properly speaking, a court at all.

The New York Times, July 2, 1979.

13. VOLUNTARY AFFIRMATIVE ACTION MEETS GOALS OF CIVIL RIGHTS ACT

The following is excerpted from the majority opinion by U.S. Supreme Court Justice William Brennan in the Weber case upholding a voluntary affirmative action agreement negotiated by the Steelworkers and Kaiser Aluminum.

Congress's primary concern in enacting the prohibition against racial discrimination in Title VII of the Civil Rights Act of 1964 was with "the plight of the Negro in our economy." (Remarks of Sen. Humphrey). Before 1964, blacks were largely relegated to "unskilled and semiskilled jobs." Because of automation the number of such jobs was rapidly decreasing. As a consequence "the relative position of the Negro worker (was) steadily worsening. In 1947 the nonwhite unemployment rate was only 64 percent higher than the white rate; in 1962 it was 124 percent higher." Congress considered this a serious social problem.

Congress feared that the goals of the Civil Rights Act--the integration of blacks into the mainstream of American society--could not be achieved unless this trend were reversed. And Congress recognized that that would not be possible unless blacks were able to secure jobs "which have a future."

Accordingly, it was clear to Congress that "the crux of the problem

(was) to open employment opportunities for Negroes in occupations which have
been traditionally closed to them," and it was to this problem that Title
VII's prohibition against racial discrimination in employment was primarily
addressed.

It plainly appears from the House Report accompanying the Civil Rights
Act that Congress did not intend wholly to prohibit private and voluntary
affirmative action efforts as one method of solving this problem.

Given this legislative history, we cannot agree with the respondent that
Congress intended to prohibit the private sector from taking effective steps
to accomplish the goal that Congress designed Title VII to achieve.

The very statutory words intended as a spur or catalyst to cause
"employers and unions to self-examine and to self-evaluate their employment
practices and to endeavor to eliminate, so far as possible, the last vestiges
of an unfortunate and ignominious page in this country's history," Albemarle
v. Moody, cannot be interpreted as an absolute prohibition against all private, voluntary, race-conscious affirmative action efforts to hasten the
elimination of such vestiges.

It would be ironic indeed if a law triggered by a nation's concern over
centuries of racial injustice and intended to improve the lot of those who
had "been excluded from the American dream for so long," constituted the
first legislative prohibition of all voluntary, private, race-conscious
efforts to abolish traditional patterns of racial segregation and hierarchy.

We need not today define in detail the line of demarcation between
permissible and impermissible affirmative action plans. It suffices to hold
that the challenged Kaiser-USWA affirmative action plan falls on the permissible side of the line. The purposes of the plan mirror those of the statute.
Both were designed to break down the patterns of racial segregation and hierarchy. Both were structured to "open employment opportunities for Negroes in
occupations which have been traditionally closed to them."

At the same time the plan does not unnecessarily trammel the interests
of the white employees. The plan does not require the discharge of white
workers and their replacement with new black hires. Nor does the plan create
an absolute bar to the advancement of white employees; half of those trained
in the program will be white.

Moreover, the plan is a temporary measure; it is not intended to maintain
racial balance, but simply to eliminate a manifest racial imbalance. Preferential selection of craft trainees at the Gramercy plant will end as soon as
the percentage of black skilled craft workers in the Gramercy plant approxi-
mates the percentage of blacks in the local labor force.

We conclude, therefore, that the adoption of the Kaiser-USWA plan for
the Gramercy plant falls within the area of discretion left by Title VII
to the private sector voluntarily to adopt affirmative action plans designed
to eliminate conspicuous racial imbalance in traditionally segregated job
categories.

AFL-CIO News, July 7, 1979.

14. THE WEBER DECISION

By James Johnson

The recent decision of the Supreme Court to turn back the challenge of
Brian Weber to affirmative action represented a major victory for Black
people, the labor movement and indeed all progressive-minded individuals in
this land.

Brian Weber, a white factory worker, contended in his suit that the
Kaiser Aluminum and Chemical Corporation and the United Steelworkers of
American illegally discriminated against whites when they set up an on-the-
job craft-training program at a Gramercy, La., plant that reversed half of
its slots for minority workers. The program was initiated to correct an
imbalance that saw only 1.8% of skilled jobs going to Afro-Americans in a
city whose population is 40% Black.

Justice William Brennan, writing for the 5 to 2 majority, stated:

"It would be ironic indeed if a law triggered by a nation's concern over centuries of racial injustice and intended to improve the lot of those who had been excluded from the American dream for so long constituted the first legislative prohibition of all voluntary, private, race-conscious efforts to abolish traditional patterns of racial segregation and hierarchy."

The court's decision dealt a major blow to racism, those who profit from it, and the main ideological weapon used against affirmative action programs, the myth of reverse discrimination.

The ruling provided clear affirmation of the immense power of public opinion, for the decision was not arrived at in the court's chambers alone. The court was forced to rule against Weber because hundreds of thousands of Americans, recognizing Weber's challenge as a threat to the working class as a whole, marched, rallied, lobbied and wrote thousands of letters in support of affirmative action.

Weber's racist challenge evoked a united response and fightback from the Black community, which spearheaded the struggle. There were other forces though which helped to make victory possible. Trade unionists throughout the land forced their leadership to take a forthright position against the Weber challenge. Consequently, the mighty power of labor which includes a disproportionately large percentage of Black workers in the basic industries, united with the Black liberation movement into a coalition which recalled the glorious days of the CIO and the civil rights movement when other major victories were won.

The women's role, especially in the trade union movement, contributed significantly to the victory. This unity of forces foreshadows the type of coalition that must be built if affirmative action and other people's victories are to be extended.

The victory, however, is not complete. The decision should be viewed as a door opener for more vigorous action. The court's decision leaves open the possibility that other affirmative action plans may be impermissible. It also failed to define what constitutes "traditional patterns of segregation."

The victory will not be complete until affirmative action moves from the voluntary to compulsory stage. Compulsory affirmative action must begin with all public sector jobs. Nor should the federal government be permitted to provide contracts to any employer who does not have the enforceable affirmative action program.

In 1952, Charles E. Wilson, the president of General Motors, expressed the sentiments of all monopolists and other reactionaries when he stated, "What's good for General Motors is good for the country." We must untiringly explain the relation of Black freedom to progress and democracy by proclaiming loud and clear, "What's good for Black folks is good for all the exploited and oppressed in this country!"

Black Liberation Journal, 3 (Summer, 1979):6-7.

15.   APPEAL OF BLACK CONSERVATIVES RINGS HOLLOW TO WORKERS, POOR

By Norman Hill

In mid-December, newspapers devoted front-page coverage to a conference of blacks in San Francisco. However, what made the conference noteworthy was not its size--there were about 100 participants--nor the range of the organizations which were represented--few of the participants could be said to represent significant black constituencies. What was special about the meeting, what made it news, was the fact that it was a gathering of black conservatives.

Of equal importance was the fact that the conference was sponsored by a conservative foundation which Ronald Reagan helped found in the early 1970s. In 1980 Ronald Reagan failed to attract a significant portion of the black vote. The overwhelming majority of black community and political leaders endorsed President Carter in his unsuccessful bid for re-election. Yet despite little black enthusiasm for Ronald Reagan, a number of black intellectuals and professionals have begun to embrace Reagan's conservative economic positions.

To some extent there is evidence to suggest that there is a small constituency for conservative political ideas in the black community. However, despite the growth of a black upper-middle class of professionals and businessmen who might be drawn to the conservative siren song of tax cuts, the overwhelming majority of blacks are workers and the poor. For them the appeal of black conservatism will right hollow, and for this reason one can confidently predict that blacks will continue to be a solid voting block which backs pro-labor candidates who support policies dedicated to a more equitable distribution of wealth.

Nonetheless, the two-day conference in San Francisco indicates that a debate will have to begin for the first time within the black community on political options. This debate, in my view, will be a healthy one insofar as it helps sharpen the arguments of black liberals and moderates.

Who, then, are the black conservatives and who do they stand for? The two leading prononents of black conservatism are Prof. Thomas Sowell, an economist from the Hoover Institution, and Prof. Walter Williams of Temple University in Philadelphia. Both are strong opponents of organized labor, which they claim limits opportunities for blacks. Their view, however, flies in the face of the evidence that organized labor, more than any other institution in American life, has opened its doors to increased black participation. Indeed, today, over 30 percent of black workers are union members. Rather than adopting a policy of exclusion, the labor movement has sought better working conditions for all its workers, irrespective of race. And, most importantly, unions effectively represent their members, who on the average receive $2,000 a year more than non-union workers and have better health and retirement benefits.

A second favorite target of Sowell and Williams is the minimum wage. They argue that the minimum wage is responsible for the inordinately high rate of black teenage unemployment and propose that it be eliminated entirely. At the least, they feel, a sub-minimum wage should be established for teen-agers. Their prescription for black teenage unemployment would be worse than the disease it is meant to cure. For a teenage sub-minimum wage would displace unskilled adult workers, a large proportion of whom are blacks with family obligations.

Under conditions of full employment, where every adult is guaranteed a job, the implementation of the youth sub-minimum wage would be of less serious consequence. Under conditions where unemployment stands at nearly 8 percent nation-wide and with figures several percentage points higher among blacks, the implementation of a youth sub-minimum wage would produce disastrous consequences for adult black unskilled workers.

Yet despite the fact that the views of Sowell and Williams are not in the interests of most blacks, the black conservatives cannot be dismissed as mere oddities. They are reflective of the sense of frustration with the state of the economy most blacks have felt in the last decade. In this way they mirror the dissatisfaction which moved many Americans to vote for Ronald Reagan.

If the conservative policies which Walter Williams and Thomas Sowell espouse are implemented by the new Administration, blacks and all working Americans will be able to judge the merits of the conservative approach. If history is to serve as any guide, these policies will be found wanting and will be repudiated in future elections.

And within the black community, those who have consistently favored progressive social programs and who have actively participated in the labor movement should welcome the opportunity to challenge the views of the black conservatives. Complacency can hardly be characterized as indicative of leadership. And the coming Reagan years give little reason for us to be complacent.

AFL-CIO News, February 7, 1981.

16. ADMINISTRATION POLICIES FAIL TO
ADDRESS NEEDS OF BLACKS

By Norman Hill

In the six months he has been President, Ronald Reagan has failed to articulate anything approaching a coherent policy on matters of racial inequality and poverty. Aside from generalities concerning the need to combat discrimination and to bolster productivity, the Administration shows no sign of having given serious thought to the plight of what has come to be called the black underclass.[18]
This underclass has been a persistent fact in the life of American society for many decades, and its ranks continue to swell.
The typical Reagan Administration response to the problem of black poverty and unemployment has been to assert that only the private sector can resolve the problems faced by blacks and others who are poor. Help business and industry, the Reagan argument goes, and you will help poor blacks and all poor Americans improve their lot. However, a glance at the recent history of black unemployment and impoverishment gives little indication that the Reagan approach will work.
Since World War II, the rate of black unemployment has stood at roughly twice that of white unemployment. This ratio has remained constant in times of economic prosperity and through periods of economic decline, through periods of inflation and periods of price stability. No matter how the economy has been doing, blacks seem disproportionately to shoulder the burdens of unemployment.
What improvement has been made by blacks in the last 35 years can be attributed to increased education. Blacks who have received adequate training and education have made tremendous strides economically. Black women college graduates, for example, today earn slighly more than their white counterparts. But the Reagan Administration has implemented massive cuts in federal aid to education and has drastically cut funding for a number of training and employment programs which seek to prepare minorities and the poor for meaningful private sector employment--precisely the initiatives one would expect the President to support.
Of equal importance is the Reagan approach of "states' rights." The Administration is a vocal proponent of block grants and of giving increased power to the states. Yet it is precisely at the regional and state level that, for historical reasons, discrimination remains a significant problem. For example, due to a variety of complex factors, black workers in the South earn 78 percent of the income of white Southerners. Throughout the rest of the country, however, the earnings of black and white workers are nearly identical.
An approach that puts emphasis on "states' rights" will prove unable to diminish the discrepancy between the earnings of Southern whites and blacks. Federal action must be a component in diminishing these differences. And it is precisely such federal intervention that President Reagan appears to oppose.
Recently, the Gallup Organization conducted a poll of the views of the black population. The results are both interesting and ominous, for they indicate a deepening division between blacks and whites, in some measure as a direct consequence of the policies of the Reagan Administration.
The Gallup study found that while 55 percent of whites were optimistic about what 1981 would bring to them personally, only 18 percent of blacks expected a better year and 48 percent expected things would be worse.
Similarly, in February a *Newsweek* magazine poll found that 52 percent of blacks expected things would get worse for them during Reagan's presidency and only 8 percent felt things would improve. In April, while President Reagan enjoyed a 74 percent approval rating among whites, only 25 percent of blacks approved of the President's performance.
In the late '60s and early '70s, when blacks were experiencing some social advancement, polls registered a significant sense of progress. In 1969, for example, 70 percent of blacks felt that the situation of blacks had improved during the previous five years. In 1981 only 30 percent felt this is true.

The Gallup survey reveals one very dangerous trend. Only the barest majority of blacks (51 percent) rejects violent protest as a means of accomplishing goals, and two-thirds of blacks agree that the only time the federal government really pays attention to blacks is when they resort to violence. This sense of frustration and rage must be confronted. Yet in the context of the Reagan Administration's retreat from necessary social programs and in the Administration's failure to confront the reality of racial inequality, there are the seeds of disaster.

Black Americans have viewed the Administration with skepticism since Ronald Reagan took his oath of office. Yet the President has made no serious effort to diminish this skepticism by developing a policy which addresses the specific needs and problems faced by blacks. Glib generalizations and assertions that the private sector will resolve the plight of the black poor do not constitute a coherent policy on black inequality. They constitute a serious failure of leadership.

In defending his economic policies, Ronald Reagan frequently asserts that "a rising tide lifts all boats." He, however, appears to have forgotten that those who are without boats may very well drown.

AFL-CIO News, August 22, 1981.

17. PROGRESS OF BLACK AMERICANS
REVERSED UNDER GOP POLICIES

By Gus Tyler

In *Source,* the official publication of the Republican National Committee, there appears an intriguing short piece under the title: "The Reagan Economic Program: An Agenda for All Americans." The brief item makes it clear that "all Americans" very specifically includes "black Americans."

Here is a word-for-word repetition of this most unusual story:

"Black unemployment declined from 10.7 percent to 6.4 percent during the '60s, but increased from 6.4 percent to 11.3 percent during the '70s.

"Black unemployment declined faster than white unemployment during the '60s, but rose faster during the '70s.

"Between 1959-59, a decade of growth and private prosperity, median black family income, in constant dollars, rose 6.4 percent—from $7,200 to more than $11,800.

"Yet, between 1969-79, the decade of public sector prosperity, real black median income declined by 3 percent."

That's the full account. It makes two points: first, that blacks did much better in the 1960s than in the 1970s; second, that jobs and income fell in the 1970s because of "public sector prosperity," whatever that means.

Now let's tap our memory banks. Who were the Presidents of the United States in the 1960s, when things were going better—jobs and income—for the blacks? For eight of the ten years, the Presidents were Democrats John F. Kennedy and Lyndon Baines Johnson.[19]

In the 1970s, Republican Richard Nixon and Gerald Ford were in the White House for seven of the 10 years. That decade of the '70s included the deep recession year of 1974-75.[20]

If any conclusion is to be drawn from the GOP figures, Democrats do better than Republicans for black America.

Putting parties aside, the '60s were characterized by expansionist policies, a desire to grow. The '70s were marked by restrictionist policies, a decision to create unemployment on the theory that, if people were out of work and could not buy, prices would not climb so rapidly.

As to that statement about "public sector prosperity," the implication that government was spending too much in the '70s seems strange since those years were dominated by Republican Presidents who were busy impounding funds and pinching pennies.

Actually, the government was tigtening up on spending in that decade. Federal employment was 4.19 percent of all wage and salaried people in 1960, but at the end of the '70s was down to 3.16 percent. Government spending (purchases) fell from 10.60 percent of the gross national product in 1960 to 8.77 percent by the end of the 1970s.

This should not come as a surprise, of course, since all three Presidents in the '70s--Nixon, Ford and Carter--believed that "cooling the economy," including the public sector, was the way to check inflation. As we know, these painful policies did not hold the price line, but they did do much damage to America, including its minorities as *Source,* the voice of the GOP, so succinctly proves.[21]

AFL-CIO News, February 27, 1982.

18.   WHERE REAGANOMICS HITS HARDEST:
MINORITIES & WOMEN

You don't have to be a statistician to figure it out. Just visit the unemployment lines in any racially mixed neighborhood and you'll see a disproportionate number of blacks, Latinos, other minorities, and women. The last hired, they're often the first fired during a recession or forced to hustle from one marginal job to another with long stretches in between.

While Reaganomics aids Big Business and the banks, working and middle-class Americans continue to suffer. What makes matters worse is that the American minorities are suffering even more. This country's lopsided distribution of wealth has a flip side: the lopsided distribution of joblessness and poverty when hard times hit.

The statistics merely confirm what you can see with your own eyes. Reagan has wrung inflation out of the economy by pursuing a deliberate policy of industrial slowdown, disinvestment, and layoffs. Record post-World War II unemployment has thrown a devastating number of white males out of work in the last two years -- but the impact on minorities has been doubly devastating. In February, when white joblessness stood at 9.2%, the unemployment rate for blacks and Latinos was 19.7% and 15.8%, respectively.

The greater job losses of blacks and Latinos stem from many causes -- the "last-hired, first-fired" syndrome, racism (including lack of educational opportunity), and the disproportionate numbers of minority workers in marginal shops and hard-hit industries.

The auto industry demonstrates some of these factors. Of the 30 largest auto plant shutdowns since 1980, all but a handful have occurred in the frostbelt or on the two coasts where Latinos and blacks have paid heavily. Minorities constituted about 11.2% of all U.S. workers in 1978-79 but held exactly twice that percentage of auto jobs; the 1979-83 auto slump has hit them especially hard. Of 270,000 indefinite layoffs in auto, 100,000 are minorities and women.

Did Reagan, David Stockman, and other White House "supply-siders" deliberately set out to make minorities pay for their trickle-down experiment? Some of them may have done exactly that. The perpetuation of a distinct, highly visible underclass of unemployed and marginally employed minorities not only tends to undercut the solidarity of all American workers, but it forces down the real wages of white workers as well. These facts are not lost on Big Business strategists.[22]

But there are other supply-siders -- and Reagan is probably one of them -- who honestly believe their massive cutbacks have been even-handed. "The Administration has reaffirmed the original vision which lies at the heart of our national commitment: an America that is color-blind," declares a recent White House defense of the Fiscal 1984 budget. Yet this belief is a good part of the problem, for the truth is that America is still more color-bound than color-blind. Blacks, Latinos, women and other minorities were never in as good a position to survive the budget cuts.

Take housing. Nearly a quarter of all black households are so poor that they have relied, until now, on some degree of federal aid for shelter.

Latinos have increasingly found themselves in the same predicament. Thus, when Reagan slashed federal housing subsidies by $20.4 billion and upped the rent that poor tenants pay, he destroyed far more minority households, proportionately, than white ones.

What about Reagan's 1981 tax cuts for homeowners? Not only did they continue the old mortgage interest deduction, but they created new tax subsidies for "gentrification" (well-to-do people moving into once-poor neighborhoods), the sale of homes by people 55 or older, and real estate speculators, while ignoring the real housing needs of minorities.

Blacks, Latinos, and other minorities were simply not as well-positioned as whites to pluck these plums. About 40% of all black families and 33% of all Latino families can be found in the bottom-fifth of all U.S. population when the measure is income; the top 50%, however, is 95% white. It is no surprise that while two-thirds of all white households own their own homes, only about two-fifths of all blacks and Latinos do.

The same inequalities mark the Administration's attack on nutrition, child welfare, job training, and health programs. When Reagan chopped $3.3 billion from the food stamp program in 1981-82, he drove a million people off the rolls. Another six million -- in particular the working poor -- had their food stamp allotments cut. Since 3 out of every 10 black families depended on food stamps for an adequate diet at the time of the cuts, blacks suffered disproportionately. So did Latinos.

Last year a million children from low-income families dropped out of the federal school lunch program; they couldn't pay the higher prices schools charged after Reagan cut back the federal contribution. We have already seen how blacks, Latinos, and other minorities are clustered in the low-income brackets. More of their children had to stop eating lunches, proportinately, than children from white families.

Black families represented 10% of the U.S. population but make up 30% of all the families living in poverty. Twice as many blacks and Latinos are unemployed, proportionately, as whites. Two-fifths of the families receiving Aid for Dependent Children (AFDC) benefits in 1981 were blacks.

Thus, when Reagan cut $1.5 billion from AFDC in Fiscal 1982-83, $1.7 billion from Medicaid, and $4.4 billion from job retraining programs, his budget axe was not "color-blind" but fell hardest, and proportionately most often, on black and brown necks.

The attack which Reaganomics has launched on the American working class has been so prolonged and severe that it has hurt the white majority more than any economic program since President Hoover's (1928-32). If proportionately the greatest impact has been on blacks, Latinos, and other minorities, numerically the greatest impact has been on whites. The basis for a multi-racial, multi-ethnic alliance of working people against Reaganomics is firmly in place.[23]

UAW Solidarity, 26, (April, 1983):16-17.

PART II

THE AFL-CIO AND THE CIVIL RIGHTS ISSUE

THE AFL-CIO AND THE CIVIL RIGHTS ISSUE

During the AFL-CIO merger negotiations, Walter Reuther announced that the CIO would insist that all affiliated unions be required to enlist members without regard to their race. Exactly what this meant, however, was unclear. The AFL had issued declarations against racial discrimination repeatedly since its formation, but it had not taken action against an affiliate on these grounds since the 1890s. In fact, the CIO's Committee on Civil Rights had refused even to recommend disciplining its own affiliates for discrimination. Nevertheless, most blacks initially were satisfied with the merger agreement's statement that the new federation would "constitutionally recognize the rights of all workers without regard to race," and that it would establish the internal machinery to guarantee non-discrimination. The statement did not specifically state by what means the principle would be implemented. Therefore, as early as the founding convention, those few black delegates in attendance demanded that the federation deny affiliation to any union that practiced racial discrimination. Their effort failed as did all subsequent efforts to pressure the federation along these lines. Thus, a long internal struggle began to force the organization to take firm action against the problem.

The leader in this struggle was A. Philip Randolph, one of two black vice presidents of the 27-man AFL-CIO Executive Council. Randolph had maintained his silence on the racism issue since the merger, but he and other black delegates came to the 1959 convention with a plan calling for the AFL-CIO's Civil Rights Department to determine the extent of discrimination and segregation in member unions, and then to initiate stern measures against those refusing to reform. Randolph demanded, however, that action be taken immediately against the railroad brotherhoods which barred or segregated Negroes for more than a half century. The resolution failed to pass under repeated confrontations between Randolph and the AFL-CIO leadership, and ultimately resulted in his censure at the 1961 convention. The chairman of the subcommittee which presented the report against Randolph was George M. Harrison, president of the Brotherhood of Railway Clerks, a union which had "jim crowed" Afro-Americans into segregated locals for decades.

The censure report also indicted the National Association for the Advancement of Colored People. The protests of black workers and their leaders had gained the attention of the NAACP, and just after the merger it announced that it would begin concentrating on the problems of Negro labor. In numerous speeches and reports, the civil rights organization attacked organized labor for its failure to correct even the most blatant forms of racism practiced in some of the member unions. The AFL-CIO executives denounced the NAACP for criticism so unrelenting that it was considered detrimental to the Negro-labor alliance.

By the mid-sixties George Meany had unveiled a stepped-up civil rights program calling for a more aggressive educational campaign, and assistance for black workers who wanted to file complaints of discrimination with the federal government under Title VII of the Civil Rights Act of 1964. This was the first step toward reestablishing the alliance forged by the CIO prior to its merger with the AFL between black civil rights workers and the more progressive labor leaders. Soon, A. Philip Randolph had been pacified as well, and the alliance again seemed secure.

THE AFL-CIO AND THE CIVIL RIGHTS ISSUE

THE AFL-CIO AND THE CIVIL RIGHTS STRUGGLE

1. AFL-CIO MERGER AGREEMENT

*AGREEMENT FOR THE MERGER OF THE AMERICAN FEDERATION OF LABOR AND THE
CONGRESS OF INDUSTRIAL ORGANIZATIONS*
Signed February 9, 1955

1. Agreement to Merge
The American Federation of Labor and the Congress of Industrial Organizations agree to create a single trade union center in America, through the
process of merger which will preserve the integrity of each affiliated national
and international union. They further agree upon the following principles and
the procedures to accomplish this end.
2. Principles of Merger
(a) It is recognized, as a fundamental basis for the merger of the AFL and
CIO, that each national and international union, federal labor union, local
industrial union and organizing committee (hereafter referred to as affiliated
union) holding a charter or certificate of affiliation granted by either
federation shall retain its charter or certificate and become, by virtue of
the merger, an affiliate of the merged federation.
(b) It is further recognized and agreed that the integrity of each
affiliated union in the merged federation shall be maintained and preserved.
In order to effectuate this principle, the Constitution of the merged federation shall contain a constitutional declaration for respect by each affiliate
of the established bargaining relationship of every other affiliate and against
raiding by any affiliate of the established collective bargaining relationship
of any other affiliate. The merged federation shall provide appropriate
machinery to implement this constitutional declaration.
(c) The parties further agree that, subject to the foregoing, each
affiliated union shall have the same organizing jurisdiction in the merged
federation as it had in its respective prior organization.
(d) The parties recognize that the above provisions may result in conflicting and duplicating organizations and jurisdictions. Where such is the
case, affiliates of the merged federation will be encouraged to eliminate
conflicts and duplications through the process of agreement, merger, or other
means, by voluntary agreement in consultation with the appropriate officials
of the merged federation.
(e) The merged federation shall be based upon a constitutional recognition
that both craft and industrial unions are appropriate, equal and necessary as
methods of trade union organization.
(f) The merged federation shall constitutionally recognize the right of
all workers, without regard to race, creed, color or national origin to share
in the full benefits of trade union organization in the merged federation.
The merged federation shall establish appropriate internal machinery to bring
about, at the earliest possible date, the effective implementation of this
principle of non-discrimination. . . .

Then we must think sobriety of our position as a nation and of the things
we like to feel are really in the tradition of America. We speak of our
freedom, we speak of the Founding Fathers, we speak of the Constitution and
the Bill of Rights. I think we have some right to be proud of those things,
to be proud of our tradition and our heritage; but I think we have no right
to complacently sit by as long as those rights are denied to any portion of
the population of this great country.
We have had striking evidence in the last few days, if we needed any such
evidence, that the Constitution of the United States and the Bill of Rights

and the civil liberties that we all like to boast of do not prevail in certain parts of our country for people whose skin is a little different in color than that of ourselves. We have men who call themselves statesmen, who are public servants elected by the people, and still who, in the interest of white supremacy, defy a decision of the United States Supreme Court in regard to desegregation. Yes, they are amending the Constitution to suit themselves insofar as its application is concerned, and what they are saying in effect is that this Constitution does not prevail in the Southland.

Proceedings of the First Constitutional Convention of the AFL-CIO, New York, December 5-8, 1955, pp. liv, 26.

2. CORRESPONDENCE TO THE MERGER CONVENTION

December 5, 1955

New York, N.Y.
President George Meany and President Walter Reuther, AFL-CIO Merger Convention, 71st Regiment Armory, Park Ave., 34th St.
The Negro Labor Committee sends you fraternal greetings and best wishes for a most successful merger convention. For twenty years the Negro Labor Committee has been the advocate of unity and has diligently practiced it. From our birth we have served all sections of labor regardless of affiliation or race or craft or creed except communism. We have survived every attempt to capture or destroy us. Your final merger will be appreciated around the world by all workers and progressives who have faith in the survival of democracy and those who brought unity about will live forever in the memory of man. Again success. Fraternally.

FRANK R. CROSSWAITH, Chairman,[24]
The Negro Labor Committee

December 5, 1955

New York, N.Y.
George Meany, President, AFL-CIO
71st Regiment Armory, N.Y.
The National Association for the Advancement of Colored People hails the birth of the AFL-CIO as a propitious step toward industrial democracy. As the free world's largest and most powerful trade union movement, the AFL-CIO now has the opportunity to demonstrate to all the peoples of the world that American labor is united in support of our nation's democratic ideals of equality, freedom and justice for all, irrespective of race, color, religion or national origin. We in the NAACP are confident that you will insist upon and adhere to these principles within your ranks and invite you to join with us in the struggle to secure for all Americans the rights and privileges guaranteed by the Constitution. As you enter this new era we congratulate you and assure you of our cooperation in our common cause of making our country a happy and prosperous land in which no man is favored or rejected by reason of such irrelevant considerations as race or religion or nationality.

ROY WILKINS,[25]
Executive Secretary

3. REPORT OF THE RESOLUTIONS COMMITTEE ON CIVIL RIGHTS, 1955

The AFL and the CIO have always believed in the principle and practice of equal rights for all, regardless of race, color, creed or national origin. Each federation has separately played a distinguished role in the continuing struggle to realize for all Americans the democratic rights promised to all by the Constitution of the United States.

The AFL-CIO is similarly pledged and dedicated to promote and defend the civil rights of all Americans. Its Constitution declares that one of its objects and principles is:

"To encourage all workers without regard to race, creed, color or national origin to share in the full benefits of union organization."

Another such object and principle of the new Federation is:

"To protect and strengthen our democratic institutions, to secure full recognition and enjoyment of the rights and liberties to which we are justly entitled, and to preserve and perpetuate the cherished traditions of our democracy."

Our Constitution likewise provides for a "Committee on Civil Rights" which:

"Shall be vested with the duty and responsibility to assist the Executive Council to bring about at the earliest possible date the effective implementation of the principle stated in this constitution of non-discrimination in accordance with the provisions of this constitution."

Thus the AFL-CIO stands dedicated no less than its predecessors to bring about full and equal rights for all Americans in every field of life.

Discrimination in Employment

Both the AFL and the CIO have been pre-eminent in the campaign to secure equality in the campaign to secure equality of employment opportunity to all workers. This campaign has several different facets.

Both federations have in the past repeatedly supported and urged the enactment of Federal fair employment practices legislation, to prohibit discrimination in employment because of race, creed, color or national origin.

During the past year several states and municipalities have enacted fair employment practice laws or ordinances, but year after year the threat of filibuster by Dixiecrat Senators has prevented fair employment practices legislation from receiving any real consideration by the Congress. This determined minority has been able to impose its will upon the Congress because Senate Rule 22 invites filibuster by making cloture virtually impossible. The authority vested in the Rules Committee in the House of Representatives has likewise sometimes enabled that Committee to act as a roadblock to progressive legislation.

In 1953, President Eisenhower established the President's Committee on Government Contracts, a revival of a similar committee which had functioned under President Truman. The Committee's function is to coordinate and assist the federal departments and agencies in the enforcement of the clauses prohibiting discrimination in employment which all government contracts are required to contain. Representatives of the AFL and the CIO were appointed and are serving as members of this Committee. [26]

This Committee has developed a strengthened non-discrimination clause, which specifically prohibits discrimination by government contractors in all phases of the employment relationship, including hiring, placement, training, promotion, tenure of employment and compensation. Since a large percentage of business firms have contracts with government agencies, this clause, if vigorously enforced, can do much to eliminate discrimination in employment. Already, on the initiative of the labor members of the Committee and with the cooperation of the International unions involved, the Committee has made limited progress toward eliminating discrimination in a number of industries and areas where heretofore discriminatory practices had prevailed.

Discrimination in employment, promotions or lay-offs because of race, color, religion, or national origin violates both the legal and moral rights of those who are discriminated against. Already substantial progress in ending discrimination in employment has been made by the negotiation and diligent policing of non-discrimination clauses in collective bargaining agreements. By giving full support to these clauses our affiliates can make a notable contri- bution toward the elimination of discrimination in a large sector of American industry. By creating appropriate internal machinery, our affiliates can assist in realizing these objectives.

Removal of Segregation in Public Facilities

One of the most notable triumphs for democracy in recent years is the progress which has been made toward ending segregation in public schools.
In 1954 the Supreme Court of the United States unanimously, and in clear and unequivocal language, declared that segregation in the public schools violates the United States Constitution. A year later it reiterated this decision, and ordered that those localities where segregation in the public schools still exists proceed with "all deliberate speed" toward its elimination. In response to these decisions of the nation's highest tribunal, a number of states and localities have already ended segregation in their public schools. The experience of these areas, and particularly of the District of Columbia with its large Negro population, has shown that there is no insurmountable obstacles anywhere to complying with the requirements of the nation's Constitution.
Unfortunately, however, some states and localities have sought to delay the end of segregation, and even to perpetuate it indefinitely, by a variety of flimsy and discreditable subterfuges and devices. We are confident that the courts will rebuke these tactics as rapidly as the cases come before them. Still worse, in one or two states the forces of racism and reaction are using the segregation issue as a rallying point for the creation of Ku Klux Klan-type organizations, such as the White Citizens Councils which seek by the vilest and most brutal methods to deny all political and civil rights to America's Negro citizens. [27]
There is every reason to expect that the Supreme Court will apply the doctrine of non-segregation to other types of public facilities, including all those which are supported or aided by federal or local taxes. It has already taken such action in the case of public parks. There have already been several lower court decisions to this effect, and even in the absence of such decisions, progress has been made in many communities in the elimination of racial barriers in trains and buses, public housing, public parks, and theatres and restaurants. The ICC has recently prohibited segregation on the nation's railroads and their facilities. In only a few years all branches of the Armed Forces have shifted from almost complete segregation to almost complete integration. Despite dire prodictions of disaster, this change has been accomplished smoothly and without incident; now, therefore, be it
RESOLVED, 1.   The AFL-CIO declares its strong support for an effective and enforceable fair employment practices act. We urge the enactment of similar legislation by all states and cities that do not now have such laws on their books.
2.   As an essential preliminary to the enactment of civil rights legisla- tion, and particularly of a fair employment practices act, we urge that the rules be so amended that the will of the Congress may not be stultified by a recalcitrant minority. Rule 22 should be changed to permit a majority of Senators present and voting to limit and close debate.
3.   Our affiliates should see to it that employers with whom they deal who hold federal contracts adhere to the letter and spirit of the non-discrim- ination clause required in government contracts. In addition, our affiliates should seek to have non-discrimination clauses included in every collective bargaining agreement they negotiate.
4.   The AFL-CIO wholeheartedly supports the decisions of the Supreme Court outlawing segregation in the public schools. We urge all of our affiliated state and local bodies to work with other liberal forces in their communities to facilitate a peaceful and effective transition to an unsegregated American educational system. We urge the Administration to

utilize the full powers of the federal government to frustrate and punish
unlawful attempts to block implementation of the Supreme Court's decision.
    5. We urge the Congress to enact legislation making lynching a federal
crime, and to invalidate state laws requiring the payment of a poll tax as a
prerequisite to voting.
    COMMITTEE CO-SECRETARY CURRAN: I move the adoption of the resolution.[28]
    PRESIDENT MEANY: You have heard the resolution on Civil Rights. The
motion is to adopt. The Chair recognizes Vice President Carey.
    VICE PRESIDENT CAREY: Mr. President and delegates, I rise in support of
the resolution. All of us, I am sure, are exceedingly grateful for this
inspiring address by Brother Marshall. In one sense, however, Vice President
Willard Townsend, Vice President A. Philip Randolph and I can feel that we were
the victims of discrimination, because doubtless everything that we were going
to say in addressing ourselves to this question of civil rights was splendidly
covered by Thurgood Marshall's remarks.[29]
    Therefore, I ask permission of President Meany and the Convention to place
in the record the statement I have prepared to give.
    I hope everyone will subscribe to this resolution so ably presented by the
Resolutions Committee and co-Secretary Joseph Curran.
    PRESIDENT MEANY: You have heard the motion and the request that Vice
President Carey be permitted to put his full intended remarks in the record.
Is there objection to that? Hearing none, we will vote on the motion with that
understanding.
    . . . The motion to adopt the resolution on Civil Rights was seconded and
carried unanimously.
    . . . Vice President Carey's complete remarks are as follows:
    VICE PRESIDENT CAREY: Mr. Chairman, I rise in support of the Resolution
before this Convention.
    The issue of Civil Rights was high on the agenda of the basic principles
that concerned the AFL-CIO Unity Committee during its negotiations leading to
this historic convention. This issue has been high on the agenda of public
discussion and political controversy for the last decade,--a decade marked by
substantial progress, undreamed of a few years ago. Also, this progress has
produced the paradoxical situation that finds many persons' civil rights being
violated daily.
    We, as a labor movement, have moved forward to carry out the principles
enunciated in this Constitution. The majority of the organizations comprising
the AFL-CIO have always believed in the principle of equal rights for all.
The labor movement has always played a distinguished role in the continuing
struggle to realize for all Americans the democratic rights promised by the
Constitution of the United States.
    The AFL-CIO is similarly pledged and dedicated. We are constitutionally
bound to encourage all workers without regard to race, creed, color or national
origin to share equally in the full benefits of union organization. However,
being practical men, we also recognize that worthy ideals and principles are
inadequate, unless we create machinery to implement and translate these ideals
into reality. Therefore, we established constitutional machinery which we
sincerely believe provides the necessary tools. In view of our experiences
and traditions, we believe the most practical kind of machinery for the
implementation of this non-discrimination policy is a constitutional committee
carefully drawn from a cross section of the new Federation.
    This kind of machinery proved effective in the CIO. In 1942, we created
the CIO Committee to Abolish Racial Discrimination which was succeeded by the
CIO Committee on Civil Rights. We discovered shortly after the creation of
CIO that enunciating a principle in a constitution was not enough. To put
that principle into effect required machinery and concentrated effort.
Without machinery, this principle would have remained a pious hope instead of
becoming one of our finest traditions.
    We found our next task was the creation of similar machinery in our
affiliated international organizations and state and city bodies. Today, many
of the former CIO unions have developed functioning machinery within their own
organizations, constantly working to extend these principles to the local
plant and community level. The next step was to recommend that our affiliated
unions include anti-discrimination clauses in their contracts with management.

This is where discriminatory patterns generally begin,--at the hiring gate, which in most instances, is management's sole responsibility.

Looking back, important milestones can be identified. One of the early milestones was the end of wage differentials based on race. This issue was fought out by a CIO union, aided by the CIO Committee to Abolish Discrimination, to a successful conclusion before the old War Labor Board.

We joined the AFL at the end of the war in lending our experience and resources to President Truman's Committee on Civil Rights. Boris Shishkin and I, working as a team, were successful in having many of the concepts that guide the labor movement accepted by this group of good citizens. The results of our efforts are reflected in the final report accepted by the American people entitled, "To Secure These Rights." Following publication of this report, the Supreme Court began to translate the Federal Government's responsibility to preserve the civil rights of each individual into decisions that are changing the patterns of American life. The Supreme Court in 1948 declared that racially restrictive covenants were no longer enforceable in the Federal Courts. The Supreme Court banned discrimination in eating places in the District of Columbia. In a series of decisions in the field of education the framework of segregation was narrowed. These decisions eloquently reaffirmed that our Constitution can and should be color blind.[30]

In retrospect, we can now see that these decisions were just a prelude to the important one. On May 17, 1954, and again in May, 1955, the Supreme Court unanimously and in clear unequivocal language, declared that in the field of public education, segregation has no place, that it is a denial of the equal protection of laws. This historic declaration promises our children a greater and more equal share in our democracy than we experienced. Moreover, the Court lost no time in applying the doctrine of non-segregation to other Federal and local tax-supported institutions and facilities. We have associated ourselves with this point of view and have implemented it with every means at our command. In this struggle, although the NAACP has taken the leadership in forging the law into an instrument of social precision to accomplish these objectives, the labor movement has always been closely associated and identified with the NAACP and other like-minded groups in this struggle. We supported amicus curiae briefs before the Supreme Court in this series of cases. But more important, we began utilizing our resources to implement these decisions through our machinery on the local level.

At the same time, we were working to put our own house in order. Our General Counsel and also a member of the Committee on Civil Rights, recommended we issue a directive that has proved to be prophetic and historic. We directed all state and city bodies to abolish segregated facilities in rest rooms, drinking fountains and other facilities. We banned separate meetings and functions on our property. This directive preceded the latest series of Supreme Court decisions declaring segregation in public facilities unconstitutional.

We next initiated a campaign to take the race tag off jobs. Working with one of our major unions, we began to develop a program designed to permit any worker, regardless of his color, to be promoted to any job which his seniority and skill entitled him to occupy. As this campaign has succeeded, we have developed tools and techniques available to other unions. This campaign marked the first time that the problems of discrimination in an entire industry had been attacked simultaneously.

We are confident that with the added strength and enthusiasm our new Federation will bring to this struggle, the advances of the last decades can be accelerated. We believe we can bring greater vitality to the task of completing democracy's unfinished business. We know in so doing we will immeasurably strengthen the American labor movement.

In view of the nature of its task, the AFL-CIO Civil Rights Committee must be regarded as the agency in the new Federation responsible for the formulation of policy in this vital area. Broadly speaking, the committee should recommend policies and programs for our new Federation. It should develop procedures and programs for the consideration and acceptance of our International Unions and state and city bodies. The committee should be the spokesman with governmental agencies, for our new Federation. It should have the responsibility of maintaining appropriate relationships with approved private organizations working in this field.

The resources and skills of the committee will always be available to our International Unions in working out the practical day-to-day problems that constantly arise as they seek to breathe life into our ideals. We must have faith--faith enough to dedicate ourselves to the realization of these values.

Also, we must clearly recognize that this task cannot be accomplished in a vacuum--it cannot be accomplished within the confines of the labor movement without, at the same time, fighting for the extension of these principles in the local communities in which we live and work.

We must constantly seek to strengthen those civic and community forces whose ideals and convictions and programs of action are consistent with ours. We must continue to support, plan and work with the NAACP, the National Urban League, the Jewish Labor Committee, and the many other organizations with which we share common ideological convictions.

The recent wave of terror and denial of constitutional rights in Mississippi and other Southern states must enlist our grave concern. They not only do violence to the rights and dignity of the victims, but they do violence to you and me. Our constitutional rights are *also* attacked. The emergence of the "White Citizens Councils" in Mississippi, the "States Rights in North Carolina," the "Tennessee Society to Maintain Segregation" and other similar organizations represent a new type of Ku Klux Klan.

We must realize that a more terrible, a new and more powerful type of Klan is attempting to rise in the South today than the Ku Klux Klan which followed the first World War. This time it is more dangerous, because it is ultra-respectable and does not hide behind sheets. This time it is openly led by prominent citizens, many of whom are elected local and state officials. This time it counts among its members and supporters: bankers, lawyers, powerful industrialists and plantation owners. It counts among its supporters state Governors, United States Senators and Congressmen.

Remember its birth! The White Citizens Councils came into being shortly after the 1954 decision of the Supreme Court outlawing segregation in public schools. Its organization was inspired by a speech made by Senator Eastland.

While this movement was organized on the surface to mobilize public opinion to delay and prevent the enforcement of the U.S. Supreme Court decisions outlawing segregation in the schools, the real purpose behind this movement is to use the desegregation issue to stop economic and social progress in the South.

There is substantial evidence that the movement is directed at trade unions. This fear stems from the AFL-CIO announcement that we will launch an effective organizing campaign among the working people of the South. This can be demonstrated by the fact that among the leaders of this new subversive movement are a number of individuals active in the anti-labor organizations who succeeded in securing enactment of "right-to-work" laws in our Southern states.

On October 23, 1955, they merged into a Southern Confederation of Pro-segregationists, under the name of the "Federation for Constitutional Government," directed by John U. Barr, who has been a spokesman for the manufacturers' associations in the South, a leader in the Dixiecrat Party of 1948, and a leader in all of the anti-labor organizations created in recent years.

In Charleston, South Carolina, a successful organizing campaign, conducted in a rubber fabric plant by the United Rubber Workers, came to an end when the local unit of the White Citizens Councils applied economic and social pressure on the white members to withdraw from the union, because it included both white and Negro workers on an equal basis. Other examples can be cited.

Every area of the South, where these councils have been organized, and have become a political and economic power, the normal process of justice has been diminished. At the same time, this campaign of terror and intimidation is showing its effect among prominent Southern liberals who are silent and lonely and have not spoken out against this menace. Many of the large Protestant church denominations have gone on record as approving the abolition of racial segregation as a public policy. However, when the local ministers attempt to put their religious beliefs into practice, they are immediately threatened and intimidated by these White Citizens Councils.

Organized labor constitutes the only other group which has economic and political influence in these major industrial centers of the South. Unless we of the trade union movement and like-minded community groups develop a program to expose this type of subversion, our liberties and future union organizing campaigns will be jeopardized. Equally important, unless we act promptly and decisively, our local unions risk being infiltrated by these organizations with their totalitarian philosophy. Such a situation could well sound the death knell to our efforts to bring the benefits of trade union organization to Southern workers.

This development has underscored the need for Federal legislation which will arm the Department of Justice to protect the civil rights of each citizen. More than one hundred civil rights bills were introduced during the last session of Congress. Not one was debated or voted upon,--a negative record consistent with that of previous Congressional sessions. The Administration continued to exercise no leadership in bringing any of these bills out of committee. Moreover, this negative performance of Congress is a total repudiation of the platforms of both parties, which have repeatedly pledged support of civil rights legislation.

The reign of terror in Mississippi, where three Negroes have already been killed under lynch law conditions, has dramatized the helplessness of the Federal government in protecting the civil rights of all Americans. Thus the United States, which has protested brutality and violence throughout the world, now stands mute and helpless when brutality and violence are used against United States citizens. This condition is the more tragic for these citizens were only seeking to exercise their right to vote and to enjoy other rights guaranteed under the Constitution. This cynical disregard of pledges by both major political parties will continue to leave our Government helpless, until we convince our elected representatives that there is a widespread demand and need for Congressional action on civil rights in the coming sessions of Congress. As President Meany has said, we must answer this challenge by increased political action.

Probably the most important event in the long history of the American labor movement is occurring in this historic convention. I am completely convinced that a united, democratic labor movement of 16 million Americans can be the greatest single force in our society for the swift expansion of civil rights and liberties in every sphere of our national life.

For the same reason our new merged labor movement should be more effective in organizing the unorganized, in legislative activity and politics because of its greater dedication and numerical strength. Our new movement must be more effective in both the quantity and quality of its efforts in the fields of civil rights and anti-discrimination.

Merger can be the threshold of a new future . . . a new future for the nation's working men and women, for the underprivileged and for minorities. Basically a unified labor movement inspires this hope!

Proceedings of the First Constitutional Convention of the AFL-CIO, New York, December 5-8, 1955, pp. 109-13.

4.   WHAT GOES ON HERE?

As the American Federation of Labor and the Congress of Industrial Organizations, totaling fifteen million workers in 145 international unions, formalize their merger next week in New York, the question of whether or not a Negro unionist becomes a member of the AFL-CIO executive council is a most pressing one.

This governing body will consist of twenty-seven vice presidents, but although Negro unionists number over 1,500,000, there seems at this writing no likelihood that any Negro will be a council member.

Alarmingly, the CIO executive committee has just voted against promoting Willard S. Townsend, president of the United Transport Service Employes and an outstanding Negro trade unionist, to a vice presidency, which would have automatically made him an AFL-CIO executive council member.

Considering that Mr. Townsend's union is a CIO pioneer and that the CIO has always boasted, with justice, of its championship of Negro labor and its vigorous opposition to racial job discrimination and exclusion, his rejection is ominous.

However, it is being rumored that Townsend was rejected because he is seeking Congressional nomination as a Republican in Chicago, while from the beginning the CIO has been the labor arm of the Democrats, through the political operations of CIO-PAC, which its members have been annually pressured into financially supporting.

The AFL, which will have seventeen of the twenty-seven vice presidents on the AFL-CIO executive council, has not named a Negro vice president either, although A. Philip Randolph, head of the Brotherhood of Sleeping Car Porters, joined the federation a quarter-century ago and is one of its most capable and honest executives.

Despite the fact that President George Meany (AFL) and Walter Reuther (CIO) expressed the desire that at least one Negro be on the executive council, nothing has been done—and the deadline is close.

This failure has understandably agitated Negro unionists who fear the new organization will be less forthright and determined in pressing for fair employment practices as a monopoly than the two groups did as competitors.

Reportedly immediate attention will be focused on organizing the millions of unorganized workers but there seems little likelihood that there will be any "Operation Dixie" approach for fear of antagonizing Southern white workers by too rapid organization and integration of Negroes.[31]

CIO unions have pledged themselves to contribute $1 per member to "organizing the unorganized" and the AFL hopes to do the same (which presages a $10-15 million fund); but that's far in the future, because the merger agreement requires that all present union officers be "frozen" into their jobs, which unduly burdens the combined treasury.

Most unions have done no big organizing since 1940, and now with the necessity for administrative economy, there will be a temptation to take the line of least resistance racially and to seek increasingly to win favor by identification with "community interests" (which in Dixie means following the racial pattern).

Nor is it reassuring that the AFL, the dominant partner in the new setup, has a far worse record than the CIO, the junior partner, in fighting labor jim crowism.

Under these circumstances, it is imperative that at least one Negro sit on the new executive council to help keep it in line with progress; and failure to elect one will intensify pessimistic speculations.

Pittsburgh Courier, December 3, 1955.

5. NEW DAY DAWNS FOR NEGRO LABOR IN AFL-CIO MERGER HERE

By Ethel L. Payne

A. Philip Randolph, president of the Brotherhood of Sleeping Car Porters and Willard S. Townsend, president of the United Transport Service Employees, were among 27 vice-presidents named to the newly merged AFL-CIO labor union last week.

The 27, together with George Meany, head of the unified body and William F. Schnitzler, secretary-treasurer, will comprise the Executive Council which will be the governing arm of the organization. And 11-member executive committee will handle the administrative details and carry out the policy.

Randolph's nomination was no surprise as a movement to get him on the council has been quietly booming for months, but it was unlikely until the eve of the ratification convention that a second Negro would be named. Townsend's appointment was virtually assured after CIO leaders emerged from an agreement caucus sparked by the news that Randolph was already in.

History Made

Thus, history was made and the significance of the rising prestige of Negroes in the American labor movement was duly paid tribute to when for the first time, two will have key policy making spots in running the affairs of an organization numbering 15 million workers, the largest in the world.

The gloom of pessimism shown by many union rank and file members that a moderate conversatism would nullify any attempts to vigorously attack discrimination within and without trade unionism was lifted somewhat when both the AFL and CIO moved decisively to assure strong action on this.

Some Grumbling

In separate conventions before the joint ratification meeting, both unions adopted resolutions against racial discrimination in all its forms. A center of interest was around the newly set up civil rights department of the unified organization. Critics of the clause in the constitution, providing for its establishment protested that it lacked authority to invoke sanctions against unions which practiced discrimination, and there was strong feeling that it would be just another token gesture. . . .

Named as chairman was James B. Carey, and selected to direct the department was Boris Shiskin, former research director of the AFL. George L. P. Weaver, assistant to Carey got the post of executive secretary under Shiskin.[32]

Following the conference between Meany and Randolph, it was learned that the committee which will direct the operation of the civil rights unit will be composed of seven AFL representatives and four CIO. Two of the AFL members it was learned are Milton P. Webster, first vice-president of the Sleeping Car Porters and Frank Evans, head of the Cleveland division of the UAW, AFL.[33]

In an exclusive interview for the *Defender* Publications, Randolph had this to say: "I believe the civil rights department of the unified labor movement can be made effective, despite its lack of sanction to be applied to unions that still maintain color bars.

This can be accomplished if Negro trade unionists will be ever vigilant and intelligently aggressive in fighting against discrimination on account of race or creed. The fight to completely eliminate color bars in trade unionism will never be abandoned by the Brotherhood of Sleeping Car Porters."

New York Age Defender, December 10, 1955.

6.   ABOUT RANDOLPH AND TOWNSEND

For the first time in the history of the American labor movement, Negroes will be included in the top echelon which will govern a huge force of more than 15 million people. Here are some thumbnail sketches of the two named last week at the ratification convention of the AFL-CIO.

A. PHILIP RANDOLPH--Now 66 years old, but handsome and erect, Randolph is a philosopher with many qualities of mysticism about him. To millions of American Negroes, he symbolizes the best in honest leadership and integrity. A life long Socialist and militant fighter, he has been crying out discrimination and injustice for more than 40 years.

Born in Crescent City, Fla., he came to New York as a young man and has made it his home ever since. With Chandler Owen, he edited and published a number of Socialist pamphlets and periodicals and lectured at the Rand School of Social Sciences. He was a struggling young visionary writer when he was approached in 1925 by a group of Pullman Porters and asked to lead them in their fight for better working conditions.[34]

Long Battle

The story of that long hard battle is a success saga, but it was literally achieved through blood, sweat, tears and harrassment. Now 18,000 strong with jurisdiction over Canada and U.S. it has over a million dollar reserve and is strong and solvent.

Randolph has used the power of his union to wage a fight on a broad front. Called the "Father of FEPC," he organized the March on Washington Movement in 1942.[35]

It grew out of the desperate need for action to break down color bars in

employment and the war industry. When Randolph threatened to lead a march of
a hundred thousand Negroes on Washington, Mrs. Eleanor Roosevelt arranged the
historic meeting at the White House with he and other Negro leaders.[36]

WILLARD S. TOWNSEND: President of the United Transport Service Employees
since its founding 20 years ago, Townsend is 60 years old. He was born in
Cincinnati but has made Chicago his home for over 30 years.

His union of about 4,000 members includes railroad, bus and airline
redcaps, Pullman, laundry and repair-shop workers, dining car employees and
tobacco workers. He attended school at the Royal College of Science in
Toronto, Canada, and worked to support himself as a dining car waiter.

New York Age Defender, December 10, 1955.

7. SOLIDARITY FOREVER

Tears flowed freely at the CIO convention during the pageant of its 20
years of existence and the thought that now it was ending.

CIO staffers -- in fact, nobody was sure what was going to happen because
the machinery for running the new organization had not even started up its
motors.

President George Meany brought some relief to worried members when he
emphasized that the small unions must be allowed to keep their independence and
not to be swallowed up by the bigger ones.

The clasped hand became the symbol of unity, and there were truce meetings
all over the New Yorker and Statler hotels between AFL and CIO leaders.

The lions and the lambs were lying down together and the quip was going
the rounds that the shotgun wedding had finally come to pass.

Disappointed office seeker was William Hartung of the CIO woodworkers, a
union of a 100,000 membership.

Reports were that he was sacrificed as a vice-president of the merged
union after word went down that a place must be made for a Negro.

Immediately after being approved as a vice-president, Philip Randolph was
named to the all-important resolutions committee by Meany.

New York Age Defender, December 17, 1955.

8. AFL-CIO RESOLUTION ON CIVIL RIGHTS, 1957

In the course of its first two years, the AFL-CIO has carried forward
with diligence and vigor its policy of equal rights and of equal opportunities
for all, regardless of race, color, creed or national origin. Our Federation
has taken firm steps to give practical application to its non-discrimination
policy and to win for it widest acceptance both within the ranks of labor and
in the community at large.

Dedicated to bring about the full and equal rights for all Americans in
every field of life, the AFL-CIO has provided leadership in the American
community in taking timely actions to affirm and to secure these rights.

The AFL-CIO Executive Council, assisted by the Committee on Civil Rights,
initiated a number of practical programs to implement the principle of
non-discrimination proclaimed in the AFL-CIO Constitution.

In this work, prior consideration was given to the removal of discrimination within the ranks of the AFL-CIO itself. For the enduring goal of our
Federation is to assure to all workers without regard to race, creed, color
or national origin their share in the full benefits of union organization.

To this end, machinery has been established to effect compliance with
the AFL-CIO civil rights policy throughout the ranks of the labor movement.
Complaints, charging existence of discrimination by an affiliate, after staff
investigation, are handled by a specially constituted Compliance Subcommittee

of the Civil Rights Committee. If, after diligent efforts to enlist the
cooperation of the affiliate concerned and, after due notice and hearing, it is
found that discrimination complained of still exists, the Committee on Civil
Rights may certify the case to the Executive Council for appropriate action to
effect full compliance with the AFL-CIO civil rights policy.

Gratifying and responsive cooperation has been extended by our affiliates
in the effectuation of this vital program. A growing number of our affiliates,
including national and international unions, as well as state and city central
bodies, have established machinery of their own to administer and further their
civil rights programs.

An important contribution to labor's progress in the civil rights field was
the calling of the First National Trade Union Civil Rights Conference by the
AFL-CIO in Washington last May. To exchange experiences, share the know-how
and to hold common counsel on the best ways and means to win broad acceptance
and support of labor's non-discrimination policy is to lay groundwork for future
progress, whether at the local union or the national level.

Of foremost concern to us also has been the assurance of equal employment
opportunity to all workers. The use of non-discrimination clauses in collective
bargaining contracts has been extended and now effectively bars discrimination
in hire, tenure, and conditions of employment as well as in advancement to a
better job, in a major portion of unionized establishments. Progress has also
been made, on union initiative, to assure equal opportunity in vocational
training and apprenticeship training programs.

We have participated in the work of the President's Committee on Government
Contracts which coordinates and assists Federal agencies in the enforcement of
non-discrimination clauses in government contracts and have pressed for
effective administration of this important program.

We have continued to back the enactment of enforceable state and local fair
employment laws and the vigorous application of such laws.

On the national scene, the last two years have seen both progress and
reverses in civil rights. The courts of the land have continued to insist that
discrimination and segregation in schools, in public transportation and in
other public facilities are repugnant to basic constitutional guarantees of
equality. Hundreds of communities have successfully implemented these
decisions. But there has also been willful defiance of the law of the land,
culminating in the disgraceful incident at the Central High School in Little
Rock, Arkansas.

Labor's reaction to Little Rock was made unmistakably clear on September
24, 1957, when the AFL-CIO Executive Council unanimously declared "that the
defiance of law and order in Little Rock by a mob of demonstrators against
school integration is completely intolerable." The Council voiced its support
of Federal troops to enforce compliance with court orders, for failure to have
used full power of the Federal Government would have meant defiance of the law
of the land, threatening national sovereignty and bringing lawlessness in its
wake.

While supporting the action of President Eisenhower's action in the
"Little Rock" situation, we nevertheless feel morally obligated to express our
keen disappointment, shared by millions of other Americans, at the failure of
President Eisenhower and his administration to provide vigorous and positive
leadership and initiative essential for the implementation of the historic
Supreme Court decision of May 17, 1954. This failure created the tragic
political and moral vacuum which encouraged the attitudes manifested in the
"Little Rock" incident.

The passage of the Civil Rights Act of 1957, won after bitter struggle,
with strong support from the AFL-CIO, is a significant forward step in the
ever-continuing struggle for human rights. The bill, as finally enacted, was
weakened by the elimination of Title III. President Eisenhower's failure to
give backing to the inclusion of Title III in the bill, led to this setback.
Despite this and other weaknesses, the new law establishes new and far-reaching
safeguards of civil rights proclaimed by the Constitution and the Bill of
Rights.

The President has appointed the members of the Civil Rights Commission
established by the Civil Rights Act of 1957. We look to the Commission and
the Department of Justice to act vigorously to carry out the objectives of the
law. It will be their responsibility to assure the enforcement of the right

to vote guaranteed to every American citizen. It will be their joint responsibility to expose the areas where civil rights are still being violated and
to study and interpret the effects of these violations. It will be the
Commission's responsibility to bring forward meaningful and practical suggestions for further action to assure inviolate exercise of civil rights by every
American.

The role of government, national, state and local, is vital to the
maintenance of freedom and democracy in our land. In the final count, however,
the triumph of human rights will be best assured by the understanding, dedication and action of the people themselves.

Labor with other liberal groups will carry on its historic struggle for
human justice in the spirit of brotherhood. As unionists, we hold affirm and
secure equal rights for all Americans in every field of life.

The AFL-CIO continue to assure to all workers without regard that
intolerance of race, creed, or color in our ranks or in our communities is
incompatible with the principles embodied in our constitution.

RESOLVED: That the AFL-CIO carry forward its historic drive to affirm
and secure equal rights for all Americans in every field of life, and that the
AFL-CIO continue to assure to all workers without regard to race, creed, color,
or national origin, the full benefits of union organization.

We recommend that our affiliates set up internal Civil Rights Committees
and machinery for effective administration of a meaningful civil rights program
within their ranks, working in close cooperation with the Civil Rights
Committee and the Civil Rights Department of the AFL-CIO.

We recommend that our affiliates insist on non-discrimination by employers
in hire, tenure and conditions of employment, and in advancement of their
employees. We urge our unions to include a non-discrimination clause in every
collective bargaining agreement they negotiate and to provide for effective
administration for such a clause.

We recommend that our affiliates take the initiative in assuring equal
opportunity in all apprenticeship training and vocational training programs.

We recommend that the President's Committee on Government Contracts
withdraw government contracts from those companies consistently guilty of
violating the Federal Government's policy of non-discrimination. We pledge
our continued cooperation with the President's Committee on Government Contracts
and ask our affiliates to make sure that employers with whom they deal holding
Federal contracts, adhere to the letter and spirit of the non-discrimination
clause required in each government contract.

We renew our support for the passage of an enforceable Federal fair
employment practices act. We also call for enactment of enforceable fair
employment practice laws by all states and cities not having such laws and for
strengthening of such existing laws where necessary to ensure their effectiveness.

We again urge that, in order to assure full and fair consideration by
Congress of proper civil rights and fair employment practice legislation,
Senate Rule 22 be changed to permit a majority of Senators present and voting
to limit and close debate.

We renew our support of the decisions of the Supreme Court outlawing
segregation in the public schools, in public transportation and in places of
public accommodation. These decisions represent a heartwarming reaffirmation
of the democratic American principles that are embodied in the Constitution of
the United States. We call upon President Eisenhower to recommend and the
Congress to enact legislation that will endorse and support, by implementing,
constitutional guarantees of Civil Rights, including those affirmed by the
Supreme Court decisions. We call upon the Executive Branch to make use of its
full authority to effect implementation of these decisions.

We urge the National Labor Relations Board to adopt the policy that the
use of race-hate propaganda during union organization campaigns is deemed to
be interference with, and coercion of, employees and constitutes an unfair
labor practice; and, further, that the use of such propaganda will be
sufficient ground for setting aside an election upon request of the union.

We call upon President Eisenhower and the Department of Justice to
launch an immediate and full-scale investigation into the activities of the
so-called citizens councils now operating in Mississippi, Alabama, Georgia,
Tennessee, Arkansas, Louisiana, South Carolina and Florida, or anywhere else

they may be operating, to determine if their activities and methods violate
any Federal statute or the Constitution.

COMMITTEE SECRETARY McDONALD: Mr. Chairman, in behalf of the Committee,[37]
I move adoption of Resolution No. 83.

. . . The motion was seconded.

VICE PRESIDENT RANDOLPH: Brother Chairman and delegates of this Convention: I rise, of course, to support the resolution and to say that since
Labor itself is not yet fully free, it is an act of enlightened self-interest
that Labor should support the principle of civil rights.

Civil rights represents democracy and democracy represents civil rights.
No individual in a state is a full citizen of that state unless he has the
attributes of citizenship, and the attributes of citizenship are involved in
civil rights and civil liberties.

The foundation of civil rights is the Judeo-Christian ethic--the Christian
tradition that the personality of every human being is sacred, that the
personality of every human being is entitled to recognition, respect and
reverence. This principle was enunciated by Jesus Christ for the first time in
human history upon his advent upon the earth. Mankind prior to that had no
concept of the dignity of the personality of an individual. The individual had
no worth as such. He had no value as such because prior to that the whole
world was under the concept of slavery, and the concept of slavery recognized
an individual as an inanimate thing, subject to use and exchange.

Therefore, the labor movement, representing great masses of workers, has
the moral responsibility for its commitment to the principle of civil rights.

I am glad to say that the American Federation of Labor and Congress of
Industrial Organizations has set a high standard on this principle; not only
have standards been set but machinery has been put into operation for the
implementation of the principles.

In this connection I want to commend the Director of the Civil Rights
Department, Boris Shishkin, for his ability and resourcefulness in carrying out
the principles of this doctrine of civil rights.

I want to also commend the Civil Rights Committee, under the splendid
leadership of Charles Zimmerman, who succeeded the distinguished leader of the
International Electrical Union, Brother Carey, as the chairman.[38]

I think this Committee is doing a splendid job. It has a small but
competent staff. Therefore, it may be looked forward to that progress will be
made in the implementation of the program of the AFL-CIO on this question.

However, it is well to say that we have just begun. While we have only a
few unions here that still have color clause in their constitutions, there are
still unions in the AFL-CIO that practice discrimination, and it shall be the
obligation and the responsibility of the Civil Rights Committee, the Civil
Rights Department, to work toward the complete elimination of all forms of
discrimination.

It is to the great credit of our movement that its head, the President,
Brother Meany, has been a consistent inspiration to the whole cause of civil
rights. He has never retreated from the position set forth in the Constitution.

It is my hope that this Committee will give consideration to the whole
field of apprenticeship training. Here we have a wide scope of discrimination
based upon color and race. The Government is also partially responsible for
discriminatory practices in this field.

May I say, fellow delegates, that there are other facets to this question.
Ordinarily we think of civil rights in connection with individuals, but today
organizations also have civil rights. The right of individuals to associate
themselves together for the achievement of certain objectives, the right to
achieve certain objectives by organization, is being denied to certain groups.

I have in mind the National Association for the Advancement of Colored
People. It has been barred from Texas, Alabama and Louisiana, and there are
a number of other States that are now beginning to develop a program to bar
this organization, because it is committed to the principle of civil rights
and is responsible for the Supreme Court decision of May 17, 1954. Now, this
is a tremendous crisis to this organization. If it does not have the right
to exist in a State, then the people for whom it is struggling to abolish
evil discriminatory practices will be the victims of discrimination. As a
result of barring the National Association for the Advancement of Colored
People, it has lost tremendous resources and is now compelled to look for

support from various groups in order that it might be able to carry on its program. . . .

So, I am glad to add my voice to the support of this resolution and to commend the work of the Civil Rights Committee and the Civil Rights Department of the AFL-CIO.

Thank you very much.

PRESIDENT MEANY: Is there further discussion on Resolution No. 83?

May I just re-emphasize the importance of one of the points referred to by Vice President Randolph, that there is a definite indication in the South that more and more of the white people of the South are coming to the conclusion that it is not good business to discriminate against the Negro. . . .

Are there any further remarks on the motion to adopt Resolution No. 83, which covers the broad field of civil rights?

. . . The motion to adopt the resolution was carried.

Proceedings of the Second Constitutional Convention of the AFL-CIO, Atlantic City, N.J., December 5-12, 1957, Vol. I, pp. 259-65.

9. AFL-CIO RESOLUTION ON CIVIL RIGHTS, 1961

RESOLUTION NO. 84--By Delegate Walter P. Reuther, Industrial Union Department. [39]

WHEREAS, The AFL-CIO constitution and the resolution on civil rights adopted at its Third Constitutional Convention in San Francisco set forth clear and unmistakable principles. It remains for us to now translate these principles into firm action; therefore be it

RESOLVED, That this Fourth Constitutional Convention of the AFL-CIO reaffirms the dedication reflected in its constitution to the achievement of a labor movement wholly free of racial discrimination and segregation of any kind; and be it further

RESOLVED, We call for the creation of a Fair Union Practices Board within the AFL-CIO that shall be armed with authority and jurisdiction over all matters of racial discrimination and segregation involving affiliates of the Federation; and be it further

RESOLVED, We urge that the President of the AFL-CIO appoint to this Board only those leaders of the labor movement who have evidenced devotion to the principles of this resolution and who are connected with trade unions which have likewise evidenced devotion to the principles of this resolution; and be it further

RESOLVED, That this Fair Union Practices Board be given the power to investigate and discover discriminatory practices or threats of such practices, with or without prior complaints, and that it be authorized to direct international and local unions to make investigations and to furnish the Board with reports thereon; and that the Board be further authorized to hold hearings and to take any other steps necessary to carry out the mandate of this resolution; and be it further

RESOLVED, We authorize the Fair Union Practices Board to enforce the mandate of the AFL-CIO Third Constitutional Convention calling upon all affiliates "to set up without delay internal Civil Rights Committees" and empower the Board to work with such committees; and be it further

RESOLVED, We further authorize the Fair Union Practices Board to certify any findings of racial discrimination to the AFL-CIO Executive Council to recommend to the Council such remedial action as may be required; and be it further

RESOLVED, Where the findings of the Board disclose practices of racial discrimination in any form on the part of an employer, and where there has

not been an earnest collective bargaining effort to correct the siutation, we
call upon the Board promptly to present its findings and recommendations to
the President's Committee on Equal Employment Opportunity.
   DELEGATE LOUIS MANNING, Transport Workers Union of America: Point of
order, Mr. Chairman. Point of order.
   PRESIDENT MEANY: State your point of order.
   DELEGATE MANNING: I would like that the entire resolution be read and
that we discuss the resolution.
   PRESIDENT MEANY: The resolution is in the hands of every delegate and
the practice of the committee to comment on the various paragraphs
rather than reading it over is to conserve time of the convention. Unless the
convention disagrees, we will follow that practice. You have the resolution
in front of you and you can read it along with the Secretary of the Committee
as he describes the various paragraphs.
   DELEGATE MANNING: And we will get a chance to discuss it?
   PRESIDENT MEANY: Of course you will get a chance to discuss it. That's
why the Committee is reporting on it.
   DELEGATE MANNING: Thank you.
   . . . Committee Secretary McDonald then summarized the balance of the
resolution on Civil Rights.

   COMMITTEE SECRETARY McDONALD: Mr. Chairman, in behalf of the Committee I
move adoption of the Civil Rights resolution.
   PRESIDENT MEANY: You heard the reading and the presentation of the report
of the Committee on Resolutions on the Civil Rights resolution. The motion is
to adopt the report. The Chair recognizes Delegate Randolph.
   DELEGATE PHILIP RANDOLPH: This resolution on civil rights was debated in
the Resolutions Committee for quite a long time. As a matter of fact, I
presented several amendments for the change of the sanctions in the interest
of strengthening the sanctions of the resolution against unions that practice
race bias. One of the amendments I presented involved a requirement that each
international and national union advise the Executive Council of the Civil
Rights Committee on the specific time it planned to initiate action for the
desegregation of its racially segregated unions, but this amendment was
rejected.
   Now, we went over this resolution in detail and I, of course, wanted that
the sanctions be stronger inasmuch as the idea of expelling the union on
account of race bias was turned down. However I agree that the structured
machinery of compliance with a view to the solution of cases of race bias is
set up with some care and some elaborateness; and I rather think that if a
strong Civil Rights Committee is appointed by President Meany that that
committee can make this resolution work.
   As I was commenting on this matter with Walter Reuther, Walter Reuther
said, "Well, the words of the resolution are not as significant as is the
strength of the committee that may be appointed to work in the interest of
implementing the resolutions."
   The resolution is not wholly satisfactory to me but I prodded the Chairman
so continuously about the matter that he finally told me, "Well, Phil, this is
the best that you are going to get." So, although, as I have said, the
sanctions are not strong enough for me, I think it is the best resolution on
civil rights that the AFL-CIO has yet adopted. And I am determined, in
connection with the Civil Rights Committee which may be appointed by the
President, and with the Civil Rights Department, with adequate personnel, to
make the resolution work. And I hope that it will.
   PRESIDENT MEANY: The Chair recognizes Brother Carey.
   VICE PRESIDENT JAMES B. CAREY: Mr. President and delegates: I consider
it highly appropriate that this matter of civil rights comes before this
convention during Human Rights Week as proclaimed by President John K. Kennedy.
It will be 170 years ago this Friday that our nation had the wisdom to adopt
the Bill of Rights. It was 80 years ago that a labor leader, starting with
Sam Gompers and others, set up the predecessor organization to the AFL. That
was Jeremiah Grandison, an American Negro, who pleaded eloquently for racial
democracy in the AFL's founding convention in 1881.[40]
   This resolution that we are considering is extremely important in terms
of the relationship of the American labor movement, not only to the Negro
community, but also to the entire community of our nation and to this nation's
relations with the world.

Mr. Chairman, I propose that the Committee's report be amended as
follows: That on page 15, under the first Resolve, the first paragraph, that
we add the words,
". . . as guaranteed in the AFL-CIO Constitution."
Mr. Chairman, I propose that on page 16 the resolution be amended to
include the following paragarph, following the paragraph starting with the
words: "In order to strengthen the procedure for compliance . . ." and ending
with the words "being practiced":--
"The President of the Federation shall appoint to the Civil Rights
Committee only leaders of the labor movement who have evidenced devotion to the
principles of this resolution and who are connected with trade unions which
have likewise evidenced devotion to the principles of this resolution. The
Civil Rights Committee shall have power to investigate and discover discriminatory practices or threats of such practices, with or without prior complaints,
to direct international and local unions to make investigations and to furnish
the Civil Rights Committee with reports thereon; to hold hearings, and to take
any other steps necessary to carry out the mandate of this resolution."
I propose the resolution should be amended to include the following
paragraph:
"We commend the non-violent demonstrators for their passionate devotion to
racial equality. We proudly identify ourselves with these dedicated groups of
Americans and we propose to make common cause with them wherever possible, for
they have provided the nation with a true example of courage and of honor. We
ask our government to exhibit the same devotion to racial equality by adopting
the necessary executive orders and legislation to bring true equality to every
corner of the land."
The resolution should be amended to substitute for the existing language
concerning the NLRB and employer use of race-hate, the following language:
"For more than four years the AFL-CIO has been on record urging the
National Labor Relations Board to find that when an employer uses race hate to
frustrate organization, he violates the federal law and such conduct should be
enjoined and any election results affected by this tactic should be set aside
at the request of the victimized union. We note that the National Labor
Relations Board has announced that it is considering establishment of such a
policy for representation election cases. We urge that this policy be
enunciated and put into effect in this area and, further, that the policy be
extended to unfair labor practice cases."
Mr. Chairman, the first three proposals made are on matters to be considered by the Resolutions Committee in strengthening the machinery to comply
with the Constitution of the AFL-CIO. But I do urge consideration for the
last proposal made, namely, that we repeat the action that we took at our convention in 1957, and again in 1959, when we unanimously called upon the
National Labor Relations Board to declare the use of race hate campaigns by
employers to be an unfair labor practice, and at the request of the union, the
results of an election could be set aside.
Mr. Chairman, I would appreciate the acceptance of especially that last
proposal by the Committee on Resolutions.
PRESIDENT MEANY: The Chair recognizes Delegate Reuther.
VICE PRESIDENT REUTHER: Brother Chairman and fellow delegates, I rise
to support the resolution and the specific amendment that Brother Carey submitted as it relates to declaring the use of materials of an anti-civil rights
or hate race basis as a basis for declaring an unfair labor charge.
Now the matter before us is a very serious one, and, like Brother Webster,
I don't think the Negroes are looking for sympathy, they are looking for
understanding. This is the deep human problem that the labor movement must
deal with, not just by adopting a resolution, but by demonstrating the will to
translate that resolution into affirmative action, not only in the ranks of
labor, but in the whole of our society wherever the ugly and immoral forms of
discrimination exist.
We have heard during this convention, and there are resolution after
resolution that we have already adopted or will be adopting talking about the
struggle between freedom and tyranny, how democracy faces its greatest
challenge in the face of the Communist thrust. I say that American democracy
will be unworthy of leading the forces of freedom in the world unless we
begin to bridge that ugly and immoral gap that separates American democracy's

noble promises and its ugly practices in the field of civil rights because
there are hundreds and hundreds of millions of people who are looking at
America, and they find it very difficult to square Little Rock and Montgomery
and New Orleans and the other areas of American life on the job front where
Negroes are denied their rightful opportunities. They can't figure how we
square that with a society that professes to believe in the worth and dignity
of every human being. Therefore, we in the labor movement have a lot of
unfinished work inside the movement and outside the movement.

I support the resolution because the resolution says that we shall intensify our efforts. This means that we are going to pursue more vigorously for
affirmative action in trying to deal with providing equal opportunities in the
labor movement and equal opportunities in the balance of our society.

As one human being, I believe in civil rights, in the right of every person
to equal opportunity as a matter of simple human decency, and as a matter of
simple moral justice. But I believe in civil rights and equal opportunity,
because freedom and equality rate, like peace, very indivisible. You can't
have them unto yourself. You can only have them, and be secure in having
them, as you share them with your fellow man and as you make them universal so
all men may share them.

George Meany and I both are serving on the President's Equal Employment
Opportunity Committee. We served together on the committee set up by President
Eisenhower, the Government Contract Compliance Committee. And it was with a
sense of deep shame that we found unions in the AFL-CIO were denying people the
opportunity to work on federal contracts because of race discrimination.

The old Nixon committee didn't do very much except issue pious proclama-
tions. But I can assure you that the committee is going to do differently now.
Arthur Goldberg is working on the President's committee. Vice President
Johnson, too. That committee now has an executive order with teeth in it, and
we intend to implement that executive order, and we intend to fight racial
discrimination on the job front in every federal contract. I want everyone to
know that that executive order has the kind of provisions that if there is
non-compliance on the part of the union or the employer or both, the committee
has the right to recommend the cancellation of those contracts. And we intend
to press for cancellation where we can't get compliance.[41]

I know something about the practical fight for equality on the job front
because the union that I have the privilege of being associated with has been
engaged in this struggle for a long time. We have not achieved perfection.
We still have work to do, but we are working at it. We learned a long time
ago in the early picket lines and when we faced the company goons and the
Pinkertons that if the employer can divide you, he will divide you.

The labor movement has to unite all people. General Motors in the early
days tried to pit the skilled worker against the production worker. They
tried to pit the American-born against the foreign-born. They tried to pit
white against black. We learned we all had the same problems and we all
shared the same hopes and aspirations in a dream about a better tomorrow, and
none of us made progress until we all stood together, skilled and unskilled,
American and foreign-born, white and black. That's how we built the labor
movement.

We have had discrimination on the job front. We have wiped it out inside
pretty much where we have contractual control. But at the hiring gate, we
couldn't make any progress. In our last negotiations we made some. In some
cases we made a great deal. In other cases we made a first step towards
beginning to fight against discrimination at the hiring gate. The companies
took the position "we decide who we hire, and after they punch the time clock
the first day and are working under the contract, then you have something to
say about it." But we have been fighting for a model fair employment clause
to eliminate discrimination at the hiring gate. We have made some progress.
The whole labor movement has got to work on this. We have made progress, no
one can deny that. No one can deny that no other organization in American
life has worked as hard on the question as has the labor movement.

But progress is a relative thing. We aren't moving fast enough. We
have to do a more effective job of getting our own house in order so that we
can make a greater contribution to the whole of our society in the struggle
for equal opportunities for all of our people.

I happen to believe, and I feel this way very deeply, as one dues-paying member of the UAW and of the AFL-CIO. We took the Communists out of leadership because they betrayed the principles of the labor movement and because they would rob us of our freedom. We opposed the crooks and the racketeers for the same reason because they betrayed the principles for which the labor movement stands and they would rob us of our money. And those people in the leadership who knowingly and willingly pursue racial policies that discriminate and violate the Constitution also betray the principles of the labor movement, and they would rob us of our dignity. One is as bad as the other in my book of values. We have to deal with all of them with equal firmness.

Dr. King says that the people in the Negro communities expect the labor movement to behave differently and more responsibly and to do more than they expect other people to do. There are people in the labor movement who haven't understood that. But we need to understand it because the Negroes of this country have a right to look to the American labor movement to join them in this struggle to wipe out the last ugly vestige of racial discrimination, because the labor movement is about people. It is about the struggle for dignity and security and human values.[42]

The NAM is not interested in these values. We have got to lead that struggle. We cannot be the symbol in America until we first take care of our own housekeeping. It is hard to conceive even if you do your best to try to understand the deep inner feelings of the Negro brother or a Negro sister, but you will never understand it.[43]

I worked in the German underground movement fighting fascism. I have been beat up by gangsters, shot at and thrown in jail, but I can't remotely begin to understand what a black human being feels deeply in his heart. He is filled with impatience because justice is too long in coming, and he is not going to wait.

And you and I who the good Lord gave a lighter skin to need to comprehend and share that impatience of our Negro brothers and sisters. Out of that deeper understanding as humans, we have to find a deeper sense of dedication because the value standards that we believe in in the world are in jeopardy because millions of people look to America and they think we don't believe in the things that we profess to believe in.

Therefore, my plea is to adopt this resolution, but then go back home and let's do something about it.

I was not at the council meeting when the report was considered. I was at the bargaining table and missed that council meeting. I have respect for my fellow council members, but I think that this document is not helpful to the labor movement, and I hope that we can reconsider it because I think that we cannot afford to divide ourselves on these issues when we need to be together. We need to be together to fight the White Citizens Council, the hate mongers. That is what we are talking about here today.

I hope this resolution can be the first step in a whole series of vigorous steps to give meaning and purpose and substance to these noble words in the resolution so we can go back home together and begin to fight the practical fight to give every American equal rights and equal opportunities and equal dignity in the labor movement and all over America.

Thank you.

DELEGATE CHARLES HAYES, United Packinghouse, Food and Allied Workers: Mr. Chairman, I couldn't sit here and live with my own conscience and not get up and at least voice an opinion on an issue so vital as this, not only to me as an American Negro, but to the trade union movement as a whole.[44]

Yesterday we heard what amounted, in my opinion, to one of the greatest and deepest addresses that I ever had an opportunity to hear at a labor convention by Rev. Martin Luther King, one who in the eyes of many people of my race in this country and in the world as a whole, is looked upon as "Mr. Civil Rights." I feel this question quite deeply because I think that there is not enough recognition in the minds of labor given to the full depth of this problem.

It is easy enough in convention after convention to pass resolutions. But somewhere along the line we have to close the gap between the adoption of resolutions and the performance of unions after adopting those resolutions.

I happen to feel this quite keenly because I come from an area--that is Chicago, Illinois--where over the past six years I have seen approximately

10,000 jobs disappear from my industry where some 8,000 people who used to work on those jobs were members of my race. Here six years later some of those people have not been able to find employment anywhere else; too young to retire, yet too old, by employer standards today, to be hired anywhere else. This I think is one of the tragedies that we don't quite recognize and certainly the situation is not looking too bright for the future. Where there are jobs, people are denied the right to those jobs, regardless of their skill, because of the color of their skin.

I heard Rev. Martin Luther King mention yesterday--I say again I think he did a beautiful job--pointing out that inescapable ally that organized labor has in the Negro people.

I don't think anyone can deny that the Negro votes in this country played a real role in electing the current administration. And I think some credence and some credit has to be given to that contribution in the form of trying to help them remain at least in the unions and in a position where they can make a living for themselves and their families. It is a tragic situation when a person is denied a job because of the color of his skin. Many people who I knew as butchers in our industry, if they have found employment today, are found at the airports as a skycap and in downtown Chicago parking cars.

A great number of those 10,000 that I mentioned can be found on the public relief rolls in the city of Chicago. They are not looking for handouts, but merely looking for an opportunity to work to provide for themselves and their families.

I say to you people here who represent leaders of the highest body of organized labor and who are leaders of different international unions, if I could do nothing more in my remarks than to arouse your consciences to the depth of this problem because technological changes which we say are fine for American society, are not only going to affect the Negro worker but they are going to affect to some extent every industry and are already doing it. And it seems to me we as organized labor have to come up with some kind of program, like we have been talking about here, designed to place some responsibility of the governmental bodies of our country and our states and our cities to come up with some kind of program that will provide a way of life for people who are thrown out of a job as a result of technological changes.

Yes, I say to you unequivocally that Negroes by and large are the hardest hit. In Chicago alone I guess the unemployment figure runs somewhere near 5 percent. When you put it on the basis of how many Negroes, it is at least 10 percent, according to statistics put out by the Chicago Urban League, and I have no reason to doubt it.

But I say to you people in closing, let's not just talk about this resolution or its content as I have heard it. A great responsibility rests on the shoulders of the Executive Council to implement the procedures outlined therein, and I would hope that it be approached with some sincerity as to the depth of the problem so that two years from today when another convention comes around for this great body that we will not have to come back here talking about what we didn't do or what we should do; we can spend our time talking about some of our accomplishments.

PRESIDENT MEANY: The Chair now recognizes Committee Secretary McDonald.

COMMITTEE SECRETARY McDONALD: Mr. President, at this juncture I speak as President of the United Steelworkers of America. I have a very short statement. It is not emotional, but I just want to try to tell the delegates something which has been done by our union, and something which I think can be done by other unions on this subject of civil rights. In order to keep it short, I am going to read just a few paragraphs.

In May of this year, I and other officials of our union met with the President's Committee for Equal Employment Opportunity and pledged the full support of our union in the implementation of the President's Executive Order No. 10925, which was created for the purpose of dealing with the problem of discrimination in employment.

Following this meeting I informed all of our local unions, staff representatives and district directors, of our action and requested that copies of the Executive Order and our own statement of policy on civil rights be posted in all union facilities and plant bulletins and that immediate steps be taken to implement both documents with the greatest possible speed.

On November 27, 1961 we took what we consider to be the most significant step yet taken by a trade union to unite the forces of labor and industry in support of a positive program for using their joint resources and influence to eradicate whatever aspects of discrimination in employment exist.

The United Steelworkers of America sent letters to every company with which we have collective bargaining agreements stating our desire to work with the several companies to implement the President's Executive Order and requesting them to join with us in signing a statement which would clearly and without question state our mutual intentions.

I would like to quote just a couple of paragraphs from the letter we sent to about 2,800 companies with which we have labor agreements:

"November 24, 1961

"As you know, President John F. Kennedy issued Executive Order No. 10925 on March 6, 1961, which created the President's Committee on Equal Employment Opportunity for the specific purpose of ending the many discriminatory employment practices which have prevailed for so long at certain companies against members of minority groups in our country.

"At the time the order was issued the President called for the full cooperation of all representatives of labor and management in implementing the principles of the directive. His appeal, of course, was not limited to those companies and unions where discriminatory practices may exist. He sought also the continued cooperation of companies and unions whose practices are non-discriminatory and consistent with the principles of the directive.

"On May 3, 1961, I and other officials of the United Steelworkers of America met with President Kennedy, Vice President Lyndon B. Johnson, Secretary of Labor Arthur J. Goldberg and members of the committee staff and pledged the union's full support of the President's program to end discrimination in employment.

"On June 27, 1961, we took the first step to implement this support within the union by formally acquainting all our officers, staff representatives, office personnel, local union officers and members regarding their individual and collective responsibility in helping to fulfill our pledge. As part of this action, copies of the Executive Order and a Statement of Principles, defining the Union's policy on civil rights, were ordered posted in all union facilities.

"We now feel that a second step should be taken to insure a realization of the full intent of the President's program.

"Accordingly, we are taking this opportunity to invite the chief executive officer of each company with which we have collective bargaining agreements to join us in signing the attached statement which forthrightly declares our mutual determination to work together to implement the principles of the President's program within the areas of industry under our jurisdiction.

"I hope that you will accept this invitation to sign this important statement and that you will further agree to have your representatives meet with the union's representatives to review the situation at your company and determine what steps, if any, may be required to realize our expressed intentions.

"I know that you and all of the officers of your company are aware of the gravity of this problem we face in our country, particularly so in view of present conditions and the position we must maintain among the free and uncommitted nations of the world.

"It is because of this that I look forward hopefully to an early and unfavorable reply from you signifying that you will join us in what should prove to be an outstanding example of the best in democracy at work.

This is the statement which we sent to the 2,800 companies:

"The _____ Corporation/Company and the United Steelworkers of America hereby pledge their individual support and joint cooperation to the President of the United States in his request to all management and labor for assistance in implementing the principles of Executive Order No. 10925 which aims to stamp out the evils of discrimination in employment wherever it may exist.

"We take this opportunity to publicly declare our intention to aid the President's Committee on Equal Employment Opportunity

in every way possible to attain the objectives for which it was
created. In addition, we will have our representatives meet to
review the situation at the plant level and determine what
steps, if any may be necessary to implement the principles of
the President's program.

"/s/_____
                              Corporation

"/s/_____
                    United Steelworkers of America"

We sent that statement out to the 2,800 companies, and I am very happy to
say that several of the most important steel companies in America have returned
these signed statements to us, and others have signified their willingness to
sit down with us and review their employment policies with an aim to correcting
any abuses which may exist.

On the afternoon of the 14th of December--this week--we will be meeting
with a number of representatives of the greatest corporations in America in
order to discuss this problem. Right now I want to say that I hope that the
affiliated unions of the AFL-CIO will consider doing something similar to what
we have done, and that we will find additional ways for working together where
the occasion permits to bring the all too-widespread discrimination in employment which still exists under control once and for all.

Mr. President, perhaps you will be happy to note that the secretary and
several members of the United Steelworkers Civil Rights Committee have already
met with the leaders of seven unions of the AFL-CIO. They had a meeting this
morning and they intend to work out something along this line, something
affirmatively for the employers, to get them to agree with us to get rid of
this terrible problem of discrimination. I think that this is an affirmative
way to approach this problem, not by emotion, but by positive action.

PRESIDENT MEANY: The Chair recognizes Delegate Curran of the NMU.

VICE PRESIDENT JOSEPH CURRAN: Mr. President, I rise in support of the
resolution. I represent a union that learned in its early life how difficult
a situation can be where there is discrimination in industry. Going to sea,
we had ships that were divided--some black, some white, some Chinese, and some
Spanish. When the whites would strike for better wages, hours and conditions,
the employes would use the blacks and the Chinese and the Spanish against them
on the basis that they were not acceptable to the whites and, as a result, the
strike was broken. This occurred for many years, and conditions were very bad
in our industry. When we formed our organization in 1937, one of the first
steps that we undertook was to write into our Constitution a "no discrimination"
clause, and it has been in our Constitution ever since 1937. We sail, we live
together, and we work together--black, white, yellow and green--on these ships,
and there are no colors in our union. They are all members of our organization.

The first collective bargaining agreement that we made in 1938 contained
a clause stating, "There shall be no discrimination on a job because of race,
color and creed." I think it is a step in the right direction, if you please.
But at this late date, it seems to me that what we are talking about as being
progress is really something that we should not discuss with any pride. The
labor movement, insofar as I am concerned, consists of workers. It does not
consist of any colors. It consists of all Americans, and it consists of all
members of unions. There should be no discrimination.

The passage of this resolution will not in effect, as the brother from the
Butchers' Union pointed out here, stamp out the evil that has infested our
country and made the image of America something for the Communists and others
to use in their drive around the world to build communism. After we leave
this convention and adopt this resolution, what will count is what we do when
we go back home.

It is not enough to get on this floor and engage in fine platitudes or
engage even in real sincere declarations unless we go out of here, as the
brother said, and come back in two years with this situation licked, so the
anti-labor elements in our country, the Communists and, yes, the Fascists,
too, and the right wingers cannot use this problem against us.

It seems to me that a resolution of this type does not need any real
discussion insofar as I can see. What it needs is the unanimous agreement of

all of us to recognize one fact: Whether you like it or not, what happens to
your black brother will happen to you. A worker is a worker. There is no
difference between the skin. If the employer is able to defeat a white worker,
he will then defeat the black worker; and if he defeats the black worker, he
will defeat the white worker. It is that simple.

We have always said that an injury to one is an injury to all. That is a
good trade union symbol. There should be no regard for color. It should be a
situation in which every worker is considered as a worker and is recognized on
the basis of his ability and his character, and not on the color of his skin
or who he knows.

Our organization fully supports the resolution. However, we are puzzled.
We have here a complete resolution on the question of civil liberties. As I
read it, it takes care of almost every problem that has been raised in the
report made by President Randolph of the Sleeping Car Porters. It takes care
of almost every problem. Yet we have the subcommittee report referred back to
the Resolutions Committee. I do not understand how we can adopt the resolution
on the one hand and have referred to the special subcommittee the questions
that President Randolph raised on this floor. I think they are one and the
same. They deal with civil liberties. They deal with rights. And I say that
we not only should adopt this resolution unanimously, but we ought to say to
President Randolph that not only is he not censored for bringing problems to
our attention, but that we agree with him wholeheartedly that civil rights and
the rights of all workers must be considered as our paramount problem if we are
going to have a labor movement.

PRESIDENT MEANY: The Chair recognizes the Chairman of the Resolutions
Committee, Brother Harrison.[45]

COMMITTEE CHAIRMAN HARRISON: Mr. President--

DELEGATE MILTON WEIHRAUCH, IUE: Do I have the floor?

PRESIDENT MEANY: Brother Harrison, the Chairman of the committee, has
the floor; you will have the floor next.

COMMITTEE CHAIRMAN HARRISON: All I want to say is that the report of the
Committee on Resolution No. 143 represents the combined best thoughts of all
of the members of the Resolutions Committee, and the resolution emerged as a
report to this convention after a series of compromises, give and take in many
respects, in the words of many of the members of the Resolutions Committee.

You heard here today the endorsement of the resolution by Phil Randolph,
although he made it plain it does not go as far as he would like the resolution
to go. But it is the opinion of your Resolutions Committee that the machinery
we have provided in the resolution for the implementation of the civil rights
that we set forth in our Constitution is good machinery that will bring good
progress.

I am confident that President Meany will appoint a good Chairman to the
Civil Rights Committee of the AFL-CIO and he will appoint good members to that
committee who will in good faith try to implement the policy of the Federation
and use the machinery.

I hope that we can approve the resolution as it has been presented by the
Resolutions Committee, and for that reason I now direct my remarks to the three
or four suggestions offered by Brother Carey. Brother Carey offered one
suggestion, to insert in the beginning of the first "Resolve" the following
language: "as guaranteed in the AFL-CIO Constitution."

I would not subscribe to approval of this suggestion, because it seems to
offer something that may create serious difficulties for all of these affiliates
if it is not carried forward.

I think the Constitution of this Federation has been accepted by all of
our affiliates, and I think every one of our affiliates is bound to observe
the Constitution in good faith and practice.

I don't think we need to say that anybody is guaranteed what rights we
have set forth in the Constitution.

We also have responsibilities set forth in the Constitution, and I would
urge that you not approve that proposal.

The second suggestion offered by President Carey was to put shackles on
the President about the kind of people he can put on the Civil Rights
Committee. And to be plain about it, Carey wants a packed jury. I want an
impartial, dedicated Civil Rights Committee that will enforce the Constitution
of the Federation.

The next suggestion that Brother Carey proposes has to do with the second to last paragraph, and the paragraph in the committee's resolution of particular significance reads, as follows:
"We deplore and denounce the use of reprehensible and venomous race hate propaganda by unscrupulous anti-labor employers. We urge that the President's Committee on Equal Employment Opportunity establish procedures whereby it can bar from government contracts any employer who engages in this contemptible practice.
"We further urge that the National Labor Relations Board carefully review every anti-labor practice case, and representation proceedings where false assertions and epithets are so used to arouse race hatred and coerce employees in their choice of a bargaining representative, or preclude the holding of a fair election."

That says everything that intelligence would warn us to say. In other words, if an employer uses false hatred propaganda that ought to be an unfair labor practice. But our Committee was advised by competent counsel that if they told the truth in their propaganda that there is nothing we can do to stop them because that is their right under the Constitution, to speak the truth.

Carey in his suggestion wants to knock out the word "false propaganda" because he makes no exceptions.

I'm not going to quarrel with Brother Carey about his language, but I don't think his language is as good or as comprehensive or as all-inclusive as the language we use in our report. If he wants to weaken our report with his language; I'm not going to quarrel with him, but I think he is making a mistake.

PRESIDENT MEANY: The Chair recognizes Brother Weihrauch of the IUE.

DELEGATE MILTON WEIHRAUCH, IUE: Thank you, Mr. President. I am under the impression that those amendments that were offered by Brother Carey were going to be referred back to the Committee and not be discussed, I thought that that was what was going to take place. However, I think we ought to recognize that this great country of ours from history on has been made up of minorities, and I think we ought to recognize that bias and discrimination and hate all go hand in hand.

I have had the experience of seeing our people call each other slanderous names. I have seen Swedish people come to the plants, and they have been slandered as "Squareheads." I saw the advent of the Irish people into the plants and they were called "Micks." Then I saw these people get a little place in the sun; and I saw the Italian people come into the plants and, boy, what names they were called.

During the war our Negro brothers came into the plants, and what trouble we had getting the white and the Negro people work side by side. I think we made our greatest step toward civil rights in that particular period, because it was our local union's position that people willing to die for this country could work together in the factory for the same country.

Now a question. What is going to happen to the advent of the new minority, the Puerto Rican? There are almost one million Puerto Ricans in the New York-New Jersey area. Believe me, are they being discriminated against! They are exploited, they are condemned to ghettos and miserable apartments with outrageously high rents.

We have to do something about this, because the whole world watches this country. They watch us, the Kremlin and the satellites watch us. They watch Alabama, Arkansas, and Mississippi, and if we don't bring our house in order we give the Communists a great deal of room for exploitation of the miseries that we don't take care of.

The question is, are we to fail the minorities in 1962 and drive them away from the AFL-CIO? If we do that, we must put these minorities on the meat chopper. They will be ripe and ready for the exploitation of the Communists, and they will be ripe and ready for the exploitation of the racketeers.

Oh, yes, the racketeers—I have seen contracts between unions and companies that have enslaved the workers. The racketeer is the twin to the Communist. What protection did the people get in these sweetheart agreements?

None. They get the lousiest wages possible, and with the collusive arrangements
and the contract for these low wages, dues must come out.
     I will tell you, Puerto Rico is ready for organization. But they think
that the AFL-CIO is trying to exploit the workers in Puerto Rico. Of course,
that is not true. But the people commute back and forth, and they see the
ghettos and the slums that their brothers work in the New York-New Jersey area.
     Our union has done some substantial organizing in Puerto Rico. Just last
year we invested about $200,000. Our income is probably ten percent of that.
But it is our fight in the field of civil rights.
     I am for this resolution, provided that we all talk the same language,
whether it be in the north and the east, where it is a bit more popular to
talk that way, in the south and in the west.
     I say that the job of eliminating discrimination primarily belongs to us.
The other organizations that are involved in this field, they are our allied
organizations, but primarily this job is ours.
     If this resolution is to be meaningful, we must have real integrated
Civil Rights or Human Relations Committees in every single local that we have.
These Civil Rights Committees shouldn't just be all one color, they must be
integrated. We must see to it that the white and the black mix together and
discuss the problems of human relations, and that is the way they get along,
and understand each other. It shouldn't be one color just talking to itself.
     It has been recognized that we are in a nuclear age, that that resolution,
to mean something, is to mean we have to have action, we have to have job
training programs on the jobs of the day and the jobs of tomorrow. It means
that we have to have apprenticeships thrown open, vocational schools thrown
open to train the minorities to do the work of tomorrow. It means that our
organizations must invest some of their treasuries in housing to take these
people, these minorities out of the ghettos. And above all, this resolution
that I have confidence in, if it is going to be meaningful, . . . and we have
to look all around this room and particularly behind the dais where we see a
symbol of the AFL and the CIO workers together shaking each other's hand, . . .
that is what this is all about. That is what civil rights is all about, that
we all work together in human relations and understanding so that we bring a
better tomorrow for all of us.
     DELEGATE LOUIS MANNING, Transport Workers Union of America: Mr. Chairman,
brothers and sisters, I have been on the board of our union for the past 27
years. In the outset, I want to say that in my union, this feeling of discrimination ranks second to none.
     What is civil rights? Civil rights coming from a Negro--and I am a Negro--
is the right to live. Is there any man or women in this auditorium who would
stand and tell me that I have no right to live? I came into this world I
should say, some 50 years ago. I had no say. I find myself here and I believe
every delegate in this house finds himself or herself here in that same manner.
     Brothers and sisters, we Negro people look toward you--and when I say
"You," I mean the labor movement--for relief. Where else should we go? We
must come to you. We are asking you here to examine your hearts and to tell
us Negro people how long will you keep us in servitude. How long will you
keep us in slavery? We are asking you to do something and to do it now, not
tomorrow, not a month from now, not a year from now, but for Jesus Christ's
sake, do it now.
     Brothers and sisters, the eyes of the world are watching us in America.
And every time a Negro is lynched and every time a Negro is denied his civil
rights, communistic Russia and the satellites are looking on. You are giving
them food and you are giving them ammunition to use against us.
     I want to see a strong resolution passed here today so that the brothers
in the back of the hall can take it back to their country and tell about it.
I am telling you, brothers and sisters, that would be selling America. If we
would do that, we would be in a position to cut out some of the grants to buy
good will. The African people are looking on and they are watching every move
that we are making.
     I say, brothers, you have to be a Negro to know what it is to be discrim-
inated against. When I walk down these streets, I wonder if they would serve
me at the lunch counter. Yet I am an American and am willing to give my life
for America, I am willing to die for America like my brothers of the past. I
say to you, fellow delegates, that the time is now; now, not next year. Don't

put it off but give us real honest to goodness civil rights.
I thank you.

DELEGATE RUSSELL R. LASLEY, United Packinghouse, Food and Allied Workers:
Mr. Chairman, there is one particular phase of the civil rights program that
I don't believe any delegate to the convention has spoken on yet, and yet I
consider it to be basic if we are to have any kind of a meaningful civil rights
program within the Federation. That is the whole question of representation of
Negroes and other so-called minority group members and all members of our trade
union life.

Look around us today in this hall and you will see only a handful of Negro
delegates present here. Over the past several years that I have been attending
conventions, which has been for quite a number of years, first in the CIO and
now in the AFL-CIO, the number of Negro delegates attending conventions has been
dropping off year by year. The reason for that is that there has been no real
push and aggressive movement to integrate Negroes into the full life of the
labor movement. And I mean by that, the code of ethics for civil rights--
written by A. Philip Randolph and to be presented to this convention now
included in the omnibus resolution--does not pinpoint exactly what I'm talking
about. In the code of ethics it shows that Negroes should be brought into
activity in the local unions and then brought up to the international union
level so that Negroes play a role as administrators and policy makers within
the Federation.

It is not enough to be only a dues paying member. It is a fact that
Negroes have the capacity and the ability to give leadership as well as be led.
And until we recognize that particular point, until we recognize the significance of this, then we will not be able to carry out a meaningful civil rights
program.

I hope that by the time of the next convention of this Federation, the
program that is intended and anticipated will bring about the result of more
Negroes as delegates to this convention, because they are in positions of
leadership in their particular local unions, federated bodies and in their
international union.
Thank you.

DELEGATE CLYDE ROGERS, International Brotherhood of Pulp, Sulphite and
Paper Mill Workers of the United States and Canada: There is one thing that I
am really happy that has come out of this convention. I am a Southerner and I
am proud of it.

In the mill where I work, I can testify to two colored men that are
printing press operators in the heart of Dixie; top paid jobs. We haven't at
any time attempted to take these men from this job. That's their job. It is
their seniority right. Their rate is the same as any others. This is in the
heart of Dixie.

A little more than ten years ago it would have been a far-fetched idea
that a colored man would have been a deputy sheriff of Mobile County, Alabama.
But I can boastfully say today that we have a number of colored sheriffs in
Mobile, Alabama.

Ten years ago it would have been a far-fetched idea to have thought about
a colored man being a city officer. But we have them on the job now that
patrol our streets every day. And I am proud of it. That's in the heart of
Dixie.

We have colored bus drivers in Mobile. That's in the heart of Dixie.

I have been sitting here and I have been having myself a field day. I
heard from Chicago, I heard from Denver and also about the problems that you
have over in other major cities. I heard from many of them and you have convinced me of one thing here today. Somebody has been talking out of both
sides of their mouth. For years and for years you have been trying to work
with the problem, trying to convince the South of how we ought to work with
it, but you haven't found the solution yet by your own testimony, and it is
the truth.

I would like to say this. I am opposed to any person being brought down
that has the right, ability, and claim to a job. Once he gets that job, he
should have the right to work on that job. I do not oppose that right. But
I think, as I have heard right here from the delegates, that you need a
Martin Luther King somewhere else, too. I would like to say this. I think a

lot of the guns are shooting at a sinking ship. I am reminded that the same
principle would be involved if my wife should come and say, "Roger, your
breakfast is ready. Everything is just right. I love you more than anybody in
the world"--and then say, "I want a divorce." It really would not make sense.
We have been talking about how we have solved the problem, and by the words of
the testimony of these men from the north and in various parts of the United
States, you have not solved the problem. You have not solved the problem.
This is a problem you have been working with for over 100 years and, mind you,
when we train our attention on a few southern states, let us not be blinded by
the problems involved in "right-to-work" laws around other parts of our country.
     There is something that we can say here on the matter of "right-to-work"
and on the subject of civil rights, President Meany. We have racial problems.
You have convinced me that you have them also, and you have not ironed them
out. You have had 100 years and you have not done so yet.
     But there is one thing that I can proudly and boastfully stand here today
and tell every one of you delegates. Our problems in some of our situations
right now would be the next thing to a Sunday afternoon picnic compared to some
of the problems that you have in Chicago. And it is the truth.
     Friends, let me say this to you today. I think that our thinking covers a
central part of the United States instead of a limited area. Every one of us
would do good and well to take some of the thinking that is written in the
civil rights resolution today back home for some real down-to-earth serious
consideration. I make that statement based upon your own words of testimony,
from the various states of this great union of ours. I wanted to hear how
you were doing in other places. I certainly feel that after hearing some of
the words of testimony from the various parts of the United States, we could
walk away from this convention saying, "The job we are accusing the Southerners
of not having been able to accomplish we have not been able to accomplish
either," which should give us the initiative to work even harder than we ever
have before in the history of this nation to prove the thing that we are
hollering about the most--that we are doing the fair thing and the right thing.
I do not think the fair thing and the right thing has been done in the other
places. It has not been proved. So the civil rights program is not being
carried out. The resolution has not been worked out. I feel that it is
something that everyone could work with if we find the solution and devote the
time and effort to prove to one another that it can work. Thank you.
     PRESIDENT MEANY: The Chair recognizes Brother Carey.
     VICE PRESIDENT JAMES B. CAREY: Mr. President, I rise to present my own
explanation of my own proposal. I am not in agreement with the way it was
presented by Chairman Harrison of the committee. I present a proposal that
was adopted by the Convention of the AFL-CIO in 1957 in the civil rights
resolution. It was reaffirmed and adopted in the 1959 AFL-CIO Convention in
San Francisco. It reads as follows:
     "We again urge the National Labor Relations Board to adopt the policy
that the use of race hate propaganda during union organization campaigns is
deemed to be interference with and coercion of employees and constitutes an
unfair labor practice and, further, that the use of such propaganda will constitute sufficient grounds for setting aside an election upon request of the
union."
     The IUD Convention, in keeping with the position taken by the AFL-CIO on
the Civil Rights question in 1957 and 1959, adopted the following:
     "We believe that when an employer resorts to racism to interfere with
union activity, it violates Federal law. We urge the National Labor Relations
Board and its general counsel to effectuate the Federal labor policy."
     Mr. Chairman, I submit that the resolution adopted on this subject by the
AFL-CIO conventions of 1957 and 1959 and the IUD Conventions of 1961 is a
sound position, despite any reference that any lawyer may have made on the
action of the AFL-CIO at two of its conventions and the IUD at its recent
convention.
     I suggest that the present resolution falls short in this respect of the
resolutions previously adopted on this subject. It says:
     "We further urge that the National Labor Relations Board carefully
review every unfair labor case," and emphasizes that the board shall find

that the use of race-hate material by an employer shall be declared an unfair labor practice. I have been charged with seeking to pack a committee. Nothing of the sort; I merely want to see this crucial committee guided by men who are solidly devoted to AFL-CIO policies."

I would suggest that the committee not have in its membership people who are not dedicated to the AFL-CIO Constitution and the precepts of this resolution. It would be unheard of to suggest that we cannot find interested people in the leadership of the American labor movement who are dedicated to the furtherance of this important objective and principle of the AFL-CIO as it is contained in the Constitution.

Mr. Chairman, I do urge the Chairman of the committee to accept at least the wording with respect to the Labor Board procedure that was adopted by two previous conventions to the AFL-CIO.

DELEGATE FRANK RILEY, International Brotherhood of Electrical Workers: Mr. President, I subscribe to the policy of Brother Harrison and Brother Curran. I have had considerable experience with the problem of the dark-skinned man in my local union in the city of Detroit. I cannot subscribe to the policies, that is, many of them, of the National Association for the Advancement of Colored People. I do not know whom they represent when they say "colored people," because the black man, in my estimation, is not a colored person. When I went to school black was not a color. We are the colored people, the white, yellow, brown, and the red races--but when they try to shove something down my throat that I cannot digest, then they are going to have trouble with me. That is what has happened in the city of Detroit.

Recently, not I myself personally, but my organization was criticized on the front page of the *Detroit Free Press* for discriminating against the Negro race in our local unions. The brother was an officer of the Wayne County Federation of Labor, a Vice President. I sat on committees with the same brother when I was a member of the Board of Supervisors of the County of Wayne, and never at any time did this brother ever discuss the problem of the Negro entering the union that I represent.

I also sat as a member of the Public Lighting Commission of the City of Detroit for 11 years, and on that Commission sat another gentleman who is a member of the Detroit Urban League. Many times we discussed the problems of the Negro in Detroit. He explained to me the policy of the Detroit Urban League and the way that they tried to help the Negro and the other colored people that may also be protected by the Detroit Urban League. He asked me if I would sit down with the Committee of the Detroit Urban League and discuss the problems of the Negro in my local union.

I said "Yes, I would be glad to," and I did sit down with the Committee of the Detroit Urban League. I sat with them for three hours. They asked me how many Negroes did I have in the local unions that I represented. I told him I did not know. And I was truthfully telling him I did not know because in our organization we do not ask the race, color, creed or nationality of any member who becomes a member of our organization. To this Committee, who were all, I think, members of the Negro race--I never asked them, but I think they were--I outlined the policy of our organization and the qualifications that they would have to meet if we were to accept an agreement with any of the Negro contractors in the City of Detroit who themselves had an organization of their own.

After I outlined the policy to them, I said, "You take this to your people. If they accept the qualifications that I am offering you, which are not any different than any other contractor--white, yellow, brown, or any other race-- I will be willing to meet with them, and if they can meet those qualifications, we will sign an agreement with them and accept them into our organization."

You know that I never heard again from that Committee until I read in the newspaper that we were accused of being discriminatory. Later on we received applications from about 14 employees of a contractor in the City of Detroit. We were asked to accept them into our organization. All we could go on was what we read on the applications that they had filled out. It was not our application. It was one that they had typed up themselves. Most of them were from Tuskegee Institute. They had had two or three years in there, which qualified them as electrical workers. Well, we did not accept them right away, but it was not long after that we were charged with discrimination. In the State of Michigan there is an antidiscrimination law. At that time I was bowing out as business agent of Local 58 for health reasons. Later on these members were accepted into our organization and we had an agreement with this contractor. As I told that committee when I sat with them in the Urban League, I did not think that they would ever be able to compete with the white contractor with the same wages and on the same basis as other contractors. They didn't believe me. But I want to tell you here that just two months ago that contractor sent a letter to our organization--at the time I happened to be president of the Executive Board in my organization--canceling the contract. He could no longer operate under the contract with our local union.

And we are accused of being discriminatory.

Now the National Association for the Advancement of Colored People on many, many occasions tried to shove people down our throat.

PRESIDENT MEANY: Frank, please get to the resolution.

DELEGATE RILEY: And we refused to accept them. But I want to say this, that I think the resolution covers this situation very thoroughly. I think the amendments and the speeches of others of the self-appointed world-savers that are vying for the front pages of the newspapers at the present time do not know what they are talking about. They are only using it as a means to obtain publicity. I hope, delegates, that you vote for the acceptance of this resolution. Thank you.

PRESIDENT MEANY: I would like to put the resolution at this time. I think we have discussed it at great length.

I would like to point out, however, first, that this is the most comprehensive resolution ever presented to any convention I have attended on this subject. I think it represents the thinking of those who feel that we can do something on this problem, do more than we are doing.

But I want to emphasize that it is not going to be done in Washington alone. We will get a good committee and we will get a good staff--we have a good staff. We will add to that staff and we will get a good committee. But when it is all said and done, it must be done at the local level with the cooperation and assistance of the international unions of the state federations and of the local central bodies. The local central bodies can perhaps be more helpful than the international union in this respect, because I have experience, and I know what is going on in the City of New York.

Puerto Ricans were mentioned. Let me say that if the Puerto Ricans didn't have the labor movement in back of them in the City of New York, they wouldn't have any friends.

For many years, the trade union movement in the City of New York has had a committee to help these people who came up from the South and landed in New York, not knowing the language in a good many cases, unable physically to cope with the climate, and they landed on relief rolls and were given the most menial jobs at the poorest wages.

The local labor movement under Charles Zimmerman and Harry VanArsdale set out to do something, and they are doing something every day in the week, with the cooperation of the city authorities. And I am proud of what they are doing.

So this calls for something more than speeches. This calls for action at the local level, the international union level and in Washington where we will have our Civil Rights Department and our Civil Rights Committee in operation.

I like the resolution. I hope that we can put it into effect so that we can come back to the next convention with a report of progress and of having eliminated a good deal of these problems.

Everybody is in favor of the resolution, but it is boiled down now to a question of substitution of language for the last portion of the resolution where the committee brings in a report urging the National Labor Relations Board to carefully review unfair labor cases and representation proceedings where false epithets are used, and so on and so forth. And Brother Carey brings in an amendment which he feels represents stronger language, in which he asks that they set aside any of these cases where race hate is being used to frustrate union organization.

So I will now put the question on the amendment proposed by Brother Carey. Those in favor of the amendment signify by saying aye; those opposed, no. The amendment is lost.

I will now put the question on the original resolution as presented by the Committee. Those in favor of the resolution as presented by the Committee signify by saying aye; contrary minded no. The ayes have it and it is so ordered.

Proceedings of the Fourth Constitutional Convention of the AFL-CIO, Miami Beach, Fla., December 7-13, 1961, Vol. I, pp. 490-516.

10. AFL-CIO RESOLUTION ON CIVIL RIGHTS, 1963

RESOLUTION NO. 116--By Delegate Walter P. Reuther, Industrial Union Department.
RESOLVED: We earnestly resolve to do whatever is within our power to tear down the barriers between us:
IN UNIONS--Trade Unions were formed to secure social justice for workers. The reason for our being is to build a free society dedicated to human dignity and happiness. The achievement of this goal is predicated on equality and brother-hood. Thus, our history and our very purpose demand that we be in the forefront of the struggle to assure first class citizenship to all people--to all colors; to all creeds; to all citizens, without regard to national ancestry.
We call upon all union members in our ranks to search out and eradicate all vestiges of discrimination and segregation in the labor movement. Labor can hardly point a finger of scorn at others when there are still segregated locals and when Negroes and other minorities are barred from apprenticeships because of race.
Time is of the essence! We cannot wait any longer.
IN CONGRESS--The moral crisis in American race relations grows worse. The President warned in June that "continued Federal legislative inaction" will result in increased "tension, disorder and division." We call this warning again to the attention of Congress and urge Congress to redouble their efforts to enact a broad comprehensive civil rights bill in the remaining weeks of this session.
While the bill approved on October 29 by the House Judiciary Committee contains significant improvements over the original bill proposed by the Administration, it can still be strengthened. While we are gratified to see an FEPC provision in the bill, we want a Commission with more power, one that could issue its own final orders, enforceable in the courts. We pledge our-selves to work for the strengthening of the FEPC provision as well as for provisions that will open all places of public accommodations to all citizens and give the Justice Department greater power than the compromise bill does, to protect peaceful demonstrators and workers for constitutional rights from harrassment and police brutality.
THE EXECUTIVE--We note with satisfaction that President Kennedy and the Admin-istration through executive action have pursued an affirmative and aggressive policy and program of achieving equality for all Americans. We applaud this achievement of the President and his Administration, but there is much more to be done. Therefore we urge the President to extend Executive Order 11063 so that it covers not only FHA and VA-insured mortgages but also conventional mortgage activities of such federally-assisted lenders as banks insured by the Federal Deposit Insurance Corporation or federally-insured savings and loan companies. We also urge him to establish by Executive Order, a Community Relations SErvice such as he originally pledged to do in his Civil Rights message of June 19. The fact that the Service has been deleted from the bill approved by the House Judiciary Committee puts an additional obligation upon the President to establish a service that would seek voluntary solutions of community relations problems arising out of discrimination.
IN THE NATION--We call upon all individuals in and out of the labor movement to speak out against discrimination and to act in their daily lives to end it. Only the hourly, daily actions of millions of us will make a brotherhood more than a platitude and launch, at last, "a great moral crusade to arouse America to the unfinished work of American democracy to the end that all Americans may enjoy the privileges of first class citizenship in all phases of our national life."

COMMITTEE SECRETARY McDONALD: Mr. Chairman, I am proud to move the
adoption of this resolution.
PRESIDENT MEANY: You have heard the reading of the resolution and the
motion is to adopt.
The Chair recognizes Vice President Philip Randolph to open the discussion
on this subject.

VICE PRESIDENT A. PHILIP RANDOLPH, Brotherhood of Sleeping Car Porters:
President Meany, members of the Executive Council, platform guests, fraternal
delegates, brothers and sisters:
We are on the threshold of what may well be the most important discussion
of this convention.   The labor movement is now called upon to take a stand on
the civil rights revolution that has gathered momentum during the past year.
I do not propose to launch this discussion with a chapter-and-verse recital of
labor's failure to keep pace with that revolution.   Nor do I propose to rehash
altercations that are better left to labor's past than projected into labor's
future.   I intend instead to analyze the plight in which the Negro finds
himself in the year 1963, and to make concrete proposals for action by the labor
movement.
Let me say that I have been very much encouraged by President Meany's
discussion of civil rights in his opening remarks Thursday.   Those remarks help
to establish an atmosphere in which we can plan constructive action.
Let me also say that our deliberations today proceed under international
scrutiny.   I am delighted by the presence here of representatives from labor
movements around the world, especially from the developing countries of Latin
America, Asia, and Africa.   They have first-hand knowledge of the American
labor movement's unshakable commitment to the development of free, democratic
institutions throughout the world.   They know that the AFL-CIO has backed up
this commitment with investments of millions of dollars, so that fledging
trade unions may achieve viability under difficult circumstances.   But, while
foreign observers are duly impressed with the achievements of the American
labor movement, as with the achievements of American technology, they sometimes
point to spiritual or moral deficiencies which we cannot defend or rationalize.
Foremost among them is the persistence of racism in American institutions.
The labor movement cannot afford to measure its achievements in the field
of racial justice by the standards of other institutions.   As a force for
social progress, we have always prided ourselves on being in the forefront.
Similarly, in assessing labor's contribution to civil rights, it is not enough
to measure how far we have come; it is not enough to compare ourselves favorably with government or management.   We must measure our achievements against
the needs of our time, the demands of our democratic creed, the imperatives of
the Judeo-Christian traditions.
The Negro is caught in a severe economic crisis.   The mass of black
Americans stand today in the same relative economic position they occupied in
the depths of the great depression.   The destructive forces that have been at
work on the American economy over the past decade have hit the Negro especially
hard.   Two out of three Negro families subsist on less than $4,000 a year.
More important, the gap between Negro and white median incomes has actually
grown wider in recent years.   The same is true of the gap between Negro and
white unemployment rates.
Thus, the Negro worker finds that, despite progress toward social and
political equality, his relative economic position is deteriorating or stag-
nating.   The desperation and frustration that this paradoxical situation
engenders is responsible for much of the militance and impatience of the
current civil rights revolution.   And that militance will not abate.   For long
ago--during Reconstruction--the Negro learned the cruel lesson that social and
political freedom cannot be sustained in the midst of economic insecurity and
exploitation.   They saw that land in an area which was the chief source of
life, they had none.   Freedom requires a material foundation.   Our recent
civil rights gains are based largely on the economic progress the Negro
registered, with labor's help, in the 1940's and early 1950's.   We are fearful
that these gains will be wiped out by the economic stagnation that has
characterized the Negro community since 1953.
This is the economic background which gives rise to much of the
apparently irrational and excessive behavior accompanying the revolution.   But

the labor movement must not ignore or ridicule those who lie down before
delivery trucks, climb cranes, or engage in other allegedly "extremist" actions.
These actions are frequently led by responsible and dedicated Negro ministers
who are determined to shake the white community out of lethargic indifference.
These ministers recognize that their actions may be only symbolic. But they
also know that, in the words of the scriptures, if they do not speak out,
"there is nothing left but the stones to cry out in their place."

Moreover, labor is no stranger to these techniques, I bid you to recall
the unbridled hysteria which greeted labor's first sit-down strikes. If the
Negro's nonviolence movement owes a great deal to Gandhi and Thoreau, it is
also indebted to the American labor movement. If the behavior of militant
Negroes baffles many white Americans, it should not baffle the house of labor.
For, more than any other segment of American society, we have intimate knowledge
of the forces blocking the Negro's stride toward freedom.

Among those forces are automation and technological change, of which
Brother Meany has spoken. Automation is destroying tens of thousands of the
unskilled and semi-skilled jobs to which Negroes have traditionally been
relegated. Meanwhile, centuries of discrimination and exploitation have
deprived Negro workers of the education and training required by the new
skilled jobs opening up. Thus, we find that approximately 25 percent of the
long-term unemployed are black Americans.

As unemployment becomes increasingly structural, the Negro is increasingly
rendered economically useless. His old job is obliterated by the machine, and
he does not qualify for new jobs. We hear a great deal of talk about the need
to accelerate our rate of economic growth, and to increase purchasing power as
a means of increasing the labor demand. These are goals to which labor is
correctly committed, just as we are committed to a shorter work week. But we
must bear in mind that these remedies are not enough so long as millions of
Americans, black and white, are not prepared for the new jobs that an expanding
economy will create. There is already a shortage of highly skilled technical
and professional workers. These skilled workers are so much in demand that
they work over-time and enjoy high standards of living, while millions of
other workers are unemployed, underemployed or unemployable. These millions
are creating what the great Swedish economist Gunnar Myrdal has described as a
vast "under-class" in American society. They are the pariahs, the exiles, the
untouchables of our economy.

The Negro finds himself trapped in this under-class. He finds himself
trapped in the growing slums and ghettoes of the big cities, while more
prosperous white workers are migrating to the pleasant suburbs. A racial and
occupational separation is taking place which dooms our aspirations for
integrated housing and schools. In fact, residential and educational segregation is actually increasing in our metropolitan centers. Deprived of decent
integrated education, how are Negro youth to acquire the skills demanded by
our technologically advancing economy?

This is the vicious circle in which the Negro finds himself. And the
Negro is not alone. Many white workers also find themselves caught short by
the profound transformations our economy is undergoing. The problem of these
workers, black and white, is not merely an economic problem. It is a social
problem. Social justice and economic reform have become inextricably
intertwined in our time. If we are to speak to the needs of these workers,
the labor movement will have to tap its wellsprings of social idealism. It
will have to renew its crusading spirit. It must move toward a new evangelical spirit to reach down and lift up the poor workers, the disinherited, those
in poverty and despair.

Our failure to meet this challenge can bring only the ugliest consequences,
of which the first signs are already evident. Make no mistake about it,
brothers and sisters, there is a growing feeling of alienation from the labor
movement in the Negro community. The Negro's traditional loyalties toward
organized labor have been put to a severe strain. The Negro-labor alliance,
needed now as never before, is being pulled apart. It is being pulled apart
not only by the persistence of racial discrimination in a number of unions,
but also by the failure of labor to throw its full weight into the civil
rights revolution in every community.

The Negro will become more critical of labor precisely because he has
learned to expect more from labor. These expectations are just and must be

fulfilled. Otherwise, I fear, brothers and sisters, that advocates of so-called
"right-to-work" laws and other anti-union legislation will receive a better
hearing from the Negro community than they have been accustomed to in the past.
And I ask you to remember the role which Negroes played in defeating "right-to-
work" laws in California and other states only a little while ago. Any alienation of the Negro from organized labor, any breakdown of the natural alliance
between the Negro and labor, can only encourage the reactionary currents in
American political and cultural life. The Negro-labor alliance is our strongest
weapon against the coalition of reactionary Republicans and Dixicrats who would
deprive the Negro of his civil rights and drag organized labor back to the
nineteenth century. The political power of this coalition must be shattered.
It must be shattered in Congress, where the seniority system and the disfranchisement of Negroes enables the coalition to exercise a stranglehold over
congressional committees. It must be shattered on the local level, where
radical right-wing groups are launching a reactionary counter-revolution against
the civil rights revolution. The coming struggle for power between liberalism
and reaction can eventuate in victory for the liberal-labor forces only if the
Negro is liberated from the thralldom of exploitation, from the remnants of a
feudal caste system. The reactionary coalition which denies us medicare, old-
age security, higher minimum wages, and other social needs--and which at this
very moment is blocking both civil rights and tax-cut legislation--this coalition can be smashed only by a strong Negro-labor alliance, which rests on a new
faith and confidence on the part of Negro workers in the AFL-CIO. For when
masses of white workers join black workers in the streets and at the polls, we
will be well on the way to the democratic political revolution which will free
all Americans from minority rule.
       Let our alliance be strengthened. It is in labor's own interest. For the
Negro's protest today is but the first rumblings of the "under-class." As the
Negro has taken to the streets, so will the unemployed of all races take to the
streets. To discuss the civil rights revolution is therefore to write the
agenda of labor's unfinished revolution. The labor movement cannot ignore this
under-class. It cannot degenerate into a mere protective association, insula-
ting the "haves" from the "have-nots" in the working class.
       And so the Negro looks to the labor movement to lead the struggle for
full employment now. We cannot accept economic policies which envision 4-1/2
percent chronic unemployment by 1980, when current trends indicate that most
of that 4-1/2 per cent may be black. We certainly need a tax-cut. But even
more, we need a massive federal works program to put all Americans back to work
at decent wages. We need higher minimum wages. We need a massive federally-
administered training program to prepare unskilled and semi-skilled workers
for the new jobs that the coming decade will bring. These are among the most
important planks of the March on Washington Movement. They must be inscribed
on labor's banner.
       I have heard many sincere criticisms of the demand for preferential or
compensatory treatment raised by numerous civil rights leaders. Rather than
debate the validity of this demand, let us recognize that it will grow louder
as unemployment continues. For history shows that as unemployment rises, the
gap between Negro and white unemployment rates widens. As this gap widens,
the Negro's demand for preferential treatment to close the gap becomes more
vociferous. But, my friends, there is no need to demand preferential treatment
in full-employment economy. To achieve a full-employment economy, in fact,
labor must be in favor of preferential treatment--not just for the Negro, but
for all the unemployed, the poor, the aged, and the deprived youth of this
nation. These groups would benefit from a domestic "Marshall Plan" organized
on the basis of need. On their behalf we must insist on a constitutional
right of every worker to a job.[46]
       As the labor movement struggles for full employment, there are immediate
tasks we can execute to strengthen the Negro-labor alliance. To accelerate
the eradication of discrimination and segregation within the house of labor,
we need better lines of communication between Negro trade unionists and
labor's leadership. I would propose the establishment of a representative
committee of Negro trade unionists and officers of the AFL-CIO to plan
programs and evolve new techniques to deal with discriminatory practices on
the local level.
       Just as we need more communication within the labor movement, so must the

labor movement establish closer official relations with the civil rights organizations. The coalition of civil rights, labor, religious, and fraternal
groups that organized the March on Washington vividly demonstrated the value of
such relations. I would therefore propose that a committee of the AFL-CIO
leadership be appointed to meet periodically with leaders of the six national
civil rights organizations to work out mutually beneficial policies and
programs that concretely strengthen and substantiate the Negro-labor alliance.
Civil rights is labor's day-to-day business, just as economic justice is the
Negro's day-to-day business. We must therefore infuse our efforts on behalf
of civil rights with the same enthusiasm and rugged determination that we
bring to the collective bargaining table. Thus, I should like to see this
committee stimulate vigorous local and national mass-action campaigns by labor
for a strong civil rights bill by Christmas!

I should like to see both these committees cooperate on a close examination
of the economic crisis of the Negro as it relates to the problems of technological change and automation—problems of urgent concern to labor. These problems
need to be clarified and solutions to them must be advanced, if the Negro
community is not to succumb to demoralization and frustration, and if it is not
to fall victim to false leadership.

All of us are heartened by the creation of the Special Task Force "to help
affiliated central bodies in community-wide drives to eliminate discrimination
from every aspect of community life." We must vigorously support and expand
this Task Force so that its influence will be felt in every city in the
country. We must give it the means of moving into communities where vigorous
civil rights campaigns are under way, to mobilize local unions on the side of
those campaigns. This Task Force must have maximum moral and financial backing
if it is to succeed in educating rank and file workers to their responsibilities
to themselves, to their black brothers, to the cause of human rights, and to
the sacred principles of free, democratic trade unionism.

But this vast educational task cannot be shouldered by the Special Task
Force alone. President Meany, Brother Reuther, and other outstanding national
leaders of the AFL-CIO must lend a hand. They must themselves be prepared to
go into areas of racial tension—into cities like Birmingham and Danville, in
Houston, in various areas of the North—and speak to the rank and file in the
moral and economic terms they can understand. The principles of labor
solidarity and of racial equality will be seriously undermined if we permit a
cleavage to develop between the rank and file and the leadership of the vital
issue of civil rights. The leadership of organized labor seems to be in advance of the membership in their comprehension and attitude toward the civil
rights resolution.

Brothers and sisters, the resolution before us is the strongest statement
of labor's position in civil rights ever to come before a convention of the
AFL-CIO. I am happy to have played a part in drafting it. It firmly commits
organized labor to a frontline role in the civil rights revolution.

The resolution unreservedly commits us to a strong civil rights bill.
That bill must contain a solid Part III, authorizing the Attorney General to
initiate injunctive civil suits against violators of any constitutional right.
Remember, brothers and sisters, that this provision will not only help protect
southern Negroes from police dogs and fire hoses. It will also protect
southern labor organizers.

The civil rights bill must also contain a strong FEPC with commission-
enforcement rather than costly court-enforcement procedures. Neither the
labor movement nor the civil rights movement has fared well at the hands of
southern judges.

Let me then commend this resolution to your solemn and undivided attention. It speaks forcefully of the wrongs of segregation, discrimination,
exploitation, and disfranchisement suffered by black Americans. And it says
in unmistakable terms:

"These wrongs cry for correction. And it is the responsibility of all of
us, individually and collectively, to work diligently for that correction.

"As trade unionists, we must work in two directions. We must set our own
house in order, removing the last vestiges of racial discrimination from
within the ranks of the AFL-CIO. Secondly, we must cooperate with our
neighbors in the general community to assure every American the full rights
of citizenship."

Brothers and sisters, it is for the purpose of expediting progress toward
these twin goals that I have proposed the establishment of two committees to
facilitate communication with Negro trade unionists within the house of labor
and with the civil rights organizations on the outside of the house of labor.

For it is not enough--though it is our task--to give resounding approval
to this resolution. We must each go forth from this historic convention determined to implement this resolution--its letter and its spirit--in every city
and town, in every village and hamlet across the country.

Let each of us individually and unequivocally embrace the Negro's struggle
for freedom, and the labor movement will rise to its full moral stature. Let
us do this, and when labor's rights are threatened, you will see an outpouring
of black Americans into the streets in defense of those rights, as they have
taken to the streets in defense of their own rights.

Let us so implement this resolution that the day will come and not be far
off when the white steelworkers of Birmingham will take the hands of black
children in the crusade to redeem the South.

Let us so implement this resolution that the mill workers of Danville
will join the struggle for civil rights in that beleaguered city--so that white
unemployed miners in West Virginia and Tennessee will march arm-in-arm with
their black brothers to transform their bleak hills into flourishing country-
sides.

Let us so implement this resolution that the dispossessed migrant farm
workers--Negro-American, Mexican-American, Indian-American, and poor white
alike--will stand together for dignity and economic justice--so that the sharecroppers and tenant farmers of Alabama, Mississippi, and Georgia will know that
decisions made this day and implemented this year sounded the deathknell of
their bondage and heralded their liberation.

In the last analysis, my brothers and sisters, the essence of trade
unionism is social uplift. The labor movement traditionally has been the only
haven for the dispossessed, the despised, the neglected, the downtrodden, and
the poor. We must pledge our lives to the social revolution which will bring
all of them into labor's crusading fold--into the pale of dignity and economic
well-being.

This is labor's ultimate faith. This is the basis of our program. This
is the challenge before us. This is the task to which we must now rededicate
ourselves.

PRESIDENT MEANY: May I congratulate Phil Randolph for a very moving,
intelligent address on a subject in which he has been a leader for many, many
years.

Before going into a general discussion of this subject, in order that this
convention will have before it all of the information which I feel is pertinent,
I would like to have a report from our own Standing Committee on Civil Rights
under the Chairmanship of Secretary-Treasurer Schnitzler. Then I will make a
very short report on the special Task Force Committee which Phil mentioned in
his address.

I would like to now call on Secretary-Treasurer Schnitzler to give a
report for the Standing Committee on Civil Rights, particularly on what
progress has been made and what plans the Committee has for solving the internal civil rights problems. That is in other words, the problem within our own
organization.

I call on Secretary-Treasurer Schnitzler.[47]

SECRETARY-TREASURER SCHNITZLER: Mr. President and delegates: the work
of the Standing Committee on Civil Rights has been with the international,
local unions, state bodies and central bodies throughout the country. While
numerous complaints have been received and processed through the Committee,
through our Subcommittee on Compliance, and through our Civil Rights Department, nevertheless the discussion through the five meetings we have had since
the last convention has been directed towards developing a mass approach to
this entire problem.

True, on many occasions we received complaints in which only one person
was involved. That received our immediate attention, but the Committee was
conscious of the fact if we were to deal only with complaints involving one,
two or three persons, we would run out of years in our life before we could
make any kind of an impact on this entire question.

I would like this morning to break down the report I am going to make in three sections. First I want to talk about some of the work that has been done in cooperation with the government.

Many of you, of course, were present at the White House conference on June 13 when over 300 of our presidents of international unions, state federations, and the larger of the central bodies were present. The President's Committee on Equal Opportunity has up until this month had three conferences throughout the country, in St. Louis, in Detroit and in Los Angeles last Thursday. In every one of these conferences the major part of the work was done by trade unionists from these respective areas.

I may point out that President Meany, at the time he was Chairman of the Subcommittee on Apprenticeship & Skilled Training of the President's Committee on Equal Employment Opportunity, proposed that minority group specialists be added to the staff of the United States Bureau of Apprenticeship. They complied with the recommendation, and five minority group specialists on apprenticeship are presently working in the offices in Chicago, New York, Atlanta, Los Angeles and St. Louis.

We had also recommended on numerous occasions that the Department of Labor expand its activities and open up what we call information centers throughout the country, centers where minority groups can go to find out the various requirements for entering the various trades, apprenticeship and so forth. There are at present in operation four centers in the cities of Washington and New York, and there are four in California cities.

In February of 1962 President Meany issued a directive to all of our state, local and the central bodies in which he laid down the policy for convening conventions, meetings, conferences, schools and seminars by those groups.

On July 22 of this year he appointed a special committee and a task force that would be engaged in community-wide racial activities.

These are reports that we have. I know somebody is going to come up and say probably, later on, that I didn't make mention what they had done. The only reason I can't mention what they may have done is because they didn't tell us about it; and one of the big problems we have had is getting the information from our affiliated organizations.

There are at present 38 state councils that have standing Civil Rights Committees that are on the job all of the time. In some of the lesser populated states the state organizations don't have the necessary income to be able to set up a committee, so the work is carried on by the officers of the organization, together with nominees or those that serve on committees that are established by the governor of the state or by the mayors of the respective cities.

We have recorded now in the headquarters that 45 of the larger central bodies throughout the country have standing committees on civil rights.

I want to point out, as I go along, some of the things that represent highlights in the work of some of our affiliated organizations. It was through the efforts of our Vermont State Council that they were able to pass an FEPC law in that state; and whenever you meet the officers of that organization they don't talk about all of their activities; they are so happy about this, which they consider to be a tremendous accomplishment on their part.

In the state of Texas, the State Council made up a half-hour film that has been shown throughout the state at various meetings, and has also been used on television throughout the state of Texas.

Since our last convention there have been desegregated conventions of state organizations,--and I don't only mean meetings, I mean for housing and health as well,--in the states of Texas, Florida, Arkansas, Kentucky, North Carolina, Virginia, Tennessee, and South Carolina. Our COPE organization reported that four area conferences in the early part of this year that were held in Tennessee, Arkansas, Virginia and Texas, were completely integrated.

The state of California has been in the forefront of receiving applause for what they have been doing and it has been through the work of our state council in California that the governor set up a statewide Committee on Equal Opportunity in Apprenticeship & Training for minority groups. Many splendid reports have come from that state of the work that has been done by this committee, which has been staffed more or less by representatives from the trade union movement.

In New York City and in Chicago, through the efforts of our central labor bodies, they have had civil rights conferences.

The states of Minnesota, Wisconsin and Massachusetts as state organizations have had a state conference on civil rights.

Let me get into some of the work of our affiliated international unions.
I want to say first that at the convention in July of this year, the Locomotive
Firemen and Enginemen removed the white Caucasian clause from their constitution by convention action, which now means that there is not a single affiliate
of the AFL-CIO that has any kind of discriminatory regulations against
application for membership in its organization.

118 of our international unions have signed agreements with the President's
Committee on Equal Employment Opportunity. In addition, 87 of those international unions have designated an executive officer as the contact man; that
is, the man that would be contacted if there would be any complaint of any kind
against any of the locals of that affiliated organization. These are mostly,
of course, the larger international unions. Among all of the smaller international unions the president of the organization serves as the contact man.

Of the 130 international unions, there are 111 at the present time that
have no segregated locals of any kind, and of the 19 international unions that
do have segregated locals left, there are only 172 out of over 55,000 local
unions in the AFL-CIO. One of the international unions in the railroad crafts
has merged 22 locals so far this year, and it always maintained that they
weren't segregated locals by color as such; rather, the segregation came about
through work jurisdiction and charters being granted in particular work
jurisdiction fields. As I go on through my report, I am going to point out
where there have been mergers recently that have come to our attention affecting
segregated locals in our international unions.

Our reports at headquarters indicate that there are five unions, the IBEW,
Bricklayers, Plasterers, Machinists and Painters, who have signed national
agreements with their employers in which they have written into the national
agreements non-discrimination clauses.

Just about two months ago, the Executive Board of the Carpenters International Union issued a directive to all of their affiliate local unions in
which they laid out a four-point program with which each local union is to
comply.

You have heard quite a lot about apprenticeship, but before I get into
that subject let me point out to you that insofar as the Building Trades are
concerned, back in the years of 1950, '51 and '52, there were approximately
168,000 apprentices indentured every year in their certified apprenticeship
programs. That has been reduced to approximately 100,000 at the present time;
and while everybody is talking about apprenticeship, they haven't had a clear
vision of the entire problem of apprenticeship.

There are only approximately 100,000 apprenticeships indentured into
certified apprenticeship programs every year, which is only two-thirds of what
it was 10 years ago. It seems to be going downhill constantly, and with the
few openings that you have in apprenticeship, there isn't any opportunity to
take care of many of the youngsters coming out of school that want to enter
the apprenticeship of the skilled trades.

In the District of Columbia, there are 104 Negroes presently serving as
apprentices in the trades in the District of Columbia; and since July 1st, 29
more have been added, so there are presently in apprenticeship service 133 in
the District, and of six other unions there are 82 out of 401 presently in the
apprenticeship programs in the District.

Brother Randolph mentioned Danville, Virginia. Based on the information
we have at headquarters, the two local unions of the United Textile Workers
voted to merge and have merged in that city. As I understand it, there are
7,000 members in the white local union. There are 1,100 members in the
colored local union. So as a merged organization that will represent over
8,100 workers in the City of Danville, Virginia, and we can look forward to
them utilizing their best efforts to get rid of many of the problems that
have plagued that city for much too long.

In June of 1963 the union presidents of the Building Trades Department
wrote a four-point program designed to grant equal opportunity and admission
to members and job referrals and apprenticeship and training, and then in
September of this year the Committee on Equal Employment Opportunity of the
Construction Industry Joint Conference adopted what they call non-discrimination

guide lines for all of the local joint and apprenticeship committees throughout the country.

In Charleston, South Carolina, through the efforts of the local union of the Retail and Wholesale and Department Store Workers, they were able to eliminate all departmental segregation and racially separate lines of promotion and seniority and eliminate whatever wage differentials existed.

There are seven Philadelphia Printing Trades unions that have signed a 12-point agreement with the employers in the graphic industry, and while I don't want to particularly keep mentioning the names of local unions, there's some I just have to.

The Tobacco Workers have been at work in merging with segregated unions that they have had. The segregation that exists in the tobacco, cigarette and tobacco companies in America was there long before the plants were organized, and it is through the direct activities of the officers of the International who are working with the officers of their affiliated local unions that I am able to report to you that in the Philip Morris plant of Richmond, Virginia, the American Tobacco Company in Richmond, Virginia, the American Tobacco Company in Reidsville, North Carolina, the U.S. Tobacco in Richmond, Virginia, the Brown & Williamson Tobacco Company in Louisville, that the ten segregated local unions in these five plants have been completely merged; and the two local unions in the Liggett & Myers Tobacco Company in Richmond, Virginia, have already voted to merge, but they haven't completed all of the details of putting the two locals together, even though it has been voted by both of the local unions involved. They are presently working on, and have favorable reports from the officers and executive boards of the local unions of Brown & Williamson in Winston-Salem, North Carolina, and the Lazrus & Brother Company of Richmond, Virginia.

Reports have come to us from the Musicians that locals have been merged in Denver, San Francisco, Sioux City, Cleveland and Hartford.

The Retail Clerks granted a charter, a new charter in Shreveport, Louisiana, in which there are 800 members of that local union on a completely integrated basis.

Reports have come to us from the various trades that work at the shipyard in Pascagoula, Mississippi; and our figures take us up now to somewhere 18 or 19 workers have been entered into the apprenticeship program in that yard.

The two segregated locals of Carpenters in Knoxville, Tennessee, have been merged, and the Buckeye Oil Company in Memphis, Tennessee, was persuaded by a local union of the Retail and Wholesale Clerks to get rid of the dual seniority list and are promoted on the basis of their qualification and qualification only. Through the work of the local of the UAW in Memphis, Tennessee, the facilities in the cafeteria and locker rooms have been desegregated, and Negro workers have been hired for the office force of that plant. In Memphis, Tennessee, also, the two segregated locals of the American Federation of Government Employees, employed at the Kennedy Hospital, have merged into one integrated local union.

Also, in Memphis, the Rubber Workers at the Firestone Tire & Rubber Company report that 21 Negroes have been indentured for the first time on tire-building machines, and the seniority rosters were merged into one roster where heretofore there were separate rosters.

The Aluminum Workers report that two segregated locals in Richmond, Virginia, were merged, and two segregated local unions in Sheffield, Alabama, were merged, meaning that there are no longer any segregated locals within that international union. Their job is now 100 percent complete.

In Atlanta, Georgia, the State, County, Municipal Employees merged two local unions at the Grady Hospital. In Baltimore, representatives of the Building Trades have gone to the vocational schools and told of their trade, the training required, the qualifications necessary, and pay scales as they go through apprenticeship, and the pay once they reach journeyman status.

As a result of their efforts, there have been more applicants from the minority groups, many of whom have been accepted into the apprenticeship programs for the first time.

The Pulp, Sulphite and Paper Mill Workers have had a number of segregated local unions in the South, and they have merged locals in Lufkin, Texas, Savannah, Georgia, and Calhoon, Tennessee. Recently, as a result of organizing campaigns, when they chartered locals in Crossett, Arkansas, North

Little Rock, Arkansas, Atlanta, Georgia, and Dallas, Texas, they chartered completely integrated locals to start with.

In Birmingham, Alabama, the Steelworkers, through their efforts in the Tennessee Coal and Iron Division, have eliminated separate lines of seniority and set up one line of seniority governing all of the workers in that plant. The Steelworkers have non-discrimination clauses in all major agreements.

In the State of Oklahoma we have a report that of 41 apprentices that are presently in the trades, there are seven Mexicans, seven Indians and 27 Negroes.

The Oil and Chemical Workers merged two segregated locals in Beaumont, Texas and in Port Arthur, Texas. Those were the last remaining segregated locals in that international union, so they have no further segregated locals and their job has been completed 100 percent as well.

In Cincinnati we have reports that seven local unions have taken in colored members either directly or in apprenticeship programs for the first time.

The ILA here in New York has merged two segregated local unions.

In the Rochester area in upstate New York 19 local unions will have taken in colored or minority group workers for the first time.

In the Batavia section there are four; in the Geneva section there are seven, and in the Syracuse-Schenectady section there are four.

In the City of Philadelphia, six local unions, and in Pittsburgh seven local unions have made agreements with the Philadelphia, Pittsburgh and Pennsylvania Human Rights Commission.

In addition to that, we have been working very closely with NILE recently --the National Institute of Labor Education--working with the Office of Manpower, Automation and Training, initiated a union-sponsored training program for unemployed and under-employed youth. I might add that the President of the Building Trades Department served on that committee and was very active in helping develop the program. Their No. 1 project will involve 100 youngsters in the District of Columbia who will participate in a training program for apprenticeship in the carpenters trade. There are two programs in Newark, New Jersey, in which 40 youngsters will be working with the Newark Paint Trades Joint Board.

IATSE Local 152 accepted into membership a Negro American. The Laundry Workers chartered a completed integrated local union in Shreveport, Louisiana. A completely integrated local union has been organized at the Atlanta Metallic Casket Company, Villa Rosa, Georgia, with single job posting and promotion lists.

Community Progress, Inc., a private foundation of which former Connecticut State Labor Council President Mike Sviridoff is Executive Director, has helped place minority groups in apprenticeship programs and reported 17 of these apprentices have been placed.

Chicago Building Trades reports placing 90 American Negroes on federal building projects in that city.

St. Louis Bricklayers' union reports 18 Negro Americans placed--two bricklayers and two apprentices. The Machinists' local of St. Louis at the McDonald Aircraft Corporation reported upgrading two American Negroes to supervisory positions.

Houston, Texas, IBEW local and the Printers' union accepted Negro journeymen into membership.

The Glazers union of Houston, Texas negotiated a contract calling for complete integration in a manufacturing plant.

The Boilermakers, Machinists, and Molders union jointly negotiated a contract with the Lufkin Foundry in Texas, calling for complete integration and upgrading and promotion.

Pantex of Amarillo, Texas, under Metal Trades Council contract is completely integrated, including promotions and supervisory jobs.

The Boilermakers negotiated contracts with the Exchange Parts Company and Stratoflex, Inc., in Fort Worth, Texas, with everyone having the same rights to promotion and higher paid classifications.

The Boilermakers in Houston, Texas, merged two segregated unions.

The Office Workers union, holding bargaining rights in General Dynamics plant in Forth Worth, have negotiated contracts covering Negroes who have been employed and they can bid for upgrading and promotion.

In Fort Wayne, Indiana, Negro apprentices have been placed in the

International Harvester Company and several Building Trades unions have Negro apprentices for the first time.
The A&P and Kroger food markets in Terre Haute, Indiana, employ Negroes as cashiers and stock workers.
These are the things that are going on.
I mentioned that many complaints have been received. They have been processed. We have at the present time at headquarters nine complaints that are being processed. Never have we failed to complete a complaint. Where it was an improper complaint, of course, it was eliminated, but where it was a proper complaint, through the help of our international unions, and local unions, state and local bodies, we have been able to make the necessary adjustment to eliminate the complaint.
Let me just enjoy a little luxury this morning and talk about ourselves.
I must say that our Director, Boris Shishkin, and his two Assistant Directors, Don Slaiman and Walter Davis, have been running back and forth across this country jumping in wherever necessary to try to carry out the obligation we had under the Civil Rights Resolution that was passed at the last convention.
In my travels throughout the country I have come in contact with many representatives of many recognized national organizations, and I have talked to them about this problem.
I have mentioned these various instances to give you an idea of the work that's going on in all of the 50 states by our trade union movement. As I examine the work that our people have been doing, there isn't anybody in this country that is more determined, that shows more good will in eliminating the discrimination as it has existed, than the representatives of our trade union movement.
I think that on this platform I ought to say we haven't done all that we should have done, but I'm certainly interested in harnessing all of your good will and your efforts, so we can move on and do the total job that our resolution calls for.
Before concluding, I want to announce that the members of the Civil Rights Committee are: Eugene Frazier, George Harrison, Dave McDonald, Lee Minton Louis Simon, Richard Walsh, Charles Zimmerman, A. J. Hayes, Ralph Helstein, Joseph Keenen, Emil Mazey, John Murphy, James Suffridge, Milton Webster, Robert Powell and Dave Sullivan. [48]

PRESIDENT MEANY: Thank you, Secretary Schnitzler.
I will have a report on this special Task Force a little later. I think at this time we should allow the discussion to proceed on the resolution itself.
The Chair recognizes Vice President Reuther.
VICE PRESIDENT REUTHER: President Meany, fellow delegates and friends:
I rise to support the resolution on civil rights and to lend my voice on the sentiments expressed by Brother Phil Randolph.
American democracy is in deep moral crisis. I believe that as a people and as a nation we face the challenge of whether or not we are equal to being true to our faith, whether we are equal to being true to America's promise of the equality of all men.
We in the labor movement share a heavy and unique responsibility in this crisis, for it has been the historic role of the labor movement to take the concept of human brotherhood out of the stratosphere of pious platitudes and bring it down to earth and give it new meaning and substance in the lives of people. The civil rights struggle is about that practical job.
For 100 years Negro Americans have been denied, they have been deprived, they have been degraded, and they have been discriminated against. Today they are on the march to achieve freedom and first-class citizenship.
As one member of the trade union movement, I share the view that the labor movement of America has the sacred duty, it has the moral responsibility and it has the historic opportunity to join in that march with Negro Americans so that freedom can be a blessing of every American regardless of race or creed or color.
Our Negro brothers and sisters will not be satisfied, nor should they be satisfied, with tokenism, because there are no half-way houses on the road to freedom. Each of us, every American of every creed, every color, of every

political persuasion, shares the responsibility for joining together so that we can build a bridge over the moral gap between what American democracy has promised and its failure to perform up to that promise in the field of civil rights.

I believe that we all recognize that we must be deeply involved in this struggle because the labor movement is about the struggle for freedom; it is about the struggle for human dignity, it is the struggle for social justice not for a few but for every man and his family.

It is our task to strip the mask from those Americans who practice what I call high octane hypocrisy, who sound off and make noble noises about human brotherhood and, having made these noble noises, they drop the "brother" and keep the "hood."

We have understood that no man is an island, that freedom is indivisible and that you can make freedom secure for yourself only as you make it universal. Abe Lincoln knew that and he said that those who deny freedom to others deserve it not for themselves and they will not long retain it.

We stand on trial before the world. The world knows we have the most productive economy in the world, that our technological progress is second to none, and that we do have the highest living standards of any people in the world. But we are not going to be judged by material standards.

We are going to be judged by moral standards, by the ability of our free society to relate its technical progress to human progress. They are going to judge us in the field of civil rights and human rights not by what we preach but by what we practice. And I believe, with the President, when he stood before the Berlin wall, which is a tangible monument to the moral bankruptcy of communism, that we are committed to defend freedom in Berlin. But I think we need to understand that we cannot successfully defend freedom in Berlin so long as we deny freedom in Birmingham, because the two are tied together.

Now, what does the resolution call for? First, it says that we shall join with men and women for good will throughout our nation to secure passage of the strongest civil rights bill, a bill with teeth in it, a bill that will give America effective tools to end the ugly forms of discrimination in every aspect of our national life.

The bill that came through the committee in the House is a move in the right direction, but we have to be eternally vigilant to work to strengthen that bill so that we can go to the Senate with the strongest possible bill.

Then we face the practical task of joining with church groups, with civil rights groups, with civic and fraternal groups in the creation of a great coalition of conscience to try to bear upon the United States Senate the total pressure of an aroused people so that we can smash the filibuster. If we do that, I say we can sweep aside the Eastlands and the Goldwaters, and we can get a civil rights bill through the United States Senate.

But after we have that bill, the job will not be done. Our job will just be beginning because we then will be called upon to implement in every state and in every community the purposes of that bill and the use of the tools that it will provide. This means we must work on the job front, on the housing front, on the education front, in the broad field of public accommodation. Then we must work to get legislation at the local and state level to fill those areas where the federal government does not have adequate jurisdiction.

Then it calls upon the labor movement to set its house in order. And I think this Convention has to say in a loud and clear voice that cannot be misunderstood that there is no room for Jim Crow in the house of American labor.

I believe that we have to say that labor's solidarity is colorblind and that we are going to build that solidarity to encompass every American, regardless of race or creed or color.

We have heard Bill Schnitzler's report. We have made progress, but progress is a relative thing. We are in the middle of a social revolution and when you are dealing with the dynamics of a revolution, people will not judge where we are or where we have come from; they will judge us based upon how far we still must go.

It isn't what we have done that is important; it is what remains to be done.

There will be many pressures. There will be much criticism. Yes, there will be times when that criticism directed against the American labor movement will be unfair, it will be unreasonable, and many times the criticism will be most sharp against the very people and the very organizations who are doing the most.

But that is the nature of the struggle to make human progress, because the people who are impatient, who are reaching out to be free, to be whole human beings, they are not going to use microscopes and work out the refinements of niceties.

They are going to look at the NAM. They know the NAM is not committed to human values, it is committed to property values. The American labor movement historically has put priority on people and not profits because we have been committed to human rights over property rights. And for this reason they are going to expect the American labor movement to do more and more and more.

The important thing today is not will we adopt this resolution. Every delegate here knows that that is precisely what we are going to do. The important thing is not what we say. The important thing is what we do to implement the purposes of this resolution. The words are good, but our task is to commit ourselves to implement those words.

It is not going to be easy to tear down the structure of hatred and prejudice that has disfranchised millions of Negro Americans. This is a hard task, but was building the labor movement an easy task? It was not. It took sacrifice, it took struggle, it took dedication, it took determination, it took courage and it took compassion.

The struggle for civil rights will require nothing less than what we put into building the labor movement in the early days when the going was rough.

What we need to keep in mind, I believe, is that the measure of our conviction and the measure of our commitment as a labor movement cannot be measured in the area of convenience and the area of comfort of articulating brave goals in an area where it is easy, where everyone agrees. That is not the best.

The test is, what do we do in those areas when we are dealing with the forces of change and challenge and controversy? Will we have the deep moral conviction to stand up and fight to do the right thing when it is hard?

That is the task on civil rights. The civil rights fight has to be won in the areas where it is difficult, not in the areas where it is easy.

Our problem in America is further compounded by the fact that we are dealing with two parallel but separate revolutions.

We are dealing with the great social revolution of civil rights, in which the structure of American society must yield to the morality and the reality of the 20th Century. Parallel to that revolution is a technological revolution which complicates the social revolution of civil rights.

We cannot solve either of those revolutions in a vacuum. We have got to find a common solution to both. What we need to avoid more than anything else is to be trapped in a dead end alley where people believe that you can solve the problem of employment opportunities for Negroes outside of a broad full employment program for every American.

We should not get ourselves boxed in where the discussion will be whether a black American walks the streets unemployed or a white American walks the streets unemployed. The position of the labor movement has got to be that there must be a job for every American, whether he is white or black or brown or yellow, because there is no other answer.

I am confident that we in the American labor movement, in cooperation with men and women of good will--and the church groups are one of the encouraging elements of this whole development--can by rational and responsible action find answers to America's and democracy's great dilemma.

If we fail to work together and find the answers in the light of reason, in the spirit of brotherhood, then the apostles of hatred will move in to fill the vacuum created by our failure. Reason will yield to riots, and brotherhood will yield to bitterness and bloodshed, and we can tear asunder the very fabric of American democracy.

This is the great challenge. Let us adopt the resolution, but then let us go back home, each of us, and commit ourselves to the practical task of implementing the high purposes of this resolution. If we do that, I believe that American democracy can be equal to this challenge. Thank you.

   PRESIDENT MEANY: Thank you, Brother Reuther.
   The Chair recognizes Vice President Keenan.

VICE PRESIDENT KEENAN: Mr. Chairman, I rise to support this resolution.
I would like to say a few words about the present. I am not ready to stand for
this labor movement being put on trial. Many of our organizations date back
some 60 or 70 years, and 60 or 70 years ago they had to meet the requirements
of that time in order to maintain their existence. The skilled trades had to
develop an apprentice system because of the conditions in the industry. Years
ago the contractors generally maintained their offices in their vest pockets,
and called the organizations for men. Then continual employment was normal.
In late years, in most of the industries, we have had full employment, and
that set up another set of circumstances. I get quite concerned every time I
pick up a newspaper and read about the discrimination in the Building Trades
or the Printing Trades.

Just a few years ago we had the Taft-Hartley Act passed. A few years
later we had the Landrum-Griffin passed, and in Landrum-Griffin they placed on
the labor organizations of this country some of the most dastardly regulations
that could be conceived in the minds of men.[49]

You all have the reporting forms. You all have the regulations for
bonding, and Bill Schnitzler, I believe, can make the greatest dissertation
on bonding that I know of.

Just some six months ago the government handed out a questionnaire asking
the unions of this organization to render detailed reports on the makeup of
their unions. I don't mind that, if it is general. But when they talk about
hiring halls, they are talking about just a small percentage of the total
membership of this organization. What about the hiring halls of AT&T and all
of the great corporations of this country?

I have been in this field for just 22 years. In 1940 I came to Washington
to serve on the National Defense Council, and this was one of the first issues
that we were faced with, on construction jobs. There were 23 international
unions with a color bar then. I can say that there has been progress all the
way along the line. Slow, yes. Discouraging at times. I spent hours in
certain cases trying to get the regulations changed, or some modification in
order that we could cope with people of other than white races on the job.
Today I would think that the time has come to look into the large corporation
and their hiring practices. This is one issue on which more people talk out
of both sides of their mouth than on any other issue that I know of. I think
the time has come that we must stand on our own feet and stop being on the
defensive.

We are known as the family of labor. Every family, no matter how large
or small, has its complications and its heartaches. I am not going to say
here today that we have been perfect. Most of us have tried to do our job.
Most of us have tried in our own way to overcome the handicaps we find in our
local unions. This is a question on which in every section of the country you
find a different flavor. I just want to say this: after we adopt this
resolution, let us implement it in this organization. We have a Committee on
Civil Rights. As the complaints come in they go to the Committee, and we will
be coming to you with those cases.

I am sure, if we all cooperate, that we can put the wording of this
resolution into effect a whole lot quicker than we now realize. I say, let
us do the job ourselves, and let this organization go out and do the job that
it is set up to do and that it is destined to do. Thank you.

PRESIDENT MEANY: Thank you, Brother Keenan. Any further discussion?
DELEGATE CLEVELAND ROBINSON, Retail, Wholesale and Department Store
Union: Brother Chairman, I rise to support the resolution. It is hardly
necessary for me to do that because, as Brother Reuther said, everybody in
this room will vote for the resolution.[50]

I do believe that there are some things that ought to be said in this
Convention which have not yet been said, because in my opinion, unless we
face the facts as they are, and unless we are prepared to tear away the mask
of hypocrisy which exists in too many places in our labor movement the job
is not going to be done.

We have heard much talk about help internationally, and I am all for it.
I am very happy to see that there are delegations here from Africa, Asia and
other nations. All to the good. It is fine when our Negro community reads
about the amount of money that our government is pouring into these countries,

and what AFL-CIO is doing, and it is very fine and heartwarming to know that
we have the ability, by the Marshall Plan for example, to restore Europe after
its devastation in war. Nobody can question the ability of the United States
when we really mean to go to work.

If we do these things, why, in 1963, 100 years after the Emancipation
Proclamation, do we have to have these despicable conditions that pertain to
the Negro in America?

This is the basic question, and to those who are talking about the
progress that has been made, let us come to one conclusion: Either a man is of
the Negro race or he is not. If he is a man, then one day more is too long for
him to suffer, and he does not want to suffer 350 years of slavery. He has
suffered 100 years since Emancipation, and as far as he is concerned, he reads
a little better today, his kids know a little more, and that is why they are
ready to fight for democracy, because it is working for everybody but them.

Let's examine some of the things we have heard here today. Brother
Schnitzler reported about the Building Trades, and he talked about the fact
that there are declines in jobs, number of apprenticeships, but there are
still 100,000 apprenticeships that go out each year.

May I ask how many of them go to Negroes--that's a basic question--in the
year 1963, and you will find what the answer is.

We hear a report a hundred and eighteen unions signed with the Vice
President of the United States that they will not discriminate. Well, I'm
informed that no more than 30 of these unions as much as published it in their
publications, said nothing about doing anything else about it. Now, I know
what we did in RWDSU. We had a doubt. We adopted a policy, and we went ahead
with the job. It is not, for a fact, perfect, but things are being done.

I don't think many unions as much as took it to their Executive Boards to
say anything to acquaint their membership with this fact. As far as they are
concerned, the day of their signing was they day they forget about it.

Are we going to have these kinds of situations? If we do, the labor
movement will continue to receive severe criticism from the Negro community,
and justifiably so, because the Negro has supported the labor movement all
down the years, and the labor movement has betrayed the Negro worker.

Let's go a little further. We talk about the fact that there are such
vast areas when Negroes and other minorities work without any kind of protection by federal laws. No unemployment benefits, no minimum wage, no workmen's
compensation and no social security. I think the figures run into the
millions. They are to be found in hospitals, working as janitors in schools,
in some instances working for state governments at wages as low as 50 cents
an hour.

This is happening not yesterday. It's happening today. It's happening
right here in New York, and one of the things I haven't heard mentioned here
is that one local union of RWDSU, under the leadership of a man known as Leon
Davis, undertook a campaign to shed some light on this picture, and, from
nothing, in less than four years, has organized some 10,000 of these Negro-
Puerto Rican workers, and has by so doing doubled their wages from $28, $30 a
week to today $60 a week, and what was the crime that this man committed?

He, along with leaders of the New York labor movement, and with consultation with state officials and in the labor movement, agreed with Governor
Rockefeller that legislation should be passed which would give the people
collective bargaining rights which they did not have before. It didn't take
anything from them. It gave them something they didn't have, and for this
this man is being punished. He is being called a criminal. He went to jail
for 30 days, the only union leader I know who has been to jail for picket
line activity in recent years, and was sentenced to another six months, and I
will say this: That if we could get others in the labor movement, other
segments of the labor movement, to move in on the millions of workers, underprivileged workers, throughout the length and breadth of our country who are
working at starvation wages, who are literally in slavery, if we could get
this to be done, it would be a fine thing on the part of the labor movement.

I must commend Brother Reuther that he saw to it that the Industrial
Union Department did give some money to support these down-trodden, forgotten
workers in their struggle for dignity. I hope that something will be done
to continue to organize these workers throughout the length and breadth of
our country.

I believe that Brother Randolph's suggestion about upping the minimum
wage is quite in order, because while the President talked of the tax cut,
there are millions of workers to whom a tax cut means nothing. They never
made enough to pay taxes in the first place, so what can a tax cut do for
them? But if we were to broaden the minimum wage law to cover these workers
and bring it up from where it is today, from a dollar and a quarter to somewhere about $2.00 an hour, this would be money which would be going to people
who would have to spend it for food, clothing and shelter, and American
business would hum.

More people would be on jobs, and the greater measure of security would
be found for these downtrodden people.

There is one other basic question we have to face. What do people do who
are in the low income brackets with education of their kids? The government
tells us it takes $6,000 or better for a family of four to live. Well, all of
us have reports about how many people are making less than $6,000, how many
are making less than $3,000, and, certainly, you know that Negroes, Puerto
Ricans and other minorities form the bulk of these numbers.

What are we supposed to do in terms of educating our kids? How can we
carry a kid through high school? We hear about the eight million dropouts.
Wouldn't it be in order that the labor movement find some way of formulating
some policy where we could pressure the federal government to grant subsidies
and loans to these families so that they can see their kids through high
school, if not through college, at least?

I think it is in order, because the money that we would advance and invest
on our kids today will pay off bigger dividends for tomorrow, and if we do not
do it now, in 1970 or 1980 our problems will be so very great that today will
be a picnic.

All in all I'd say that we have a big problem ahead of us, and the labor
movement, I believe, can do a big job. In some areas some unions are doing a
fine job. In other areas it must be said that less than a fine job is being
done.

I tell you that when upwards of 250,000 people marched on Washington on
August 28th, with the churches in the vanguard, with the civil rights organizations in the vanguard, and with the official labor movement not approving
it, the Negro community was very, very disappointed.

I hope that this will not happen in the future. I think that the official
body of the AFL-CIO missed the boat despite the fact that many fine trade
unionists, including Walter Reuther and others, found ways and means to support
this to the hilt. But this was a fine demonstration of what is necessary if
we are to put a minority on the road to success, to freedom and equality for
all. Thank you.

DELEGATE FRANK EVANS, Allied Industrial Workers of America: Certainly we
are happy to have a resolution coming from the Resolutions Committee on Civil
Rights, and there is no question in any of the members of organized labor's
minds as to how far organized labor has gone into the field of civil rights.
I think I can stand here today and say that organized labor has gone further
into this field of civil rights than any other organization in America, but at
the same time say that we are not satisfied with resolutions. We do want
resolutions passed, but we want agencies that are able to support and back up
the positions that are outlined in the resolution.

We know that this body here cannot hand down orders to local unions where
discrimination prevails in the lower echelons of organized labor. I do know
that this Convention can give orders to international unions, national unions
and city central bodies, but the international unions will have to order the
local unions that are discriminating against Negroes to stop discrimination
and do the job that is outlined here in Convention.

I want to say that we should do the thing that was done in Cleveland
this year, during July and August, on the question of discrimination in the
trades, by calling in all the executive boards of the local unions, the
representatives of the local unions, and in some cases of the international
unions, and sit down around the table to negotiate this question to a
satisfactory conclusion. While on the floor, Mr. Chairman, I'd like to point
out that when Brother Cruikshank and I, went into Chicago in 1962, meeting
with the convention of the National Medical Association, and we got passed

in that convention a resolution on aid to the aged in spite of the AMA's position on that question. After getting this resolution passed, we then had, for the first time in the history of America, for doctors of America to say to you that I went with a delegation of doctors to the offices of the AFL-CIO, met with Brother Meany on this question, and there we did receive the aid and assistance for these doctors who had filed suits against some 56 hospitals and medical organizations in Cook County, Illinois.

I don't want to say too much on this question at this time, because they're in litigation, but I can say to you that we are now in the process of a settlement agreement on the question of discrimination against Negro doctors and Negro patients who could not get into these hospitals in Cook County, Illinois, and I can say I'd like to commend the Executive Council of the AFL-CIO on their position in getting this thing passed. I thank you.

DELEGATE LEO SMITH, IUE: Mr. Chairman, I rise in support of the resolution. Let me say that the Negro is fed up with delay and indecision. Let me say that we want jobs. We want freedom, and let me say that the time is now. Let me point out to the delegates of this Convention that all of you have a stake in the Negros' fight for first and not second class citizenship.

Let me point out that three-fourths of the world's people are members of the so-called darker races. Yet they say also that despite this sweetness and light there is a tremendous bout being waged for the controls of the minds of men in the United Nations.

Let me also say now racial difficulties are being phonographed in sound and are being played by Russia all over the world. This is used to blacken the name of America: the snarl of the police dog as he rips the flesh, the filthy language of the police as they turn water hoses on our people.

Let me say that the concept of nonviolence has grown very, very thin; that the Negro is at the breaking point and that unless our elected officials from President Kennedy on down assert themselves in the cause of freedom, then we are going to witness a blood bath that will make the purge of Adolph Hitler look like a tea party.

Let me say again, in support of the resolution, that I urge each delegate to this convention to go back into their communities and do their part in implementing it. Thank you.

DELEGATE H. S. BROWN, Texas AFL-CIO: As one of the states represented at this Convention South of the Mason-Dixon Line, Mr. Chairman, I rise in full support of the remarks and full support of the resolution.

I do this not on my own individual action, but with the unanimous decision of the state convention, which concluded without a dissenting vote on August 29 in the great city of Houston, to support the fullest and strongest civil rights measure than can be passed by the Congress of these United States, and calling upon eliminating from our membership any local union that has any form of discrimination.

It requires that every central body shall have an active civil rights committee that shall meet on a regular monthly basis and shall submit its grievances to the State Committee with the right to suspend that organization from its membership.

In addition to that, however, and in support of the remarks of Brother Randolph and Brother Reuther, I think that we must take this matter from this Convention to the local level. In our state, it is not just the Negro. There are two million Latin Americans who receive less than 50 cents an hour.

This resolution is applicable in South Texas where 100,000 Mexican citizens cross the bridge every day as so-called commuters and take jobs in Laredo and in Brownsville and in El Paso where the trade union movement is non-existent today except for a few crusaders. It means that the employees who are working, the maids in the biggest hotel in one of the national chains, are working 60 hours at $11 a week. Many of you in this hotel carry a carte blanche card to that kind of an operation.

We will take our stand with the Negro, with the Latin American, or ten years hence we will not stand at all in our state, and I don't know about yours.

We called on the governor of our state of Texas five times in five weeks to call a special session of the legislature to denounce all forms of discrimination, including the damnable "right-to-work" law, which is a device

and a scheme that is being peddled to our minority friends as a way in which
they can be guaranteed a job--and 268,000 Texans are looking for a job today
with a phony set of Texas Employment Commission figures that says that there
are 3.9 percent unemployed but fail to mention the people over 50 that can't
get a job, and, therefore, not being in the labor market are not reported in
the official unemployed statistics.

These are the conditions of which we speak when we talk about civil
rights. Not Negro, not Latin American. It's jobs and decent wages with a
collective bargaining agreement, with a right to be heard, with a right to be
grieved.

There are a half million Negroes in our state working for less than fifty
cents an hour. There are nearly a million unorganized Latin Americans in our
state working for less than fifty cents an hour, so when we put our TV show
that Brother Schnitzler talked about on every station, we didn't talk about
color. We showed an actual family of Juan Hernandes and nine kids trying to
live on 31 cents an hour, and that a union contract would mean decent wages
and decent conditions.

Ask the ILGWU what happened in San Antonio, where they once had 4,000
members in eleven plants, and today, under right-to-work and the prejudice of
one person against another, not a single member is left, not a single union
contract.

Ask Brother Potofsky of his fight in El Paso today to organize 50,000
garment workers who are working under pitiful substandard conditions.

Civil rights means more than just doing something for the Negro. Politically we can't win in Texas against the money changers that run the temple,
called the state government, with just organized labor. We formed, Brother
Randolph, the alliance you speak of a year ago then known as the coalition,
and if you are interested in how it works, come and see our movie, a second
one we are producing for state-wide TV. It will be shown at four o'clock today
in the Georgian Room of this hotel.

It is a premiere, and we would like for other states to take the hand of
the Negro, the Latin American, the Indian, whatever he is, if he is a worker,
and he is not making at least $2.00 an hour. That is the brother that we need
to get with and win the kind of progress we are talking about. And we are
proud to support the resolution. Thank you very much.

DELEGATE MARY CALLAHAN, IUE: I rise in support of the entire civil
rights resolution. However, on the implementation I think there was one thing
that could have been brought out a little more clearly and something that I
think every one of us can address ourselves to. We who are parents and
teachers, who are delegates here today, we have a message to take into our own
homes. We don't want ten years hence to have another social revolution,
because we have been remiss in our duties and responsibilities in not following
through on the precepts of equality and equal rights for all peoples.

Therefore, we can sort of make up for our remissions and omissions of the
past by starting out with our children in our homes and in the schools and
teach brotherhood of people and children, because children aren't born, you
know, with hatred and discriminatory practice. They learn it somewhere.

Should we examine our consciences and see if maybe we who are standing
here today and applauding and preaching have done our job? It is not too late.
If our children are grown up, certainly we have grandchildren whom we can
reach. I think this should be part of the resolution, Mr. Chairman.

PRESIDENT MEANY: The Chair recognizes Vice President Walsh.

VICE PRESIDENT WALSH: Mr. Chairman and delegates: I rise in support of
the resolution. But in support of that resolution, I would like to call to
the attention of the delegates and to the governmental agencies that we, the
international unions, need help. Too long now the government of this country
has been enacting laws which have been tying the hands of the international
unions and then sending them out to do jobs with their hands tied behind
their backs.

Not too long ago the AFL Convention suspended an organization from the
American Federation of Labor, and very shortly thereafter in an election
which was held the same people were designated as the bargaining agency for
that organization.

As an international president, I want to see segregation wiped out in
our international union.

I want, as president, to have the power to instruct our local unions to
comply with the action of this Convention, and if they don't comply with the
action of this Convention, I want to discipline them, even to the extent of
removing the charter of that organization, if necessary. But I would like a
promise from the people who are handling the laws of this country, especially
Taft-Hartley, and Landrum-Griffin, to give a promise to our international
unions that when we discipline a local union because they will not carry out
the mandates of this Convention, that they won't certify the same people as
the bargaining agent for the people whom we expel from our international union.
I think we are entitled to that support.
     From this platform today I say to the agencies, give us the help to help
us to stop segregation in our international unions. Permit us to discipline
the people who won't carry out the orders, and we'll try to do the job.
     Thank you.
     DELEGATE MATTHEW GUINAN, Transport Workers Union of America: I rise in
support of the resolution on civil rights, and also in support of the
expressions of Brother Randolph and Brother Reuther, and particularly Hank
Brown from the State of Texas, because I think the job that Hank Brown is
doing in Texas deserves a great deal of credit, because they are doing it under
great difficulty.
     The Transport Workers Union has never taken a back seat to any union or
any other organization in the country when it comes to the fight for civil
rights, because from its inception in 1934 we adopted principles for equality
and for anti-discrimination against all minorities, not just Negroes.
     I am happy to stand up here before this Convention today and am proud to
say that we have practiced these principles that we adopted back in 1934 and
have continued to practice them. We distributed this pamphlet that we put out
here this morning, so it gives you a record of the Transport Workers Union on
the question of civil rights over the past 25 years.
     But, Mr. Chairman, I have been at many conventions and listened to resolu-
tions on the question of political action, on the question of civil rights, and
I'm sorry to say that to this day I have never seen effective implementation of
these resolutions of the past.
     I know, Mr. Chairman, it is in your heart at this moment to see to it that
this resolution has effective implementation.
     There is just one thing I would like to add, Mr. Chairman. I think that
it is most important in the fight on Capitol Hill to get out a strong civil
rights bill that we mobilize the full labor movement to lobby on Capitol Hill
to bring about an effective bill.
     I say that some people here perhaps feel that the progress is too slow.
I particularly refer to Cleve Robinson, who thinks that we are not going fast
enough, and I agree that perhaps we are not going fast enough. But this,
Cleve, is one of the major problems that faces the labor movement today.
     We,you, say that the labor movement had the full support of Negroes right
from the beginning, going back many years, let's not talk too freely about
that, because I've seen the problem in my own organization--and we went through
some rough times from 1937 until 1950. I'm sorry to say that many of the
Negroes did not join our organization when we had the open shop. But I'm glad
to say that they are getting more sense, they are coming into the organization,
and we're giving them every support in fighting for their civil rights and all
of their rights.
     Thank you, Mr. Chairman.
     DELEGATE HERRICK S. ROTH, Colorado Labor Council: I would like, if this
is seconded, to move an amendment to the resolution, Mr. Chairman, which
would add the remarks of Brother Randolph as the preamble to this resolution
and the recommendations of Brother Randolph to the resolves of this resolution. If it is seconded, I would like to indicate why.
     PRESIDENT MEANY: You are moving to amend the report of the Committee.
     DELEGATE ROTH: Yes, sir.
     PRESIDENT MEANY: Is there a second?
     A DELEGATE (Name not given): Second.
     PRESIDENT MEANY: Who seconds the motion? Give your name.
     DELEGATE EVANS: Evans.
     DELEGATE MAZEY: Mazey.

DELEGATE ROTH: Evans and Mazey, among others.

PRESIDENT MEANY: Very well.

DELEGATE ROTH: Brother Chairman, I think perhaps one of the most
eloquent speeches we have had here on the floor was by my good brother, Hank
Brown, from Texas, and illustrates why Brother Randolph's remarks themselves
are even more stirring than this resolution. The trouble, I suppose, with
resolutions is that we don't often get down to statistics. Brother Randolph
gave a number of specifics that keyed to the kind of thing that's going on in
Texas and that some of us in some states, I think, are trying to do at our own
levels, because we are not going to solve this, I know, without getting to the
grass roots.

I want to make it perfectly clear that the AFL-CIO and our own state
organization are working harmoniously on this with the full support of President Meany. The thing is that in the specifics, Brother Randolph mentioned at
least two things that, if you adopt this amendment, would be added that are of
great importance from our point of view, after trying to tackle this at the
grass roots pretty hard for the last four months.

One of these specifics is that we need a coordinating body between the
leaders of the minority communities and the labor movement in every town and
city in this country. If we did this at the top level officially, which
seems to me his remarks would direct us to do and which I am certain will be
done anyway, this would convey the sense of this Convention and would not just
be another committee report. The sense of the Convention then would say, do
this not only at the national level, but at the local level.

Then I think, too, in his remarks, as he was emphasizing the importance
of this communication, that we will find that we will begin to open up job
opportunities. Right now we aren't talking to the people in business and
industry who have job opportunities, but the nice part about it is that when
you do this, you do it exactly as Brother Brown has said, you find that your
building trades people want to expand the apprentice program and not cut it
back in job opportunity. You find that leaders of business and industry
decide that it is worth working with the labor movement to give this kind of
opportunity.

I think the last reason, though, that we should really support this is
that over the years Brother Randolph within the labor movement and on the
outside has been a key spokesman not just for the Negroes but for the Latin
Americans, the Spanish Americans. Better than ten percent of the population
of our state is in this category; less than three percent is in the Negro
category. But this is the great unemployed, the great underemployed, the
great undereducated segment of our society.

Nobody but the labor movement can do this. The NAACP over the years has
not done it until this sudden movement of peoples. If they had harkened to
Brother Randolph long ago historically, even we would have done more in the
labor movement.

So I would like to suggest that we add this, and I would say fittingly
as a preamble, and with the recommendations as part of the resolve to this
report, because it makes concrete sense and comes from the great leader within
our own movement and would, therefore, be strong support of this Convention for
it. I urge your support of the amendment.

PRESIDENT MEANY: Now, Brother Roth, you spoke of the idea of the AFL-CIO
doing something at the local grassroots level in conjunction with other groups
of citizens. I said at the beginning of this discussion, after the resolution was read and Phil Randolph made his address, that I had a report to make
on a special committee, a special task force committee. I am rather surprised
that Brother Roth is unfamiliar with this, because his city is one of the
cities where we have already gone to work. He must know that we are doing
this work, because we have not only gone to work there, but we are helping
the Denver local central body finance this activity.

Last July, after a meeting at the White House of a number of trade union
leaders, the question came up as to the best way to accelerate progress in
the field of civil rights, with the idea of placing more reliance on community
action.

In the final analysis, this problem is an old one of about a hundred
years, more than one hundred years. We have to do something more than pass
resolutions and use the weight of the labor movement and pass laws. We have

to change the thinking of a great many people in this country, people who do
not think of themselves, if you please, as being segregationists or being
anti-Negro, but people who don't hate, don't think of themselves as having
prejudices, but who have gotten into a certain way of life that excludes any
recognition of those with a different color of skin. There is sort of an
indifference on the part of a lot of people. They don't think in terms of this
being their responsibility.

So we in the labor movement felt that we have to go to the local level,
that it involves all Americans, that all Americans can be adversely affected by
this business of race discrimination. So we set up a Special Task Force of the
AFL-CIO, consisting of Secretary-Treasurer Schnitzler, Vice Presidents Randolph
and Reuther, President Haggerty of the Building Trades Department and myself.

The purpose of this committee is to assist AFL-CIO local central bodies
to initiate the establishment of bi-racial human rights committees, or civil
rights committees, whatever they want to call them, in the major cities across
the nation; where none exists, to initiate the action, and where they do exist,
to help support and strengthen these committees.

The idea was to have a broadly based committee involving every important
segment of the community, with labor in the forefront, with labor initiating,
labor pushing for action, parent-teacher associations, religious groups, civic
leaders, and so on, right down the line.

This is to fight discrimination every place, not just on the job, but in
the schools, in housing, in stores, in theaters, in local recreation areas;
and this, of course, means the full cooperation of the entire community.

We have started. July is not so long ago, but we got started. I assigned
two assistant directors of the AFL-CIO Department of Civil Rights to head this
committee staff. We have already begun work in eight cities in the brief time
since our August Executive Council meeting.

Our staff leaders have met with local central bodies in Boston, Cincinnati,
Washington, D.C., Milwaukee, Oakland, San Francisco, Denver, Houston and other
places. We have plans under way in practically all of these places.

We have received a tremendous fine response from the local labor movement.
They like the idea of our staff people coming and assisting to set up these
meetings, and here at a meeting of the five-man committee the other day we
decided to double the staff; in other words, instead of having a two-man team,
to have two two-men teams, because in each of these cities, when they go there,
it takes at least two or three days.

The success of this program will play a large part, I think, in this
field, because it gets right down to the local level. This is where you have
got to eliminate discrimination. You have got to eliminate it right down at
the local level, right at the grass roots level, and we can use the assistance
of every national union, the national representatives throughout the country,
the state federation people, and the central body people. I think this will be
a definite contribution to this problem.

I would like to talk very briefly on the resolution. If you read the
resolution you will find that it covers a wide range of activities, legislation, action within the unions, discrimination, apprenticeship, all the way
down the line.

I recall when we didn't have such an active interest in this field. Oh,
yes, I recall when Phil Randolph, Milton Webster, and two or three of us would
sit down during a convention and see how far we could go. We had Matt Woll,
Dave Dubinsky, and Bill Green, who carried the ball on this for many, many
years, convention after convention of various international unions, meeting
with the officers, pressing officers to reach down and bring about the
elimination of these clauses. [51]

We had in the AFL in 1940 23 national unions with a color bar in their
constitution. Whether we should be proud of that or ashamed of it is hardly
the question today. We did have it. It was there. It was a fact. It has
been eliminated.

Of course this represents progress of some kind, but we are told that
this doesn't mean much today. I think it means something. I know that Phil
Randolph came here year after year after year, and made his speech, made his
plea. He didn't have too much help. There wasn't too much activity in those
years as we have seen this past summer.

I had an old friend who came in to see me just a few days ago, a fellow

by the name of George Hunton, head of the Catholic Interracial Council. He is
over 80 years of age. He came in and I talked to him. I have known him for
many years. He said, "You and I remember when this was kind of a lonesome
field. We didn't have any bishops talking about this. We didn't have the
great religious communities." Yes, we had clergymen here and there, but we
didn't have the top people in those days. We had the Catholic Interracial
Council. We helped finance it. It didn't have much money. It did the best
that it could.

So, as I say, my mind goes back in this field, and I refuse to accept the
idea that the American trade union movement should be scolded and berated
because it is not doing enough, because I remember the time when this was the
one segment of American society that was out in the front and fighting in this
field, and we didn't have too much help.

I know the Negro is impatient. I know he has a right to be impatient. He
has a right to say he wants these things, and he wants them now. He has
waited a long time. I can understand that perfectly, but I can't understand
the idea that the way to get these things is to abuse your friends. The way
to get these things is not to abuse the International Ladies Garment Workers
Union, the one union that stood out in this city over the years, and hold them
up for abuse. I don't buy this idea at all. I think the White Citizens Council
should be abused, I think the big corporations, who give lip service to this
idea of equality should be abused, and I think the trade unions should be
criticized wherever there are shortcomings, but I don't get the idea that it is
good policy to abuse the people who are doing the most for you, to get them to
do more, on the ground that you are wasting time criticizing those who are
fundamentally opposed to you.

I think we can do a job. I am confident that we can do a good job in this
field. I don't know of any time where I have seen the American trade union
movement, right down to the very grass root level, more conscious and more
awake on this particular problem. We have to do it from a trade union point of
view. It has got to be the trade unions, and there is no reason why it
shouldn't be trade union action, because the fundamentals of this American
trade union movement, the fundamental principles upon which we are founded,
indicate that this activity is a normal activity of the trade union movement.

I am quite sure that the resolution covers the subject very, very well.
The committee that has considered this resolution includes in its membership practically every president of every fair-sized international in this
Federation, and I am sure that they went over this resolution with a great deal
of care. I think it represents the sentiment of the convention. I think it
gives us a program that we can well set our minds to carrying out, and if we
carry it out, I think we will do a really good job.

I realize that you have an amendment before you, and I would suggest, if
the resolution is not satisfactory, rather than vote for that amendment, that
you send it back to the committee, because if we are going to consider those
amendments, I would like to talk to the committee about it.

I think the proposals made in Philip Randolph's speech will certainly be
given consideration by the officers of the Federation, and by the Executive
Council. I think the portions of this resolution which direct action on the
part of the officers and the Executive Council certainly can be carried out,
and I am certain that all the members of the Executive Council will put their
best efforts forth to carry them out.

As I say, you have before you the question of amending this resolution
or of passing it as is, so I would like to first put the question before you
and take a vote on the amendment to the resolution proposed by Brother Roth
and seconded by Brother Evans. Those who favor the amendment signify by
saying aye; those opposed, no.

The amendment is lost.

You will now vote on the resolution as presented by the Committee. The
amendment was rejected and you are now going to vote on the resolution as
presented by the Committee, signify by saying aye; contrary, no.

The motion has carried and it is so ordered.

I would like to announce for the record that the resolution was adopted
unanimously.

Proceedings of the Fifth Constitutional Convention of the AFL-CIO, New York,
November 14-20, 1963, Vol. I, pp. 204-41.

11. AFL-CIO RESOLUTION ON CIVIL RIGHTS, 1965

RESOLUTION NO. 95--By Delegate Walter P. Reuther, Industrial Union
Department.
The industrial unions of America have long been in the forefront of the
civil rights movement. Through the years, they have joined with others in
helping to make the important progress of recent years possible. But to
achieve real civil rights for all our citizens, much more remains to be done.
The Civil Rights Act of 1964 and the Voting Rights Act of 1965 transformed
into law the beliefs of the Declaration of Independence and the promises of the
post-Civil War constitutional amendments. The Civil Rights Act of 1964 opened
up the public accommodation of the nation, provided for the desegregation of
all facilities receiving federal funds and sought to guarantee equal employment
opportunities for all. The Voting Rights Act of 1965 provided the means to end
discrimination at the ballot box. We commend President Johnson for his
courage, his skill and his leadership in securing the passage of these laws--a
truly historic code of freedom and equality.
But laws do not enforce themselves. Laws form the basis of change; only
enforcement produces change. The challenge now is to convert these laws into
solid and continuing accomplishment; unfortunately this challenge has not been
fully met.
The Voting Rights Act of 1965 provides for Federal registrars in counties
where there is discrimination against Negro registration and voting and against
registration and voting by other minority groups. Today almost four months
after the law took effect the Justice Department has sent registrars into only
thirty-two counties; Congress has provided a ready and effective means for
breaking through the voting discrimination pattern but unless registrars are
promptly appointed in every county where discrimination exists the 1966
elections will once more see massive disenfranchisement of Negroes. After a
hundred years of delay we cannot wait longer for "voluntary" compliance; the
tools for the enfranchisement of Negroes are at hand and they should be used.
Nor has the Department of Health, Education and Welfare protected the
school desegregation rights recognized and enforced by the 1964 Civil Rights
Act. What the Supreme Court required in its historic 1954 decision was public
school desegregation; that is what Congress has required HEW to foster through
the withholding of federal school aid. Yet instead of requiring desegregation,
HEW is accepting so-called "freedom of choice" plans permitting the Negro child
to choose white or Negro schools. But the choice is illusory; the option to a
Negro child in the deep South is only freedom to invite harassment. Whatever
may be the virtues, if any, of freedom of choice in areas of the country free
of intimidation, freedom of choice in the deep South today is nothing more
than laundered segregation.
But this is not all. There remain urgent civil rights areas where we
have yet to make even a significant beginning. Every day new all-white suburbs
spring up in metropolitan areas and tighten the white noose around the
deteriorating central city with its Negro, Latin-American, Puerto Rican and
other minority ghettoes. For all the promise of desegregation in employment,
education and public accommodations, the pattern of segregation in housing
continues unabated as we create new apartheid communities.
And there are other fronts on which action is vitally necessary if we are
to make equality a reality in America. It is high time to begin the reform of
judicial administration in the South. The judicial system in some of our
southern states today is racially segregated and discriminatory in purpose and
effect at every significant stage. The courts themselves--from the judge to
the prosecutor to the marshals--all these are "for whites only." Negro
citizens in these localities cannot obtain fair treatment from the courts when
their most fundamental rights are at stake--to purchase property, to have
their contracts honored, to be protected from physical assault. Moreover,
Negroes continue to be denied participation in the jury system; a Negro
charged with a crime thus comes before "twelve good men and true" drawn
exclusively from the hostile white community in a discriminatory and
segregated fashion.
Thus Negroes cannot use the courts either to preserve and vindicate their
rights or to obtain a fair trial when they are accused of violating the rights

of others. And possibly worst of all, those who dare to stand up for the
protection of the Negro in his civil rights are assaulted and attacked, and
even murdered in cold blood while the southern system of "justice" fails to
operate or actually protects the white citizens who perpetrated the crime.
The unpunished killings of William L. Moore, Medgar Evers, four young girls in
a Birmingham church, James Chaney, Michael Schwerner, Andrew Goodman, Colonel
Lemuel Penn, Jimmy Lee Jackson, Reverend James Reeb, Mrs. Viola Liuzzo and
Jonathan Daniels demonstrate that southern prosecutors, judges and juries will
not or cannot punish cold-blooded murders of Negroes and their civil rights
supporters.

The rule of prejudice in many southern courts is destructive of our basic
precepts of justice and strikes at the fundamentals of a free and civilized
society. Government by the lawless, by the ruthless night-riders of the Ku
Klux Klan and their ideological allies, must come to an end!

But even when the last law providing for equality has been passed and when
the full resources of the federal government are put behind the enforcement of
all the laws, there will still be a gigantic task ahead. Centuries of discrimination have left Negroes and members of other minority groups disadvantaged to
a degree that even full legal rights cannot overcome. Undereducated, under-
housed and underemployed, the alienation and hopelessness of many Negroes and
others is the fault of a society too long indifferent to their cause. A massive
poverty program—on which we have made only a small down payment—is the
responsibility of a society which has permitted this alienation and hopelessness
to take place.

We do not urge this massive program out of fear of repeated Watts-type
riots. We urge it as the responsibility of civilized society to see that none
shall be denied where means exist to help. This is no time for a slow-down in
civil rights; speed must be the watchword until the job is done. And, as we
call upon the nation to redouble its efforts toward equality, we pledge to
speed up our own work to bring full equality to all within the ranks of
labor. . . .

RESOLVED: 1. We call upon the Administration to move forward with the
implementation and enforcement of the 1964 and 1965 civil rights laws with all
the vigor and resources at its command.

2. We urge President Johnson to extend the 1962 Housing Executive Order
to cover not only FHA and VA insured mortgages, but to cover mortgage activities
of all federally-assisted or federally-insured bank and savings and loan
companies.

3. We strongly recommend the passage in the next session of Congress of
legislation making acts of physical violence against persons attempting to
exercise civil rights or to peacefully protest the denial of civil rights
federal crimes to be tried in the federal courts. And we call for immediate
federal criminal prosecution of local law enforcement officers who by condona-
tion, conspiracy and inaction deny equal protection of the law to citizens.

4. We urge that the federal government enforce civil rights laws to the
limit of its ability, especially in curbing the vicious lawlessness of the Ku
Klux Klan and its sympathizers among public officials and private citizens.
Federal agents should be ordered to act promptly to arrest violators of all
federal laws. Federal prosecutions should be multiplied. Better appointments
of judges will make those prosecutions more likely to result in justice.

5. We urge that jurors in both federal and state courts be chosen from
jury rolls made up completely by chance selection, so that systematically
all-white juries in both federal and state courts in the South will become a
thing of the past.

6. We pledge to continue our past close cooperation with men, women and
organizations of good will outside the labor movement who seek wholesome and
democratic solutions to the vexing problems of discrimination. The hope of
the future lies in the continuation of this alliance of labor with other
groups and individuals in search of justice. Together we can find the way.

Proceedings of the Sixth Constitutional Convention of the AFL-CIO, San
Francisco, Calif., December 9-15, 1965, Vol. I, pp. 210-13.

12. STATEMENT BY THE AFL-CIO EXECUTIVE COUNCIL
ON CIVIL RIGHTS ACT OF 1966

Chicago, Illinois
August 23, 1966

On September 6, the Senate will begin consideration of the Civil Rights
Act of 1966 (H.R. 14765), which meets the major objectives of the 1965
AFL-CIO convention's civil rights resolution.

This bill is not as strong as we would like but it is a positive step
forward in the achievement of full and equal opportunity for all Americans.

The bill contains provisions assuring non-discrimination in the selection
of federal and state juries; broadening federal laws against acts of racial
violence, and authorizing federal court injunctions against anticipated
violence or intimidation.

Probably the single most important section of the bill is Title IV,
establishing for the first time a federal guarantee of the principle of fair
housing. We wish this section were stronger but the hard, practical fact is
that this was the strongest possible title that could have been passed in the
House of Representatives.

As passed by the House, this section does guarantee the principle of fair
housing. It does provide an important first step in implementing that
principle. It applies to an estimated 40 percent of the nation's homes (about
23 million dwellings) as well as to all new housing developments and high-rise
apartments.

We would have preferred 100 percent coverage but such a proposal would
not have passed. We supported, without apologies, the Mathias amendment as an
acceptable compromise to insure passage of this title. Without it, the title
would have been defeated and there would have been no open housing section at
all.

The compromise contains less than we wanted and less than justice demands,
but by establishing the principle of fair housing it makes a significant start.

However, the fight is far from over. In the Senate, a determined filibuster is planned by those who traditionally oppose any civil rights measure.
That filibuster must be broken before the Civil Rights Bill of 1966 can become
law.

We intend to do everything in our power, in cooperation with others who
believe in full civil rights, to break the filibuster and pass the bill. We
earnestly solicit the support of all in America who believe in the principle
of open housing. Certainly the inhumanity of the ghetto, the injustice of
segregated housing, the denial of equal opportunity to Negroes is just as
reprehensible when it occurs in Northern cities as in the South.

Therefore we urge the Senate to pass H.R. 14765 with speed and without
crippling amendments.

AFL-CIO press release. Copy in possession of the editors.

13. BLACK POWER AND LABOR

*An Exchange of Views Between Jerry Menapace, Executive Secretary
of Local 117, Amalgamated Meat Cutters and Butcher Workmen, and Abe
Feinglass, Vice President and Director of the Fur and Leather Dept.
of the A.M.C.B.W.*

July 21, 1966

Abe Feinglass, Vice-President
A.M.C. and B.W. of N.A.
2800 North Sheridan Road
Chicago, Illinois 60657

Dear Brother Feinglass,

I write at this time because I am disturbed and disillusioned by the change in direction of the Civil Rights Movement.

As you know, Local 117 has always supported the movement, vocally, physically and financially, and our Union meets C.O.R.E.'s standard as a "good" organization. [52]

When C.O.R.E. selected Baltimore as its Target Project, I was pleased, and I felt that those of us in Labor who are and have been genuine friends of the Civil Rights Movement could join hands with C.O.R.E. and clean up the stinking injustices which still prevail in certain sections of Baltimore, including certain all-white Local Unions in the Building Trades.

The Building Trades elected a new President, a young, active and rough former Iron Worker, and they rented offices in our building. Largely through my efforts at getting close to this new President and convincing him that he must use his position to break down the barriers to minority groups, he has embarked on a bold, new (for Building Trades) program to integrate his Council, and in less than a year, he has accomplished more integration than anyone could have predicted. We used our influence on him and on one of our Employers who happens to be Negro to settle a dispute between them as to who would construct a new plant. We also were responsible for the Building Trades hiring a Negro girl as private secretary to the President.

All of this was done only to improve Labor's image with the Negro community, and especially with C.O.R.E.

Then came the introduction of what's called the Maryland Freedom Union. As in a few other areas, this so-called Union is attempting to organize workers in all-Negro plants or stores, in all-Negro areas, and using the emotion-charged momentum of the Civil Rights Movement to accomplish their goals. The Freedom Union began by organizing a small department store employing twelve or fifteen Negroes, which, of course, brought loud cries from the Retail Clerks Union here.

Our Central Labor Council's Civil Rights Committee, acting on a letter from the Clerks, recommended to the Council (of which I am Secretary) that we condemn the actions of the Maryland Freedom Union. Not wanting to put our Council in the position of opposition or condemning any legitimate effort to organize workers, especially an all-Negro effort, I successfully amended the Civil Rights Committee's report to refer the entire matter to the Council Executive Board, of which I am an Officer, and forbade the press in the meeting to print any reference to the battle which took place on the floor.

Subsequently, I met with leaders of the Maryland Freedom Union, one of whom is a full-time C.O.R.E. activist and a very intelligent, dedicated young man, in an effort to learn more about their purpose and goal. They assured me and the Amalgamated Local 117 that we were a "good" Union and that they would not attempt to organize in our jurisdiction. They agreed further to turn over any leads that might pick up in our jurisdiction, if we would agree to help them financially and oragnizationally.

I explained to them that as an Officer of the AFL-CIO Council and as head of the fourth largest Local Union in the Baltimore area, I could not help them organize workers in other Union's proper jurisdiction, but if they could assure the Council that their goal was to organize workers into legitimate Unions and not to perpetuate this Freedom Union in direct competition to Locals of our Council, I was sure that together with C.O.R.E., we could set this town on its ear.

I am sad to say, not only would they not give this assurance, but they went right to the task of raiding two Unions affiliated with our Council, using the "black brother" approach.

Then came the much publicized Baltimore C.O.R.E. Convention, which I attended as "Community Observer." I'm sure you have read the results.

The day after the Convention, two leaders of C.O.R.E. came to my office to ask for *financial* support for their "Baltimore Project." I underscore "financial" because they no longer want my personal *physical* support and their reasoning makes me doubt very seriously the moral and practical application of "Black Power."

These two C.O.R.E. leaders told me quite matter-of-factly that they do not intend to accept white liberals in positions of leadership in their movement. That Negroes must develop "their own" leaders, even if it means serious and costly mistakes in the process. That Negroes cannot continue to "accept the patronage" of white liberals, because to do so somehow leaves the Negro feeling inferior and unable to do for himself.

When I suggested that this new concept was "separatism" of a different color, and that the phrase "Black Power" would undo much of the work that had been done by so-called white liberals like myself, I was politely told that I was afraid of Black Power, I never was a true friend of the Civil Rights Movement.

It took a few seconds to let my blood cool down, then I not so politely told the young gentlemen to get the hell out of my office.

Abe, I am very disappointed. And, from reading the remarks of Dr. King, Roy Wilkins, and several of our Baltimore Negro leaders, I'm not alone.

The problem for me is one of mixed emotions at this moment.

I agree wholeheartedly with the goal of true equality for all Americans. But I find myself in complete disagreement with this new "Black Power" approach. And I am incapable of defending C.O.R.E.'s actions, because they have neutralized me to the point of complete apathy insofar as Community Action is concerned.

Please give me the benefit of your thoughts, Abe, because I feel that I have not deserted the cause of Negro rights, rather the cause has deserted me.

Fraternally,
Jerry Menapace,
Executive Secretary

July 28, 1966

Mr. Jerry Menapace,
Executive Secretary
Local Union No. 117
1216 East Baltimore Street
Baltimore, Maryland 21202

Dear Brother Menapace:

I have your letter of July 21st, and have read it carefully.

It is clear that the problems you raise are serious, and do complicate our efforts to play a role in the struggle for Civil Rights. Nevertheless, it seems to me that the fight we have developed, and which people like you have carried forward, to achieve equality and integration was motivated by our own conscience, and our own understanding that a great wrong had been committed against the Negro people. We have the responsibility of attempting to correct it.

Nothing that any Negro leader or organization does changes this fundamental premise or justifies the abandonment of this worthwhile cause. It is a fact of life that in all revolutionary causes and upheavals, there develop some mistaken and distorted policies. These usually reflect inevitable responses to delays, sellouts, frustrations and continued massive exploitation.

I am sure that you will recall from reading recent history that in the years after the Automobile Workers were organized, there were hundreds of wildcat strikes all over the country. You will also recall the arguments of the employers and many public officials who said that although they could understand these outbreaks prior to an agreement, now that machinery had been established for the solution of grievances, these wildcats were indefensible.

Our answer was that you cannot spoon feed liberty. We asked for understanding, however illogical individual acts were.

I am confident that you understand that there are many in the labor movement who do things that we cannot accept as proper. Nevertheless, we would fight against anyone who would deny the decent objectives of all of labor because of some actions of a union or a few unions.

I do, therefore, believe that this period requires the greatest understanding of those of us who are really concerned with the whole struggle. I cannot, in good conscience, on the basis of what you tell me in your letter, recommend that you give money to CORE's present community project. This would be to support the long term goal of a labor movement divided along lines of color.

On the other hand, I would suggest even more energetic activity by our

Local Union and other local unions in bringing opportunity for employment to
Negro workers everywhere in the area. I would suggest development of even
stronger Negro leadership inside the ranks of our own and other local unions.
Only by developing such a Negro leadership within our own ranks can we carry
forward the fight which can be successful only as a joint and common effort --
the elimination of bigotry, racism and all Jim Crow practices.

Beyond that, by developing a Negro leadership within our Union, there is
the hope that such a leadership can play a role in bringing clarity to the
Civil Rights organizations whose basic purpose we honor and share, but whose
current tactics we believe, frankly, to be mistaken.

I hope this letter will help you in clarifying your own thinking on the
matters you raised with me.

With best wishes and best personal regards, I am

> Fraternally yours,
> Abe Feinglass, Vice President
> Director, Fur & Leather Dept.

Labor Today 5 (December-January, 1966-67):16-18.

14. AFL-CIO EXECUTIVE COUNCIL REPORT ON CIVIL RIGHTS, 1967

How can we explain riots and eruptions in cities and the emergence of the
black power slogan after civil rights victories in the courts and in the
Congress?

There are those who say nothing has happened except a few token steps in
eliminating discrimination and segregation. There are others who say too much
freedom has been routed too fast.

At the February 1967 executive council meeting we said:

"Sweeping changes have taken place on the American scene
in the area of civil rights over the past few years but the
forward momentum has clearly slowed . . . Yet the problems of
civil rights remain and continue to affect basic components
of our social fabric--schools, jobs, housing and other urban
problems."

It is true that the public accommodations issues which generated the
sit-ins and the freedom riots have been all resolved and that some progress
has been made in the areas of employment, voting, hospitals and school
desegregation.

There is still a long way to go in ending the dual school system in the
South. De facto school segregation in the North exists as well. Equal
justice and freedom from intimidation have still to be finally won. The
struggle to end discrimination in housing has barely begun.

It may be safe to say that, but for housing, legal remedies exist for most
practices of segregation and discrimination based on race, color, national
origin and religion. However the country, white as well as nonwhite, expected
that with the acceleration of the pace by which segregation and discrimination
were being eliminated, minority group citizens would move up the economic
ladder into the mainstream of American life.

From 1939 until the Supreme Court Decision in 1954, the gap between the
average income of minority group citizens and the population as a whole
narrowed slowly but steadily and perceptively. Indeed it did so on an
average of one percent a year, so that by 1955, the average income of minority
group citizens had moved from 45 percent of the national average to 60 percent.

Since discrimination and segregation were a substantial reason for that
gap, it was logical for many to assume that a more rapid elimination of
discrimination would lead to a more rapid elimination of this gap.

While for many individual minority group citizens the dropping of
barriers led to better jobs, better education and better housing, for large
masses of minority group citizens it did not. In the last decade, during a
period of rising standards of living for the population as a whole and for

many minority group citizens as well, the median income of minority group citizens has not kept pace with that of the population as a whole. Not only has the gap not narrowed at a faster pace, it has not narrowed at all. Our great urban centers have developed overcrowded, decaying center cities with high unemployment rates, and increasing problems and difficulties in providing adequate education, housing, and social services.

In the last few years, we have reduced unemployment to 4 percent and lower. Minority group unemployment has also come down from 11-12 percent to between 7.5-8 per cent. However it remains double that of the national average and minority group youth unemployment has maintained itself at between 21 to 30 percent. In the hard-core ghetto areas it is as high as 35 percent.

Here is the powder keg. Legal guarantees have been established, expectations have risen. But for many, no significant, tangible benefits have been experienced.

Earlier this year this council said:

"Equal opportunity in employment requires full employment and education and training needed for higher-skilled and better-paid jobs--in addition to the elimination of discrimination. Equality of opportunity in education requires that sufficient funds are provided to raise the quality of our schools, North and South, to meet present day needs as well as that these schools be integrated.

"Equality of opportunity in housing requires that we eliminate slums and build up the homes that are needed for all of America's population--in addition to eliminating discrimination in sale and rental of housing. Indeed we must make our cities a healthy and decent place to live and repledge ourselves to the elimination of poverty in America."

However it has become increasingly clear that to accomplish the foregoing requires complex and massive action.

To start on this monumental endeavor it is necessary that Congress enact the civil rights legislation put before it by the President and adequately fund model cities, anti-poverty, housing, education and job training legislation.

In addition, there is a crying need to enact an emergency job creation bill which would provide employment in public services in our cities for a million unemployed, largely unskilled, workers. Finally Congress and the nation must develop a comprehensive program for the reconstruction of our cities that will end slums and urban decay while providing fruitful employment at adequate incomes.

It is only on this base that we can expect the "Fulfillment of These Rights."

In August 1967, the AFL-CIO participated in the Urban Coalition Conference convened by the U.S. Conference of Mayors. At the Conference, the delegates, consisting of representatives from labor, business, civil rights and religious institutions called for such a program.

The AFL-CIO Compliance Program

While government action is essential, there is an important role for voluntary institutions: business, labor, civil rights, religious and others. We in the AFL-CIO have long assumed a responsibility not only to help get legislation but to help work for its effective and intelligent implementation. We have also acknowledged the responsibility of working in our own house to eliminate discriminatory practices that may exist.

The program that was developed by the AFL-CIO after the passage of the Civil Rights Act of 1964 to help bring about compliance with the act still provides a meaningful guide.

Point One was an education campaign in regard to civil rights problems. This is a continuing program. The AFL-CIO through its departments of civil rights, legislation, education, public relations, community services, publications and political education does a year-round job in this area.

Civil rights programs are conducted at summer schools of international unions and state federations, at conferences and special education institutes. In the spring of 1966 a third four-week staff training institute for full-time southern union staff members was held at the University of Georgia. There was a full week on civil rights problems, and Roy Wilkins, Executive Director of the NAACP, was a guest speaker at the institute.

Following the 1966 elections, the November issue of the *Federationist* was devoted fully to civil rights, with articles by President Meany, A. Philip Randolph, Roy Wilkins, Whitney Young and Bayard Rustin. It also carried articles by the directors of the Civil Rights and Education Departments and by Professor Ray Marshall, well known authority in the area of labor and civil rights. This issue had an additional run of 80,000 copies by now exhausted because of requests and orders by unions and others.

In addition to other AFL-CIO pamphlets and material, 100,000 pamphlets on "Right to Work, A Trap for America's Minorities," prepared by the A. Philip Randolph Institute, and 30,000 pamphlets on President Johnson's civil rights message to the 90th Congress have been distributed.

The Civil Rights Department also makes monthly mailings of important material on civil rights to key union leadership.

Another point of the program called upon the labor movement to observe the workings of the Civil Rights Act, "so that any inadequacies which may develop in practice can be presented to Congress for further legislative action."

We have, following this mandate, supported and helped get enactment of the Civil Rights Act of 1965 and are now supporting various proposals before Congress in the areas of equal protection under the law, fair housing and the strengthening of the Equal Employment Opportunity Commission. President Meany testified in August 1967 on fair housing legislation.

Next, the AFL-CIO pledged to support adequate funding of effective implementation of existing legislation. We have continued to support adequate budget requirements for those federal agencies entrusted with the responsibility of implementing existing legislation.

We have also worked with the compliance committee of the Leadership Conference on Civil Rights, both in helping and pressing these federal agencies.

Liaison Programs

Most importantly as we have said before, "The promotion of equal opportunity in employment is a major concern of unions. Unions, of course, do not control the overwhelming majority of hiring, but unions can . . . make a significant contribution to achieving voluntary compliance with this section of the law."

It is significant that the recent survey of the Equal Employment Opportunity Commission and other studies show that the employment area that has been least penetrated by minority groups is that of white collar. This area also has been much less penetrated by unionization.

Another growing segment of the labor force is that of government. In some sections of the country, especially in state and local government employment, minority group representation is extremely low. It is for this reason that the AFL-CIO recommended that Title VII be extended to state and local government employment.

Even prior to the appointment of the Equal Employment Opportunity Commission, President Meany had asked each international union president to appoint an officer to work on fair employment problems with the commission and the AFL-CIO Department of Civil Rights. Today, some 85 international unions have assigned an officer to work in this area.

Shortly after the appointment of the EEOC, the Civil Rights Department obtained an agreement with EEOC that a copy of all discrimination charges which involved local unions would be sent to the Civil Rights Department and to the international union whose local was involved. Many similar agreements have since been obtained with a number of state fair employment practices commissions.

In the past two years the work of the AFL-CIO Civil Rights Committee and its Subcommittee on Compliance has increased tremendously. In many cases international unions, working with the Civil Rights Department, have helped the Equal Employment Opportunity Commission to conciliate complaints with local unions and have also been able to provide staff investigators with an understanding of why some charges were not justified.

Since December 1965 the Civil Rights Department has received notification of over 350 charges of discrimination involving AFL-CIO affiliates.

Besides work on individual complaints, there are complicated policy problems which the AFL-CIO attempts to help the commission to resolve. An

all-day meeting between the commission and a representative group of international unions on problems of seniority and a second similar all-day conference on problems of sex discrimination have been held.

In February 1967 the EEOC published in the Federal Register an announcement of an open hearing to discuss proposed reporting forms to be issued to
unions and joint apprenticeship committees.

The AFL-CIO Civil Rights Committee devoted a good portion of its March
meeting to a discussion of these proposed forms. The AFL-CIO testified at the
public hearing and asked that the commission take the forms back for review
because some questions were unclear, some unnecessary. This was done. Although
there is still not complete satisfaction with these forms, significant improvements have been made.

Shortly after the Equal Employment Opportunity Commission became operative,
Walter G. Davis, then assistant director of the AFL-CIO Civil Rights Department,
became deputy executive director of the commission on a temporary basis. He
helped develop its field office structure and, even more importantly, he helped
familiarize the commission and its personnel with the structure and policies of
the labor movement.

Since his return to the AFL-CIO and the resignation of Winn Newman, a
labor liaison officer, who is now with the United Steelworkers Union, the EEOC
has appointed two labor liaison officers.

The Civil Rights Department, working with labor liaison officers and
regional EEOC offices, has helped to promote a series of conferences for key
union leadership at regional and state levels. Two fruitful conferences have
been held this year, in Cincinnati, Ohio, and in Washington, D.C. Others are
scheduled.

At the same time, the staff of the AFL-CIO Civil Rights Department has
begun a series of visits to the various regional offices of EEOC and one and
two-day conferences for EEOC staff. The purpose of these conferences is to
provide background and information about union structure, principles of
collective bargaining and union policy.

Although the EEOC has had difficulties with turnover in staff and with
budget and has experienced many problems, being a new agency, there have been
some important achievements.

The AFL-CIO has fought long and hard for a FEP law and we will continue
to work with EEOC for effective and intelligent enforcement of the act, as we
continue to work with our affiliates in maximizing the elimination of discriminatory practices that may exist in local unions.

In addition to work with the EEOC, the AFL-CIO Civil Rights Committee has
seen a need to develop avenues of cooperation with other government agencies
such as the Office of Federal Contract Compliance and the Justice Department.

The Civil Rights Department is attempting to develop a procedure for
conciliation between international unions and these two government agencies.

The last point of the 1964 program was a call upon our state and city
central bodies to work with other groups in the community to help solve civil
rights and related problems at the grass roots level. The need for this is,
if anything, far greater than even before.

Mergers of Segregated Locals

The AFL-CIO began working on problems of discrimination before there was
a Civil Rights Act.

At the founding merger convention, the Civil Rights Committee was established.

At the 1959 convention, the various types of discrimination that were
known to exist within the labor movement were identified. The convention
called on all affiliates to cooperate with the Civil Rights Committee to solve
such problems.

One such problem is that of segregated locals. Affiliates were asked to
effect mergers of such locals, separated because of race.

Many of our affiliates that had segregated locals responded to the AFL-
CIO convention mandate calling for merger with all possible speed before the
Civil Rights Act was on the books.

The first interpretive guideline issued by the Equal Employment Opportunity Commission stated that separate locals and separate lines of seniority

based on race were a violation of the Civil Rights Act. President Meany responded immediately by stating that the AFL-CIO was in agreement with this guideline and that it was perfectly consistent with the AFL-CIO policy.

Since that time there has been acceleration in the activity of affiliated international unions in effecting mergers of segregated locals. The American Federation of Musicians for instance has assigned James C. Petrillo, its former president, to work with local unions in bringing about mergers. He has been successful in effecting mergers of separate locals in Baltimore, Md., Washington, D.C., Norfolk, Va., Chicago, Ill., and other cities. [53]

The Molders International Union earlier this year instructed separate local unions in Virginia and Alabama to appoint committees to work out satisfactory merger agreements in compliance with the law and with AFL-CIO policy. This has been successfully done in Holdt, Anniston, and Mobile, Alabama and in Richmond, Virginia.

The Chemical Workers, Oil Workers and Tobacco Workers also have completed the mergers of all their remaining separate locals.

Other affiliates have successfully completed mergers and continue to work on those still existing.

Out of the 60 thousand-plus local unions that our affiliates have, at the latest count 142 racially segregated locals remain. Plans for merger of many of these are presently under way.

Apprenticeship Programs

Although there are less than 250,000 registered apprentices in the U.S., approximately half of which are in the building and construction trades industry, access to these jobs by minority group youth has generated a very high degree of interest.

This is understandable because these apprentice openings lead to skilled and well-paid jobs and frequently to supervisory and business opportunities. Since the technological revolution we are going through is eliminating many semi-skilled and nonskilled jobs, entry into the skilled and technical job section of the labor force becomes even more significant. What is involved is not merely finding better jobs but being left increasingly in low-paid service jobs or finding no job at all.

It was assumed by many that if nondiscrimination was assured, significant numbers of minority group youth would automatically find their way into large numbers of apprenticeship openings.

Nondiscrimination regulations were enacted by the Bureau of Apprenticeship and Training. Apprenticeship was specifically covered in Title VII of the Civil Rights Act, and regulations were adopted by the contract compliance agencies as well.

We have discovered however that unless special efforts are made to bring information about apprenticeship opportunities, actively recruit and motivate minority group youngsters and frequently help them prepare for admission to programs, very little progress results.

However, in the last couple of years some government and private efforts have been successful in bringing significant numbers of minority group youngsters into skilled apprenticeship jobs.

The Apprenticeship Information Center of the Employment Security Office in Washington, D.C. has placed some 500 Negro youngsters in apprenticeship openings since June 1963, almost 400 of these from June 1965 to June 1967, as printer, bricklayer, carpenter, cement mason, electrician, plumber, steamfitter, ironworker, sheetmetal worker and plasterer apprentices.

The Labor Department has established information centers in more than a score of other cities and while none have worked as effectively as the one in Washington, the one in Chicago has achieved some significant results. It has placed over 100 minority group apprentices in the last year alone. It is hoped that other centers will increase their effectiveness.

In New York City, the apprenticeship program of the Workers Defense League and A. Philip Randolph Education Fund has been successful in placing over 250 minority group youngsters within the last two years—as electricians, carpenters, steamfitters, iron workers, stone derrick men, metal lathers, plasters, sheet metal and elevator construction operators.

This program has been funded by the Labor Department to expand its

activities into New Rochelle and Buffalo, New York; Cleveland, Ohio; and
Newark, New Jersey. It has already placed electrical, plumber and bricklayer
apprentices in New Rochelle and Westchester County. In Buffalo, New York,
where the program has only been in operation since May, it has placed apprentices in sheet metal; other youngsters have made application and are being
prepared to qualify for steam fitters, roofers and ironworkers programs.
     It helps willing youngsters to apply and prepares them to qualify and
brings information to the schools and the community and it has, by demonstrating its competency, received cooperation from the trades and the contractors.
     In Baltimore, Maryland, the Urban League has received a grant to develop
the same type of program and has also received the cooperation of the Baltimore
Building Trades Council and its affiliated unions in carrying out such a
program. The goal of at least 30 minority group youths placed as apprentices
by the first of the year, has already been reached in such trades as iron
workers, steam fitters, operating engineers and carpenters.
     In Detroit, Michigan, a similar grant has been made to the Trade Union
Leadership Council, which has signed a contract with the support of the
Detroit Building Trades Council to recruit and refer minority group youth in
the coming year.
     In Oklahoma City and Tulsa, the Building Trades Council has cooperated
with community groups to insure opportunities for minority group youngsters.
In the past few months Negro apprentices have been placed in sheetmetal,
roofers, operating engineers and carpenters.
     In Philadelphia, Pennsylvania the Opportunities Industrialization Center,
in cooperation with the Building and Construction Trades Council, the Negro
Trade Union Leadership Council and the Urban League has referred and placed
65 Negro apprentices in the lathers, sheet metal workers, plumbers, roofers,
carpenters, bricklayers, electricians and iron workers programs.
     Although the number of jobs involved can have no great impact on overall
Negro youth unemployment figures, these job openings, for the reasons we have
mentioned above, have more than symbolic significance. It is for this reason
that Secretary-Treasurer Schnitzler, Chairman of the Civil Rights Committee,
assigned a good portion of his speeches to the subject of equal opportunity at
the Southern States Apprenticeship Conference in New Orleans two years ago and
the Mid-Atlantic States Apprenticeship Conference in Norfolk, Virginia this
year. Director Don Slaiman of the Civil Rights Department did the same at
the Southern States Apprenticeship Conference in Biloxi, Mississippi this year.
     Although not receiving as much publicity as the question of apprenticeship
entry and that of merging segregated locals, the AFL-CIO and its affiliates
continue to work on other matters pertaining to the elimination of discrimination and the expansion of equal opportunity for all.
     The following are some of these areas: Equal access to membership, equal
wages and conditions of work, elimination of discrimination in seniority and
promotion systems, nondiscriminatory representation and finally union initiatives to expand equal opportunity by negotiation of nondiscriminatory clauses
in collective bargaining agreements and other affirmative measures, including
helping workers to file complaints with government agencies where necessary.
     The organization of minority group workers into unions is in itself a
very significant step towards expanding opportunities, increasing wages and
improving working conditions for these workers.

Proceedings of the Seventh Constitutional Convention of the AFL-CIO, Report
of the Executive Council, December 7-12, 1967, Vol. II, pp. 158-66.

15.   AFL-CIO RESOLUTION ON CIVIL RIGHTS, 1969

     Fifteen years ago, the Supreme Court ruled that racial segregation in
schools violated the Constitution and called for its ending with all
deliberate speed. But compliance with the law came very slowly. After ten
years, only 1% of Negro children were going to integrated schools in the
South. Today, the figure is still far from satisfactory.

During the Kennedy-Johnson Administration, Congress passed comprehensive civil rights legislation to end discrimination in all aspects of American life --public accommodation, voting, education, employment, housing and in the administration of justice.

Today, we can see the results of substantial progress not only in this fight against discrimination but in bringing minority group citizens into the mainstream of American life.

But despite this progress, there are no grounds for complacency. The increasing crisis proportions of problems in our cities, the abnormally high rates of unemployment among Negro and other minorities and the remaining pockets of discrimination are festering sores. It would be idle and tragic to ignore them or pretend that they will go away.

Indeed, it cannot be stressed too strongly that the country as a whole, and we in the labor movement in particular, must pay greater attention at every level--national, state and local--to bring about sound, effective and democratic solutions to these problems.

In fact, since the last election, the momentum for sound progress has slowed.

It is no exaggeration to say that the great gains that have been made as a result of the efforts of the civil rights movement, the American labor movement and religious and liberal organizations are in peril today.

The Nixon Administration has failed to provide forthright and unambiguous support or adequate and consistent implementation of the laws.

The United States Civil Rights Commission recently observed that "for the first time since the Supreme Court ordered school desegregation, the Federal Government has requested, in court, a slowdown in the pace of desegregation."

This is no isolated incident. In failing to oppose the Whitten amendment in the House of Representatives and by moving from established, successful regulations to complete reliance on the courts, the Nixon Administration is permitting a major threat in the struggle to achieve meaningful school desegregation.

Another example is in the area of voting, where the Voting Rights Act of 1965 aided by vigorous implementation by the Department of Justice under President Johnson resulted in 800,000 new Negro registered voters in those states where voting discrimination had been most onerous. But here too, the Administration has failed to press for a simple five-year extension of the Voting Rights Act of 1965 that would insure that the clock not be turned back.

Nixon Administration officials are covering this retreat in civil rights enforcement by trying to make a whipping boy of unions, especially those in the building trades. They have resorted to an unsound double standard in attempting to deal with the legitimate problem of expanding the opportunities for minority group workers in higher paid skilled and technical jobs.

It is part of a calculated strategy of accommodating conservative elements in the South while, at the same time, trying to divide minorities, labor and liberals who have been the backbone of the effort to achieve progress in the civil rights area.

The unity of these forces for equality are vitally necessary today to maintain the gains that have been made and to start a new march forward toward the goal of an integrated society with equal opportunity and equal justice for all.

The AFL-CIO is proud of its record in the struggle for civil rights and we have particularly sought to end discrimination in employment. The AFL-CIO played a major role in getting a Fair Employment Practice section into the Civil Rights Act of 1964 which covered unions as well as employers. It has worked with its affiliates to attain compliance with the law. Today, it strongly supports efforts to strengthen the Equal Employment Opportunity Commission by giving it cease-and-desist powers needed to make it more effective. The Administration is opposed, seeking enforcement in the federal district courts. Here as in the school desegregation situation, the Administration moves in a direction that the civil rights movement can only view as dilatory and ineffective.

Nor has the AFL-CIO limited its efforts to the legislative front. It has taken the initiative to work with affiliates in developing affirmative action programs on a sound basis that would bring significant results, whether required by law or not.

Specifically in the construction industry, the AFL-CIO has worked with the Building Trades Department, international unions, local building trades councils and groups like the Workers Defense League--A. Philip Randolph Education Fund Committee, the Urban League's LEAP Program and other community groups. The results obtained speak for themselves.

By July of 1969, 4,248 minority group apprentices were placed by Outreach Programs. Of these, 3,958 were in building and construction trades apprenticeship programs. The bulk of these were not in the so-called "trowel trades." Electricians, carpenters, iron workers, plumbers, steamfitters and sheet metal workers accounted for 2,293 of these apprentices.

Minority group apprentices in the construction industry have moved from less than 2.5% in 1960 to 7.2% in 1968. The majority of regular apprentices in federally serviced programs are in the construction industry. The percentage of minority apprentices is higher than in metal manufacturing, non-metal manufacturing and public utilities and transportation.

At its last Convention, the AFL-CIO endorsed the Outreach Programs that then existed in sixteen states and recommended that these programs be emulated in other states. Today, Outreach Programs for recruiting, motivating and preparing youngsters for building trades apprenticeship programs have been founded by the U.S. Department of Labor in fifty-five cities after agreement by local building trades councils for full cooperation.

This is an excellent example of a sound policy being designed and implemented with effective results.

The AFL-CIO is encouraged by the policy statement of the Executive Council of the Building and Construction Trades Department, which was passed unanimously at its recent 1969 Convention. This statement reaffirms the Building Trades policy of non-discrimination and calls for the acceleration and extension of apprenticeship Outreach Programs which have proved successful in actual operation. Moreover, it does not limit itself to these successful programs.

It also outlined a program for increasing minority group participation outside of the apprenticeship route, saying:

"We make flat and unqualified recommendation to local unions throughout the United States that for a stated period of time they should invite the application of qualified minority journeymen for membership in their respective local unions and should accept all such qualified minority journeymen provided they meet the ordinary and equally administered requirements for membership."

It also recommends for study by local unions the establishment of training programs for minority workers who are not either qualified journeymen or eligible for apprenticeship. The statement says:

"We also recommend that the local unions and the local councils explore and vigorously pursue training programs for the upgrading of minority workers who are not of apprenticeship age. Such programs should be developed in such manner as to prevent under-cutting the established apprenticeship programs. The recommendations which have been previously made on model cities should furnish an appropriate guideline for development of these journeymen training programs."

The implementation of this excellent statement is a sound basis for bringing increased participation by minority group workers in skilled jobs in the construction industry, especially in those locals which now have low participation rates. The use of quotas is a bad substitute for sound, effective programs. It is not only of questionable legality under the Civil Rights Act, but it does not even insure permanent skilled jobs for minority workers.

The Administration's so-called "Philadelphia Plan" sets up unsound procedures used in no other industry, segment of the labor market or in government itself. The excuse for this is the low percentage of Negroes and other minorities in the construction industry. In most cases, the figures that have been used for justification have been erroneous. For example, in Philadelphia, government officials implied that less than 2% of building trades membership were minority group workers. The facts are that over 30% of Philadelphia Building Trades members are Negro, and excluding Laborers, 12% of all journeymen are Negro.

Government figures on white collar occupations and in industries, such as
textile, banking and newspaper, show far less overall minority group participation than in construction and no higher percentages in skilled categories. In
these industries, employers unilaterally do the hiring. Unions have little
if any, say. There is no excuse for the Administration to play a "numbers
game" as they did in the Philadelphia Plan publicity. Falsely portraying the
facts won't help minorities get jobs or end discrimination.

The AFL-CIO urges that vigorous efforts be made to expand opportunities
for minority group youth and workers in the better-paid and more skilled jobs
throughout our economy, including the building and construction trades
industry. But we urge that it be done on a sound, fair effective continuing
basis and we are opposed to making a political football out of an issue as
important as the issue of ending discrimination in employment--everywhere, in
all kinds of employment, for all time.

Discrimination and deprivation are problems not only of the American
Negro, but of other minority groups. Americans of Mexican descent are the
second largest minority. Puerto Rican, Indians, Japanese, Chinese, Eskimos
and Aleuts today face problems of discrimination.

Some of the Spanish-speaking minorities have a disproportionate number of
people unemployed, under-educated, and below the poverty line in income.

The AFL-CIO especially and its state federations in those areas where
these minorities are concentrated must pay increasing attention to their
special problems. We are proud of our efforts and those of our affiliated
unions in helping the farm workers, under the leadership of Cesar Chavez, to
bring dignity and an end to exploitation to this segment of the working poor.
The AFL-CIO is also proud of the increased participation by minority group
workers in the trade union movement and of the contributions that they are
making.

The AFL-CIO reiterates its dedication to the principle established in its
Constitution--when the merged federation was founded--equality and equal
benefits of union membership for all workers regardless of race, creed, national
origin or sex. We urge that all international unions, state federations and
central bodies insure that their civil rights committees be active and work
with the Civil Rights Department of the AFL-CIO toward the end of eliminating
any vestige of discrimination that may remain in labor's house.

We must--and we will--continue our fight for full civil rights.

We will continue to measure progress and not seek to hide it. We will
continue to delineate shortcomings and move to eradicate them. We will continue the unity of labor, liberal and civil rights forces.

We stand firm in the conviction that has brought us this far--our belief
in the dignity of a man, the worth of an individual, the classlessness of
citizenship.

The answer is the keystone of the trade union movement--brotherhood.

Proceedings of the Eighth Constitutional Convention of the AFL-CIO, Atlantic
City, N.J., October 2-7, 1969, Vol. I, pp. 460-64.

16.   THE FIGHT FOR CIVIL RIGHTS IS ALIVE AND WELL

Thanks to the Leadership Conference on Civil Rights--25 Years Old

Several hundred trade unionists, civil rights leaders, church leaders,
community leaders and members of Congress recently gathered on the Senate
side of the U.S. Capitol for a very special occasion.

They were marking the 25th anniversary of the Leadership Conference on
Civil Rights--the vast coalition, now made up of 135 national organizations,
that spearheaded the successful drives for national civil rights legislation
during the 1950s and 1960s.

It has been through the LCCR that organized labor has been able to play
a significant role, itself, in the civil rights fight. Today, in addition
to the AFL-CIO, 24 labor organizations are affiliated with the Conference.

The Amalgamated Clothing Workers of America was one of the first to join.
At the 25th anniversary reception on the Hill, two of the three top founding leaders were on hand, Roy Wilkins, the executive director of the National Association for the Advancement of Colored People, and Arnold Aronson, an official of the National Jewish Community Relations Advisory Council. Wilkins is chairman of the LCCR and Aronson the secretary. The third founder, AFL-CIO Vice-Pres. A. Philip Randolph, was unable to attend; but he was surely represented in spirit by Bayard Rustin, director of the A. Philip Randolph Institute, and chairman of the LCCR executive committee.

As Wilkins licked the white icing of the birthday cake off his fingers, he exclaimed, "If anyone tells you civil rights is dead, say you saw it alive tonight."

Civil rights was very much the topic as the LCCR held its annual board meeting during the day.

The meeting affirmed the present focus on the civil rights movement. The general consensus is that what is needed, more than new civil rights laws, is the *enforcement* of the laws now on the books.

"When a law is passed," said Clarence Mitchell, who serves as legislative chairman of the LCCR, "opponents take the second line of defense." Enforcement is critical, he said, noting that "some people thought that everything was done when the Emancipation Proclamation was signed."[54]

In addition to enforcement, the LCCR stresses economic issues.

Rep. Andrew Young (D-Ga.), a one-time aide to Dr. Martin Luther King, said that "the civil rights movement made life better for those who have always done fairly well. We have still not helped those who are excluded from the economic mainstream."

He said that in Atlanta mass transit was not presented as a civil rights issue although poor blacks would benefit from the system.

Along this same line, the latest LCCR memo to participating organizations listed the pending Congressional issues of concern: legal service, genocide convention, busing, education, voter registration, budget control, minimum wage, Labor-HEW appropriations, manpower and D.C. home rule.

This was an entirely different ball game from 1949 when Randolph, Whitney Young, Wilkins, Walter Reuther, Aronson and others first formed the Leadership Conference. It was motivated by a 1948 report of a panel named by President Truman entitled, "To Secure These Rights." It recommended legislation not just on fair employment practices but in other areas such as voting rights, education and housing.

The Leadership Conference had its first major success with the passing of the 1957 voting rights bill. That law had severe limitations but did provide for setting up the Civil Rights Division in the Department of Justice and the U.S. Civil Rights Commission.

In 1960 and 1962 further civil rights progress was made in voting rights and outlawing the poll tax.

It was in 1963, following the tragedies of Birmingham, Ala., that President Kennedy called for across-the-board civil rights legislation. However, it was after his assassination that President Johnson signed into law the Civil Rights Act of 1964 which prohibited discrimination in public accommodations and in programs receiving federal assistance or by unions or employers and set up the Equal Employment Opportunity Commission.

A stronger voting rights law was passed in 1965 and, in 1968, a bill prohibiting discrimination in the sale or rental of about 80 percent of all housing.

About the time that the drive to support the Kennedy legislation was starting, organized labor's central role in the LCCR began to show itself.

The AFL-CIO, which had been cooperating with the LCCR, formally affiliated, adding considerable weight. Also, Walter Reuther and Jack Conway, then director of the Industrial Union Department, agreed to assign a staff member to the Conference.[55]

The IUD move proved to be a particularly fortunate one. Marvin Caplan, a respected Washington newsman who had worked in fair housing programs, was assigned to the Conference and named director of its Washington office.

For the first time in its history the Leadership Conference had an office and full-time director. With its growing number of affiliated organizations, it has played a decisive role in the civil rights legislation of 1964 to date.

Five task forces were set up in employment, housing, federal programs, education and federal regulatory agencies. Later task forces were established on health, veterans' affairs and women's rights.

The Leadership Conference rarely gets into the headlines. It brings together lobbyists from its affiliated organizations and works quietly but effectively.

Its broad front ties in closely with trade union goals. Of its 15 executive committee members, four are from organized labor—AFL-CIO Legislative Director Andrew J. Biemiller, former AFL-CIO Civil Rights Director Donald Slaiman, AFSCME Pres. Jerry Wurf and ILGWU Vice Pres. Wilbur Daniels.[56]

The Leadership Conference on Civil Rights has changed with the time but its prime goal has always been to make this democracy work for all its citizens through the democratic process.

The Advance (April, 1974):12-13.

17. AFL-CIO EXECUTIVE COUNCIL REPORT ON CIVIL RIGHTS, 1975

Since Congress passed the Civil Rights Act of 1964 and President Lyndon Johnson signed it into law on July 2, 1964, its widespread, positive effect on social behavior and employment practices in this country has been heartening.

It became law at a time when many symbols of racial discrimination remained, such as water fountains marked "white" and "colored." Blacks and other minorities were denied hotel accommodations and meals in restaurants solely because of their race or color. Libraries, public parks, swimming pools and other government-owned facilities were also segregated. In employment, most low-paying jobs were relegated to minorities and women, and very few blacks held public office.

With implementation of the various titles of the Civil Rights Act of 1964, many of these symbols of discrimination vanished within a decade and, hopefully, remain relics of the past. At the present time, most jobs are no longer designated on the basis of race and sex. Lines of progression and seniority rosters are devoid of racial and sexual designations.

The entree to higher job classifications through upward mobility programs grew at an accelerated rate until equality of aspirations and opportunity became a victim of the economic mismanagement that cast America into a depression.

There can be no denial that some slippage has occurred in civil rights progress. A number of important social programs, enacted during the Kennedy-Johnson years, were dismantled by the Nixon Administration through callous vetoes and heartless impoundments of congressional appropriations. Discriminatory allocation of revenue-sharing funds at the state and local levels has likewise had a negative impact on much-needed social programs.

Therefore, it is important to make sure that local and state governmental agencies disburse and allocate revenue-sharing funds in a non-discriminatory manner. The labor movement should concern itself with the programs for which these funds are allocated, and seek to preserve those social programs beneficial to the poor, minorities, elderly and handicapped.

Jobs and Manpower Training

Depression-level unemployment has hit all workers, but is particularly devastating in its impact on minorities and women. The unemployment rate for blacks at this writing was a frightening 14.6 percent and certain to go higher and remain high for many months to come. The official figure for unemployed black teenagers was an alarming 40.2 percent.

In spite of the economic crisis, some progress has been made in civil rights, but much more remains to be done. Minorities cannot get a room in the inn, or put food on the family table, or send their children to school

properly clothed, unless they have jobs.   Jobs are important to everyone.
Therefore, full employment is as essential to fulfillment of civil rights as
it is to a healthy economy.
     The problems of blacks and whites are not the same in 1975 as they were
in 1963.   Today's problems have little to do with racial attitudes and prejudices.   Blacks and whites share concern about crime.   Both races are emphatic
in their feelings about law and order.   Mutual concerns among both blacks and
whites include housing, drug addiction, transportation, education and, above
all else, jobs.
     Emergency unemployment legislation enacted by Congress in late 1974 in
order to create thousands of public service jobs has been grossly underfunded,
perpetuating atrocious inner-city jobless rates.   The government must become
the employer of last resort for all workers--of all colors, at any age, for
both sexes.   The AFL-CIO has been in the forefront of those calling for full
employment in this country.   We recognize that this nation has the manpower to
work and the technology to open the job market.   What is needed is governmental
leadership to achieve full employment.
     The affluent have fled the cities, taking with them expansions of major
industrial plants.   This exodus to suburbia eroded the tax base of central
cities, and many municipal governments are unable to provide some essential and
necessary services.   Rising unemployment also reduces tax revenue for local
governments, forcing layoffs of civil servants, and among those hardest hit
are minorities and women.
     In the private section, plant closing and reduction of work forces affects
all workers, including minorities and women.
     The remedy proposed by friend and foe alike in order to curtail layoffs,
especially as they effect women and minorities, is creation of alternatives to
layoffs by seniority.   These so-called alternatives include, among other things
Work-sharing imposed by law; "phantom seniority," and proportionate layoffs on
the basis of race and sex not seniority.
     The issue of layoffs by seniority is now before the U.S. Supreme Court.

Council Recommendation

     The seniority system is a cornerstone of the American labor movement.   It
is a contractual right.   Seniority itself is color-blind.   American workers,
regardless of race or sex, must not be compelled by government to surrender a
portion of the work to junior employees.   Workers must not be forced to accept
alternatives to seniority unless the decision is a voluntary one, arrived at
through the free collective bargaining process.
     Therefore, the AFL-CIO pledges its total, emphatic commitment to the
support of seniority systems that grant each member of the workforce his or
her "rightful place."   The AFL-CIO will also continue its unflagging opposition
to any effort to dilute the rights of any employee by granting others preferential treatment.
     We reaffirm our commitment to affirmative action programs designed to
eliminate discrimination in hiring, training, upgrading and promotion, and
urge our affiliates to utilize the services of the AFL-CIO Civil Rights
Department when necessary for assistance in the implementation of civil rights
policies and programs, including state and federal laws relating to equal
opportunity.   Further, we commend those affiliated unions with manpower training programs which assist in upgrading their membership for all job opportunities.
     Apprenticeship and journeyman outreach programs, endorsed by the AFL-CIO
and its building trades affiliates, have proven their worth in recruiting and
preparing minority youths to enter the skilled trades.   A new dimension was
added to these programs in 1974 when women began to be recruited for skilled
trades through these programs.   Outreach programs are coordinated basically
by three contracting organizations: the Recruitment and Training Program
(RTP, Inc.) of the A. Philip Randolph Educational Fund/Workers Defense League;
the National Urban League Labor Education Advancement Program (LEAP); and the
Human Resources Development Institute (HRDI).   A number of other local
organizations also participate in outreach activities.   Currently, programs
are functioning in 120 locations throughout the United States.   The success
of these programs depends largely upon the amount of construction going on in

the community. Without a doubt, the depression in the construction industry
has adversely affected these work-related programs.

Despite the present gloom, we must think in terms of a healthy economy
that will create additional training and employment opportunities for young
people desiring to become skilled in the building trades. It is essential,
then, that we reaffirm our commitment to provide opportunities for young people
to enter the trades, regardless of race or sex. Thus we commend the efforts
of RTP, LEAP, HRDI and other organizations in the implementation of outreach
programs and for the placements they have achieved.

The struggle for a society free of discrimination based on race, sex,
religion and national origin is a continuous one. It is a battle which must
be constantly waged as a national endeavor until the last vestige of discrimination is eliminated. However, this country must be mindful of the progress
made in the last decade through the efforts of government and voluntary organizations.

We in the AFL-CIO are proud of our involvement in the struggle for equal
opportunity for all. Many problems remain unresolved largely because of continuing high unemployment. Full employment and civil rights go hand-in-hand.
Without full employment, civil rights are empty indeed. America's twin
problems of unemployment and discrimination are not resolved by pitting worker
against worker for the right to be unemployed. That is why the best weapon
against discrimination of any form is a healthy full employment economy.

Equal Employment Opportunity Commission (EEOC)

Fair employment practices was a national goal of the labor movement for
many years prior to enactment of federal legislation. AFL-CIO civil rights
policy for the elimination of segregated local unions, segregated lines of
progression, seniority lists based on race, and providing full membership in
unions and admittance to apprenticeship programs for minorities predates the
Civil Rights Act of 1964.

Despite our commitment to assist in implementing Title VII of the 1964
law, the AFL-CIO has met stubborn resistance from the EEOC to providing adequate notice of alleged violations to the AFL-CIO Civil Rights Department and
the respective affiliated union. National or international unions should be
automatically advised by the EEOC when one of their locals is charged with a
violation. Copies of charges should be provided to the parent union and the
AFL-CIO Civil Rights Department to facilitate our efforts to achieve voluntary
compliance. Failure to give adequate and expeditious notice is a major reason
for the excessive backlog of unresolved allegations languishing in the Commission's archives.

The AFL-CIO Civil Rights Department and the EEOC have discussed the
problem for 10 years. A tentative agreement was finally reached to conduct a
pilot project to expedite the handling of backlogged cases and to develop a
speedy procedure for investigating allegations and to provide remedies without
jeopardizing the charging party's rights to full relief under the law. But
the proposed agreement was never considered on its merits by the EEOC.

The AFL-CIO Civil Rights Committee formed a subcommittee and called upon
EEOC commissioners to indicate their concern about the ever-increasing backlog
and the apparent indifference on the part of the commission.

It is our hope that this attitude of the commission majority will change
immediately. The charging party is entitled to speedy relief under the law
if the charge has merit. On the other hand, the respondents have the right to
know the nature of the charges within a reasonable period of time.

Council Recommendation

The AFL-CIO commitment to fair employment practices predates the law
itself. Title VII of the Civil Rights Act of 1964 requires the EEOC to seek
resolution of complaints through the conciliation process before litigation.
Yet unions are being bombarded by litigation, rather than conciliation by the
commission. The manner in which this law is presently being implemented
certainly reflects a lack of sensitivity toward unions on the part of the
EEOC.

We call upon the commission to expand its conciliation efforts, reserving
litigation for those respondents who refuse to comply with the law or who fail

to recognize that all men and women are entitled to equal opportunity to earn
a living.

We strongly urge the EEOC to provide unions and the AFL-CIO Civil Rights
Department with the necessary information to develop a speedy procedure for
investigation and achievement of voluntary compliance as suggested in the
proposed agreement between EEOC and the AFL-CIO.

Further, we urge our affiliates to call upon the AFL-CIO Civil Rights
Department to assist in matters involving EEOC and state commissions whose
concerns are to eliminate discrimination based on race, sex, religion or
national origin.

Proceedings of the Eleventh Constitutional Convention of the AFL-CIO, San
Francisco, Calif., October 2-7, 1975, Executive Council Report, pp. 214-18.

18.   REAL EXERCISE OF CIVIL RIGHTS LINKED TO FULL EMPLOYMENT

*The following remarks by AFL-CIO President George Meany were made in
accepting the Social Responsibility Award of the Martin Luther King, Jr.,
Center for Social Change. They were delivered by AFL-CIO Vice President
Murray H. Finley.* [57]

This award belongs not to me but to the entire AFL-CIO--the men and women
who have worked so hard for social justice for all Americans.

It is not a culmination, but a continuation of a shared dream that has
always bound the labor and civil rights movement together.

Dr. King himself said it best: "Our needs are identical with labor's
needs," he told the 1961 AFL-CIO convention, "decent wages, fair working conditions, livable housing, old age security, health and welfare measures, conditions in which families can grow, have education for their children, and
respect in the community."

Today, we have reduced that phrase and that dream to two words--"full
employment"--because "full employment" is absolutely essential if civil rights
are ever to be fully enjoyed and exercised by every American.

"Full employment" is not just a black issue or a labor issue. Yes, a
far higher percentage of the unemployed are black. And yes, when unemployment
is used as a tool of economic policy it is workers who suffer most.

Full employment is truly a human rights issue. It is the issue of the
last quarter of this century. Because, without jobs for every American who is
able and seeking work, the American dream--the dream of Martin Luther King, the
dream of Samuel Gompers, the dream of Phil Randolph--will remain a dream--an
unrealized dream.

We have an opportunity--in our lifetime--to take a giant step toward
making that dream a reality. The Humphrey-Hawkins Full Employment & Balanced
Growth Act would, in my opinion, take its place beside the Civil Rights Act
of 1964 and the Voting Rights Act of 1965 as legislation which frees America--
not just black Americans. It would free all Americans from the archaic theory
that when workers are set against each other for available jobs--through
artificial divisions such as race or sex or national origin--those with jobs
will work harder for less money, fearing an unemployed worker standing at the
plant gate waiting for their job. That is, of course, exploitation of the
cruelest form.

Thanks to Arthur Burns and the Nixon-Ford Administration, there is a new
segregation in America. A segregation as bitter and brutal as the one outlawed by the Civil Rights Act. It is a segregation based on whether or not
an individual has a job--those always working and those always jobless. Like
segregation based on race, this new segregation must go. [58]

So passing the Humphrey-Hawkins bill is essential. We are pleased that
President Carter has committed himself to this fight by endorsing the amended
bill. We in the labor movement and the Center for Social Change share a keen
interest in this bill, but we know it is only a first step. It must be backed
up with effective, extensive programs and we intend to keep fighting for such

programs. To us, the Humphrey-Hawkins bill is the foundation on which to
build, the necessary base for realizing our dream.

There is one other important piece of legislation, which, in my opinion,
is equally vital to economic and social justice in America. That is labor law
reform, now before the Senate.

It is a measure of great importance to black workers, who are union
members in greater percentage than their percentage in the workforce generally,
because they have found in the labor movement a vehicle for social change, for
a strong voice in their own destiny.

During the hearings in the House and Senate on labor law reform, it was
clearly evident that employers who are the most flagrant violators of workers
rights to form unions usually have an almost identical record of violations
of equal employment opportunities. The unorganized worker--is very often
black, very often a woman, always underpaid and almost always afraid.

Mrs. King has eloquently testified to those facts and her support for the
protection of the rights of all workers to form unions has been invaluable.
We know, as she knows, that Martin Luther King, Jr., was murdered in a march
for workers rights to form a union.

That the labor movement shall never forget. And that is what makes
receiving this award such a great moment for me personally and for the entire
AFL-CIO.

In accepting this award, we are not expressing satisfaction for what we
have done in the past. Rather we look upon it as an emblem of intention of
what we shall accomplish together in the future.

AFL-CIO News, January 28, 1978.

19. MEANY HAILS SOLIDARITY OF CIVIL RIGHTS ALLIANCE

Louisville, Ky.--Much remains to be done in the struggle to achieve social
and economic justice for all Americans, AFL-CIO President George Meany said in
a message to the NAACP's 70th annual convention.

He noted in a letter to NAACP Executive Director Benjamin L. Hooks that
progress has been made in the past 25 years toward racial justice through the
cooperative efforts of the labor-civil rights coalition.[59]

"Working together, the labor movement and the civil rights movement have
largely succeeded in wiping out the legal and legislative sanctions that
perpetuated injustice," Meany observed.

"But we are painfully aware of how much remains to be done to secure equal,
quality education for all our children and to secure equal rights, equal opportunity and a decent measure of economic justice for Americans of both sexes
and all races.

"The AFL-CIO remains fully dedicated to achieving these goals," Meany
declared. "We are convinced that no more effective instrument exists for
pursuing them than the mutual understanding and unity of purpose that have
been forged between the leaders and members of the AFL-CIO and the NAACP."

He said the coordinated efforts of the two organizations in voter registration and voter education campaigns have become a vital force for social and
political change. "And we intend to do all we can to make them more effective."

Warning that the progress workers and minorities have made "is menaced by
a revival of reactionary forces ranging from the Ku Klux Klan to 'Proposition
13' evangelists to professional union busters," Meany said it's essential that
"we present a united front against those who would tear down the social and
economic programs designed to move America ahead."[60]

He said the AFL-CIO and NAACP must jointly continue the fight against
bigotry while stepping up the fight against the dismantling of educational
and social programs.

"We have to work together for job-creating programs aimed at full employment and equal opportunity for all," Meany declared.

"Together," we can do much that neither organization could ever do alone.

I have every confidence that in the future, as in the past, our two organizations will unite in the struggle to make the American dream of justice and
equality a reality."

AFL-CIO News, June 30, 1979.

20.   LABOR'S CIVIL RIGHTS GOALS LINKED TO DEMAND
FOR FULL EMPLOYMENT

The best possible affirmative action programs is full employment, the
AFL-CIO declared in pledging to continue its support for integration, outreach
programs and enactment of ERA and for allies who share those goals.

While reaffirming support for affirmative action, the convention vowed
that "we will oppose any efforts to destroy the seniority system" and hailed
recent court decisions for taking those two issues out of an either/or confrontation.

In a separate convention action, the AFL-CIO urged enactment of the Fair
Housing Act of 1979, legislation written in the wake of a national survey
finding that a "black person has a 62 percent chance of encountering discrimination in the purchase of a home and a 75 percent chance in the rental of one"
and similar problems are faced by Hispanics, Asian-Americans, women and the
handicapped.

Included in the bill, which the convention said would finish the job of
the 1969 law by the same name, is a provision for federal enforcement powers
on behalf of blacks or handicapped persons "after a full hearing establishes
discrimination."

Some of the measures advocated by the convention included reaffirmation
of longstanding AFL-CIO goals or programs. Among them are:

* Continued emphasis on the outreach principle to recruit blacks, women
and minorities, "which has been so successful in the construction trades and
should be expanded into new sectors of the economy."

* ERA enactment, which entails holding off right-wing attempts to have
state referenda undo the recent congressional gain of deadline extension to
1982.

* The community groups to which the AFL-CIO pledges support and urges
affiliates to do the same include such longstanding labor allies as the A.
Philip Randolph Institute, Leadership Conference on Civil Rights, NAACP and
National Urban Coalition as well as such relatively new organizations as the
Coalition for Labor Union Women and the Labor Council for Latin-American
Advancement.

* Designation by every affiliate of a person to work with the AFL-CIO
Dept. of Civil Rights on relations with the federal Equal Employment Opportunity Commission. The federation pledged continued cooperation with the EEOC
"wherever it's possible to find efficient and equitable solutions to employment discrimination charges."

Cooperation from the EEOC under the Carter Administration was judged by
the Executive Council to be an area of major improvement in the two years
between conventions.

AFL-CIO News, November 24, 1979.

21.   A COALITION FOR PEOPLE
AFL-CIO President Lane Kirkland to the NAACP Convention [61]

The coalition between the labor and civil rights movements is the most
effective and most constructive alliance in American political and social
history. In the struggles of the 1940s, the'50s, and the '60s, to break

down the legal sanctions that perpetuated racial discrimination in America, this alliance brought about a political and social revolution.

Millions of youngsters are now growing up without ever having seen a "whites only" sign over a public drinking fountain, and without ever having seen a fellow citizen turned away from a restaurant or a college admission office or an employment office solely because of race. To that extent they live in a different world--and a better one--than their mothers and fathers knew.

Yet those youngsters are also learning that while discrimination is unlawful, it has not ceased to exist.

None of the rights guaranteed under these laws has any meaning, except to those--black or white--who have the resources and the opportunity to exercise them.

Equal education is attainable only for children whose parents can afford to keep them in school. Equal accommodations are available only for those who can pay the dinner check or hotel bill. Fair housing laws hold meaning solely for American families who have not been priced out of the market. Equal employment opportunity is an empty promise to nearly 10 million American workers of both sexes and all races and colors who need and want jobs and cannot find them.

Inequality in America, in the 1980s, is not statutory. It is economic.

What is needed is a program to educate the politicians. If the American people are given the facts about who will benefit and who will suffer as a result of the current budget-balancing and tax-cutting proposals, I am convinced that they will teach the politicians. Getting these facts to the public is the most important task we face.

Our many years of working together toward mutual goals have taught us something about teamwork and coordinated effort. In the Budget Coalition that was formed in April to oppose the budget-cutting madness on Capitol Hill, we have helped lay the foundation for a far larger alliance of organizations, some of which have never before been aroused to political and social action on a national scale.

They include other civil rights organizations, labor organizations that are outside the AFL-CIO, women's groups, religious organizations, family farm organizations, youth groups and senior citizens, the National Conference of Mayors, consumer groups, environmental groups and more than a hundred others.

What they have in common is that they genuinely represent the interests of people, rather than the interests of those whose chief concern is to maximize profit at the expense of the public.

That is the foundation on which we must build in order to remind our nation's leaders that public interest is paramount to corporate interest.

AFL-CIO News, July 5, 1980.

22. LACK OF OPPORTUNITY THWARTS STRIDES TOWARD RACIAL JUSTICE

The following is from an address by AFL-CIO Sec.-Treas. Thomas R. Donahue to a Catholic Interracial Council dinner in New York honoring Federation Vice President Frederick O'Neal and lawyer William Shea.[62]

For the moment, the immense strides that were made toward racial justice and social unity during and after the civil rights revolution--in which the church and the labor movement played so large a role--have come to a standstill.

I say "for the moment" because I know well that all progress toward these goals is ultimately irreversible. This country will move ahead again, but meanwhile we have to fight with all our energy to retake ground that is being lost.

Bull Connor's dogs and clubs are a thing of the past. I never expect to see again, in any public place, a sign that says "White only," or even "No Irish need apply."[63]

But there will be no end to discrimination in housing until there is
enough housing to go around. There will be no end to discrimination in education until all parents can afford to provide their children with all the
education they can possibly absorb. And there will be no equal employment
opportunity until there is opportunity for all, until there is a job for every
man and woman who is able and willing to work.

For the moment, what we face is the undoing of the progress we have made,
and the division of the American people along economic lines or racial lines
or sex lines or age lines or any other lines that are handy, and the restoration of the frozen, unjust social and economic order of the past.

The vital question is, "Am I my brother's keeper?" The church and the
labor movement have always answered with a resounding yes. But those who
preach the gospel of supply-side economics say the question is irrelevant.

They have no wish to talk about public health, public education, public
welfare as human values or even as public capital investment that enriches and
enlarges the society of which we are a part. They think of these things only
as consumer expenditures that increase public spending and reduce the return
on private capital.

When irresponsible tax concessions to the rich and the corporations have
sent the budget deficit into orbit, their solution is to shoot down $40 billion
in social security benefits--or at least it was until the Senate rebelled at
that solution.

With 10½ million human beings desperately looking for jobs that do not
exist, they cut emergency job programs, job training programs, public service
jobs and unemployment compensation programs, and promise only that things will
get better soon.

It was actions like these that led Congressman Henry Reuss of Wisconsin
to say that these policies are "not just mistaken; they are wicked." To that
I would add that they are deeply, shamefully frivolous.

The real capital of this nation is its human capital. No wealth has ever
existed that is not the product of human hands and minds and hearts. To
squander that capital by deliberately denying human beings the opportunity to
develop to their highest potential is not only morally wrong but something that
those responsible look upon as a far worse sin: Imprudent business management.

The American labor movement and the church have long stood together on the
questions of this nation's human capital--not really as "capital" but as
"humanity."

We have shared the simple goals of equality for all and the recognition
of the dignity of every person. Actually those goals are not simple at all.
They are simply stated--but their fulfillment has been a central occupation of
labor and the churches for many years.

We need the laws and the courts, most assuredly, to set a legal framework
for dignity and equality, but we need to shape the minds, hearts and acts of
people--we need to truly love one another--if we are ever really going to
"assure these rights." We have to keep pressing for dignity and equality and
have to keep on pressing against the "outer limits."

After Dec. 13, when the Polish government moved to crush Solidarity, the
amazing analyses by some of our commentators was that those brave Polish trade
unionists had pressed against the outer limits and tried to achieve too much.
It's a line that never made a bit of sense.

For people who seek reform, for those who would disturb the status quo,
for those who seek dignity and equality, there are only outer limits. There
are no inner limits which fall easily. Every push is against an outer limit
that some other person or force has set.

When a worker joins a union and seeks recognition of his dignity on the
job, he or she presses against the outer limits of the boss's authority.

When a black seeks the full measure of equality, in any form, he or she
presses against the outer limit of some ancient prejudice. When the Poles
sought a voice in their state, when the black South African seeks a voice on
the job, when the South American peasant fights for land, they all press
against the outer limits that some person or group seeks wrongly to impose.

It has to be our business to continually press against those outer limits
until they all finally crumble.

AFL-CIO News, June 12, 1982.

A. PHILIP RANDOLPH: "GENTLEMAN OF ELEGANT IMPATIENCE"

23. AFL–CIO SEATS TWO NEGROES

A. Philip Randolph, Townsend Named to Union's Exec. Board

By Harold L. Keith

A. Philip Randolph and Willard S. Townsend will be seated on the executive
boards of the newly merged AFL and CIO as a result of actions taken at the
founding convention of the organization in New York City.

Mr. Randolph is president of the International Brotherhood of Sleeping Car
Porters (AFL) and Mr. Townsend is president of the CIO United Transport Service
Employes Union.

Both men are Negroes and their appointments were hailed by labor leaders
as "evidence" that labor intends to back up its "pledges" against segregation
and discrimination in employment.

Mr. Randolph will be one of seventeen AFL vice presidents, and Mr. Townsend will be one of the ten representatives of the CIO on the AFL–CIO executive
board.

Mr. Townsend's appointment was made possible by the defection of Mike
Quill, International Transport Workers Union. Mr. Quill had dissented regarding
the merger on several key issues. Oddly enough, one of the things which led to
Mr. Quill's refusal to take a vice presidential seat was his insistence upon a
more strongly worded clause against segregation or discrimination. [64]

Mr. Quill had protested strongly against other provisions of the merger
agreement and then announced that he would not take a seat on the executive
board "under any circumstances."

However, Mr. Townsend was not without opposition. Many of the executives
within CIO ranks had ripped into his appointment on the grounds that Mr. Townsend's union did not have enough members.

They claimed that there were other CIO unions with larger and more representative memberships who should have received representation.

They noted that Mr. Townsend's union has a membership of a little more
than 10,000 spread out over the nation, while there are many CIO local unions
with more members.

The CIO Executive Board in two separate sessions held prior to the New
York meeting had turned down Mr. Townsend as an executive board possibility.

But, the big industrial union was faced with the practical necessity of
having Negro representation on the board and Mr. Townsend was the only choice.

George L. P. Weaver, long-time stalwart of the CIO Civil Rights Committee,
had been mentioned as a possible choice but overtures made in his behalf met
with so many objections that Mr. Townsend ended up with the prize.

Mr. Townsend was recommended for the post by David J. McDonald, president
of the CIO United Steelworkers of America.

Mr. Randolph's appointment was a foregone conclusion. Long one of the
most eloquent among the AFL's leadership, he like Mr. Townsend was the only
possible choice for appointment to the board.

His appointment was made despite his outspoken opposition to what has
been termed the "mousy, mealy-mouthed" anti-segregation provision of the
AFL–CIO merger constitution.

Mr. Randolph has staged rallies in New York and Cleveland on this issue
and is expected to continue to fight for a more positively worded clause with
punitive provisions for unions which discriminate.

The merger means that the combined strength of the nation's biggest labor
group is now 15,000,000 members with only the Mineworkers of John L. Lewis
and several independent unions outside the folds. [65]

Pittsburgh Courier, December 5, 1955.

24.   RANDOLPH SAYS NEGRO NOT FREE

Calls for "Complete Equality"

Speaking at an Urban League "Sound-off" luncheon last Tuesday, A. Philip Randolph, militant vice-president of the newly merged AFL-CIO, said "the Negro is not free" and called upon President Eisenhower to send armed troops into Mississippi and South Carolina to ease the "cold war" waged against Negro citizens of those states.

He also said President Eisenhower has "a moral obligation to make a major statement in the interest of Negro freedom."

"The Negro has got to take what he gets," the veteran civil rights leader said, "not by violence, not by the gun; but by continuous protest, continuous demands and continuous organization. Negroes want complete equality and first class citizenship and they want it now. Gradualism is no answer."

Michael J. Quill, president of the Transport Workers Union of America, followed Randolph to the speakers' rostrum and said that labor has material to win the battle for civil rights. Remarking that 1956 can be a historic year, he said that "the strangest kind of characters are running for President."

"Some of them come from the deep South," he said, "where they believe in one toilet for whites and another for Negroes. When they come to Washington they are democratic. In Philadelphia they are liberals and when they get to New York they are rip-roaring progressives. Then by the time they get to New Hampshire they are ready to do away with the white toilet."

The "Sound-Off" luncheon was held in the Georgian room of the Hotel Picadilly, 227 W. 45th St., Manhattan. The luncheon was chaired by Theodore W. Kheel, impartial chairman of New York City's private transportation industry and a member of the board of the Urban League. Other guests on the dais included Mrs. Ruth Whitehead Whaley, secretary to the New York City Board of Estimates; Frank Crosswaith, Harlem Trades Union; Lloyd Garrison, former president of the National Urban League; Mrs. Sophi Yarnall Jacobs, League president; and Monsignor Cornelius J. Drew, St. Charles Borromeo R. C. Church.

New York Age Defender, January 28, 1956.

25.   AFL-CIO REPORT ON CIVIL RIGHTS, 1961

PRESIDENT MEANY: I have a special supplementary report to submit to the convention on behalf of the Executive Council on the specific question of civil rights in the AFL-CIO which has to do with a memorandum submitted by Brother Randolph to the Executive Council at its meeting last June, and answered by the subcommittee of the council at its October, 1961 meeting. This material was not prepared in time for inclusion with our full report, and is submitted at this time to the attention of the convention.

Before referring to the committee, however, I want to ask the special permission of the Convention for Brother Philip Randolph to make a statement on this matter.

Is there any objection?

Hearing none, I recognize Brother Randolph.

VICE PRESIDENT A. PHILIP RANDOLPH: Thank you, Mr. President.

Fellow Delegates, I rise to make some observations on this report inasmuch as it is based on the memorandum which I submitted to the Executive Council at its meeting in Unity House, Pennsylvania in June of this year. My report included a number of proposals concerning the question of advancing the movement of civil rights in the house of labor. It also included a number of charges.

One was that the basic status of workers in the labor movement who are non-white is that of second class citizenship. Of course this does not mean that in various areas of our American industry and in various communities Negro workers, some of them, are not admitted into a number of unions and some of them occupy places on policy-making bodies. There are about a million and a half Negroes in the labor movement. But I am talking about the broad

status of the Negro workers in the labor movement as such.   That status is that
of second class citizenship.
     The delegates of the Brotherhood of Sleeping Car Porters are basically
concerned about that question.   We indicated that evidence of this charge consisted in the fact that there are exclusionary policies applied to non-white
workers by some unions, either in the form of color bar or in the form of
tacit consent.   Of course the color bar has been eliminated in practically all
of the unions except one.   But still workers of color are excluded from some
unions by tacit consent.
     This is not an exceptional affair.   As a matter of fact, you will find
this to be practically general in various communities with respect to craft
unions.   You will find that in one community Negro workers may be admitted to
a Carpenters' local union.   In another community, they may be excluded.   The
same thing is true with respect to the Electrical Workers' Union or the
Plumbers' Union or the Bricklayers' Union.   So that we are basically interested
in the broad position of the Negro worker in the labor movement, and we are
concerned about the development of a program that will meet that condition and
solve it.
     Other evidence of the status of the Negro is the fact that Negro workers
in the possession of skills are 100 years behind their white brothers.   This
is due to race bias, and the problem today is for the Negro workers to catch
up.   The only way by which they will be able to catch up is for these barriers
preventing them from entering apprenticeship training courses to be broken
down.   That is really the essence of the struggle of the delegates of the
Brotherhood of Sleeping Car Porters against race bias in the labor movement and
also of the Negro American Labor Council which was recently organized for the
sole purpose of eliminating race bias in organized labor.
     Another evidence of this second-class citizenship is the existence of
racially segregated unions.   This is a question which has not altogether been
squarely met because the position has been set forth to the effect that if you
have a Negro union in a given community and a white union covering the same
jurisdiction in the same community, and if the Negro union has officers and
members who want to maintain a Negro union, that they ought to be permitted to
maintain that union.   We disagree with that position.   We hold that just as
you will not permit a union under Communist domination or under corrupt influences to maintain its position, a union which practices racial discrimination
should not be permitted, whether the officers or members want to maintain the
union or not.   It should not be permitted to continue to exist.
     These are some of the problems that I set forth in my memorandum.
     The result of race bias in the labor movement and in management and in
the government, according to various economists,--Elmer Roper, for instance,--
the results are that Negro workers lose about $30 billion a year in income.
Over a decade they lose $300 billion in income.   It is estimated that the
Negro wage rates are just about half the wage rates of the average white
worker.   Therefore, this matter involves the question of economic survival,
economic security.   That is one of the reasons and the basic reason why the
delegates of the Brotherhood of Sleeping Car Porters have presented this
question upon the floor of the conventions of the American Federation of Labor
for practically a generation.   That is the reason why we have continued to
carry on the struggle, because we are concerned about increasing the income of
the great masses of black people in this nation who work for a living.
     We are living in a day when automation is beginning to exercise vital
influence upon the whole system of American production.   The work force is
changing.   The tools are changing.   It is estimated that by 1970, the population of this country will be around 208 million people and that it will require
about $700 billion to sustain this population.   In order to sustain this
population by the production of commodities and services, the tools must
change and the work force must change.   But if the great masses of Negro
workers do not have access to apprenticeship training courses, they cannot
get the skills and the training that are necessary to play their role in our
modernized industrial society.
     The great drives that we are making today are to break down these barri-
ers against the admission of Negro workers into apprenticeship training
courses.   The recent Civil Rights Commission set up by President Kennedy or
President Eisenhower, recently made a report, and that commission indicated

that there is widespread discrimination based upon race and color with respect to opportunity of black workers to get training, not only among the craft unions, but also in the giant mass production industries of the country. This then presents a crisis to the Negro masses of the country and the Brotherhood of Sleeping Car Porters has addressed itself to this problem.

We have also charged that the approach to this question has been one of tokenism and gradualism. I know that the leadership of the American Federation of Labor and Congress of Industrial Organizations has indicated that they are working and doing the best they can to change this situation. But time is moving and the industrial revolution is moving. The radical technology is changing American life, and Negro workers haven't the time to wait for people to make up their minds to give them justice. That is the reason for the movement to bring about rapid change giving the opportunity to all peoples of color to acquire information and training in order that they may become a factor in this automated world.

We also made the charge that the leadership has not a deep enough sense of urgency of this problem. That is no reflection on the sincerity and the good faith of the leadership. But it has been my opinion that our unions have not yet grasped the significance and the depth and the magnitude of the civil rights revolution which is going on in this country.

The United States is covered today by uprisings of young Negroes who are sitting in in protest against the violation of the dignity of their personality.

Hundreds are on buses going into southern communities to assert their constitutional rights as American citizens, to enjoy the privileges and immunities that other American citizens enjoy. They are even willing to absorb brutality and violence from the police in order that they may exercise their rights. Many of them have languished in the jails of Jackson, Mississippi. They are still going in large numbers.

Therefore, this gives you some idea of the fact that the civil rights resolution was not caused by myself or by the delegates of the Brotherhood of Sleeping Car Porters, but rather it is the result of the fact that the Civil War revolution was never completed. The 13th, 14th and 15th amendments were virtually nullified following the Civil War by a rising Confederate counterrevolution.

The National Association for the Advancement of Colored People, the National Urban League, the Southern Christian Leadership Conference led by Dr. Martin Luther King--all of these agencies are concerned about completing an uncompleted revolution in order that the Negro citizens of this country may have first-class status. That is what this matter is all about.

May I say I have the highest respect and regard for the President of the American Federation of Labor-Congress of Industrial Organizations. The delegates of the Brotherhood of Sleeping Car Porters are not mad at anyone. However, we have a responsibility to work in the interest of eliminating all vestige, all forms, all remnants of racial discrimination.

In addition to that, I presented in my memorandum a number of demands and indicated what ought to be done, and on the basis of this my proposals were rejected. I was condemned and denounced because of the presentation of the proposal.

Now, of course, anyone who is in the labor movement and has gone through some 40 years of struggle in the labor movement is not thin skinned. Consequently, I am willing to go through the fires in order to abolish second-class status for black people in this country. It must be done and it must be done now--not tomorrow. We cannot wait for tomorrow. In a nuclear age, tomorrow may never come. Consequently these are some of the demands that I presented in my memorandum:

1. Abolish barriers to Negro membership in unions, whether they be the color bar in constitutions or rituals, or by tacit consent.

2. Desegregate racially segregated unions whether the officials and membership desire it or not, just as the expulsion of Communist-dominated unions or unions under corrupt influences is carried out by the AFL-CIO without regard to the wishes of the officials or members of the unions.

3. Abolish barriers to your workers' participation in apprenticeship training programs because of race or color.

4. Desegregate southern state AFL-CIO bodies and their conventions.

5. Desegregate southern city central labor bodies in all of their varied activities.

6. Integration of Negro trade unionists in departments and on staffs more equitably in the national headquarters and in national and international unions, state federations and city central bodies.

7. Seek and urge equitable placement of Negro trade unionists on the Executive Council, and policy-making bodies of national, international and local unions.

8. Reorganize the Civil Rights Committee and Civil Rights Department as follows:

(a) Assumption of the chairmanship of the Civil Rights Committee by President George Meany or Secretary-Treasurer William F. Schnitzler, to give it stature and prestige.

(b) Increase the number of Negro trade unionists as members of the committee to give its interracial composition reality.

(c) Place an eligible Negro trade unionist, sound on labor's rights and civil rights, as Director of the Civil Rights Department. A trade unionist is needed in this post who does not only know the problem of race bias but also feels it. Moreover, if the federal government can appoint a Negro as head of a major department, the AFL-CIO should follow suit since it did not lead the way.

(d) Place an additional Negro trade unionist, sound on labor's rights and civil rights, as one of the assistant directors.

(e) Place a southern native-born white trade unionist, sound on labor's rights and civil rights, on the staff as one of the assistant directors.

(f) Integrate the office force.

(g) Hold national and regional civil rights labor conferences, and invite the National Association for the Advancement of Colored People, Jewish Labor Committee, National Urban League, Southern Christian Leadership Conference, Congress of Racial Equality, American Jewish Congress, American Jewish Committee, Workers' Defense League and the Negro American Labor Council, to send fraternal delegates, with voice, if no vote.

9. Adopt a Code on Fair Trade Union Racial Practices, comparable to Code of Ethical Practices for trade unions of the AFL-CIO, the pattern of which was included in my Memorandum on Civil Rights submitted to the Executive Council at Unity House, Pennsylvania, June, 1961.

If a Code on Ethical Practices is necessary, desirable and effective in helping to eliminate corruption, by the same token, a Code on Fair Trade Union Racial Practices is necessary, desirable and can be effective in helping to eliminate race bias.

10. Develop its own survey of race bias in unions to determine its nature and extent, since any survey of discrimination and segregation even when made by a federal agency or the National Association for the Advancement of Colored People, is promptly branded "anti organized labor," which, of course, is not true. The survey should not only seek to disclose racial discrimination wherever it may be, but also disclose evidence of progress which has been made by unions in dealing with the problem, such as cases of Negro trade unionists serving as officials in unions and as members of policy-making bodies, wherever they may be.

11. Take the initiative in getting a bill for Federal Fair Employment Practice legislation introduced in the next Congress, and place the full weight of the AFL-CIO back of it. While the AFL-CIO should wage a veritable crusade for the enactment of a federal FEPC, this is not to be construed to mean that the federation does not continue to bear the responsibility to rid the house of labor of every vestige, remnant and survival of race bias. It still has the responsibility to wage a continuing warfare against racial discrimination and segregation even if, as, when a federal FEPC is achieved in the Congress, because the law must be enforced.

12. The value and validity of target dates to mark the time when specific action should be taken to deal with a specific case of race bias, such as the desegregation of a jim-crow union, should be recognized as sound and practical, since target dates have been used with respect to cases involving the merging

of state AFL–CIO bodies, city central bodies and the expulsion of unions under corrupt and Communist influences.

13. In order to resolve the crisis of confidence between the AFL–CIO and Negro trade unionists and the Negro community, a conference between President Meany and with officers of unions appointed by President Meany and a group of Negro trade unionists selected by myself, should be held in order that this crisis in confidence may be resolved and that there may be a deeper sense of cooperation, of consultation and concern about the problems of organized labor.

These are some of the proposals I presented, and I hope and feel that it is possible for them to be realized.

And so, brothers and sisters, I wanted to make these few remarks to you in connection with this report, and to indicate that our organization represents the highest order of social ideals, economic and political; that we are committed to the basic values of human advancement and freedom and justice and equality.

Our organization has suffered, it has sacrificed and struggled for the realization of these ideals. We could not be a trade unionist and be anti-white, or anti-Semitic or anti-Catholic. Our organization is fighting to remove these barriers in our social life, and certainly, we would not be a party to practicing any kind of discrimination against anybody.

It was said that we have not negotiated a non-discriminatory clause in our contract for the Pullman Company. We had no reason to negotiate one. I have never known of a case where a white worker was denied a job by the Pullman Company because he was white.

Have we come to the time when the black workers have the responsibility of taking up the burden of freeing the white workers from job color bias? Well now, you know that is fantastic. It is a fabricated fiction. It has no basis in reality, and as a matter of mere humor it becomes comical.

So I wanted you to know the position of our organization on this question, because we stand by whatever we have done; we stand by the proposals we have made, and we will continue to fight for them. But we are going to fight for them in the house of labor. We have no desire to leave the American Federation of Labor and Congress of Industrial Organizations. We have no plan to organize any black federation of labor. But there are intimations in this report that we are black nationalists, and hence want to oppose everything that is not black. This is nothing more than a travesty upon common sense, an insult to decency.

This is the reason why I wanted to make my comments and my position and the position of my colleague M. P. Webster and also all the members and officers of the Negro American Labor Council clear to this convention.

Thank you very much.

PRESIDENT MEANY: Again, with the special permission of the convention, I would like to give the floor for a few minutes to Brother Webster of this same organization.

If there is no objection Brother Webster will have the floor.

DELEGATE MILTON P. WEBSTER, Brotherhood of Sleeping Car Porters: Mr. President and delegates of the AFL–CIO Convention: I want to reaffirm the remarks made by International President Randolph on this matter. When this report was read to our international Executive Board a few days before we came down here, they were quite disturbed. They instructed us to come to this convention and protest this report with all our energy and influence, this report which has created a false impression of the Brotherhood of Sleeping Car Porters.

Since I have been in this convention I have had delegates ask me if we were anti-white. As stated by Brother Randolph, we are by no means a new organization in the American labor movement. We came to the old AFL some 30 years ago, and we have had difficulty ever since we came in here. Objection was made to bringing us in because we didn't have the white leadership, but we got in.

Then a couple of years after we got in, our jurisdiction was given to a white organization that had a color clause in its constitution. We got out of that. And all during the years we have stood upon the floors of these conventions and protested these discriminatory practices that have existed in many of the unions over the years.

But the subject wasn't as popular as it is today. We never got any headlines in newspapers; we never had any press conferences and, as a rule, nobody but we made the protest. But we carried on the protest just the same, and we believe that some results have been obtained.

We have never said at any time that there hasn't been any progress made on this question in the labor movement, but we can't rest on our laurels. It is still here. It is here, probably here more subtle than it was when many unions had color clauses in their constitutions.

We have been loyal to the labor movement, despite our serious handicaps. We have participated in everything that unions are interested in; on any matter of fundamental labor principles we are always there. As a matter of fact, not too many years ago several of the railroad unions pulled a strike against the L & N Railroad. Some of those unions had color clauses in their constitution, but we wouldn't let our men cross the picket line, and we lost thousands of dollars, as a matter of fact. So, we have made our contribution to the American labor movement on the same plane as has anybody else. And over the years, we believe we have made as great a contribution as anybody.

Only recently, as a matter of fact, one of the large railroad companies in a program to start to cut wages started on us, and they cut the wages $50 a month. As a result of the brotherhood's negotiations, the $50 a month was not only brought back, but an additional $11 a month of fringe benefits were included. I don't think other organizations in this organization have been able to do any better job than we have done.

And so, this is one part of this report today that the Brotherhood of Sleeping Car Porters. I might say that we are not looking for any sympathy, we are not looking for sympathy on this. And we don't expect any sympathy. We don't appreciate the patronizing attitude of some of the members of this organization towards the Brotherhood of Sleeping Car Porters.

Shortly after the convention in San Francisco, we had many people come to us and try to tell us what we ought to do and ought not to do about this proposition of race discrimination. I take the position that it is very difficult for a man who is white to understand and appreciate the disadvantages of discrimination.

For several years I was a member of the President's Committee on Fair Employment Practices, appointed under the late President Roosevelt. I always had arguments with the management side of the committee that I was too impatient, too sensitive, and too bitter. I think I might refer to you the same suggestion that I referred to them, white men don't feel the sting and the disadvantage and the humiliation of discrimination in this country. And if you want to know how to feel about this thing, black your face up as black as mine and walk around New York, Chicago, Philadelphia and any other place, and then you will come back here more impatient than we are. There's no question about that at all.

This is the point we want you to understand, that we are committed to the idea of fighting these racial policies within the labor movement and outside the labor movement.

Now, there are two points of disagreement in this statement here which Brother Randolph touched on that affects us quite drastically. The first is they claim that in Vice President Randolph's own headquarters staff, in his own union, the employees are non-white, his employment policy on his own staff does not seem to be without regard to race, creed or color. I don't know who wrote this report, but certainly they never made any investigation. The largest amounts of money we pay out today are paid out to white people. How anybody can say that we are prejudiced against white people is a difficult thing, and I think you ought to be practical about this thing.

We hire most of our people in the national office in New York and our office in Chicago. And our office in New York is located on 125th Street, in the heart of Harlem. The office in Chicago is located on the South Side, the heart of the so-called black belt. A stenographer, the type that we have to have, draws approximately $80 to $105 or $110 a week, and I think it is fantastic to think that white girls qualified to fill that kind of a job would come up in Harlem or come out on the South Side of Chicago to look for a job. I have advertised in the *Chicago Tribune*. I would have taken any kind of stenographer that I could get. We got seven or eight replies, two of which I believe were white, according to where the telephone number was. And they would talk over the telephone, but they would never show up. And I think it is fantastic and really going out of the way to point out the fact that we don't hire any white people.

As a matter of fact we have about half the people we used to have, but there was a time when we had to go out in the street and hire new people. Over half the new people we hired were white.

Whoever wrote this report surely hadn't taken it upon themselves to make any investigation of this matter or they wouldn't have made the serious blunders that they did.

One other point, and then I am through; and that is on this question of discrimination in the employment of Pullman porters. I never knew that a white man ever wanted the job of Pullman porter. Not too many years ago an official of the old AFL came to speak to us when we were organizing. He said, "You know the sleeping car Pullman job is a black man's job." Well, now, you know what a black man is supposed to be, don't you; low pay, long hours and a mean boss man. And that job included all of them. It is rather amusing at this late date that somebody would come around and ask why we haven't urged white people to come into the movement.

In conclusion I want to say we have in our organization men of many nationalities. The Pullman Company, as oldtimers know, was one of the hardest nuts to crack in the labor movement, and we believe we are the first ones to crack it. All the crafts that work for Pullman are unionized now. But when we started to organize, they had an open job situation out there. They had company unions. We started on our campaign and were successful to a large extent. We had eight or nine hundred Filipino attendants. And they tried to make the Filipino believe he is a step above the Negro; he is not to associate with them. And we had about 150 Mexicans down in San Antonio. We had to walk out of the conference and threaten to strike until we made them include the Filipinos in our contract. The Mexican is supposed to be white. That's what they tell me down in Texas. In fact, they can go places that I can't go, so they must be white. We took the Mexicans in. We not only took them in, but we saw to it that they were given places of responsibility on our staff in order that every phase of our organization would be represented. One of our Filipinos who is now retired and has gone back to the Philippines to live was a member of our board for 15 or 20 years.

The Pullman Company went out on the street and hired about 25 white barbers. They put them on the train up in the Northwest and they doubled up that job with the club car porters. We went out and organized them. They stayed there until the job was abolished.

I don't know yet who wrote this report. I hope to find out sooner or later. I am sure some of the members of the council didn't have anything to do with the writing of it--but whoever wrote this report, if they had only taken a little bit of time to make inquiries about the matter, I don't think they would have made themselves look as ridiculous as they have been made to look by putting out this kind of report against an organization that has shown its loyalty to the labor movement.

We have no desire to get out of the labor movement. We don't want to see anybody else put out of the labor movement.

There was some comment on Brother Randolph's contention that certain organizations ought to be put out. Well, the record of the Brotherhood is against putting people out. We were one of the few delegations that stood on the floor of these conventions when they were eliminating the unions that subsequently set up the CIO. We became very unpopular, so much so that they made wise cracks that: "The Pullman Porters have to get their tips from John L. Lewis." We don't like to see the Longshoremen put out of the organization or any other people, because we felt if you could put people out because they violated other principles and programs of the Constitution, we don't see any reason you can't put them out for violating the civil rights position.

Therefore, we have brought this matter to this convention. We want you to know how we feel about it. And, as Brother Randolph says, we have no intention of leaving the Federation of Labor. We are not mad at George Meany or anybody else. Newspapers have made a great big hullabaloo about the feud between Randolph and George Meany. But there is a principle involved and we differ. As a matter of fact, brothers and sisters, we have had controversies in this labor movement that were far more bitter than this. The only difference is that the civil rights program wasn't as popular then as it is now and we never hit the front pages. So we bring these things to you in order that you might know how we feel.

We intend to carry on our campaign. We don't scare easy. If we scared
easy we wouldn't be here. But we are here, ready and willing to work with
the AFL-CIO and with any other organization. There are men sitting in this
convention now that know we have cooperated with them in any matter that
concerned organized labor as such. So we feel that some reconsideration
ought to be given to this matter.

Therefore, Mr. President, I want to make a motion that this report be
referred back to the Executive Council for reexamination. I so make that
motion, Mr. President.

VICE PRESIDENT RANDOLPH: I second the motion.

PRESIDENT MEANY: Brother Webster, I cannot accept your motion.

This is a very unusual procedure we have just gone through. A report
submitted to this convention for reference to a committee was discussed under
special permission of the convention to the officers of the union involved.
To refer it back now would mean this motion, if accepted, would not be
debatable. It would mean that discussion would be shut off on this matter
for the rest of this convention.

Therefore, I refuse to accept your motion. It is out of order on a
number of points, and I refer this to the Committee on Resolutions for consideration and a report back to the convention so that those people who
wrote the report will have their opportunity to defend the report and so that
the delegates to this convention will have the report in their possession
and know what we are all talking about.

Proceedings of the Fourth Constitutional Convention of the AFL-CIO, Miami
Beach, December 7-13, 1961, Vol. I, pp. 463-75.

26. COUNCIL REJECTS RANDOLPH CHARGES,
BACKS AFL-CIO RIGHTS RECORD

NEW YORK--The AFL-CIO Executive Council has rejected charges by Vice
Pres. A. Philip Randolph that the federation has failed to come to grips
with the problem of racial discrimination in unions.

The council adopted over Randolph's lone opposition vote a 20-page
report by a subcommittee set up in June to review a memorandum on civil
rights in the AFL-CIO submitted by Randolph. The detailed and documented
report answers Randolph's charges and concludes that the "purport" of his
memorandum is to have the AFL-CIO set up a "punitive program" in the civil
rights field.

The council-adopted report, signed by Vice Presidents George M.
Harrison as chairman, Richard F. Walsh and Jacob S. Potofsky, declares:

"Mr. Randolph loses sight of the fact that the AFL-CIO has been, and is
today, a major and foremost force in the land for the elimination of all
forms of race discrimination, segregation and racial injustice."

The "major" responsibility for the "gap that has developed" between
organized labor and the Negro Community, the report declares, falls "upon
Mr. Randolph himself."

AFL-CIO Pres. George Meany, terming the report "very factual and constructive," told reporters that the consensus of the council during discussion
was that Randolph should cooperate in trying to solve the problems of civil
rights rather than attack the labor movement.

He commented that Randolph appears to be on the "other side of the table"
against the AFL-CIO instead of on "our side" helping to work out solutions.
Randolph's attacks, he added, prevent the federation from making even faster
progress.

In a general analysis of the Randolph memorandum, the council report
notes that the AFL-CIO has an estimated 1.5 million Negro members, and that
the federation's civil rights policy "is forthright and unequivocal"that there
must be no denial of benefits of union membership to any worker because of
race, creed, color or national origin.

Among the multitude of organizations in the AFL-CIO, it notes, there are
"many imperfections and shortcomings with respect to non-discrimination." The
report then details the intensified activities in affiliates and state and
local organizations on civil rights.

The AFL-CIO, it says, has only one form of punishment--expulsion--which
does not "cure the offending practices," but rather removes the membership of
the expelled organization from "corrective influences from the parent body
through education and persuasion."

In a detailed consideration of Randolph's memorandum the report makes
these points:

* The charge of racial exclusion from craft unions by tacit consent is
based on one local union case which is receiving "diligent attention" and is
nearing solution. Randolph, says the report, has cited "the exception that
proves the rule."
* The charge of racial exclusion from apprenticeship training programs is
laced with "inaccuracies and misstatements." It cites Meany's recent testimony
before Congress supporting legislation to deny federal assistance to apprenticeship programs where discrimination is practiced.

The report notes the charge that there are no Negro apprentices among
Masons in Washington is in error, citing a top apprenticeship award presented
to a Negro member of the union.

Randolph's implied charge of discrimination in hiring of the AFL-CIO
headquarters staff was tagged "false" by the report. It cited numerous positions filled by Negroes on the staff and clerical level, noting that "on the
other hand" Randolph's own headquarters staff at the Brotherhood of Sleeping
Car Porters, the union of which he is president, is all "non-white" and that
his agreement with the Office Employes Union, covering the staff, "does not
contain a non-discrimination clause."

The charge of racial barriers to occupation status, says the report, is
not supported by the facts as it concerns motion picture operators in New York
City. The report lists the names of Negro operators holding top jobs as
projectionists.

In the Hotel and Restaurant industry, Randolph leaves the impression that
the Hotel & Restaurant Workers Union discriminates against Negroes, the report
says, whereas the discrimination in fact is practiced by employers who do the
hiring. The subcommittee report says that the union has "one of the strongest
and most comprehensive civil rights programs anywhere."

The report terms "false and gratuitous" Randolph's charge that "not one
single step has been made to desegregate and integrate Jim Crow unions" that
belong to AFL-CIO affiliates. The report cites a number of specific cases in
Washington, Baltimore, Cleveland, etc., where such integration has been
accomplished.

It adds that "there is no evidence of any effort" by Randolph to get the
Pullman Co., with whom he negotiates contracts, to agree to employment without regard to race or color. The company, says the report, employs only
non-whites in the U.S.

To the charge that Meany has failed to place "the moral weight of his
office" behind the federation's Civil Rights Committee and Dept. of Civil
Rights, the report declares "this is simply not true," citing the numerous
awards from Negro and other groups, statements, speeches and activities by
the federation president.

To charges that the federation has not effectively mobilized for civil rights and that there has been a loss of faith in labor by Negro community, the report replies:

"The record shows that when false charges and unwarranted attacks have been leveled against the AFL-CIO, untruthfully accusing it of weakness in the pursuit of civil rights, these charges and attacks have been met with silence from Mr. Randolph. This silence and tacit consent on Mr. Randolph as a vice president of the AFL-CIO have lent plausibility to these charges and attacks in the eyes of the Negro community . . . the major share of the responsibility for the 'gap' that has developed between organized labor and the Negro community, therefore falls upon Mr. Randolph himself."

To Randolph's recommendations for a national conference of union presidents and creation of civil rights committees and departments in affiliated unions, the report details actions already taken in this area. To the complaint that not enough unions elect Negro delegates to their conventions or the AFL-CIO convention, the report notes that democratic practice provides for free choice, not directions or suggestions from "the top."

The report defends the competence of the director of the AFL-CIO Dept. of Civil Rights in reply to Randolph's demand that the department be headed by a Negro, and it cites also the need for professional knowledge. It defends the AFL-CIO's educational and publications program on civil rights and objects strongly to Randolph's target date approach to compliance, with expulsion as the remedy. It reviews a charge brought against the Molders union, noting an intensive investigation by Meany that showed no evidence of discrimination.

Finally the report analyzes the role of the Negro American Labor Council, concluding that it has "neither offered nor given any cooperation" to the AFL-CIO civil rights program and that its record is one of "words rather than action."

AFL-CIO press release, October 13, 1961. Copy in possession of the editors.

27. ALONG THE N.A.A.C.P. BATTLEFRONT

NAACP Decries Randolph Censure

Roy Wilkins branded the AFL-CIO "censure" of A. Philip Randolph, president of the Brotherhood of Sleeping Car Porters and the only Negro vice-president of the labor federation, as "an incredible cover-up."

The complete text of Mr. Wilkins' statement follows:

The National Association for the Advancement of Colored People believes that the AFL-CIO's 'censure' of A. Philip Randolph is an incredible cover-up. The so-called report made to the Federation's Executive Council by a three-man subcommittee is simply a refusal to recognize the unassailable facts of racial discrimination and segregation inside organized labor, as well as an evasion of the part of the AFL-CIO leadership of its own responsibility in fighting racism within affiliated unions.

The perfume used by the AFL-CIO to try to smother the malodorus racism in labor's ranks fades before the ironic fact that the spokesman for the Executive Council's Subcommittee which rebuked Mr. Randolph was George M. Harrison, president of the Brotherhood of Railway Clerks, an international union which, for over half-a-century, has 'Jim Crowed' Negro railway workers into segregated locals in the North as well as in the South. It has limited their job rights by negotiating discriminatory promotional clauses in collective bargaining agreements.

The attack upon A. Philip Randolph can only be regarded as a further indication of the moral bankruptcy of the AFL-CIO leadership.

We of the NAACP certainly believe in cooperation between the Negro community and organized labor but such cooperation cannot be based upon Negroes remaining silent regarding racist practices within trade unions.

We reject the Federation's statement that A. Philip Randolph caused 'the gap which has developed between organized labor and the Negro community.' If such a 'gap' exists it is because Mr. Meany and the AFL-CIO Executive Council have not taken the required action to eliminate the broad national pattern of anti-Negro practices that continues to exist in many significant sections of the American labor movement, even after five-and-a-half years of the merger and the endless promises to banish Jim Crow.

We know that the entire Negro community will rally to the cause of Mr. Randolph which is the cause of all who struggle for a truly democratic labor movement committed to social justice and equality of treatment for all who toil.

The Crisis, 68 (November, 1961):566.

28. "TAKE WHAT'S YOURS--AND KEEP IT!"--RANDOLPH
'You May Look and Think Free'

A. Philip Randolph, president of the Negro American Labor Council and vice-president of the AFL-CIO, called Monday, for "an aggressive, militant, working class movement among black workers for completing the liberation" of Negro-Americans from the domination of white financial and industrial interests.

His prescription for the achievement of this goal was "power." He said, spelling it out in capitals, "Power, coming from organization." Effective exercise of power by organized Negroes would lead to the achievement of equality with white Americans.

Organize

Mr. Randolph was the main speaker at the annual community service held at Siloam Presbyterian Church, 260 Jefferson Ave., Monday, Jan. 1, in celebration of the Emancipation. It was sponsored by the Interdenominational Ministers' Alliance of Brooklyn and Long Island and supporting community organizations.

Stressing the need for organized power among Negroes, Mr. Randolph pointed out that in the American economic milieu, "there are no reserved seats. You keep what you can take." Thus if the Negro can't take or keep anything, economically, he would continue to be dominated by those who can."

Unequal

Mr. Randolph showed that Negroes were getting a small and inequitable portion of the wealth they created. That was the reason for the struggle of the mass of Negro labor.

The NALC, he said, was engaged in a war to increase the purchasing power of Negroes by ensuring them higher wages. The ultimate aim was to build a strong economic foundation under the black community, he stated.

Mr. Randolph praised those who participated in the Sit-Ins and the Freedom Rides. He asserted that they illustrated "the determination of black Americans to be free, and to be free now and tomorrow."

The Same

Another speaker, Kelly M. Alexander, an executive member of the North Carolina NAACP warned, "You may look free, think you are free, but you are just as subordinated as we in the South."

He emphasized the need for effective use of the vote by Negroes. In North Carolina, he said, Negroes had organized and were able to communicate their strength to the white power structure.

As a result not only did Negroes defeat anti-NAACP legislation in the state legislature, but also they elected six Negroes to offices recently. He urged the audience to vote into office liberal whites and Negroes.

Support

Representatives of supporting organizations at the service were, George Fleary, NAACP; Hardy Franklyn, Brooklyn Public Library; Russell Service, YMCA;

Wendell Roye, Urban League; Henry Ballard, Church Ushers Association of Brooklyn and Long Island; Richard Green, Carver Federal Savings and Loan Association; and Nathaniel Rogers, Ancient and Accepted Scottish Rite Free Masons.
     Rev. Milton A. Galamison is pastor of the church. Rev. Joseph H. May
presided.

New York Amsterdam News, January 6, 1962.

29. AFL-CIO RESOLUTION ON
NEGRO CIVIL RIGHTS-LABOR ALLIANCE, 1965

     RESOLUTION NO. 120--By Delegates A. Philip Randolph and C. L. Dellums,
Brotherhood of Sleeping Car Porters.
     WHEREAS, The alliance between labor and the civil rights movement was a
major force, together with the church forces and the great legislative genius
of President Lyndon Baines Johnson, in winning the enactment of the Civil
Rights Act of 1964 and the Voting Rights Act of 1965, and
     WHEREAS, The enemies of civil rights, namely, the John Birch Society, Ku
Klux Klan, White Citizens Council, and a growing group of reactionary rightist
forces are also the enemies of the trade union movement, led by the AFL-CIO;
therefore, be it
     RESOLVED: That this Sixth Constitutional Convention of the AFL-CIO go on
record to support a Negro-labor alliance and that it be expanded and
strengthened as a basis of a broad coalition of conscience composed by the
three faiths, Jewish, Catholic and Protestant, to fight for labor's rights
such as the repeal of Section 14 (b) of the Taft-Hartley Act, higher minimum
wages and extended coverage, and the implementation of civil rights legislation.
     COMMITTEE SECRETARY ABEL: Mr. Chairman, the Committee on Resolutions
moves the adoption of this resolution, and I so move.
     . . . The motion was seconded.
     PRESIDENT MEANY: You have heard the report of the Committee on Resolu-
tions on Resolution 167, Civil Rights. The Chair recognizes Vice President
Randolph.
     VICE PRESIDENT A. PHILIP RANDOLPH: President Meany, fellow delegates to
this convention: It has been two years since I last stood before this convention. These have been eventful and dramatic years for the civil rights
revolution. Indeed, the social and political landscape of the entire country
has been changed.
     We have won the passage of two historic pieces of legislation--the Civil
Rights Act of 1964 and the Voting Rights Act of 1965. Thus, after centuries
of slavery, segregation and discrimination, the American people have spoken
out unequivocally--not merely on behalf of the Negro but in the name of
democracy itself. For when men are denied, on grounds of race, the elementary
rights of due process and the right to vote, the moral foundations of that
society are in doubt.
     These victories are, first and foremost, the fruits of the struggle of
the Negro people themselves. History will record that our gains, like those
of labor, were not handed down from above but were wrested from reluctant
hands through courage and sacrifice, often to limb and life.
     Medgar Evers, William Moore, James Chaney, Michael Schwerner, Andrew
Goodman, Lemuel Penn, Jimmy Lee Jackson, Mrs. Liuzzo, Reverend James Reeb,
Jonathan Daniels, the four young girls of Birmingham--these are but some of
those-- black and white; Catholic, Protestant and Jewish--who have made the
ultimate sacrifice, in the cause of freedom. President Meany, I request that
this convention rise for a moment of silent tribute to the memory of these
freedom fighters. . . .
     Brothers and sisters, we know that more than courage and determination
were required to secure the civil rights legislation. Mass action had to be
mobilized. The great Selma-to-Montgomery March, which captured the conscience
of the nation and the attention of the world, generated the dynamism behind

the Voting Rights Act of 1965. I am proud to tell you, brothers and sisters, that perhaps no single group was so distinctively and honorably present on that occasion as the representatives of the labor movement. President Meany sent Don Slaiman, director of our Civil Rights Department, with a delegation that included, among others, Dave Sullivan, Robert Powell and Charles Zimmerman.

And so, on the very steps of the capitol of Alabama, labor's voice was raised high and clear in the name of freedom. President Meany, I participated in that historic event, and I can tell you that nothing so inspired the embattled Negroes of Alabama with courage and confidence as the visible and dramatic support of the labor movement in those glorious days.

Not only in Alabama but in Washington, the political power and skill of the Negro's allies were indispensable. The fact of the matter is, brothers and sisters, that the AFL-CIO--under the able and forthright leadership of President Meany, Brother Reuther and the Executive Council--did a yeoman's job of lining up congressional support for the civil rights legislation of the past two years.

Special recognition is due to Andrew Biemiller who, working side by side with Clarence Mitchell, of the National Association for the Advancement of Colored People, and Joseph Rauh, Jr. of the Industrial Union Department, co-ordinated labor's lobbyists on Capitol Hill. Without their tireless efforts, we might not have won the battle. Let these hard facts be properly noted by the hostile critics of the labor movement who profess sympathy for the cause of racial equality. [66]

Brothers and sisters, the Resolution on Civil Rights which is before you is a commendable document which reaffirms labor's commitment to racial justice and equality. It emphasizes what labor knows from experience--that the passage of good laws is not sufficient, that the laws must be vigorously and effectively enforced. The agencies responsible for administering the laws must be given the resources to discharge their responsibilities firmly. Where necessary, the laws must be strengthened through amendment.

But we also know that the work of the civil rights movement has just begun. We rightly demand of the government that every barrier to the Negro's full participation in the nation's political life be struck down. Once those barriers have fallen, however, it is our task to mobilize the masses of Negroes at the ballot box.

This is labor's task as well. For when the full political potential of the Southern Negro is realized, the face of Congress will be radically changed. The Dixiecrat politicians who have joined with conservative Republicans in opposition to labor's legislative demands will have to sing a different tune-- or find other jobs. Moreover, brothers and sisters, I submit to you that the continuation and expansion of the Negro voter registration campaign in the South lays the foundation for labor's drive to organize the unorganized in the South.

The last two years have plainly demonstrated that the Negro-labor alliance is not a one-way street. Virtually the entire national Negro leadership has put its weight heavily behind the congressional campaign for repeal of 14(b), for a 2-dollar minimum wage, for extension of the Fair Labor Standards Act, and for other labor demands. They have testified before congressional committees and their testimonies have been published and widely distributed by the Randolph Institute.

When the Negro leadership speaks out for labor's demands, they are not merely making a gesture in return for labor's support of civil rights. Rather we are bound together in a coalition of mutual interest.

Negro workers need and demand the repeal of 14(b) now! And they know why they want it. They know that repeal of 14(b) helps clear the way for unionization of the South. They know that repeal of 14(b) is a step toward economic security and better living standards. They know that repeal of 14(b) means greater dignity on the job--freedom from exploitation and intimidation.

And they know full well where the die-hard resistance to repeal of 14(b) is coming from. It is coming from the greedy profiteers and the reactionary politicians who have tried to block the Negro's advance every step of the way. That is why, in Oklahoma and other states, the Negro vote was decisive in defeating so-called right to work laws. And I can promise you, brothers and sisters, that throughout this land, the Negro revolution will join hands with labor in saying to the next Congress: Repeal 14(b) now!

And we say, too, that if there is any single step that will raise Negroes out of poverty, it is labor's demand for a national 2-dollar minimum wage. In this land of affluence, in the year 1965, two out of every three Negro families live in poverty and deprivation. In part, this fact reflects the astronomically high unemployment rates in the Negro community. But in most cases, the head of the Negro family is working--forty hard hours a week. He does not need to be lectured about self-help. Give him a decent wage, and he will be able to help himself. He will be able to keep his family together, to educate his children, to contribute to the well-being of the community. And he will be in a stronger position to struggle effectively for the dignity and the rights which he has been denied.

A national 2-dollar minimum wage, extended to millions now uncovered, would redress a shame of the nation. It would mean a revolution in southern racial and economic relations. It would weaken the position of runaway plants that locate in the South in order to escape unionism and exploit a cheap labor market. In many southern towns and cities, such companies become entrenched in the local power structures and fiercely resist civil rights efforts to change the status quo. The impact of a 2-dollar minimum wage on the ghetto-entrapped Negroes of the North would be no less revolutionary.

In short: if the civil rights revolution is to have meaning outside of the South--in the teeming slums of the cities, in the industrial centers of the nation--the needs of the dispossessed Negro masses must be hitched to the economic demands of labor.

More and more, the Negro leadership recognizes that of all the mass institutions in the nation, the labor movement holds out the greatest hope for progress in the daily conditions of life in the Negro community. Yet they do not forget for one moment that labor's own house is not yet entirely in order, that segregated locals and discriminatory practices still exist in some unions. The eradication of these conditions, noted in the resolution before you, must be high on your priority list in the coming year. We must not permit the existence of any barriers to expanded cooperation between labor and the civil rights movement; and we must not give any ammunition to labor's enemies.

The Civil Rights Department is to be congratulated for the vigor and effectiveness with which it has labored to eliminate the remaining discrimination in our ranks. Even before Title VII, the fair employment section of the Civil Rights Act, went into effect, the department was hard at work preparing international unions to cooperate in obtaining compliance with the law. At the same time, the AFL-CIO has called for a strengthening of the enforcement machinery of Title VII.

But more than your congratulations, Don Slaiman and the Civil Rights Department need your active support. Union locals must be encouraged to utilize the valuable technical assistance the department can provide.

Brothers and sisters, two years ago when I stood before you, I spoke of the impact of the technological revolution and its economic dislocations on the Negro community. I said then that large sections of the community, unskilled and uneducated, were being rendered economically obsolete and deprived of social dignity. I spoke of a growing underclass, lacking hope and leadership, bereft of any sense of a stake in the total society. And I said then that, if we listened carefully, we could hear the rumblings of that underclass.

I do not need to tell you that in these two years those rumblings are exploded into thunderous and wildly destructive violence, from the tenements of Harlem to the slums of Watts. That violence cannot be excused or defended, for it took a larger toll in life and limb than has the nonviolent movement in the South--and with less to show for it. But it serves no purpose simply to denounce the riots without trying to understand their causes. For, of this much we can be certain: if those causes are not identified and uprooted, radically and finally, we will be courting disaster.

Let me say that I have been greatly encouraged by President Johnson's speech at Howard University and by the Department of Labor's study on the Negro family. Both move in the right direction of pinpointing the social and economic roots of the Negro's discontent. To further explore these roots, the President has, as you know, scheduled a special White House Conference, of which I have the privilege of serving as honorary chairman.

This conference will give special attention to the problem of Negro family instability. This, brothers and sisters, is a major problem with deep historical roots. Under two centuries of slavery, the Negro family was systematically destroyed. The right of Negroes to marry is barely one hundred years old. Following slavery, a system of segregation was introduced which denied the Negro family, particularly the Negro male, even the rudiments of economic security. To this very day, many of our welfare laws encourage family desertion by Negro males.

I do not have to tell you how family breakups encourage delinquency, crime, school drop-outs, and many forms of destructive, anti-social behavior. But when all of this is said, the question remains: How do we strengthen the Negro family and the fabric of the Negro community?

Here again, I think the labor movement knows the answer at least as well as the sociologists and psychologists and other experts. The answer is jobs—decent jobs at decent wages. We know that when the Negro unemployment rate dropped during World War II, so did the Negro rate of divorce, of illegitimacy, and other indications of family instability. And so, brothers and sisters, the answer to Negro family instability and to Watts is the enactment of labor's programs for full and fair employment.

The record of the last ten years will show that we cannot look to the private sector of the economy to achieve the goal of full employment. But we can meet that goal through expansion of the public sector—through meeting the vast unmet social needs of the country. We can put the unemployed back to work by clearing our slums and rebuilding our cities, by building schools and hospitals, by modernizing and expanding mass transit facilities, by investing in flood control and by combating air pollution. We can open new jobs for the poor by expanding our social services.

We can achieve full employment by tearing down the physical environment of poverty and building a great society in its place. It was with this concept in mind that I proposed, at the planning session of the White House Conference, a national freedom budget of 100 billion dollars. This is a feasible and realistic budget, which has the support of leading labor economists. We have the means; we lack only the social imagination and the political will.

This is, above all, an imperative budget if we are serious about building the Great Society. As President Meany has said, "We must not let money stand in the way." Either we decide upon massive social investments now, or we face the incalculably more costly alternative of social disintegration and violence. In the long run, it is the budget-balancers and the tight-money boys who will prove to be the most impractical. Let me say right here that the recent action of the Federal Reserve Board may do more to dry up job opportunities for Negroes—not to mention whites—than the most overtly racist discrimination.

Brothers and sisters, I cannot close without commenting on a great danger that may lie ahead. In times of war or international crisis, as you know, there is a tendency to divert attention away from crying domestic needs and problems. Even now there are those who would exploit the perilous situation in Viet Nam for their own narrow political purposes. Already we have heard the reactionary voices of Senators Stennis and Russell and other segregationists. They call for a cutback in the war on poverty; they would push the struggle for racial equality off the stage of history; they feel strengthened in their opposition to labor's struggle for industrial democracy.[67]

These tendencies must be vigorously fought. As President Meany has said, our efforts to resist Communist totalitarianism will require sacrifices and impose burdens. But those sacrifices and burdens must be evenly distributed. We must not place the heaviest loads on those least able to bear them—the poor and dispossessed, black and white. We must not now dash their new hopes for a place in the sun. We must press forward the struggle for justice and democracy at home while we pursue it abroad.

In recent weeks, the Negro leadership has gathered together to discuss the objectives and directions of the civil rights movement during this difficult period of transition. They have concluded that we need to press forward on three major fronts. First is to achieve economic security for the Negro family through full and fair employment. Second is to see to it that the civil rights legislation is vigorously implemented. Third is to secure full protection of individuals in the exercise of the constitutionally-guaranteed rights. There must be an immediate end to the brutalization and

murder of civil rights workers, and to a discriminatory jury system which
makes a mockery of justice.
President Meany, the resolution before us speaks forthrightly and directly
to these concerns of the Negro leadership. Not coincidentally, but by indis-
putable social logic, the forces of labor and civil rights again find themselves on the same side of the struggle for justice.
Brothers and sister, I urge the adoption of the Resolution on Civil
Rights.
Thank you.

PRESIDENT MEANY: Thank you, Brother Randolph, for a clear statement of
position supporting the AFL-CIO.
Is there further discussion? Those who favor the motion to adopt, signify
aye. Contrary? It is carried and so ordered.

Proceedings of the Sixth Constitutional Convention of the AFL-CIO, San
Francisco, Calif., December 9-15, 1965, Vol. I, pp. 213-20.

30. A "FREEDOM BUDGET" FOR ALL AMERICANS
Prepared by the
A. Philip Randolph Institute

Foreword

After many years of intense struggle in the courts, in legislative halls,
and on the streets, we have achieved a number of important victories. We have
come far in our quest for respect and dignity. But we have far to go.
The long journey ahead requires that we emphasize the needs of all
America's poor, for there is no way merely to find work, or adequate housing,
or quality-integrated schools for Negroes alone. We shall eliminate slums for
Negroes when we destroy ghettos and build new cities for *all*. We shall
eliminate unemployment for Negroes when we demand full and fair employment for
all. We shall produce an educated and skilled Negro mass when we achieve a
twentieth century educational system for *all*.
This human rights emphasis is an integral part of the Freedom Budget and
sets, I believe, a new and creative tone for the great challenge we yet face.
The Southern Christian Leadership Conference fully endorses the Freedom
Budget and plans to expend great energy and time in working for its implementation.
It is not enough to project the Freedom Budget. We must dedicate ourselves to the legislative task to see that it is immediately and fully
achieved. I pledge myself to this task and will urge all others to do likewise.
The Freedom Budget is essential if the Negro people are to make further
progress. It is essential if we are to maintain social peace. It is a political necessity. It is a moral commitment to the fundamental principles on which
this nation was founded.

October 26, 1966   *Martin Luther King*

Introduction

The "Freedom Budget" spells out a specific and factual course of action,
step by step, to start in early 1967 toward the practical liquidation of
poverty in the United States by 1975. The programs urged in the "Freedom
Budget" attack *all* of the major causes of poverty -- unemployment and under-
employment; substandard pay; inadequate social insurance and welfare payments
to those who cannot or should not be employed; bad housing; deficiencies in
health services, education, and training; and fiscal and monetary policies
which tend to redistribute income regressively rather than progressively.
The "Freedom Budget" leaves no room for discrimination in any form, because
its programs are addressed to *all* who need more opportunity and improved
incomes and living standards -- not just to some of them.

The "Freedom Budget" differs from previous worthy efforts to set forth similar goals because it fuses general aspirations with quantitative content, and imposes time schedules. It deals not only with where we must go, but also with how fast and in what proportions. It measures costs against resources, and thus determines feasible priorities. It is not only a *call* to action, but also a *schedule* for action.

The "Freedom Budget," however, is not self-executing. It defines programs around which can be rallied all those individuals and groups who favor these programs and their objectives. But even with this convergence of forces, these individuals and groups will need to assume the political task of impressing upon *their* Government the obligation to undertake promptly the needed legislative and Executive programs. As is stressed throughout, improved operations under the Employment Act of 1946, commencing at once, must be the first focal point of the implementation process. The "Freedom Budget" is thus an imperative call to *national action -- now.*

Why do we call this a "Freedom Budget?"

The language evokes the struggle of the civil rights movement, its vision of social justice and equality, its militant determination that these goals be rapidly and forthrightly achieved. This is the vision and determination that underlies the "Freedom Budget" and must propel any genuine war on poverty. The moral issues in this war are no less compelling than those of the battle against racism.

We call this a "Freedom Budget" in recognition that poverty and deprivation, as surely as denial of the right to vote, are erosive of human freedom and of democracy. In our affluent nation, even more than in the rest of the world, economic misery breeds the most galling discontent, mocking and undermining faith in political and civil rights. Here in these United States, where there can be no economic nor technological excuse for it, poverty is not only a private tragedy but in a sense a public crime. It is above all a challenge to our morality.

We call this a "Freedom Budget" because it embodies programs which are essential to the Negro and other minority groups striving for dignity and economic security in our society. But their legitimate aspirations cannot be fulfilled in isolation. The abolition of poverty (almost three-quarters of whose U.S. victims are white) can be accomplished only through action which embraces the totality of the victims of poverty, neglect, and injustice. Nor can the goals be won by segmental or *ad hoc* programs alone; there is need for welding such *programs* into a unified and consistent *program.*

The main beneficiaries will be the poor themselves. But in the process everyone will benefit, for poverty is not an isolated circumstance affecting only those entrapped by it. It reflects -- and affects -- the performance of our national economy, our rate of economic growth, our ability to produce and consume, the condition of our cities, the levels of our social services and needs, the very quality of our lives. Materially as well as spiritually, a society afflicted by poverty deprives all of its citizens of security and well-being.

In this war, too, we encounter the pessimists and the tokenists, those who counsel "gradualism" and those who urge piecemeal and haphazard remedies for deep-rooted and persistent evils. Here again, "gradualism" becomes an excuse for not beginning or for beginning on a base too small to support the task, and for not setting goals; and the scattered, fragmented remedies, lacking priorities and coordination, often work at cross purposes.

In the economic and social realm, no less than in the political, justice too long delayed is justice denied. *We propose and insist that poverty in America can and therefore must be abolished within ten years.*

The means toward this end are spelled out in the following pages, prepared in cooperation with some of the nation's outstanding experts. There may be minor disagreements with regard to statistical data, analysis, and policy proposals, even among those endorsing the "Freedom Budget" in this publication. These individuals subscribe only to the broad directions of the "Freedom Budget," and are too imbued with a sense of urgency to cavil about the details. But this limitation is not intended to imply lukewarmness in terms of urgency, nor to question that in its *major* aspects the "Freedom Budget" is essentially sound and imperative.

The "Freedom Budget" contends that this nation has the resources to
abolish poverty, for the first time in human history, and to do so within a
decade. Indeed, the very process of abolishing poverty will add enormously to
our resources, raising the living standard of Americans at all income levels.
By serving our unmet social needs -- in slum clearance and housing, education
and training, health, agriculture, natural resources and regional development,
social insurance and welfare programs -- we can achieve and sustain a full
employment economy (itself the greatest single force against poverty) and a
higher rate of economic growth, while simultaneously tearing down the environment of poverty. All of these problems interact, whether viewed as causes or
results, and they are in truth both.

Only such a massive and sustained program -- which sees poverty in terms
of the national economy, and not only in terms of the personal characteristics
of the poor -- can bring success. Goals must be set, along with timetables for
achieving them. We must plan the allocation of our resources in accord with
our priorities as a nation and a people.

The economic impact of the war in Vietnam and the attendant question of
inflation are discussed subsequently and need not be taken up here, except to
point out that the "Freedom Budget" is not predicated on cutbacks in national
defense nor on one or another position regarding the Vietnam conflict, which
is basically a thorny question to be viewed in its own terms. The fundamental
proposition is that the broad approaches of the "Freedom Budget" can and should
be implemented, whether or not an early termination of the Vietnam conflict is
achieved, or even were there to be substantial increase in its economic and
financial burdens.

Clearly, however, there are those who would use the Vietnam war and the
issue of inflation as sharp weapons to force cut-backs or dangerous slowdowns
in the needed rate of expansion of domestic social spending. Their cries
might attract more notice had they not, in too many instances, been vociferous
opponents of Great Society programs prior to the stepped-up American involvement
in Vietnam. And as for the problem of inflation, to the extent it augments,
the Federal Government has at its command selective measures to combat it which
do not require impairment of Great Society programs of needed magnitudes. If
the progress of inflationary pressures should indicate that we are trying to do
more than our rapidly-advancing productive resources will support, then a
legitimate effort against inflation means cut-backs of the relatively nonessen-
tial, not of the vital. A simulated campaign against inflation which punishes
those who need help most reveals the crocodile tears of those who bewail how
inflation hurts the unfortunate. It is important that thinking Americans
recognize the selfish character of any assault on needed domestic programs.

As we reject these selfish pleas, so must we reject another argument
emanating from different quarters, to the effect that the termination of the
Vietnam conflict is the prerequisite for acceleration of domestic social
programs. We all desire that termination, on safe and honorable terms; nonetheless, the argument just cited, no less than that of economic conservatives,
would hitch the aspirations and long-denied needs of the poor to the outcome
of the Vietnam war -- a dependency which, we repeat, is neither economically
necessary nor morally defensible.

Those drafting this "Freedom Budget" have sought to outline, objectively
and fully, the steps required for the abolition of poverty in America. It may
be argued that the "Freedom Budget" is too ambitious to be "politically
feasible." We contend that the proper question is whether the persistence of
poverty is any longer feasible. Can we afford another Watts, and what has
happened since? How many examples of seething discontent do we need before
we move earnestly to provide jobs for all, clear the slums, rebuild our
cities, overcome the shortages of schools and hospitals, and reverse the
neglect of our other social needs?

Who, only a few short years ago, would have acknowledged the "political
feasibility" of the tremendous legislative victories of the civil rights
movement in our own day?

These breakthroughs were not won by those who thought narrowly of what
was "politically feasible," but by those who placed the moral issues squarely
before the American people. Having stated the issues clearly, they forged a
mighty coalition among the civil rights and labor movements, liberal and
religious forces, students and intellectuals -- the coalition expressed in
the historic 1963 March on Washington for Jobs and Freedom.

Social progress is always the trusteeship of those battling constantly
to lift the level of "political feasibility." A nation can decay, as all
history shows, if the level of "feasibility" is kept too far below what is
required to survive and advance. We must ask, not only what is feasible *by*
whom, but also what is *needed* by whom.

To the full goals of the 1963 March the "Freedom Budget" is dedicated.
Within this coalition of conscience the strength must be mobilized for the
implementation of this "Freedom Budget" for all Americans.

A. Philip Randolph

I.   The "Freedom Budget" In Brief

Basic principles

The "Freedom Budget" stems from seven basic principles:

(1)   Freedom on the American scene must include what Franklin D. Roosevelt
called "freedom from want." This can be achieved, not by the power of any one
group, but by the power of a fully-employed U.S. economy plus the power of the
aroused conscience of the American people;

(2)   "Freedom from want" for an increasing majority of our citizens is
not good enough; it must embrace all. Our economy is rich enough, and should
be just enough, to reject as intolerable the ghetto within stone's throw of
the duplex apartment; the alien worlds of slums and suburbs; the unemployment
rate four times as high in some localities as in the nation at large; the
millions receiving substandard wages despite many thousands of millionaires;
the low-income farmers despite luxury restaurants; the poverty among 34
million and the deprivation among another 28 million, in a land where median
family income is now close to $7,000, and where the families in the top income
fifth have eight times as much income as the families in the lowest income
fifth. We have already received tragic warning that there is no prospect for
domestic tranquility in a nation divided between the affluent and the desperately poor;

(3)   The U.S. economy has the productive power to abolish "freedom from
want" by 1975, not by pulling down those at the top but by lifting those at
the bottom, if we start *now* and do our best. What we have the power to do, we
will in fact do, if we *care* enough about doing it. The real issue is neither
economic nor financial, but moral;

(4)   Our economy is now too abundant for the poverty or deprivation still
afflicting almost a third of a nation to be explained mainly by the personal
characteristics of the victims. True, personal deficiencies have a bearing
upon the economic condition of many individuals. But it is even more true that
deficiencies in nationwide policies and programs, evidencing a default in the
national conscience, spawn and perpetuate these personal deficiencies. Just
as malaria has been stamped out more by clearing swamps than by injecting
quinine, the main attack upon poverty and deprivation must deal more with the
nationwide environment than with the individual. Beyond this, the modern
technology has advanced to the point where every American should enjoy "freedom
from want," regardless of personal characteristics;

(5)   While "freedom from want" by 1975 will require action at all levels,
private and public, the leadership role must be taken by our Federal Government.
It alone represents all the people. Its policies and programs exert the most
powerful single influence upon economic performance and social thinking. We
accept this principle without question during a total war against external
enemies. A "*war* against poverty" establishes the same principle on the
domestic front;

(6)   A war against want cannot be won with declarations of intent. It
cannot be won with token or inadequate programs which identify areas of need,
but apply policies and programs which only scratch the surface. It demands
specific quantitative goals, fully responsive to the need, and commitment to
their attainment;

(7)   This war against want must be color blind. Negroes will benefit
most relative to their numbers because, for reasons not of their making,
want is most heavily concentrated among them. But in absolute numbers, the

vast majority of those yearning for release from want are white. And those
already free from want, both white and nonwhite, cannot enjoy fully the benefits of economic progress and the blessings of democracy until "freedom from
want" becomes universal throughout the land.

Basic objectives

Founded upon these principles, the seven basic objectives of the "Freedom
Budget" are these:

(1) *To restore full employment as rapidly as possible,* and to maintain
it thereafter, for all able and willing to work, and for all whom adequate
training and education would make able and willing. This means an unemployment
rate below 3 percent by early 1968, and preferably 2 percent. Full 40 percent
of all U.S. poverty is due directly to inadequate employment opportunity, and
involuntary unemployment is corrosive to the human spirit;

(2) *To assure adequate incomes for those employed.* About 20 percent of
all U.S. poverty is among the working poor (including their dependents) who
receive substandard wages. In addition, millions of farm families and others
in rural areas have substandard incomes. Treatment of these problems depends
primarily upon Federal legislation;

(3) *To guarantee a minimum adequacy level of income to all those who
cannot or should not be gainfully employed.* About 40 percent of all U.S.
poverty is among those who cannot or should not work because of age or other
disabling factors. More than 13 percent of all U.S. poverty is among families
headed by women who should not work. Until, under Federal auspices, we achieve
such a guaranteed income, there should be immediate and vast improvements in
all Social Security and welfare programs, with much larger Federal participation;

(4) *To wipe out the slum ghettos, and provide a decent home for every
American family, within a decade.* Foul housing is both cause and consequence
of poverty. It breeds resentment and unrest. Housing and urban renewal, on a
scale matching the need, would also make the largest single contribution to
job creation in the face of job displacement by technological trends elsewhere
in the economy. It would accent the types of jobs most suitable for absorbing
those now most vulnerable to unemployment;

(5) *To provide, for all Americans, modern medical care and educational
opportunity up to the limits of their abilities and ambitions, at costs within
their means.* The shortage of personnel and facilities upon enactment of
Medicare (which helps *only* the aged portion of the population) speaks for
itself. Many schools in our great cities are a shambles;

(6) *To overcome other manifestations of neglect in the public sector, by
purifying our airs and waters, and bringing our transportation systems and
natural resource development into line with the needs of a growing population
and an expanding economy.* This, too, would provide the types of jobs most
suited to reducing unemployment. Along with housing and urban renewal, it
would immensely improve the living conditions even of those who already enjoy
"freedom from want" in a more limited sense;

(7) *To unite sustained full employment with sustained full production
and high economic growth.* This is essential, in order that "freedom from
want" may be achieved, not by robbing Peter to pay Paul, but under conditions
which bring progress to all.

The key role of our Federal Government

The "Freedom Budget" sets forth the above seven basic objectives in
specific and quantitative terms. It sets time schedules for their accomplishment. It establishes their feasibility by means of a balance sheet of all of
our needs and resources, with due allowance for all of our other private and
public undertakings and aspirations as a nation and a people.

In this way, the "Freedom Budget" is a call to action. But the response
to this call must take the form of national programs and policies, with the
Federal Government exercising that leadership role which is consistent with
our history, our institutions, and our needs. The six prime elements in this
Federal responsibility are now set forth.

(1) *Beginning with 1967, the President's Economic Reports should embody the equivalent of a "Freedom Budget."* These Reports should quantify ten-year goals for full employment and full production, for the practical liquidation of U.S. poverty by 1975, for wiping out the slum ghettos, and indeed for each of the seven basic objectives set forth in the "Freedom Budget." With due allowance for private and public performance at other levels, but with a firm determination by our Federal Government to close the gaps, all major Federal economic, financial, and social policies -- including the Federal Budget -- should be geared to attainment of these ten-year goals, starting at once in realistic magnitudes;

(2) *The bedrock civilized responsibility rests with our Federal Government to guarantee sustained full employment.* The Government should at once and continuously lead in organizing and financing enough job-creating activities to close the gap between full employment and employment provided at other public and private levels. None of these Federally-created jobs need to be made-work, because our unmet needs in the public sector are large enough to absorb beneficially this Federal effort. Training programs, to be effective, must be synchronized with job creation;

(3) *The Federal Government should exert the full weight of its authority toward immediate enactment of a Federal minimum wage of $2.00 an hour, with coverage extended to the uppermost constitutional limits of Federal power.* This would be a moderate start toward eradication of substandard living standards among millions of those employed;

(4) *A new farm program, with accent upon incomes rather than prices, should focus upon parity of income for farmers and liquidation of farm poverty by 1975.* More than 43 percent of all farm families now live in poverty, contrasted with only 13 percent of all nonfarm families;

(5) *To lift out of poverty and also above deprivation those who cannot or should not be employed, there should be a Federally-initiated and supported guaranteed annual income, to supplement rather than to supplant full-employment at decent pay.* The anti-poverty goal alone involves lifting almost all multiple-person families above $3,130 by 1975. Pending this, there should be immediate and vast improvements in all Social Security and welfare programs, with greatly enlarged Federal contributions to all of them, including old-age insurance and assistance, general public assistance, special-purpose public assistance, unemployment insurance, and workmen's compensation;

(6) *Fiscal and monetary policies should be readjusted to place far more weight upon distributive justice.* The massive Federal tax reductions in recent years tended to redistribute income with undue concern for those high up in the income structure, and inadequate concern for those lower down. State and local taxes and indirect taxes are so regressive -- they bear with such excessive weight upon low-income people -- that we should make the Federal income tax much more progressive than now. The decision to rely so heavily upon tax reduction and so little upon increased domestic spending to stimulate the economy was undesirable; it lowered our capacity to serve some of the greatest priorities of our national needs which depend upon public spending and are hardly helped by tax reduction. The current monetary policy does little to curb the excesses in the economy, and places a severe handicap upon activities of utmost urgency, especially housing. The sharply rising interest rates help those most who need help least, and hurt those most who need help most, because it is the lower income people who depend most upon borrowing. We cannot afford to neglect equity and social considerations in fiscal and monetary policies which transfer billions of dollars every year from some to others. Improved income distribution also helps the whole economy.

The "economic growth dividend" in the "Freedom Budget": uses of this dividend

We cannot enjoy what we do not produce. The "Freedom Budget" recognizes that all of the goals which it sets must be supported by the output of the U.S. economy. This output should grow greatly from year to year, under policies designed to assure sustained maximum employment, production, and purchasing power in accord with the objectives of the Employment Act of 1946.

With such policies, our total national production (measured in 1964 dollars) should rise from about 663 billion in 1965 to 1,085-1,120 billion by

1975. This would mean, for the ten years 1966–1976 inclusive, a level of total national production *averaging annually* 231.5–244.2 billion dollars higher, and *aggregating* over the ten years 2,315–2,442 billion dollars higher, than if total production remained during these ten years at the 1965 rate. This aggregate ten-year figure of 2,315–2,442 billion dollars is the "economic growth dividend" upon which the "Freedom Budget" draws to fulfill its purposes.

The "Freedom Budget" does not contemplate that this "economic growth dividend" be achieved by revolutionary nor even drastic changes in the division of responsibility between private enterprise and government under our free institutions. To illustrate, in 1965, 63.7 percent of our total national production was in the form of private consumer outlays, 16.5 percent in the form of private investment, and 19.8 percent in the form of public outlays at all levels for goods and services. Under the "higher" goals in the "Freedom Budget," these relationships in 1975 would be 63.5 percent, 16.9 percent, and 19.6 percent.

But while the "Freedom Budget" will not be regarded as socialistic, it is indeed socially-minded. It insists that we must make deliberate efforts to assure that, through combined private and public efforts, a large enough proportion of this "economic growth dividend" shall be directed toward the great priorities of our national needs: liquidation of private poverty, restoration of our cities, abolition of slum ghettos, improvement of rural life, and removal of the glaring deficiencies in facilities and services in "the public sector" of our economy. The "Freedom Budget" thus has moral as well as materialistic purposes.

The use of only a fair and moderate portion of this "economic growth dividend" to support the great priority purposes in the "Freedom Budget" makes it clear that even those who are already affluent or wealthy would not be penalized in any way in order to accomplish these great priority purposes. Entirely to the contrary, they would continue to enjoy what they have now, and also share largely and directly in the "economic growth dividend" itself. They would also benefit indirectly in multiple ways by the portions of the "economic growth dividend" used to support these great national priorities.

A few examples will serve to prove the point that only fair and moderate portions of the "economic growth dividend" would be used to support these great national priorities. To cite one outstanding example, based upon the deplorable conditions in our cities and the slum ghettos and rural slums, the "Freedom Budget" proposes that total private and public investment in residential structures and related community improvements (measured in 1964 dollars) average annually during the ten years 1966–1975 about 53 billion dollars, or about 530 billion in the aggregate for the ten years. On an average annual basis, this would be about 23 billion dollars higher than about 30 billion of such investment in 1965, and over the ten years it would aggregate about 230 billion dollars higher than if such investment were maintained throughout these ten years at the 1965 rate. This 230 billion dollars would be less than *one-tenth* of the economic growth dividend of 2,315–2,442 billion dollars. This is a very moderate share of that "economic growth dividend" to apply to a program which would come close to obliterating the slums and providing a decent home for every American family by 1975, and would make the most powerful single contribution toward the rescue of our cities and the creation of employment opportunity.

The portion of this investment in residential structures and related community improvements which would be galvanized by the public subsidies (at all levels) needed to rehouse those among the poor and deprived who live in slums would average annually during the ten years 1966–1975 about 10 billion dollars, or about 100 billion dollars in the aggregate for the ten years. On an average annual basis, this would be about 9 billion higher than about one billion of such investment in 1965, and over the ten years it would aggregate about 90 billion higher than if such investment were maintained throughout the ten years at the 1965 rate. This 90 billion dollars is in the neighborhood of *one-twenty sixth* of the "economic growth dividend."

To take another very significant example, the term "transfer payments" is used to describe those programs such as Social Security and other welfare payments which are designed in the final analysis to transfer a fair portion of the national income toward those who need help most. The "Freedom Budget" proposes that these transfer payments average annually during the ten years

1966-75 close to 23.8 billion dollars higher than the 1965 rate of 38.5 billion, or aggregate during the ten years about 238 billion higher than if the 1965 rate were maintained during these ten yeras. This 238 billion dollars is only in the neighborhood of *one-tenth* of the "economic growth dividend."

To take a third example, the "Freedom Budget" proposes a wide variety of programs, private and public, which would come close to the liquidation of U.S. poverty by 1975. In the final analysis, whatever means may be adopted, the liquidation of poverty depends primarily upon increasing the incomes of those who are now poor. It has been estimated reliably that the 34 million American poor would need to receive annually about 13 billion dollars more in income than they now receive to be lifted out of the poverty cellar. In the aggregate during the ten years 1966-1975, this would come to about 130 billion dollars. This 130 billion dollars is only in the neighborhood of *one-eighteenth* of the "economic growth dividend."

These three illustrations make it clear that the accomplishment of these high priority goals, and the other priority goals set forth in the "Freedom Budget," would involve so small a portion of the "economic growth dividend" that there will be room and to spare despite these priority programs for enormous progress for all. More than that, every program designed to eliminate "freedom from want," including home construction and increasing the purchasing power of our senior citizens and of the poor generally, will contribute to economic growth and enlarge opportunities for private investment and profits.

Responsibilities of the Federal Budget

While the "Freedom Budget" is based upon combined private and public efforts, the Federal Budget is the most powerful single instrument of national economic and social policy. It profoundly influences the economic climate in which private enterprise operates. It speaks for the needs and aspirations of all the people, and identifies our great national priorities to a degree that they cannot elsewhere be identified.

The "Freedom Budget" proposes a Federal Budget which (measured in 1964 dollars) should rise from 104.045 billion dollars (112.8 billion in current dollars) as contained in the original fiscal 1967 Federal Budget (which is several billions too low) to 135 billion dollars in calendar 1970, and 155 billion in calendar 1975.

The proposals for national defense, space technology, and all international do not represent independent determinations in the "Freedom Budget," but merely reflect the composite judgment of informed experts, *and make liberal allowances for increases now in prospect*. All of the other proposals are based upon determinations within the "Freedom Budget" as to what part of our "economic growth dividend" should be devoted to priorities which depend upon the Federal Budget.

Total proposed Federal outlays include a Federal contribution of one billion dollars in 1970, and two billion in 1975, to help increase benefit payments to the aged under the Old-Age, Survivors, Disability, and Health Insurance program.

The following table reveals the "Freedom Budget" proposals for the Federal Budget (measured in 1964 dollars).

	1967 (Actual)		1970		1975	
	Total Bil.$	$ Per Capita	Total Bil. $	$ Per Capita	Total Bil. $	$ Per Capita
All Federal Outlays	104.1	521.79	135.0	645.93	155.0	685.84
National Defense, Space Technology, All International	64.6	323.77	77.5	370.82	87.5	387.17
All Domestic Programs	39.5	198.04	57.5	275.12	67.5	298.67
Economic Opportunity Program	1.5	7.39	3.0	14.36	4.0	17.70
Housing and Community Development	0.1	0.57	3.4	16.03	3.8	16.81

| | 1967 (Actual) | | 1970 | | 1975 | |
	Total Bil. $	$ Per Capita	Total Bil. $	$ Per Capita	Total Bil. $	$ Per Capita
Agriculture and Natural Resources	5.9	29.75	10.5	50.24	12.0	53.10
Education	2.6	13.10	7.0	33.49	9.5	42.04
Health Services and Research	3.3	16.74	4.8	22.97	7.0	30.97
Public Assistance; Labor, Manpower, and Other Welfare Services	4.4	21.92	6.6	31.58	7.5	33.18

The above proposals for the Federal Budget will seem excessive only to
those who do not appreciate the growing productive powers of the U.S. economy,
under conditions of sustained full employment and full production.

For the ten years 1966-1975 inclusive, Federal outlays as proposed in the
"Freedom Budget" would *average annually* about 35.5 billion dollars higher, and
over the ten years *aggregate* about 355 billion dollars higher, than if the
Federal Budget remained stationary during these ten years at its 1965 size of
98.7 billion (calendar years, 1964 dollars). This 335 billion dollars would
be only about *one-seventh* of the "economic growth dividend."

Moreover, when the outlays for national defense, space technology, and all
international are excluded from the proposed Federal Budget, the "Freedom
Budget" proposals for all domestic programs in the Federal Budget would
average annually only about 18.5 billion dollars higher, and over the ten years
aggregate only about 185 billion dollars higher, than if Federal Budget outlays
for these domestic programs remained stationary at their 1965 size of 37.7
billion. This 185 billion dollars would be only about *one-thirteenth* of the
"economic growth dividend."

Allowing for some proposed *decreases* in Budget outlays (e.g. lower interest
rates), about *8 percent* of the "economic growth dividend" is earmarked by the
"Freedom Budget" for increases, above the 1965 level, for all programs in the
Federal Budget addressed to the war against want. This is modest indeed. It
should also be noted that this about 8 percent, or about 18.7 billion dollars
on an annual average basis, comes to only about *2 percent* of the 184.2-906.9
billion dollars which our total national production should average annually,
1966-1975. What could better illustrate that the whole question of whether
we "can afford" the "Freedom Budget" is a moral question and not an economic
issue?

The proposed Federal Budget would be only 15.38-15.51 percent of the
total national production in calendar 1970, and only 13.84-14.29 percent in
calendar 1975, contrasted with an average of 16.16 percent during the fiscal
years 1954-1967. Thus, the size of the Federal Budget relative to the size
of the total economy would tend to decline somewhat. However, Budget outlays
for all domestic programs would rise from 5.65 percent of total national
production in 1954-1967 to 6.55-6.61 percent in 1970 and 6.03-6.22 percent in
1975.

In short, the Federal Budget as proposed in the "Freedom Budget" would
not at all distort our traditional concepts of the appropriate relationships
among Federal public outlays at State and local levels, and private outlays.
It would not distort our traditional concepts of a "mixed economy," based
upon responsible free government and responsible free enterprise. It would
merely use the Federal Budget as a primary instrument toward balanced economic
growth and improved social justice.

Looked at even more broadly, the whole program set forth in the "Freedom
Budget" would not subtract from the income of anyone. It would facilitate
progress for practically all, but with accent upon the dictates of the social
conscience that those at the bottom of the heap should make relatively the
most progress.

Specific full employment goals

The first imperative step toward utilizing in full our productive potentials is to restore full employment by early 1968 at the latest, and to
sustain it thereafter. This must take care of population growth. It must deal
not only with full-time and officially-recorded employment, but also with the
full-time equivalent of part-time unemployment and the concealed unemployment
which results from those who are not participating in the labor force (and who
therefore are not counted as unemployed) because of scarcity of job opportunity.
For example, in late 1966, full-time unemployment of about 4 percent meant a
true level of unemployment of about 5½-6 percent. This means that, compared
with 1965, total employment (measured in its full-time equivalent) must be
about 4.6 million higher in 1967, 9.3 million higher in 1970, and 16.6 million
higher in 1975. The total number of new jobs which must be created is much
greater, to allow also for those who will be displaced from old jobs by technological changes.

Specific goals for liquidation of U.S. poverty

Designating the benefits of sustained full employment and full production as a *means* towards all other objectives, the first *end* priority in the
"Freedom Budget" is the practical liquidation of U.S. poverty. Moving adequately toward this goal in every year *beginning now,* the poverty of about 34
million people in 1964 can and therefore should be reduced to only slightly
more than 2 million in 1975. The rest of the goal can be achieved shortly
thereafter.

The anti-poverty program, stemming from the Office of Economic Opportunity, should be improved qualitatively and greatly augmented quantitatively.
But at best, this program touches only one small aspect of the poverty problem
as a whole, which requires for its solution the coordinated utilization of all
major national economic policies. This is true both with respect to a full-
scale war against poverty in the form of enlarging the private incomes of the
poor, and a full-scale war against poverty in the form of programs in the
public sector.

Programs designed to improve income distribution are vital to the
liquidation of poverty. From the purely economic viewpoint, full resource use
cannot be sustained if the situation persists as it was in 1964, when the
highest income fifth of all U.S. multiple-person families received 41 percent of
total multiple-person family income, and the highest two-fifths 65 percent,
while the lowest fifth received only 5 percent and the lowest two-fifths only
17 percent. In terms of social justice, such maldistribution is intolerable.
Practically all major national economic policies affect income distribution,
and should be used to affect it progressively, not regressively.

Specific goals for wiping out the slum ghettos

The most fundamental approach to "freedom from want" is guaranteed full
employment, plus guaranteed annual incomes for those who cannot be employed.
But other efforts in the war against want are essential.

The first of these is to wipe out the slum ghettos which are both the
roots and offshoots of poverty, while their replacement would also make the
largest single contribution to sustained full employment and the rescue of the
urban environment from deterioration and decay.

Traditionally-financed private housing for middle-income and high-income
families should average about 1.3 million a year. But we should start moving
upward now toward about 400,000 starts of lower-middle income housing in 1968,
and about 500,000 in 1970 and on through 1975. This calls for large increases
in public outlays for land acquisition and some other purposes, use of Federal
loans or credit and other action to drive interest rates downward, and a
long-range planned program. Above all, housing starts for low-income families,
with annual subsidies to bridge the difference between the annual cost of what
these families can afford to pay without excessive strains upon their overall
budgets and what decent housing costs, should be lifted year by year to at
least 400,000 in 1968, and 500,000 in 1970 and on through 1975, compared with
less than *one-tenth* this amount in most recent years. With about 21 million
new homes, 1966-1975 (inclusive), almost all American families should enjoy

decent homes by 1975. Allowing for feasible increases in State and local
efforts, the basic thrust in this connection must come from Federal financial
assistance.

Investment in health services, education, and training

Public responsibility, especially at the Federal level, must move immediately and at an accelerating rate toward increased investment in our human
resources in the form of health services, education, and training.

Granted the advance represented by Medicare, we need approximately to
double within ten years the annual rate of outlays for hospital construction,
and to increase at least 50 percent by 1975 the annual number of physician
graduates. Seriously inadequate medical care, due to the cost factor, still
handicaps about 40 percent of our population. The battle should now be
resumed for a nationwide system of health insurance.

For at least six years ahead, we need a construction program very con-
servatively estimated at more than 100,000 public school classrooms (with
related facilities) a year, requiring outlays of about 27 billion dollars.
We need about 100,000 new teachers a year in the public schools. We need vast
enlargements in facilities and also in teachers at higher levels, accompanied
by public financial aid to hundreds of thousands of young people who possess
every innate endowment to go to college but lack the means.

Many types of training programs, including vocational, should also be
expanded greatly. But we have learned from World War II experience, and
experience during other periods of full employment, that the problem of training is reduced to manageable proportions when job opportunities are not lacking.
Moreover, a ten-year projection of the volume and structure of full-employment
requirements would show us better what to train people for. Training them for
jobs which do not materialize adds to frustration and discontent.

Lifting our welfare services to meet the need

This summary cannot detail all of the deficiencies in the nationwide medley of welfare services. Many of them are both inadequate and degrading. They
institutionalize poverty instead of fighting it. The largest group of those
dependent upon organized public payments are our senior citizens. About two-
thirds of them live in poverty, and receive benefit payments (upon which most
of them depend almost entirely for their livelihoods) averaging somewhere
between one-third and one-half of the income required to lift them above
poverty.

With large Federal contributions to offset in part the undesirable features of payroll taxes which take away with one hand in order to give with the
other, the average old-age insurance benefits should be approximately doubled
within five years. Other types of welfare payments should be increased in
similar manner. *As already indicated, we should start working now toward
replacing this medley of inadequate efforts with a more universal and unified
system of guaranteed incomes for those who cannot or should not be gainfully
employed.*

Improving rural life

The extraordinary concentration of poverty in rural America, the economic
disenfranchisement of a majority of our farm people, and the lag in public
services in rural areas even relative to the gross deficiencies in urban
areas, call for both general and specialized approaches. Most of these point
ultimately to Federal responsibility, both in the form of a drastically recon-
structed national farm policy and Federal equalization policies designed to
help the poorer areas of the nation serve public needs. Underemployment is
rife in agriculture. Hired farm workers, especially migratory, are among the
most neglected and exploited people in America.

How to contain inflation

The "Freedom Budget" is not neglectful of the problem of inflation. Its
attainment would not generate the classical type of inflation which results
from attempting to do more than our productive resources can support, because
the "Freedom Budget" goals for economic growth are based upon reasonably

conservative estimates of the growth in the civilian labor force and in productivity. The high degree of price stability 1961-1965, compared with re-
current inflationary trends during 1953-1961, indicates that an adequate rate
of economic growth is more conducive to price stability than an inadequate
rate of economic growth punctuated by recessions. The reappearance of considerable price inflation 1965-1966, at a time when the real rate of economic
growth was beginning to slow down, and when idleness of manpower and other
productive resources was still too high, indicates in the main that the
selective price inflation during this period was not due to excessive pressure
upon our productive resources but rather to business decisions to increase
prices which were not justified in view of very high profit levels. Indeed,
some of these price increases may have reflected the desire of some industries
to "get while the getting was good" in the face of some important signs of
economic softening. The remedy for this type of selective inflation is to
take selective measures to curb it, not to abandon the essential goal of
adequate economic growth and full employment and production.

But even if this analysis is not entirely correct, this would not negate
the urgency of achieving all of the great priority programs quantified in the
"Freedom Budget." It would simply mean that we should use tax policy and
other measures to restrain marginal enjoyments instead of sacrificing what we
need most. There is plenty of room in the U.S. economy for social justice;
and if the total productive powers of the economy are hard-pressed, that is
all the more reason to put first things first. We did not starve munition
production to fight inflation during World War II; we should not dull the
weapons in the war against want if we need to fight inflation now.

The challenge, 1966-1975

If the "Freedom Budget" becomes the living law of our national economic
and social goals, policies, and programs, we can convert an abundance which
already exceeds the most fanciful expectations of a decade ago into an America
by 1975 where poverty has come close to total abolition; where every American
enjoys a decent home in a suitable living environment; where our cities have
become places in which to live instead of places to move out of as rapidly as
possible; in which the educational and health services enjoyed by all of the
people will be abreast of the advances in knowledge and science; in which the
poisons will have been extracted from our airs and waters; in which our natural
resources and means of transportation will be conserved and replenished; and
in which the incomes of all, while by no means equal, will be equal to the
requirements for living without want or economic fear, by virtue of employment
for those willing and able, and by other appropriate methods for those not
able to be employed.

Most important of all, we shall have recognized that the foundation of a
Great Society is a Just Society. The "Freedom Budget" does not ask for the
moon, but only for justice here on earth, in a land so well able to afford it.

II. Why We Need A "Freedom Budget"

Identity of our domestic and international purposes

The American people today are torn by two seemingly conflicting purposes.
On the one hand, they have been stirred to their depths by the "war against
poverty" and by other splendid goals of the Great Society. They want to move
forward toward these goals, and regard this properly as an essential economic
and social follow-through on recent progress toward civil rights in racial
relations. On the other hand, many of them believe that we must slow down
instead of speed up the practical pursuit of these objectives, because of the
war in Vietnam and the rising costs of national defense and related activities.
Current national policies and programs, in the main, embody this viewpoint.
So long as this seeming conflict is not resolved, we the American people
remain divided among ourselves.

A. Philip Randolph Institute, *A "Freedom Budget" For All Americans: Budgeting
Our Resources, 1966-1975 To Achieve "Freedom From Want"* (New York, 1966),
pp. i-24.

31. MINUTES

A. Philip Randolph Institute
National Executive Board Meeting
Monday, September 19, 1966
Hotel Roosevelt
New York City

Present: A. Philip Randolph, presiding; David Bazelon; Irving Bluestone;
Robert Gilmore; Ralph Helstein; Vivian Henderson; Norman Hill;
Rachelle Horowitz; Tom Kahn; Leon Keyserling; Isaiah Minkoff;
Eleanor H. Norton; L. D. Reddick; Bayard Rustin; Donald P. Slaiman
and Whitney Young

I. *Discussion: Crisis in the Civil Rights Movement*

The opening discussion was on the nature of the civil rights movement
and its effects on the work of the Institute. Commentary among the group
was, in essence, as follows:

Irving Bluestone felt that the emergence of the black power concept
and the failure of society to meet the needs of the Negro people has
created a crisis of strategy and tactics. At the present time the coalition has essentially fallen apart. We are concerned with helping to
develop the talents of young people. It is imperative for the Institute
to establish a concrete program on which all groups can cooperate, i.e.,
the Freedom Budget.

Vivian Henderson agreed that we do have a crisis and ought to recognize it. There is an absence of program which creates a vacuum. He is
not convinced that the local political leadership has a program. The
mayor of Atlanta did not address himself to the program and conditions
that led to violence. We must get programs not only at the federal level,
but also at the local level.

Don Slaiman said that the civil rights movement has to move from protest to politics and work for implementation of existing legislation.
Unless the federal government moves, there is going to be less done by
private groups. There has to be increased attention paid to continuing
and expanding the job of implementation on the federal level and the grass
roots level. He raised the question of how to revitalize the coalition
between labor, liberals and civil rights.

Ralph Helstein stated that we need local grievance committees to work
at the implementation of civil rights legislation. The Freedom Budget is
essential, but there is another question. What do you do at the local
level, in terms of organizing the communities? The Freedom Budget is not
enough; there must be something more. Civil rights leaders need to look
at themselves and ask themselves if they are doing the kind of job that
needs to be done in mass movements. At a meeting in Chicago on fair
housing, no effort was made to reach people on a logical basis.

Irving Bluestone raised several questions: Where do you go from
here? The ability to get finances is receding and it takes money to run
a revolution. How do you mobilize broad organizational support? Is the
Freedom Budget and the approach beyond the intellectual reach of the
average person? He felt that people are getting scared and disaffected
and, as a result, money is drying up. The Institute should call a meeting
to discuss ways and means of rallying around the Freedom Budget.

Bayard Rustin said that along with implementation we must also fight
for new legislation.

II. *Annual Report*

Mr. *Rustin* continued with a report of the activities of the Institute during the past year, including meetings and consultations held,
publications prepared and issued, and statements drafted.

He reported that the Institute has prepared and published testimony
on behalf of the $2.00 minimum wage, extended unemployment benefits,
Repeal of 14B, and the 1966 Civil Rights Act. More than 150,000 copies

of the joint testimony has been distributed to labor unions and civil
rights organizations.

The Institute conducted a week-long workshop for 500 students going
into the south to work on voter registration.

The Institute mobilized both Negro rank-and-file and leadership in
support of the labor movement in Atlanta during the Scripto strike, in New
York during the Taxi Workers organizing drive and the Welfare strike, in
Philadelphia in behalf of the AFT organizing drive, and in behalf of the
grape workers strike in Delano. It advocated a Negro-labor alliance in
speeches before countless religious, liberal, community and student groups.
The staff addressed a number of international union conventions and
prepared papers advocating the alliance for the White House Conference on
Civil Rights and for the John LaFarge Institute, and at off-the-record
meetings of civil rights leaders. It also brought civil rights people and
trade unionists together to map out joint programs.

The Institute has cooperated with the Urban League and the Workers
Defense League in getting Negro and Puerto Rican youth into Apprenticeship
Training Programs and has met with Brennan, VanArsdale and vocational
counselors as well as civil rights people. It has advised unions
organizing Negro and Puerto Rican workers.

The Institute found 300 jobs for youth in Harlem who stopped in the
office, helped about 25 return to school, and referred 150 more to Workers
Defense League programs.

Robert Gilmore, Treasurer, then presented the Financial Report and
spoke of the budget for next year.

*It was moved and seconded that the report of the Treasurer be adopted.
The motion was passed unanimously.*

III. *Freedom Budget*

The predominant issue of the Freedom Budget was next discussed as
follows:

Leon Keyserling began by discussing the need for the Freedom Budget.
The Budget stems from the idea that at some time it will become apparent
that the civil rights movement will have to be implemented in ridding a
large part of the population from want. The Freedom Budget is based on
the idea that when you develop a program you must get action; to get
action you must get legislation; to get legislation you must have education. The Budget is to educate the thousands who are badly lacking in
program. He said that he and others have been working a long time on the
Budget and it is now ready to go to the printer. This raises several
questions: How many are going to be printed? Who are they going to be
sent to, and how? How are the leadership people going to be brought
together to find out what they are prepared to do? Schools, libraries,
economists, the Congress, are all good sources for the distribution of
the Budget.

Don Slaiman expressed the feeling that the Budget should be published
when more sponsors are obtained among the civil rights, labor and liberal
leaders. The consensus, however, was that the Budget should be published
as soon as possible.

Bayard Rustin suggested that the day the Freedom Budget is published
there should be a coalition of leaders in Washington, D.C. to (1) take the
first copy to the President; (2) call on Senators Kennedy and Javits to
present Mr. Randolph to the Senate to explain the significance of the
Freedom Budget; and (3) hold a press conference. The economists who
worked on the Budget should hold a press briefing to inform the press of
the contents of the Budget. The Budget should go to the NAACP, Urban
League and other civil rights organizations, church leaders, congressmen,
Leadership Conference groups, heads of sociology and economics departments
of colleges and universities. He also suggested that meetings explaining
the Freedom Budget be held in Philadelphia, New York, Boston, Atlanta,
Cleveland, St. Louis, Chicago, Denver, Los Angeles and San Francisco.

A meeting will be held later this week to determine the amount of
copies to be printed. The Industrial Union Department is turning over
the plates of a simplified version of the Budget to the Institute. The

IUD will devote one issue of its publication, AGENDA, to the Budget. Dr. Vivian Henderson and other economists will hold conferences on the Budget at schools and universities, and a young Negro staff member of the Institute will visit campuses to get college groups in promoting the Budget.

Isaiah Minkoff said the Freedom Budget should come out with great dramatic impact, and that a large first issue should be printed.

Whitney Young said that the time for the Freedom Budget is now. The Marshall Plan for Negroes, which was a precursor of the Freedom Budget, never got off the ground, but the country is now ready for the Freedom Budget. We desperately need to put the civil rights struggle back on the offensive. The Freedom Budget will be helpful in putting the civil rights struggle back in perspective.

It was suggested that Mr. Rustin contact Whitney Young and, together, they would attempt to involve top public relations people in publicizing the Budget.

It was moved and seconded that the report of Mr. Keyserling be adopted and that Mr. Rustin be authorized, together with his committee, to publish the document for distribution. The motion was passed.

It was moved and seconded that the endorsers' list be broadened, if possible. The motion was passed.

It was moved and seconded that appreciation be extended to Leon Keyserling, the economists, and others for the very magnificent job done on the Freedom Budget. The motion was passed.

IV. *Future Program*

General consensus was that it is important to have a conference of labor and Negro leaders in the South on southern politics and a conference of northern civil rights leaders to enlist support of the civil rights movement to help organize the unorganized. A conference should be held between civil rights leaders and the leaders of the building trades on how the two groups can work together for the Freedom Budget.

There being no further business before the Board, the meeting was adjourned at 4:50 p.m.

Minutes, A. Philip Randolph Institute National Executive Board Meeting, September 19, 1966, New York, Box 65 Committee Affiliations 1967, Whitney Young Papers, Columbia University.

32. $100 BILLION FREEDOM FUND

By A. Philip Randolph

Mr. Randolph's $100 billion Freedom budget, originally proposed at the Planning Session of the White House Conference "To Fulfill These Rights," November 17-18, is a blueprint for a brave new approach to a solution of the economic and social problems now being faced by Negroes in America's ghettos.

The Freedom budget is essential if Negroes are to have first-class economic and social citizenship. This budget is not simply a special plea on the behalf of the narrow self-interest of a minority, because our proposal is that Negroes make their full contributions to the creation of a Great Society. And creation of the Great Society will benefit all Americans. Achievement of this goal depends in large measure upon the aroused conscience of America. And that conscience, as President Johnson has nobly said, knows no color line.

But how fast this flame of conscience succeeds in consuming the evils against which it protests depends upon how boldly and quickly we translate it into massive program action. If we yield to any tendency to let the towering size of our troubles, and the cost of overcoming them, lead to an indecisiveness or faltering measures, then we will indeed be letting our consciences make cowards of us all.

The very nature and meaning of these manifold troubles must be defined

in terms of our economic, social, and political capabilities to overcome them.
The Negroes in Watts today may be better off in material terms than their
counterparts of 50 years ago, or very large segments of the American people
during the depths of the Great Depression 30 years ago. But the profound difference is that the unemployment and poverty of those earlier times were merely
a tragedy, because we had neither the economic resources nor the know-how to
deal with them. Today, because we have both the resources and know-how, the
millions of unemployed and the far more than 30,000,000 living in poverty take
on also the aspects of a national crime.

The situation in Watts erupted in volcanic form because the people there
knew or felt that their deep troubles were interlaced with manifest injustice.
And this eruptive potential is seething just under the surface in portions of
every large city within the United States, awaiting only some slight additional
pressure or some unpredictable incitement to propel the explosion.

Because of the very nature of this newly-developing problem, the very advances in general prosperity and in employment, which may breed complacency in
some quarters, are multiplying the fundamental pressures by the contrasts which
they sharpen. Although unemployment as customarily measured is now said to be
lower than at any time within eight years, the crucial fact is that at no time
within these eight years has it been less than two times as high as it ought
to be. When account is taken also of part-time unemployment, and of the concealed unemployment -- concealed because hundreds of thousands or millions of
young people and Negroes have been turned from the labor force to the pool
rooms and to the dope and knife gangs because the jobs they need are not there
-- unemployment is really about twice as high as officially measured. And
where it is most heavily concentrated is even more menacing than these figures
indicate.

About 34,000,000 Americans live in poverty, and about an equal number live
above the poverty ceiling but far below the requirements for a minimum health
and decent standard of living. One-fifth of the nation still lives in slums,
as our cities continue to deteriorate and become increasingly the homes of the
poor. Perhaps 40 percent of our people still lack adequate medical care at
costs within their means. More than a quarter of a million of our American
poor are among our senior citizens, who are poor because we have hardly com-
menced to bring our social security systems into line with changes in the
price level since 1935 and the mandates of the increased per capita productivity and wealth of the population as a whole. Millions of people working full-
time, are being paid abysmally substandard wages. Millions of broken families
are not receiving the welfare payments which would represent the basic concept
of some decent floor under incomes and living standards, a concept already embraced in some countries far less rich than we are. The concentration of
poverty is extraordinarily high among our farm people.

I am passionately convinced that our attempts to deal with these problems
are handicapped by dividing them into too many subcompartments. This makes the
solutions appear even more complex than they are, and leads to fragmentary and
random solutions. Fundamentally, the unemployment problem, the poverty
problem, and the others which I have mentioned, are all *one* problem. They all
mean simply that we are not bringing into use our full resources and directing
them toward purposes responsive to the great priorities of our needs which
bespeak the social and moral conscience of the nation.

We talk about a *total* war against poverty, and this concept is fraught
with ultimate meaning if properly applied. When we were in a total war against
external enemies, we made a budget of our total resources, a budget of our
total needs, and then used policies and programs to bring the two together
under a defined set of priorities, both civilian and military. The one additional ingredient which we added was the principle of equity. Because we did
just this, during the World War II era, we maintained full employment, and in
addition lifted living standards and reduced poverty more rapidly than ever
before, even though we were burning up half of our productive resources in
fighting our external enemies. If we now benefit by this lesson, what could
we not accomplish in the few years ahead, when only about 7 percent of our
current production is being devoted to national defense?

I believe that the time has come to make meaningful the concept of total
war, as we are now expressing it, for humane purposes on the domestic front.
I believe that the first step toward this end would be for the Federal

government through appropriate agencies:

(1) to set forth specifically the magnitudes of full employment for the next ten years, which means less than three percent and preferably only two percent unemployment as usually measured, and to commit itself fully and explicitly to the attainment of full employment within a year's time and its maintenance thereafter;

(2) to define what patterns of utilization of this fully employed labor force would produce the goods and services most responsive to the great priorities of our national needs, even while adding to the living standards of those already so affluent that their new wants relate to luxuries rather than to necessities;

(3) guided by this ten-year projection of our productive resources and needs, which might be called goals, we should identify and set in motion those policies and programs, sufficient in quantity as well as in quality needed to translate what we *can* do into what we *must* do.

When we do this, I believe that much of the arid and futile debate as to whether unemployment is a demand problem or a structural problem, and as to whether poverty is due to something wrong within the individual or something wrong within the society, will disappear. Necessary problems of training and education will then have ten times the utility they now have, because we will know what to train and educate people for. We cannot afford to cling to the notion that training automatically creates a job, or that self-improvement automatically eradicates poverty. We need to encircle the problem, instead of touching it at a few points only.

I have been a life-long believer in the essentiality of community action and grass-roots participation, and in both the role of private enterprise and public action. But the very nature of a *total* war against unemployment and poverty and all their manifestations calls for greatly increased emphasis upon adequate Federal programs and huge increases in Federal expenditures. Increases in private incomes alone, while necessary, cannot themselves, at appreciable speed, channel a large enough part of our resources into the clearance of slums, the recruitment and adequate pay of teachers and nurses, and many other major elements now being articulated as the aspirations of the Great Society.

Within the next few months I shall, on the basis of more adequate preparation, specify in much greater detail the main components of what we should do in the years immediately ahead. I earnestly hope that these may help to give direction and content to the successor conference to this great conference. But there are a few specifics which I feel compelled to set forth without delay.

If our productive powers are marshalled as fully as they should be, our national product in 1975 will be considerably more than $400 billion higher than it is now. This is an average increase of more than $40 billion for each of the next 10 years, or an aggregate of more than $2.2 trillion more during the next decade than if output were stabilized at current levels. I submit that, as a first step toward channeling these vast increases in productive output toward the purposes we need most, the Federal budget, as the most important single embodiment of national purpose and program, should be lifted in 1975 to about $60 billion higher than it is now, or lifted about $6 billion a year. This would aggregate a lift of about $330 billion over the decade. Taking account of the transfer payments which enter into such programs as Social Security, but do not enter into the conventional budget, and taking account also of feasible increases in State and local outlays, total public investment in 1975 should be at least $100 billion higher than now -- and perhaps much more than that. As this would represent an average increase of about $10 billion a year, the total public investment over the decade ahead would aggregate about $550 billion above what would result from stabilization at current levels.

There are many ways of measuring the practical realism of this goal. If our total national production rises by an average of about $40 billion a year over the next 10 years, we will enjoy during the decade as a whole about $2.2 trillion of total national output. I think that the allocation of about 25 percent of this to those great priorities of our national needs which require increased public investment is entirely sound and essential.

Another measurement: We are told reliably that the increased tax revenues accruing each year to the Federal government from economic growth at

existing tax rates may lift Federal tax collection by about $10 billion a year
on the average, during the next 10 years, or additional tax collections aggregating about $550 billion over the next 10-year period. This would far more
than cover the financial costs ($330 billion, see above) of the proposed in-
creases in Federal outlays in the Federal budget, and the balance could be
devoted to help the States and localities which are much harder pressed in
financial terms than the Federal government.

Still another measurement: We have since 1962 undertaken tax reductions,
by legislation and administrative action, having an annual value in the
neighborhood of $20 billion. Even without allowing for the increases in the
size of the revenues foregone by this tax reduction which will result from
economic growth, the aggregate tax reductions thus calculated will have a value
of about $200 billion over the next 10 years. Certainly we can and must afford
during the next decade to put about $330 billion additional Federal outlays
into vitally important purposes. While this is not the time nor place for me
to quarrel with the tax reduction policy, we all know that a very substantial
part of it is going to those who need help least, that it is a very imperfect
weapon for those who need help most, and that only to a trickle-down extent do
tax reductions address themselves to the servicing of the great priorities
which I have mentioned, and with which we are all so deeply concerned.

The problem of freeing one-fifth of our people, of every color, from the
slum ghettos in which they now live in our cities, and to a degree elsewhere,
is of prime importance. In the slums are concentrated many of the causes and
consequences of poverty. Vast programs of housing and urban renewal would not
only make war on this poverty at its very roots, but would also make war against
a whole congeries of social evils, and would restructure employment opportunity
so as to take care of perhaps half of the job problems facing us over the next
decade. This is the central answer to the thrust of the new technology and
automation, and would provide a uniquely high product mix of semi-skilled and
relatively unskilled jobs, the achievement of which is the real hope for a
preponderant portion of the unemployed.

By 1970, the annual level of non-farm housing starts should be lifted to
at least 2,250,000, compared with about 1,600,000 in 1965, and maintained at
this higher level at least through 1975. This would represent an average for
the decade of more than 500,000 more starts per year than we are now achieving,
and in the aggregate more than 5,000,000 more starts over the decade than would
result from stabilization at current levels. As I do not believe that we can
maintain indefinitely the current level of starts for upper middle-income and
high-income groups, we ought to build 6 or 7 million new homes during the next
decade for lower middle-income and low-income people, with a higher annual rate
than 600 to 700 thousand during the years immediately ahead.

The 10-year program of more than 5 million more housing starts than would
result under current programs might involve an additional 10-year investment
above current levels, considering costs in urban areas, of about $50 billion
which might be lifted to the neighborhood of an additional $100 billion above
current levels by the community facilities and public improvements of all
types which would be necessary to, and following in the wake of, the needed
housing effort. Considering the high multiplier effect of housing investment
upon almost every type of economic activity, the reason appears why I estimate
that these levels of housing effort might take care of about one-half of the
25 million new jobs which need to be generated over the next 10 years.

What is the role of the Federal government and the Federal budget in this
enlarged housing and urban renewal effort? We all know that, despite the good
housing legislation of 1965, Federal assistance to some 35,000 units per year
of housing for low-income people is merely a token program. It, therefore,
combines some laudable results with frustration and hostility. The annual
contributory system under the Federal program holds the annual costs remarkably low relative to the benefits to be achieved. Taking into account the
profits made by the Federal government on some of its housing programs, the
government is now spending almost nothing net on housing and urban renewal.
I think that these Federal budget outlays for housing and community development should be lifted to at least $4 billion per year by 1975, as an essential
part of lifting the total Federal budget by about 60 billion dollars by 1975.
In view of the paramount urgency of this housing and urban renewal need, the
most rapid acceleration should commence now, and I feel that Federal budget

outlays for housing and community development should be lifted to about 2
billion dollars in the Federal budget to be submitted next January, and to
considerably above $3 billion by 1970.

The American Negro will benefit more, in proportion to his numbers, than
others from these efforts. This is not because he is a Negro, but because he
suffers now so much more than others, again relative to his numbers, from unemployment and poverty in all aspects. But in absolute numbers, there are far
fewer Negroes unemployed and living in poverty in the U.S. than those of
lighter skins. In absolute numbers, those of lighter skins will benefit far
more than the Negro. The Negro's greatest role in the attainment of the Great
Society is not as a beneficiary, but as a galvanizing force. Out of his greater suffering and deprivation, he has fairly-fully awakened the American conscience with respect to civil rights and liberties. The debt which the whole
nation and Detroit are more immediate. The preliminary work of reorganization
will begin at meetings scheduled to convene in each city before the year's end.[68]

Additional cities on tap for more than one chapter include Philadelphia,
St. Louis, Cleveland, Boston, Baltimore, San Francisco and Miami. Plans also
call for New York City to get a few more branches.

No innovation is ever received without its opposition. And the multiple
branch plan has its opponents. Nevertheless, in those cities where it has
been effected, and in those where the actual reorganization has been started,
a revitalized spirit of support for the NAACP has been noted. The rejuvenated
interest is attributed to the fact that NAACP branches in those cities are now
closer to the communities to represent and obtain leadership from those communities.

The Crisis, 73 (January, 1966):18-23, 53.

33. COMMENTS ON A "FREEDOM BUDGET" FOR ALL AMERICANS

By Andrew F. Brimmer[69]
Member of the Board of Governors
of the
Federal Reserve System

The "Freedom Budget" reiterates the depressing details of poverty in
America, and urges programs which will "attack *all* of the major causes of
poverty -- unemployment and under-employment; substandard pay; inadequate
social insurance and welfare payments; bad housing; deficiencies in health
services, education, and training; and fiscal and monetary policies which tend
to redistribute income regressively rather than progressively." The "Freedom
Budget" makes the claim that it differs from previous efforts to establish
social goals because it "measures costs against resources" and sets out a
"schedule for action."

The "Freedom Budget" justified its proposals and the impact of these programs on the economy on both a moral and a statistical level. The attempt to
quantify our potential output and distribute the increment according to social
needs is a useful approach and produces a meaningful base for testing the differential impact of alternative programs. It is probably true, that whatever
the level of expenditures for Vietnam or the possible inflationary impact of
the "Freedom Budget," the programs presented could still be carried out -- if
the American people were willing to assign these social programs a sufficiently
high priority, and forego other expenditures. But given the present demands
on economic resources, it also means that we would have to assign an even more
powerful role to the Federal government and intervene much more directly in
the economy in terms of wage and price controls than would be necessary if
the proposals were being carried out at a time when there was a large backlog
of unused resources and a more stable or declining price pattern. Thus, in
effect, timing considerations and the size of the program without clear priorities for its various parts, render the "Freedom Budget" more radical than
many of its liberal proposals taken individually.

Misleading use of figures, some questionable economic theory, and a lack
of modesty mar the presentation. For example, a questionably large increase
in GNP growth over the next ten years (which probably cannot be attained
without substantial inflationary pressures) is presented in such a way that it
implies that these increases are somehow "new found," and can thus be allocated
to the "Freedom Budget." Little account is taken of the fact that much of the
anticipated rise in output will be absorbed just by larger population requirements and growth of current programs. The proposition that full-employment by
itself promotes higher productivity increases is also debatable when experienced
manpower resources are scarce and investment is being pushed beyond sustainable
levels. In addition, the authors claim that it is the first attempt to measure
social goals against resources overlooks several other excellent studies of this
sort.

Apart from these analytical considerations, the "Freedom Budget" is disappointing as a document of persuasion. The presentation is discursive and
appears unrealistic because of its wide ranging and seemingly excessive demands
proposed in the present economic environment. Actually, a great many of the
ideas are before Congress at the present time or have been passed into law in
somewhat less bold form. For example, minimum wage legislation at $1.60 an
hour by 1968 has been signed into law and will be reviewed again in a few
years; a bill extending unemployment insurance coverage and higher benefits
may pass; and provisions for more direct employment by the Federal government
of people who cannot find private employment is in the Administration's anti-
poverty bill. The Housing Act of 1965 has provisions for rent subsidies and
more job training and economic opportunity could and probably would have been
expanded under existing programs, if additional money were made available.

Equally disappointing is the failure of the "Freedom Budget" to live up to
its promise to provide a "schedule for action." It presents GNP forecasts for
1970 and 1975 and the percentage of GNP which should go to the "Economic
Opportunity Program," "Agriculture and Natural Resources," "Education," "Health
Services and Research," and "Public Assistance; Labor, Manpower, and other
Welfare Services." But these broad categories are not broken down and no
specific price tags are assigned to easily identifiable programs. The projected
increase of real GNP at an annual rate of over 5-6 percent per year, for the
next ten years, built on top of current rates of resources use and price trends,
would imply continuing intensive inflationary pressures. This problem is dismissed lightly despite the fact that a 5 percent rate of growth has over the
past few years produced inflation once unutilized resources were absorbed. An
annual growth rate of 4-4.5 percent over the next decade would be a much more
realistic forecast for planning purposes.

Many old ideas are, of course, good ideas. But what is needed at the
present time is a more objective analysis in detail as to how and when these
programs might be put into action. All of us will agree with "The Freedom
Budget" that we need more public housing and greater provision for moderate
income homes. But just saying there is a need for so many additional units a
year and citing the "seriously deficient" housing figures from the 1960 Census
is not particularly helpful. We need some new approaches if we are to get the
local authorities actually to build the houses for which money is voted. In a
similar case, there is no discussion of specific plans which might be expected
to produce a workable income maintenance scheme.

It is, thus, relatively easy to be critical of the "Freedom Budget" --
because of its excessive demands, lack of priorities, statistical manipulation,
lack of candor in regard to high priority competitive domestic and international
requirements, and its almost complete disregard of the problem of price
stability. Nevertheless, the issues presented are real -- the goals of continuing full-employment, high growth rates and eradication of poverty are now
largely accepted by all who are concerned. But the apparent promise of an
easy solution to the poverty problem in ten years can only lead to unfilled
expectations.

What is, it seems to me, now needed is a clear and realistic restatement
of goals and the specific programs required to meet them which will take into
account the current strained economic and military situation. Such a restatement would assure the continuation of current programs and would stress that
progress will be stepped-up as resources become available in an economic
framework of full-employment and stable growth. The current problem of the

trade-off between low levels of employment and stable prices is a real one,
and should not be dismissed casually. Otherwise much of the hoped for gains
will also disappear in the winds of rising prices.

Andrew F. Brimmer to Mr. Whitney Young, January 31, 1967, Box 65 Committee
Affiliations, 1967, Whitney Young Papers, Columbia University.

34. PHIL RANDOLPH, THE BEST OF MEN,
TOUCHED AND CHANGED ALL OF US

*AFL-CIO Sec.-Treas. Lane Kirkland delivered the following remarks at a
memorial service for A. Philip Randolph at the Metropolitan African Methodist-
Episcopal Church in Washington, D.C.*

Phil Randolph was the best of men, because he sought to make certain that
no person was better than any other.

In the labor movement, we call him "our own Phil Randolph"--just as, I
am sure, the civil rights movement claims him, too, for their own. In truth,
he was even more than both of ours, for Phil Randolph belonged to all of us--
people were his constituency.

Better, perhaps, than any other individual who ascended to a leadership
position--much less the leadership of two great movements at the same time--a
feat as rare as the individual himself--Phil Randolph understood, in his own
words, that "social and political freedom cannot be sustained in the midst of
economic insecurity and exploitation."

He knew that the freedom he sought for blacks was, in the final analysis,
freedom for whites as well. Fear and prejudice had bound his nation, and
prevented it from achieving the fullest measure of its greatness for all its
people.

That greatness could not occur, can not occur, with poverty and deprivation in our midst--no matter whether that human misery is caused by discrimination based on the color of a person's skin or the color of the collar they
wear to work.

In the trade union movement, Phil Randolph found a vehicle to fight racism
and poverty. It was not a popular choice. Capital, in the form of the Pullman
Company, fought him. Other blacks, too, opposed Randolph's decision to work
within the established trade union movement. Some because they preferred a
black-only labor movement. Black newspaper publishers and academics denounced
"Negro unionism," but for a different reason: they argued that the best
interests of blacks would be served by "standing with capital."

Phil Randolph knew that both extremes were wrong. Blacks could not overcome their oppressors by either adopting their tactics or standing by their
side.

And he persisted. He persisted with style. His manners have been described as Edwardian, his oratory Shakespearean, his language biblical. He
was unfailingly gracious, courteous and polite. But he persisted--no one could
ever mistake his civility for weakness.

For this was a strong, stubborn, tough, proud, unrelenting fighter.
George Meany once called Phil Randolph a "gentleman of elegant impatience."

Adjectives describe the person, but achievements make the man. Leadership was Phil Randolph's crowning achievement, and he didn't earn it by age or
longevity. He earned it by leading:

By leading against Marcus Garvey's "Back to Africa" movement and against
W. E. B. Du Bois' elitist concept of the "Talented Tenth" in the early 1920s.

By leading the struggle against the Pullman Company to organize the
Brotherhood of Sleeping Car Porters. [70]

By leading the fight against Communist infiltration of the National Negro
Congress in the late 1930s.

By leading the 1941 March on Washington movement, which moved President
Roosevelt to issue Executive Order 8802 banning discrimination in defense
industries and government. [71]

By leading the battles against racial discrimination and segregation within the labor movement itself.

By leading the triumphant 1963 March on Washington for Jobs and Freedom. And long after his death, Phil Randolph will still be leading as the A. Philip Randolph Institute carries on his work by leading successful voter registration and political education programs in the black community. And the Recruitment & Training Program continues to bring minority apprentices into the skilled trades.

Phil Randolph has left us more than memories. He left us a vision. He took a country divided by segregation and brought people together. He took a good labor movement, marred by discrimination, and made it better. He brought two movements together, overcoming the efforts of those who would keep us apart.

He touched all of us. He changed all of us--and with us, he changed history.

He was the best of men.

AFL-CIO News, June 9, 1979.

35.   RANDOLPH'S VISION RECALLED TO NATION

By Rex Hardesty

President Jimmy Carter described him as a man of "dignity and tenacity." AFL-CIO Sec.-Treas. Lane Kirkland recalled him as a "gentleman of elegant impatience."

And Bayard Rustin spoke of "a gentle but iron-willed radical."

Thus was A. Philip Randolph remembered for the nation in a memorial service at the Metropolitan AME Church in Washington. Randolph, founder of the Sleeping Car Porters, longtime AFL-CIO vice president and civil rights leader for 70 years, died May 16 at the age of 90.

The national memorial service drew a standing room crowd of 3,000 to the church described by the pastor as the "church of Frederik Douglass," the abolitionist and Negro leader who died in 1895. Metropolitan Op-Leontyne Price sang, with Miss Prices's powerful rendition of the Lord's Prayer provoking a standing ovation.

Similarly, Rustin's recollections of "The Chief," as the Pullman car porters called Randolph, brought tears, most notably to Rustin himself.

He recalled a black newspaper editor and Harlem street corner orator of pre-World War II America whose "leadership flowed from the depth of his humanity."

"Mr. Randolph was a successful and uniquely gifted labor and civil rights activist, precisely because he was a sensitive, unselfish and dignified human being," Rustin said. "He did not study organizational behavior, his leadership flowed from the depth of his humanity."

Consequently, the cruelty of segregation and exploited workers set Randolph on a course from which he never varied, and President Carter likened the civil rights movement that bore fruit 50 years later to "building a nation."

So from a loneliness of being a pacifist, a democratic socialist and integrationist before 1920, Randolph rose to national recognition by building a union. He came to global attention with his 1963 March on Washington.

But, Rustin explained, at any point along the way he would revert to the lonely agitator, because he would reject the "fads, the easy answers and the separatist illusions that had too frequently plagued movements for liberation."

Rustin recalled Randolph urging him to aid Japanese-Americans detained during World War II or to help the refugees from Southeast Asia. One of his last expressions of concern before he died was the plight of refugees from Haiti.

"His universal moral concern compelled his resistance to any tendency anywhere in the world which defended unjust acts in the name of justice or excused wrongdoing--either by blacks or whites--because it was done in the name of some particular freedom, or in the name of democracy, or of anti-colonialism," Rustin said.

The tax collector who visited Randolph's apartment soon after he died found a net worth of less than $500, Rustin said. Randolph's most valued possession was a battered watch once given him by Pullman car porters.

President Carter cautioned that, in remembering the gentility and idealism of Randolph, future Americans should not forget that "he faced down four Presidents," in his pursuit of peace (Wilson), a national fair employment practice law (Roosevelt), integration of the armed forces (Truman) and the 1963 march (Kennedy) that helped produce the 1964 Civil Rights Act.

The Louisiana state legislature also honored Randolph with a joint House-Senate resolution taking note of the Sleeping Car Porters as the first all-Negro union. The resolution also cited President Johnson's 1964 presentation to Randolph of the Medal of Freedom.

At the national memorial service, Kirkland traced the leadership of Randolph in 50 years by standing up against Marcus Garvey's "Back to Africa" and W. E. B. DuBois' "Talented Tenth" elitism of the 1920s; the Pullman Company in the 1930s; and the federal government in quest of the executive orders signed by Roosevelt and Truman in the 1940s.

"Phil Randolph has left us more than memories," Kirkland said. "He left us a vision. He took a country divided by segregation and brought people together. He took a good labor movement, marred by discrimination, and made it better."

AFL-CIO News, June 9, 1979.

36. A. PHILIP RANDOLPH MEMORIAL

The death of Asa Philip Randolph on May 16, 1979, is a great loss to the entire nation and the labor and civil rights movements in particular.

For more than half a century A. Philip Randolph devoted his entire energies to securing dignity and freedom for all. He believed that the "principle of social equality is the only sure guarantee of social progress."

Against the racism of hostile employers, Randolph led and gave vitality to the Brotherhood of Sleeping Car Porters--organized the industry in a racist environment and built an effective union. He worked hard and long to free the labor movement from racial discrimination, and he played a key role in achieving equality throughout our nation.

In Randolph's unending struggle for dignity and justice for blacks and labor, he was a genuine friend to all of labor, helping workers in every trade and industry in the nation throughout the difficult early days of building unions; therefore, be it

RESOLVED: That the AFL-CIO carry forth the message and goals of America's great civil rights and social activist, A. Philip Randolph; that the AFL-CIO work with other organizations to honor the memory of A. Philip Randolph by continuing to build a labor movement where workers of all races, struggling side by side, can achieve dignity and respect; and that Congress be urged to authorize that a medal be struck in his honor.

Proceedings of the Thirteenth Constitutional Convention of the AFL-CIO, Policy Resolutions, adopted December 1979, pp. 131-32.

37. HOUSE VOTES GOLD MEDAL HONORING PHIL RANDOLPH

The House voted to issue a gold medal honoring the late A. Philip Randolph for his "lifelong advocacy of peaceful change on behalf of workers and minorities."

It passed and sent to the Senate a bill authorizing the President to present the medal "in the name of Congress" to the A. Philip Randolph Institute, which carried on the work Randolph began in his twin role as a trade union and civil rights leader.

The bill was taken up under a no-amendment procedure which requires a two-thirds vote. Rep. John Rousselot (R-Calif.) led an effort to defeat the bill but it passed with bipartisan support on a 333-61 rollcall. [72]

During the debate, both Democrats and Republicans spoke in admiration of the profound impact that Randolph had on his times.

AFL-CIO News, March 22, 1980.

THE NAACP AND THE AFL-CIO

38.   THE NAACP HAILS THE AFL-CIO MERGER

The Crisis hails the merger of the American Federation of Labor (AFL) and the Congress of Industrial Organization (CIO). We think this is a step in the right direction for organized labor, although it may pose problems in leadership and, for the AFL, in race relations. Many AFL unions bar Negroes from membership or otherwise discriminate against Negro labor, and attempts to make them change their policies have usually been futile. On the other hand, the CIO as an industrial union has welcomed every worker regardless of his race or origin.

This naturally poses the question of the status of the Negro union member in the merged organization. What is the AFL-CIO now going to do about its racially exclusive unions? Unless this problem is attacked head-on it is going to be around to plague organized labor for many a year to come.

The Crisis, 63 (January 1956):35.

39.   RACISM WITHIN ORGANIZED LABOR: A REPORT OF
FIVE YEARS OF THE AFL-CIO
1955-1960

Labor Department
National Association for the Advancement of Colored People

The elimination of racism within trade unions was one of the major goals for organized labor announced at the merger convention of the American Federation of Labor and the Congress of Industrial Organizations in December, 1955. This was welcomed by many civil rights agencies and especially by the National Association for the Advancement of Colored People which offered its full support to the labor movement.

Today, five years after the AFL-CIO merger, the national labor organization has failed to eliminate the broad pattern of racial discrimination and segregation in many important affiliated unions. Trade union activity in the civil rights field since the merger has not been marked by a systematic and coordinated effort by the national labor federation to eliminate discrimination and segregation within local unions. This is especially true of the craft unions in the building and construction trades where the traditional anti-Negro practices basically remain in effect.

Efforts to eliminate discriminatory practices within trade unions have

been piecemeal and inadequate and usually the result of protest by civil rights
agencies acting on behalf of Negro workers. The National AFL-CIO has repeatedly
refused to take action on its own initiative. In too many cases years have
elapsed between the filing of a complaint by an aggrieved worker and acknowledgment and investigation by the Federation, if indeed there is any action at
all.

Discriminatory racial practices by trade unions are not simply isolated or
occasional expressions of local bias against colored workers, but rather, as
the record indicates, a continuation of the institutionalized pattern of anti-
Negro employment practices that is traditional with large sections of organized
labor and industrial management.

The pattern of union responsibility for job discrimination against Negroes
is not limited to any one area of the country or to some few industries or
union jurisdictions but involves many unions in a wide variety of occupations
in manufacturing industries, skilled crafts, railroads and maritime trades as
for example, the Seafarers International Union which operates union-controlled
hiring halls on Great Lake ports such as Duluth, Chicago, Detroit, Cleveland
and Buffalo. As a systematic practice this union will dispatch only Negro
workers for menial jobs as messmen in the galley departments of ships operating
under S.I.U. collective bargaining agreements. Over the years Negro members of
the Seafarers International Union have repeatedly protested this practice, but
to no avail as the union continues discriminatory job assignments in its hiring
halls.

On occasion one or two Negroes have been admitted into an all-white local
union as token compliance with a state or municipal fair employment practice
law as with the International Brotherhood of Electrical Workers in Cleveland;
the Bricklayers in Milwaukee and the Railway Clerks in Minneapolis, but this is
essentially a limited and strategic adjustment to community pressure and
represents very dubious "progress."

Certainly the token admission of a few Negroes into an electrical workers
union in Cleveland can no more be regarded as integration than can the token
admission of two or three Negro children into a southern public school. There
are also many instances where unions have removed the "lily-white" exclusion
clause from their constitutions as public relations gestures but continued to
exclude Negroes from membership by tacit consent.

As long as union membership remains a condition of employment in the
building trades, on the railroads and elsewhere and qualified Negroes are
barred from union membership solely because of their color, then trade union
discrimination is the decisive factor in determining whether Negro workers in
a given industry shall have an opportunity to earn a living for themselves and
their families. This is especially true in the construction industry where
AFL-CIO building trades unions exercise a high degree of control over access
to employment.

AFL-CIO affiliated unions are today guilty of discriminatory racial
practices in four categories: outright exclusion of Negroes, segregated locals,
separate racial seniority lines in collective bargaining agreements and exclusion of Negroes from apprenticeship training programs controlled by labor
unions.

As for the Federation's Civil Rights Department, its performance would
seem to indicate that its major function is to create a "liberal" public relations image rather than to attack the broad pattern of anti-Negro practices
within affiliated unions. The Civil Rights Committee of the AFL-CIO is the
only standing committee in the Federation whose chairman is not a member of
the Federation's Executive Council and/or the president of an international
union. The rigid protocol of the national labor federation indicates that
such a person is not in a position to impose a policy upon an international
or local union but must confine himself to issuing declarations and to exercising such persuasion as he can muster. More often than not, his efforts
are fruitless.

Organized Labor in the South

The threat of several local unions in the South to organize a Southern
Federation of Labor has clearly not materialized, however, one is forced to
note that the White Citizens Councils began taking control of some local

AFL-CIO affiliates soon after the Supreme Court decision of 1954 in the school segregation cases. Because the national leadership of organized labor has made it a practice to avoid as much internal conflict on racial issues as possible, the Ku Klux Klan and White Citizens Council forces, especially in Alabama, have moved into many local unions and made them, in effect, virtual extensions of segregationist organizations.

As a result, Negro workers throughout the South are experiencing an acute sense of alienation and rejection from organized labor. This becomes increasingly evident in an analysis of Negro voting behavior in union certification elections conducted by the National Labor Relations Board. Although it is not possible to get an official breakdown of election results by Board regions, election results are known and are discussed in union circles.

At the South Wire Company, Carrollton, Georgia, where several hundred workers were involved, the International Brotherhood of Electrical Workers Union recently lost an NLRB election by eight votes. It has been stated by the union organizers that the decisive vote was cast by the forty-five Negroes in the election who voted against the IBEW.

Early in 1960 an election was held in Aiken, South Carolina at the Savannah River Atomic Energy Project with seventeen unions of the Metal Trades Department of the AFL-CIO seeking certification by the NLRB as bargaining agent. Thirty-one hundred workers were involved. Six hundred of these were Negroes. It was stated by union organizers that the six hundred Negroes voted almost as a solid bloc against the union and the election was lost.

The active recruitment of trade union members for White Citizens Councils, Ku Klux Klan and other segregationist organizations accounts for much of the loss of influence that the AFL-CIO has suffered among Negro workers throughout the South. News of this activity has come not alone through word of mouth but frequently from newspaper advertising in local communities plainly to be seen by Negro workers themselves.

In a number of localities such as Savannah, Georgia, public notices have appeared stating that the Ku Klux Klan or the White Citizens Council will hold a meeting in a union hall. Newspapers have also printed reports and pictures of union officials speaking at such meetings and the point has not been lost on the Negro worker. Moreover, they are aware that the National AFL-CIO has permitted its civil rights declarations to be ignored by many affiliated unions.

The correction of this mutually damaging situation would seem to demand action directly by the AFL-CIO leadership and by the international unions involved. At the very least what is required is that AFL-CIO members and local affiliates not be active participants in segregationist attacks upon the Negro's struggle for basic citizenship rights.

Segregated Local Unions

The Brotherhood of Railway and Steamship Clerks which maintains many segregated local lodges in northern as well as southern cities is among the important international unions which maintain a broad national pattern of segregation. In the Brotherhood the existence of more than 150 segregated all-Negro locals with separate racial seniority rosters limits job mobility and violates the seniority rights of thousands of Negro union members.

This union has persisted in its racist practices despite repeated protests from Negro workers and community organizations. On April 30, 1967, the New York State Commission Against Discrimination ordered the merger of the "lily-white" George N. Harrison Lodge (783) and the all-Negro Friendship Lodge (6118). The white union refused to comply and the local lodges remain segregated to this day. Similar situations exist in Chicago where Negro workers are in segregated local lodge 6132 and in Tulsa, Oklahoma, where they are in local 6257. In East St. Louis and St. Louis there are 14 all-colored lodges and 14 all-white lodges which function through segregated joint councils.

The practice of segregation is so well institutionalized in this union that the designation of the Negro lodges over the country begins with the numeral "6." It is ironic to note that the president of the Brotherhood of Railway and Steamship Clerks, George M. Harrison, is a member of the Civil Rights Committee of the AFL-CIO and a Federation Vice President.

The Brotherhood of Railway Carmen of America maintains segregated locals in California, Florida and in many other states. Recently Negro workers filed charges jointly against this Union and the Sante Fe Railroad with the California Fair Employment Practices Commission. The Commission has announced that it will conduct a public hearing on January 9 on complaints that the company and the union have acted in collusion to discriminate against Negro workers.

In Jacksonville, Florida, Negro workers employed on the Atlantic Coast Line Railroad belong to Local 690, a segregated all-Negro unit, while white workers employed on the same line hold membership in Local 509, an all-white unit of the Brotherhood of Railway Carmen. In addition the white local prevents the all-colored local from participating in negotiations with management and insists that it "represents" the colored local. Similar practices occur in other cities where this union operates segregated locals.

Racially segregated locals are today characteristic of many building trades unions in the North as well as in the South. The United Brotherhood of Carpenters and Joiners is quite typical of building trades unions in its treatment of the Negro worker. This union, for over a half-century has been among the most important of all the building trades unions, and, with very few exceptions, organizes Negroes and whites into separate locals insofar as it permits Negroes to join the union at all. In the South there seems to be no exception to this rule and it is most often followed in northern cities as well.

The white locals are in control of the union hiring hall and, because of frequent arrangements with municipal and county political machines, all hiring for major public as well as private construction projects is done through the "lily-white" union hiring hall. In many instances, the white local will import white workers from other cities rather than allow local Negro members to share in attractive work opportunities.

Quite frequently Negroes are excluded altogether from work in white neighborhoods. This means that Negro carpenters are restricted to marginal maintenance and repair work within the Negro community and that they seldom are permitted to work on the larger construction projects. The same practices are true for other building trades unions in many cities throughout the country.

The Hod Carriers, Building and Common Laborers Union is currently defendant in a suit brought by Negro construction workers in Chicago, charging that the Hod Carriers Union bars them from desirable jobs within this union's jurisdiction. In other cities Negro workers charge that white locals controlling job assignments in federal construction projects refuse to accept "travelling cards" issued by colored locals.

The International Brotherhood of Pulp, Sulphite and Paper Mill Workers has agreed not to issue any new charters to segregated local unions and has indicated that action will be taken to merge segregated locals wherever possible, as well as to eliminate separate racial seniority lines in collective bargaining agreements. This occurred after representatives of the NAACP appeared before the Union's General Executive Board and made a presentation on behalf of Negro union members.

Unfortunately, the United Papermakers and Paperworkers Union refused the request of the NAACP Executive Secretary to confer with the Executive Board of the Papermakers Union regarding the matter of segregated locals and separate racial seniority lines in union contracts.

On the positive side we note that the American Federation of Musicians has merged segregated locals in some 16 cities and that the International Ladies Garment Workers Union with the requested assistance of the National Association for the Advancement of Colored People merged separate white and Negro sections of the Atlanta local into one unit.

Racial Exclusion Practices

Today in virtually every large urban center in the United States Negro workers are denied employment in the major industrial and residential construction projects because they are, with some few exceptions, barred from membership in the building trades craft unions. This includes the International Brotherhood of Electrical Workers, the Operating Engineers, Iron and Structural Steel Workers, Plumbers and Pipe Fitters Union, Plasterers and Lathers, the Sheet Metal Workers Union, the Boiler Makers, etc.

The basic fact of craft unions in the building trades industry is that they control access to employment by virtue of their rigid control of the hiring process. In this industry unions perform certain managerial functions, especially the assignment of union members to jobs. The refusal to admit Negroes into membership simply denies Negro workers opportunities to secure employment.

This is true in many cities across the country such as Terre Haute, Indiana, Washington, D.C., St. Louis, Mo., Dallas, Texas, Cleveland, Ohio, East St. Louis, Ill. and Dade County, Florida, etc. (Chicago, Ill., appears to be a partial exception, perhaps because of the Negro's effective use of his growing political power). Because the National Labor Relations Board has done little to enforce the anti-closed shop provisions of the Taft-Hartley Act, building trades unions affiliated to the AFL-CIO in most instances are closed unions operating closed shops.

Local 26 of the International Brotherhood of Electrical Workers in Washington, D.C. is a typical example of how union power is based to completely exclude Negro workers from securing employment in vast federal construction projects. For many years Negro workers have been attempting to secure admission into Local 26, which controls all hiring for electrical installation work in the nation's capital. They have filed complaints with the President's Committee on Government Contracts which over three years ago brought this matter to the attention of the National AFL-CIO.

As of January 1, 1960, there were still no Negroes admitted into membership in Local 26. However, after the Justice Department threatened action and as a concession to pressure from other government agencies and to protests from Negro civil rights organizations, one Negro electrician, James Holland, was reluctantly permitted by the union to work in a government installation.

Soon after the merge in 1955 two international unions were admitted into the Federation with "lily-white" exclusion clauses in their constitutions although this action was clearly in violation of the policies announced at the time of the merger agreement between the AFL and the CIO. They were the International Brotherhood of Locomotive Firemen and Enginemen and the Brotherhood of Railroad Trainmen.

Since then the Brotherhood of Railroad Trainmen has removed the "Caucasian Only Clause" from its constitution but in November, 1958, the Brotherhood of Locomotive Firemen and Enginemen successfully defended its exclusion of Negroes from union membership in a suit brought by Negro firemen in the Federal District Court in Cincinnati, Ohio. Despite many appeals the National AFL-CIO refused to intervene or make any public comment and this union continues to exclude all Negroes from membership.

For almost a generation qualified Negro plumbers have been attacking the racial exclusion practices of the Plumbers Union (United Association of Journeymen and Apprentices of the Plumbing and Pipe Fitting Industry of the United States and Canada, AFL-CIO). On December 4, 1958, Frank T. Lyerson submitted an affidavit to the AFL-CIO Civil Rights Department charging that Local 630 of the Plumbers Union in East St. Louis, Illinois refused membership to him and other qualified Negroes. Although Local 630 limits membership to white persons exclusively, the National AFL-CIO has not taken any action on this or on other complaints against the Plumbers Union.

The practices of other building trades unions in the St. Louis-East St. Louis area are typical of the racial exclusion practices of many old-line craft unions. At the present time qualified Negro workers are barred from securing employment in the large harbor improvement project in St. Louis as well as in the vast federally-financed construction program in East St. Louis because of the exclusionist practices of unions affiliated to the Building Trades Council of the AFL-CIO.

Local 309 of the International Brotherhood of Electrical Workers, AFL-CIO, in East St. Louis is an all-white local and has consistently refused to admit qualified Negroes, including Jethro Smith who filed an affidavit with the National AFL-CIO. Henry Densmore filed a similar affidavit against the Operative Plasterers and Cement Masons Association, Local 90, which also maintains a rigid policy of excluding Negroes from membership.

Negro firemen for the first time were admitted into the International Fire Fighters Association, AFL-CIO, Local 734 in Baltimore, Maryland, during 1959. This occurred after action by the National Association for the

Advancement of Colored People in support of Negro firemen who filed a complaint
with the Baltimore Fair Employment Opportunity Commission against the union.
However, Negro firemen who applied for admission into the Fire Fighters Union
in Washington, D.C. during November, 1960, were refused admission into the
"lily-white" Association of Fire Fighters in the nation's capital.

At its 1958 convention, the National Transport Association amended its
constitution to admit Negroes and since then has enrolled some Negro workers
within its jurisdiction in several states.

Separate Racial Seniority Lines in
Collective Bargaining Agreements

Many major unions affiliated to the AFL-CIO have negotiated into their
collective bargaining agreements separate lines of seniority promotion. These
limit Negro employment to unskilled or menial job classifications which deny
Negro workers equal seniority and other rights and prevent them from developing
job skills which permit employment in more desirable classifications.

Although some few isolated actions can be reported as having eliminated
separate seniority lines such as that of the United Automobile Workers of
America at the General Motors Fisher Body plant in St. Louis, Missouri (UAW
Local 25), the action of the Oil, Chemical and Atomic Workers at the Magnolia
Refining Corp., Beaumont, Texas, and at the Phillips Petroleum Corporation in
Kansas City, Missouri, as well as the limited action by the United Steelworkers
of America in response to a law suit filed by Negro members at the Sheffield
Steel Company in Houston, Texas, the pattern of such discrimination remains
practically intact in southern industrial operations where trade unions hold
collective bargaining agreements.

At present, many thousands of Negro workers who are members of AFL-CIO
unions in southern paper mills, chemical plants, pulp works and oil refineries
as well as steel plants and in the textile industry suffer the acute disadvantages of separate lines of progression for Negro and white workers in union
contracts.

Examples of trade unions that have entered into collusion with management
to deny Negro workers equal seniority rights in the paper manufacturing and
pulp and sulphite industry in the South are to be found at the Union Bag-Camp
Paper Corp., Savannah, Georgia, where all the Negro workers are limited to
membership in two segregated locals, Local 601 and 615, affiliated to the
International Brotherhood of Pulp, Sulphite and Paper Mill Workers.

All white workers hold membership in Local 388 and 435 of the same union
and Local 408 of the United Papermakers and Paperworkers Union. Similar conditions exist at the Crown Zellerbach Corp., Bogalusa, Louisiana; Hudson Pulp
and Paper Company, Palatka, Florida; and at International Paper Company plants
in Mobile, Alabama; Georgetown, South Carolina; Moss Point and Natchez,
Mississippi and Bastrop, Louisiana.

In these and many other paper mills throughout the South these two unions
hold joint collective bargaining agreements and maintain a rigid pattern of
racially segregated local unions with separate seniority lines limiting Negro
employment to laborer classifications.

At the American Viscose Corporation plant in Front Royal, Virginia, where
the Textile Workers Union is the collective bargaining agent, the union has
approved a supplemental agreement to the contract which limits Negro employees
to unskilled and menial job classifications that violate their basic seniority
rights.

A similar condition exists at the Atlantic Steel Company plant in
Atlanta, Georgia where after years of protest by Negro union members, the
United Steelworkers Union has only partially eliminated those seniority provisions which limit Negroes, no matter how well qualified, to common laborer
classifications.

A typical example of how separate seniority lines based on race in
collective bargaining agreements prevent Negro workers from bidding for more
desirable job occupations is to be found at the United States Phosphoric
Company in Tampa, Florida. Over 200 Negro workers have repeatedly complained
to the President of the International Chemical Workers Union, AFL-CIO,
regarding the supplemental agreement to the union contract which contains

rigid promotional lines for white and Negro workers limiting Negro workers to undesirable menial job classifications and preventing upgrading into production classifications.

The International Union of Operating Engineers, the Lake Charles, (La.) and the Galveston (Texas) AFL-CIO Metal Trades Councils hold collective bargaining agreements in several large oil refineries and chemical plants in the Gulf area. These union contracts contain provisions limiting Negro employment to some few menial jobs, a wage differential based upon race, and separate lines of seniority progression for white and colored workers.

Apprenticeship Training

The continued exclusion of Negroes from apprenticeship training is particularly disturbing because of rapid technological changes in the nation's economy. Because of the disproportionate concentration of Negroes in the unskilled sections of the labor force there has already been a disproportionate displacement of Negroes as a result of technological change. Continued exclusion of Negro youth from major apprenticeship training programs in the North as well as in the South endangers the future economic well-being of the entire Negro community.

It is important to note that in the ten-year period from 1950-1960, in the State of New York, the increase of Negro participation in building trades apprenticeship training programs rose only from 1.5% to 2%. In most of these programs the role of the labor union is decisive because the trade union usually determines who is admitted into the training programs and, therefore, who is admitted into the union.

Recent studies clearly indicate that no large scale significant advances have been made by Negroes into those craft union apprenticeship programs which have historically excluded non-whites. The railroad craft unions as well as the railroad operating Brotherhoods remain adamant in their opposition to Negro craftsmen and bar apprenticeship opportunities to Negro youth.

Almost equally exclusive are the printing trades unions with exceptions being found in some areas of the Assistant Printing Pressmen Union and the Lithographers Union. Open access to plumbing and pipe fitting apprenticeships controlled by the Plumbers Union is a rare experience for a young Negro in the North as well as in the South. Similarly Negro youth are almost completely excluded from apprenticeship programs operated by the Sheet Metal Workers Union, the Ornamental and Structural Iron Workers, the Glass Workers, the Tile Setters, the Machinists or the Bricklayers Union.

The NAACP secured the admission of a Negro for the first time into the Sheet Metal apprenticeship training program in St. Louis, Missouri. In an unusual procedure the Association secured certification from the Bureau of Apprenticeship of the U.S. Department of Labor for a non-union firm owned by a Negro after Local 36 of the Sheet Metal Workers International Association had refused to admit Negro applicants into its apprenticeship training program and had refused to permit the participation of the Negro-owned company in training programs conducted by the union. The owner of Kennedy and Sons Sheet Metal Shops offered to have his employees join Local 36 of the Sheet Metal Workers Union but the membership applications of the Negro workers were refused by the all-white local affiliate of the AFL-CIO.

Recent action by the New York State Attorney General acting at the request of the National Association for the Advancement of Colored People made possible the admission of the first Negro into the apprenticeship training program operated by the Plumbers Union in the State of New York.

A sustained program of activity by the Oregon Fair Employment Practices Commission and the State Apprenticeship Council resulted in the admission of Negroes for the first time into various apprenticeship programs conducted by unions affiliated to the Oregon AFL-CIO Building Trades and the Metal Trades Councils. These isolated actions, however, are completely inadequate as they do not eliminate the broad national pattern of Negro exclusion from apprenticeship training programs.

Increasingly, apprenticeship and other forms of technical training become the heart of fair employment practices. The continued exclusion of Negro youth from such programs, especially those controlled by AFL-CIO craft unions in the printing industry, the building and metal trades and in other craft jurisdictions prevents thousands of young persons from realizing their human potential and dooms them and their families to a marginal economic existence. It is in this area that the disparity between the public relations pronouncements of the AFL-CIO on civil rights and the day-to-day reality for Negro workers is most sharply outlined.

Many traditional sources of Negro employment (the nation's railroads and mass-production industries, for example), are rapidly drying up as a result of automation and other technological changes in the economy. Today the status of the Negro wage earner is characterized by drastic change and crisis. Thus, the virtual exclusion of Negroes from apprenticeship and other training programs forces them to remain as marginal employees in the economy. They are the ones who are hired last and who can be dispensed with easily with the added advantage that their displacement can be rationalized in terms of lower attainments in craft skills.

In addition, the appreciable lack of skilled Negro craftsmen directly affects the economic well-being of the entire Negro population as it removes potential sources of high income occupations from the group. The devices outlined briefly in this report operate effectively to concentrate Negro wage earners in those jobs which suffer the highest instances of unemployment.

The concentration of unskilled, low-paying jobs with a lack of employment stability together with other income limitations such as denial of access to union hiring halls in the building trades, and separate racial lines of seniority promotion in collective bargaining agreements all contribute to an explanation of why Negroes constitute a permanently depressed economic group in American society.

Staff report reviewing conditions previously cited by the NAACP, but summarized here at the end of five years of the merged AFL-CIO. Delivered by Herbert Hill, NAACP Labor Secretary at the Association's Annual Meeting, January 3, 1960, New York City. Copy in possession of the editors.

40. THE NAACP VS. LABOR

By J. C. Rich

The present anti-labor campaign of the National Association for the Advancement of Colored People, accusing well-known labor leaders of discriminatory practices, provides Southern yahoos with absolution for their sins from an unexpected quarter. Whatever noble purpose the NAACP may have in mind, one immediate result of its actions has been to cloak racists of the stripe of Governor Ross Barnett and Senator James Eastland of Mississippi in a garment of social respectability. For how could lily-whites of the backwater South be wrong if prominent Northern labor leaders also discriminate against blacks?[73]

The NAACP charges have been made against such men as David Dubinsky, President of the International Ladies Garment Workers Union (ILGWU); David McDonald, President of the United Steelworkers; Walter Reuther, President of the United Automobile Workers; and Paul Hall, President of the Seafarers International. In at least one instance, the organization found itself so far off base that it had to beat a hasty retreat to the norms of ordinary courtesy. The NAACP stated that it had not meant to offend Reuther, and regretted that some of its labor activities had outraged him. But it has not granted the same dispensation to McDonald, and certainly not to Dubinsky.[74]

Yet according to newspaper speculation—possibly "leaked" speculation—Reuther has been put on notice that there is a Negro caucus within the United Auto Workers. Presumably, the NAACP believes it is entirely proper to maintain a special Negro grouping within a union, although it justifiably condemns racial segregation when practiced by whites in certain unions.

The course which the NAACP has set for itself is a tragic and self-defeating one. For the American labor movement has long worked toward the same goals as the NAACP. To be sure, some local unions and some union workers, like their non-union neighbors, have adopted the mores and habits of the

communities in which they live. But the national organizations are more
sophisticated and more responsive to the call of justice and social equality
than their various branches in the South. Thus, building a racist--or anti-
Semitic--case against the labor movement because of the actions of a particular
union violates fact and verify so completely it is nothing less than a trespass
on integrity.

And it is this violence to integrity, as well as the malice inherent in
the NAACP assault on the labor movement, that has disturbed the labor and
liberal-minded community. It is absurd to imply that Dubinsky is no better
than Mississippi's meanest bigot, and it is equally absurd to suggest that
McDonald runs a Jim Crow union.

Negro steel workers labor side by side with their white shopmates; their
wages, hours, seniority rights and other prerequisites are protected by the
union with equal diligence. In the garment union, the administration of David
Dubinsky has been notable for the degree of acceptance and affectionate regard
accorded by whites to Negroes and Negroes to whites. The conflicts and antagonisms of which NAACP spokesmen have made a Federal case are never seen in the
market or in the shops. Differences occur, but nobody in sound mental health
thinks that one has to go to court about them.

Notice to the effect that the NAACP intended to drag unions to court came
last August, when news stories quoted Herbert Hill, the Association's labor
secretary, as saying: "We will not be satisfied until discrimination is
completely eliminated and we will continue to make progress in a trade-union
way undeterred by outsiders."

This statement reveals more about Herbert Hill than it does about union
practices. Hill seems to believe that discrimination, or any other evil, can
be "completely eliminated." But who is to judge whether in truth there is
discrimination and to what degree it prevails? Who is an "outsider" and who
an insider in judgments of this sort? And by what prerogative does Hill consider himself an insider in the pursuit of justice, while relegating men like
George Meany, Dubinsky and McDonald to the limbo of outsiders?

In the NAACP's battle against labor, Hill has distinguished himself on
another score as well. While on lend-lease from his organization to the House
Labor and Education Committee, headed by the redoubtable Congressman Adam
Clayton Powell (D.-N.Y.), Hill composed a bill of indictment against the
ILGWU. The subcommittee to which the indictment was presented refused to grant
it the dignity of acceptance because it lacked substantive evidence. More
knowledgable specialists in this sort of infighting saw in Hill's document a
diatribe similar to those the Communists used to spread in the market against
the ILGWU in the days when they were striving to capture the needle trade
unions. Hill is no Communist, but unconsciously he repeated a charge originally
made some 20 years ago by the labor editor of the *Daily Worker*. The charge was
that not a single Negro member was to be found in the huge Dressmakers Local 89,
managed by ILGWU Vice President Luigi Antonini.[75]

This was true 20 years ago, and it is still true. Yet the absence of
Negro members in Local 89 has nothing to do with an anti-Negro bias or any
other invidious prejudice. Local 89 is a "language" local composed of Italian
dressmakers. It was originally founded with the aid of Jewish trade unionists
in order to facilitate the unionization of Italian workers who were streaming
into the needle trades.

The *Daily Worker* knew this and so, presumably, does Hill. The supporters
of the NAACP might well wonder whether it was fair to slander a friend and
ally in the cause of civil rights. Antonini, a bitter-end anti-fascist even
in Mussolini's heyday, certainly deserves better at the hands of libertarians
than to be tarred with bigotry.

Charles Zimmerman, a leader of the ILGWU's Dressmakers Union who has
resigned from the NAACP after years of active participation in its work,
pointed to still another barb in Hill's anti-union agglomeration. "The most
shocking thing in Mr. Hill's entire statement," Zimmerman recented declared,
"is its slurring reference to the 'ethnic composition' of the ILGWU leadership.
The NAACP . . . has now endorsed this kind of attack, and in my judgment there
is no longer any place in it for anyone who believes that the struggle for
equal opportunity for Negroes is part of the struggle against bigotry and
discrimination in all forms and in all places."

The "ethnic composition" in Hill's bill of complaint is a Nice Nelly way

of saying that the top leadership of the ILGWU is Jewish. Negroes may draw
their own derogatory inferences from this reflection. Perhaps Dubinsky should
apologize to Hill for being Jewish, and to the heads of the NAACP for being
president of a union.

The charges against the ILGWU; the hearings conducted by Congressman
Powell's Congressional crony. Representative Herbert Zelenko (D.-N.Y.); the
inquisition Powell himself has threatened to pursue--all at base seem to have
one finding: Despite the many Negroes and Puerto Ricans among the ILGWU's
New York membership, there are no Negroes or Puerto Ricans in its top leadership.[76]

This too, of course, is fools' gold when considered as evidence. The
impulses that bring leadership to the fore anywhere also have their own
inertial force. Congressmen dearly cherish the inertial force that propels
them to office election after election. The composition of their constituencies may change, but if they are responsive to these changes they continue to
retain office.

What has happened to the NAACP, it appears, is that it has not been
responsive to change. Negroes have joined unions and have acquired status in
many communities, but the NAACP remained its old somnolent self until it was
prodded into action by its more dynamic members. What is more, new Negro
organizations have arisen to challenge its exclusive holding on liberal sym-
pathies.

The NAACP's great achievement has been in court procedures. This was as
much the achievement of Thurgood Marshall, the organization's chief counsel for
many years, as it was of the Association as a whole. Since Marshall's judicial
appointment, the NAACP has reverted to Hill's juvenilities and the anti-union
bias of some of its directors.

Ironically, in doing so the NAACP has assailed not the old-line unions
which flagrantly impose Jim Crow restrictions on Negroes, but the progressive
unions with a leadership famous for social insight and a sense of public
decency and responsibility. The social attitudes and administrative conduct of
Meany, Reuther, McDonald and Dubinsky are so well known they are part of the
very air we breathe. Dubinsky has been on public view for more than 50 years.
He could not, even if he wanted to, keep his behavior a secret from the liberal
community which cherishes him as friend of every progressive cause.

Liberals may well therefore ask: Why vilify a man with fabrications that
are as outrageous as they are preposterous? What purpose other than an appeal
to the basest prejudices of Negroes is there in stating that even the most
renowned whites, the most respected labor men, the most articulate spokesmen
of liberalism are racist bigots at heart? Is it really a service to Negroes,
really a service to the cause of civil rights to put Dubinsky *et al.* on a par
with the white supremacists and the ILGWU with the White Citizens Council?

Scandalized and dismayed, many in the progressive trade-union community
are determined to examine the liberal credentials of the NAACP anew. If the
Association intends to pursue an anti-union course, it will have to do so as
an open enemy of labor, not as a member of the liberal coalition. Liberals
and labor unions have had long experience with open enemies and know how to
deal with a new recruit to intolerance. This should be clear from George
Meany's announcement that the AFL-CIO has withdrawn its long-standing support
of the NAACP.

The New Leader, 45 (November 26, 1962):20-21.

41.   REFLECTIONS ON THE NEGRO AND LABOR

By Daniel Bell

Some years ago, an older friend, an official of one of the out-of-town
locals of the International Ladies' Garment Workers' Union and a Socialist,
complained to me about the apathy of most of the members in his local, and,
in some cases, the resentment of a minority against the union leadership. "I

don't understand it," he said. "I work hard for them. I spend long hours negotiating for them. I don't let the boss get away with a nickel. But they don't appreciate it."

I was reminded of his remarks recently on reading the charges made by Herbert Hill, the Labor Secretary of the NAACP, of racial discrimination in the Garment Workers' Union, and the outraged rejoinders by David Dubinsky and other ILGWU officials. Like most of the young Socialists who were active in the Young People's Socialist League in the '30s, I have long had a warm feeling for, even an emotional identification with, the ILGWU. The union supplied us with some of the best jokes (copies supplied upon request) about the radical movement. It provided intermittent employment for many of us (I did "educational work" and editorial chores for Local 62 during my graduate-school days). Through generous contributions, it supported most of the Socialist institutions during the bleakest days of the depression and after. Its record of progressive leadership in a variety of areas is too well documented to need repetition. The idea, therefore, that the ILGWU practiced racial discrimination seemed absurd.

Hill's statement, compiled originally for a Congressional subcommittee, stated that Negroes were excluded from the higher-paying jobs in the garment trades (specifically in the cutters' local); that certain locals excluded Negroes; that a predominantly Negro local (composed primarily of shipping clerks) was attached to a larger local of pressers and was thus deprived of full citizenship rights in the union; and that Negroes and Puerto Ricans were under-represented in the union's leadership, which was, and remains, predominantly Jewish.

The ILGWU's answer, which appears in the Fall 1962 issue of *New Politics,* was prepared by Gus Tyler, the union's political director. It is, I think, quite convincing as a rebuttal to the specific charges. Hill's statement was sloppy (Local 89, accused of rebuffing Negroes, is an Italian-language local, and accepts only Italian members--a hangover from an early organizational structure), his figures were often incorrect, and his portentous social analysis (*e.g.,* that the Jewish labor leaders have more in common with the Jewish employers than with the rank-and-file membership) was a piece of pseudo-sociology.

It also seems clear that the original occasion for the statement was unfortunate, since the Congressional hearings were being conducted, in New York rather than in Washington, during a primary campaign by a Congressman who had been denied endorsement by the ILGWU-dominated Liberal party in New York. And for anyone who knows the long devotion to liberal causes of such men as Charles Zimmerman, the manager of the union's Dress Joint Board, the idea of their condoning overt racial discrimination, even for reasons of expediency, did not ring true.

Yet, wrong as Hill's charges are in detail, deeper problems remain, problems that have been obscured by the stridency of charges and replies. The first is symbolized by my friend's observations about the apathy and ingratitude within his local. But this is only part of a broader, more vexing issue: the propriety of attacking one's friends, rather than one's enemies, as the Negro organizations are now doing. And this, in turn, is part of a still larger question which few persons have cared to discuss openly: whether in his fight to overcome second-class status, the Negro should receive not merely equality of opportunity but, in order to establish himself as a full citizen, preferential treatment as well.

The first problem (which has been caricatured by the charge of racial discrimination) is really, in its way, the familiar family chronicle of the original generation that built an institution (or a business or a store) and won't let go for the next one. The telling phrase in the complaint that my old Socialist friend made was the reiterated "for them." He was doing a good job, for them. He had negotiated a good contract, for them.

But as I tried to tell him at the time, sometimes people like to do things for themselves, even if they do them less well. His reply, on reflection, was that the workers could not negotiate a contract: They did not possess the skills, the boss would outmaneuver them, they would not be too exorbitant in their demands, they did not understand the economics of the industry, etc. When I asked him if they could not learn--after all, *he* had come up from the shop--his answer was that they are not interested, that in his generation the talented people had gone into the shop because there was nowhere else for immigrants to go, but now the more educated ones did not go into the union, and so on.

My friend was no fool. He knew all about Robert Michel's "iron law of oligarchy," had read Will Herberg on union bureaucracy, was aware of the growing gulf between the leadership and the rank-and-file, and his reply reflected an awareness of being trapped in this disparity. "Besides," he said, "I am 55 years old. Am I supposed to get out of the union now, after 30 years of service, because the new membership, which had little to do with building the union, is ethnically different from me?" He had helped build a useful social institution, and had identified himself so completely with it that he found it hard to conceive of its continuing without him, and others like him.

And in a way he is right. Once the older generation passes, the ILGWU will be a different union. The tragedy is that the change is going on now, amid circumstances of growing resentment rather than of honor. Clearly, there is no easy answer.

The other problems are of equal difficulty, going far beyond the dilemmas of the ILGWU. It is startling to realize that in the quickened pace of the Negro effort to gain higher status in this country, the liberals (Dubinsky, Walter Reuther and even George Meany), rather than the reactionaries, are the ones who find themselves under the gun in the Negro community. Why does the NAACP pick on us? a friend in the needle trades recently asked me. Why doesn't it go after the building trades, the electrical unions (apart from Local 3 in New York) and other places where Negroes can't even get jobs, let alone leadership positions, because of union discrimination? One reason, he said, answering his own question, is that the NAACP is itself under fire from the more militant sections of the Negro community, and to maintain its own position it picks on the liberal unions because they are more vulnerable.

Wasn't this, I asked, exactly the reaction that the Jewish employers in the needle trades had 50 or more years ago, when the ILGWU was first trying to get a foothold in the industry? The Italian bosses ran worse sweatshops, they said, yet the unions pick on us because they can shame us in the Yiddish press. But precisely because the ILGWU was able to do so, the union succeeded in winning such victories as the establishment of arbitration councils under Louis D. Brandeis and other prominent Jewish spokesmen. Such tactics are bound to be repeated, and they are understandable.[77]

What is it, then, that the Negro community wants, and why so much more demandingly from its liberal friends? The fact is--and this is the "bite" in Hill's charges--that the Negroes are underrepresented in the leadership of many of the unions where they form a significant portion of the membership. In the case of these unions, what the Negroes want is "recognition" at the level of top leadership and a growing share of the spoils of office.

Demands such as these are usually voiced behind closed doors rather than openly, because they fly in the face of the American mythos that all individuals are equal and there is no such thing as a group identity. And they usually provoke the response (which Reuther, for one, has articulated) that this is Jim Crow in reverse, that a man ought to be judged on the basis of individual merit and not for any "extraneous" capacity. Yet there is a curious paradox in this "democratic" response. For one thing, the realistic political process in the United States, at least in the northern urban centers, has been one of ethnic groups advancing themselves precisely in this fashion: by organizing on bloc lines, electing their own kind, and using the patronage system to enhance the wealth and status of their group.

A second, more complex fact is that the basic existence of the labor movement is rooted in the conception of "group" rather than individual rights. Legally, the individual's protection on the job--where, for example, a union shop exists--is based on the "collective" contract, not on his individual right. (Thus, under an old NRLB ruling, employers are forbidden in certain circumstances to give individual workers merit wage increases on the ground that this may be a form of favoritism and would violate the group's rights). How far down does the group right extend *within* the union? Often a union recognizes certain "functional" groupings (for instance, the skilled trades in the United Auto Workers) as legitimate claimants to its own rights of representation. Does the Negro community--if it so organizes itself--have a legitimate claim for representation in group terms?

This has to be answered in a still wider context, which is the unspoken premise that "equality of opportunity" is an inadequate springboard from which the deprived sections of the Negro community--that is, the overwhelming majority--can advance economically and educationally. The phrase "equality of opportunity" has meaning if the competitors are roughly equal from the start (which is why there are handicaps in a horse race). But in many instances, even if a genuine equality of opportunity--for jobs, school places and the like--prevailed, the Negro would still lose out, with harmful social consequences for the community, simply because of extra, inherited handicaps he bears.

Admission to an elite public school like New York's Bronx High School of Science, for example, is by competitive examination, a matter purely of merit. Yet the number of Negro children in that school is scandalously low, and this failure to get on the first step of the educational escalator becomes a self-reinforcing vicious cycle as regards future opportunities. The solution is not necessarily a double standard, wherein Negro children with lesser qualifications are admitted on a quota basis; it may require the creation of special classes to coach bright but culturally deprived Negro children, in order to allow them to compete on a better footing.

But why even blink at the "double standard?" Why should intellectual merit alone be the determining basis for entry into an elite school? Ivy-league colleges such as Harvard, Yale and Columbia maintain geographical quotas in order to gain a representative national student body, on the ground that such mixtures are more valuable to the educational process than those selected by grades or college-board scores alone. On the same basis, a larger proportion of Negro children in the elite schools would both act as a spur to these children and "broaden" the experience of the other students.

All this may seem a far cry from my opening story; yet there is a consistency and a connection. The implicit demand of the Negro community is for special efforts and even special treatment in order to win basic social rights. It arises for the same reason that Tocqueville noted in all revolutionary movements: Increasingly radical demands are made not when one's lot goes from bad to worse, but when it goes from bad to better. For what may have been formerly accepted as destined and inevitable now, with the possibility of improvement in sight, becomes intolerable; and the demand for improvement quickens.

But the demand for special treatment is nothing new in the United States. It is the very basis for existence of the labor movement. The preamble to the Wagner Act points out that equality of bargaining is a necessary aspect of social justice, and in order to redress unequal power, the workers have to be given the added protections of the law to organize, to compel the employer to bargain, and so on. Farmers receive price supports, subsidies, mortgage insurance and the like. In economic and educational opportunity, the Negro is in a position of inequality, and the government is bounden to help him move ahead. But doesn't the trade-union movement have a *special* obligation to help redress the balance?

To return to my original tale, the tragedy of old institutions is that they are like Cheshire cats: The image remains after the body has disappeared. In the end, the image without the body is insubstantial, and quickly fades away. Or, to change the metaphor, and make the issue more plain: The "genius" of American democracy is that the society survived because the older ruling groups learned to share their power instead of resorting to class war, most notably in the acceptance by employers of collective bargaining in the factories. How curious that the labor leadership which benefited from that historical lesson should so plainly fail to see the virtue of applying it to its own institutions.

The New Leader, 46 (January 21, 1963):18-20.

42.   AFL-CIO SAVES NAACP

If the National Association for the Advancement of Colored People had to depend exclusively on the black public to save it from utter destruction, it would have had to hoist a black mourning flag as a symbol of its untimely demise. The NAACP chapters around the country, fell far short of raising the money needed to challenge a Mississippi court decision.

The Association has consecrated 67 years to a titantic struggle for civil rights, for elimination of restrictive covenants in home ownership, for abolition of lynching, for equal employment opportunity, for job equity, for elimination of segregation in the Armed Forces, and for desegregation of the public schools. It has won most of these battles through costly legal proceedings depleting its treasury.

The victories have helped to establish the claims of U.S. blacks to the guarantees of equality as vouchsafed by constitutional provisions. Without them, citizenship for black Americans would be devoid of substantive meaning. Without them, Lincoln's historic emancipation of the slaves would have meaning only as an abstract document to be preserved on library bookshelves for posterity.

The 14th and 15th Amendments which struck a final blow to slavery as an American social institution, would have been useless. The NAACP fought tooth and nail to safeguard the intent, the identity as well as the application of those constitutional warrants which sustain this nation's commitments to its black citizen and the principles of a democratic society.

Despite this long, costly and imposing history of the NAACP's unflagging struggle for justice and equality, 25 million blacks were not moved by the threat of its dismemberment posed by a Mississippi court ruling.

On Aug. 9, a Mississippi court awarded a hardware company $1.25 million in damages against the NAACP. The ruling was on a lawsuit filed by a group of white merchants who contended that they suffered severe financial losses because of a 1966 boycott organized by the NAACP.

That 25 million blacks could not or would not raise such a comparatively small amount is cause for serious introspection. It shows a lack of social responsibility; it points to a mournful state of moral bankruptcy lessening the validity of the eternal hymn sung to black pride.

The Association had to call on the AFL-CIO, a predominantly white federation of labor to raise the sum of $800,000 dollars, the balance needed to save it from dissolution.

With that SOS call outside its own membership of nearly half a million, the NAACP loses its status as a completely independent civil rights organization. It is a quasi entity. Its souls has been mortgaged.

Pittsburgh Courier, October 26, 1976.

43.   BENJAMIN HOOKS, EXECUTIVE DIRECTOR, NAACP, TO THE AFL-CIO CONVENTION, 1979

Once again it is an honor and a privilege for me to represent the NAACP at a meeting of the AFL-CIO. It is indeed a joy to be back. I was with you in your 12th Constitutional Convention at the Bonaventure two years ago at Los Angeles, and I am proud and happy to have the occasion to be with you again.

It is also a great personal pleasure to pay tribute to George Meany, your retiring President, who has given his life to the organized labor movement and who in his dedicated service to the rights of the worker has touched the hearts and improved the lives of millions.

George Meany is no ordinary man. He is a determined and vigilant fighter for the working man. He is a careful and deliberate champion of human and social justice. He is a close and dear friend of civil rights and a passionate advocate for the under class.

In history of the great men of the American scene who have shaped the world events and the national spirit, George Meany stands tall and prominent. What errors he may have made in the body politic, he has given attention to the special needs of the unionized worker. In this area he was not only always right, but he was always basically and always forthrightly right, and the best exemplification of labor leadership in my generation. In fact, his name has become synonymous with organized labor, and it is to him that we gladly extend our thanks, appreciation and congratulations. (Applause).

George Meany's position was not, as in the case of some political leaders, vulnerable. He could and he did make tough decisions and honest choices. He has been a leading human and civil rights advocate.

Every piece of civil rights legislation in this country was enacted with the active support and leadership of George Meany and organized labor. You name it--the Civil Rights Act of 1965, the Fair Housing Act of 1968, and the Equal Opportunity Employment Act of 1972. None of these acts would have become law without the strong and vigorous support not only of George Meany, but of the house of organized labor. For that America will always be grateful. (Applause).

He has been a strong advocate of women's rights, approving the addition of language in Title VII of the 1964 Civil Rights Act to prohibit discrimination because of sex. He was a leader of the fight for positive equal rights amendments, and has been in the forefront of the successful struggle to extend the time for states to ratify ERA until June, 1982.

Mr. Meany, along with Walter Reuther, then President of the CIO, was among the first persons to speak out in support of the landmark Supreme Court decision in Brown versus Board of Education 25 years ago, stating then that the Supreme Court has reaffirmed the basic philosophy of the American way of life, that all citizens are equal, regardless of race, creed or color. He also remarked that the decision against segregation in the public school system was a matter of simple justice.

We are grateful to the leadership of organized labor and George Meany when you backed the NAACP to survive the 1.6 million dollar judgment awarded to a group of merchants in Mississippi. And it was labor unions across the nation that helped put the word out that the threat of such court decisions, couched in the misapplication of secondary boycotts and the string of trade laws, could have a disastrous effect on organized labor's activities, to apply economic pressures on the labor unions. It is, therefore, with great pride that we recall that organized labor was prepared to put up $800,000 to make sure that the NAACP did not go out of business.

Our relationship with the labor movement is across the board. We have been given tremendous support by the NAACP Ad Hoc Labor Committee, co-chaired by Roosevelt Watts, Secretary-Treasurer of the Transport Workers Union of America, and William Oliver, Director of the United Auto Workers Fair Practices Department. And I want to publicly express the NAACP's deep appreciation to all the unions represented on that committee for the moral and financial support they have given NAACP.

We have also received extensive support and cooperation from the AFL-CIO Department of Civil Rights nationally and through our branches across the country. The NAACP has the good fortune to have your civil rights director, William E. Pollard, as an effective, active, elected member of our national Board of Directors.

Then I want to say a word about Lane Kirkland. I understand that you are to be the new President of AFL-CIO, and I want to congratulate you ahead of time. (Applause).

If this were an NAACP convention I would be definitely afraid to congratulate anybody until he had been elected and certified. But since you are an orderly and constructive convention and everything is in apple pie order, I have the privilege to congratulate you three days ahead of time. So, right on, Brother Kirkland, and may your tribe increase.

And to my good friend, Tom Donahue, and to the good people of the labor movement who had the good sense, intelligence and foresight to elect two of the finest men that labor has ever been able to afford to these important and prestigious jobs, we look forward to working hand in hand, heart in heart, arm in arm, to keep the cause of human progress and human rights moving forward.

Congratulations, again. I wish you well.

I appreciate the opportunity to be here because America's position today domestically and in the foreign affairs of our world is in serious trouble. Our position abroad as a great power has been substantially weakened just as we are caught up in a domestic income struggle of life and death. The candidates for public office and incumbents have recognized that inflation is a major concern of the American public, but too many see the solution to inflation in cutbacks in federal spending in social and human services. They countenance the solution to inflation in terms of massive layoffs of public employees.

Many people have forgotten that since Proposition 13 passed in California we have lost 134,000 public service jobs. These are men and women who have lost their jobs to the tax-cutting fever that not only cuts fat but cuts bone and muscle and gristle. Unless those of us who are concerned about progress come together and exercise our muscle to stop the conservative trend in America, all of us will soon be in serious trouble. (Applause).

As I look about this country today and I see the rise of the Nazi party, when I see the Ku Klux Klan, when I see the enemies of human progress everywhere raising their ugly heads, I know that this nation is in trouble. There is a round of conservatism which threatens to undo much of the progress that has been made. We seem to be living in an age when there are a lot of people who want to get all they can, call all they get, and then sit on the can.

We must be alert to that and remind them that America was built by the struggle, the sweat, the toil and the tears of millions of people who believe that not only must they make a way for themselves but they have an obligation to reach out and help others. It is one of the enduring triumphs of the labor movement that you have been great, because not only have you worked for yourselves, but you have not forgotten the rest of America. When you work for a minimum wage law, most of organized labor is not really affected, but you are affected in the sense that you are helping millions of others who have no way to express themselves.

I want to congratulate you for this spirit. I want to congratulate you for recognizing that quite often there has been bigotry and segregation and prejudice within the house of labor as it related to blacks and Hispanics and Asian Americans, and as it related to women in the work force. I want to congratulate your leadership for moving forthrightly to try to right those wrongs, to recognize them, to speak to them and to keep working until every vestige of discrimination and segregation, prejudice and bias should be run out of the house of labor; and you will continue to move forward recognizing that every American regardless of race, color, creed, sex or previous condition of servitude must have a right to make their contributions to the well-being of American life.

Therefore, today I call on the American labor movement, I call on Lane Kirkland and Tom Donahue and the presidents of the 105 international unions that find their homes in labor's house to help the NAACP to implement the full and broad meaning of the Weber decision. For in that Weber case a great union, the United Steelworkers and a company, the Kaiser Aluminum plant, forged a voluntary affirmative action plan that can bring into the mainstream of American life those who have been left out, those who have been put on the sidelines, those who have been forgotten, those who have been called unemployable, and those who have been called folk who didn't want to work.

I believe, Lane, that in the years ahead we can forge a working relationship that can reach out our arms and our hearts and embrace into it the whole panoply of the American working force so that every man and woman, boy and girl in this nation, who wants to be employed, can have a decent job and have a chance to make a living.

This is a job that I would call upon the American labor movement. Move into the ghettos of Harlem, the central areas of Watts, look at the south and west sides of Chicago. Go down into the barrios of Los Angeles, look at

the exploitation in such corporations as J. P. Stevens, and you understand
that we still have a long way to go.

In the words of the poet Robert Frost, "The woods are lovely, dark and
deep, but we have miles and miles to go and promises to keep before we sleep."

We must not let anything separate that fine historical alliance between
the NAACP and organized labor. We should not forget our heritage.

You know, it is easy for a people to get a little fat and lazy. As I
look around the labor movement, as I look around at some of my brothers and
sisters at the NAACP conventions, they have moved from the agony to the avenue
and from poverty to prosperity, from neck bones to T-bones and sometimes we
forget where we come from. I would beseech, brothers and sisters of the labor
movement, let's not forget the deprivation, the trials, the bloodshed of many
of our brothers and sisters who died to build the labor movement. They died
believing that the labor movement one day would speak to the problems of the
people. You are the heirs of the promises and you are also the keepers of the
dream and generations yet unborn will look back to see whether you were faithful to the promise.

I remember in Memphis, Tennessee, seeing leaders of the labor movement
being beat down in the street like wild dogs, but they would not let anybody
turn them around.

I remember the boss of Memphis, Tennessee, saying that labor organizations
would never come to pass in Memphis, Tennessee. He dared organized labor to
come across and they had the guts to fight until victory was won, and you must
not forget your history. You must not forget your heritage. You must not
forget where you come from.

We must not become so lazy and indifferent to the cries of labor, the
poverty-stricken and the powerless. We must not become so concerned about our
own power that we forget the brothers and sisters who are still laboring in an
environment where there is so little for too many. They look to us to reach
down and help them.

So, today I pledge for my part, and I am sure that Lane Kirkland pledges
on his part, that the NAACP and the labor movement, working together for the
passage of labor law reform acts in the Congress, will succeed. (Applause).

We shall work for the implementation of the Hawkins-Humphrey bill. We
shall work wherever that ugly monster raises its head to defeat the so-called
right-to-work laws. We have already been to Missouri to fight it, and we are
going to Louisiana to see that it is repealed because those who want to see us
progress have an amazing way to get good-sounding words such as "right to work."
We know they are a damnable lie and it has to be told.

We shall work together to defeat those who would hold us back, and to
march on until victory is won in the J. P. Stevens fight. We shall work to
make sure that there will be no exploitation of foreign labor at the expense
of American laboring men and women, to have a fair trade law that means that,
and to make sure that multinational corporate interests don't move the jobs
of American working people beyond the boundaries of the Atlantic and the
Pacific, in order to exploit cheap labor and bring the goods back here.

We shall work together for labor legislation; we shall work for the
election of decent candidates at the local, state and national level, and then
we are going to have a report card on them, to make sure that if they are
elected with our support, they will vote like they promised to vote. If they
don't do it, we are going to say to them, in the language of the Old Testament,
in Job, "The Lord giveth and the Lord taketh away, and if we give it to you
and you don't act right, we are going to take it away from you." (Applause).

We are tired of elected people who forget about us as soon as they get
in office and I don't care a rap whether it is a representative in a state
house or the President of the United States. They have got to be responsible
to the people who put them into office and do what they promised to do when
they are running.

We shall work to eliminate the Nazi Party and the Ku Klux Klan, that they
will not rear their ugly heads and divert the cause of Jesus Christ and change
the meaning of Judeo-Christian heritage, because we understand that those who
put on night sheets and pillow cases and ride down the streets with grips and
gloves and shotguns are trying to destroy the spirit of progress in America.
Even though they may come after blacks in the morning, remember, they will be
after labor in the afternoon.

So, they never seem to know for whom the bell tolls.

I believe that we can forge an alliance. I believe that we can build a momentum in this nation that will inexorably move forward.

I believe we are inextricably bound together and that the things that bring us together are stronger than the things that keep us apart.

So, in so many physical ways we must be prepared to move to New York and look at the beautiful Statue of Liberty that stands there in the harbor with that marvelous light beckoning to those poor and oppressed people from across the water, saying, "Give me your tired, your huddled masses, the young, to be free." Every night we must turn that statue on a pedestal so that not only she pleads to Europe and lands across the sea, but to the barrios of California, the ghettos of Watts and Harlem, and the Appalachian foothills and wherever people are suffering for freedom. We can say to Americans of every race, color and creed, "Give me your tired, yearning to be free." Then the day will come when from every mountainside, black and white Americans, female and male Americans, Jew and Gentile, will be able to sing, "My country 'tis of thee, sweet land of liberty. Of thee I sing."

God bless you. (Applause).

Proceedings of the Thirteenth Constitutional Convention of the AFL-CIO, Washington, D.C., November 15-20, 1979, pp. 198-203.

44. NAACP TO JOIN LABOR'S SOLIDARITY DAY PROTEST

DENVER--The NAACP voted enthusiastic endorsement of the AFL-CIO's Solidarity Day demonstration and called on more than 2,200 local branches to take part in the Sept. 19 rally in Washington "for jobs, justice and equity."

Nearly 5,000 delegates to the 72nd annual convention of the nation's oldest civil rights organization applauded and adopted a Solidarity Day "emergency resolution" that was brought to the floor at the opening session of the convention.

Other special resolutions adopted at the same session with the support of the NAACP board sharply criticized Reagan Administration budget cuts and pressed for renewal of the Voting Rights Act. A few hours later, delegates sat politely but silently through a speech by President Reagan.

The Solidarity Day resolution and a message from AFL-CIO President Lane Kirkland stressed the long and close alliance between the trade union and civil rights movements.

In endorsing Solidarity Day, the NAACP cited the attempts by the Reagan Adminstration to "diminish or destroy" programs to help "the aged, the poor and the disadvantaged."

The resolution, adopted by voice was without dissent, welcomed the initiative taken by the AFL-CIO and the federation's invitation to the NAACP and other concerned organizations "to participate in this timely demonstration."

UAW President Douglas A. Fraser, one of the speakers at a labor luncheon held during the convention, said his union is going all out to make Solidarity Day a success.[78]

"Let's make this the greatest demonstration since people of all walks of life and all colors marched in Washington in support of civil rights in 1963," Fraser urged.

Kirkland's letter to NAACP Executive Director Benjamin L. Hooks expressed confidence and determination that hard-won progress will not be reversed.

He cited the "fundamental changes" that the labor and civil rights alliance helped bring about.

"We have swept away the age-old legal codes and legislative sanctions that perpetuated racial discrimination in our schools, in housing, in public accommodations and in the world of work," Kirkland said.

Equality is closer to becoming "a fact of daily life, as well as of law," he noted. And labor remains committed "to affirmative action programs necessary to open doors previously shut to minorities and women."

But Kirkland voiced concern at signs of retreat. "Violations of civil rights laws that would have been unthinkable even a year ago have already begun to surface in states where our opponents eagerly anticipate the demise of the Voting Rights Act," he warned.

And there is suffering ahead, he said, "as the Administration seeks to close one door after another in the face of those who need jobs, food, housing and the educational, medical and social services their government will no longer supply."

The AFL-CIO is devoting its energies and resources to preserve a just society, Kirkland affirmed.

"We are heartened," he said, "to know that the NAACP is at our side."

AFL-CIO News, July 4, 1981.

45. ROY WILKINS PROVIDED STRENGTH DURING
CRITICAL CIVIL RIGHTS ERA

By Bayard Rustin

Roy Wilkins was a gentle man with a strong will. He was a man of keen judgment and open-mindedness, a man who was willing to change his mind. In a very real sense he was the statesman of the civil rights movement.

He was not a man of charisma. He was not a speaker who could electrify crowds with his rhetoric. His strength and his lasting contribution to the civil rights movement rested in his thoroughness, his quiet determination, and his organizational talents.

It was under Roy Wilkins' aegis that the true black Declaration of Independence was written. It was not a single document such as the one drafted by America's founding fathers. Rather, it was the immense project of legal proceedings and test cases which were initiated by the NAACP, which included the Brown v. Board of Education decision, and which continued far beyond it.

These decisions won rights for blacks in enclave after enclave of American society.

I first directly collaborated with Roy Wilkins during the planning stages of the 1963 March on Washington, which was initiated by A. Philip Randolph, the great black labor leader.

At first, relations between us were somewhat strained because Wilkins, a cautious man by nature, was troubled by my personal history of involvement in socialist and other radical causes. Yet despite initial misunderstandings, once we had begun working together and had come to understand that our goals for the black community were similar, we formed a close bond of friendship.

Despite his initial coolness to the idea of a March on Washington for civil rights and economic justice, once Roy Wilkins was convinced of the project's merits, he and the NAACP were to give the endeavour the strongest financial and organizational support it was to receive.

That the march was a great success was in large measure due to the organizational network Wilkins had established. And it was at Wilkins's insistence that Martin Luther King, Jr. was chosen to be the final speaker at that march and there delivered his historic "I Have a Dream" speech.

Because Roy Wilkins had a keen sense of what blacks wanted and because of his effectiveness in expressing the needs and desires of black Americans, he was frequently vilified by a minority of black extremists who sought to arrogate for themselves the right to speak in the name of all blacks.

Wilkins played a central role in leading black community opposition to the black power and separation movements which did so much to weaken black political power and to heighten racial tensions. He was a committed integrationist and he battled all the way with such extremists as Stokely Carmichael and H. Rap Brown, who today are mere footnotes in the history of black political life.

Wilkin's contributions were great and lasting. They have survived him, above all, in the form of the NAACP, the organization which he helped build into a network of 400,000 members. His stewardship of the NAACP encompassed the period of the 1950s and early '60s in which the civil rights movement made its greatest progress. He, likewise, led his organization in the more difficult and frequently disappointing period which was to follow.

The death of Roy Wilkins marks the final chapter in a great era in the history of the civil rights movement. It was an era of great visionaries and leaders--Martin Luther King, Jr., A. Philip Randolph, Whitney Young, and Roy Wilkins.

We are now, without question, firmly entrenched in a new era, an era whose outlines are not yet easy to perceive. The civil rights movement stands at the crossroads. Today, its influence is lower than at any point since its inception. It confronts the dangerous problems of a hereditary and ever-growing underclass of black poor, of economic inequality, and of an administration which is indifferent to the plight of the poor and working poor.

The civil rights movement is at a crossroads. One can only hope that new Roy Wilkinses will emerge to lead that movement down the proper path.

AFL-CIO News, September 19, 1981.

46. DELEGATES HIT REAGAN ON CIVIL RIGHTS RETREAT

Hollywood, Fla.--The AFL-CIO reaffirmed its strong commitment to ending discrimination and guaranteeing civil rights to all Americans.

The convention stressed in a resolution that the federation will continue to "vigorously oppose" attempts by the Reagan Administration to "annihilate" generations of civil rights progress.

So-called voluntary action in civil rights touted by conservatives will not work, the AFL-CIO said. The battle for equal opportunity, the resolution said, "can be won only through strong enforcement action by executive agencies and the courts."

The Administration, the AFL-CIO charged in its Executive Council report, has supplemented its attempts to wipe civil rights laws off the books with such tactics as lagging enforcement, appointing people with anti-civil rights stands to key positions to weaken enforcement, gutting of social, educational and equal employment programs, tearing down of affirmative action programs, foot-dragging on a wide variety of anti-discrimination cases, such as in housing, as well as damaging internal reorganizations of agencies and "regulatory reform" which amounts to gutting protective provisions.

Services available

Key sections of the resolution urged AFL-CIO affiliates to use the services of the federation's Civil Rights Committee and Dept. of Civil Rights, and to appoint union staff to work on programs to guarantee civil rights to all Americans.

The resolution called for support for "strong, viable civil rights agencies" such as the Equal Employment Opportunity Commission, the Office of Federal Contract Compliance Programs, the U.S. Commission on Civil Rights and the Justice Dept.

The resolution affirmed the need for non-discriminatory seniority systems, coupled with the use of the collective bargaining process to "open employment doors for women and minorities."

Employees should not be subject to discrimination or harassment in any form because of sexual orientation, the resolution said, calling for federal, state and local laws to eliminate such abridgement of civil rights.

The AFL-CIO urged affiliates to continue to support and strengthen educational programs to alert union members to the dangers posed to the labor movement and the nation by the propaganda of the Ku Klux Klan and other extremist and hate groups.

Community work

The value of the work in communities toward equal opportunity and social and economic justice by coalitions representing the interests of the labor movement and blacks, Hispanics and women was stressed in the resolution. The AFL-CIO will continue to support and work closely with the A. Philip Randolph Institute, the Labor Council for Latin American Advancement, the Coalition of Labor Union Women, Frontlash and the National Council of Senior Citizens.

Although a 25-year extension of the labor-supported Voting Rights Act was signed in 1982--in spite of repeated attempts by the Administration to weaken it--there are still pockets of resistance to the law in some parts of the country. The resolution pointed out that the Justice Department must be expected to pursue strong enforcement of the civil rights law.

At the same time, the AFL-CIO said, organized labor will be pressing voter registration and "get out the vote" programs to see that all Americans take advantage of this right.

Worst record

Federation Vice President John Sweeney, president of the Service Employees, branded the Reagan White House "the most anti-minority Administration in the history of our country" in calling for adoption of the resolution.

"We in the labor movement don't believe civil rights is a 'special interest,' it's all our interest," Sweeney said.

Fred O'Neal, an AFL-CIO vice president and head of the Actors & Artistes, urged all affiliates to work closely with the federation's Dept. of Civil Rights and to appoint staff members within their own unions.

Delegate John Sturdivant, executive vice president of the Government Employees, told the convention the resolution was important to the morale of many dedicated government workers whose efforts to do their jobs--carrying out civil rights laws--are being hampered by the anti-civil rights attitudes of the Reagan Administration.

Also speaking in support of the resolution were Delegates Marc Stepp, vice president of the Auto Workers; William Olwell, vice president of the Food & Commerical Workers; Evelyn Dubrow, vice president of the Ladies' Garment Workers, and Steve Edney, vice president of the Seafarers.

AFL-CIO News, October 15, 1983.

BLACK CIVIL RIGHTS LEADERS SPEAK BEFORE
AFL-CIO CONVENTIONS

47.   THURGOOD MARSHALL

*Special Counsel, National Association for the
Advancement of Colored People*

Mr. Meany, officers and friends: On behalf of the National Association for the Advancement of Colored People and those we represent, I want to say that it is more than a pleasure and a privilege to be here this afternoon. I have condensed what I want to say on paper for a very simple reason: that is the only way I know to get something over in short fashion. I hope you will bear with me in reading, because I for one consider this one of the most important periods in our lives insofar as the actual practice of the survival of democracy is concerned.

We in the NAACP salute the merged AFL and CIO as an example of further consolidation of forces seeking justice for all Americans. The additional strength from this merger will most certainly be used for the benefit of the country in general. A large measure of the success in the fight for human dignity that has come about has resulted from the recognition by organized labor of the need of extending labor's fight from inside the plant to the community in general. So, those of us in the fight for justice for Negro Americans can now depend upon an even stronger support from this new consolidated arm of organized labor.

While great progress toward removing racial injustice from American life has been made in the past two decades, we have found that the real task is and

will be the job of bringing established principles of law into everyday practice in local communities. Experience during the past two years has made it
clear to everyone concerned that real opposition to law and order is being
built up in areas of the South. This opposition is being built up on the
local level.

In backward areas of the South, the so-called "good people" of these
states have banded themselves together in organizations such as the White
Citizens Councils of Mississippi and other similar organizations. These local
groups have grown during the past six months into state organizations and will,
in short order cross state lines. While these organizations are set up for the
ostensible purpose of *"using every lawful means"* to preserve racial segregation
and other forms of discrimination including the denial of the right to vote.
In truth and in fact these organizations are creating the type of atmosphere
which now makes it possible to run Negroes out of business, to discharge
Negroes from employment and even to threaten and murder poor defenseless
Negroes in Mississippi. Of course, the White Citizens Councils deny any
responsibility for these murders. However, they cannot deny that they have
created the atmosphere of disregard for the established law of the land. This
atmosphere makes it possible for murderers to go free and unpunished. This
atmosphere of lawlessness must be changed.

The murder of Rev. G. W. Lee in Belzoni, Miss., for insisting on his right
to vote, the murder of Lamar Smith for insisting on the right to register and
the unprovoked murder of little Emmett Till has focused nation and worldwide
attention on Mississippi. These murders and other forms of intimidation point
up but definitely the complete absence of protection of civil rights for
minority groups in the South. Of course, those of us who have been in this
fight for any period of time have known of this lack of protection for Negroes
along with similar lack of protection of the rights of organized labor in many
areas of the South. It is a sad commentary to realize that many of us require
cold-blooded murders in order to rally us to action. The whole vicious program
against Negroes in the South will without doubt lead to further violence and
pressures against organized labor. One of the biggest jobs ahead for this
consolidated bloc of labor leaders is to organize the unorganized in the South.
Recent developments of lawlessness and opposition to voting and desegregation
of education makes it clear that organized labor must insist not only on
organizing in the South but must insist that it be done throughout the South
on a completely integrated basis without any compromise in the slightest detail
to the segregated policies prevalent in areas of the South.

The Negro in the South has refused to compromise on the question of racial
segregation in public education and other public facilities. Organized labor
must refuse to compromise in its organizing even in the South. Between the
two, we can rally other good forces of the South to the end that justice will
prevail.

However, the inability of the United States Department of Justice to bring
to justice those guilty of denying constitutionally protected rights to Negroes
in the South points up the need for adequate Federal legislation to protect all
of us in the exercise of our rights throughout the South. In other words, we
must have Federal protection of the right to live, to speak out, to organize,
and to insist upon our constitutionally protected rights. States such as
Mississippi have demonstrated their unwillingness as well as inability to
protect these rights. Therefore, we must use our combined strength to secure
from Congress adequate anti-lynching legislation, anti-poll tax legislation
and a strengthening of the Federal Civil Rights Statutes as a bulwark against
unprovoked violence in our every day work. We must, in addition, insist upon
strong FEPC legislation and necessary safeguards in Federal appropriations in
schools, housing and other facilities which will prevent Federal money from
being used to continue segregation in opposition to the law of the land.

It should also be noted that this vicious anti-Negro program extends to
white citizens who dare to speak out for justice for Negroes. It is highly
significant that in many areas of the deep South organized labor is being
bracketed in the same position as the Negro.

In this great expansion program of bringing great industries into the
South, organized labor has a more important task than ever before in seeing
to it that the plants involved are not only organized on a completely non-
racial basis but that the communities surrounding these plants are run in a

democratic fashion which today means, according to the law of the land, the absence of racial segregation. Anything short of this will merely mean that the expansion program in the South will become a further example of extended racial discrimination on an even larger scale. At this late date, it goes without saying that organized labor has a terrific stake in vigorously opposing racial segregation in community life whether it be in the North or South.

Despite all of the organized opposition to desegregation, it is important to remember that the solid South is broken for the first time on the question of race. As of today, twelve of the seventeen Southern states are now admitting Negroes to graduate and professional schools. Some thirty-odd private universities opened their doors to Negroes and it is just a short matter of time until all will be opened up.

It is also worthy of note that on the elementary and high school levels portions of either of the seventeen Southern states and the District of Columbia have moved toward integration of public schools and this has been accomplished in less than two years. This is the type of progress that has solidified the unreconstructed areas which are now more determined than ever to do everything possible to prevent integration of public schools.

In the latest drive toward desegregation as a result of recent Supreme Court decisions we have found that the good people of the South are either afraid or unwilling to oppose the pro-segregationist groups. We find that most of the Southern press is against integration of public schools. We find that church organizations for the most part will go no further than to merely adopt innocuous resolutions in favor of desegregation.

If the desegregation job is to be done, it will have to be done on the local level. If we are to be successful in this task we will need more than ever before the support of organizations such as those here represented who are in a position to transform resolutions into action programs on the local level.

The type of diehard opposition now being built up in the South will not disappear overnight and we cannot blow it away. It will only be removed by intelligent cooperative leadership of those Americans who have more at stake than others. Together we can do the job.

PRESIDENT MEANY: In your behalf I wish to thank Mr. Marshall for his address this afternoon and to express to him the opinion that the organized labor movement of this nation will be able to more effectively carry out its tradition of non-discrimination and of civil rights for all, and that through this merged organization we will be able to carry on the principles both organizations in the past have adhered to, and implement those principles much more effectively than we have in the past.

Proceedings of the First Constitutional Convention of the AFL-CIO, New York, December 5-8, 1955, pp. 107-09.

48. DOCTOR MARTIN LUTHER KING, JR.

President, The Southern Christian Leadership Conference

President Meany, distinguished platform associates, delegates to the Fourth Constitutional Convention of the AFL-CIO, ladies and gentlemen:

I need not pause to say how very delighted I am to be with you today. It is a privilege indeed to have the opportunity of addressing such a significant gathering. I have looked forward to being with you with great anticipation.

At one time I thought the forces of nature wouldn't cooperate with me enough in order to be here, for I left Los Angeles early this morning. When I got to the airport, I discovered that the flight that I was to take out of Los Angeles had been canceled because of weather in Dallas and in Atlanta. But I was lucky enough to get a flight through Chicago and certainly that was a joyous moment when I heard that I could go another way and get here. Of course the flight was rather bumpy all the way from Chicago to Miami and I was very happy when we landed.

I don't want to give you the impression that I don't have faith in God in the air. It is just that I have more experience with him on the ground.

But it is a delightful privilege to be here and I want to express my great pleasure to President Meany and the committee for extending the invitation.

Less than a century ago the laborer had no rights, little or no respect, and led a life which was socially submerged and barren.

He was hired and fired by economic despots whose power over him decreed his life or death. The children of workers had no childhood and no future. They, too, worked for pennies an hour and by the time they reached their teens they were worn-out old men, devoid of spirit, devoid of hope and devoid of self-respect. Jack London described a child worker in these words: "He did not walk like a man. He did not look like a man. He was a travesty of the human. It was a twisted and stunted and nameless piece of life that shambled like a sickly ape, arms loose-hanging, stoop-shouldered, narrow-chested, grotesque and terrible." American industry organized misery into sweat shops and proclaimed the right of capital to act without restraints and without conscience.

Victor Hugo, literary genius of that day, commented bitterly that there was always more misery in the lower classes than there was humanity in the upper classes. The inspiring answer to this intolerable and dehumanizing existence was economic organization through trades unions. The worker became determined not to wait for charitable impulses to grow in his employer. He constructed the means by which a fairer sharing of the fruits of his toil had to be given to him or the wheels of industry, which he alone turned, would halt and wealth for no one would be available.

This revolution within industry was fought mercilessly by those who blindly believed their right to uncontrolled profits was a law of the universe, and that without the maintainance of the old order catastrophe faced the nation.

History is a great teacher. Now, every one knows that the labor movement did not diminish the strength of the nation but enlarged it. By raising the living standards of millions, labor miraculously created a market for industry and lifted the whole nation to undreamed of levels of production. Those who today attack labor forget these simple truths, but history remembers them.

Labor's next monumental struggle emerged in the thirties when it wrote into federal law the right freely to organize and bargain collectively. It was now apparently emancipated. The days when workers were jailed for organizing, and when in the English Parliament Lord Macauley had to debate against a bill decreeing the death penalty for anyone engaging in a strike, were grim but almost forgotten memories. Yet, the Wagner Act, like any other legislation, tended merely to declare rights but did not deliver them. Labor had to bring the law to life by exercising its rights in practice over stubborn, tenacious opposition. It was warned to go slow, to be moderate, not to stir up strife. But labor knew it was always the right time to do right, and it spread its organization over the nation and achieved equality organizationally with capital. The day of economic democracy was born.

Negroes in the United States read this history of labor and find it mirrors their own experience. We are confronted by powerful forces telling us to rely on the good will and understanding of those who profit by exploiting us. They deplore our discontent, they resent our will to organize, so that we may guarantee that humanity will prevail and equality will be exacted. They are shocked that action organizations, sit-ins, civil disobedience, and protests are becoming our every day tools, just as strikes, demonstrations and union organization became yours to insure that bargaining power genuinely existed on both sides of the table. We want to rely upon the goodwill of those who oppose us. Indeed, we have brought forward the method of non-violence to give an example of unilaterial goodwill in an effort to evoke it in those who have not yet felt it in their hearts. But we know that if we are not simultaneously organizing our strength we will have no means to move forward. If we do not advance, the crushing burden of centuries of neglect and economic deprivation will destroy our will, our spirits and our hopes. In this way labor's historic tradition of moving forward to create vital people as consumers and citizens has become our own tradition, and for the same reasons.

This unity of purpose is not an historical coincidence. Negroes are almost entirely a working people. There are pitifully few Negro millionaires and few Negro employers. Our needs are identical with labor's needs, decent

wages, fair working conditions, livable housing, old age security, health and
welfare measures, conditions in which families can grow, have education for
their children and respect in the community. That is why Negroes support
labor's demands and fight laws which curb labor. That is why the labor-hater
and labor-baiter is virtually always a twin headed creature spewing anti-Negro
epithets from one mouth and anti-labor propaganda from the other mouth.

The duality of interests of labor and Negroes make any crisis which
lacerates you, a crisis from which we bleed. As we stand on the threshold of
the second half of the twentieth century, a crisis confronts us both. Those
who in the second half of the nineteenth century could not tolerate organized
labor have had a rebirth of power and seek to regain the despotism of that era
while retaining the wealth and privileges of the twentieth century. Whether
it be the ultra right wing in the form of Birch societies or the alliance which
former President Eisenhower denounced, the alliance between big military and
big industry, or the coalition of southern Dixiecrats and northern reactionaries
whatever the form, these menaces now threaten everything decent and fair in
American life. Their target is labor, liberals, and the Negro people, not
scattered "reds" or even Justice Warren, former Presidents Eisenhower and
Truman and President Kennedy, who are in truth beyond the reach of their crude
and vicious falsehoods. [79]

Labor today faces a grave crisis, perhaps the most calamitous since it
began its march from the shadows of want and insecurity. In the next ten to
twenty years automation will grind jobs into dust as it grinds out unbelievable
volumes of production. This period is made to order for those who would seek
to drive labor into impotency by viciously attacking it at every point of
weakness. Hard core unemployment is now an ugly and unavoidable fact of life.
Like malignant cancer, it has grown year by year and continues its spread. But
automation can be used to generate an abundance of wealth for people or an
abundance of poverty for millions as its human-like machines turn out human
scrap along with machine scrap as a by-product of production. Our society,
with its ability to perform miracles with machinery, has the capacity to make
some miracles for men--if it values men as highly as it values machines.

To find a great design to solve a grave problem labor will have to intervene in the political life of the nation to chart a course which distributes
the abundance to all instead of concentrating it among a few. The strength to
carry through such a program requires that labor know its friends and collabo-
rate as a friend. If all that I have said is sound, labor has no firmer friend
than the 20 million Negroes whose lives will be deeply affected by the new
patterns of production.

To say that we are friends would be an empty platitude if we fail to behave as friends and honestly look to weaknesses in our relationship. Unfortunately there are weaknesses. Labor has not adequately used its great power,
its vision and resources to advance Negro rights. Undeniably it has done more
than other forces in American society to this end. Aid from real friends in
labor has often come when the flames of struggle heighten. But Negroes are a
solid component within the labor movement and a reliable bulwark for labor's
whole program, and should expect more from it exactly as a member of a family
expects more from his relatives than he expects from his neighbors.

Labor, which made impatience for long-delayed justice for itself a vital
motive force, cannot lack understanding of the Negro's impatience. It cannot
speak with the reactionaries calm indifference, of progress around some obscure
corner not yet possible even to see. There is a maxim in the law--justice too
long delayed, is justice denied. When a Negro leader who has a reputation of
purity and honesty which has benefitted the whole labor movement criticizes it,
his motives should not be reviled nor his earnestness rebuked. Instead, the
possibility that he is revealing a weakness in the labor movement which it can
ill afford, should receive thoughtful examination. A man who has dedicated
his long and faultless life to the labor movement cannot be raising questions
harmful to it any more than a lifelong devoted parent can become the enemy of
his child. The report of a committee may smother with legal constructions a
list of complaints and dispose of it for the day. But if it buries a far
larger truth it has disposed of nothing and made justice more elusive. Discrimination does exist in the labor movement. It is true that organized labor
has taken significant steps to remove the yoke of discrimination from its own
body. But in spite of this, some unions, governed by the racist ethos, have

contributed to the degraded economic status of the Negro. Negroes have been
barred from membership in certain unions, and denied apprenticeship training
and vocational education. In every section of the country one can find local
unions existing as a serious and vicious obstacle when the Negro seeks jobs or
upgrading in employment. Labor must honestly admit these shameful conditions,
and design the battle plan which will defeat and eliminate them. In this way,
labor would be unearthing the big truth and utilizing its strength against the
bleakness of injustice in the spirit of its finest traditions.

How can labor rise to the heights of its potential statesmanship and
cement its bonds with Negroes to their mutual advantage?

First: Labor should accept the logic of its special position with respect
to Negroes and the struggle for equality. Although organized labor has taken
actions to eliminate discrimination in its ranks, the standard for the general
community, your conduct should and can set an example for others, as you have
done in other crusades for social justice. You should root out vigorously
every manifestation of discrimination so that some internationals, central
labor bodies or locals may not besmirch the positive accomplishments of labor.
I am aware this is not easy nor popular--but the 8 hour day was not popular
nor easy to achieve. Nor was outlawing anti-labor injunctions. But you accomplished all of these with a massive will and determination. Out of such
struggle for democratic rights you won both economic gains and the respect of
the country, and you will win both again if you make Negro rights a great
crusade.

Second: The political strength you are going to need to prevent automation from becoming a moloch, consuming jobs and contract gains, can be multiplied if you tap the vast reservoir of Negro political power. Negroes given
the vote, will vote liberal and labor because they need the same liberal
legislation labor needs. To give just an example of the importance of the
Negro vote to labor, I might sight the arresting fact that the only state in
the South which repealed the "right-to-work" law is Louisiana. This was
achieved because the Negro vote in that state grew large enough to become a
balance of power, and it sent along with labor to wipe out anti-labor legislation. Thus, support to assist us in securing the vote can make the difference
between success and defeat for us both. You have organizing experience we
need and you have an apparatus unparalleled in the nation. You recognized five
years ago a moral opportunity and responsibility when several of your leaders,
including Mr. Meany, Mr. Dubinsky, Mr. Reuther and Mr. MacDonald and others,
projected a two-million dollar campaign to assist the struggling Negroes
fighting bitterly in handicapped circumstances in the South. A $10,000 con-
tribution was voted by the ILGWU to begin the drive, but for reasons unknown
to me, the drive was never begun. The cost to us in lack of resources during
these turbulent, violent years, is hard to describe. We are mindful that many
unions thought of as immorally rich, in truth have problems in meeting the
budget to properly service their members. So we do not ask that you tax your
treasuries. Instead, we ask that you appeal to your members for one dollar
apiece to make democracy real for millions of deprived American citizens. For
this you have the experience, the organization and most of all, the understanding.

If you would do these two things now in this convention--resolve to deal
effectively with discrimination and provide financial aid for our struggle in
the South,--this convention will have a glorious moral deed to add to an
illustrous history.

The two most dynamic and cohesive liberal forces in the country are the
labor movement and the Negro freedom movement. Together we can be architects
of democracy in a South now rapidly industrializing. Together we can retool
the political structure of the South, sending to Congress steadfast liberals
who, joining with those from Northern industrial states, will extend the fron-
tiers of democracy for the whole nation. Together we can bring about the day
when there will be no separate identification of Negroes and labor. There is
no intrinsic difference as I have tried to demonstrate. Differences have been
contrived by outsiders who seek to impose disunity by dividing brothers because
the color of their skin has a different shade. I look forward confidently to
the day when all who work for a living will be one with no thought to their
separateness as Negroes, Jews, Italians or any other distinctions.

This will be the day when we shall bring into full realization the

American dream--a dream yet unfulfilled. A dream of equality of opportunity, of privilege and property widely distributed; a dream of a land where men will not take necessities from the many to give luxuries to the few, a dream of a land where men will not argue that the color of a man's skin determined the content of his character; a dream of a nation where all our gifts and resources are held not for ourselves alone but as instruments of service for the rest of humanity; the dream of a country where every man will respect the dignity and worth of human personality--that is the dream.

And as we struggle to make racial and economic justice a reality, let us maintain faith in the future. We will confront difficulties and frustrating moments in the struggle to make justice a reality, but we must believe somehow that these problems can be solved.

There is a little song that we sing in the movement taking place in the South. It goes something like this, "We shall overcome. We shall overcome. Deep in my heart I do believe we shall overcome." And somehow all over America we must believe that we shall overcome and that these problems can be solved. They will be solved before the victory is won.

Some of us will have to be scarred up, but we shall overcome. Before the victory of justice is a reality, some may even face physical death. But if a physical death is the price that some must pay to free their children and their brothers from a permanent life of psychological death, then nothing could be more moral. Before the victory is won some more will have to go to jail. We must be willing to go to jail and transform the jails from dungeons of shame to havens of freedom and human dignity. Yes, before the victory is won, some will be misunderstood. Some will be dismissed as dangerous rabble rousers and agitators. Some will be called Reds and Communists merely because they believe in economic justice and the brotherhood of man. But we shall overcome.

I am convinced that we shall overcome because the arc of the universe is long but it bends toward justice. We shall overcome because Carlisle is right when he says, "No lie can live forever." We shall overcome because William Cullen Bryant is right when he says, "Truth crushed to earth will rise again." We shall overcome because James Russell Lowell was right when he proclaimed; "Truth forever on the scaffold, wrong forever on the throne, yet that scaffold sways the future."

And so if we will go out with this faith and this determination to solve these problems, we will bring into being the new day and the new America. When that day comes, the fears of insecurity and the doubts clouding our future will be transformed into radiant confidence, into glowing excitement to reach creative goals and into an abiding moral balance where the brotherhood of man will be undergirded by a secure and expanding prosperity for all.

Yes, this will be the day when all of God's children, black men and white men, Jews and Gentiles, Protestants and Catholics will be able to join hands all over this nation and sing in the words of the old Negro spiritual: "Free At Last, Free At Last. Thank God Almighty We Are Free At Last."

Thank you.

(Standing ovation).

PRESIDENT MEANY: I am sure it would be superfluous for me to tell Dr. King we appreciate his address. I am sure everyone here is moved by his splendid outline of a philosophy for human rights and human decency.

We appreciate beyond words his presence here and his most stirring address on a subject dear to our hearts. Thank you very much, Dr. King.

Proceedings of the Fourth Constitutional Convention of the AFL-CIO, Miami Beach, Fla., December 7-13, 1961, Vol. I, pp. 282-89.

49.   ROY WILKINS

Executive Director
National Association for the Advancement
of Colored People

Thank you, George Meany, and thank you, delegates to the Convention.
I am pleased to bring greetings to the delegates to this Convention of
the American Federation of Labor and Congress of Industrial Organizations from
the National Association for the Advancement of Colored People.

I bring the thanks of our members for the clear pronouncements of President Meany and for the invaluable service of the AFL-CIO and its skilled
legislative staff to the work of the Leadership Conference on Civil Rights.
Also for the support labor has given at the major political party conventions
to the civil rights items in the platforms. In addition, many units of
organized labor have aided campaigns on the local level involving state and
municipal projects for housing, health, public education, employment and welfare. We are proud of this partnership in the civil rights field.

We join labor in its apprehension over the beginning of a trend away from
liberalism. The civil rights campaigns, like those in behalf of the prime
goals of organized labor, cannot make progress in an area of suppression and
reaction.

We are sure you share with us an uneasiness at the racial crisis that has
been presented sharply by the civil disorders and riots of the past four
summers, the worst of which was the summer of 1967. Much more is at stake than
a mere be-kind-and-be-just-to-the-Negro situation. The future of democratic
government could well be at stake also.

This is a time, then, for plain talk--not diatribes, but truth, unpleasant
though it may be.

Organized religion is facing up to the challenge. By and large, the courts
are recognizing a new day. The universities are taking a fresh look. When we
see that the National Association of Manufacturers, no less, is concerned about
Negro unemployment and is pushing a program to open doors to Negro applicants,
we realize that the business community, a large part of which hitherto has
remained indifferent, is awake and stirring on wholly new paths of activity.

The executive branch of government, along with the judicial has made a
definite turn. Only the legislative branch has been reluctant. On riot control it has been eager and determined, generous with appropriations, united
and expeditious. On other matters in the civil rights and general welfare
fields it has been slow, carping, partisan, parsimonious and hostile. One has
only to examine congressional action on the education bills, anti-poverty
legislation, the iniquitous Social Security Bill.

And here we have a bill that the AFL-CIO and other organizations, including my own, I am proud to state, has condemned and asked the senators to reject
the conference report. In the words of your telegram from President Meany to
every senator, this is a bill that ought to be rejected because the provisions
in the welfare section, the provision regarding mothers, leave no alternative,
as the *New York Times* said, to either sterilize the mothers or starve the
children. We can't have this kind of legislation in the Congress of the
United States. Now, by this sort of procedure the riots and events of last
summer persuaded apparently our Congress not only to deny a reward to rioting
but to abdicate their proper role in the forward movement of our country.
They have definitely forgotten that the rioters are but a small fringe of the
country.

Each American, in this crucial time, will have to live with his conscience
and the collective conscience of the organized bodies of which he is a member.

In the rapid movement of the currents of democracy, no institution is
more sensitive to change than the American labor movement. Although it may
choose, for reasons which seem good to it, not to act at certain times,
nevertheless, it is not unaware of developments.

The crisis of our day involves the denial of equality of opportunity,
citizenship and human rights to our Negro citizens more than a century after
they were emancipated from slavery.

As far as the AFL-CIO is concerned, the stark, bald issue is jobs. As
far as causes of riots go, the stark, bald issue is jobs.

In many cases unions control access to employment, so equal employment opportunities for Negroes falls into the AFL-CIO orbit. As we ask ourselves why we had riots in more than 50 cities and what can be done to prevent this from tearing our country apart, let us look frankly at some records of the past business-as-usual years in the job market.

At the outset I wish to state in the clearest possible terms that nothing --absolutely nothing--ever done by the NAACP is intended to be anti-labor; but it is pro-Negro. To the degree that our number of priorities are different, to that degree will there be some within organized labor who misunderstand, either honestly or otherwise, our activities on behalf of Negro wage earners.

We are, of course, aware that some progress in eliminating discriminatory practices within organized labor has taken place since the merger in 1955, but given the worsening job crisis of the Negro worker and the racial turmoil in our urban centers, we are forced to conclude that the rate of progress has been far too slow. The specifics are not cheerful items.

In Cleveland, for example, in 1966 at the end of a decade of demonstrations, the filing of complaints, of negotiations with union representatives and the attempts to secure enforcement of federal executive orders, the five major craft locals in the building trades, according to data revealed by the U.S. Commission on Civil Rights had exactly four Negro apprentices. This is certainly, in the words of the Supreme Court, deliberate speed.

The assumption that the rate of progress is minimal in securing the admission of Negroes into skilled craft unions is further confirmed by the August 1967 report of the U.S. Department of Labor entitled "Manpower, Automation, Research Monograph No. 6," and it contains this significant sentence:

"Indeed the 1960 census showed only 2,191 Negro apprentices in all the trades throughout the country. That figure was one more than had been recorded in the 1950 census ten years before."

Cincinnati was the scene of racial disorders last summer. On July 24, 1967, the U.S. Department of Justice filed a lawsuit against Local 212 of the International Brotherhood of Electrical Workers in the U.S. District Court in Cincinnati charging them with excluding Negroes from employment. The plaintiff was Anderson L. Dobbins, a college graduate and a certified journeyman electrician. Although the Equal Employment Opportunity Commission found reasonable cause, the local union refused to admit Mr. Dobbins, and although he served as an electrician in the U.S. armed forces, and in private industry for more than ten years, he stands rejected by Local 212.

In the summer of 1963, the NAACP and other Civil Rights organizations picketed the construction site of Barringer High School in Newark, New Jersey, protesting the exclusion of Negro workers there. A year later they picketed also the Rutgers University Law School Extension construction site in Newark, and finally, the State University of New Jersey on February 9, 1965, filed formal complaints against the five locals of the International Association of Bridge, Structural and Ornamental Iron Workers. The local unions eventually entered into a stipulation with the commission in December of 1966 and agreed to admit Negroes for the first time into the union-controlled apprenticeship training programs.

But four years after the initial demonstrations, three years after the filing of complaints with the Division against Discrimination, and a year after a stipulation that the locals would admit Negroes, not a single Negro has been admitted into any of the five locals. Nor is there a single Negro employed within this union's jurisdiction in the extensive public and private construction in Northern New Jersey.

We can anticipate with the new public construction beginning next year on West Market Street in Newark, and on the edge of the Negro ghetto, just what the feeling will be, and the question inevitably arises, "What did we learn from the terrible riot in Newark last year?"

The Brotherhood of Railway and Steamship Clerks had traditionally operated segregated locals in many northern as well as southern cities, but they now have changed all of that. Union agreements provided for separate racial classifications which limited Negro job mobility and the seniority of the Negro members, but in 1966, after a request and a threat of a suit, the Brotherhood of Railway Clerks abolished several segregated local lodges. But they did this by reclassifying the traditional Negro job classifications and declaring them to be within the jurisdiction of the white local. In practice

this meant, for example, that Negro freight handlers were replaced by less
senior white workers who had been in the all-white baggage clerks seniority
line.   In other words, we will abolish the segregated local but now everybody's
seniority will count, and the whites who had seniority over here in their
separate local have more than Negroes that have been abolished and taken in,
and they have no seniority in the white local, and therefore their jobs are
out.
       Another example is to be found in the Brotherhood of Locomotive Firemen.
This union did not remove the provision in its constitution that banned
Negroes from membership until only three years ago, 1964.   But as Arthur M.
Ross, Commissioner of Labor Statistics observed, and I quote:

       "The Brotherhood of Locomotive Firemen -- removed a Negro
       exclusion clause from its constitution in 1964, after the
       railroad 'work rules' arbitration had made it virtually certain
       that few, if any, additional firemen would ever be hired on
       American railroads."

Other industries, of course, where unions continued over-discriminatory
practices a decade after the merger were in paper and pulp manufacturing,
chemicals, oil refining, skilled metal trades, and so forth.
       Now, the record in Cleveland serves to point up all of this.   The record
of repeated efforts of Negro workers to breach the color bar in craft unions
in Cleveland, Ohio, in the decade following the merger illustrates the limited
nature of the progress that has been made.
       In 1955 charges were filed with the Cleveland Community Relations Board
against Local 38 of the International Brotherhood of Electrical Workers, and
this local traditionally controls all of the work, electrical work in the
Cleveland area.
       Although it did not agree to accept, after being ordered to admit workers,
it did not agree to accept the plaintiff in the case, but it did accept some
other Negroes as members of their race.
       But in 1966, eleven years after the original charges were filed with the
Cleveland Community Relations Board, Local 38 has admitted exactly two Negro
electricians to work in Cleveland.
       As a result of the mass picketing at the Cleveland Municipal Mall Con-
struction site, an agreement was entered into on August 4, 1963, between
Plumbers Local 55, the City of Cleveland, the United States Department of
Labor and the United Freedom Movement, consisting of local civil rights groups.
Local 55 agreed to admit Negroes and to sign labor agreements with the Negro
owned contracting companies -- they did admit one Negro plumbing contractor
with his four journeymen but that is as far as they went.   The Cleveland story
was wrapped up in a hearing before the United States Commission on Civil
Rights in Cleveland in April, 1966, and the lineup reads something like this:

       The International Brotherhood of Electrical Workers, Local 38 with a
total membership of 1258 had 2 Negro members.
       Ironworkers Union, Local 7, with a total membership of 1786 had no Negro
members.
       Plumbers Union, Local 55, with a total membership of 1482 had three
Negro members.
       Pipefitters Union, Local 36, with a total membership of 1319 had one
Negro member.
       Sheet Metal Workers Union, Local 65, with a total membership of 1077 had
45 Negro members.

       The Sheet Metal workers were far in advance in numbers and in proportion
to the others.
       Now, my friends, we find that going west might have been good for Horace
Greeley but it wasn't very good for Negroes in the labor movement.
       Recent data from the Bureau of Census indicate that there are now more
Negroes in the San Francisco-Oakland East Bay Area than there are in Birmingham, Alabama.   The rate of long-term unemployment among Negro males in Oakland
exceeds the general rate of unemployment for the entire nation during the
Great Depression of the 1930's.   In every survey of the national scene, Oak-
land is listed as a "powder keg" city.   But the November 1967, report of the
U.S. Commission on Civil Rights details the exclusion of Negroes in union

controlled employment in the federally-financed Bay Area Rapid Transit System
(BART) construction which will employ approximately 8,000 people at peak construction times.   This is a one billion dollar project.   The Office of Federal
Contract Compliance reports that as of May, 1967, there was not a single Negro
among the 106 electricians, ironworkers and plumbers engaged on BART construction.

In the coming year more than $76.5 billion will be spent nationally for
construction, much of it in the public sector.   How much of this huge sum will
go into the paychecks of Negro workers?

At the present time NAACP attorneys are representing Negro workers in five
separate court suits in Alabama against the U.S. Steel Corp. and the United
Steelworkers of America on the issue of separate racial lines of seniority and
promotion.   Although these cases were originally filed with the Equal Employment Opportunity Commission which found "reasonable cause" to credit the
allegations in the complaints, both the company and the union have thus far
failed to comply with the law in eliminating discriminatory promotion procedures
based on race.   After a decade of attempting to resolve this matter by fraternal discussion and negotiation, as a last resort the NAACP has had no choice
but to file suit.

A similar record might be traced with other unions maintaining discriminatory classification systems involving seniority and job promotions.

An illustration that comes to mind is Crown-Silver Box in Bogalusa,
Louisiana.   But there has been progress.

For example, on May 18, 1966 at a meeting of the New York Furriers Union
Joint Council, affiliated with the Amalgamated Meat Cutters and Butcher Work-
men, the 40 year-old Greek Fur Workers local was dissolved.   The 1500 local
union members transferred to other locals affiliated to the Furriers Joint
Council as a result of action by the international union to comply with Title
VII, the Equal Employment Opportunity section of the Civil Rights Act of 1964.

Other AFL-CIO locals could well imitate the Amalgamated Meat Cutters and
some other labor organizations which have successfully acted to disband
nationality locals.

A list of unions which have gone beyond mere ritualistic gesture on racial
matters would include the American Federation of Teachers which successfully
eliminated segregated locals by offering its southern locals the choice of
either integrating or disaffiliating; the United Packinghouse Workers of
America which even in the Deep South has carried out its commitment to racial
equality at the work place as well as within the union; the American Federation
of State, County and Municipal Workers and the Retail, Wholesale and Department
Store Union.   Also, of course, the great industrial unions whose good policies
and acts serve to highlight the derelictions cited.

What is urgently needed now is not simply a repetition of previous commitments to justice, but rather a new definition, a new standard that will
require a new set of enforcement procedures within affiliated unions themselves.
Minimal change in labor and in American life generally will no longer suffice.
What might have been regarded as progress in 1940, 1950, or even 1960, can no
longer be so regarded.

For the most part voluntary compliance does not work.   This is true for
labor unions as it is true for industrial corporations.   There now exists a
comprehensive body of civil rights law relating to discrimination in employment.   The American Federation of Labor-Congress of Industrial Organizations
and its affiliated international unions have a clear obligation to secure much
greater compliance with this body of law than has been obtained in the past.

In conclusion, I would like to say that I lay this record in your lap
because the errant children of the AFL-CIO, the international unions and their
locals are your children.

They have thus far chosen to ignore the forthright resolutions of your
council and of this convention.   If they have not ignored what you have voted
and what your chief, George Meany, repeatedly has called for, they have paid
only lip service to the policy.   It has been a conversation piece.   It has
been observed by powerful and important unions only in the breach, or, at
best, with a grudging, foot-dragging tokenism.   The proud policy of the AFL-
CIO is not being followed.

Some of them are deliberately ignoring and some of them are ignoring it
through a shoulder-shrugging gesture.   But the Negro citizen and the Negro
children of the country are determined that employment will be opened by

massive employment activity by the government itself, but some by a change in
labor practices. Negroes must have more than bread and clothing and shelter.
They must have access to the comfort, the security, and even the affluence
that is America. On this there is now no debate. The debating and the backing
and filling days are over. The techniques of unfilled promises and of post-
ponement are transparent and useless in today's hard necessities.

The AFL-CIO can rise to this challenge honestly, as it has to many others.
New thinking, embracing all Americans in the work force at all levels, is
required.

Failure to devise a fresh formula is unthinkable; the very future of a
whole people and their system of enterprise and of individual liberty rests
upon a turning and upon a victory. Thank you.

(Applause).

PRESIDENT MEANY: I wish to thank the Director, Roy Wilkins, of the NAACP
and to say to him that we are completely aware of the problem that he poses,
that we have a civil rights department, that we have the cooperation of practically every national and international union in this field. However, you
will not change conditions over night. We keep trying. And in a good many of
the organizations we have a problem of securing Negro boys as apprentices to
take the test that these organizations prescribe and which they have prescribed
for many years.

I can say to Mr. Wilkins that we in the AFL-CIO are not satisfied with the
progress that we have made. I feel we are making progress--perhaps not fast
enough--but I can assure him that the AFL-CIO and its national unions will continue to apply ourselves to this problem, and I want to say to him, very
frankly, that I, for one, do not resent in any way the report that he has given
us today. He presents us with a challenge I think we have to meet, and we shall
meet that challenge. Thank you very much.

(Applause).

Proceedings of the Seventh Constitutional Convention of the AFL-CIO, Bal
Harbour, Fla., December 7-12, 1967, Vol. I, pp. 419-27.

50. MARY MOULTRIE

President, Local 1199B, RWDSU

President Meany, members of the Executive Council, distinguished guests,
and delegates of this great convention. First, I want to tell you how happy
and proud I am to be able to speak to this great convention on behalf of the
hospital workers in Charleston, South Carolina.

I want to express our heartfelt thanks and appreciation to the officers
of the AFL-CIO, to the officers of our international union, the Retail, Wholesale and Department Store Union, and to the leaders and members of the
hundreds of international and local unions in the AFL-CIO for the moral and
financial support they gave us during our great struggle in Charleston.

Hundreds of our brothers and sisters from AFL-CIO unions marched side by
side with us on the picket line. AFL-CIO members in South Carolina went to
jail with us. In addition, we will always remember the help and guidance we
received from Brother Bill Kircher, the national organizational director of
the AFL-CIO, who was with us in Charleston as the personal representative of
the AFL-CIO Executive Council.

Nor will we ever forget the fact that the threat by the Longshoremen's
International Union to close down the port of Charleston in support of our
fight played a very important role in helping us achieve our victory.

We won in Charleston. And we won the hard way. We were forced to strike
for 100 days just for the right to have a union. We suffered and sacrified
to put an end to poverty wages of $1.30 an hour. We marched and we went to
jail because we were sick and tired of being sick and tired.

We, 400 hospital workers--almost all of us women, and all of us black--
were compelled to go on strike so that we could win the right to be treated

as human beings. In this struggle, we had to take on more than just the managements of two hospitals.

We had to fight the entire power structure of the state of South Carolina. And when I say the entire power structure, I don't only refer to the Governor, or to Charleston's not-so-distinguished congressman, Mendel Rivers, or that great defender of the 18th century, Senator Strom Thurmond. I'm talking about the textile bosses, the men who really run our state, as well as all of the other reactionary racist forces which have kept South Carolina as the state with the lowest literacy rate, the lowest per capita income, and the lowest percentage of unionized workers in the entire nation.

But that's not the whole story. We had to face 1,200 national guardsmen armed with tanks and bayonets, and hundreds of state troopers. All because 400 black women dared to stand up and say we just were not going to let anybody turn us around.

And we never stopped fighting for a single day. We suffered. But we kept on marching. More than 1,000 of us went to jail. But we kept on fighting. The hospital bosses and their supporters thought we'd just die out after a day or two of marching. They thought we'd just give up and scratch our heads and shuffle back to those hospitals. They thought we'd just say, "sorry, boss," and put those handkerchiefs back on our heads. Well, they sure were in for a big disappointment. Because we learned in the course of our struggle that only the strong survive. And we sure are strong today in Charleston.

And as a result, something new and beautiful has come to Charleston--a powerful, democratic union--Local 1199B.

Of course, it would be ridiculous to think that we did it all by ourselves. Nothing could be further from the truth. We received support and assistance from decent-minded people all over America. First, from our own black community--from our ministers, our students, our old people and our young people. Everyone in the black community made our cause their cause. They struggled with us and they suffered alongside us. Because like hospital workers, they, too, were sick and tired of being sick and tired. They joined us in daily marches and nightly rallies. They joined us in standing up to the tanks, to the armored vehicles, the tear gas and the mace. They did so because they shared our determination to be free. And together we faced this armed strength with our bodies, with our souls and with our hearts--unarmed in a non-violent demonstration, massively organized and militantly conceived in the true spirit of Dr. Martin Luther King.

And we could not have survived if it had not been for the wholehearted support and the brilliant leadership provided by the Southern Christian Leadership Conference headed by Reverend Ralph David Abernathy. Reverend Abernathy, his entire staff and Mrs. Coretta Scott King, who is the honorary chairman of our hospital organizing campaign, provided the leadership for a massive boycott in which black people refused to buy anything except food and medicine at white-owned stores. Many of our supporters refused to even buy a newspaper during the boycott. Others went without needed clothing and shoes. But they just kept on keeping on.

And we could not have survived and we could not have won if it had not been for the tremendous support given us by organized labor through the AFL-CIO Executive Council's Charleston Strike Fund. Unions from all over America sent us contributions to help feed the strikers and help us pay the rent. You know when the announcement was made that the AFL-CIO Executive Council was setting up the Charleston Strike Fund with a startling contribution of $25,000, the South Carolina papers called you outside agitators. I want to say here what we said then. We believe from the bottom of our hearts that we hospital workers have more in common with you steel workers in Pittsburgh, with you packing house workers in Chicago, with you clothing workers in New York City, with you transport workers in Philadelphia than we have with the hospital bosses and the people who own and run the textile mills in South Carolina.

So you can see we won because we were able to forge a coalition of union power and soul power--a winning combination of organized labor and the civil rights movement.

And we won wage increases ranging from 30 to 70 cents an hour for all state workers. This adds up to $10 million in wage increases in the pockets of poor black and poor white workers all over South Carolina. We won a real grievance procedure, a credit union through which union dues will be deducted.

In other words, we have won de facto union recognition. And we are building
a strong, effective, democratic union. Local 1199B. And we intend to keep on
fighting until we have all the same rights, the same wages, the same benefits
as all other unionized workers up north.

Right now we are conducting a voter registration campaign together with
the SCLC, and I am happy to report to you that since the strike we have
registered more than 1,500 new voters in Charleston, South Carolina.

We suffered much. But we learned a great deal. We learned that poor
people do not have to suffer endless abuse and punishment without fighting
back. We learned that when we stick together, when we are united, we are
somebody. We learned that when workers are ready to fight for their rights,
other workers will come to their support. We learned that we have the capacity to fight, the willingness to suffer for what is right and in the course
of this struggle, we have acquired the experience, the dedication to become
leaders and true fighters for freedom.

We intend to continue to build our union behind the banner of the AFL-CIO.
We intend to move forward to build an organization of hospital workers everywhere to follow our example of rallying poor and exploited workers everywhere
to organize into unions, and to unite all workers, black and white, into one
union.

A year ago, nobody ever heard of us. We were forgotten women, second
class citizens. We worked as nurse's aides. We cleaned the floors. We
prepared the food in the hospitals. And if it had not been for the union, we
would still be forgotten people.

Today we are somebody. Thanks to the AFL-CIO, thanks to the SCLC, thanks
to the RWDSU, thanks to Local 1199, our brothers and sisters in New York City,
we are not alone. And we are not afraid.

We have demonstrated to the city of Charleston, to the state of South
Carolina, and to people all over America that we can and we will overcome.
And nobody, just nobody, is going to turn us around. And Charleston and the
rest of the south had better believe it.

PRESIDENT MEANY: May I add my appreciation for the thoughts expressed by
Miss Moultrie, to all of the international unions, local and central bodies,
and the state feds throughout the country, who joined with us in helping these
workers achieve a trade union which will improve their conditions in the
future. Thank you very much, Miss Moultrie.

Proceedings of the Eighth Constitutional Convention of the AFL-CIO, Atlantic
City, N.J., October 2-7, 1969, Vol. I, pp. 198-202.

51. BENJAMIN HOOKS

Executive Director, NAACP

Thank you, Mr. Meany, for that very generous introduction. And to all of
you who are gathered here today on this very momentous occasion, may I say to
you as the milk cow reputedly said to the farmer on a very frigid morning back
in my home state of Tennessee: "Thank you for that very warm hand."
(Laughter).

It's a great joy to be here. I recognize that you have a lot of business
to attend to; that you have been engaged in a lot of important work. Therefore, I will try not to keep you too long, although as a Baptist preacher it's
very difficult to look at an audience this large without bringing out my
longest speech. But my wife reminded me before I left Memphis that one does
not have to be eternal to be immortal. So, I'll try to do my best, Mr. President, to keep these remarks within some decent time frame.

When I was on the FCC, I had some good jokes, and I'll just tell one of
them. It doesn't fit, but I will tell it because it usually makes folks laugh
and it sets the stage.

When I was regulating radio, television, and all the various things we
regulate as FCC commissioners, you know, the broadcasters would complain about
the fact that we were hard to get along with, difficult to deal with. In fact,

they said it couldn't be done. But I would remind them that it was possible
to get along with the FCC. In fact, it wasn't difficult at all. It was like
making love to a gorilla. It could be done, but it absolutely had to be done
on the gorilla's terms. (Laughter).

It's not difficult to get along with the labor movement so long as you do
it on their terms. It's not difficult to get along with the NAACP as long as
you do it on our terms.

It is my pleasure and honor to have this opportunity to address this convention of the AFL-CIO. I'm especially grateful to greet and hail George
Meany, your president and the dean of organized labor. We of the NAACP salute
and congratulate George Meany for his uncompromising and fearless stands in
defense of civil rights and social justice. History will record that hardly a
significant advance has been made on the civil rights front without the active
involvement of organized labor and the magnificent leadership of George Meany.
(Applause).

We are particularly grateful to him for his unbridled tolerance. In an
age when it is fashionable in politics to engage in docile talk, Mr. Meany
insists on rejecting the so-called favorable theory, and he calls them like
he sees them. We in the civil rights community do not take kindly to the abuse
and cheap shots being hurled at this great leader by persons jealous of his
stature, impatient with his cadence for justice, and frightened by his staying
power. Hail George Meany and long life. And may your enemies always miss
their mark. (Applause).

It is also good to be in a convention where there are so many members of
the NAACP. We cherish your support and encourage you to join us. And if
you're not already NAACP members, we have folks with us who will be glad to
separate you from the dollars that you have in your pocket, that you might
become members of this great organization.

As the Executive Director of the nation's largest and oldest civil rights
organization, I bring you greetings on behalf of the more than 1,700 branches,
more than 450,000 dues-paying members. Labor and the civil rights movement
have had a long and marvelous involvement, and it is certainly our hope that
this kind of involvement will continue and grow stronger as the days and years
roll on.

In 1949 I went back to the City of Memphis, Tennessee, to practice law.
I use the term "I went back" advisedly because even though I was born and
raised in Memphis and had received my elementary and college education there,
had been drafted into the Army, had spent almost three years in the Armed
Forces, served as a combat veteran, had been decorated; when I came back to
Memphis, I found the conditions almost like I left them. The great City of
Memphis, the sovereign State of Tennessee did not provide any place for a
black person to receive a legal education, and so I had to go to Chicago, leave
my family, my friends, my acquaintances to go there to receive my education.

While I was in Chicago, I ran into many people who were friends of my
family, and they advised me to stay in Chicago, and told me how well I could
do. But I had made a commitment that I wanted to go back to Memphis, to a
rigidly closed and segregated society; I wanted to go back to Memphis where I
had seen with my own eyes in the '30s labor organizers beat down in the
streets of that city. I wanted to go back where every acre was a drop of
blood and every step was a tear. I wanted to go back to do my part to help
make Memphis an open society.

When I got back there, when I would go into the courtroom to practice law,
I was never treated with respect. I can remember just like it was yesterday
when I had the occasion to visit the jail to see my clients that I was treated
like a common criminal myself.

I remember the segregated restrooms. On one particular day when I was
engaged in a very heated lawsuit, I called for a recess and went into the law
library, only to be informed that this law library located in the courthouse,
where the guardian of justice sits on that seat supposedly with blindfolds on
her eyes, that because I was black I could not use that library. And I
remember asking the reason why, and the librarian in a rather shame-faced way
handed me a little booklet. When I got back to the office that day I read
it, and it said, "This bar association shall be open to all white lawyers
practicing in the vicinity of Memphis and Shelby County." And then they told
me I could make some private arrangements to use it. But I want to say to

you that I never used that library until the day came when I could walk up into it openly as a full-fledged lawyer and as a human being. (Applause).

So, I became active again in the NAACP. I joined the voter rights registration efforts, Masons, Elks, civil rights groups. We put on some gigantic voter registration drives.

Mr. Meany, I shall never forget how labor, COPE, and other groups from labor came into Memphis and helped us greatly to move the black registration from 7,000 to more than 127,000 people in our county. And I remember how we used to vote people in office and vote some out of office. We put some rascals in and we also put some rascals out. But we kept moving. Sixteen years after I went back to Memphis, Tennessee, to practice law, I remember on the first day of September that I walked into the courthouse and did not stand before the bench but went behind the bench, put on a black robe. The judge who had had that courtroom, did not even want me to practice law in his courtroom, died, and the Lord had taken him home to wherever he takes judges (Laughter), and I stood behind his bench, put on a black robe, and held up this right hand and I swore to uphold the laws of the state of Tennessee and the United States of America.

I remember even then the courthouse was lily white: All the other judges were white, the jurors were white, the baliffs, the clerks; all of the lawyers were white. In my courtroom, the only thing black was a thin row of defendants sitting in the second row with blue jail uniforms on their way to the penitentiary.

But I'm happy to report to you today when I left that courthouse five years later it was no longer lily white, but it looked like the keyboard of a piano. And I had even the staid, conservative jurors singing with me, black and white together, "We shall overcome some day." (Applause).

It is because of this that I have faith that America can overcome these challenges. I do not stand here to recite the dreary facts and figures of segregation and discrimination and racial prejudice out of bitterness or vindictiveness or hatred, but I repeat them because it is so easy to forget where we came from. The great English historian Toynbee has said that people who forget the lessons of history are doomed to repeat the mistakes of history, and I think it's important that we remember where we have come from so as we march forward into a bright new future we can take cognizance of the many things we have already overcome and remember that while we have come a long way we still have a long way to go.

NAACP was founded in 1909 as an interracial organization. It has remained in that position. Roy Wilkins, who led this organization through some very difficult years, was criticized and called an Uncle Tom because he insisted that we should not join in the many of "hate Whitey." We believe that you should judge a man or a woman on the content of their mind and their character rather than on their sex or the color of their hair or the texture of their skin, and we still subscribe to that belief. (Applause).

We have seen lots of changes in this country. I have been on the back end of the streetcar and the front of the train. I have been all over this country when I could not get a hotel accommodation, could not use the restroom. I've felt in my own body the stings of arrows, of the outrageous discrimination which was practiced. But because we have seen the changes, it gives me confidence that we can make some changes if we don't forget where we've come from.

To those of you who are in the labor movement, it would be so easy for you to forget the kinds of victories that labor has already won. And I fear, Mr. President, as I move around, that many younger members of labor have forgotten the days of the lockout and the goon squads, when blood literally flowed in the street.

They've forgotten the gallant sacrifices of those who were fired and had to go for months without a job. They've forgotten about the days when you went to work it was dark and got home after it was dark. They've forgotten the days when they said if you don't come to work on Sunday, don't worry about coming to work on Monday. They've forgotten about the days when there was no unemployment compensation, no social security, no minimum wage.

It was organized labor that led the fight that changed the whole landscape of America, and whatever you accomplish from this go forward, remember that you stand on the shoulders of men like Gompers and Green and Lewis, who

did without that you might go forward, and you will always be in their debt so
long as the labor movement goes forward. (Applause).

But how quickly we can forget where we've come from. It was with the help
of the labor movement that we were able to get in the '60s in the presidency
of Lyndon Johnson, one of the truly great presidents of our nation, those five
monumental civil rights bills which were passed. It was because of the fact
that this nation felt it was intolerable for a whole segment of this population to be locked out of jobs and opportunites. We had a commitment, and I
can remember the days of Selma, and Birmingham, and Montgomery, when I was
working with Dr. King, and I see faces here that I recognize that marched with
us, that said solidarity forever, whose marching feet and thumping hearts
helped to bring forth a new day in this land. And I stand here today with the
pundits and the critics, and all of the members of those who would like to see
both labor and the civil rights movement dead, proclaiming that the coalition
has come to an end. There are those who would like to see us fall out and
fight with each other.

It is true there will be some issues upon which labor and the civil
rights movement do not agree. NAACP will maintain the independent status and
posture. We will insist on speaking out with a loud voice on those things
which affect us particularly. Likewise, we expect labor to be protected and
zealous about its own interest. But in spite of whatever disagreements we may
have, the things that bind us together are so much greater and so much more
important than the things that will separate us, that we can say to those who
would criticize the coalition and who proclaim its untimely death, like the
late Mark Twain is reported to have said, the reports of our deaths have been
greatly exaggerated.

I think my presence here today is eloquent testimony to the fact that we
of the house of civil rights and the house of labor will continue to march
together until the great American dream shall become a reality for every citizen, regardless of his race, regardless of his color, regardless of his creed,
regardless of his previous background, we shall work to see that the fruits of
democracy are extended equally to every American citizen. (Applause).

This is our job. This is our goal, and this is our dedication.

Now, I remind Mr. Meany, because when the fervor over busing had reached
fever heat, and when emotions had overtaken much from the white community, the
one consistent voice that was raised across this country in defense of quality
integrated education was that of George Meany, quite often not with applause
of everybody, but he had the intestinal fortitude--if you let me put it in my
own language, he had the guts--to stand up for that which he believed to be
right. When all the world went the other way, he was marching to the tune of
a drummer who proclaimed that justice was on his side, and I think he deserves
a great hand for the kinds of stands he has taken across the years in the
persual of human rights and justice. (Applause).

Bill Pollard, who works with Mr. Meany, is a member of our board. There
are many other members of organized labor who sat on the council of NAACP when
we were having our problems in Port Gibson, Mississippi, problems which proved
to be a blessing, for they tried to destroy us, and all it made us do was to
live a little longer.

It was organized labor that came to our rescue. So we are indebted to
you, and I just want to take this opportunity to say publicly, thank you for
your support. And if we need you again, we hope you will be equally forthcoming.

We are making an appeal to the many parts of organized labor for some
rather steady contributions, because somehow we find that money is the name of
the game.

We need you and you need us.

We are facing, I think, a conservative era, when the forces of the new
right are constantly asking what is it that blacks and labor want? But let
me assure you that we shall not be deterred by the cries of our enemies. We
shall work together. But I think you ought to sometimes pat yourself on the
back. Perhaps there are only 15 or 16 million members of organized labor.
But when you work for minimum wage, when you work for Social Security, when
you work for unemployment compensation, and some decent work hours, every
working man in America, every working woman in America, whether they are
members of organized labor or not, benefitted from the effort you made, and

we ought to remind the world that this nation is in debt to the whole forces
of organized labor for making this a better place in which to live and to work.
(Applause).

So, we come today saying that while the civil rights laws of the 60's have
been passed, the job now is implementation. We come seeking to extend and
renew and invigorate that partnership which has been so important. We come to
remind you that we face some common dangers, and some common enemies, and we
come to say that we want to work together on the things that are worthwhile.

I would remind you that the NAACP has historically taken many, many posi-
tions that were favorable to the house of labor. Our Washington representative,
Mr. Clarence Mitchell, testified in favor of the situs picketing bill.
(Applause).

Mr. Mitchell also served as the co-chairman of the Coalition for A Fair
Minimum Wage.

We have taken a position in favor of labor law reform. We share the
painstaking effort that has gone into the whole question of the passage of
labor laws, and the time demands our constant examination.

Mr. Mitchell also testified for the NAACP in favor of repeal of Section
14(b).

So, in so many ways we have had common goals and common objectives, and
we've come to continue that.

And, Mr. President, and to the members who are gathered here today, we are
gathered today to say that we must continue the fight for full employment in
this nation. We come to reaffirm our support for the Humphrey-Hawkins bill.
(Applause).

We are tired of those who have their PhD degrees, who live in two-car
garage homes, who are saying that we must have an unemployment rate of six and
a half percent. When you translate that into human terms, that is six and a
half million people who get up every morning without a job and go to bed in
hopelessness and despair. We maintain that is too many people to be without
a job. We think that a more acceptable level has to be reached.

And when you talk about a six and a half percent unemployment rate in the
general community, you're talking about more than 15 percent. I am convinced
today that the unemployment rate is more than six and a half percent. I would
think if the truth were told, it's closer to 10 percent, and in the black
community it's 20 percent, and among black teenagers, it's 40 and 50 percent.
This is an intolerable condition, and we must do whatever it takes to make
sure that this nation is dedicated to the proposition that everybody who wants
to work can have a job and will have an opportunity to work. (Applause).

We must be equally determined that those who cannot work can receive a
decent welfare check; that unemployment compensation meets the level of living
standards, and we must give it without sniffing down our noses or looking down
at those who are blind, disabled, halt, crippled or maimed, mentally defective,
or whatever it is that prevents them from working. We must give them charity
with love and open arms. We must remind this nation that the woods are dark
and deep, but we've got promises to keep and miles and miles to go before we
sleep.

And I think we can count on your support for positive, affirmative action
programs. The NAACP has never been in favor of rigid quotas, but we do believe
in goals and timetables that will bring into the mainstream of American life
those who have been artificially and systematically excluded from it.

If this nation could spend billions of dollars on a foreign Marshall
Plan, somehow we can revitalize our cities and give life and hope to those who
live there. And if we can revitalize our cities, we can provide the jobs that
give adequate livelihood to millions of people who are now without jobs. And
we understand that the best affirmative action program anybody can have is a
program that will guarantee for everybody who wants to work a job, and if we
have that none of us need fear about being laid off because somebody else is
being hired, but there will be jobs for everybody.

I think this nation can afford it. But I don't think we can afford not
to have it.

We are concerned about a national health insurance program that will fix
it so that a major illness will not be a financial catastrophe.

We are concerned about the provisions of our international law that
permit dumping so that so many thousands of American working men are being

laid off because of cheap imports that are uncompetitive, and because so many tax incentives have been devised to let multinational corporate entities take the work from America and land it all over the world.

We are concerned about protecting the rights of American working men to produce the kinds of goods and services that we know we can do. We will join you in that endeavor. (Applause).

We are concerned about equality for women. We are concerned about a Congress that is growing increasingly conservative. We are concerned about people that we put into office and as soon as they get there, they turn their backs on our justifiable and legitimate demands.

We would like to join you in a mammoth voter registration campaign during 1978 so that we can meet them at the voting place and to say to those who come to us pretending to be our friends and yet turn their backs when we need their help, that as Vernon said the other day, the Lord giveth and the Lord taketh away, and the blacks and labor unions can also give and we can also take away. (Applause).

These are the kinds of concerns that we have. We are concerned that we can march together to the end that men and women shall enjoy the good life.

I would like to say to you that while I can criticize America, I still recognize the goodness of this land, for in spite of all its defects, whenever I leave here, Mr. President, to go anywhere abroad, I always buy a round-trip ticket, because I recognize that only a very few times and places in history have men and women enjoyed the rights that we have.

We said in 1776 that all of us were created equal, and we have come now to demand that that promise be kept.

As black folk we tended your babies, planted your corn and picked your cotton. We fought in every war. We fell in Bunker Hill. We were with you in the War of 1812. We joined Andrew Jackson in 1835. Three hundred thousand strong we put on the blue coats of the Federal Army so that woman could write, "Mine eyes have seen the glory of the coming of the Lord." We plunged with Theodore Roosevelt up the rough slopes of San Juan Hill. We died by the thousands going across France and Germany in World War I. We were faithful in World War II, Korea and Vietnam.

We have got an uncashed check in our pocket. We now come to the bank of justice demanding that it be cashed, and we don't want to hear any foolishness about insufficent funds. (Applause).

In that great and noble endeavor we solicit your support.

I recognize, Mr. President, as I close today, that sometimes labor gets a little tired of hearing evangelical exhortations of us who come asking you for more. I know there are those of you who can say, "I have lost friendships, I have lost positions, because I have spoken up for black folk." I know some of you have been called nigger lovers. I know some of you have been run out of office and been threatened. But in spite of that, the times demand that you continue to do that which is right.

And I know that labor gets a little tired. I know you want to tell me about all the things you have done, but there are still miles and miles to go before we sleep.

It was in the dark and dreary days of World War II when Winston Churchill constantly summoned his fellow country people to greater and more enduring efforts. Time and again he got on the radio and asked them for blood and sweat and toil and tears. He asked them to fight in the cities, on the beachheads, but never to surrender. On one occasion he said to them, "I hope you will so conduct yourselves that if the beleaguered island empire of Britain should endure for 1,000 years, that historians will look back and say this was your finest hour."

And then when the very skies of Europe were lighted up with the bodies of those who were being burned alive in the concentration camps while America stood on the sidelines vacillating as to what they should do, when it seemed that the tyranny and madness of Hitler would destroy the whole of the civilized world, once more Winston Churchill took to the airways and said, "I know I have called on you for inhuman sacrifices, for blood and sweat and toil and tears. I have called on you to fight on the beachheads and in the cities."

And I know that labor has been called upon so many times to do the impossible, but I close today by reminding you of the stern words of Churchill at the height of the Battle of Britain as he called on the words of a great

Jewish rabbi spoken hundreds of years before then, "The time is now. You are called upon to render this great expectation. And if not now, when? If not you, who?"

Peace. (Standing ovation).

PRESIDENT MEANY: May I say that it is difficult to find words to express my deep appreciation to Mr. Hooks for that very, very inspiring and intelligent approach to our problems.

We in the AFL-CIO count the NAACP among our best friends.

Mr. Hooks mentioned Clarence Mitchell. We have been with Clarence Mitchell down through the years, back in the days of the Johnson Administration on the civil rights bill. But when our building trades felt that as a matter of justice they should have the same rights as other trades to picket, in the situs picketing campaign, the bill for situs picketing, Clarence Mitchell stood by our side. In the campaign for a minimum wage, Clarence Mitchell chaired our citizens committee. Clarence Mitchell went with me to the White House to try to convince the President of the United States that his figure was too low. Well, the President didn't come up to our figure, but he did come up, and we got the best minimum wage bill that we have ever had since the law was placed on the statute books in 1938.

Clarence Mitchell stood with us in labor law reform, acted on our committee. We stood with him back in those days when the voting rights was before the Congress.

I'm delighted to welcome Mr. Hooks here as his first appearance at an AFL-CIO Convention, with deep appreciation for the long friendship we and the NAACP enjoy.

I recognize, and I am sure he recognizes, that there are many, many, many grave problems that the American labor movement and the NAACP must face together, and I can assure him that we are going to do our best to help in the future, as we have in the past, together to solve those problems.

Thank you very much. (Applause).

Proceedings of the Twelfth Constitutional Convention of the AFL-CIO, Los Angeles, Calif., December 8-13, 1977, pp. 442-51.

52. VERNON JORDAN

Executive Director, Urban League

Mr. Chairman, Escort Committee, platform guests, ladies and gentlemen: I consider it a great pleasure to be here to address my brothers and sisters in the great American labor movement.

I do think it appropriate to relate to you this one story, one story dealing with my friend to my right, Lane Kirkland. When some months ago I had a conversation with him about the future presidency of the AFL-CIO, I asked him if he would be a candidate and if he would be running and he simply responded thusly:

He said, "If nominated, I will not run. If elected, I will not serve, but if defeated, I will demand a recount."

There is a great bit of advice being passed along to presidential candidates these days. The Urban League is a nonpartisan, non-exempt, elemosynary institution, and we don't endorse political parties; but the following situation might be helpful to those who are seeking the presidency.

In 1964, when Lyndon Baines Johnson was opposing Barry Goldwater, Louie Martin, who now works for President Carter, then worked for President Johnson, sent some pollsters to Harlem to ascertain how the brothers and sisters were going to vote. They went to 125th Street and 7th Avenue. A brother came by, and they said, "Mister, we are pollsters and we would like to ascertain your presidential preference for the 1964 presidential campaign."

The brother said, "Fine."

The pollsters said, "If you had a choice between Jesus Christ, Martin Luther King, Jr., and Lyndon Baines Johnson for the presidency of the United States, for whom would you vote?"

The brother said, "That's easy. I'd vote for Lyndon Baines Johnson."

The pollsters said, "You mean to tell me if you had a choice between Jesus Christ, Martin Luther King, Jr., and Lyndon Baines Johnson for the highest office in the land, you would vote for Lyndon Baines Johnson?"

The brother said, "Yes."

The pollster said, "Why?"

He said, "Number one, Jesus Christ said, 'Seek and you shall find.' Martin Luther King says, 'Ask and it shall be given unto you.' And Lyndon Baines Johnson says, 'Stay home, boy, and I'll send it to you.'" (Laughter and applause). So that for those who choose to either remain or to replace, they might take that into consideration.

This is an historic convention. It marks the passing of a great era in the pages of labor's history, and the start of a new one.

As my friend George Meany steps down from his post as your President, he carries with him the fervent thanks of America's working people, for whom he has fought so long.

And black Americans know that George Meany led the labor movement's strong support for civil rights. His tenure was marked by strong gains in the unionization of black workers. George Meany's voice has been raised forcefully against racism and discrimination, and against the misguided economic policies that fight inflation with mass unemployment and with greater hardship for America's poor.

I well remember last year's struggle to save federal social service programs that were in danger of being sacrificed to the budget-balancers. George Meany spoke up then--loud and clear. Nobody's going to be dancing in the streets if you balance the budget, he said. But they will dance in the streets if you have full employment and a decent job for everyone who wants work.

America needed the strong voice and the strong leadership of George Meany --and it got it.

And America will continue to get that kind of forceful leadership from organized labor. Your new President, to be elected momentarily, if he can muster the necessary votes, Lane Kirkland, is an articulate spokesman for the hope and aspirations of America's working people and her poor people.

Black Americans are especially impressed by his unswerving support for black needs and for black efforts to be full partners in this America of ours. And I want to express my personal admiration for his dedication and his long identification with the Urban League movement. Lane Kirkland serves on the board of trustees of the National Urban League and is, therefore, one of my bosses; and I hope that he will continue to be as good to me as you are going to be to him. And I know that under his leadership the AFL-CIO will be a dedicated fighter in the coalition to end poverty and discrimination.

Black people and unionists must stand shoulder to shoulder in the fight for an integrated, open, pluralistic society. The fiftieth anniversary of the start of the Great Depression is a grim reminder to us all that we can't take economic growth for granted.

The past decade has seen rising inflation rates, permanently high unemployment, and more people thrown into poverty. Now we're moving into another recession. And all the while, black people have been in a permanent economic Depression.

Back in the 1930s, one out of four people in the labor force could not find work. That is how the Depression is most often defined--not by the stock market crash, but the mass unemployment that reached into every corner of our stricken nation.

But today, in 1979, almost one out of every four black people who wants a job is unemployed. About half of them are officially unemployed; the government counts them as such. The other half are discouraged workers who no longer qualify as statistics, much less as recipients of unemployment compensation.

While the Depression may mean bad memories for some or a nostalgic look at the distant past for others, it is a clear and present reality for the black community.

And that same community is being whipsawed by inflation. Everyone talks about the high inflation rate. But for America's affluent it just means that the vacation to the south of France will be a little more expensive, or that the fur coat will cost a bit more.

For the middle classes, inflation means a different kind of belt-tighten-
ing: a cheaper, less fashionable vacation resort or putting off buying a new
car until next year.
But for the poor, it means hunger. I do not exaggerate. Inflation is
strongest where the poor are weakest. It hits hardest in prices for housing,
heating, health and food.
The poor can't tighten their belts because they can't afford belts at
all. The poor can't buy cheaper cuts of meat because they're already on the
way to becoming involuntary vegetarians. We've always eaten rice and beans,
and now some of us can't even afford that.
And the terrible Depression that hits America's poor people hasn't led
to one tear dropped on their behalf in Washington, our Capital. In fact, the
response to their plight borders on obscene callousness.
The poor are faced with the grim choice of heating or eating. And the
so-called "silent majority" goes its own way, scrambling to gain advantage,
retreating into selfish privatism, ignoring the life and death needs of poor
people.
National policy is obsessed with the fight against inflation. This is
reasonable, because inflation is devastating. But it is using methods that
have been tried before, methods that invariably lead to sharply higher unemployment and tremendous suffering by poor and minority people.
Economists differ about what causes inflation, but the nation's
economic policymakers are busy penalizing poor and working people. The Federal
Reserve's tight money and tight credit policies have led to interest rates that
were illegal in some states just a few years ago. We are faced with the
familiar scenario of tight money, high interest rates, job layoffs, lower production, decline in housing, cuts in public services, more people on welfare
rolls, and sharply lower living standards.
Then, when it's all over, when the official announcement says the recession is over and we're in a period of expansion, we will find a higher permanent rate of poverty and unemployment in the black community.
We can't let the ugly scenario play itself out. We can't let the 1980s
become the decade in which the gains of the 1960s are finally wiped out.
I am here to say that if the issue of black equality was right in the
1960s, it's right in the 1980s.
If it was a cause for national concern that black people faced discrimination and disadvantage then, it should be a cause for concern in the 1980s.
If racism was wrong then, it is wrong in the 1980s.
If equality was right then, it is right in the 1980s.
So, we have to coalesce, the labor movement and black people, in the 1980s
to make it a decade in which black people finally enjoy full equality. We
must organize behind an agenda for the 1980s. An agenda that includes a
national full employment policy; a massive drive for affirmative action in
all aspects of national life; a national youth development policy that gives
hope and skills to young people denied both; a national health policy that
assures high quality health care for all, and a housing program that assures
a decent living environment for all. (Applause).
The black agenda for the 1980s transcends race, sex and region. It is
"black" only in the sense that blacks are disproportionately poor. Our agenda
is directed at helping all of America's poor and deprived citizens--most of
whom are white. It is an agenda that is in the national interest--an agenda
that will make America a strong, better nation.
To that end, the black community and the labor movement must cement their
alliance and stand fast as the cutting edge of America's progressive thrust to
ensure better lives and hopes.
But there is something else that the labor movement, the civil rights
community and all Americans must stand fast on, and that is the situation that
we face this morning in the Middle East, the situation that we face in Iran.
Let me say on behalf of the black community, on behalf of the National Urban
League, just this about what is happening today in Iran.
The freeing of the black and female hostages in Iran is a cynical attempt
to divide the American public. (Applause).
Black Americans refuse to be pawns in the Ayatollah Khomeini's insane
game.
The black hostages were held because they are Americans, not because

they are black.   Black people struggling for equality resent the use of our
misfortunes by a foreign dictator only concerned to embarrass the United States
of America.   (Applause).

We join with all Americans in demanding the release of all the hostages.
We join with all Americans in demanding our government stand firm against
terrorism and blackmail perpetrated by the Ayatollah Khomeini.

Thank you.   God bless you all.   (Standing ovation).

Proceedings of the Thirteenth Constitutional Convention of the AFL-CIO,
Washington, D.C., November 15-20, 1979, pp. 273-77.

PART III
RADICAL BLACK WORKERS

RADICAL BLACK WORKERS

Just as the civil rights revolution of the early sixties played an important role in nudging organized labor toward a more affirmative stand against racial discrimination, the Black Power Movement of the late-sixties also served as a powerful catalyst. To most militants, usually young urban males, "black power" in the unions meant demanding a place in the power structure of the unions. Some of the more radical among them, however, went even further, rejecting white leadership altogether in locals where membership was primarily black. Others argued that black power could be achieved through all-black unions, and still others maintained that the goal of labor organizations should be to act as the vanguard of a black revolution that would transform the United States into a nebulously defined marxist state.

Of all the developments which symbolized the emergence of black radicalism in the unions, the most widely publicized was the black worker insurgency in Detroit. It came as a shock to white and black liberals alike to hear the Dodge Revolutionary Union Movement (DRUM), for example, reject the United Autoworkers as racist. After all, the NAACP had acclaimed the union as the most progressive on the question of race. At least one-third of the black auto workers in Detroit were under thirty, had been influenced by the civil rights struggles, and exposed to the ideas of Malcolm X, Frantz Fanon, and Karl Marx, and were admirers of the Black Panther Party. DRUM demanded, among other things, a significant increase in the number of blacks in official positions in the UAW, and in the company hierarchy. Soon other revolutionary groups were formed after the fashion of DRUM at Ford (FRUM), Jefferson Avenue (JARUM), Mack Avenue (MARUM), General Motors (GRUM), and Eldon Avenue (ELRUM).

Because wildcat strikes and demonstrations failed to achieve their demands, these groups decided to broaden their revolutionary base by expanding into other industries. This led to the formation of the League of Revolutionary Black Workers, which sought to unite black workers, students, intellectuals, and the multitudes of black youth described as the "street force." The League was convinced that attempts to gain black power in the UAW through the electoral process was futile. Therefore, the League issued a long list of demands including the firing of Reuther, election of a black UAW president, one black vice president, an international staff composed of 50 per cent blacks, and recognition of the League as official spokesman for black workers empowered to negotiate demands with the company and the union.

For once in complete agreement, company, union, and government officials believed that these were the fulminations of a "handful of fanatics" and "black fascists" bent on the destruction of American institutions. Although the radicals did not realize their goals, of course, they did put such a fright into UAW union leaders that much needed reforms were instituted which pleased the moderate black reformers, if not the radicals.

Similar developments were experienced in other industries where black workers were under-represented in the union hierarchy. As in the UAW, other union officials decided that the best way to cope with the black radicals was to open up more staff jobs to moderate blacks. To most workers the radicals' demands perfectly illustrated Eugene V. Debs's famous remark: "There is a difference between class consciousness and class craziness." When confronted by the radicals, labor leaders found the moderate civil rights reformers the eminently more acceptable alternative.

THE BLACK WORKERS CONGRESS

1. THE BLACK LIBERATION STRUGGLE, THE BLACK WORKERS CONGRESS
   AND PROLETARIAN REVOLUTION

History of the Modern Black Liberation and the
Black Workers Congress - Summed-Up

In the year 1955, in the old southern city of Montgomery, Alabama, a
Black woman by the name of Rosa Parks stood up, and then sat down. Then
masses of Black people kicked off the modern Black liberation struggle.[80]
The NAACP filed over 55 desegregation suits in 1955. Emmett Till was
lynched in Mississippi while Roy Wilkins was named to succeed Walter White as
head of a hounded NAACP throughout the south. Black veterans were, by and
large, home, or on their way back from Japan and Korea telling stories of how
they had seen those courageous Chinese troops fighting a much better equipped
American Army. The ruling class and Joe McCarthy had just finished the job
of catching the CPUSA disarmed and flabby the results of a criminal, revisionist policy unable to have been turned around. White mobs lined up to block
school doors throughout the south. The battle of Little Rock broke after the
people of Montgomery had defeated the Montgomery Bus Company's Jim Crow Policy.[81]
1957 was the year of Ghanian independence and the founding of SCLC. Members
of the elite wing of the Black bourgeois and petty bourgeoisie proudly talked
about going to Africa to serve the Ghanian government. The struggles of the
African, Asian, and Latin American peoples revealed more concretely to masses
of Black people here the lie of the "colored peoples inferiority." On through
Tent City, the lynching of Charlie Mack Parker, massive voter registration
campaigns, the bursting upon the scene of the heroic, young Black students,
Robert Williams and the people of Monroe, N.C., demonstrating the lie of
"natural negro passivity," expressed through 'non-violence', and the Black
liberation movement surged onward. Toward the last couple of years of the
'50s, the Black masses were hit with an unemployment they were to never recover
from. The face of the Black community would reveal more and more growing
numbers of unemployed youth and their underemployed fathers and brothers of all
ages. This is what was happening brothers and sisters.
       By 1960 only 59% of Black people resided in the South. Outside and
inside the south Black people lived overwhelmingly in large metropolitan areas.
The same year saw the birth of SNCC and the election of the ruling class
politician-JFK who wanted to "lead" the Black liberation movement (into the
lion's den). Black people unfolded mass struggle against every stronghold of
Jim Crow, using sit-ins, freedom rides, legal suits, etc., while defying white
mobs, dogs, and lying, "benevolent" politicians.[82]
       Malcolm X! Black Patriot! Malcolm summed up the decade 1955 to 1965,
and even though the ruling class murdered him, his ideas and spirit are with
us now. He articulated the aspirations of the period, even though many of us
couldn't understand what he was saying then. On the heels of tumultous mass
struggle, Black people shouted: "Black Power"! as they learned that the
Federal government was not really their friend but their enemy from top to
bottom. In the last half of the 60's Black people proclaimed straight up that
if we were to be mashed into the dirt any longer, then the government needed
its Army, Navy and police, but no unruly band of civilian whites would insult
Black people, north or south, ever again. The chips were down. The
"American system" was on the line. There was no where to run, no place to
hide, except maybe one--the Uncle Toms of the Black bourgeoisie, and the
right opportunists, like the CPUSA.[83]

The Leading Role of the Black Liberation Struggle

Let's back up a few years or so. During the entire period the Black peoples
struggle baptized a generation of white youth and progressive white Americans
in a wave of mass struggle and ruling class violence, opening the eyes of Americans of every class and strata to the hypocrisy of "American Democracy," more
so than any other mass movement with the possible exception of the mass peoples
struggle against the imperialist war in Indo-China. And the Black peoples
struggle played a key role in helping to launch the struggle against the aggression in Vietnam. The Black peoples struggle was a huge inspiration to the
Chicano and Puerto Rican peoples whose struggles also shook U.S. society. The
Black peoples struggles exposed the good-for-nothing CPUSA and all their foul
deeds. The Black peoples struggle was objectively anti-imperialist from the
'Git,' and in the late 60's it was becoming consciously anti-imperialist.
This new, anti-imperialist force reached its height at that time, with the
birth of the Black Panther Party. The Black peoples struggle for liberation
shook American imperialism to its knees throughout the 1960's, giving birth to
a host of anti-imperialists; black, brown, yellow and white, many who evolved
into a small sector of conscious, anti-revisionist Marxist-Leninists.[84]
By 1967, almost 50% of Black people lived outside the south and almost
90% of Black people lived in metropolitan areas of over 250,000 in population.
Black people were overwhelmingly an urban people, a proletarian people. Black
workers caucuses sprung up in practically all the basic industries. These
caucuses aimed their fire at the fact that Blacks held the dirtiest and lowest
paying jobs and were excluded from active participation in the unions.
The mass struggle of Black people burst forth before the Black proletariat
was class conscious or organized enough to play the leading role. Consciousness
of the necessity for revolutionary class struggle, a struggle against the Black
bourgeois forces dominating the movement, of the need for independent organization which represented their class interests and could lead them into action agai
the imperialist system, only penetrated into a very small circle of Black
workers in the early sixties. Therefore the crisis of the Black liberation
struggle which became apparent in the late sixties, revealed itself more and
more as a crisis of the leadership. With each advance of the struggle the
bankrupt leadership of the Black bourgeoisie and the vacillating influence of
the Black petty bourgeoisie became clear to the masses of Black people. For
almost a decade and a half of active mass struggle, every coalition and organization in the Black community was led by preacher so-and-so or attorney so-and-
so. They carried on "negotiations" with the ruling class whites for "reforms":
civil rights legislation, programs for housing, education, economic assistance,
etc. NOT A SINGLE ONE OF THESE PROMISES HAVE BEEN KEPT! These promises turned
out to be simply gestures to hide the exploitative nature of the present system
and the class interest of the Black bourgeoisie, who knew how to use the
militancy of the masses for their own selfish ends.
But it has been the Black masses themselves, 90% of whom are part of the
laboring masses, who have been the driving force of the Black liberation
struggle. They have taken to the streets, to the marches, and to the barri-
cades demanding jobs, better housing, better education, increased wages and
an end to the "heavy hand" of the state, especially in the form of "police
brutality." It was these demands and this reality which must be taken as the
starting point in understanding the storms unleashed by the valiant Black
people in the latter half of the sixties. Though the Black bourgeois and
petty bourgeois classes assumed what it thought was its natural 100 year old
right to leadership, the Black masses literally set fire to America in the
60's after a decade of prattling about "non-violence" by these bourgeois
forces.

Ruling Class Strategy: Carrot and Stick

In the midst of the sweltering cities the working class content of the
Black peoples demands could not be mistaken, nor could they be altogether
denied. In the face of such storms the ruling class showed that it knew how
to use the carrot as well as the stick--they knew how to bribe and flatter,

and who to run to. Under the guise of "economic self-development," and "Buy
Black," "Do our own thing," etc., the monopoly capitalists pumped literally
millions of dollars into Black enterprises--banks, cooperatives, farms, fran-
chises, night clubs and insurance companies, with the accumulating wealth of
the Black bourgeoisie jumping from $500 million in 1965 to $1.6 billion in
1973! The Black petty-bourgeoisie on the other hand, was rewarded with a host
of new positions in the corporate structure, and the proliferating "poverty-
programs" popped up in every Black ghetto in the country. Nevertheless,
these bourgeois and petty bourgeois forces maintained their leadership of most
of the major Civil Rights organizations--SNCC, CORE, SCLC, the URBAN LEAGUE,
and the NAACP. Even where militant, younger forces had come forward to
challenge the old guard forces, as in SNCC, it was the radical wing, by and
large, of the petty bourgeoisie speaking, a younger, radical wing who would
vacillate between continuing the revolution or capitulating to the Ford Foundation, the "liberal" bourgeoisie, and the Democratic Party.
        The reasons the Black bourgeoisie took the course that they did were not
accidental:
    1) Their objective was economic position in society--small and medium size
        capitalists who wanted a "bigger piece of the action" of imperialist
        America, and a chance to exploit more of the 'Black Market'!
    2) The fear of arousing and bringing into revolutionary action "their
        own" deprived peoples, many who already recognized the need for
        destruction of the present system as the only way out.
    3) Fear of the working class and communism in general, especially
        frightened by the victories of the heroic Vietnamese peoples whose
        examples were an inspiration to oppressed peoples everywhere,
        including Black people in the U.S.

                                The Black Panther Party

        The Black Panthers became the first to see through this unholy alliance,
and from the far off shores of the Bay Area California, gave the call for
Black people to continue to fight against U.S. imperialism and racism. They
helped to expose the treacherous activities of the Black bourgeoisie who were
ready to sell out Black people for a few pieces of silver. They raised the
banner of Marxism-Leninism as the only ideology for Black people, and conducted
merciless criticism of cultural nationalism, mysticism, and Pan Africanism of
the Black bourgeoisie. They raised the banner of armed struggle as the final
answer to any oppressed peoples situation and actively participated in the
armed self-defense of several Black communities. Because of the Black Panther
Party, the ruling class was unable to douse the flames of the Black liberation
movement that many thought was already dead.
        But the BPP made some serious mistakes. Foremost among them being the
idea the lumpen, or street elements of the Black community were the vanguard
of the struggle. Responding to who they saw as the main elements in the city
rebellions of Detroit, Newark, Harlem, Cleveland, and Watts, the BPP concluded
that it was the unemployed and semi-employed youth that were the main force
in the Black community. They were unaware of the powerful Black proletariat
in the big industrial cities, and the leading role of the proletariat in
general, which was just beginning to stir. Also, the Panthers were reacting
to the revisionist line of the CPUSA which was advocating the "peacful transition to socialism," and who had already sold-out the working class in the U.S.
and condemned it to a state of disorganization and disarray. The desperation
and despair of the unemployed youth, which made up the BPP, was real, as was
their revolutionary fervor. Undoubtedly, this element of the Black community
will play an extremely important role, but again, only the proletariat, with
its ideology and its vanguard, a Communist Party, can lead. Despite the
mistakes, the BPP played a tremendous role in raising the mass struggle of
Black people to a new level, and paved the way for the Black proletariat to
play the role it is historically destined to play.
        The political situation within the Black liberation movement had seen
the temporary lulling of the momentous mass struggles of the 60's and the
earlier part of the seventies. Repression was aimed like a killer knife at
the Panthers, though all Black people were the target. But in the early

1970's rebellion after rebellion began to rock the prisons from Folsom to
Attica. Inflation was already choking the American people; unemployment was
astronomical in the ghettos. The Nixon-Kissinger gang in Washington was fran-
tically pursuing their Nazi-terror in Vietnam, while lashing out at the people
here at home. The ideological and political confusion caused by all the militant rhetoric of the "Black Power" days was dispersing the militants of the
Black liberation struggle, and sending the "white radicals" back to their
campuses. At the same time Black workers in basic industry were building
militant rank-and-file organizations to combat the oppressive conditions of
plant life and the racist, sell-out policies of their "union leaders." Within
the working class, strike after strike hit the monopoly capitalists where it
hurt most--in their pocket book--workers' strikes caused a loss of 51.6
million man hours in 1970.

Revolutionary Upsurge Among Black Workers

In 1969, the first revolutionary Black workers organization of the modern
era -- The League of Revolutionary Black Workers -- was formed in Detroit. As
we stated before, there is a close connection between the mass anti-imperialist
uprisings of the Black masses, especially the Black Panthers, and the awakening
of the Black proletariat with the formation of the League. Without the Civil
Rights struggle and the mass rebellions in the cities, the struggles of Black
workers and the formation of the League would not have taken place when it did.
The formation of the League, in turn, greatly influenced the Black struggle and
the entire revolutionary movement of the proletariat in the U.S.
    This is what Mike Hamlin, Chairman, and one of the founders of the League,
had to say about the League's program:
    "The League of Revolutionary Black Workers is dedicated to
    waging a relentless struggle against racism, capitalism, and
    imperialism. We are struggling for the liberation of Black
    people in the confines of the U.S. as well as to play a major
    revolutionary role in the liberation of all oppressed people
    in the world."
    The formation of the League represented an important new turn, the
beginning of a new stage in the anti-imperialist struggle of Black workers and
masses of Black people. Before the League, Black workers had participated in
the mass struggle, but not as an independent and organized force, merely as
another "interest group," following the leadership of another class. The
formation of the League marks the beginning of the transition where the Black
liberation movement merges with the revolutionary movement of the proletariat
as a whole. And who but the Black sector of the proletariat was in a better
position to lead such a transition? Indeed, the major question which confronted the League was precisely -- Who will assume the lead of the next high
tide in the Black struggle? After 1969, only sheer opportunists, or people
who didn't know any better, could place any hopes in the revolutionary capacity
of the Black bourgeoisie. The radical Black petty bourgeoisie, represented in
the main by SNCC, were splintering, some going to the Ford Foundation, others
to Africa, others underground, and still others, nowhere. A few had made
attempts to link up with the BPP, but that didn't work either.
    In response, the League put forward the following position: The sole
class which owing to its objective position, is capable of leading the Black
liberation movement is the proletariat! The League proved this by causing
major shut-downs in the big auto plants of GM and Chrysler, which rekindled
the spark of the working class movement. Thousands of Black workers walked
off their jobs to protest the racist and brutal treatment they received at
the hands of both the company and the union. These struggles, which were
also supported by many advanced white workers, scared the hell out of the
giant auto companies which dominate the economy of the United States. Additionally, these struggles had a particularly profound effect on the workers
and Black revolutionaries everywhere. The Black working masses had become
active and revolutionary (at least in Detroit) and were led by an openly
revolutionary organization -- the League! In light of these struggles, not
only the national oppression, but the class exploitation of Black people was
more clearly revealed, striking another blow at the bourgeois nationalism of

those Blacks who said we are only fighting against "all white people." Though
the social-political activity of the bourgeois-led Civil Rights movement had a
stimulating effect on the Black sector of the working class, the open treachery
of the Black bourgeoisie discredited it in the eyes of this sector of the Black
population, and in turn, stimulated the Black workers to organize themselves
independently. The formation of the League, and its subsequent development,
marks the point where a new current of events was to be observed in the Black
movement:

- Considerable numbers of the masses of Black working people, industrial
  proletariat, bagan to break away from the "bourgeois nationalist"
  leadership of the bourgeoisie and petty bourgeoisie.
- The deeping of capitalist relations within the Black community, spurted
  by the development of the Black bourgeoisie and the growth of the
  Black proletariat, polarized the Black community even more as the
  struggle over "who will lead" the Black people intensifies. Class
  struggle within the Black Nation sharpens.
- The growth of Marxism-Leninism Mao Tse Tung Thought among the Black
  proletariat and the radical wing of the Black petty bourgeoisie,
  signals the wanning influence of bourgeois nationalism among the
  advanced sector of the Black population.

The League played a key role in inspiring the Black Liberation Movement
and spreading Marxist-Leninist ideas among Black workers and workers in
general, as well as other progressive sectors of the population. However, due
to weaknesses in proletarian ideology, the League made mistakes in regards to
succumbing in many respects to bourgeois nationalism and syndicalism.

Today the Black sector of the proletariat, though far from being leadership of the Black liberation movement, is nevertheless making its presence
felt. The great storm that was the mass struggle of the Black masses brought
forth many individuals and organizations, each claiming to represent the
"truth," leading Black people to their "final place in the sun." Most of these
organizations showed the determination and fighting capacity of Black people,
but in the main they have come and gone with little trace of their presence
left behind. This only has proven what we've been saying all along. Only the
proletariat, and within the Black liberation movement, the Black proletariat,
is capable of leading all classes and strata in the final assault against U.S.
imperialism and monopoly capitalism, to peace, liberation and socialism.

Formation and Development of the Black Workers Congress

The mass upsurge of Black people during the sixties--the Civil Rights
Era, the rebellions in the cities, the Black Power era, the community and
prisons struggles and the development of militant rank-and-file Black workers
movement--largely spontaneous in nature, provided a real meaning and real
basis for the calling of a Black Workers Congress. The masses of people knew
that rebellions, no matter how militant and destructive they were, could only
go so far without leadership and organization. The Panthers had been routed
with their leadership split and their local organizations riddled with
informers. There was no thought of turning to the Black bourgeoisie, and even
less so to the CPUSA and various white "revolutionary" groups. The League
was there but it was a local organization centered in Detroit, and was unable
or unwilling to expand. Therefore, the desire for an independent Black
worker's organization, with a clear revolutionary line, that was national in
scope, was a general aspiration of the advanced sector of the Black population.

Various Black worker's organizations like the League, the United Black
Brothers in Newark, caucuses in Baltimore, Milwaukee, Chicago, Cleveland and
Gary, Indiana, together with "movement activists," students and revolutionary
intellectuals from various backgrounds and experiences in the Black struggle,
former members of SNCC, and the Black Panther Party, formed the Black Workers
Congress, on December 2, 1970. Combined, these forces represented a sector
of the most advanced wing of the Black liberation movement, some with wide
experience through all the stages of the struggle. There were about 30 delegates representing a dozen or so organizations, divided more or less equally
between worker and revolutionary nationalist groups. The overwhelming

majority of the delegates and groups were working class, but the leadership
was clearly in the hands of the intellectual elements, and those who had little
or no experience in the workers movement, or in organizing workers. As such
the character of the founding conference was mainly petty bourgeois in its
ideological and political outlook.

The ideological basis of this new, national organization was only super-
ficially touched on. A draft Manifesto was passed out. James Forman, organizer of the conference made a speech on the importance of organizing Black
workers. Discussion of the Manifesto was light. The League representatives
were hesitant and expressed concern as to whether such an organization could
be built. The representatives of the United Black Brothers, however, pushed
for the formation of a national organization, as did most of the other delegates. A continuations committee was formed and a second conference was
scheduled for Chicago in January to review the work of contacting other workers
in different parts of the country, and make further decisions. In the interim,
the Manifesto was published on newsprint for distribution.

The Congress developed in a contradictory way. A fairly rapid tempo of
organizing work, which pushed the organization into nearly 20 cities in a few
months, began under the conditions of an emerging internal struggle. The
United Black Brothers was to attend only one other meeting before leaving over
a struggle about the "ratio of workers to activist on the central committee."
SNCC and the Third World Women's Alliance attended no more meetings, apparently
because they objected to Forman's leadership of the new organization. The
United Front of Cairo, although always open to the BWC attended one or two
meetings later on, but they never really participated in much work of the
organization. At just about every meeting there were long discussions and
struggles on the questions of Marxism-Leninism Mao Tse Tung Thought, the
National Question, how the organization was to be built, the political line of
the BWC, the nature of the Black liberation movement, the "white left," etc.

Without a doubt, the Manifesto of BWC reflected, especially in its
demands, some of the aspirations of Black people, Black workers and the general
anti-imperialist movement at that time. But demands are not a program, and the
ideological and political basis of the organization was left unclear. For
instance, the BWC in its Manifesto, stated its ideological basis in this manner:
"The systematic study of *revolutionary theory* and experiences
of movements and socialist nations so that we might learn from them,
but in our learning we must at all times remember that we must apply
all theory to the concrete realities of the U.S."
It was very difficult to tell what the BWC was guided by since Trotskyites, Revisionists, Anarchists, all claim to have a *revolutionary theory* in
the world. What we needed was not All Revolutionary Theory, but Marxism-
Leninism and the Thought of Mao Tse Tung, which is the only *genuine revolutionary theory* in the world. It was easy to see why the BWC was ransacked with
ideological struggle, because its vague and opportunist line left room for all
sorts of political tendencies which kept the organization from becoming
politically and ideologically unified. This was demonstrated clearly by subsequent events.

Throughout the years 1971 and early 72 the BWC was engaged in a tremendous organizing campaign in about all the major cities in the U.S. from Los
Angeles to New York, New Orleans to Chicago. Dozens of conferences were
called in an effort to find anti-imperialist forces (individuals and organizations) and future cadres for the organization. This effort proved more than
successful as hundreds of new revolutionary elements came to the fore thirsting
for a revolutionary organization they could belong to. Though most of them
were revolutionary students and youth, many advanced workers were contacted
and joined the BWC. This also energized potential Black revolutionaries
and communists, who had not participated in the mass upsurge of the sixties,
but who became inspired to revolutionary activity by what they had seen, heard,
and read about those struggles. More than anything else, this organizing
activity helped dispel the myth that Black people "were not ready for Marxism,"
and were "politically backward," were "demoralized" by the Panther experience
so on and so forth.

The early experience of the BWC proved that not only was the Black liberation movement alive and well, but that its real potential had hardly been
tapped. For the masses of Black working people, here was an organization

dedicated to working for their interest, around the concrete day-to-day issues of their lives, and not some pie-in the sky Black thing. The masses of Black people were tired of all the rhetoric of the Black Power movement which promised them everything and gave them nothing. Indeed, the Congress saw as one of its main tasks, the spreading of Marxism-Leninism among the masses of Black working people who were clearly ready for it.

The sharpening of class contradiction between the Black masses and the imperialists, expressed most sharply in the "Law and Order" Nixon-Agnew Team, led to an intensification of the revolutionary struggle of Black people and the working class as a whole, particularly the strike movement of the working class in the early 1970's, and the mass prison rebellions throughout the country. For example, in 1972, during the first seven months alone, there were over 4,500 strikes in the U.S. in which 3 million workers took part. Many of them, like "Oneita Strike" in South Carolina, were led by Black workers. Since 1970 there have been numerous struggles involving Black workers in Steel, Aero Space, Rubber, Transportation, Communications, Longshore, etc. etc. The most important aspect of these struggles, however, was that in many cases, political rather than economic demands were put in the forefront as in the Longshoremen's strike in Louisiana, who refused to unload chrome from Rhodesia.

The BWC was able to play a good role in the prison struggle through the Harriet Tubman Prison Movement which it directed. This organization of activists and ex-prisoners also covered the country, and generally heightened the awareness of the masses to the nature and character of the prison movement which was sweeping the country. Harriet Tubman set up many organizing committees of community people to build outside support for the prisoners' struggle and aided the prisoners inside with legal and political education, and also set up many Marxist study circles inside the prisons themselves. At the time of the Attica Uprising, the BWC in coordination with Harriet Tubman, called many significant mass demonstrations, rallying the Black community in support of the prisoners' demands. In Buffalo, for example the largest demonstration in the history of the Black community was called--over 4,000 angry Black people gathered![85]

Around the end of 1971 the BWC was in a very good position to build a mass anti-imperialist movement in the Black community as well as in the plants and factories, since it had a good deal of cadres, and was the only national organization that was beginning to sink some roots within the Black sector of the class. Additionally the organization had a year of organizing experience behind it with people who were really respected and known amongst the masses. The organization was just beginning to come out of its cocoon, so to speak, and was beginning to spread its revolutionary wings.

But this potential was not realized. At least not then, anyway.

"The creation and advocacy of revolutionary theory plays the principal and decisive role in those times as Lenin said: 'without a revolutionary theory there can be no revolutionary movement.' When a task, no matter which, has to be performed, but there is as yet no guiding line, method, plan or policy, the principal and decisive thing is to decide on a guiding line, method, plan or policy." Mao

Just as the greatest political opportunities for the BWC began to mature, the organization became bogged-down in an intensified ideological struggle over just what was its principal and chief task, its "guiding line, method, plan or policy." The continuing struggle, which was waged mainly within the leadership of the organization and was a reflection of the political and ideological differences within the organization and movement, paralyzed the organization in almost every respect. The leadership of the BWC, in the later half of 1972 and early 73, could not claim to have any unity on any of the burning questions of the revolutionary movement--the National Question, Party Building, the United Front, the Student and Youth movements, the Women Question, you name it. Naturally, this state of affairs could not continue for very long without something coming to a head. It did. The objective demands of the revolutionary movement along with better grasp of Marx-Leninism compelled the BWC to make the necessary criticism and self-criticism, compelled us to learn from our mistakes, compelled us to make the changes that were necessary if the organization was to go forward.

The struggle centered around the following question: "What is the
principal problem facing the BWC and what is the solution to this problem?"
On this question the leadership split, and two lines began to emerge. There
was one line which said the principal problem of the organization was the
absence of a unified proletarian ideological and political line, and the
presence of a bourgeois and petty bourgeois line dominating the organization.
The other position said that "administration" and "structure" and "incompetent
personnel" was the principal problem. To get to the truth, it was necessary
to sum-up the experiences of the organization and see whether or not its
original ideas, theories, plans, and programs corresponded to what came to
pass.

Early History

Armed with a minimum amount of ideological unity, the BWC spread itself
over the continental U.S. in a matter of a few months. The main way the
organization was to build itself, was through the mass conferences we spoke of
earlier. Reality turned out to be quite different. No more than 5% of any who
attended those conferences became members (not altogether a bad thing). These
conferences were open, mass events and anyone could attend, regardless of
political outlook. Now these conferences were good for making contacts and
meeting people, but it is just not the way to build a communist organization.
Even then, the organization failed to establish any on-going committees that
could maintain links with the masses after the conferences were over. All in
all, the conferences turned out to be good rap sessions, and showed the
organizing abilities of many of the BWC cadre, but they were all too expensive
and really not worth the effort. Why then, did the BWC pursue its political
and organizational work in this way?
       The BWC operated with an erroneous and opportunistic concept of how to
build a revolutionary communist organization. The Congress was to be simultaneously both a cadre and a mass organization. The concept was developed by
James Forman and was called "cadre/mass." In practice, this broke down to
mean that some people in the BWC had to accept Marxism-Leninism while others
did not. Forman, and the BWC leadership at that time, thought that the main
problem of the communist movement was "sectarianism," and in order to combat
this, what we needed was a communist organization of thousands, even millions
of people. Therefore, the BWC followed this line, the line of building the
organization as a "mass" organization "with cadres." The BWC was to be a
group that was simultaneously a mass Party and a cadre Party. Forman predicted
we would have 5,000 cadres by "1975." In the final analysis, this was pure
ideology, politics, and organization.[86]
       The BWC operated with the view that the main problem of the Communist
movement was not of an ideological and political nature, but merely one of
"organization." What was wrong with the Communist movement was "too small,"
rather than that it lacked a unified political line and program on which to
unite all the genuine Communists into one organization, a new Communist Party.
From its incorrect appraisal of the objective and subjective factors of the
revolutionary movement, the BWC's plans and programs were put together with
the expansion of the membership of the organization as more important than
anything else. To facilitate this, the organization's structure was made so
loose, that one only had to agree to the mixed-bag of points in the "Manifesto"
to be a member. To make matters worse, never were any of these "organizing
drives" carried out with an understanding of our ability to service and educate these new members. Thinking we could solve ideological and political
problems through "organization," the BWC only wound up disorganizing itself!
"Organization" only becomes key in the final analysis after there is ideological unity and clarity around the basic political line.
       Of course, the Communist movement is small in the U.S., too small. But
it must be clear that the mass character of a Party and its influence with the
masses, is not determined above all by its LARGE MEMBERSHIP but primarily by
the CLOSE TIES WITH THE MASSES, by the Party's POLITICAL LINE, which defends
the interests of the masses, and how it carries out this political line in
practice. The CPUSA, for example was at one time 100,000 strong, but that
didn't help it become a genuine Communist Party, which never happened.

Because of the lack of a correct line, the mistakes in the organizational
field reflected themselves primarily in a mass, loosely structured organization
with no centralized leadership. Thus the leading bodies of the BWC were unable
to give firm direction and discipline. Unified political action, even on a
local scale sometimes was impossible, as was the proper selection and training
of cadres. As a result, many of the members became demoralized, cynical and
finally left the organization before it had a chance to correct these errors.
The collective leadership of the organization was undermined as a further consequence as each section of it operated semi-autonomously, each "doing their
own thing."

Internally, the incorrect organizational line manifested itself through
Liberalism--the lack of a critical attitude towards the leadership by the
members, and among the "leaders" themselves. It more or less had become a
tradition that everything the leadership said was right, even though many of
the directives were ignored anyway. Everyone would pat each other on the back.
Programs (especially those proposed by Forman) were rubber-stamped, without
being first discussed and thoroughly thought over. A correct Leninist style
and method of work was consistently ignored for a style of helter-skelter
campaigns which were started and stopped at a moment's whim. Besides the
liberalism prevailing within the organization, this lack of a critical attitude was due, among other things, to the theoretical weaknesses, which again
stemmed from the lack of clarity around a basic line, a necessary foundation
upon which to refute any erroneous views, whether from the leadership or not.
This naturally lead to a lot of unprincipaled struggle (gossiping, rumor-mon-
gering, etc.) and factional intrigue inside the organization, because again,
in the absence of a unified ideological and political line how can principaled
struggle unfold in an organization? If for some reason a comrade is in error
or out of step, it is on the basis of the organization's ideological and
political line that he has struggled with-against either right or "left" devia-
tions. How can such a process occur in the abstract? And what if a comrade
attacks the line itself? Well, in all cases that is what right and "left"
errors amount to, an attack on the line, but in direct assaults on the line we
have the right to demand that the comrade prove his position concretely. It
is on such a basis that changes are made or rejected inside Communist organizations. Of course there are certain Marxist-Leninist tenets which are not
open for a vote or debate, like the dictatorship of the proletariat, etc.
The experience of the BWC in organizational work proved once again, that the
best "organizers," if not armed with a correct political line, will get bogged
down and not be able to carry out any serious political work.

Because of the bourgeois and petty bourgeois nature of its own line, the
BWC fought the "sectarianism" of the Communist movement with "spontaneity."
Genuine revolutionary organizations cannot defer or bow to spontaneity, and
must prepare ideologically, politically, and organizationally for any mass
work and in the most serious manner possible. They must keep in close contact
with the masses, who after all are the real makers of the revolution.

The Struggle Between the Two Lines

It became clear to more than a few members of the organization that what
was passing for a guiding line and political program did not reflect an understanding of the unity of Marxism-Leninism-Mao Tse Tung Thought with the concrete practice of the Black liberation movement nor of the worker's or
communist movement. All were agreed on this, but again there was no unity
within the leadership as to how to resolve the problem.

In the meantime Nixon mined the harbors of Haiphong. A program called:
"The Vietnam Summer Offensive," was put together and hurriedly written, then
rubber-stamped by different sections of the leadership under pressure from
Forman who was "morally-outraged" at what was happening in Vietnam. The
Offensive was an entire package. The first event was to be an Emergency
Summit Conference of Third World People held in Gary, Ind. In the meantime
another conference was being held in Buffalo by the BWC for Vietnam Veterans,
this being done without even the knowledge of the local BWC leadership. After
cadres were exhausted, and everyone had gone home, what could be said about
the blitz of conferences was not more than some more good "rap" sessions.

NOT ONE CONCRETE PROGRAM CAME FROM ANY OF THIS! Again the BWC had substituted digging deep roots within the working class for the glimmer and shimmer of the movement spotlight!

On July 8th 1972, the Central Committee called an extended meeting (Plenary Session), to be used primarily as an educational conference for the rank-and-file. What began as an educational conference developed into a full blown ideological struggle between two sections of the leadership over the nature of the organization's problems, its present condition, and its future development. From that meeting on, what was becoming clearer and clearer to the majority of the members of the leadership was the clear-cut ideological struggle in the BWC between proletarian and bourgeois and petty bourgeois ideology. It was not enough to just list what the contradictions in the organization were--over-extension of cadre, lack of unity within the leadership, no positions on the burning questions like Party Building, the National Question, and so forth; for that had been done before, only to reappear again at another meeting. It became necessary to get to the bottom of these problems, to examine their social, historical, and ideological roots, and the class forces behind them. During the July 8th conference itself, almost every cadre present spoke about how his or her work was affected because there was no ideological and political center in the organization; on how the work suffered because there was no single part of the organization that knew anything about the work of any other; on how there were no unified positions on a number of important organizational and political questions around which disputes between individual members could be settled and work carried out; on how demoralizing it was to watch different individuals within and outside the leadership set their own agendas; on the shameful manner in which the membership's education was handled; on how criticism and self-criticism was unfolded in the organization; and finally, on how the work of the organization, as fragmented and disjointed as it was, was never properly analyzed and summed up.

As the process to rectify the organization began, some elements of the leadership, led by James Forman resisted. They continued to maintain that "administration" and "incompetent personnel (meaning the rest of the leadership)" was the problem. According to Forman the ideological struggle which had unfolded, was no more than a "jockeying for power," by a "factional majority," that was "trying to seize absolute power" in the BWC, and were out to "wreck me personally and politically."

The struggle inside the BWC was indeed a struggle for power. Not so much between a "majority and minority faction," as Forman and his people contended, but a struggle to promote the leadership of the working class over that of the petty bourgeoisie and bourgeoisie, to promote the interest of the revolutionary class over all the rest. There is no such thing as a struggle in class society --be it inside an organization, a family, between friends, etc.--that takes place isolated from the political and ideological tendencies of different classes. The struggle inside the BWC was only a reflection of the same class struggle taking place everywhere in the U.S. society. As Lenin said:

> "Every trend in Social Democracy (genuine revolutionism) receives the adherence of a greater or lesser number of not purely proletarian but semi-proletarian, elements, how rapidly it rids itself of the other trends, how rapidly it successfully combats them."

Intellectuals, Petty-Bourgeois and Proletarian

It wasn't so much Forman the individual that was the problem, but the class tendencies he brought into the working class. Forman was an intellectual. He was part of the intelligentsia--the doctors, lawyers, writers, journalists position in capitalist and revisionist countries. Subjectively, they regard themselves as being superior to working people. They generally come from the petty bourgeoisie and bourgeoisie, but in the U.S. many have working class and even "peasant" backgrounds. Intellectuals play an important role in these societies because of the division between mental and manual work which gives them a monopoly of the word and pen. During revolutionary times, many intellectuals come into the worker's movement in large numbers. This is

both a good thing and a bad thing. On the good side, the proletariat needs
revolutionary intellectuals because of their many skills and their wide knowledge. But the proletarian intellectual, is an intellectual of a new type. He
is a transformed intellectual, or one who is sincerely trying to integrate with
the workers and peasants, one who gets rid of his or her bourgeois and petty
bourgeois baggage.

He integrates himself with the masses and learns from them as well as
teaches. Over a hundred years ago Marx said:

"If people of this kind from other classes join the
proletarian movement, the first condition must be that they
should not bring any remnants of bourgeois and petty prejudices
with them but should wholeheartedly adopt the proletarian
outlook."

On the bad side, intellectuals, especially those in the U.S. bring into
the worker's movement all sorts of bourgeois and petty bourgeois prejudices,
especially subjectivism; petty bourgeois radicalism. While this subjectivism
takes many forms—empiricism, pragmatism, anarchism, individualism, etc., in
essence it's the same, an approach to reality that is dogmatic and one-sided
and is based on wishful thinking, "feelings" and imagination, rather than on
concrete analysis of a concrete situation. Generally these tendencies lead to
"left" and right opportunism in political and organizational work. The
bourgeois and petty bourgeois intellectual is generally removed from the masses
and has little faith in their ability to make revolution. They are generally
impatient and are apt to spontaneous activity.

The Expulsion of James Forman

These are the type of individuals which dominated the leadership of the
Black Workers Congress, and whose ideological influences have played havoc
with the organization. "Their way of appraising a situation was to take individual incipient, indirect, one-sided, and superficial phenomena favorable
to their viewpoint and magnify them into something widespread, grave, direct,
all-sided and essential, and they were afraid to acknowledge or were blind to
all the facts not in conformity with their viewpoint" (Mao). During and after
the July 8th Conference, the more proletarian elements in the leadership waged
a bitter struggle against the petty bourgeois tendencies and the opportunist
line of James Forman. Forman and his group turned a deaf ear to the honest
criticism as "unjust" and "incorrect." Never once did he admit to doing anything wrong, attributing all the organization problems to "the historical
conditions of the time." His egotism was so strong, that he walked out of a
central committee meeting while being criticized by other C.C. members, again
refusing to acknowledge he was guilty of anything. This together with the
tremendous problems his line caused the organization, precipitated his expulsion, together with a few of his followers. On April 4, 1973 James Forman was
expelled from the BWC for refusing to criticize his opportunism, his elitism,
and bourgeois individualism.

Forman's expulsion did not end the struggle against petty bourgeois and
bourgeois tendencies, however. Marxism-Leninism Mao Tse Thought teaches us
that the law of the unity of opposites is universal, that there will always be
contradictions in anything. Inside parties and organizations will be manifested in ideological struggle against "right" and "left" tendencies, and will
only be a reflection of the class struggle going on inside the society at
large. Liberalism, opportunism, revisionism, and subjectivism, will remain
dangerous tendencies that the developing worker's movement in the U.S. will
have to wage a bitter struggle against, at each twist and turn, in the
revolutionary movement.

The BWC Today

The temporary setbacks the BWC suffered only hastened the resolution of
the problems of the organization. Subsequently, the organization has continued to consolidate a proletarian line by summing up its revolutionary

experience, the experience of the communist movement in the world and in the
U.S. and the experiences of the Black liberation struggle. Though not a very
large organization, we have dedicated and able cadres throughout the East,
Mid-West and Southern United States who are carrying out revolutionary work
within the Black sector of the class, the workers movement as a whole, and the
anti-revisionist Communist movement. As an organization of Black communists
we are fully dedicated to joining with, arousing and leading the U.S. proletariat and Black people in general, and other national minorities in overthrow-
ing U.S. imperialist rule and building socialism in the U.S., under the dictatorship of the proletariat and its revolutionary, multi-national Communist
Party.

Summary

        In summing up the experiences of the BWC--the first national revolutionary
Black Communist organization in recent history--the first stage of its existence
was characterized by the penetration of bourgeois and petty bourgeois ideas in
both mass and organizational work. In this stage too, the organization expanded tremendously, picked up many new forces, and sunk some roots in the working
class and Black community. The second stage was characterized by the struggle
against the bourgeois and petty bourgeois influences in ideological, political
and organizational work. In this stage, the organization consolidated itself,
and placed more emphasis on training its existing cadres, rather than recruiting new ones. The third and present stage is characterized by the consolidation of a more proletarian line, though the struggle against alien class
influences is still continuing. And during this stage also, while we will
deepen and expand our work and influence among the black sector of the proletariat, and black people generally, we will also give primary attention to the
ideological, political and organizational problems of the Communist movement
as a whole. All in all, we can say that the future is bright though the
struggle is full of twists and turns and beset with many sacrifices.
        In summing up once again the class struggle inside the BWC, we can say
that the penetration of bourgeois and petty bourgeois ideas came from at least
the following sources:
        First, from the very class nature of the original leadership who were
Black intellectuals and "movement activists," and whose objective position
in U.S. society is in between that of the proletariat and the bourgeoisie, and
whose subjective outlook naturally tends to be a vacillating one between
revolution [incomplete sentence].
        These intellectuals were not armed with the Marxist-Leninist stand, view-
point, method and outlook, but instead interjected their own petty bourgeois
and bourgeois theories. Secondly, from the bourgeoisification of the proletarian elements in the organization who were greatly influenced by and followed
the leadership of the petty bourgeoisie. But even more so, what caused the
proletarian elements not to exert their leadership was their own inadequate
grasp of Marxism-Leninism-Mao Tse Tung Thought and the experience and reality
of the United States and the communist movement as a whole. Third, these
errors and alien influences were due to the uneven development of the Black
liberation struggle and workers movement in different parts of the country,
and the lack of experience and traditions of Marxism-Leninism within the Black
community. And finally, to the lack of a genuine Communist Party in the
United States, which has caused the necessity to build a new Communist Party
that is armed with the theory of Marxism-Leninism-Mao Tse Tung Thought and is
free from subjectivism, opportunism and modern revisionism, has a correct
political line which includes a revolutionary solution to the problems of
black people and oppressed national minorities in making proletarian revolution, has a thorough understanding of the problems of strategy and tactics of
revolutionary struggle in the U.S., masters the main form of struggle at each
stage, as well as secondary ones, and is capable of uniting all who can be
united in a revolutionary united front against U.S. imperialism under the
leadership of the working class, has deep roots among the masses of the people
and consists of the most trusted and experienced cadres from the ranks of the
revolutionary movement!

The revolutionary cadres of the BWC have acquired a better understanding of the Marxist-Leninist proletarian line as applied to the concrete situation of the U.S. and have raised their fighting spirit to an entirely new level. We have learned from our own experience the truth and wisdom of Comrade Stalin's teachings: "The Party becomes strong by ridding itself of opportunist elements." At the same time, the BWC cadres know full well that truth does not fall from the skies, nor is it hatched in the brains of some great man of history. No! Mao Tse Tung Thought teaches us, and life, our own experiences, have fully confirmed:

"Truth develops through its struggle against falsehood. This is how Marxism develops. Marxism develops in the struggle against bourgeois and petit bourgeois ideology, and it is only through struggle that it can develop."

Mao Tse-Tung

SMASH OPPORTUNISM, MODERN REVISIONISM AND IMPERIALISM!
UP WITH THE DICTATORSHIP OF THE PROLETARIAT!
BUILD A GENUINE MULTI-NATIONAL COMMUNIST PARTY! . . .

*WHY WE NEED A "NEW" COMMUNIST PARTY AND THE
ROLE OF A BLACK COMMUNIST ORGANIZATION*

The Role of the Black Workers Congress

As we stated in the beginning sections of this pamphlet, the Black Workers Congress--a national communist organization--developed as a result of the revolutionary national movement of Black people.

Though we are a predominantly Afro-American communist organization, we see the central and immediate task today as uniting all genuine communists and advanced workers into one revolutionary party regardless of nationality.

We arrived at this conclusion because we realized that though there are historical reasons for such a communist organization as the Black Workers Congress--the scattering of communist forces after the revisionist betrayal of the CPUSA, and the national character of the Black liberation struggle, we do not intend to raise this aspect of our history to a principle. After 1957, and through the sixties, there was a period of disunity and isolation among the communist forces the main reason communists played little or no role in leading the mass upsurges of those periods. The spontaneously awakening mass movements (Black liberation, student, youth and women's movements) thus developed in a period of historically evolved isolation (further increased by our sectarianism and isolation from Marxism-Leninism). Some groups, (like the New Left) elevated this "independence" to a principle--proclaiming this isola-tion and disunity a permanent feature of the U.S. revolutionary movement--'American Exceptionalism'!

On the other hand, some say because we are a "national form" we cannot be a communist group. They try to compare us to the Jewish "Bund" in Russia. They would like us to liquidate ourselves and join their "multi-national" form or group. Again we would like to make clear we are for the fusion and unity of all Marxist-Leninists into one Communist Party. This is the only basis on which we unite--"multi-national forms" are not the multi-national party. All Marxist-Leninist organizations will have to "Liquidate" themselves (we like the world "unite" better) if they intend to be members of the party, not just the "national forms." Prior to the party, no particular "form of communist organization" is higher or "lower" than any other (that is, unless some groups think they are the party already?)--all are affected with the same narrowness and amatuerishness one has, but whether or not one is willing to openly and resolutely admit its short-comings and to move towards genuine unity, away from the path of isolation and sectarianism to the path of uniting on the basis of Marxism-Leninism and the building of a new, genuine, revolutionary Communist Party.

Only such a party (national in scale, Bolshevik-type) can lead the working class and its allies to power and socialism and guarantee the com-plete emancipation for the Afro-American, Puerto Rican, Chicano, Asian, and

Native American (Indian) peoples. Only such a party can liberate women from their age-long oppression and guarantee them full equality with men in the struggle. Only such a party can release the full energies of the youth and allow full-play to their ambitions and talents. In a word, only such a party can bring proletarian revolution to America.

Again we want to stress the importance and decisive necessity for building the new Communist Party now! In the United States today the objective conditions for revolution are more than ripe. The ever deepening economic and political crisis seen in the "energy crisis" and the 'Watergate' scandal point to the doom of American imperialism. Massive unemployment, the deteriorating living standards of American working people, the increased repression directed at the oppressed nationalities and working class generally, is a testament to this fact. While the ruling class mounts offensive after offensive, shifting the burden of their economic and financial crises on the backs of the people, the proletariat is disarmed without revolutionary leadership and organization. What is worse, some "Communists" would like to enshrine this present state of affairs while they go about saying "we must build this and that mass movement! Genuine Marxist-Leninists must liquidate this present state of affairs by concentrating our forces, first of all, on building a revolutionary Party and not scattering our forces by seizing on tasks which we are in no position to carry out.

In Party building we recognize both the ideological and organizational aspects. The ideological unity of Marx-Leninism Mao Tse Tung Thought as the ideological basis for their actions and integrate it with the concrete situation of their country. Organizationally this unity may be achieved through the medium of a National Political Newspaper of the Iskra type or some other forms yet unknown.

Ideological unity must eventually take an organizational form, the Party itself; no matter what all the steps that must be taken in advance. One guiding principle should be, QUALITY OVER QUANTITY, at this time, so that when the Party does come into being it will be able to build a closely-knit organizational structure with iron discipline (a minimum necessity given the tremendous tasks that face us and the strength of the enemy) and which will enable it to be closely bound up with the masses and mass movements and organizations. Party building must be closely linked to the political line (or program) for revolution in America.

We unite with genuine Marxist-Leninists in the struggle to build the 'New' Communist Party. In the interim (Party building is a process of struggle and not a single act), the Black Workers' Congress has set basic tasks for itself, the successful completion of which will advance the whole Communist movement:

> 1) Help build a genuine Communist Party of a new type composed of the most courageous and revolutionary elements of the class--black, brown, yellow, and white, male and female, young and old.
> 2) Bring Marxism-Leninism Mao Tse Tung Thought to the advance elements in the national-revolutionary struggle of the Afro-American people and black sector of the proletariat (though not exclusively).
> 3) Fight for the hegemony of the black proletariat in the black liberation movement and the leading role of the proletariat in general, to isolate the treacherous influence of the Black bourgeoisie in the black liberation movement and the influence of the bourgeoisie in the working class in general. . . .

The Trade Union Question

The development of capitalism, particularly the industrial revolution, marked the entrance into history of the working class, a class that was totally propertyless, having no way to earn a living except to sell its ability to work for the capitalist or property-owning class. In return for selling its labor the working class receives "wages" -- only partial payment for the value it created, and barely enough to return back to work another day, to produce more value and profits for the capitalist.

The nature of capitalist society is such that the capitalist always tries to minimize the cost of production and maximize his profits. This can only be done at the worker's expense, the worker that finds himself constantly the victim of attempts by the capitalist to lengthen the working day, or speeding up production and reducing wages.

Trade Unions arose in the era of modern industry.

"The Trade unions were a tremendous progressive step for the working class in the early days of capitalist development inasmuch as they represented a transition from disunity and helplessness of the workers to the rudiments of class organization." V. I. Lenin, *Left-Wing Communism*

The workers and capitalist do constant battle over the level of wages, the price of "labor." A long time ago, when the individual worker attempted to present his grievances to the capitalist, he was laughed at and crushed.

The emergence of modern, large-scale industry meant the increased socialization of the working class. A few workers scattered in many small shops because a mass of workers concentrated in a few large shops. Coupled with the practical experiences of day-to-day struggle against the employers, the working class had learned that in order to get their grievances met, they would need an organization that would represent their interest and would improve their chances of winning struggles. Thus developed the first form of mass working class organization, the Trade Union. The trade unions would fight over such issues as the *intense exploitation of the working class, shorter working hours, better working conditions, speed-ups and increased wages, etc.* But the trade unions had their limitations.

Trade Unions Have Their Limitations

"Trade Unions work well as centers of resistance against the encroach-ments of capital. They fail partially from injudicius use of their power. They fail generally from limiting themselves to a guerilla war against the effects of the existing system, instead of simultaneously trying to change it, instead of trying to use their organized forces as a lever for the final emancipation of the working class, that is to say, the ultimate abolition of the wages system." Marx, *Wages, Prices & Profit*

The trade unions see their struggle as one waged primarily inside of the capitalist system for the improvement of the worker's condition. The trade unions fight around contracts serves as an excellent example of the role and limitation of the unions. Instead of really using contracts to improve the worker's condition, the unions, when they do "negotiate," act like people at a trading fair, like businessmen at an auction, rather than representatives who are supposed to "protect" the interest of their people. But even a "good contract" still simply means the worker has only won a better deal for the selling of his labor power, the fundamental cause of this problem still exists--the capitalist system.

This is why it is important not to confuse the trade unions with the revolutionary *Party of the proletariat*, the highest form of working class organization. The party not only fights for the day-to-day interest of the working class (low wages, speed-up, poor working conditions, etc.) it attacks the fundamental cause of these problems--the capitalist system itself. Frederick Engels in his series of articles on the British Labour Movement, sums up the relationship of the trade unions to the struggle to abolish the capitalist system in this way: "Trade-Unions should not be seen as an end in itself but only a means, a very necessary and effective means, but only one of several means towards a higher end: the abolition of the wage-slave system itself." But trade unions are not what they used to be in Engels time.

Trade Unions Under Imperialism

The development of capitalism into monopoly capitalism, to imperialism, has also been felt within the worker's movement. The super-profits obtained by the monopoly capitalists from their super-exploitation of oppressed peoples at home and abroad enabled them to bribe the upper sections of the working class in the capitalist countries, especially the trade union bureaucrats. The notorious Samuel Gompers and the AFL of the early 1900's are the classic examples. Gompers was the one who coined the phrase: "What's good for American business is good for the American worker."

Today the trade union movement is controlled by these types of bureaucrats--labor lieutenants of the capitalist class within the worker's movement. These people like George Meany and Leonard Woodcock, no more represent the worker's interest than David Rockefeller or Richard Nixon if they were president of the AFL-CIO or the UAW. Almost to the man, these traitors and their lap dogs down the union scale, "bargain" the workers lives and security away at every contract time, refuse to deal with any of the concrete issues that workers on the line, in the pit, or on the road face, refuse to deal with the question of the unorganized worker in a serious way, refuse to fight racism and discrimination on the job or in the union, at the same time as they mumble rhetoric about "equality" and go around shaking the hands of "civil rights leaders," and buffoons like Bayard Rustin who no more represent the interest of Black workers than they do white workers, or any worker for that matter. The unemployed worker is not a problem to them because he pays no dues. And they work overtime to make sure that whatever little democracy is left in the union is stamped out fast. The average salary for these criminals is $50-$100,000 a year, with "expense accounts" equal or past that sum! If anybody knows would you please tell us, what do these opportunists have in common with the average American worker, black or white, who barely makes enough to keep him and his family alive?

The more and more the rank-in-file has found itself up against the wall by the capitalist, the more it has found its "labor leaders" acting and talking more like "management." This situation has given rise to the militant struggle going on in almost every union in the country, between the rank-in-file and the bankrupt union leadership. This struggle is a key aspect of the overall struggle between capital and labor, between revolution and reaction. It is literally impossible for workers to struggle against a given contract and management without at the same time waging a militant struggle against the companies' agents within their ranks--the class collaborationists union leadership.

"If things are as they say," some may ask, "why then do you continue to work in these unions?"

Communists work inside the unions controlled by these enemy agents in order to win the workers of these unions by mobilizing and building rank-in-file organizations, developing the consciousness and unity of the rank-in-file, and getting them to rely on their own strength to get things done. Communist work inside these unions not in order to "push the leadership to the left," or into the struggle period, but in order to "kick these traitors out of the workers movement! Communists work inside these unions only in order to win the workers to revolutionary struggle, and not to inspire the masses with the spirit of obedience and loyalty to the trade union bureaucracy like the CPUSA still does. Communists work inside unions to win the masses of the workers and not to "gain control" of the trade union machine, and the trade union officials like the CPUSA still does. Communists work inside these unions in order to learn to lead day-to-day struggles of the proletariat so that they can link this struggle to the total revolutionary movement and raise it to its highest level to proletarian revolution and not to reformists campaigns like the CPUSA still does.

Super-Exploitation, White Chauvinism and Racism in the Trade Union Movement

Because the U.S. is a multi-national imperialist state which oppresses people within its own borders as well, as outside, Black and Third World workers (Puerto Ricans, Chicanos, Asians, etc.) find themselves excluded from some jobs altogether, at the same time, again because of racism and national discrimination, find themselves locked into the worst and hardest jobs at the lowest pay in the labor market. Not only are they the "last hired, first fired," but are victims of discrimination and racism; in job placement,

promotion, security, classification and retirement. By forcing Black and other
Third World workers into a limited section of the job market, namely the bottom
of the barrel and exclusion from some jobs altogether, namely the highly
paid-highly skilled ones, the bourgeoisie wields a double weapon. First,
it has a tremendous reserve of labor power willing and ready to work at any
price whenever there is a labor shortage, thus driving down the wages of all
workers the monopoly of the higher paying, highly skilled jobs, and thus
easing the competition they have to face on the labor market. Over the years
the U.S. ruling class has shown how skillfully it can use both whenever
necessary. Additionally, Black and other Third World workers are forced to
work for a smaller wage for the same work as white workers, thus enriching the
bourgeoisie even more. In 1969 it was estimated that Black workers earned
$3,000 less per year than white workers in the same job category. With at
least 10,000 Black workers in the labor force, this means an extra
$30,000,000,000 (30 billion) for the bourgeoisie. Who says discrimination
doesn't pay?

Union bureaucrats, because they receive the most from this bribery (which
usually takes the form of the high salaries and "expense accounts" we talked
about) have a material stake in keeping racism and the national oppression of
Black and other Third World workers alive and well. For example, do they ever
use the strength of the union to deal with the question of job discrimination?
Of course not. Take the U.S. Steel workers union which has somewhere in the
neighborhood of 250,000 Black workers, or about 30% of the total membership.

A study made of Black employment in basic steel by the Pittsburgh Equal
Employment Opportunity Commission in 1968 observed that "negroes comprise
12.27% of laborers, 12.93% of the service workers and 10.86% of the semi-
skilled operatives, while holding only 3.21% of the total work force, while only
7% of the higher paid jobs within these industries are held by Blacks, while
25% of the lower paid jobs within these same industries are held by Blacks --
this situation is not due to the fact that Blacks are not unionized! In
fact we find that 35% of Black males are unionized as compared to 30% white and
within the female workforce, we find 14% Black women are unionized as compared
with less than 13% white! The explanation and heart of the problem lies in
the fact that racism and national discrimination are profitable and that the
labor bureaucrats are loyal to the capitalist class, and are the enemies of
all works.

These criminal labor bureaucrats who do the bidding of the bourgeoisie
in the Trade Union movement, obviously also advance the policy and practice
of racism and national discrimination within the unions themselves. Some
unions in fact most of the craft unions, exclude Blacks from membership or
have only a handful of token members. Unions where Black workers are found
in large numbers, notably those like UAW with 350,000 blacks and USSW with
250,000 blacks virtually hold token positions at best.

Moreover, Black and Third World workers are forced to provide the prime
fodder for the increased extraction of surplus capital, the accelerated rate
of exploitation which Nixon and his ruling class cronies currently plan for
the American working class.

The Black workers have traditionally played the role of the most
exploited brutally oppressed, and the most profitable source of labor, that
was so cheap that they received no renumeration for their work, except that
required for bare subsistence--minimum food, clothing and shelter. That
source of cheap labor was so productive that it earned huge profits for the
white overloads of yesterday and today. Basically, from the billions and
billions of dollars ripped from the hides of our forebearers the American
capitalist class accumulated the necessary capital to build the American
empire.

Since slavery, Black labor has continued to assume particular importance
in the development of both domestic capital and international imperialism,
primarily because Black female and male workers are the final prop, the
ultimate mainstay, onto which capitalism shifts its weight in order to survive. Black workers have remained a source of the cheapest, most productive
labor. First as agricultural labor, then as miners, merchant seamen, government, transportation, and service workers, dock and warehouse workers, etc.
and finally as the most exploited section of the proletariat in light and
heavy industry. Today Black and other Third World workers are still solidly
entrenched at the base of production.

So we see that Black workers still are:
- the lowest paid sector of the working class
- Forced into the worst jobs in the labor market except when needed to suppress the wages of "higherpaid" whites
- Subjected to the most hazardous working conditions, higher mortality rate (2½% more than whites) and higher rates of industrial disease
- Subjected to harsh regimentation and discipline on the job
- In a position of having little or no control, influence or power in their unions
- Leading the struggles of the working class against these as well as other conditions that affect the working class as a whole, by militant rank and file struggles inside the plants and factories as well as within the unions.

Trade Unions in the Declining Stage of Imperialism

With the sharpening of general crisis of capitalism, imperialism makes a last ditch effort to save itself. It moves more and more to open terroristic rule, discarding its own "bourgeois democracy," in favor of fascism. Crucial to this development are the trade unions. In the declining stages of imperialism, the government moves to bring the trade unions more *directly* under its control, *transforming them from organizations designed for struggle against the capitalist class, into organizations and agencies for the planning of production and for "industrial peace."*
Let's look at what's happening inside the trade unions today. In 1971 the United States Steel Worker's Union under the class collaborationist leadership of I. W. Abel, "negotiated" a 3% wage increase over a three year period. In the same contract, the USSW leadership agreed to work with the steel industry in setting up "productivity committees" which would increase the "productivity of the worker"! The year 1973 will go down in history as the year the U.S. working class was caught with its pants down -- wages frozen by the government, forced over-time, increased speed-up, "meat crisis," "milk crisis," "wheat crisis," "energy crisis," etc., and a cost of living reaching the sky! 1973 caught the U.S. economy staggering with inflation, recessions, high unemployment, tax increases, funds cut from health and welfare services while corporate profits reached unheard of records.
All the while this is happening the bourgeoisie is steadily tightening up its faithful, time-tested lackeys, the labor bureaucrats, giving some of them cabinet posts with one hand and with the other, beating down the insurgent movement of the rank and file and trying to smash out of existence the few remaining "progressive unions." The appointment of the racist, hard-hat supreme--Peter Brenan--former head of the N.Y. Building Trades Council to Secretary of Labor, and the other offers of the Nixon administration to appoint more union heads to official government posts, is part and parcel of the policy to use these traitors to do the work of the government and police in stopping the militant rank and file movement.
Over the past ten years we have witnessed a great upsurge in the workers movement expressed among other things in the development of militant rank and file workers organizations, and in particular in Black worker's caucuses like--DRUM (Detroit), the United Black Workers (Newark), Concerned Transit Workers (Chicago), HRUM (New York), Fight Back (N.Y.) etc., only to mention a few that have played a major role in this development. Not only have these worker's organizations struggled around economic issues such as speed-ups, discrimination in hiring, harassment of Black and Latin workers by racist foremen, low wages, etc., but have raised anti-imperialist demands like "U.S. out of Indochina," "No chrome from Rhodesia," "Stop police brutality of Black people in the community," "End the oppression of women," Support the struggle of the Palestinian people, fight Israeli aggression, etc. etc.
Another type of caucus that has developed during this period and is based primarily on the discontent of the rank and rile with much of its present class collaborationists leadership, are caucuses like--'United

National Caucus (UAW),' Youngstown Steel Workers Group (Ohio), and the 'Miners
for Democracy (West Virginia).' In the main these caucuses directed their
struggles around the lack of union democracy and the corruption of the union
leadership, like the Tony Boyle case. Through genuine rank and file organizations with good mass membership, these caucuses are led by reformists, and
would-be union bureaucrats, or in the case of Miners for Democracy--by a
bourgeois lawyer! These caucuses are usually national or industry-wide, but
very seldom if at all, lead and develop local or for that matter, national mass
struggles around issues facing the rank and file. At the end of every issue is
the would-be union bureaucrat or reformist crying: "Elect me and I will get
things done!" These caucuses are nevertheless progressive to the degree that
they do challenge the class collaboration of the union leadership, but are weak
in the sense that the reformist leadership and the basic programs have not and
cannot make any essential changes in things or develop the workers' consciousness to a higher level.

The third type of caucus found in almost every union are the "election
coalitions," which usually come to life around election time and usually have
no life outside of the election period. These caucuses are merely more often
than not, political machines for the local union politicians or would be
politicians and are used by both black and white bureaucrats. However, many
honest and sincere workers join these caucuses because they see nothing else
around or because they are dissatisfied with the present leadership.

Our strategy in the Trade Unions and worker's movement generally is
simply to unite all those who can be united around the immediate political and
economic issues of the workers. Our task is to raise the level of spontaneous
consciousness of the workers to revolutionary working class consciousness by
introducing socialist consciousness and taking the lead in the day-to-day
struggles of the working class and by proving to them in practice that communists are their real leaders and the real fighters!

In approaching our work we start from the concrete, day-to-day issues,
political and economic, facing the masses of workers; while at the same time
raising this struggle to higher levels by pointing out to the workers how the
immediate problems are related to the overall system of monopoly capital and
the revolutionary movement as a whole. We do not lie to the workers like the
opportunists in the CPUSA, or give them the illusion that their problems can be
solved simply by improving an abuse of the capitalist system, like the CPUSA
does. But we prove this to them by participation in mass struggle and not just
by handing out leaflets at the plant gates. Because only through the course of
revolutionary mass struggle do the masses learn the necessity for revolution.
Today at the present stage of the revolution our task is to win over the
"vanguard (i.e., build up cadres, create a Communist Party, work out the
programs, the principles of tactics)." STALIN[87]

We do this mainly by organizing propaganda, political exposures --
introducing socialist ideology to the most advanced sectors of the working
class, but also by participating in and building Black workers caucuses,
multi-national rank and file caucuses in the plants and unions, anti-imperialist worker's organization, organizing the unorganized (bringing in unions into
an unorganized shop) as well as by experimenting with new forms of revolutionary struggle as they arise. As Black communists, interested in building a new
Communist Party, we need to sink deep roots in the black sector of the class,
as the best and most expedient means of building the revolutionary unity of
the working class as a whole at this time.

The defense of the day-to-day interest of the working class is just as
much a job for communists as is the struggle for socialism. Karl Marx and
Frederick Engels wrote "that communists have no interests separate and apart
from the proletariat as a whole, they always and everywhere represent the
interests of the worker's movement as a whole."

In our work in the workers movement we must do four things:
-- develop cadres from the ranks of the advanced workers for the BWC,
   and other genuine communist organizations, and the future Communist
   Party.
-- raise the consciousness of the workers to revolutionary class
   consciousness
-- struggle to defeat a given policy of the imperialists
-- help merge the national and class struggle by holding to the right

-- to political secession of Black people and equal rights for the other oppressed nationalities.

In the Trade Union movement our task is to win the ideological, political and practical leadership of the proletariat in the trade unions, the revolutionary proletariat.

Our political task in the trade unions today means first of all winning the advanced elements of this struggle to communism, and then developing the rank and file workers movement into a revolutionary class consciousness workers movement. We do this by persistently interjecting socialist consciousness into t workers movement and by seriously involving ourselves in the day-to-day political and economic struggles of the working class, particularly the struggles of Black workers, in order to direct and lead these struggles to higher forms, and to merge the national and class struggles of oppressed and working people generally into one mighty fist directed against imperialism. This task can only be fulfilled by strengthening our ties with the masses of workers in the trade unions, especially the most advanced; by organizing them into anti-imperialist worker organizations in the plants and unions and those that may spring up in the future. These anti-imperialist worker's groups, must be organized around a concrete *political program,* including a strong Marxist-Leninist study program. They must, in order to advance and link themselves with the masses of the workers, engage in *mass revolutionary struggle;* against wage cuts, racial and national discrimination, imperialist aggression abroad, police brutality, unemployment, compulsory overtime, inflation, organizing the unorganized, etc., etc. And they must especially conduct merciless and unremitting criticism and exposure of the traitorous trade union bureaucrats, revisionist, and Trotskyites, so that the workers can be able to distinguish genuine Marxism from sham Marxism.

While engaging in trade union work, we must be especially on guard for the errors of economism and right opportunism. Even within the anti-revisionist communist movement these tendencies are making themselves felt. Among communists generally, they are manifested in a tendency to "hide" our politics from the workers and shying away from political and ideological struggle in the union and plant. This is especially true in regards to struggles that take place outside of the workplace and do not have an obvious "economic character" -- like police brutality, imperialist aggression, community struggles and so forth. The flip side of the coin is to raise these "other" struggles in an scholastic and abstract manner so that the workers can't possibly get the connection. But the main tendency is not to raise them at all. For 'white' communists in particular, right opportunism is expressed in a definite tendency not to raise the national question among white workers while acting in a paternalistic manner towards black workers. In this way, they wind up alienating themselves from both white and black workers who are in general not interested in revolutionary phrase-mongering, not backed up by revolutionary deeds. Since many do not know how to even raise the struggle against chauvinism and racism among the white workers, they end up not raising it at all, and thus fall into opportunism and "economism" (issues that white workers "can relate to"). They have to realize that they cannot shy away from this struggle against chauvinism and racism even if it means "going against the tide," at present. "Going against the tide is a Marxist Leninist principle." Otherwise, they fall into chauvinism themselves, even if this chauvinism takes the form of "Liberalism," and wind up, in practice, following the CPUSA's revisionist line.

For Black communists in the trade unions, there is a tendency not to understand and apply the proletarian line on the national question. They shy away from developing the leading role of Black workers in the trade union movement and the Black liberation struggle generally. They especially shy away from struggle around the relationship between Marxism-Leninism Mao Tse Tung Thought and the Black liberation movement, revolutionary nationalism and anti-imperialism and the struggle against Black bourgeois influences. Many black communists suffer from the disease of "black leftism," and in their efforts to develop the "pure proletarian class struggle," negate or don't understand the revolutionary role and significance of the mass, anti-imperialist struggle of Black people and the leading role of the Black proletariat. They must always keep in mind the prophetic words of Mao who said that the Black liberation movement was a clarion call to the entire working class and oppressed in America.

The struggle for the revolutionary unity of the working class in the trade unions is the job of all genuine communists in the U.S. But revolutionary unity can only be built from an understanding of the causes of disunity. The revolutionary unity of the working class in the U.S. is hampered by the splits in the U.S. labor movement, which are objective and real, and cannot be wished away. This split is due primarily to opportunism and white chauvinism. It has been compounded by the revisionist betrayal of the CPUSA and the strong traditions of "social democracy" within the U.S. communist movement. Marxism-Leninism teaches that where the labor movement is split (and it is split in every capitalist country), a bitter and determined struggle for its UNIFICATION should be conducted. But, in order to do this, our work in the trade union in the present period must be linked to the necessity to build a genuine communist party. We say that NO CONCESSIONS can be made in regards to white chauvinism and opportunism, they have to be thoroughly rooted out and liquidated. This can only be done during the course of a long mass struggle, but it must be done steadily and systematically. Only then can the historic role of the great U.S. proletariat be fulfilled.

The Black Liberation Struggle, The Black Workers Congress, and Proletarian Revolution: A Comprehensive Statement by the Black Workers Congress, pp. 20-32, 38-39, 43-48. Pamphlet in possession of the editors.

2. EXCERPTS FROM THE BLACK WORKERS CONGRESS MANIFESTO

Our Objectives:

1) Workers' control of their places of work--the factories, mines, fields, offices, transportation services and communication facilities--so that the exploitation of labor will cease and no person or corporation will get rich off the labor of another person, but all people will work for the collective benefit of humanity.

2) An elimination of all forms of racism and the right of self-determination for African people, Chicanos, Puerto Ricans, Asians and Indians who live in the United States and Puerto Rico.

3) The elimination of all forms of oppression of women in all phases of society, on the job and in the home.

4) The right of all people to express and develop their cultural heritage throughout the United States.

5) The right of all people to express and develop their cultural and religious views without fear of prosecution.

6) A halt to the growing repression and increasing fascism of the United States, the militarization of the police, the arming of right wing forces and the repeal of all repressive legislation that abolished the right of people to assemble, to speak freely, to have privacy and to publish their political views.

7) The replacement of all class collaborators in the trade union movement with leadership that will fight for the international solidarity of all oppressed people, a leadership that will fight all manifestations of racism, white skin privilege, capitalism, and imperialism (the sending of money, armed forces and Christian missionaries from one country to another for the purpose of exploiting and oppressing its workers). This leadership must demand real equality for women in employment.

8) The creation in the labor movement of revolutionary Black caucuses, Chicano and Puerto Rican revolutionary caucuses, Third World labor alliances, independent revolutionary union movements and other forms of revolutionary labor associations that will break the strangle-hold of the reactionary labor bureaucrats and the capitalist class collaborators that help to prevent the working class people from understanding their historic role in controlling the means of production.

9)   A twenty-hour work week where all the people of the United States will be employed and have the necessary funds for food, clothing, shelter and the right to improve their standard of living and enjoy the benefits of an industrialized society.

10)   Thirty days of paid vacation time each year for all workers including women in the house and the use of all resort areas and the creation of new ones for working class people and the elimination of special privileges at resort areas for any group of people.

11)   An elimination of speed-up, compulsory overtime, unsafe working conditions, inadequate medical facilities on the job, brutality and terror in the mines, factories and industrial plants of the United States and Puerto Rico.

Siege: National Voice of the Black Workers Congress, Vol. 1, No. 1 (1971):12.

3.   ORGANIZE THE REVOLUTION DISORGANIZE THE STATE!

300 Attend National Conference

The first national conference of the Black Workers Congress was convened in Gary, Indiana over the Labor Day weekend. Approximately three hundred Black and other Third World workers and students participated in this conference, an historic first.   The thrust of this conference was to pull together the efforts of Black and other Third World Workers in a unified struggle against U.S. imperialism and its lackeys.

The conference began on Saturday morning with opening remarks by Michael Hamlin, Chairman of the Black Workers Congress. Following these remarks came a speech by John Watson on the Objective Conditions of Black and Other Third World Workers Today (text herein). The speech gives an analysis of the crisis that capitalism is in today, of how Nixon's wage-price freeze is used as a tool of economic sanction to capitalist business and how this new economic policy further exploits working people, Black and other Third World workers in particular. Watson's speech ended with a call for workers to organize and struggle against economic oppression.

Other delegates to the conference gave brief speeches of solidarity to the concept of Black Workers and other Third World people moving against Imperialism and industrial repression. Representatives from the Chicano, Puerto Rican, and Asiatic oppressed communities spoke to the need to escalate struggles against imperialism.

Workshops were convened on organizing workers, youth, and women. A cross section of workers shared their experiences in struggling against imperialism. The workshops focused on how to build struggle around the concrete issues which workers face, and how to mobilize and involve workers in day to day issues of struggle. Another important topic was building working class unity, through actions against plant atrocities especially when workers are murdered due to unsafe conditions in plants.

The Black Workers Congress Women Commission is organizing to fight imperialism as it exploits Black and other Third World women on the job or excluded from the job; to fight imperialism as it controls Black and other Third World women on welfare rolls; to fight imperialism as it keeps the wives of Black and other Third World workers locked economically and socially into their households or that they don't recognize and move against the common enemy; to fight imperialism as it uses capitalism, racism, and anti-woman propaganda and practices to oppress Black and other Third World people, the rest of the working class, and oppressed people around the world.

A highlight of the conference was a film "The Red Detachment of Women" made in China released in 1970 over three years after their Cultural Revolution. This precedent-setting film depicts the role of women in revolutionary struggle. This detachment of women was given the task of struggling politically and militarily with the Chinese landlord class.

The Women's workshops were greatly inspired by this movie as well as the organizational experiences shared with them by other Black and Third World women and men.

A proposed constitution for the Black Workers Congress was presented and accepted in principle.

Siege: National Voice of the Black Workers Congress, Vol. 1, No. 1 (1971):1, 10.

4. CONDITIONS FACING BLACK AND THIRD WORLD WORKERS

Speech given by John Watson at the first National
Conference of the Black Workers Congress
Gary, Indiana, Sept. 5, 1971

Brothers and Sisters:

It is a great honor and pleasure to address you at the first National Conference of the Black Workers Congress.

Black and other Third World folk, who have always been available whenever American Capitalism needed victims to exploit are now being made the primary victims of Nixon's New Economic Policy.

Whenever capitalism is in a period of acute crisis and sees its vital interests threatened, the ruling class forces the working class to bear the burden and make the supreme sacrifice to overcome the crisis.

Thus, under the guise of patriotism the ruling class herded millions of working class youth into the armed forces to fight and die in the unjust imperialist war in Vietnam, and now it calls on the working class to tighten its belts and bear the lion's share of the suffering caused by the present Wage-Price Freeze. And just as the Black and other Third World workers have been forced to take a disproportionately high rate of casualties in Vietnam, today they will be forced to bear the greatest brunt of the economic austerity program of the ruling class.

Moreover, Black and other Third World people are forced to provide the prime fodder for the increased extraction of surplus capital, the accelerated rate of exploitation, which Nixon and his ruling class cronies currently plan for the American working class.

The Black worker has traditionally played the role of the most exploited, brutally oppressed, and the most profitable source of labor that was so cheap that they received no remuneration for their work, except that required for bare subsistence, minimal food, clothing and shelter. That source of cheap labor was so productive that it earned huge profits for the white overlords of the day. Basically, from the billions upon billions of dollars of profits ripped from the hides of our forebears the American capitalist class accumulated the surplus capital necessary to build the American industrial empire.

Indeed the mighty industrial fortresses of General Motors, IBM, U.S. Steel, etc., are all laid on a foundation of Black and Brown blood, sweat and tears.

Since slavery, Black labor has continued to assume particular importance in the development of both domestic capital and international imperialism, primarily because the Black female and male workers are the final prop, the ultimate mainstay, onto which capitalism shifts its weight in order to survive.

Black workers have remained a source of the cheapest and most productive labor. First as agricultural labor, then as miners, merchant seamen, government, transportation and service workers, dock and warehouse workers, etc., and finally as the most exploited section of the proletariat in light and heavy industry. Today Black and other Third World workers are still solidly entrenched at the base of the proletariat.

In the building trades, for instance, only 4.3% of the operating engineers are Black and Puerto Rican, whereas they accounted for 39.3% of the laborers' union.

Blacks have always been the major source of the reserve army of labor, that vast body of men and women who find themselves unemployed, semiemployed or often permanently underemployed and used by big business to suppress the general level of wages. From 1958 to 1968 the official black unemployment rate never dropped below 6.4% and for half of that period the rate was never lower than 10.2%. Today Black unemployment has climbed astronomically, with unemployment rates 40% higher for Black and other Third World workers in many large cities. With unemployment so high, Black and other Third World workers remain a prime source of cheap, highly productive labor, facing a continual suppression of wages due to increased competition for jobs, especially in the service sector, fast foods, and related industries.

This suppression of wages is expanding broadly throughout all areas of the economy.

In the past, the ruling class used the tactic of divide and conquer against the working class. First they denied jobs to blacks, then used blacks to break white strikes. They constantly pitted white against black labor through the use of racism and white skin privilege. Eventually the unions recognized they could not exist without Black workers and the accommodation of blacks into these unions was brought about under the guise of equality, but in reality we are still the victims of the virulent racism of both the companies and the unions.

Moreover the companies still attempt to use Black labor as a wedge to force wage levels down.

For instance, the capitalists are faced with a squeeze in the construction industry, where white racist unions have forced wage levels upward through the practice of restricting entry of Black and Brown workers into these crafts. The capitalists answer this practice by calling for the integration of the building trades using such schemes as the Philadelphia plan, as well as through the introduction of prefabricated and modular housing construction techniques employing low paid Black and other Third World labor in factories. They have also established a wage-price stabilization board for the construction industry.

So we see that Blacks still are:

1. The lowest paid sector of the working class.
2. Forced into the worst jobs in the labor market except when needed to suppress the wages of overpaid whites.
3. Subjected to the most hazardous working conditions, higher mortality rate ($2\frac{1}{2}$ times that of whites) and high rates of industrial disease.
4. Subjected to discrimination on job placement, job upgrading, and classification.
5. Subjected to harsh regimentation and discipline on the job.
6. In a position of having little or no control of power in their union.

Of course these conditions have the subsidiary effect of maintaining such substandard conditions in Black working class communities as inadequate education and health care, inferior recreation facilities, police brutality, delapidated housing, and so on. Being relegated to the lowest paid, dirtiest jobs (as important as these jobs are to the U.S. economy) Black and other Third World workers often are forced to struggle for survival against both the unions and the companies. This continual struggle coupled with the rise of consciousness brought about by the civil rights movement and the rapid spread of revolutionary ideas has created in Blacks the most militant, class conscious, politically advanced and volatile section of the working class.

However it has been lack of organization that has prevented the power of Black and other Third World workers from being used to the fullest extent. Yet, generally without leadership, training, or organizational experience, Black working class organizations, caucuses, rank and file committees, and ad hoc groups have sprung up all over the nation in an amazingly wide variety of industries.

These groups are challenging both companies and unions on the issues of their racism, exploitation, and their generally class-collaborationist policies on health, safety, etc.

The reaction of the bourgeoisie to the rising militancy of Blacks has been the usual carrot and stick game.

On the one hand they have created a Black national bourgeoisie, new jobs as consultants on minority relations, personnel offices populated with Black tokens, minority training programs, etc. On the other hand the response has

been stepped-up repression of militant organizations, caucuses and their
leadership, the use of economic sanctions (firings, suspensions, etc.), the
use of court actions and injunctions, blacklisting, slander and threats of
violence--sometimes carried out--and the like.

None of this has stemmed the rise in class consciousness on the part of
Black workers, however. In fact given the objective situation in the world,
the steady rise of revolutionary consciousness, the African, Indo-Chinese, and
Latin American anti-imperialist struggles, it is impossible to prevent the
onward development of class struggle among all workers, much less among blacks.

The ruling class has thus attempted to prevent the development of conscious organization, especially, where it is under Marxist-Leninist leadership,
resolutely dedicated to the anti-imperialist movement, and to deny the resources,
skills and knowledge necessary to prepare and sustain organizational forms for
revolutionary struggle.

While Black labor has reacted predictably to its objective conditions of
existence (that is increasing militancy, national pride and class consciousness,
and increasing resistance to oppression) the American capitalist class also has
been beset by its own set of contradictions and has responded predictably.

Since World War II the U.S. has assumed the role of the dominant figure in
the western imperialist system. As a result, a series of phenomena have led to
political, economic and military disaster for imperialism's top dog, the U.S.A.
Some of these phenomena are:

1. The U.S. had consistently exported capital and currency through the
   use of foreign investment, foreign aid, maintenance of armies abroad,
   expanded tourism, and importing foreign goods.

2. The U.S. dollar had become the foundation (reserve currency) of the
   western monetary system while the U.S. accepted the gold standard
   (the price of gold was set at $35 per ounce). Foreign governments
   accumulated billions of dollars for which the U.S. did not have the
   gold to back them up. Consequently, the dollar became the object of
   regular recurring speculation by international currency dealers to
   force the U.S. to devalue, and giving the speculators a sizeable
   profit on the money markets.

3. The U.S. had expended vast sums of money on the defense of international imperialism, squandering dollars all over the world which
   were picked up by imperialism's allies, i.e. Japan, West Germany,
   Israel, South Vietnam, etc.

4. The fact that the dollar was overvalued in the world money market
   led to a huge deficit in the balance of payments position of the U.S.
   and led to the first U.S. deficit in the balance of trade since 1893.
   In a word U.S. imperialism had stretched itself thin.

5. With the continuation of the war in Vietnam, the general pattern of
   inflation developed with prices continually rising, unions pressing
   for higher wages, and the development of a wide range of wage levels
   throughout the working classes, and a general pattern of falling
   rates of profit for capitalists.

Caught in the contradiction of over-production, an adverse trade balance,
recession, galloping inflation and falling prices, the ruling class began
screaming for drastic policies to stabilize the economy. In recent months,
the capitalists began to experience panic between the competitive squeeze of
foreign industry, economic gains won by major unions, the pressures of the
international monetary system, and the Vietnamese war. . . .

With the government stepping in to enforce wage restrictions on the
brink of banning strikes, the role of the class collaborationist union
bureaucrats could be finished. They may be forced to fight--not in the
interest of the workers, but to prevent the ruling class from using its
direct powers to police workers thus eliminating the functional role now
played by the established union leadership. Let there be no doubt that the
Wage-Price Freeze is a gigantic giveaway to business at the expense of labor
--especially Black workers.

The Wage-Price Freeze puts no limit on the interest that banks charge,
creates no excess profit (as was the case in World War II), abolishes the

excise tax on autos, creates a 10% surcharge on imports, and revives the
investment tax credit allowing business to deduct 10% of their income tax.
There is, however, no freeze on the rise of professional fees, and the freeze
does not apply to the price of stocks. In fact, the stock market rose sharply
immediately following Nixon's announcement, and many corporations, mutual
funds, insurance companies, banks and other capitalist institutions reaped
millions in an orgy of profit taking.

This policy, coupled with $84.7 billion cut in non-military federal ex-
penditures means long term layoffs and long term wage freezes for lower level
governmental employees (Blacks). Nixon's current proposals call for a nine
billion dollar tax cut for industry against a two billion dollar cut for
individual tax payers (which will primarily benefit wealthy individuals).

The wage freeze will be enforced by a chorus of cheering corporate leaders
while there is no real enforcement mechanism on the price freeze. Corporations
plan price schedules in anticipation of deferred wage increases won by labor
in contracts signed months or even years ago. As a result, workers are losing
the increases they struggled for, while many companies have increased their
price schedules in advance. The United Farm Workers lose their 5 cent an hour
raise negotiated last year and due this October while prices were raised in
advance.

There is little doubt that there will be a continuation of the freeze in
one form or another after November. There will most certainly be the creation
of some kind of Wage-Price stabilization board to ride herd over the economic
demands of workers. Currently the capitalist press sees no return to the old
economic system: in fact, the *Wall Street Journal* predicted that the freeze
would end "sometime less than infinity," but the system would return to old
ways.

Perhaps most sinister, yet least publicized, are Nixon's plans on productivity. In the final analysis, the excess profits will once again be
squeezed out of the backs of workers.

The steel settlement, described by I. W. Abel U.S.W. president as, "one
of the most successful, if not the most successful contract negotiation" in
the union's history, won a 30% wage increase over a three year period, as well
as a renewal of the previously lost escalator clause. At the same time, an
agreement was made to set up "joint committees on productivity" to tackle the
"major problem" in the industry, lagging productivity. Both Secretary of
Labor James D. Hodgson and R. Health Larry, U.S. Steel Vice President (head of
the management team), cited this provision as having the most potential impact
of any in the agreement.

Immediately after the signing of the steel contract, Nixon slapped a
freeze on wages. But there was no freeze on production rises, on increased
regimentation, on the use of time or motion studies. Moreover the price
freeze did not effect the steel industrial corporations. They were allowed to
quietly raise the price of steel 8% after the freeze went into effect. Nixon's
call for the establishment of productivity boards on a national level is a
clear step to increase the exploitation of workers.

We can expect working conditions to continue to decline, safety conditions
to deteriorate even more and production to speed up to an even more exploitative rate.

The number of casualties resulting from the stepped up class warfare
brought on by the "New Economic Policy" will increase in coming months and
years. Accidents, disease, fatalities and injuries will increase, as will the
harassment of workers by foremen and other supervisors. Disciplinary actions,
suspensions and firings will increase, and workers in this country will respond
to this violent pressure with increasing violence (for example James Johnson of
the Chrysler Eldon Plant in Detroit or Ike Jernigan at Lockheed Plant in L.S.).
Federal cutbacks in domestic spending will further exacerbate the problem of
inadequate housing and education, inferior health care, the pollution of the
environment and the many other insidious effects of a panicky capitalist
system galloping wildly in a frenzied search for more profits.

The working class will move to defend its interests because it has no
choice. The burden of capitalism is becoming too heavy for the workers to
carry, and we can easily predict that Black and Third World workers who are
most victimized by this new capitalist offensive which escalates that class
war, will be in the vanguard leading the counterattack against imperialism.

But from where will these workers derive their leadership? Who will guide them into battle? Who will raise the slogans of class warfare? Who will unmask and expose the infinite tricks and duplicity yet to be used by business to satisfy its rapacious appetite for profit? Who will clarify the issues, and expose the sell out class-collaborationist union leadership?

Who will organize, call national demonstrations which raise the clarion for total class solidarity, for general strikes in which the power of workers at the point of production to seize control of industry is shown?

Who will put an end to the clique of madmen who presently manipulate the political and economic resources of this country so as to bring havoc and destruction to the world's people?

Due to the years of class-collaborationist policies the established unions are hopelessly paralyzed when it comes to real class struggle.

The old left has long ago given up revolutionary practice for reformist and revisionist policies which are totally out of touch with present reality.

The new left is fragmented and demoralized and barely understands the role of the Black and Third World working class anyway.

The Black Workers Congress armed with a correct analysis and program, coupled with its projected activity being national in scope, is the only currently existing organization that promises to provide the leadership necessary in the upcoming struggle.

We must rise to this historic task. We must put forth the revolutionary slogans.

We must organize the broad masses to understand the necessity of building socialism.

We must train and educate a highly developed cadre of workers.

We must develop broad class solidarity and prepare to lead massive demonstrations and strikes.

We must relentlessly lay blow upon blow on our vicious class enemy to end the perpetuation of racism, capitalism and imperialism. Blow upon blow to these racist murderers and ruthless oppressors, blow upon blow to their repressive state apparatus, to their courts, their army, their police and other military and para-military forms, their foremen and executives, their corporations and all of their flunkies, high and low.

And we must continue to battle them until they are wholly, completely, resolutely, and utterly destroyed, and their evil influence is eradicated forever from the face of the earth.

John Watson

Siege: National Voice of the Black Workers Congress, Vol. 1, No. 1 (1971):9-10.

5. BLACK WORKERS DELEGATION IN VIETNAM

In 1924 a young Vietnamese journalist named Nguyen Ai Quoc wrote an angry and brilliant article condemning the common American practice of lynching Black people. He began that article with these words, "as it is commonly known, the Black people are the most oppressed people in the world."

Nguyen Ai Quoc made that statement and launched his campaign against the brutalization of black people in America on the basis of his own personal knowledge. He lived for a while in the United States where he made his home in Harlem and became the the the close friend of many Black people, among them Marcus Garvey, the father of modern day Black Nationalism.

Nguyen Ai Quoc later changed his name to Ho Chi Minh. By that name, Ho Chi Minh, his memory is loved and revered by the Vietnamese people as the father of the Vietnamese Revolution and the first president of the Democratic Republic of Vietnam.

True to the memory and heritage of Ho Chi Minh, the people of North Vietnam and the revolutionary fighters in the South Vietnamese Liberation Army still maintain their understanding, support and sense of brotherhood with Afro-American people and other oppressed people inside the United States.[88]

In North Vietnam our delegation was greeted and treated like visiting relatives. Not only by Vietnamese officials, but also by farmers, factory workers, students, women and even young children who met and played with us on the streets where we wandered at our leisure without any guides, guards or escorts.

In complete honesty we must say that we found the Vietnamese leaders to be better informed, more factually up-to-date and more sympathetic to the plight of our people than any of the rich, white politicians who are sending our brothers to Indo-China to die - any of them, from Kennedy to Agnew, from Longstreth to Rizzo!

As a Black person who has lived in the ghettoes of Chester and North Philadelphia as well as in the racist wilderness of Mississippi, I must also say that at night on the streets of Hanoi and in the country side of North Vietnam, I felt perfectly safe and unafraid for the first time in my adult life. In North Vietnam there are no street gangs, no trigger-happy, nigger-hating cops, no pushers, no junkies, no unemployment, no children dying of malnutrition and deteriorating neighborhoods except in those areas where American bombs have left homes, schools, hospitals, farms, nurseries and churches in ruins.

But the Vietnamese people are rebuilding their country in the North even while defending their country in the South. Nothing less than the total nuclear destruction of Vietnam will bring the U.S. government and the U.S. military anything but defeat, defeat and more defeat. The Vietnamese will win. Our task, as Black people and as peace-loving people of any race, are: 1) to step up the movement against the war, 2) demand that Nixon withdraw all of the troops, and 3) to demand that not one solitary penny of our tax money goes to support the Uncle Tom Saigon puppet administration.

Most important, the task of Black people is to totally refuse to partici-pate in the war in Vietnam: to stop letting Nixon make murderers and corpses out of our sons, and to encourage Black G.I.'s (who make up 50% of the battle-field forces in Vietnam) to either put down their guns or to turn their guns on our real enemies instead of the Vietnamese.

Similarly, we would do well to learn from the experiences and determina-tion of the People's Republic of China, the nation to which Richard Nixon sent Henry Kissinger on a beggar's errand just a few days before our own very pleasant, non-secret visit which I hope we can discuss in more detail.[89]

Siege: National Voice of the Black Workers Congress, Vol. 1, No. 1 (1971):11.

AUTO

6. BLACK WORKERS IN REVOLT

By Robert Dudnick

Black, White Together?

Something is happening in the ranks of American labor and neither the bosses nor the generality of union bureaucrats are pleased.

Militant black workers are on the move, demanding an end to racial oppression in the unions as well as in the shops. This development, mush-rooming in Detroit, must be given complete support by the radical movement. It is one of today's most significant struggles.

The privileged position of the white worker is the material base of white working-class racism. The white worker must be convinced to renounce this privilege. As long as millions of black workers are forced to endure double oppression--as workers and as blacks--often with the connivance of

white workers who have accepted and even defended white privilege, the working
class will be divided and class solidarity unobtainable.

Institutionalized racism, white supremacy, benefits only the ruling
class in the end. But the short-run economic and social benefits of white
supremacy are nonetheless real for many white workers. These privileges are
false, not because they do not exist but because they lead white workers to
line up with the boss against the rest of the working class. In many situations, white workers will have to fight against these short-run self-interests
to win their class interest and establish class solidarity.

In conducting militant agitation against racism, the black workers in
Detroit--forming themselves into such groups as the Ford Revolutionary Union
Movement (FRUM), Dodge Revolutionary Union Movement (DRUM) and so forth--are
striking a blow for eventual class solidarity. And if they have to do so by
fighting and organizing against the "liberal and progressive" leadership of
the United Auto Workers, so be it.

One of the UAW locals coming under fire from FRUM recently characterized
the militant black workers as "black bigots." This is a lie. The black
workers are struggling for their minimal rights in a racist union in a racist
company in a racist society.

White supremacy in the unions and the working class must be attacked as
the basis for developing class consciousness and the solidarity necessary to
battle the ruling class. This is a precondition. There can be no such thing
as victory--even a reformist victory--if blacks, as blacks, are kept one degree
below whites.

There used to be a slogan about "black and white together." This was an
illusion. How can there be "togetherness," for instance, when a 20% across-
the-board wage increase, or seniority rights, means one thing to the white
worker and quite another to the black, who is paid less for similar work; who
is the last hired, first fired; who is rarely promoted; who is forced to live
in a ghetto; who is systematically miseducated; who is discriminated against
in every aspect of life?

Storm in Auto

A specter haunts Detroit that tomorrow will haunt the nation. It is the
specter of black revolution in basic industry--the unity of national struggle
and class struggle. A week of investigation here indicates that the Detroit
black workers movement is the most important revolutionary action in the
country.

All the elements are here. The vanguard is here. The workers are here.
The guts of monopoly capitalism's production are here. And the conditions
are worsening in Detroit's auto plants.

The League of Revolutionary Black Workers operates from an office at
9049 Oakland in one of the city's black ghettos. It is made up of three
black worker organizations--the Dodge Revolutionary Union Movement (DRUM), the
Ford Revolutionary Union Movement (FRUM), and the Eldon Ave. Revolutionary
Union Movement (ELRUM), at Chrysler Corp.'s only gear and axle plant. Joining it soon will be JARUM, the Jefferson Ave. Revolutionary Union Movement, at
another Chrysler plant.

Since DRUM started at Dodge Main in Hamtramck, a suburb surrounded by
Detroit, the movement has caught fire to the extent that the league plans to
organize black workers wherever they are--not only in Detroit and not only in
auto.

But the black insurgency would have a tremendous effect even if it were
limited to this city's auto plants. If they can be shut down, steel, rubber
and glass will totter, too. And there is enough black muscle here to shut
them down tight.

Those in the driver's seat of the multibillion dollar auto industry are
worried. The United Auto Workers union, run by Walter Reuther from the sleek
Solidarity House here, is also worried. Both have tried to buy off the
workers.

"We have also been informed by a reliable source that the company [Ford]
has instructed some union officials [of UAW Local 600] to kill one of our
people as an example and they have promised that the Dearborn police will not

even arrest them," Mike Hamlin of the league's central committee said.

Two factors appear to have led to the black labor insurgency. One is the general black liberation movement, which has increased its pace and deepened its analysis since the old civil rights movement. The other is DRUM, FRUM and ELRUM's ability to link that struggle to immediate conditions facing black auto workers.

In the Engine Plant

At Ford's Rouge complex in suburban Dearborn, a company town even worse than Dodge's Hamtramck, there is particular concern about the engine plant, where some of the hardest work is done. Before FRUM, conditions were so bad that some workers who are part-time preachers were holding prayer meetings during breaks with company consent. One assembly line is supposed to have a maximum production of 136 units an hour. But it often runs as much as 172 units an hour. Even the lower figure is considered dangerous to health and safety.

The UAW, born of violence and militancy in the 1930s, finally organized Ford in 1942, the last major auto producer to sign a union contract. Since then, it has done nothing for the black worker. In the Ford engine plant, for example, few grievances are filed for black workers. The contract says shop stewards are supposed to work the line four hours a shift and attend to union business the other four hours. But in return for not filing grievances, the company allows them "to spend the entire eight hours doing nothing," a FRUM spokesman said.

Meanwhile, conditions at Dodge Main had led to five wildcat strikes before some young blacks helped lead a walkout on May 2, 1968. Although Detroit's black revolutionaries had always had a working-class outlook, they had not had much success until that month.

Vanguard elements were grouped around the *Inner City Voice,* which started publication in September 1967 after the city's black rebellion as the successor to the *Black Vanguard,* which ceased in 1964. The tiny *Voice* group had a long history in the black struggle and was able to mobilize its base around the paper.

Nine assembly workers came to the *Voice* group in 1968 and began working with a staff member who was fired from an auto plant for participating in a wildcat. They developed a revolutionary analysis and began publishing the DRUM newsletter.

At first the newsletter was written entirely by the workers, exposing conditions in the plant. But because, as one of the *Voice* staff members put it, "you can't build movements on exposes," the *Voice* group began "integrating ourselves with the workers" and writing political articles for the newsletter. Blacks from the streets and the *Voice* group distributed the newsletter at the plant, leading the company to charge that the Northern-style cotton choppers were being stirred up by "outside agitators."

Union in Chaos

"By the eighth week of the newsletter," Hamlin recalled, "the plant was in an uproar." Black workers were screaming for a strike and DRUM membership was growing. "The company began to walk softly and the union was in chaos," he said.

The leadership agreed with the demand to strike and Dodge Main was hit on July 8, 1968. The nine workers and the *Voice* staff mobilized militant community elements and manned picket lines, with the in-plant leadership talking to workers 100 yards from the picketers. Had they been any closer at that stage, they would have been fired.

The picketers stopped only black workers—about 70% of the workforce—and the wildcat was a "tremendous success," closing the plant Friday and Monday. This was possible because nearly all black workers stayed out.

"We are learning," Hamlin said. "We struck because the workers demanded a strike," but did not continue past the two days because DRUM did not have the organization to run a protracted strike. The strike was seen as a test of what DRUM could do.

A surge of membership hit DRUM after the walkout--from Dodge Main and
other plants as well. The organization went into a "very serious" effort to
tighten structure while increasing organizing activities.
Meanwhile, DRUM began to move on the UAW another way--in Local 3 elections.
Although DRUM considers itself an independent black workers organization, not
an old-fashioned caucus, it tries to keep its tactics supple to fit the situation. DRUM entered union politics to demonstrate its power and race consciousness.
DRUM candidate Ron March led in the preliminary election for trustee,
winning 563 votes to 521 for Joe Elliot, a white man backed by the Local 3
leadership. But even this was in doubt--DRUM charges many votes were stolen
from March.
Cars with March posters were ticketed and delayed on election day by
Hamtramck police. Cops swept through bars near the union hall, beating black
workers. White workers and cars bearing other posters were not harassed.
About 50 black workers went to the Local 3 union hall to talk it over.
The police, led by UAW official "Cannonball" Selpski, invaded the hall and
maced the workers. They also used ax handles.
March lost the Oct. 3, 1968 runoff by what Local 3 claimed was about 700
votes. Local 3 has 10,000 members, of which 60% are black. But the local
managed to mobilize more than 1300 white retirees, who are allowed to vote in
UAW elections even though they no longer work.
From the beginning, DRUM had included workers at the allied Huber Ave.
Foundry because they also belong to Local 3. Workers from other plants also
attended DRUM meetings. "We took plants as workers came to us," Hamlin said,
and workers at several area plants are beginning to organize against the auto
industry's Big Three.
FRUM started when Ford workers who had been attending DRUM meetings came
out with their own newsletter. The situation there was more difficult, however, because Dearborn is a company town. Ford even owns the highway into the
plant. The factory is hardly as accessible as Dodge Main. "The few copies that
were able to be distributed prompted an immediate and vicious reaction by the
plant and the union," a central committee member said. Aside from the
kill-and-go-free deal, one FRUM organizer was challenged to a duel and some UAW
shop stewards have taken to waving guns in work areas.
ELRUM, the next unit, was started by one man. "We began with this one
fellow," Hamlin said, "and we started publishing a newsletter at the plant.
The response was the same; as a matter of fact, the response was even greater
than at Dodge."
Some problems developed in ELRUM--the workers did not at first have the
theoretical background of the DRUM leadership and their tactics showed it.
Furthermore, ELRUM grew too fast for the structure to keep pace. But conditions were bad enough so that ELRUM had to take a revolutionary line.
Things came to a head about two months ago, when, during the eighth week
of the ELRUM newsletter, 300 black workers descended on UAW Local 961 and
demanded to be heard. The local's president tried to fob them off, but the
workers presented a list of demands anyway.
The local adjourned its regular executive board meeting and the bureaucrats, with the 300 workers, went into a general meeting which lasted long
enough for those on the afternoon shift to miss starting time.
When they returned to work the next day, 66 of the 300 were disciplined
immediately and more were hit later. The discipline ranged from five days to
a month off. The workers struck, using the same tactics that had been employed
at Dodge. "The plant was stopped cold, meaning that if we had shut it down for
a couple of days, Chrysler would have had to start shutting down plants all
across the country," Hamlin said. Chrysler has no other gear and axle plant.
"It was just one day to let Chrysler feel the impact of the workers' strength."
"Chrysler moved immediately. They discharged 26 workers. Now, mind you,
none of the workers at Eldon manned any pickets," Hamlin said--the support
cadre did that. Among those fired were four workers with at least 20 years
seniority each.
Workers, joined by black and white radicals, resumed picketing at
Solidarity House. Chrysler headquarters in Highland Park also has been
picketed.
Additionally, a national boycott of all Chrysler products is being mapped

so that by 1970 anyone who drives a new Chrysler Corp. car through any black
ghetto "will be placing himself in grave danger." Hamlin predicts that 90% of
Detroit's black people will support the boycott.

Most intensive organizing has been at Dodge and the company has threatened
to move the plant—built in 1924 from Hamtramck. "Wherever they build these
plants," Hamlin said, "the nature of the work is such that black people will be
required to do that work because the white people will not do the hard-ass
work." Besides, he added, it is more profitable to use cheap black labor than
to automate because there is more surplus value extracted from live labor than
from a machine at this point.

The league is an umbrella group for DRUM, FRUM, ELRUM and JARUM. It does
not dictate policy to any of them (or to its high school affiliate, *Black
Student Voice*), but provides a broad framework in which they can operate.

The league's central committee handles technical assistance and resembles
a working general staff. Within each revolutionary union movement, however,
there is a structure which covers everything from the department to the overall
plant. Constituent organizations are represented by the central committee, the
members of which are responsible for specific areas—editorial, treasury,
intelligence and security, internal education and so on.

The leadership plays down personalities, learning from the experience of
some other black organizations. Central committee members teach each other
whatever particular skills they may have to develop leadership depth.

What makes it all go, however, is the base. "DRUM has no intention of
abandoning the man on the line," central committee member John Watson said,
"because the man on the line *is* DRUM; the man on the line is the basic unit of
DRUM."

Caste and Class

While there have been plenty of bread-and-butter and antibureaucracy
rebellions in latter-day American labor history, nothing much has happened in
a radical way since the formation of the CIO in the 1930s. Now, however, what
could easily turn into a revolutionary kick in the pants for the left is
developing among black workers.

Why? It is not merely a question of correct practice. Behind the practice lies a conscious theory, an ideological concept put into the mold of
black requirements.

Its most powerful attraction is that it combines the struggle of domestically colonized Afro-America with the class struggle.

"Well," said Mike Hamlin, a main spokesman for the League of Revolutionary
Black Workers, "I think it's inevitable that there has to be a revolution in
this country, that the ruling class has to be overthrown, and I think eventually that at least all black workers will recognize this."

"Most of our people probably see it as a caste struggle as opposed to
class. I think that's a natural development at this time," he continued. "I
think that in a protracted struggle it will become more of a class struggle.
However, I don't see much movement among white workers to begin to wage any
kind of struggle. . . . We think that a certain kind of development is inevitable, given the actual situation in terms of the masses of people involved;
there's only one direction they can go."

The caste and class terminology is a restatement of the position that
black people are oppressed as workers, and also as colonized subjects of white
America. In the latter instance, black people therefore must be approached on
a national basis, as blacks. This can unite all sectors of the black community in an anticolonial struggle, in somewhat the same way the Chinese fought
the anti-Japanese war while they fought the class war.

But the class analysis, which must develop after the caste approach, can
sift out black workers from other black strata. It can also enable black
workers to struggle together with white workers on a strictly class basis—if
white workers ever get organized.

At this time, however, the league does not see any chance of that. "If
you're talking about a working class in this country," a league leader said,
"at this point you can only talk about black workers. We don't see any identification of white workers with any kind of class movement. We know that

white workers occupy a privileged position within the working class—at least
they think they do—and they enjoy a great number of benefits."
    Although the league and its constituent groups work with all militant
black groups here, there are sharp differences over theory. The league is not
a cultural nationalist organization, although some people apparently think so.
What the league does is to use black identity and anticolonialism—which are
legitimate concerns in the first place—as part of a more general struggle.

Where the Buck Is

    For example, central committee member John Watson, speaking of the ruling-
class New Detroit Committee's attempts to buy off black liberation, said: "If
you simply have a ghetto analysis, you would think that when you begin to see
all these black things in the ghetto—community centers, schools, that kind of
black nationalism thing—that black people are actually getting somewhere.
But when it gets down to the level of production, the level where the Man is
actually making the buck off the black people, nothing is being done."
    Racism is seen as a product of economic and other forces. "I think it's
a bit of both," one militant said, "more having an economic base, but I think
racism has existed in this country for so long . . . that it has some of the
other [cultural psychological] aspects in it. . . . Europeans in general have
some kind of deeply rooted racist strain." But this can be wiped out, he
added, in the heat of the struggle.
    What appears to make the league different from other groups is its stress
on exploitation at the point of production. Even its national-form organizing
is done there, rather than in the basically powerless "community." Other black
groups have paid some attention to point-of-production considerations. But
they have asked or demanded more and better jobs. The thrust of the league's
ideology points to worker control of the means of production.
    Revolutionary theory often is one thing and immediate practice something
else. The league does not consider this to be a problem. "We think that our
long-range objectives are inevitable and anything we do is just a step toward
that end," Hamlin said. He also said that black workers here have gone all
the reformist routes and found them to be dead ends—a revolutionary line is
the only clear road. The concept seems to be one of engaging the struggles on
reformist issues which will clearly lead to revolution, rather than engaging
in reformist battles simply for reformist ends.
    Another central committee member said the league's internal education
program stresses Marxism, but takes from it what is most applicable to Afro-
America. A similar process is used with the writings of Frantz Fanon who,
while addressing himself to colonial liberation of peoples of color, did not
write much about the peculiarly American condition in which the colonized
people is a numerical minority oppressed by natives of the same land.

New Marxist Language

    It is interesting to note that the league shuns the elitist position of
some older leftist groups that confine themselves to internal debate. The
league does not consider the workers stupid, but realizes that people who work
on an auto assembly line 40 or more hours a week are not likely to sit through
a session dead-weighted with heavy Marxist terminology. So those who conduct
internal education "reinterpret Marxism in the language of the community."
    A DRUM leader outlined what probably is the basic ideological view: the
working class can change society at the point of production. But there are
two working classes at this stage of American capitalism—black and white.
The blacks form a "subproletariat." They can be organized on a caste basis,
but can work revolutionary change on a class basis.

It's Pure Hell

Anybody who thinks workers are bought off with color television and two cars hasn't worked on an auto assembly line lately.

You can make maybe $130 a week on the line. But you'll bust your ass doing it. Compulsory overtime is as certain as model changeover layoffs. And if you're black, it's three times worse.

Rose Logan, a black woman, worked in Dept. 25 of Chrysler's Eldon Ave. gear and axle plant here. She was run down by a forklift driven by a white man. The company doctor gave her a quick examination and sent her back to Dept. 25. Rose Logan finished out her shift, then went home.

A few weeks later she died from her injuries.

There is more. Injuries, racism and wanton firings occur every day in every plant. The following is a review of some instances:

One Friday night, Curtis Lee, a black man, was crossing the street in front of the Dodge Main plant in Hamtramck when he was hit by a car and thrown 100 feet. Plant guards refused to help, saying they did not know if the bleeding man in the street was a Dodge employe. Black workers went to his aid, but Hamtramck city cops told them to "move along." When Lee finally got to the hospital, he was in critical condition from internal injuries, a fractured skull, three broken ribs, a broken arm and two broken legs.

On the night of Sept. 7, 1967, Willie Brookins, father and auto worker, was returning to Dodge Main from his lunch break. He had a paper bag with two sausages in it and showed the contents to the gate guard. Inside the property, a second guard demanded to see the contents, hinting that Brookins had a bomb stashed in the bag. Brookins ignored him and went up the elevator to his third-floor work area. The guard and his captain went up too, took the sausages from the bag, threw them to the floor and stomped on them. A fight broke out. Brookins was sent home. On Sept. 11, 1967, he was fired and denied unemployment compensation.

A white superintendent at Dodge named Little had a black worker, Floyd Daniels, suspended for sleeping in a rest area. A month later, Little caught a white union steward named Syl sleeping in a first-floor work area. No action was taken.

In Dept. 9160, where 60% of the workers are black, Dodge supervisory personnel locked the door to their office during the hottest part of the summer. The reason: their office had the only working Coke machine in the area.

There are other little things. Dodge suspended Ray Johnson for leaving a pair of safety glasses in a lunch area. John Matthews, Jr. was fired for being seven minutes late. Plant guards at Dodge Main are packing Mace.

These are individual manifestations of general company and union policies. To get the broader picture, it helps to know that Ford, for example, fires about 600 black workers a week, who then hire on at other auto plants to be fired again. This gives the companies a revolving pool of desperate workers. It also allows Ford to replace the 600 with 200-300 new workers, thereby doubling and tripling the workload of those who are left. The 600 discharged workers usually are fired on their 89th day of employment, one day short of gaining seniority. Meanwhile, the United Auto Workers has already taken out its $20 initiation fee and three months dues ($7 a month). This means the UAW is getting at least $30,000 a year in all plants from 89-day-and-goodbye black workers.

On top of that, Ford and other companies collect poverty-program money for training "hard core" people, parolees and welfare mothers. They are told to do the job or have their parole revoked or welfare cut off. There are women working underneath cars on the line in pools of oil and grease. DRUM calls all this "niggermation."

Until recently, the only acceptable excuse for absence was a doctor's note saying the worker was ill and under treatment. Black workers needed two notes. The policy has been changed somewhat: Ford no longer accepts notes from black doctors.

Chuck Wooten, one of the founders of the Dodge Revolutionary Union Movement who was fired from Dodge Main, worked in the body shop there, making components for Dodge Chargers. He had to assemble three pieces of stock and do 24 spotwelds. "Now, most of the metal in the body shop is very sharp and gloves are hard to get, you understand," he said. "See, what it is, foremen

get a bonus—I think it's on a quarterly basis-for the less safety equipment
they have to use, such as gloves and aprons, and if you've got a foreman that's
profit-conscious, you're gonna have hell getting gloves." Gloves sometimes
last a week, when you can get them.

"On the spotwelding line upstairs on the seventh floor," Wooten said,
"there's a heavy concentration of smoke and workers are constantly inhaling
this day in and day out. You might be working over a hole in the floor [the
plant was built in 1924], you're constantly working, you have to avoid the
hole in the floor."

Down in the Pit

Many jobs involve making several spotwelds on cars from the bottom. This
means the worker stands in the pit, bent over backward, reaching above and
behind him, all day. Between 56 and 64 cars come through the pit each hour.
There are four workers in the pit. Each handles two spotwelding guns. They
do this for the entire shift, except for lunch and two 23-minute breaks.
"Usually on these jobs there's not time enough to even light a cigarette. This
is a fact," Wooten said.

"The thing that sticks in my mind mostly," he said, "is the incident that
happened two years ago where there was a black inspector who worked next to me,
inspecting the stock I put on the line . . . and they came up to him one day
and told him that 'We're laying you off because there's an overabundance of
inspectors and we're going to put you on the line.' And the next morning he
was on the line and the next morning there was also a new white hiree on his
job as inspector." The white man had never worked in an auto plant.

In the four years Wooten worked at Dodge Main, he saw the assemblyline
chain break at least 15 times. This is the chain that propels the cars on
dollies down the line in somewhat the manner a carwash chain works. When the
chain breaks, the force hurls the dollies together at 60-80 miles an hour.
Many workers labor in the foot and a half space between the dollies. Last
time the chain broke, a foreman was caught between dollies. Both his legs
were cut off below the knees.

And so on.

The White Workers

Where do white workers stand in relation to the black revolt in the auto
plants? How can whites be organized? Should they be organized? There are a
lot of opinions.

The Ford Revolutionary Union Movement, part of the League of Revolutionary
Black Workers, gave this advice: "We as black people do not need white people
to move in behalf of us, but they move because they are oppressed too, and we
of FRUM do not see that type of action at present so we say to the other
[white] groups—keep up the nibbling and we'll do the chopping."

Among white radicals in and out of the plants, opinion is divided. Jim
Jacobs of the National Organizing Committee's Detroit collective believes that
auto production will be all black in the next 40 years, with whites in all
skilled classifications. Meanwhile, however, he sees white workers as "caught
in a terrific bind"—real wages are down, speedups are increasing and younger
whites intensely dislike factory work.

As basic industry turns black, Jacobs reasons, white workers will increasingly go into service work, thus fragmenting them and breaking down the
socialization of labor upon which revolutionary action is based. He believes
it will take far sharper objective conditions to move the white working class.
But from the present conditions it is possible to recruit and develop
organizers.

Jacobs and Detroit NOC believe sharper contradictions are not impossibly
far off. In a position paper presented at a general NOC conference in
Chicago Feb. 22-23, the Detroit staff said, "Profits once made on expansion
must now be made on speedups, increased productivity through heavier automation and wage controls or layoffs" because of developing world recession.

"The effects on older, skilled workers may be serious too," the draft document declares. "But young workers and blacks with less seniority in the shop and less capital invested in their skills will be hit hardest and first. The blacks have their movement but there is no equivalent for young whites-- only George Wallace."[90]

Martin Glaberman, national chairman of Facing Reality, an organization grouped around author C. L. R. James, takes a somewhat different view. He says that white workers are in a minority here and it no longer really matters what they do. Elsewhere, however, Glaberman adds, organizing white workers is crucial.[91]

He sees the white working class as both inherently revolutionary--and racist. "People were educated into racism," he says, "and conceivably they can be educated out of it" as long as it is understood that black demands will not be submerged in the process.

Detroit's black workers are vital, he believes. Glaberman recalls something many have forgotten: the 1967 black rebellion here shut down the auto plants in addition to burning out some ghetto merchants. This had an effect on white workers as well as blacks. When auto plants shut down, a lot of American industry quivers.

Another view is expressed by Art Fox, head of the United Caucus in UAW Ford Local 600. Altough United Caucus leaders have taken individual antiracism stands, he says, the caucus itself has no official position on FRUM. "Most of us see the need for a combination of forces," but FRUM does not, he complains. "Racism unfortunately cannot be a primary" aspect in organizing white workers, Fox believes. On the other hand, he says, "racism is the key to the whole business" and FRUM sometimes indiscriminately attacks white workers for the same kind of racism displayed by company and union personnel.

(A *Guardian* reporter, however, read a mountain of revolutionary union movement literature and could find no more than four or five such instances, apart from the use of words "honkie" and "Polish pig." In the overwhelming majority of cases, white racism was discussed in terms of supervisory and union personnel).

Fox, whose United Caucus is centered in the skilled trades, holds a view at sharp variance with that of other white organizers. NOC's Jacobs believes racism must be attacked first so that white privilege can be knocked down. Glaberman thinks racism should be quickly handled.

Must Begin Now

Jim Griffin, a Marxist toolmaker apprentice in an auto plant, says that white radicals have "got to start now because the black struggle is not going to stop for anyone." But he also says that racism will not disappear before captialism goes and it is necessary to attack the root before the leaf. He fears that as the black struggle spreads to other cities where the Detroit savvy does not exist, there may be a tendency for blacks to take a strictly nationalist line in addition to the tone they use toward white workers.

Mike Hamlin of the League of Revolutionary Black Workers looks at it as a matter of no-choice survival. "We have got to do our thing, which is to organize blacks to carry out the struggle, and in order to insure that history doesn't repeat itself we have to move in this way. Progressive elements in the white populace will understand because of their knowledge of this history."

The history he refers to is the general submergence of black interests to white bread-and-butter issues during the days of the old left's caucus approach to rank-and-file insurgency.

How are white workers reacting to the black movement? Opinions differ here too.

"There have been two reactions," Hamlin says. "The majority of them have become passive and there's another segment that has become reactionary; they're frightened, they're carrying guns. They're reacting in various ways, including supporting Wallace, but they don't do that openly too often, depending on whether or not they constitute a majority in the plant."

Griffin, who worked on the assembly line before his apprenticeship, thinks that the white reactions will break down this way when the black people get up even more steam:

1--Surprise, with some expression of racism, but general passivity.
2--Behind that, a feeling of admiration of black courage.
3--A learning of lessons, some private conversations, and a few whites moving into supportive roles, especially if there are white radicals around who "always drive the basic lessons home" about racism.

White racism from workers, Chuck Wooten of the Dodge Revolutionary Union Movement says, "used to be a problem before DRUM . . . until we started organizing black workers around the issue of racism. . . . I think it's a question of more respect for the black workers now. Like it would be nothing for a general foreman to run up and immediately start harassing the black worker for making some type of mistake, when now they're usually met with as much argument as they give. In a few instances, we've had some ass-kicking done."

This ties in with Griffin's factory experience that workers want people to "prove that you have a backbone--that you know what you can get away with."

Griffin believes there is a sharp need for white factory organizers. "Hell, let's face it," he says, "a lot of white radicals are floating around doing nothing." If those radicals with working-class politics want to get into carefully selected factories, "it's time to start doing it now," while maintaining the campus strength the white movement has built," he says.

Hamlin seemed to sum it up: "A conscious proletariat cannot be racist."

A Working Town

When it comes to Midwestern cities, Chicago may be hog butcher to the world, as the poet said, but it took Detroit wheels to get the hogs on their way.

Detroit has several other industries--chemical, some rubber and electric-- but the town rises and falls with auto. A B. F. Goodrich advertising sign along a freeway tells you at a glance what the year's to-date auto production is. Men riding home on the bus talk more about welding than the stock market; they carry little yellow lanterns instead of attache cases.

It's a working town with dirt under its fingernails. Downtown closes early--people have to get up early.

Detroit has a reputation as a good town for black people. It's not true.

The main black ghetto runs along 12th St., but there are many other black areas scattered across town, starting from the old ghetto near downtown and the Detroit River. The area has become an urban renewal target and the houses, a few of them still occupied, look a lot like those in the black area of Greenwood, Miss. The only difference seems to be that a school on East Lafayette has been named for the late Rev. Dr. Martin Luther King Jr.

The July 1967 rebellion sent funnels of smoke high into the air and white Detroit didn't quite know how it happened. Many white people went across the river to Windsor, Ont., to look at the burning skyline. Some even moved there. The new vantage point does not seem to have improved their perception much.

But Martin Glaberman, a white radical, has an unusual view of what happened here. He says the rebellion stemmed not from "despair," but from a positive sense of black power. The civil rights movement left some impression on Detroit and the city's ghettos are populated by workers to a high degree. The last point is confirmed by black leaders.

For a look at how the ruling class does its duty here, John Watson of the Dodge Revolutionary Union Movement and the *South End,* Wayne State University student paper, puts it this way:

"The ruling class here has been making certain kinds of moves designed to coopt the revolutionary movement and designed to buy off revolutionary leaders. The most obvious example of this developed immediately after the revolt. What's happened is that you've had a two-poled movement here going at the same time. One is a movement to organize an independent base of black workers which has been developing out of the conditions black workers face in the plants, and the other is an attempt by the ruling class to develop all sorts of progressive-sounding programs . . . and give all sorts of people positions and money and projects to run. . . ."

The white left is rather unusual here. Detroit has been a stronghold of Trotskyism; there are several groups which split from the Socialist Workers

party in addition to a barrelful of independent ex-Trotskyists. The Communist
party, once a power, no longer has any independent influence, but does hold
some strength in parts of the Democratic party. SDS at Wayne State is small,
but is trying to look toward the working-class and community colleges. The
whites appear to be trying to get themselves together.

The media are among the worst in the nation's big cities. The evening
Detroit News is heavily slanted against black people, the morning *Free Press*
less so. WJBK-TV also slants the news.

Combatting this is the *South End,* the Wayne State University student
newspaper, which is controlled by black and white militants, an underground
FM station, WABX, and the *Fifth Estate,* which tries to steer a course between
hard politics and hippie culture. A black daily paper is being talked about.

Detroit is also the hometown of the White Panthers, headed by John
Sinclair. The White Panthers sound like the extreme left wing of the Yippies.
They do a pale imitation of Black Panther rhetoric and see revolution as a
cultural event. Although not considered a serious force, some sources say
they have helped discredit the white left among black militants.

'Why I Joined DRUM'

*Chuck Wooten is one of the original nine workers who founded the Dodge
Revolutionary Union Movement here. Speaking with the Guardian, he told why:*

My thing for getting in DRUM was that from the first day I got hired in,
I noticed immediately that the day I was hired there were about 60 of us hired
at the same time and we were all taken to the body shop. And out of that
number, about 40 were black. Out of this group, I think it was between seven
and 10 of the white workers that went into the body shop went into inspection
and the others [whites] were systematically given light jobs on the sixth
and seventh floors.

The area of the line I went into, it was putting fenders and doors on the
cars and, well, the door job was the worst job in that area. And from the time
I started in there until I left that area, until I went on days, every time a
new black worker came in he was given that door job. All the time I stayed in
that area I never saw a white worker work that job.

We constantly used to talk about these things, you know, but in all the
time I was there up until the start of DRUM, this was my main thing: what are
we going to do about the way black workers are treated in here? And it took
almost four years for me to find anybody else that was really ready to do
something about it and this is where DRUM came from.

During the wildcat strike of May 1968, upon coming to work that morning,
there were picket lines established which, ironically, were manned by all white
workers at the time and as a result of this all the black workers received the
harshest disciplinary actions.

A few workers and I went across the street and sat in the bar, sitting
there drinking. We were sitting at that table talking and it was here we
decided we would do something about organizing black workers to fight the
racial discrimination inside the plants and the overall oppression of black
workers. Well, this was something I'd been trying to get started in the body
shop for the four years I was in there, but I just never ran into anyone who
was conscious enough to really take some steps about doing something about this.
And this was the beginning of DRUM.

Beyond Detroit

What can the radical movement learn from Detroit's black auto workers?
The answer, I think, is plenty. The lessons seem to boil down to two
essentials:

1--Capitalism can only be killed where it lives: at the point of production.

2--Contrary to all the fears of certain tattered fringes of the white
left, Detroit emphatically demonstrates that the national form of struggle

has been a necessary prelude to a general class-line assault by Afro-America
on the holders of power.

It is no longer necessary to belabor the first point. The movement is
beginning to realize, as much of it did not before, the central role of production in any revolutionary endeavor. For several years, the white and black
movements concentrated on "community organizing." The general failure of this
line of attack has obliged us to look to more powerful crowbars of change. It
has been comparatively cheap for capitalism to handle the issues raised by
community organizers. If all the rats and roaches, all the pot-holed streets
and all the rest of it were cleaned up in the "community," capitalism would
still stand because only one or two of its fingers would have been amputated.
The heart would still be intact. From cops to welfare, the strictly "community"
issues are only secondary aspects of capitalism: they are used as control
devices, but they are not a system of themselves. That system is production
for profit.

This should not be taken to mean that the radical movement should ignore
community issues, for no revolutionary movement can ignore the immediate conditions of the people in whose name it operates. But a conclusive solution to
these conditions--one which ensures that they will not recur--demands production of, by and for the workers. If production is the central arena in which
captialism will be slain, therefore, it follows that the hand that holds the
wrench shall be the hand that holds the gun.

The *black* community, however, nonetheless has had an amazing impact on
America. The courageous rebellions and the general ferment have by and large
been the result of (a) objective conditions and (b) increased black awareness
as a development of national struggle. The national form was necessary and
therefore inevitable. No oppressed people can develop a politics without self-
definition of the group, especially in the case of black America, which has
suffered from a pattern of psychological warfare too extensive and too well-
known to go into here. The Detroit movement indicates that the group is being
welded together and that the black national aspects are becoming part of a
higher level of struggle.

The developing unity of class and national struggle presents some considerations of tactics. What strikes the observer in Detroit and elsewhere is
that dual unionism--the establishment of independent workers' organizations--
is arising out of the ashes into which "organized labor" dumped it years ago.
There is promise here.

Since black interests have consistently been submerged to more general
trade union questions "to avoid splitting the working class," the development
of independent bases of black worker power should surprise no one. Black dual
unionism can provide a powerful force for the most oppressed sector of the
working class by giving it instruments which, if truly democratic, would be in
hock to no one else. Certain tactical freedoms would be possible. The League
of Revolutionary Black Workers in Detroit, for example, considers itself to be
such an independent base, but also has engaged in United Auto Workers politics
as the tactical situation demanded.

Perhaps the most important problem involved in the black dual union
approach--given the existence of a *class* struggle--is its relation to the
movement of white workers, when that happens. It is not much of a problem now
because there is very little motion in the white working class. But should
white workers start to move, and many white organizers think they will, the
problem could become acute. Would each movement take its own course, as the
white student and black movements of today have done? If so, how may they
become parallel movements? Will white racism, even among workers who are in
motion along more or less radical paths, still stand in the way of true class
solidarity? Will black workers realize that it will take *all* workers to
overthrow the system that lies at the root of black oppression? Will white
workers understand that, in addition to class interests, black workers must be
supported in their legitimate drive for self-determination?

So much depends on what white workers and their vanguards--self-appointed
and otherwise--do. If the traditional caucus-style struggle can be modified
to provide a parallel, in-union form to the black dual union, there is the
possibility of class solidarity. But if caucus organizations continue to be
based on the "black and white, unite and fight" slogan, they will entirely
miss the correct and irreversible mood that is growing among black workers.

Dual unionism is a much more difficult undertaking for the white working class. Black dual unions will have a previously mobilized community behind them. The white "community" has rarely been organized as such and experience shows that when whites are organized along these lines racism is strengthened. Whites are not colonized subjects in America. Without community support, white dual unions can be smashed by the superior financial power of the established unions. Who is going to join a new union that has no strike defense fund? The answer is no one except a black worker who knows that a community initially organized on a national basis will contribute to such a fund.

Like the Detroit black workers, white workers will have to approach dual unionism with tactical suppleness. There appear to be some possibilities of dual unions among white workers, especially welfare employes, but this group is not basic to production.

Some white factory organizers are complaining that the insurgent black workers have no class analysis and that this makes their job among white workers more difficult. Aside from the obvious fact that it is not the black man's job to make things easier for white organizers, what needs to be asked is, what do these white organizers think their job *is?* To gain a little more money for the skilled trades? The job of white organizers, rather, is to build explicit class consciousness and defeat racism. In this sense, white workers have far less class consciousness than black workers. The black people, as seen in Detroit, have been doing their job. Our turn is long overdue.

Black Workers In Revolt: How Detroit's New Black Revolutionary Workers are Changing the Face of American Trade Unionism, pp. 1-15. Pamphlet printed by *The Guardian* (N.D.) in possession of the editors.

7.   WILDCAT!

By Detroit NOC

A wildcat strike is an act of defiance, a clearly illegal action directed at the union as well as management. It occurs when the everyday tensions of industrial conflict burst into collective struggle. The workers, in order to express their power, attempt to stop production.

Since wildcats are primarily spontaneous movements of workers, they are often confused struggles that are easily crushed. When they first walk out, workers are permeated with a feeling of power, "we actually shut it down." Later, as the wildcat continues, management threatens to fire them, and the international union bureaucracy moves to place the local under discipline. The struggle becomes grim. Workers are unsure how long they can hold out. They begin to feel economic pressure from loss of a weeks pay. Management moves to "negotiate the issues" providing the workers return. Many of the older men, who have experienced walkouts before, begin to predict its demise. Wildcats that do not develop leadership at this point are usually crushed through the collective resources of management and the unions.

Back at work the immediate issue is "solved" through negotiations and everyday life returns to the shop. Workers feel little has been achieved, yet take no action. All is calm until the tensions build again--the sell-out contract, deteriorating working conditions, safety hazards, the arrogance of the foremen, the compulsory overtime, the years of frustration of hard work just to break even economically--this oppression surges into the minds of the workers and another wildcat begins over some ordinary worker-management confrontation.

The walkout at the Sterling Stamping plant was similar to the above sketch, except for one important difference. On the side of the workers was the active participation of organizers and students who placed the wildcat into the context of political struggle. Through their efforts, the wildcat became more than an industrial dispute. If nothing else was gained at

Sterling, many workers learned to respect the students for turning out to support their strike. Hopefully, out of the wildcat will emerge a cadre of revolutionary workers who see their role as organizers laying the ground work for a mass-based working class movement in Detroit.

This goal is the thrust of NOC's work in factories and it guided our actions during the Sterling struggle. As a cadre of organizers, the National Organizing Committee seeks to develop groups of politically conscious white workers in the shops. These groups will provide the outreach into the plant through literature, production and struggle. While our factory work is very limited (we only began four months ago), the wildcat at Sterling provided us with some experience and insights into organizing workers in basic industry.

The Plant

Opened in 1955, the Sterling Stamping Plant is a relatively recent addition to the Chrysler empire. Employing over 3,500 production and skilled workers, the 80 million dollar plant sprawls over 1/2 mile of land in the white working class suburb of Sterling Heights. At Sterling, hoods, frames and fenders are made for almost all Chrysler models. Engineers are proud of the plant's flexibility: stamping dies can be moved in and out of the 167 major presses, changing the whole line in less than six hours. The Sterling plant is critical to the auto parts supply of the four major Chrysler assembly plants in Detroit: Lynch Road, Hamtramck, Warren Truck and Jefferson.

Of all the Chrysler plants, Sterling Stamping is one of the few containing a clear majority of white workers. At least 70% of the workers are white, mostly Polish and Italian, with some Southern white. Ethnic loyalties are strong in the plant: there are "Dago" and "Pollack" production lines. Since Sterling is such a new plant, a good majority of the production workers are young guys between 18 and 30, most of whom are married.

Although Sterling Stamping is a new plant, the working conditions are very poor. The presses leak oil, making the floors slippery; hi-los often break down; aisles are cluttered with razor sharp scrap metal and machine parts; and the conveyor belt, used to take metal scrap from the presses to the bailing room often breaks down. In the past five years many workers have been injured. A few of them have lost their fingers or hands under the huge presses.

The local leadership of UAW local 1264 has always been a militant thorn in the sides of management and the international UAW. During the 1967 contract ratification process, workers remained out over a week refusing to settle on plant working conditions issues. It wasn't until UAW International Board member Douglas Fraser threatened to put the local under receivership that the men returned to work. Last summer, two wildcats occurred over the lack of ventilation in the plant. In all instances the local leadership, which is supposed to maintain its side of the contract and discipline the ranks, supported the wildcats. Given this militant leadership it would be in the interests of management to crush the local.

The need of Chrysler to keep its workers in line is particularly pressing in the spring of 1969 as the auto industry suffers its first effects of what might be a long-term economic stagnation. Sales are down substantially, increasing inventories to the highest in automobile history (at the time of the wildcat there were 1.7 million cars unsold). Production is being cut back. During February production was slowed down as many assembly plants were shut down for a week. Overtime became scarce and there were plans for an early model change this year.

Of the big three, Chrysler is in the worst economic position to sustain any possible recession. In 1961, the company almost went out of business. Through a re-organization of dealerships, a new five-year warranty plan (revoked on 1969 models), and industrial diversification (Chrysler is now moving into the plastic industry, and is also purchasing over 2 million dollars worth of real estate a week) Chrysler has maintained 17% of the domestic auto market. At the time of the Sterling Wildcat however, Chrysler held almost 400,000 unsold cars, an 83 day supply according to recent sales rates and the highest in the industry. If inventories remained that high, it would be necessary for the auto company to cut back production in June.

During these lay-offs, the corporation would have to pay 95% of the base pay of all workers with one year seniority. The wildcat at Sterling, which idled 35,000 workers for eight days, served to keep production down, while management could blame the workers for the disruption and save money by not paying any SUB benefits to those laid off.

In addition, the wildcat was a golden opportunity to harass the union leadership. As profits grew less in a period of slow expansion, capitalists make up for losses in sales by forcing more labor out of workers. After experiencing the power of the League of Revolutionary Black Workers at Dodge Main and Eldon Gear and Axle, Chrysler was very anxious to keep industrial discipline tight. Workers should not be able to cut into production, nor a local union leadership be permitted to encourage the challenge to discipline. The workers of Local 1264 needed to be taught a lesson--a wildcat strike would enable management to fire some of the plant militants as well as force some of the local leadership into dealing with the power of the International. Thus, it is very likely that Chrysler, because of its high inventories and its need to assert industrial discipline, provoked the incident which initiated the wildcat strike.

Wildcat

The wildcat began over safety conditions. On Wednesday, April 2nd, workers were ordered to clear out 12 feet of scrap metal which had piled up because the conveyor belt had broken down. The metal was razor sharp, and with the floor slippery from spilled oil, the job was clearly a dangerous one. When local union officials advised workers that they did not have to clear out the basement, Chrysler fired all the stewards, committeemen and union officials on the spot. The walkout began as workers learned they had no union representation against management. Picket lines were established and until Thursday, April 10th, no production was turned out at Sterling Stamping.

During the first night of the walkout, scabs driving through the picket lines were attacked and cars smashed. Thirty-four workers were arrested. After that, except for a few isolated incidents, the lines remained firm. Solidarity between the plant workers and the Chrysler truckers, who take the auto parts to the assembly plants, was strong. None of the big blue trucks crossed the picket lines.

NOC organizers arrived on Thursday morning and found solidarity in the ranks very high. Most workers were militantly anti-Chrysler and anti-UAW International. They were pissed off at the arrogance of management for poor working conditions and continual mistreatment. They were angry at the UAW International for not supporting their actions. Workers supported their local officers and most sought to build a strong local union. The men on the picket lines were primarily young guys, and most of the stewards and committeemen, generally a bit older, were also present. The wildcat was headed by the union president and vice-president, both politically sophisticated and able men.

Union Consciousness

Not surprisingly the workers militance stayed at the level of trade union consciousness. While the men disliked Chrysler, few supported the concept that they should control the company. Many looked toward an "honorable settlement" of their grievances. The issues of safety conditions and firings were treated as demands unrelated to other struggles in the auto plants. Many workers said that Sterling, in comparison to plants in the Detroit areas, was basically a good plant to work in, except for some problems with working conditions and a few foremen who were bastards. Yet in discussions they revealed the common problem affecting all auto workers. Although most guys saw a broader struggle of management everywhere trying to crush militant workers they were uncertain how to relate to it. For the workers at Sterling, the wildcat was primarily an action to achieve better conditons in this particular plant.

As militant unionists, workers had little understanding of the role of the state. Even after the police arrested 34 workers, most guys did not perceive the partisan role the cops played in class conflict. For them there were good and bad cops. Although many guys served in Vietnam and were profoundly influenced into an anti-war position, they did not relate it to their struggle with Chrysler. Finally, the wildcat leadership (local president and v.p) is involved in the activities of the local Democratic party making them unwilling to see struggle except through existing institutions. As the wildcat continued, the politics of the leadership presented a problem to our efforts in organizing.

Finally, most workers were unable to deal with white supremacy. When we asked why weren't any blacks on the picket lines, the standard reply was, "those guys don't care, they are just over at the union hall." Many guys felt that whites were given the more difficult jobs in the plant because management would know it got done properly. Yet, when pressed on their feelings, workers admitted that there was no equality in the shop. Although 30% of the plant is black, there are no black stewards or committeemen. Even the most racist southern workers admitted that there is a problem when they said the skilled trades department is all white. Some even saw the need to relate to groups like DRUM and ELRUM in their fight against Chrysler.

We spent the first days on the picket lines trying to put the issues of the wildcat into political perspective. We ran down stuff on the UAW—how it does not fight for better working conditions in the national contract, how the contract screws local union power, how grievances are settled from the shop floor, etc. We provided legal counsel for the local union officers in their attempts to head off a threatened Chrysler injunction on picketing. Finally, we began to place the wildcat into the larger context, laying out Chrysler's reasons for provoking the strike. Much of our analysis was confirmed when on Sunday, management fired 69 guys for strike activity. Many of the firings were arbitrary; some, however, were against the most militant workers who had been identified from photographs taken by foremen escorted out to the line by plant pigs to identify picketers.

Role of NOC

We came on hard about our politics, telling guys that NOC was interested in workers taking power, the right of workers to control the production process and the state. We passed out fist buttons which were gobbled up immediately. We were very hard on white supremacy, making it clear to guys that they should support the demands of black workers for if they really wanted to beat Chrysler, they would need to unite with the League of Revolutionary Black Workers, and this could not be accomplished unless white workers accepted the legitimacy of black demands.

We raised questions concerning the relationship of guys to their wives. Were they telling their wives about the strike? How come very few of their wives were on the line? Through these raps, particularly on white supremacy, many workers disagreed violently with our analysis. Yet, almost everyone recognized and accepted us as "agitators," "organizers," or "anti-establishment people" who had been active in the student movement, black liberation struggle, or worked organizing poor people.

Our leafleting efforts were modest, as we placed heavier emphasis on personal contact with workers on the picket lines. There were several difficulties with this approach. At night great quantities of beer and dope were consumed as many workers transformed the picket lines into a party-like atmosphere. While remaining solid in preventing any scabs from crossing the lines, guys were certainly not interested in political raps. Another problem with personal contact was, except for a small group of guys who were there most of the time, the same workers did not show up. During the eight days of picketing very few of the workers came regularly. In fact, as the wildcat continued, the personnel changed rapidly. Many guys we talked to at the beginning of the wildcat simply didn't show up as picketing became pretty much a routine affair. Finally, since the plant was in the suburbs, there were very few cafes or bars nearby, making it difficult to bring a few workers together for some long political raps.

At one point when it appeared that management was going to break through the lines to get at some of the auto parts remaining in the plant, we prepared a leaflet that was to be distributed in the community by high school groups working with NOC. The leaflet listed the demands, gave an analysis of why the wildcat (Chrysler's desire to crush the leadership as well as save money while inventories are high) and called for community solidarity with the strikers. The leaflet was not distributed however, as Chrysler backed away from confrontation with the workers. In retrospect, our decision not to turn out more leaflets for the community and the workers may have been a tactical error. Leaflets might have overcome some of the problems inherent in the personal contact approach. Yet, in all cases contacts with workers on a face to face level were extremely important.

Tactical Error

Perhaps the most important tactical error we made was not engaging students in the struggle from the outset. At first we felt that students would turn off the workers. Their life-style is so different and their knowledge of the issues so limited that we anticipated workers would be hostile to their participation. Yet, on Sunday, independently of our actions, SDS chapters began to appear on the line. Our analysis of student participators was incorrect. In fact the presence of students was critical to the continuance of the wildcat.

By Sunday, the wildcat had reached the fifty day. After the first two evenings, very few scabs attempted to cross the picket lines, and marching around the plant exit gates became an uneventful chore. Fewer and fewer workers began showing up on the line. Those that did appear grew increasingly uncertain of whether the wildcat would last.

The diminishing worker support for the wildcat would be critical at the first shift change Monday. Since the wildcat began right before the Easter holiday, many workers took advantage of the strike to have an extended weekend vacation. They were ready to return to work on Monday. Without a strong show of pickets the wildcat would be broken.

On Monday morning only a handful of pickets appeared, but bolstered by about 75 SDS people from the University of Michigan, cars were turned away. The wildcat continued and the spirits of the workers rose. Guys began showing up on the line again, partly because they were interested in meeting the students. The older workers were disturbed by the presence of the students on the line; one brought up a razor and shears to cut some of their hair. However, the younger workers were open to the students and interested in talking with them.

Through their discussions, workers learned about the movement. They clearly understood what students were about for as one worker put it: "the students are always on the side of the underdog." Many workers stated flatly that the students made the difference when the fate of the wildcat was in doubt on Monday. In general they were very open to political discussions with students.

On the other hand, most students simply don't know enough about workers and the issues effecting them to lay out some concrete analysis. Their rhetoric had little relationship to the lives of these young workers. Even though many of the guys at Sterling were the same age as the students they were in a world altogether different than college students. Most were married, faced with consumer problems, raising children and attempting to find ways to exist for a lifetime in a factory. They were not pissed off at the pigs. The war and the draft had little direct impact on them. Most of their problems were centered around dealing with industrial discipline. They were working hard (some had been working seven days since Christmas) and finding the money they earned was just enough to make ends meet. For them the students were visions of people which only their children might become. Regardless of the effect of the students on the attitudes of the workers, the mere visible signs of students manning the picket lines with workers forced the UAW into action.

International Seduction

The International union played a subtle role in forcing the wildcat to
end. In the beginning of the strike the International's pressure was absent.
However, as the wildcat continued and students joined the workers the UAW
pushed quickly for a settlement. On Monday, the UAW summoned the local union
leaders to Solidarity House, the UAW headquarters. During this meeting the
UAW bureaucarts told Local 1264's union representative that if they did not
order their men back to work the local would be taken into receivership by the
International. That afternoon the local was put into receivership and Douglas
Fraser, executive board member and head of all of the UAW's Chrysler division,
ordered all of the workers at Sterling Stamping back to work.
The next morning, to the surprise of many, they refused. Many men were
confused and started to go to work, but when they saw the picket line they
turned around and went home. Fraser's response was to call a mass meeting for
the Local 1264 members.
At the meeting the UAW used all the traditional ploys. The vast majority
of the rank and file came to the meeting feeling angry and militant. Fraser
and others, who spoke about ending the strike were booed and heckled. When
Fraser first called for a strike vote, only a handful voted in favor of
returning to work. Fraser started to put down the presence of students on the
picket lines and guys shouted back: "The students did more for us than the
International!" Still, Fraser monopolized the microphone and dragged the
meeting out for two and a half hours. Many workers left disgusted. In
essence, Fraser said that the only way to get the 69 fired workers' jobs back
was to go back to work and let Fraser, as the UAW representative, bargain with
the corporation. He said the only alternative was more firings, more people
laid off at other plants. He then introduced a fired worker who got up and
told the rest of the workers to go back. The meeting was controlled by the
careful selection of speakers and by the refusal of the chairman to let militant workers effectively question Fraser. Finally, on the third ballot Fraser
pushed through a return to work vote, primarily by promising to allow a regular
strike vote in the plant on the next Monday. Many workers, however, were
confused and did not vote at all.
Workers went back, only to overwhelmingly sanction an official walkout for
May 8th. Yet, the last minute negotiations produced an agreement in which
Chrysler agreed to keep oil off the floors, repair the conveyor belt, and fix
some of the machines. Sixty-five of the men were re-hired, most punished
through loss of back pay, and the jobs of five men remain contested in binding
arbitration. Although the local leadership fought for the settlement, it was
a sell-out as the union did not even win amnesty for all the men. In a ratification vote, the local membership approved the settlement, 1,380 to 794.
Since the wildcat we have been meeting with guys who expressed an interest
in working with us. We aided one worker in putting out a leaflet that named
the scabs. During the wildcat guys promised to get the scabs after the strike
was over. A good number of the car windows have been broken and tool boxes
crushed in the presses since the leaflet. One problem we have been facing is
the inability to get all our contacts together to plan collective action.
Sterling works on three shifts and since the wildcat many guys have been
working seven days a week as Chrysler planned for a local strike that would
shut down operations until the summer. There has not been a single day when
everyone was off. In addition, workers are spread all over the suburbs and
eastern half of Detroit, making it difficult to select a central meeting place.
We hope, however, to have a group of workers attending educationals and
planning activities on a regular basis in the near future.
The struggle the wildcat initiated will continue in the shops. The
critical need for us is to evaluate our efforts in dealing with some problems
in organizing in a wildcat situation. It is to these questions we now turn.
Essentially the problems we encountered focused around four areas: a)
the ability of young workers to organize; b) white-black worker relationships;
c) the woman question; and d) relationship with local union officials.

Young Workers

The emphasis in NOC's work has been on young workers for the following reasons: 1) since they are just being integrated into the shop young workers are the most likely to rebel against industrial discipline; 2) young workers are less ensconced in a life style and family pattern which will impede their development as organizers; 3) young workers are the most oppressed by the seniority rules, wage levels, unemployment compensation and lay-offs; and 4) young workers grew up after the Depression making them a different view of solely wage and fringe benefit increases than their fathers. At Sterling we found that young guys were interested in our politics.

Yet, so pervasive is the bourgeois notion of individualism that most of the workers have not experienced collective work. During the wildcat we found continually that guys did not know how to organize. There was no leaflet distributed to all workers explaining the reasons for the wildcat. The picketing was unorganized; it was assumed workers would show up to fill each shift. Although most workers were interested in getting publicity for their actions, the idea of passing out leaflets in their communities never occurred to them. All through the 8 day walkout, there was no communications center as most business was conducted in a haphazard fashion. Had some of the militant workers organized themselves for the Wednesday meeting with Fraser, the outcome might have been considerably different.

In part, the failure of the workers to organize themselves was due to the local president and vice-president. The rank and file were denied information during the wildcat by these union officials who kept negotiations with the UAW International or Chrysler a deep secret. The local would not even give names and telephone numbers to workers to get guys out on the picket lines. Both these union officials were very capable men and could have easily organized groups of militant workers to carry-out the business of the wildcat, yet because of their politics, they refused to see this as a desirable end.

Elitism

One of the very important orientations of the American union is to keep workers systematically deprived of the skills by which they can organize themselves. In the UAW, it is the International structure that is responsible for organizing drives. Working through the local leadership, the International passes on its elitist politics: keep the rank and file in the dark as much as possible, then there will be no disruptions. They do not understand the nature of contemporary capitalism. At Sterling the local president and vice-president, no matter how much they thought of themselves as anti-establishment, conformed to that rule. As the UAW applied pressure, both through threat and reward (the local leaders were told that if they did not urge the men back to work their careers with the Democratic Party would be over, at the same time, jobs on the International staff were dangled before them for their help in stopping the walkout), the local leadership began to urge the end of the strike. The stewards and the committeemen however, remained loyal to the wildcat, reflecting the division between the vice-president and president who stayed outside the plan, and those officials of the union on the shop floor.

We tried hard to counter the lack of organizing ability by first getting guys to see how important it was to be together. Continually we would ask: what are you going to do when the wildcat is over? How are you going to take-on Chrysler with all its resources? How can you even take control of your own local, let alone the International? As best as possible, when guys expressed interest in organizing, we attempted to pass on techniques.

For example, if a leaflet is to be passed out in the shop we stressed the need for a distribution system where workers pass along material from department to department. This prevents management from singling out one individual for handing it out, and also engages many workers in an action, establishing new contacts for a plant caucus. Any leafleting of plants should recognize the importance of an internal distribution system. It is much more efficient to give a worker 50 leaflets, if he will hand them out inside, then dispose of 500 during a shift change.

White Supremacy and Male Chauvinism

We faced another key problem at Sterling with the lack of black participation on the picket lines. While many blacks hung around the union hall, very few went out on the lines. For most of the white workers the lack of black participation was proof, "they didn't care about the strike."

At the wildcat we were unable to deal with this problem in concrete terms. We did talk to a few black guys about the League of Revolutionary Black Workers, and the League is now in contact with them, but there was little racial interaction during the wildcat. Our experience at Sterling indicates how important it is to raise black demands that will involve black workers in the struggle. Otherwise it is likely that most black workers tend to view the struggle as a white man's affair. In other plants, however, black and white have worked together on wildcats, so the Sterling situation is not universally applicable.

If our handling of the problem of black workers was insufficient, the way we dealt with male supremacy was a disaster. Although we talked about these issues to workers, as in the case with the black workers, little concrete organizing was accomplished. NOC women should have visited the homes of workers to talk to their wives about the strike. We failed to reach the significant minority of women workers in the plant. Although there were very few women workers on the picket lines, at the union meeting with Fraser many did show up and some contacts should have been attempted.

Our failure to deal with the question of male chauvinism in concrete terms reflects a blind spot particularly present in working class organizing: you go to the bar and talk to the guys. Of course the women are supposed to fall in line behind the men. In part, our attempts at Sterling suffered from that perspective. To counter this dangerous tendency NOCs women's sub-collective has been established to deal with organizing working class women both in the factories and the communities.

Leaders vs. Rank and File

Finally, during the walkout we had many problems with the local union officials. While they accepted our aid (when faced with the threat of attack from both management and union, they would have accepted anyone's aid), they became suspicious of our intentions, particularly as the UAW pressured them into urging the rank and file back. As already stated, there were political reasons why the leadership would support the UAW International.

Adding to different political perspectives was the complication that in order to help the wildcat during its initial stages we provided independent legal counsel for the local. A very important area of any working class organizing in factories is knowledge of labor laws. Unlike the university, the internal behavior of unions is subjected to a variety of federal and state laws that can lead to court action by management or the union. We also gave advice on strategy and tactics. This placed us in close contact with the leadership, while at the same time we had little hopes for them remaining anything but reformist during the struggle. Throughout the wildcat we remained in uneasy contact with the leadership not sure how much to work with them or how much to be independent. This problem has still not been resolved as the present union leadership has asked we help them in the next union election.

Our experience suggests keeping away from specific dealing with the local leadership. On the other hand, the in-plant leadership, union stewards and committeemen, seem very open and willing to move. The goal should always be to remain with the rank and file. We went up to the picket lines at Sterling with the idea that the wildcat would be crushed, and it was important that the struggle, initiated by the action would be carried on in the plant through a Solidarity caucus. Our time aiding the local leadership was important in terms of contact and access to information about conditions within the union, yet involvement with the leadership was always risky, for even the most militant do not have the same interests as radical organizers and they could crush whatever actions we had begun.

One observation that ties together our experiences at Sterling is that most workers are without a political perspective. Deprived knowledge of an anti-capitalist analysis, workers are often unable to deal with the forces oppressing them. Many guys at Sterling were extremely pissed off about how the bosses screwed them, but became frustrated because they didn't know how to move. These workers were some of the first to walk out of the meeting with Fraser. Workers cannot be expected to be able to cope with the contradictions they face every day on the job without the placing of these contradictions in a general political framework. The UAW International plans its political actions carefully. Workers can only respond with a gut action--a wildcat--but cannot sustain a struggle. It is our job to begin that process of political struggle. The working class is in motion; it always has been. The task is to develop the political program and ideology that will mobilize workers into a struggle against capitalism and imperialism.

The Movement, 5 (June, 1969):12-13, 21.

8. CONFRONT THE RACIST UAW LEADERSHIP

WHERE: COBO HALL   WHEN: 11:00 O'CLOCK AM

SUNDAY, NOV. 9   BE THERE

JOIN THE LEAGUE OF REVOLUTIONARY BLACK WORKERS

Our basic demands of the U.A.W. are:

1. Halt U.A.W. racism. 50% representation for black workers on the international executive board. Fire Reuther and elect a black president and one black vice president, 50% of all international staff members should be black. Open skilled trades and apprentices to any black worker who applies. Recognition of the League of Revolutionary Black Workers and its affiliates as the official spokesman for black workers on the local and national level with the power to negotiate black demands on the company and union and the power to call officially sanctioned strikes.

2. We demand that the grievance procedure be completely revised so that grievances are settled immediately on the job by the workers in the plant involved. The grievance procedure is used to prevent workers from using their strike power to fight abuses from management. Since the procedure completely ties the hands of workers and basically serves company interests it should be scraped and replaced by a completely new system.

3. Elimination of all safety and health hazards in the auto industry. This means cleaning the air in the foundry and redesigning dangerous machinery and cut back in production on hazardous jobs.

4. The union must fight vigorously against speed up and increases in production standards. The companies should double the size of their work force to meet the present workload. There were 650,000 production workers in auto in 1947 producing 4.5 million vehicles. In 1966 650,000 workers produced nearly 10 million vehicles loaded with accessories and options. We are working two and three times as hard for the same real income. With today's technology production standards can easily be cut to reasonable humane lines.

5. The union must fight for a five hour work day and a four day work week. The profit level of industry is high enough to allow for more leisure time for workers.

6. The union must fight for an immediate doubling of the wages of all production workers. Since 1960 wages of black workers have risen less than 25%. Yet profits have risen more than 90%. The pitifully small increase the black production workers have received has been completely wiped out by inflation. We know how wealthy the company is. We know how low their labor costs presently are. In fact, we know that it costs less than $100 in labor

to produce a $3,000 car. We say increase that labor cost to $200. per car and double the wages immediately.

7. We demand a cut in union dues. The union already collects $10 million a month from its members and can't defend the rights of the workers.

8. We demand the end of the checkoff of union dues. While the check off was progressive in the 30's today it prevents workers from disciplining poor union leadership.

9. We demand that all U.A.W. investment funds be used to finance economic development in the black community under programs of self determination. The union now holds over $90,000,000 in strike funds in white banks. They lost over $1,000,000 in strike funds when a bank in California folded two years ago. We demand that all such money be held in black institutions and used in the black community.

10. We demand that the union end its collusion with the United Foundation. Black workers should contribute only to black controlled charities working for the benefit of the black community.

11. We demand that all monies expended for political campaigns by the U.A.W. be turned over to the League of Revolutionary Black Workers and the Black United Front for black controlled and directed political work.

12. We demand that the U.A.W. end its collusion with the C.I.A., the F.B.I. and all other white racist spy institutions.

13. We demand that the U.A.W. end all interference in the political, economic, social and cultural life of the black community. That community and the black workers in it are to exercise self determination in all political, economic, social and cultural activities and are to use black contributed union funds in any such activities. This means that the UAW end its affiliation with MDCDA, New Detroit, and other such programs and place all administration authority and funds in the hands of the black community.

14. We demand an end to the harassment of black revolutionists and their leaders by the auto companies with U.A.W. Cooperation.

15. We demand that the U.A.W. use its political and strike powers to call a general strike to demand immediate:

    a. An end to the Vietnam war and withdrawal of all American troops.

    b. An immediate end to all taxes imposed upon workers.

    c. Increases in profit and industrial property taxes to make up the difference.

    d. Reallocation of all Federal monies spent on defense to meet the pressing needs of the black and poor populations of America.

The League is calling for all concerned black people to support and participate in this action.

There are several things you can do to help:

1. Lend your name to the list of supporters of the Nov. 9 action.

2. Have your organization endorse the demonstration and encourage members to support.

3. Help publicize the demonstration by passing out literature, word of mouth, announcements at meetings, etc.

4. Come out on Nov. 9th and bring as many people as you can.

A brother from the League will contact you soon to get your signature on a support petition. In the meantime call us at the League office 865-8184 for more information.

League of Revolutionary Black Workers circular (November, 1969) in possession of the editors.

9. BLACK WORKERS PROTEST U.A.W. RACISM

MARCH ON COBO HALL

The leadership of the United Automobile Workers Union has concocted another plot to increase the wealth, power and prestige of the big time white racist union bureaucrats at the expense of the black community and the rank and file black union member. Walter Reuther and his company owned henchmen have called for a special U.A.W. convention to be convened on Nov. 8 & 9, 1969, at Cobo Hall.

The excuse the Reuther clique has given for holding this convention is "to raise strike benefits." Now we are all in favor of higher strike benefits for brothers struggling against the tyranny of the auto bosses, but we know that Reuther and his boys really are not concerned with the welfare of their own rank and file members. Quite to contrary, workers who attempt to strike and carry on strong struggles against racism, for higher wages and better working conditions, find that they must fight their own union leadership as resolutely as they do the company. As a result, most strikes are wildcats in which the union provides neither strike benefits or fight for the rights of workers who are suspended, fired or otherwise face disciplinary actions.

We recognize that the real reason for holding this convention is to provide an excuse for the raising of your union dues!

The record of the Reuther gang does not even warrant a continuation of the present level of union dues. While profits have risen over 50% in the last ten years, wages have not even kept pace with the rise in the cost of living. Speed up and increases in production standards have made automobile labor a living hell. Reuther is running a sweetheart shop. Hand in hand with Chrysler king pin Lynn Townsend , billionaire Henry Ford II, and G.M. dictator Edward Cole, the Reuther clique helps extract billions of dollars in profits for the white racist monopoly capitalists of the automobile industry.

Reuther doesn't need anymore of our hard earned, blood and sweat drenched money. He needs to be overthrown, deposed and disposed of along with the cheap gang of cut throat thugs, bureaucrats, crooks and sellout politicians who hold on to his coat tails for dear life.

The U.A.W. needs a special convention. It needs profound changes in its leadership, its tactics, strategy and overall goals. A special convention should address itself to the pressing needs of the black production worker, and the black community. Any so called union convention which does not should be attacked and attacked vigorously by the Black community and the black working class. The time has come for the people to put a permanent halt to the sell out, power made games played by the Reuther bureaucrats at our expense.

The U.A.W. Must End All Racist Practices Within the Union and Fight Racism in the Company.

Walter Reuther and his henchmen are a bunch of phoney bigots. Reuther shed alligator tears when Martin Luther King was assassinated and piously marched to Selma, Alabama for "Negro Rights." Yet how many times has he cried over the bodies of black workers who have died in industrial accidents in Detroit auto plants, how many times has he marched for the rights of Black workers in his own back yard. The Reuther concern for civil rights is a cheap facade designed to prevent black U.A.W. members from seeing clearly the deplorable record of the U.A.W. in establishing and maintaining racism in its own shops.

Early in the history of the U.A.W. racism was an established fact. In Chrysler and G.M. plants blacks were often denied employment in all fields except janitorial service. Henry Ford recognized the labor value of the "big black buck" and hired thousands of black men to work in his sweatshops before the U.A.W. was organized. When the U.A.W. first tried to organize Ford Rouge, under the leadership of Reuther and others of his ilk, one of the white unionists demands was that all black men be excluded from employment. It wasn't until the black workers made it clear that if they were to be excluded that there would never be a U.A.W., that the Reuther clique relented and allowed integration of the hardest, dirtiest and lowest paying jobs. The

racist union leadership only made this concession after black workers broke
picket lines set up by racist white union organizers. After the U.A.W.
gangsters promised equality inside the union black workers joined, fought and
died to win the struggle for unionization.

The union's promise of equality was, of course, a hollow one. The big-
shots first bought out a few of the more weak kneed black labor leaders.
"Buddy" Battles, president of the foundry unit at Local 600 once led black
workers through U.A.W. picket lines as a protest against union racism; but
today Battles is a paid agent of Reuther, active in stifling militant black
action in and outside of the plants. Once a few colored "brothers" had sold
out the rest of the black workers were set up as easy prey for the company.
"Token" integration of the union leadership didn't allow blacks the political
power to effectively demand equality. Even today with 45 to 50% of the U.A.W.
membership black, only two of 26 international executive board members are
black, and only about 75 of over 1,100 international representatives are black.
The few blacks in the hierarchy understand that their jobs depend, upon their
jumping in rhythm with Reuther's tune. They are the most conservative element
in the leadership of the black community, and the least independent.

Under control of Reuther's racist machine, the black worker has fared no
better inside the plant than he has in the union. Racism has been the calling
card. Blacks are first of all systematically excluded from the skilled trades,
white collar jobs, and all but the lowest level of management. Blacks are
employed under the most dangerous conditions. In the foundries, for instance,
95% of the workers suffer from sillicosis and other lung diseases and have
their life expectancy cut 15 to 20 years short. Black workers are found in
great numbers in the stamping plants where fingers and toes are severed almost
daily. Black workers are found in the shops, the body shops, spot welding on
final production lines, and anywhere else where men drop dead from exhaustion
fighting never ending, constantly accelerating production lines.

Under the Reuther machine black men 50 years old are tied to the production lines while 20 year old white boys get jobs as clerks in the stock dept.
or in transportation; and the white youngsters are soon promoted to supervisory
or other white collar jobs. For the black worker the pressure of production
never ceases. In fact, because of the super exploitation of black labor,
profits in autos have soared. A process called "niggermation" is more pervasive than automation. Often new black workers are forced to do the work of
two white men. An investigation by members of the League of Revolutionary
Black Workers uncovered a typical case at the Ford engine plant where a young
brother was producing over 120 units an hour on a job previously worked by two
men at a pace of 70 units an hour; the previous men had exercised seniority
to get off the job because it was too strenuous.

Black workers earn billions of dollars of excess profits for the white
racist corporations because of U.A.W. sanctioned and enforced racist practices.
As long as the official representative of black workers perpetuate their continued enslavement we can make no progress; therefore we must use whatever
pressure and force we can bring to bear to end all racist practices in the
union and demand that the union movement fight to the end against racist
practices of the company.

The Union Must Fight Speed-Up and Win Better Working Conditions.

The fault of the U.A.W. doesn't end with racism. Even privileged white
workers suffer because of the neglect of duty of the Reuther gang. Speed-up,
safety hazards and unhealthy working conditions have become regular fare for
all auto workers. Through cooperation with the company in increasing production, Reuther and his gang have made millions for the auto barons at the
expense of the worker. In 1947, the auto industry produced 4,800,000 cars
with a production labor force of 626,000. In 1966 the industry produced
10,560,000 cars and trucks with a production labor force of 668,400. Moreover, the late model cars are bigger and have more accessories and options
than anytime before in our history. So black workers are now producing at
least twice as much as auto workers twenty years ago.

On the sweat and muscle of black workers the auto companies have doubled
and tripled their stock. In 1946 Chrysler was worth $283 million, today they

are worth over $2 billion, and only 10% of this rise came from the sale of
stocks. The rest was squeezed from the backs of black workers. G.M. rose in
capital worth from $1.4 billion to $8.7 billion with less than 10% new investments; and Ford increased its value from $771 million to $4.8 billion with
less than one half of one percent in new money. Since 1960 average wages have
increased about 25% for black workers; during the same period profits for the
white owned and controlled corporations rose 77%, dividends rose 60%, personal
interest income rose 80.6%, and undistributed corporate profits rose 83%.
While wages rose to an average of $3.50 hr., inflation wiped out any real rise
in our income and we are often forced to work overtime or extra jobs simply to
make ends meet. So speed up has reaped untold fortunes for the white auto
capitalists while we barely manage to survive. Who's interest do the Reuther
gang really represent?

End Harrassment of Black Workers and Black Revolutionists.

As if the record wasn't bad enough, the Reuther gang cannot leave the
black worker to his miserable job. Black people are constantly harrassed and
intimidated by the company with the full cooperation of their union "representatives." Brothers are forced to contribute money to the white controlled
United Foundation for instance. If they refuse they are usually punished by
some petty unofficial form of discipline. Black men who wear beards or
dashikis, tikis, naturals or other symbols of black pride are often intimidated
by their supervisors. This harrassment must end, and the union must quit siding
with the company, or must be recognized and destroyed as an agent of the company
and replaced by a viable organization representing the most progressive sector
of the labor movement.

Fiscal Responsibility to the Black Community.

The U.A.W. collects over $10 million every month from its membership. This
money, the bulk of it from the pockets of black workers is used to provide
salaries, staff and facilities for the U.A.W. sellout leadership. Millions of
dollars are used by Reuther and his bunch for their pet projects and for
investment purposes. The projects, however, are never designed to benefit the
black community. Millions are squandered on political campaigns for special
conferences and conventions and do nothing for recreation and reform programs
in the inner city as well as the suburban areas. But the money (our money) is
rarely used to support black candidates (except for known Reuther flunkies) or
invested for black economic development, or for independent community organization in the ghetto. Millions of dollars which black Detroit area workers pour
into the union coffers every year could be used to build new homes, schools,
universities, libraries, recreation and social centers, rifle ranges, food
co-ops, small industries, etc. Instead Reuther supports further blackmail of
the black workers by social faggots like the United Foundation. We pay enough
in union dues to provide 10 black controlled United Foundations. The money now
taken from black workers and administered by the U.A.W. must be turned back
into the hands and control of rank and file black U.A.W. members. We have
already spent too much in supporting the needs of white America, and we want
the white ruling class, also Reuther and the auto barons, to keep out of the
business of the black community.

The Union As a Political Force.

A union of workers is power. They can, if they so decide, control the
economy of a country as large and powerful as the U.S.A. simply by calling a
general strike. When workers are abused by a racist capitalist controlled
government, they can respond by closing down the economical heart of the nation.
Black workers are drafted, have incredibly high income taxes, state taxes, etc.
We are brutalized by the police, and robbed by corrupt politicians, but because
of the Reuther leadership we cannot use our natural power to strike, for

political reasons. As a result the war goes on, taxes increase, inflation, spirals, cops shoot at children, our schools are undereducating our children and our community rots in decay. Yet, Reuther does nothing more than preach his "love" for "civil rights." Black workers make up 35% of the industrial labor force as represented by production workers. Our hands actually create the wealth of America, and without us the nation could not continue its existence. This is power, real power, in the very hands of black labor. Because Walter Reuther and his henchmen hold the leadership of "our" union with the sweethearts of G.M., Ford and Chrysler, we have been unable to join together to use our power in our own interest.

The time, however, is coming near. The U.A.W. will either respond to the needs of black folk, or we will move independently of the official unions to exercise the power for our own benefit rather than for the auto bosses and their friends.

This is the crux of the matter. Black U.A.W. members are overworked, underpaid, abused, misused, and usually refused when they ask for redress. Yet Reuther is calling a convention to raise a strike chest larger than the $90 million on hand (to be invested by white capitalists). The strike benefits should be raised if the union is really going to struggle against the system. But the Reuther clique isn't interested in the black worker, or his family or his community, he only wants more of your money to do with as he pleases. This policy must stop; the Reuther gang must be confronted, the U.A.W. must begin to represent the interests of black workers.

> Join us in the movement to free the black workers from the final chains of slavery to the chain gangs of Chrysler, G.M. and Ford. Join us in our exposure of the Reuther clique of white hearted bandits. Demonstrate with the League of Revolutionary Black Workers.

CONFRONT THE RACIST U.A.W. LEADERSHIP

COBO HALL

NOVEMBER 9, 1969

League of Revolutionary Black Workers circular (November, 1969) in possession of the editors.

10. LEAGUE OF REVOLUTIONARY BLACK WORKERS GENERAL POLICY
STATEMENT, LABOR HISTORY, AND THE LEAGUE'S LABOR PROGRAM

As the betrayal of Blacks became more of a reality, and capitalism became entrenched in the society, white labor became more outrageous. Strikes were numerous and most of them were against the hiring of Black workers. Observe the following list of strikes from 1882 to 1900:

1882	Against Employment of Negro Men	2	0	2
1883	Against Employment of Negro Men	2	1	1
1885	For Discharge of Negro Employees	1	1	0
1887	Against Working w/Negro Men	1	0	1
1887	For Discharge of Negro Employees	1	1	0
1888	For Discharge of Negro Employees	6	0	6
1888	Against Employment of Negro Men	1	0	1
1889	Against Working Under Negro Foremen	1	1	0
1890	Against Working w/Negro Men	1	0	1
1891	Against Working w/Negro Men	1	0	1
1892	Against Working w/Negro Men	1	0	1
1894	For Discharge of Negro Employees	2	1	11
1896	Against Negro Employees Doing Journeymen Work and for the Discharge of Negro Men	11	0	1
1897	For Discharge of Negro Employees	1	1	0

1898	Against Employment of Negro Men	1	1	0
1899	Against Obnoxious Rules and For Discharge of Negro Waiter	1	0	1
1900	Against Employment of Negro Men	5	3	2
1900	Against Employment of Negro Girls	1	0	1
	Total:	41	10	31

Aside from the fact that white workers were racist, we can't ignore the fact that the rise of imperialism worked hand in glove with buttressing the demands of the white labor. In essence, white workers had the following ideals:

American labor talked of spiritualism of labor; talked of merging labor with the rising monopoly class, the class that was brutally exploiting Blacks, Whites and the world; spoke for the annexation of other territories.

This was the level of consciousness of the white worker and many times their leaders; he ignored slavery, refused to acknowledge the Blacks as vanguard in struggles, fought for expansion of slavery and concomitant to this, worked hand in hand for the rise of imperialism.

It's important to understand that the move by America to annex Santo Domingo, Philippines, and other places enhanced the polarization between Black and white workers. The support of the capitalist system by the white worker granted them certain privileges that blacks were and still are denied.

The labor movement as represented by United Mine Workers, Steel Workers, UAW, AFL-CIO, etc., are all the antithesis of the freedom of black people, in particular, and the world, in general. For the most part, at this stage, white labor must be viewed as an enemy because of the positions it holds in working hand in glove with the imperialists.

The UAW and AFL-CIO, as well as other major unions, support imperialist, fascist wars in Vietnam. Labor supports strong legislation against "crime in the streets," but says nothing about organized crime or the crimes against the people of Vietnam, etc. Nor do they protest the past and current crimes against black people. Aside from white labor's political stance, they are at best, pressure groups to obtain bourgeois rights. They request wage increases, living allowances, etc., but say nothing about worker control of plants, production and the state. Such bourgeois demands exemplify a desire to live in this burning house.

In reality, the white worker is moving more and more to think of himself as a middle class suburbanite than as a worker. Many white workers are living in small towns surrounding large cities and are involved in forming militias against the so called threat of black rioters, as well as fight against legislation for welfare and education for the cities.

The exploitation of working class youth for a racist, imperialist war in Vietnam, the high cost of living coupled with increasing taxes and lower real wages, has caused the white worker to lose a good deal of his previous privileges. The contradictions within the system are forcing him to struggle against it and those in real control of the factories, state and system.

Another major factor is to understand that the development of imperialism in the late 19th century and its subsequent decay in the twentieth century, has to be recognized and evaluated. Capitalism's pacifications via privileges for white labor are decreasing because of the revolutionary actions around the world against capitalism and its concomitant, exploitation. Privileged positions and benefits are being taken away via taxes, wars, and other factors that deny whites their excuse for racism and failure to act with working class consciousness.

The revolutionary fronts around the world, as represented by Zanzibar, Congo, Brazzaville, Frelime, China, the NLF, the French workers and students, and the black liberation groups in the U.S., are all demanding the immediate destruction of a burning house. White labor, on the contrary, supports the very obstacles to freedom of blacks, and ironically enough, to their own freedom from capitalist exploitation of their labor.

The one outstanding factor at this point is that as long as white workers think of themselves as white workers or white middle or lower class, they will be counter to the struggle, and will retain white consciousness as opposed to class consciousness. To think in those terms means a struggle for the

decaying privileges that buttress the system of racism and exploitation instead
of for the liberation of all working people.
    It is without question that white labor will be forced to shift gears.
Currently, however, the liberation struggle of blacks is moving at a quickening
pace.   It is our contention that the key to the black liberation struggle lies
with the black workers.
    As previously stated, the black liberation struggle is part and parcel of
a world struggle of the oppressed against the oppressor. However, we must
carefully scrutinize which groups in the struggle are the most important in
changing a society and stopping its functioning the way it is.   That is the
group most able, due to their position in production, to lead and carry on the
revolutionary struggle.
    We say black workers, but this group must be defined better.   There are
many "workers" among our people, like small shop owners, professionals, service
workers, and also the factory and mine workers.   It is the latter group that we
speak of as the backbone of the revolutionary forces.   Specifically the mine
and factory workers, because they do the jobs that grant the most profits to
capitalist, the ruling class.
    Auto plants, mine companies, chemical corporations, steel, aluminum, etc.,
all make their billions at the expense of foundry, assembly, etc., workers, all
of whom work for far below the wages they should get in relation to work done
and, in fact, do most of their work so the owners can pocket the profits.
    These blacks comprise the majority of the workers among the black working
class.   It is also significant to note that this class is the most organized
group.   The organization of black labor dates back to the late 1860's early
1870's, as a direct result of manipulative use by the monopoly capitalist class
of white labor's racism.
    Aside from numbers, organization, viability, and strength, this group
(along with all workers in the plants and mines) are in direct conflict with
the owners of the means of production.   Just as the peasant in South America,
the black mine worker in Africa, the worker in Europe, are the backbones of
production in their countries, blacks have been and still are, the backbone of
exploitative labor in this country.
    Union management means labor versus boss or exploited versus exploiter.
Another significant factor is that this monopoly capitalist system's major
apparatus for control does not serve the black worker at all.

Overall Position of Black Workers:

    Even based on government statistics, the position of the black worker in
the labor force is clear.   In 1970 the total civilian labor force was approximately 84,617,000 with a total black force of 9,560,000 or 10.1% of the total
labor force.   The total labor force represents a 59.6% participation rate by
the entire white population and a 62.4% participation rate by the total black
population.
    Unemployed statistics show that there are 2,214,000 or 3.1% of the white
labor force out of work as compared to 523,000 or 6.1% of the black labor force
out of work.
    In concluding the findings of these tables we state that black workers make
up a significant section of the reserve army of the unemployed and that the
rate of unemployed among black workers is twice as high as that amongst whites.
The labor participation rate percentage categories demonstrate that blacks as
a people, are more of an integral part of the proletariat than whites and
would even have a greater labor participation rate if jobs were not so hard
for blacks to find.
    Tables further indicate that black workers are disproportionately located
in blue collar and service worker positions.   In blue collar positions black
workers are mainly operatives and laborers working on the hottest, dirtiest,
and most dangerous jobs.   In this category black workers comprise 23% or
nearly 1/4 of all positions.   Figures fall to present an adequate picture in
the industries and plants like Dodge Main, Eldon Avenue, Ford Rouge, etc.,
black workers make up 70 to 85% of the work force and have the ability to
bring all production to a halt, by methods of closing down the hot dirty
foundries, steel mills, and production plants.   Whites working in the operatives and laborer category are able to gain the fruits of their white skinned
privileged positions by being placed in the easiest jobs such as stock chasing,

transportation, and light assembly positions, leaving black workers make up
only 3.1% of all apprenticeship positions which is directly related to the
lack of upward mobility from the operative blue collar sector. In skilled
trades sector black workers once again are heavily concentrated in dirty, hard
positions, they comprise 12.3% of all masons, tilesetters and stonecutters,
22.8% of all plasterers, lathers, and cement finishers placing them at the
bottom of the building trades. Black workers make up 23.8% of all furnacemen,
smelters, and pourers, and 25% of all metal molders are found in the smog and
polluted air of the foundries.
     To the contrary, the percentage of white craftsmen and foremen is double
that of blacks and a definite product of the white skinned privilege which
degrades black workers, especially in the area of promotions.
     One half of the white working force is employed in white collar positions,
as compared to one quarter of the black working population. But even in
these categories perform the hardest and steady physical work, 11% of black
workers in this sector are tied to low clerical positions categorized by low
pay and constant physical work. Black workers are employed to such a degree
in the clerical sector that once again, they are essential to many industries
and have the power also to bring all work to a standstill.
     In the service sector black workers are employed three times to the
degree of whites and have a near monopoly in household services. Whites working the service sector enjoy the luxuries of homes of the ruling class barons
and earn lucrative salaries for their services; mainly the management and over-
seeing of black service workers.
     In the farm worker sector, black workers perform mainly the migrant em-
ployment categorized by next to slave wages and subhuman living conditions by
the families of those involved. While whites in this sector are mainly owners
of the land and the farm products being produced.
     The tables finally show that black workers are systematically excluded
from all decision making positions--judges, lawyers, and administrators and
are left virtually in a powerless position not only in industry on the job,
but also at home in the black community. Black workers find themselves as
paupers as the white skinned privilege outside the places of work takes the
form of white racist domination in order to maintain the resolute privileged
position occupied by white racist anti-black and backward administrators who
only carry out those policies which are in opposition to the interests of
blacks.
     Because of the positions which blacks occupy as workers which are charac-
terized generally by hard work and low pay, they are forced into a position
of perpetual suffering, economically. The wives of black workers are very
often forced to take extra employment in order to meet basic family needs.

Economic Situation of Black Workers

     Categories in which white workers are heavily concentrated are areas of
highest pay and power. Professional positions, categories in which whites
are employed heavily, represents the areas of highest pay. Management and
skilled positions in which whites are employed up to five times the degree of
blacks also, are the recipients of high pay scales.
     In comparison, the economic position of black workers, in their areas of
highest concentration, blue collar service, lower clerical and farm workers,
represent the lowest position of the wage scale. The combination of the dual
oppression of black workers of the hardest, dirtiest jobs, and at the same
time, receiving the lowest pay, has had the effect of raising their political
consciousness more and more to the point of open class war at the point of
production. The struggle of black workers has been systematically stifled by
the overall political economy of poverty. The ruling class has systematically
dressed up the realities under which black workers live. Through constant
streams of propaganda, in the form of advertisements, they have been able to
some degree, to foster false hopes and dreams in the minds of black workers.
The educational system has perpetuated false notions in terms of understanding
the fundamental characteristics of life under monopoly capitalism.
     Both the unions and the companies have denied blacks the knowledge of the
fundamentals for organizing techniques and propaganda skills which has
fostered strong feelings of individualism and personal gain.

The ruling class has acted as though it was seriously addressing itself
to the problems of black workers by extending its rolls of non-productive
employees in order to have more troops to dupe the already confused and unorganized black workers. The companies have created hard core programs and
backed certain community organizations and propagandized heavily about them
via the mass media. They have mixed repressive techniques with soft-lined
measures in order to crush and stifle rebellion simultaneously. Many reform
groups and civil rights organizations have attempted to gain purely economic
reforms without addressing the importance of the political economy of poverty.
The monopoly capitalist class has to maintain a system of strict poverty
domestically. It cannot afford to spend the billions of dollars thrown away
annually on imperialist wars here, at home, for fear of it changing the objective power relationships between itself and the proletariat. During a few
lucrative months during 1966, before the rising inflationary prices and high
taxes had begun to deplete the wage gains of workers, it became necessary for
many companies to stop paying afternoon shift workers on Thursday, which has
been a long ago established standard, because over half of the workers would
not come to work the following Friday. Once black workers had earned enough
to meet their immediate objective necessities, the extra day gave them time
to explore organizing methods or hire organizers to buy guns which they in
turn, could use in their struggles against the ruling class.

The monopoly corporations have placed great emphasis on the political
aspect of the economy of poverty. They have done everything possible except
slow down the level of production and raise the economic level of workers,
which is the reality which has sparked class struggle amongst black workers
inside basic industry.

So that reality still exists, black workers are the main producers in
this society. It is the bare hands of black workers which turn raw materials
into finished products. They are transforming those raw materials far out of
proportion to what statistics show they are producing in increasingly greater
numbers as production becomes harder and faster. Black workers are toiling
under more and more severe working conditions while black children and wives
go hungry because of the low wages, inflationary prices, and increased taxes.
They exist as the most oppressed and exploited section of the proletariat and
have the power to bring all of industry to a schreeching halt. Their only hope
can be seen through open class war and the potential of carrying out a Black
General Strike which would bring the entire U.S. productive capacity and its
monopoly capitalist owners to their demise.

Inner-City Voice (official organ of the League of Revolutionary Black Workers),
3 (February, 1971):10-12.

11. DRUM BEATS WILL BE HEARD

In the beginning of 1970 we characterized the coming year as the "year of
the struggle." Indeed, in retrospect 1970 can truly be considered the year of
the struggle. But, now we are confronted with the harsh realities of 1971.
The overall condition of black, non-white, and poor white people in America
had developed into a situation fraught with serious and far-reaching consequences. Intense recession, accompanied by high unemployment especially
for young black workers is imminent. Inspite of the insidious rhetoric of
President Nixon forecasting the gradual decline of the unemployment rate, one
has only to note the ever increasing unemployment lines. The unemployment
rate rose to a five year high of nearly 5.6% last year. An atmosphere of
repression has reached a crescendo reminiscent of Germany of the 30's
witness the vicious assassinations of Ralph Featherstone, Fred Hampton, Bro.
Chaka, and in the same breath let us not forget to raise question with
regards to the mysterious disappearance of our beloved brother H. Rap Brown.
Consider the unjust and inhumane incarcerations of Martin Sortre, Soledad
Brothers, Bobby Seale, James Johnson, Cleveland Sellers, Fred Ahmed Evans,
and especially Angela Davis, who is presently facing the gas chamber in

California. The educational institutions are in utter chaos. Already this year there have been reports where black and white high school students have erupted into violent confrontations. Black students across the nation are demanding an end to the racist nature of these institutes of "learning." They are proving stubbornly defiant in their heroic efforts to re-evaluate the entire educational process. What is most significant to note is that they are not just demanding a more "relevant" education for blacks (i.e. Black history, black music) but are challenging the very fabric of these institutions.

The numerous federally funded reform programs such as jobs, C.A.P., and Model Cities have virtually gone for naught. These short lived programs served the suffering black masses, in the decade of the 60's. The proliferation of literally hundreds of "hope" programs were supposed to placate the volatile urban areas. The failure of these programs, which were inevitable, in turn have ironically served to manifest the latent frustrations and angers which had for so long remained tacit.

Amidst the miserable conditions of a people whose legitimate struggle had for over 400 years been stifled by the forces of oppression rose the murmur of D.R.U.M. beats. D.R.U.M. beats could be heard in the wildcat strikes, and union elections at Dodge Main (strike 68, Trustee Election, and DRUM slate election 68, 70). D.R.U.M. beats rapidly permeated to other plants; such as Eldon Gear and Axle, and Ford Rouge. As far away as Mahway, New Jersey (United Black Brothers) and Cambridge, Massachusetts (Polaroid Workers Revolutionary movements) similar beats could be heard.

The increased militancy on the part of black workers found both the bureaucratic unions and management unprepared. But, with great resilience on the part of these reactionary elements they were able to a certain degree impede the tangible development of these black workers movements. In 1970, towards the end of a two day union election held in Detroit at the U.A.W., workers who had served as voting challengers were forcibly removed from the union hall by union officials and the local police with three voting booths left open. As a result of this violation of election procedure the U.A.W. functionaries were able to maintain their strangle hold on the local.

Now the D.R.U.M. beats are sounding the tune of International Black Appeal. The International Black Appeal is a charitable fund apparatus, which is attempting to address itself to the problems of the black, non white, and poor white workers. It has five major areas of concern (1) Emergency food and Health Centers: This component speaks firstly to the severe nature of hunger and incorrect diets of the black and poor people. We will have use of churches and our churchmen to provide services in minimizing this problem. Information about the conditions and a stringent effort to support groups to combat this problem. In addition, and equally important, we seek the immediate construction of medical neighborhood clinics which will provide immediate emergency relief. This would also identify and assist in developing drug centers to alleviate the problem as much as possible. (2) Labor strike and deals with the problems of black and poor worker's families who because of circumstances many times beyond their control, find the worker of the family is fired, laid off, or becomes severely ill. We want to address ourselves to the families of these needy workers and assist the worker in combating his problems (i.e. stamping out racism in plants, better work conditions, safety conditions, etc.). Familes of the black and poor feel these problems in an economic and social order thats overflowing with racism and class preferences. (3) Legal Defense services: Black and poor people are the greatest victims of racism and unequal justice under the law. Here again, the problems of families are affected many times by the loss of the bread winner, inadequate or non-existent money for bail, equally little money for good lawyers, etc. It is within this realm that the fund wishes to address itself. (4) Welfare system: Here the fund shall address itself to groups of organizations that attempt to make the welfare system and its agencies more responsive and cognizant to the needs of the black and poor communities. (5) Housing and Recreation: This field of endeavor is crucial to the black and poor people's areas. Many problems occur because of the inadequacy or lack of both these facilities. The fund shall seek out organizations to involve itself in combating these problems.

Albeit the I.B.A. is still in its initial stages, however black workers from many of the Detroit area plants have given it their full support. Already many of these workers have spent invaluable time working for I.B.A. Black workers such as Rufus Burke (Great Lakes Steel), Ron March (Dodge Main), Fred Hosley (Eldon Gear and Axle), and many others have made presentations on the program of I.B.A. on various local black programs. Soon they will begin to distribute literature at the various plants. It is incumbent upon black and poor people to take an interest in the development of a program, which like no other program in the history of America is geared to operate in their interest. Black workers, especially must make resolute their determination to insure that in 1971 D.R.U.M. BEATS WILL BE HEARD.

Inner-City Voice (official organ of the League of Revolutionary Black Workers), 3 (February, 1971):3.

12. BLACK WORKER RAPS

This is an interview with Brother Rae Johnson, a member of DRUM, and a former worker at Dodge Main. He like so many other black workers have been fired because of his attempts to bring about a change in the unbearable working conditions at the plants, and the racist repression leveled against black workers.

Q. What was your job at Dodge Main, brother Rae?
A. I was, at the time I was fired a spot welder, which is one of the most dirty jobs in the plant body shop. But before that I had worked in many parts of the plant, being switched around often because I couldn't get along with the racist practices and bad conditions in these different areas.
Q. What is the feeling or the mood of Black workers at Dodge Main?
A. Well they are pretty disturbed about the racist foremen, and all the penalties they are issued by them; they are also upset about the mess they got over the contract settlements because they realize that they didn't from them. They also realize that since the Union doesn't represent them, that they don't have anyone to fight for them, and that they put their jobs on the line everytime they try to speak up for some kind of change.
Q. What kind of harrassment do the workers get, are you speaking of fines, penalties, and this type of thing?
A. Yea, this and other things. For example if a man works ten hours a day six days a week, or maybe seven days, then naturally he wants to take off, but what happens is if he takes off and comes back, if he doesn't have a doctors excuse, then he can expect penalties as large as 30 days lay off or maybe being fired, depending on who you are, and your record, that they have on you. But a man doesn't have to be physically sick, to be sick of that line, you're just tired as hell.
Q. Are White workers harrassed like the Black workers?
A. Not to the degree that Black workers are. For instance the places in the plant where the dirtiest jobs are, there are predominantly Black workers doing them, like the foundry for instance, and the body shops. I know when I came here in 1964, that most of the Blacks that came in were sent to these dirty and dangerous jobs, and these are the areas that Blacks catch the most hell, and this practice is still going on today.
Q. What kind of grievance procedure if any, does the union cut Blacks into, or does the worker have any way of airing his grievances?
A. There is a grievance procedure, but it has been proven insufficient especially for the Black worker. You have problems when a Black worker is being treated unjustly because he's Black, and the union doesn't address themselves to this at all. Plus you have the working conditions, you can tell them that the working conditions are unsafe but the Union doesn't seem to address themselves even to this. In fact if you worked where the job was so bad that you wanted to walk out in protest, like most Black workers do, then you stand a chance of getting fired quickly, and the UAW has not to this day backed up the men in this respect.
Q. What are the strengths and the weaknesses of the various contracts that have been signed?

A. Well there are two contracts that were signed, one was a National contract, and the other a local contract, but as I said it doesn't matter because in reality you don't get anything from either one. The National contract supposedly gave the men better fringe benefits and wages, and other junk but nothing at all about better working conditions, and this is the most important issue. The raises they give you don't amount to anything, like you're supposed to get about a fifty cent raise, but actually when that fifty cents is broken down what you really have is about thirty three cents cost of living from the old contract, then you had about 11 cents raise that will come if you speed up the production, so actually this will come to about a 6 cents raise which is only about 20 dollars a year, and with the cost of living gone up twice that, this doesn't amount to anything at all it's just a game they play to make the workers think they're getting something, and the strike serves to sell the surplus of cars they already have.

Q. So it's all just a sham then?

A. Yeah, and then you go down to the local level where they claim that they are really supposed to be dealing with plant conditions and they really didn't do much of anything, except made a couple of political moves that will probably help them in the next election. As for working conditions in the plants, they are just as bad, if not worse.

Q. Working conditions, what exactly do you mean when you speak of the working conditions in the plants. Do you mean, like for instance when I was working in a plant on the line, they didn't have suspension brakes for the high-lows, and grease from axles was all over the floor, things of this nature?

A. Yes, you have that kind of problem in all plants where they don't fix the machines and machines are run unsafely. Like for instance in our plants where you are running cars on a line, gas fumes are rapid in fact just a couple of weeks ago they had to put everybody out because of a fire that started because of the gas, in fact a worker lost his life trying to put out the fire, and at the time of the fire the fire extinguishers were not working. So the safety thing at Dodge Main is just ridiculous. About a year ago they had another explosion in skill trades and many men were burnt badly, so this type of occurrence is quite frequent.

Q. You were fired because of your actions and affiliation with DRUM, is that right?

A. When I did start moving with DRUM, management really started to come down hard on me and some of the leaders of DRUM that worked at the plant. The foremen and management would start saying things like they were going to discipline me for being one minute late, and any other petty thing they could get a hold of. Things of that sort that a White worker or one of these guys that just does anything they want him to do without giving them any, what they call trouble, could do, and never get into trouble for. I would continuously be harrassed and they would try to make me attack them so they would have a reason to fire me, but I wouldn't fall for that.

Q. What exactly did they fire you over?

A. Well this job I had was a key job, because it can slow the line down, and they never did like this because they want as much production as possible. However, they claim they also want quality, so they say, and if you've been on a line you know that on the line you can't get quality and the kind of speed in production that they want. So if I got the speed they would come down on me for the quality, so I slowed down the line to give them that good "Chrysler quality" but they didn't go for that and anything I did they would attack me. Like I was in this pit, which was a safety hazard in the first place, and you are under the car, and what they want to do is run the car over you, while you do what your supposed to do to it, and this way they can speed up production. But this time they hadn't been doing that, they were just bringing the car in and you adjust the car like you supposed to, the front end is what I had to work on and then start it up and move it down the line. However, one day they decided that they would speed up production, and keep the car running while I worked on it, you know underneath a running car isn't the safest thing, but damn the man down in the pit, this way was cheaper and more expedient and this way they wouldn't have to take the time to start the cars up after the man finished his part, because sometimes the cars wouldn't start and this would cost them a few minutes in time trying to start the car again. So I raised a lot of hell over this, called down the plant safety men and told all the

other brothers in the plant, what was going down, and really did whatever I
could to bring this to the light. But what made it so bad on me I was the only
one in that pit complaining about what was going on. So they didn't go for
that because the safety men found it was a safety hazard, and I had called
them. The way I understand it now is that the union has got a new ventilation
system and all this time its been costing the plant plenty bread, and you know
they don't go for that. All this time I had been going to the union and complaining to the board of trustees at the meetings it has been stated that it
was the unions doing that got this ventilation system and I've been fired.
     Q. So they fired you because you were trying to bring about some safety
conditions?
     A. Yeah, safety conditions and them not getting the production they
wanted out on the line, and do it just happen that these racist foremen, all
of the foremen are White, even though most of the workers are Black, felt that
they weren't getting enough production and it was my fault. So what he did
was one day come up to me about five minutes before quitting time, and charged
me with walking off the job five minutes before the whistle blew. This I may
add is a common practice for the workers around the plant. Especially the
White workers, so if they fired people for doing that, there wouldn't be anybody in the plants because like I said it is common practice, even the foremen
do it. But, what was really bad is that I didn't walk off the job five
minutes early, so it was an out an out racist act. I feel that they are going
to have to take me back though because the charge is so ridiculous, if they
make it stick, that will be one more example of the bullshit that goes down in
the plants.

Inner-City Voice (official organ of the League of Revolutionary Black Workers),
3 (April, 1971):3.

13. NATIONAL WORKERS PROGRAM

Black Panther Caucus

     1. Organize the Unorganized
There are more than 71 million workers in the U.S. Only 20 million of them
(28%) are union members. In order for the workers to have the strength and
unity we need in fighting the bosses, we must organize all workers into unions.
     2. Shorter Work Week
The work week should be 30 hours per week (with no compulsory overtime) at 40
hours pay, or fewer hours if necessary to guarantee full employment.
     3. Stop Runaway Shops
When a boss decided to move his shop, all workers must be given the choice of:
a) going with the shop at the same wages and conditions (with transportation
paid by the boss), or b) taking 3 years severance pay with continuation of
health and welfare plans for 3 years or until they find new jobs. The union
contract must go with the shop to its new location.
     4. Women Workers
One third (1/3) of the workers today are women. Unions must lead the fight
for an end to discrimination against women. Women must have equal rights to
jobs and must receive equal pay for equal work. Unions that represent women
workers must guarantee leadership positions to women. As part of the struggle
for these ends unions must demand child care centers to be provided by the
companies and the government for the children of working women.
     5. Automation
The unions must fight to win the right to negotiate all automation with the
company before it takes place. The unions shall set the conditions of automation so that there are no lay-offs and job safety is guaranteed.
     6. Health and Welfare
Every year in the U.S. 14,500 workers are killed on the job; over half a
million fall ill with occupational diseases; 7 million are injured; and 2
million are disabled.

Unions must fight for the right to set and enforce health and safety standards
on the job.
Unions must fight to win fully paid medical and dental coverage for all workers
and their families. At the same time, labor must struggle for free medical
and dental care for all the people.
      7. Anti-Labor Laws
Labor must take the offensive against anti-labor laws by demanding their repeal
and defying them when they are used.
      8. End Racism
The labor movement must struggle against racism in the unions in order to
effectively combat racism in the society. The unions must educate the workers
to understand that racism serves the bosses by dividing the workers and preventing the development of class consciousness.
      9. End the War
Labor must demand an end to the war in Vietnam and all aggressive imperialist
wars. This must be coupled with a struggle in this country against racism
and growing fascism.
      10. Union Sell-Out
All of the problems we have outlined can be blamed in part on the sell-out of
union leadership to class collaborationist, cold war, and racist policies.
We must rebuild a militant trade union movement by combating these policies
through the formation of rank-and-file caucuses and the fight for class
consciousness.

Auto Workers Focus (rank and file newspaper of the Black Panther Caucus), 1
(August, 1970):8.

14. BLACK WORKERS--DUAL UNIONS

      I'd like to take this opportunity to define what "dual unions" are and
what role they will play in the black workers liberation struggle. The position black workers must take on such a question, I will try to relate in this
article.
      First let us examine the Communist Party's position on dual unions. The
clearest example of that was in Chicago at the rank-and-file conference. I
was a witness to a verbal attack on a black rank-and-filer because he's trying
to build a dual union that will serve the true needs of the workers in his
union (New York City Transit Authority). The event took place at the start of
the panel discussion on racism. The panel was headed by an old black cat who's
in the CPUSA, and it seems he allowed a white dude to get up and run his thing
against dual unions, then sit down with a shit-eating grin on his face.
      When the brother from NYCTA tried to present his side, he was told to be
quiet and sit down--that white dude had done his thing. The Community Party's
historical position on dual unions has always been dogmatic and backwards. And
black workers must be clear on this point.
      To illustrate. Workers know that union leaders wish them to remain
ignorant on all political issues because these misleaders have spent years
building their power and they are not about to let some small group of young
cats beat them at their own game.
      The time will come when these brothers will have to break away from the
racist unions as they exist today and form their own rank-and-file union to
protect themselves and their interest which is not only based in the union but
also in the black community. Our union leaders have us thinking that we as
employed are better than the unemployed or lumpenproletariat. We do not own
any means of production, thereby we have nothing to protect in those factories,
so how can we be better than the street brothers?
      In labor today there is a strong right-wing leadership (AFL-CIO George
Meany; Frank Fitzsimmons, Teamsters; W.A. Boyle, Mine Workers; C.J. Haggerty,
Building Trades; and, last but not least, L. Woodcock, Auto Workers), and when
I hear somebody talking about we should not get away from these racists, and
that I should work within the framework of the present leadership, I say later

for them racist bureaucrats and I suspect their friends in the Communist Party.[92]
We've heard the echoes of "work in the framework" before, and there's no difference between the Nixons and Kennedys, Wallaces or Unruhs, Agnews or
McCarthys, Reagans or Daleys of our time.[93]
    We say the friends of our enemies are our enemies and there is no thin
line, and when our so-called friends echo the words of our class enemies, then
we must deal with our so-called friends, because it is clear they only want to
replace the "bad guys" with their "good guys" who have every intention of the
union structure remaining.
    The time to move is now. The examples have been shown to us by Brothers
"Ike" Jernigan, L.A., California, and James Johnson, Detroit. These brothers
dealt with the bosses and the union leaders in the only manner they have left.
    Dual unions are necessary for all oppressed workers and anybody who stands
in the way of this must be shown the method Jernigan and Johnson showed their
oppressor.

                                        Free Jernigan
                                        Free Johnson
                                        Free All Political Prisoners

                                        Kenny Horston
                                        Chairman, B.P.C.

Auto Workers Focus (rank and file newspaper of the Black Panther Caucus), 1
(August, 1970):3.

15. AUTO MONGERS PLOT AGAINST WORKERS

By William Allan

    DETROIT--It's expected soon that the Big 3 of auto, General Motors, Ford,
and Chrysler, both in the U.S. and Canada, will drop their boom (their reply
to the United Auto Workers demands) on the 1-1/2 million member UAW. Certainly
the modest demands of the UAW for a "substantial" wage increase, reported to
be around 15 per cent, will encourage the profit-swollen Big 3 to come forth
with even more modest offers backed up with lots of hookers.
    Long ago the GM moguls laid down the line for the 1970 negotiations, which
was that before any money was to be transmitted commitments would have to be
forthcoming on a weakened grievance procedure and increased productivity to
"cut costs."
    The time is getting near. The flim-flam of TV lights, radio reporters,
the extraneous questions of the pencil and paper reporters, has gone, and now
it's down to the nitty-gritty bargaining and to see how much the corporations
can get away with.
    The auto moguls are also encouraged by the lack of mobilization of the
UAW's militant rank and file, who are eyeing uneasily the "15%" reported
demand of their union leaders.
    Leonard Woodcock, UAW president, at present making the rounds of the
boondocks speaking at many meetings to get better known, is feeling the uneasiness and concern of the workers at the disquieting lull in the negotiations.
    Woodcock is telling the membership if the companies agree to pay 26 cents
owing the workers because of increased cost of living, plus a package increase
of 8 per cent, "the union would tell them they are getting warm." The 8 per
cent would cover a pension of $500 a month with 30 years seniority, and other
fringe demands. But the word coming back from the rank and file gatherings
Woodcock is speaking to is that he wants the 26¢ plus something in the
neighborhood of an additional 12 per cent.
    Workers that reporters of the *Daily World* spoke to say that isn't enough
because the 26¢ is not "new money," but old money, and a mere 12 per cent
from companies who between 1947 and 1969 made a total of $82 billion in
profits before taxes, is not even crumbs.

But the main hammer being quietly used in negotiations against the workers is on working conditions. A sample is the demand by the companies for the right to discharge employees after three days of absenteeism if they don't notify the company they are ill. Also the companies want the right to have their own doctor examine a sick worker to decide if he is ill.

This will affect in great numbers black workers, who because of working in the dirtiest, hardest, hottest, most disagreeable jobs in the industry, the racetrack, gutbusting jobs have to lay off from sheer exhaustion. In this summer heat of 90 degrees outside and 110 inside many sicken and collapse.

This demand of the companies is a racist attack on the black workers and means the companies want to use this to wipe out many of the militant sections of workers, bypassing the grievance procedure. What's alarming is that a UAW spokesman, Nelson Samp, Ford UAW team, was quoted in the press as saying, "We can go along." The companies of course say absenteeism is heaviest on weekends, insinuating workers are off for a weekend somewhere.

While 41 papers have been presented by the UAW on the 1970 demands, not one that we can learn of has been delivered on working conditions, the main problem facing the workers in the plants.

The companies are making moves also to shift local plant demands and negotiations into higher echelon negotiations figuring that in this way they can avoid rank and file strike action unless local demands are won. In the past scores of plant strikes have held up national ratification until these shop demands were won. They are the real nitty-gritty demands, like speedup curbs, health and safety, curbs on overtime, fighting discrimination, equal pay for equal work for women, streamlining the grievance procedure. For example, in the giant Ford Rouge plant, it's learned that 450 grievances from that plant alone are before the national UAW-Ford empire. With scores of Ford plants in the U.S. and Canada, the amount of grievances could run into many hundreds more. Any mobilization by top UAW of rank and filers would send these shop demands into major issues, which they are. Failure to mobilize the workers on these fundamental issues takes the heat off GM, Ford, Chrysler and leaves the union open for a smasher of an attack and weakening. No 12 per cent package could remedy that. That's why the present lull is disquieting; it helps management, not the cause of the workers. The negotiators need rallies, marches, demonstrations to put on the heat.

Auto Workers Focus (rank and file newspaper of the Black Panther Caucus), 1 (August, 1970):1.

16. BLACK WORKER SHOOTS FOREMEN:
RESOLVE PROBLEM WITH MANAGEMENT

On Wednesday evening, July 15, James Johnson, Jr. responded to months of harassment and years of oppression and shot to death two (2) foremen and one (1) job setter at the Eldon Ave. Gear and Axle Plant. Dead were Hugh M. Jones, 44, a black production foreman; Gary L. Hinz, 32, a white production foreman; and Joseph Kowalski, a white job setter.

Bro. James Johnson was a conveyor loader in Dept. 78, the Brake Shoe Dept. and had been so employed for the past three (3) years. Eldon Ave. Gear and Axle Plant, the home of ELRUM, has some of the worst working conditions of any plant in existence. The plant is so unsafe that all of its 4,500 employees are risking their lives when they walk through the gates. In Dept. 72, there is an inch and a half of oil covering the floor of the aisles. The oil comes up over the soles of the workers' shoes. The entire ventilation system is inoperative. The jitney trucks have no brakes, lopsided tires, no horns, and no lights. The aisle-ways are blocked by skid boxes, axles and scrap iron. Drill presses, cutters and grinders do not have safety guards. The management at Eldon is one of the most backward managements in town and totally nonresponsive to the just cries of black workers. The plant is the only gear and axle plant the Chrysler Corporation has and is the key to continued production of the entire Corporation. Unlike assembly plants where lost production can be

made up, overtime or lost time at Eldon means a slow down at assembly plants.
Working conditions are so bad that black foremen have been employed for over
10 years in order to moderate racial conflict at the point of production.
     All the hourly employees are represented by Local 961 of the U.A.W.-C.I.O.
The union President is Elroy Richardson, a former black Vice-President who
rode the tide of black consciousness to the presidency in the spring of 1969.
The local executive board consists of a group of loyal flunkeys in the service
of every qualm of the President. Local 961 is a backward local with none of
the so-called reforms which some other locals have. It has no education
department and no good and welfare fund and the union hall is locked more than
open. Elroy Richardson is the only Local President out of over 3000 locals to
attend the 22nd Annual Constitutional Convention as a Sergeant-of-Arms in
Atlantic City in April of this year.
     For over the last six (6) months, the already oppressive conditions
worsened with the increase in layoffs and accompanying speed-ups of gear and
axle production. The first open manifestation of these conditions took place
on April 16, 1970, on the midnight shift in Dept. 73, when a white foreman
named Ervin Ashlock threatened to bash Bro. John Scott's head in with a pi-
nion gear. Scott then informed his committeemen and the following procedure
ended in the discharge of Bro. John Scott. Elroy Richardson, the Union
President, sent his union Stewards into the shop and ordered the workers out
on a wildcat strike. The strike lasted two (2) days and the President got
cold feet and ordered the workers back to work. Two weeks later Chrysler
Corporation responded by discharging fourteen (14) Union Representatives and
once again the plant went on an unauthorized strike. This strike also lasted
two (2) days and the workers were sent back to work without any Union representation.
     No Union Stewards were reinstated until about mid-May, which means the
workers were forced to toil without any representation whatsoever. During this
period the racist management at Eldon took extreme advantage of the situation
by arbitrarily forcing workers to perform two (2) jobs, attempting to provoke
them to the breaking point. The workers had been beaten down and their spirits
defeated by two (2) unsuccessful strikes. They had seen their Stewards discharged in mass and nothing was done about it and if the Chrysler Corporation
was bold enough to discharge fourteen (14) union representatives, it was
obvious that individual workers' jobs meant nothing. Hope was gone and each
worker feared arbitrary discharge for disobeying foremen orders. It was this
period of time that witnessed the death of two (2) black workers arising out
of harassment from the Medical Department and unsafe working conditions at
Eldon. Sister Mamie Williams died in the hospital after being forced back to
work by a Chrysler Corporation doctor, which was contrary to the orders of her
private physicians who had ordered her to bed. Precisely two (2) weeks later
Gary Thompson, a 22-year-old Vietnam war veteran, was crushed to death under a
two (2) ton skid box which fell off of his faulty jitney truck. On June 2,
1970, Gary Thompson was buried and both Local 916 and Chrysler Corporation
responded merely by sending representatives to his funeral services. In the
weeks since the 1st of June, the Eldon management has continued its wanton
arbitrary discharges and suspensions while some of the discharged Stewards are
still in the streets.
     Needless to say, these are the precise and particular conditions under
which Brother James Johnson had toiled under in his last six months at Eldon
Ave. Gear and Axle Plant. The events around his personal existence as a black
employee at Eldon are intricately intertwined with the overall objective conditions mentioned above. James Johnson's dept. is Dept 78, which is brake
shoe dept. in which new conveyor belts were added in February. The new
conveyor belt ran at such a rate that it threw brake shoes all over the floor,
adding extra work for James Johnson, the conveyor loader on afternoon shift.
On the afternoon shift Dept. 78 is under Steward District 11 which is covered
by Clarence Horton, who ran unopposed in the last election for steward.
Clarence Horton represents three (3) departments: 78 (brake shoe), 80 (brake
assembly), and 83 (brake drum). Clarence Horton is a poor union steward who
is not even very knowledgeable about union procedure. He is a very poor
spokesman and a loyal supporter of Elroy Richardson, the Union President.
Clarence Horton was discharged along with thirteen (13) other stewards on
May 1st, and was not reinstated until the 2nd week in June. For six (6)

weeks James Johnson was employed at Eldon with no union representation. In the early part of May, James Johnson was involved in an automobile accident and he himself being placed under doctors care. The medical officials at Eldon Ave. ordered him back to work over and above the recommendation of his own private physicians. These were the same officials who ordered Mamie Williams back to work, which led to her death one week later. James had signed up for his vacation time for mid-May. After being ordered back to work, he left the plant on his two-week vacation time which he had previously been granted. James returned to work in the first week in June and was discharged without reason and his vacation pay was denied. At the time of his 1st discharge his union steward was himself discharged. His first discharge was so flagrant that management was forced to reinstate him two (2) days later on its own initiative. After his reinstatement James Johnson became the object of constant surveillance and harassment. All of the foremen in Dept. 78 are merely high school graduates and very blatant and bold in the manner in which they exercise their authority. Management has set out consciously to attempt to provoke James into committing an act for which they could discharge him.

On Wednesday evening, July 15, James Johnson was taken off his job as conveyor loader and replaced by a worker with two (2) weeks seniority. He was then placed on the brake oven job which consists of placing brake shoes in bake ovens which bakes the coating on the brake shoes. The entire operation is done in 120-degree heat. It was at this point that Bro. James Johnson spoke out in protest at being removed from his job. He was taken to labor relations office with his steward, Clarence Horton, and his General Foreman, Jim Rhoades, at which point he was suspended for insubordination and told by his steward to go along with their decisions. Management had reached its long-awaited objective; they had provoked Bro. James to speak out against his treatment. James Johnson was then escorted out of the plant by plant protection guards. He returned shortly, armed with a 30-caliber carbine, in a desperate search for his General Foreman, Jim Rhoades. He supposedly asked all of his fellow workers to stand back for he was not going to hurt them. En route, in pursuit of James Rhoades, he encountered his foreman, Hugh Jones; a foreman in an adjacent dept., Gary Hinz; and a jobsetter who tried to disarm him. Johnson then supposedly threw his weapon down, saying, "I'm satisfied," and walked back to the guard shack, where he was apprehended by the Detroit Police Department.

Bro. James Johnson has moved the Black Workers struggle at the point of production to a new and higher level. As we have stated over and over, the oppressive and inhumane working conditions inside the auto industry, coupled with the sellout and class-collaborationist unions, have sparked open rebellions in basic industry. Often times in the past black workers have been driven to the point where they could stand no more and have lashed out viciously at their tormentors. In February of 1969, Bro. Rushie Forge was driven to the breaking point and lashed out, stabbing a black Labor Relations Representative, William Young, at Dodge Main. Bro. Chuck Wooten reached his breaking point minutes after Rushie by stomping Dick Prallie, a white General Foreman, in Dept. 9110 at Dodge Main. In August of 1969, Bro. Sid Lewis was likewise driven to that point and lashed out at his foreman, Howard Lewis, in Dept. 9130 at Dodge Main. In July of 1969, Bro. Ike Jernigan, employed at Lockheed Aircraft in Los Angeles, California, lashed out and shot and killed his foreman, his Union President, and another Union official. In September of 1969, another black worker in Dept. 9150 at Dodge became outraged and locked his foremen in the trunk of a car on the assembly line. Individual outrages at the point of production represent only one form which the struggle of black workers has taken. There have been individual acts of sabotage against property and all forms of wildcat strikes and numerous caucuses have been formed--all in response to the monstrous oppressive conditions that exist inside basic industry. As black workers rise up we have nothing to lose but our chains, we have nothing to lose but our jobs, our homes, our families and our future, our automobiles and our television sets. The owners and operators of the means of production own our jobs, our homes, and our families. We have neither security nor hope for the future. They control our places of employment, the schools that our children attend, decide what our wages shall be, and what kind of society our children will live in. They tell us when, where and how long and how hard we shall work. They own everything of value.

Brothers, they even think that they own us. The owners and operators of the
means of production may cause one brother to lose his job, but they can't
fire one thousand. They can take away one man's home, and one man's car; but
they can't steal from one hundred thousand. They cannot repossess from one
million. They can wreck one family, but they cannot wreck the unity of one
million families. They can enslave thousands, but they cannot enslave the
unity of millions. And they can defeat one armed enraged black worker, but
they cannot defeat a million armed black workers or the unified mass of 20
million.

Auto Workers Focus (rank and file newspaper of the Black Panther Caucus), 1
(August, 1970):4-5.

17. MARUM NEWSLETTER

The Pig Is Back

We understand the Pig is back to work (Stanley Vaske) doesn't it strike
you funny that the pig got caught stealing and was paid off by labor relations
a very short time ago, well he sure got back to work awfully fast, just goes
to show what these honkies will do, if it were a black worker paid off he
would stay off for a long time but if its a honkey worker he gets back to work
in less than a month. Of course you know we have a honkey labor relations man
and he looks out for all wrong doers if they are white, there are many black
brothers stay out much longer for less crimes, but then that is some of that
Mississippi justice Georgie boy is dishing out. We want to remind labor
relations of one thing and that is this shit is playing out and you don't have
very long to straighten it out. If he thinks he can continually get away with
this double standard shit he is badly mistaken, we don't see how he sleeps
nights but we know he does although he have cause some bread winners to suffer.
When we start our bargaining with upper management one of our first demands
will be that Georgie boy Doty and Kiel must go they are not fit to manage
nothing, they don't know how to treat people especially if they are black.
To show you that the union are in co-hoots with the corp. there is no way
in the world the pig could have gotten back to work this quick if there hadn't
been a deal made. It's funny how he got back and no one else in the history
of the union got back that fast. Between the two racist Dorman and Georgie
Boy some dealing went on, and we are aware of what went on. We know that the
union gave away quite a number of grievances. They give away all the workers
problems just to get that greedy ass Vaske back. What if the pig had been
black? He would be two years getting back.

Sweat and Blood

We give our sweat and blood to this racist outfit, we even buy what we
build trying to make it strong and what do we get in return? We get a hard
way to go, we can't go into the better jobs because of racism, and all this is
in co-hoots with the UAW, no black workers can make a mistake without paying
for it. Labor Relations doesn't give a black worker a chance. What ever the
situation is the black pays. It is a double standard type justice going on
and this includes the top of the Personnel right down to the lowest foremen
in the plant. A foreman can claim a black worker does something and without
trail or investigation Georgie boy stamps his doom seal on the worker, the
foreman don't even have to be present, just leave a note and labor relations
goes to work.
To show you that this corp. don't mean black people any good they say
they don't discriminate yet if a supervisor commits a wrong against black
workers and have to be dealt with he not only don't get punished, he gets a
better job, which in turn gives other whiteys the incentive to mess over
black workers. Underwood and Polite wound up with better jobs just because

they mistreated some black workers. We are damn sick and tired of this double
standard shit and the next time this racist ass corp. does something like that
they will remember it a long long time. We are giving this corp. a chance to
stop this bull, and if they don't we will inform you of another course of
action. Look at the situation in Pittsburgh, first they say black people are
lazy and when they try to get into a better job then they say what do they
want. This has been going on for the past four hundred years, first you are
lazy and when you try they want to know what do you want, and that is how that
damn Welfare started.
    We say one thing and that is the hell with the welfare and to hell with
this double dealing shit, everything in the United States is just as much ours
as it is theirs and we intend to get it.

Fools Set Foolish Examples

    There is one of our brothers that is the biggest Tom in the plant, and to
top it all off this clown is a young fellow, we refer to one conk head BRADY.
If he were an old man you could expect Tomism but this country ass fool is a
young man. Look at some of the things this fool does. He cooks and brings
honkey Joe Williams breakfast every morning and spreads it out on the table,
could it be that honkey Joe is screwing him. He sure acts like his wife and
when he is not playing wife to Joe he is stuck up in the Canfield Bar hoping
to get something from that honkey broad that runs the joint. Maybe he has a
double thing going but we don't think so. The thing he better watch is Joe
and the broad may have a thing going. Another thing is very plain to see and
that is that broad hasn't got him on the back side of her ass. He had enough
nerve to say he was going to run for chief Steward, well if a vote came
between him and a toilet stool we would have to vote for the stool.
    YOU CAN TAKE TOM OUT OF THE COUNTRY BUT! YOU CAN'T TAKE THE TOM OUT OF
BRADY.

A Word to Bobby Bell

    A few weeks ago Bobby Bell was suspended for allegedly pushing a foreman,
we know he wouldn't be dealt with fairly because right away that double
standard practice went into effect. Now who even heard of a worker hitting or
pushing a foreman that he doesn't even know, he had never seen this bum before
but he still was fired. What about the foreman? What did he do to provoke
this action. The double dealing Corp. sent Bell a letter saying he was fired
instead of a suspension, they suspended him first and that was to get him out
of the plant and then they sent him the letter saying he was fired.
    We still want to know what did that foreman do to provoke this? We also
want to know why labor relations fire people without hearing both sides of the
story. Of course we knew Bobby wouldn't be dealt with fairly because he happened to be a black man and on the other hand georgie boy double standards
must prevail.
    We wonder how labor relations sleep nights after having put a working
Father with children in the streets. Maybe he thinks black children don't have
to eat.

Progress: Means to Look Ahead

    Now progress means to go forward and to go forward means to look ahead,
but in order to look ahead one must have foresight and when we look at the
jokers running the local all we see is Hindsightedness.
    Honkeys like Dorman and Zappa and Toms like Ghant and Marshall aren't
capable of running a local. What have Dorman done since he has been president
other than put the racist ass Britten in the local when the local was already
full of honkies. What has Joe Zappa done and has he been around the local
quite awhile. About the only thing he ever did was to help keep blacks out
of the skill trades.
    It was bad enough that we weren't getting any representation at the mack
plant but then they had to go and assign that Tom ass Bill Marshall to represent the mack plant, this Tom isn't capable of representing a hens ass much
less talking about people. He will sell his soul out for a dime. Hank Ghant

isn't any better because he already said what ever the honkies do or tell him
to do is alright with him.

There is one thing we must do right away and that is get rid of these
Toms, we also told you guys in 1970 that if you want to progress that you
would have to get rid of Stanley James and Sambo Weary, in the first place
they are not capable of representing you and secondly they are playing games
with your bread and butter. These Toms make deals but the deal is not in your
favor.

MARUM

The UAW sneaked into the plant and left a pink leaflet (just like the
sneak's they are) and they are trying to get your mind off of the real issues
just like they have been doing for years, they are talking about electing
management personnel and all that bunk and the vacation pay, etc., well we
don't give one damn about this crap they are talking. We want EQUALITY AND
DIGNITY: What good is all this shit if you have to go into the back room to
have yours. Lets talk about the real issues since they brought us the subject,
that is concerning the Chrysler Corp. and the UAW.

CHRYSLER: What about better jobs for black people, how come there are no
black UP-GRADERS in tool and die, how come there are no Superintendents in the
plant, and how come there are no black people on good jobs as a whole? The
reason is simple that racist corp. works real hard at keeping black workers
down, and these double standard double dealing policies they have must go and
the time is running out.

UAW: Lets talk about throwing rocks at someone else when you live in a
glass house yourself. There are more PREJUDICE in the UAW than there are in
the Chrysler Corp. although they are in collusion with each other. Lets look at
some facts. You have over one thousand international Reps and less than one
hundred are black, you have a dozen or more reps from Local 212 and only one
(1) is a black, the same thing applies to the local.

Now you tell us what the above statement has to do with pensions,
insurance, etc. The fact of the matter is these honkys don't want to see black
people with a damn thing. They want your dues but they don't want you to
participate in the management of the affairs of the union. So the Hell with
the UAW, all we want from you is OUTVILLE, and this came from Mack Ave. not
Wayne.

MARUM (Mack Ave. Revolutionary Union Movement), Vol. 1, No. 2. In possession
of the editors.

THE PROGRESSIVE LABOR PARTY

18. BLACK WORKERS: KEY REVOLUTIONARY FORCE

January 1969

Imperialism has one primary need--to amass maximum profits. Therefore,
the oppression of Black workers at home and the domination of oppressed
peoples in Asia, Africa and Latin America is not merely an aberration of
deranged imperialists, but the necessary operation of imperialism.

Racism is the political expression of imperialism; it organizes and
justifies such brutal exploitation at home and abroad that the exploitation of
Black workers is the most profitable domestic business of U.S. imperialism.

Wage differentials between Black and white workers each year amount to
$22 billion. In addition, billions more are saved by denying Black Americans

the vital social services necessary for survival; this is the enormity of
Black oppression.

Imperialism as a system must perpetuate racism in order to thrive; it
must continue to reap the super-profits derived from the "racial inferiority"
thesis it has drummed home into both Black and white workers.

Consequently, the ability of the working class to reject racism is crucial
to its ability to end class oppression. U.S. imperialism cannot exist without
the brutal super-exploitation of Black people and, therefore, will never grant
equality to Black workers.

The fact of this $22 billion of super-profits raked in by the bosses in
this country permeates every aspect of life. It leads us to the conclusion
that unless an all-out fight is made against the racism that permits this
robbery--a battle waged by revolutionaries in the first place and by the working class in general--then (1) the workers will be unable to make any basic
advances in their class interests and establish a Left-Center coalition to
lead their fight against the bosses; (2) the danger of fascism will increase;
(3) the hacks who serve the ruling class at the head of the trade union movement will continue to ride roughshod over the interests of the rank and file;
and (4) no Marxist-Leninist revolutionary party will succeed in the United
States.

The basic industries on which the U.S. ruling class depends for its very
existence are increasingly using Black workers as a source of labor power. In
the auto industry, which affects one out of every seven jobs in this country,
there is a growing Black minority. No longer limited to 10 or 20 percent of
the work force, it now makes up 35 to 50 percent, and in many plants Black
workers are in a majority. In the steel mills the Black work force has reached
about 35 percent of the total. In the next 8 to 10 years the present 500,000-
man work force in basic steel is expected to dwindle to 200,000 if the $2
billion annual capital investment plans of steel bosses produce their planned
results. Since the preponderance of Black workers are among the unskilled--
those most likely to be affected by such plans--a fierce struggle involving
tens of thousands of Black workers is looming.

The transportation industries are gaining increasing numbers of Black
workers, since this is another area that hires many unskilled workers. In
many metropolitan mass transit systems, Black workers form a majority. This
is also true in other "vital city services" such as sanitation where Black
workers compose from 30 to 70 percent of the work force.

Thus, though Black workers compose only 10-15 percent of the population,
their presence--and militancy--in such vital areas of the economy as basic
industry, the key unionized sectors, and key industries in big cities, gives
them a far greater importance than their numbers suggest; in fact, a decisive
importance.

Consider New York City, for instance: Black and Latin workers make up
25 percent of the population but are a majority, or near it, in mass transit,
sanitation, garment, post office, welfare department, and are sizable
minorities in teamsters, railroad, longshore, distribution and city government.
Though New York's white workers form majorities in some of these industries,
most of them are in the skilled crafts and in the white-collar sales areas.
Black workers, therefore, being either a majority or sizable militant minority,
can bring the city's politicians and their bosses to their knees.

The above example can be repeated in other large cities where Black
workers make up an even larger percentage of the population--up to 40 and even
50 percent in places like Chicago, New Orleans, Newark, and Detroit.

Since capitalism as a system creates racism, there is more to the problem
than just the effects within the working class at the point of production.
The ruling class-created ghetto so permeates every area of life that white
workers--and the middle class--can no longer escape its growing effects.
During the New York school shutdown, a racist fight affected every neighborhood
in the city as Black parents demanded better education for their children.

But the effects of the ghetto spread far beyond education: super profits
to banks grow from mortgages on ghetto housing; rebellions begin to shape the
uses of the army and national guard as well as local police forces; the flight
of whites to surrounding areas makes Black people a greater force within the
cities and creates sharper contradictions about "who pays" for the running of
the city, since the remaining Black workers are the lowest paid; the

hopelessness of ghetto life leads Black youth to enlist in the armed forces or
await the draft, making for a less stable military to depend on in foreign
imperialist wars and in domestic rebellions. The increasing revolts among
Black servicemen in Vietnam and here at home attest to this instability. The
special oppression also leads to a greater resistance to being drafted by many
Black youth. Both types of opposition to the military creates a greater need
for the ruling class to figure out ways to put more pressure on white youth
to "serve their time," resulting in all kinds of new gimmicks to maintain a
standing army. Again the special oppression of Black people sharpens the contradictions for the whole population.

Of course, the ruling class has many "answers" for these problems:
"community control"; breaking up present slums with middle-class housing and
relocating Black people in new slums; making welfare clients into case-aides
and eliminating caseworkers, who cost more money; hiring more Black cops and
national guardsmen, as well as turning militant Black youths in the ghetto into
local police forces over Black workers ("community control of the police").

Though it's been said that fascism will come to the U.S. in the guise of
democracy, it is more important to say that racism will be the main tool the
ruling class uses to turn white workers and the white middle class to fascism.
The bosses will try to present the Black workers as the main enemy in every one
of the situations already cited, thereby preventing the specially oppressed
Black workers from leading the whole working class in revolution against the
bosses.

Recent Experiences in Labor Movement

The central importance of the fight against racism--and the potential for
working-class victory if the fight is successful--is reflected in the fact that
it is fast becoming the burning question in just about every major trade union
and community struggle now taking place.

In the New York City school shut-down, the Shanker leadership of the
United Federation of Teachers has done the bidding of the bosses by calling a
racist walkout directed essentially against the Black and Latin working-class
parents of the city. The split between white and Black workers in New York has
not only hurt any common class struggle against these bosses, but has set
rank-and-file white teachers fighting ghetto parents, and generally taken the
heat off the main enemy--the ruling class's Board of Education. (For a full
analysis of this struggle see *Challenge,* October 1968 and the section of the
Black Liberation Program on community control, in this issue).

In a recent major rank-and-file-led strike in New York's largest industry,
garment (see PL, October 1968), racism was the tactic the bosses tried to use
to split the Black and Latin workers. This was a particularly important
gambit for the garment bosses because these workers were setting an outstanding
example to the 250,000 workers in the garment center and could become of
decisive importance in breaking the boss-banker-ILGWU-Mafia-police hold on
those workers. Nor did the ruling class lose sight of the fact that half of
these quarter-million workers live in the ghetto and could bring in special
organized leadership because of the experience gained in their struggles
against the bosses at the point of production.

In recent auto wildcats, the issue of racism assumed an increasing
importance. First there were the King assassination walkouts, led by Black
workers, which shut down the plants; in some cases the companies tried to
forestall the movement by voluntarily closing down "in memoriam" before the
Black workers walked. Then there were disorganized attempts by white workers
to walk after Kennedy was killed, but these were racist reactions. (If "they"
could shut it down for one of "their own" why can't we do the same for one of
"ours"). For the most part these failed to shut the plants.

In two wildcat strikes in Chicago--Railway Express and bus drivers--again
it was Black workers in the lead, with the bus strike contributing to the
disruption at the Democratic convention.

And there have also been welfare client demonstrations. Since these were
generally led by government anti-poverty forces, the caseworkers were on the
spot. They had to find a course of action that would neither be directed
against the clients nor seek out the cops as allies but would, at the same
time, help build the union against the city, not against the clients and also

defeat the racism existing among both white and Black caseworkers.
These struggles--involving either the leadership of Black workers, the
fight against racism by Black and white workers or the use of racism by the
ruling class to divide and weaken the working class--follow many battles of
a similar nature in the past year: a wildcat at Ford's Mahwah (N.J.) assembly
plant when Black workers walked out with the support of white workers after a
white foreman called one Black worker a "Black bastard" (see *Challenge,* May
1968); the historic Memphis sanitationmen's strike, which fought the whole
ruling class structure of that deep Southern city for union recognition and
decent pay and conditions, setting a fighting example for unorganized workers
all over the South (see *PL,* June 1968); the wildcat strike and two-day rebellion of 15,000 Black and white workers at Newport News (Va.) Shipbuilding and
Dry Dock Co., initiated by 200 Black workers over oppressive working conditions and discrimination, and joined by the rest of the workers, a majority of
whom are white (see *PL,* Oct.-Nov. 1967). No doubt still more examples both
inside and outside the trade union movement could be cited to prove the point
that racism and the fight against it, especially when led by Black workers
over class issues, has become the all-pervading issue in the country.

Ruling Class Reactions

That the ruling class recognizes the importance of maintaining racism is
evident from its latest actions. A two-pronged drive has unfolded raising
racism among white workers to new heights and also pushing anti-working class
Black nationalism to an unprecedented degree.
The ruling class made "law and order" (meaning shoot Black people) the
main issue in the recent elections; it gave Wallace tremendous publicity to
bring out the worst racism among white workers; under the guise of "community
control" it provoked a school shut-down in New York City designed to weaken
and destroy the teachers' union as well as whip up racism among white people;
it is attempting to use professional workers such as teachers and welfare
workers--people with middle-class backgrounds, aspirations and ideology--as a
base from which to launch strong attacks on Black and Latin workers and the
class consciousness of workers generally; and it is using every anti-working
class Black nationalist it can create or buy as a target for white people to
vent their racism on.
And that is the other side of the ideological coin: the capturing of the
Black movement by anti-working class nationalism, using the very increase in
Black consciousness itself as a weapon against both Black and white workers.
The ruling class is afraid of the class leadership Black workers in Black
caucuses can give to white workers, setting them in motion against their
sellout leaders. Thus, the big pitch for "Black capitalism" (a major plank of
Nixon's campaign), or "sitting down with the Black Panthers," or "making
contact" to keep things cool--meaning buying off any Black militants, an
approach increasingly used by mayors such as Alioto of San Francisco and
Lindsay and his "urban task force" in New York, and "community control"; in
other words, anything to prevent Black workers from developing a revolutionary,
Marxist-Leninist outlook.
The ruling class "lieutenants" in the labor movement are busy, too. It
is no accident that Reuther is forming a second labor federation at this time.
In addition to the unions considering joining (UAW, teamsters, chemical
workers, rubber workers--all with large numbers of Black workers), it will
probably include unions such as District 65, the drug and hospital workers'
Local 1199 and the UFT in New York, as well as many ex-left-led unions that
are having plenty of trouble keeping their increasing Black memberships in
line. Reuther, himself, sees the handwriting on the wall in the UAW, with
Black workers increasing in membership and in leadership of rank-and-file
actions.
Therefore, what better way to create the illusion of action than to set
up a safety valve for more militant workers to "fight the Meany old guard,"
which, of course, includes the "fight for civil rights." As things stand now,
the Alliance for Labor Action may have four million members. It will be
looking for--and feeding--Black nationalists and sellouts to join the payroll
and become the leaders of the militant Black workers. In other words, the
main feature of this new federation will be to contain the rising rank-and-file

militancy in the labor movement, of which the Black workers form a crucial part. The organizers are even "sponsoring" (unofficially, of course) Black caucuses in their own unions (Reuther in the UAW, Shanker in the UFT) to steer the workers down the wrong road.

Fighting Racism: Principled Struggle

In PLP's Black Liberation Program we stressed the necessity of organizing Black workers in the shops and at the "point of production." Here, we have emphasized the role of Black workers in certain key industries and the all-pervading influence of racism and the fight against it in every important people's struggle now occurring. From this it must be concluded that unless an all-out fight is made against racism within the working class (which, of course, includes our own members), a Marxist-Leninist party cannot grow or succeed in the United States. Furthermore, the ability to defeat a ruling-class move to fascism will be seriously weakened. We will not even be able to construct a Left within the trade union movement, let alone a real Left-Center coalition.

It is not only crass racism to conceive of building this Left and this coalition without major emphasis on the role of Black workers in leadership of of—it is also impossible. In the past, many of us have coupled the correct idea of the Black Liberation Movement being the "vanguard of the revolutionary process" in the U.S. with the false notion that this meant the Black people as a whole were in advance of the white workers, especially in basic industries. And, further, that while the Black people could not wait for the white workers, at some time the white workers would catch up and assume their rightful place (being the majority, after all) in the leadership of the working-class movement. It is time to bury this theory, for it is now clear that the trade union movement—and any budding Left-Center coalition within it—will be smashed unless it decisively includes Black workers in its leadership as well as, of course, in its rank and file. Therefore, the Black workers (not the "all-class" Black population) are an essential part of the revolutionary potential of the U.S. working class and in a quality and quantity far exceeding their percentage in the population. Without the Black workers, no rank-and-file movement of workers in any key area of the trade union movement can succeed for long, if at all.

The fight against racism is inseparable from the fight of rank-and-file led unions, from working class solidarity. We can thus define the New York school shutdown as a racist action, not a strike in the class interests of workers. And we can oppose "solidarity" in the abstract by asking "solidarity with whom and for what?" In New York it was solidarity with the teachers' bosses, and administrators and principals, to say nothing of the cops necessary to "protect" teachers' "job security" in the schools. That's about the last place to look for job protection—to the police whose job is to break the class actions of workers.

Contradictions such as these are going to increase. We must prepare to analyze every action led predominantly by white workers from a class viewpoint that considers racism an anti-working class factor. We must carefully determine if the action is building solidarity against the ruling class or for racism.

From all this we must conclude that the question of fighting racism is a principled question, a question of strategy, not tactics. Building a base for revolutionary ideology and for a Marxist-Leninist party, rather than a base "for the union" or a personal base for ourselves, can only succeed if the fight against racism is made a central task of the Marxist-Leninist party.

This problem is most clearly revealed among teachers in New York because the class struggle is a lot hotter, at the moment, on the school issue than it is in many other trade union situations. But when the battle heats up in other industries and areas of working-class struggle, we will be faced with the same ruling-class drive to raise racism to a fever pitch. We could then easily give in to it (since to fight it "isolates me") the way some teachers did.

Such behavior stemmed from the confused idea that the struggle was for solidarity in a trade union class struggle, rather than a racist action; therefore, any opposition might lead to isolation from one's fellow teachers.

Yet, in nearly every instance where the class analysis of the action as racist
was put forward, some teachers--and parents--were won over to that understanding, and won over on a higher level than ever before. This is building a base
for a Marxist-Leninist party, for a revolutionary ideology. To "defend the
union" under any and all circumstances, without examining the class content of
that defense, is economism, not Marxism; and in this case was also racism.
Such a defense will have the opposite result: It will destroy the union as a
viable weapon of class struggle for rank-and-file teachers. In such a situation Black and white workers (in this case, Black parents and white teachers)
who see "going into school or staying out" as a purely tactical question are
thinking of racism itself as a tactical question. Here we see, in sharp
relief, the inseparability of class-conscious trade unionism and the fight
against racism, since in not fighting racism in a principled way the union, as
an organization that is supposed to fight in the class interests of its members,
is being destroyed.

We cannot adopt an approach that says: "Racism is a tough question; it
splits workers if you fight on it too soon. Therefore, fight on other not-so-
tough economic questions first." With racism staring us in the face now in
just about every situation we encounter, the "too soon" approach will tend to
make the fight against racism a tactical question. This would be a disaster
for a Marxist-Leninist party. We must make the fight against racism a cardinal
principle. Of course, this doesn't mean that the first time one meets a
particular racist white worker he should be fed the entire Marxist-Leninist
analysis in one swallow. But it does mean that the path of how to--and the
necessity to--fight racism every step of the way is laid in concrete discussions in our PLP clubs, in caucuses, and in all organs of people's struggle.

For our part, in PLP, we must re-emphasize the struggle to win over the
white workers, away from racism and to a class line. Not to do this would be
to all into the trap of: "All white workers are racist; therefore develop
relations with only Black workers." It is possible to make progress among most
white workers, as we have found from our own experience. Even more important,
we must develop the kind of mutual trust and confidence among workers that goes
into their understanding of us as communists. Such a relationship will go a
long way to helping us get listened to and break down racism among white
workers. The main concentration for white communists is still among white
workers.

Black Communism Reflect Anti-Racism

A real measure of whether we're fighting racism among the masses is whether
we're recruiting Black workers to a Marxist-Leninist party, which in turn is a
reflection of how well we're fighting racism among white workers. No Black
worker can be expected to join such a party unless it is actively fighting
racism among white workers who are racist. Thus, recruiting Black workers
becomes a key question and forces white communists to measure up to what
they're doing among white workers as well. For instance, are white workers
being recruited to a line that doesn't include fighting racism as a principled
question?

There are, of course, many special aspects to the fight against racism.
For example: People who come from middle class or student backgrounds acquire
a special brand of racism over and above the brand developed among white
workers, a certain class snobbishness that is directed against all workers but
that becomes a racist attitude when it involves Black workers.

Another problem concerns teachers. Teachers have a particular problem in
fighting racism because they are involved not only with their fellow workers
but also with the children and parents in the large cities where a high
proportion of the population is Black or Latin. Though an auto or garment
worker may not like his work, this doesn't necessarily reflect itself in racism
towards his fellow workers. But if a teacher doesn't like children, he will
inevitably adopt racist attitudes toward the ghetto children similar to the
racism of his fellow teachers. Teachers deal mostly with the children of the
working class and in a high percentage of cases with the children of the
specially oppressed Black and Latin workers. Under these circumstances, to
dislike children will inevitably result in anti-working class and racist
attitudes. If the cornerstone of any strong teachers' union is an alliance

with parents, and if these parents are part of specially oppressed groups--
victims of racism--certainly a dislike of children that becomes racism will
defeat the aim of any teacher attempting to fight in the class interests of
his fellow teachers or of the working class as a whole.

Racism is the main tool the ruling class has to divide the working class.
In every instance where its use has been successful, all workers have been
set back, no matter how much a privileged group of white workers think they've
gained, because the united struggle of workers as a class has been weakened.
And in all the instances cited in this article, where racism has been forced
to take a back seat, the class interests of all workers--Black and white--
moved forward.

To root this cancer out of our Party and the working class is a first
order of business. We must make a qualitatively renewed effort to study the
questions of racism and nationalism as they reveal themselves in our everyday
relations with white and Black workers. We must oppose racism whenever and
wherever it bursts forth, in the smallest incident as well as the biggest
strike or working-class struggle.

The fight against racism is a life and death matter in the United States.
To succeed means to bring the militant and revolutionary leadership of the
specially oppressed Black workers to the working class as a whole in the total
fight against the same exploiter--the bosses who own and run this country.
It means to build a base for socialism within the trade union movement, and a
Left-Center coalition that will toss out the present sellout misleadership
and work in the class interests of the rank and file. And it means that a
truly revolutionary Marxist-Leninist party will be built in the U.S., one
that will not in any way accommodate itself to the ideology of the class
enemy.

Therefore, for the working class to emancipate itself and all oppressed
people, for it to eventually seize state power as a class, with a Marxist-
Leninist party in its vanguard, the racism that splits the working class must
be buried.

Progressive Labor Party, *A Plan for Black Liberation* (New York, N.D. 1969?),
pp. 19-25.

19.   BLACK WORKERS MUST LEAD

The most important question facing the Black Liberation Movement is who--
what class--will give leadership to the movement. Everyone and all classes
cannot lead. There must be a focal point, a leadership, a guiding force, a
section of the people that must give leadership.

That focal point and leadership must be a CLASS since all societies are
class societies. This means that in all societies there are the people that
rule and the people who are being ruled. They are the different classes. In
the U.S. today the ones who rule are the boss class (called the bourgeoisie),
and they rule over the working class--the overwhelming majority of the people.

The working class and the bourgeoisie are constantly in a struggle. For
the moment the ruling class (the bourgeoisie) has the upper hand. As a
result we are forced to work for them for low wages, forced to live in slum
housing, forced into inferior schools, forced into the army, etc. If any
have the illusion that they are not FORCED into these conditions they should
consider how workers are treated by the cops, the national guards, the courts,

the jails and prisons, etc. This rule depends on FORCE and is properly called
the DICTATORSHIP OF THE BOURGEOISIE.
    The dictators--the "ruling class" or bourgeoisie--is the group of bankers,
bosses and landlords who own the large industrial plants, factories and farms,
and buildings. They actually determine who will be president, governor, mayor,
police chief, judge, etc. This class of rich people that run this country are
the exact opposite of us and are our enemy and as long as they run the country
we will never be free!
    The working class ("proletariat") are the people who must sell their
labor-power in order to live. They own no means of production.
    AMONG THE BLACK PEOPLE there are similar divisions into classes. But the
Black bourgeoisie exists more as a state of mind, as something they would like.
Most of these people are cheap imitators of the white bourgeoisie, the "Ebony
magazine type Negroes"--with or without "naturals."
    Thus, what is called the "Black bourgeoisie" is in reality a member of the
lower middle-class that WANTS to be in the ruling class and share the gravy of
exploiting the working class. Many of these people work for a living (sell
their labor power) just like any member of the working class. The major
difference is that their *loyalty* is to the ruling class and not to the working
class.
    These social climbers will use any method to achieve their ends. They may
yell to the skies "Black power!" "Black capitalism," "We have to do our own
thing," "Buy Black," "Support your own" (meaning themselves) and on and on.
The key question is whether their program and action is for the liberation of
the Black working masses--not just themselves and their few class brothers.
We must ask who are they trying to organize and for what? And when we examine
these questions we find that their class position is clear.
    They talk and act in a manner that says clearly, "We are the educated
class and we know what's good for the movement." They talk down to the Black
workers, and, in fact, hold the Black working people in contempt! If they ever
speak to the Black workers it is for the purpose of getting them to support
some project whose main benefit will be just for themselves or their class.
NATURALS AND DASHIKIS CANNOT HIDE THEIR BASIC PETTY-BOURGEOIS CLASS POSITION!

                              Sitting on the Fence

    Most of these would-be members of the "Black bourgeoisie" have been
college trained. What effect does this have on them? Let's examine.
    The ruling class has selected a handful of Blacks to send to college to
be trained to carry out the policies that the ruling class has made. These
students have been educated in middle-class values and, yes, trained to be
white middle-class in Black skins! It is quite similar to the imperialist
countries training local civil servants, teachers, police, etc. to carry out
its policies in the colonial countries.
    WITH THE TREMENDOUS UPSURGE of the Black rebellions and the increasing
fighting spirit among large sections of the Black workers, these middle-class
trained Blacks are caught in the middle. Many do not know which way to turn.
Should they line up on the side of the Black workers or on the side of the
"Black bourgeoisie" and the ruling class?
    Many of them, at this point, have decided to try to straddle the fence.
They don't want to give up anything and at the same time they want to be
identified with "the movement." At no point do they change their "in" way of
life, their aspirations or their relationship to the Black workers.
    Sometimes they may change their outward appearances, but this is because
they have no strength unless they get some support from the working class--
which is 90% of the Black people. So they become the loudest talkers about
"Black capitalism" and "Black culture," etc. They claim this is "speaking
to the needs of the Black people." THE NEEDS OF THE BLACK PEOPLE ARE
HOUSING, SCHOOLS, DECENT EDUCATION, JOBS, AN END TO POLICE BRUTALITY, END
IMPERIALIST WARS. THE NEED IS TO END EXPLOITATION OF MAN BY MAN--TO DESTROY
CAPITALISM--TO ACHIEVE SOCIALISM: IN OTHER WORDS--TO MAKE REVOLUTION! THIS
WORKING CLASS RULE IS THE OPPOSITE OF WHAT WE HAVE NOW AND IS CALLED THE
DICTATORSHIP OF THE PROLETARIAT!
    When leaders speak about and organize around these issues then they will
be "speaking to the needs of the Black people!" But what most have been

attempting to do is to *hide* their class position and their bourgeois world outlook in a lot of talk about Black this or Black that--to hide the fact that the things THEY want would be a sellout of the struggles of the vast majority of the Black people--the Black workers!

Who Must Lead?

For many years the Black Liberation Movement has been led by the so-called "Black bourgeoisie--in the name of preachers, students, nationalists, athletes, entertainers--in a word, by everyone EXCEPT the people whose interests all of this leading is SUPPOSED to be serving--the Black working people! Why do these mis-leaders get the spotlight? The reason is that when a true Black workers' organization emerges the ruling class does everything in its power to smash it. But the RULERS will HELP the NON-working class leaders to flourish, by giving them money, giving them publicity, etc.

A clear example is the Black rebellions. The young workers and the unemployed have been doing the fighting and organizing the resistance to oppression, but it is the would-be Black bourgeoisie "spokesmen" that appear afterwards and get handouts. The ruling class helps them "feather their own nest" because this is the cheapest way to make sure that 90% of the Black people--the working class--the fighters--get nothing!

The so-called "Black bourgeoisie" cannot lead the Black Liberation Movement at this level of the movement's development! When our movement was at a lower level of development some of the "Black bourgeoisie" did help by stirring things up. But now that the movement is very much alive the need is for much clearer leadership and they mess us up. Now it is up to the working class to seize the leadership. Leaders not in the working class will change with the wind and can be counted on to put their personal interests above that of the mass of the Black people--the workers.

YES, THE CLASS THAT MUST LEAD is the Black working class! This is the class that daily suffers at the hands of the bosses and the slumlords. This is the class that daily fights, in a thousand and one ways, to protect its class interests against the bosses. This is the class that controls production (the factories, the transportation system, the shops, the mine pits, etc.). They are the ones that can organize to hurt imperialism where it will hurt most --at the source of profit.

The Black workers have the organizing skills that they learn in the shops and in the unions; and it is in their most direct interest to overthrow U.S. imperialism because as long as imperialism exists they will never be free. U.S. imperialism CANNOT BUY OFF the entire working class (this would mean the end of their profits); whereas it is not difficult to buy off a handful of the so-called "Black bourgeoisie."

The Black working people are stable and the chance of them wavering or straddling a fence very small. What fence is there to straddle? What is there to waver about? They have been born into the working class, have become workers and the odds are that they will always remain workers. This should be a source of pride because no economy or system can exist without the working class. The ruling class, through its propaganda machinery, always try to downgrade the people who use their hands to earn a living. They glorify the white collar workers and try to say that only the "misfits," "those who can't make it," etc. wind up as workers with their hands. This is a lie and part of their attempt to keep our working men and women in slavery!

IT IS THESE WORKERS THAT ARE the most militant and that strike fear in the hearts of the ruling class. It is the working class, and the working class only that can properly lead the Black Liberation Movement. They have accumulated years of experience and have developed hatred for the ruling class and the bosses.

Students and the more advanced sections of the small bourgeoisie can join this leadership by serving the people--by putting their talents into the service of the working-class revolution.

Black Workers Organize!

The Black workers must kick out the fakers and pimps and bloodsuckers! Their leadership has meant sellouts and compromise. It has meant leaders

accepting deals when the ruling class comes in with a higher bid. It has meant
lining up with the ruling class--the enemy of the Black workers!
    BLACK WORKERS, ORGANIZE the workers in your shops and plants against the
corrupt union leadership and against the bosses, around your class demands!
Where there is no union organize one that will represent the interests of the
workers in the shop.
    Organize in your communities against the slumlords, against police
brutality, for a decent education for our children, against the dope traffic--
organize to protect and save our communities against "Black removal."
    Organize to kick out the fakers who call themselves "leaders" but feather
their own nests.
    BLACK WORKING MEN AND WOMEN: ORGANIZE, ORGANIZE, ORGANIZE! You must take
your rightful place at the head of the Black Liberation Movement!
    Without your leadership there will be no freedom or liberation for the
Afro-American people!

Progressive Labor Party, *A Plan for Black Liberation* (New York, N.D. 1969?),
pp. 54-56.

MORE BLACK LABOR RADICALISM

20. RACISM AND THE WORKERS' MOVEMENT

Philadelphia Workers' Organizing Committee

How the Few Rule the Many

    Working people make up the vast majority of the population in this country.
We, through our labor, create the wealth of this nation. Yet it is a small
handful who exercise control over how that wealth is used and distributed.
This handful, who own the mines, mills, and factories, possess vast wealth and
power while those of us who created that wealth make just enough to scrape by
and have little say in the important decisions that shape our everyday lives.
We are the victims of inflation, layoffs and lousy, often dangerous working
conditions. We endure a government that overtaxes and underserves us. We are
sent off to fight wars to protect the investments of big business. We get
empty gas tanks while the oil companies quadruple their profits. All these
problems and many more that go together to make up our day to day life stem
from the basic fact that this society is set up to serve the few at the expense
of the many. It is based on the exploitation of the majority, the working
people, for the enrichment of a small minority, the owners of the big corpora-
tions--the monopoly capitalists.
    The monopolists, through their control of the educational system and the
mass media, attempt to make this state of affairs seem like the natural order
of things. By a trick of language they turn the profit system, which in
reality is based on the exploitation of labor, into the "free enterprise"
system and seek to convince us it works for our benefit. They reduce wars,
unemployment, inflation and crime to just so many "kinks" to be ironed out.
Or even worse, they try to tell us that we, ourselves, are the creators of
these problems. This barrage of ideas, which we get in school and now get
daily from the newspapers and television, is one important way in which this
minority of exploiters seek to maintain their rule over the majority of
exploited.
    The employer class, realizing themselves to be in a small minority, do
everything they can to keep us in the dark about the real roots of our
problems. But in spite of these efforts working people know they're getting

the short end and have no choice but to fight back to protect their basic
interests.

Knowing this the monopolists long ago realized that their best line of
defense of their profits and privileges was to keep the working class divided
against itself. If the struggles of various workers can be isolated from
each other or better yet pitted against each other then the power of the
working class, its power in numbers and in its position at the heart of
production, can be neutralized. Whenever there has been this kind of unity
in the history of our country the working people have made tremendous strides
forward and the employers have had to beat a retreat. The Nineteen Thirties
is a good example. The workers, through a militant unity, built the CIO
unions, won unemployment compensation, social security, and many other concessions from the reluctant, but frightened monopolies and their agents in
Washington. Thus it has always been almost an article of faith with the
employers that they must prevent the creation of such unity and do everything
in their power to break it once it does develop.

The single most important weapon in the arsenal of the bosses for
dividing the workers is white racism. The employers discriminate against the
Black workers (and Puerto Rican, Chicano, Asian and American Indian workers
as well) and reap greater profits as a result of this discrimination. But
more importantly they seek to instill fear, prejudice and hostility in the
white workers toward their black counterparts. They seek to turn the white
workers against the black struggle for equality. They count on the resentment
this breeds among the black workers to lead to their blaming the white workers
for their situation. The biggest reward they hope to reap from the sowing of
racist ideas is the divisions this will create among the workers' ranks.
Without black-white unity the black workers will be unable to mount an effective
challenge to discrimination. Without black-white unity all the workers will be
unable to wage a successful fight for their interests. To the extent racial
conflict can be created among the workers, class conflict, this is conflict
with the employers, is averted. . . .

Racism Provides Superprofits

Within the U.S. this intensification of oppression of peoples abroad was
paralleled by the stepped up oppression of the Afro-American people. Just as
the cheap labor of the peoples of Latin America and Asia brought the monopolies
super profits, so the labor of Black workers here in the U.S. was employed
for the same end. The drying up of large scale European immigration underlined
the need for new sources of cheap labor. The expanded production brought about
by the First World War accelerated the demand for black labor. Thus from the
early years of the twentieth century down to our own time, the U.S. has
witnessed a great internal migration -- the movement of Black people from the
agricultural Southlands to the industrial cities of the North, Mid-West and
Far West. This movement of Blacks from a farming people to an urban wage
earning people was accompanied by continuation of racism. The inequalities
of the plantation were transferred to the Northern ghettoes and factories.
The features of this inequality must now be examined.

Racism: The Great Wedge

Workers Pitted Against Each Other

Great as these benefits of racism to the capitalist are, the single greatest service it renders him is its power to divide the mass of white workers from the black workers and mislead them into the employer's camp. The white worker, as we have seen, is not profiting from racism. On the contrary, he too is threatened very directly by its effects. The white worker's real interests lies in uniting with the black worker to put an end to the inequality between them . . . an inequality that enables the employer to oppress black labor, threaten the white worker, and pit the one against the other. But the white worker so often does not grasp this and instead views the black worker, rather than the employer, as the cause of his problems. This blindspot is the product of years of conditioning and of centuries of history. The idea of white supremacy has been cultivated in the white worker by a capitalist controlled culture, a culture that has developed to justify and smooth the way for the exploitation of labor and its division into two antagonistic racial camps.

To the extent the white worker leans toward racial conflict with the black workers as opposed to class struggle against the employers, he benefits not himself, but his boss. A good general example of this is the situation in the South where racism has served to lead many white workers into defending Jim Crow discrimination and to oppose the black struggle for equality. The result--disunity between black and white--has enormously aided the efforts of Big Business and their flunkey politicians to maintain the South as a capitalist paradise and a worker's nightmare. No unions, low wages and the worst social services in the nation -- these are some of the fruits of racism for the white as well as the black workers. In that stronghold of white supremacy, Mississippi, the average hourly wage of production workers is $2.77/ hour, the lowest such average in the country. Compare this with Michigan, a state with a strong labor movement, where the average is $4.94/hour and the point is made even clearer. . . .

Black Workers and the Class Struggle

Rank and File Movement Grows

The importance of black-white unity is underlined when we look at the role black workers are playing in the trade unions and the struggles of working people generally.

In the unions in the last few years we have seen the development of a broad rank & file movement that takes a stand for a democratic, militant brand of unionism in opposition to the bureaucratic, sell out policies of the AFL-CIO leadership. Rank & file caucuses in auto, steel, transport and other basic industries have formed around the elementary need of workers for a union that genuinely represents them and fights for their interests. These caucuses have grown up in response to a union leadership that has collaborated with management to speed up production and improve "efficiency" at the expense of the workers . . . a union leadership that has by and large caved in before the joint demand of big business and government for wage controls in a period of escalating prices . . . a union leadership that has sat on its thumbs while our jobs are exported to unorganized low wage areas and a union leadership that has failed to challenge and even cooperated in the employer's practice of racial and sexual discrimination. These misleaders have been able to carry out their disastrous policies in large part because they seek by fair means or foul to keep the rank & file out of the arena of decision making. Thus the caucuses have called for a return to rank & file worker's basic interests.

Another side to the upsurge of rank & file activity is the development of new unions like the Hospital Workers and Farm workers unions and new organizing drives by old unions like the Amalgamated Clothing Workers which are bringing thousands of previously unorganized workers into the ranks of organized labor and setting an example for the rest of the unions through their militant struggle.

Role of Black Workers

At the heart of this rank & file upsurge stands the black worker. In basic industry much of the leadership and initiative for the rank & file movement has come from the black workers. This leadership has taken many forms-- black caucuses, revolutionary black workers' organizations, and multi-racial rank & file groupings. While the black workers have naturally and quite correctly made the demand for equality and an end to racism a central concern of this movement, they have also been in the forefront in waging a fight for better wages and working conditions, union democracy and the full range of worker's concerns. The situation in the United Steel Workers is a good example. USW president I. W. Abel and the bureaucracy he represents have a long history of collaboration with management in maintaining racial discrimination in the plants, consigning Black workers to the dirtiest, most dangerous and lowest-paying jobs. At the same time the USW is one of the most top down, undemocratic of unions. Recently Abel has taken his collaboration with the employers another step by going along with company inspired productivity schemes and by signing away the right to strike in the interests of profits and labor peace for the steel monopolies. A massive rank & file movement has developed in steel in response to these sell out policies and it has been the Black workers who have been most militant in fighting not only the racist discrimination policies, but the productivity plan and the no-strike pact as well.

Black workers have also been a key force in pushing the unions to take a broader view of their tasks--to see themselves not as narrow pressure groups, but as the fighting arm of the whole working class, battling on the political as well as the economic front. This phenomena too has taken many forms. Black longshoremen in the East, West and Gulf coast ports have taken direct action against the pro-business, racist foreign policy of the U.S. government by refusing to unload goods from the white supremacist states of South Africa and Rhodesia. Predominantly Black unions like the Hospital Workers actively mobilized their memberships in mass demonstrations against U.S. aggression in Southeast Asia.

In taking these actions Black workers demonstrated an understanding of the common interests of workers throughout the world as well as grasping the cost to U.S. workers of the government's militaristic and aggressive policies. Solidarity with the struggles of other workers here in the U.S. is another side of the same spirit as when West coast Black longshoremen recently refused to load scab produce in support of the striking farmworkers. Black led rank & file struggle has also been characterized by an understanding of the need to link struggles of workers on the shop floor with struggles in the community. In Detroit, for example, the League of Revolutionary Black Workers, a group based in the auto plants, joined forces with working people in the community in the fight for better education, health care, law enforcement and other concerns. This in turn made it possible to mobilize community support for struggles in the plant.

Why Black Militancy?

The militancy of the Black worker certainly has much to do with the nature of the conditions he or she faces. Since Black workers generally have the most oppressive jobs they have been hit the hardest by the speed up drive and the general attack on working conditions that the bosses have launched. Lower wages and the greater likelihood of a layoff slip, harassment by racist foremen, barriers to upgrading and a hundred other factors combine to make up the extra burden of oppression the Black worker carries. But oppression doesn't automatically translate into resistance. The Black worker, concentrated in areas of heavy industry where labor is highly social and cooperative, learns the capacity for collective action from the job itself. Also the Black

worker has been moved and educated by the growing intensity of the Black
Freedom struggle over the last two decades. The Civil Rights Movement, the
urban rebellions, and the various struggles of Black students, welfare recipients, tenants, and prisoners have all contributed to the political consciousness of the Black worker. These struggles generated a spirit of resistance in
all Black people. For the Black worker this spirit has increasingly taken the
shape of an across the board struggle against the forms of class exploitation.
As has already been made clear the demand for equality and an end to racism is
itself a demand that serves the whole working class, white and black. But
what is also important is that the Black workers have been in the front lines
of almost every struggle to better the way of life of all workers.

Labor and Black Liberation

    The Labor Movement in its effort to protect the living standards of
workers and push forward toward a decent society for working people needs
allies. It needs staunch friends outside the trade unions. Black people
generally, that is Black people outside the labor movement in civil rights
organizations, welfare rights groups, Black political organizations and community groups have been the most consistent ally of the trade unions and have in
fact often been far ahead of the AFL-CIO in fighting for the interests of the
working class. This has taken many concrete forms--the fight for a minimum
wage and a guaranteed annual income, for more jobs through expanding socially
useful production of housing, schools, hospitals and the like, for improved
social services, consumer protection and many other reforms all of which
serve the needs of working people. Black organizations were far in advance of
the AFL-CIO in opposing the Vietnam War and spiraling military spending. The
Black Liberation Movement has, besides being a struggle for full equality, been
a movement that necessarily embraces the full range of concerns of the working
people, a reflection of the fact that the overwhelming majority of Blacks are
workers (94%) with interests that unite them with the whole working class.
    Thus in two fundamental respects the Black people's interests and struggle
coincide with the interests of the working class. First the struggle for
equality is a struggle that serves all workers in that it aims at eliminating
a powerful weapon of the exploiters--a means for greater economic exploitation
and a wedge for dividing the workers against each other. Secondly, this
struggle, given the class character of the Black people, not only concerns
itself with ending discrimination, but demands across the board improvements
in many other areas that concern working people as well.
    All this throws into sharp relief the importance of Black-white unity.
It makes clear why the bosses value their old friend Jim Crow above all others.
Racism does not simply divide Black from white--it divides the white workers
from the workers who have generally been the most militant and most conscious
of the whole class's interests, that is the Black workers. And it divides the
workers movement from its most important ally, the broader Black movement that
consists of Black people outside the work places as well as the Black workers
and trade unionists.

The Road to Victory Over Racism--Class Unity and Class Struggle

Unity

    Given that racism is very profitable to the bosses, both economically and
politically, it should be clear that they will not give up their practice of
racial oppression easily. Black people have waged a stubborn and heroic
struggle against their oppression from the time the first slave ship docked in
the New World to the present. In our time we have witnessed this struggle at
a high point of intensity. Through mass organization and action Black people
have succeeded in eliminating the most blatant legal forms of Jim Crow. They
have scored some gains in the areas of employment, housing and education. In
the course of waging these struggles Black people have come to a greater
understanding of their history and culture and attained a new degree of
national pride and self-respect, qualities that the racist rulers have always
sought to deny them. But still after almost two decades of intense struggle

the situation of the mass of Black people is not greatly altered. The brutal
every day realities of ghetto life remain intact and the overall pattern of
racial discrimination survives.
    The frustrations that this failure to uproot racism have created has led
some Black people down politically self-defeating paths. Religious cults,
separatist or Back-to-Africa movements, and isolated terrorist groups are some
of the forms that have flourished in the wake of these frustrations. The
basic reason for the failure to lick racism is again the successful splitting
tactics of the employers who have been able to largely isolate the Black movement for equality and pit a substantial section of white labor against it.
The plain fact of the matter is that it takes Black-white unity, the unity of
the working class, to really beat racism back. Only a united, fighting working
class has the numbers and social power, a power inherent in the worker's role
as the producer of all social wealth, to force the struggle against racism
beyond its present stalemate.

Class Struggle

    The road to defeating racism is the broad highway to class struggle. This
means the demand for an end to racism has to be taken up as part of the overall
demands of the whole working class. It has to be put forward as a demand that
is vital to the interests of all the workers. To successfully defeat racism
means relying on the working class as the main force. And this means projecting
the struggle against racism from a working class viewpoint.
    The struggles of the Black workers demonstrate an advanced grasp of this
viewpoint. In spite of the indifference and hostility of many white workers,
the Black workers' movement has generally placed the demand for an end to
discrimination in the context of a broad program that speaks to the interests
of the mass of workers and has promoted Black-white unity. This understanding
grows out of the actual experience of the Black worker on the job. It is
obvious to most Black workers, at least in plants that are multi-racial, that
the support of the white workers cannot be mobilized on the basis of abstract
moral appeals against racism or still less by calling them "hunkies" or
"devils." They can only be won through demonstrating that racism hurts all
workers. They can only be drawn into struggle on the basis of a clear program
that puts forward demands that speak to the grievances of the mass of workers.
These are the lessons that the actual struggle of Black workers against racism
and exploitation teach. And these lessons are of vital importance for the
larger Black Liberation Movement.

Workers Must Lead Black Movement

    The Black People's Movement is not of one mind on how Black people are to
achieve freedom in America. These differences grow out of the reality that
Black people, like white people, are in different social classes. While the
vast majority of Black people are part of the working class, there is also a
small but influential Black middle class. This middle class, composed mainly
of small businessmen and professionals, is the social base for the ideas of
separatism and so-called Black capitalism. This class tends to think of
expanded business opportunities for themselves as the road forward for Black
people. Separatist thinking is strong among this group because it seeks to
develop and control a Black market in opposition to White owned business.
Among the professions separatist thinking takes the form of promoting various
poverty programs or "community control" projects that will enhance the
opportunities and power of this strata.
    It is important to recognize that the Black middle class is victimized by
discrimination and racism. There can be no question that Black businessmen
and professions should have equal rights with their white counterparts. The
Black middle class is a legitimate part of the larger Black Liberation movement. But this class cannot be counted on to lead the Black movement. It
cannot provide leadership for the mass of working class Black people for the
basic reason that the working class viewpoint so necessary to the successful
development of the struggle is alien to this class of small capitalists and
independent professionals.
    Their whole program of expanding Black business is no solution to the

problems of Black workers. Black owned businesses are generally small retail
and service operations that employ a handful of workers and have little
economic importance. In an era of monopoly when it takes millions to start a
major enterprise, these small businessmen can never hope to become owners of
large scale industry. Even if they could this would leave the Black worker in
a position where he was now exploited by a Black capitalist instead of a white
one. The Black middle class cannot be counted on to consistently put forward
a program that genuinely serves the Black masses. Nor can the black middle
class be expected to champion the cause of Black-white class unity when it so
often perceives its interests in terms of narrow nationalism and separatism.

The Black middle class has provided much of the leadership of the Black
movement in the past. For this reason its influence and the strength of its
ideas are very great even among the masses of Black workers. But to move the
struggle against racism beyond its present stalemate it is the Black workers
who must take the leadership of the Black Liberation movement. This is essential to building the unity between Black and white workers, the whole working
class and the whole Black people. This does not mean that all Blacks from the
middle class must be thrust out of leadership and only workers can occupy these
positions. It means that the working class viewpoint must prevail over the
ideas of separatism, narrow nationalism and Black capitalism. It is for the
most part the Black workers who will carry forth this struggle for the working
class stand. For it is the Black workers who have the clearest, most direct
and most urgent stake in building a united working class movement against
racism and the whole system of capitalist exploitation.

Can the White Worker Be Won to the Struggle Against Racism?

But, of course, the main block to going forward in the fight against
racism is on the white and not the Black side of the fence. No matter how well
organized, no matter how well led, no matter how politically conscious the
Black Movement is, it can only go to a certain point without the full force of
the whole working class being brought solidly onto the side of Black Liberation.
The main problem and the primary task is to win the white workers to an understanding of the effects of racism on the workers' movement and to gain the
white worker's active participation in the struggle for full equality. It is
the special responsibility and obligation of the class conscious white workers
to see that this urgent task is carried out.

In many rank & file movements there is a tendency to want to play down
demands against racism on the grounds that "they divide people." What this
really means is that these demands will alienate sections of the white workers
and thus weaken the struggle. What it also means, by way of implication, is
that it is less important to alienate the Black workers by ignoring their
oppression. Many white workers who make this argument may be sincerely
interested in unity and unconscious of the racist bias it reflects. Some
Black workers will even subordinate their own special concerns in order to
make it easier to mobilize white workers because of the need for unity on what
are seen as common concerns. In both cases this argument is fatally wrong.
The source of disunity among the workers is not the struggle against racism
itself. The struggle only brings racism out into the open. There is no way
around it. The white workers must be won to this struggle. They must be
convinced that it is vital to their interests. And they can be! The view,
common to many Black workers as well as many progressive white workers, that
the mass of white workers cannot come to take up this struggle is a denial of
the possibility of class struggle--a denial that workers can understand their
own collective interests and act on this understanding. It is also a view
that is contradicted by both history and current events in the labor movement.

Historically racism has indeed been a powerful and destructive force
within the labor movement. But there are also numerous examples of Black-
white unity in opposition to racism. The Industrial Workers of the World
(IWW) was a militant revolutionary industrial union in the early years of this
century. The "Wobblies," as they were called, were unique among the trade
unions of the time in that they actively fought racism. In their organizing
drive among Black and white lumber workers in the South the IWW created
racially mixed locals, which were unheard of at the time and condemned by the
craft minded, racist American Federation of Labor (AFL). In spite of a

vicious propaganda campaign waged by the employers to split the white workers
away from the Blacks, the ranks remained united. The appeals to the white
workers to uphold "white supremacy" by refusing to strike with Black workers
fell upon deaf ears. Efforts to break strikes by getting other Blacks as well
as Mexican laborers to scab also failed. The southern timber workers were
finally crushed only through the organized violence of the state. The employers could not allow this example of fighting class unity to succeed because
it threatened the whole foundation of white supremacy on which the capitalist
house of cards rested.

During World War I revolutionary elements in the AFL succeeded in launching a successful organizing drive among the Chicago Packinghouse workers.
This campaign, which breached the employer's open shop dike in basic industry,
brought thousands of Black workers into the AFL. The Packing trusts sought to
wreck this campaign by splitting the workers racially. When the union sought
to hold a march and rally, the city government acting for the Packers, refused
to give the union a permit unless they would agree to separate Black and white
marchers and rallies. The union compromised by agreeing to separate marches
but holding a single rally. The white march went through the black community
where the Black people cheered the marchers. The white workers carried
placards making their opposition to the segregation of the marches clear. One
white worker carried a sign that read: "The bosses think that because we are
of different color and different nationalities we should fight each other.
We're going to fool them and fight for a common cause -- A Square Deal For All."
Later the bosses fomented a violent race riot. The police and National Guard
acted more to intimidate and brutalize the Black people than to restrain white
racist mobs which were encouraged in their pillage by the Packers. The union
played an important role in ending the riot and defending the Black community
from racist outrages. At one point the union struck the Packers to bring the
riot to an end.

In the late nineteen twenties the Trade Union Unity League, a Communist
led group of industrial unions, made the demand for Black equality a central
part of its program. The TUUL not only opposed racism on the job but agitated
for social equality for Black people in all aspects of American life. The
best known campaign in which the TUUL played an active role was the fight to
free the Scottsboro Boys, nine Black youths who had been framed on a rape
charge in Scottsboro, Alabama. The TUUL sought to educate the workers through
this campaign and succeeded in mobilizing white as well as Black workers to
oppose this legal lynching.

The unemployment struggles of the thirties are another important example
of Black-white unity. The Unemployed Councils, which led and organized the
struggle for jobs and relief, fought against discrimination in the administration of relief as well as in employment practices. The Councils also fought
evictions and in numerous instances mobilized white unemployed to join with
Blacks in opposing evictions of Black unemployed by ghetto slumlords. Black
workers made up approximately half the membership of the Councils and were
prominent in their leadership.

Nor is this kind of Black-white unity just ancient history. In the
fifties the American Federation of Teachers, responding to the civil rights
movement, expelled all its segregated locals in the South and supported
integration of schools in that area. In 1965 District 65 of the Retail,
Wholesale and Department Store Workers Union conducted a successful strike
involving over two thousand employees in New York's textile converting
industry for the specific purpose of opening up more jobs for Black and Puerto
Rican workers. At the last conference of the United Steel Workers, which
focused on upcoming contract demands, a substantial number of white workers
joined with the Black fellows in calling for the elimination of racist
practices in upgrading. In Fremont, California last year the Brotherhood
Caucus swept the elections and won control of a UAW local. The Brotherhood
Caucus, which successfully united Black, white and Chicano workers, included
in its program a demand for a discrimination committee for each shift with a
full time union representative and the power to redress grievances for
discrimination. Even in the deepest South there are examples. A long strike
against the Masonite Corporation in Laurel, Mississippi saw Ku Klux Klan
members join with Black workers in common struggle. In the course of the
strike the white workers dropped the Klan and spoke out against segregation
at the Masonite plant.

This is not to underestimate the depth of the problem. The dominant reality is that the mass of white workers, both historically and currently, have not taken up the struggle against racism. But what these examples illustrate (and countless others could be cited) is that the white workers *can* be won to this struggle. The ruling employer class has sought to create the impression that the white workers are implacably hostile to Black people. They have suppressed the true history of working peoples, including the instances of class unity, in order to further this impression. They have tried to place the responsibility for racism in the U.S. on the white workers and not on themselves. The famous Kerner Commission Report, issued after the series of rebellions that swept the Black communities in the late sixties, is a good example of this. The report fully acknowledges and documents the existence of white racism, but it places the responsibility for this situation on "White America" --in other words on the mass of white working people. The report implies that it is their racist attitudes that hold Black people down. This, of course, lets the big monopolies and the politicians who serve them neatly off the hook. The institutions of government and business only reflect the attitudes of the white majority according to the Kerner view. The practical implications of this analysis are to focus on "education" of the majority rather than change of the institutions.

The mass media constantly reinforces the ruling class's version of who creates and sustains racism. The "All in the Family" show is a good example. Archie Bunker is a stereotyped version of the white worker--an ignorant bigot. It is the Archie Bunkers, we are led to believe, who are the problem--their ignorance lies behind the racial oppression of Black people. There can be no denying that ignorance and bigotry exist among white working people (although Archie Bunker is by no means the "typical case" as the producers of this show suggest), but is this really the source of Black people's oppression? Why are there no T.V. shows about David Rockefeller, whose Chase Manhattan bank makes millions from investments in the Apartheid industries of South Africa? What about the owners of General Motors who daily crush the life out of Black workers on their sped up assembly lines? Where, indeed, are all the big employers who daily wring millions of extra dollars out of the toil of black labor? They are faceless and invisible. The owners of public communications like TV are in solidarity with owners everywhere. What corporation will sponsor a TV show that exposes the real enemy--the monopoly corporations themselves?

This brainwash that the problem of racism is the creation of the white masses as opposed to the white ruling class must be countered. It is similar to that which is employed to explain all other social problems. (Pollution is not caused by the profit hungry monopolies but by the people who litter our highways and drive pollution making cars--war is the product not of the drive for more markets by the big corporations but by the "aggressiveness" of the people, etc.). This lie can best be exposed by the active involvement of masses of white workers in the struggle against racism. History shows this can be done. The interests of all working people demand that it be done.

The Fight Against Racism in the Trade Unions

Unions: Strengths and Weaknesses

The trade unions are the largest and most powerful mass organizations of the working class. Over twenty million workers are organized into unions, including most of the workers in basic, heavy industry. The union's ability to make improvements in the wages and working conditions of its members is a matter of proven fact. The unionized worker makes an average of 2,000 dollars more a year than his unorganized counterpart. Pensions, health insurance and other fringe benefits are the ordinary fruits of trade unionism.

At the same time the trade unions as they exist today reveal serious weaknesses. They are dominated by a high paid, privileged bureaucracy that seeks to conciliate the employers at the expense of the rank & file. This leadership has traded away at the bargaining table many of the hard fought gains workers have won over the years--gains that include protection from speed up and the right to strike. Moreover this leadership has either gone along with or offered only token resistance to the various anti-labor policies of the Nixon administration. The unions have by and large failed to organize the unorganized and stem the flow of jobs to cheap labor, non union areas. Finally the unions have, again in general, failed to seriously challenge racial and sexual discrimination or even worse have practiced it directly themselves.

This is a sharp indictment of the present union leadership and the policies they represent. Unions do not have to be this way. And they can be changed. In spite of their bureaucratic character, unions are generally sufficiently democratic so that a strong and well organized rank & file movement can oust union misleaders and change union policy. The recent housecleaning in the United Mine Workers where the corrupt Boyle machine was sent packing by the rank & file is a good case in point. The new Miller leadership has taken important steps forward by restoring union democracy and adopting a more militant stance toward the coal operators.

Because of the immense real and potential power unions possess to wrest gains for the workers from the employers they are a central arena for any movement aimed at general improvements in the conditions of working people. For all rank & file workers the struggle to make the union a more democratic, fighting instrument is of vital importance. And for all workers the transformation of the unions from their present racist stagnation into genuinely anti-racist organizations is a must.

The racist practices of the trade unions grow out of the existence of a labor bureaucracy that is tied to the employer class in a number of ways. The bureaucracy receives large salaries and privileges that tend to separate them from the rank & file and tie their outlook to that of the employers. By and large they are saturated with a class collaborationist philosophy of trade unionism--the idea that conciliation of and cooperation with the employers is the best path for the labor movement. Since racism serves the interests of the employers, since it is vital to maintain the stability of their system of their high level profits, racism inevitably becomes part of the outlook of these agents of the employers within the ranks of the worker's movement. It is important to understand that the labor bureaucracy is racist not by way of misunderstanding their interests, but rather because their interests are so closely tied with those of the employers.

The Case of the ILGWU

The case of the International Ladies Garment Workers Union (ILGWU) is a good concrete illustration of the interrelationship between bureaucratic class collaborationism and racism. The ILGWU has a reputation as a progressive union (unlike the racist building trades unions which everyone knows are politically backward). This reputation is the product of its dim, distant past when it was truly a fighting union and of the clever public relations campaigns of its leadership. In terms of its actual trade union practice the ILGWU is rotten to the core.

The ILGWU consciously works to keep wages down and cool out worker militancy. For example in 1967 the union's politically powerful leadership opposed a minimum wage bill for the city of New York, where the garment industry is centered, and used its muscle to defeat the bill. Wages of the mass of garment workers have fallen sharply over the years relative to that of other workers and at least for some years they have even fallen absolutely. The development of this policy coincides with the period in which the garment industry in New York became predominantly Black and Puerto Rican in terms of the workforce. The Union argues that wages cannot be improved because this would cause employers to fold or move with the consequent loss of jobs. In other words the union has become a force for holding down wages for the benefit of the employers.

Scuttles Democracy and Promotes Racism

In order to succeed in carrying out such a blatantly class colloborationist policy the union necessarily cannot allow rank & file democracy for if it did the mass of workers would clearly reject such a program. Thus the ILGWU in its constitution bans any form of rank & file organization. There can be no caucuses except for a short period prior to national conventions.

Furthermore through an involved series of undemocratic eligibility requirements
the ILGWU restricts the right of the rank & file to run for and hold union
office. In 1967 only one-fifth of one percent of the ILGWU's 442,318 members
were eligible to run for the General Executive Board (GEB), the union's governing body, and only one twentieth of one percent were eligible to run for
President or Secretary-Treasurer. Out of the union's 145,000 Black and Puerto
Rican members only four or five of them were eligible to run for the GEB and
not a single Black was eligible to run for President. Furthermore under former
President David Dubinsky all union officers had to submit a signed but undated
letter of resignation to him as soon as they took office. Thus the ILGWU
leadership is grossly unrepresentative of the workers and is completely sub-
servient to the top. There is not a single Black on the GEB and virtually no
Blacks and Puerto Ricans in leadership positions at the local level.
     The garment manufacturers have sought to exploit the cheap labor market of
New York City which is predominantly Black and Puerto Rican. The ILGWU is their
accomplice in this undertaking. There are some well paying job classifications
in the industry but these are restricted to whites. The union has maintained
that upgrading Blacks and Puerto Ricans into better paying job classifications
is not its concern. Until very recently the ILGWU maintained segregated locals.
In short the policy of putting the employer's interests first has inevitably led
the ILGWU leadership to scuttle union democracy and defend and promote racism.
     In order for the rank & file movement to develop its full potential--for
it to become a force that really can transform the trade unions, these weaknesses
must be corrected. The struggle against racism must become a conscious thrust
of the *whole* movement, not simply the activity of Black caucuses. All rank &
file groups must take the involvement of Black and other minority workers in
leadership as well as in all other phases of activity an absolute priority.
Rhetoric about wanting to involve Black workers is not the road to achieving
this priority. Instead a program that raises the demand against discrimination
must be developed and implemented. This is the key to building Black-white
unity in the rank & file movement and transforming what are now predominantly
white groupings into genuinely multi-racial organizations.
     The exact content of an anti-racist program can't be spelled out in
advance. It depends on the concrete circumstances in each industry, shop and
union. What may make good sense in one situation may be disastrous in another.
But certain general concerns and demands are basic to virtually all job situations in at least some form. The following, then, outlines the general elements
of a rank & file trade union program to challenge racism on the job.
     The implications of this for the broader trade union movement are clear.
The case of the ILGWU, while somewhat extreme, describes a problem that is common to most unions in one form or another. The fight against racism must be
part and parcel of the fight to unseat the labor bureaucracy and defeat its
policy of class collaborationism.
     The rank & file movement as it presently exists within the trade unions
has included the fight against racism as one of its major thrusts. But the
movement is also very uneven in terms of this struggle. Black caucuses or
rank & file formations with strong black leadership have been the most consistent
fighters against discrimination. Here there has sometimes been a failure to
place the struggle against racism in the context of black-white unity and the
overall class struggle. The class interests of the white workers in defeating
racism have not always been understood. In general, though, the Black workers
have promoted a class struggle outlook in the fight against racism. In caucuses
where Black participation is weak, the fight against racism has been correspond-
ingly weak or even non-existent. This points to the failure of the bulk of
militant white workers to grasp the import of this struggle. The reason there
is little participation on the part of Black workers in these caucuses is precisely because of the failure of the white workers and caucus leadership to
develop an active program that speaks to the racial oppression of the Black
workers. This is one of the key areas of weakness in the rank & file movement.

     1) End Discrimination in Hiring. The forms of discrimination in
     hiring are many and varied, ranging from companies that simply do
     not hire blacks at all to firms that hire substantial numbers but
     only in the lower job categories. The union should expect that
     Blacks be represented in all job classifications proportionate to

their numbers in the labor market in the area. In other words
if Blacks make up 50% of the work force in the community then
the company's hiring policy should reflect this in that roughly
half the workers hired for all job categories should be Black.
The union should demand that discriminatory educational
requirements, unrelated to ability to do the job be eliminated.
When there are legitimate qualifications that Blacks, because
of discrimination in education, may be at a disadvantage in
meeting, the company should be responsible for providing training.
The union should create a watchdog committee to monitor company
hiring practices. Many companies constantly violate existing
civil rights laws in practicing discrimination. The union,
besides taking action on its own, could make sure these violations
are caught and get the Human Relations Commission or the appropriate
government body to act to correct these abuses.

2) *End Discrimination in Upgrading.* Black and minority workers (as
well as women) are kept in low paying, often dirty or dangerous job
classifications through discrimination in upgrading or promotion
policies. The forms of this discrimination also vary widely. In
some industries (Men's Clothing and Ladies Garments for example)
there is no established procedure for upgrading and the bosses
promote whomever they wish. In industries, like steel, the device
of the double seniority trial has been used. Seniority is the
basis for upgrading but only within a particular department--thus
minority workers can be restricted to certain departments, generally
the dirtiest, dangerous and lowest paying ones. Finally the device
of apprenticeship or training programs is used. These programs often
are discriminatory in the kind of qualifications they demand for
entrance. To correct these abuses the union must insist on the
principle of plant wide seniority as the basis for upgrading. All
job openings should be posted and all workers should be able to bid
with the job being awarded to the worker with the most time in.
In cases where special skills or training is demanded, entrance to
apprenticeship programs must not be discriminatory. Educational
qualifications, testing and other requirements must be evaluated
with this in mind. Unless the knowledge required is job related it
should be dropped from the requirements. (You don't need to understand European history to set dies or lay bricks). Here too the
union must oversee the whole upgrading program and make sure that
equal opportunity is really being offered. The only real test of
the program is that over a reasonable period of time the inequality
in the distribution of jobs disappears. As long as there are job
classifications that are disproportionately white the problem still
exists.

3) *Stop Racist Harassment.* Racist foremen or supervisory personnel
can and do harass Black and minority workers. Insulting racist
language, discriminatory job assignments and a racial double standard
in evaluating quality of work and job performance are common forms
of harassment. The demand of the Brotherhood Caucus of UAW local
No. 1364 in Fremont, California is a good example of the kind of
measure unions need to take to deal with this problem. Point nine
of their program calls for a Discrimination Committee for each
shift with power to deal with discrimination on the shop floor.
The UAW in many locals have Fair Employment Practices Committees.
At one time many of these committees really functioned to fight
racism but in recent years they have been eliminated in many locals
or have become nothing more than window dressing to hide the do
nothing policy of the UAW leadership. The Brotherhood caucus is
demanding a revival of this committee by making its chairman a
full time official.

4) *Equality in Union Leadership.* A union's leadership at all
levels should reflect the composition of the union's membership.
If it does not, something is obviously wrong. While in the last
few years substantial numbers of Black workers have been elected
to union office, the situation remains grossly unequal. Here too

the problem varies from union to union. The previously cited
example of the ILGWU, a union with huge minority membership with
a lily white leadership is one kind of situation and not a unique
one. In some other unions like the UAW there is much more minority
representation, although the top echelons remain disproportionately
white. A rank & file movement must push for more minority
participation at all leadership levels of the union. Obviously
more Black leadership is not, in and of itself, a total solution
to the problems of Black workers. But representative union
leadership is an elementary part of union democracy and white
support for Black union candidates is an important step in the
process of forging Black-white unity. Since a number of unions
have tried to cool out rank & file insurgency on the part of Black
workers by adding a few more Blacks to their slates without
altering their racist policies, it is always going to be important
to stress that leadership, both actual and potential, be judged
by the content of their program.

Not all anti-racist demands deal directly with discrimination. Many demands
around wages and working conditions are blows against racism to the extent they
aim at improving the conditions of minority workers and narrow the inequality
between Black and white. For example the rank & file movement in steel, by
pushing for improvements in working conditions in the coke ovens, which are predominantly manned by Black workers, is taking up the fight against racism while
at the same time taking steps that will improve and protect conditions of all
the workers. The anti-racist content of any rank & file program will undoubtedly
consist in some large part of demands of this sort that speak concretely to the
problems of the workers victimized directly by racism.

The rank & file movement must not only adopt anti-racist demands as part of
its program. It must actively struggle for them within the union. These demands
must be seen as educational tools to deepen the broader rank & file's consciousness of the importance of the struggle against racism. This aspect is particularly important with the white workers who must be convinced of the need to
struggle for these kinds of demands. A program is only as good as its author's
willingness to fight for it.

While the bedrock of any rank & file organization is a program that deals
with questions of immediate concern to the workers on the job, there is also a
need to take up broader political concerns. We as workers cannot solve all our
problems within the framework of collective bargaining. Our experience with
Nixon's new economics of frozen wages, spiraling prices and mounting shortages
is an illustration of this. The war in Vietnam, which gravely affected working
people in the U.S., is another. The rank & file movement must take up these
political questions as part of an effort to broaden the political horizons of
the union--to make the union a fighter for the working class in all its battles
as well as its defender on the shop floor. The unions must break out of the
trap of relying solely on the two capitalist parties and take political action
on their own. Nor should political action be limited to electoral activity and
lobbying. The unions should take direct action--demonstrations, marches and
political strikes.

Similarly the struggle against racism cannot be limited to the fight between
the union and the company over wages, working conditions and other immediate
concerns. The labor movement must take up the agenda of the Black liberation
movement and adopt it as its own. This must occur if an alliance between these
two forces is to be forged. And it is exactly such an alliance that is the
cornerstone of the strategy to end the system of class exploitation and racism.
The trade unions should join the fight for equality in education, housing and
law enforcement. The drive of the Welfare Rights Organization for a guaranteed
annual income should get the full support of labor. The unions must actively
oppose the racist foreign policy of the U.S. which supports the white supremacist
settler states of South Africa, funds the attempt to maintain Portuguese
colonialism in Africa and lends support to Zionist aggression in the Middle East.
Again the activity of the trade unions on these vital issues cannot be limited
to resolutions at conventions. The trade unions must mobilize their ranks for
mass action towards these goals. The key to moving the trade unions in this
direction is the organized pressure of the rank & file. It is the task of the
rank & file movement to take up these issues as part of the overall program for
transforming the trade unions.

Organize!

Throughout this section we have talked about the tasks of the rank & file movement in relation to the trade unions. Finally we want to discuss the forms of that movement--the way it needs to organize itself. Rank & file organizations of all sorts exist. Many of them have no real program. They consist of those disgruntled with the union leadership who want to see some kind of change. These caucuses which lack any political and programmatic definition are likely to fall victim to careerist elements who will play on the real grievances of the ranks to get themselves elected to union office and once in power will continue business as usual. A rank & file group that is really going to make a difference can't be built around simple opposition to the current leadership or around the personalities of a few of its leaders. It has to be built on the basis of a program that reflects the interests of the mass of workers and can draw them into struggle. It has to be a mass, democratic organization open to all rank & filers. It has to hold its own leadership accountable for upholding its principles and program.

Class Struggle Program

What should such a program be? It must be a *class struggle* program. In other words a program that proceeds from the assumption that the mass of workers have interests that are distinct and antagonistic to that of the employers and that the workers have to struggle *against* the bosses to get what they need. This kind of class struggle unionism is in opposition to the dominant business unionism in the country today which preaches cooperation with the conciliation of the employer as the road forward for workers. The broad content of the class struggle program has already been touched on in various places in this article. The union must fight for job security, better wages and improved working conditions instead of helping the company to justify speed up, low wages or the elimination of jobs. The union must be a genuinely democratic organization accountable to its membership. The union must take a stand of solidarity with workers everywhere--in other unions, in other cities and in other countries. The union must militantly represent the interests of the working people in the political arena as well as in the shop. And as we have stressed throughout--the union must resolutely oppose racism and champion the cause of freedom for all oppressed minorities. This is the kind of unionism that flows from an understanding that there is a struggle going on between the employer class and the working class. It is a union that expects the union, a worker's organization, to choose the worker's side. It is this kind of program that the rank & file must organize itself around in order to win back and transform their unions.

Representative Groups

Besides having a solid program the rank & file caucus must be broad. It can't speak for the mass of workers if it only consists of a handful of people. It must not only draw in large numbers but it must be truly representative of the union's composition in terms of race, sex, occupation and job classification. This need underlines the importance of developing the kind of concrete program that can appeal and activate the broad ranks.

Black Caucuses?

In many cases, as we have already mentioned, Black workers have organized their own organizations--all Black caucuses. Some may wonder is this not in contradiction to the need for broad all inclusive organization? The answer is that the very existence of a separate Black caucus indicates that there is not an immediate base for a broad, multi-racial or multi-national group. It indicates that the struggle against racism on the part of the white workers is at such a low ebb that the Black workers feel no confidence or trust in the white workers. In such a situation Black-white organizational unity would be at the expense of the Black workers. It would be a unity without principle. In these circumstances a Black caucus is not only justifiable, but correct and healthy given that the alternatives would be no organization or an unprincipled

or unworkable alliance. While Black caucuses thus are a legitimate and necessary form within the rank & file movement, there can be no justification for a
white caucus. Whites have no separate interests to unite around as whites.
When whites do form a white organization it is always to protect their imagined
racial interests and racial privilege. A white caucus is by definition going to
be a racist form.

Black-White Unity

While recognizing the legitimacy of Black caucuses, our goal must be to
build united Black-white caucuses. In a situation where a Black caucus already
exists and there is no other form, the task is to raise the level of struggle
against racism on the part of the white workers to a point where the Black
workers in the separate organization feel confident that they can participate
in a multi-racial form without compromising the fight against their racial
oppression. The responsibility for advancing this struggle and laying the
groundwork for Black-white unity is firmly on the shoulder of the class
conscious white worker. At the same time the class conscious Black workers
have a special responsibility to fight against separatism--the idea that even
principled unity with the white workers is wrong.

The achievement of a united caucus on any principled, lasting basis is
possible only on the firm ground of a serious, programmatic struggle against
racism. Within the caucus as well the struggle against racism will and must. go
on. White workers, even the most class conscious, will not automatically shed
all their blindspots overnight nor can they be expected to. Black workers will
not overcome a distrust based on centuries of racial oppression in a minute
either and they certainly cannot be expected to. Unity and progress will take
large measures of both struggle and patience--the patience born of the understanding of our common interests as a class and our common need for a better
life and a new world.

Racism and the Workers' Movement, Philadelphia Workers' Organizing Committee,
Class Struggle Unionism Pamphlet No. 1, pp. 1-39. Pamphlet in possession of
the editors.

21. UNITED COMMUNITY CONSTRUCTION WORKERS, 1971

Manifesto

WHEREAS   GOVERNMENT (FEDERAL, STATE, MUNICIPAL) HAS CONSISTENTLY APPEALED
           to political expediency rather than to the law of the land or to
           a sense of justice, history, or morality; it is painfully clear that
           Black workers have no redress or grievances or protection under the
           law from either the legislative or judicial systems.

WHEREAS   WE, AS ENLIGHTENED BLACK MEN DEEM IT NECESSARY TO SHED ALL vestiges
           of modern colonialism in order to maintain and exact survival, it
           is hereby declared that we, and we alone, will determine our own
           destinies; our own economic and vocational fates. That the right
           to work, bring sustenance to our families and rebuild our own
           community is our basic right and reason for being and that this
           right will not be abridged, amended, manipulated, or dictatored to
           by anyone, regardless of prior claims.

THEREFORE FROM THIS TIME FORTH, THOSE AREAS KNOWN AS THE SOUTH END Roxbury,
           North Dorchester, Mattapan; the domicile of third world residents,
           are deemed "Off Limits" to racist unions, non-functioning compliance
           officers, discriminatory contractors, planning agencies, bureaucrats,
           and all others who have not initiated creditable prior consultation
           with those directly affected.

THEREFORE LET IT BE KNOWN THAT ANY AND ALL CONSTRUCTION WORK TO BE performed
           in the third world community will be performed by third world
           persons on a ratio of no less than fifty percent of the skilled
           workers and that the total unskilled labor force will emanate from
           that community.

WHEREAS   IT IS RECOGNIZED THAT EXISTING TRADE UNIONS HAVE SYSTEMATICALLY
initiated barriers to employment based on racial lines, sophisticated
these barriers as institutionalized policy and procedure, solicited
governmental sanction of same, expended energies and resources to
maintain the status quo to the determent of the common good, and that
government has made but token and mere strategic adjustment to just
protest, it is incumbent upon Black workers to reject all efforts by
unions and government based solely on their so-called "Good Faith"
resolves intended to correct existing abuses.
THEREFORE WE REAFFIRM OUR COMMITMENT TO ESTABLISHING AND MAINTAINING our own
Black unions so that we may best determine our own destinies in and
for our own community.

Leaflet in possession of the editors.

22. BLACK WORKERS FIGHT IMPERIALISM:
POLAROID CORPORATION

The image of Polaroid Corporation as a liberal company and an "equal rights
employer" is under sharp attack by a group of black employees, the Polaroid
Revolutionary Workers Movement. On Wednesday, October 7, more than 200 people--
most of them workers--gathered at Tech Square in Cambridge to hear spokesmen for
the group denounce Polaroid's trade and investments in South Africa.

They demanded: (1) That Polaroid announce a policy of complete disengagement from South Africa. (2) That the management meet the entire company and
announce its position on apartheid (South Africa's rigid policies of segregation
and white supremacy) in the U.S. and South Africa simultaneously. (3) That the
company donate all its profits from South Africa to the recognized African
liberation movement in that country.

Although the vast majority of South Africans are black, the white supremacist government denies them basic political, civil and simple human rights. For
a black person to move from one part of the country to another, they must first
obtain approval from the government. Every black African must carry a pass book
with official identification including his photo, legal residence, name of
employer, and permits to live and work temporarily outside a "native area."
Polaroid admits that its film is used for passbook photos and also that its
South African distributors have supplied 66 ID-2 systems to S. African military
and industry since 1967.

Low wages and tight control of the work force make South Africa a haven for
big corporations in search of super-profits. Average profits there are higher
than anywhere else in the world, except Middle Eastern oil fields. And Polaroid
has not hesitated to take advantage of this situation. Polaroid sunglasses are
now manufactured in six countries outside the U.S., including S. Africa. Because
of the higher profit rate, companies like Polaroid prefer to open new plants
where labor is cheap--as in South Africa. In this way, the exploitation of
black workers thousands of miles away threatens our jobs as well.

Polaroid's development of personnel security systems is an even more direct
threat to workers in both countries. The system now used in defense plants can
easily be used in the future to monitor the coming and going of workers in
other industries. Security systems will be used to prevent workers from ripping
off some of the surplus value the companies make off our sweat. Security
systems enable employers to blacklist job applicants who have been fired on a
former job, have been thrown in jail, run up debts, been political activists,
union militants, etc.

In an interview with *THE MASS STRIKE,* Ken Williams, a member of the
Polaroid Revolutionary Workers Movement, accused the company of using black
people as window dressing, giving them front office jobs and showing pictures
of black employees prominently in all their public relations material. At the
same time, the company's international sales department is lily-white, and
Polaroid's money and ID system help to stabilize the most vicious, racist

government in the world. The man responsible for Polaroid's involvement in South Africa, former vice-president Stan Calderwood, is now head of WGBH, and has been strongly criticized by Boston's black community for the station's racist censorship and cancellation of the "Say, Brother" program.

Black workers at Polaroid are fighting back. They are blowing the whistle on a "liberal" company whose activities in fact bolster racism, imperialism and fascism, in South Africa and here at home. As workers we have the duty to demand that the products of our labor serve the needs of the world's peoples-- not lead to further oppression. Polaroid workers are showing the way, living up to their responsibilities to their brothers and sisters in South Africa. We enthusiastically support them. It's our fight, too!

Leaflet in possession of the editors.

23. BOYCOTT POLAROID

The Polaroid Workers Revolutionary Movement calls upon everyone who believes in freedom and justice to help the people of South Africa by boycotting all Polaroid products until the following demands are met: (1) That Polaroid announce a policy of complete disengagement from South Africa. (2) That the management meet the entire company and announce its position on apartheid (South Africa's rigid policies of segregation and white supremacy) in the U.S. and South Africa simultaneously. (3) That the company donate all its profits from South Africa to the recognized African liberation movement in that country.

Polaroid, the "humanistic corporation," the "equal opportunities employer," has been doing business with racist South Africa since 1938. They sell film, cameras, sunglasses and identification systems through a local distributor.

Hundreds of American corporations do business with South Africa. Many have opened manufacturing plants there because profits are higher than anywhere in the world except Middle Eastern oil fields. The reason for these superprofits is obvious: Black people, who are the vast majority of South Africa's popula- tion, are paid an average of thirty cents a day and work under concentration camp conditions.

Polaroid knows this. We quote from "The Polaroid Newsletter" of Nov. 2, 1970: "The black native is treated as an unwelcome foreigner in his own country. His activities and movements are arbitrarily restricted. He is required to carry a passbook whenever he is in any of the work centers or cities and is subject to imprisonment without trial if caught without it. It is a crime for a black African to go on strike, to criticize the government's racial policy, or to use a 'white' entrance instead of the 'natives only' entrance."

Polaroid has agreed to prevent the use of its film for passbook photos. BUT IT REFUSES TO CUT OFF ALL ITS BUSINESS WITH SOUTH AFRICA. It refuses to stop selling ID-2 systems to the military, the backbone of apartheid, to the aircraft companies that make planes for the military, to the mining companies that profit from the forced labor of black workers. It refuses to stop the sale of cameras, film and sunglasses even though no black people could possibly afford them, even though any business with South Africa helps to stabilize that system and to give it a cloak of legitimacy. It refuses to turn its South African profits over to the African people's freedom movement.

The United Nations has called for a total economic boycott of South Africa. As employees of Polaroid we demand that the company honor that position. And if Polaroid refuses to put the welfare of people over profits, then it is up to all thinking people to boycott Polaroid.

Leaflet in possession of the editors.

24. POLAROID BLACKS ASK WORLDWIDE BOYCOTT

By Parker Donham

A group of black workers at Polaroid Inc. yesterday called for a worldwide boycott of the company's products until it ends all sales to South Africa.

The Polaroid Revolutionary Workers' Movement (PRWM) said the boycott would continue until the Cambridge firm discontinues sales of its patented polarized sunglasses to Frank and Hirsch Ltd., its licensed franchiser in South Africa.

Last week, in response to PRWM demands, the company said it was discontinuing sales of its ID-2 photo identification system, and film used in the system, in South Africa.

Polaroid's manager of community relations, Robert Palmer, who acts as press spokesman for the company, last night said he has been instructed by company officials not to respond to the announcement of a boycott. He said a statement would be forthcoming "in a few days."

The month-long dispute centers on the dissident workers' contention that Polaroid's sales in South Africa constitute support for the country's official policy of separating the races, known as Apartheid.

Palmer said Polaroid's total sales in South Africa last year were "in the neighborhood of $1 million," but he said he could not break down the sales of the photo identification system and the sunglasses.

He said last week's announcement that the identification system would no longer be sold in South Africa was a "symbolic first step," but added that the company was continuing to discuss the issues raised by PRWM.

Boston Globe, October 27, 1970.

PART IV
THE NEGRO-LABOR ALLIANCE

THE NEGRO-LABOR ALLIANCE

The revolutionary black workers placed a severe strain on the alliance between blacks and organized labor, but ultimately their actions strengthened that relationship and helped to elevate it to a higher plain. Moderate black unionists also sought to increase the power of black workers in the unions, but by integration, not separatism. Their goals were more readily achievable, and stood as a confirmation, rather than a refutation, of organized labor.

The struggle against racism in the labor movement for a long time concentrated on opening membership to blacks. Since the rise of the CIO, however, the battle against racism increasingly became one against discriminatory practices in hiring and promotion, and for greater black participation in union leadership. Since the promise held out to blacks by the AFL-CIO merger remained largely unfulfilled, black caucuses within the various unions sought to achieve a "fair share" of the benefits of membership for blacks. This concern for more "black power" in the unions was not just a matter of racial pride. In the late sixties only about a dozen unions had so much as one Negro on their governing boards, even though approximately 2 million of the 14 million union members in the AFL-CIO were black. Since Afro-Americans were so under-represented in union officialdom, their grievances were frequently neglected, and may have been co-participants in the discrimination.

One of the most prominent of the black caucuses seeking black power through integration was the Negro American Labor Council. Founded in May 1960, the NALC made it clear at the outset that it was a black organization, although whites were not barred, whose goals were to increase union membership among black workers, to increase their chances for promotion on the job, and to integrate them into the executive and staff levels of the union administrations. The delegates elected A. Philip Randolph president, and Cleveland Robinson of District 65 vice president. It was on behalf of the NALC that Randolph presented charges of racial discrimination to the AFL-CIO Executive Council, an action which ultimately led to his censure in 1961. In addition to its efforts on behalf of black workers, NALC played an important role in the civil rights movement, for it was under the leadership of this group that the historic 1963 March on Washington was planned. Even though the AFL-CIO Executive Council condemned the demonstration, the March represented a high point in the history of the Negro-labor alliance up to that time. The federation's Industrial Union Department defied the Council and strongly endorsed the demonstration, and over 40,000 unionists were mobilized for the event. Two key union leaders, Randolph and Reuther, were on the March's leadership committee.

By the early 1970s many blacks were convinced that despite the good work peformed by the black caucuses, the elimination of racism on the job and in the unions would require a unified effort by black unionists on a national scale. The Coalition of Black Trade Unionists succeeded the NALC and assumed this mission at a 1972 conference of 1,200 black union members and officials. From its inception the new organization made it clear that it intended to deal specifically with the concerns of black workers, and would "insist that black union officials become full partners in the leadership and decision-making of the American labor movement."

BLACK POWER AND THE NEGRO–LABOR ALLIANCE

NEGRO LABOR ASSEMBLY

1. MINUTES OF THE NEGRO LABOR ASSEMBLY
OCTOBER 14, 1959

Harlem Labor Center - 312 W. 125 St.

THE MEETING of the Negro Labor Assembly was called to order at 7:30 p.m. with Brother Richard Parrish, presiding.

Present were:

Oscar Clarke	Paper Box Makers, Local 299
Mildred Simmons	Plastic & Novelty Workers, Local 132
James Walker	Cafeteria Employees, Local 302
Estella West	Blouse & Waistmakers, Local 25
Howard Scott	Children's Dress, Local 91
Ollie Austin	Skirtmakers Union, Local 23
Richard Banks	Children's Dress, Local 91
Ruby Rowley	Negro Labor Committee
Allan Jackson	Dress & Waist Pressers, Local 60
Richard Parrish	N.Y. Teachers Guild, Local 2 and N.L.C.
Frank P. Crosswaith	Negro Labor Committee
Edith Ransom	Dressmakers Union, Local 22

EXCUSES: Elizabeth Knight, Frame & Novelty, Local 111; Winifred Gittens, Negro Labor Committee; Mabel Fuller, Priscilla Timpson, and Martin Forrester, Undergarment and Negligee Workers, Local 62.

BRO. PARRISH welcomed the delegates at the first meeting for the Fall, and said, "that he hopes they have returned with renewed vigor to work and plan together for a very constructive year, in which the Negro Labor Committee will continue to work tirelessly in bringing more workers into the trade union movement. . . ."

COMMUNICATIONS:

FROM THE City of Hope, honoring Peter Ottley for his dedication to the labor movement and to his race. Bro. Ottley is Sec'y-Treas. of the Hotel & Allied Service Union, Local 144. Bro. Parrish reported that to date the affair was moving very slowly – and urged that the labor movement should pay more homage to a man who has given many years of service to the cause of labor. BRO. CROSSWAITH then suggested that because of the low finance of our Committee, it was impossible for us to participate, but a telegram be sent on the date of the dinner. The delegates adopted the suggestion.

FROM THE American Committee on Africa; the National Sharecroppers Fund, and many others asking for donations. Again because of our low finances we are unable to make a contribution at this time.

FROM THE Federation of Negro Civil Service Organizations, sponsoring a rally on Oct. 29th, the proceeds of which will be donated to the NAACP, and the Southern Leadership Conference. The delegates were urged to attend and get their friends to do likewise.

FROM THE Trade Union Salute, a celebration of the NAACP 50th anniversary, to be held Dec. 5th, 1959. The Committee recognizes the assistance given to the NAACP but will not be able to participate because of low finances. It was suggested that a letter be sent to these organizations expressing our regrets, and wishing them continued success.

THE FOLLOWING telegrams were sent to the Brotherhood of Sleeping Car Porters, and the AFL-CIO, conventions, respectively.

To A. Philip Randolph President
Brotherhood of Sleeping Car Porters, Convention.

"The Negro Labor Committee sends you fraternal greetings and best wishes for a successful convention.

May your deliberations and decisions in this convention bring us closer to that day when human exploitation and racial and religious prejudices will be no more.

Signed: Frank R. Crosswaith, Chairman

To George Meany, President
AFL-CIO Convention.

"On behalf of the Negro Labor Committee, we send you fraternal and personal greetings for a constructively successful convention.

In the struggle between the forces of dictatorship and democracy, the labor movement must remain united and insure the triumph of democracy for the workers of the world, regardless of craft, creed or color.

Signed: Frank R. Crosswaith, Chairman
and Richard Parrish, Exec-Sec'y."

THE DEATH of Bro. Isidore Nagler, Vice President of the ILGWU, and Gen'l Manager of the Cloak Jt. Board, was brought to the delegates attention by Bro. Crosswaith who sent a letter of condolence to the family. The letter was read, and the Assembly stood for a two minutes silence to honor the memory of the deceased.

IN REFERENCE to the recent flare-up at the AFL-CIO convention between Bros. George Meany and A. Philip Randolph, the following letter was sent to the press.

Dear Editor:

"Mr. Meany, the head of the AFL-CIO, recently asked profanely what right A. Philip Randolph, the head of the Brotherhood of Sleeping Car Porters had to represent the Negroes of America, when Mr. Randolph was pressing him to start ending racial segregation and discrimination in those unions -- luckily a minority where it still exists. This kind of attack will do organize labor no good. For it will tend to make some Negroes anti-labor at a time when organized labor needs all the friends it can get. Mr. Randolph was only asking that the AFL-CIO carry out the pledges against racial discrimination which it had repeatedly made, by trying to get the two unions affiliated with it which still bar Negroes from membership by constitutional provision, to change their constitution -- to try to get other unions some of whose locals still discriminate against Negroes to stop that practice and to eliminate segregated locals altogether.

Organized labor has done much for Negro workers. In those states in the North and West where civil rights legislation like fair employment practice laws, fair educational practice laws, or legislation against racial discrimination in housing have been enacted, organized labor has given substantial help in getting the laws passed. And such Negro organizations as the National Association for the Advancement of Colored People has in turn helped substantially in labor's campaign to defeat anti-labor legislation. Yet the labor department of the NAACP has well documented instances where cases of racial discrimination against Negro workers have been called to the attention of unions, yet nothing has been done. Organizations working for the rights of racial minorities need the help of organized labor, and organized labor needs the help of Negro workers. It will be a great pity if any permanent rift between them should develop.

Signed: Frank R. Crosswaith, Chairman
The Negro Labor Committee."

THE DELEGATES voted their opinion and regretted the incident. Bro. Crosswaith then said, "nothing would hurt the Negro more than an attempt to withdraw from the labor movement. This is a time to strive for greater unity. . . ." The delegates also agreed that this is the time for greater unity and action among Negro trade unionists in bringing the thousands of unorganized workers into the labor movement.

BRO. PARRISH then reported that, "Bro. Randolph is going ahead with the formation of a national Negro Labor Committee, in which all Negro trade unionists will be asked to become members. This organization will concentrate on helping to erase discriminatory practice within organized labor. It will not lessen the work performed by each member in the local unions, but will help to step up their activities. We can no longer sit back and let the chips fall where they will, but must be united in a democratic fashion and be dependent on each other for leadership and guidance. . . ."

BRO. JACKSON then asked what significance will this new organization have on our present Negro Labor Committee.

BRO. PARRISH replied, "this new organization will in no way deprive or weaken the present Negro Labor Committee who is dependent on the unions for its support, and has enough of its own work to do. The new organization will be independent of the influence of these unions whose discriminatory practices prevents the full participation of Negroes in their activities. The members will be charged yearly dues which will help to defray the expenses of the organization. . . ."

ON SEPTEMBER 22nd Bro. Joseph Fox, President of the Cafeteria Employees, Local 302, requested Bro. Crosswaith to send an appeal to the Horn and Hardart workers who were holding an election on Sept. 30th for union recognition. The message was read to the delegates and approved.

BRO. WALKER of Local 302, reported that the Local lost the election by a margin of 3 to 1 votes against the union. The Negro Labor Committee then pledged continued support of Local 302 until victory is achieved.

FINANCIAL STATEMENT for September was read: - Receipts $580.00; Disbursements $585.62.

DELEGATES REPORT:

BRO. PARRISH reported that he attended the Brotherhood of Sleeping Car Porters, Convention, and "that during the deliberations the delegates adopted the resolution to work together for greater unity and the abolition of racial discrimination and segregation within the labor movement." He also attended the United Automobile Workers, Convention.

BRO. CROSSWAITH reported that "despite the fact that he is no longer with the New York City Housing Authority, many persons come daily to the office to seek his advice and aid on how to get into the projects -- also many come seeking jobs or the possibility of getting into a union of their trade. . . ."
HE ALSO reported that Sister Gittens was still at home recuperating from her recent automobile accident which occurred last July. It was suggested that the Negro Labor Committee write to her officially expressing our regrets and wishing her a speedy recovery.

BRO. PARRISH then reported on the "Frank R. Crosswaith Scholarship Awards" which were given last June to four students of Junior High Schools 136, 139, 120 and 188; amounting to $100.00 each. One of the students John Pressley who is attending Fashion Institute has requested financial aid to help him purchase equipments for school. An allotment of $20.00 was drawn from his account with the Carver Bank.

BRO. JACKSON then suggested that delegates who are delinquents in attending the Assembly meetings should be brought to the attention of their Local Manager after missing three consecutive meetings. This suggestion was agreed upon.
HE ALSO suggested that the delegates and their friends regardless of Party affiliations should vote for Samuel Pierce for Judgeship in the Nov. election. As "he is a very capable lawyer and is worthy of our support."

BRO. PARRISH then commented that "never before in the history of this city were Negroes so ill-informed about the benefits derived from the trade union movement. In this community there are still one-half of the Negroes who know nothing of the Negro Labor Committee and the work it is doing. It is important that we establish an educational program to bring these facts to the people, and bring more community workers into our organization. Laws on the books will not solve our problems. This is a question of color prejudice and Negroes will have to solve them by becoming more alert and more united on social, political and economic goals."

HE THEN suggested that in the near future we will call a special meeting of the delegates to make arrangements for an affair to raise funds for the Negro Labor Committee.

AFTER MUCH discussions under "Good and Welfare" the meeting adjourned at 9 p.m. The next Assembly meeting will be held on November 11th, 1959.

Respectfully submitted,

THE NEGRO LABOR COMMITTEE

Negro Labor Committee Record Group, 1925-1969, Schomburg Collection, New York Public Library.

2.   MINUTES

NEGRO LABOR ASSEMBLY
held on
September 30, 1965
at
HARLEM LABOR CENTER

The meeting of the Negro Labor Assembly was called to order by the Chairman, Allan Jackson, at 7:15 p.m. Members present were: Helen Boyd, Local 23-25; A. C. Bell, Local 302; Christine Scott, Local 23-25; Estella West, Local 23-25; Richard Banks, Local 91; Edward Fagan, Local 99; Hazel Allen, Local 22; A. C. Jolly, Local 302; Allan Jackson, Local 60-601; L. Joseph Overton, Local 338.

The Chairman read the proposed program policy as set forth in the letters sent to the members. The proposed program is:

1. A drive to enroll at least 100,000 new registered voters prior to the coming election.
2. A conference on community activities and the rebuilding of better relations.
3. To urge the Department of Sanitation for a ten day clean up program of all Harlem streets and the enforcement of Sanitation Codes prohibiting the placing of garbage in the streets by commercial establishments.
4. To discuss ways and means of how we can assist the public schools in our area diminish attacks on teachers by students.
5. Report of the action taken to date by the Executive Director in connection with our proposed Housing Project (Frank R. Crosswaith).

The Chair stated he wanted this organization to be recognized City and Statewide. The organization should stand for unions, better race relations and as a guiding light to the labor movement and the entire community and must be recognized City, State and Nationwide.

L. Joseph Overton, Executive Director, reported on several meetings and conferences he had held with Chairman H. Evans of the Redevelopment Board and Chairman Leo Brown of Marine & Aviation and also correspondence was read between he, architects, coordinator and others pertaining to the Frank R. Crosswaith Housing Development. Mr. Overton reported that Herbert Evans stated the Negro Labor Committee would probably receive approval. Commissioner Leo Brown of the Marine and Aviation said there are certain things which must be

included. They want to have the property developed with a boat marina and
amusement pier. Under this condition we can have a lease for the land. The
project has also been approved by the Housing Commission. The organization
is now in a bottleneck between Housing and Marine Aviation over which will
have jurisdiction of the project after it has been developed.

The Housing Authority wants figures showing the project will rent for
not more than $27.50 per room. This had been reported to them by our archi-
tects indicating the feasibility of this being done as they are more interested in rentals than cooperatives because people have to borrow the down-
payment. However, they have not said we could build a combination of both.

The Body extended commendations to L. Joseph Overton for his work on the
project.

Mr. Overton then continued to read correspondence between himself and
contractors, builders, etc., involved in the housing project, also further
correspondence was read by the secretary.

MOTIONED by Mr. Banks that the correspondence presented here by Mr.
Overton along with all actions taken to date be approved and accepted by the
Body. Same was

SECONDED by Mrs. Boyd and unanimously approved by the Body.

Mr. Overton stated he would like to have brochures sent out to all Locals
about the Housing Project. We would allegate equal amounts of the projects to
all affiliates to sell or rent as they choose. If an affiliate cannot dispose
of their allocation it should revert back to the organization for redistribution among those that can. We are trying to get 100% financial backing from
the Federal Government and if, by an unfortunate occurrence, our proposed
plans do not materialize, the Negro Labor Committee Treasury will not have
been affected for the risk money which is being spent now and is coming from
the contractors and engineers who wish to have a part in building the project.
When the apartments are available the monies needed for security and advance
rent will be determined by F.H.A. Specifications not by the Negro Labor
Committee.

The members of this organization were asked at one time to keep the
housing project as quiet as possible. This is no longer necessary and may be
discussed with whomever you desire since we are the only sponsors applying
for this location and the danger of others applying for the same location has
now been resolved. The affiliates who have only been advised through our
minutes should definitely be given a detailed report of our actions and position. There has been considerable publication already by newspapers, etc.
The Honorable Paul Screvane and Borough President Constance Motley have
already given their approval.

Mr. Overton believes approval from all agencies will be forthcoming
within the next two weeks. This is the reason he would like to set up
brochures so you may take it to your locals with all procedures and actions
in it.

The capacity of the project will be a minimum of 2,553 units, a 32-story
house with four different structures, from efficiency apartments to three
bedrooms.

The Chairman stated that we should try to do things to bring glory to
the N.L.C. We must move ahead with the times and fight. Rededicate ourselves
to programs going on today as we did when we first started -- to further Negro
labor causes.

Mr. Overton said "What needs to be done by the Negro Labor Committee is
to preach the gospel about trade unions if you can't do anything else. We
need the job done now more than ever. It is not that we have no leadership
-- it's that the leaders are not organized -- they don't know when a riot
occurs if those people participating are members of their own unions or not.

I was able to pull people out of the street during the riots because I
was a labor leader. The people know and trust me. Some people are against
laborers. Everyone wants to associate with those with degrees. We must
stop this. People must know who we are and if it wasn't for labor they would
not be able to exist without labor paying for it. We must tell them everytime we get a chance that the toothbrush they use every morning came from
labor. Every service, every device they use comes through a laborers hands
first.

Some girls want to work in stores while going to school and we give them jobs. When I ask them where their mother works they tell me in a factory. When I ask what union they belong to they can't tell me. They will say they don't belong to a union. However, I know there aren't that many non-union shops. This shows me that not even the parents are telling their sons and daughters about unions and their importance.

We then have to show them the importance and involve them so they will want to become a part. When they see union men making $2.00 an hour and they can only receive $1.25 an hour they begin to realize what a union is.

Unions are for workers. Black men are workers and they must be a part. We have a big job to do if we take the time and responsibility. We must get to the people and tell them. The unions are ready now.

We must have unity. We must get mileage in the community by participating in anything that comes up -- the Negro Labor Committee must be a part of it. The members of the Negro Labor Committee must support their leaders regardless of who they may be. The Negro Labor Committee does not have money in their treasury to pay a full time executive secretary to run their projects. There are jobs the members and committees can do themselves. When you report back to your locals have something to report that the members can do. Be present and take part in community affairs and learn to do some of the work yourselves. One operation could be to have a center for people so when they go out looking for a job they will know how much they are worth. Learn to organize the unorganized people. Stop looking for excuses. There is plenty to do if we only do it.

We're going to clean up Harlem in the name of the Negro Labor Committee. Bring people up to 312 even for social hours, with refreshments in the name of N.L.C. The first time you may only have 35 people, the next time it may be 50, etc. The work we do is for the organization and organizations affiliated with the N.L.C. and not just for individuals who may be participating in the program. I want glory for N.L.C. not for any individual."

Mr. Banks said "We haven't met for a long time and we don't know what's happening. Why don't we charter a way of how to do things and plan for it and then do it. I propose: 1. An election for the N.L.C. 2. Each officer elected told, in a meeting his duties and responsibilities. 3. This is to be taken care of as soon as possible."

Mr. Jackson remarked "When voting a person into office you must go by the guidelines of the duties outlined for the particular office so you can determine who you want for that office by the person's capabilities and qualifications. Also, a person cannot take away another persons duties if they are spelled out.

We should establish a group of permanent committees -- duties outlined -- when this is done then you are ready for an election regardless of present personalities. We should compare the structure of International Unions Constitutions and take out what we need for the constitution."

Mr. Bell: I have asked about duties of elected officers many times. I suggest the Chair appoint a committee to draft the constitution.

MOTION: Mr. Banks -- "I move 1. N.L.C. has an election. 2. Each officer elected told, in a meeting, his duties and responsibilities. 3. This is to be taken care of as soon as possible."

AMENDMENT by Mr. Overton: "The drafting of by-laws outlining the specific functions and duties of all officers be implemented with all due haste."

SECONDED by Christine Scott and motion unanimously approved.

Mrs. Scott said the N.L.C. should take a big part in voter registration. Let's make a concentrated effort to get everyone out to vote.

The Chairman then reread the proposed program for N.L.C.

After a lengthy discussion it was moved by Mr. Jolly and seconded by Mr. Bell that we approve the program as read. Motion was unanimously accepted.

Mr. Jackson, Chairman: Summary -- Tonight we endeavored to set down policies to strengthen N.L.C. Our road won't be smooth. But if we can be united as N.L.C. WE SHALL OVERCOME.

Mr. Overton: Mr. Chairman, I suggest you appoint a committee tonight for the purpose of taking inventory of all the Negro Labor Committee's

assets and liabilities. The Chair should appoint a committee for the purpose
of restoring Frank Crosswaith's office, now used as a storeroom and set it up
properly as an office we may use for business. An organization should have a
place for the Head to use for business and have meetings.

The Body agreed the establishment of committees should be postponed until
the next meeting.

Mr. Johnson read condolences sent by the Negro Labor Committee to Mr.
Overton upon the passing of his Mother and Sol Green.

It was motioned by Mr. Bell and seconded by Mr. Banks that the meeting
be adjourned.

Mr. Johnson stated the next meeting would be the second Wednesday in
October.

The meeting was adjourned at 10:15 P.M.

                              Respectfully submitted,

                              PATRICIA BELL
                              Acting Secretary

Negro Labor Committee Record Group, 1925-1969, Schomburg Collection, New York
Public Library.

                         NEGRO AMERICAN LABOR COUNCIL

                   3. KEYNOTE ADDRESS TO THE SECOND ANNUAL
               CONVENTION OF THE NEGRO AMERICAN LABOR COUNCIL,
                              NOVEMBER 10, 1961

                            By A. Philip Randolph

        In the mid-twentieth century black labor is one hundred years behind
white labor. Black labor is behind white labor in the skilled crafts. They
are behind in trade union organization. They are behind in workers' education. They are behind in employment opportunities.

        Why? The answer is not because white labor is racially superior to black
labor. Not because white labor is more productive than black labor.

        In the race between black and white labor in American industry, black
labor never had a chance. How could it be otherwise when Negro workers began
as slaves while white workers began as free men, or virtually as free men?

        In addition to a quarter of a thousand years of captivity in the labor
system of chattel slavery, black labor, even after emancipation, has been a
prisoner for a hundred years of a moneyless system of peonage, sharecropper-
plantation-farm laborism, and a helpless and hopeless city-slum proletariat.

        No greater tragedy has befallen the working class anywhere in the modern
world than that which plagues the working class in the South. Both white and
black workers turned against their own class, to subject them to sharper and
sharper exploitation and oppression.

        Verily, black and white workers did not fight each other because they
hated each other, but they hated each other because they fought each other.
They fought each other because they did not know each other. They did not
know each other because they had no contact or communication with each other.
They had no contact or communication with each other because they were afraid
of each other. They were afraid of each other because each was propagandized
into believing that each was seeking to take the jobs of the other.

        By poisonous preachments by the press, pulpit and politician, the wages
of both black and white workers were kept low and working conditions bad,

since trade union organization was practically non-existent. And, even today, the South is virtually a "no man's land" for union labor.

There is no remedy for this plight of the South's labor forces except the unity of the black and white working class.

It is a matter of common knowledge that union organization campaigns, whether under the auspices of the old American Federation of Labor, or the younger Congress of Industrial Organizations, or the AFL-CIO, have wound up as miserable failures.

The reason is not only because the southern working class is divided upon a basis of race, but also because the AFL, the CIO, and the AFL-CIO never took cognizance of this fact. They never built their organization drives upon the principle of the solidarity of the working class. On the contrary, they accepted and proceeded to perpetuate this racial-labor more, the purpose of which was, and is, the perpetuation of segregation--the antithesis of trade union organization.

Thus, they sowed the winds of the division of the workers upon the basis of race, and now they are reaping the whirlwinds.

The leadership of the organized labor movement has at no time ever seriously challenged Jim Crow unionism in the South. White leaders of labor organizations, like white leaders of the Church, business, government, schools, and the press, marched together, under the banner of white supremacy, in the Ku Klux Klan, to put down and keep down by law or lawlessness, the Negro. . . .

While, before Emancipation, the Negro only had job security as a slave because he toiled for nothing, so, following Black Reconstruction, black freedmen labored within the framework of a peonage-sharecrop, labor-barter commissary system for, perhaps, a little more than nothing.

And, despite the Thirteenth, Fourteenth, Fifteenth Amendments, clear commitments to the protection of the freedmen, the Negro laboring masses have never fully broken through the barrier of the ethnic-labor mores of the South, which were hardened into a racially segregated order by the celebrated *Plessy v Ferguson* decision of the U.S. Supreme Court of 1896. Moreover, like the proverbial locusts, the doctrine of least ethnic-labor costs, or a racial sub-wage differential, spread in every area of American industry.[94]

Thus, Negro workers are not yet fully free in the South. By the same token, white workers in the South are not yet fully free, because no white worker can ever become fully free as long as a black worker is in southern Bourbon bondage. And as long as white and black workers in the South are not fully free, the entire working class, North, East, South and West, is not and will not become fully free. There is no principle more obvious and universal than the indivisibility of the freedom of the workers regardless of race, color, religion, national origin or ancestry, being based, as it were, upon the principle of least labor costs in a free market economy.

This is why the racial policies of the American Federation of Labor and Congress of Industrial Organizations have so devastatingly weakened, morally, organizationally, and politically, the American labor movement before the Congress, the public, and the world.

One has only to note that while trade unions, such as the Amalgamated Clothing Workers, Ladies' Garment Workers, and United Textile Workers, are building up decent wage rates and sound rules governing working conditions in New York, Massachusetts, Pennsylvania and Illinois, corporate capital, highly sensitive to the least threat to high rates of profits and interest upon investments, promptly takes flight into the land of non-union, low wage, low tax, race bias, mob law, and poor schools, namely, Dixie. Southern mayors, governors, and legislatures make special appeals in the northern press to industries to come South for non-union, cheap labor.

But this anti-trade union condition in the South is labor's fault. It is the direct result of the fact that neither the old AFL, nor the CIO, nor the AFL-CIO ever came to grips with the racial-labor problem in the South. Instead of meeting the racial-labor issue head on, organized labor has always adopted a policy of appeasement, compromise and defeatism. The evidence exists in the fact that it has recognized and accepted:

(a) The Jim Crow union
(b) The color bar in union constitutions, rituals, or exclusionary racial policies by tacit consent

    (c) Racially segregated seniority rosters and lines of job progression
    (d) Racial sub-wage differential
    (e) Indifferent recognition, if not acceptance of the concept and practice
        of a "white man's job" and a "black man's job"
    (f) Racial barriers against Negro participation in apprenticeship training
        programs
    (g) Failure to demand Negro workers' participation in union democracy
    (h) Racially segregated State conventions of the AFL-CIO in southern
        cities
    (i) Racially segregated city central labor bodies of the AFL-CIO

Is there anyone so naive or cynical as to believe that these forms of race bias are not organizationally and economically disadvantageous to the black laboring masses? Not only has the long system of color caste condition in American industry thrust the Negro workers to the lowest rungs of the occupational hierarchy, but it tends to reinforce the accepted inferiority hereditary position of black labor, which drastically limits their economic mobility and viability.

Although not unaware of the fact that racial discrimination in trade unions affiliated to the AFL-CIO has existed for almost a century, no profound concern is now manifest by the leadership about this dreadful evil.

Instead of becoming aroused and disturbed about the existence of race bias in unions that affect employment opportunities and the economic status of the Negro worker, AFL-CIO leadership waves aside criticism of the movement's racial policies, as pure exaggeration unworthy of dispassionate examination.

Such was the reaction to a memorandum on race bias in trade unions, together with corrective proposals, I submitted to George Meany and the Executive Council at Unity House, Pennsylvania, June 1961.

Instead of giving the memorandum a painstaking, rational analysis to determine if it contained any meritorious suggestions, it became the occasion of voluminous rebuttal and attack upon, and censure of, myself.

The rebuttal was not only innocuous, barren and sterile of a single new, vital, creative and constructive idea with which to grapple with the menace of race segregation and discrimination, but was a distressingly vain effort to justify a "do little" civil rights record in the House of Labor. . . .

Just a word now about the objective effects and results of race bias in trade unions and industry in two major cities that are generally considered to be relatively liberal, New York and Detroit.

In New York City, as well as throughout the State, non-white persons make up a very large part of those who live in poverty; a poverty that is frequently related to discriminatory racial practices that force Negroes into a marginal position in the economy, even though opportunities may increase for other groups within the community.

The two major industries in New York City are garment manufacturing and printing and publishing. The printing and publishing industry alone employs more than 160 thousand workers, or about nine percent of the manufacturing labor force. In both garment manufacturing and printing, however, we find that Negroes and Puerto Ricans are concentrated in the low paid, unskilled job classifications.

The Graduate School of Public Administration of Harvard University recently conducted a series of case studies in New York metropolitan manufacturing and concluded that in the New York garment industry Negroes and Puerto Ricans "were largely to be found in the less skilled, low-paid crafts and in shops making the lower priced lines, and in this industry their advancement to higher skills is not proceeding very rapidly. In the higher skilled coat and suit industry the new ethnic groups have hardly made an appearance."

The New York metropolitan region has twenty percent of the nation's employment in printing and publishing. In a survey made by the NAACP of Negro employment on the seven major New York City newspapers we find that, with the exclusion of building service and maintenance, less than one percent of those employed on the seven major newspapers are Negroes. Virtually all of the Negroes that are employed on these newspapers are within the white collar jurisdiction of the New York Newspaper Guild.

We estimate that less than one-half of the one percent of those currently employed in the newspaper crafts outside of the Guild's jurisdiction are Negroes. This includes printing pressmen, compositors, photoengravers, stereotypers, paper handlers, mailers and delivery drivers.

In the past decade very little progress has been made in eliminating the traditional pattern of Negro exclusion and discrimination in the Plumbers and Pipe Fitters Union; the Iron and Structural Steel Workers; the Plasterers and Lathers; the Sheet Metal Workers; the Boiler Makers; the Carpenters, as well as the Bricklayers, Masons and Plasterers Union, and others.

In New York City, Negro waiters and bellboys are more noted by their absence than presence in the hotels and restaurants except, perhaps, in a token form at some banquets. However, Negroes are members of the Hotel and Restaurant Employees Union. One will need the proverbial microscope to discover a Negro bartender anywhere in the city except in a Negro community.

Negro motion picture operators have no job mobility. They are chiefly confined to the second-class motion picture theatres in Negro communities where they receive a sub-wage differential paid operators in this class of theatre.

At present there is a broad exclusion of Negro youth from major apprenticeship programs jointly conducted by industrial management and labor unions in the City of New York. For many occupations the only way a worker can be recognized as qualified for employment is to complete the apprenticeship training program. This is true for the printing trades, among machinists and metal workers, the construction industry, and others.

The role of the labor union in these occupations is decisive because the trade union usually determines who is admitted into the training program and, therefore, who is admitted into the union. This is especially true when the union controls access to employment.

In the New York metropolitan area there are many apprenticeship training programs in the building trades. Apprenticeship programs provide essential training for a wide variety of skills in their important area of the region's economy. These include apprenticeship programs for asbestos workers, electrical workers, glaziers, ironworkers, latherers, painters, plumbers and sheetmetal workers.

A recent study by the NAACP clearly indicates that less than one percent of the apprentices in the construction industry throughout the nation are Negroes. Unfortunately, the number of Negroes in apprenticeship training programs in the New York construction industry differs little from the national pattern.

The lack of apprentice-trained Negro craftsmen directly affects the economic standing of Negroes as a whole. Data indicates that craftsmen command substantially higher incomes than unskilled workers. If, then, Negroes are not employed in such occupations in large numbers, a potential source of high income is removed from this group. When this is coupled with other income limitations it becomes apparent why Negroes constitute a permanently depressed segment of American society.

"The Struggle for the Liberation of the Black Laboring Masses." Reprinted by permission of A. Philip Randolph.

4.   UNLESS SOMETHING SPECIAL HAPPENS

By Whitney M. Young, Jr.

Before the Third Annual Negro American Labor
Council Convention, New York City
Friday, November 9, 1962

Mr. Overton, Toastmaster Randolph, President Meany, Distinguished Guests, Members and Friends of the Negro American Labor Council:

I bring you greetings from the National Urban League, and wish especially on this occasion to pay tribute to Phil Randolph -- who on November 19th will receive the National Urban League's EOD Award for distinguished service as a labor leader, one who has made an outstanding contribution to the concept of equal opportunity.

Race relations in America stands today at the crossroads. For both white Americans as well as Negro Americans, the moment of truth has arrived. The direction we shall move from this point on depends upon both of these groups of citizens, and their leadership recognizing the certain realities which face us in this celebration of the Centennial of the Emancipation Proclamation. For white Americans, these realities are as follows:

1) The widely-heralded progress which the Negro citizen is supposed to have made, is more fantasy than real, more intangible than tangible. The evidence for this can best be seen when we view the extent to which the gap has been closed in the areas of economics, education, health or welfare, between the Negro American and his fellow citizens. The facts reveal little change in the last ten years. For example the average income of Negro families is 53% that of white families as compared with 1952 when it was 57%. There are 2½ times more unemployment among Negro workers, and in cities like Detroit the unemployment rate is as high as 60% although Negroes represent only 20% of the total population. Housing is actually more segregated than it was ten years ago. According to the 1960 Census one out of six homes in which Negroes live is dilapidated, as compared with one out of thirty-two homes for white citizens. Of the one million new homes built annually during the last ten years less than 3% have been made available to Negro citizens. In education our children still receive 3½% years less; and in the matter of health our parents still die seven years sooner.

2) Another reality that Americans must face is the fact that the day has passed when the Negro citizen can be relied upon to react to his abuses and injustices with despair, resignation, or feelings of inferiority. From this day on his reaction to these inequities will be one of resentment, bitterness and hostility.

3) The disappearance of old barriers and the establishment of new laws or even the adopting of the more polite language will not in and of themselves, substantially erase the 300 years of deprivation, and certainly not for many years to come, unless something special happens. The back wheels of a car cannot catch up with the front wheels unless something special happens. I have insisted that if those who make the decisions in this country are really sincere about closing the gaps, then we must go further than fine impartiality. We must have, in fact, special consideration if we are to compensate for the scars left by 300 years of deprivation, which actually represented special consideration of another type. Equality for a while, therefore, is not enough. We must have better schools, better teachers, better facilities, and all else being equal the Negro should be given special priority in employment, including apprentice jobs.

This is not an original idea, since we recall that after World War II veterans were given a ten-point preference in Civil Service exams because they had been out of the mainstream of American life for four years. Certainly those of us who have been out of it for 300 years are not being unrealistic when we ask for similar consideration.

4) The alternatives to positive and accelerated action in this field are becoming quite clear. Either the Negro citizen will be helped to become a constructive, productive consumer, proud of his citizenship, or he will become a disgruntled, chronic dependent through indifference or casual treatment. Either long-time experienced organizations in the field, like the Urban League,[95] will be given support to provide effective, responsible and most certainly inexperienced. Finally, our choice is between spending millions for programs of prevention, education, and rehabilitation, or billions for social disorganization and international loss of prestige.

For the Negro citizen, he must reflect his new maturity by also facing certain realities:

1) That no individual member of a minority group, however secure and privileged at any given moment, is ever permanently secure and advantaged until the least among these, our brothers, know and feel that same security.

2) That monolithic approaches to the solution of our problems, and no single leader will guide us into the Promised Land. Those who think this, are as naive and out-dated in this jet age as the horse and buggy. It is not a question of whether we need an NAACP or CORE or the Negro American Labor

Council, or the Urban League. The issue is whether we are sufficiently informed on the nature of our problems to recognize the value and the unique contributions which each of these groups can make if sufficiently supported both morally and financially.

3) History has taught us that the struggle for dignity and first-class citizenship must always begin with protest and activities that dramatize the injustices and mobilize public opinion. These are also helpful in the removal of barriers, and the opening of new opportunities. But history has also taught us that this guarantees us only the opportunity. It does not assure us of the desired status.

This is why the organization I represent, the National Urban League, is so crucial and so important at this moment in history. And this is why, though much younger, the Negro American Labor Council can be so important. For, while both of us were born in a climate where protest and righteous indignation were appropriate, and had been the proven formula of other minority groups throughout history; and, while to a degree we must never lose our divine discontent -- we, nevertheless, must face in a responsible way, the total challenge which is ours.

The Urban League sees its challenge beyond that of protest, to assist a citizenry that has been scarred, discouraged, and in many cases demoralized, to take a second look at a new destiny and their role in helping to share that destiny. Toward this end, we therefore make no apologies for concentrating our efforts largely in the area of counseling and guidance of youth, activities designed to strengthen family life, programs of education to stimulate Negro youth and adults to improve themselves through re-training, adult education, and better use of their economic resources. We shall no longer be embarrassed or intimidated by the charge that we are negotiators -- for the mature person must certainly know by now that unless we are represented at the level of policy-making; unless we are there to shape the rules and regulations which implement the new laws; and unless we screen very closely those who have the responsibility to carry out new policies -- then all of the legal changes, the legislative changes, and even the new vocabulary which is so now in vogue, become meaningless platitudes and pious hopes.

Finally, we will no longer be sensitive about the fact that our 350 staff people located in 62 strategic American cities where 70 percent of the Negro population lives, are professionals, and highly-trained and skilled in the areas of research, social science, education, and industrial relations. For today we know, as the labor union has so-well learned, that in order to bring about effective social change, one must be able to compete educationally with those whose policies he would seek to change.

The challenge to the Negro American Labor Council, is also to go beyond the protest stage, and to see to it that every Negro first understands the benefits of union membership; and, secondly, that he participates actively in all meetings and programs of his union. I cannot help but feel that when more than 20 or 30 percent of the membership of the union happens to be Negro, and there are problems of discrimination and lack of representation on the policy-making body -- then a great deal of that blame rests squarely on the shoulders of the Negro members themselves, who have become masters in the art of protest, but remain naive babies in the art of planning and organization.

May I conclude by saying, as forceably and with as much conviction as possible, that it is imperative that we always keep in proper perspective, whatever discontent we in the Urban League, or any other organization in the field, or the Negro American Labor Council itself, may have with organized labor as an institution in our society. Our activity must be clearly focused on a specific and well-documented act of discrimination.

For, in the final analysis, on those basic rights which affect the health, welfare, and social and economic status of the masses of Negro citizens, organized labor has been the institution which uniquely and almost without exception, has been standing by our side.

I am therefore pleased, as a representative of the National Urban League, to join with you on the occasion of your Third Annual Convention, and symbolically associate the Urban League with the objectives of the House of Labor.

At this crucial moment in history, we mutually seek for every citizen his God-given right to dignity and equality of opportunity.

Speech delivered at the third annual Negro American Labor Council convention, New York, November 9, 1962, Box 123 Speeches, Whitney Young Papers, Columbia University.

5. RANDOLPH FEARS CRISIS ON RIGHTS

By Raymond H. Anderson

YONKERS, May 28—A. Philip Randolph expressed concern here today over what he called a "crisis of relaxation" in the civil rights movement.

Mr. Randolph, speaking at a convention of the Negro American Labor Council, said that the passage of the Civil Rights Act of 1964 had led some Negroes to believe that the struggle for equal rights had been won.

"Thus, there is a tendency of the civil rights revolution to lapse into a state of relaxation, as shown by a loss in membership and a deficit financial condition of civil rights organizations."

The Negro American Labor Council opened a three-day convention today at the Westchester Town House, 165 Tuckahoe Road. Mr. Randolph, who is president of the five-year-old group and also head of the Brotherhood of Sleeping Car Porters, delivered the keynote speech at the meeting of about 100 delegates from throughout the country.

"The civil rights revolution, though indispensable to endow Negroes with full, first-class citizenship and with political potentiality to help shape and direct the course of the American government, is wholly inadequate success-fully to grapple with the basic economic and social problems of black Americans," the labor leader declared.

"In the struggle of Negroes to solve the problem of unemployment, they must fashion a new weapon with which to fight," he said. "This weapon must consist of the alliance of the Negro and labor and the black poor and white poor. This is an alliance which has a natural basis because neither the Negro nor labor is fully free."

Mr. Randolph urged that the Federal Government invest billions of dollars in public works.

At an evening rally at the Messiah Baptist Church, the delegates heard the Rev. Dr. Martin Luther King plead for more equal incomes. "Call it what you may," the civil rights leader said, "call it democracy, or call it democratic socialism—but there must be a better distribution of wealth within this country for all of God's children."

The New York Times, May 29, 1965.

6. NEGRO JOBS FOR A STRONG LABOR MOVEMENT

Following are excerpts from the address of Cleveland Robinson, national president of the Negro American Labor Council, to the Council's national economic conference in Washington last month. Robinson is also the secretary-treasurer of District 65, Retail, Wholesale and Department Store Union, AFL-CIO.

The Negro American Labor Council came into existence as the result of the clash between A. Philip Randolph, president of the Brotherhood of Sleeping Car Porters, and George Meany, AFL-CIO president, at the AFL-CIO convention in the Fall of 1959.

At the convention Randolph cited the failure of the AFL-CIO leadership to lend its full weight to the struggle of the Negro workers, or to insist that certain unions abolish their lily-white practices and accept Negroes as equal partners.

Meany rejected Randolph's proposals in arrogant and insulting fashion.
This brought an angry reaction from Negro trade unionists throughout the
country and the NALC was formed in 1960.
The NALC founding convention was based on the conviction that the essence
of the civil rights struggle is an economic revolution.

We realize that segregation, discrimination and the denial of basic human
rights means for Negro masses joblessness, low wages and other forms of depri-
vations. Thus in the midst of the struggle, while we join forces in the broad
civil rights fight, we place emphasis on the economic plight of our people.
The fact remains that despite all the progress that has been made thus
far, economically the Negro masses have made no real progress in terms of
their every day needs. As a matter of fact, statistics could very well prove
that we are worse off today than we were a decade or more ago. In the midst
of unprecedented affluence, and a national output of close to 800 billion
dollars per year, Negro unemployment is still more than twice that of whites.
And unemployment among Negro youth is rising at an alarming pace. Whereas in
1953 average wages for Negro workers was 59 percent that of whites, today's
figures places average wages of Negro workers to be 53 percent that of whites.
The advent of automation and cybernetics, and the lack of basic skills amongst
masses of Negro workers makes him not only an unemployed worker, but too often
an unemployable worker. But perhaps of greater significance is the fact that
in the areas where masses of Negroes are to be found working, their wages are
abominably low and working conditions deplorable.
The fact is that despite headlines from the employer-controlled press about
the strength of the labor movement, less than 20 million of the working people
of the nation are organized. Upwards of 50 million are unorganized and the
unorganized are to be found, in the main, among that 70 percent of the nation's
work force who are not industrial workers, but in service industries.
Our people are to be found in service. Masses of us work in the laundries,
in the hospitals, in the educational system, in the hotel and restaurants, in
the stores and in the fields. We perform services in the homes of the rich.
We perform services which are vital and essential to the life of our community
and our nation in these areas. Yet our jobs are often described as menial.
In most instances we have no unions. We are unorganized and have no way
of determining for ourselves what our salaries should be, what our hours of
work should be, or whether we work or we do not work. It is a fact that
except in rare instances the mainstream of labor has not seen fit to put forward efforts necessary to organize in these areas.
Therefore, it is my proposal that through the initiative of Negro trade
unionists and the NALC, in every community throughout the nation, and especially
in our large urban communities, we convene conferences of all forces concerned
with our struggle. Conferences for the purpose of mapping plans for the organization of our people into unions, unions which we will control, unions that
will be democratic institutions, unions whose programs will respond to our
needs, unions which will be a force to be reckoned with.
It is my belief that with this kind of determination and with this kind of
effort, we will receive the backing of many fine unions now with the AFL-CIO,
or even some independent unions. But it will be up to the people in given
localities to decide with whom they affiliate, or whether they will affiliate
with anyone at all.
Knowing that in unity there is strength, it would therefore be to our
greatest advantage to maintain affiliations and alliances with unions and
organizations whose workers, programs, and philosophies are compatible with
ours.
We of the NALC know that in this society, and in this system under which
we live, strong trade unions are essential for the welfare of working people.
Where there are no unions the people will surely perish. The failures of
certain unions and union leaders to live up to their trust, of necessity had
to be highlighted, and this of course has gotten more publicity in the press
than the good things the unions have done.
For example, there have been more headlines about the discriminatory
practices of certain craft unions and their exclusion of Negro workers from
their ranks or of the collusion between certain union leaders and employers
in signing "sweetheart" backdoor agreements, thus exploiting Negro workers

and others, than there have been of the fine work that has been done by the
vast majority of our unions in elevating wage standards, providing health and
welfare benefits, vacations, pensions and job security for workers.

This has brought about a situation where Negro workers and other oppressed
minorities such as Puerto Ricans and Mexican Americans have looked upon unions
with a certain amount of suspicion and mistrust, and in too many instances have
acted against their own interests by not joining legitimate unions, and fully
participating in the lives of their unions. This situation we cannot permit
to continue.

It is up to us through such conferences as I have proposed in our localities, and by other measures to bring home to the masses of our people the basic
truth that unions are essential, and that in a large sense it is the people,
the workers themselves who really make the union; and that their physical
participation in the life of the union is as necessary as their financial
support.

In these days when there is so much talk about power, I think it is fitting
and proper to state unequivocally that we need power and we must have power.
Our oppressors would want us to believe that we are powerless. The slogan
BLACK POWER has been distorted and taken out of context by people on both sides
of the aisle -- friends and foes alike. And I am here to say that the organization of our people along the lines we are now projecting will be the greatest
manifestation of power ever to be realized by us. Power to demand -- power to
negotiate -- power to decide. Power to make decisions, politically, economically and socially. Unquestionably with this kind of power at our command,
alliances with other groups sharing our views and our objectives will first be
meaningful.

It is my belief that in the same manner and method that we organize ourselves for the eradication of low wages and exploitation, we organize ourselves
so that we can deal effectively with the cancer of discrimination, and adequate
programs for the training of our people for today's job market.

Low wages and exploitation, job discrimination and unemployment carries
with it inherently the social problems so prevalent in the communities from
which we come. These are basically in the areas of housing, health and recreational and educational needs.

In the meantime the administration and Congress, despite declarations to
the contrary, are making it crystal clear that they are not ready to appropriate anything resembling adequate funds for the needs of the millions who are
living in poverty and deprivation. Can we imagine how many jobs could be
created if in our urban areas there was a massive program for building decent
homes, hospitals, schools and facilities for recreational and cultural activities? Certainly if this were done our building trades unionists would have no
fear for jobs since there would be more than enough for everyone who wanted to
enter these trades.

We have to make it clear what we believe our priorities ought to be. If
we believe that our priorities and our national interest and our moral standing
in the world community rests with a continuation of our current foreign policy,
which today is resulting in the expenditure of countless of billions for a war
in Vietnam, and thereby stymieing from a practical point of view any realistic
expenditures at home in these areas which are of vital concern to us, then
those who keep silent or give support to the administration's foreign policy
are correct; but they should have no illusions that through government efforts
there will be any meaningful change as long as this situation continues to
exist.

But if on the other hand, we believe -- as I do -- that our priorities are
here at home, that our nation will be immeasurably strengthened when we have
closed the gap between the fine words articulated in our Constitution and our
Bill of Rights, and our day to day performances, then our prestige with the
world community will grow by leaps and bounds when we have erased from our
society racism and its effects. And that nations will be more quick to emulate
us because of these things, than because of our ability to wipe them out of
existence by our military might.

Hence -- our current foreign policy is wrong from a moral as well as a
practical standpoint. Then I believe it is our obligation to press for this
priority which means in the first place that we demand an immediate end to
the killing and war expenditures, and that we provide for our nation's youth,

real opportunity and hope for life, liberty and the pursuit of happiness instead of the dismal outlook of death on a Vietnam battlefield.

But here again, experience will indicate that the voices of the masses of
people must be heard, and this we can only do through organization. Let us not
forget that organized labor as a force has been responsible for many of the
fine things which today have become a part of our national life. Yes -- there
was a time when the leadership of organized labor was not the conservative and
complacent image that by and large it represents today.

We must profit from these experiences of the past, because then the masses
of the people who constituted organized labor were lowly paid, they knew what
joblessness and exploitation were. They were hungry and they were angry and
therefore, they knew they had to fight. The leadership which arose from their
ranks were men dedicated to their struggle who were prepared to fight all
enemies, employers or government, and to give their lives if necessary to the
cause of the people they represented.

Today we are the jobless, the exploited, the hungry and the angry -- and
what we need is to learn to fight, and fight we must.

The steel workers, the automobile workers, the workers in the coal mines
all have a history. A history replete with violence meted to them by harsh,
vicious and unconscionable employers. But a history made rich by the fact that
they were smart enough to stand together and fight together, thereby winning
for themselves and their families, dignity and self-respect, good wages and
security. So now -- we the black masses must look to ourselves for some of the
answers to the problems that we face today -- and that our children must face
tomorrow.

The Worker, June 25, 1967.

7. FRUSTRATION IN THE GHETTOS: A NATIONAL CRISIS

*Pleas by a Northern Negro Union Leader
and by a Southern Group*

A Northern Negro union leader and a Southern interracial group have responded to the outbreaks in Negro ghettos with statements built on the same
theme: the poverty, discrimination and degradation imposed upon the Negro
people must be ended if riots are to be eliminated and the entire society is
to progress.

Cleveland Robinson, Secretary-Treasurer of District 65, Retail and Wholesale union and president of the Negro American Labor Council, in an article
in the August issue of his union's paper, makes a strong argument for white
to join the Negro in his struggle for equality, "in which whites, too, will be
the gainers."

The Southern Regional Council, an interracial Atlanta-based organization
formed in 1944, issued a statement titled "On the National Crisis," which
itself indicates the council's contention that the problem of the ghetto is
the product of the whole country. "We are compelled . . . to speak to the
nation," said the council, "urging that it act against the causes of the riots
and not merely with repressive force to end them." Below are excerpts from
both statements.

Following are excerpts from Cleveland Robinson's statement:

Whether we like it or not the strife raging in many cities of the U.S. is
on the rise. Some explain it as just a matter of lawlessness, or simple
frustration, or rampant police brutality.

Others blame it on resentment against segregation and poor housing, or
job discrimination, or poor education, or ghetto conditions, or plain ugly
race hatred.

While it is recognized by most people that all of these and other factors
are elements in the picture, many black people are coming to the conclusion
that these elements are really by-products rather than causes. Many who see

things thus have referred to the events of Newark, Detroit and elsewhere as a
rebellion. There is amongst the black people a strong belief that a basic
historic force is revealed in the clashes, and that this very force is the root
cause of what we see.

It stems from a growing self-esteem among dark races everywhere and amongst
the descendants of the African slaves in America. We see ourselves as resisting aggression which we contend America has waged against us for centuries.
We are, in effect, demanding that the U.S. confess its historic crime, agree
to make amends for its sins, and repair the damage it has inflicted upon more
than a dozen generations of black people.

An individual white person who sincerely believes that he personally never
did a black man any harm, who may have contributed to "Negro causes" who perhaps even joined civil rights demonstrations, feels that he is not guilty and,
therefore, not responsible for the conditions of Negro life. He even agrees
to fight to correct these conditions. But he tends to resent what appears to
him as ingratitude, lawlessness, irresponsibility, and, perhaps worst of all,
race hatred in reverse.

Whites will continue reacting this way if they maintain the illusions
which have been obscuring the picture. Can anyone deny that this nation brought
Africans here in chains and forced them into slavery? For whose benefit did
these slaves toil if not for the benefit of white America? And, are not white
workers members and beneficiaries of this America, whose prosperity was at
least in part, eked out of the sweat and blood of the black man?

If the black man feels he is unjustly oppressed why should he obey laws
which are designed to oppress him? Would whites play according to rules in a
game where the cards are stacked against them?

But above all, what good is done, what contribution is made towards a solution of existing problems, by reacting negatively to the black man's efforts to
escape his condition, even though some of these efforts tend to irritate?

Would it not be better to insist that those conditions not be permitted to
continue for a single day? Should you not aim your resentment against those
who talk of war on poverty, but wage war on the poor; who find billions for
guns, but mere pennies for people; who come up with unlimited incentives for
fat corporations, but never a hope for frustrated youngsters?

It is impossible for the black man in America to accept his fate without
resistance. His spirit of rebellion is a positive thing even though his
methods may at times be self-defeating. The reaction to it can make him an
enemy or can make him the initiator of a wonderful surge of human progress.

Undoubtedly the job that needs to be done is gigantic, almost impossible.
In fact it can't be done unless you really remake the nation. Somehow, white
workers seem to have forgotten that the enemy of the black workers is the
enemy of all workers; that their own human needs can never be fully met unless
the very nature of our society is changed. If the black man's rebellion will
hasten recognition of such a need, isn't he making a contribution to all?

If he irritates occasionally as he tries to master the complex technique
of rebellion, is that too great a price to pay for a victory in which the
whites, too, will be the gainers? A nation good enough for black people to
love will be a nation where whites, too, will walk in dignity, in confidence,
knowing that their prosperity, their humanity is not built at the expense of,
but in partnership with, all Americans.

Following are excerpts from the statement by the Southern Regional Council:

As an organization of Southerners of both races dedicated to equal opportunity for all, the Southern Regional Council has watched with profound grief
and alarm the riots that have occurred during this first half of the summer of
1967. But far more destructive than riots would be the failure of the nation
to recognize riots as a symptom of profound failure--social and economic--of
American society to provide a chance for a decent and constructive life for
vast numbers of its people, North and South, white and Negro.

Fully aware of the need for tact and sympathy in doing so, we are compelled
as Southerners, out of a knowledge of our own region's tragic history of
racial antagonism, to speak to the nation, urging that it act against the
causes of the riots and not merely with repressive force to end them.

We would also urge the South, as it continues to strive to restructure its
society to conform to laws of equality and racial justice, to look upon these

322 THE BLACK WORKER VIII

riots which have occurred in Northern cities as a severe object lesson in the
tragic consequences of not achieving these objectives fully for all citizens.
    . . . historically, the South has exported people of both races not
properly prepared for life in a complex modern nation, and with them have
developed new variants of the deprivation and racial antagonisms that have so
long crippled the South. And we can only look about our own region and know
that the same conditions which have exploded into riots exist in many places
in the South.
    The starvation-level poverty in many parts of the rural South is a par-
ticular problem of ours, more severe and punishing probably than any other
poverty in the nation.
    We must note too another grave factor in our current crisis. There now
are millions of Americans outside our economic system, neither contributing to
it or benefiting from it. This must realistically be seen as a serious threat
to the economic system.
    We continue in the conviction that for the South and for the nation, the
only realistic and moral goal in regard to race relations is the full integration of Negroes and other minority groups into the American society. We
recognize and applaud efforts of such groups to develop legitimate methods of
gaining objectives of self-interest, economically and politically. But we
continue to oppose racism and separatism as antithetical to everything America
stands for. It is our belief that Southerners, white and Negro, have moved
and are resolved to continue to move toward the kind of society, one of equal
opportunity and human dignity, made possible by the Constitution of the United
States.
    It is toward this high goal rather than to the absence of riots that we
must look.

The Worker, September 10, 1967.

8. NALC HEAD ASKS LABOR AID MARCH OF POOR

    YOUNGSTOWN, O.—Cleveland Robinson, president of the Negro American Labor
Council, called on the organization to "play a vital role in the remaining
days" of the Poor People's Campaign in Washington.
    He urged the NALC to "carry on the struggle throughout our unions and our
communities to mobilize the poor and oppressed people, and their allies to be
fighters in this cause."
    Addressing the NALC's annual convention here last week Robinson declared
that "this nation is facing a crisis of untold proportions."
    "Our calls for justice by and large have gone unheeded, many times un-
noticed," he said. The "root cause" of the "tragedy of our times" is "white
racism," he added.
    For the past two years, he said, the NALC "has continued to wage limited
struggles in the fight for equality of job opportunities, with some limited
success."
    "The fact is that our work and our activities are still not welcome in
large sections of the labor movement. Maybe, in a way, this is a credit to
us because it means that we are facing issues head-on. We reject compromise,
and tokenism, and we continue to tear away the mask and expose the hypocrisy
that still exists in far too many places."
    "However, there remain areas where our black full-time trade unionists
and rank and file leaders are not full participants in our movement. This we
must view with deep concern, and seek ways and means to encourage and enhance
their participation."
    "This is a time for us to reassess our goals, and make new demands on
ourselves, on the labor movement and on the nation."
    "When we raise quite sharply the question of jobs, meaningful wages, the
breaking down of discriminatory barriers, meaningful training programs, and
show our distaste and impatience, we are so often told or reminded that much
progress has been made, and that black workers are better off today than they
were ten or 15 years ago."

"Is this so—really?" he asked.

"Isn't it a fact," he asked, that

* "the wage gap between black and white has widened not narrowed?";

* "unemployment amongst Negro youth is four to five times higher than among white groups?";

* "with automation and cybernetics all the way from the farms to the factories, thousands of our people are now hopelessly unemployed, and are among the ten million who are going to bed hungry each night, not knowing where the next meal is coming from?"

We know that things are not better, he said.

"For thousands, yea, millions of our people, and others, poverty, deprivation and misery is the way of life," he said.

"So in reassessing our goals we must come to the conclusion that the elimination of poverty and disease and misery, and the bringing about of conditions whereby all may share in the abundance that is available without regard to race or color or creed, must be our nation's highest priority."

"This means demands upon the Congress, upon State Legislatures, upon industry, for radical changes. And it means demands upon our labor movement, that it once again put itself in the vanguard of the struggle for the most oppressed."

"Our first demand upon the Congress, must be the appropriation of funds—funds that will make possible a decent home for every American at prices he can afford to either own or rent."

He called, also for—

* "Complete health care for every American."

* "A job for every worker at meaningful wages."

* Abolition of the current welfare system.

* A pension, equivalent to a living wage, for the "infirm and the disabled, dependent children and widows."

* A "guaranteed annual income at a living wage," for "those Americans who cannot find work" who "can turn their attention to the improving of the academic or vocational skills" while they are unemployed, "thus making them available for today's job market."

* Improvement in social security "to provide pensions for senior citizens on which they can live."

"Six percent of the gross national income," said Robinson, "approximately 50 billion dollars per year is the price tag for these unmet needs."

"We must here take note," he declared, "that today our nation is spending in excess of 30 billion dollars on the war in Vietnam. And an additional 85 billion dollars for defense appropriations."

"This nation must now face squarely the question as to whether it can continue to wage war in Vietnam. A war in which the poor do the fighting and the dying, and the black youth of this country are fighting and dying in Vietnam in high disproportionate numbers. A war in which the Pentagon is spending 71 million dollars to kill rice crops and starve the Vietnamese people. And napalm bombs are killing thousands of innocent women and children. An unjustified war, an illegal underclared war."

"Our demand," he said, "is: stop the fighting, make peace, and spend the money, the talent, and the energy of the nation in creating, prolonging and sustaining the lives of our people here at home, as well as helping other oppressed people."

"This, we believe, is America's best and first line of defense."

"We must make other demands on the Congress and on our nation's executives," he declared. "Too long have we seen the spectacle of corporations and contractors who are practicing discrimination, being rewarded with fat government contracts. We say an end must be put to this."

"We must demand that Congress and the Executive Branch see to it that no corporation, no contractor, does business with the government or performs work where Government funds are involved, where there is not clear cut fair employment to practice on all jobs, and all training programs, and in all hirings pertaining to such firms or contractors."

"We cannot, as workers sit by and see our brothers, Mexican Americans and Puerto Ricans, or our black brothers in the fields," Robinson said, "toiling at starvation wages, exploited as slaves, having no laws to protect them."

He demanded that Congress "pass laws giving collective bargaining rights to all workers," "see that all such workers are protected under laws governing workmen's compensation, fair labor standards, child labor and so on," and "enact minimum wage legislation covering all workers." Such minimum wage at this time should be no less than $2.50 an hour, he said.

"There may be some who feel that the demands outlined are unachievable. To this I must say, it is not our job to determine what is achievable."

"Our job is to determine and place before the nation what is needed. Let the Congress and our nation's chief executive, and the industrialists, those who hold power, let them know what is needed."

"We know what this nation can afford, and that our people are entitled to these things and more, not as charity, but as a right."

Robinson charged that the AFL-CIO executive council "has not seen fit to wage an effective struggle for the most oppressed."

"The dynamic, progressive, demanding, and dissatisfied voice of labor is nowhere present in the top echelons," he said.

"Nor do we find," from the top body of the labor movement, directives or calls for total mobilization of all of labor, to the cause of the oppressed in a manner where the strength of the labor movement, in its totality, including its rank and file, can be brought to bear on a given issue.

"Instead, too often we find this leadership is prone to be satisfied with what 'is possible', and hail mediocre victories and compromises as evidence of progress, when to the victims of discrimination, the oppressed and the have-nots, such results are totally unsatisfactory."

"We believe that the time has come for a change in the structure of the top body of the labor movement," he said, in order "to make possible representation from the most oppressed, the Negro, Puerto Rican, and the Mexican American, in the highest councils of labor."

"We are not asking or suggesting that anyone be replaced," Robinson said, "we are suggesting that the leadership be broadened, for this is the time when people must speak for themselves."

He urged that the AFL-CIO "make available funds to aid in the organization of the most oppressed workers, and develop leadership from their ranks in full-time positions, so that an effective war against poverty can be waged on behalf of such workers."

Robinson called for the building of NALC chapters "in every city and in every community."

"In every union where our black brothers are to be found, strong caucuses must be developed so that an effective struggle can be waged, not only on the broad programs we outlined, but on the basic day to day grievances and problems which our people face."

"We must help our people to get into decent unions, and be good union members, and to develop leadership from their ranks for us workers, progress cannot be made in a real sense without unionism."

"Where we cannot get the help from organized labor" he added, "we can encourage the formation of independent unions of such workers wherever they may be."

The Worker, June 2, 1968.

9. SOMETHING NEW IN THE HOUSE OF LABOR

By Gene Grove

A black-led union of 40,000 workers of all races has set out on its own war on poverty . . . championing and organizing the unorganized, the under-paid, the underemployed. . . .

The minutes dragged by in the stifling afternoon in Suffolk, a little town between Norfolk and Newport News, Va., and although the air conditioning wheezed manfully it was fighting a losing battle, as were the some 100

delegates deadened by the heat and the mounds of ham and Southern fried chicken
they had eaten for lunch. It was a meeting of labor union leaders, and the
people in the room represented some 40,000 workers scattered across the country,
most of them considered unskilled, most of them among the lowest paid, most of
them in what are regarded as menial jobs, half of them black. They had trekked
to this little town to register their final protest against what they regarded
as the irrelevance of their union, the Retail, Wholesale and Department Store
Union, and of the AFL-CIO itself.

When the meeting at last got under way a minister pronounced a benediction
and led the delegates in *Jesus Keep Me Near the Cross,* a good hymn which most
of the black delegates seemed to know and to which most of the white delegates
listened with studied interest. They all continued to listen with care as, one
after another, men approached the speaker's stand to denounce their union.
Then a large, impressive black speaker with a musical accent and glasses like
the bottoms of Coke bottles rose and said, "We belong to the house of labor,
but when the house becomes so rotten and dilapidated that the walls crumble and
the roof leaks and the floors sag, then it's time to get out and build a new,
clean house," and the delegates exploded at last with fervor that brought a
sense of purpose to the room.

As a matter of fact, the speaker, Cleveland Robinson, admitted later that
he had used that same phrase once before, in 1962, as a threat which helped
pry some concessions--which later had proved, Robinson thought, ephemeral--
from AFL-CIO President George Meany, and the *New York Times* had thought it
striking enough then to print it as the newspaper's quotation of the day.
Robinson, too, thought enough of it on reflection to use the words again, and
this time not as a negotiating tactic. Minutes after he sat down, workers
voted to renounce their affiliations with the RWDSU and AFL-CIO and to strike
out on their own as an independent union -- the National Council of Distributive Workers.

The *Times* seemed to have something of a predilection for quoting from
people who were to turn up at this small, even obscure, gathering in Virginia.
Only a few weeks before the meeting it had used another of the speakers, David
Livingston, for its quotation of the day. Speaking of labor's failure to
organize black and Puerto Rican workers, he had said: "To say you're for
civil rights is not enough any more; everybody is for civil rights. The oppressed want power and some share of the responsibility and they have not
generally found relevance in the labor movement." Relevance is a much over-
and mis-used word in these times, but it is a fact that the union officials
meeting in Suffolk were prompted to build anew in what Robinson called "the
house of labor" primarily by the race issue. The immediate causes were contained in a statement read to an RWDSU meeting--and subsequently ignored--which
referred to the "restlessness of the oppressed in our midst," as well as the
Kerner Report's identification of white racism and the necessity for unions to
organize and develop full-time leadership among Negro, Puerto Rican and Mexican
workers. The statement also proposed that the RWDSU, whose national officers
all are white, "rearrange and/or expand its national leadership to include
outstanding Negro trade unionists in its highest echelon of authority and thus
provide inspiration and stimulus to the organization efforts of black working
people." The dissatisfaction went beyond that specific, though, to a general
unease about the direction of organized labor: various spokesmen complained
that many international unions had refused to let down their racial bars and
the AFL-CIO had done nothing effective to force them down, that Negroes were
not admitted to the top echelons of union leadership, that the unions had
failed to recruit and train members of minority groups and that they had
failed to try to organize the poor and the dispossessed. The labor movement,
the spokesmen insisted, no longer was relevant (to again use that word) to the
needs and aspirations of the minorities, the unorganized, the underpaid, the
underemployed, the oppressed.

They punctuated their dissent and convictions, after they had voted to
disaffiliate, by electing Cleveland Robinson president of the new union, an
election which made him the first black president of a multi-racial union in
American labor history, if one remembers that the Brotherhood of Sleeping Car
Porters, led by Robinson's good friend, A. Philip Randolph, is an all-black
union. And if the fledgling union of 40,000 sounds small by the standards of,
say, the Teamsters, the Mine Workers or the Steelworkers, already it is far

larger than such established unions as Randolph's Porters, the American Newspaper Guild or a host of others. Nominating Robinson, Livingston said he would
be "glad and proud to serve in a union with black leadership. We will tell our
members that they must accept the democratic principle. This will be the first
union in America where black leaders are proud to follow." Including Robinson,
four blacks were elected to office, as were one Puerto Rican and three whites.
     The trail that led these 40,000 to break away from the RWDSU and the
AFL-CIO is somewhat winding and the nuances of all the relationships are not
always clear, but the final reason, the one they flung at the delegates to the
convention, was simplicity itself. "It is clear to all," said Livingston, who
is president of what was District 65 of the RWDSU before the break and now is
District 65 of the National Council of Distributive Workers, "that the AFL-CIO
has not faced up to the fight against racism and for liberation."
     Accepting the new national presidency, Robinson put it at some greater
length:
     "The minorities," he said, "are left out of the mainstream of American
life. There are 57 million unorganized workers in the United States, and the
AFL-CIO is not relevant to their problems. The only real war on poverty is
the war of workers organizing for a living wage: for the right to say if they
work, when they work and for what they work. Without a living wage you can't
take advantage of any other rights. The failure of the AFL-CIO to organize the
poor and dispossessed . . . means for the poor whites hungry bellies and for the
poor blacks degradation. . . .
     "We intend to organize near everybody who is now excluded from the labor
movement, and if the AFL-CIO attempts to interfere with our locals we shall not
let them rest. When the poor black and the poor white are liberated, America
will be liberated."
     Robinson's talk comes out rather tougher in print than it sounds when
listening to him. He is a big man who nevertheless gives an impression of
gentleness. His voice, naturally soft, is softened still further by the accents
of his native Jamaica. And the syntax of his speech, a considerable improvement over the extemporaneous offerings of most union laeders, is made the more
impressive by the fact that he retains only a hint of vision after a losing
10-year fight with glaucoma and, as a result, cannot read his speeches. He is,
perhaps, the least known of the significant movers and shakers of the civil
rights movement of the past dozen years, certainly less widely known than
Randolph, Martin Luther King, Jr., Roy Wilkins, Jesse Jackson, Whitney Young,
James Farmer and the rest, less known even than Bayard Rustin, whom Robinson
hired to help him organize the 1963 March on Washington. Yet Robinson is, for
example, president of the Negro American Labor Council, a long-time advisor to
and recently elected a regional representative of the Southern Christian Leadership Conference and a member of the New York City Commission on Human Rights.[96]
He came to this country in 1944 from Jamaica (where he had been, at various
times, a schoolteacher and a policeman), found himself in jobs that paid in the
neighborhood of 30 cents an hour, and within a year was participating in the
struggles to organize the clothing wholesalers and warehouses where he worked.
     "Aside from whatever dedication came to me from a sensitivity to my own
problems and those of my fellow workers," he says, "I was angered at the discrimination I saw when I came to this country, discrimination I didn't see in
the West Indies. There you could aspire to the heights. A man knew there that
the best gift he could give his son was a good education--men would sacrifice
all their lives to send their sons to Oxford--because you knew that if your
son got a good education he could use it to the best of his ability. You didn't
know that here then, and you still don't."
     The union in which Robinson found himself showed its social conscience
quite early. District 65, the union of which Livingston is president and of
which Robinson remains secretary-treasurer while serving, too, as president of
the new Distributive Workers union, began life as a union for Jewish dry goods
workers on Manhattan's Lower East Side. It participated in the great organizing drives of the '30s and through mergers with other locals, such as the shoe
workers, and efforts to organize such as the city's textile workers, its
membership had risen to perhaps 10,000 by the time Robinson joined it and its
ethnic composition was changing rapidly. Within a year after Robinson joined
the union he was made an organizer and not long after that the union leadership, then entirely Jewish, made its first efforts at adjustment to the

altered facts of its life by backing Robinson and an Irish Catholic, Bob Burke, for election as vice-presidents of the union. It later helped form the Distributive, Processing and Office Workers union and took over many of the locals of the Food and Tobacco Workers and the United Office and Professional Workers when those unions collapsed. This, plus the continuing pursuit, as far as Phoenix and Los Angeles and Kansas City, of runaway shops from New York, succeeded in transforming what had been a New York local union into District 65, with shops scattered throughout the country.

Robinson is fiercely proud of his union and, conversely, contemptuous of unions which haven't done as much for the underprivileged. With 25,000 out of the new Distributive Workers' total of 40,000 members, District 65 naturally provided the impetus and leadership for the breakaway, and it was partly to take the focus away from New York that the founding convention was held in the hall of Local 26 of Suffolk. District 65 has some 10,000 black members in its 25,000, while some 70 per cent of the 15,000 members in the 10 locals which joined it in disaffiliating from the RWDSU and the AFL–CIO are black. The members, black and white, remain largely the economically disenfranchised. District 65's big drive right now seems modest enough: its hiring hall is refusing to send workers out to jobs in which the minimum pay is less than $100 a week. Its headquarters remind one as much of the Rev. Leon Sullivan's self-help school in Philadelphia as they do of a union headquarters: there is a co-op drugstore, for instance, a dental clinic, classrooms for the teaching of language and arithmetic skills and, for the Puerto Rican members, English itself. Beyond that, there is instruction in community action, how to get improved bus service and police protection and so on.

The new union didn't begin, naturally, without considerable preparation, all of it directed by District 65. Before they arrived in Suffolk the delegates were assured of a loan of $120,000 from the United Auto Workers to help them get started and of organizing help from both the Auto Workers and the Teamsters.

"If any of the unorganized workers in the country ask for our help," Robinson said, "we are going to help them. We are going to become the vehicle through which they cross the barrier to dignity and full citizenship in this country. We are going to organize the Mexican-Americans, the black Americans, the poor whites and the American Indians. We extend our hand and our strength to those who have seen the door of opportunity slammed in their faces." The union is working on plans for organizing campaigns in 50 cities, in cooperation with the Alliance for Labor Action, a new group headed by the Teamsters, who were thrown out of the AFL–CIO, and the Auto Workers, who quit.

The sort of blanket jurisdiction to organize anyone who is unorganized, primarily the poor and disenfranchised, which the union has arrogated to itself is the reason for its new name, the Distributive Workers, a name broad enough to cover anyone this side of the American Medical Association and necessary, too: already the union has such disparate groups as loggers in Virginia, clothing workers in North Carolina and sanitation workers in South Carolina under its aegis, as well as the people who pack the peanuts for your cocktail party and the people who make the buttons for your dresses. It is, then, neither a craft union in the tradition of the old AFL nor an industrial union in the tradition of the old CIO, but a union willing to be all-encompassing in its style.

In his New York office seven floors above Astor Place at the northern edge of the Lower East Side--where the Bowery begins and just across the street from Cooper Union, the ancient school where Abraham Lincoln made the speech which started him on the path to the presidency, Robinson spoke one day recently of himself and his union.

"Generally, in the labor movement, they say they'd really like to have blacks and Puerto Ricans in positions of leadership but that they've got no one qualified for the job. And it's even worse in industry. In other unions they once in a while give Negroes a title but it's only window dressing and they never see that they do a job. Now, when I was first with District 65 I was placed in charge of 10 or 15 organizers and every one of them knew more about organizing than I did. If they'd have waited for me to have the experience I'd never have made it. It was the same when they made me secretary-treasurer. I was treasurer in name only after I was elected, but I worked in every department--as a bookkeeper, as a teller in the credit union--even if I was the secretary-treasurer, to make myself qualified. What I'm trying to say is that you can take a raw, dedicated guy and train him for the job if you really want to, and that's what has to be done. You can't wait for a person to be qualified because he never will be if he doesn't get the chance and the responsibility."

Robinson by now is quite comfortable with responsibility. Among his many other jobs, he is a founding member and currently is president of the Negro American Labor Council, an organization of unionists dedicated to the elimination of racial bias in the labor movement and in industry. "The only black in the highest councils of the AFL-CIO," he says, "is A. Philip Randolph. In 1959 he documented the racist character of the labor movement and called for action. And George Meany asked: 'Who appointed Randolph spokesman for Negroes and the labor movement?' Well, we showed him." Negro labor leaders formed the NALC, elected Randolph president and Robinson vice-president and by 1962 were threatening to picket the AFL-CIO convention unless someone paid attention to them. Meany agreed to meet with 18 of the blacks--six of them from District 65--before the convention.

"The night before the meeting," Robinson remembers, "there were some who felt we should be docile and polite and they called their own meeting. I learned of it and went and read the riot act and the next day, instead of being polite, we presented a list of angry demands. Meany was totally unprepared. He said of Randolph: 'I don't know what's happened to the old man lately. He seems to be getting senile.' [Meany himself is in his 80s.] We told him off. We pointed out the irrelevance of the labor movement to the oppressed workers. Instead of helping them, the unions and employers, especially in the craft unions, are in a conspiracy to keep the blacks out." (Meany advanced to his present position from New York's Local 2 of the plumbers union which, two years after the confrontation with the NALC, struck the Bronx Terminal Market construction when an employer tried to comply with the state's fair employment practices law by hiring a Negro and three Puerto Ricans who were not union members. The union later said it was not segregated: it had 16 Negroes among its 4,100 members. What was heralded as a concentrated drive to recruit minority group members ended a year later with four Negroes added to the membership, raising the proportion of Negroes to something less than 0.5 per cent).

"We told Meany he must change or the blacks would find a new home," Robinson says. That was the first time Robinson used his analogy about the house of labor. "Meany made some concessions and wound up saying he had misunderstood and at the next convention of the NALC he was the guest speaker. But nothing meaningful resulted from it all. Meany would make speeches and use the proper terms but they just weren't relevant, not in the building trades in particular. Over a period of a year and a half the best they could show was an increase of one or one-and-a-half per cent in the number of blacks."

It was this agitation within the ranks of labor that was the genesis, a little-known footnote to history, of the March on Washington. The NALC convention in the Fall of 1962 projected a march on Washington for jobs and freedom for the late Summer or Fall of 1963, preferably Labor Day, with the emphasis heavily on the demand for jobs for Negroes and an end to industry and union bias. Then the Spring of 1963 saw an outbreak of civil rights activities and the accompanying violence, the freedom rides, the spectacle of Bull Connor's police dogs in Birmingham and all the rest. In late Spring, the Rev. Dr. Martin Luther King, Jr. called on Robinson and Randolph and asked them to move the date of the march up to August and to expand the aims of the march to put pressure on Congress to pass the pending civil rights legislation which became the Civil Rights Act of 1964.

The relationship between King and District 65 was neither sudden nor casual. It dated back to the Montgomery bus boycott in 1956, when King first became a national figure. District 65 had contributed heavily to the boycott-- not from union funds but from gifts solicited from the membership--and through the years had given as much to King's Southern Christian Leadership Conference as all the rest of organized labor together. King attended every District 65 convention from the days of the bus boycott and announced to a Chicago meeting of labor leaders a few months before his murder that he, too, was a union man, "ever since Cleve Robinson and Dave Livingston made me an honorary member of District 65, about 10 years ago." The union's contracts now call for a holiday on Dr. King's birthday. Speaking at one of the conventions, King once said:

"As against the many massive international unions you are small, but only in one dimension. A deep look into your quality shows that you are like a diamond in a massive vein of coal. You have brought your fighting tradition into the present, and wherever there is a battle of decency you have made yourself a part of it. There may be bigger unions, but none with a larger heart and conscience. In a day when all too many unions have lost their vibrant identity of the '30s, District 65 is a refreshing ray of hope. Indeed, you are the conscience of the labor movement. When the day comes that your example is the theme of all in the labor movement, the dream of brotherhood of men will begin to live in the world around us."

After the appeal from Dr. King, the NALC leaders talked with other civil rights leaders and by June word of the March was out. "Whereupon," Robinson remembers, "the pressures began to grow in Washington to forestall the march. All the top civil rights leaders were called into the White House and asked to call it off on the grounds that it would be uncontrolled and that there would be violence. But we went ahead, the NALC and Jim Farmer from CORE and the SNCC people. Early in June we hired Bayard Rustin, four weeks before the announcement of the March, and for those four weeks he was paid out of District 65 funds while he planned the March.

Robinson, by now an accomplished treasurer, took care of the money and shocked everyone by announcing after the March was over--as they waited anxiously to learn how much more than the $150,000 which was raised had been spent and how much more they would have to cough up--that there was a balance of $16,000. Part of the balance could be attributed to Robinson's refusal to pay a bill from the City of Washington for $6,700 for portable latrines. "I was going to pay it," he recalls, "when someone pointed out to me that American Legion parades and such were never billed for latrines, so I said, 'The hell with it.'" Robinson took personal charge of the balance and used it up in contributions to other civil rights activities such as the New York City school boycott and the Poor Peoples' March on Washington. When Randolph retired as president of NALC in 1966, Robinson was elected in his place.

His final defection from the AFL-CIO is explained by Robinson with a certain sadness. "There are grave contradictions in our nation," he says. "It is the richest country in the world but there are millions who work a full day and live in abject poverty, grossly exploited, and you can add to them the millions who are simply barred from their rightful place in society. The government's response is to talk about the war on poverty but in large measure that's a farce. It cannot address itself to the real problems. The only real war on poverty takes place when those who are exploited have organized themselves and achieved power on the basis of the collective bargaining of their wages and working conditions and have determined as an organized group what course they will pursue."

"The AFL-CIO is not relevant to these basic issues. By and large, the masses of Puerto Ricans, blacks and whites have grave distrust for the AFL-CIO despite the fact that they know organization is their only hope. They distrust it because they don't see themselves reflected at all, even in those unions where the majority is black or Puerto Rican. What we have done in the Distributive Workers is to take cognizance of that and to share the power in a real sense. We're determined to use our dues money to help the poorest, those the other unions have disregarded, to organize and control their own unions and to become masters of their own destiny. This is a multi-racial organization in which all will share power, in which our aims and aspirations are to organize the poor, not those who already are in the middle class. The Poor Peoples' Union would be a good alternative name. There are millions of such people, unskilled mostly, doing tasks which in most instances are of the greatest importance in terms of community welfare, subsidizing a rich, affluent society with their blood and sweat."

"I say the only thing that makes a job menial is the wages. People need wages that make them proud and for good wages they are good jobs: for menial wages they are menial jobs. The jobs we're talking about go directly to the health and welfare of a community, distributing food or collecting garbage, for instance. If the doctors in a community go on strike for a week, few people would suffer, but let sanitation men strike or the food processors and distributors, and the community would collapse."

Tuesday Magazine (March, 1970):6, 7, 20, 21, 24.

10.   NALC DELEGATES WARN AGAINST REDBAITERS

By J. J. Johnson

NEW YORK, Nov. 17--Black trade unionists arriving at the Hotel McAlpin for the ninth convention of the National Afro-American Labor Council, which opened today, are meeting at a critical junction in the struggle of Black workers. Many have expressed anxiety about the convention's outcome.

According to some of NALC's New York members, Black workers, who voted overwhelmingly against Nixon, do not have to be warned of the dangers he represents.   The question is, How best to fight him?

The AFL-CIO leadership, headed by George Meany, has been trying to undermine the conference by, among other things, redbaiting the NALC.

According to NALC officials, Bayard Rustin of the A. Philip Randolph Institute, is being employed by Meany to spread his venom.   It was Rustin who recently asserted that all-Black organizations are not needed in the labor movement, since, he said, the AFL-CIO has been taking care of its Black members.

A young worker told the *Daily World;* "The objective problems facing NALC are immense, yet forces within the organization have chosen to place further obstacles in its already difficult path."

Redbaiting Clause

He was referring to Point Seven of the organization's Objects and Principles, which reads: "In pursuit of the abovementioned objects and principles, the National Afro-American Labor Council herewith announces its unalterable opposition to racism, communism, fascism, corruption and racketeering in the trade union movement and the NALC."

Many workers, including young workers, are baffled as to how the NALC can equate the struggles against racism, fascism, corruption and racketeering with the struggle against communism.   Historically, it has been the Communists in the labor movement who have been the staunchest and most consistent fighters against these evils, racism, fascism and racketeering, in or out of the labor movement.

Daily World, November 18, 1972.

11.   NALC CONVENTION URGES POLITICAL ACTION

NEW YORK, Nov. 20--The ninth convention of the National Afro-American Labor Council (NALC) took place at the weekend at the Hotel McAlpin.

About 100 delegates from different sections of the country participated.

Among those who attended or sent messages of support were Percy Sutton, Manhattan Borough president; Rep. Herman Badillo, (D-NY); Nelson Jack Edwards, United Auto Workers vice president; Amy Terry, deputy regional director, U.S. Dept. of Labor, Bureau of Apprenticeship and Training; Dr. Cleveland A. Chandler, chairman Department of Business and Economics, Morgan State College; Harold Gibbons, Teamsters vice president; and Rep. Charles Rangel (D-NY).

William Lucy, Secretary-Treasurer of the American Federation of State, County and Municipal Workers, AFL-CIO, addressed the Saturday evening banquet.

Three Workshops

Three workshops on economic action, community action and political action, were held Saturday afternoon.   The next day, the delegates heard the reports from the workshops.

The political action workshop stressed the need for Afro-Americans to participate in the electoral process.   Reference was made to the fact that 87 percent of the Black community had voted against President Nixon.   The fact that 46 percent of eligible voters, a large percentage Black and Brown, did not vote was also emphasized.

Anti-Communist Clause

Charles Wilson, a member of Local 719, UAW, in Chicago, called for removal
of the anti-communist clause in the constitution. He recalled how anti-
communism was used to destroy a 500-member NALC branch in Chicago.

Cleveland Robinson, NALC's president, replied, "Anti-communism is a constitutional matter and not a subject of debate. For practical and organizational
reasons, the executive body of this organization saw fit to include this clause.

"We do not redbait. We condemn redbaiting and will exclude no one for
political beliefs. But we will not be controlled by anybody, right of left.
When the gavel goes down, the majority rules. We changed the constitution two
years ago and eliminated what we felt was unnecessary."

Jobs for Youth

The economic action workshop took up the questions of full employment,
minimum wages, the organization of the unorganized and areas of discriminatory
practices.

A report by Beverly Pyron, of the Young Workers Liberation League, on
unemployment among youth brought cheers from the crowd.

"A deep crisis," said Pyron's report, "faces the young people of our
country, particularly Black youth. . . . Throughout the country we witness
brutal attacks against Black youth. The slaying of two Black youths in Baton
Rouge is only one of many brutal attacks. These attacks have resulted in a
rising tide of unpunished police. FBI and National Guard attacks, and frameups
against Angela Davis, the Soledad Brothers and other militant figures."

". . . The generation gap concept is used to keep young and old apart in
the movement when the only gap is between working people and the bosses. We
address our resolution to the following problems.

"1) On the job training with pay.

"2) Unemployment insurance for first job seekers.

"3) Job programs for Vietnam veterans and ex-prisoners.

"4) Open admission with remedial programs.

"5) Equal minimum wage for youth.

"In order to meet these problems we would like the convention to go on
record as a supporter of the concept of a National Youth Act."

A resolution urging a $2.50 an hour minimum wage law was passed by the
convention.

Community Action

Jim Davis, head of the Youngstown, Ohio, chapter delivered the community
action report. He called for building autonomous community groups and establishment of an educational program within each group.

A young worker from Philadelphia attempted to open discussion of the anti-
communist clause, but he was called out of order.

Leo Rabouine, president of the New York Chapter, stressed the need to
fight for guaranteed pensions. He cited the case of a worker in his local
(Brewery, Teamsters) who retired but was unable to collect his pension.

Felicia Coward, a young electrical worker from Philadelphia, spoke of the
dangers of runaway shops to Black workers and the entire labor movement.

A delegate told the *Daily World,* "We have a good program and the workers
are ready. We must now organize to implement that program."

Daily World, November 21, 1972.

COALITION OF BLACK TRADE UNIONISTS

12.   CONFERENCE PROCEEDINGS, COALITION OF
BLACK TRADE UNIONISTS

Chicago
September 23-24, 1972

OPENING SESSION
SATURDAY, SEPTEMBER 23, 1972

MR. HAYES:

Ladies and gentlemen, will you please clear the aisles and take your
seats. We are ready to proceed with the first annual Conference of Black
Trade Unionists. Please clear the aisles. Will the Sargeant-at-Arms please
clear the aisles.[97]
(PAUSE)
This is a very historic occasion. Assembled here today is one of the
single largest gatherings of black trade unionists in the history of the
American Labor movement.

MR. HAYES:

Before we proceed further let me call on someone who is a civil rights
activist and certainly a friend of the Trade Union movement, one with whom I
served as an Executive Board Member of Operation PUSH nationally, and who is
pastor of Monumental Baptist Church here in Chicago. I give to you The
Reverend D. E. King for the invocation.[98]
Reverend King.
(The audience rose for the invocation).

THE REVEREND MR. KING:

Thou Who hast made us in Thy image and after Thy likeness, O God, we
come acknowledging Thee and all Thy ways, for Thy ways are right and altogether
holy.
We come to acknowledge Thee in all our ways, for our ways are not always
right, nor are they always holy, but in whatever way we find ourselves, we
acknowledge Thee, for we know that we were not made by blind chance or by unthinking dust, but we were made after Thy Supreme Intelligence.
As we come, we pray that Thy wouldst forgive us for not making of ourselves all that we should be, for not making our respective communities all
that they should be, for not making of this nation and of this world what
they should be.
Forgive us for not pressing our claim to the highest and best in humanity
and as trustees of Thy creation. We thank Thee for these Union leaders and
members from the various states, and we pray for them as they assemble here
for their convention.
We especially pray that they might be sensitive to the unnamed and unap-
preciated masses who merely exist trying to live, working for others who live
by the sweat of their brows.
We pray that they may be sensitive to the unexpressed emotions and to the
inaudible sentiments, and we also pray, O God, that Thou wouldst help these
leaders and these members of this Union to speak for people who cannot speak
for themselves, and to act for people who are unable to act for themselves.
May all of us, whether we are of religious persuasion, or civic, or
political, help us to unite in one common bond of leadership to give leadership to those who need us.
We pray Thy blessings upon the President, upon his corps of officers and
workers. We pray Thy blessings upon the homes of those who have come to
Chicago. Bless their families, and bless their labors back home, and may Thy

peace and love abide with us throughout this meeting, and we will give Thee the praise and the glory and the honor due Thy name.

We will be trustees of Thy creation and of the work that hast been assigned to our hands. In the name of Jesus Christ who came to save the masses and to make us free, we pray. Amen.

MR. HAYES:

On your behalf I want to say to Reverend King that we are appreciative of his taking time out from his busy schedule to give us those words of wisdom and to express words of blessing over our conference here.

We would like to extend to him a welcome opportunity, if his schedule will permit, to spend as much time during our deliberations at our conference as he so desires.

Now, to those of you who don't know me, I am Charles Hayes, Vice President of the Amalgamated Meat Cutters and Butcher Workmen of North America; one of the convenors of this conference; one who has the honor and privilege of making a few remarks in the opening of this historical conference and extending to you some words of welcome, those of you who are from out of town.

Let me say at the outset, personally, I want to thank each and every one of you for being here. You don't know what it might mean in terms of results your coming here to this kind of conference.

We have people here from every corner of this United States -- North, South, East and West, -- who are Trade Unionists, who have responded to our call to be here today and tomorrow.

What you have done here has superseded anything that I ever dreamed that we had any right to expect.
(Applause)

Some of you have come here with great sacrifice. Some of you here didn't come with the umbrella or the blessings of your own organization. You have done so on your own, because you recognize the need to get together and have some dialogue on some of the problems that are of deep concern to black people who are in the Trade Union movement.

We also have among our midst some white Union leaders who feel the same as many of us do when it comes to recognizing the kind of problems that need immediate attention on the part of the members and leaders of the Trade Union movement.

Most of us realize and want to say it in a most profound way that the leadership of the AFL-CIO certainly did not reflect our views when they came out with a position of neutrality in this year's Presidential Election.
(Applause)

There are many white Trade Unionists who share that view. Many of us realize, too, that we have to begin to give some profound thought to some kind of an ongoing structure that stretches beyond the November elections and reaches out into the bowels of the Trade Union movement to give some guidance and sense of direction in helping us to overcome some of the shackles that are around our ankles within the movement.

We are deeply concerned about the failure of many unions to recognize the need for the elevation of blacks and other minorities into policy-making positions and we intend to try to change this. It is only through organization that we can hope to do it.
(Applause)

Let me hasten to say that I am not suggesting or telling you that it is the purpose of this conference to form and leave here with a structure designed to compete with existing Trade Unions.

We intend to organize and work within the effectuate certain reforms, just like the Democratic Party did in Miami Beach.
(Applause)

During our two days here we are going to be quite hard at work in workshops, panels, and we have tried to select people who will be able to impart to others some of the knowledge and expertise that they have on the given subject matter.

We certainly aren't going to discourage full participation on the part of the people who are here in the discussions. However, let me caution you that we will not be able to permit monopolization of discussion on the part of any one or two individuals.

(Applause)

I know that many of us are orators in our own rights (Laughter) and have one weakness. The only thing we need is an audience, and when get it we are hesitant about turning it loose. (Laughter)

Well, we don't intend to, but we haven't provided you with a forum for you to turn loose the whole ball of wax on people. Express yourselves as concisely as possible, as briefly as possible, and understand that we will not be able to conclude a conference here that will please everybody, or satisfy every whim or wish, or every idea.

Whatever decisions we finally arrive at will, in our opinion, be decisions which will be couched against a backdrop of what is best for the whole. This is the only way we can look at it -- not individually as such.

We are pleased to have with us this afternoon a representative of Congress who is a member of the Black Legislative Caucus, and even before he went to Congress he stood on the side of organized labor, and more recently, has been making his voice certainly heard in the civil rights arena, particularly in the area of brutality of police against citizens here in the City of Chicago.

He has gotten out of favor, to some extent, with the Establishment because of his positions, but this is in recognition that his first allegiance is to his constituency, the majority of whom are black like us.
(Applause)

So it is with a feeling of great honor and pleasure that I give to you now a friend of mine, a leader in the political arena, Congressman Ralph Metcalf.[99]
(Applause)

CONGRESSMAN METCALF:

Thank you very much, Charlie Hayes, for that very splendid and very elaborate introduction.

To the members, the convenors of the Black Trade Unionists, in addition to Charlie Hayes who very modestly omitted telling you that he is the Chairman of the Labor Committee of the First Congressional District of the State of Illinois, which I am proud to represent.
(Applause)

Also, he is an advisor on labor matters; a very distinguished and dynamic Bill Lucy, Mr. Jack Edwards, Mr. Cleve Robinson, and Mr. Bill Simmons, all convenors. I would like for you to know that I am right-handed, and I want to now give recognition to my right arm. That is Mrs. Addie Wyatt, Addie, will you stand.
(Applause)

Platform dignitaries, delegates, my brothers and sisters in the labor movement, my brothers and sisters of the Black Trade Unionists, I am most appreciative of the invitation to come and address you this afternoon.

But, Charlie, if you had only said, "Ralph, would you stick your head in the door and just see this outpouring of dedicated Black Trade Unionists," my afternoon and my day would have been complete without me having said a word.
(Applause)

This is indeed an inspiration to me, and we all need to inspire others, because the tasks before us today and tomorrow are monumental. I compliment you on your concern about the oncoming election, your desire to have a massive registration. And I hope that massive registration is being thought of in terms of 100 percent.

I am where I am because I am a team member. I listen to my advisors, and then I am frank with those that I talk with, and I am going to be frank with you.

Sometimes we want to pat our chests and take a great deal of pride before we are really entitled to it, and, therefore, we dilute our real effort in the goal that we are seeking -- which is to bring about meaningful changes in the Trade Union movement, to eliminate discrimination, and to make all of us free.

What we really need to face up to is the fact that you and I have not been successful in encouraging and urging the vast majority of our people to register and vote.

Let me tell you what the Establishment thinks -- I am no longer of the Establishment -- Charlie and Addie Wyatt have made me free.

(Applause)

They look upon us as just a minority, a minority who casts fewer votes than any other ethnic group. And if you want to prolong the struggle that we are confronted with, then keep our voting record down to the level that it has been.

But if you want to really have recognition and then move in the right direction, then it will be the numbers that count, for there are those who work on strategy -- and President Nixon is one -- who say that the blacks don't come out and vote in sufficient numbers to warrant his really programming for us.

This, to me, is one of the challenges that I think all of us must accept. Certainly, you are to be complimented as Black Trade Unionists for working toward the goal of bringing the vast number of minority group members who are presently excluded from participation into the economic life of our country, into areas where they have, and are still being excluded.

You are to be complimented for working toward the cessation of inequities that bring about the discrepancies in the hiring of our people, and thus we have the unfortunate statistic of being more unemployed than the national average.

I say to the Black Trade Unionists that while you have come a long, long way -- for I remember when you emerged, Charlie, out of Operation Breadbasket[100] -- to a very viable and a dynamic force. You are today only at the crossroads.

There is a new black man, and there is a new black woman, and there is a new white person who thinks as we do, and we have new and truly great black leaders, which is terribly important.

I read an article in the paper recently where some of the white fathers discouraged some of the black brothers and sisters from attending this convention. I would want them to come here today, see who is here, see the prestigious group that is here, see what we are talking about, and let them catch up with the changing times.

(Applause)

For we are emerging from that state. I don't see a handkerchief on anybody's head here today.

(Applause)

I see men and women, and they only reflect strength and determination, and that is the way we are going to achieve it. We want to send the word out that we are capable of making decisions, of selecting our own leaders, and participating at the decision-making level.

(Applause)

I raise the question, and I haven't had a chance to talk with my labor advisor, but I want to know how many black people were involved in the decision-making when George Meany decided that AFL-CIO will be neutral.

(Applause)

Well, this is our answer to him. No longer -- no longer are we content to be taken for granted. No longer are you to tell us what to do, but you are to discuss with us, and we will make our own agreements.

(Applause)

I have said over a period of time that every election is different. It is different because you have different candidates. You have different issues, and the times are different.

But this is a unique election like I've never seen before. There is this idea of neutrality that they are trying to encourage us to witness. They don't tell you that those who are going to vote for President Richard Milhous Nixon -- the suburbanites, the upstaters, the downstaters -- will be coming out for the minority party while we stay home.

I must refresh those of you in the State of Illinois with what happened a few years ago, and I think that history is good to let us know where we have been, but to prepare us for today and tomorrow.

We had a great liberal in the United States Senate. His name was Paul Douglas, a proven liberal. He had the nerve, the audacity, to be democratic and to bring about change. He had the nerve and audacity to appoint a black man, Henry Magee, as the Postmaster of the world's largest post office, here in Chicago, and that position had heretofore been awarded to a white German-American.[101]

And they resented it. So, when election time came, a little rain fell, and our people just didn't bother to come out and vote.

(Applause)

At that time I was the Chairman of the City Council's Building and Zoning Committee. I inherited and welcomed the support of my administrative assistant, who was Polish, and who was also at that time a ward committeeman.

He related to me what happened, that as he would go into the black precincts, the judges would be sitting there twiddling their thumbs with no one to vote. He went into the Lithuanian precincts and into the Polish precincts, and he found them standing out in line with raincaps on waiting to get in and vote against this liberal, Paul Douglas.

Now, what does that say to us?

We want to make sure that we know where our raincaps are on November the 7th.

(Applause)

And we want to remember that if we are to have more friends who are liberal -- be they black or white -- then we have got to come out and reward them for what they have done for us.

So, our problem is that of indifference. Black youth are not sufficiently motivated, and this world is theirs, after we prepare them for it, and they ought to be exercising the right to vote.

I was one of those who fought for that right to vote, but we have not motivated them. Rather, we stay in the area of "The party ain't no good," or "The white man ain't no good," you know, instead of saying we are going to bring about changes.

So, we get right back into this old thing called neutrality, call it apathy or indifference, and Dante said in his *Inferno*, "The hottest places in Hell are reserved for those who in times of great moral crisis maintained neutrality."

And that is our position.

(Applause)

We are confronted with the problem of being neutral, or of being active. I've seen a lot of pieces of literature, but let me tell you that while I was waiting for you to convene I had a chance to read this.

I ask you -- I beg you -- not to read it as a piece of literature, but rather to read it as information that you can take with you and that can motivate you, and you, in turn, can motivate others to do the job. I endorse every word in this particular piece of literature, including that part that says we can't depend upon the Democratic Party machine bosses to defeat Nixon. We've got to do it ourselves.

(Applause)

You know, you are going to hear me making some strange sounds soon at the proper time about a certain candidate that is running for a high County office which I am very much opposed to and will try to do everything that I can to bring about this defeat.

He happens to be a Democrat, but he "ain't in my corner" and he "ain't in your corner," and therefore, we are going to work against him.

(Applause)

I think what we've got to recognize is that if President Nixon, whom everybody in Washington says is the biggest politician ever to sit in the White House, is allowed four more years, he will ruin us. He will absolutely set us back.

I am not a great historian, but I do know what happened during Reconstruction days. There are those of you who think that we in the Congressional Black Caucus are doing a marvelous thing. We have thirteen members -- a mere pittance of what we ought to have. That is not even as much as we had during Reconstruction days.

We have only one black United States Senator. We had two at that particular time. So we are still really playing catchup, and when you see what he -- President Nixon -- has done in stacking the Supreme Court with strict constructionists -- you know what that means? "Racist."

(Applause)

And I know of no President who has not during his four years in office had a chance to name at least one or two more members to the Supreme Court. And the Supreme Court makes the law of our land. Let us quickly review.

There are some of us who believe that we started our ascendancy up when the Supreme Court ruled that there should be no discrimination in education, but I submit to you that there was a momentous decision that was passed down before that.

That decision was that racially restrictive covenants shall not be enforceable in the courts of law, which means that we, by Constitutional rights, have a right to move and have our being and live wherever we can afford and have a desire to live.

Then, of course, came the 1965 Voting Rights Act, and look today at the number of black elected officials that we have. Over two thousand of them spread out throughout the width and breadth of the United States, and it is still but a pittance of our percentage of the population.

So, we cannot afford four more years of Richard Milhous Nixon, and we cannot look forward to eight years of dominance and catering to special interests and disregarding the labor man, the black man, the minorities, the liberals, those who want to move ahead.

Already as you have seen, as I did, viewing the Republican National Convention, that they cut down those handful of liberals who wanted to follow the Democratic Party program of opening up the party to women equal to their population, to minorities equal to their population, to youth equal to their population.

If we don't give our youth a chance to participate in the early years, they won't be prepared to do it when they get into adult life.

At the Republican Convention they set the stage for Spiro Agnew to be the Republican nominee four years from now. Mrs. Pat Nixon said already that he was her candidate for the Presidency in 1976, and you know she wouldn't be talking unless she had conferred with Richard. (Laughter)

You talk about credibility, and this is something that all of us have to be really on our toes and wide awake about, that we really look at the word "credibility," where the Republicans are trying to show that our very champion of democracy, our champion of the rights of all people, Senator George McGovern, lacks credibility.

I say, to the contrary, he is a man of great courage and determination, and he has taken some very calculated risks for the principles that he believes in.

(Applause)

Contrast that, if you will, with the statement that was made by General Dwight David Eisenhower -- and he got away with it -- when he said just some few weeks before he ran for election, that if elected, "I will go to Korea."

He was elected. He did go. But I ask you what the hell did he accomplish?

But the American people were moved by that, and four years ago the American people were moved when Richard Nixon said, "I have a secret plan to end the war in Vietnam."

Well, he didn't say when, and it is still a secret, and we are still spending $24 million an hour to keep up the escalated war in Indo-China, when that money ought to be spent domestically.

I have voted against all of these military appropriations.

(Applause)

I think that money ought to be spent domestically. Then, when we see the expose of the alliance between the Republican Party and the donations given by ITT, it was so hot they had to leave San Diego and move to Miami to let it cool off.

We see the President still favoring the favored few by tipping off the world market in wheat in Russia and, therefore, they made a killing on that. And they talk about "credibility."

Here we catch red-handed members high in the Republican Party coming into the Democratic headquarters at the Watergate Hotel in Washington and bugging it. Where can we have any sense of security, any sense of privacy?

They stop and search and frisk us, a typical example of the fears that we have today, and we have a Governor here who said, when he was campaigning, "I will not raise the taxes."

As those of us in Illinois know, the first thing that he did, the first year, was to raise the taxes and insult the intelligence of the electorate by thinking that if he did it right away, they would forget it three years from now, which will be 1972, but we haven't forgotten it.

So, we must recognize that we have to reorder our priorities, and we have to be looking at labor as it truly is in the present situation and devoting our time to education, to housing, to a reduction of crime.

But who is going to do that? It is going to have to be you, the labor leaders, the leaders of our community, the ones that we depend upon to lead us and bring us victory.

Don't be caught up with this negativism about polls. We remember what happened when they said that Truman couldn't win. And I tell you this, that he did win by one vote per precinct in the United States.

John Fitzgerald Kennedy won by less than one vote per precinct. And we can be the difference. I don't ask for us to be the difference between his winning or losing. I ask that we be a part of the main body to pile up the votes so that we can have a victory not only for George McGovern, not only for Sarge Shriver, not only for liberal members of the Congress, but for liberality in itself.[102]

Then, and only then, can we have aspirations of truly being free.
(Applause)

MR. HAYES:

Thank you, Ralph, for giving us those inspiring and informative remarks.

At this time I have an important announcement to make.

There are some people who have taken the liberty to park their automobiles outside of the hotel and proceeded to become participants in this conference. I may already be late, because I forgot to tell you when we first started that the hotel has held them off as long as they can.

The first procedure when you park in a no-parking zone in the downtown areas of Chicago is to place a ticket on your car. And if that doesn't move you quickly, the tow truck will be along and move it for you.

Then you will have to pay the cost of the ticket, plus the expense of towing and storage when you retrieve your car.

Now, let me make a few introductions. To my extreme left is the International Vice President of the Textile Workers Union, Brother Ed Todd.[103]
(Applause)

I want to introduce -- you have heard from Congressman Metcalf. The next person will be introduced by someone else. This young lady here is Mrs. Gwen Hemphill, the secretary to Brother Bill Lucy. I just can't help but introduce her.
(Applause)

On the extreme right is a representative of the United Steelworkers Union, Brother John Thornton. Would you stand, please.
(Applause)

Next, sitting to him, to his left, is Brother Tom Turner who heads the Wayne County AFL-CIO Council, and is also a member of the Steelworkers Union. Brother Turner.
(Applause)

I see we've got some Steelworkers out in the audience. I notice the manner in which they leap up.

Next to Brother Turner is the Director of the State, County and Municipal Workers here locally, Brother Neil Bratcher.
(Applause)

The norm would have been to have you hold your applause until the end, but I thought it was just unfair not to permit some of you to let your steam off. (Laughter)

Next is a leader of the United Automobile Workers Union, Sister Lillian Hatcher.
(Applause)

Next to her, to her left, is a Vice President of the Distributive Workers Union who operates not only out of New York but all over, particularly in the South, Brother Cleveland Robinson.
(Applause)

Now it is my great pleasure to introduce to you your Conference Chairman, who is one of the convenors of this conference and certainly is well represented here by members of his organization.

He recognizes full well what unity of purpose means. His International Union has for many, many years exemplified by action what the struggle for human and economic rights means for working people.

This dynamic leader of the Trade Union movement, while he concerns himself with the problems of collective bargaining, certainly finds ample time to participate in the political struggles and the social struggles which take place not only within the Trade Union movement but within the communities in which we live.

He is a big leader in more ways than one, not just physically, but in terms of his sphere of operations. So it gives me a great deal of pleasure to present to the conference your Permanent Chairman, International Vice President of the United Automobile Workers Union, Nelson Jack Edwards.[104]
(Sustained applause)

CHAIRMAN EDWARDS:

For those very kind remarks, I recognize Charlie's remarks as being the high point of the day, so far as I am concerned. If I would now take my seat and you believed all that Charlie said about me, my day would be a great day.

But Charlie didn't use a piece of equipment that I think is very, very great, because Bill Lucy decided that the old gavel that he chairs AFSCME meetings with, or the gavels that we have chaired many of our Local Union meetings with, was not sufficient for a new beginning, and he went out and bought a new gavel.
(Applause)

This gavel -- this gavel someday generations down the road I hope, will be in a museum, and the youngsters of our posterity will understand why we bought it and what it achieved.
(Applause)

Now we have had several meetings, obviously, to get this kind of outpouring, and we thought we had overshot our field when we said that we would go for a goal of one thousand Trade Unionists from across the length and breadth of this country, that was in total disagreement with Mr. Meany's neutrality.

At this point we said this, many of us thought that if we have a session and only have five hundred people there, it's going to look bad for us. It will signify the fact that maybe we are disturbed and our colleagues are not.

Well, I want to report to you that we have already registered 950 delegates to this conference and we are still registering.
(Applause)

I am sure that before the day is over the figure of one thousand will be down the drain, because it could very well go down the drain with my next statement.

Over in the Century Room is a room that we were able to secure for guests. We had expected to have space in this hall to house non-delegate members to this conference.

You need not take my word. Just look around. There is no space for one guest. We are going to be cramped for space for delegates. But over in the Century Room is a group of guests that came here to be with us in this conference, and I am going to predict that there are fifty or more over there, so the one thousand figure has been achieved already.
(Applause)

Now we come together here today voluntarily. No one twisted your arm to come. No one twisted our arms to call you to come. We decided in Miami -- Bill Lucy and I and Charlie Hayes and others -- always keeping in mind the Old Pro, Cleveland Robinson, that somewhere along the way labor representatives must rise to the point of demanding respect and recognition.

Now, in Miami that was a big convention. The track was fast, and everyone was doing his thing there, and no one thought about you or the representatives you sent there. You had more lawyers speaking for labor people than ever before. You had the clergy there telling what was good for all of you, and we never got a chance to say a word.

We had technical, professional people there saying what was good for you that never associate with you, never know a thing about your hopes and aspirations, but they spoke for you.

We decided that it was about high time that the labor movement stand on its feet and say that there is a section of the labor movement that was ignored -- the black section -- that the next Democratic convention, we will go into that convention united and we will demand respect and no one will take it away from us.

(Applause)

Now, Chicago is a great city, for many, many reasons. But Chicago is a symbolic city if you look at the purpose for which we came here. In 1890, a conference was held in this city, and the delegate attendance was 145 delegates.

The delegates came into this city and formed the Afro-American League of the United States. And the purpose that brought them here is the same purpose that brings us here today.

I will read to you, quoting from the stencil history of that conference:

"They gathered themselves for the purpose to protect against unfair taxation, to secure a more equitable distribution of school funds, to insist upon a fair and impartial trial by a judge and jury, to resist by all legal and reasonable means mob and lynch law, and to insist upon the arrest and punishment of all such offenders against their legal rights."

Now, you can say, if you will, that you are from a certain section of the country, and that while lynch mobs and that sort of thing is passe, is no longer with us, that if you are from Michigan, you can say that. If you are from New York, you can say that. If you are from Ohio, you may say that.

But I can tell you that I am a seed from Alabama, and I wouldn't want to write that off at this conference. We had better prepare to fight against it coming upon us again, because it has not disappeared from the American scene.

A growing mentality in this country suggests that in Alabama, Georgia, Mississippi -- where my good friend Charles Evers can't see the difference between the two candidates -- I don't know what's blurring his eyesight.

I see very clearly the difference between the two.

(Applause)

One is against us and the other is for us. But let's be candid about the whole subject. We have never had in the history of this country, to my knowledge, and I have read about evil men in the White House to a degree, but we have never had a man in the White House that fanned the flames of hate and racism against us.

When Tilden and Hayes made the great compromise in 1886, President Tilden didn't do a thing for us. The deal had done enough against us, and he went on through four years of doing nothing except what he was told.

And you can read into your history, looking for the guy in the White House that said no blacks ought to be housed in the suburbs because it's not good for the nation. Blacks ought not to have integrated schools, after the Supreme Court says separate but equal means inherently unequal, and he says no, we ought not integrate our schools.

The Congress prepares a bill to deal with unemployment, and he says, "I can't sign that bill, although it is passed by the Congress. It is inflationary."

You send a kid to school that is out of a home that is a welfare home, and he has built the welfare rolls higher than they have ever been in the history of this country, but he vetoed the bill to give them milk and food in the classroom.

If you can't see the difference between that man and Mr. McGovern, I suggest that we ought to all go home and die early so our posterity can bury us.

(Applause)

Now it is fairly obvious that when things are bad in this country, it is always worse for us. We are never on the same plateau no matter how bad things are. But even when things are good in this country, they are not good for us in many cases.

And the unemployment figures that run through the fabric of this country suggest that Mr. Nixon is really wrestling with bringing down unemployment. 5.6 percent of the population that is in the work force is unemployed, but that tells you nothing about what we have in our section because we help to magnify that 5.6 percent, but if you pull us out of that, it becomes 5.1 percent.

And if you look at what happens to us if you separate us from that figure, it then becomes 9.7 percent nationally, and if you bring in our younger people, it goes up to 25 percent.

I can tell you that I worked for a living for a long time in a lot of places, and nothing is more wrecking and discouraging to young people that are looking for jobs and praying that some employment manager will hire them than to have them constantly turned away and told there is no need for your services.

Think of the demeaning value in that alone, and that ought to be enough to make anyone wake up and speak out in behalf of his children. Never mind what's happening to me that's good. I have children and I know what's happening to them in many cases, and you have children, too.

So what we must do here today and tomorrow is to find out how we can collectively bring about a cohesive movement that will say to all concerned, "Don't take us for granted. We are not automatic. And if you think we have no place to go, we will give you desolation and you won't have any place to go because you're not going to use us as a rung."

Now, finally, I am going to give you what the Congress can talk about, and then I'm going to go on with the program.

Thurgood Marshall, one of the greatest jurists, I think, this nation has ever known, was speaking in Washington at a White House Conference in 1966, and he had this to say about the law.

Before I give you the quote, I think you ought to understand that we have only two areas that are available to us to make progress in behalf of ourselves and our families in the political-judicial area.

If we fail in politics, it is almost obvious that we're going to fail in the courts, and especially when a court is stacked against us, such as the Supreme Court is now stacked against us.

So Thurgood has this to say. He said, "Some lessons for the future is the history of the struggle for Negro rights."

Marshall went on to say, "What is striking to me is the importance of the law in determining the condition of the Negro." "He was effectively enslaved not by brute force, but by a law which declared him a chattel of his master, who was given legal rights to recapture him even in free territory."

Now if you think the law doesn't bear upon us, you kid yourself. We can't win in that area yet, but I'll tell you where we can win, where we can make progress, and that is in politics, and that is why we are here.

We all have received great equity from collective bargaining, or otherwise you wouldn't be here. You are leaders and activists in that area, and if we do what this conference was designed to do, and that is have every one of you become a missionary of good will, because our communications system basically differs from this updated, elite system that TV pawns are trampling around and picking up guys. They are not going to pick us up here.

They care less about us, because we are against Mr. Nixon. If this was a black conference in behalf of Mr. Nixon, you would have TV strewn all across these aisles.

(Applause)

What we must do -- what we must do is go back home and never mind the tom-tom drums. We have other ways of doing it now. We sold those, got rid of them. They were not effective enough.

We must go back home as missionaries from this conference and decree that no matter what happens on November 7th, we shall not cease our efforts, and what will happen, I think, on November 7th can greatly be determined here today and tomorrow in this conference.

(Applause)

Now, it is my job to move this program, but I just had to say something. I am going to bring to you now a young man that I have a great deal of respect for. All working class, no matter what their color have a great deal of respect for him.

No matter where you hear the name, if men and women have heard of work that he has done, they say, "Oh, he is great. I'd love to meet him."

Well, many of you here today will meet for the first time this great labor leader, the Secretary-Treasurer of AFSCME, Mr. William Lucy.

(Sustained applause)

MR. LUCY:

Certainly one of the great labor leaders of our time is Nelson Jack Edwards, and I am pleased, first of all, just to be introduced by him, and secondly, to hear the very kind things that he said.

I see Charlie Hayes up here. You know, Charlie almost had the shakes here a little bit ago, because Charlie started talking about what the Lord said do.

I am supposed to tell you why we are here and how we hope to move this movement from the arena of discussion into the front lines of action. We want to talk about what is important to us and maybe contrast that to what has been happening to us.

Like the Congressman, like Charlie, and like Jack, it is awful hard to look out upon this crowd without really just taking a swing at the present incumbent in the White House, because, you see, this crowd is what really raises the questions in your mind as to which way can he be thinking.

Now, we are Black Trade Unionists, and I think -- and I hope you agree with me -- that it happens to be a worthy combination, worthy of respect, and certainly worthy of admiration, and worthy in the same sense as one would call himself a doctor, a lawyer, an engineer.

We have a profession, and we ought to be doing it. We've got to get about doing our work. I just want to add to the voices who have already said it, and I don't want to review the record too much, but I see no way that Black Trade Unionists, black workers, black people, poor people, can support the candidacy of Richard Nixon. There just isn't any way.
(Applause)

When Charlie, Cleve, Jack, myself and others of us met down in Miami and said we were going to give some thought to putting this kind of meeting together, I want to tell you that folks went straight up the wall.

They said, "What are you all trying to do -- create a separate thing?"

We said, "No, we're not, but it has always been separate anyhow."
(Applause)

What we want to do is define our role in whatever it is. What we want to do is point out to you that you have become more involved in making decisions that affect our well-being, and you don't even remind us orally about it anymore. You let us read about it.

Shortly after our convention, where some of us were lucky enough to get ourselves elected, I suppose a whole lot of folks thought that what we would do now is like we always have done, go into our hole.

When we started to talk about this thing, folks came to me and said, "You are going to mess up your credentials."

I said, "I have no credentials."

They said, "If you do this, your constituency might not like that."

Well, you see, my constituency didn't know where I was coming from -- What's going on there?

(Shouts of "Can't hear")

Well, I will have to holler, then.

My point is that there are those in high places in the Trade Union movement who said that we shouldn't do this. My point -- and I think it was supported by the rest of the Planning Committee -- is that it is time for it to be done. Time has moved by us, and we have not come together and said to ourselves what we are and where we ought to be going.

I want to also say, and nobody has touched on this yet, but I think we ought to do it, that those of us who are workers and who are poor, and those of us who are black and who are hungry, and certainly those of us who have walked the long road from Selma to Montgomery can't help but look with contempt -- and I want to say "utter contempt" -- for those of us who claim to be black leaders and yet by endorsement give credence to the program that Nixon has been running down for three and a half years.
(Applause)

When it is made for the promise of maybe a few -- and I want to point out -- "uncollectible" dollars, or maybe just for the right to get one of those grinning photographs taken next to the man (Laughter), and in the minds of so many people who believe in them, that Nixon is all right.

But, you see, we've got a mission to perform, and we've got a job to do, knowing that those grins and HEW loans and HUD loans to a bunch of those who have just decided that now is the time to get into what they call black capitalism are not "where it's at." We've got a job to do in that respect.
(Applause)

I think we have to ask them where is their blackness, where is their sense of integrity, and where is their commitment to millions of black folks and to poor folks who had confidence in trusting them. You see, we have to call the roll before we get out of here; I think we've got to do that.

Because, you see, the time has come for the folks in this country to understand the sense of commitment to each other. Now, I know Sammy Davis has got a bunch of money. Lots of money. I want you to know that he is free to support any candidate he wants to, but why wasn't he doing it earlier? Why wasn't he doing it before the convention and on national television?

I know that Jim Brown, one of the greatest football players we have ever seen -- and I am proud of that -- but he is one of the worst political analysts that I've ever seen.
(Applause)

There is a fellow in Washington, D.C. I think his name is Paul Jones, or something like that. He is responsible for bringing together the black leaders for Nixon.

They had a $100-a-plate dinner down there, and they got more news coverage than a general session of the United Nations. Do you know why? Because that was a rare occurrence.

But that isn't rare. Black Republicans have been supporting the Republican administration for I don't know how long. But I want to make one distinction here, that I would like to see them down in the bayous and the ghettos digging our votes for Richard Nixon.

They have served their purpose. (Shouts of approval)

Now, some of us -- and I know the cat from Philadelphia is going to be waiting to see -- and I know from Cleveland, from Detroit -- we are all going to be waiting to see when the $100-a-plate cats come down and convince our folks as to why they ought to be voting for Richard Nixon.

You see, we also ought to keep in mind a couple of things, and then I'm going to get off Nixon. You see, we for a long time have been acting out of emotion, and I think we ought to deal with that a little bit.

A long time ago, my father used to say, "I don't have to worry about getting involved in the issues because I sure go to church on Sunday morning and they shall be explained to me."

And right in the midst of a sermon, as the minister goes for his thing Up There, his arm shall come down upon the issues. It's not like that anymore.
(Applause)

It's not like that anymore, because, you see, we are starting to act out of our interests. We are beginning to look at the record. I think Jack was running it down, and Charlie was, and, you see, we can just find enough in the record to convince everybody as to why they should be opposed to Nixon.

Now, we must not make one mistake, though. We must not lie about it, you see, because we quickly believe a lie, and that gets the thing all out of kilter. What we have got to do is tell the truth, because it is the truth that he is at his worst.

You see, when he talked in his Labor Day speech about the "Work Ethic" versus the "Welfare Ethic" and people ate that up because people, in our society, want to have somebody to look down at.

He talked about the fact that we've got to control the welfare rolls, yet since his administration came into office they have added six million people to it.

He talked about the fact that all these people ought to be put to work, yet he has eliminated two and a half million jobs in three and a half years.
(Applause)

And then he does the ultimate thing: In this big proclamation that we ought to all go to work, then he vetoes a Public Service Bill that would have created enough jobs to offset the two and a half million that he wiped out.

And then he does the one thing that is terrible in the sense of the high office that he holds: He refused to spend $5.6 billion that was appropriated by Congress for an accelerated public works program.

Now, let me just say one thing on that score. We know where we work, most of us. When you start talking about building highways and roads and things like that, that is us. That is us. (Laughter)

Now, you see, if you were talking about designing a space shuttle, that is none of us. Now, you notice what happened to the space shuttle -- right? When you talk about designing fancy airplanes like Lockheed and others do, that is none of us.

You know they got $250 million just to keep them going. And when you start talking about doing in Penn Central Railroad, that is none of us either. (Applause)

Now I want to point out something to you. In summary, let me say that this President has run up the highest budget deficit since the close of the Civil War. This year he will have a budget deficit of $22.3 billion. That is more than me and Charlie make in a week. (Laughter)

The point, then, there is an absolute lack of concern for the things that affect us. But there is an absolute commitment to the corporate interests of this country. When this administration came into office it had no problem in immediately declaring itself in support of the oil depletion allowance.

Do you all know what that is? Well, let me take a moment on that.

That is where the government will grant oil seekers money to go out and look and then will give them more money if they find it, and will give them some more money to pump it, and then will pay them for that that is gone.

Now, I think they have no problem making sure that the big grain exporters understand that they can cut a big deal with the Soviet Union, and that the grain exporters should move out into the country and buy from the farmers when the prices are down here and then sell to the Soviet Union for the prices up here, and then everybody claims they know nothing about it.

But one month before, the man who was cutting the deal now works for the grain people. You see, there is a strange system in this administration. It is known as "Socialism for the Rich and Free Enterprise for the Poor." (Applause)

Yet, I want to point out to you that there are some people in the labor movement who can't tell the difference between them.

Well, I want to tell you that some of us can. You see, our union -- and we have a member on that illustrious body known as the Executive Council -- frequently winds up in the position of being on the short end of votes. 29 to 1.28 to 2, when Charlie's union joined us.

But it is always like that, because we are talking about what is important to folks. We served notice on Mr. Meany and his council that we were moving out across the country to try and tell people what's going down. (Applause)

And it doesn't matter if they don't like it because we have been sitting on the sidelines for all these years and stuff has been happening and they didn't care if we didn't like it.

We are saying -- and the Congressman said it so well -- "If you all don't do it, we'll try it." And I think that together we can tell this country something. We can tell them that it may well be that the politicians, both in the White House and on the Executive Council, have something in common.

Maybe we ought to tell folks that one of the total concerns of the labor movement is not tied up around whether the Iron Workers can do this and laborers can do that -- because, you see, when the Wage-Price Freeze hit, it hit both of us.

You see, there is a thing in the industry called the Construction Stabilization Board. Have any of you heard of it? You see, they have their separate pay board, and they haven't turned down anything yet. (Applause)

Everybody thinks that a worker is a $10-an-hour plumber. That's not the way it is. So our people are trying to get a five percent wage increase, and he calls that inflationary. They say we can't do that because it would contribute to the bad economic situation in the nation.

Well, if it is as bad as it is, we can't help but make it a little bit worse by giving people enough to eat. There's nothing wrong with that. You see, I see something wrong when they give Stennis and Eastland thousands of dollars not to plant food and then tell me that it is inflationary just to give me enough to try to buy some.

I think that the Trade Union Movement, that powerful institution that affects and holds sway over practically everything we do, chose this time, like it did when Roosevelt ran against Hoover, to sit this one out. Some of you all remember that, I believe.

It seems like they have to have a situation at its worst in order for the Trade Union Movement to perform at its worst. But we're going to do what we

can do. It doesn't matter what the Executive Council says now. The impact is
there.
(Applause)
        There were some of us who talked about whether we, out of this conference,
ought to ask them to reconsider their positions. Well, I voted against that.
I would like for them to announce their position as loud as they can, because
what's going to be coming after them is us.
(Applause)
        You and the rest of us are going to have some time to discuss the issues.
We are going to have some time to get our minds together, so that when we go
back where we come from, we've got a message.
        You see, we are not going to talk about any second labor movement. There
is no point in that. We are going to do everything we can possibly do to
maximize support for Senator McGovern and the Democratic ticket. We're going
to do that.
(Applause)
        Then, we are going to set out to organize the neighborhoods. You see,
there is only one organization that spans the complete neighborhood -- that's
us.
(Applause)
        We are going to run into some trouble, though. But that's the way it is,
and we've got to do that. I think it is commendable, and I am proud to be a
part of the group that called this together. You see, one cat jumped up and
said, "Who gave you all the authority to do this?"
        "Nobody."
(Sustained applause)

        We've got a job to do, and we are prepared to do it. Lerone Bennett, in
an article in a recent *Ebony,* pointed out a bit of history of black workers,
about black workers in this society. He pointed out very clearly and very
accurately that they had historically been a cheap source of labor, and one to
be used if there was ever any problem with the other part of labor.
        You know, they would run in a bunch of cats on you in a minute, to work
for half of what we were working for, that is true. You see, we are getting
ourselves together now. We don't perform as strike breakers no more. No, we
will never be looked upon again as subjects in a total labor market, because
when we come out of here we are going to have impact both on the labor market
and on the labor movement.
(Applause)
        At the present time, we occupy a very important and critical position in
the politics of this nation, both in terms of the Trade Union Movement as well
as the political parties of this country. I am going to reiterate what
Congressman Metcalf said, and I hope and I believe that I will get concurrence
from the rest of the group, that we are in nobody's pocket, do not intend to
get in anybody's pocket, and we are going to assume a position of full partners.
        You see, we don't want anybody to be making decisions for us any longer,
because we are quite capable of making decisions ourselves.
(Applause)
        That doesn't mean that we are going to be right all the time. But it
doesn't mean they are going to be right all the time either. And to the extent
that we agree, we will go the same route. To the extent that we disagree, we
will go our separate ways.
        We don't want to be a thorn in anybody's side, but we don't want to be a
pivot for anybody's heel. What we are saying is that illustrious body known
as the Executive Council -- not criticism of it -- and I want to be clear, no
criticism of the Trade Union Movement, because if our economic and certainly
our social well-being is going to be protected, there is a need for that
institution.
        But what we are going to do is make it honest. We are going to make it
concerned with what its social goals used to be, or else they are going to
have a hard time explaining why they're not.
        My organization contributes to that worthwhile enterprise to the tune of
$65,000 a month. That is a lot of money out of our union, and it seems to me
that we ought to have a voice for that amount.
        I know that others will do the same thing. And I want to point out to
you that since they didn't see fit to consult us on their position of

neutrality, I saw fit to take a position not to give them nary another quarter because of it.
(Applause)

Now, they get upset about that, but do you know what? They don't elect me. That's true.
(Applause)

We will use what resources we have to move our own program. We will use what resources we can gather to move this program. And I am sure, with the support of the other unions, we are going to do something.

Now, they may ask, "Where are you all going to get your money?"

"The same place you get yours."
(Applause)

You see, because, I want to tell you that within the confines of Solidarity House they've got some wise cats with pencils and stuff. And I know that at Charlie's place over there they've got some guys that have been plotting and scheming for years. (Laughter)

We are not short on them. We can do it, you see, because we don't have to ask anybody for anything now. We have already overcome one problem. We have developed a sense of commitment.

A long time ago -- when I was talking about the preacher a minute ago -- some ministers weren't free because they had to depend on somebody. I want to tell you that the most free cat in the world is a black preacher. He is responsible to nobody except who's Out There.

And what we are saying is, "If you will allow us to serve and work with you, we are responsible to nobody except those who are out there. That's all."

To the extent that we can develop a program that you can agree with, and to the extent that we can develop some ideas and concepts that you agree with, that is where we're going, and everybody else has to either get with it, or get out of it, one or the other.
(Applause)

The challenge that is before us is to organize. I think that John L. Lewis said one time, "It is the job of the union to organize." And what does the union want more? And the cat says, "What does that mean?"

And he said, "Well, you sit around until you figure it out. We want our fair share of the benefits of this society, both as workers and as citizens."

I think that for too long we have not been a part of the institutions that have brought about change in this society. As the Trade Union Movement has been a haven for others, it is also going to be one for us. If it can be made to move on behalf of others, it is also going to be made to move on behalf of us.

And across the country in the black and poor communities of this land we are going to say to folks, "Join hands with us, and we jointly will see if we can do something about what's going down."

Now, we don't want you all to go back home after we get through spending these few hours and talk about what a great time we had listening to the speeches, because that's not doing it. You see, we want to develop a program that when some of us come together, maybe after the first of the year, and take a look at it, maybe then we will be coming out across the country, to Cleveland, to Philadelphia, and other places and stretching the program out in front of you and saying, "Let's think about it."

You see, we don't want any hit-and-miss and half-steps. What we've got to have is a concrete thing that is going to stand the test of time. As we were talking this morning, a lot of them have tried and for one reason or the other have failed.

But as Black Trade Unionists, I think we have a special obligation to get into the game and stay. We have a readymade constituency that is going to benefit from the expertise that we've got.

And I say to you as we move out of here and go into the workshops -- and we want full participation because we are searching for something, and we want to find that. We have no problem knowing what to do with it, because, you know, we've been doing it for somebody else for a long time.
(Applause)

Now we are going to try and do it for ourselves. We've got a good chance to make it work, too, because I want you to know that this is no small local union sitting up here.

We've got Cleve's union. We've got the historical and mighty Textile.
We've got Amalgamated Meat Cutters. We've got some Teamsters in the house,
too. We've got some Steel Workers down here.
(Applause)
    We aren't much in State-County -- we've got 550,000.
(Further applause)
    Every week we organize 1200 more. Here is the point that I'm making. The
point that I'm making is that we've got the resources, we've got the commitment,
and among even the people allowed to bring this together we've got the dedication.
    What we need to hear you say is: "Put the thing together."
(Applause)

MR. EDWARDS:

    Now you know what I meant when I said the people all across the country
want to meet this dynamic young man, a great, courageous, articulate man.
    We have on the agenda -- we may be running a little behind, but we don't
want you to violate our commitment. We had promised a coffee break. If you
are desirous of a coffee break, we will break now for coffee.
    If you would prefer that we continue the program, we will continue.
(Supporting applause)
    You know, many of you are acting in the manner of youngsters that grew up
during my time. There was a story about coffee which said that you don't want
coffee because it makes you black. (Laughter) You're not against it for that
purpose, I'm sure.
    I am told now that if we don't drink the coffee, we're going to have to
pay for it anyway -- (Shouts of disapproval) -- AFSCME ordered the coffee, the
commitment is made. I want to recognize your wishes, but I am told by others --
    In order that we keep pretty close to our agenda, which requires us to
get out of this room early enough so it can be arranged for our dinner -- we
will have to keep our program moving.
    I have the privilege of introducing to this conference a man that needs no
introduction. If you have been around where labor was involved in a struggle,
this personality has always been there.
    If it was a civil rights march or a civil rights struggle, this young man
has always been there. He was crying aloud for organized Black Trade Unionists
to get together ten years ago.
    Every time we have had an affair of this sort, that was dedicated to the
purpose of advancing the best interests of those that work for a living, this
fellow has been with us.
    I would like to introduce the panel that will be working with him, because
if I introduce him now and not introduce the panel, it would be a bit unfair
because this young man will make the trail very fast and very hot for anyone
that comes after him.
    So we have for the next panel operation three people -- in fact, four. I
will give out a bit of information on each of them in terms of their contribution to the labor movement and the cause for freedom, and if you will hold your
applause, we will try and give you the five names that will operate on this
panel and you may recognize them and give your expression of appreciation that
time.
    The gentleman I have made reference to so far is Mr. Cleveland Robinson,
President of the Distributive Workers of America. He is also Secretary-
Treasurer of District 65 and National President of the Afro-American Labor
Council.
    Serving on the panel with Brother Robinson is Neal Bratcher, Director,
Council 19, AFSCME. Now, I am told -- I don't know Mr. Bratcher personally,
but based upon those that know him and his work, they tell me that he is doing
an outstanding job in the field of helping to advance the best interests of
all workers.
    We have also serving on this panel Mr. Hilton Hanna, International Vice-
President of the Meat Cutters Union. And anyone who knows anything about the
Meat Cutters Union knows that to ascend from the ranks of Vice President, you've
got to be doing many, many good things, because that is a mighty tough contest.
    So, we have a man that we can salute in this position.[105]

Now, the person that I know best that will be serving on the panel is a very dear friend of mine and has been across the years. It is a female, and females today are fast proving that we have been wrong in deciding what kind of involvements we ought to allow them to engage in.
(Applause)

When it comes to politics, they boast -- and rightfully so, and this young lady stands out in this area -- that we will do as much political action work as any male in your section, including the candidate that is running for President, and this young lady needs no defense from making that kind of statement because she has proven it.

When it comes to economics, she is outstanding in that area because she knows, in this country, that females own more money than males, and most men don't believe that. But if I were a businessman and had a choice between dealing with males or females, I would take females because they have the money.

But from a Trade Union position, this young lady serves on the staff of our International Union in the Women's Department and has done an outstanding job there protecting the working of both genders, masculine and feminine.

She has done an outstanding job in the area of collective bargaining. She has articulated the purpose and the goals of the union wherever she has gone.
I now would like to announce the great woman of the UAW, Mrs. Lillian Hatcher.
(Applause)

Now, coming on to take the chair at this time will be my great friend, your friend, a fighter that never quits, one that has visions that I believe well should have waited for a few years so that some of us could get wise enough and devoted enough to join in and help them be carried into fruition -- I give to you now my friend Cleveland Robinson.
(Applause)

MR. ROBINSON:

Thank you my good friend Nelson Jack Edwards.

Soul Brothers and Sisters and allies, to me this is an occasion that I long dreamed for. I do not want to go too far back in our history and our struggles, but allow me to tell you that in my time this has not been the first occasion.

And before my time there have been other attempts. I think that to make it plain that the black worker of America from the days of slavery was never content in his lot, and he has always been trying to find some way to break the shackles, whether it was during the days when the shackles were of iron, or today when they have certain complexities and niceties so that you can't even locate them.

I can remember back in the Forties and Fifties the Black Unionists' attempts to meet, and they did meet and form some kind of organization, and it was short-lived. Our white counterparts said then that we were Communists. They did not talk about dualism then. That word did not reach their vocabularies.
We were Communists, they said.

In the Forties they set up other organizations to counteract us, because they could always find what the young people called the "house slaves."

Then, in the Sixties, after George Blue had blasted Philip Randolph in the convention in San Francisco we met in Detroit, a strong body, and we said that this is the time, then, that Black Trade Unionists must come together.

And we came together. But some of us dropped by the wayside. At that time, it was dual unionism, and those of us who chose to remain were called Mau-Mau's. At that time, of course, it was felt that to associate with anything from Africa would be degrading.

But thanks be God today we know Africa to be our homeland. We are not afraid of being identified as Afro-Americans anymore.
(Applause)

Yes, men were instructed to stay away, and so they did. But we struggled on, and I thank God today when I look around and see the array of people, including those young leaders who have come forward, many of whom have been brought within the ranks of leadership as a result of the struggles that have been carried on.
(Applause)

And I am here as one who has participated in some of those struggles, as one from a union that has been sensitive because we are a union of poor people

-- blacks, Puerto Ricans, other Latins, poor whites.

We are not from the big craft unions, and we have been struggling all along for unity and understanding and sensitivity to the problems that beset poor working people in this country.

And say thank God today that we can have a meeting such as this, and maybe if there is one good thing which Richard Milhous Nixon has done is to just let us know where it is so that we can't be silent any longer.
(Applause)

I remember 1963 when there were those of us who had to confront George Meany in Miami Beach, Florida. We threatened to picket the AFL-CIO Convention on the very issues on which we are meeting here today.

I remember him telling us of the senility of Philip Randolph, but the next year he came to our convention, and he started beginning to say that he understood. But I will tell you something: the leopard never changes his spots.

He has not understood us yet, and the unfortunate thing is that today we have a situation where even once enlightened leadership -- white leadership -- in the labor movement has now succumbed and sat by and echoed the reactionary backward sentiments that he expresses, whether it be on the war in Vietnam or the current political situation.

It is a matter of survival, Brothers and Sisters, because I say today -- 1972 -- if we were to be silent, who would cry out? Something has to be done. Not enough can be said for the trials and sufferings of our people.

No longer can those of us who think we probably have it made sit by and think we've got it made.
(Applause)

It is late in the day. I tell you, as one who goes out in the field, when I today have to negotiate for people who are making $1.60 an hour, even if they are driving 40-foot trailer trucks, black people, when the employer says "5.5 percent is all you're going to get, because that's what Mr. Nixon says," you know something has got to be wrong somewhere.

When workers who are toiling, who by their productivity are producing the kind of profits for big corporations that are unprecedented in our history, and when such workers can have leadership that today can say they have to be neutral, when a man in Washington is there sitting down, setting a wage board that will stop you from getting the wage increases after you've gotten them from your employer, something has got to be wrong, Brothers. Something has got to be wrong.

It is my prediction that we are able to change things around. This administration and the people who are supporting them -- and I am going to make it clear by saying that is George Meany, He is not neutral because he is supporting Nixon --
(Applause)

That is a fact, and now I am making it plain. Maybe there are some people whom others cannot tell them that it is wrong for us to spend our tax dollars making bombs and napalm and all kinds of instruments of destruction, and to be wiping out a country 10,000 miles away.

Maybe some of us are impervious to that kind of immorality. Maybe there are those who believe that it is right for blacks to be underpaid while whites get higher wages so that they continue to perpetuate racism and support Mr. Nixon's call for continued racism.

We've got to make it plain that when Richard Milhous Nixon gets on nationwide television and condemns the courts because of their stand on integration he is telling people to be racists. That's what it is, and maybe there are those who feel that it is all right.

They don't want to ask the working men and women, whether they be Steel or Auto or anything else. You tell me that you are saying it is all right for the man to stop your wage increases?

Well, if anybody has an illusion, they can look at the record, because the Longshoremen on the West Coast got a damn good increase, and Mr. Nixon cut it in two. The Longshoremen in New York got a wage increase, and Mr. Nixon cut it in two.

After that was done, the President of the Longshoremen in the East went to the Executive Board and recommended that the Executive Board endorse Nixon. Of course, the board members turned him down. Something is rotten in the cotton.

(Applause)

Today we've got to understand what we face. We are facing one of the worst conditions in our country because racism reigns supreme. Racism makes it so that people cannot think straight anymore. This is what it's all about.

Why are they so upset about the Democratic convention? Because black and poor people and women now have a say in it, so that it's going to be a little more democratic, and black and poor people's programs have to be attended to, and the man McGovern was the one who called for the reforms.

But even so-called Democrats decide that they've got to abandon him, and so they met with Mr. Nixon yesterday in Texas eating steaks while our people are going about not having the next meal.

We can't allow that to happen anymore. So 1972 for us is a year of decision. We have got to make a decision as to where we go from here. Let me say that it is not enough to cheer. It is not enough to say, "Why don't we?" You've got to put your money where your mouth is.

Now, Nixon has all the money and he is getting more and more. They can't even reveal where it's coming from. And I tell you, the first thing we've got to do, aside from what the good brothers have told us here before, our registration, is that we've got to dig in our pockets and put some dough on the line so that McGovern's program can go across and labor's program as we see it can go across.
(Applause)

Now, I am not telling you what I am paid to do. Because, at least in my New York union, we have taken the approach that every staff member pays 12 percent of a week's salary, and every local officer gives at least five bucks, and every worker, if you work on the staff of the union, you have to give six percent because we have endorsed McGovern, and it is a real fight.
(Applause)

Let me say one thing further. We can talk about building an organization, but we cannot unless we are prepared to make some sacrifices. I have had experiences over the years, at least the last decade-plus, of working within the confines of what is known as NALC. Many of you know it. Many of you might have heard of it.

The purposes for which we set up that organization are the very purposes for which we are meeting here. And I am telling you here now that we didn't do so well, because we did not capture the imagination of the broad masses of the rank and file and black leadership.

I am saying here, if we are to set up an organization, we have got to make up our minds that it has to be a broad coalition, that it must encompass all of us, irrespective of our affiliation, within and without the AFL-CIO.

We meet as black people with a common concern. That is what we have to do.
(Applause)

Certainly we are going to support it, because I want to tell you that not many unions are going to give as you believe they are going to give to support it. We have got to be prepared to support it.

Now, some unions will. Let me make no mistake about it. There are fine unions. Some of us belong to some fine unions. But others will not. Moreover, I will tell you something: we've got to pay our way. We've got to learn to shoulder our responsibilities. We cannot expect freedom without fighting for it.
(Applause)

In this respect we must remember the words of Dr. King. "There are those who are waiting for freedom to be handed them on a silver platter." It is not going to happen.

We have to struggle and fight and sacrifice and, yes, sometimes we are going to be kicked around. Some of us pay the price of losing jobs, but I will tell you one thing: right must, and will, prevail. And that has to be our watchword.

I have every confidence that we can move forward, and that in moving forward our very strength will protect us. If we fall by the wayside, I have to say bluntly that an organization such as this, where fulltime black leadership exists in every union, if he participates he is more safe than if he is isolated.

(Applause)

In this kind of unity there is strength.   In this kind of unity there is
a recognition.   In this kind of unity you have the ability, if you please, to
stand up and talk because you know you have people behind you and organizations
behind you that will back up what you say.

Moreover, I will tell you that the days of the Nervous Nellies and the
Uncle Toms and what have you are gone.
(Applause)

I will tell you that this is the day of the Bill Lucys.
(Applause)

Young bright men and women who are going to come forward and not be so
worried about the titles and the positions that they hold are going to use
their positions and their titles to enhance the progress of their people.
(Applause)

And this is the new thing about it, and when you have this, when you feel
tired -- and I'm not getting any younger, believe me -- we feel a sense of new
direction.   We feel that we now can make it.

And above all, let us understand something.   McGovern must win the
election, should win it, but if he doesn't, we've got to live with it, against
evil, the great odds of Nixon for four more years of Agnew waiting behind him.

Brothers and Sisters, we've got to live.   This country is what we have
built by blood and sweat and tears.   We made cotton King.   We built the
castles.   We were the construction workers when there was slave labor.

Today we need picks and crowbars and hammers to break the bonds that are
holding us back.   Thank you.
(Applause)

END OF SESSION

BANQUET SESSION

SATURDAY, SEPTEMBER 23, 1972

MR. EDWARDS:

May I have your attention please.   Ladies and gentlemen, may I please
have your attention.   We are ready now to begin this session of the program
and we have a real treat in store for you.   We have with us tonight some very
important people who will be introduced to you a little bit later in the
program.

Right now I would like to take this time to again present to you a young
man who this afternoon gave us a very inspiring presentation and who I am sure
we will hear a lot from in the months and years ahead.   He will serve as
chairman and presiding officer for tonight's program.

Brothers and Sisters, I now turn the program over to Brother Bill Lucy,
the Secretary-Treasurer of the American Federation of State, County and
Municipal Employees Union.
(Applause)

MR. LUCY:

Thank you Jack.   We are going to move right along because we have quite
a bit to get accomplished in the very short time we will be in Chicago.

Before we introduce the brothers and sisters on the platform up front,
I would like to acknowledge and give credit to those people, those members of
the combined staffs who worked so hard putting together today's meeting and
putting together tonight's dinner, and doing the behind the scenes things
that are so necessary and so vital to putting together a meeting and
conference of this type.

Let me, if I can, do it very quickly.   If they are present they can
stand.   If they are not, forget it.   I will just run through some names for
you, because these individuals have really given time and effort and energy
to trying to make things both comfortable for you and certainly meaningful
for you.

I don't know where Frank is, but Frank Cowan, who is a special representative in the office of the President of our union -- Frank has done a tremendous
job in putting together the things necessary to make this thing work. I don't
know where Frank is, but let me just run through the list.

I would hope that you would give the entire crew a great hand, because
they've done a great job.

Working with Frank has been Tony Harrison from the National League of
Cities.

Certainly, from the great union of the Auto Workers, Horace Sheffield, who
has been representing Nelson Jack Edwards. Charles Brooks, sitting down here
somewhere.

Chris Nelson from our convention coordinator's office.

Brenda Cote, who is Chris Nelson's assistant.

Edith Moore -- I saw Edith around somewhere just a moment ago.

Prince Moon from the United Auto Workers.

Whit McCrae from the Auto Workers.

Al Hyde from the staff of State-County.

And just a tremendous group of people who put a lot of time and effort
trying to make things work for us here.

Oh, I almost forgot my good buddy, the one who keeps my office straight,
Gwendolyn Hemphill.
(Applause)

I would like now to introduce to you those sitting at the head table.

On my far right, the reverend who gave us such a tremendous and moving
invocation, Reverend Claude Wyatt, from the Vernon Park Church. Reverend Wyatt,
would you stand up again for us, please.
(Applause)

And sitting next to Reverend Wyatt, whom everybody had a chance to go to
church with this morning, the big, really moving person and the moving spirit
in the Amalgamated Meat Cutters and Butcher Workmen of North America, Vice
President Charles Hayes.
(Applause)

And the brilliant young lady who did such a tremendous job as part of
the panel this afternoon, and as she put it, catching up, a member of the
International Staff of the United Auto Workers, Sister Lillian Hatcher.

And next to Sister Hatcher -- and I think it is fitting, and no more
fitting than this moment, to sort of recognize some people who made some
tremendous sacrifices, both for themselves and for others --

You know, when Charlie Hayes goes around the country doing his thing,
somebody has got to stay home and mind the store. You see, Charlie's right arm
is sitting next to Mrs. Hatcher -- Mrs. Charles Hayes.
(Applause)

Sitting next to Mrs. Hayes, one seat over, is our chairman, the one we
call the "Maximum Leader" and who has presided over this session today and
really has brought us a moving presentation and a great program. I want Jack
to stand once again. The great Vice President of the United Auto Workers,
Nelson Jack Edwards.
(Applause)

I'm going to skip this cat right here for the time being and go down
there next to the far left end and bring to you someone who, again, along with
Sister Hatcher, has played a tremendous role in the panel discussion that took
place, who sort of came to us in terms of what he thought and what he felt.
The Director of District Council 19 of the American Federation of State, County
and Municipal Employees, Neal Bratcher.
(Applause)

Sitting next to Neal is someone from the Amalgamated Meat Cutters, a
tremendous representative and one who has made a tremendous contribution over
the years on behalf of working people -- Sister Addie Wyatt.
(Applause)

Sitting next to Addie is the dean of activists, who is a mover, who has
made contributions that we all like to think that we could make in years to
come, one who gave us a very moving and a very stirring presentation today,
the great President of the Distributive Workers of America, Cleveland Robinson.
(Applause)

It seems like all great people sort of sit and stay together. Sitting next to him is a man who is a mechanic. You know you think a mechanic is one who turns wrenches, but this is one who makes things come together and makes them work.

A couple of years ago a great organization came into being and sort of sprung up on the scene and started to do things. They called it in the District of Columbia "nationwide," the Congressional Black Caucus.

You know the Congressmen go around and make all the speeches and get all the glory, but it is the cats back in the trenches who do all the work. I want to present to you now the Executive Director of the Congressional Black Caucus, Howard Robinson.
(Applause)

You see, in our union, just like in the Amalgamated and all the other great unions, we have our beautiful men, too. You see, we have not only those who are beautiful but also are moving, knowledgeable, and have the ability to project where we're coming from.

I want to introduce to you now, from the great City of New York, the Associate Director of District Council 37, Lillian Roberts.
(Applause)

We also have with us, from the State of Michigan, representing the Secretary of State of that Great State, Dick Austin, we have his representative Walter Elliot. Walter, where are you sitting?
(Applause)

We also have a number of other prominent people who have come out to share in this occasion with us. We have representatives from various governors' offices. I have lost the name now, but I believe we had a representative from Governor Gilligan's office from the State of Ohio, and he may be here somewhere. I apologize for not having the name. If you are here will you please stand.

I think that takes care of the introductions. We are fortunate to have with us tonight someone to speak to us who doesn't have to talk about Trade Unionism after reading it out of a book.

We have one with us tonight whose background, whose activities, and whose outlook is shaped by his involvement in the very things we talked about today. I was handed a long list of plaudits earlier this morning, and it was said that this was a biography of the one I'm going to introduce to you now.

It was my feeling that long sheets of paper don't nearly speak to the contributions that people have made on behalf of the working people of this country. We are fortunate to have someone with us who comes out of the movement that we are concerned with.

We have someone with us who spent a number of years representing the interests of workers such as you and I. In 1959 he was elected as an Alderman in the City of St. Louis and served with distinction for a five-year period.

In St. Louis, for somebody like this fellow to be elected, takes a little bit of doing. After spending some years on the aldermanic board of the City of St. Louis, Mr. Clay moved on to some bigger things, one of which, I might add, was having been a staff representative for the State, County and Municipal Employees, which in itself ought to be enough to do something.

Several years ago on the scene in Washington, D.C., came one Bill Clay, elected from the First Congressional District in St. Louis, and certainly a new face and a shining star in the House of Representatives in Washington, D.C.

Now, some cats, if they had got elected about the time that Bill did, would have come in and tried to be cool so that they would have got some decent appointments to committees. They wouldn't have made any noise, and that way they wouldn't have had anybody mad at them.

You know, they say that a freshman Congressman can't be "for" anything -- he can only be "against" something. He is not allowed to speak -- he is only allowed to be seen.

I want to say that that is not the case with Bill Clay. He has been a friend of working people. Some of the immediate things that he did, and particularly on behalf of public employees -- he immediately introduced into Congress a collective bargaining bill for the public employees.

That bill was joined in by some seventy-seven other Congressmen, and to those of you who are not in public employment, you don't understand what it is to struggle without a legal means to do that.

Those of us -- and particularly from the American Federation of State,

County, and Municipal Employees -- hold Bill in the highest esteem, not because he introduced the bill, but because he talked about what was relevant on behalf of workers.

I want to say to you -- and we can go on and on and on talking about his accomplishments, talking about his commitment, talking about the fact that he along with maybe one or two other people have welded together an organization in the Congress of this country called the Congressional Black Caucus, who has done a tremendous amount on behalf of poor people and working people throughout the country.

Some of you may remember right at the time that our illustrious Mr. Nixon was elected that the 13 members presented to him an agenda of items that they considered relevant to the black community.

I would suggest to you that Bill made a magnificent contribution to that agenda, and he was one of those who felt very strongly about the sit-out at the President's address to the joint houses of Congress.

It is a pleasure for me, both as a friend and as a Trade Unionist, to bring to this gathering the Congressman from the First District of St. Louis -- William Clay.[106]
(Applause)

CONGRESSMAN CLAY:

Well, first of all, I'm glad that Bill Lucy told you a little bit about me. You know, sometimes after you appear on programs like Meet the Press and on the cover of *Newsweek* you begin to believe that everybody knows who you are.

And I found this not to be true a couple of months ago when I went home to my District in St. Louis and decided that I would go down into the old neighborhood that I grew up in.

I saw three guys sitting in the alley there drinking some wine, so I said here's a chance to get three votes. I'll sit down and drink some wine with them. And we started talking, and one guy said:

"Say, your face is familiar. Did you use to live in this neighborhood?"

I said, "Yes, I lived here for twenty-three years."

He said, "Yes, I thought so." He said, "What are you doing now?"
(Laughter)

I said, "Oh, I'm working for the federal government."

He said, "You at the Post Office, too?" (Laughter)

You know, white folks have got a lot of fixations about black folks, and one of them is that black people can fill a hall like this for a dance or a party, but they can't fill it for a cause.

And we've got approximately 1100 black people at this convention.
(Applause)

And I've never been to a meeting of 300 black people unless I could look around and point out at least two or three people who were there to spy for the white folks. So what I want to say to the five or six spies who are here (Laughter) is that when you go back Monday morning, just report one thing: that there were wall-to-wall niggers there. (Laughter and applause)

You know, a lot of people are disturbed because we see such prominent names like Jim Brown and Sammy Davis, Jr., and all of the rest -- Wilt Chamberlain -- out supporting Nixon's effort for re-election.

But it doesn't disturb me, because I knew there were some niggers that kept Dr. King's dream.
(Applause)

I happened to be speaking last month in St. Louis at the Urban League's affair, and right in the middle of my speech one of those kinds of pimps walked up to me with a big pamphlet with pictures of all the black people that Nixon had appointed to office, and I'm sure you've seen that garbage that they're passing out.

At first I didn't know how to react. He just interrupted my speech. So finally I grabbed it and I took a look at it, and I said, "What's this?"

And he said, "Well, those are the black people that Nixon has appointed to office."

And I looked at it again, and I said, "Hell, more niggers in my block have lost their jobs since Mr. Nixon took office."
(Applause)

I got a little disturbed last week. I was reading *The Washington Post,* and they said that Vice President Spiro Agnew had an IQ of 145. It really upset me, because that's getting close to a genius.

So I called the editor to find out about it. And he readily assured me that somebody left out the decimal point. (Laughter)

Last summer I had the good fortune of following our Vice President through Africa. I guess I was about a week and a half behind him. You remember when he made those infamous statements about black leadership in this country.

When I arrived in Kenya, I happened to meet the official interpreter for the Vice President. And I wanted to know what the reaction of black people in Africa was to the kind of vicious attack that Agnew had made on black leadership in this country.

He started telling me, and at first I was greatly disturbed, because he said that Agnew was a very articulate speaker, and that he was able to arouse the people that he was speaking to, and the day he was in Kenya and made the statement, he was speaking to about 400 Africans in an open field.

They said that as he began his attack on black leadership, they started a chant, "Ungawa, Ungawa, Ungawa."

And as he continued and escalated that attack, the chant continued and escalated, and when he finished they were all on their feet hollering, "Ungawa, Ungawa, Ungawa."

That kind of disturbed me, until he told me that one of the Secret Service agents informed the Vice President that they were running late for the next appointment, and that from the way the crowd had reacted to the speech, they would probably be there for an hour congratulating him and they would never be able to make the next appointment.

So, the Vice President looked at his interpreter and guide and said, "Is there a way that we can get out of here without going through the crowd?"

And the interpreter said, "Well, we can cut across that open field there, which is a cow pasture. But be careful, and don't step in any ungawa." (Laughter and applause)

Let me say from the outset that I am deeply honored and consider it a privilege to have the opportunity to participate in this what I consider to be an historic occasion.

Bill Lucy has told you about my background of experience in the labor movement, and it coincides with my background and experience in the political movement. I started in the labor movement thirteen years ago in the State, County and Municipal Workers Union, and during that period and since I have done special organizing work for the Seafarers and the Electrical Workers.

My most recent job before I came to Congress was as educational coordinator for the Pipe Fitters Local 552 in St. Louis. So I have approximately thirteen years in the labor movement and fourteen years in the political movement.

I come here not as a neophyte in either, and I think that when I say that this is truly an historic event, I think I know from which I am speaking. Even though it may take a little while for many to realize it, history is being made here tonight.

This group, in a sense, has sounded the clarion trumpet of rebellion to charge the archaic Bastille of dictatorial one-man rule in the labor movement. (Applause)

What you have done is to launch a program based on the concept of manhood for blacks in the field of labor, and by taking up the gauntlet at this time and in this manner, you are saying in no uncertain terms that Black Trade Unionists have a responsibility that exceeds those narrowly defined interests of labor generally.

You, in a sense, are saying what black politicians are saying from one end of this country to the other, that we have no permanent friends, no permanent enemies -- just permanent interests. And no one can deny that it is the interests of blacks and poor working people in this country to oppose the re-election of Richard Milhous Nixon this year. (Applause)

Never in the history of our nation has the working people suffered so adversely from the policies and the programs of a President and his administration. What working man, in all honesty, could let Mr. Nixon win by default?

The interests of labor are more than that of wages and working conditions.
Mr. Nixon has sabotaged many programs that would have helped laboring people.
He was the one who advocated Day Care Centers, yet he vetoed the bill that
would have made them possible. Welfare mothers have particularly suffered from
this maniac in the White House.

He isn't concerned about them. He once said that they ought to be
scrubbing floors, because that is employment with as much dignity as employment
as President of the United States.

I think his record speaks for itself. He vetoed funds for education and
health programs which laboring people are interested in. He vetoed a bill that
would have increased hospital construction, and one that would have provided $3
billion for housing programs.

He vetoed a $9 billion bill for manpower training which would have pro-
vided thousands of jobs. He vetoed a bill that would have trained many family
doctors, and he vetoed a proposal to raise the pay for blue collar government
workers.

But in contrast, Mr. Nixon and his administration gave financial assistance to Penn Central and Lockheed and proposed a depreciation allowance that
would save big business more than $3 billion in taxes and imposed a wage-price
freeze that left high profits untouched.

He has proposed strike-breaking legislation to stymie every national
strike since I have been in Congress. He has advocated that families of
striking people or striking workers not be entitled to food stamps and other
subsidies.

He is opposed to increases in Social Security benefits, and he is
presently fighting a minimum wage bill in the U.S. Congress, and we black
people have suffered more under this man than anybody else in this country, and
we cannot afford the luxury of neutrality in this election.
(Applause)

And neither can we be taken in by the fuzzy talking and thinking of those
who say that we can stand another year or another four years of Richard Nixon.
It is imperative that we dispel the notion that the Democrats are taking us for
granted.

As Julian Bond said recently, and I quote: "If my choice is between a
Democrat like George McGovern and a Republican like Richard Nixon, I would
rather be taken for granted than just plain taken."[107]
(Applause)

As long as our country is suffering the drastic efforts of this racist
society led by a racist President, black people cannot condone neutrality.
(Applause)

As long as our country is beclouded with internal unrest and beset by
external war, neutrality is "ungawa."
(Applause)

As long as this country has five and a half million alcoholics, three and
a half million drug users, twenty-five million poverty stricken, fifteen
million on the welfare rolls, six million unemployed, fifty million who go to
bed hungry and undernourished -- neutrality must be considered "ungawa."
(Applause)

Mr. Nixon, who promised to bring this country together, has torn it
asunder. He has aroused and encouraged the racial fears and prejudices of the
bigots, and the once subtle words for "keeping us in our places," such as "law
and order," and "Make the streets safe," has suddenly grown full bloom into
overt racist epithets.

Those slogans have generated specific policies which threaten to set us
back in our cause by one hundred years. How could our President, in the name
of fair play, decree that quotas be abolished. In the name of racism, yes,
but in the name of fair play, no.

Merit employment is a euphemism for discriminatory hiring. There never
has been any merit employment in this country, and there never will be. The
definition for merit itself totally eliminates blacks from consideration.

The nation has thrived on the concept of white superiority. How, in
Sammy Davis's name, can a black person ever --
(Sustained applause)

Many Americans find most distasteful the regretful aversion for truth
which afflicts Mr. Nixon and his party -- an aversion which has shown up in this

administration and one which has attempted to create the impression that all is
well in our country.

You know, they don't refer to slums and ghettos any more as "slums" and
"ghettos." They are now low-income housing areas. Unemployed people are not
considered as individuals any more. They are weapons in the fight against
inflation.

And you know, the people who are starving and going to bed hungry -- they
aren't "poor" anymore. They are what we call the "near-poor."

And white racist attorneys who are appointed to the federal bench and the
Supreme Court aren't "racists" anymore. They are rigid constructionists. It
is perfectly all right to keep black people out of suburban areas, because you
aren't discriminating against them because they are black -- you are discriminating against them because they fall within an economic category.

This is what Mr. Nixon is doing to this country. But no matter how hard
he tries to make it appear that this country is made up of well-dressed, well-
fed, middle-age and upper-income Americans, the true picture of America will
show through.

The real face of America shows the anguish of the poor, the struggle of
the minorities, the frustrations of the unemployed, and the tragedies of the
war victims. In all fairness to Mr. Nixon, it must be noted that the GOP
convention represented the President's interests and reflected that interest
in black Americans. Only three percent of the convention was made up of black
Americans.

Twenty-five of the GOP state delegations had no blacks at all. And in an
attempt to make up for the conscious, conspicuous absence of blacks at the GOP
convention, Nixon made conspicuous use of our own Sammy Davis, Jr.

His play upon the conversion, the miraculous conversion of Little Sammy
will not enlarge the black audience of either Nixon or Sammy. I know Sammy
personally, and I know that he's not the type of person that will sell out for
one invitation to the White House. It takes at least three.
(Laughter and applause)

Our President has worked miracles with those invitations to the White
House. He invited Pearl Bailey. She sat in a rocking chair that broke while
she was sitting in it, and he gave her that rocking chair. The next week she
was on television rocking in the chair that the President gave to her.

He invited Ethel Waters to one of his prayer breakfasts, and when it was
over he offered her a doggie bag. But to her eternal credit, she informed him
that she did not have a dog.

You know, it has been tradition in this country for the little girl who
happens to be chosen as the Poster Girl for Multiple Sclerosis to have her
picture taken with the President of the United States, and that poster is
placed all over the country.

Mr. Nixon didn't think that he should invite her to the White House for
the picture, and last year our little black girl had her picture on the poster
without the President of the United States.

But for fifteen months the Congressional Black Caucus was seeking an
invitation to sit down at the White House and discuss some very important
problems with our President. He refused for a fifteen-month period, and during
that fifteen-month period he extended three invitations to our wives to come
over for tea and crackers.

Fortunately, our wives declined because they knew there would be more
crackers than tea --
(Laughter and applause)

I don't think that our people can sit idly by and let a man whose own
contempt for us be re-elected without a struggle. If I had to list three
persons who posed the most dangerous threat to the freedom and equality of
the blacks in this country, I would have to list them in this order:

Number one, Richard Nixon.

Number two, Richard Nixon.

Number three, Richard Nixon.
(Applause)

My personal opinion of the man -- and I may be a little prejudiced --
is that he finds security in the past and popularity among those who seek to
repeal the Thirteenth Amendment.

He has not made himself, or he has not distinguished himself by expanding the war in Asia, regardless of what he says about winding it down. He has attempted to stall school integration by destroying constitutional protection of blacks with his busing bills.

He has appointed racists and reactionaries to the Supreme Court and has attempted to sabotage the 1965 Voting Rights Act. In regards to the Voting Rights Act, he took the position, and he argued, that all sections of this country ought to be treated equally and fairly.

Therefore, he wanted to take half of the federal voting registrars from Mississippi and assign them to the State of Utah. (Laughter) Now, I don't want you to get me wrong. I don't think Mr. Nixon hates blacks. In fact, you can ask some of those who are supporting him for re-election.

The fact is, I think, is that Mr. Nixon not only does not hate blacks, he loves them so well that I think he would like to see every American family own one.
(Applause)

Under his leadership, the whole concept of representative government has been destroyed. This nation was founded on the idea that every section, every segment, every group, every interest was entitled to positions of authority in the decision-making bodies. That is why the House of Representatives is apportioned according to population, and that is why the Senate is apportioned two persons per state, regardless of your size.

Tradition and custom has dictated that labor and management, Jew and Gentile, rich and poor, farm and urban dwellers have a voice in our government. But under Nixon all of this has changed.

He did not appoint to his cabinet a Jew, a Catholic, an Italian, a Spanish-speaking American, a woman, a farmer, a labor representative, or a black. Eighty percent of the American population is voiceless in this administration.

Now, what did he do? Instead, Mr. Nixon surrounded himself with those that I have referred to as Nixon's masses, and they have taken over. The storm troopers and the Gestapo. The Zieglers, the Hartovans, the Erlichmans, the Schultzes, the Kissingers, the Klines, and all those others of German descent.[108]

You know, if Dick Hatcher did that in Gary and appointed only blacks, the newspapers would castrate him, and you know it.
(Applause)

Now, he only attempted to justify one of the people that he left out, or one of the races that he left out, and that was the blacks. Mr. Nixon said he did not appoint any blacks to his cabinet because he could not find any who were qualified.

Now, that's remarkable, isn't it. In view of the fact that some of his best friends are black. (Laughter) More astonishing is the fact that this nut went on television in an attempt to justify why he did not appoint any blacks to his cabinet, and he said there was a vain attempt to find qualified blacks, and that he went to the campuses of Yale, Princeton, and Harvard (Laughter), and much to his surprise he did not find many blacks at those institutions.

Well, anybody in his right mind would not expect to find many blacks at Yale, Harvard, or Princeton. Anybody who knows anything about the educational system knows that the tuition at Yale, Harvard, and Princeton is in excess of $4,000 a year.

And anybody who knows anything about economics in this country knows that the median income for blacks is less than $4,000 a year. So why would any fool expect to find blacks in overwhelming numbers at those schools?

Further, Mr. Nixon himself did not attend Yale, Princeton, or Harvard. Now, Nixon has implied and has actually said that those of us who oppose the war in Southeast Asia are unpatriotic.

But to those who say that opposition to that war is unpatriotic, I say that Americans spend $72 billion on defense and only $4 billion on education. Some Americans have spent $5 billion for one plane and less than $2 billion on poverty.

I say it is not American to spend $40 billion on space exploration and only $300 million for cancer research.

I say it is un-American to spend $20 thousand for the ammunition just to kill one Viet Cong and only $73 a year to educate each American child. This country is wasting our money.

Last year this government spent $3 billion in tax money to subsidize rich farmers. Four thousand farmers collected more than $100,000 each for not growing food, and this summer our government paid one farmer in California $10 million not to grow food.

We pay some not to grow food while others go hungry and undernourished. And actor John Wayne, who supported Mr. Nixon, received $810,000 from the federal government for not growing food.

And that conservative ass has the gall to attack welfare recipients. (Applause)

Mississippi's Senator James Eastland got $166,000 of our money last year for not growing food. But in the State of Mississippi a child on welfare receives $9.50 a month, or $114 a year. And in Alabama a person on welfare gets $1.40 a week for food, and in Mississippi, 80 cents a week for food, or four cents a meal.

President Nixon continues to label the helpless welfare recipients as freeloaders, lazy no-good vultures. He wants workfare for the poor and welfare for the rich.

Another thing about our President -- he has become a renowned world traveler. He has traveled 750,000 miles since he took office, 150,000 miles in foreign lands. He has been to the Philippines, Indonesia, Bangkok, Thailand, South Vietnam, Midway, India, Pakistan, Rumania, France, England, Russia, China -- he even went to the Vatican.

He is truly the Marco Polo of the White House, or the Genghis Khan of the West. He is really the San Clemente globetrotter.

I say that his traveling would be meaningful if at the same time he had traveled to Watts and Harlem and Fillmore and Anacostia. (Applause)

But he hasn't seen the ghettos of this country. He hasn't seen the suffering and the deprivation. He hasn't seen the 23 percent unemployment for black males in the ghettos of our nation.

He hasn't seen the 42 percent unemployment of black youth in this country. He hasn't seen the black children dying from lead-based paint. He hasn't seen the rat-infested houses in the slums.

He hasn't seen black babies dying from rat bite at a rate eight times as great as white babies. He hasn't seen black mothers dying in childbirth at a rate four times as great as white mothers.

I just can't understand anybody talking about neutrality in this race. (Sustained applause)

There are some black people saying that we should not criticize the President. They said we didn't support him, and he doesn't owe us anything. You know, I happen to believe that the President of the United States is the President of all the people.

He should have the capacity to rise above political considerations. I think by the very nature of his office he is obligated to serve the interests of the entire country.

Now, when a United States Senator says that poor people should help themselves, and he helps himself to a large chunk of federal farm money by doing nothing, should we be neutral?

When our President insults black Congressmen, ridicules black welfare recipients, makes buffoons of black entertainers, leads the fight to return us to our previous condition of involuntary servitude -- we would be damn fools to take a neutralist position. (Applause)

Yes, we can be neutral. But if we are, we will never achieve total freedom, economic equality, and social justice. We must take a stand. We must keep on unifying and expanding our goals. This is a practical reality, not an impossible dream.

Let this be the first day of the new reality for black unions, the day when black working people say to America, "We have united, united to make real, to bring into reality now those things so long promised but so definitely denied the 25 million black Americans."

We witness here tonight by your presence a manifested broad base of black unity in the union movement, a unity of black pride and black confidence, and with this unity we can and we will bring into being not only a basic change in attitudes but also a change in basic positions.

I call upon you to work for the building of a greater foundation upon which we can maximize our level of achievement.

This foundation which I call upon you to help build is made of black votes and black participation in the making of new institutions, and to be sure there are alterations to those so long outdated.

What you are suggesting here assumes one thing, and it implies another. It clearly assumes that there is a developing black political power in the labor movement, and it definitely implies that it will be operative in this Presidential year.

I suggest that both the assumption and the implication are accurate.   So let's take this occasion to devise a plan of single purpose to obtain through the exercise of black political power the reality of economic equality, social justice, and political manhood.

If you are to accept nothing less than meaningful participation at the center of power, then you as black labor leaders must be united.   This is the objective of this meeting -- full participation in labor's decision-making process must be the basis of our unity.

It must also be our purpose to achieve this goal now.   We must seek not only for the present, but as a group we must develop and demand for the future.

What has to be the positive assumption of this group assembled here is that the achievement of our goals is essential for the maintenance of an orderly labor movement.   No longer can Black Americans silently accept the present degenerate calibre of white leadership.

No longer can we passively tolerate the immorality and the insanity that permeates this country.   Our obligation is a challenging one.   We must assume the mantle of leadership and direct this nation to the path of moral humane consciousness.

We must become the spearhead in the movement to eradicate racism in private and public institutions, and if you please, labor unions.

We must become the vanguard in the struggle to provide every man in this country with a decent living and a decent home, every child with a quality education, and every person with a job commensurate with his training and his ability; every person must be afforded fair and impartial justice.

Every business must be guaranteed a fair share of public funds, and every community must have full participation in determining how tax dollars are to be spent.

These goals are attainable.   They are attainable now if only we can unite and dispel our fears, frustrations, and the indoctrinations that we have been the victims of for too many years.

Who convinced us that we must subjugate the interests of black people to the interests of this nation?   I contend that what is good for black people is also good for this nation.

(Applause)

That must become our political rationale.   We are the only group of people that I know of who are so concerned and so interwoven in the struggle to protect the interests of other groups that we have neglected our own.

If our politics of the Seventies is to be productive and meaningful, then it must be consistent with the rules of the game.

If we are to play the political game, then we must learn those rules. Rule No. 1 says that we must be practical and selfish.   We must put the interests of no group before the interests of ours.

And Rule No. 2 says that we must take what we can and give up only what we must.

(Applause)

Rule No. 3 says that you take it from whomever you can, however you can, and wherever you can.

(Applause)

Now, if we are not ready to abide by these rules, then we have not reached the age of political maturity, and all of our talk about the new black politics is just an exercise in frustrated futility.

The power exists in black America today.   If we go to that well in November and come back with our buckets empty, we have no one to blame but ourselves.   We must realize that we have real power.   We have the balance of power in many instances and the power to negate in many others.

And let me say as I close this evening that I hope that we will not be

influenced by how many black babies a candidate kissed in Harlem or how many
black entertainers are invited to the White House or how many government
contracts one black businessman receives.

I think we have reached the point of no return. I think the next two
months will determine the course and the impact of black political power for
the next fifty years.

Thank you.

(Standing applause)

(Whereupon, the banquet session was concluded with the Benediction).

SUNDAY SESSION

SEPTEMBER 24, 1972

The Sunday session was devoted to work on resolutions. Following are the
adopted resolutions, each voted on unanimously.

Resolution On The Formation Of A National
Black Trade Union Organization

There are nearly three million black workers who are members of American
trade unions. This number constitutes approximately one-third of the total
black workforce and a sizable political and economic force within the unions
and the black community. For example, the United Auto Workers, with 1.5
million members, has 500,000 black members. The International Brotherhood of
Teamsters has 200,000 black members out of a total membership of 1.8 million.
Two hundred thousand of the 1.2 million members of the United Steel Workers
are black. AFSCME with over 550,000 members has approximately 180,000 black
members.

Delegates at the Conference of Black Trade Unionists represented the
single largest gathering of black union members in history. Throughout the
two-day meeting, both union officials and rank and file members voiced considerable displeasure with the neutralist presidential stance adopted by the
AFL–CIO without apparent consideration of the consequences of this action on
blacks and poor working people. The participants also expressed dissatisfaction with their roles and involvement in the shaping and implementation of
union policy at the national and local levels.

THEREFORE BE IT RESOLVED: That the original convenors of the Conference
(Nelson Jack Edwards, UAW; Charles Hayes, Amalgamated Meatcutters; William
Lucy, AFSCME; Cleveland Robinson, Distributive Workers; and William Simmons,
AFT) form a five-man steering committee to develop a structure and program for
a permanent national organization for black union members, and that the
committee be expanded at the earliest opportunity to provide for participation
by women, youth, and representatives from other national and local unions.

BE IT FURTHER RESOLVED: That the steering committee convene a second
national conference in the spring of 1973 to adopt an organizational structure
and by-laws.

BE IT FINALLY RESOLVED: That the organization be temporarily referred to
as the "Coalition of Black Trade Unionists" which will operate within existing
trade union structure, but function as a collective body of black trade
unionists in the promotion of the interests of black workers and the labor
movement in general.

Resolution On Political Action

Black voters have proven to be a potent force in past presidential
elections. Their claims upon the political parties in 1972 are backed by
strong evidence that in a close election, they could again hold the balance
of power.

Practically every victorious presidential candidate since 1936 has
carried the black vote in northern central cities. In at least nine major

states -- California, New York, Illinois, Indiana, Michigan, New Jersey, Missouri, Ohio and Pennsylvania -- the black has had an enormous influence on large blocks of electoral votes. In the South, blacks make up an even larger proportion of the population in many districts, and aided by the Voting Rights Act of 1965, they have become a sizable portion of the electorate. As in the past, the black vote will be crucial in deciding the outcome of important national, state and local electoral contests.

THEREFORE BE IT RESOLVED: That the Conference opposes the re-election of President Richard Nixon and will do everything within its power to assure his defeat.

BE IT FURTHER RESOLVED: That the Conference declares the AFL-CIO's position of neutrality in the presidential election "alien to our best interests" and in no way representative of the position of the great majority of black workers.

FURTHER RESOLVED: That the two major political parties establish as their first priority the increase in the number of elected black officials at all levels of government, and encourage the appointment of blacks and other minorities in policy-making decisions in all local, state and federal agencies, and

That the Conference urge the creation of machinery for a black political movement which will develop political sophistication within black and poor communities.

That each delegate at the Chicago Conference return to his local community and become actively involved in the political process and build a local political base within his union and community by working in concert with other political leadership and organizations; and

That black union members be encouraged to run for elected public office wherever such opportunities exist; and

That black unionists demand from their respective unions funds and resources necessary for establishing viable national and local political organizations.

Resolution On Voter Registration And
Getting Out The Vote

The U.S. Bureau of the Census estimates that 57.6 percent of the black voting age population actually voted in the 1968 presidental election, compared to 69.1 percent of eligible whites. In the north and west, 64.8 percent of potential black voters actually voted, while in the south the figure was 51.6 percent.

THEREFORE BE IT RESOLVED: That black trade unionists mount a massive national voter registration and get-out-the vote campaign utilizing every available resource in their unions and communities.

BE IT FURTHER RESOLVED: That coalitions be formed between unions and civil rights and civic organizations like the NAACP, Urban League, A. Philip Randolph Institute, Masons, Elks, fraternities and sororities, and church groups.

FURTHER RESOLVED: That the black press be enlisted to help publicize voter registration and get-out-the vote programs; and

That large union halls be used for youth entertainment programs to encourage youth voter registration; and

That "dial a registrar" programs be established in the various communities to help facilitate voter registration; and

That black trade unionists take full advantage of the considerable number of pamphlets, posters, films, and other resources made available -- political parties, the AFL-CIO, the A. Philip Randolph Institute, and other political organizations.

Resolution On Job Opportunities
And Organizing Workers

Under the pretense of curbing inflation, the Nixon administration has

permitted unemployment to consistently hover around six percent -- the highest
unemployment rate in ten years -- with nearly 5.5 million workers without jobs.
Hardest hit by the Nixon unemployment program are blacks whose rates of unemployment run as high as 40 percent in many inner-city and ghetto areas.

In spite of the chronic unemployment problem, President Nixon vetoed major
legislation which would have provided $5.6 billion for an accelerated public
works program and $9.5 billion to assure employment and training for the Nation's
unemployed and under-employed citizens.

Wage controls were established by the Nixon Administration which froze the
wages of workers while permitting prices, profits, and dividends to remain
unchecked.

Black citizens who now complete on the average nearly 11 years of schooling, still find themselves earning little more than half the average income of
their white counterparts.

Of the 80 million or more workers in the American workforce, only one-
fourth of them are organized. Few concerted efforts have been made to organize
workers in domestic and service occupations, farm labor, and the public sector.

In 1966, the latest year for which figures are available from the Census
Bureau, 42.5 percent of all persons engaged in manufacturing were union members.
The corresponding figure for blacks was 57.8 percent. In durable goods, the
figures were 44.3 percent and 65.9 percent; for the metal industries, 51.3 percent and 74.1 percent; and in the manufacture of transportation equipment,
including the auto industry, the figures were 54.2 percent and 89.5 percent.

THEREFORE BE IT RESOLVED: That the Conference urge the labor movement to
use its full powers to solidify trade union coalitions which will work to
elect a Congress and national administration whose objectives will be equal and
full employment and a decent standard of living for all Americans.

BE IT FURTHER RESOLVED: That organized labor be urged to expand its
efforts to organize the unorganized, particularly workers in domestic, service,
farm and public service employment.

FURTHER RESOLVED: That funds for the Vietnam War be redirected to programs
creating jobs and job training opportunities for the unemployed and underemployed;
and

That the Conference support the expansion of minimum wage coverage to all
workers; and

That the Conference urge change in educational systems which would
emphasize teaching young people how to think as opposed to memorizing data.

Resolution On Community Development

Since he took office, President Nixon has shown a callous disregard for
the welfare of millions of black and poor Americans. Under his Administration,
the number of individuals and families with incomes below the government defined
poverty level has increased for the first time in more than a decade.

The President has been slow to develop meaningful and reasonable programs
to help resolve the many domestic problems currently facing the nation. Instead
of improving living and working conditions for the Nation's poor, President
Nixon's record shows that he has:

Proposed regressive and punitive welfare reform proposals.

Refused to spend monies appropriated by Congress for the school
lunch program providing nutritious meals for needy children.

Vetoed comprehensive day care and child development legislation.

Vigorously opposed the creation of a strong independent consumer
advocate program within the government.

Opposed adequate cost of living increases under Social Security.

Advocated a policy of "benign neglect" toward black citizens and
minimized federal civil rights enforcement efforts.

Reopened the nation's racial wounds by developing negative policies
on such sensitive issues as busing, job quotas, and federally subsidized
low-income housing for suburban communities.

The domestic policies of the Nixon Administration have proven disastrous
for workers, minorities, and poverty-stricken families.

THEREFORE BE IT RESOLVED: That the Conference of Black Trade Unionists work cooperatively and actively with church, social, civic, education, and civil rights organizations to improve the living conditions of black and poor families, and that black trade unionists seek out opportunities to serve on local boards and commissions in order to maximize the participation and influence of black and poor workers in community decision-making.

The following organizations were represented at the first Conference of Black Trade Unionists, held in Chicago, Ill., on September 23-24:

Allied Industrial Workers of America, AFL-CIO
Amalgamated Clothing Workers of America, AFL-CIO
Amalgamated Meat Cutters and Butcher Workmen of North America, AFL-CIO
American Federation of Government Employees, AFL-CIO
American Federation of Musicians, AFL-CIO
American Federation of State, County, and Municipal Employees, AFL-CIO
American Federation of Teachers, AFL-CIO
American Postal Workers Union, AFL-CIO
Bakery and Confectionary Workers' International Union of America, AFL-CIO
Bricklayers, Masons, Plasters' International Union of America, AFL-CIO
Communication Workers of America, AFL-CIO
Distillery, Rectifying, Wine and Allied Workers' International Union of
     America, AFL-CIO
Distributive Workers of America
Food Packers Association
Hotel and Restaurant Employees and Bartenders International Union, AFL-CIO
Illinois Union of Social Services' Employees
International Association of Machinists, AFL-CIO
International Association of Marble, Slate and Stone Polishers, Rubbers, and
     Sawyers, Tile and Marble Setters Helpers and Terrazzo Helpers, AFL-CIO
International Brotherhood of Electrical Workers, AFL-CIO
International Brotherhood of Teamsters
International Ladies' Garment Workers Union, AFL-CIO
International Longshoremen's Association, AFL-CIO
International Woodworkers of America, AFL-CIO
Laborers International Union of North America, AFL-CIO
Laundry and Dry Cleaning International Union, AFL-CIO
National Education Association
Newspaper Guild, AFL-CIO
Office and Professional Employees International Union, AFL-CIO
Retail Clerks Workers Union of America, AFL-CIO
Retail, Wholesale, Department Store Workers Union, AFL-CIO
Seafarers International Union of North America, AFL-CIO
Transport Workers of America, AFL-CIO
United Auto Workers
United Cement, Lime, and Gypsum Workers International Union, AFL-CIO
United Steel Workers, AFL-CIO
United Textile Workers of America, AFL-CIO

Coalition of Black Trade Unionists, *Conference Report* (1972), pp. 1-58.
Pamphlet in possession of the editors.

13.   BLACK UNIONISTS FORM COALITION

*Organization Will Work for McGovern But
Will Not Disband After Election*

By Philip Shabecoff

WASHINGTON, Oct. 2--Black trade unionists, reacting to the decision of the American Federation of Labor and Congress of Industrial Organizations to remain neutral in the Presidential campaign, are forming a permanent national organization.

The organization, called for by over 1,200 black union members and leaders at a meeting in Chicago last week, will initially concentrate on registering black voters and getting out the vote for Senator George McGovern.

But William Lucy, Secretary Treasurer of the American Federation of State, County and Municipal Employes who is spokesman for the new group, said in an interview that the organization would be made permanent "to deal with the peculiar problems of the black trade unionists."

"It's obvious that the A.F.L.-C.I.O. is not doing its job for black workers. The federation may consider the problems of poor blacks, but it doesn't understand those problems," Mr. Lucy said in an interview.

The Chicago meeting elected a five-man steering committee to draft a constitution for a group to be called the Coalition of Black Trade Unionists.

Workers and the Poor

The coalition will conduct a membership drive to enlist black union members throughout the country, Mr. Lucy said. It will also embark on an intensive effort to organize poor blacks, he added.

There are about 2 million black members of trade unions. The total number of blacks in the work force is estimated at 9.8 million.

The new coalition will not be a black "separatist" or even a "civil rights" organization, Mr. Lucy explained. It will work within the trade union framework for black workers and the black community, he said.

"But before now there has been no forum for black militancy within the trade union movement," he asserted.

The decision by George Meany and the executive council of the labor federation to refrain from endorsing a Presidential candidate this year was the catalyst that created the move toward a national black labor organization.

Nixon Impact Cited

"The A.F.L.-C.I.O. decision did not take into consideration the negative impact that Nixon has on the poor, especially the black poor," Mr. Lucy said. "There is no way black unionists are going to remain neutral in this election," he declared.

However, the goals of the new coalition go far beyond this year's election, and will deal with matters of particular concern to black workers he said.

For example, the new organization would not support the President's continuation of the war, as the leadership of the A.F.L.-C.I.O. has done, Mr. Lucy said.

"The war is using up money that is required for rebuilding the cities, for schools, for medical care and other things of vital concern to the black community," he declared.

The coalition will play an active role in bringing more black workers into the trade union movement, he said. It will prepare a "positive" program for raising the percentage of blacks in construction jobs, a task, he insisted, that has not been adequately performed by the labor federation.

The coalition would also serve as a link between the trade union movement and the black community -- and with poor communities in general.

The black communities, he declared, do not understand and do not trust the trade union movement. Meanwhile, organized labor has not done enough in the development of the poor black communities, he asserted.

At the labor federation's headquarters, Donald Slaiman, director of the group's civil rights department, denied Mr. Lucy's charges of inadequate concern with the problems of black workers. Mr. Slaiman also expressed doubt about the need for a national organization.

Mr. Slayman said that the A. Philip Randolph Institute, which is headed by Bayard Rustin, deals on a continuing basis with problems relating to workers and to the black community. Moreover, a large and growing number of unions are electing black officers, he noted.

"The number of officers may lag behind the number of minority union members, but it takes time to develop leaders."

Mr. Slayman said that the A.F.L.-C.I.O. had done an effective job on behalf of black workers and minorities in general. Its member unions have done "a tremendous job" in organizing the poor, he added.

"It's true there is still a lot to be done, but the record shows we haven't done badly at all," he said.

New York Times, October 3, 1972.

14. A GIANT STEP TOWARD UNITY

By Jacoby Sims

During two cool days in Chicago last September, 1,200 African-American trade unionists gathered to form the Coalition of Black Trade Unionists. The attendance far surpassed the initiators' dreams. One unionist said, "The sleeping giant is awakening."

There are some three million African-American trade unionists in the U.S. This is one-third of the total Black labor force. If they were all organized, their influence would be sizeable, both in the labor movement and in government. Members of the Coalition feel that the demands of Afro-American labor must be felt in those two areas.

Rank-and-filers and union officials from 37 unions throughout the nation attended the conference. Prior to a national constitutional convention planned for this spring, there will be regional conferences in New York, Chicago, Detroit, Washington, D.C., Cleveland and, possibly, San Francisco or Los Angeles.

On January 19, I interviewed William Simons, a member of the Coalition's steering committee and president of Local 6 of the Washington Teacher's Union, AFT, in the offices of his union.

Mr. Simons, besides his organized labor activities, has been involved in the struggle for equal rights with such groups as the National Urban League and the NAACP. He has also been active in the movement against U.S. intervention in the affairs of people of the "Third World."

Q: Mr. Simons, what is the Coalition of Black Trade Unionists?

A: The Coalition of Black Trade Unionists is a group that was organized this past summer. The purpose of organizing at that time was to express our displeasure to the position taken by George Meany and the executive council (of the AFL-CIO) on the elections, that of neutrality.

The group was also concerned about the fact that much needs to be done in the labor movement to eradicate the racist practices, the discriminatory practices, which still exist within certain unions.

And we felt that if we could organize, we would then be able to demonstrate that there are real concerns to which the labor movement is not addressing itself. We want the labor movement to address itself not only to the concerns of Black trade unionists but to those of all trade unionists.

Q: Who participated in the conference?

A: In the formation of the group there was Bill Lucy, Secretary-Treasurer of the American Federation of State, County and Municipal Employees, Nelson Jack Edwards from the United Auto Workers, Charlie Hayes from the Amalgamated Meatcutters, myself and there were one or two others.

There were members from both the AFL-CIO unions and from non-AFL-CIO unions. We had our initial meeting in Miami in August and we had additional meetings in Washington and we laid plans for the September conference.

Since that conference there have been three meetings. Their purpose was to try to put together a constitution and a structure in order to mobilize trade unionists around the country.

While the name of the organization is the Coalition of Black Trade Unionists, we do not by any means intend to limit it to Black trade unionists.

At our last meeting, we discussed taking our positions to the Secretary of Labor designee, Peter Brennan. We sought to have a conference with him simply to raise certain issues, to get his feeling about how he is going to use his position to further the growth of labor in the United States. Unfortunately Mr. Brennen did not see fit to meet with us.

Today we testified before the Senate Subcommittee holding hearings on the confirmation of Mr. Brennan. We raised these questions with the sub-committee. The sub-committee agreed it would place these questions before Mr. Brennan and elicit responses from him concerning the issues we raised. We did not take a position for or against Mr. Brennan, we simply indicated there were some concerns that we would like the sub-committee to investigate thoroughly before they arrive at any decision with respect to his confirmation.

Q: Who testified for the Coalition?

A: Bill Lucy read the main statement. Dick Parrish, respresenting the New York Distributive Workers of America, made some comments and I also made a few comments.

Q: You just stated that the Coalition is not limited to just Black workers and Black trade unionists. Who else can participate?

A: We have not drawn up our constitution as yet. But we envision that any trade unionist who is concerned with the same problems as the Coalition will be eligible for membership. I might point out that out of the 1,200 delegates in Chicago, there were at least 200-300 non-black, and other minority delegates. And they had full participation in the deliberations of the conference.

Q: When will the constitutional conference take place?

A: We are shooting for a date some time this spring, possibly in April. That has not been finalized.

Q: Is there a preliminary constitution?

A: No, we only have working papers, documents not in finalized form. We are working on a structure and quite frankly we intend to just about parallel the same kind of structure that the AFL-CIO has. That is, with the central body or executive committee or whatever name we give to it -- with state federations and local bodies with each body being autonomous -- within the framework of being bound by only the constitutional guidelines that are going to be established.

Q: How will rank-and-file participation be encouraged?

A: Rank-and-file participation will be encouraged at the local and state levels. Each local jurisdiction can organize -- have membership. And then each local jurisdiction would send delegates to the state federation. And then of course the governing body would be elected by the entire membership at the convention.

Q: Will you be working with the same unions involved in the original conference and will the group be expanded?

A: It's going to expand. Hopefully, we will get a broad-based participation from the whole spectrum of the labor movement, from those unions which are in the AFL-CIO and those which are not.

Q: What is the purpose of the Coalition?

A: The purpose is to identify the problem that exists in the labor movement as a whole. And to bring whatever pressures we can to try to get these situations corrected, so that all workers can get a fair share of the pie in the labor movement. We are not going to be a watchdog, in terms of practices that exist in individual unions. In other words, a member cannot bring a grievance to the Coalition and expect the Coalition to take action. That is not our purpose at all.

We are looking at the overall trends and, for example, we are trying to influence the decisions made by the executive council of the AFL-CIO. We will try to influence broad policy decisions of internationals.

Also, we intend to concentrate not only on problems in the labor movement per se, but also problems in the community and country.

Q: Could you specify some of the problems which U.S. workers face?

A: For example, I think we had a clear indication just yesterday, when we learned that the American Telephone and Telegraph Company has been ordered to pay some 38 million dollars to upgrade the salaries of women and other non-white workers against whom they were discriminating.

This is the kind of thing we would call attention to in other companies. This practice has been condoned by the Communication Workers (of America) over

the years. They represent the majority of the employees in the telephone system.
There are also some workers organized by the IBEW (International Brotherhood of
Electrical Workers).   Condoning discrimination has been the policy of the
union leadership.   These are the kind of things we would call attention to.

Q: In the September conference, rank-and-file workers are particularly
concerned with methods whereby they could get more Black elected officials in
their locals.   Could the Coalition lend support here?

A: Yes, in terms of working with groups of workers and acquainting them
with their union structure and how officials are elected.   And if a structure
is democratic enough -- and many unions do have a democratic process -- we will
tell the Black workers they have to begin organizing on a political basis and
be able to mobilize their voting strength at conventions or meetings or wherever
voting takes place.

Q: Are there any qualifications for membership in the Coalition? Is it
open to trade unionists regardless of political affiliation?

A. The only qualification will be that the person is a member of a
qualified union.

Q: What about President Nixon? Since he is a lame duck President, what
might he unleash on the Black worker, and workers in general?

A: Of course we have already seen how the wage-price guidelines have
affected workers.   I suspect there will probably be some efforts on the part of
the administration to try to curb the bargaining power of unions.

I do not expect that we are going to get very much in the way of positive
action by the President to lift up the workers in this country.   It has not been
the pattern in the past and I can see nothing that will project that in the
future.

Q: Will the Coalition continue to stress independent political action,
such as trade unionists running for elected offices?

A: Very definitely we would stress that kind of action.   It is absolutely
essential that there should be representatives of the workers in legislative
bodies in order to try to help shape the legislation that will benefit the
workers.

And also we would support those candidates in state legislatures as well
as Congress who have a sympathetic viewpoint toward the problems which the
working man faces. . . .

World Magazine, February 10, 1973.

15.   NEWEST BLACK POWER: BLACK LEADERS
BUILDING MASSIVE LABOR COALITION INSIDE UNIONS

By Victor Riesel

WASHINGTON--Not in many, ofttimes fiery decades has black militancy--
which is as different from extremism as a winch from a wench--been on the move.

This is a new black movement--within a movement.   Black labor men and
leaders who see their strategy as structural, quiet, organizational, motiva-
tional, and finally, a powerful massive pressure "group" far beyond the "old"
era of civil rights.

This is the Coalition of Black Trade Unionists (CBTU).   This is a movement
of men, mostly black union officials, who see themselves and the entire three
million black rank and filers as the force which will make the national labor
leadership "black conscious."   Such consciousness is not, and was not there
during last week's national labor high command meeting in Bal Harbour, Fla.,
say the CBTU's leaders, some of whom flew directly from the watering place in
sunny Florida to frigid Chicago.

On Feb. 24, they met with some 100 black labor leaders there--men and
women from western Indiana, Ohio and Michigan.   This was one of the regional
conferences which gradually will lead to the official national black, infra-
structured membership organization of unionized workers.   There will be

regional conferences in Cleveland March 10, Detroit March 31, and New York April 14.

Then with a provisional constitution in hand, the five CBTU leaders--officials of some of the nation's most influential and swiftest growing unions in the land--will make final plans for a national convention of black workers in Washington, May 25-27.

They will sing "Solidarity." They will sing "We Shall Overcome." They will be militant. But they will not bolt the AFL-CIO, or the independent United Auto Workers and Distributive Workers to which the black workers belong.

Instead, they will push for more influence, more "relevancy," more high echelon officials, more representation in the highest councils--including the AFL-CIO Executive Council--and more members on the boards of such unions as the United Steelworkers.

Man, the jargon will be different. But not the spirit of national and ethnic pressure groups gone by--powerful organizations of yesteryear which now are tiny bands of workers who have survived assimilation, tradition and the silent slippage of time.

Ever since the first dues stamp, there have been pressure groups of newly arrived proletarians. There have been--and quietly in some corner of the remnant of New York's lower East Side there still are--the one-man offices of the United Hebrew Trades, the Italian American Labor Council, German "vereine" and other groups still speaking their native tongues.

They once were powerful. They once were the force behind some of today's national labor leaders and some who have only recently retired. Some of these men actually launched movements which made Presidents of the U.S. and changed this nation's social action.

They worked mostly inside the labor movement. Now in that old tradition, though one would hardly note it amid the rhetoric of today's black speakers, the Coalition of Black Trade Unionists quietly is structuring itself. And may well have the success of its ethnic predecessors.

Actually the young (there even are some middle-aged) organizers spring from the very same unions which spurted the old movements--unions whose leaders have "graduated" from the garment industry and those in the American Federation of State, County and Municipal Employees, the Amalgamated Meatcutters and Butcher Workmen, the United Auto Workers (UAW), the American Federation of Teachers, and the Distributive Workers.

From these unions come the men on the CBTU's five-man Steering Committee, especially the municipal employees' secretary treasurer Bill Lucy, the meatcutter's Charles Hayes and the UAW's Nelson Jack Edwards.

They are neo-(Franklin) Rooseveltians, worshippers at the Kennedy's shrine and newly arrived militants. They are anti-NIXON, anti-Republican and even determined to needle Secretary of Labor Peter Brennan. They have demanded that he be recalled to Sen. Harrison (Pete) Williams's Labor Committee--not for a rehearing on his confirmation, but to get some promises from him. They want support from the former president of the New York State Building and Construction Trades Council for a universal law guaranteeing civil service workers the right to bargain collectively and to strike.

They want Brennan to pledge the beefing up of the Labor Dept.'s Office of Federal Contract Compliance (OFCC) to reinstate the black quota system of hiring by those who do business with the government. They say that the OFCC has been cut to 45 employees though 112 positions have been authorized.

They are swinging into the fight to keep the Office of Economic Opportunity (OEO) going, also the mechanism of other groups which once policed the old "Philadelphia Plan."

But mostly they want militant black representation on the AFL-CIO Executive Council, and on the executive boards of their unions. They are saying to the labor movement, match your actions with your official oratory and resolutions. In the lead is Bill Lucy, actually the highest placed black official in the labor movement--secretary treasurer of Jerry Wurf's municipal employees.

There's a labor song which says, "We'll thunder high the battle cry."
The CBTU plans just that, not only at its second national convention in May
but in street rallies in the big cities with heavy black populations--Detroit,
Philadelphia, New York, Washington, Atlanta. The big cities where once the
civil rights extremists roared soon will hear the calmer, but more powerful,
voices of black militancy attempting to march upward inside their own movement.

Press release dated February 26, 1973. Copy in possession of the editors.

16. BLACK CAUCUS IN THE UNIONS

By Stephen C. Schlesinger

As the emotions stirred up by the AFL-CIO's decision to stay neutral in
the 1972 election have gradually subsided, the labor movement is beginning to
awaken to what that election year blowup actually accomplished. One result is
a new liberal coalition of the unions which defied Meany in 1972 and endorsed
McGovern. Another is the pro-McGovern Coalition of Black Trade Unionists
(CBTU) which came into being to give black workers a voice in future federation endorsements.
        Autonomous liberal unions within labor, though they have been few and
their coalition is still informal, have been around before. But the
appearance of a unified black caucus within the portals of the AFL-CIO is
striking in several particulars: it marks the first time that an influential
segment of black unionists has identified itself as a separate body within
the federation; it exposes a division among progressive and cautious blacks
in labor; it intensifies the split between the liberal and conservative
wings of the federation, and it is affecting the way the whole labor movement
approaches such issues as race and party reform.
        The decision to establish the Coalition of Black Trade Unionists
originally followed George Meany's attempt to enforce labor neutrality in
the 1972 Presidential campaign. The fact that no black union leaders were
consulted by the AFL-CIO at a time when blacks total 3 million of the 20
million unionized workers in the country brought home to many black unionists
the limits of their power in the federation.
        Angered by Meany's edict, black activists organized to defy the federa-
tion's hands-off stand. A call went out to liberal black unionists around the
country to come together in Chicago for a conference in late September 1972.
Bill Lucy, secretary-treasurer of the American Federation of State, County and
Municipal Employees (AFSCME), was one of the most persuasive forces behind the
convocation. He recalls that many people responded because of their appreciation that the Executive Council's position was "absolutely in contrast to the
needs and aspirations of black workers and the black community." An unusual
1,500 men and women from thirty-three unions showed up in Chicago.
        The intensity of feelings triggered by the neutrality issue was evident
at the time in the comments of participants. Said Cleveland Robinson, president of the Distributive Workers union, George Meany "has not understood us
yet, and the unfortunate thing is that today we have a situation where even
once enlightened leadership--white leadership--in the labor movement has now
succumbed and sat by and echoed the reactionary, backward sentiments that he
expresses, whether it be on the war in Vietnam or the current political
situation."
        But the coalition deliberately refrained from trying to create a separate
labor movment for blacks. Instead, it agreed to organize within the AFL-CIO
and agitate for change in labor's highest councils. Bill Lucy announced at
the meeting: "But what we are going to do is make [the Executive Council]
honest. We are going to make it concerned with what its social goals used
to be. . . ." The coalition passed a tough resolution calling the AFL-CIO's
neutrality "alien to our best interests," but, aside from authorizing the
black trade unionists to work for McGovern, it carefully talked about "reform-
ing" the AFL-CIO "just like," as Charles Hayes, vice president of the
Amalgamated Meat Cutters and Butcher Workmen union said, "the Democrats did
in their party."

The Black Trade Unionists have since held several other conferences, the most recent being in Washington last May, when twenty-seven national unions and nine nonunion organizations appeared. The coalition now comprises thirty-three unions representing more than a million black workers, and on its steering committee are such black unionists as Nelson Jack Edwards (UAW), Charles Hayes (Meat Cutters), Cleveland Robinson (Distributive Workers) and Bill Lucy.

After one year, the coalition has become, according to one's angle of vision, a powerful irritant or a powerful stimulant inside the AFL-CIO. It has challenged George Meany on a number of issues. In addition to the dispute over McGovern, the federation and the coalition have locked horns over the appointment of Peter Brennan to be Secretary of Labor (Meany favored it), revenue sharing (the coalition approved it because poor blacks form the core population of most cities; Meany opposed it because he felt it lacked federal controls over the moneys), and affirmative action programs in the Democratic Party's selection of delegates (the coalition favored affirmative action with compliance monitored by the party; the AFL-CIO opposed anything which remotely resembled quotas, including most forms of affirmative action). Bill Lucy concedes that, because of these wrangles, many labor people "accused the coalition of being separatist, anti-AFL-CIO, antagonistic, a protest movement. But we never had a quarrel with the AFL-CIO. We just felt that blacks should have some input into decisions." Incidentally, the CBTU did support the AFL-CIO on the Burke-Hartke bill.

However, it does seem rather uppity for blacks to be acting this way now in the AFL-CIO, since for years they led lives of benign passivity within the federation. They upset no applecarts and behaved with pleasant resignation in the face of blatant discrimination by many unions within the AFL-CIO. Even in 1963, when A. Philip Randolph, head of the Brotherhood of Sleeping Car Porters, had the gumption to promote the March on Washington, Meany lambasted him and kept the AFL-CIO well away from the demonstration.

The characteristic federation black of recent days has been Bayard Rustin. Ironically, he was the master strategist behind the Washington March. Now, as director of the A. Philip Randolph Institute, a Meany-funded and Meany-controlled operation which has done work on voter registration and political education, Rustin has become a Meany apologist. He has, for example, preached the AFL-CIO position against the quotas in the Democratic Party's delegate selection; he favors affirmative action, but many observers find his position ambiguous and laced with Meany-type rhetoric. Rustin has earned the furious contempt of many black unionists with whom I talked.

The coalition leaders are younger than Rustin, uncowed by Meany, on the payrolls of unions which themselves act independently; they are outspoken. The only puzzling thing about them, in fact, is why as a group they waited so long to organize the coalition--long after the sit-ins, the civil rights marches, and the elections of blacks to office in the 1960s and early 1970s.

For the black presence in organized labor has, after all, been remarkable. One-third of the black work force is in unions, primarily in the monster industrial unions like the United Auto Workers (500,000 blacks out of 1.5 million members); the Steelworkers (200,000 out of 1.2 million members); the Teamsters (200,000 out of 1.8 million members); and the large white-collar unions like the AFSCME (180,000 out of 615,000 members). The industrial mode of unionization, gulping whole markets at a swallow, has proven to be color-blind. It has subverted racism and created large pools of middle-class black labor.

The successful integration of these unions, in turn, has highlighted the restrictive policies of the craft or building trade unions, whose limited work markets have fostered rigid job controls that lead to the exclusion of blacks. For instance, the most recent figures for the building trades in New York City (where most of the construction unions are concentrated) shows that blacks have actually lost ground in jobs in proportion to their presence in the city's population. In the years 1960 to 1970, blacks increased 60 per cent in population but black construction workers increased only 33-1/3 per cent.

The disquieting fact is that this meager representation of blacks in the building trades has for years provoked little protest from blacks within the AFL-CIO (though outside organizations like Fightback and the NAACP have for more than a decade fought discrimination in the construction unions). Only now,

with the tardy formation of the Coalition of Black Trade Unionists, will these
aggravations over the lack of black membership in the craft unions be highlighted and will the black membership in the larger industrial unions become
more militant. The latter effect is already apparent with the formation of
strong black caucuses within unions like the International Association of
Machinists (IAM).

The coalition's role will become more important in the next few years as
blacks continue to grow in number in the AFL-CIO unions. According to the
Labor Department's Bureau of Labor Statistics, blacks are today more likely
than whites to take a unionized job. As long as union membership remains
static (it is about the same today as it was in 1955, when the AFL merged with
the CIO--slightly less than 15 million), black membership will rise more
quickly than white membership. This means that blacks will strengthen their
influence in the labor movement as a whole. And those unions which deny them
jobs, especially the building trades, will find less sympathy from other unions
and become increasingly isolated within the movement.

The division between wings of the labor movement over the issue of race has
already shown up in symbolic ways. CBTU has been endorsed by thirty-three
unions within and without the AFL-CIO; and twenty-one unions bought tickets to
the September dinner of the Congressional Black Caucus in Washington, including
some of the CBTU endorsees, and others like the IAM, the Electrical Workers, the
NEA, the Oil, Chemical and Atomic Workers, the National P.O. Mail Handlers
union; Pocketbook Workers Local #1, the Fire Fighters union and the AFL-CIO
Board. Other AFL-CIO unions and non-federation unions have not endorsed the
CBTU and did not attend the Black Caucus dinner. Many unions still feel no
need to make overtures to any black political bodies for various reasons: lack
of social involvement, absence of black members, a desire to discourage black
activism within unions and outright racist feelings.

Black unemployment remains a festering wound in American society. Unemployment is twice as high for blacks as for whites; black teen-agers have a 33.5
per cent unemployment rate. And 33 per cent of all blacks live below the
poverty line while only 9 per cent of whites are that poor. Indeed, poor blacks
increased by 300,000 in 1972, a year when a million Americans rose out of
poverty.

These chilling statistics have had their consequences. Blacks today are
becoming more cold-blooded about their own interests. The creation of the
Coalition of Black Trade Unionists, like the establishment of the Congressional
Black Caucus, is a recognition that in a pluralistic society like the United
States, and in a federation of many unions like the AFL-CIO, only a raw form of
interest-group liberalism can achieve recognition and influence.

The coalition is beginning to push hard on a few demands: more blacks in
union leadership; educational programs to teach blacks in communities about
unions and vice versa; a national legislative and political action lobby for
blacks; expanded union organizing for blacks, other minorities and whites;
in-depth studies of subjects like the impact of technological changes on the
black labor market, etc.

The AFL-CIO's present tactic seems to be to brush the coalition off
politely. This may change as events overtake the federation, but Meany's
neutrality in 1972 did not quite envisage the counterrevolution which has been
triggered within the federation. What is happening now, slowly and awkwardly,
could portend a new liberalization of the AFL-CIO, or it could split the
AFL-CIO wide open. Either way, the power of blacks in labor has become a small
whirlwind which the trade unions can no longer contain or suppress.

The Nation, 218 (February 2, 1974):142-44.

BAYARD RUSTIN

17. MORALS CONCERNING MINORITIES:
     MENTAL HEALTH AND IDENTITY

By Bayard Rustin

It would appear that the public morality in America at the present time
is being dominated, to an alarming degree, by a concern with technological and
corporate priorities. This concern, quite naturally, ignores the problems and
aspirations of the ordinary individual, particularly the individual who is not
equipped either by spiritual inclination or technical training to participate
in the processes and values in which these priorities are pursued. A humane
culture as we have imagined it and dreamed of it in America, and which at
certain periods of our history has appeared possible, seems today to be on the
verge of being sacrificed to the special exigences of the marketplace: That
is to say, as the new technological and organizational obsession spreads, the
possibility of our creating an engaged social conscience recedes further and
further into the background, leaving more and more people, particularly our
minorities, stranded and neglected in a deepening mire of social and economic
problems. . . .
     At the heart of this problem -- the dehumanization, demoralization, and
exclusion of the individual from the prevailing concerns of our society -- is
the problem of our minorities. And increasingly today the heart of our
minority problem is being located in the urban centers of our nation. None
of us -- even those who are least interested in solutions -- can have escaped
the sense of fear and frustration that are building up in our cities, perhaps
towards an explosion whose effects we might not be able to control. And none
of us can deny that this situation is being brought about by the gradual
diminution of social morality and social concern for the value of the
individual. . . .
     As minorities are driven to the cities in search of a better life,
those in a position to help them fulfill these aspirations shrink from them
to the greener suburbs, leaving behind growing reservoirs of helplessness
and misery.
     This is by no means an excessive estimate. An objective profile of what
the cities will look like in the year 1980, or even 2000, gives no less cause
for concern. In a paper written for the Center for the Study of Democratic
Institutions, Victor Palmieri, president of the Janss Corporation, states:

          Within the next two decades -- probably in 1980 -- the core
          area of almost every major metropolitan city of the United
          States will be a racial -- predominantly black -- island.
          This is not a speculatiln. It is already very largely a
          fact in Washington, Chicago, and New York City. It is
          rapidly becoming a fact in Detroit, Philadelphia, and Los
          Angeles. Three established factors -- the rate of popula-
          tion growth among minority groups (almost three times that
          of the white population in the City of Los Angeles); the
          increasing income level and mobility of middle class white
          families; and the resulting domino effect on racially
          impacted school districts -- will maintain the velocity of
          the trend and virtually guarantee its ultimate concern. . . .

     It is in the face of this situation that white majorities become fearful
of their mental and economic security and the minorities become more and more
frustrated. The privileged majorities either retreat into pockets of
resistance or flee to the suburbs, a flight, incidentally, which the government has been subsidizing for years now by the building of new highways and
the establishment of suburban housing. While the white majority has been able
to find these outlets for their fear, there has been no outlet for minority
frustration except in rioting. The cycle seems so vicious and I'm convinced
that this whole problem -- the problem of our minorities and of our cities --

grows out of one source, and that is fundamental social immorality in our
society; the failure or unwillingness to establish humane priorities; the
absence of a major public commitment to eradicate poverty and slums. . . .

I myself wrote in the November 1966 issue of *Federationist* magazine
that a vicious cycle was being set in motion:

> Failing to deal with the social and economic roadblocks to
> equality, we stoke the fire of frustration in the ghetto;
> violent riots and cries of "black power" in turn feed a
> white backlash which makes constructive solutions to the
> problems of blacks and whites more difficult. Finally,
> backlash only confirms Negro isolationists in their
> hostility toward white America. We are today at the
> crossroads. Within the next 50 years, if the cycle of
> fear and frustration is not broken, if the just economic
> demands of the labor movement are not coupled with the
> democratic aspirations of the Negro people, and if men
> of goodwill do not join in the fight for programs such
> as the Freedom Budget for all Americans, which would end
> poverty within the next ten years in this country, then
> we may very well be propelled into a racial nightmare.
> And not only the ethnic minorities will benefit from
> the Freedom Budget; 75 percent of the poor white. All
> of us are affected by the persistence of poverty -- in
> the conditions of our neighborhoods and schools, in our
> tax rates and public services, in the quality of our
> lives. . . .

Minority Poverty and Joblessness: The white immigrant waves of the
nineteenth century and early twentieth centuries faced ethnic and religious
prejudice but they were never confronted, as today's ethnic minorities are,
with an organized system of race hatred with its own laws and myths and
stereotypes, its own economy. Those of the older generations of the white
poor who fought their way out of poverty could thus assimilate into American
life as soon as they acquired money, education, mastery of the language, and
so forth. Also, the older white immigrant came into an economy which could
put grade school drop-outs to work. The minorities who are struggling today
are faced with an entirely different problem; they must compete not only
within race prejudice but also against machines.

Moreover, the unemployed rates today are much higher than they were even
during the worst years of the great depression. As James McGregor Burns
points out, 20 percent of the population was then unemployed. Today, a U.S.
Department of Labor study estimates that in the 12 largest areas unemployment
rates between 14-and 19-year-olds range from 18.4 percent in Washington, D.C.,
to 36 percent in Philadelphia, with the rate running about 30 percent in
seven areas. The rate of nonwhite girls is somewhat higher than for boys
(over 40 percent in Philadelphia and St. Louis).[109]

I believe, therefore, that, in the same way the society provided the old
immigrants with opportunities to lift themselves and play a meaningful role
in the American social and economic order, so also it is obliged to find a
way to provide today's minorities with the opportunity and potential to lift
and save themselves: And, in keeping with our present circumstances, any
program which is conceived to help our minorities out of their present plight
must include, first and foremost, a program for full and fair employment,
i.e., federally guaranteed jobs for all those -- whether members of minority
groups or not -- who are eligible or can be made eligible for employment in
the production of goods and services in the public sector. Gerhard Colm of
the National Planning Association is correct when he suggests that such a
program of full employment *per se* will not solve all the problems of poverty,
and especially not the racial problems, but it would contribute substantially
to the solution and would create the best conditions for attacking the
residual problems. Secondly, the program must include a two-dollar minimum
wage; and, thirdly, a guaranteed annual income for those too old, too young,
or too sick to work.

We need federally financed public works programs for the creation of the
necessary physical institutions -- more schools, more hospitals, more roads,

more clinics, more psychiatric facilities, more libraries. Not only should
the poor benefit from the increased services of these physical facilities,
they should also participate in building them -- acquiring skills while being
paid. This is especially important if we are going to convince young minority
group members to take advantage of training or retraining programs. One
cannot train young people in a vacuum and expect to win their seriousness,
their hope, or their cooperation; in other words, one must show them that the
jobs exist for which they are being trained, and that they can work on those
jobs even while they are being trained.

Part of any program for full employment is the need for a "redefinition
of work." This is necessary to make up for the inroads which automation has
made into areas traditionally served by human labor. That is to say, we must
redefine work around those kinds of efforts which the technological revolution
cannot affect. What are some of these efforts? They involve creating a whole
new hierarchy of non-professional workers to help the professional perform
some of the functions he now performs. . . .

There must be creation of new opportunities for human services. Academic
study should be redefined as work and paid for. Many functions which are
performed today by underprivileged people but which do not have the stamp of
prestige should be redefined as prestigious labor and be paid for at dignified
wages. All of this, of course, must be part of a grand plan to solve poverty
and to create new motivations and liberate new energies by which minorities
can achieve a new sense of belonging and a new sense of identity in American
life.

I would make the two-dollar minimum wage the next major priority. That
alone could do as much as the entire poverty program in terms of helping
people rehabilitate themselves through their own lucrative labor. . . .

Even the passage of a two-dollar minimum wage is modest. It guarantees
an income of $4160 for a year's work, and that is roughly $2000 less than what
the government has computed to be a "modest but adequate" urban family budget.
We should not be satisfied until every American family has at least that
"modest but adequate" income. For now, however, an increase of the minimum
wage to $2.00 is a responsible and reasonable step in the right direction.

Here, I would like to discuss the most common argument against extending
wage coverage and against raising the minimum wage itself to $2.00. Rising
labor costs in unskilled and semi-skilled work, it is said, provide an incentive to employers to mechanize or even to automate. The results will be the
elimination of precisely those marginal jobs which now provide at least an
employment opportunity for unskilled Negroes, young people, and others who are
not qualified to compete in the modern economy. There is some truth in this
argument. If Congress simply amends the Fair Labor Standards Act and lets it
go at that, then the result could be negative. That is why we cannot regard
minimum wage as a panacea. That is why my proposals make sense only within
the framework of a national commitment to generate new jobs.

I would then add a guaranteed annual income. But let us consider a few
figures. As recently as March 3 this year, Joseph Alsop wrote in his syndi-
cated newspaper column:

> At present, a million American families with
> 3,200,000 children are living on welfare. In addition,
> another 3,600,000 American families with 11,800,000
> children, though not caught in the welfare trap, are
> subsisting in grinding poverty that mocks and
> dishonors our national influence.

Now, obviously, we need a bold social and economic innovation to end the
pathetic dependence of so many millions of our citizens on the caprice of
welfare agencies, and I would suggest that the innovation ought to be a
guaranteed annual income for those who are too old, too young, or too sick to
work; or mothers or families who cannot or should not work.

I do not believe that the way to deal with man is to deal with him only
as an economic person. . . . We cannot keep on handing out checks like leaflets. A man needs to feel that the check he gets is a wage for services to
the society and, given the nature of our Western values, I do not believe
that he can feel dignity and humanity by simply having checks given to him
periodically. . . .

The foregoing are some of the basic areas in which minority mental health and identity have suffered in the past, and are still suffering, but in which they should be protected from suffering in the future. And, as I suggested earlier, the creation of a more humane future -- a more humane 21st century -- for these people requires a commitment in social morality such as we have not had at any previous period of our history.

And here I should like to say a word about one or two of the possible ways in which the minorities themselves can help to generate or set in motion the sweeping social changes that the coming decades demand. Without going into the Freedom Budget, I may say I believe the programs it puts forward represent the most urgent demand for economic change in the lives of the poor in America, and provides a rallying point around which millions of America's poor and excluded can mount a massive campaign in behalf of their own future.

Which brings me to the point I really want to make: the need for organization and coalition. As stated earlier, the only elements among the minorities that are in any significant motion are the Negroes and Spanish-American minorities. This is a serious problem because these groups do not have sufficient political power to deal with any of the stubborn economic problems in the society. The only way in which these problems can be dealt with is through the creation of a political coalition made up of Jews, Catholics, Protestants, the labor movement, liberals, the students, intellectuals, civil rights, and other minority groups. And I believe one of the key partners in this coalition has to be the labor movement, particularly because it has been the most successful voluntary organization for the abolition of poverty in American history.

Elizabeth Wickenden points out that "such a coalition will become effective when there is a wide-spreading network of mutual interest. This involves a very delicate balance of what is particular to one group and what is the common interest of many groups. . . . More members of the majority need to recognize their own interests are jeopardized by an excluded submerged minority, not through fear but through real understanding."

The economic challenge that now faces minority groups gives the labor movement an opportunity to face up to a new and profound challenge. Almost half of the heads of poor families work hard and long -- yet they are still poor. Some of them are denied coverage under the nation's collective bargaining policies -- especially Mexican-American farm workers -- others lack Social Security, some work at sub-poverty wages, and many work in unorganized shops. Therefore, I believe the labor movement's program for increasing minimum wage and extending its coverage can constitute a major step forward for the working poor. I also believe that the labor movement must bring its unique skills -- organization and collective bargaining -- to the unorganized poor. Some trade unionists have already suggested that strong, stable internationals and locals should "adopt" organizing campaigns among workers who are so poor that they cannot pay the cost of organizing themselves, at least at the outset. Others have indicated that union organizing experience can make a major contribution to help organize the poor for "maximum feasible participation" in the war against poverty.

While I have no doubt about the value of maximum feasible participation in solving problems of poverty, or any other problems, I would just like to add that we ought to look at maximum feasible participation as broadly and realistically as possible. More than anything else it should represent from here on one of the vital features of the grass-roots relationship to the political institutions of the society. In other words, I am all in favor of maximum participation if it means participating as fully as possible in the political decisions of the entire society. Finally, in whatever way one interprets maximum feasible participation, it should not relieve political parties and other social institutions of their obligation to act with courage, commitment and responsibility in solving people's problems. That is to say, maximum participation of the people in the solution of their problems should not be an excuse for the traditional political institutions to shirk their own responsibilities to seek and propose remedies for the ills of the people.

All of which takes me back to the need for coalition -- a coalition of effort, a coalition of conscience, a coalition of social morality, and a coalition of concern. I have no crystal ball, I have no way of knowing whether

the new century that we create in America will be the one that ought in all
justness to be created. But I do know that we can at the present moment ask
no less. I do know that it will be a tragedy if we cannot find social answers
to the problems created by the progress of technology and automation. So we,
therefore, ought to fight for what is right, now. And in doing so we have to
work to weld behind us a broad coalition of morality, now. For if we reject
the possibility of this kind of coalition, or if we despair that it will ever
come about, then we are rejecting and despairing of the only viable democratic
alternative that is available. We cannot look any longer to third political
parties. No third political party could do what Catholics, Protestants, Jews,
intellectuals, students, civil rights workers, labor organizations, Puerto
Ricans, Mexican Americans and other minorities did for the passage of civil
rights bills, voting rights bills, public accommodations bills, and the March
on Washington. If we cannot build that force again, this time around economic
and social priorities for the excluded members of our society, then we are on
our way to a social cataclysm that we will not be able to control except
perhaps by tyranny.

Speech prepared for the Conference on "The Next Fifty Years," sponsored by
the American Institute of Planners, Box 65 Committee Affiliations 1967,
Whitney Young Papers, Columbia University.

18. ADDRESS TO THE 1969 CONVENTION OF THE AFL-CIO
BAYARD RUSTIN
Executive Director, A. Philip Randolph Institute

President Meany. Lane Kirkland, members of the Executive Council,
brothers and sisters, and particular greetings to our guests from overseas.
I am going to deal this morning with a very difficult, trying and agonizing
problem which is facing America, that is the problem of justice for all of
our citizens, regardless of color, race or creed. But before I do, I would
like to congratulate Brother Meany on his analysis of Mr. Haynsworth in his
speech yesterday, to point out something to our visitors which I know they
will see, but which I would not want any one of them to fail to see, and that
is that when there were millions of people in this country who were prepared
to let the Haynsworth appointment go unchallenged, there were two groups of
people who stood up. The first one was George Meany, representing the labor
movement, and the other was Roy Wilkins representing the civil rights movement.
I am convinced that we are going to get this man, but even if we do not,
President Meany, the civil rights movement and the trade union movement
deserves profound credit for pointing out to the American people the nature
and the danger of his campaign, and for this I congratulate all of you in
whose name Brother Meany acted. (Applause).
I would like to secondly point out to our visitors from overseas that
COPE, the political arm of the AFL-CIO performed a miracle in the 1968 elections, for history will record that when the ship of progress and liberalism
in this nation was sinking it was again the labor movement and the Negro people
who in coalition stood up and held the banner of justice; and it's a pity,
George, they beat us by a couple of votes.
Now, friends, if anything decent is going to happen in these United
States, as has been the case since the time of Franklin Delano Roosevelt, it
will be because the trade union movement and the black people of this
country do not permit themselves to become divided but stick together.
(Applause).
My friends, alliances are not made in the way in which one marries his
wife; alliances are not made out of affection; alliances are made out of
mutual interest and, although there will be difficult times for us, we must
remember that this mutual interest does in fact exist and we must hold on to
it.
Finally, let me salute the AFL-CIO for the work it has done for the sanitation workers in Memphis, for the farm workers in Delano, and for the
hospital workers in South Carolina. Then let no man say that together we are

not fighting poverty, for that is precisely what we are doing, more effectively than any other combination of forces.

I note also, and I hope the *Wall Street Journal* will take note and the *New York Times* will take note, that there was a magnificent march in Raleigh, North Carolina, a few weeks ago, with 12,000 men and women, white and black, demonstrating in solidarity, and that was organized by the North Carolina AFL-CIO and the Building and Construction Trades Council. There was unity there and, therefore, half of you don't even know about it because the press does not like unity. It records only discord and ugliness. (Applause).

My friends, I did not come here to make a congratulatory speech. I came here to talk to you about what I consider to be two of the most serious problems this nation faces. We are in a difficult period and I think that you know this better than I do, for you are working daily with the people in the streets, in your neighborhood, and your factories and shops. Therefore, you know more about it than the journalists and the television commentators and the politicians.

What is the difficulty? It is called by many names, but the reality is there has been so little done to meet the needs of the American people that we have cropped up with two twin evils, and I want to say a word about these evils.

One of them is black rage and the other is white fear. We hear all about black rage and riots but the newspapers are not telling us about the fantastic fear of many white people, a justified fear in many respects.

These two things feed on each other and they set this nation on a collision course. I believe there are people in this country who want us to be on a collision course. First there is a small handful who want this collision because they see it as the first act of a revolutionary drama of their fantasies. But they are small and sick and a sorry lot with an inflated notion of their strength which comes from seeing themselves too often on television.

But there are more powerful groups. They are not the Left but the Right. This group knows that revolution by fanatics will not succeed, but they would use this threat as a pretext for an assault--and do not misunderstand me--not only on black people but first of all on the trade union movement, on social legislation, on civil liberties, and on black people, and they will work hard at it. They would seize on the fear of the future to draw us back into the past. If they succeed then the American dream will be shattered.

My friends, this need not happen. We can get off this collision course, and to do that we must understand what makes for black fear and rage and what makes for white fear.

There are those who say black people have made no progress, we have won no gains in the last decade. But they don't know what they are talking about. Of course we have made much progress. Our long struggle has not been for nothing. The problem that we face is that progress is all that's relative, as every trade unionist knows.

For example, I could say that across the country union wages last year raised 5, 6, 7 or 8 percent, or what have you, but every trade unionist knows that these are related to prices and you know that many of your workers have been robbed of this net gain by spiraling prices. Therefore, they are resentful, they are afraid, and they are angry.

Despite this progress that black people have made, there are also many parts of our ghettos in which unemployment is double, and there are more rats and roaches in the slums than ever before. Fifteen years after the Supreme Court decision there are more Negro children in segregated schools than there were before that decision.

Now, my friends, no matter what some of the black militants and white intellectuals say, the fact is that segregated education is an inferior education and we must not permit anyone to say differently. But you know these things. You know the anguish that comes when men have hopes which have been dashed.

My friends, there is another misery. It has nothing to do with black people but with white people. And that is that they are up to here in mortgages. They appear to own homes which are not paid for; they do not have enough money to feed their families; therefore these white people have as much fear because they are afraid of losing what they have, as black people have raged because they do not have what they feel they should have.

For millions of these white people their jobs and their homes are all they have got. Because their position is so dangerous they feel threatened by the demands of black people for justice because, they argue: "This nation says we will not have enough houses. Therefore, I fearfully cling to mine lest my black brother get it. This nation says there will not be enough jobs. Therefore, I nervously cling to my job lest my black brother get it."

Now, my friends, the only answer to that is adequate housing, adequate jobs, adequate education for all. Then white fear and black rage can be contained.

Now, my friends, I maintain that we have got to build. We have got to build and rebuild. I propose that we tear down all that is dying and dead, all that is ugly and divisive, all that breeds hate and misery, and I propose that we put new towns and cities in their place, new schools in their place, new neighborhoods in their place, fresh air and clean water. I say, friends, let us build.

But the minute I use the word "build," I get right into the middle of a problem which is on all of our minds and which none of us can sweep under a rug. My friends, to use the word "build" brings a subject to the foreground which has caused much controversy and intensely strong feelings, I refer, of course, to the events that have recently occurred in Pittsburgh, Chicago, and other cities, about which I would now like to have a word and would like to have you listen carefully.

The problem raised by these events, the problem of minority participation in the building trades is difficult and dangerous, but let those of you who are in the trade union movement not mistake the problem. It is not the problem of the building trades. It is the problem of all organized labor that to this date, while we have done much, none of us has done enough to completely solve the problem, and we cannot make a scapegoat of any segment of the trade union movement, of any segment of the civil rights movement. This is a fight where we are all in together and nothing can be done without the cooperation and effective action of all.

There is no doubt in my mind that the events of Chicago and Pittsburgh are a source of tremendous satisfaction to the powerful enemies of the black movement and the labor movement. Read, for example, what was written in last Friday's *Wall Street Journal*. You know, the *Wall Street Journal* is an interesting paper. The big boys who read that want the truth. There are seldom lies in the *Wall Street Journal*. They don't want to lie to themselves.

The *New York Times* lies, but not the *Wall Street Journal*.

(Laughter).

This is what the *Journal* says to its people. "It is no accident that the civil rights groups have chosen this particular time to press their attack on the building trades. They clearly are betting that contractors beset by spiraling wage costs and the public in general will be sympathetic to demands for expansion of union hiring and training efforts in the hope that it might slow inflation in construction by increasing the supply of workers."

I don't know whether you got that, because that is a very fancy sentence. But let me proceed.

You and I understand perfectly well what is meant by that delicate and articulate little language--"slow inflation in construction by increasing the supply of workers." Baby, that simply means, let's cut some wages, let's use the building trades to do it, and let's aggravate the Negro to attack them in order to achieve that little bit. (Applause).

I do not for one minute believe that a single civil rights group would want to take such a position, for we know that it is pointless and self-defeating to get more Negroes into the industries where there are skilled jobs and well-paying, only to have the wages in that industry decline. What the hell you want in for then, only to have the wages drop?

After all, one of the main reasons why black workers are now attracted to these jobs is because the pay and the benefits are the best. They didn't get that way because contractors did it, as the *Wall Street Journal* would have us believe, or because the public in general somehow uplifted the building trades. It got that way because the building trades fought hard to make it so. (Applause).

So I want to say a word to my fellow freedom-fighters in the civil rights movement. We must continue to press vigorously for greater minority

participation in the building trades. We will not let ourselves become stooges
for those powerful economic interests that would use our struggle to depress
wages and standards, or to cripple the unions that won them. (Applause).

We black Americans have struggled too hard, come too far and learned too
much. We are not dumb niggers now sitting on a cotton bale playing the guitar.
We have learned too much to be exploited ever again by the capitalist classes
of this country.

There is a great Negro spiritual which says, "No more auction block for
me," and along with Brother Randolph I say, "No more union busting, either."
(Applause).

Some unscrupulous interests have mounted a propaganda campaign to blame
labor for the high cost of home building and other socially needed construction. They want to divert attention from the profiteering of the large
corporations and the tight-money bankers and the real estate interest--and,
if I may say so, from the economic policies of the Nixon Administration. They
would divert us and our attention from the dismal record in integrating black
Americans into the decision making process.

Now, baby, let's look where the real money is. The real money is in the
500 major corporations in this country. Look at those corporations, and if
you can find a black face in any one of them I will give you what money I
have. It won't be much, but you can have it.

Look at the *Wall Street Journal* and the *New York Times*. How many black
faces have they got amongst their reporters, editors, and managers? Not
enough to make a black power movement, and today you only need two people to
make a black power movement. (Applause).

Well, my friends, having said this I want to say a very serious word to
any of our friends who still have a problem left with their unions, and for
this opportunity I take off on what has happened with the building trades. I
read with profound interest of your recent 55th Convention. I must say that
I especially noted your policy statement, which I want to quote.

"We favor the acceleration and expansion of the apprenticeship outreach
programs which have proved successful in actual operation.

"We make the flat and unqualified recommendation to local unions throughout the United States that for a stated period of time they should invite the
application of qualified minority journeymen for membership in their respective
local unions and should accept all such qualified minority journeymen provided
they meet the ordinary and equally administered requirements for membership."

I note further a final quote. "We also recommend that local unions and
local councils explore and vigorously pursue training programs for the upgrading of minority workers who are not of apprenticeship age."

My friends, I believe that to be a statement of importance and a statement on which we can base profound progress. But one of the problems is that
black people have had 350 years of statements where often things did not
really happen. Therefore, today many people are the victims of that unfortunate history, though their hearts are totally in the right place. We also
know that in the past there has been reluctance on the part of some local
unions to comply with such policy statements. This has happened not only in
the building trades but throughout that there has been foot-dragging and
evasion, and there has been also some implementation. There must now, if our
alliance is to remain firm and beautiful, be forthright action. There must
be visible results, and now, for policy statements are never read in the
ghetto and they cannot close the credibility gap. Action, and action alone,
will.

I believe the time has come when such action will be taken. I believe
that there will be translation of these words into deeds. I know that for
many unions there will be serious obstacles in the face of shortages, but I
sincerely believe that you have the leadership, the power, the commitment,
and the belief in democracy to overcome whatever those problems are.

I believe this, my good friends, because I know that you have already
made progress, in cooperation with the apprenticeship outreach programs of
the Urban League, the Worker's Defense League and the A. Philip Randolph
Education Fund, and of other groups.

I know that in many cities the building trades themselves have taken the
initiative to initiate such programs.

Now, let me give you a few facts. These programs are now operating in 52 cities, and since their inception in 1967, they have brought in 3,862 apprentices. The fact that over 1500 were recruited in the first six months of this year alone indicates that the pace of these programs is accelerating. I was most impressed to learn that of all the apprentices enrolled in the first half of 1968, over 9 percent came from minority groups. This is nearly four times the percentage of 1960. This is progress. This is moving in the right direction. As my grandmother used to say to me, "Son, it is not so important how far you get, the real question is, are you headed in the right direction." (Applause).

We know that it is possible to find and train qualified young Negroes and other minority youth to become apprentices. We have done it, and we have done it with the help of the AFL-CIO and the building trades themselves.

What we are saying is we need to do a hell of a lot more of it. . . .

My friends, it is precisely because we have made such progress, which no one believed possible a few years ago, that we now know, and everybody else knows, we can do more, and we can and we must.

Proceedings of the Eighth Constitutional Convention of the AFL-CIO, Atlantic City, N.J., October 2-7, 1969, Vol. I, pp. 104-12.

19. THE BLACKS AND THE UNIONS

By Bayard Rustin

Which way will the blacks choose—-to fight to eliminate all segregation in the trade unions, or to become pawns in the conservatives' games of bust-the-unions?

One of the main articles of faith in liberal dogma these days is that the interests and objectives of the American trade-union movement are in fundamental conflict with the interests and objectives of Black America. One can hardly pick up any of the major journals of liberal opinion without reading some form of the statement that the white worker has become affluent and conservative and feels his security to be threatened by the demand for racial equality. A corollary of this statement is that it is a primary function of the labor movement to protect the white worker from the encroaching black. Furthermore, the argument runs, since there are no signs that the blacks may be letting up in their struggle for economic betterment, a hostile confrontation between blacks and the unions is not only inevitable but necessary.

It may well be that historians of the future, recording the events of the past five years, will conclude that the major effect of the civic turbulence in this period has been in fact to distract us from the real and pressing social needs of the nation. And perhaps nothing illustrates the point more vividly than the whole question of the relations between blacks and the unions.

This question itself, however, cannot be properly understood except in the larger context of the history of the civil rights movement. Negro protest in the Sixties, if the movement is in its turn to be properly understood, must be divided into two distinct phases. The first phase, which covered something like the first half of the decade, we one in which the movement's clear objective was to destroy the legal foundations of racism in America. Thus the locale of the struggle was the South, the evil to be eliminated was Jim Crow, and the enemy, who had a special talent for arousing moral outrage among even the most reluctant sympathizers with the cause, was the rock-willed segregationist.

Now, one thing about the South more than any other has been obscured in the romantic vision of the region—-of ancient evil, of defeat, of enduring rural charm—-that has been so much of our literary and intellectual tradition: for the Negro, Southern life had precisely a quality of clarity, a clarity which while oppressive was also supportive. The Southern caste system and folk culture rested upon a clear, albeit unjust, set of legal and institutional relationships which prescribed roles for individuals and established a modicum of social order. The struggle that was finally mounted against that system was actually fed and strengthened by the social environment from which it emerged. No profound analysis, no overriding social theory was needed in order both to locate and understand the injustices that were to be combated. All that was demanded of one was sufficient courage to demonstrate against them. One looks back upon this period in the civil rights movement with nostalgia.

During the second half of the Sixties, the center of the crisis shifted to the sprawling ghettos of the North. Here black experience was radically different from that in the South. The stability of institutional relationships was largely absent in Northern ghettos, especially among the poor. Over twenty years ago, the black sociologist E. Franklin Frazier was able to see the brutalizing effect of urbanization upon lower-class blacks? ". . . the bonds of sympathy and community of interests that held their parents together in the rural environment have been unable to withstand the disintegrating forces in the city." Southern blacks migrated north in search of work, seeking to become transformed from a peasantry into a working class. But instead of jobs they found only misery, and far from becoming a proletariat, they came to constitute a *Lumpenproletariat,* an underclass of rejected people. Frazier's prophetic words resound today with terrifying precision: ". . . as long as the bankrupt system of Southern agriculture exists, Negro families will continue to seek a living in the towns and cities of the country. They will crowd the slum areas of Southern cities or make their way to Northern cities, where their family life will become disrupted and their poverty will force them to depend upon charity."[1]

Out of such conditions, social protest was to emerge in a form peculiar to the ghetto, a form which could never have taken root in the South except in such large cities as Atlanta or Houston. The evils in the North are not easy to understand and fight against, or at least not as easy as Jim Crow, and this has given the protest from the ghetto a special edge of frustration. There are few specific injustices, such as a segregated lunch counter, that offer both a clear object of protest and a good chance of victory. Indeed, the problem in the North is not one of social injustice so much as the results of institutional pathology. Each of the various institutions touching the lives of urban blacks --those relating to education, health, employment, housing, and crime--is in need of drastic reform. One might say that the Northern race problem has in good part become simply the problem of the American city--which is gradually becoming a reservation for the unwanted, most of whom are black.

In such a situation, even progress has proved to be a mixed blessing. During the Sixties, for example, Northern blacks as a group have made great economic gains, the result of which being that hundreds of thousands of them were able to move out of the hard-core poverty areas. Meanwhile, however, their departure, while a great boon to those departing, only contributed further to the deterioration of the slums, now being drained of their stable middle and working class. Combined with the large influx of Southern blacks during the same period, this process was leaving the ghetto more and more the precinct of a depressed underclass. To the segregation by race was now added segregation by class, and all of the problems created by segregation and poverty--inadequate schooling, substandard and overcrowded housing, lack of access to jobs or to job training, narcotics and crime--were greatly aggravated. And again because of segregation, the violence of the black underclass was turned in upon itself.

If the problems of the ghetto do not lend themselves to simple analyses or solutions, then, this is because they cannot be solved without mounting a total attack on the inadequacies endemic to, and injustices embedded in, all of our institutions. It is perhaps understandable that young Northern blacks, confronting these problems, have so often provided answers which are really non-answers; which are really dramatic statements satisfying some sense of the need for militancy without even beginning to deal with the basic economic and political problems of the ghetto. Primary among these non-answers is the idea that black progress depends upon a politics of race and revolution. I am referring here not to the recent assertions of black pride--assertions that will be made as long as that pride continues to be undermined by white society --but to the kind of black nationalism which consists in a bitter rejection of American society and vindicates a withdrawal from social struggle into a kind of hermetic racial world where blacks can "do their thing." Nationalists have been dubbed "militants" by the press because they have made their point with such fervent hostility to white society, but the implication of their position actually amounts to little more than the age-old conservative message that blacks should help themselves—a thing that, by the very definition of the situation, they have not the resources to do.

The same is true of black proposals for revolution. For to engage in revolutionary acts in contemporary America—where, despite a lot of inflammatory rhetoric, there is not even a whisper of a revolutionary situation—not only diverts precious energies away from the political arena where the real battles for change must be fought, but might also precipitate a vicious counterrevolution the chief victims of which will be blacks.

The truth about the situation of the Negro today is that there are powerful forces, composed largely of the corporate elite and Southern conservatives, which will resist any change in the economic or racial structure of this country that might cut into their resources or challenge their status; and such is precisely what any program genuinely geared to improve his lot must do. Moreover, these forces today are not merely resisting change. With their representative Richard Nixon in the White House, they are engaged in an assault on the advances made during the past decade. It has been Nixon's tragic and irresponsible choice to play at the politics of race, not, to be sure, with the primitive demagoguery of a "Pitchfork Ben" Tillman, say, but nevertheless with the same intent of building a political majority on the basis of white hostility to blacks. So far he has been unsuccessful, but the potential for the emergence of such a reactionary majority does exist, especially if the turbulence and racial polarization which we have recently experienced persists.[111]

What is needed, therefore, is not only a program that would effect some fundamental change in the distribution of America's resources for those in the greatest need of them, but also a political majority that will support such a program. In other words, nothing less than a program truly, not merely verbally, radical in scope would be adequate to meet the present crisis; and nothing less than a politically constituted majority, outnumbering the conservative forces, would be adequate to carry it through. Now, it so happens that there is one social force which, by virtue both of its size and its very nature, is essential to the creation of such a majority—and so in relation to which the success or failure of the black struggle must finally turn. And that is the American trade-union movement.

Addressing the AFL-CIO Convention in 1961, Martin Luther King observed: "Negroes are almost entirely a working people. There are pitifully few Negro millionaires and few Negro employers. Our needs are identical with labor's needs—decent wages, fair working conditions, livable housing, old-age security, health and welfare measures, conditions in which families can grow, have education for their children and respect in the community."

Despite the widely held belief that the blacks and the unions have not the same, but rather irreconcilable, interests—and despite the fact that certain identifiable unions do practice discrimination—King's words remain valid today. Blacks *are* mostly a working people, they continue to need what labor needs, and they must fight side by side with unions to achieve these things.

Of all the misconceptions about the labor movement that have been so lovingly dwelt on in the liberal press, perhaps none is put forth more often and is farther from the truth than the unions are of and for white people. For one thing, there are, according to labor historian Thomas R. Brooks, between 2,500,000 and 2,750,000 black trade unionists in America. If his figures are correct, and other estimates seem to bear them out, the percentage of blacks in the unions is a good deal higher than the percentage of blacks in the total population—15 per cent as compared with 11 per cent, to be precise. And since the vast majority of black trade unionists are members of integrated unions, one can conclude that the labor movement is the most integrated major institution in American society, certainly more integrated than the corporations, the churches, or the universities.

Moreover, blacks are joining unions in increasing numbers. According to a 1968 report by *Business Week,* one out of every three new union members is black. The sector of the economy which is currently being most rapidly unionized is that of the service industries, and most particularly among government employees, such as hospital workers, sanitation workers, farm workers, and paraprofessionals in educational and social-welfare institutions. This category of worker is, of course, both largely nonwhite and shamefully underpaid. . . .

Thus, it is clear why unions are important to black workers. What may
perhaps seem less obvious and must also be sharply emphasized is that the
legislative program of the trade-union movement can go a long way toward satisfying the economic needs of the larger black *community*. The racial crisis, as
we have seen, is not an isolated problem that lends itself to redress by a
protesting minority. Being rooted in the very social and economic structure of
the society, it can be solved only by a comprehensive program that gets to the
heart of why we can't build adequate housing for everybody, why we must always
have a "tolerable" level of unemployment, or why we lack enough funds for education. In this sense the racial crisis challenges the entire society's capacity to redirect its resources on the basis of human need rather than profit.
Blacks can pose this challenge, but only the federal government has the power
and the money to meet it. And it is here that the trade-union movement can
play such an important role.

The problems of the most aggrieved sector of the black ghetto cannot and
will never be solved without full employment, and full employment, with the
government as employer of last resort, is the keystone of labor's program. One
searches in vain among the many so-called friends of the black struggle for a
seconding voice to this simple yet far-reaching proposition. Some call it
inflationary, while to others, who are caught up in the excitement of the black
cultural revolution, it is pedestrian and irrelevant. But in terms of the
economic condition of the black community, nothing more radical has yet been
proposed. There is simply no other way for the black *Lumpenproletariat* to become
a proletariat. And full employment is only one part of labor's program. The
movement's proposals in the areas of health, housing, education, and environment
would, if enacted, achieve nothing less than the transformation of the quality
of our urban life. How ironic that in this period when the trade-union movement
is thought to be conservative, its social and economic policies are far and away
more progressive than those of any other major American institution. Nor--again
in contrast to most of the other groups officially concerned with these things
--is labor's program merely in the nature of a grand proposal; there is also an
actual record of performance, particularly in the area of civil rights. Clarence
Mitchell, the director of the Washington Bureau of the NAACP and legislative
chairman of the Leadership Conference on Civil Rights, a man more deeply
involved in Congressional civil rights battles than any other black in America,
has said, "None of the legislative fights we have made in the field of civil
rights could have been won without the trade-union movement. We couldn't have
beaten Haynsworth without labor, and the struggle against Carswell would not
have been a contest."

Labor's interest in progressive social legislation naturally leads it into
the political arena. The Committee on Political Education of the AFL-CIO, the
Political Action Committee of the UAW, and the political arm of the Teamsters
were active in every state in the last election registering and educating
voters and getting out the vote. This year trade unionists were more politically
active than they have ever been during any off-year election. The reason for
this is clear. With so many liberal Senators up for reelection, and with
political alignments in great flux, 1970 presented itself as a year that would
initiate a new period in American politics--a period which would see the re-
grouping of liberal forces or the consolidation of a conservative majority.

One of the important factors determining the kind of political alignments
that will emerge from this period of instability will be the relationship
between the trade-union movement and the liberal community, and today this
relationship is severely strained. Differences over the war in Vietnam are
frequently cited as a major cause of this division, but there has been a great
deal of misunderstanding on this issue. The house of labor itself is divided
over the war, and even those labor leaders who support it have enthusiastically
backed dove Congressional candidates who have liberal domestic records, among
them such firm opponents of the war as Mike Mansfield, Edward Kennedy, Vance
Hartke, Philip Hart, Howard Metzenbaum, and Edmund Muskie.[112]

A better understanding of the trade-union movement by liberals may be
developing, but for the present the antagonistic attitudes that exist cast an
ideological pall over the chances for uniting the democratic Left coalition.
It must be said that the vehement contempt with which the liberals have come
to attack the unions bespeaks something more than a mere political critique of

"conservatism." When A. H. Raskin writes that "the typical worker--from construction craftsman to shoe clerk--has become probably the most reactionary political force in the country"; or when Anthony Lewis lumps under the same category the rich oilmen and "the members of powerful, monopolistic labor unions"; or when Murray Kempton writes that "the AFL-CIO has lived happily in a society which, more lavishly than any in history, has managed the care and feeding of incompetent white people," and adds, "Who better represents that ideal than George Wallace"; or when many other liberals casually toss around the phrase "labor-fascists," one cannot but inevitably conclude that one is in the presence not of political opposition but of a certain class hatred. This hatred is not necessarily one based on conflicting class interests--though they may play a role here--but rather a hatred of the elite for the "mass." And this hatred is multiplied a thousandfold by the fact that we live in a democratic society in which the coarse multitude can outvote the elite and make decisions which may be contrary to the wishes and values, perhaps even the interests and the prejudices, of those who are better off.

It is difficult not to conclude that many liberals and radicals use subjective, rather than objective, criteria in judging the character of a social force. A progressive force, in their view, is one that is alienated from the dominant values of the culture, not one which contributes to greater social equality and distributive justice. Thus today the trade-union movement has been relegated to reactionary status, even though it is actually more progressive than at any time in its history--if by progressive we mean a commitment to broad, long-term social reform in addition to the immediate objectives of improving wages and working conditions. At the same time, the most impoverished social group, that substratum which Herbert Marcuse longingly calls "the outcasts and the outsiders," has been made the new vanguard of social programs. And it is here that liberals and New Leftists come together in their proposal for a new coalition "of the rich, educated, and dedicated with the poor," as Eric F. Godlman has admiringly described it, or in Walter Laqueur's more caustic phraseology, "between the *Lumpenproletariat* and the *Lumpenintelligentsia*."

This political approach, known among liberals as New Politics and among radicals as New Leftism, denotes a certain convergence of the Left and the Right, if not in philosophy and intent, then at least in practical effect. I am not referring simply to the elitism which the intellectual Left shares with the economic Right, but also to their symbolic political relationship. Many of the sophisticated right-wing attacks on labor are frequently couched in left-wing rhetoric. Conservative claims that unions are anti-black, are responsible for inflation, and constitute minorities which threaten and intimidate the majority reverberate in the liberal community and are shaping public opinion to accept a crackdown on the trade-union movement.

While many adherents of the New Politics are outraged by Nixon's Southern strategy, their own strategy is simply the obverse of his. The potential for a Republican majority depends upon Nixon's success in attracting into the conservative fold lower-middle-class whites, the same group that the New Politics has written off. The question is not whether this group is conservative or liberal, for it is both, and how it acts will depend upon the way the issues are defined. If they are defined as race and dissent, then Nixon will win. But if, on the other hand, they are defined so as to appeal to the progressive economic interests of the lower middle class, then it becomes possible to build an alliance on the basis of common interest between this group and the black community. The importance of the trade-union movement is that it embodies this common interest. This was proved most clearly in 1968 when labor mounted a massive educational campaign which reduced the Wallace supporters among its membership to a tiny minority. And the trade-union movement remains today the greatest obstacle to the success of Nixon's strategy.

The prominent racial and ethnic loyalties that divide American society have, together with our democratic creed, obscured a fundamental reality--that we are a class society and, though we do not often talk about such things, that we are engaged in a class struggle . . . and its outcome will determine whether we will have a greater or lesser degree of economic and social equality in this country.

Pamphlet reprint by the A. Philip Randolph Educational Fund, 1971. Copy in possession of the editors.

20. LABOR'S HIGHEST AWARD HONORS BAYARD RUSTIN

By James M. Shevis

New York--The AFL-CIO honored veteran civil rights leader Bayard Rustin with its highest honor, the Murray-Green-Meany Award, for his years of struggle to end racial discrimination and oppression the world over.

The award, named for pre-merger presidents Philip Murray of the CIO and William Green of the AFL and for George Meany who presided over the merged organization for 25 years until his death in January, was presented at a dinner here in conjunction with the 20th national AFL-CIO Community Services Conference.[1]

Rustin is best known as the organizer of the massive 1963 March on Washington, which drew over a quarter-million Americans to the nation's capital to press for adoption of the landmark 1964 Civil Rights Act. He was a close associate of Dr. Martin Luther King, Jr. But, as AFL-CIO Vice President Peter Bommarito noted in his presentation address, Rustin's cause has not been the cause of blacks alone.[114]

Rustin led the first Freedom Rides in the late 1940s, incurring a 30-day sentence on a North Carolina chain gang, Bommarito observed. As a result of that experience, he wrote an expose for a New York newspaper, which led ultimately to abolition of that practice.

"This was not a political achievement but a humanitarian one," said Bommarito. During World War I, Rustin went to California to help Japanese-Americans who had been interned because of the color of their skin and their ethnic heritage. He also found time to help hospital workers, teachers, and sanitation workers build unions, to work with Mahatma Gandhi in India, to rally support for the democratic state of Israel, and to travel throughout Africa in behalf of independence movements there.[115]

More recently, Rustin went to Indochina to draw Americans' attention to the plight of the Boat People and the thousands of starving Cambodians. Only two weeks ago, he returned from Stockholm, where he participated in an international tribunal to focus attention on the continuing imprisonment and persecution of Soviet dissident Anatoly Scharansky.[116]

"But lest you think that Bayard is a mere gadabout who hops from one problem to another, bear in mind that he also created a durable organization that is very close to the heart of the labor movement--the A. Philip Randolph Institute, which has opened a new two-way channel of communication between the black community and the trade union movement," Bommarito told the 300 dinner guests. Rustin is chairman of the institute.

AFL-CIO President Lane Kirkland praised Rustin's "extraordinary organizing talents and ability to articulate the aspirations of black Americans," and pointed out that he was among the first black leaders to recognize that the gains of the civil rights revolution could not be secured unless they were rooted in economic progress for the black masses.

"Along with A. Philip Randolph, he argued that such progress could only be made through a movement dedicated to full employment at decent wages for all Americans," Kirkland observed. "And at the heart of such a movement, he repeatedly insisted, were the trade unions of America. He was right then. He is still right."

A moving tribute to Rustin came from actress Liv Ullmann, who joined him and a dozen other prominent persons in Indochina in February in a march to draw world attention to the plight of the Cambodian refugees.

"Being with you in Thailand, visiting the refugees from Cambodia, left me with images of your wonderful laughter, your deep and sincere commitment to the homeless, your striding as if you were the freest man in the world, the warmth of your handshake, your fight against injustice, your compassion and commitment, and your happiness to be alive," she said, "always looking like you lived comfortably within yourself with such pride and, as we all know, at the same time, far, far outside yourself."

In accepting the award, Rustin paid tribute to Randolph, who died a year ago, and to Meany.

"Whatever I've been able to do has begun with that great and marvelous man, A. Philip Randolph, on whose shoulders I stood eternally," Rustin said of his closest associate during decades of struggle for civil and human rights.

Of Meany, "he believed in me, and this helped me to grow," said Rustin. He also credited Meany for his role in enactment of the 1964 Civil Rights Act.

There would not have been a meaningful law if Meany had not prevailed upon President John F. Kennedy to put an effective enforcement provision into the statute, Rustin told the gathering.

Rustin had some sobering comments on the recent racial rioting in Miami as well as the influx of refugees into the U.S. from Cuba and Haiti.

"It has been an agony for me to learn of blacks and whites killing each other in Miami," he said. "If we do not deal with our problems at home, sooner or later the President and the Congress will be crippled in helping those who suffer abroad."

As for the debate over whether to let Cubans and Haitians find asylum in the United States, he observed: "If America is ever so cruel as not to allow these people in, she will never be able to deal with those in the black community."

AFL-CIO News, May 24, 1980.

UNITED STEELWORKERS OF AMERICA

21. STEELWORKERS FIGHT DISCRIMINATION

By David J. McDonald
President, United Steelworkers of America

Men can work together and they can live together.

This is the creed of the United Steelworkers of America. We believe in civil rights on the job and off the job. We know that life and work are synonymous and that we cannot afford the atomization of our people that inevitably accompanies any denial of civil rights. Ours is not a Sunday or holiday creed. Throughout the year we work to make a reality of our great American ideal of equality for all.

We know that men work together because they do so daily in the mines, mills, and plants of the steel industry. We are confident that men can live together in harmony and on equal terms outside the work-place, as well as inside.

We know that there are problems—that bigotry and suspicion will not of themselves break down and evaporate. Nevertheless, there is no room in our democracy for ghettos of any kind—racial or religious. We call upon all segments of American life—labor, management, churches, civic groups, government—to unite in a common and continuing effort to eliminate such ghettos and the hurt they bring to millions of our citizens. The United Steelworkers of America pledges full cooperation with all who will work with good will in this effort without regard for any differences of view on other aspects of our national life.

In the Plant

Some time ago I visited a big steel plant. In one area, I noted a crane operator manipulating a ladle of molten metal at the end of his crane-hook. As the metal streamed from the ladle it was poured by hand into pigs by a brawny white worker. Beside this worker there stood a husky Negro youth whose job it was to scrape the scum from the surface of the metal as it was being poured. Nearby, another Negro worker was repairing some defective equipment.

As the ladle on the crane-hook gradually emptied of metal, it became necessary to manipulate it manually. Without a word from anyone, the Negro repair worker brought over a two-by-four which he placed in the loop at the end of the ladle handle. The white man and his colored helper, both of whom were stripped to the waist, pulled hard on the ladle to get out all the molten metal.

Finally, the Negro repairman left his work to lend a hand. The white crane operator also came down. It was a hot operation, made even hotter by the heat of the molten metal. Together, they accomplished the job. All the metal was poured into pigs.

There was no attempt to enforce segregation on this job. No foreman rushed over to order the men to separate nor did any mill superintendent order all operations halted. Industry has not built segregated production facilities because they would be entirely uneconomic--it just wouldn't make good sense. If segregation doesn't make good sense on the job, it doesn't make good sense anywhere.

Obviously, the Negroes, the Puerto Ricans, and other minority groups have been and are today discriminated against in employment opportunities and at the job level. We have sought earnestly to eliminate this discrimination in our industry. We have been quite successful. I do not mean by this that our success is total or that we have no remaining problems. The important thing is that we recognize our problems, and we are working actively to overcome any difficulties that we may find.

In a Southern plant some time ago, such a difficulty was called to the attention of the international union. This plant employed 5,100 white workers and 900 non-whites. There were dual lines of promotion and seniority. This resulted in the by-passing of longer service workers in promotions and in the retention of both whites and non-whites of lesser seniority on the job during layoffs while longer service workers of both groups were laid off.

When we learned of this situation, we sent a representative of our international to meet with the all-white local executive board. After we clearly explained the international's policy, the local board agreed to promotions according to qualifications and seniority as well as to a layoff procedure entirely in accordance with contract provisions.

We then called upon the company to end discriminatory practices. While the company did so, it handled the matter poorly. It took eighteen months of dealing with this company to get the problem finally cleared up. Today, this Southern plant is fully integrated. Initial resentments among the workers have been forgotten. The union is better off and so is the company, since there are fewer grievances on the job and fewer production hitches.

Equal Rights in Union

We built the Steelworkers as an integrated union all the way. So far as we are concerned, all members have equal rights and it has been that way from the start. We do not tolerate Jim Crow locals or Jim Crow meetings. Our international policy has been firmly established by convention after convention.

In 1954, the United Steelworkers met bigotry head on at the key employment level. The three chief officers of our organization directed a letter to our staff members and to every local union calling for full compliance with the law and with union policy in employment practices.

The constitution of the United Steelworkers, we pointed out, dedicates our union to uniting all workers in the industry regardless of "race, creed, color, or nationality"; grants membership on equal terms to all of these workers, and obligates the union "to establish through collective bargaining adequate wage standards, shorter hours of work, and improvements in the conditions of employment for the workers in the industry. . . .

"Thus this union stands unequivocally opposed to discrimination of any

sort, shape or form. That policy applies specifically to discrimination in
employment. This union is flatly opposed to discrimination in hiring, promotion, layoff, or any other term or condition of employment. Any collective
bargaining contract which either by its terms or actual operation permits
discrimination on account of race, creed, color, or nationality violates the
policy of this union.

"It is not only the policy of this union to fight job discrimination
because of race, color, creed or nationality; it is its legal duty to do so.
The United States Supreme Court, the lower federal courts and the National Labor
Relations Board have all held that when a union acts as exclusive bargaining
representative of employees in a bargaining unit, it is the union's legal duty
to represent every employee in that unit fairly and equally, and in such a manner that no discrimination results because of race, creed, color or nationality."

In the United Steelworkers, no contract, which by its terms or operation
permits discrimination against any member, is approved. This is and has been
our union policy. Because we have made this clear and because we oppose and
fight discriminatory practices, the matter of equality at the job level is
settled affirmatively in the United Steelworkers of America.

Equality Is Indivisible

Long ago we learned that the fight for civil rights cannot begin in the
morning when a man enters the factory gates and end when he leaves at night.
When a union member is deprived of adequate housing because of his color, creed,
race, or nationality, his standing as a citizen, a union member, and worker is
adversely affected. When equal educational opportunities are denied, the productivity of America is lowered to the detriment of union members and all
Americans. When discrimination of any kind occurs in the community, fundamental
freedoms are under attack, including the freedom of workers to unite into unions
of their own making.

The fight for freedom and equality must proceed simultaneously at all
levels of our lives, since freedom itself is indivisible. Long ago, we of the
United Steelworkers recognized this--out of our experiences and through the
long hard years of building our organization. In 1948, we formed a United
Steelworkers National Civil Rights Committee which has been provided with the
staff necessary to work at the job throughout the year. At our recent convention, this Committee was able to report that as the result of union policy "many
categories of employment heretofore closed to non-whites have opened in the past
two years in the steel industry." It noted, nevertheless, that discrimination
in employment will finally be eliminated "only with the passage of a Federal
Fair Employment Practices Law, with adequate finances and personnel to administer
it effectively." Once again, at this convention, the United Steelworkers called
for federal legislation to end discrimination on the job and in the community.

Our civil rights program is carried forward in four basic areas--in employment, housing, community, and education. We have sought to build for a human
relations or civil rights committee in each local. Such committees are concerned with the civil rights and civil liberties of our members on the job and
in the community. While they do not function perfectly, they have proven to be
of tremendous value in our work. We coordinate the work of these committees
through our districts, through our National Civil Rights Committee, and through
our union educational work.

In the Community

Our national Civil Rights Committee is represented on the executive or
advisory boards of national and local agencies devoted to the fight for civil
rights and civil liberties, since we recognize the value of working with other
groups in this key area. In the City of Pittsburgh, for example, we are one of
15 participating organizations in the Mayor's Commission on Human Relations and
we have representation on the Commission's Fair Employment Practices Committee,
which is concerned with enforcement of Pittsburgh's local fair employment practices ordinance.

In Pittsburgh, we joined with the public school system, the Carnegie Museum,
and the Commission on Human Relations in sponsoring a booklet called, "We Humans."
This booklet deals with the races of man. It is used widely in the junior and

senior high schools. In Los Angeles, we are now working with the school board
in an effort to establish a similar project.

A slum clearance project in the Bunker Hill area of Los Angeles will
necessitate the relocation of 16,000 low income families, many of whom are nonwhites. The Civil Rights Committee of our union is now working with housing
authorities to obtain resettlement of these families without discrimination
because of race, color, creed or national origin.

So that there may be greater understanding among our members, our union
sponsors human relations institutes and seminars, both as part of our regular
education program and as part of our work in civil rights and civil liberties.
We have worked with university experts in this field to learn how we can better
work with each other to promote greater understanding. We have developed and
circulated widely within the union and in the community literature combating
discrimination.

When a trouble spot develops, we act. Where a situation requires cooperation with other unions, we seek that cooperation. Our district directors have
unequivocally condemned mob action against integration in their areas and we
have combated bigotry in such areas by following up fast with meetings and conferences aimed at the maintenance of good race relations.

The United Steelworkers is doing its part in the battle against discrimination. The AFL-CIO and its unions are bearing their share of the load. Many
religious and civic groups are also in the fight and can be depended upon to
continue their work at the national and community level until discrimination is
wiped out.

Management Has Responsibility

It is time, however, for management and enterprise to take a forthright and
positive stand. I call upon the National Association of Manufacturers, the
Chamber of Commerce, and their local bodies to move. Their power is great.
They know that all discrimination is costly and uneconomic. I ask them to take
a stand with us against the appalling waste of human resources that grows from
segregation and discrimination.

More, I ask the managements of American corporate enterprise and individual
businessmen in our communities to take an affirmative stand. I ask that they
show by example that all Americans are equal. I ask that they work with us to
end discriminatory practices in the plants and to end racial and religious
ghettos in the community.

The plant manager in a smaller community is a very important person whose
word often causes local politicians to tremble. But this man, like the unskilled
factory worker, is subject to orders from top management.

Top management in steel, textile, furniture, chemical, and all of our great
industries usually are men who live in the North. I urge them to begin educational work against discrimination among their local managers, North and South.
This is an obligation of industry. It is not labor's role alone and not alone
the role of the political parties to uphold the Supreme Court's edict on education. With the practical help of corporate management, school integration could
be carried out more effectively and more smoothly everywhere.

I will make management an offer: If top management will agree, the district
directors and staff representatives of the United Steelworkers will work with
local managements in programs of education at the plants and at the community
level. I cannot speak for all labor, but I will do all I can to get all of our
unions to go along, and I am quite certain that almost every one will work
effectively in putting over such a program. With the help of management, we
can enlist community organizations of all kinds in the work--PTA's, veterans'
organizations, Kiwanis Clubs, Rotary and many others.

Together, we can eliminate second class citizenship once and for all. All
Americans will benefit. In the words of a delegate at our last convention, "the
problem can be solved if we only get together and be sensible and reasonable
about this thing--much easier than you think if we just make up our minds that
we want to get together."

Industrial Union Department (AFL-CIO) *Digest,* 2 (Winter, 1957):3-9.

22. USWA'S CIVIL RIGHTS PROGRAM WINS PRAISE

District 15 Delegates Urged to Fully-Integrate Communities

The United Steelworkers of America under the leadership of President David J. McDonald, has done more to solve the problems of civil rights and bring about social justice than any other union in the United States, according to the Rev. Charles Owen Rice, Pittsburgh.

Father Rice, pastor of Immaculate Conception Church, Washington, Pa., addressing the annual conference of District 15, United Steelworkers of America, quoted the late Pope John XXII regarding the rights of people and their duties.

"Go after your own rights--live up to your full potential," Father Rice urged. "These people (the minority groups) must go after their rights-- it is our duty not to interfere," Father rice told the more than 350 delegates attending the conference at Mountain View Hotel, Greensburg.

"We, as members of the United Steelworkers of America, must help them-- we must accept them completely in our own communities."

"We must not only be good members of the United Steelworkers of America but also we must be good members at heart, too," Father Rice declared. "If our labor communities are not integrated in every way--our homes, our hearts, what chance has the United States of America?" Father Rice asked. "If you do not believe that the man working next to you is as good as you--then God help America," Father Rice added. "Peace is gone in our country until that problem is settled," he continued.

Director William Hart of USWA District 19, following the theme set by Father Rice, also lauded President McDonald's leadership and said that the United Steelworkers of America has expended more monies on the problems of civil rights than any other union in the United States.

Supporting this claim, he said, is the fact that the United Steelworkers of America has the "ablest Committee on Civil Rights in existence"; that seminars conducted at major universities emphasize the importance of civil rights and that, finally, the entire program of the USWA is aimed at social justice for all people regardless of race or creed or national origin.

Director, Hart, president of the Allegheny County Labor Council, said that, as president, he had established a Civil Rights Committee for the first time in the council's existence.

Attacking the problem of unemployment in Allegheny County, Director Hart cited the fact that the county needs 130,000 new jobs to attain the national employment level.

"There is need," he said, "to engage in warfare to promote the United Steelworkers of America--to change the image that Pittsburgh is a center of labor strife."

He said that news datelines carry the name "Pittsburgh" because so many national contracts are signed in the city and that people elsewhere get an erroneous opinion when they read the agreements have not been reached.

Director Hart also called for all-out support of the County Labor Council's political action program and he cited instances where federal and even state appropriations and contracts are going elsewhere because of the weak support from elected politicians.

Director Paul Hilbert, chairman of the conference program, listed the steady drop in employment in the steel industry in District 15 -- that employment which once was 45,000 had dropped last February to 23,000 -- then bounced back to 31,000 in May. Automation and technological advancement was blamed for a good part of the decline.

In summarizing the USWA program in District 15 during the past 12 months, Director Hilbert launched the Community Services Committee which he called the "silent service" because most of the help arranged by this committee remains secret . . . and recipients of union help are not embarrassed as is so often the case in public relief or charity.

He also praised the blood donor program and the eye care program.

Guest speakers included Roland Sawyer, USWA housing consultant, who outlined the Four Freedoms Inc. program providing low-cost housing for senior retirees and their wives. He said that the USWA's pamphlet -- "Housing

After 60" -- had been widely acclaimed by other unions and by housing authorities throughout the nation. He disclosed that, at the present time, the Steelworkers have 107,000 retirees.

Other speakers at the one-day conference included Maurice Schulte, who represented Vice President Howard R. Hague; Director Paul Normile of USWA District 16 and Charles Ford, USWA legislative representative at Harrisburg.

Mr. Schulte, member of the International staff, traced the course of current Human Relations Committee talks and lauded the "wisdom" of President David J. McDonald and other top officers, including Mr. Hague and Secretary-Treasurer I. W. Abel, in anticipating the inroads of automation and technological advancement which had led to widespread replacement of manpower in the mills.[117]

He cited the 13 weeks extended vacation plan in the can industry and the supplemental unemployment benefits (SUB) program which has helped during long periods of layoffs and is now creating new job opportunities for Steelworkers.

Mr. Ford rapped the leadership of Republican Gov. William Scranton who imposed a five per cent state sales tax--highest in the nation--and cited the fact that 71 per cent of the state revenue now comes from the "bottom" --the little people, so-called. Prior to this, corporations and machinery taxes made up the lion's share of the tax. He rapped the state's antiquated educational system and constitution and declared that "Pennsylvania is fast losing status--it is not up to par with other states."[118]

The Wage Policy election highlighted the day's festivities with the following elected to represent District 15:

Pete Latin, Local 1407, James Betters, Local 1514, Sigmund Balogh, Local 2227, all basic steel; Francis Scumaci, Continental Can Local 4337; Matt Brulja, National Tube Salaried Local 2316 and Anton Bon, Vesuvius Crucible Local 3730.

Steel Labor (July, 1963).

23.
ADDRESS BY
VERNON E. JORDAN, JR.
EXECUTIVE DIRECTOR
NATIONAL URBAN LEAGUE
AT
SIXTEENTH CONSTITUTIONAL CONVENTION
(UNITED STEELWORKERS OF AMERICA), 1972

This great union is convened at a time when the precious, hard-won rights of black Americans are under massive attack. By implication, this means that labor, too, will soon come under a similar attempt to tear from it, its own bitterly-won advances, for history shows us that America's actions towards its black citizens is a barometer of its eventual actions towards its organized working men and women.

Black people sense today that the Second Reconstruction -- that remarkable stride toward equality made in the 1960s that benefited labor and white people no less than black -- is on its deathbed, fatally ill from the diseases of reactionary vindictiveness and liberal withdrawal.

Those who would strip from black people the gains of recent years are also

intent on using the labor movement as a pawn in their struggle. The extent to
which they have been successful in changing the image of the labor movement from
one of progressive activism is readily seen.

Unions, striving to win decent wages and better working conditions for
their members are condemned as selfish and affluent. Since when does a factory
worker's income of $8,000 or so make him affluent? Since when do attempts to
catch up with galloping inflation become "selfish?" And how can the limited
power of unions be compared with the massive power of giant corporations?

But those who would split the mutually beneficial alliance of liberals,
labor and blacks go beyond their relatively mild attacks on the labor movement
to slander the decency of working people and of ethnic groups. Workers are
Wallacites, they say. Poles -- or Slavs, or Italians -- it doesn't matter,
pick your own sample ethnic group, are anti-black, they claim. Working people
and union members are stigmatized as hard-hat bigots. The Archie Bunker-ization
of the American working man is a myth fed by the media, by the enemies of both
working people and black people, and by those who roll the clock back to the
good old days when blacks knew their place and unions weren't recognized.

I believe this new mood of anti-black, anti-labor feeling represents a
dangerous threat to labor and to black people. If the labor movement is split
away from its natural allies in the civil rights movement it will itself become
weaker and more liable to direct attack. And to the degree that the general
public is convinced that labor is selfish and bigoted, the labor movement will
lose the moral standing and public goodwill it needs to succeed in its aims.

What I have outlined here is not science fiction or futurist fantasy -- it
is a clear and present danger that threatens us both. I care profoundly about
this situation because I believe that the cause of black Americans would be
seriously weakened if the labor movement became less active in the alliance
that has benefited us both. And I care profoundly because if the labor movement is significantly weakened, then the black working man, who has joined
unions to a greater degree than any other group, is also significantly weakened
in his chances for a better life.

I would contend that unless black Americans are brought back to center
stage in this nation's affairs, everyone will suffer, but most especially, the
union movement and the average working man. The problems of black people have
been shunted to the back of the bus, once again ignored and invisible. And
all the while our cities are deteriorating and the thrust toward social reform
and greater equity is fading.

This can be seen clearly in this election year. The campaign thus far has
centered around charges and countercharges, to the exclusion of serious discussion of the issues of importance to black people. Neither candidate has come
up with proposals for better housing, for penal reform, for welfare reform.
The issue of education is totally ignored, except for the code-word phony issue
of "busing." The value of paychecks is shrinking and the rights of black people
are systematically eroded and the cities are sinking fast, but none of those
basic issues is getting the considered attention they -- and we -- deserve.

An example of a new issue recently injected into the campaign -- one that
spells serious trouble for black working people -- is the issue of so-called
quotas. Both candidates have declared they are opposed to quotas. It appears
too, that because of the President's opposition to quotas, the Philadelphia
Plan may be greatly modified to remove numerical and percentage benchmarks for
employment of blacks in construction work. Such a step would be a transparent
attempt to drive a wedge between black people, who have historically been denied
the right to work and to join unions in the construction industry, and the
labor movement. Such an attempt dishonors the labor movement by publicly
assuming that the handful of unions that practice discrimination in the building
trades are representative of the bulk of the labor movement, which is integrated
and which opposes discrimination.

Anyone -- from the man with the shovel to the men contending for the White
House -- knows that without some sort of effective numerical guidelines, no
affirmative action plan can work. Already there are self-satisfied statements
coming from people in the construction industry about how the removal of firm
guidelines will mean they won't have to integrate their union or their work
force. An end to the Philadelphia Plan spells an end to the only moderately
effective effort to open job opportunities for black workers, but it also

spells the end of the very many voluntary hometown plans jointly formulated by
the civil rights movement, government and the building trades locals.

Let us not forget that this country has always had negative quotas against
black people who were barred from jobs, schools and homes. Black people today
seek no special treatment as special Americans, but assurances that we will not
receive the special treatment we've received throughout the history of this
nation. For blacks *have* been special Americans -- singled out for discrimination and oppression in the past and today singled out for the special treatment
of isolation and withdrawal. By labelling goals and guidelines as quotas and
by refusing to admit the realities of the necessity of federal enforcement of
civil rights laws, the nation once again threatens black people with enforced
poverty and inequality of job opportunity.

The real obscenity here is that groups have been set squabbling amongst
each other for the scraps from the table of the affluent society; that there
are not enough jobs and employment opportunities to go around in this, the
richest nation in the world's history, and that political expediency is being
allowed to obscure the driving need for black equality in our economy.

The quota issues has come to prominence at the same time that we have
seen the emergence of what might be called "The New Minorities" -- groups of
Americans who, most of them for the first time, have forged a self-consciousness
and a realization that they too, have not fully shared in America's bounty.
Among these "new minorities" are various ethnic groups, women, students, and
others.

In general, I believe this is a healthy development. It has resulted in a
creative ferment that stresses the true pluralism of our country and rejects
the melting pot myth that deprived millions of people of their culture and
heritage. If there is a negative side to this development however, it is in
the way the just demands of various groups for equality of results tends to
obscure the priorities necessary to enlightened social reform. And those
priorities must be those that will reverse the basic racism that deprives the
largest and most impoverished minority -- black Americans -- from a rightful
share of the country they helped build.

The new minorities arose only after the civil rights movement matured and
showed the way. Their rhetoric, tactics and strategies are direct copies of
those used by the civil rights movement. Their very existence is an indication
of the positive moral effect the black movement has had on the rest of the
nation. But it is just clear that the establishment is striving to accommodate
the needs of the new minorities at the expense of blacks. Instead of baking
a bigger pie and giving everyone decent portions, they're slicing the same old
pie of economic opportunities thinner.

I believe that unless blacks return to the spotlight of social change in
America; unless activists and reformers recognize the basic truism that as
blacks go, so goes the nation, all of us will lose out. The issues the black
people are raising and the aims of the civil rights movement are issues and
aims that will benefit all. The tactic of settling the claims of the new
minorities to counter the aspirations of black people is a tactic designed to
drive another nail in the coffin of the Second Reconstruction.

White Americans, and especially the working people, have a lot to lose if
the Second Reconstruction is allowed to die an ignoble death. If we look at
some of the issues of importance to black people, we see that if we lose, white
working people join us in defeat.

The current vicious welfare measure under consideration, for example, will
affect more white people than blacks. Black people are disproportionately poor,
but two-thirds of all poor people are white and a true reform of the welfare
system that corrects the inequities of the economic system will benefit everybody.

If the civil rights laws now on the books were adequately enforced, black
Americans would have their fair share of the rewards and responsibilities of
American life, and that could only result in an expanded economy that helps
white people as well as black. It also would result in an America in which
there is domestic peace and mutual concern for justice, a nation in which the
resources now wasted in keeping the lid on black people can be diverted to the
benefit of all.

The Supreme Court's about-face from the landmark decision of the Warren
Court affect us both. On the very day that the court split for the first time

on a civil rights case involving school desegregation, it also handed down a
decision sharply limiting labor's rights to communicate with the public and
with prospective union members. Once the Court places property rights above
human rights, we both -- labor and the black man -- get it in the neck.

This goes too, for political liberals who are compromising on the just
claims and rights of black people. Historically, we have seen that black people
are but the first to be deserted. Union-busting traditionally follows retreat
from principles. Today it is the black man's rights that are being compromised.
But I can promise you that the next steps will see the revival of right-to-work
laws, curbs on strikes, and other anti-labor measures. If there is any doubt
on that score, just look at who was the target of the economic freeze and the
policies of Phase Two.

The suburban housing freeze that shuts out low and moderate income
families is something that hits white workers as well as blacks. Many communities think their zoning laws will keep them lily-white, but those same local
restrictions in many instances make it impossible for working people of all
colors to live in the towns in which they work. The labor movement has been
alerted to the dangers of international companies relocating manufacturing plants
in foreign countries; it has still to become fully aware of the need to protect
its members from losing their jobs or from having to commute four or five hours
a day because of relocation to sites that don't have adequate housing opportunities for families that earn average or below-average incomes.

And the busing issue is one that has been used to divert many working
people from the real issues of concern to them. The use of busing is only one
of many ways in which quality education can be achieved through ending the
illegal and unconstitutional system of segregated schools. Many white Americans
have been diverted from their true interest in economic gains and in a more
equal society through emotional and irrational appeals to their latent prejudice.
The right to equal educational opportunities is a right sanctioned by our Constitution, and if black people's rights to desegregated schooling are compromised,
then white people's rights to organize into labor unions and to enjoy other
Constitutional guarantees will be compromised.

On nearly all points of the economic and social compass, our mutual
interests converge. A full-employment economy with meaningful jobs for everyone
who wants to work must be the cornerstone both of the labor movement's desire
for jobs and the black community's need for economic empowerment. A total re-
structuring of our health, welfare, and housing system is on both of our agendas.
In a multitude of areas, we both know that our mutual dependence is our mutual
strength; that together we will overcome, divided we will succumb to our common
enemies -- the enemies of the working man and the enemies of the black man.

It sometimes seems as if the tide against us is irresistible, but we should
remember that often what seems irrestible is only the unresisted. I am here
today to ask you to join us in resisting those who would weaken us both.

Black people have been excluded from the fruits of this society for four
hundred years, and in a thousand ways, white people have been held down because
of our exclusion. Black demands for inclusion in our society and white worker's
demands for security and peaceful progress are identical. Together we can build
a new, better society; together we can create an America that is in tune with
its ideals.

Black Americans have not yet renounced America, for all the hatred and
deprivation that have been lavished upon us. It is increasingly clear that to
the extent that there is among the citizenry hope and faith in the American
ideals, they are held by those who have suffered most and benefited least.

Black people, for all our righteous anger and forceful dissent, still
believe in the American dream. We believe today as we once believed in the
dungeons of slavery; as we once believed in the struggles of Reconstruction,
and as we held our faith through the dismal days of separation and segregation.

Black people have a claim on this land. We have fought in its every war
-- even in segregated armies -- and are dying today in disproportionate numbers
in Vietnam. Our sweat and blood have created its wealth, as our faith and our
hope have given it a soul. This nation must find within its innermost being
the understanding that our needs, our dreams, and our sacrifices must be shared
and that together, black and white, we can build a society that is humane, that
is civilized, that is a true community in every sense of the word.

Many years ago, Samuel Gompers was asked: "What does Labor want?"
"What does Labor want?", he replied, "We want more school houses and less
jails; more books and less arsenals; more learning and less vice; more
leisure and less greed; more justice and less revenge; in fact, more of the
opportunities to cultivate our better natures, to make manhood more noble,
womanhood more beautiful, and childhood more happy and bright."

And that, my brothers and sisters of this great American labor union,
is what black people want!

Address by Vernon E. Jordan, Jr., at the Sixteenth Constitutional Convention
of the United Steelworkers of America, Las Vegas, Nevada, September 19,
1972. Reprinted with permission of Vernon E. Jordan, Jr.

24. HISTORY OF THE UNITED STEELWORKERS OF AMERICA: STEEL UNION BUTTRESSES RACISM

By Staughton Lynd

I. W. Abel, the present president of the Steelworkers union, defeated
David McDonald in 1965 partly because he was supported by black members of
the union. Once elected Abel would not even grant black spokesmen an
interview.

The incident was part of an historical pattern: first, of management
deliberately setting blacks, Latins and whites against one another; second,
of white union politicans making election-time promises to members of
minority groups which they forget after election day.

Blacks and Latins entered the steel industry in large numbers during
and just after World War I. Previously the industry had recruited its
workmen from American whites and from Eastern European immigrants. As one
supervisor put it, the two groups were combined in a "judicious mixture"
tp prevent effective group action.

The outbreak of World War I stopped immigration from Europe. Blacks
from the American South, and later Mexicans, were solicited in their place.
By the mid-1920s blacks and Latins together made up about 25 percent of the
steel labor force.

The steel companies fostered race hatred among these new workers just
as they had among the old. The city of Gary, Ind., is an example.

When U.S. Steel laid out the city of Gary in the early 1900s, it
build homes only for its skilled, white, American-born workers. Unskilled
laborers, both Eastern European and blacks, had to fend for themselves.
There was a severe housing shortage for all poor people. As a result, they
lived not only crowded but also very mixed. White and black rented rooms
from each other in the same houses. One early resident recalls:

"If you had a house with an apartment on the street and an apartment
in the back, in a lot of cases you and your family took the apartment in the
back and rented the front out to black people, because the front apartment
paid a little bit more. During the hot weather you and your tenants and
their family would share in the front porch and the front yard."

Blacks Stayed Below

In this early period, immigrants and blacks had pretty much the same jobs.
Later the immigrants moved up the ladder and the blacks were held in the
hardest, dirtiest jobs. After World War I the immigrant population of Gary
slowly began to move out of the poor area. U.S. Steel's man on the Realty
Board did everything he could to discourage residential integration.

The steel strike of 1919 hastened the emerging racial antagonism. Blacks
had little reason to support the strike because 20 of the 24 craft unions
involved excluded blacks. Whites were offended when the company imported
Mexicans and 30-40,000 blacks as strikebreakers to Gary, it is remembered:

"The mills brought black people in here from deep parts of the South in
box cars. They promised the black workers promotions and good jobs. Some of

them did work on some of the jobs, until the strike was broken, and then they
went back to work at the end of the line."

The incident made use of by the Gary authorities to bring in federal troops
to crush the strike began when white workers tried to pull a black scab off a
streetcar carrying him to the mill. The CIO organizing drive in the 1930s over-
came to some extent the division among blacks, Latins and whites. A black
worker says:

"Black workers rushed in in large numbers because they were like drowning
men. The white workers kind of hung out. Some of the white workers said,
'Well, I don't want to be part of something that is going to give a black worker
as much right as I have.' But all people don't think alike no matter what race
they are. If you are going to elect some officers, and some folks are active,
that's who you are going to elect. The first election in the Tin Mill we had
a black worker for recording secretary. We had a black worker vice president.
We had a black worker grievance committeeman. The foreman called a meeting one
day of all the white workers. His remarks were, 'Men, the union might be all
right. But why in the hell do you have to have a Negro to represent you?' One
of those men spoke up and said, 'You might call him a Negro but we call him a
brother union member and we are sure that we trust him in all that he has done.'"

After the union was organized, according to this man, "blacks and whites
alternated at jobs so that everyone could take a coffee break, pitched in for
anyone who didn't have lunch money, played softball together at Roosevelt Park
and brought their families."

Racist Union

The spirit of brotherhood evident during the organizing drive has faded,
along with the democracy and militancy of that period. The international union
itself is demonstrably racist. Today blacks are about a third of the Steelworkers' membership and in some plants they are a majority. Yet there has
never been a black member of the international union executive board. The same
is true of the union's appointed personnel.

According to the Ad Hoc Committee of Concerned Steelworkers, a caucus of
black steelworkers formed in 1964:

"Of more than 1000 employes of the international (in 1968), less than 100
are Negroes. Of 14 departments of the international, only two have Negro personnel. One of these two departments is the Civil Rights Department (obviously).
Blacks were in the forefront during the formation of this union 25 years ago.
Through the acceptance of crumbs down through the years instead of our just
deserts, we now find ourselves hindmost."

More significant than the exclusion of blacks from leadership positions in
the union is their concentration in dirty, unhealthy, poor paying jobs in the
mills. True, blacks now work in areas of the mills from which they were previously barred. But departments like the coke plant, sintering plant and blast
furnace continue to be all-black in most mills and the black worker's ability
to move into better jobs continues to be less than the white's.

A study made in Youngstown, Ohio, in 1964 concluded that "given the same
seniority and education, the white employe's chances for advancement are substantially greater than are the Negro's and that is true at all levels of
seniority, at all levels of education, and at all job levels." A study of
black employment in the basic steel industry of Pittsburgh made for the Equal
Employment Opportunity Commission in 1968 observed that "Negroes comprise 12.27
percent of the laborers, 12.93 percent of the service workers and 10.86 of the
semi-skilled operatives, but only 3.21 percent of the craftsmen."

The union has a direct responsibility for this situation because of its
failure to insist on plant-wide, rather than departmental seniority. Placed in
traditionally all-black departments by the hiring practices of the companies,
black workers hesitate to try to transfer to other departments because they
must give up their accumulated seniority in (say) the coke plant and start all
over again.

Also, in every economic recession blacks who had found their way into a
previously all-white department tend to be squeezed out. A white worker in
the open hearth in a mill in Youngstown, Ohio, who has worked for years to
integrate his department, puts it this way:

"Our department was desegregated and blacks moved into all the jobs. I

didn't hear any complaints at all. But now, with the recession again, it is
an all-white department for all practical purposes. People are getting
bumped according to seniority. How does a black person break through and
become a machinist when the youngest machinist has 30 years in the plant?"
     Discrimination in job assignment can literally be a death sentence. It
has recently been established that a person who works on top of the coke
ovens for more than five years is 10 times more likely to get lung cancer
than are other steelworkers. Coke oven workers are almost all black.

Guardian, April 11, 1973.

25.
NATIONAL AD HOC COMMITTEE OF CONCERNED
STEELWORKERS ANNUAL MEETING, 1972

BLACK STAFF ON PAYROLL OF UNITED STEELWORKERS

	BEFORE AD HOC	AFTER AD HOC
DISTRICT DIRECTOR	0	0
ASST. DISTRICT DIRECTOR	0	0
INTERNATIONAL REPRESENTATIVE	1	2
DEPARTMENT HEAD	0	1
ASST. DEPARTMENT HEAD	0	1
STAFF REPRESENTATIVE ASSIGNED TO PITTSBURGH	3	12
SUB-DISTRICT DIRECTOR	1	5
KEY STAFF REPRESENTATIVES	0	5
STAFF REPRESENTATIVES	31	62

     The National Ad Hoc Committee has been instrumental in increasing the
number of international representatives, the number of sub-district directors,
and the number of black staff representatives in the steelworkers union.
     The National Ad Hoc Committee has also been a contributing factor in the
promoting of five (5) black staff representatives to the position of key
staff.
     Through the efforts of the National Ad Hoc Committee the Civil Rights
Department has been reorganized with a black man as the Director. There is
also a black Assistant Director of the Contract Administration Department.
     Out of twenty-eight (28) departments in the Pittsburgh office, ten (10)
now have black staff representatives as members.
     There are still eighteen (18) departments that need integrating. In the
steelworkers union, we still do not have a black person on the executive
board of this union.
     The purpose and intent of the National Ad Hoc Committee will remain the
same until the United Steelworkers has been completely integrated:

OUR PURPOSE AND INTENT is to secure our rightful share of all the
benefits our Union has to offer including employment in all levels.
This Committee has embarked on a Three Point Program to achieve
this goal.

     1. Negroes on the Executive Board.

     2. Full integration on all levels within the various
         districts and National offices as department heads
         and policy makers.

     3. Reorganization of the Civil Rights Department has
         been dealt with.

     Prior to 1964 a National Ad Hoc Committee was a dream; something hoped and
longed for. This dream was cherished in the heart of many black steelworkers.

These brothers had met in convention after convention trying to unfold their
dream in reality. At the 13th Constitutional Convention of the United Steelworkers in Atlantic City, New Jersey, these brothers joined themselves together
and molded their dream into three demands. These demands were presented in both
candidates aspiring for the office of President of the International Union.

    1. There must be blacks on the Executive Board.
    2. There must be blacks in every Department.
    3. The Civil Rights Department must be integrated with a Black Director.

I am happy to have been one of the founders of this great committee.

This national committee has organized local branches in eleven (11)
States: Gary, Ind.; Chicago, Illinois; Baltimore, Maryland; Birmingham, Alabama;
Cleveland, Ohio; Youngstown, Ohio; Detroit, Michigan; Philadelphia, Pa.; Pitts-
burgh, Penn.; Houston, Texas; Los Angeles, California.

This brochure will give a report of the progress made in those eight (8)
years. Many Ad Hocers have moved up into the International Union as International
Representatives, technicians, sub-district directors, assistants to department
heads.

I have had the privilege to serve two (2) years as Secretary-Treasurer and
four (4) years as National Chairman, during these years; I have had the pleasure
of visiting every branch.

In this 16th Annual Convention, my term of office will expire. The guidelines prohibit a national officer from succeeding themselves more than once.
Coupled with the fact that 1972 makes it possible for me to retire from physical
labor, under our labor agreement; this I have taken advantage of.

       I appreciate the cooperation given me by the various branches.
       I hope that the Ad Hoc Committee will carry on until every vestige
of segregation and discrimination has been eliminated.

                            Fraternally yours,

                            Rayfield Mooty, Chairman
                            National Ad Hoc Committee of
                            Concerned Steelworkers

After Abel's election as International President, the Committee tried for
four years without success to meet with him. Finally, convinced that it was
time to use labor's strongest weapon against labor leaders, black steelworkers
confronted Mr. Abel with a picket line at the 14th Constitutional Convention in
Chicago's International Amphitheater in 1968.

After three days of demonstration and publicity Mr. Abel was forced to
meet with the Committee and discuss the three point program. Some progress
had been made. The Civil Rights Department had been reorganized and some
departments had been integrated (tokenly). But there was still no black
department heads, the number of black employees was less than 100 of a total
of about 1200, and the Executive Board was still all-white.

Mr. Abel promised that the Board was planning to support Mr. Leander Simms
for District Director. The demonstration was called off. The Committee made
an all-out effort to help Mr. Simms in District 8. But this was a handicapped
race: every one knows that you can't start in September to run for District
Director the next February. Mr. Simms lost the election. Mr. Abel won. He
has never met with the Committee since.

          THE AD HOC COMMITTEE OF CONCERNED STEELWORKERS ALSO JOINS
              OTHER RANK-AND-FILE STEELWORKERS IN DEMANDING;

1. *No Neutrality in the Presidential Election!* The membership cannot
    afford to stand in the middle of the road while vital decisions are
    being made. The rank and file is accustomed to look to the Inter-
    national Union for leadership in national politics. If that leader-
    ship is not forthcoming, the rank and file will act on its own.

2. *Eliminate the Productivity Clause From the Contract!* The union was
    started in the first place mainly to keep the company from defining
    jobs and arranging work schedules as it pleased, eliminating jobs any
    time it wanted, and generally pushing people around on the job. In
    the last contract the union agreed to help the company do these things.
    It takes all the strength out of the union when local presidents and
    grievance committeemen are required to help the company do its dirty
    work.

3. Amend the Constitution of the USWA to provide for a referendum ballot
    of the membership on all contracts.

4. Seek immediate inclusion of our contracts of a clause which gives our
    members the right to strike for reasons of health and safety, against
    speed-up, racial and sex discrimination, and company violation of the
    contract after a 30-day waiting period.

5. Adopt as the top priority goal of this union the fight for the 6-hour
    day, 30-hour week at 40 hours pay to make room for a FOURTH six hour
    shift in the 24-hour day, thereby increasing employment to the poten-
    tial of 25% and returning part of the benefits of new technology to
    the working people.

6. Provide that pension funds be invested in loans to union members at
    the same rate of interest given to large borrowers, that portable
    pensions be instituted so that total time in the steel industry is
    the basis for retirement pensions, and that the pension funds give
    full disclosure of all investments.

7. Provide a full quarterly disclosure of the membership in each company
    of the current status of the SUB funds, that all interest accrued from
    such funds be plowed back into the fund, that all workers be included
    in the fund from the first day on the job, and that senior workers
    shall have the option to take a layoff instead of younger workers.

8. Repeal the Wage Freeze.

National Ad Hoc Committee of Concerned Steelworkers, annual meeting and election
of officers, Convention Hall, Las Vegas, Nevada, September 18-22, 1972. Copy
in possession of the editors.

26 . BLACK STEELWORKERS' PARLEY
SPURS REPRESENTATION FIGHT

     LAS VEGAS, Sept. 28 -- There was more than one convention of steelworkers
in this city last week. While the United Steel Workers of America was holding
its Constitutional Convention, Black members of the USWA from all parts of the
country held a meeting which will no doubt have a great impact on the future
direction of the union.
     The Black steelworkers' meeting elected officers and discussed plans for
further breaking down the discriminatory practices that still exist within the
union's structure. Also they were concerned about the bias against Blacks in
the plants, as well as the union's position in the overall struggle against
discrimination.

Jim Davis Chairman

     Elected chairman of the Ad Hoc committee of Black steelworkers was Jim
Davis, 43, member of the Youngstown, Ohio, grievance committee in Local 1462.
     The new secretary of the committee is Charles M. Cavness, Richmond,
California, who is chairman of the grievance committee of Local 51.

Other officers elected were Charles Brown, Baltimore, first vice-president; Eddie Leonard, Detroit, second vice-president, and John Fair, inside guard (sergeant at arms), Baltimore.

A key leader of the Ad Hoc Committee was Rayfield Moody, who served as its secretary-treasurer for two years and was chairman for four annual terms. He has reached the retirement age in the industry, and he could not, as a national officer, run for office this year in the Ad Hoc Committee but he called on the committee to "carry on until every vestige of segregation and discrimination had been eliminated."

Staff members of the United Steelworkers can only be honorary members of the Ad Hoc Committee although since the committee was formed the number of the union's black staff representatives has risen from 31 to 62.

There are still no black district directors or assistant directors, however, and in the last eight years the number of international representatives has only increased from one to two.

There are now 12 black staff members assigned to the Pittsburgh office to the union, compared to three when the Ad Hoc Committee began its pressure.

There are now five black sub-directors and five key staff representatives compared to only a single black sub-director and no key staff representatives in the pre-Ad Hoc period.

Stand on Elections

Ad Hoc has no firm plan for backing any of the Blacks running for union office in the 1973 elections, Davis said, but he added that it will "consider supporting" Samuel Stokes, former president of Local 1200 in Columbus, Ohio. Stokes has been on the union staff since 1946 and has been a key staff representative since 1969.

Another Black running for office who will "very likely" get Ad Hoc support, is Al Wellington in District 26, northern Ohio counties. According to Davis this district has a 30 percent black membership and Wellington, who will be running against director Lester Ganich, has considerable support among white workers.

Davis said that while the Ad Hoc Committee has "no direct ties" with the leaders of other rank and file organizations in the union -- RAFT (Rank and File Team) and the National Steelworkers Rank and File -- they may "work jointly on issues."

At the Convention there appeared to be a working relationship among all of the rank and file groups, each of which had its operating center in Las Vegas.

Davis said the Ad Hoc Committee will continue to press its three-point program, which includes demands for a Black member of the present all-white-all male-executive board of the union, for Blacks in every department of the union, and for fully integrating the international's civil rights department with a black director.

"Blacks make up about 25 per cent of the union and we expect no less representation than that in the union," Davis said. "We pay 25 per cent of the dues and we want 25 per cent of the jobs."

The black caucus movement reportedly has bases in Pittsburgh, Baltimore, Philadelphia, Birmingham, Youngstown, Cleveland, Detroit and Chicago.

Daily World, September 29, 1972.

27.   THE FIGHT AGAINST RACISM IN THE USWA

An Interview with Rayfield Mooty

There is no union, with the possible exception of some in the Building and Construction Trades Department of the AFL-CIO, where the leadership has such a long and inglorious record of accommodation to, and cooperation with, racism and racist practices as does the "Official Family" of the United Steel Workers of America.

This long history of racism in the USWA has been countered by an equally long campaign by rank and file steelworkers to overturn these policies and

practices. White as well as Black and Latin steelworkers have been a part of
these struggles but Blacks--as they have since the struggles against chattel
slavery--have played a leading and decisive role in those struggles.
   The 19th Constitutional Convention of the United Steel Workers of America
is an important event, not only for steelworkers but for workers everywhere.
One of the biggest challenges before the Convention will be the struggle to
unite the steelworkers union in preparation for the sharp economic and legislative battles that lie ahead. This, in turn, requires a new level of unity
between Black, Latin and white steelworkers--and a sharper struggle against
racism within the steel industry and within the United Steel Workers of America.
   The 19th Constitutional Convention will mark the 10th anniversary of the
Ad Hoc Committee of Concerned Steelworkers' picket line at the 1968 convention
of the USWA. Rayfield Mooty led that picket line. *Labor Today* spent a day
talking to him about the event and about the struggle for Black representation
within the ranks of the steelworkers union. We think it's a story worth
sharing.

*I see that one of the signs you carried at the 1968 convention says, "Integrate
all departments." Just what did you hope to accomplish when you decided to
picket the place?*

   That was just one of our demands. We had three. Our first was that there
be Blacks on the International Executive Board. Our second called for reorganization of the Civil Rights Department and our third was for full integration in
all levels of the union so that Black steelworkers would be represented at all
levels where policy was determined. We called it our Three Point Program.
   There's another thing that you must remember--we did not begin our activity
in 1968. The Ad Hoc Committee of Concerned Steelworkers grew out of the Negro
Steelworkers Leadership Committee that had been established at the 1964 convention in Atlantic City. This was the group that set up the Three Point
Program. Ad Hoc was just continuing the work that had been started earlier.
   Also, we didn't end our activity with the 1968 picket line. We picketed
the International office in 1970 and we went back to the 1970 convention. But
none of these had the same impact as our picket line in Chicago. How could it?
After all, how many times before that had members of a union set up a picket
line at a convention of their own union--to say nothing about the fact that
this was a picket line established by Black workers.

*You say that the Ad Hoc Committee of Concerned Steelworkers grew out of the
Negro Steelworkers Leadership Committee. What happened to that group?*

   I've learned one very important thing in the 42 years since I joined the
Steel Workers Organizing Committee in 1937: Events sometimes force you to take
action before you are prepared for it, before you've been able to think everything through. That's the way it was in 1964 when we organized the Negro
Steelworkers Leadership Committee.
   Don't forget, the United Steel Workers of America was organized in 1942
and before that we had been the Steel Workers Organizing Committee for six
years. And in all of those thirty years, fewer than thirty Blacks had been
hired by the International Union--despite the fact that the USWA employed, and
still employs, between 1,200 to 1,500 people.
   In 1964 there were no Blacks in any position of decision or authority.
There were no Black department heads. There were only a handful of Blacks on
staff and very few working as clerks, secretaries or bookkeepers.
   Blacks had been burning over this discrimination--it was racism, pure and
simple--for years and we finally decided to do something about it. We organized ourselves at the convention, drafted our program, a statement of intent,
and went to work.
   As we traveled around the country building support for our program, we
came to understand that the concept that gave rise to the Negro Steelworkers
Leadership Committee was too narrow. We realized that we would have to
establish an organization that would allow white participation as well. So,
we dissolved the Leadership Committee and reorganized ourselves as the Ad Hoc
Committee of Concerned Steelworkers. Although few whites joined Ad Hoc, they
could have if they wanted to. There's nothing wrong with changes if they are

necessary, just as long as you don't forget what you're all about—that's
another thing I've learned.

Labor Today (September, 1978).

MUNICIPAL WORKERS

28. UNION BATTLE WON IN MEMPHIS

*Editor's Note: We are reprinting this article (slightly modified) from MDS
Newsletter, Box 2647, New Orleans, La. 70116, because we feel it can serve
several useful purposes. It is a vivid lesson in building wide community
support for workers' struggles and in going beyond strictly trade-union forms
of struggle. Memphis is also a case study in the sources of the recent ghetto
uprising which go deeper than the bullet that killed Martin Luther King.*

By Fred Lacey

A titanic union struggle in the city of Memphis, Tenn. is over and the
workers have come out on top. City sanitation workers stayed out on strike
for 65 days. They defied a court injunction demanding their return. They
braved police terror which included mass arrests and the widespread use of
mace, tear gas, and police clubs against them. And they defeated a city administration which brought in scabs by the truckload from the bordering states
of Mississippi and Arkansas in an effort to break their strike.

The strike began on Feb. 12, in the wake of the sanitation workers' strike
in New York City, and was sparked by a typical action of job discrimination
against black workers (black workers make up over 1,300 of the city's 1,600
sanitation workers). On a rainy morning a good number of black workers were
sent home, while a smaller group of favorites, including white workers, was
told to stay by the trucks. Later, the weather cleared up and those who were
told to stay got in a full day's work. The workers sent home demanded that the
city pay them for the lost day, but the administration refused to give the men
more than two hours compensation. Piled on top of all the other rotten working
conditions, the men decided that they had taken enough, and walked out on strike.

Some of those other conditions that led up to the strike include: (1) no
bathrooms, no washrooms, and no showering facilities for the men to clean up
with after work, and no protective work-clothing, which meant that all workers
had to go home in the same clothes they had been working in all day; (2) no
place for the men to lunch, which meant a situation that one worker described
as "having a sandwich in one hand and a garbage can in the other"; (3) job
discrimination against black workers, who were consistently denied job promotions; and (4) no pension or retirement system.

Besides this, the sanitation workers were not listed as regular city workers,
and therefore did not qualify for workmen's compensation. Early in January of
this year, two men were crushed to death by a defective packer in their truck.
The men's families received a "gift" from the city of $500 for "burial expenses,"
and one month's pay. Nothing more.

Wages were another factor causing the strike. The city administration
hired mostly older men with families for the job, and paid them 5¢ over the
minimum wage to start, with the maximum wage rate set at $1.80 per hour. This
pay scale, averaging between $53-$60 a week after taxes, came nowhere near to
supporting the men's families. Forty per cent of the sanitation workers
qualified for and were drawing welfare checks in addition to their sanitation
pay to support their families before the strike. Many more workers were on the
food stamp program as well.

Long Organizing Effort

Memphis is one of the many big Southern cities that the freedom movement never really organized. But there is no question that the battles of Mississippi, Alabama, and Georgia and the early Memphis sit-ins had a major impact on the city's black workers. Their response to this tide was to move and try to organize against what was oppressing them the most, which began in 1963 for the sanitation workers when they threatened a strike. Another strike was planned in 1966. But on both occasions the city administration immediately got an injunction against the threatened strike, fired the most militant workers, and promised to fire any man who dared to walk out on strike. These tactics of the city stopped the walkout those years, but nothing changed for the workers, and in 1968 they were ready to fight.

One reason for this lies with a man named T. O. Jones. He was fired by the city in 1963, after six years on the job, for leading the workers to strike. Later that year he was hired by the American Federation of State, County, and Municipal Employees (AFSCME) to continue organizing among his former co-workers.

The Opening Guns

On the first day of the strike, T. O. Jones appeared with a committee of sanitation workers at the office of the city's director of public works demanding a pay increase and action on many of the job conditions the men were fed up with. When the public works director refused to commit himself to improving the conditions or raising wages, and insisted that the strike was illegal under the 1966 injunction, T. O. Jones pulled out a brown paper bag, took off his dress clothes in the director's office, and put on what he called his "jail clothes." He then told the director that they could throw him in jail if they wanted to, but that the strike was definitely on.

The next night, the city's mayor, Henry Loeb, addressed a union meeting of over 800 striking workers. He told them that this was not New York City and that "nothing will be gained by violating our laws." He also said that the walkout was posing a grave "health menace to the city" -- the men laughed at him. He sternly told the men to go back to work and then there would be negotiations -- the men laughed at him again. . . .

The Movement (June, 1968).

29. MEMPHIS: KING'S BIGGEST GAMBLE

March Was Out of Hand Before It Even Started

By Robert M. Ratcliffe

MEMPHIS, Tenn. -- Martin Luther King took the big gamble here last Thursday, and lost: his prestige went on a nosedive and his image was dented and cracked.

Dr. King put his international fame on the line when he dared lead 10,000 or more on a march that was already out of hand before it started.

First sign of trouble popped up when Memphis' handful of "black power" youngsters and "the invaders" rushed to the front of the march ahead of Dr. King. They refused to move back and shouted: "King is not our leader, we want Carmichael."

Anticipating serious trouble, the Rev. James M. Lawson, Jr. of Memphis, advised King to get into a car and move out of sight until the "black power" group could be brought under control. It was learned that Rev. M. Lawson would have called off the march if given the necessary encouragement.

King's aides reportedly recommended that he go on with the march through downtown Memphis, and off they marched.

What happened a few minutes later made international headlines.

The widely ballyhooed march, composed of thousands of junior and senior high school students who had cut classes and hundreds of adults who took a day

off from work, was to have been a peaceful one in behalf of 1,300 negro sanitation workers on strike nearly two months.

The mass of humanity, taking up all street and sidewalk space, moved off
around 11 a.m. from in front of historic Clayborn Temple AME Church, up Hernando
to famed Beale St. and then west on Beale to Main St.

Smashing of store windows and looting began on Beale just as march leaders
turned into Main St., and there was more window-smashing and looting for one
block on Main St.

It was at this point that Dr. King and local march leaders agreed that the
thing was out of hand. The more than 600 policemen on duty were called into
action. Tear gas was squirted into faces of fleeing marchers, many of the
looters, and those who couldn't run fast enough, were beaten with police sticks.

Meanwhile, King was hustled down a side street where he and his lieutenants
bummed a ride back to his suite in the fabulous Holiday Inn-Rivermont.

King and the local march leaders denied that they deserted. Beale St.,
the street famous with his blues, was in a shambles, broken glass, sticks,
placards, stolen items and blood littered the pavement and sidewalks.

The innocent as well as the guilty were clubbed by policemen. Clayborn
Temple, where it all started, became a rallying point for "black power" and the
AME church administration building next door to the church became a temporary
hospital.

Police soon cleared out the entire area and sealed it off. But window-
breaking and looting continued throughout the city. A 16-year-old schoolboy,
Larry Payne, was killed a mile away from Beale St. He was accused of looting
a Sears branch store. Policemen said the boy had a knife in his hand and that
the killing was in self-defense. Witnesses said the boy had no knife. That
both of his hands were in the air when the officer shot him.

Mayor Henry Loeb set up a curfew Thursday night, 7 p.m. to 5 a.m., and
this continued throughout the weekend. State troopers and 4,000 members of the
National Guard rolled into town to help keep order. Whiskey stores were closed
and no beer was sold.

Pittsburgh New Courier, April 6, 1968.

30. ECONOMIC BOYCOTT IN MEMPHIS TO CONTINUE

MEMPHIS -- The Memphis sanitation strike of some 1300 Negro workers which
took the life of Dr. Martin Luther King, Jr. was settled last week but the Rev.
James Lawson, one of the leaders of the economic boycott which has cut white-
owned business profits 80 per cent said the "Poor Peoples Campaign" here "is
just starting."

"We've just begun," he added. "We want to get to the point where every
poor person in this Shelby County of ours will be able to walk on their own two
feet. The battle is not over. We've got a fight on our hands."

Along this line, the Memphis City Council was to meet this week with Negro
leaders and discuss remaining civil rights issues, including police brutality.

Thus the Southern Christian Leadership Conference, now headed by the Rev.
Ralph Abernathy, moved to concentrate more time on its national "Poor Peoples
Marches," of which the Memphis campaign is but one part.

That the agreement for an across-the-board wage hike of 15 cents per hour
bringing the wages of most of the men up from $1.50 to $1.75 and those of
drivers and supervision leaders to $2.20 per hour was a victory, it was agreed.

The City Council voted 12-1 to accept the agreement, including its features
of union recognition and dues check-off. The garbage workers okayed the settlement by giving a unanimous vote at their meeting.

Moreover, J. O. Patterson, one of three Negroes on the Memphis City Council
pointed out that the final agreement which settled the strike was practically
the same one that had been voted by City Council even before the strike.

Councilman Patterson said: "Seven weeks ago, we agreed to the main issues
almost identical to those before us today and then a majority of the Council
changed its mind, . . . refused to take any action on this matter and a lot of

hell broke out across this city and across the nation. We could have avoided
all this including the death of Dr. King."
    The resistance against recognition of the union and a settlement had been
placed by most Negroes at the door of Mayor Henry Loeb, long-time leader of
white hard-line resistance in the city to civil rights legislation.
    Some Negroes would stereotype Mayor Loeb as the man who vetoed the appoint-
ment of a Negro to the Metropolitan Transit Authority during Mayor Loeb's first
term from 1960 to 1963. They also point out that he was against the chosen
Negro because he had taken part in civil rights desegregation cases.
    Mayor Loeb in last year's primary also defeated a wealthy Negro, A. W.
Willis, in a city which is more than 40 per cent Negro in its population.
    For this reason much of the economic boycott's fire was directed against
the chain of laundries, restaurants and other stores owned by the Loeb family,
although Mayor Loeb was said to have sold his interests several years ago.
    Typical of the new issues of race and economic uplift in which Memphis
Negroes are now interested is the suit filed in the name of Colie Jennings, a
car man helper, against the Illinois Central Railroad, in behalf of all Negroes
in Tennessee employed by the railroad.
    This suit in Federal Court charges that the railroad discriminates against
Negro employees and others in the areas of promotions, restrooms, locker facilities and time clocks.

Pittsburgh New Courier, April 27, 1968.

31. THE STRUGGLE IN MEMPHIS

By Bayard Rustin

    One of the great exhibitions of Negro unity, political courage and economic
power is now taking place in Memphis, Tennessee. It is a struggle that should
inspire every black person in the United States and one that all of us should
support, because it is at once a struggle for dignity, for bread and butter,
and for the right of Negro institutions in our society to organize and be
recognized.
    I was there two weeks ago, and found it a memorable and moving experience.
Along with Roy Wilkins of the NAACP and several other national civil rights
and labor leaders, I addressed a rally of more than 9,000 Negro citizens, one
of the largest indoor meetings I have ever spoken before.
    All the memories of the great protest movement floated back; I was reminded
of Montgomery, Birmingham, and Selma, scenes of some of the most creative moments
of the civil rights crusade of the early 1960s. The Memphis AME Temple resounded
with the familiar strains of We Shall Overcome. Young people and college students of all social and economic levels filled the balconies. The leadership
of the great civil rights coalition of the early 60s were present: civil rights
groups, liberals, labor unions, students, and clergymen.
    What was it that stirred black Memphis into such unified action? It all
started on February 12, when 1300 garbage collectors and sanitation workers --
almost all of them Negroes -- went out on strike, and when the Mayor of Memphis
refused to recognize either their demands or their union. In fact, the Mayor
has refused to recognize the Union -- Local 1733 of the American Federation of
State, County and Municipal Employees -- for the entire 2½ years since it was
chartered. In the meantime, he has recognized and bargained with all other
unions with a majority of white workers.

Distort Demands

    Though the white-owned newspapers have distorted the Negro sanitation men's
demands and have inflamed white opinion against them, these demands are fair
and simple. They are: 1) Recognition of Local 1733 as bargaining representative of the Negro sanitation men. 2) Establishment of meaningful grievance
procedures. 3) Payroll deduction of union dues. 4) Fair provisions for promotions. 5) Health, hospital and life insurance. 6) A uniform pension program.

7) Sick leave, vacation, and overtime pay. 8) Meaningful negotiations to
improve the extremely low wages of laborers and drivers.

Not only do these demands seem fair, they represent the minimum rights and
privileges enjoyed by millions of other unionized white sanitation workers
across the nation. Yet the response of Mayor Henry Loeb has been nothing short
of repressive and racist. He has refused to recognize the existence of the
Union. He has turned a deaf ear to the demands of the workers. And he has
stood by while union leaders were arrested and thrown in jail, and while the
police attacked Negro strikers with billy clubs and mace.

In the face of such brutal resistance the will of many other groups would
have been quickly broken; but in one of the inspiring shows of unity and
courage, the whole Negro community of Memphis has rallied behind the embattled
strikers. Daily rallies and marches are held. Food and money are donated to
help the workers take care of their families. And a boycott of downtown
merchants and newspapers has resulted in a 40 percent decline in business

Real Power

This is an illustration of the real power of black people, and an indication that one of the most effective ways of affirming their dignity and
identity is by unifying behind and struggling in behalf of the issues that
affect them. But the strikers will require more massive assistance if their
struggle is to continue, for at the moment they receive no more than $20 a
week to pay their rents and take care of their families. I therefore urgently
appeal to anyone who reads this column to send financial contributions now to
COME (Committee On The Move for Equality), care of Clayborn Temple, 280 Herndon,
Memphis, Tennessee.

There is no doubt that this is one of the key political struggles of 1968,
one in which the entire Negro population in the South has a stake. As the Rev.
James Lawson of SCLC has said, "This is a significant turn in the civil rights
movement and for a new chapter in labor history. Never before has a union
been backed by a whole community." Therefore, as the Montgomery bus boycott
was the beginning of a ten-year campaign across the South in demand of the
franchise and public accommodations, so the Memphis struggle may be the real
beginning of the campaign for Negro economic democracy in the South and other
large cities in the nation.

New York Amsterdam News, April 6, 1968.

32.
IN MEMPHIS: MORE THAN A
GARBAGE STRIKE

By J. Edwin Stanfield

This report is written and published as the strike and accompanying Negro
protest -- the old civil rights movement still alive -- in Memphis continues.
Perhaps by the time this report reaches the reader, the strike and turmoil
will have been settled. This is to be wished -- but only if the settlement is
honorable, if it reaches honestly to the issues, from the surface economic ones
to the deep-lying ones of human dignity. Otherwise -- as in the past in
Memphis and all too many other southern and American locales -- the time of
danger and of disaster will have only been postponed, with an ever-increasing
store of anger and loss of faith. There is the real possibility, too, that
the situation in Memphis may have deteriorated into violence and repression.
If so, this report can only contribute to the record, so badly misread and
misunderstood in America, of how such tragedy comes about, and of how it might
be averted. In simplest terms, avoiding such tragedy was in Memphis and
across America merely a matter of government and society living up to their
responsibilities to all citizens.

There have been at work through the time of tension in Memphis forces and
influences for positive and intelligent action meeting the highest obligations

of society and government. Such forces and influences come from both races of
men in Memphis. It remains a problem in all of American life how such positive
people and institutions might be supported and encouraged. It is toward that
end, primarily, that this report is submitted.

The Strike

On Monday, February 12, 1,375 men (mostly sanitation workers but also other
employees of Memphis' Department of Public Works) went out on strike.

The walk out originated over a sewer workers' grievance. Twenty-two
employees of that department who reported for work on January 31 were sent home
when it began raining. White employees were not sent home and, when the rain
stopped after an hour or so, were put to work and paid for the full day. The
Negro workers complained. The city then paid them two hours' "call up pay."
When they saw their pay envelopes at the end of the week, they called a meeting
of Memphis Local 1733 of the American Federation of State, County, and Municipal
Employees (AFL-CIO). Local 1733 is all Negro. The local had no official
status, a result of the city of Memphis' policy of not recognizing a particular
union as bargaining agent for municipal employees. The question of recognition
of the union was to become a central issue in the strike.

Mayor Henry Loeb, who was elected in October, 1967, took the position
that the strike was illegal and that the strikers had to return to work before
their grievances could be discussed. He declared that he would never sign a
contract, that the city could not recognize a particular union as bargaining
agent for municipal employees, and that he would not agree to a dues check-off.
The union insisted that federal precedent supported its demand for recognition.
Indications were that the mayor would not be adamant on any of the other points.

Coming even as it did in the shadow of the devastating, nine-day strike in
New York City, the Memphis strike received little notice outside the state. It
did not create a "newsworthy" crisis as the New York strike did. The reason is
simple: Memphis has a population of just over 500,000. Using non-union workers
and supervisors, the city managed to keep picking up garbage and trash downtown
from vital institutions, such as hospitals. They also kept enough scab crews
operating to pick up in designated residential sections each day. The daily
papers printed maps showing which neighborhoods would get service on that day,
and the location of city dumps so that citizens could dispose of their own
accumulations, if they wished. The garbage problem was kept below crisis proportions.

Mayor Loeb, a tall, big-boned, darkly handsome man, spoke of plans he
still had in reserve, such as one to place garbage trucks at shopping centers
to which citizens could bring their garbage. When 317 men reported for work
on the seventeenth day of the strike (108 non-strikers, 62 strikers who
returned, and 147 new men) the mayor was delighted and spoke of the possibility
of tapering off on hiring as soon as the force "gets high enough to provide
once-a-week pickups."

The strike was merely a symptom of Memphis' larger problem.

More than 200,000 of the city's citizens are Negroes -- about 40 per cent
of the population. The 80,000 Negro voters were almost solidly against Loeb
when he was elected last October; but Negroes failed to vote in a bloc for any
other candidate, including A. W. Willis, Negro representative to the Tennessee
House. Mayor Loeb's handling of the sanitation strike, with concurrence of the
City Council, apparently triggered the release in the Negro community of built-
up resentment over low wages generally and under-employment of Negroes in local
government. Their resentment was heightened by disappointment, for there had
been hope that the new mayor-council form of city government (changed from
commission form in January) and a new police commissioner would mean a change
for the better.

On February 16, the local chapter of the NAACP threatened massive demonstrations unless the city met the demands of the strikers. A group of Negro
ministers, with the Reverend James Lawson as chairman, became interested in
the strike, since many of the workers were members of their congregations.
They began by sponsoring a series of meetings between city and union officials.

On Monday, February 19, while the second of this series of meetings was
in progress, representatives of the NAACP and some of the strikers picketed in
front of city hall. Little progress was made in the negotiations. The demonstrators continued their vigil through the night and left at dawn without
incident.

The "Sit-In"

The City Council's Committee on Public Works scheduled a public hearing for Thursday at 10 a.m. Some 100 people, including union officers, ministers, and sympathizers were present when the hearing began. Fred Davis, committee chairman, hinted that the union representatives might not be speaking from the viewpoint of the strikers. "We are going to pay particular attention to what the men themselves have to say on the issues," he declared. "We are concerned that the men as individuals have not been able to bring out their views."

With that, union officials called the Rubber Workers' Hall, where the daily rally of strikers was to begin at noon. In a short time, roughly dressed sanitation workers began to drift into the City Council's chamber. Soon the room, which has a seating capacity of 407, including chairs for councilmen, clerks and reporters, was crowded with about 700 people, mostly sanitation workers.

Chairman Davis insisted that the rank and file were being misrepresented. Officers of the union local insisted that they were the proper spokesmen, not some unlettered member chosen at random. Mr. Davis declared that due to over-crowding of the chamber contrary to fire laws, the committee would recess.

The workers and their leaders and friends said that they would remain in the hearing room until they got satisfaction. Speaker after speaker exhorted the workers and voiced grievances of the strikers in particular and of Memphis Negroes in general. There was singing of spirituals, patriotic songs and the anthems of the civil rights movement. "The plush, red-carpeted council chamber," reported the Memphis *Commercial Appeal,* "was jammed with strikers who vaulted across the railing onto the dias reserved for city officials."

Since no one had eaten lunch, union leaders sent for bread, bologna, cheese, luncheon meat, ham, and mustard. The city attorney's table was appropriated for making sandwiches. "The usually immaculate carpet for the chamber," the *Commercial Appeal* complained, "soon became spotted with bread crumbs and tiny pieces of paper despite the small trash cans placed in each aisle for refuse."

Meanwhile, Inspector Sam Evans of the Memphis Police Department had 142 officers converge on city hall. They remained parked within a block, five to a car, with car motors running.

The committee eventually capitulated. It reopened the hearing and finally, about 5:30, agreed to recommend that the city recognize the union and agree to "some form of dues check-off." A newsman asked Councilman Davis what the mayor replied when told of the committee's recommendation. "He maintained a polite silence," said Mr. Davis. The recommendation was to be presented to the City Council in a special meeting at 2:30 p.m. the next day.

A cartoon published in the *Commercial Appeal* on Friday, February 23, after the sit-in at city hall on Thursday, silhouetted a fat Negro sitting atop a garbage can surrounded by a pile of rubbish and overturned receptacles. The garbage can was labeled, "City Hall Sit-In." Wavy lines indicated an odor rising from the garbage from the garbage heap and the black man. Above his head these fume-lines formed the legend, "Threat of Anarchy." The cartoon was titled, "Beyond the Bounds of Tolerance."

"Memphis garbage strikers have turned an illegal walk out into anarchy," said an accompanying editorial, "and Mayor Henry Loeb is exactly right when he says, 'We can't submit to this sort of thing!' . . . When the Council deals with the problem today it should not be intimidated or stampeded into imprudent decisions by yesterday's belligerent show of force." (Ironically, on Wednesday evening, scarcely twenty-four hours before that cartoon and editorial were published, *Commercial Appeal* Editor Frank R. Ahlgren had received a brotherhood award at the annual affair of the local National Conference of Christians and Jews).

The February 23 March

On Friday afternoon, so many people showed up for the Council meeting that it was moved to a municipal auditorium. (The Memphis *Press-Scimitar* estimated one thousand. An observer sympathetic to the strikers estimated two thousand. Estimates of crowds at meetings and marches by the two Memphis dailies were, with notable consistency, about half those of Negro leaders).

In view of what ensued, the Negro ministers and union leaders wondered why they bothered. The meeting was called to order at 2:30 p.m. with the traditional cry of the sergeant-at-arms: "Oyez, this honorable City Council of the City of Memphis is now in session. All persons having business to transact or matters to bring before the City Council draw nigh, give attention, and ye shall be heard." The Public Works Committee's resolution was never heard. Another resolution, obviously prepared and discussed by the councilmen in advance, was substituted and passed by a vote of nine to four. (The four opposed were three Negro councilmen and one white man who thought the recommendations too compromising). The substitute resolution suggested concessions by the mayor on all points, except the vital issues on a contract recognizing a union and a system of union dues check-off. After passage of this resolution, Council Chairman Downing Pryor announced that members would not, at that hearing, hear citizens -- and the Council was adjourned at 2:45.

This had an electric effect on the assembled strikers and their leaders. As on Thursday, union officers and community leaders, including some recognized even by the white press for the "responsibility," got to their feet to express anger and resentment. T. O. Jones, president of Local 1733, was quoted by the *Press-Scimitar* as saying, "We are ready to go to their damned jail." Dr. Vascoe A. Smith, Jr., a Memphis dentist and NAACP leader, was reported in the press to have said, "Don't let them hoodwink you. You are living in a racist town. They don't give a damn about you. . . ."

A march along Main Street was quickly organized after the meeting and an understanding was reached with the police that marchers would stay on the west side of the street.

For several blocks all went smoothly. Then, in the marchers' version, a police cruiser edged over the center line, bumping and nudging the marchers, crowding them closer to the curb. The *Tri-State Defender* reported that the car stopped on a woman's foot and the marchers tried to push it off. Other accounts were that it ran over the woman's foot, and in anger, marchers tried to shove it back over the center line. The white press questioned whether the car even touched the woman's foot. Whatever the case, marchers were under the impression that it had; there was pushing of the police car.

Indeed, in the police version it was claimed that (for unspecified reasons) an attempt was made to overturn the squad car. Officers quoted one marcher as yelling, "Let's turn the patrol car over," and said that men then started rocking the car. At any rate, five policemen jumped from the cruiser and, joined by other officers, began spraying the marchers with Mace, a new tear gas-like chemical causing temporary blindness and severe facial discomfort. They sprayed not only the men in the immediate vicinity of the squad car, but other marchers up and down the block. In the ensuing confusion, they gassed a number of bystanders and even fellow officers.

Jacques Wilmore, staff director of the regional office of the U.S. Civil Rights Commission, whose office is in Memphis, saw the police grab a man in the crowd, pulling him toward the curb. According to Wilmore, "a third policeman came up and just cracked the man across the head. I walked up to them and pulled out my identification. That's when they squirted me two or three times directly in the eyes with Mace." Bobby Doctor, another employee of the Civil Rights Commission, and Baxton Bryant, Executive Director of the Tennessee Council of Human Relations, were with Wilmore at the time and were sprayed in the same sweeps of the gas canister.

Gerald Fanion, director of the Shelby County Community Relations Commission, a Negro, said he was helping a woman out of the ruckus when a policeman walked up to him and squirted him in the face. "I told him who I was and that I was acting as liaison for the county and he squirted me again," said Fanion.

P. J. Ciampa, white field director for the striking union, was sprayed repeatedly. On the following Monday he still had raw, peeling skin under his left eye. He was treated for abrasions and bruises inflicted by the police. "I've never seen such brutality," said Ciampa.

The *Tri-State Defender*, a Negro-owned weekly, published a page of photographs of the fray. One showed a policeman sprinting directly toward a camera, club in hand. The cameraman reported that a few seconds after he snapped the picture, the policeman yelled, "Gimme that camera, nigger," and chased him into the crowd.

The lead editorial in the *Press-Scimitar* on February 24, the day after police broke up the march, lamented that "leaders of the union have shown no respect for Tennessee law. . . ." It continued:

On the other hand, Memphis can take deep pride in the
prompt and efficient way its law enforcement officers handled
the volatile situation. Police were on the job as the strikers
and their leaders boiled out of the meeting and started a march
on Main Street.
    They had guns, but they didn't shoot.
    They had Mace, the new irritant gas which incapacitates
but does not permanently injure -- and they used it. They went
into action as soon as fired-up marchers attacked a police
car . . .
    How much better to do it this way than to be late and soft
as were police in Detroit and other places . . . letting
disturbances grow into full-scale rioting.

The use of Mace and billy clubs by the police resulted in unprecedented
unity among Memphis Negroes. According to residents, Negro ministers who in
other years were often leaders of divisive factions were virtually unanimous
in calling for support of the sanitation workers and the union.
    The ministers cancelled a demonstration scheduled for Saturday and had a
strategy meeting instead. Next day they went into their pulpits and called for
a boycott of (1) all downtown stores; (2) the two daily newspapers; and (3)
every establishment doing business under the name of "Loeb." (Mayor Henry
Loeb's brother, William, owns a chain of barbecue and fried chicken restaurants,
and a laundry chain). They also announced downtown marches in support of the
strikers and the boycott for both Monday morning and Monday afternoon, and a
mass meeting at Clayborn Temple AME Church on Monday night.
    The action of the police greatly strengthened the strikers. It made the
preachers mad, and preachers still have influences among Negroes in the South.
One of them, still furious on Monday night, urged the boycott of all Loeb
businesses in this manner: "Somebody tried to explain to me that William Loeb
who owns the cleaning places is just Henry Loeb's brother. I don't care if it
is his brother or his sister or his mother or his father or his uncle or his
auntie or his cousin -- if it says 'Loeb' on it, you stay out of there! If it
says 'Loeb' on the sign or on the front of the store or on the back of it, on
the side or on the top or on the bottom of it -- you stay out of there!"
    The boycott was effective, and again the actions of the police had helped.
Downtown streets and stores were virtually empty throughout the next week.
Clerks straightened and restraightened stock, arranged and rearranged window
displays. Negroes apparently were supporting the boycott. Speculation was
that white people stayed away from town out of fear of another melee.

Demonstrations

    In spite of Friday's bitter experience, marches were conducted daily
throughout the following week (February 26 - March 2).
    In Monday's march, which was typical of others during the week, most of the
demonstrators were adults and nearly all were Negroes. There were four white
girls from Southwestern at Memphis and a couple of young white men from Memphis
State. Not many Negro youngsters were in the lines. Quite a few were on the
sidewalks, watching and chuckling.
    Some of the signs were neatly stenciled and carried pointed, but judicious
messages: "Dignity and Decency For Our Sanitation Workers," and "Keep Your
Money In Your Pocket," and "Jim Crow Must Go," and "We Are Together Once And
For All."
    Others were crudely lettered and blunt: "Only God Is King, Henry," and
"Watts Also Waited Too Late," and "Watts Also Fired Negroes," and "Sign
Contract Blue-Eye Soul Brother."
    The march moved slowly up Beale Street and turned north on Main. Trying
to keep two car-lengths apart, as instructed, the marchers moved past the pawn
shops on Beale; past dozens of fashionable shops on Main. All but a few of the
stores were empty. So were the streets, except for clerks who had stepped out
to watch and people waiting on corners for buses.
    Asked how the boycott was affecting business, a dime store clerk answered,
"Well, it ain't helping any. People stay away from fear of getting involved."
    An elderly woman carried her sign and faced straight ahead, lips pursed
and eyes darting from side to side. She was dressed simply, but neatly, and

wore a hat. Asked if she were a member of a striker's family, she answered,
"No, I'm just a church member and a friend. It's easier for me to march
because I am alone now, and don't have children to take care of. I could be
home in bed. But I remember. I been there. I've been without work. And
I've been too poor and hungry to go to work when I had it."

On Saturday, March 2, 400 to 500 college and high school students
picketed downtown stores all day. That afternoon there was a joint march by
the young people, the ministers and their followers, and the sanitation men.
The papers estimated 1,000 people in that march; again observers sympathetic
to the strikers guessed twice that many.

Meanwhile, on the day after the use of Mace on marchers, Mayor Loeb and
City Attorney Frank B. Gianotti decided to seek an injunction against the
strike in Chancery Court. Chancellor Robert Hoffman issued an injunction
prohibiting engaging in a strike against the city; picketing city property
and coercing the city by striking, picketing, or other means by recognizing the
union as bargaining agent. Officials explained that it would be difficult to
enforce the injunction so as to require the men to return to work, but 23
persons specifically named could be cited for contempt and jailed for up to
ten days. These included Jerry Wurf, president of the union international;
P. J. Ciampa, the union's field director; T. O. Jones, president of the
local; and other national and local officers.

City Council Meeting - February 27

The City Council agreed to give Jerry Wurf thirty minutes at its regular
meeting on Tuesday, February 27, to present the views of the union and the
purposes of the strike. Even as they sought to do well, however, insensi-
tivity and, perhaps, fear caused the Council to wound the feelings of Negro
citizens.

Mr. Wurf was scheduled to appear at 3:30 p.m. Strikers at the noon
rally were urged to fill the Council chamber. The daily march from Clayborn
Temple was timed to arrive at city hall just before the council session began
at 2:30. Police had ruled that the public seating capacity of 407 would not
be exceeded, stating that fire laws prohibited standing in the aisles. But
strike leaders wanted a show of strength and determination and urged the men
to fill the lobby outside the chamber. Loud-speakers were arranged so that
persons in the lobby could hear the proceedings.

Shortly before 2:30 the doors of the chamber were opened and people
started filing through the two entrances. Four to six policemen were stationed at each, counting the people going in, murmuring, "If you will go in
two by two, we would appreciate it." Neat cardboard signs scotchtaped to
the marble wall beside each door stated, "Council Chamber - Public Seating
Capacity 407."

The first hour of the session was taken up with bone-dry business having
to do with licensing and zoning. Then Council Chairman Downing Pryor observed
that it was time for Mr. Wurf's presentation and he had received word Wurf
was delayed, so there would be a recess until he arrived.

Pryor did not tell the crowd that Wurf, along with other union officials,
had been cited for contempt and summoned to Chancery Court. The summons had
come, Wurf said later, just as he arrived at city hall for the Council
meeting. Aware that he was to appear in court at precisely 3:30, he had
asked Councilman Pryor if it would be possible for him to make his presentation
earlier in the meeting. Pryor told him the agenda of the Council was fixed by
law, but assured him that the Council would recess and stay in session until
he completed his business at Chancery Court -- unless, of course, he was sent
to jail for ten days. (At the mass meeting that night, telling the crowd the
Council should be credited with decency about this matter, Wurf said when two
members of the Council made him that promise, the attorney for the city told
them *they* might be in contempt of court).

When the recess of the council meeting was announced, people began milling
around. After an hour of growing restlessness, Baxton Bryant, with others,
persuaded Chairman Pryor that it would relieve tension if some of the ministers
were allowed to speak while the audience was waiting for Wurf. Pryor called
the meeting back to order and nervously laid down the rules. Each speaker
would be limited to five minutes, a standing rule, he said, and not new for
the occasion. If Wurf arrived, the person then speaking would be allowed to

finish, then Wurf would speak. If he had not arrived after thirty minutes,
the council would recess again and wait for him.

With only five minutes apiece, the preachers wasted no time on amenities.
The clerks sat round-eyed, spellbound, giving the impression that they had
never heard anyone address the Memphis City Council in such tones before --
certainly not Negroes.

The Reverend S. B. Kyles said that all the policemen at the door and the
five or six "emergency cars" outside made him think he was in Russia. He
resented the thirty-minute time limit -- "I'll tell you, we have all night!"
He rebuked spokesmen for the ministers for agreeing to speak to the Council
on the Council's terms: "We aim to talk to you on *our* terms."

"If you don't settle it here," he told them, "it is going to be settled,
anyway. You may have to settle it down where we are."

The Reverend James Lawson, chairman for the group of ministers, said he
was so flustered and angry that he hardly knew how to begin to express
himself. Negroes, he said, are still the victims of two "sticks": (1) the
police -- "those symbols of repression" guarding the door and (2) rigid
structure. "If you dont' beat us over the head with a night stick, you hit
us over the head with an agenda!"

"Some of us want to settle this in this council," he told them, "but if
we can't, we may just go back to our studies, perhaps just go fishing, and
let whatever happens happen! Just forget it! This is not a threat, because
Memphis is a part of this country, and this country is in turmoil, whether we
like it or not!"

It was during Lawson's speech that Wurf arrived. During the preachers'
speeches, the police had moved along the sides of the chamber and stood there,
watching. One had a two-way radio, another a bullhorn.

"I planned to come here to make a humble statement," Wurf began.
"Posturing does more harm than good. In the interim some of us have been
arrested . . . and now it is a temptation to try to prove one's manhood. But
I am going to forego that and simply state our goals."

He reviewed the objectives of the strike and negotiations with Mayor Loeb.
"The mayor has made much of the fact that he will not sign a contract," Wurf
told them. "It has become a posture which is more important to him than the
substance of the issue." He concluded with the suggestion that the Council
should not abandon its responsibility entirely to the city's chief executive.
The meeting was adjourned.

Legal Actions

At the request of counsel for the defendants, the hearing on the contempt
citation had been postponed until Friday morning, March 1. On Thursday, union
attorneys filed a petition to have the matter shifted to federal district
court, arguing that the injunction violated the First and Fourteenth Amendments,
the rights of free speech and due process of law. On Friday morning, Chancellor
Robert Hoffman refused to relinquish jurisdiction voluntarily, but did grant
a continuance until Tuesday, March 5. On Friday afternoon, the federal court
refused to take jurisdiction. Subsequently, the leaders were given sentences
of 10 days in jail and $50 fine in state court. They were freed pending
appeal.

Legislative Action

In the state capitol at Nashville, meanwhile, Senators Joe Pipkin and
Hugh Stanton of Memphis had introduced three bills aimed at the strike. The
bills were rushed through the Senate committee system and scheduled for a vote
in only three legislative days.

One bill, passed by 21-10, provided a five-year prison sentence for persons disrupting public communication with police and fire departments. (There
had been some talk in Memphis of tying up police and fire department telephone
lines).

The other two bills would have outlawed strikes against police, fire, and
sanitation departments and prohibited union dues check-offs from government
paychecks. Little opposition had been expressed to them, perhaps because of
the speed with which they were sent through the legislative machinery. Then,
on the night of the 26th, according to the Nashville *Tennessean,* "Organized

labor . . . descended on the legislative halls . . . and appealed to each
senator." Matt Lynch, president of the State Labor Council, said "all
elements of organized labor" opposed the two measures. The bills were defeated, in effect, by referring them to a committee.

Thus, in the first two weeks, a pattern was set which was not in signif-
icent degree to change through subsequent meetings of the City Council, protest confrontations of strikers and their sympathizers with police, and
negotiating sessions with city officials. In effect, the Negro community,
unified as probably never before around the issue of the garbage strike, met
and became increasingly aware of stubborn resistance from the city's top
official, and less stubborn but vacillating and ineffective response from
the City Council, this accompanied by abrasive encounters with police and
harsh criticism from the press. A measure of support unprecedented in the
South had come from white union members who marched some 500 strong with the
strikers on March 4. But beyond that, the other elements of white power,
including clergy and businesses, the latter hard-hit by the boycott, had not
effectively entered the crisis on either side, a not unusual situation in the
South. With each passing day of inability of the city (and beyond it, the
state and the nation) to deal realistically with the simple terms of the
strike and the larger issues of Negro rightful demands, tension in Memphis
mounted.

By March 7, such whites as Baxton Bryant, who had played a valuable role
as a trusted intermediary between the Negro community and the city, began to
doubt the utility of their function. It seemed to them that the city officials
retained the imperturbable, immemorial southern charm and willingness to
discuss the problem, but that in fact they were not yielding an inch. Perhaps
he should cease walking through open doors which led only to closed minds,
Bryant suggested to the Reverend Starks, president of the black Interdomina-
tional Ministers Alliance, over breakfast that morning. "Oh, no," responded
Starks. "Somebody's got to talk to them; some channels have got to stay open.
And we can't do it. We've got nothing to say to them any more."

But a man as positively disposed toward life as Reverend Starks has
difficulty in persuading himself of his own counsel of despair. He decided
to join Bryant and a reporter in interviews with the mayor and Downing Pryor.
In both interviews, Bryant tried to convey his sense of the dangerously
escalating hostility between the solidified Negro community and the city
officialdom. He cited the report of the National Advisory Commission on
Civil Disorders. Memphis was becoming a perfect example of two alienated,
antagonistic communities tensely confronting one another, he said. The mayor
responded with great personal warmth, repeated his unalterable opposition to
dues check-off, now the crux of the conflict. In the large, beautifully
appointed, softly shaded office, the anguish expressed by Bryant and reflected
in the tense faces of Starks, seemed incapable of passing to the other side
of the executive desk.

But if the mayor was unmoved, he was not inactive. He wanted so much to
"keep talking" to the Negro leadership and he was so happy Starks had come.
Could he not return later; the mayor would be happy to clear his calendar.
Was it not the utmost importance "that we keep talking to each other?" The
group was rising to leave, but it looked as if Starks were rising alone. He
drew himself up to his full height and said, "No, mayor. I cannot come to
see you. Our community has taken a position and I stand with them. You have
to talk to all of us." There was no sign that the mayor had heard the death
knell of plantation politics for the duration of this crisis.

Downing Pryor tried to express his personal concern, and the helplessness
of the Council. Any action by the City Council would require six weeks to
hurdle a mayoral veto -- surely that was too late? But Starks did not let
him off so easy. A pro-union resolution by the Council would not only hearten
the Negro community, but show them that there was now an independent agency
at city hall, capable of redressing their grievances. Pryor evaded this
challenge, describing instead the bold new fair employment resolution promul-
gated by the Council: Increased hiring of Negroes until their number in city
jobs equals their percentage in the population, accompanied by the necessary
placement and training services. It sounded like a serious piece of legislation and there was little doubt that it had been hastened, if not inspired,
by the mobilization of the black community behind the sanitation workers.

The Issues

The objectives of the strike were outlined by Jerry Wurf, president of the AFSCME (AFL-CIO) as follows:

(1) Union recognition and a contract with the city.
(2) Effective grievance procedures ("So if it rains they don't send a man home like a dog without wages -- or worse, send you home and give the white man "wages.")
(3) Union payroll deduction, or dues check-off.
(4) Merit promotion -- without regard to race.
(5) Equal treatment in the retirement system.
(6) Payment for overtime.
(7) Decent wages.

Something like accord was reached early in the strike on all of the strikers' demands except union recognition and dues check-off. At the start of the strike, wages averaged about $1.70 per hour, and the strikers were demanding $2.35. The mayor and councilmen made an offer of a five per cent raise immediately, with another five per cent scheduled for the next fiscal year, and the sanitation men seemed willing to accept this. The other points apparently did not present insurmountable problems, either. As previously noted, Mayor Loeb said publicly that he would never sign a contract and could not agree to a dues check-off. The union tried to give him a face-saving way out by suggesting an exchange of letters between him and the president of the union in lieu of a contract, and collection of dues through the independent employees' credit union. It was reliably reported that the mayor was considering such a letter, but when a news report labelled the projected letter a "compromise," the mayor was incensed and resumed his stance.

After the Negro community, led by the preachers, got into the fight other issues were defined. Dr. Ralph Jackson, director of the Department of Minimum Salary of the African Methodist Episcopal Church, was principal speaker at the mass meeting on Monday night, February 26. "We're going to march until the sanitation workers say 'Satisfied'!" he told the crowd, and the crowd shouted its affirmation. "But I have news for you: We're going to march *after that!*" And again the crowd let it be known that he was speaking for them. He listed the following issues:

(1) Police treatment.
(2) Housing. ("The housing authority has announced plans for 12,000 units -- 8,000 for whites and 4,000 for Negroes. Well, they'll never get off with it!")
(3) Jobs. ("And the days of the *one* Negro are over. You know what I mean, -- one here, one there, and one over yonder -- and look what we've done for you!")
(4) Wage scales.
(5) Justice in the schools.

The Police

"Almost invariably," says the Report of the National Advisory Commission on Civil Disorders, "the incident that ignites disorders arises from police action. Harlem, Watts, Newark, and Detroit -- all the major outbursts of recent years -- were precipitated by routine arrests of Negroes for minor offenses by white police. But the police are not merely the spark. In discharge of their obligation to maintain order and insure public safety in the disruptive conditions of ghetto life, they are inevitably involved in sharper and more frequent conflicts with ghetto residents than with the residents of other areas. Thus, to many Negroes police have come to symbolize white power, white racism, and white oppression. And the fact is that many police do reflect and express these white attitudes. The atmosphere of hostility and cynicism is reinforced by a widespread perception among Negroes of the existence of police brutality and corruption, and of a 'double standard' of justice and protection -- one for Negroes and one for whites."

Obviously, the police spark was present in Memphis. The injudicious use of Mace seemed the worst excess of the first month. It was far short of the injudicious use of rifle fire by state police against rampaging students at Orangeburg, South Carolina, at about that same time, but something less than

even-handed and cool-headed protection of all citizens, including those exercising constitutional rights of protest.

At the mass meeting on Tuesday night, February 27, after the Reverend
Mr. Kyles' impassioned speech before the City Council, the Reverend Malcolm
Blackburn thanked Mr. Kyles for "calling attention to our blindness."

"We have been blind to conditions of life in America," he told the crowd,
"for none of us noticed or questioned how we were surrounded by police in the
Council chamber this afternoon, and counted like cattle as we entered our
chamber. . . .! If none of us can stand in the aisles or around the walls
because of the fire laws, then next time we ought to see to it that the police
do not, either, because we don't need them!"

Then, pointing into the ranks of upturned faces, all black, he added,
"We don't need them watching us in this mass meeting, either!"

"And we don't need two or three policemen on every other corner during
our marches," he went on, "or helicopters circling overhead, when we have
shown that we can march peacefully and with dignity without some damned
cop . . .!" His arm shot out for emphasis and the end of his sentence was
lost in applause.

Bishop J. O. Patterson attempted to deal gently with the Negro policemen
who apparently had been singled out, but in so doing he made the point again.
"I feel sorry for our Negro policemen," he said. "Most of them are nice
fellows. But now they have been assigned a task that is contrary to the Bible.
The Bible says that the law is for sinners, not the righteous."

The police were always very much in evidence before and during the
marches downtown or when workers and sympathizers attended meetings at city
hall. They talked back and forth on walkie-talkies. They cruised in police
cars with shotgun muzzles visible above the dashboards.

Little wonder the crowds were sparse for the marches. Rumor had it that
the mayor was greatly pleased at the report that only 120 people showed up for
one of the marches, and concluded that the strike would play out. But at the
union hall, when no police were in evidence, the meeting places were packed
and jammed.

One other police incident during the first month was noteworthy. On
Thursday night, March 1, three policemen -- two patrolmen and a lieutenant --
arrested two Negroes outside the church where a mass meeting was being held.
They charged them with jaywalking. One of those charged was Gerald Fanion,
and the other was Edward Harris, photographer of the Tri-State Defender.

Police commissioner Frank Holloman personally appeared in city court the
next day and asked that the charges be dropped. "We have been trying to keep
the peace in our community," he explained, "and if a mistake is made the best
thing to do is to admit it and try to correct it."

Judge Ray Churchill granted the motion and commented, "I think this is
a wonderful step forward. In all my experience I believe this is the first
time anything like this has happened."

Police Chief J. C. MacDonald announced that the three officers had been
suspended and said they had made an "error in judgment."

"I never have, and I never will tolerate harassment of citizens by
police," he said.

The past record of the Memphis Police Department in this crucial area of
relations with Negro citizens has not been a notably bad one, as these things
go in the South and the nation. In a special report of the Southern Regional
Council on Memphis as among southern cities which had made most progress by
1964, Benjamin Muse wrote: "In few cities have the police been so largely
and favorably identified with the civil rights advance. Public order has been
maintained in Memphis -- tranquility in which negotiations could quietly
proceed and insurance against disorder which enabled desegregation steps to be
confidently taken. With small exceptions, police brutality, which is incompatible with any durable public order, has been absent, but the police 'mean
business,' and the public knows it." But, perhaps ominously for the crisis
that was to come in 1968, the report pointed out that in the sit-ins of 1961,
police were deployed in numbers that some considered excessive, arrests were
made in great quantities with very many of the cases subsequently dismissed,
and complaints of rough handling of demonstrators were numerous. All of this
was under a former police commissioner, but it is indicative of the kind of
police relations with Negro citizens that underlay the outburst of feeling

against police in 1968. In that same 1964 report, incidentally, the Memphis
press was praised for its role in fostering successful desegregation, but
once more an ominous note was sounded: " . . . Those demonstrations [of
1960-61] were larger and more disruptive than many realized -- owing to the
policy of the Memphis press of minimizing the publicity."

Incredibly, albeit incidentally, it was reported on February 27 that
3,000 Tennessee National Guardsmen were to bivouac in Memphis on March 9 for
one day of riot control practice. Other drills were to be staged simultaneously in Nashville and Knoxville. The practice was planned to acquaint
Guardsmen with the topography of the city and identify potential trouble
spots. Details were not revealed. The Guardsmen would be outfitted, the
report said, in full field gear, including weapons.

The drill took place on schedule, but without incident. The Guard
avoided "areas of existing tension."

Dignity As An Issue

Negro citizens' complaints against police and the newspapers were only
a part of the problem in Memphis. The attitude of public officials was the
common demoninator of the preachers and the garbage collectors in their
struggle. If one were required to say in a word what the strike and the
marches and the mass meetings in Memphis were all about, that word would have
to be *dignity*. One can read in the narrative of events of those days in
Memphis a chronicle of indignities suffered by Negroes at the hands of the
Public Works Department, of the City Council, and of the mayor. Early in the
strike, the people began calling him "King Henry."

Dr. Ralph Jackson was by his own admission a conservative minister. But
he happened to be marching in support of the strikers when the police broke
up that march and his ministerial standing meant nothing: he was gassed with
all the others. Preaching at one of the mass meetings, he let it be known
that the Mace had opened his eyes:

I have a confession to make. For thirty years I have been
training to hold myself in check. I couldn't understand what
made some people lose control of themselves and fly off the
handle. I never thought it would happen to me. But I lost
thirty years of training in just five minutes last Friday!

A union official said, concerning negotiations for a settlement of the
strike, "I don't think Mayor Loeb has any objection to seeing the men get
more money. But he wants them to continue in dependency. It's a strange
social system he is trying to preserve."

Jesse Epps, another official of the union who is a young man, looked out
over the rally of more than a thousand black men at the Rubber Workers' Hall.
Most of them were in their upper thirties or older. "We have to win this
one," he told them. "This is the last chance for many of us to be men." The
willingness of the men to hold out so long when they could have settled for
better wages, grievance procedures, and everything else except the dignity of
collective bargaining with the mayor, suggests that they agreed with Mr. Epps.

Jesse Epps is the AFSCME's staff man in charge of the southern region.
Highly capable, he is a union organizer who recites poetry ("Heaven is not
reached at a single bound . . .") and quotes the Bible accurately. In one of
those quiet, two-men-in-a-room conversations that do not lend themselves to
posturing, he said matter-of-factly and with a far-away look, "I don't think
I've ever been so hurt as I was when the City Council walked out last Friday
afternoon without hearing the people." This was Jesse Epps the man, the
black man, talking -- not Jesse Epps the union organizer. "The basic issue,"
he continued, "is not pay, but recognition of the union. There has never been
the unity in the Negro community of Memphis that there is now, and the reason
is that recognition of the union involves recognition of the workers as *men*.
The mayor wants to say, 'Go on back to work and then we'll do right about your
complaints; you know our word is good as our bond.' Just as if Memphis were
a Delta plantation."

A Coalition?

There is much talk these days about coalitions, and particularly a
coalition of the labor movement and the civil rights movement. What happened

at Memphis seems, at first glance, anyway, to be an example of the kind of coalition that is so much discussed. Union men readily acknowledge that, if it were not for the Negro ministers and the unity of the Negro community behind them, the sanitation workers "wouldn't have the chance of a snowball in hell." On the other hand, the union has provided the sort of know-how (and money) that seems to be necessary these days to come to grips with a not-so-simple issue around which to rally liberal and minority-group forces. AFSCME officials did this without preempting -- and, in fact, encouraging -- local leadership of the strike. "This is a new day for these ministers and these churches," said one observer.

As noted, organized labor forces torpedoed anti-strike legislation in Nashville. That was fine, according to coalition strategists, for, while it was obviously a matter of self-interest, it happened to be supportive of an all-Negro local and the black community of Memphis backing that local.

In Memphis, labor forces were standoffish at first. The rank and file were all for better wages and working conditions for the sanitation men, but did not care for the civil rights overtones. As late as the fifteenth day of the strike, an AFSCME official commented that he had heard from only three white men representing local labor unions. There had been a few relatively small checks for the strike fund, he said, but helpful as that was, he needed some white faces at the union hall rallies to let the sanitation men know that they had labor's support.

The evidence of support came on March 4, at the beginning of the fourth week of the strike. Under leadership of Tom Powell, head of Memphis' AFL-CIO Central Labor Council, and Dan Powell (no kin), Southeastern Regional Director of the AFL-CIO Committee on Political Education, five hundred white labor unionists joined Negro ministers and sanitation workers in the daily downtown march. It was a red-letter day for the strikers.

It remained to be seen whether the AFSCME or other unions will find in the Memphis experience anything like a standard procedure for organizing in the South. Perhaps conditions in Memphis were unique, so that there would be no way of approximating the developments there in other cities. Moreover, the American Federation of State, County, and Municipal Employees is not just a union of sanitation workers. It seeks to include all municipal employees, "from city engineers on down." But as one union official put it, it is hard to get white Southerners to join a black man's union.

Nevertheless, the coalition of civil rights forces with organized labor in Memphis, however brief or singular, was noteworthy. President Wurf had the candor to acknowledge at one mass meeting that some parts of the AFL-CIO have given Negroes less than a fair shake. "But we see this labor struggle as part of the basic struggle of the Negro community for decency and dignity," he said.

A few minutes later he added, "Memphis has been, for me, one of the most moving experiences of my life."

It was unusual, labor observers said, for a national president of a union to put so much of his personal prestige on the line in a situation as unsure of victory and unpredictable in tone as that in Memphis. Mr. Wurf's union does have a large number of Negro members across the nation, and they might be expected to be pleased with his role in Memphis. But beyond that, he seemed genuinely involved in the demand for dignity that transcended the practical and pragmatic aspects of the struggle in Memphis.

Outcome in Doubt

The outcome of the strike remains doubtful. At the end of the fourth week, both city officials and strikers were standing firm, despite pressures building up on both sides.

On Thursday, February 29, Mayor Loeb, in a letter to the strikers, could still only "restate the city's position." The letter offered eight cents an hour pay increase and, in general, met demands of the workers on insurance, retirement plans, a grievance procedure, and hours and overtime. But the mayor still refused union recognition, refused a dues check-off and insisted that "as a precondition to any rearrangement of wages and working conditions, the strike must end." He concluded:

I assure you of fair, dignified treatment. As I have
said many times, there will be no reprisals. In fairness
I should remind you that some of the regular jobs have been
filled and others are being filled daily. Your jobs are of
the utmost importance to you and your family and I am
sincerely interested in your welfare.

Next day strikers assembled in Rubber Workers' Hall rejected by a
thundering, unanimous vote an offer from the City Council that proposed a
raise of ten cents immediately and five more cents in July, but made no
concession on union recognition or dues check-off. The morale of the men
was good.

"But they're getting hungry," admitted one union officer. "On the other
hand, it was warm and sunny today, and the garbage is getting noticeable.
All in all, I'd say the city is in as bad shape as we are."

By that time, as obligations mounted, the strike was costing the union
$2,000 a day, up from about $400 a day at the beginning, to provide the
absolute necessities of the men and their families. Collections at the mass
meetings were running $600 to $800, but $2,000 per day was hard to come by.

Just the logistics of aiding the strikers was a problem. Some of the
men were in debt to more than one loan company; some owed several months'
back rent; some reported demands for immediate payment or payment in advance
of rent. An older worker summed it up: "The man came for the payment on my
burial insurance. I told him that right now I'm just trying to keep alive.
Reckon I can let somebody else worry about it when I die."

Tragedy Waiting in the Wings

In the midst of all the drama in Memphis, the excursions and alarms,
one sensed tragedy waiting in the wings.

For one thing, there was a strong undertone of alienation, even among
the ministers, whose basic attitude toward the society is positive. "This
country has given us a bad check" one of the preachers said. "It bounced.
They had the money. They just didn't put it in the bank."

Dr. Jackson, who seems to have become the semi-official money-raiser for
the strikers, told the audience one night, "I'm going to New York on Monday
to talk to some of these white folks who keep talking about their consciences."
He mentioned the National Council of Churches. "I don't guarantee we will get
the money. But if we don't, this whole nation is going to know that they've
just been *lying* about their consciences!"

That was not the only hint of deepening disillusionment. Another
minister told of receiving a letter from the Memphis Ministerial Alliance
asking him to contribute toward a $1,700 ad titled, "An Appeal to Conscience."

"Well, where are they now?" he shouted. "They would do better to give
the $1,700 to the strikers' fund, make their appeal to conscience from the
pulpits of their own churches, and come to the meeting to show their support."

He was followed by the Reverend John W. Aldridge, the assistant minister
of Idlewild Presbyterian Church, who also happens to be chairman of Memphis
Presbytery's committee on social concerns. He was the only white preacher
present that evening, except the Reverend Malcolm Blackburn, only white
minister of the African Methodist Episcopal Church. Aldridge read a resolution of support which had been adopted by the Presbytery's committee.

The Catholic Council of Human Relations, like the Memphis Council on
Human Relations, passed a resolution calling upon the mayor to meet all
stated demands of the sanitation workers. The Catholic Council on Human
Relations is affiliated with the National Catholic Council for Interracial
Justice, a voluntary association of laymen and clergymen concerned about
intergroup relations.

Otherwise the white churches and churchmen of Memphis were not notably
involved. Jerry Wurf made a poignant statement in his talk at one of the
church meetings. "I'm a Jewish boy from Brooklyn," he said. "I've stood in
a lot of Protestant pulpits in times of stress and trouble. It just occcurs
to me that these have always been the pulpits of Negro churches. You have
always made me feel welcome and at home."

"The ministers are in this thing until it is proven beyond the shadow of
a doubt that our way won't work," said the Reverend Malcolm Blackburn on

another occasion. "Then, as one minister said yesterday, we shall just have to go fishing."

Another preacher said that the ministers were committed to nonviolence as a way of life. "But if we ministers, leading the people our way, cannot get results, we have no alternative but to withdraw and. . . ." The end of his sentence was lost in an approving roar, in the midst of which he turned and pointed into the balcony where three or four young black men, self-proclaimed radicals, stood watching. They broke into broad grins.

Bishop J. O. Patterson said he believed completely in nonviolence. But he added, "Someone asked me, 'What would you do if somebody was standing on your foot?' I said, 'Well . . . I *got* to have my foot!'"

The Reverend W. Herbert Brewster preached on Wednesday night. An orator of the old school, he admonished the crowd: "Don't reduce yourself so low that you will hate any man. I feel sorry for any man who is a little man in big times, because a little man in big times is a loser."

When he had finished his sermon, Dr. Jackson came to the pulpit to direct the taking of a collection for the strike fund. "Dr. Brewster better go on back and pray some more," he said, "because he hasn't got me liking Loeb yet. . . ." The crowd loved it.

"When he was up here talking about loving Loeb," he continued, "Bishop Patterson passed me a note that said, 'He didn't get a whiff of that gas, did he?'" The crowd loved that, too.

"You better be careful, Doctor," he concluded. "You might be up here calling for water while the rest of us are calling for fire!"

With that he pulled an object out of his pocket and held it up for the crowd to see. It was a gold-plated cigar lighter.

That Monday night meeting was drawing to a close. It had been in progress for three hours, which is not unusual for civil rights mass meetings. Before the Reverend Mr. Blackburn pronounced the benediction, he introduced a tall young black man wearing a light, olive-colored jacket with the word "INVADERS" across the back.

"I'm a radical," the young man began. "I'll tell you just like that. I'm a radical . . .

"Before Henry Loeb will listen, the garbage has to be in the street . . . not in your back yard. As long as those trucks are allowed to roll, they can keep it picked up wherever they want it picked up . . .

"Preaching and money raising are fine. Somebody has to do it. But there are some *men* out there, we've got to do some *fighting*. Not marching—fighting!

"And when you talk about fighting a city with as many cops as this city's got, you better have some guns! You're gonna need 'em before it's over!"

When he sat down the minister who had been presiding throughout the evening returned to the pulpit and said he apologized for not recognizing the young radical. It is a free country, he said, and while he did not agree with the brother, he certainly granted him his right to say what he thought. Then he reminded the crowd, "We have chosen our weapons. These are the weapons of nonviolence."

The incident was discussed later by a small group at the front of the church. Someone commented that the sentiments expressed by the young man were a new wrinkle in mass meetings. "Yes," replied Blackburn, "but I felt we had to let it wrinkle to keep it from tearing. We may be in trouble this way, but if we did not recognize this mood as part of the picture, we most certainly would be in trouble."

"Yea," someone else added. "One of the young folks said to me, 'You old folks are barking up the wrong tree. But we'll wait and let you bark a while longer.'"

And so at this writing, with the strike a month old, the tension mounting (in the fourth week, there were incidents of brick throwing by Negroes, of garbage being set afire, of a sit-in at City Council with 121 Negroes arrested and released on their recognizance, of a policeman brandishing an over-sized club gleefully and just as gleefully being laughed at scornfully by Negroes), the outcome was highly uncertain in Memphis -- both as to the immediate issues of the strike, the deeper one of dignity, and the awesome one hanging

over America in 1968 involving the danger of massive violence and police-
state repression.

Out of the impasse, these points, with meaning not merely in Memphis
but for all the nation, seemed clear:

1. Spiritual as well as physical needs are imbedded in Negro protest
and agitation and, indeed, anger. The demand for dignity as well as better
pay was the most profound and moving quality of the Memphis garbage strike.
In all of its floundering with the problems of race and poverty, America
has seemed unable to grasp that there are hurts in deprivation to the psyche
as well as the stomach. Organized labor, in many of its modern manifestations, has seemed to miss this point, also, concerning itself with economic
security rather than social needs of people. The excellent performance of
labor in Memphis, like the old Operation Dixie, and the current efforts to
organize textile plants in the Carolinas and farm workers in Texas, served
to point up how rare such attention to the underdog by labor has become.

2. Black power, for all its ambiguity and sometimes irrationality, is
a psychological force at work in such a situation as that in Memphis, not by
any means all negatively. Indeed, the most positive, constructive meanings
of the phrase were implicit in Negroes' demand for dignity. That this demand
was made in a context of nonviolence and in the traditional framework of a
labor strike should serve to give new insight into the semantics and
psychology of black power as an influence on Negro thinking and emotion.

3. The impetus to violence by Negroes is also a factor to be reckoned
with in such a situation as that in Memphis. In the simplest terms of human
anger, the capacity and ability of Negroes in such a situation to espouse and
practice nonviolence was extraordinary. For here as in nearly all other
southern locales, there had been the beautiful spirit of the Negro movement
of the early 1960's met with hostility and force and arrests when all that had
been demanded was the most basic rights of American citizenship. And here as
in nearly all other southern locales, eight years after the sit-ins and four
years after passage of the 1964 Civil Rights Act, the demands were the same
ones of basic rights -- for an end to discrimination in education, jobs,
housing.

Those who have pronounced the civil rights movement dead and buried may
want to take a second look at such phenomena as Memphis. "Well, well," said
an old man there, shouldering a protest sign and moving out of the church for
a demonstration, "marchin' again." The tone and much of the spirit of the
old movement was newly alive in Memphis, and its impetus still lives in
Negro communities and hearts across the South's cities, towns, and farmlands.
One of the very most hopeful things about such new manifestations of the
movement as Memphis has been the absence of exploitation from afar for less
than local interests of the braveness and beauty and belief of the local
people who are the strength of the movement. It was to be hoped that such
exploitation would not be attempted in Memphis.

Maintaining nonviolence among masses of untrained and volatile demonstrators was never easy. The implicit threat of the nonviolent leaders in Memphis
to "go fishing" and leave things in the hands of "radicals" was a mark of the
loss of faith, the frustration and the despair that has come to so many
Americans of good will and pragmatic common sense out of the failures on every
level of government and through all elements of American society to answer
the most elemental needs of race and poverty.

Two Negro women waiting for a bus during one march were asked by an
observer if they were supporting the boycott. "We sure are," one of them
declared. "I ain't buying nothing!" She glanced at the man's white face,
looked down at his notebook, then straight into his eyes. "I don't know who
you are," she said firmly, "but we're tired."

4. Failure was on prominent display in Memphis. The city government,
the press, the business community, the white church, all the institutions,
seemed for the first month simply incapable of coping with what was at once
a fairly clear-cut demand, and also a highly dangerous situation. The role
of the police in such crises is of particular concern. The danger of Negro
violence exploding out of all the failure of the government and society was
matched by the danger manifest across the nation of overreaction and

repression by police. Instead of agencies for maintaining peace and order, police departments in racial encounters have become themselves direct and dangerous influences toward disorder. In Memphis (and this is not an uncommon situation in the nation), there seemed to be a failure of men on the force to carry out the police commissioner's generally enlightened racial policies and methods aimed at avoiding violence. If the pay of garbage collectors in Memphis was a surface issue, reflective of unmet problems confronting cities the nation over, a less obvious but far more fundamental problem was that of the pay of policemen -- the need that such pay and the standards and quali- fications for police services be greatly increased. But it was a paralysis of the normal function of the city and society to resolve the strike and its issues and its dangerous potential, rather than a will to confront basic problems that characterized the first month of the strike in Memphis. An observer felt that those in positions of power never seemed to grasp the reality of the situation, its danger, or its promise. And this same sort of paralysis seemed to afflict the other agencies of government, state and federal, which might be expected to act toward mediation and reconciliation when a city did not.

Special Report, Southern Regional Council, Atlanta, Ga., 1968, Box 31 Administrative Files, Whitney Young Papers, Columbia University.

UNITED AUTO WORKERS

33.
ADDRESS OF WALTER P. REUTHER BEFORE THE
ANNUAL CONVENTION OF THE NATIONAL ASSOCIATION
FOR THE ADVANCEMENT OF COLORED PEOPLE,
DETROIT, MICHIGAN
JUNE 26, 1957

Mr. Chairman, friends, it's difficult for me to tell you how happy and proud I am to be here, because when I come to an NAACP meeting, I have a feeling that I belong here. I'm home here. And I can never escape the same reaction every time I hear that wonderful song, "Lift Up Our Voices and Sing." It always gives me a sense of renewed faith and dedication, because I feel that a people who can sing that song cannot lose.
I'm proud to belong to the NAACP, because it is made up of people who are dedicated in a great crusade to make America true to itself. This is what this is about. Make America live up to its highest hopes and aspira- tions and translate those hopes and aspirations into practical, tangible reality in the lives of all people, whether they are white or black, whether they live in the North or in the South. I say that each of us is blessed that we can be engaged in this crusade, in this struggle for justice for human dignity--in this struggle to wipe out in every phase of our national life, every ugly and immoral kind of discrimination.
A couple of years ago I had the privilege of attending an ADA meeting in Washington and Roy Wilkins was the principal speaker. And I want to say that Roy did himself proud that night. He was reporting on some of the struggles in the South. He had just returned from a speaking tour in a number of the Southern states, and he said there are three organizations that are being held responsible for the drive for civil rights and human dignity in the South. He said there is the NAACP. There is the ADA, and there is the CIO. Mrs. Roosevelt was my dinner partner and I said to her, "No wonder I'm having trouble. I'm an officer of all three of those organizations."
Now why did they come together? Well, because they shared the same values, the same respect for human dignity. They shared the same hopes and the same aspirations. And they dreamed the same dreams about the bright new tomorrow that we're working and fighting to build. A tomorrow where

discrimination will be no more. Where Jim Crow will be buried for keeps in
every phase of our national life. A bright tomorrow where every child,
regardless of race, creed, or color, all created in the image of God, will
have equal educational opportunities so that every child can grow, intellec-
tually, spiritually, and culturally, limited not by a segregated schoolroom,
but limited only by the capacity that God gave each child to grow.

But the NAACP and the American labor movement do more than just dream
about that better tomorrow. And that's why you can preach about the brotherhood of man from morn til night, and the Eastlands and the Talmadges and the
bigots will never raise their voices in protest. But when you begin to work
to translate the brotherhood of man into practical fulfillment, that's when
they begin to fight back. They are fighting us because we are working, trying to give practical substance and meaning and purpose to the noble concept
of the brotherhood of man.

We had a distinguished churchman, Bishop Oxman, who addressed the UAW
convention some months ago. He said, you know there is a lot of noble talk
about the brotherhood of man, but there are some people who keep the hood and
drop the brother. And those are the people who are fighting us. And because
they are fighting us, we meet at a time of great crisis. The challenge is
compelling, but when the burden is heavy, always remember that the reward is
so great and wonderful in terms of basic human values that it's more than
worth the struggle and the sacrifice that go into winning the reward. Since
you meet in the city in which the headquarters of the UAW is located, I am
sure you will permit me to bring to you the fraternal greetings and the best
wishes from the one and a half million members of the UAW, and I would like
to say for them that we are with you all the way until victory is ours in
this fight for civil rights.

You have come back. You were here in 1943. Detroit was the great
arsenal of democracy. We were turning out more weapons of war with which to
fight Hitlerism, totalitarianism, than was any other city in the world. But
unfortunately, this city went wrong and we had tragic, ugly race riots back
in that period. But one of the things that we have always been proud of
about the UAW is that when the people of Detroit were rioting and destroying
and killing each other on the streets, white and Negro workers worked side by
side in brotherhood in the plants under our contracts. Because they had
learned to know the meaning of human solidarity, of brotherhood, because they
had learned through the hard experience of struggle that when the employer
can divide you and pit white against black, American-born against foreign-born,
he can divide and rule and exploit everyone. And we learned a lesson that
only in the solidarity of human brotherhood, only as you stand together with
your fellow man can you solve your basic problems.

That's the lesson the whole of America needs to learn. I've often
thought--why is it that you can get a great nation like America marching,
fighting, sacrificing, and dying in the struggle to destroy the master race
theory in Berlin, and people haven't got an ounce of courage to fight against
the master race theory in America? We need the same sense of dedication, the
same courage and the same determination to fight the immorality of segregation
and racial bigotry in America as we did in the battlefields against Hitlerism.

We've made progress in Detroit since you were here in 1943. We haven't
made enough progress, but we have made great progress, and I think that we can
take great satisfaction and encouragement from the progress that we have made.
The delegates to this convention in 1943 were treated as second-class citizens,
and you were put in second-class hotels. This time you are in the best hotels
where you ought to be.

We made progress on the FEPC front. The NAACP, the trade union forces,
the church groups, civic groups worked together, and despite the overwhelming
opposition of the Republicans in our State Legislature, we finally got an FEPC
law on the books in the State of Michigan. Negro workers have made progress,
but we still have not broken down the barriers to equal job opportunities in
every phase of our economic life. They are in the factories, but they are not
in the offices, where they have a right also to equal job opportunities.

And just as the Negro workers have proven themselves in the factories and
on the assembly lines, Negroes have proven themselves in the field of public
service. Since 1943, we have elected four Negroes to important political
positions in the City of Detroit. They were elected by tremendous majorities,

have demonstrated the good judgment of the people who put them there, by
dedication and by a high sense of public trust and service. We're proud of
the fact that the Honorable Judge Wade McCree sits in the highest court in
the City of Detroit. And we are proud that another Negro, the Honorable
Judge Davenport sits in another court of Detroit. And we are equally proud
that in the City of Washington from the Thirteenth Congressional District,
a Negro, the Honorable Charles Diggs, is in that position. And we are proud
that a distinguished Negro doctor, Dr. Remus Robinson, sits on the Detroit
Board of Education. Because of the outstanding public service and the sense
of dedication that these four outstanding Negro citizens have demonstrated in
the public positions to which they have been elected, I would like to predict
that in the fall election of 1957 in Detroit, we will elect a prominent Negro
to the Common Council where we need one.[119]

I think we all realize that the world is troubled--that we live with
crisis in America and the people of every nation are living with crisis in
the world. I have been saying for a long time that the crisis in the world
is not economic or political or military. Essentially, the crisis in the
world is a moral crisis. It's a reflection of man's growing immorality to
himself. Of man's growing inhumanity to man. The H-bomb is the highest and
most terrible destructive expression of that growing inhumanity.

And in a sense our crisis in America, the crisis in education, the crisis
in civil rights is not political, it is moral. We've got all that it takes
to solve these problems. But we haven't demonstrated the moral courage to
step up to solving these problems, and this is our basic problem. America
is in crisis, not because it lacks economic resources, not because it lacks
the political know-how, not because we don't know how to do the job of
squaring democracy's practices with its noble promises. We just haven't
demonstrated the moral courage. And until we do, we will not meet this basic
crisis in civil rights and in education.

And I believe that the civil rights issue--and I don't say this because
this is an NAACP convention, I have been saying this wherever I go, because
I believe it--I believe that the question of civil rights must be made the
top priority item on American democracy's unfinished business in the twentieth
century. Civil rights is not a political issue, because when a matter or
issue is essentially a moral matter, it must transcend partisan politics.
This is exactly the approach that we have been making together. We have been
trying not to play politics with civil rights, but to put the civil rights
question in its proper focus and mobilize people from all political parties to
try to adopt legislation and to take necessary steps to implement an effective
civil rights program.

We have been saying that there are three basic reasons why we support
civil rights. First, we support it as a matter of simple justice. As a
matter of human decency. As a matter of dignity and as a matter of basic
morality. Secondly, we fight for civil rights to make them universal, because
as Joe Rauh said in his speech, civil rights and human freedom are indivisible.
You cannot have those things unto yourself. You can be free only as your
neighbor is free. You can be free only as you share freedom with the people
you live with. Hitler taught us that when he jeopardized the freedom of the
smallest country in the world, he jeopardized our freedom. And when Mr.
Eastland and the Dixiecrats and the bigots in the South jeopardize the Constitution and deny Negroes their freedom, they are putting my freedom in
jeopardy, even though I live in the City of Detroit.

Those people who can't understand the first two basic reasons that ought
to put America on the highroad in the struggle for civil rights at least to
understand the third reason: that civil rights is no longer a domestic
question confined to the geography of the United States. The question of
civil rights in the United States is an international issue. As a matter of
fact, there are more people thinking about it abroad than there seem to be in
America thinking about this problem. Because more than one-half of the people
in the world are dark of skin, and they look at America, and they brush aside
our noble slogans about the virtues of American democracy. They brush aside
our economic indexes which say that we are the richest country in the world.
And they say, yes, but how do you square your noble professions with your ugly
practices in the civil rights field?

Mr. Eastland sits there in his Committee, and you would think that he is really trying to fight the Communists. He doesn't know anything about what makes a Communist. What he does not understand are the great social, dynamic forces sweeping the world. This struggle between freedom and tyranny is not an old-fashioned struggle for geography. This is a struggle for the hearts and minds of people. And you can't win it with an H-bomb, even though you need one to defend yourself. You can't win the struggle of ideas and ideals with guns, although we as a part of the free world must of necessity be strong on the military front, in order to meet the challenge of aggression no matter where it may raise its ugly head. But what we need to understand in the world is that military power is the negative aspect of a dynamic foreign policy, and that if you want to win the struggle of ideas and ideals for the hearts and minds of men, you have got to wage the struggle on the positive basis, and civil rights is the key issue in the world. Mr. Eastland and his associates and the association of bigots don't understand this. We need somehow to get through to the dark corners of their small mentalities on these kinds of things.

My feelings on this are not based upon reading a book. I have been in Asia, India, and North Africa. I have talked to people--workers in the big cities, intellectuals, businessmen, government officials. I have gone into the mountain villages. I am here to tell you that they know what's going on in America. I went up into the foothills of the Himalaya Mountains in Northern India, in a little village of three hundred people, and we had a meeting, and I talked about America--what we were doing trying to bring to fulfillment the great promise of America. They didn't want to know about how many Chevrolets General Motors made last year, or whether the Chrysler fins had a bigger sweep than the Cadillac fins. They asked me about Montgomery, Alabama. Just sit down on a doorstep with a peasant in a village of Northern India and take on the task of trying to explain to him why America, conceived in freedom and dedicated to the proposition that all men are created equal, a nation that can split the atom, that can make a pursuit ship go three times as fast as sound and yet, in this twentieth century, we can't live together in brotherhood and we continue to discriminate against Negroes. It will tax your ingenuity, and you will give them no answers. You can only give them excuses. And excuses are not good enough, if we are going to win the struggle of freedom in the world.

I came back more convinced than ever, after talking to people in North Africa and India and Asia, that America's immorality in the field of civil rights could be the Achilles' heel of American democracy in the struggle against Communist tyranny. Because when you have to put footnotes to try to explain in a feeble way why American democracy fails to meet the challenge on the civil rights front, when you have to make excuses, you are in serious trouble, and we are in serious trouble, because the people of the world are not going to judge America by the number of tons of steel that the U.S. Steel Corporation can roll in a year, by the number of shiny new automobiles with more chrome that we turn out every year. They are not going to judge us by these things. They are going to judge us by what we do about basic human problems. Not how modern is our plumbing, but how modern is our civil rights program as it affects people. These are the things they will judge us by, and if this Congress would step up to its responsibilities and pass a civil rights bill in it, with effective enforcement machinery, that civil rights bill would give America a moral force in the world more powerful than all the H-bombs that we will ever make in the fight against Communism.

And yet we have enemies. I get a lot of literature, you know. I don't read it all, but I read a couple that came over my desk the other day. Here's one: "Behind the Plot to Sovietize the South." And on the back it tells you in summary what this pamphlet is about, and I'll quote it to you: "This booklet tells about the activities of Walter Reuther and his collaborating white and Negro Communist, Socialist and Marxist kind of labor agitators who are mobilizing a massive offensive to impose an insidious civil rights program on the South." I want to say to the people who put out this kind of literary trash that the NAACP, the AFL-CIO, and all of the good people who are joined together in the fight for civil rights, we do more to fight the Communists in one week, than all these people would do in their whole lives put together.

We need to understand that this fight between freedom and tyranny is for keeps. It's the only world series in which there is only one game. No

play-offs, no return matches, no next year's season. You either win the
first game, or you lose for keeps. That's what we are in. Now you would
think that in that kind of a game you would put your best team in, and Mr.
Eastland and Mr. Talmadge and those fellows shouldn't even be on the scrub
team. We've got to put our best team in, because we've got to demonstrate
not only that we have great economic muscle, but we have the sense of moral
responsibility to find a practical way to equate economic muscle with social
and political morality in terms of the lives of everyone, because, you know
if we were just a little country, no bigger than Luxembourg, it really
wouldn't be tragic if we were doing so badly. But in truth, America is the
last hope of freedom. If we can't make freedom and democracy work in America,
then it can't be made to work any place in the world. And I say we are going
to make it work in America, because it must be made to work.

Now the task ahead is a difficult one. We will need to mobilize all of
our forces. We will need to pull together men and women of good will and
good faith--people in the NAACP, our good friends in the churches, the labor
movement, the liberal people who are willing to stand on the side of morality
in this struggle. We need to broaden our efforts to get more allies in the
leadership conference that has been working so effectively in the past. And
we need to have the courage to tell both political parties that they both
should be ashamed of the shoddy record that they have registered on the field
of civil rights.

The Supreme Court is living in the twentieth century and the Congress is
still somewhere back in the dark nineteenth century. It's about time they
catch up. You know, these fellows are the same fellows who passed the Taft-
Hartley Act. The same people who fight against civil rights are the same
people who fight against social progress. Well, I want to say to these people
in Congress that they have been on the longest sit-down strike in the history
of America--eighty long years. And we think it's about time that they
terminate that sit-down strike on civil rights and begin to turn out some
legislation. Now the bill has passed the House, but that's nothing new.
That's happened many times, but now it's over in the Senate, the graveyard of
civil rights legislation. I think that we've got a job to do. It can be
done. We must mobilize the American people, and we must translate their moral
will into practical pressure and say to that Senate, "Stay in there. Outlast
the filibuster, if it takes all summer and all fall, until the next Congress
meets in January." And if these evil men who use the right of unlimited
debate to block the will of the majority, if they know that the majority is
going to stay put through the hot summer into fall, and into the winter months,
maybe they won't try so hard, because they know it will not succeed. And the
only people in America who can see to it that the filibuster does not succeed
are the American people, and our job is to mobilize the American people, so
that their will and their moral pressure will exert itself upon the Congress.

We also must make it clear there can be no compromise on the jury trial
provision. We don't want a civil rights bill in name without any substance.
We don't want a civil rights bill that looks good on paper, that has no
enforcement machinery, and these people who talk aobut the jury trial, they
are using that only to try to destroy a civil rights bill that can be enforced
through the federal government and the federal courts.

Then we have the long-range fight on Rule 22. Because even though the
present limited civil rights bill is adopted, this is only the beginning,
because there are many other areas in which the ugly forms of discrimination
are working every day in the lives of millions of Americans and Rule 22 is the
key that will open the door in the Senate so that majority rule can prevail
and the filibuster can be ended. We have been saying a long time that the
right of debate does not mean the right to prevent the majority from acting.[120]
Debate is not an end. It is the means to an end, and the end must be
legislative action.

We are very happy that the UAW was able to join forces with the NAACP in
originating the original approach to changing Rule 22. We helped finance
some of the constitutional lawyers who went back to the Hamilton papers and
the early constitutional papers and developed the whole case to prove that the
Senate was not a continuing body. Therefore, every new Senate on the day of
its organization can adopt its own rules and, any new Senate can abolish Rule
22 and substitute in its place a rule providing for majority rule. And

because we participated in that historic effort, with the NAACP, we have
received many brickbats from the people in the Senate who believe that filibuster is their best line of defense.

Now we made progress on Rule 22. In 1953, we only got twenty-one votes.
We had fifteen liberal Democrats with us. We had five liberal Republicans,
and we had Wayne Morse, the Independent. In 1957, we got forty-one votes,
seven votes short of what we needed. I say we need to intensify our efforts
between now and the January date in which the new Congress in 1959 is
organized to get those other seven votes, so that we can abolish the filibuster
in the United States Senate for all time.[121]

We are continuing to work on this matter. As a matter of fact, hearings
are being held now. Friday morning, June 28, 1957, I'm going to testify on
Rule 22 before a Subcommittee of the United States Senate dealing with rules
of procedure. But Rule 22, let us always remember, has been the shovel with
which the Dixiecrats and reactionary Republicans have always dug the grave
for our civil rights legislation. And until we abolish Rule 22, we will
never be able to translate our civil rights program into practical legislation
and implementation.

We have the question of FEPC. Yes, thirty-eight major cities have
adopted the local FEPC ordinances. Fifteen states have state FEPC laws. We
have made progress, but no one should kid us into believing the answer to
FEPC can be found either locally or at the state level. Tell me how you'll
get relief in Mississippi, at the state level, where you need it most. The
only way that we can get a comprehensive FEPC law on the books is to do it
in Washington, D.C., and to bind the forty-eight states in the process.

Well, there are some mighty fine people in America who tell you, yes they
are against discrimination in every phrase. They are opposed to it in terms
of job opportunities. They are opposed to it in terms of education. They are
opposed to it in terms of transportation. But, they say, legislation is not
the way to do it. Education. You've got to educate people. You've got to
get hatred out of men's hearts. Well, we agree. Education is important.
But you can't educate this problem out of existence by education alone. You've
got to work both on the educational front and the legislative front. And
you've got to parallel those two activities right down the line.

I have told a story on other occasions which I think bears repetition
beacuse it's the simplest way to illustrate what I think to be a very fundamental point. These people who talk about education as the answer to FEPC,
and these other problems, I ask them to look to see what happens in America
in about ten days from now. We're going to have a Fourth of July weekend.
There are going to be millions and millions of Americans in their automobiles
driving all over America. And on the Friday before the weekend, the National
Safety Council will launch its comprehensive, intensive educational program.
They'll be on the radio networks, the TV networks, and the newspapers. Everybody is going to be told and warned to drive carefully, don't exceed the speed
limit. Don't go through a red light. Observe all the traffic regulations.
We're going to just saturate America with education on traffic safety, but no
one would propose that that's where we end. In addition to this educational
program, we have thousands of fellows on motorcycles in blue uniforms. And
when you go through a red light or exceed the speed limit or violate some
other traffic law, the motorcycle officer pulls you over to the curb. He
gets a book out, and he gives you a ticket. It costs you ten bucks, and that
speeds up the educational process like nobody's business.

So we say let's educate and educate and educate. But let's expedite the
educational process by some effective legislation. And if an employer will
not give a qualified Negro, or a qualified Jew a job, because of prejudice,
let's take that employer into court the way you go into court when a cop
catches you going through a red light. And you will see how fast the educational process picks up. Now these good people who are all for education and
opposed to legislation don't think it's wrong to have this fellow on the
motorcycle. They think that's perfectly proper, perfectly fine, and yet,
when you're dealing in a field of basic human values of human rights of basic
morality, they just want the educational process to take its own course.
We've got to keep pressing and pressing and pressing until we get a federal
FEPC law.

We're proud in the Auto Workers Union of the progress we've made. Other unions have made great progress in breaking down discrimination in the factories. But we haven't got one single major contract, although we've got one and a half million workers under contract, and although we try and try and try at the bargaining table in which the employer has agreed to a clause prohibiting discrimination because of race or creed or color at the hiring gate. They say to us, "Oh, you don't represent the workers until we employ them. We aren't going to let you say anything about whom we hire. After we hire them, then you can talk about their work, their conditions of employment, their wages." Well, we believe that the question of the policy at the hiring gate is important, and if we can't do it at the bargaining table, then we have to do it in the halls of Congress.

Now there are many other things we need to be thinking about. I want to say to this convention of the NAACP, the American labor movement is not a fair-weather friend of yours in the fight for civil rights. I want to say for the AFL-CIO, its leadership, George Meany, and the people involved in directing that organization: "We are with you all the way, and we are going to stay with you all the way until we get on the statute books of America effective civil rights legislation in all of these fields, not only in FEPC, but in every other aspect of our national life."

We want an America in which every citizen is equal when he walks into the polling place to cast his ballot. We want an America in which every child has educational opportunity, an America in which every citizen has equal job opportunity, equal rights to the use of all public facilities, the right to live in a decent neighborhood, in a decent house.

It's about time we look at this problem of clearing the slums in our major cities. We're not clearing the slums. We're just modernizing them. We're just creating new ghettoes. I say it's about time we had some courage to build decent communities in which all Americans can live on an integrated basis as decent citizens living together in a wholesome community.

Now these are not matters of special privileges. These are basic rights to which every American is entitled. And no American should be satisfied with less.

The task is difficult. The struggle will be hard, but let us always remember that human progress has never been served to mankind on a silver platter. The history of the world shows chapter after chapter that men of faith and courage have had to fight to bring to fulfillment their dreams and their hopes and their aspirations. What we need to do is to keep the faith. Keep the faith in ourselves. And when the going is rough, as it will be, let us remember that the test of one's convictions is now how did you behave, how did you stand up when it was convenient and comfortable. The test of one's convictions is: do you stand up for the things that you believe when it takes courage? Do you stand up in the face of adversity, in the face of great controversy? This is the kind of fight we are engaged in. That's why when the going is rough, always remember that there are millions of us, and that together we can move mountains, and that together we can solve this problem and make America in the image of what it really stands for.

So I say to you, we pledge our hands and our hearts, we pledge our all to you in this struggle, because we believe that this is the most important struggle that America must win, if it is going to be true to itself and provide leadership to the free world. And if we mobilize our multitudes, if we mobilize all the people of good will and good faith in America, I say that we can do the job, and together we can build that brave new tomorrow that we dream about and fashion it in the image of peace, freedom and justice, and human brotherhood.

Henry M. Christman, ed., *Walter P. Reuther: Selected Papers* (New York, 1962), pp. 195–208.

34. THERE'S NO HALF-WAY HOUSE ON THE
ROAD TO FREEDOM

In the two years since our last convention, this nation has made more progress in achieving civil rights for all citizens than was made in all the years since the period of Reconstruction following the Civil War.

Yet this progress, historic when measured against the habits and hostilities of the past, falls short when measured--as we must measure it-- against the prejudice and discrimination that remain and the goals of equal rights and equal opportunity that must yet be attained.

The UAW, true to itself as a union whose strength is derived from the solidarity of all workers and to its mission to make progress with the whole community, played a prominent role in the historic 1963 Washington rally and in efforts to obtain the strongest possible civil rights law from Congress.

These efforts were climaxed with passage of the Civil Rights Act of 1964, a sweeping law attacking segregation and discrimination on a broad front, including public accommodations, jobs, education and the right to vote.

However, the voting rights section of the law left intact much of the southern pattern of systematic denial of voting rights to Negroes; it equiv- ocated in the matter of literacy tests and made no provision for Federal voting registrars in states and localities where Negroes were deliberately kept from registering.

The Negroes of the deep south were terrorized by southern officials and the Klan whenever they attempted to exercise their rights. They mobilized early in January, 1965 under the direction of the Rev. Martin Luther King's Southern Christian Leadership Conference to assert their constitutional right to register and vote. As this campaign of nonviolent demonstration progressed, the violence against Negroes intensified, reaching a climax of calculated terror in March.

I had the honor that month of leading a UAW delegation to Selma in support of equal rights and in protest against the brutality of southern racism. UAW members from every region participated in that freedom march.

The Montgomery march was shadowed by the tragic murder of a northern civil rights worker, Mrs. Viola Liuzzo, wife of a trade union official, who was shot by Klansmen on the highway. The failure of all-white southern juries to return murder convictions in the Liuzzo case and in the trial resulting from the earlier slaying of the Rev. James Reeb brought to national attention another aspect of southern injustice which requires further Federal legislation.

In June, 1965, as work went forward in and out of the Congress to shape a strong voting rights law, President Johnson made an historic address at Howard University, dealing with civil rights legislation in the broader con- text of the entire struggle for equality of opportunity in a society that professes to be free and democratic.

He opened up for national discussion and public action an aspect of the civil rights revolution which the UAW had long been concerned--its economic aspect. For us in the UAW, the chief interest of the President's address lay in his emphasis on what he called "the next and the more profound stage of the battle for civil rights"--that of reinforcing legislative gains by an across-the-board attack on the unemployment, poverty and deprivation which hit the Negro hardest but affect millions of whites as well.

The rioting in the Watts section of Los Angeles that occurred in August, 1965 soon after enactment of the Voting Rights Act, was a clear signal to the nation of the urgency of our getting on with economic solutions.

The bitterness of frustrated hopes gave rise to the destructive and senseless violence of Watts. We cannot approve or condone violence, for the futility of violence born out of bitterness will solve no problems. But it is not enough for the advantaged to condemn the violence on the part of the disadvantaged. The advantaged must work harder to help the disadvantaged to achieve equal rights and equal opportunities in every phase of our national life.

The UAW was actively involved in efforts to fight unemployment and poverty in the Watts area before the rioting, through the Watts Community Labor Action Committee. We were working with other AFL-CIO unions to find jobs for Watts' residents, to help set up a Head Start program and a problem clinic, and to campaign for greater health facilities.

Throughout the UAW, and in all the communities where our members are concentrated, we are making an expanding effort on behalf of equal rights and equal opportunity. New state, area and local fair practice councils have been established in several regions.

We are participating in a registration drive in southern communities where Negroes under the 1965 law are protected in the exercise of rights long denied them.

In Boston, we joined in an attempt to end a regime of entrenched bigotry on the board of education. In Pontiac, Mich., we have been working with the county AFL-CIO council to overcome municipal opposition to sorely needed additional public rental housing.

In Detroit, the Citizens Committee for Equal Opportunity--which we were instrumental in founding in 1963 with the cooperation of religious, business, civil rights and other civic leadership in the metropolitan areas--has worked effectively in creating understanding and proposing reasonable action in all the sensitive areas of race relations.

Nationally and in many cities, we are active in cooperation with human relations councils and through local union educational programs in fostering equal opportunity in housing.

This is not to say that civil rights legislation will not continue to be of basic importance. Laws already on the books must be strengthened as experience dictates.

Senators Douglas of Illinois and Case of New Jersey have already introduced a bill proposed by the Leadership Conference on Civil Rights, in which the UAW participates, which would have the effect of integrating southern juries and would provide Federal protection for civil rights workers and Negroes exercising their constitutional rights.

The point is that we must press forward on all fronts toward full citizenship and equal opportunity for all our people. Centuries-old prejudice dies hard, but we have to understand that there can be no half-way house on the road to freedom.

UAW Solidarity (May, 1966).

35.   WATTS: WHERE THEY MANUFACTURE HOPE

By Alvin Adams

At the age of 14, he had saved enough money to buy a train ticket that would take him as far as Meridian, Miss. as he could get.

In Los Angeles, he washed cars, steam-cleaned engines and managed to finish high school. He learned something about the police by being one: an Army MP.

For something like 25 years, he was one of the unspectacular citizens of Watts. In 1949, employment at Ford's Los Angeles plant and his resultant membership in the UAW brought out leadership talents he admits he didn't know he had.

Early in 1965, Ted Watkins became a UAW International representative. After a day and a half in the Region 6 office and long conversations with UAW Director Paul Schrade, he went to the Watts section of L.A. "to bring some activities." He hasn't been back.

Watts, where he went to work, is the predominantly-Negro area of some 150,000 people at the south central edge of Los Angeles that gained world-wide notoriety as a result of racial rioting in August, 1965. The Kerner Commission, established to study the rash of riots since that time, said the Los Angeles riot "evoked a new mood in the ghettos around the country."

Before the riot, Watkins and other trade unionists who wanted to put their union skills and experience to work in the improvement of their home community laid the groundwork for a unique combination of labor and community forces: the Watts Labor Community Action Committee.

As full-time administrator of WLCAC, 45-year-old UAW "rep" Watkins directs a staff of 150 persons in the programs of the organization, which is

chartered by the state of California. The scope of the program has grown
beyond the traditional borders of Watts to include surrounding territory.
    With the eyes of a man surveying his own neighborhood, Watkins sees the
problems in human terms:
    "The people of Watts have no community economic base. They have no
major food markets; no major department stores; no theater; no hospital.
Whatever they need, they have to go outside the community--sometimes, miles
away. The buses are expensive, and slow, and many of our cars don't always
run right.
    "And Watts is boxed in by housing projects at each corner. This is a
concentration of poor people, a concentration of problems, a concentration of
families without fathers, a concentration of mothers on welfare, a concentration of kids who don't have any male images or anything to go by," Watkins
said.
    The consumer action office of WLCAC goes right to the heart of many
problems.
    "Any problem that the resident might have, whether it be contract buy-
ing, food stamps, welfare, lighting, street maintenance, sweeping--just about
anything that affects the consumer, we work directly with them," said former
UAW Local 509 mechanic Ollie Taylor, director of the office.
    "A car dealer will sell you a car and know that in three months you can't
keep up the $122 a month payments," Taylor's staff tells people. "So he gets
your trade in, the extra money you had to borrow on the side to complete a
down payment and the car back."
    Often the help needed is legal, and WLCAC refers such cases to the
Neighborhood Legal Services of the anti-poverty program.
    Other problems require direct action. And a delicate touch.
    "People will come in and say the store on the corner has high prices.
Run him off," Taylor said. "Unless this man is just a regular gyp artist,
you've got to try to establish some communication to see why his prices are
so exorbitant, what he can do to bring them down, before you do anything to
him. We find in this community, a lot of people have everything they own
invested in one of these little stores. I think it would be wrong to chase
him out of business before trying to relate to that individual.
    "You have to try to solve the consumer's problem and the merchant's
problem."
    Such are the cool heads at work in the once-hot Watts.
    Along with advice on spending, WLCAC now offers advice on saving through
the newly-opened WLCAC federal credit union, chartered with the international
unions' support.
    The credit union's trained, nine-member board of directors which raised
$2,000 to get started, include UAW members E. J. Franklin (a retiree from
North American Local 887) who serves as president; Ellsworth Freeman, also of
Local 887 and WLCAC program director George Williams, UAW Local 923 member and
credit union treasurer.
    In its first six months of business, the credit union acquired $8,000 in
180 accounts, many of which were opened by WLCAC-paid workers. Payroll deduc-
tions now bring in $1,400 a month. In the same six months about $5,000 was
loaned, in amounts from $25 to $200.
    "Loans are made for every reason that banks and finance companies would
not lend money," said credit union manager Melvin D. Streator, "such as if a
man had his utilities shut off, he got arrested last night, or--who knows
what."
    "Nobody would make loans on these grounds, but we do. Just because we
know that they're telling us the truth and we know the circumstances."
    Although the underlying factor in all the problems of the Watts area,
economics is not always easy to get at, thus WLCAC has found itself reaching
out in nearly every direction to build a better community.
    Significantly, the first success of the brand-new organization was a
drive to have built a new hospital to serve the area.
    (The need for hospital facilities was involved in the spark which ignited
the six day of rioting, which cost 35 lives, $200 million in damage and was
called the worst U.S. riot in nearly a quarter century.
    (Rioting broke out in Los Angeles after a white policeman, two miles from
Watts, stopped and shot to death a Negro motorist Leonard Deadwyler who was

rushing his expectant wife to County General Hospital).

With the nearest hospital 15 miles from Watts, the McCone Commission--created to study causes of the riot--recommended that a hospital be built to serve the community. WLCAC spearheaded a hospital referendum drive, which failed, but "we went before the commissioners until they finally got tired of looking at us and pushed that hospital through," said Watkins.

Construction is now underway on the 470-bed, $24 million structure, renamed the Dr. Martin Luther King Jr. Hospital, to serve the Watts-Willowbrook area which has a population of 347,000. Watkins has been named a vice president of the permanent South Los Angeles Hospital Authority Commission.

WLCAC next turned its attention to the kids of Watts.

With understanding no outside organization could muster, WLCAC realized: "Much of the mischief and more serious trouble that our youngsters get into is a desperate cry for help, for attention."

Watkins observed: "The process of socialization that our boys and girls are exposed to from the time they begin to crawl is a very tragic one.

"The destruction of our family structure has been effective to the point where the father has been driven out of the home (because of his inability to provide for his family) and the mother has been forced to become dependent upon the welfare system, which stifles drive, ambition and motivation."

A father in the family can be a proud possession.

One teenager, enthusiastic about his WLCAC activities, described his family: "two brothers, one sister, a mother--and a father."

Ferman Moore, a husky 19-year-old, is typical of many Watts youth.

In the days immediately following the riot, Ferman Moore was "full of animosity."

"I had a lot of problems. I disagreed with a lot of things that were going on. I talked and tried to advocate a lot of violence; a lot of no good."

He was talking in a barber shop when he met Ted Watkins, who asked if he needed a job. "I said yeah, I need a job."

At the age of 17, he went to work as a WLCAC crew chief, supervising a group of young workers. But first, "I had to change my image, so the young brothers and sisters would grow up and want to be the right type of young men and women."

The work with the youth of Watts has been one of the most rewarding aspects of WLCAC for Watkins.

"The month we started working with kids we had 1,700 with us--cleaning up the community, going on trips, taking hikes," he recalled. "We found that these kids had never gotten any positive attention. It gave them some real, new kind of feeling as far as being somebody."

Obtaining funds from government anti-poverty programs to augment support from labor and other sources, WLCAC was able to engage once-idle youths in work-education-recreation projects and, at the same time, launch services beneficial to the community at large.

Enrollees are paid wages, whether their work is to help construct buildings or to clear a vacant lot of weeds and debris. They are not paid when they do not work. From the beginning it was clear that they would not be content with "make work" activities. They wanted skills, training, real jobs.

Both job training and transportation were tackled when WLCAC obtained from the government broken-down trucks and buses. The motor pool not only serves as a NYC-enrollee mechanics training school but also as a transportation center using the 60 repaired vehicles.

Just as the problems of Watts are interwoven, attempts to solve a given problem may begin to unravel others.

The seemingly single task of cleaning and beautifying the community led to the concept of "vest pocket parks," the utilization of scattered, home-sized vacant lots as playgrounds. Some 23 parks, including at least one to have swimming facilities and one for senior citizens, are near completion.

Attractive parks required, in addition to playground equipment, shrubbery and WLCAC persuaded private business to contribute half a million dollars worth of street trees, shrubs, ground cover and flowers. Then, for a place to cultivate these plants until they are planted throughout the community, WLCAC turned to the Los Angeles Dept. of Water and Power. In an unprecedented move, the department leased to WLCAC 12 blocks of fenced land beneath gigantic power lines and provided free water and thousands of feet of pipe for irrigation.

Providing training of CCC and NYC work crews, the "growing grounds" project is directed by Duane West, a landscape architect who said youths have an opportunity "to learn what it takes to grow a plant, how to water it and care for it. Most of them have never done this before. Then they realize that plants are a part of the visual improvement of our community."

A second service station recently was put into operation by WLCAC after officials of Mobil Oil described the volume of sales at the organization's original, eight-month old station at 103rd and Central Ave. as "fantastic." That station sells 65,000 gallons of gasoline a month and performs minor repairs through a program that offers training to 34 young men and women ages 16 to 21, said former longshoreman Lehman Copeland, WLCAC staffer and Mobil-trained general manager of the station.

The trainee program at service stations includes young women as well as males. Although this program works well, WLCAC discovered that young women in the area generally are more difficult to work with than the young men. "Their future expectations, based on their observations of their mothers and older sisters, are self-defeating," one adult explained. To meet this need, special girls' programs, including grooming courses designed to revive a sense of feminity, have been established.

Another youth training and money making venture launched by WLCAC is a poultry ranch located on an acre-sized lot outside the city limits. Equipped with incubators, cages and additional equipment, the ranch is stocked with 5,000 fowl and produces about 70 dozen eggs a day. Manure from the ranch is aged, chemically treated and used for fertilizing the portion of Water and Power Dept. land cultivated for the growth of farm produce.

Under the direction of Vertis Hayes, former chairman of the Dept. of Fine Arts at Le Moyne College in Memphis, Tenn., and one time product designer for a California-based maker of house and gift wares, young people work in ceramics, paints, pastels, papier-mache, soap carving and other methods of creative expression.

"In order to develop a person totally and well, you must help him to feel free to express himself," is the belief of Hayes, who, as a young man, entered the field of art against the advice and best wishes of persons who warned that as a Negro he would never be able to make a living.

"The art talent, though," observed Hayes, "is one of those strange things that sees fit often to visit across the railroad tracks, and we find it everywhere." In his project, one portion of the remediation program which includes math, English, grammar and social science, he has found "a great deal of talent, a great deal indeed."

A maker of miniature race cars contracted to have WLCAC put together the 15-piece section of track which counts the tiny car's revolutions around the track. Eight to 10 17-year-olds complete the production in a small-scale assembly line operation, expected to last two months and turn out 4,000 pieces.

The list of activities will go on--undoubtedly has been expanded even as this report is published, for WLCAC has gained that toehold which has eluded similar-intentioned groups in other communities.

Solidarity (August, 1968).

36. A BLACK CAUCUS FORMED IN AUTO UNION

By Jerry M. Flint

DETROIT, Sept. 30--A black caucus has formed within the United Automobile Workers and is demanding "full equity" for Negroes within the big union.

The group is called the National Ad Hoc Committee of Concerned Negro U.A.W. Members and is headed by Robert Battle 3d. Mr. Battle is a vice president of Local 600, the union's largest, at the Ford Motor Company's Rouge works in Dearborn, Mich.

A committee of the Negro group, including Mr. Battle, met Sept. 18 with Walter P. Reuther, president of the 1.5-million-member union. A report on the meeting was given yesterday at a session of the caucus. Mr. Battle said he expected to meet again with Mr. Reuther in a week to 10 days.

There had been reports that Mr. Reuther was unhappy with the complaints of the group. "He is only half as unhappy as we are," Mr. Battle said yesterday.

In a written statement of complaint to Mr. Reuther, the Negro group warned that unless the problems were solved and Negroes received their "full equity" in the independent union, "others" would stir action and "chaos could ensue."

The groups said that Negroes made up one-fourth of the union's membership but that only 75 of 1,000 U.A.W. international representatives, or 7.5 per cent, were Negro. The group also complained that of more than 100 key staff jobs in the union, only seven were held by Negroes.

Vital political decisions affecting Negroes are "determined and dictated by white" union officers, the caucus said. This "must be ended now," the group declared in its statement to Mr. Reuther.

The caucus said it represented Negroes ranging from the most moderate union activists to black revolutionaries. As many as 100 U.A.W. members, many of them in local leadership positions, have attended meetings of the group.

In submitting its complaints, the group said that Mr. Reuther's own integrity and commitment were not at issue. The statement said:

"It is precisely because of our faith in your integrity and commitment that we seek to resolve these matters with you at the conference table, rather than, as many powerful voices have suggested, take the issue to the streets and the public press."

The New York Times, October 1, 1968.

37.   OUT OF STRUGGLE--SOLIDARITY

By Cornelius Cobbs

The Solidarity Caucus at International Harvester's Tractor Works plant was formed three years ago to fight to regain and maintain decent working conditions and to educate the new, young members about their rights under the union contract. Our symbol is the clenched fist. It means that if we all stick together against International Harvester like a clenched fist, we can't be broken like the fingers of an outstretched hand.

From "All-Black" to "Solidarity"

The caucus had its origins when many of the militant blacks at International Harvester formed the New Breed Democratic Trade Union Caucus to try to break the white monopoly on skilled trades jobs. Last year some whites first asked to join the caucus because they also disliked what was going on in the shop.

They felt that our group was carrying on the best fight against the company, so they asked to be part of it. We believed we would be strengthened by their participation, so we agreed. Of course, the first thing people would catch when they saw New Breed was "all black," so we changed our name to Solidarity. The name is closer to labor's goals.

Of the 2400 workers at I.H., about 60% are white and 40% are black, but the leadership in the caucus remains black.

We work under one of the best contracts in the UAW chain. It comes from the fighting tradition of the plant, which dates back to the struggle for the eight-hour-day in 1886. Then, the plant was the McCormick Works Reaper Division, and the week was 60 to 80 hours long. It was the police brutality during the strike for a shorter day that called out the famous Haymarket demonstration 83 years ago.

A Fighting History

Ask any "old timer." He will tell you about the company goons, the vicious role of the police, the techniques used by the company to break strikes, the harassment, the bloody, cracked heads, the guerilla movement within the shop, the infiltrators and informers, the wildcats and sit-down strikes, the unity forged in struggle.

He will tell you about the speed-up, the dirty conditions, the company favoritism, the dangerous equipment, the impossible work loads and the polluted air.

Pace-setting Contract

The union tradition was developed and fought for by minority-group whites . . . Poles, Italians, Bohemians, Irish, new immigrants who gave leadership to the others. They were members of the old Farm Equipment – United Electrical Workers union (FEUE), and the contracts they won set the pace for the industry. We brought their old contract with us intact when FEUE merged with the United Auto Workers in 1955.

The contract is unusually good in several ways. For example, we have never had compulsory overtime. Almost all of the auto industry contracts require it. We would never accept it. Second, we have one of the best piece-work systems in the Chicago area, and an excellent safety clause, because we can strike on it. Older workers in particular benefit from the contract because of the recent emphasis on pensions, vacations, holidays, medical benefits, and so on.

What the 'Old-Timers' Don't Say

Union tradition and the contract have established the local as a leader in the fight for good working conditions. But the story the "old timers" don't tell is how white racism or black exclusion was never dealt with. The blacks and other non-white minorities in the early days were put into the foundry . . . the heaviest and filthiest jobs in the plant. They were almost totally excluded from the skilled apprentice trades such as tool and die, millwrights, machine repair, and so on. These latter were the highest paying in the shop.

Under FDR, the union won a Fair Employment Practices clause in its contracts, but the problem of white racism remained. Today probably not more than one tenth of 1% of the apprentices or skilled workers are black or Spanish-American. This is one of the main reasons why we formed the Solidarity Caucus.

Contract Weakened

The second major reason for the Solidarity Caucus is because of the inroads made by the company on the hard-won gains of the past. Although the contract is advanced compared to others, Harvester has knocked big holes into it. For example, formerly there was no prohibition on strikeable grievances. Now, these are limited to health, sanitation and piece-work prices. Before, we had a 52 week-maximum benefit period for workers injured on the job. This has been slashed to 26 weeks.

The list of grievances includes the harassment and speed-up of the piece-workers, the severe discipline imposed for minor violations of company rules, the refusal or delay by the company in controlling smoke pollution in the welding departments and the severe breakdown in the processing of grievances.

An example is the speed-up and harassment of piece workers that affects blacks and whites. Last June we had a sit-down on the Department 55 line, where earth-moving tractors are made, because Harvester tried to put another tractor on the line without adding more men. Traditionally, a new tractor on the line has meant 100 additional new men at the Personnel office. So when they try to sweat more work out of us, we have to use the slow-down or sit-down to make them appreciate the meaning of the contract.

Speed-up Increasing

The piece-work departments are especially vulnerable to speed-up. For example, where a lot of fellows had to do 9 to 10 pieces before, they have to do almost 20 pieces now to make the rate. And if you do not make the rate in

30 days, you are disqualified. They will put you in a lower grade or put you on another job. The company literally wants to tie you to a machine.

Company Harassment

Or take the piece-work count. Anyone can make a human error. If you have 500 pieces to do, you count them. You might count 500, but maybe a checker will come around later and find only 490. You get a 30-day suspension! They say you are cheating. What we are trying to do is to put a stop to this harassment.

Or take vacation dismissals. The fellows want to get off at 12:00 to start their vacations early. Well, the foreman would not issue them personal passes, so they went home without them. When they came back they were suspended, some for three days, five days, seven days. Company harassment.

One fellow got 90 days off for a roll of tape. They found a roll of masking tape which he left in his work clothes going out the gate.

The Harvester Company Is Flexing Its Muscles

Health and safety are both affected because the plant is kept short of maintenance men and janitors. For example, the snorkel-exhausts for welding and cutting break down faster than the maintenance men can get to them for repairs, but the company won't hire any more men . . . their way of cutting down on overhead. The foremen say they have got to stick within their budget.

Another example: The company would not hire any more janitors, so they had to close up the toilets on the ground floor. Often it is very inconvenient for a fellow to run upstairs to use the toilet. Those that remain open were not cleaned up until the union threatened to bring in the state inspectors.

Right to Ban Overtime Was Lost

Most serious is the question of overtime. As I mentioned, we have never had compulsory overtime. But with every contract the company is coming closer and closer to it. In the last contract the union allowed the elimination of its power to completely ban overtime as a hammer in the grievance demands. Prior to this, the union could ban all overtime if there were outstanding, unresolved grievances. It was one of the most important protections we had.

Sit Down in Allied

Probably the most effective action we have taken was the sit down last fall in the Allied Building, where most of the cutting and welding operations are done. By one o'clock the afternoon of the action, the smoke from the welding machines was so thick you could cut it with a knife. You could not see your hand before your face.

What has been happening is that Harvester has been converting from the old steel-electrode welding to MIG (metal-inert-gas) welding. These machines work much faster. While the old ones had a ten-inch per minute burn-off rate of the electrode, the new machines burn at the rate of 160 inches per minute! They not only increase the workload down the line, but they also give more heat, smoke, and a gas called ozone, which is suspected of causing lung difficulties such as bronchitis and more colds.

The snorkel-exhausts on the machines do not remove the gas fast enough, and the flexible plastic hoses do not last under piece-work conditions. We had been promised fans to help remove the thick smoke, but we never got them. So we decided to stop all the machines. We sat down. Nobody worked. The whites and blacks together. Then we went to the Superintendent's office and stayed there, even though we were told to go back to work. The men stuck together until we won a concession: the company promised to install fans. Today several fans are in place.

Education for Young Workers

The Solidarity Caucus, I think, has played an important role in educating the workers. We have a program of education which we are trying to build around the young workers in the shop. Many of these kids have never been in labor before and they have just come out of the high schools, a few from college. They constitute at least one third of the force. On the day shift,

250 workers are being retired this year, making room for many more youngsters.
    For most of the men over forty or fifty, who fought in the battles of
the early days, struggle is just a romantic notion, although they like to
reflect on it and feel good about it. They just get up once in a while and
have a testimonial to themselves and the good old days.
    Of course we are not trying to build another union within Local 1301, so
we do not have a highly organized form. Anything that the leadership brings
up that is good for the members, we support. The leadership has participated
in the civil rights marches to Selma, they have donated money to various
organizations, and these things stand to their credit, as far as they go.

Caucus Runs on Program

    Basically the caucus is not so much political as it is educational.
When we ran a black for grievance man, it was because there was insufficient
black representation from the membership. We want to choose our own leaders.
And when we ran a white southerner for grievance zoneman, we were not "running
a white." We were running a program. A man will vote for us if he accepts
our program whether he is black or white, and whether our candidate is black
or white. The main reason Solidarity takes the form it does, of black-white
unity from the rank and file itself, is because of the need to put the greatest
possible pressure on the company to regain and maintain our contractual gains.

Proportionate Representation Needed

    Another big thing that is very important here is that we are demonstrating
that blacks can become leaders, too. Here we are trying to show that when
blacks are in control, whites are willing to follow that leadership because it
speaks for them. When we formed a black-white coalition, we blacks joined it
as equals. We were not underdogs in this coalition.
    It is hard for some people to accept this. You see, this is something
that had never happened before. Usually they had mixed caucuses, but blacks
never led them. At one time it was good that a small number of blacks were
allowed to participate in the leadership of the union. Even tokenism had its
place. Today, however, what is needed is not for someone to accept the "black
position" in the leadership, but proportionate representation from the rank
and file.
    The future coalition, I think, will be the Appalachian whites who are
the most dispossessed of the whites and the blacks and Spanish-Americans. The
Solidarity Caucus can provide for the whites and blacks the proper trade union
focus to trade union problems that have been neglected for years. And we can
prove to many of the militant blacks that it is not the white guy who is on
his back, who is chaining him to the ghetto, because the poor white does not
own any ghettos.
    In a way you might say that the black workers in the union are helping
lead a fight with their white brothers to keep alive and to update the traditions of this plant . . . black and white unity, rank and file democracy,
Solidarity against International Harvester.

The Caucus is Fighting on the Issues

By Bill Foster

    I support the Solidarity Caucus and ran on the Solidarity ticket for
grievance zoneman, because the caucus is fighting against a lot of things that
are going on at Harvester that I don't care for.
    Right now the piece workers, especially, are in terrible shape. Harvester
is cutting prices so you just can't make it anymore. Piece-work grievances
are piled over my head, nine or ten months behind. They are not doing anything
with them. After a year or so they just throw them out, and in the meantime
the piece-workers take the brunt.
    They are not giving the black workers a fair shake. In the skilled
trades they might take one in, here and there, every so often, but I know that
more are qualified. Harvester will tell how you did, but they won't let you
actually see the tests. This makes it easy for them to discriminate against
black workers.

It does not bother me that the leadership of the caucus is mainly led by black people. Why should it? I think they have basically the same interest I have.

The opposition knows we are there. When we write a leaflet on some issue, they always come out with something a little more militant! I am sure there will be changes in the next few years, because the union is not serving its members as it should, but the caucus is fighting on the issues.

Investments in Slavery

Every month the company mails us their slick-printed magazine, *IH News*. Its purpose is to make us feel we are part of a great, modern family, to fill us with pride so we will come in and bang out those tractors. Every month they have a story about one or two of their plants. They try to show labor and management working together in harmony for everybody's benefit.

But one plant they never write about. One plant they don't even want us to know about is their plant in South Africa.

Conditions in South Africa are a worldwide scandal. By now, most people know something about a country where three million white colonialists ride on the backs of twelve million Africans and one million "coloreds" -- East Indians and people of mixed blood.

In South Africa, the Africans are restricted to 10% of the land and the most menial jobs. They are denied education, and are not permitted to join or organize unions or political parties.

To show how they have been made prisoners in their own country, all Africans must carry a pass which they must show at any time to any white who demands it, or go to jail. In order to hold a job, travel in the white area or move from town to town, an African must have his pass specifically stamped.

Since 1948, five million Africans have been convicted of "pass violations." In the Sharpeville Massacre of a few years back, 109 Africans were shot down and their bodies stacked up like steel pipe -- for the "crime" of refusing to carry a pass.

We think all Harvester workers should know the truth about how big corporations, including IHC, are involved in the looting and enslavement in South Africa.

IHC South Africa has operations in both production and distribution, centered in Johannesburg. In January of 1968 they sold 120 machines, so you can see it is a going concern. They manufacture farm implements to fit imported tractors, and may be producing Scout trucks as well. (Facts are hard to come by -- they don't let their secrets out). Including Pan-African Industries, which they bought out in 1962, IHC South Africa now employs about 1000 workers, two-thirds African.

Wages and working conditions are governed by South African rules: strict apartheid (segregation), no Africans in unions, and so forth. Average wages in manufacturing in 1963 were as follows: whites $2,881, Africans $590 per year.

Now get this -- here they are in Chicago with their "New Start" program, trying to show how concerned they are with the problems of black people, and there they are in South Africa with their teeth sunk into the neck of the black people.

Did you ever wonder why there are so few black workers in the skilled trades and higher classifications at Tractor Works? It's all part of the same policy.

Give one group (whites) a few miserable crumbs to make them feel better than the rest. That's company policy.

What's our policy? Is the old union principle "An injury to one is an injury to all" out of date?

Solidarity Committee Caucus, UAW Local 1301.

Labor Today (May, 1969).

38. BANNON URGES MORE OPPORTUNITY FOR
MINORITIES TO ENTER TRADES

CINCINNATI, Ohio--New programs are bringing an increasing number of
blacks into the ranks of UAW skilled tradesmen at Ford Motor Co. but far
greater progress is urgently needed, according to UAW Vice President Ken
Bannon. [122]

Bannon urged 100 delegates at a meeting of the UAW Ford skilled trades
subcouncil here to work for expanded opportunities for non-whites in the
trades.

Of the 20,525 UAW members in the apprenticeable trades at Ford, 864--4.2
per cent--are members of minority groups, Bannon said. The ratio in non-
apprenticeable trades is 6.9 per cent of the 4,000 workers.

Bannon, director of the UAW Ford Dept., and Jeff Washington, assistant
director of the UAW Manpower Development and Training Dept., outlined ways in
which local unions may increase opportunities for nonwhites in the skilled
trades.

Washington detailed Project Outreach, a program under which classes are
set up in local unions to provide intensive instruction and counseling to
workers who want to take skilled trades apprenticeship tests.

Other actions taken to increase opportunities for minorities and for
workers disadvantaged by inadequate education include a pre-apprentice program
at several Ford plants. This program allows an applicant who fails a portion
of the apprenticeship tests to undergo instruction aimed at overcoming his
deficiencies.

The UAW also won agreement from Ford to test only current employes,
halting the practice of bringing in new skilled trades apprentices from outside. Testing procedures were changed, allowing greater supervision by the
UAW Ford joint apprenticeship committee. Notices of the tests and the procedures for applying were posted more widely in all plants.

Washington told the skilled tradesmen that while upwards of 30 per cent
of the UAW membership consists of minorities--blacks, Chicanos, Puerto Ricans,
Indians and Orientals--less than five per cent are tradesmen.

"This is the most serious internal problem facing our union today," he
said, adding: "In many areas, if the union doesn't eliminate racial imbalance,
the government is going to do it."

While aimed at improving opportunities for minorities, Project Outreach
has trained more than 1,500 workers, of whom 53 per cent were Caucasians.
Washington noted: "If a member, regardless of color, needs the training, it's
available."

UAW Solidarity (September, 1972).

39. BLACK CAUCUS BUILDS BLACK-WHITE
SOLIDARITY AT CHRYSLER PLANT

By Johnny Woods

"This election wasn't easy--the victory wasn't easy. Racism was used
against the slate. Some of the union officials told the workers the Progressive Slate was an all-black slate. But our candidates for the Election
Committee, three black and three white, ran on the issues, and we won four
out of six spots."

Building Unity

A group of auto workers were talking about the first stage of an election
in their union, Local 110, United Auto Workers, at the Chrysler truck plant in
St. Louis. The Progressive Slate referred to was the outgrowth of what began
as a Black Caucus in the local, expanded to include white workers, and fielded
a slate led by a Black candidate for president and a white candidate for vice
president. The caucus promises to be a growing, dynamic force in the union.

The brothers and sisters told *Labor Today* how the Black Caucus used to discuss racism, speed-up, health and safety--all issues--at their meetings: "We found out as we went along that the problems in the shop were problems that had to be dealt with from a *worker's* point of view. We found out we had to reach out and pull *all* workers together--female, male, Black and white."

Strengthen the Union

Using leaflets written in clear, powerful language aimed right at the brass-tacks issues concerning all workers at the plant, the slate won quick popularity.

But company and some union officials felt threatened by leaflets head-lined: "Only a STRONG UNION can Break the Chains of layoffs, cutbacks, oppression, speedups and unjust firing."

Leaflets declaring: "What we need are candidates who are going to fight against the wage-price freeze, right-to-work laws and other anti-labor legislation . . . And this can only be done with candidates running not on friendship, color, or being a good guy, but on the candidates' knowledge of the issues, as well as willingness to fight for us once elected. *And let it also be added that it is only the rank and file workers that can create this willingness to fight on the part of the elected official.*"

The Whispered Lie

A whispering campaign was launched against the slate. Rumors that it represented a Black group seeking Black control of the union, or even planning to form an all-Black union, began to be heard in the plant.

The Slate answered this and other slander with more leaflets. They showed that the six candidates for the Election Committee were divided not only into three whites, three blacks, but also three day-shifters and three night-shifters.

"We didn't know how effective our leaflets would be," a leader of the Black Caucus said. However, a white worker candidate who was attacked the most by local union officials and some racist white workers for being associated with the so-called black slate--anyway, after the results were in, he had the most votes. A black candidate came in second and the slate finished one, two, three, four out of the six spots."

Progressive Slate

Next came the general elections. The Slate ran 28 candidates. The plat-form dealt with problems faced by all segments of the local. "For instance, we had women workers who were being placed on jobs some men weren't being assigned to because of physical limitations." A perverse "concern" for women's equality found the company putting women on these heavy jobs. And union officials did nothing about it.

They also proposed that the educational committee conduct orientation programs for new workers informing them of the history of unions and the role unions have played in the labor movement.

Racism Dies Hard

But despite--or, really because of--this broad platform aimed at problems shared by all workers, the "all-Black takeover" rumor flew thicker and faster in the general election last June.

The facts of the matter there were only 700 blacks out of 3,000 in the local, and none of the union officials was Black.

"But there was somewhat of a breakdown of sorts in terms of fighting racism," a candidate on the Progressive Slate told *Labor Today*. "Some of the white workers became concerned about their own race (for election) in certain departments. But we had some white workers who stayed with it and who really got out there and fought racism to the end. And we won something like 8 out of 28 races."

The Case of Sister Brown

The Progressive Slate and the Black Caucus did not fight racism in the abstract. "There are so many anti-worker practices underlying racism at the

Chrysler plant and others across the country that any union worthy of the
name should be fighting on this front of the local and international level
every day."

For example, at Local 110 there was the case of Gloria Brown, who was
discharged because she rejected the advances of her foreman.

The foreman "wrote her up" as unable to do her job--a difficult job she
had been switched to after refusing to date him on two occasions. She went
to the union, which had already deducted $80 in dues and initiation fees
from her paychecks.

"They told me there was nothing they could to--I didn't have my 90 days
in."

No One Safe

Sister Brown went to the Black Caucus and a week or two after she was
discharged a leaflet was issued. The leaflet headlined "No One Safe," pointed
out that no worker could be secure in his job if management was permitted to
get rid of a person in the manner in which the foreman McCullough reportedly
discharged Sister Brown.

"It was only after she stood and defended her dignity as a woman and a
worker that she was found to be unsatisfactory."

The leaflet called for Sister Brown's reinstatement and the firing of the
foreman. (Her case is still pending).

The Issue Is Joined

The second half of the leaflet defended the rights of Danny Burns, a
white worker unjustly fired from another department in the plant.

Alonzo Bimbo, a foreman, threw his helmet at Burns, the leaflet charged,
with the intention "not only to harass Danny but also to do bodily harm."
Bimbo was angry because Burns, through no fault of his own, had run out of
material.

About 50 workers saw the incident and signed a petition to the union,
demanding action. They also notified the Black general foreman, Willie Walker,
because, as the leaflet stated, they "felt that he would act to straighten out
the issue because . . . he was once a worker, and being Black, had received
some of the worst treatment."

Stick Together

But Walker stood with the "wrong-doing foreman." And the leaflet
concluded:

"Now all the workers fully understand that company men stick together, no
matter what color the workers are. We as workers must stick together too,
stick together and demand the firing of Bimbo and the firing of McCullough."

Enforce the Contract

The caucus is also demanding strict enforcement of contract provisions
for in-plant promotion.

One leader of the Black Caucus said: "They have hired directly off the
street in order to avoid putting a Black in the skilled trades area. I have
put in for the skilled trades--carpentry--and I have my apprenticeship hours
in. But I never heard from management and they have hired directly off the
street since my application's been in. It would be more than a dollar an hour
for me if I were in carpentry."

Selling Us Short

The Black Caucus also feels the UAW is selling out to management in the
area of so-called productivity. As one brother put it: "The first thing they
say when they sit down at contract time with management is that management
reserves the right to run the plant. It's about the first thing they (union
leaders) agree on when they go up to bat."

As a result, in the speed-up and the use of smaller work forces to do more
and more producing, the dispensary and even the morgue fill up."

"They have millwrights," one Chrysler worker said, "so when a line breaks
down from too much stress and strain and too many hours running, they have men
to come and get it back in operation.

"Your body performs so many hours and you don't have anybody to come put it back in operation. And after 10 hours a day, six days a week, if you have to just, like, rest it, and take a day off because you're exhausted, that's not good enough unless you have a doctor's statement."

"They want you to have a heart attack."

Bored, Hell! We're Tired!

Another worker agreed: "If they don't fight for these things at contract time this time, we're just in trouble all over again. When I first started with the UAW, I thought things were supposed to get better. I thought we were supposed to progress. With automation the job should get easier over the years, for everybody.

But it ain't working like that. When I started, we were on eight hour schedules. But now, as far as I'm concerned the eight hour day is just non-existent. It's just on the books. We're working ten hours a day--and more often than not, six days a week!" Hooting at Woodcock's harmony proposal, he said: "We're out there on the line and they're up there in the office. No way we can get together and play 'hand-shakey'!"

Bright Future Ahead for the Union

A veteran member of the caucus described the election campaign as "historical." He went on to say: "We had a Black candidate for president who got the most votes on the first ballot, although he lost in the run-off. Our candidate for vice-president won. We had Black and white candidates running for offices throughout the structure. And a Black won election for a plant-wide office--the first time."

This brother sees greater successes ahead, and a bright future for the union: ". . . because the caucus is concerned with the well-being of *all* workers . . . By educating the workers, making them more aware, I think we started on the road to make a progressive union. Because we gave leadership, some of the incumbents, and some of the people elected on their slate have come to the Black Caucus and agreed to work with us on Standing Committees."

"The recently published positions of the union officials who have just won, are very similar to the ones that the Caucus presented prior to the election."

"We're breathing down their backs. We're not really opposing them. We're just trying to make them more progressive.

Labor Today (July, 1973).

40.   BLACK-WHITE CAUCUSES WIN UAW LOCAL OFFICES

By Ted Pearson

CHICAGO, July 19--"There is a movement developing, if this year's local elections in the United Auto Workers Union are any indication, that's going to shove the 'harmony clause' somewhere other than down the throats of the workers" declared Fred Gaboury, national field organizer for the National Coordinating Committee for Trade Union Action and Democracy (TUAD).

The *Daily World* interviewed Gaboury in his office here seeking the view of the workers related to TUAD, on the negotiations opened last week (July 10-18) between the UAW and the auto and farm equipment manufacturers.

Official union demands at the bargaining table, important as they may be, are only part of the story, according to Gaboury. The attitude represented by the so-called harmony clause is deeply resented. It states that "the growth and success of the company are of direct interest to the workers and their union, and the growth and success of the union are of direct interest to the company."

In St. Louis, Milwaukee and Chicago, to name but a few, major UAW locals have either dumped or strongly challenged old leadership that imitates this attitude.

First Black President

At the Chrysler Truck Plant in St. Louis, for example, Bill Robinson, the first Black candidate for president of UAW Local 126, compelled a run-off election, and carried eight of his Black Caucus running mates (some of whom are white) to victory.

The Black and white slate of the "Black Caucus" ran on a hard-hitting campaign which attacked both racist and sex discrimination against Blacks and women. Their literature lacks the polish of professional union politicians, but its message comes through loud and clear, with case-by-case calls to action on behalf of individual Black and women workers who have been harassed or abused by the company and its foremen.

A record 2,000 of the 3,000 members of Local 126 voted in the election. One of the Black Caucus candidates who won was Chet Lundstrom, for vice president. Lundstrom is white.

Black Trustee

Another is Willard Anderson, who was elected on the Caucus ticket as trustee. He is the first Black worker to win a plant-wide office in the union.

In Milwaukee, at the American Motors Body plant, Ted Silverstein piled up 750 votes for vice president in an election in which 2,400 of the shop's 3,000 workers voted. Running on the "Black and White Get It Together" Caucus ticket (B&WGIT), Silverstein and his two white and two Black running mates struck great interest among the rank and file. They campaigned against speed-up, disciplinary discharges and racist discrimination against Black workers in the skilled trades. Their rallies drew more than local union meetings. Their house meetings were jammed.

Local 75's incumbent leadership itself does not have such a bad reputation for taking up grievances (even if it doesn't win too many), so the B&WGIT vote takes on even greater significance.

Training School

Local 75 recently set up a pre-apprentice training school in order to qualify Black and Latin workers for company apprentice programs in spite of racist tests. When the company opened up the apprentice program before the school was completed, the B&WGIT Caucus asked the union to demand that the company wait. Instead, many white stewards were observed scurrying to sign up white workers in the apprentice program in order to keep those enrolled in the school from having a chance.

Of the 36 workers in the school, 18 were white and 18 Black. The union brass sacrificed both to keep the skilled trades lily-white. This made a deep impression on both Black and white not alone the 36 to whom had been promised the apprenticeships. It was no small factor generating support among white and Black for the B&WGIT slate.

In Local 6 at the Melrose Park plant of International Harvester near Chicago, a strong commitment to rank and file demands for substantial wage increase, ending speed-up and compulsory overtime and ending racism carried Norman Roth into the presidency. Roth's Black and white caucus did not carry any others on his slate with him however, although their vote was significant.

As in the other two locals mentioned, Roth's campaign hit hardest at do-nothing leadership. His majority was based among the Black and Latino workers, with important sections of whites.

"To sum it up," concluded Gaboury, "the demands for an end to compulsory overtime, for a cost of living clause that doesn't leave the workers behind and for '30 and out' are being made because the rank and file are demanding them. But as these elections show, they are demanding much more, and could upset the applecart yet under conditions of Nixon's Phase IV."

Daily World, July 20, 1973.

41.   STEPP NAMED FIRST BLACK UAW
HEAD AT BIG 3 PLANT

By William Allan

DETROIT, June 8--Mark Stepp, Black vice-president of the United Auto
Workers, has been appointed to head the union's Chrysler department. This is
the first time a Black UAW leader will head one of the union's departments at
the Big Three firms.
Douglas Fraser, newly elected UAW president, held his first executive
board meeting here and proposed Stepp to succeed him as top negotiator at
Chrysler.
Stepp was elected international vice president by the executive board in
1974 and was reelected at the recent Los Angeles convention.
Fraser also named Martin Gerber, a new UAW vice-president, to be in
charge of technical, office and professional organizing work. Gerber was also
appointed by the Board to be in charge of organizing work for the UAW, formerly
handled by vice-president Pat Greathouse.
In the last three years the UAW has recruited only a little over 60,000
new members.
Fraser will retain command of the skilled trades department of the UAW.
In addition, he will be the new chairman of the national Community Action
Program (CAP), the union's political arm. During the debate in the Los
Angeles convention on reaffiliation with the AFL-CIO, delegates active in CAP
registered loud beefs about having to work with AFL-CIO top leaders. Specif-
ically they mentioned that in New York State and New Jersey AFL-CIO COPE
leaders were consorting with Rockefeller types, and fear exists amongst UAW-
CAP activists that reaffiliation with the AFL-CIO could mean that CAP will be
swallowed up by COPE.
Fraser, in a wrapup press conference in Los Angeles, said he would advise
state and local CAP organizations to "keep their options open" with the AFL-
CIO.
In Michigan where the UAW has an estimated 600,000 members, the AFL-CIO
about 300,000 and the Teamsters 100,000, the COPE and CAP and DRIVE organizations have worked together for some years. Fraser together with Robert Holmes,
International vice president of the Teamsters, and Bill Marshall, state head
of the AFL-CIO along with the State Building Trades Council, formed a United
Labor Coalition some years back and helped elect Coleman Young as Detroit's
first Black mayor.

Daily World, June 9, 1977.

42.   LABOR, BLACKS MEET, MAP POLITICAL PUSH

By Geoffrey Jacques

DETROIT, Oct. 17--Representatives of 95 national organizations met here
today to organize a counterattack against the political right and to demand
action by the Carter Administration for the people's welfare. The meeting was
initiated by the United Auto Workers.
Rep. Ron Dellums (D-Cal.) gave a program for "turning things around," as
the principal speaker at the morning session. [123]
"We here have a common frame of reference," Dellums said. "We 95 organizations have spoken up against racism, against exploitation, against the
bloated military budget. We must fight for the people who are not being
served by the system -- the Blacks, the Hispanics, the elderly, the women."
Dellums stressed that the country was not moving to the right.
"It's just that we have let the right articulate the issues," he declared.
The emerging labor-liberal coalition, he said, could develop a program
that can "unite the middle class and the oppressed peoples."

Fraser's Statement

At a crowded news conference at Cobo Hall this morning, Douglas A. Fraser, UAW president stated:

"We're on a collision course with the Democratic Party and they ought to be put on notice about that.

"The politics of personality and not the politics of principle are being practiced in Washington," Fraser continued.

This meeting, which included leaders of 20 national unions and 75 national civil rights, environmental, and women's organizations, will demand both "accountability and responsibility" from the Democratic Party, Fraser said. . . .

Daily World, October 18, 1978.

BUILDING TRADES

43. NAACP BATTLE FRONT

A delegation of representatives of the NAACP met separately with state and city fair employment agencies on January 26 in an effort to obtain firm commitments that Negro skilled workers will be employed in the construction of new school buildings in New York City.

The meetings were arranged in response to telegrams sent by Herbert Hill, NAACP Labor Secretary, to George Fowler, chairman of the State Commission for Human Rights and to Stanley Lowell, chairman of the City Commission on Human Rights.

Mr. Hill and W. Eugene Sharpe, chairman of the New York State NAACP labor committee, headed the Association delegation.

Citing Federal, state and municipal statutes and executive orders banning racial discrimination in publicly-financed construction work, Mr. Hill charged that the city "will be a direct party to the continuing pattern of discrimination against Negroes if city contractors are permitted to use 'lily-white' union hiring halls as sole source of labor recruitment in violation of the law."

The NAACP labor secretary asked for an "immediate conference to discuss specific enforcement of anti-discrimination laws before construction is begun on municipal school contracts." He further warned that "refusal of the Commission to enforce fully the law can only lead to public protests by unemployed Negro workers in New York City who are the victims of systematic exclusion from skilled craft jobs in the New York building and construction industry."

Mr. Hill's telegrams were dispatched Monday, January 18, following announcement that Mayor Robert F. Wagner had approved $14 million in construction contracts for four new schools.[124]

In another development, Mr. Hill met with New Jersey Governor Richard J. Hughes in Trenton on January 27 to protest the use of public funds in the construction of state buildings on which skilled Negro workers are not employed. John F. Davis of Newark, a member of the NAACP national Board of Directors, joined Mr. Hill in the conference.[125]

Backing up the protest was a 75-person picket line at the construction site of the new Rutgers University Law School in Newark. Included in the line were members and supporters of the Newark NAACP Branch. Picketing of the site of the state institution began on January 20.

Meanwhile, in Cleveland, Ohio, the Iron and Structural Steel Workers Union agreed to admit the first five Negro applicants into the union's apprenticeship program. Agreement was reached after action by the Cleveland

NAACP Branch to secure cancellation of the $32 million contract for construction of a Federal Office building.

CLOSED SHOP, CLOSED UNIONS

The craft unions in the construction industry are "closed unions operating closed shops," Roy Wilkins, executive director of the NAACP, charged in an address at the third national conference of Plans for Progress held in Washington, D.C., on January 26.

In addition to Mr. Wilkins, Vice President Hubert H. Humphrey and Whitney Young Jr., participated in the conference called by the President's Committee on Equal Employment Opportunity and attended by 500 top executives of the nation's major corporations.

The Vice President called for an all-out effort by big industry to curb the "massive unemployment among nonwhite workers in our cities." Mr. Young warned that Negro unemployment is "approaching a catastrophe."

"Construction unions," Mr. Wilkins said, "have imposed de facto closed shop arrangements that give the union effective job control. As far as the Negro worker is concerned, the skilled craft locals in the building and construction trades are closed unions operating closed shops.

"This, of course, is clear violation of the National Labor Relations Act as well as of executive orders banning racial discrimination. The excuse of unemployment in this industry is not valid." He cited a recent New York City report indicating an increase of 20,000 jobs in construction in that city.

The NAACP leader reviewed the efforts of the Association to level the color bar in construction industry employment in Philadelphia, New York City, Cleveland and elsewhere. Also cited were the more than 900 complaints filed by the NAACP with the President's Committee alleging job discrimination in plants of some of the country's largest corporations.

"The history of government contract compliance in relation to anti-discrimination provisions indicates that so-called 'voluntary compliance' is an inadequate approach," he said. Plans for Progress was instituted as a means of securing voluntary compliance with executive orders requiring non-discrimination.

"The encrusted traditions of anti-Negro practices by employers and certain powerful labor unions have become the traditional pattern in many industries and is deeply resistant to change," he asserted.

"If real significant gains are to be made for Negroes, not just token and symbolic breakthroughs, then something much more vigorous and pattern-oriented than the hesitant approach that is suggested by the term 'voluntary compliance' is required," Mr. Wilkins told the industry leaders.

Recent rulings by the NLRB holding "that discrimination by a labor union is an unfair labor practice" were hailed by Mr. Wilkins as a "new note of progress." He cited also a noticeable increase of Negroes in higher-paying positions in government, industry, films and television.

The Crisis, 72 (March, 1965):164-66.

44. NY BUILDING TRADES UNIONS FACE DISCRIMINATION HEARINGS

William H. Booth, chairman of the N.Y. City Commission on Human Rights said he will ask a full meeting of the civil rights body on March 30 to set public hearings to determine whether the building trades unions have made progress against discrimination since the 1963 hearings.

Booth's announcement came after Peter J. Brennan, president of the Building and Construction Trades Council of New York told newsmen in Washington he had no plans to submit reports on discrimination conditions in the council's affiliates requested by Booth. He said Booth should request each local for such data.[126]

Booth said last Sunday he set a week's deadline for submission of the reports in letters to Brennan and to Harry Van Arsdale, president of the

Central Labor Council, after the two told him progress had been made in integrating some of the lilywhite areas, and promised him reports within two weeks. But such reports never came, he said.[127]

Brennan, attending the Building trades legislative conference in Washington, termed Booth's action "political."

Booth said his move in the unions parallels his letters to 15 major suppliers to the city in which he asked them why they don't employ more Negroes and Puerto Ricans.

Booth said he is seeking an executive order from Mayor Lindsay directing companies to comply with equal job opportunities laws on pain of cancellation of contracts with them.

Booth appeared to be dissatisfied with the rate of integration in the apprenticeship program of Electrical, Local 3, a union that has been cited for comparatively more advanced efforts to get Negro and Puerto Rican youths into its apprenticeship program. Recently, said Booth in an interview, Van Arsdale took him to the apprenticeship school of Local 3.

"Sure enough," said Booth, "there was a sprinkling of Negroes among the apprentices. But I told him that didn't prove anything, I'd have to see figures."

The 1963 hearings, an aftermath of the wave of civil rights demonstrations at construction projects that year, showed that certain building trades unions were almost 100 percent lilywhite, notably in sheet metal, plumbers and iron workers.

The Worker, March 27, 1966.

45. BUILDING TRADES TAKE SOLID
STAND AGAINST DISCRIMINATION

Bal Harbour, Fla.--Delegates from AFL-CIO Building Trades unions voted unanimously here that "we wholeheartedly support apprenticeship programs and selection procedures which are nondiscriminatory, uniform and fair."

Members of 18 unions representing 3.5 million tradesmen in the U.S. and Canada made it clear that "we oppose and will not tolerate discrimination" and, while favoring efforts to encourage the entry of minority-group members into the skilled trades, they will continue to oppose any lowering of the standards each trade has maintained over the years for the admission of new members.

Delegates to the 54th convention of the AFL-CIO Building & Construction Trades Dept. acted on the subject of hiring practices and apprentice training regulations in two resolutions affirming that:

* The department endorses generally the "principle of affirmative action to assist Negroes and other minority group persons in finding suitable employment" and invites Labor Dept. officials to discuss the matter in depth with B&CTD representatives "in the hope that sources of conflict may be diminished and a higher degree of cooperation obtained."

* Delegates condemn the use of the Office of Federal Contract Compliance, a Labor Dept. agency, of such a formula as "minority representation in every craft in every phase of the work" on every federal building project. Such formulas are "often impossible of fulfillment and destructive of working conditions and performance standards."

* The construction unions call on contractors to join in opposing such "unrealistic approaches and unsound formulas which could destroy the efficiency and flexibility of an industry which historically has met the needs of the country in war and peace" and "can continue to meet those needs totally and without discrimination."

A convention committee drafted a resolution detailing labor's objections to proposed regulations for federal apprentice training programs which find the unions "guilty before trial" of discriminatory practices, and destroy the voluntary character of training programs supported by Building Trades unions and the contractors who hire their members.

Labor Sec. W. Willard Wirtz, a convention speaker, said he had read the resolution on the proposed changes and "while I don't go along with everything" in the department's list of objections, "I think it is an error" to talk in terms of "one or more Negroes or whites or anybody else as being required" on every single construction job.

Wirtz said he will talk further about the apprenticeship rules at a January meeting with a departmental committee of union presidents.

AFL-CIO Pres. George Meany, noting that the federation has a policy against racial discrimination "to which I completely subscribe," said he was "quite sure" the Building Trades Dept. adheres to that policy. In today's world, which is largely non-white, it is "just a matter of good common sense, as well as a matter of decent human relations, to eliminate discrimination," he declared.

He asked the 255 delegates "how do you get these new members that they say it is desirable to have? How do you get colored boys into these highly skilled trades? Well, you get them in the way you have always gotten" union members.

Meany recalled that he had had to pass an examination as a journeyman 50 years ago to join his local union of Plumbers in New York City, he added "I don't mind telling you that I failed the first examination. And it was on the level because my father was president of the union."

Meany said his father was "just as sore as hell--not at the examining board that turned me down, but at me. And I had to wait six months and serve another six months as an apprentice" before taking another exam.

There is "no other way" to meet the problem of screening untrained applicants for membership than by the apprenticeship route, and "no short cut," the AFL-CIO president declared. "And when we bring them in as apprentices," he asked, "do we lower the standards? I say absolutely no. We do not compromise the standards."

Meany was strongly applauded when he said "I think we should say to all government agencies that we are prepared to follow the AFL-CIO policy of non-discrimination but that we are not prepared to lower the standards of our industry or trade to do that."

The convention received greetings from Pres. Johnson in a message and heard major addresses from two members of his cabinet--Wirtz and Sec. Robert C. Weaver of the Dept. of Housing & Urban Development. Other speakers included Pres. Paul Hall of the Seafarers, Dr. Donald Shulman of the AFL-CIO Dept. of Civil Rights, and Deputy Dir. Joseph Rourke of the federation's Committee on Political Education.[128]

New four-year terms in office were voted without contest for Dept. Pres. C. J. Haggerty and Sec.-Treas. Frank Bonadio, and two-year terms for the department's 10 vice presidents, all top officers of affiliated unions.

Bonadio reported that, since the 1965 convention, the department chartered 22 new councils and issued more than 1 million quarterly membership cards to building tradesmen whose unions applied for them.

In other actions, the convention voted to support the present Administration policy on Viet Nam but strongly condemned the activities of two government departments--that of the comptroller general for assertedly advising the Atomic Energy Commission and other federal agencies that they need not observe prevailing wage rates set by Wirtz for contractors on federal construction jobs, and the Office of Federal Contract Compliance, which was accused of trying to force hiring quotas for a specified number of minority-group members on contractors and unions.

Weaver praised Haggerty for welcoming the opportunity to provide workers and to train new workers for the model cities program and other programs designed to rebuild rundown neighborhoods in 63 demonstration cities. Weaver also proposed that organized labor help raise $1 billion to match the amount pledged by U.S. insurance companies to "create new and rehabilitated" housing.

Slaiman reported that in the civil rights area "we are making progress." Building Trades councils and local unions are "taking in large numbers of minority group youngsters into apprenticeship trades," Slaiman said. He cited two examples--120 Negroes and Puerto Ricans were in the graduating class recently of 800 journeymen and apprentices sponsored by New York Local 3 of the Intl. Brotherhood of Electrical Workers; and the Washington, D.C. Bricklayers local has 800 Negro journeymen in its ranks.

Rourke warned of the need for extensive COPE campaigns and the collection of badly needed COPE dollars in coming election campaigns. He said
"there are at least 10 friendly senators who could go down to defeat unless
we do the job." He added: "If we lose 30 more congressmen--and it can
happen--we'll have the book thrown at us" in the form of punitive laws.

Earlier, Haggerty had advised local unions to seek qualified craftsmen
in city areas and start trainee programs "for those area youths who show an
interest and an aptitude."

Hall reported that the Maritime Trades Dept., which he also heads, is
preparing to release a detailed study of the adverse impact of the Landrum-
Griffin Act and the way it is used against unions. A similar study will be
made of the National Labor Relations Board, Hall said.

He reported that in the South and some other areas, employers can get
an "ex parte injunction" against unions any time they want one, and receive
prompt action from NLRB regional officials while unions must wait "anywhere
from three months to six months" for decisions that could be made in a few
days or a week at most.

Pres. Thomas J. Murray of the Chicago-Cook County Building & Construc-
tion Trades Council gave the oath of office to the top officers and the
following vice presidents: M. A. Hutcheson, Carpenters; Gordon M. Freeman,
Intl. Brotherhood of Electrical Workers; Peter T. Schoemann, Plumbers &
Pipefitters; Edward J. Leonard, Plasterers; John H. Lyons, Iron Workers;
Russell K. Berg, Boilermakers; Hunter P. Wharton, Operating Engineers;
Thomas F. Murphy, Bricklayers; Peter Fosco, Laborers, and L. M. Raftery,
Painters.[129]

AFL-CIO press release, December 4, 1967. Copy in possession of the editors.

46. BUILDING UNIONS BOILING OVER GOV'T.
HIRING RULING

MINORITY WORK GAIN SIGHTED

PHILADELPHIA -- A rapidly accelerating showdown between industrial
building unions and the Federal government's new policy of having regional
Federal agencies pools insist on population-proportionate hiring of Negroes
on all roads, buildings or other contracts using federal money, was developing here this week.

The new Federal agency pool policy of immediately and fully ruling on
minority hiring and subsequent cancellation of contracts, without months of
red tape, has infuriated both contractors and building trades unions.

The plan has been put into practice in Cleveland first, where much of
the current racial peace has been attributed to the program, and later in
Philadelphia.

In Philadelphia in recent weeks, it has resulted in cancellation of a
$37.7 million contract to a builder to construct a new U.S. Mint. It has
voided contracts for $97 millions in U.S. aided road construction and the
re-allocation of millions of dollars more being planned for roads in
Pennsylvania next year.

The not-yet-allocated millions of dollars for such road work will be
used to appeal House Ways and Means Chairman Wilbur Mills' demand that
federal domestic spending be cut in light of threats of inflation and Vietnam war demands, it was said.

It has also resulted in cancellation for $19 millions worth of federally-
aided building construction.

The regional Office of Federal Contract Compliance said that it will
also affect another $50-million to $75-million in Federally-funded construction, outside of road work, within the next three or four months.

That is, said the OFFC official, if contractors fail to provide an
unequivocal commitment and proof that they have hired the proper share of
minority workmen at most levels.

The impasse has produced "crash" training programs for Negro youths who are to be paid apprenticeship wages while learning in both Philadelphia and Pittsburgh.

Last week a Philadelphia Councilman, W. Thatcher Longstreth, asked the Federal government to institute a three-month moratorium on the Regional Pool of Federal Agencies Plan in Philadelphia. He also asked for an immediate summit conference among unions, contractors and Federal officials.

The new program of the Regional Federal Agencies Pools follows quickly on a report made by NAACP labor secretary Herbert Hill the first week in April in which he stated he had evidence of a secret agreement of officials of the U.S. Labor Dept. with contractors and unions to institute a "token" training program for Negroes in crafts union trades. The NAACP's Hill said the agreement purported that the Federal contracts would continue "lily-white" despite the token training program.

All this seems to be changed now, as far as the Government is concerned, although Hill has threatened that the NAACP will file suits over the issue.

In light of the cancellations and the new practices, James Loughlin, business-manager of the 30,000-member Philadelphia Building and Construction Trades Council which includes 55 local unions, said:

> "The feeling in some of our unions is that if they try
> to put non-union members into these jobs, our people will
> just walk off the job."

Loughlin said he feels that the new Regional Federal Agencies Pool program is "only a move to destroy the apprentice programs and standards we have developed over the past 50 years."

He said he believes the plan is illegal in that it "infers a quota system on a race basis for hiring."

He blasted OFCC coordinator Bennett O. Stallworth, who is director of the Regional Federal Agencies Pool, for "only talking to the Trades Council once in 19 months."

His views were supported by Joseph F. Burke, president of the Sheet Metal Workers Local 19, which has a membership of 1400, of which only three are Negroes.

Burke said his union had tried to enlist Negro apprentices but the results have been "disappointing." He said that since 1963 the union took applications from 1148 persons, of whom 99 were Negroes.

Out of the 99 he said 88 qualified to take the entrance test. However, when the tests were given only 60 showed up.

Out of the 60, only 11 passed and were invited to start the apprentice program, but only three showed up.

He did not say how small the number of Negroes was expected to be when the Negro apprentice group reached the journeyman stage.

Burke said this was a typical experience in dealing with getting Negroes into the industrial unions programs.

Meanwhile, Bayard Rustin, outstanding Negro civil rights leader who is executive director of the A. Philip Randolph Institute, said: "The unions are certainly the only major institution that wholly subscribes to, and substantially embodies in its own programs, the proposals and priorities outlined in the Freedom Budget for All Americans."

The Freedom Budget, which had been endorsed by such other Negro leaders as Dr. Martin Luther King Jr., the Urban League's Whitney Young and others is the ultimate goal of the "Poor People's Campaign" set to converge in May from all parts of the nation on Washington D.C.

The Freedom Budget is a program devised by Leon Keyserling, who served as national budget director for President Truman and a task force of the nation's best national economists, as a formula for ridding the United States of both poverty and racism in the next ten years by a budget of $185 billions and a $2-per-hour national minimum wage.

Pittsburgh Courier, May 4, 1968.

47. OPPOSITION TO PHILADELPHIA PLAN

RESOLUTION NO. 187--By Delegate Maywood Boggs; Metal Trades Department, AFL-CIO.

WHEREAS, The building trades in its efforts to meet the growing demand for skilled craftsmen have in the past worked hand-in-glove with the federal government to select and train the most qualified young men for the skilled trades, and

WHEREAS, This training program has become selective due to the higher skills needed to perform the highly diversified tasks within our industry requiring more education and dedication, and

WHEREAS, The building trades through its own efforts has made progress and its participating in projects which will give minority groups more equal opportunity based on fair and impartial qualifying examinations, and

WHEREAS, The Philadelphia Plan is high-handed, ambiguous and is trying to be enforced without due process, and

WHEREAS, The contractors through the competitive bidding process and government specifications are required to have the best craftsmen possible in order to meet competition and specifications, and

WHEREAS, the Philadelphia Plan can in no way produce instant mechanics regardless of color, and

WHEREAS, This plan can only increase the cost to the contractor and cause detriment to all effected trades, and

WHEREAS, The revised Philadelphia Plan is in definite conflict with the Civil Rights Act of 1964 whereby quotas for Negro or other minority employment are disallowed by law, and

WHEREAS, The Civil Rights Act of 1964 can be searched in vain for authorization to require such programs; therefore, be it

RESOLVED: That the AFL-CIO use all the power and persuasiveness at its means to defeat this plan, to the point and including the withholding of all manpower from any federal project perpetuating this plan, and be it further

RESOLVED: That this Convention prevail upon the Congress to enforce the Civil Rights Act of 1964 by striking down the Philadelphia Plan as not meeting the requirements of the act; and, be it further

RESOLVED, That this Convention prevail further upon Congress to withhold funds from any federal projects where this Philadelphia Plan, or similar plan, is being enforced.

Proceedings of the Eighth Constitutional Convention of the AFL-CIO, Atlantic City, October 2-7, 1969, Vol. I, pp. 472-73.

48. REVISED PHILADELPHIA PLAN

RESOLUTION NO. 270

WHEREAS, The Building and Construction Trades Department (AFL-CIO) has been engaged in a program of practical affirmative action to increase the employment of Negroes and other minority groups in the building and construction industry which has produced substantial, concrete results, and

WHEREAS, The Building and Construction Trades Department (AFL-CIO) at its 55th Convention in Atlantic City, New Jersey adopted a Statement of Policy which strengthened and expanded its affirmative action program, and

WHEREAS, The department's Statement of Policy declared that:

"We are convinced that the goal of increasing Negro and other minority worker participation in the building and construction trades can be accomplished with due regard to the rights of the existing organized work force. We think such an approach is preferable to unthinking actions which tend to pit one part of the population against the other." and

WHEREAS, The Amended Revised Philadelphia Plan is a part of a pattern of conduct formulated by political strategists in the Nixon administration to divide the labor movement while slowing the process of implementing the civil rights program on voting and education in the South, and

WHEREAS, The Revised Philadelphia Plan was adopted after an admittedly improper procedure which was described by the Assistant Secretary of Labor in charge of the Office of Federal Contract Compliance as follows: ". . . in Philadelphia we announced the Plan then did the hard research." and

WHEREAS, The "hard research" consisted among other things of describing as "Surveys Conducted by Agencies of the United States Department of Labor" a memorandum to the files by one government employe quoting another government employe's "conservative estimates" of "minority manpower available." On the crucial question of minority manpower available, the Philadelphia Order is based also on a single typewritten sheet of "estimates" which apparently became a "Manpower Administration Survey" by writing those words in pencil in the upper right hand corner of the typewritten sheet, and

WHEREAS, the unsubstantiated statistics in this matter raise a serious question as to whether the high standards applicable to the fact finding processes of the Department of Labor have been fulfilled, and

WHEREAS, the Comptroller General of the United States, a non-political officer, who cannot be accused of partiality toward the labor movement, ruled the Philadelphia Revised Plan illegal (August 5, 1969) as in conflict with the Civil Rights Act of 1964, and

WHEREAS, There is doubt as to the validity of the after-the-fact ruling of the Attorney General on the said Revised Philadelphia Plan issued September 22, 1969, and

WHEREAS, The Amended Revised Philadelphia Plan continues the quota system under new legal verbiage, and

WHEREAS, It is clearly evident that the Department of Labor is approaching the question of employment opportunities in the construction industry in a manner highly discriminatory to that industry and unlike the government's approach to other industries such as the textile mills in the South as evidenced by the approved affirmative action program of the J. P. Stevens Company where the "goals" are determined by the company rather than the government and where it is specifically stated that these goals and timetables "will not be interpreted as numerical quotas . . .", and

WHEREAS, The Amended Revised Philadelphia Plan in addition to its illegality and lack of foundation in fact is impracticable and unworkable.

RESOLVED: That this Convention go on record as opposing the Philadelphia Plan, the Revised Philadelphia Plan, and the Amended Revised Philadelphia Plan.

RESOLVED FURTHER: That the Secretary of Labor is requested to make a personal inquiry into the fact finding and other procedures leading to the issuance of the Amended Revised Philadelphia Plan to ascertain their consistency with the otherwise high standards of the Department of Labor and to take appropriate action on the basis of such inquiry.

The Committee recommends adoption of Resolution 222, and I so move.

. . . The recommendation of the Committee was adopted.

Proceedings of the Eighth Constitutional Convention of the AFL-CIO, Atlantic City, October 2-7, 1969, Vol. I, pp. 472-73.

49.   BLACK CLAIMS BIAS IN UNION TRAINING PLAN

By Martin J. Herman

Randolph Hughes signed up for a six-month program to learn how to operate heavy equipment three years ago with a belief he would be making $15,000 a year after completion.

Hughes finished confident he could operate a wide variety of construction equipment. But his dream of a high salary never materialized.

It took him nearly a month after graduation to find his first job. And his first-year salary was $6,900. This year he's made even less -- about $2,500.

Discrimination Charged

The reason for his frustration, Hughes, a black man, claims, is racial discrimination by Local 542 of the International Union of Operating Engineers which ran the now defunct training program.

Hughes said in one year he was referred to 23 different jobs by Local 542. Some lasted a few days; others several weeks.

Some, he said, were long distances from his home, 6253 Old York Road, and most were of the lowest paying in the union, which has a top rate of $8.13 per hour for cherry picker and back hoe operators.

Class Action Suit

Hughes, 30, and several other program graduates, spoke at a press conference called by Community Legal Services Inc. and Attorney General J. Shane Creamer to announce a class action suit seeking to remedy discrimination against blacks by Local 542, four contractors associations and a private contractor.

The suit, filed in U.S. District Court, alleges that the defendants have consistently discriminated against blacks and other minority groups to keep them from union membership and high-paying jobs that are available to whites.

The suit specifically lists 12 black persons, most of whom attended the press conference at 311 S. Juniper St. But it seeks to represent the entire class of persons who are so discriminated against.

Claimed 900 Black Members

It alleges that Local 542 was exempted from the Philadelphia Plan for Negro hiring on the basis of its claim that it already had 900 black members and an agreement that the union made with the Federal Government. The agreement was that the local would take more blacks into the union and add blacks to its apprenticeship program and upgrade the existing skills of black members then on union roles.

The suit states that the union actually has 193 black members and undertook to provide these benefits through two training programs which were financed by the state and Federal governments. Pennsylvania paid 80 percent of the cost of the programs which cost $1.2 million.

The money went to rent obsolete equipment at "prime rates," and to pay white instructors also "prime rates," the suit alleges.

'Non Marketable Skills'

"In reality the blacks were trained on obsolete equipment and taught non-marketable skills, and only a handful ever received union membership," the suit claims. The suit asked the court to supervise recruitment and job training programs of the union.

Hughes said yesterday that some of the trainees have not yet gone to work.

Those blacks who did get job referrals, he claimed, were those "who went along with anything the union said." Hughes said he could not operate all types of equipment.

'Because I Was Black'

"I don't think I was discriminated against because of my inexperience," he added. "Only because I was black."

Howard Goodman, a CLS lawyer, said the union refers candidates to jobs through a hiring hall and that this is one way the union performed some of the discrimination. He claimed that a chronological system of referring men should be established.

Creamer said he believed it was the first time such an action had been taken against a labor union by the state. He said after investigating the allegations the state felt it was "in the public interest" to join with the CLS in the suit.

Tighter Controls Needed

William H. Wilcox, secretary of the state Department of Community Affairs, said tighter controls will have to be instituted to see the problem

does not occur again. He said the program did not provide the help expected
for training the hard-core unemployed.

In addition to the union, the other defendants are the General Building
Contractors Association, Ind., Contractors Association of Eastern Pennsylvania Excavating Contractors Association and Glasgow Organization.

The Evening Bulletin (Philadelphia), November 9, 1971.

50. LEAP

PROJECT LEAP TO ADD JOURNEYMEN COMPONENT

As announced in late January, USDL's Manpower Administration awarded
1.6 million dollars to the National Urban League to extend LEAP's national
contract until August 31, 1971.

The late Whitney Young's subsequent surprise visit to the White House
netted an additional award of 1.8 which brings the total package to 3.4.
These additional monies are to be used to expand LEAP projects in 10 new
cities. More important, though, it provides for a journeyman training
component for eleven existing LEAP projects. The new component to be implemented as a unit under current outreach structures establishes a new route
of entry into the building trades for minorities. The JTP will recruit,
prep, and follow-up on two new groups. Skilled craftsmen who heretofore
were unable to secure journeymen status and semi-skilled craftsmen, mechanics
who are unable to meet Apprenticeship requirements, who with additional
training can achieve journeyman status.

Cities designated by USDL for the journeymen training program are cities
where Hometown Plans have not been developed: Akron, Atlanta, Baltimore,
Columbus, Dayton, Hartford, Milwaukee, Minneapolis, St. Paul, Omaha, Port-
land, St. Louis and Tacoma. Although New Orleans has a hometown plan it has
been added to the list because the plan is under sponsorship.

Priority cities on USDL's list for new LEAP projects are: Albany, New
York; Louisville, Kentucky; Rockford, Illinois; Toledo, Ohio; Springfield,
Illinois; Pueblo, Colorado; and Jefferson City, Missouri.

"WHY APPRENTICESHIP OUTREACH FAILS"

At the Atlanta Conference site, Don Slaiman, Director, AFL-CIO Civil
Rights Department, discussed conclusions he has drawn after carefully
assessing current apprenticeship outreach programs.

"The reasons they fail" said Slaiman, "has to do with three critical
factors. First, the savvy and determination of outreach staff. Second, the
cooperation of local joint apprenticeship committees." He cited examples of
good cooperation as providing information as to when and where apprenticeship
openings are available, being fair with applicants, providing a calm, positive atmosphere during joint apprenticeship committee interviews. "Finally,"
Slaiman explained, "NOTHING is as important as jobs and job openings."

OFCC CONDUCTS HEARINGS IN ATLANTA

Because Hometown Plan negotiations have been at a standstill since
January, OFCC conducted hearings, March 31 - April 2 to uncover reasons for
the breakdown. Co-convenors for the Minority Coalition, Lyndon Wade,
Executive Director of Atlanta Urban League, and Vice Mayor Maynard Jackson
requested from two weeks to a month to resume negotiations and come up with
a plan. OFCC is considering an imposed plan.

These events seriously hamper efforts to get the journeyman training
component off the ground.

NEW ORLEANS PLAN AWAITS DOL APPROVAL

Although two key locals, Sheet Metal Workers Local No. 11 and Plumbers
Marine and Steamfitters Local No. 6 are not within the scope of the New
Orleans Plan, the Urban League of Greater New Orleans, sponsor of the plan,

is awaiting Department of Labor approval. Though signed last June, the plan
was sent back twice for additions: a year-by-year breakdown of the numbers
of minorities going into the locals and a budget proposal. According to
Henry Braden, Director, Project LEAP, the unreasonable delay as far as he
can see, can only be attributed to U.S. Attorney, John Mitchell's delay in
signing the agreement regarding actions planned by his staff.

Another reason, perhaps more significant, is the fact that the National
Urban League carries the prime contract for all affiliates with outreach
programs. The Urgan League of Greater New Orleans is the first affiliate
sponsor of a hometown plan. Will OFCC approve the plan if the National
Urban League carries the prime contract for the outreach component?

HARTFORD URBAN LEAGUE CONVENES COALITION FOR HARTFORD

Under the capable leadership of Hartford Urban League Executive Director,
Bill Brown, Norm Wright, Economic Development and Employment, and Roy Dixon,
Director Project LEAP, the Urban League convened a group of representatives
from CAP agencies, Civil Rights groups, and social service agencies, to form
a coalition for the development of a Hartford Plan. The final draft is being
completed by Norm, who will then submit it to the coalition. No input from
the trades or employers has been enlisted thus far. The position of the
coalition is that it would be better to approach the trades and the contractors with a working document, an established base for negotiating, as
opposed to entering negotiations cold.

BREAKFAST HELD IN HONOR OF BALTIMORE APPRENTICES

The Baltimore Urban League, the Baltimore Building Trades Council, and
the Association of General Contractors co-sponsored a breakfast honoring
more than 400 apprentices and new indentures placed through Project LEAP.
Following breakfast, speeches were given by cooperating union and management
officials, Travis Vauls, Executive Director, and Tom Waters, former project
director for Baltimore, LEAP's senior project.

"Some very important issues were raised later during the question and
answer period," said Project Director, Joe Washington. Primary issues
raised by the apprentices centered around:
- Going through the formal apprenticeship system, meeting the age
  and educational requirements, and finding that whites coming in
  through the back door who were not required to go through the
  same process nor do they meet the formal requirements like,
  education and age that the blacks had to meet.
- Class training, another prerequisite, is seldom work related.
  "One of the good things that came out of the meeting," Washington
  added, "was the need to establish a 'buddy system' within the
  Project itself. We have guys who are new indentures who don't
  know the 1st and 2nd year guys in their same locals because of
  different job sites and schedules."

Saturday morning sessions will be held to implement this buddy system
where indentures will be assigned to older apprentices in the same craft as
well as to discuss and resolve general problems confronted by new indenture.

The Builder (National Urban League), 1 (No. 1, 1970):1-2.

51.   COALITION DEMANDS HIRING OF
MINORITY WORKERS

The need for fundamental change at Boston State College has led to the
formation of a coalition of progressive forces. The Coalition includes the
Black Student Association, the Radical Action Union, several student representatives of S.G.A., the faculty of the New University Conference, the
Fenway Campus Ministry and the Metropolitan Ministry in Higher Education.
These groups and individuals have organized the coalition to establish a
working relationship amongst themselves in order to confront issues which are
of common concern.
    The coalition is dealing with the complex issues surrounding the im-
pending construction of a twelve story, $15.6 million dollar building at the
Huntington Avenue Campus. The primary concern of the Coalition is that the
building not be constructed in a vacuum, ignoring the crucial political,
economic, and moral issues involved. Specifically, the coalition is determining to work with the surrounding community to insure that Black and other
minority group workers are represented in significant numbers at the job
site. We are also concerned that minority contracting firms receive their
fair share of the contracts for the building. To this end, the coalition
has begun to work with groups from the surrounding community, especially the
United Community Construction Workers (U.C.C.W.). This union of Black
workers has been struggling against racism and job discrimination in order
to provide work with dignity to its members.
    None of this will occur unless the building trades unions, the contract-
ing corporations, the State, and the college are forced and pressured into
making it happen. The coalition recognizes this fact. This recognition
rests on a number of things, most importantly the collusion of all of the
above in perpetuating a destructive situation for Blacks and other minority
groups.
    The building trades unions have traditionally been exclusionary in
nature, especially discriminating against Blacks. The racism of these unions
is evident today when one recognizes that a minute percentage of the membership is non-white, despite the fact that Blacks have worked for and demanded
entrance into these closed unions for a long time. The unions have preferred
to keep their ranks confined to small numbers of skilled workers to try to
raise the wages of their members. So some workers "make it" while most
others are forced to fight for jobs, let alone decent wages. These unions
have lately delved into tokenism, to satisfy federal compliance laws.
But, tokenism does nothing for the mass of workers.
    The contracting corporations perpetuate this situation. They are solely
concerned with profits. They prefer to bargain with small numbers of
skilled workers, giving in on some wage demands, the cost of which they
simply pass on to whomever is paying for the construction project. Thus
they continue to make their huge profits and continue to manipulate a
situation where black and white workers are divided and fighting each other.
There is little chance then that the construction workers will confront them,
for fundamental changes in their work situations; some having been bought
off, some fighting each other, and most excluded from construction work by
this alliance between unions and contractors.
    The State and the college simply want this building up. They are not
concerned if minority workers are excluded from the job, if they are
unemployed, or if the repercussions from this affect the entire Black and
minority communities.

While they supply the money to the contractors with one hand, with the other they exude pious declarations against racism. In the contracts that have thus far been signed between the State's Bureau of Building Construction and Contractors, there is a weak and meaningless anti-discrimination clause. It supposedly commits the contractors not to discriminate in the hiring of workers, but says nothing about the unions. In effect, there is no affirmative action demanded by the State to end racism on the job site, and no intention of forcing compliance against discrimination.

What is needed, the coalition believes, is strong and affirmative action by the State and the college to force the unions and contractors into hiring significant numbers of Black and other minority group workers. The commitment of the coalition, of U.C.C.W., and of the community is clear. This construction project can become an opportunity for Boston State to reverse its traditional non-concern with the welfare of the surrounding community, and to work effectively against racism and poverty. If the coalition cannot convince the college of the need for this, then we are prepared, along with others, to do anything necessary to see justice prevail.

No less than thirty percent (30%) of the labor force in all the construction trades, skilled and unskilled, employed on the construction sites of Boston State College will consist of Black and other minority workers. The general contractor and subcontractor shall meet this minimum requirement. The general contractor shall be held responsible for the compliance of all subcontracts.

Minority employment efforts are to be coordinated through and monitored by the United Community Construction Workers Union and the Boston State College Coalition. The UCCW's efforts will be directed towards their membership and other sources of minority employment and training. They will provide recruiting mechanisms for the training and placing of new construction workers, skilled and unskilled. In those trades where there is not thirty percent minority employment available, the United Community Construction Workers will provide minority persons to be trained on the job in the various trades where such deficiencies exist.

Minority persons placed for training by the UCCW shall be counted toward the thirty percent requirement. The UCCW and the Coalition will provide a regular compliance check on the general and all subcontractors. In the event that a subcontractor(s) or the general contractor are found to be in violation of this affirmative action program at any time, this determination being made by the UCCW and the Coalition, they will be given twenty-four hours to bring their employment condition up to the standards provided in this contract. At the end of twenty-four hours the UCCW will again determine whether they are in compliance. If they are not in compliance, but the UCCW and the Coalition has been satisfied that adequate and sufficient steps have been taken to meet the requirements as soon as possible, then the UCCW and the Coalition may permit them to continue on the site with the understanding that the employment requirements for minority workers will be met within no more than five working days. If at the end of five working days the contractor is still not in compliance then he will be required to withdraw from the job and the construction site immediately. Any financial loss resulting from the non-compliance of the contractor will be paid to Boston State College and minority workers who were available to work, skilled, unskilled and/or for training, by the contractor found in violation and forced to withdraw from the site.

To enhance the full participation of the minority community in the construction industry, minority owned and operated construction contractors and subcontractors will be used wherever possible on the construction site. Minority contractors within and around the Boston area shall receive no less than thirty percent of all contracts and/or subcontracts to be given out for construction at Boston State College.

The same minority employment and training requirements shall be enforced against the Black and minority contractors employed on the construction sites at Boston State College. Boston State College agrees to allow the U.C.C.W. to enforce the terms of this affirmative action program on its behalf at the expense of the College.

The U.C.C.W. shall also coordinate and monitor the use of minority owned construction companies. They shall determine compliance and non-compliance

with regard to all requirements set forth in the affirmative action sections
of this contract. When there is a determination that there is non-compliance
with regard to the employment and use of minority construction (subcontract-
ing) companies, the general contractor shall be given five working days to
comply. If there is no compliance within five working days, but sufficient
steps have been taken to insure compliance (as determined by the U.C.C.W.)
then the general contractor shall be given no more than eight additional days
to be in compliance or to present and put into effect an acceptable alternative for that particular segment of the construction. This section applies
to minority construction companies as subcontractors. Acceptability of all
alternatives will be made by the U.C.C.W. and the Coalition.

United Community Construction Workers (Boston) flier (n.d. 1972) in
possession of the editors.

52.   THE BRICKS AND MORTAR OF RACISM

By Paul Good

They swarmed over the construction site like a people's crusade, black
and Puerto Rican men, women and children with posters waving, their hands
clawing down wooden cement forms and setting them aflame.

The setting was the excavation of a $37-million Family and Criminal
Court building in the South Bronx, a New York City project going up in a
minority enclave. The posters told the demonstrators' story: *"Pare La
Obra,"* they read, "Stop The Work," "End Construction Industry Discrimination."

To make certain the message got across to the predominantly white work
force, the invaders who came from the surrounding community told individual
workmen to lay down their tools. "If we don't work here," they said, "you
don't work here."

A white laborer wheeling a load of mortar objected, "I ain't gonna stop,"
he said. "I got a family to support."

"We got families, too," replied a black youth as he tipped over the
wheelbarrow.

Some workmen waved shovels in defiance. The demonstrators picked up
rocks and pipes. Police arrived. A few arrests were made, and work on the
courthouse stopped.

A few weeks later, the scene was duplicated in Spanish Harlem. This
time it was private construction, a union-sponsored $80-million housing
development where 110th Street meets First Avenue. The blocks leading to the
site look like stage sets left over from "Dead End," that all-white New
York slum drama from the days when blacks and Puerto Ricans did not preoccupy
the metropolitan mind.

Again, nearly everyone working on the site was white, nearly everyone
protesting was not. But this time, police and demonstrators fought, and
there were injuries on both sides. Two stumpy Irish-American workmen,
brothers, watched and when a foreman announced work was suspended, one said
bitterly: "Those black bastards. My brother here had to wait 12 years to
get into the union. We worked like hell for everything we got. And now
these bastards want it all handed to them."

These recent incidents were skirmishes in a growing battle by minorities
to get jobs in New York City's multibillion-dollar construction industry. It
is a struggle--also occurring in other big cities--that could provoke open
job warfare, and its cause traces to an elemental fact of municipal life:
Virtually every building ever constructed in New York, from the newly
completed mammoth World Trade Center down to a one-family house in Queens and
including schools, hospitals and cathedrals in between, rests on what can
only be described as a foundation of racism.

"It's a result of the systematic racism of America," says Jim Haughton, the black director of Fight Back, a Harlem-based group that uses everything from cajolery to flying raids like the First Avenue sortie to get minority members into the construction trades. "And New York is the epitome of racist political hustling. I deal with all the intricate layers of it while City Hall and Albany duck their responsibilities and let the unions and contractors get away with murder. And at the end of the line is that poor, lone black guy looking for a job or justice."

Haughton's charge of systemic racism can be measured in various ways. For example, a close reading of two recent issues of leading industry magazines for this area--*Construction Equipment* and *Constructioneer*--showed not a single black or Puerto Rican worker in any ad or article. Similarly, a photo of the annual meeting of the New York General Contractors contained 100 all-white faces.

Minorities, comprising more than 30 per cent of the city's population, hold but 2 per cent of union membership in the skilled trades, such as sheet-metal or elevator construction work, in which a journeyman can make $15,000 a year. But the vast majority of minority workmen are jammed into less-skilled, lower-paying categories where they earn half that. It is the kind of income differential that buys one man a house in the suburbs and pens another in a ghetto flat.

The union card or book is the key to the hiring hall, where job assignments are supposed to be made. The book can be a guarantee of benefits, work continuity, a safe-conduct pass through the economic battleground of construction. Without it, a man is at the mercy of contractors, scrambling each day. But even with it, minorities often find no guarantees. Instead, there is deceit on one hand, distrust on the other.

One cold spring morning, Haughton leads an Alabama-born black plasterer, Joe Strickland, to a building going up on Williams Street, in the financial district. Strickland, father of eight, belongs to Plasterers Local 60 but was laid off last December. Outside the contractor's trailer, he meets contractor Joe Giamboi, his former boss. Giamboi, dressed in camel-hair coat, Italian sandals and light blue pants, tells Strickland: "I brought you colored guys up from the South. You were one of my best men. Then somebody put bad ideas in your head."

When Giamboi leaves, Strickland says: "They brought us up when plasterers were in demand. They worked us like a bunch of damn hogs, then we'd be first let go in a slump. The union takes your dues but doesn't listen. He says I got bad ideas because I spoke out against conditions."

In the trailer, another contractor puts it this way: "We have to keep the Irish and Italians from laying off blacks and hiring their friends. You know the unions; we have limited control. If you think you can get the Irish and Italians to give it up, God bless you."

But a foreman named Louie announces that all eight carpenters on the job are black. Carpentry is one of the lower-paying trades that whites are quitting. Still, Haughton would like to see for himself.

He borrows a hard hat and rides to the 13th floor, where great sheets of white plastic to block the wind billow like sails between naked girders.

He finds five black and two white carpenters. "I thought you said eight out of eight, Louie?" Haughton says. "I made a little mistake on the number," Louie replies.

Racial numbers in construction remain lopsided despite numerous laws banning discrimination. The state's first such law goes back to 1935. Federally, there are Executive Orders--some of which originated with the Franklin Roosevelt Administration--the 1964 Civil Rights Act and fair employment provisions currently written into every contract. Mayor Lindsay's administration has the most potent regulations in the nation, on paper at least, and now administers what is called the New York Plan. The plan is supposed to increase the number of minority workmen dramatically by putting trainees to work. In 16 months, it has resulted in about 300 minority trainees at a time when ghetto unemployment equals the white rate during the Depression. Minority critics, however, call the plan a farce.

Most laws and plans provide penalties against unions and contractors that defy them. But the stigma of second-class minority citizenship adheres to most minority legal safeguards, producing second-class law enforcement while law-and-order remains a majority shibboleth.

Local 28 of the Sheet Metal Workers Union is a clear example, though not a unique case, of the law's delay in ending discrimination in the building trades, and it provides legal perspective on the current crisis. In 1948, the State Human Rights Commission ordered the local to stop excluding Negroes. In 1964, the commission found it still was excluding them and the State Supreme Court issued a cease-and-desist order. The union claimed there were no qualified black journeymen and that no blacks passed the apprenticeship tests. In 1966, minority rights groups tutored black apprentice applicants. But the union called their test scores "phenomenally high" and scrapped the test results. The State Supreme Court issued a restraining order and the union promised to let in qualified Negroes.

Two years later, there still were no blacks in Local 28, and the city held up $6-million in contracts affecting metal workers until the union began compliance. Today, nearly a quarter of a century after the first legal action, there are 20 blacks in Local 28--out of 3,300 journeymen. Last year, the state sent black trainees to work on the State Office Building in the center of Harlem. Local 28 refused to let them work and the men were forced to sit in a construction shack, getting paid for the time.

Local 28 is the only union that refuses to have anything to do with the New York Plan. Yet it is working on public construction throughout New York, and because the demand for sheet-metal workmen is great, it often winds up working on ghetto projects. As far as can be determined, no public construction project anywhere in the country has ever been canceled because of civil-rights violations, as required under Federal law, although dozens of courts have documented violations. One example may show the kind of priorities governing enforcement and help to explain why demonstrators feel they have to knock over wheelbarrows and fight with the cops.

The Federal Government accounts for nearly $1-billion of the $2.6 billion worth of construction under way in New York. The Office of Federal Contract Compliance (O.F.C.C.) is supposed to ensure that contractual job pledges are carried out. The Equal Employment Opportunity Commission (E.E.O.C.) is supposed to process minority complaints. E.E.O.C. has a national backing of 40,000 cases and the New York office admits it has no current minority statistics. The O.F.C.C. office here consists of its director, Kenneth Smallwood, one assistant and a secretary. This is the total staff assigned to supervise the performance of individual compliance officers in Federal agencies holding myriad construction contracts.

But wait. Mr. Smallwood and his assistant must also check compliance throughout the rest of New York State, New Jersey, Puerto Rico and the Virgin Islands!

"It's tragic," says Herbert Hill, national labor director of the National Association for the Advancement of Colored People. "We have all the law anybody needs but the only result is the triumph of tokenism. Nationally, despite vaunted Federal outreach programs, the latest Washington E.E.O.C. figures show that minority membership in construction unions actually *declined* to 6.8 per cent from 7.4 per cent the previous year.

"In New York State, under Rockefeller, we've witnessed the demise of the strongest state antidiscrimination law in the nation. Peter Brennan-- president of the A.F.L.-C.I.O. Building and Construction Trades Council of Greater New York--has always been a big Rockefeller supporter, along with Ray Corbett, the head of the State Federation of Labor. Rockefeller repays political debts to the unions and contractors by the administrative nullification of the law in relation to construction. His calculated sacrifice of principle and law borders on the criminals.

"And Lindsay, at the beginning of his term of office, said all the right things and gave hope that change was possible. But Lindsay has compromised with those who are responsible for the racist pattern, as witness his support for the defunct New York Plan. Tragic is the only word to describe it."

Jim Naughton puts it more succinctly: "The only contract compliance in New York is when the brothers throw up a picket line."

The situation in New York is as complex as it is critical. There are more than 100,000 members dealing with about 10,000 contractors and subcontractors. Construction, it would seem, should be a manly, even noble, undertaking -- the raising up of edifices where people can learn. But in

New York, its history is dog-eat-dog.   Contractors have exploited workmen
and workmen exploited one another.   Italians, who later came to control many
unions, started out beneath blacks.   A wage schedule for Croton Reservoir
construction in 1895 listed daily pay:

COMMON LABOR, WHITE
$1.30 TO $1.50

COMMON LABOR, COLORED
$1.25 TO $1.40

COMMON LABOR, ITALIAN
$1.15 TO $1.25

Slowly, painfully, as the 20th-century skyline rose, the various trades
carved out their separate union fiefs.   Italians, whose struggle was power-
fully described by Pietro di Donato in "Christ in Concrete," developed their
construction cosa, the Irish their clan.   But blacks were excluded, as they
were excluded from Congress, newspapers, churches and other institutions.
And the unions by their own nature -- racism aside -- were exclusionary.
At the mercy of weather and prevailing economic winds, a tightly controlled
membership was a hedge against labor surpluses.   The apprentice system
evolved along the lines of medieval guilds, designed to let a trickle of
favored applicants get past entrance requirements and serve apprenticeships
that today extend up to five years.   Consider, for example, the fact that
the Air Force can train a jet pilot in 18 months, while it takes a union
five years to train a pipe fitter.   During such long periods, more than half
the trainees drop out.
      The Plumber's Union, which has fewer than 1,500 blacks nationally out
of 170,000 members and a 2.3 per cent minority representation in New York's
Local 2, now requires a high-school diploma or equivalent.   Given that
stricture, George Meany--president of the A.F.L.-C.I.O.--never could have
qualified as an apprentice for his first union card, though that may not
have mattered.   Prof. Russell A. Nixon, labor expert at Columbia University's
School of Social Work, estimates that 75 per cent of construction journeymen
get their union books without becoming apprentices.   Relatives and friends
train them on the job at salaries well above the low apprentice rate.   Meany
was a high-school dropout when he joined Local 2 half a century ago.   His
father, Mike, was then its business agent.
      The apprentice system works in conjunction with prevailing union nepotism:
dad getting in his son, somebody telling the business agent that Pat or Tony
or Olaf sent him.   But nobody ever sent around Booker because nobody knew him
or wanted to.
      Federal Judge Marvin E. Frankel ruled that one New York trade union with
only 13 blacks among 1,500 members must give "compensatory lost pay to
victims of forbidden discrimination."   He described the union in terms applicable to many others: "There is a deep-rooted and pervasive practice in this
union of handing out jobs on the basis of union membership, kinship, friendship and, generally 'pull.'   Numerous blacks, often with substantial relevant
work experience, vainly shaped the hall day after day during the summer   ,
months, at a time when inexperienced students, other inexperienced white men
and similarly situated whites got jobs through people they knew."
      That New York suit, began on complaint of a black who belonged to the
Wood, Wire and Metal Lathers Union in Daytona Beach, Fla., revealed another
dimension of discriminatory practices by New York locals.   When the man moved
here, Local 46 refused to transfer his book, thus keeping him out of the
local--and out of work.   Many skilled Southern blacks coming north in search
of work and not welfare are similarly stymied.   The anomaly is that, while
most Southern locals provide an opportunity for blacks to become journeymen,
some Deep South cities show better minority percentages in many unions than
does New York, where locals technically are not segregated.
      A black counterattack began in the mid-sixties, when both the tempo and
the possibilities of protest increased.   Groups like Fight Back began
picketing public construction sites or sitting in.   Their logic was plain:
White and black tax dollars were paying for new facilities.   So blacks and
Puerto Ricans should get their share of building jobs, particularly in the
ghettos.

The tactics drew headlines and token response. The contractors and unions "checkerboarded" the few existing minority card holders, moving them from site to site, from one hot point of jobs-rights protest to another. But minority anger and frustrations were beyond the reach of such public relations tactics.

While militants developed direct action techniques, more traditional routes of redress were pursued by others: The N.A.A.C.P. concentrated on the courts, helping to establish a body of antidiscrimination law with clout. The Workers Defense League (W.D.L.), an old-line job rights group nurtured by the A. Philip Randolph Fund, sought to pry open the apprentice programs, working closely with the federally funded Joint Apprentice Program (JAP). JAP started in a Brooklyn storefront 5 years ago, directed by Ernest Green, the first black to graduate from Little Rock High School. It has produced success stories like Curtis Alexander.

Alexander, 25, holds union card No. 082 40 2459 in the International Brotherhood of Electrical Workers, Local 3. He is a Class A journeyman in a union about 5 per cent minority. Other blacks and Puerto Ricans in his union lack Alexander's Class A book. They are relegated to "M" card status, hundreds of them permitted to work only on low-paying rehabilitation jobs, but barred from new construction and prime journeyman's pay of about $8 an hour--plus liberal overtime.

"You get no respect without this union card," says Alexander, a short, intense man never far from anger. "With it, you get hired by shaping up at the union hall and most times they send you into a black community--it could be two boroughs from where you live. But without the book you've got nothing. You pick up jobs from day to day at the mercy of the system."

In 1964, after graduating from vocational high school, where he studied electrical installation, he filled out an apprentice application at I.B.E.W. They said they'd call. Alexander would still be waiting except that the JAP program finally got him an electrician's apprenticeship at $2 an hour.

"I remember," he says, "a white foreman told me, 'I'll teach you, but we once had a colored fellow here who didn't want to learn.' I asked him what the hell that had to do with anything. After I got my book, I been on jobs with 300 white faces and one other black. There were jobs you could only talk to the foreman because everybody else spoke Italian. How long were they in this country, I wonder?

"I received a lot of racism. How many times you got to be called 'boy' or 'kid' or 'Jack' when you got 'Curtis' stenciled on your helmet? And jobs- like World Trade Center, where you can stay up for a year and rack up the overtime, we don't see them."

Alexander says his father was a baggage handler for the Pennsylvania Railroad who "started from scratch" like his father before him. "But that will stop with me," he says. "There's a lot of other brothers out there wiped out where they could've made it if they had one real shot like I got. That is going to stop now too."

JAP has 19 offices throughout the country and claims to have placed 4,000 minority members as apprentices, with roughly 1,400 in New York. How many of these have dropped out, how many are working with union books is impossible to tell. But given the present inadequate minority percentages in the skilled trades, even if the unions began accepting minority apprentices proportionate to their population ratios, the best estimates are that it would be well into the 21st century before any parity was achieved.

The trainee concept is a tacit admission that the apprentice system, at best, cannot produce results fast enough. Trainees do not have to meet apprentice standards of age, education and lack of prior criminal record. They are supposed to advance to journeyman as rapidly as their talent and dedication permit.

Mayor Lindsay, who courts minority support, does not have any black adviser among the top-level men around him. So it is not known how he settled on James Norton, a black, to run the City's enforcement agency, called the Office of Contract Compliance. The choice has been controversial. A pro-Lindsay official who is a building-trades expert generally respected by militants and moderates says: "Norton is and was a disaster. Lindsay's executive orders constitute the strongest antidiscrimination program in the country. But he picked the wrong guy to run it. He never asks contractors

for enough in the preawards bidding, and he doesn't follow up to see if
they're even delivering their pittance. A contractor can act as a pressure
point on the unions. He can tell a union he likes a man's work--so give him
the book."

Norton, in his Broadway office across from City Hall, is wary during an
interview. "If you talk to unions and contractors, I'm a bastard," he says.
"Minority groups think I'm a bastard too. They don't see enough evidence of
change to give me a good-guy award. Now, there's a need for the Jim
Haughtons--but for all his talk he can't deliver skilled craftsmen. There
aren't that many because they never had a chance to be trained.

"Then you've got this problem of communities wanting only their people
on the job, like up at the Bronx Courthouse. Should a black worker from
Harlem be laid off there so somebody from South Bronx gets the job?"

How do he and his staff of four inspectors covering five boroughs write
minorities into contracts and check on complaints? "There's no real figure
I have in mind as a percentage," Norton says. "You bargain and try to get
what you can."

But if the law is the law, isn't that like bargaining with a man over
whether he'll pay his traffic tickets or income tax? "Listen, it's not
exact. No one has ever defined exactly what compliance is. Most of the
time, we try for 15 per cent and up. Then we try to keep an eye on particular sites to make sure the number is being maintained. The pace isn't fast
enough to suit me or the man who wants the job. But there aren't enough
openings for all those who want jobs."

Norton adds that "although we have a helluva lot of minority unemployment, we don't have a helluva lot who want to go into construction," a
statement that would seem to be contradicted by the facts of at least one
recent hiring experience. Under court orders, the Lathers union had to
accept 50 apprentices, starting at $3.40 an hour. More than 2,000 applica-
tions were received, mainly from minorities, and a court lottery was held to
eliminate 1,950.

As far as job opportunities go, figures are sanguine if not conclusive.
Nationally, construction work is running $18-billion ahead of last year, and
for the mid-Atlantic states, including New York, it is up 5 per cent in 1972,
for a record $31.4-billion. Milton Musicus, chairman of the City Construction
Board, says $800-million in new city awards by the end of the fiscal year
will make it "the biggest construction year in recent history and provide
the equivalent of 20,000 man-years of work for the industry."

What 20,000 man years translates to in jobs is anybody's guess. But
it's known that annual construction turnover through death or retirement
runs about 6 per cent. With union membership at more than 10,000, that
makes 6,000 annual journeyman vacancies in the present work force, with
2,000 at most coming out of apprenticeship ranks. And the State Department
of Labor says that 80,000 additional construction workers will be needed in
the state during this decade, with perhaps a quarter of those in New York
City. With that kind of bullish job market, the work will be there. Who
will get it is the question.

The New York Plan was supposed to supply much of the answer. It
evolved during 1970, at a time when the Nixon Administration, faced with
mounting big-city ghetto unrest, began insisting on "hometown" plans to
satisfy antidiscrimination requirements in laws governing Federal construction funds. Otherwise, Labor Secretary George Shultz warned, the Government
would impose the so-called Philadelphia Plan in New York and elsewhere.
Under that plan, that city is supposed to bring minority participation in
building trades to 20 per cent within five years. The prospect chilled
Peter Brennan and the 100 unions he represents as head of the New York
Building and Construction Trades Council. So he and a protege, Donald Rogers,
devised the New York Plan. The view of the minority groups is that if ever
foxes were sent to guard the henhouse, this was it.

Rogers was director of the council's Urban Affairs Fund, a management-
labor mechanism dominated by Brennan and dedicated to the status quo. A
sketch of Rogers's background is necessary to appreciate what took place in
this Alice-in-Constructionland saga.

Rogers was recording secretary of Local 15 of the Operating Engineers,
a union with no formal apprentice program and an almost nonexistent skilled

minority membership. When, for example, was the last time you saw a black
bulldozer driver or crane operator? In 1963, after racial violence and 800
arrests around city construction sites, Rogers was named chairman of an
employer-union committee to get minorities into the trades. His committee
screened 3,000 applicants. Thirty one--about 1 per cent--got into the
unions.

The New York Plan, as devised by Brennan and Rogers, seemed so inadequate that even the O.F.C.C. director in Washington, John L. Wilks, could
not approve it. It called for on-the-job training for a maximum of 800
trainees. It set no minimum wage. It ran for only one year, expiring this
June with no guarantee of continuation, although extension was assumed.
There was no pledge to admit any trainee into the unions. And it contained
a clause that any contractor signing it was "automatically" deemed in compliance with Federal, state and local antidiscrimination laws without
requiring proof. A nine-man administrative committee, with unions and
contractors in the majority, was to run the plan.

Brennan, a good friend of Governor Rockefeller, hurried down to
Washington to see President Nixon when the O.F.C.C. held up approval. It
was during a period when construction workers supporting the Vietnam War
were tangling with peace demonstrators in New York. Brennan gave Nixon a
hard hat and pledged union support of the war. Immediately thereafter,
Wilks wrote Brennan approving the plan, although every civil-rights group
in New York, with the significant exception of the Workers Defense League,
denounced it. Wilks said that a craft-by-craft breakdown of trainee goals
had persuaded him. "As you know," he wrote, "approval of the plan is only
good-faith efforts to meet craft-by-craft commitments to specific goals."

Then, after the governor and mayor had signed the plan on Dec. 10, 1970,
three key unions announced they would not participate: Plumbers, Electrical
Workers and Sheet Metal. Mayor Lindsay reacted decisively in March, 1971,
by freezing $200-million in city construction awards. The freeze lasted
seven months, while communities howled that schools and hospitals weren't
being built. Finally, the Plumbers and Electricians signed independent
agreements outside the plan to take on 100 trainees each. Sheet Metal Local
28 refused to agree to anything. Nevertheless, antidiscrimination law being
what it is, the freeze ended and the plan was under way with a total trainee
goal of 1000 by this June 30.

What has it achieved? The plan itself has placed 217 trainees, 64 of
them holdovers from the old Model Cities program, with another 100 trainees
taken on by the freelancing Plumbers and Electricians. An April check of
the craft-by-craft breakdowns that so impressed the O.F.C.C.'s Wilks shows
for example, 13 elevator construction minority trainees out of 60 assigned
slots, 8 engineers out of 73 slots, 10 steamfitters out of 90, etc. The
city's own Public Works Department, with 12 construction projects under way,
has exactly two such trainees. Voluntary cooperation from the private
sector -- companies like Consolidated Edison, Bell Telephone and hundreds
of others -- has produced nine trainees. While the plan produced these slim
results, the U.S. Bureau of Labor Statistics was reporting that in seven
ghettos teen-age unemployment alone was running 42 per cent and a total of
27,900 young and adult males were out of work.

What went wrong? Depending on whom you talk to, nothing much or everything. The N.A.A.C.P.'s Hill calls the plan "stillborn" and the State
Advisory Committee to the U.S. Commission on Civil Rights has prepared a
highly critical report. But Deputy Mayor Edward Hamilton says it's the best
program in the country. Hamilton cites many reasons for the poor numerical
showing to date: a late administrative start, last year's construction
freeze, budgetary problems, failure of city agencies to notify the plan of
the construction projects.

"I don't care how much general law you have," Hamilton says, "unless you
get contractors to promise a specific number of jobs nothing will happen.
This is what the plan does. Some people say to break union opposition by
frontal attacks, the by-God-you-will-comply approach. And they get their
noses bloodied. We could fight in the courts but it would create ill-feeling.
Lawsuits should be the court of last resort."

Hamilton may be right. But the single greatest minority gain in New
York's construction history came this January when Federal Judge Dudley

Bonsal ordered Steamfitters Local 638 to transfer 168 minority workers from
a lower-job branch to one of full journeyman status. The case grew out of
protests at the World Trade Center.

New York Plan director Eddy Johnson, a lanky young black, holds his job
at the pleasure of the administrative council. He has a staff of nine.
Johnson defends the plan, although he thinks the most important thing for
unemployed minorities is to "develop the right attitude."

"I'm not so much concerned with the past," he says, "because what's
dead is dead. I don't know what somebody means when he talks about unions
holding guys back. That's isolated cases. We've found no difficulties
with unions. And after they train one of our men for four years, it's gonna
be pretty damn rough for them to say he's not qualified for a card."

Johnson stresses that the plan is not merely for jobs but primarily for
training. For example, dropout trainees lacking math receive simplified
instruction off the job. "Like to teach inverting fractions," he explains,
"we cite Lew Alcindor and Bob Cousy, larger and smaller, top and bottom."
It was the first time in years that an interviewer had heard Alcindor called
anything but his chosen black name of Kareem Abdul-Jabbar.

James MacNamara, director of the city's Building Trades Training
Program, thinks Mayor Lindsay's antidiscrimination executive orders were the
best in the business. But MacNamara, a former union organizer with a
reputation for square shooting, feels Lindsay was misled into accepting the
New York Plan. Still, he is hopeful overall:

"In 10 years I don't think discrimination in the trades here will be a
major issue. All we have to do is keep up the pressure and get good administrators. Attitudes are changing. I went to a Bricklayers meeting recently
where an Italian foreman said, 'Why should these guineas get the jobs when
these niggers have been here all these years'."

A tour of Harlem construction sites--even allowing for the fact it is
black and Puerto Rican turf--reveals changes in the old order. The guide is
Bob Scott, a tall young black in a shin-length coat and full-blown Afro, who
is a Workers Defense League trouble-shooter. He moves confidently into
construction sheds he would probably have been thrown out of a few years ago.

The first stop is a State Urban Development Corporation middle-class
housing project at 131st Street and Eighth Avenue. Even the name--Lionel
Hampton House--represents some kind of progress. A few years ago, the city
built a housing project in Harlem and renamed it after Stephen Foster. "We
got good cooperation here," Scott says. "Only two of 13 trainee slots are
operating. But that's because certain jobs haven't opened in the building
sequence. Forty per cent of the regular work force is minority."

The white superintendent, interrupting a sandwich lunch to talk, is
friendly without going overboard. "Nobody's going to do anything without a
prod," he says. "You can preach how good you are racially but you have to be
pushed to deliver. I really don't think most contractors have to use the
power of the almighty buck to lean on people."

To the west, there is a problem at the city's Martin Luther King High
School site at 65th Street and Amsterdam Avenue. There have been problems
there from the start. When construction began last spring, there were only
one or two minority workmen on a building named for the country's foremost
civil rights leader. Fight Back demonstrated. There were dozens of arrests,
work was temporarily discontinued and today there are five trainees for 95
journeymen jobs, with more to come. One of them, a neat black of 30 with a
West Indian accent and wearing new mustard-color workshoes, is the current
problem. His name is Al and he has been fired without any notification to
the New York Plan.

"Mon, it's a jungle in there," he tells Scott, his voice pitched high
and with outrage. "They are so arrogant. They call me stupid and nigger.
No matter what I do, I can't please them. I try to live with this and
continue to the end of the training because, you know, I have five children.
But they won't teach me anything about plumbing. All I do is hold the
ladder.

"The other day, one picked up a pipe to hit me and I picked up a
spanner. A jungle. I argued with a journeyman and the foreman told me I
should apologize. I said, 'I'm sorry.' The man said, 'I don't care what
you are, I'm not getting paid to train you.'"

They go into the construction trailer. "A contractor is not allowed to fire a trainee without notifying the plan," Scott says. "That's irresponsible." The atmosphere is chilly. There is the unspoken assertion in the face of a grizzled white carpenter: Whoever got notified when I was fired?

While Scott and Al wait to see the foreman, an elderly site superintendent for the contractor says: "If they said we had to put on 10 more trainees tomorrow, we'd be in real trouble. Racism? Listen, since I started to work there's always been colored on the job. And this goes back 50 years." A minute later he adds: "They been shut out, yes. It's a father-and-son thing in the unions, so they couldn't get in."

The foreman, Kenny, arrives. He's in his early 30's, tall with a mod auburn mustache and looks much like a Marlboro model in his white hard hat. "From the start," he says, "Al didn't understand things like going for coffee. Low man on the totem pole does it. I did it. We had trouble with five white apprentices last month, said they didn't want to do it. The business agent told them: 'It's not in the contract but it's in the system.' But Al took it as a personal racial thing."

Al admits the coffee charge. But he's adamant about other abuse and the refusal to train him. "Look, Al," Kenny says, "guys don't want to teach anybody their trade. They're protecting it." But there've almost been swingouts with Al. "All right, one of the guys was an idiot and we fired him. I switched you around but there was no harmony in your gang. I laid off two other men you had trouble with."

"They were from New Jersey and they had to go anyway," Al says. "Always when there was trouble you didn't believe me. I was always praying for the next day to come when I wouldn't have to work with such men."

After some calls to plan headquarters, it's decided that Al will be switched to another site. Scott cautions him to cool it.

With minority nerves raw from discrimination and white egos bruised from the belief they are being pushed around, "rights" remain in direct conflict. And there is a ready battleground in New York. The city is glutted with private office construction. But there are voluminous blueprints for housing, schools and other civic projects. Much of it will be in or near minority neighborhoods.

There is, for example, the massive North River Pollution Control Plant to the west of Harlem, the largest competitively bid nonmilitary construction in U.S. history, covering 10 city blocks and costing $3-billion to $4-billion. How can minorities get their share of this work that will stretch over years. Norton's compliance office has yet to hold a preconstruction conference with the major contractor.

The N.A.A.C.P.'s Herbert Hill says: "There is only one way--numerical goals. You can call it quotas or ranges, but it must be fixed in writing. Not a token 1,000 trainees in some amorphous scheme to get them books, but so many union journeymen working by such a date. And the bid specifications for contractors must reflect population percentages."

A precedent for ranges has already been established in the Metal Lathers suit mentioned earlier. Judge Frankel, faced with union intransigence, ruled in March that "the following ranges shall be established as the standards for minority employment in the work jurisdiction of Local 46:

1972	1973
9-13%	13-17%

1974	1975
16-20%	19-23%

This formula is the result of litigation that began four years ago in the U.S. Attorney's office at Foley Square. The office is the most active in the country in prosecuting discrimination violations but the case illustrates the enormous and time-consuming difficulties. All this for one small union. And the union is appealing the decision, which could drag the case on further.

The zeal of the Nixon Administration in prosecuting unions and forcing hometown plans is not regarded as an unmixed blessing by some minority observers. They feel it is a tactic to break union strength at a moment when

historical circumstance suggests inevitable unwhitening. Thus, goes their
reasoning, blacks will eventually inherit unions which--like many of the
other things they inherit--are second hand and second class.

Ultimately, it seems, the job discrimination crisis must be resolved
through a combination of governmental action, social commitment and minority
pressure. After community people in the South Bronx stormed the courthouse
site, the number of trainees there was suddenly trebled. But that still was
regarded as insufficient and the day is approaching when militant groups
will draw their issue plain: In minority sections, white men must be laid
off to make places for blacks and Puerto Ricans.

This was the issue at a recent meeting in Fight Back's Harlem headquarters. The office is one long, narrow room painted the thin poverty
green of tenements. More than 100 blacks and Puerto Ricans were crowded in
to hear the weekly address of Fight Back's director, Jim Haughton. His
speeches combine the fervor of old-time unionism with soul appeals to the
brothers to get themselves together. There were old black men in the
audience with worn boots and tired faces, young ones with Afros and uncal-
lused hands. A Puerto Rican father held his sleeping son in his arms and
listened uncomprehensively to Haughton's rapid-fire English.

"We couldn't tighten them up at the World Trade Center," he said.
"But we're entering a new ball game now. They have to build in Harlem, East
Harlem and Bedford-Stuyvesant now, and they build without us if we let them.
We can't say much about downtown or way crosstown. But we'd be less than
men if we don't control our own part of town. Are we ready to do business?"

The men responded: "Right on!" and Haughton continued:

"We have to learn more about the nature of our struggle, the nature of
their oppression. We have to make our brothers sharp and wise in the ways
of the system which has been prospering at the blind sufferance of black and
Puerto Rican communities.

"Because it is not going to bend lightly to our demands. There is going
to be pitched battle. They will bring in police and National Guardsmen to
oppose us. There will be heavy struggle ahead this summer. But the days
will be exciting and meaningful as long as all the brothers struggle
together. Are we ready?"

The "Right on!" seemed to shake the building's foundation. It may echo
in other foundations before this year is out.

New York Times Magazine (May 21, 1972):24-25, 57-58, 60, 62, 64, 68-69.

53. CIVIL RIGHTS AND CHURCH LEADERS WARN OF
ATTACKS ON BLACK PEOPLE

Within a period of a few days I came upon two articles which reported
the latest propaganda of the non-union segment of the construction industry,
this time aimed directly at black people. One article was by Bayard Rustin
in a news release from the A. Philip Randolph Institute, the other article
was by Msgr. George G. Higgins from the NC News Service. Rustin's article
was titled "A Sneak Attack On Black Construction Workers," and Msgr. Higgins
column was titled "Dog-Eat-Dog Job Competition Prescribed for Black Workers."

Let me first quote from Rustin's article:

"Today, much of the bombast, crudity, and overt racism of the recent
past has disappeared. Discussion of racial issues has become more refined
and civilized. But this 'cooling off' of racial rhetoric raises a new and
perplexing problem: many, almost invisible assaults on black people now slip
by us unnoticed and therefore unchallenged. Such a 'sneak attack' on black
people is now underway within the construction industry.

"Blacks have finally begun to obtain their fair share of good-paying,
relatively secure jobs in the unionized skilled trades. But now, just as we
begin to see encouraging advances, we also witness the emergence of a bold
movement among employers to undermine the wages, job security and working
conditions of their new black workers by promoting something known as the
'merit shop.'

"What exactly is the 'merit shop' and how does it effect black workers? The merit shop is nothing more than a non-union shop in which the employer--and the employer alone--sets wage rates, working conditions, vacations, fringe benefits, and work rules. Workers (in merit shops) lack the protections afforded by a solid collective bargaining agreement. . . .

"It is no surprise--and certainly no coincidence--that the lowpaying 'merit shops' have become so popular in areas with large black populations and high unemployment rates which make labor cheap and docile. . . . All of this is just the beginning for the 'merit shop' proponents who are organized in the Associated Builders and Contractors (ABC). This powerful, well-balanced organization now hopes to significantly increase the number of 'merit shops' in urban areas. By focusing its anti-union, wage-cutting efforts in the cities, ABC will be undermining the position of black workers, workers who have enjoyed the benefits and high wages of union jobs.

"If we ignore this sneak attack on blacks, we will be openly accepting the cruel destruction of opportunity for the black working class, a group which has overcome numerous obstacles in the long struggle for equality and security," Rustin concluded.

Msgr. Higgins is very disturbed about the essay of a college professor, published in the *Wall Street Journal*. Walter E. Williams, associate professor of economics at Temple University, declared that blacks don't need a 'political savior--what they need is the opportunity to compete in the market.' But what the professor means by that is that the federal minimum wage law, the Davis-Bacon Act, and all other laws that 'restrict competition' in the workplace should be repealed. He also says, in effect, that black workers would be better off if there were no unions because unions limit competition in the marketplace. Msgr. Higgins said that such policies as Professor Williams favors would condemn black workers to the same kind of dog-eat-dog competition that all workers were exposed to in this country before trade unionism and before the enactment of protective labor legislation.[130]

True to form, Professor Williams furnishes the National Association of Manufacturers' pet argument that employment inevitably declines after increases in the minimum wage go into effect and that black workers are the main victims. (The fact is that civilian employment was 4.3 million higher in March 1979 than in December 1977 just prior to the increase in the minimum wage. There were 25,000 more black teenagers employed in March 1979 than in December 1977, and unemployment of black teenagers declined by 46,000).

Msgr. Higgins has stated that Professor Williams' arguments against trade unions insult the intelligence of black workers. In fact, black union members fare considerably better than non-union blacks and within the ranks of union members the income gap between blacks and whites is less than among non-union workers. Fortunately, black workers know far better than Professor Williams does which side their bread is buttered on, he said.

Our thanks to both Bayard Rustin and Msgr. Higgins for calling attention to the latest propaganda of anti-union forces against the black workers of America. We agree that their nonsense should be exposed for what it is at every opportunity.

General President

The Laborer (Laborers International Union), August, 1979.

PART V
1199 AND THE BLACK WORKER

1199 AND THE BLACK WORKER

It seems fitting to close this series on the black worker with Drug and Hospital Employees Local 1199, Martin Luther King's favorite union, and a dramatic example of the potential power in an alliance between the civil rights and labor movements. Started by Jewish drug store clerks in Harlem and the Bronx in 1958, Local 1199 undertook to organize workers in New York's voluntary hospitals, a group conventional labor savants considered to be unorganizable. The workers were nearly all uneducated blacks and Puerto Ricans whose wages were so low that they needed supplemental welfare relief in order to survive. Moreover, they were barred by state law from collective bargaining, and were not covered by the minimum wage or unemployment compensation laws. Nevertheless, Local 1199 effectively organized these workers because the black community gave the union its strongest support, and its drives were endorsed by the NAACP, the Urban League, and the Southern Christian Leadership Conference. Black activists as diverse as Ruby Dee, Ossie Davis, A. Philip Randolph, Malcolm X, and King lent their personal prestige to assist 1199. In fact, it was from a picket line of the Newark hospital strikers that King left for Oslo, Sweden, to receive the Nobel Peace Prize in 1964.

No strike for union recognition more cogently demonstrated the alliance between 1199 and the civil rights movement than the struggle to organize the nearly all-black Charleston hospital workers in 1969. Initially the hospital administrators treated the union with contempt, and fired their local leaders. Companies such as J. P. Stevens feared that they too would become the targets of unionizing drives if 1199 succeeded, so they gave their complete support to the hospitals. Local and state political leaders also worked closely with hospital officials, and the police and national guardsmen handled the mostly black women brutally, arresting hundreds of the desperately poor strikers. Even during the strike's darkest hours, however, the workers never faltered, for civil rights activists transformed the struggle into one for human rights and dignity. SCLC field staffers, including Ralph Abernathy and Andrew Young, remained in Charleston with 1199 officers, and Coretta Scott King inspired the strikers to go on, while Walter Reuther and George Meany donated thousands to the cause. By the end of April the city had become the scene of mass meetings, daily marches, rallies in churches and union halls, boycotts, and mass arrests. To many it seemed more like the early days of the civil rights movement than a fight for union recognition. Victory finally came through the intervention of the federal government, and Andrew Young summed up the importance of the effort: "We won this strike because of a wonderful marriage--the marriage of SCLC and Local 1199."

Finally, no assessment of 1199 would be complete if it confined itself to bread and ignored the roses. In fact, "Bread and Roses" are inseparable features of 1199's activities, and its unique and imaginative cultural program is called just that. In a union where so many workers were uneducated, theater, poetry, music, and other art forms practiced by the workers themselves, became an essential part of the union's educational campaign. But it is much more for Bread and Roses also offers its members inspiration, and the opportunity for personal development. The modern labor movement could take a few lessons from 1199 if it wishes to become more than a movement for bread alone.

OVERVIEW

1. TWENTY YEARS IN THE HOSPITALS: A SHORT HISTORY OF 1199

1959 was a relatively quiet year for most American trade unions. Not only was organization practically at a standstill, but union membership in many major industries actually declined. Much of the nation was still gripped by the complacency and conformity that typified the 1950s.

Against this unpromising background, a small local union of drug store workers in New York City--the Retail Drug Employees Union, Local 1199, affiliated with the Retail, Wholesale and Department Store Union (AFL-CIO) undertook an organizational drive in New York City's voluntary hospitals that was to shake the foundations of the nation's health care system and provide the labor movement with an inspirational example that it *was* possible to organize the unorganized and forge an unshakable alliance with the rising civil rights movement.

If one were looking for the industry most unlikely to be organized in 1959, the New York City voluntary (private, non-profit) hospitals would have been high on the list.

The workers in these voluntary hospitals had been accurately described as "the most underpaid and poorly benefitted workers in the richest city of the richest nation of the world." They had been forgotten by their employers, the unions, the government, and the public. They included nurses aides, orderlies, dishwashers, porters and laundry and dietary aides. Most were black and Hispanic women, and were poor. Their pay was as low as $28 for a work week of six and seven days and as many as 50 hours. Skilled technicians with Ph.D. degrees were receiving $60 a week. There was no job security and little chance for advancement. Thousands of full-time employees were compelled to apply for supplementary welfare assistance in order to support their families.

It was indeed ironic that New York's voluntary hospitals were staffed by thousands of "involuntary philanthropists" who enabled the hospitals to balance their budgets through substandard wages and working conditions. They were denied such elementary rights as minimum wage protection, unemployment insurance, disability benefits, and, most important of all, the right of union representation.

There had been some sporadic efforts to organize these workers prior to 1958, but for the most part, they had been shunned by the organized labor movement. There were several reasons for this. First was the fact that the voluntary hospitals were controlled by rich and powerful trustees. Their rosters read like a "Who's Who" in New York's financial power structure. Then, too, the unions knew that hospital workers, lacking bargaining rights, would have little leverage other than to strike--and that was considered unthinkable. Finally, and sadly, few unions were willing to undertake the organization of large numbers of black and Hispanic women workers.

In 1956, Doris Turner, now executive vice president of District 1199, but then a dietary worker at Lenox Hill Hospital on the upper East Side of Manhattan, took home $29.71 each week. In order to survive, she recalls, she had to shop in second-hand clothing stores. Other workers were even worse off. "A man who worked there 30 years had diabetes," she remembers, "and had to have his legs amputated. All they gave him was two weeks' pay. . . . Then a woman who'd been there five years was hurt accidentally by an orderly pushing one of those heavy trolleys. They fired her, just like that."

Al Kosloski, a maintenance worker at Montefiore Medical Center in the Bronx since 1937, remembers how he was expected to be available on Saturdays or even on hospital time to help a supervisor or administrator build his driveway or make other home repairs. "Your job depended on being cooperative," Kosloski recalls.

A Montefiore cook who was sick of this treatment recalls "most of the workers were scared to join a union, afraid to be fired. We belonged to our stomachs."

The union that defied all the odds and undertook the formidable task of organizing these "unorganizable" workers--Local 1199--had been formed in 1932 under the leadership of Leon J. Davis. By 1958, it included some 6,000 pharmacists, porters, clerks and other drug store workers. Although relatively small, Local 1199 had a long record of success in organizing campaigns, and an equally long record of opposition to discrimination.[131]

It would be difficult to overestimate the importance of the role played by the late Elliott Godoff in spearheading the organizing drive. Godoff, a former hospital pharmacist with more than 20 years experience in organizing hospital workers, joined the 1199 staff in 1958. So, when 1199 made the decision to throw its resources into this new "crusade," it was able to call upon the man who was probably better qualified to lead it than any other trade union leader in the city. When Godoff moved into 1199, workers he had organized earlier at Maimonides Medical Center in Brooklyn decided to accompany him. Thus Maimonides became the only hospital in the city which had recognized the union when it began its hospital organization campaign.

That summer, 1199 decided to organize Montefiore Hospital in the Bronx. President Davis assigned Godoff and Theodore Mitchell, a former drugstore porter who had become the union's first black organizer, to Montefiore. They worked for months signing up 600 of the hospital's 900 workers. "I walked all night with cards in my pocket getting them signed up and the bottom of my shoes burning like hot peppers," recalls Montefiore cook Kenneth Downes, a member of the original organizing committee. In December 1958 the workers voted overwhelmingly for the union, and shortly thereafter the tremendous gains of the historic contract between 1199 and Montefiore Hospital were made public.

More important even than the contract provisions themselves was the fact that the union was able to negotiate a contract with the hospital. The news of this had a truly electrifying effect on workers in voluntary hospitals throughout the city.

Davis and his colleagues recognized early that a crucial factor in the organization of the nonprofessional workers in New York City's voluntary hospitals, the majority of whom were black and Hispanic women, was the need for a working coalition between the union and the civil rights movement. 1199 brought good credentials to such a coalition. In addition to its early record of fighting discrimination against black pharmacists in Harlem, the union had solicited funds from its membership a support of the Montgomery, Alabama bus boycott in 1956. In the process, 1199 established a relationship with the boycott's leader, Martin Luther King, Jr., that was to continue until King's assassination in 1968. On more than one occasion, King called 1199 "my favorite union."

Even as the Montefiore contract was being negotiated, 1199 was organizing workers from other hospitals all over the city. Hundreds of drugstore 1199ers joined "crack-of-dawn brigades" and distributed leaflets at hospitals at 6 a.m. before going on to their regular jobs. 1199's midtown headquarters was alive night after night with organizing meetings of hospital workers asking questions, getting answers, taking on responsibilities.

By Feb. 4, 1959, President Davis was able to announce that the organizing drive had "brought 6,000 new members into Local 1199 in one month." He sent letters to the directors of seven major hospitals where the union had signed up a majority of the workers. The letters requested union recognition and contract negotiations. Management refused. The union then demanded elections at the seven hospitals. But the trustees, confident that their exemption from collective bargaining legislation made their position impregnable, insisted that "nonprofit hospitals are no place for unionization." When The New York Times, in an editorial supporting "Unions for Hospital Workers," raised the question as to why hospital workers should be asked to accept wages lower than those offered in private employment, Dr. Henry N. Pratt, director of New York Hospital, replied, "There is no compulsion to work for a hospital."

Strike votes took place on the sidewalk outside all seven hospitals, with the workers casting secret ballots in portable voting booths. The result was a pro-strike majority of 2,258 to 195.

On May 8, 1959, 3,500 hospital workers walked off their jobs. At 6 a.m., in defiance of a State Supreme Court order, picket lines were set up at Mount Sinai, Beth Israel, Flower Fifth Avenue, Brooklyn Jewish, Bronx and Beth David Hospitals. The next day, the workers at Lenox Hill made that hospital the seventh to join the walkout.

The leaders of 1199 perceived early in the strike that their only chance for success lay in rallying the conscience of the public behind *"la cruzada"* (the crusade)—as the city's Spanish-language newspaper, *El Diario*, referred to the hospital campaign. In spite of the militancy and determination of the strikers, they could be replaced on a temporary basis, and the professional and technical workers, including the nurses, were not part of the strike.[132] This, combined with the awesome power of the hospital boards, made it imperative that the union arouse public opinion to demand a settlement. The union used every possible means to bring the pressure of prominent public figures like Eleanor Roosevelt and Herbert H. Lehman, as well as of the media, to bear on the hospital managements. Coordinating this effort was Exec. Sec. Moe Foner. His effectiveness in this area was recognized by the American Public Relations Association when it gave its 1959 award to Foner for his role in conducting the union's media and public relations during the strike.

Interviewing pickets during the third week of the strike, *New York Times* labor reporter A. H. Raskin wrote:

> They seem determined to carry on indefinitely. They say they are tired of being "philanthropists" subsidizing the hospitals with their labor. One girl picket said: "Whenever we feel disheartened, we can always take out the stub of our last paycheck and get new heart for picketing." She pulled out her own and showed that it came to $27 in weekly take-home. . . .
>
> Financial hardship has been a part of their life for so long that the prospect of higher pay is less of a goal for many than the pivotal issue of union recognition. They feel for the first time that they "belong"—and this groping for human dignity through group recognition is more important than more cash.

This was particularly true for the women, who had to endure sexist as well as racist exploitation. It is not surprising that they were the most militant of the strikers, battling police and going to jail.

A decisive role was played by New York City Central Labor Council President Harry Van Arsdale. Under his leadership, more than 160 local unions, joint boards, and joint and district councils contributed over $100,000 to the support of the strikers, in addition to participating in picket lines, donating food, and providing other services.

Black and Puerto Rican leaders rallied to the support of the strikers. "Your effort to organize the voluntary hospital workers," said Thurgood Marshall, NAACP leader and later Supreme Court justice, "could well be one of the most important organizing campaigns this city has ever seen." Congressman Adam Clayton Powell led members of his congregation to the Mount Sinai picket line and shared a street meeting platform in Harlem with Leon Davis. Joseph Overton, president of the New York NAACP, expressed gratitude to 1199 for its efforts on behalf of New Yorkers of "Latin American and African descent."

On June 22, 1959, the bitterly-fought 46-day strike came to an end. Even though a justice of the New York State Supreme Court told the hospital managements that their refusal to recognize the union was "an echo of the nineteenth century," he could not budge them. To the end, they refused to grant union recognition. However, they did accept impartial grievance machinery and arbitration through outside representatives of the workers' choosing. They also agreed to include in the settlement the provision that "there shall be no discrimination against any employee because he joins or remains a member of any union or because he has presented a grievance under the grievance procedure." The agreement also included a minimum wage of $1 an hour, wage increases of $5 a week, a 40-hour week with time-and-a-half for overtime, seniority rules, job grades, and rate changes.

The settlement was known as the "PAC Agreement," named after the "Permanent Administrative Committee," which was established under the agreement. The PAC was a body of six management representatives and six public representatives. None had any connection with the labor movement. The Hospital Association, confident that under such an arrangement it could continue to dominate the scene, agreed to accept the PAC, and 37 hospitals signed the statement agreeing to the establishment of the grievance machinery.

On a hot June Monday afternoon, the hospital strikers jammed the non-air-conditioned ballroom of the Hotel Diplomat. The heat was intensified by the lights of the television cameras. The strikers listened intently as Leon Davis urged them to accept the settlement even though it provided only "back-door recognition" of the union. "Don't worry," he assured them, "We'll be in the front door before long." The strikers enthusiastically accepted their leaders' recommendation.

The hospitals, however, were not through fighting. They rehired the strikers one by one, in some cases over a period of six or seven weeks. The majority of hospitals which accepted the machinery for reviewing wages and grievances soon made it clear that their acceptance did not mean abiding by the terms. In September, 1959, the union reported that only in the hospitals in which the workers were organized were the provisions in effect. And even in those hospitals that were living up to the terms of the settlement, "there was no way for the union to resolve anything directly with management."

When management at Beth-El Hospital in Brooklyn (now called Brookdale Hospital Medical Center) tried to avert an election in June 1962, the non-professional workers struck. They were later joined by workers at the Manhattan Eye, Ear and Throat Hospital, who also struck for union recognition and higher wages. Because he refused to call off the strikes, Leon Davis was jailed for 30 days for "contempt of court."

A short while after the strike began, 50 black and Puerto Rican civic and religious leaders met at the offices of A. Philip Randolph. The Committee for Justice to Hospital Workers which emerged from the meeting pledged to organize wide strike support in the black and Puerto Rican communities. Co-chaired by Randolph and Joseph Monserrat, and with Bayard Rustin playing a key organizational role, the Committee grew in numbers to 235 black and Puerto Rican leaders, including Dr. Martin Luther King, Jr., Roy Wilkins of the NAACP, James Farmer of CORE, Whitney Young, Jr., of the Urban League, novelist James Baldwin and Judge Emilio Nunez. In a letter to *The New York Times* supporting the hospital strike, Randolph, Monserrat, and Baldwin wrote:

> As leaders of the Negro and Puerto Rican communities, we believe that the hospital strikes symbolize in most dramatic form the second-class citizenship status and sweatshop wages of all minority group workers in our city.
> The hospitals' refusal to agree to such a simple request as a secret ballot election and the elementary right of union representation is unreasonable, unjust and cruel. Such refusal constitutes nothing less than a determination to perpetuate involuntary servitude among the minority group workers at the bottom of the economic ladder. . . .[133]

The situation became even more potentially "explosive" when the union threatened 11 additional walkouts for higher wages and union recognition by July 31. Governor Nelson Rockefeller intervened. He promised to recommend to the Legislature the passage of a law granting collective bargaining recognition to the workers in New York City voluntary hospitals, provided that the union call off the strikes then in progress and abandon the threat to call out 11 more hospitals. In the words of *The New York Times,* Rockefeller was promising "for ill-paid hospital workers collective bargaining rights which workers in most other industries have had for more than a quarter of a century."

On the basis of Rockefeller's assurance, the union, after 62 days, called off the strikes at Beth-El and Manhattan Eye, Ear and Throat Hospitals. Martin Luther King, Jr., hailed the strike settlement as "historic" and said of the struggle of hospital workers:

> It is part and parcel of the larger fight in our community against discrimination and exploitation, against slums, against juvenile delinquency, against drug addiction--against all forms of degradation that result from poverty and human misery. It is a fight for human rights and human dignity.

The struggle for collective bargaining rights for the workers at New York City's voluntary hospitals, so pivotal to their right to genuine union representation, was followed with great interest in the press and throughout the labor movement. *New York Post* editorial writer James Wechsler wrote:

One feels a special elation about even the limited victory the hospital workers have won because they were fighting against such seemingly hopeless odds. Some of the most respectable, affluent and untouchable figures in the community were arrayed against them. But the miracle of democracy is a continuous one. . . . It was a large affirmation that no good cause is a lost cause. . . .

On Sunday, July 21, 1962, East 72nd St. between Second and Third Avenues was jammed with a cross-section of New York's black and white communities. Speakers at the 1199 rally included Socialist leader Norman Thomas, Roy Wilkins, District 65 President David Livingston, Malcolm X, Bayard Rustin, Father George B. Ford, Representative William F. Ryan, A. Philip Randolph and Leon Davis. [134]

By the beginning of May, 1963, the state legislature had passed and Governor Rockefeller had signed the law extending collective bargaining rights to hospital workers, but limiting its geographical coverage to New York City. This legislative victory was extended in 1965 to cover the entire state. The 1965 legislation followed a bitterly-fought eight-week strike for recognition by 1199ers at Lawrence Hospital in Bronxville, N.Y., a wealthy Westchester County suburb.

With the way cleared for them to organize into 1199, thousands of hospital workers signed up. One after another, the workers voted in elections for 1199, and the voluntary hospitals recognized the union as the collective bargaining agent. A few weeks after the legislation had amended the state labor law to cover hospital workers, *The New York Times* described Local 1199 as "the nation's largest organization of hospital workers, with contracts covering 8,500 employees at 24 voluntary hospitals."

In 1964, a campaign was launched to bring a new category of hospital employees into 1199. The drive began with the formation of 1199's Guild of Professional, Technical and Clerical Employees, directed by Jesse Olson, a former pharmacist and one of the 1959 strike leaders. The growth of the Guild not only brought the benefits of union membership to new members, but also strengthened immeasurably the bargaining position of all other workers in the hospitals.

By 1965, 1199 had scored a number of important achievements. Union membership had grown from six thousand in 1959 to 30,000. Wages had more than doubled, and health coverage for workers and their families, paid for by the hospitals, had been won in union contracts. Workers also enjoyed paid vacations, sick leave of 12 days a year, and the 40-hour week (and in a number of contracts, the 35-hour week), with time-and-a-half for overtime. There were three days' funeral leave in the event of death in a worker's immediate family, and, to top it off, two days' matrimony leave.

On March 23, 1968, three weeks before his assassination in Memphis, Tennessee, Martin Luther King, Jr. told an 1199 rally: "You have provided concrete and visible proof that when black and white workers unite in a democratic organization like 1199, they can move mountains." One such "mountain" was moved shortly thereafter. In full-page advertisements in the leading New York City newspapers, 1199 announced "A Hospital Crisis," and informed the public "that starting midnight, June 30, when our contracts expire, we will no longer work unless we win a minimum wage of $100 a week."

The campaign was a success. Under the new agreement, workers who had been earning from $70 to $76 a week were to receive $88 immediately and $100 a year later. (Most of these workers had been earning $32 a week less than ten years before). In addition, for the first time, the contract included employer-financed pension and job training and upgrading funds.

In 1970, 1199 moved from a three-story building on Eighth Avenue to a 14-story structure two blocks south on 43rd St. named the Martin Luther King, Jr. Labor Center. The building's entrance was dominated by a mosaic mural including the words of 19th century black abolitionist Frederick Douglass: "If there is no struggle, there can be no progress." [135]

At the ceremonies dedicating the new headquarters, Congresswoman Bella Abzug, herself one of the pioneers in opposing America's involvement in Vietnam, praised 1199 for being "one of the first unions to cry out against the horrible, immoral war in Vietnam." The union's record justified this tribute. In July, 1964, President Leon Davis had warned against the "aggressive and dangerous foreign policy we are pursuing in South Vietnam." In November, 1965, Executive

Secretary Moe Foner played a key role in organizing the Labor Leadership
Assembly for Peace gathering in Chicago, where over 500 leaders from 50
international unions vowed to "seek to express the underlying and deeply-felt
peace sentiment of American workers."[136]

1199's spectacular success in 1968 in winning the $100-a-week minimum
for nonprofessional hospital workers in New York City climaxed a decade of
dramatic progress in its organizing efforts and sent shock waves through unorganized hospitals throughout the nation.

During the 1960s, there had been some limited beginnings in organizing
in New Jersey, Connecticut, Long Island and Westchester county. Many of these
campaigns were led by Vice Pres. Len Seelig, who took responsibility for the
Connecticut area in 1968 but who died in an auto accident in 1971 at the age
of 41. The $100-a-week victory, coupled with 1199's success in organizing
professional and technical employees, placed the question of extending organizing efforts to other parts of the country high on 1199's agenda.[137]

Even the realization was being fully absorbed by the leaders of the
union. President Davis received a telegram from Mrs. Martin Luther King.
It read:

> I have always admired what your union has been doing to
> eliminate poverty wages and win dignity for hospital workers. My
> late husband also admired your substantial achievements. I am
> particularly interested in your current campaign because so many
> hospital workers are women—Black women, Spanish-speaking women,
> and white women—often the main supporters of their families. My
> husband used to say that they were forced to work at full-time jobs
> for part-time pay. May I suggest that when you have succeeded in
> winning a new contract with a $100 weekly starting wage for hospital
> workers in New York, that you undertake a new responsibility—the
> task of organizing the many thousands of unorganized hospital
> workers in the major cities of our nation. I believe that such an
> organizing crusade would represent a major contribution to the
> struggle to eliminate poverty.

The union announced in October 1968 the formation of the National
Organizing Committee of Hospital and Nursing Home Employees, with Coretta
Scott King as its honorary chairperson. Just at this time, events were un-
folding in Charleston, South Carolina, which would become central to 1199's
national organizing effort.

In the spring of 1968, Charleston hospital workers, most of them black
women earning $1.30 an hour, began holding meetings to organize. They tried
to talk about union recognition with Dr. William McCord, president of Charleston Medical College and director of its hospital, a state institution. They
were denied an opportunity even to meet.

The Charleston hospital workers got in touch with 1199. Local 1199B
was launched to represent hospital workers in the city. When 12 union members
were fired on March 17, 1969, 400 workers at Medical College Hospital walked
off their jobs. A week later, 90 workers at the Charleston County Hospital
walked out in sympathy. Demands included union recognition, a wage increase,
a grievance procedure and rehiring of the 12 fired workers.

The hospital administration treated the strikers' demands with contempt.
Dr. McCord, for example offered to give the workers, almost all of them black,
an additional holiday—the birthday of Confederate General Robert E. Lee. But
contempt soon gave way to naked force. An injunction limited picketing to
"ten people . . . at a time—twenty yards apart," and no closer than eight
blocks from the hospital. The workers defied the injunction and conducted mass
picketing around the hospital site. They were promptly arrested. By the end
of the first week of the strike, 100 of them were in jail. The strikers, and
particularly the staff members of Local 1199, were also attacked by vigilantes.
The room of Henry Nicholas, assistant director of the National Organizing
Committee, who had come in to assist the local organization, was fire-bombed.
The workers had to organize a security guard around the building as well as
around their union hall.

With arrests piling up, staff members of both the Southern Christian
Leadership Conference (SCLC) and 1199 arrived to direct the battle. Andrew
J. Young coordinated SCLC activities and worked closely with 1199ers Nicholas,

Elliott Godoff and Moe Foner. They made the nation aware that the strike of
the black hospital workers in Charleston involved, in the words of a *New York
Times* editorial, "values as fundamental as those in the original battles for
school desegregation and equal employment opportunities."

By the third week of April, Charleston had become the scene of mass
meetings, daily marches, evening rallies in churches and union halls, and
boycotts of stores and schools. It also became the scene of daily confrontations and mass arrests as the Charleston power structure, headed by J. P.
Stevens, owner of 23 textile mills in South Carolina and an implacable foe
of unionism, struck back. South Carolina Governor McNair quickly let it be
known that the state would never recognize a public employees' union, and
Dr. McCord emphasized the same point in his contemptuous remark to a *Business
Week* reporter: "I am not about to turn over the administration of a five
million dollar institution to people who never had a grammar school education."[138]

The governor sent 600 state troopers and National Guardsmen into
Charleston and announced a 7 p.m. curfew. Mass arrests were stepped up.
Hundreds of police, state troopers and National Guardsmen with fixed bayonets,
paraded the streets. One of the strikers, Edrena Johnson, kept a diary of
her nine-day stay in jail. On April 25, she recorded the following:

> As I lie here in a cell at the Charleston County jail, I
> feel the sympathy of all who are fighting for what is right.
> We, as black people in South Carolina, have awakened to the fact
> that we are no longer afraid of the white man and that we want
> to be recognized, not because of our race, but because we are
> human beings and we have a right--a right which we shall fight
> and go to jail for. We, the black people of South Carolina, will
> no longer sit back and be counted. We're going to stand up for
> what is right. We're soul from our hearts, and soul power is
> where it's at.

The national heads of nine civil rights organizations and five elected
black officials issued a joint statement in support of the strike. They
noted that it was the first time black leaders had come together on a single
issue since Martin Luther King's assassination a year earlier.

The signers were headed by Coretta King, who throughout the strike gave
herself entirely to the cause of the hospital workers. On May 1, *The New
York Times* carried a full-page advertisement with a picture of Mrs. King on
one side and on the other, the statement: "If my husband were alive today,
he would be in Charleston, South Carolina."

National television newscasts brought Charleston's marching blacks,
with their blue-and-white 1199 hats, courageously parading under the guns of
Guardsmen, into millions of American homes.

Unions across the country sent delegations to march with the strikers.
United Auto Worker President Walter Reuther joined the demonstrations in
person and presented a check for $25,000 to Local 1199B. The AFL-CIO donated
an additional $25,000.

The daily demonstrations and the nationwide publicity that the strike
was receiving, most of it favorable to the strikers, finally persuaded
Charleston's businessmen to begin discussing a settlement.

The strike lasted 113 days, during which 1,000 persons, including
1199 President Leon Davis and Reverend Ralph Abernathy, were jailed. In the
end, union power and soul power produced what the *Richmond Times-Dispatch*
called "an unbeatable combination."

The workers at the Medical College Hospital won wage increases of 30
to 70 cents an hour. They also won the establishment of a credit union and
a grievance procedure in which the union could represent them. All workers
were to be reinstated, including the twelve whose firing had started the
strike. It was, to be sure, a compromise settlement; the union did not win
recognition as a bargaining agent. But, as Mary Ann Moultrie, probably the
first rank-and-file delegate to address a national convention of the AFL-CIO,
told the delegates to that organization's 1969 convention:

> We 400 hospital workers--almost all of us women, and all of
> us black--were compelled to go on strike so that we could win the
> right to be treated as human beings. We had to fight the entire

power structure of the state of South Carolina. . . . We had
to face 1,200 National Guardsmen armed with tanks and bayonets,
and hundreds of state troopers. All because 400 black women
dared to stand up and say we just were not going to let anybody
turn us around. A year ago, nobody ever heard of us. We were
forgotten women, second-class citizens. We worked as nurses
aides. We cleaned the floors. We prepared the food in the
hospitals. And if it had not been for the union, we would
still be forgotten people.

At a rally toward the end of the strike, Coretta King had brought a
large audience to its feet cheering when she said: "We won this strike
because of a wonderful marriage--the marriage of the SCLC and Local 1199.
The first of many beautiful children of this marriage is Local 1199B here in
Charleston, and there are going to be as many more children as there are
letters in the alphabet."

In August, 1969, again with strong support from the SCLC, including
Mrs. King, and the black community, Local 1199E, the second "child" of the
marriage, compelled Johns Hopkins Medical Center in Baltimore, Maryland to
agree to a representation election for 1,500 service employees, mostly black
women. The union won by a two-to-one margin.

Other victories followed, in Baltimore and elsewhere. The Hopkins
victory in Baltimore led to successful elections at other major hospitals
there and to the eventual creation of District 1199E, which now has 6,000
members in Maryland and Washington, D.C. under the leadership of Pres. Ronald
Hollie. In Philadelphia, 1199C won elections at several major hospitals and
laid the basis for the current powerful district of 10,000 members headed by
Pres. Henry Nicholas, 1199P began organizing elsewhere in Pennsylvania and
now has 5,000 members in 25 different communities under the leadership of
Pres. John Black, 1199 W. Va organized in West Virginia, 1199H organized in
Ohio, 1199 Mass. organized in Massachusetts. During the same period, 1199 won
elections covering 4,000 workers in New York, New Jersey and Connecticut.

The National Union of Hospital and Health Care Employees was created
in 1973 at a founding convention in New York. District 1199 in the New York
City metropolitan area became the largest of several districts and areas with
a combined membership of 100,000 in 14 states and the District of Columbia.
Continued growth up the present finds members from Rhode Island to Iowa in
seven districts and in areas that will become financially self-supporting
districts when they organize enough members to make this practical.

The two newest districts--Connecticut and New Jersey--are outgrowths
of the original Local 1199. When they became big enough to stand as self-
sufficient districts, their members voted to do so. District 1199J in New
Jersey became a district in 1977 under the leadership of Pres. Aberdeen
David. The former Connecticut Area of District 1199, headed by 1199 Vice
Pres. Jerry Brown, is now completing the process of becoming District 1199
New England. The new district will include 10,000 members now under contract
in Connecticut and Rhode Island, plus whatever new members are organized in
Maine, New Hampshire and Vermont.

The hospital and nursing home industry which the new national union
first proposed to unionize in the early 1970s was the third largest employer
in the country. Non-professional hospital workers were 90 percent unorganized,
and administrators intended to keep it that way. Workers in voluntary hospitals
had been excluded from federal law giving workers the right of union representation. There was neither National Labor Relations Board machinery for
conducting union representation elections nor legal definitions of unfair
labor practices. Hospitals were not legally required to recognize the union
as the official bargaining agent of the workers.

The new national union pressed for federal legislation granting hospital
workers collective bargaining rights. Victory on this front came on July
11, 1974, when Congress passed legislation extending the coverage of the
National Labor Relations Act to employees of non-profit hospitals and nursing
homes.

As the national organizing effort progressed, a considerable portion
of 1199's energies, finances and personnel were devoted to it. At the same
time, progress continued in New York both in the Hospital Division headed by
Exec. Vice Pres. Doris Turner and the Guild Division headed by Exec. Vice
Pres. Jesse Olson.

An impressive display of strength came June 13, 1972 when 25,000 members of 1199 jammed onto Murray St. next to City Hall in lower Manhattan as a prelude to expiration that month of their contract with the League of Voluntary Hospitals.

Wearing their blue-and-white hats and chanting "We want a contract!", the demonstrators carried signs stating "We can't make it on $130 a week," "Don't force us to strike the hospitals" and "Don't blame us for rising hospital costs."

The latter was a reference to a development reported somewhat later by the President's Council on Wage and Price Stabilization. The Council found that hospital workers' wages were not responsible for the dramatic rise in hospital costs over the previous decade. It noted that wages were a steadily decreasing percentage of hospital costs and that other major elements in hospital budgets were rising faster than wages.

"We're here today to let everybody know that hospital workers are not the forgotten people or the invisible people," Exec. Vice Pres. Turner told the June 13 rally. "The jobs we hold are some of the most important jobs in the world. Without us, the hospitals would not run."

Addressing himself to the city as a whole, Pres. Davis told the huge crowd:

> This is a better city because of us. We are not making impossible demands, but only that which we need to take care of our children, our families. We will not permit anyone to destroy our dignity as an organized group of men and women who insist on the right and power to influence our own lives. We know all too well what it's like to have things shoved down our throats. Well, no one is going to shove anything down our throats ever again!

Three weeks later, a citywide hospital strike was averted when a two-year contract brought raises to 33,000 workers of $24 a week or 15 percent, whichever was greater.

The first half of that raise was due July 1, 1972. But President Richard Nixon's three-year-old Cost of Living Council, which discriminatorily imposed mandatory wage controls on 10 percent of the nation's workforce, including hospital workers, held up the raise for 11 months. Members in dozens of other communities experienced similar delays at the hands of the COLC. The second New York raise was due July 1, 1973. Infuriated over their long wait for the first raise, New York 1199ers set a Nov. 1 deadline for COLC approval of the 1973 raise. When that date came and went without action in Washington, 30,000 members struck for one week. The result was a compromise. 1199ers did receive a second year increase, but it was less than what they had originally negotiated. Nevertheless, the union won respect across the nation for its courage in taking on Nixon's arbitrary and discriminatory wage control apparatus. Part of the price the union had to pay for standing up to Nixon was an unprecedented $725,500 fine for violating a federal court anti-strike injunction. But most 1199ers shared the summary of striker Moshe Goldberg of Brooklyn Jewish Hospital. "Even though the money we lost by striking will be lost forever, the strike had a point. We cannot let them dictate to us," he said.

New York 1199ers were forced to strike again for 11 days in July 1976 when the League of Voluntary Hospitals not only refused to negotiate for wage increases, but refused to agree to take the dispute to binding arbitration. A strike highlight was a rally of 10,000 strikers outside the opening session July 12 of the Democratic Party national convention at Madison Square Garden. In the face of the determination of 40,000 strikers and widespread public support for an arbitrated settlement, management finally capitulated. The disappointing award by arbitrator Margery Gootnick that came two months later convinced many 1199ers that in the future they should rely on their strength on the picketline rather than arbitrated decisions.

The early 1970s were a period of organizing growth for 1199 in New York City as well as in new areas. The biggest success came at the nation's largest voluntary hospital, Columbia Presbyterian in upper Manhattan, when workers voted 878-507 for 1199 on March 1, 1973. Subsequent victories at St. Luke's Roosevelt and Methodist Hospitals reduced those major New York voluntary hospitals without 1199 contracts to a very few conspicuous holdouts.

But perhaps the most dramatic new organizing effort of the 1970s came in an entirely new field. The nation's two million registered nurses had become increasingly militant. They were tired of being ignored by the predominantly male medical power structure when they asked for better salaries and a voice in patient care delivery. They were frustrated increasingly by the inability of the American Nurses Association and its state affiliates to represent their interests effectively.

A few nurses in several states had joined 1199 over the years, but the big breakthrough came in 1977 when 650 RNs at Brookdale Medical Center in Brooklyn voted for 1199 representation and then struck for two days to win their first union contract. A significant factor in the strike victory was the cooperation of the 2,000 other 1199ers already under 1199 contract at Brookdale.

With the Brookdale victory, a fourth division of District 1199 became a reality. Joining the Hospital, Guild and Drug Divisions was the League for Registered Nurses, directed by Exec. Vice Pres. Sondra Clark, a former Brookdale RN who led the organizing drive there.

The 1199 RN Division now has 3,000 members at 35 institutions, among them major hospitals such as Brookdale and Beth Israel Medical Center in Manhattan. An additional 2,000 RNs are under 1199 contract in other districts and areas. Some, like the 160 nurses at Fairmont General Hospital in Fairmont, W. Va., displayed tremendous unity and widespread membership participation in winning union contracts. The Fairmont RNs struck for 45 days to win their contract.

"Our people really stuck together because they finally got tired of years of having no say and being ignored," said Fairmont RN Mary Shafer. "Women were held down in the past, but today they're more ready to speak out on things."

In addition to winning better salaries and working conditions, nurses in 1199 have quickly become involved in a variety of professional programs, ranging from RN Committee lectures and conferences on subjects such as the 1985 proposal or cancer care to the successful fight against the arbitrary voiding of the year's RN licensing exam by New York State.

Another major development was the successful organization during the past year of 6,400 employees at 40 state-run health institutions in Connecticut. The new members include 1,800 professional employees in categories such as doctor, dentist, social worker, psychologist, RN and chaplain. The state employees, organized under the leadership of 1199 Vice Pres. Jerry Brown, form a major portion of the membership of the new District 1199 New England.

Elsewhere, 1199 organizing in the late 1970s slowed somewhat. Reasons included consistent unemployment nationally and retrenchment by many hospitals, a vicious offensive by hospitals willing to spend hundreds of thousands of dollars for anti-union "consultants," and frustrating delays by the National Labor Relations Board in processing applications for representation elections.

In spite of this, election wins brought unionization to new thousands of hospital workers in such widely separated communities as Gary, Ind., Davenport, Iowa; Huntington, W. Va.; Philadelphia; Detroit; Rochester, N.Y.; Portsmouth, N.H.; Aliquippa, Pa. and Providence, R.I. Following Elliott Godoff's death in 1975, organizing drives were conducted under the leadership of National Union Director of Organization Bob Muehlenkamp.

By the end of the 1970s, unionization had brought about an unprecedented transformation in the lives of New York hospital workers. The average wage in the lowest paid job category was $230 a week, or more than seven times the wage received only 20 years earlier. Average weekly salaries in higher-paid categories at the end of 1979 were $315 for radiologic technologists, $258 for LPNs, $281 for laboratory technicians, $414 for pharmacists and $339 for beginning social workers. On top of this, a three percent raise was due to 1199ers at League of Voluntary Hospitals institutions on Jan. 1, 1980.

The union's pioneering Benefit, Pension and Training and Upgrading Funds, financed entirely by management payments but administered jointly by the union and management, had become models in their fields. The Benefit and Pension Funds were directed from their beginnings by 1199 Sec. Treas. William J. Taylor, a former drug store luncheonette worker who retired last summer after 42 years in 1199.

Under the self-administered Benefit Fund, workers and their dependents could be assured of hospitalization, surgical benefits, medical care benefits

in both their homes and the doctors' offices, an optical plan, disability
pay of two-thirds of their salary, diagnostic services including x-ray and
laboratory work, maternity benefits, life insurance coverage, dental and free
prescription coverage. Each year, the Benefit Fund also sends hundreds of
members children to all-expenses-paid three-week summer vacations at camp and
provides college tuition aid on the basis of need to hundreds of members'
children. In 1979, for instance, 460 children of members utilized the summer
camp program. The tuition aid program has assisted 4,500 children of members
since 1967. Its 1979 budget is $675,000.

The Pension Fund dispersed nearly $1 million to more than 6,000 retired
National Union members this year. And Retired Members Division in New York
and Philadelphia have been cited by government and private agencies for their
outstanding role in providing retirees with a wide variety of programs to
enrich their retired years. These have included classes in arts and crafts,
languages, photography and film-making. A highlight of 1979 was a handsome
exhibit of photo-essays of and by retired members, shown at District 1199 and
at the Brooklyn Museum.

The Training and Upgrading Fund aided more than 1,700 New York members
who studied for better health care jobs last year. Among graduates of full-
time training programs were 32 registered nurses, 15 radiologic technologists
and eight respiratory therapists. Full-time students receive tuition, a sti-
pend of 85 percent of their net pay up to a maximum of $150 a week and costs
of textbooks. Part-time Fund programs include tuition assistance for health-
related courses, basic education, high school equivalency, English as a second
language and college preparation. The program is widely recognized for its
success in providing avenues to better pay and more challenging positions for
workers previously stuck in dead-end jobs.

A democratic structure emphasizes the crucial role of rank-and-file
delegates elected by secret ballot every two years by the membership. Currently, 2,000 New York delegates handle thousands of grievances each year and
meet in monthly delegate assemblies to discuss and act upon all important union
affairs. The delegates spend one weekend every other year at a training
session in the refreshing rural atmosphere of Pawling, N.Y.

The union's staff contains a high proportion of former hospital workers
who rose from the ranks to take on responsibilities as organizers and officers.
Typical of this process was Vice Pres. James Boykin, who died of a heart
attack in 1976 at the tragically early age of 48. Boykin was a Flower-Fifth
Ave. Hospital cook who became an 1199er in the 1959 strike and served as an
active delegate before joining the staff as an organizer in 1963. He was
appointed acting vice president and Hospital Division Bronx-Westchester Area
Director in 1972.

The union's growing attention to legislative affairs was illustrated by
its success in building a coalition that won decisive support from political
leaders in the effort to prevent the closing of Brooklyn Jewish Hospital. The
district's legislative director is Judy Berek, a former Kingsbrook Jewish
Medical Center laboratory technician.

Many 1199ers are living in the prize-winning 1,590-family cooperative
1199 Plaza housing development in East Harlem. *The New York Times* called the
development "superb" and "one of New York's most architecturally significant
housing projects."

Many of the New York district's initiatives in social, cultural and
educational affairs were matched in newer National Union districts. A leader
in this area was District 1199C in Philadelphia, where a new training program
has won national recognition and where the district plays an important role in
the city's political scene.

For many years, 1199 members have participated in a wide variety of
social, educational and cultural activities designed to demonstrate that a good
union doesn't have to be dull. These include dances, picnics, moonlight sails,
live theater programs with Broadway stars, film festivals, Christmas children's
parties, art exhibits at Gallery 1199, annual health care conferences, and
regular meetings of special committees of pharmacists, RNs, LPNs, dietitians,
radiologic technologists, laboratory technicians and therapists. The union
produced three award-winning documentary films and a book of poems by staffer
Marshall Dubin on the hospital strikes. Its monthly publication, 1199 News,
has been among the most consistent award winners in the labor press.

Building on this base, 1199 during the past year developed the Bread and Roses cultural project, called by *Business Week* magazine "the most significant program ever undertaken by a U.S. union to bring culture to its members." The program's name is taken from the banner in the 1912 Lawrence, Mass. textile strike on which young mill women proclaimed "We want bread and roses, too."

Supported by grants from federal and state cultural agencies and a number of private foundations and individuals, Bread and Roses offers cultural events to members inside major hospitals and nursing homes, at 1199 Plaza and at union headquarters. Its events include drama, music and poetry programs by professional companies; art and photography exhibits; a Labor Day Street Fair attended by 75,000; an original musical revue based on members' oral history accounts of their own lives; conferences and seminars; videotapes and films; and much more.

Directed by National Union Exec. Sec. Moe Foner, Bread and Roses has already attracted favorable comment by newspapers and magazines across the nation. It is widely recognized as a prototype for the entire labor movement.

Earlier this year, two people with long 1199 associations paused to look backward in articles in 1199 News as the union celebrated its 20 years in the hospitals.

Actor, playwright and director Ossie Davis has been closely identified with 1199 for 25 years as writer, performer and volunteer organizer. He and his wife, Ruby Dee, are "deeply proud of our continuing involvement with the union," Davis said. He added:[139]

There is a spirit about 1199 that comes from a tradition of struggle. Being aggressive and feisty when the cause is right, 1199 didn't hesitate to jump into any fight where peace, civil rights, race prejudice, corporate greed, bureaucratic stupidity or political indifference were involved.

Edna Mallon, a central service aide at Flushing Hospital in Queens since 1962, recalled the union struggles that brought her wages from 75 cents an hour to her current $260 a week, "with beautiful benefits and the prospect of a nice pension."

"The mural on our 1199 headquarters building tells the story of what we hospital workers were and what we have become, said Mallon. "If there is no struggle, there can be no progress."

1199 News: A Special Issue, 14 (December, 1979): 3-47.

2.

LOCAL 1199 MAKES REALISTIC GAINS FOR ITS NEWLY-ORGANIZED MEMBERS

By Moe Foner

A crusade to organize 35,000 workers in New York City's eighty-two voluntary, non-profit hospitals has focused public attention on Local 1199, Drug and Hospital Employes Union, affiliated with the AFL-CIO's Retail, Wholesale and Department Store Union.

When the campaign started, early in 1958, few New Yorkers were familiar with "1199" whose 6,000 members, employed in some 1,800 retail drug stores in the metropolitan area and Long Island included 2,100 registered pharmacists. Increased public interest in the local was demonstrated in the course of a ten-day period this past summer.

Across the desk of its president, Leon J. Davis, came inquiries from union leaders in several states and far off Ghana requesting details on the local's experiences in organizing hospital workers, and invitations to lecture at several schools and colleges including Harvard University's Graduate School of Economics. Simultaneously, a feature article on the hospital campaign appeared in *Fortune Magazine*.

Local 1199 made headlines when 3,500 newly organized members in seven hospitals struck for forty-six days during the Spring and Summer of 1959.

The nation's first major walkout of hospital workers, the strike climaxed a whirlwind organizing drive that had enrolled 6,000 members in a one-month period.

Led by Harry A. Van Arsdale, Jr., head of the New York City AFL-CIO Central Labor Council, the entire labor movement rallied behind the strikers. Thousands of trade unionists turned out daily on the picket lines, tons of food were collected and 162 local unions contributed a total of $167,000 to aid the strikers in a display of labor solidarity unprecedented in New York City history in the memories of some of the oldest members of the labor movement.

Public support for the strikers came in the form of food, funds and resolutions from community, civic and religious groups, including the formation of a sixty-five member Citizens' Committee headed by Dr. Reinhold Neibuhr and A. Philip Randolph.

When Local 1199 decided to organize voluntary hospital workers, few labor leaders held out hope for success. Except for a handful of abortive efforts in the massive drives of the 1930's, unions had largely left the voluntary hospitals alone. The thousands of workers required to run them were truly "the forgotten men and women" of New York City--forgotten by unions, employers and the public. Within the shining hospital walls, there had simmered in silence thousands of unprotected workers whose daily tasks are essential for the hospitals' maintenance. They were cooks and dishwashers, nurses' aides and technicians, laundry workers and clerks, porters, housekeeping and maintenance workers.

These workers earned as little as $25, $30 and $32 for a six-day, forty-four workweek. Overtime pay was non-existent, split shifts prevalent. In some cases, to eke out a bare existence, many were compelled to seek supplementary relief assistance from New York City welfare agencies. Because they worked for charitable, nonprofit institutions, they were excluded from coverage under New York State's Labor Relations, Unemployment Insurance and Disability Benefit laws.

While workers at city-owned hospitals in New York City have been organized for years, labor had shied away from the nonprofit hospitals. Denied collective bargaining protection by law, it was felt that voluntary hospital workers could not be organized. Some said that hospital workers would never unite in a common fight as members of trade unions. Still others feared that organization might create conflicts between hospital trustees and labor leaders who often sat together at trustee meetings of community and social agencies.

Some eyebrows were raised in December 1959 when Local 1199 scored its first major breakthrough at Montefiore Hospital in the Bronx with a decisive 628-31 vote in a secret ballot consent election and quickly expanded its campaign to thirty hospitals throughout the city. Assisted by stories and editorials in *El Diario de Nueva York* and *The Amsterdam News,* the largest Spanish language and Negro newspapers in the city, "La Cruzada de Local 1199," as it was termed in *El Diario,* the drive soon resembled the mass organizing efforts of the 1930's.

Dan Wakefield, a reporter who covered it from the beginning, described this aspect in an article in *The Nation* magazine, March 14, 1959:

"To walk into one of these organizing meetings is to walk back into a time of the five-and-a-half and six day week, the wages under a dollar an hour, the fears of firing from the boss for 'talking union,' and the almost revival-meeting enthusiasm of workers suddenly awakened out of their plight."

Soon, *The New York Times* and *New York Post* took up the cudgels for the hospital workers. In an editorial on March 7, 1959 *The Times* called attention to the financial plight of the hospitals, but added: ". . . Why should workers performing the same kind of jobs as in private employment be asked to be philanthropists by accepting much lower wages and the human sufferings that follow. And why should collective bargaining be denied them when it is a policy overwhelmingly approved by the American public?"

Actively assisting in the campaign were some 500 drug store members of Local 1199. Recognizing that success depended on massive rank and file participation to distribute leaflets at hospitals throughout the city, pharmacists, clerks, sodamen, porters and cosmeticians enrolled in "1199's" "Crack of Dawn Brigade." At least once a week, these volunteers appeared at hospital gates at 5:30 A.M., distributed leaflets and talked union until it was time for them to report for work at the drug stores.

Today, Local 1199's Hospital Division has a membership of 8,000 and holds
collective bargaining agreements covering 3,200 nonprofessional, technical and
office employes at voluntary hospitals and homes in the metropolitan area.
The Statement of Policy issued by thirty-seven subscribing hospitals at the
close of the 1959 strike was improved considerably this past July.

While it does not include union recognition, the revised Statement of
Policy provides for a truly impartial board of six public members known as
the Permanent Administrative Committee, appointed by the Chief Judge of the
New York State Court of Appeals with six consultants equally divided among
hospital trustees and labor. An improved grievance procedure has been established with the PAC acting as final arbiter of all disputes and the PAC will
make annual reports on all issues affecting workers in the subscribing hospitals.

Since the union entered the scene, wages, still below standard, have
improved markedly. Hiring rates, formerly as low as $25, $30 and $32 for a
forty-four-hour, six-day week, are now $45 with some hospitals already plan-
ning to go to $50 for a normal forty-hour, five-day week. Overtime pay is a
normal practice and split shifts have been eliminated.

*Activity on the legislative front also has paid off for hospital workers.
Bills were enacted in the New York State Legislature last year bringing non-
profit institution employes under the State Disability Benefits Law and a
$1-an-hour minimum wage for the first time in the State's history.*

But what kind of union are hospital workers joining? The local that
defied the warnings about the impractical and impossible task of organizing
hospital workers is an outstanding example of professional organization. Its
largest segment consists of registered pharmacists but also includes sodamen
and women, drug clerks, cosmeticians, porters and deliverymen.

Local 1199 was established at the height of the depression in 1932 when
a small group of pharmacists met in a dingy room in downtown Manhattan. Among
them were Leon J. Davis, "1199's" president for the past fifteen years. At
that time those fortunate to be employed earned as little as $20 for a sixty-
six-hour, seven-day work week. Their professionalism included sweeping, mop-
ping and dusting floors as well as filling and delivering prescriptions.

The meeting coincided with the appearance of an editorial in the *American
Druggist* warning that: "Unions in pharmacy will fail because pharmacy is a
personal service profession and no drug clerk wants forever to remain a clerk.
The job of organization is hopeless."

But history confounded the experts. The pharmacists, prime movers in
forming the union, soon recognized that their best interests lay in extending
organization to the rest of their fellow employes. Through the long climb
back to prosperity and since, improvements in working conditions and status
have come to members in all categories. The starting rate for pharmacists is
now $130 for a forty-hour, five-day week, in addition to welfare and pension
benefits.

More than 85 per cent of New York's drug stores have been organized by
Local 1199. Unionization extends to such chains as Whelan's and Liggett's
individual stores employing up to sixty workers and small owner-operated stores
with only one worker employed for as few as fifteen hours weekly. Contracts
are negotiated with seven major employer associations, individual stores, and
the managements of the chains.

No local union, particularly one where most members work in one- and
two-man stores alongside their employers, can long maintain vitality and
effectiveness without membership participation. From the start, "1199" has
sought to encourage such participation as decisive to the existence of the
union.

The backbone of the local are its stewards. They are the line of communication with the membership, its grievance agents, and its spokesmen on the
job. Some 300 stewards--roughly one for every fifteen members working in the
same store or vicinity--provide the real leadership of "1199."

Elected by secret ballot every two years, the stewards meet monthly as
the Drug Division Council to debate and act on pending union affairs. Their
actions, normally accepted, are subject to final approval and veto by the
membership itself. Because they possess real responsibility and power in the
union's administration, their job has become one of commanding respect. For
this reason, the steward structure functions efficiently and democratically.

Divided into geographical areas, usually on a borough-wide basis, the membership meets every other month. Meeting attendance averages about 40 per cent, with more than 60 per cent turning out at union-wide meetings called to discuss contract issues.

Local 1199 has never negotiated dues checkoff in its contracts with drug stores. Its members take the position that each "1199er" should make his dues payments directly to the union, helping to create a spirit of direct involvement in union affairs. The union has never had any difficulty in collecting dues in this manner.

Long ago, the local was faced with definite choices concerning its activities and progress. Its experience clearly indicated that if activities were limited to collective bargaining and grievance processing, internal life and participation would decline. What was needed, its leaders decided, was to bring together its widely dispersed membership into welfare, educational, social and cultural activities that would strengthen union bonds.

Before health and welfare plans became commonplace, "1199ers" decided to pool their resources in a mutual aid venture. In 1940, the local approved a sick benefit plan of its own. Each member contributed twenty-five cents a week, and in return was eligible for benefits for $10 weekly for a maximum of five weeks. In 1940 this was regarded as a very considerable benefit for store workers of any kind.

Out of this beginning, there came demands for employer support to a sick benefit plan and in 1945, agreement was reached with employers for establishment of a fund based on 3 per cent of payroll. Since then, it has been improved and expanded. Supervised by a union-employer Board of Trustees, its director is William J. Taylor, "1199" vice president and a former sodaman. Today, employer contributions have been increased to 3.5 per cent of payroll to cover a comprehensive program of sickness, accident, hospitalization, surgical, maternity and death benefits. A similar amount is contributed to the Local 1199 Pension Plan, established in 1950, which permits older workers to retire with a measure of security. Both plans are self-administered and self-insured paying no commissions to outside agencies and permitting savings to be translated into improved benefits and reserves.

Benefits have been increased to a maximum of $65 weekly for twenty-six weeks, something unheard of for drug store workers a few years ago. Under consideration today is a medical reimbursement program whereby members and their dependents would be reimbursed for doctors' visits.

Since 1945, the Local 1199 Benefit Plan has paid out a total of $5,216,000 in benefits to 26,650 members and their families and has reserves of $1,450,000.

The local has developed a diversified program of educational, social and cultural activities to meet the needs and interests of members and their families. Its class program, the Local 1199 "Unionversity," offers courses to meet the on-the-job needs of members. To better equip them to service the growing number of Puerto Rican customers, classes in Spanish are conducted. Members interested in obtaining information on cosmetics products attend special courses in that subject.

For soda fountain workers, special classes are arranged in cooperation with the Food Trades Vocational High School. Latest developments in pharmacy are available to members at classes in Pharmacology and Management Problems taught by leading educators, including Dr. Arthur G. Zupko, dean, Brooklyn College of Pharmacy, who conducted an eight-session course last year attended by 180 members, the largest of its kind ever offered outside a college of pharmacy. Since the "Unionversity" program was organized in 1954, more than 2,300 members have attended courses at nominal fees to cover costs. Classes for stewards and new members are also an important part of "1199's" educational activities.

Because the union recognizes that social and cultural activities play an important role in promoting unity among all sections of the membership, "1199" organizes such annual events as its Negro History celebration, Salute to Israel, and Latin-American Fiesta. These programs are attended by standing-room-only crowds and feature original dramatic-musical presentations with such stage and screen stars as Sidney Poitier, Ricardo Montalban, Sam Levenson, Ossie Davis, and Ruby Dee among others.

Children of members get into the act, too. Small-fry holiday parties and the local's unique program of monthly socials for teenage sons and daughters of members, Teen Time at 1199, are regular events at union headquarters. Each year, through its camp program, the local has been sending forty children of members to all-expenses paid summer vacations at leading camps.

This program has been expanded to include the awarding of two annual college scholarships of $1,000 each to children of members. One award is for general college education while a second is for use at a recognized college of pharmacy. Selections are made by the "1199" College Scholarship Board, consisting of prominent educators headed by Dr. Hugo H. Schafer, dean emeritus, Brooklyn College of Pharmacy. The Camp-Scholarship Program is financed by annual voluntary contributions from thousands of members and hundreds of employers.

Local 1199 members also maintain their own Blood Bank and Credit Union. Arranged in cooperation with the American Red Cross, hundreds of "1199ers" donate blood each year on Blood Bank Day and are eligible to draw from the common pool in case of emergencies affecting themselves or their families. Its Credit Union, where members may borrow and save without red tape, has loaned almost $600,000 to 3,000 members in the past eight years.

The unusually high degree of participation in these activities led to strong support for a proposal that the union purchase its own headquarters. In 1958, the local opened its own auditorium, used as a meeting hall and for social events. Purchase and renovation of the building, located at 300 West 45th Street, was made possible when members oversubscribed to $175,000 of local building fund bonds.

Most drug store owners agree readily that Local 1199 has brought a measure of order and stability to the industry. Over the long pull, everybody has gained from the union, the owner and the general public, and, of course, the worker.

Local 1199's Committee on Pharmacy has helped to advance the special interests of its pharmacist members and the entire profession. Through classes, forums and at regularly scheduled meetings, the committee constantly advances suggestions and programs designated to enhance the profession. "Professionalism" is not dead within Local 1199, but it has been integrated into the life of a union dedicated to the needs of drug store and voluntary hospital employes.

This year, two separate and independent divisions were established, one for drug store members and the other for the local's newly organized hospital workers. The members of each division meet separately and make their own decisions on all matters affecting their interests. Over-all union decisions require a majority vote in each division. Thus, the rights and interests of both divisions are fully protected.

Hospital workers, still in the early stages of building a union, know from their own experiences that there is no magic to the organization and administration of a union. They are tapping a rich reservoir of experience from their fellow members in the drug stores, experience which indicates that the best answer to continued progress lies in democratic trade union principles and practices.

Industrial Bulletin of the New York State Department of Labor (November, 1960), reprint in District 1199 Archives.

3.   LOCAL 1199 SPARKS NATIONAL UNION FOR HOSPITAL, NURSING HOME WORKERS

America's 2-1/2 million hospital and nursing home workers, most of them black and almost all scandalously underpaid, finally got a national union of their own this weekend.

The three day founding conference of the National Union of Hospital and Nursing Home Employees, a division of the Retail, Wholesale and Department Store Union, AFL-CIO, began yesterday (December 12) in a Manhattan Hotel.

The new union grows out of the national organizing drive conducted by New York-based Local 1199, Drug and Hospital Union. It has its roots in the historic 100-day strike last spring and summer of black hospital workers in Local 1199B in Charleston.

"Opened The Door"

Coretta Scott King, honorary chairman of the new union, said recently the victorious Charleston campaign "opened the door to a new day for all hospital workers." The new union, she said, will lead the effort to "wipe out poverty wages and win justice, dignity and human rights for all hospital workers."

Mrs. King's concern for hospital workers is similar to that of her late husband, Dr. Martin Luther King, Jr., who often referred to Local 1199 as "my favorite union."

6,000 Organized

Hospital organizing is off to a lightning start in Baltimore, where NUHNE's Local 1199E organized 6,000 members in less than four months. Most prestigious of the 16 institutions unionized there is world-famous Johns Hopkins Hospital. Elections are upcoming at 10 more Baltimore institutions employing 1,000 workers.

1199E organizer Fred Punch is typical of the up-from-the-ranks leadership in the rapidly-growing new union. Until a year ago, Punch was an orderly at St. Barnabas Hospital in the Bronx. He discovered 1199 when the union organized service and maintenance workers at St. Barnabas in the summer of 1968. Last week, Baltimore's NAACP gave the 32-year old former orderly its annual "Man of the Year" award for leading the crusade to end poverty wages for Baltimore hospital workers.

Growing in Pittsburgh

In Pittsburgh, where racial tensions simmer after recent confrontations between white construction workers and civil rights groups seeking jobs for blacks, Local 1199P nevertheless is growing fast among both black and white hospital workers. Management at major hospitals like Presbyterian is trying to undercut black-white unity by labeling 1199P "Black nationalist" in propaganda aimed at white workers. But NUHNNE Secretary-Treasurer Henry Nicholas says this hasn't worked and he expects quick organizing success in Pittsburgh.

From Charleston to Durham to Baltimore to Philadelphia--the hospital organizing drive has been based on the formula 1199 Union Power Plus SCLC Soul Power Equals Victory. Southern Christian Leadership Conference President Ralph Abernathy, who went to jail during the Charleston strike with Local 1199 President Leon Davis, has pledged his organization's continued support in bringing union and human rights to all hospital workers. The link between the SCLC and 1199 has been seen by many commentators as an historic-joining of forces by labor and civil rights movement.[140]

An example of the new organizing techniques the 1199-SCLC cooperation produced occurred this summer outside of Johns Hopkins Hospital in Baltimore. Hundreds of employees leaving work were thrilled to find Mrs. King waiting on the sidewalk to greet them personally and urge them to vote for 1199E. "I was convinced right on the spot that there's something special about this union," said a middle-aged nurses' aide.

Hospital workers in New York first heard about Local 1199 ten years ago. Although hospital workers are the third largest employee group in the country --four times larger than steelworkers, for instance--they had been completely ignored until Local 1199 began organizing them here in 1959. With pioneering journalistic assistance from the Amsterdam News, the union grew to include 42,000 hospital workers in New York, Connecticut and New Jersey. Symbolizing this growth is the union's new 15 story headquarters on 43rd Street off Eighth Avenue, scheduled for occupancy this spring.

New York 1199ers showed the way for many other city unions when they won the $100-a-week minimum wage last year along with a management-financed training and upgrading program, solid health and pension plans and other fringe benefits.

The union has also made an impact outside the world of the bargaining table. It was the country's first union to oppose the Vietnam war and sent the largest labor delegation to the November 15th anti-war March on Washington. It provided strong support for Mayor Lindsay's reelection and opposed last year's teacher strike.

"The voice of organized hospital workers has been a major force for justice and dignity in New York. Now we have a chance to make this force felt throughout the country. We must not fail," said NUHNHE Executive Vice President Elliott Godoff yesterday.

Amsterdam News (N.Y.), December 13, 1969.

HOSPITAL WORKERS ORGANIZE

4. HOSPITAL STRIKE IS SETTLED; $40 MINIMUM, OTHER GAINS WON

The great strike of 3,000 workers in seven hospitals ended June 22 with a victory for all hospital workers. This was the first such strike in history-- the first time that hospital workers ever joined together in a union to fight for justice for themselves and their families. With representation through their union won, as well as important wage and hour gains, the workers of the seven hospitals voted at a huge mass meeting at the Hotel Diplomat to accept a settlement of the strike worked out with Mayor Wagner, and go back to their jobs. Some managements have already begun to violate the settlement by discriminating against strikers returning to work. Local 1199 Pres. Davis immediately announced that the union would defend every single striker who is unfairly treated. He pointed out that Local 1199 has the right to take any violation of the agreement to arbitration, and every grievance will be pressed through to arbitration if that is necessary to make the managements live up to their word.

Terms of the settlement cover not only the seven struck hospitals--Mount Sinai, Beth Israel, Bronx Hospital, Beth David, Lenox Hill, Brooklyn Jewish and Flower-Fifth Avenue--but also will cover any one of the 81 hospitals where the workers organize into Local 1199 and elect their own representatives.

The agreement provides the following terms:

1. No workers will receive less than $40 a week (which comes to $173 a month). No worker will receive less than a $2 a week raise, and in most cases the raise will be bigger, running as high as $17 a week in some cases.

2. The work week will be 5 days a week, 40 hours a week.

3. Time and a half will be paid for overtime.

4. Wherever the workers are organized in Local 1199, they have the right to take up grievances through their own elected representatives of Local 1199. And if the union representative cannot settle the grievance with the hospital management, an impartial arbitrator will make the final decision. *Never again --wherever the workers are organized in Local 1199--will management have the final say as to whether a worker is fired, or demoted, or anything else.*

5. Wherever the workers are organized in Local 1199, they can present requests for wage increases and other benefits every year through their elected representatives to a committee which includes public members. At least three of the six public members must approve the wage rates and other conditions decided upon. Never again will the managements have the final say on how much you should earn, or how little.

6. The first review of wage rates and job classifications takes place next October. Wherever the workers are organized in Local 1199, they are assured of representation to set job classifications which will guarantee that they are properly paid for the work they do. *This is important for all hospital workers, but especially for x-ray and lab technicians, social workers and clerical workers.*

7. The agreement clearly states that every employee has the right to join the union and remain a member of the union; and that no employee will be discriminated against for being a union member.

Accomplishments--But Only the Beginning

These are great accomplishments for so short a time, but they are only the beginning in the hospitals of New York. Because of the fight put up by the strikers and their union, Local 1199, the eyes of the entire city--and in fact the entire country--were on the hospital workers and the terribly low pay they received. For the first time, people learned about wages of $32, $34 and $36 a week, no time and a half for overtime, long hours and no unemployment insurance.

Many improvements have already been made and promises made, but through Local 1199 hospital workers have a guarantee that promises will be kept--and that progress will be made steadily to bring up the wages that are still very low. Through their union, hospital workers proved that they have the courage to fight for their rights. The managements used to treat hospital workers like dirt, but wherever the workers organize solidly in Local 1199, things will be changed. Management now has respect for the fighters of Local 1199. They will have respect for their workers wherever they organize in Local 1199 and elect their representatives.

1199 Hospital News, July 9, 1959.

5. ONE BIG UNION ESTABLISHED FOR ALL HOSPITAL WORKERS: LOCAL 1199 HOSPITAL DIVISION, AFL-CIO

The powerful Hospital Division of Local 1199--with thousands of members who have come through a tough and victorious strike as a base--has now been set up as a functioning, active organization.

These workers understand that Local 1199 has been able to win substantial improvements for every hospital worker. They recognize that no other union has accomplished anything for hospital workers; that the "vultures" who did little else but pass out leaflets are now attempting to divide the workers and prevent them from achieving what is needed now--one big, united union of hospital workers, Local 1199.

At the meeting June 22 which settled the strike, Local 1199 President Leon Davis announced that the hospital workers will now run their own organization, although he will continue to give it leadership, as he has since the organizing drive began in the hospitals. However, he said, the organizers who had been "on loan" from the Drug Division of Local 1199 during the strike will now return to their duties in that division.

President Davis said that leading strikers were being added to the staff that has been directing the organizing drive, and together they would make up the top leaders who would continue the big job of organizing all voluntary hospital workers in New York. As the campaign expands, and more workers are organized, additional leaders will be brought on the staff from the ranks of hospital workers, he said.

The Hospital Division will function as a separate part of Local 1199, Davis said, with its finances coming from the dues of the hospital workers themselves. Dues for hospital workers are $3 a month, of which 50 cents is paid for a life insurance policy of $500 for each member during the first year and $750 in the second year of membership.

Membership cards for Hospital Division members will be issued every month. When a member pays his $3 dues at the union headquarters nearest his hospital, or at the main Local 1199 headquarters at 300 West 45th Street, he will be given the membership card for that month, which will show that he is a paid-up member.

1199 Hospital News, July 9, 1959.

6.   MORE HOSPITALS ORGANIZING INTO LOCAL 1199

The campaign to build one great big union of 30,000 hospital workers in Local 1199 is moving ahead at a fast pace as the message of unionism goes out to more and more thousands of workers in many hospitals. The best organizers for 1199 are the workers in the seven hospitals where the historic strike took place. They have been handing out 1199 Hospital News and "talking union" to workers in dozens of hospitals, with good results.

Here are developments in some of the newer hospitals being organized into Local 1199:

Organizer Elliott Godoff reports three more hospitals in Upper Manhattan either with majorities organized, or about to be:

Daughters of Israel: The results of organizing the overwhelming majority of the 125 employees into 1199 are: A $1 an hour rate ($173 a month) is now in effect, as well as the 5-day, 40-hour week and time and a half for over-time. In this hospital rates were $108 and $110 a month for 44 hours a week. Godoff said the union would see to it that the hospital stops the 6-day week which it is still maintaining for some workers, and will discuss with the management the charges for 3 meals a day. The workers want to stop eating meals at the hospital. A committee has been elected to represent all depart-ments.

Joint Disease: Workers here are taking advantage of the strike settle-ment to set up their organization as part of 1199, so that they will be re-presented by elected persons for grievances and other matters. Although the hospital is paying the $40 a week minimum and meeting other conditions of the settlement, it is not yet paying time and a half for overtime. The union has asked workers who put in overtime to bring their paychecks to the union office at 1421 Madison Ave., so that this can be corrected.

In the Bronx, Organizer Ted Mitchell reports:

Mount Morris Park Hospital has been organized, and the management has agreed to the $1 an hour rate and other conditions. Wages here were from $32 to $38 a week. The workers are becoming full-fledged members of 1199 by electing their representatives and taking out their July membership cards. Chief Steward is Ella Scott. Other stewards are Leotha Becknell, Bernice Godfrey, Luevena Sanders and Joyce Alvarenga.

In Brooklyn, Organizer Horace Small reports:

St. Johns Episcopal Hospital: The organizing drive is sweeping through the hospital, with entire departments signing up. Wages here are $32 and $34 a week for 40 and 44 hours, with no time and a half for overtime. Meetings of the workers are electing stewards for each department.

Lutheran Medical: The organizing drive here is doing very well as the workers sign up to improve wages as low as $32 a week.

1199 Hospital News, July 23, 1959.

7.   STRIKE SETTLEMENT SETS STAGE FOR ORGANIZING
DRIVE TO BUILD STRONG 1199 IN HOSPITALS

The most dramatic fight conducted by the labor movement in the past 30 years, the strike of 3,000 workers at seven voluntary hospitals under the leadership of '1199,' ended on June 22 after 46 hard-fought days on the picketline with a victory for hospital workers throughout the city.

The end came at an inspiring and enthusiastic mass meeting of the strikers at the Hotel Diplomat where they cheered a report on the terms of the settle-ment worked out at City Hall meetings leased on proposals of Mayor Wagner's appointed committee.

Terms of the settlement, reported to the strikers by 1199 President Leon J. Davis, cover not only the seven struck hospitals but will apply to any one of the city's 81 voluntary hospitals where the workers organize into 1199 and elect their own representatives.

These terms provide:

1. A $40 a week minimum wage, raising the incredibly low pay scales of $30, $32, and $38 a week and a minimum raise of $2 a week. In most cases, workers will receive raises of $5, $10 and in some instances as high as $17 a week.

2. A 5-day, 40-hour week, with time and a half for overtime. Many workers put in 44 hours and longer work weeks before the strike; few received overtime pay.

3. A review of job classifications, wage ranges, sick leave and holidays on October 1, and annual reviews thereafter. A Review Board, made up of six hospital representatives and six public members appointed by the Chief Justice of the State Court of Appeals was established. At least three of the public members must agree with whatever wages and conditions are established, thereby giving greater weight and influence to their views than those of the hospitals representatives.

4. A grievance procedure which permits a worker to choose a union representative to speak for him with hospital management and provides also for arbitration of any unresolved disputes.

5. Reinstatement of all strikers to their jobs.

The settlement was interpreted in the press and labor circles generally as a major victory for the strikers. Pres. Davis hailed the terms as "backdoor recognition," and stated in press and television interviews that "we will be at the front door soon." He noted that the hospital trustees had earlier vowed that they would never recognize and deal with representatives of the union; that they would never rehire the strikers (who had been "fired" repeatedly during the strike); and they would never surrender their "right" to make all decisions on wages, working conditions, and grievances in the hospitals.

Davis paid tribute to the strikers for conducting "a heroic struggle that had won the respect and admiration of the entire labor movement and the community at large, and awakened the city to the brutal oppression of hospital workers." He also expressed the profound thanks of the strikers to Central Labor Council AFL-CIO President Harry Van Arsdale for "mobilizing the support of hundreds of thousands of trade unionists to this great crusade and making it the concern of the entire labor movement.

Among the scores of unions that had contributed funds, food and forces to aid the strikers, Davis paid particular tribute to District 65 whose Organizational Director Bill Michelson and participated in City Hall talks and which had loaned 14 full time staff members to '1199' during the strike. The members of '65'collected over $10,000 for strike relief.

Hardly had the strike ended when a new wave of organization was in full progress with hundreds of hospital workers in all parts of the city joining the union. Encouraged by the important gains made as a result of the tremendous fight in the struck hospitals, large numbers of other workers signed up in '1199.'

At one hospital, Daughters of Jacob, all but a few of the 150 workers joined the union and an '1199' committee met with management to work out representation rights. The $40 minimum and 5-day, 40-hour week went into effect early this month bringing wage increases of $20 to $40 a month.

Another important development was the union's announcement of the establishment of the Professional, Technical and Office Section of the Hospital Division, seeking to enroll x-ray, lab technicians, social workers and office workers as a prelude to win improved standards for these employees. Despite stories in the press about "non-professional workers on strike," large numbers of professionals took part.

Concrete plans are also under way to set up the Hospital Division as a self-sustaining part of the union, with its own staff and all other independent features. Dues collections from the hospital workers are scheduled to begin with July and Pres. Davis announced that a full discussion of all phases of the organizational structure of the Hospital Division will take place at membership meetings in September.

Commenting on the results of the strike at a union-wide membership meeting on contract preparations, Davis declared: "These workers deeply appreciate the contributions 1199ers have made in building a union in the hospitals. Every 1199er can be proud that he has won the everlasting admiration and gratitude not only of the hospital workers but of the entire labor movement, locally and nationally.

"By extending aid and assistance to these workers, 1199ers have helped
expose the unholy alliance responsible for inhuman wages and working conditions in our hospitals. These workers are now engaged in a campaign to
build a powerful organization, to stand on their own feet, maintain themselves financially and bring the benefits of organization to others like
themselves. They will forever be grateful to you in '1199,' and you can say
with pride, "I was one of those responsible for helping the hospital workers."

You have demonstrated through your aid to these exploited workers that
you believe in the best traditions of our nation, that we are our brother's
keeper, that wherever suffering and indignity exist we will not turn aside but
will join in the fight to eliminate injustice.

"This strike was the most sincere and most decent thing that has taken
place in this city in some 25 to 30 years. It makes me feel prouder of our
union than ever before. People who think that we went into this fight looking
for personal glory are way off base. They can only see things reflected in
their own small images. Our union has emerged from this fight as a great and
wonderful organization. We have won thousands of new friends, practical
friends who can be counted on to help all of us move forward to join in the
drive to make ours a better and finer nation."

1199 Drug News, (July–August, 1959):9.

8. THE CHALLENGE OF BRONXVILLE: 1199 TAKES IT UP WITH
ALL-OUT DRIVE TO WIN LAWRENCE HOSP. STRIKE

The seven-week-old strike at Lawrence Hospital in Bronxville, N.Y., has
become a challenge to all members of Local 1199. The challenge comes from
a stubborn and aloof management with contempt for the human as well as the
union rights of its employees and from the wealthy and exclusive Bronxville
community, where Negroes and Jews are not welcome as citizens and only toler-
ated as workers.

In the face of this challenge, Pres. Leon Davis told the Hospital Delegate Assembly, "The one thing we can do is to bring masses of our members into
Bronxville, to show them they can't ignore us and our problems. It is the
one thing we must do to shake the hospital management out of its plantation
approach to its workers."

The numbers who have come to Saturday demonstrations during the past few
weeks have obviously not been enough. Davis said, in calling for a really
massive outpouring for Saturday, March 6. If necessary, he said, massive turn-
outs would be repeated Saturday after Saturday until the Lawrence Hospital
management agrees to a fair settlement.

The strikers, even after pounding the pavement for seven weeks in some
miserable weather, are determined to carry on the fight. The civil rights
movement, including all top national leaders as well as local leaders, has
strengthened its support. The metropolitan press, including the *New York
Times,* the *Amsterdam News* and *Journal-American,* and radio stations WMCA and
WINS, have given strong editorial support.

The Lawrence Hospital workers' battle, like some others in the history
of 1199's Hospital Division, is having and will have results that are important
to many more hospital workers than those at Lawrence. Under the pressure of
the battle of Bronxville, Governor Rockefeller has announced his support for
legislation extending collective bargaining rights to hospital workers all
over New York State. Vital support has also been assured by the leadership
of the Democratic majority in the State Legislature, which has before it the
Berking-Sutton Bill which implements extension of labor law coverage.

These developments recall the struggle of Beth-El Hospital workers in
Brooklyn and the Manhattan Eye and Ear Hospital workers several years ago.
It was through the determination of these workers that the first historic
breakthrough in hospital employees' union rights was won.

The Bronxville strike began on Jan. 16 when the Lawrence Hospital
management refused to recognize 1199 as the union the workers have chosen to
represent them. The hospital is located in one of the wealthiest and most

fashionable communities in the United States. It is also a lily-white community, which only permits Negroes to come and work there, mainly at the more
menial jobs. And Bronxville's citizens like to pretend that the poverty wages,
poor working conditions, and discrimination in their midst just don't exist.

But even in Bronxville there are some who couldn't remain silent about
these conditions. Mr. and Mrs. John Richardson, Jr., and Mr. and Mrs. Harold
Turner are four such people.

The Richardsons and Turners have joined the strikers on the picketline,
invited them to their homes and organized the Concerned Citizens Committee
in support of the strikers' demands.

Both couples have withstood countless threatening phone calls in the
middle of the night and other abuses and insults. The Richardsons' family
doctor, who is also an attending physician at Lawrence, told them that he
will no longer care for their five children because of the parents' support of
the strikers.

CORE, NAACP, Negro American Labor Council, Urban League and church
groups from neighboring New Rochelle, Yonkers, Mt. Vernon and White Plains
have also rallied to support the Lawrence strikers. These forces are being
coordinated by Joseph T. Jackson, head of the Westchester NALC.

Actor-playwright-1199er Ossie Davis, who lives in New Rochelle, and
Wyatt T. Walker of Yonkers, former assistant to Rev. Martin Luther King, are
co-chairmen of another support group, the Citizens Committee to Aid the
Lawrence Hospital Strikers.

On five straight Saturday afternoons 1199ers and others have traveled
to Bronxville to participate in mass demonstrations. They came face-to-face
with hundreds of armed and helmeted cops, sheriffs and troopers, imported
from all the surrounding town. The police were stationed in the streets, on
top of the hospital and on the roofs of other buildings.

As the demonstrators have marched, hundreds strong, through the streets
of Bronxville, they chanted, "No contract, no work" and "Jim Crow must go."
Black and white supporters walking hand-in-hand sang "We Shall Not Be Moved"
and "We Shall Overcome."

The curious and upset population of Bronxville lined the streets and
stared. The town had never seen anything like it before.

1199 Hospital News, 7(February, 1965): 1.

9.   THE BRONXVILLE STRIKE

On January 16 service and maintenance workers at Lawrence Hospital in
Bronxville, Westchester County, began a strike aimed at securing union recognition. It is now eight weeks later and this strike continues.

Seeking its end, Governor Rockefeller recently reiterated his support
of extension of collective bargaining rights statewide to workers in voluntary
hospitals; such a law, passed in 1963 and containing a no-strike clause, was
mistakenly limited in its application to New York City. The Democratic
leaders of the Legislature have now promised to make it statewide.

The Bronxville strikers want to go back to work. They are even ready to
withdraw their demand for union recognition, pending legislative action, if
promised there will be no reprisals. But--they say--the hospital will take
back only a few of the strikers, declaring that the remainder of the struck
jobs have been filled.

The issue in Bronxville is important. Other hospitals in the suburban
areas and farther upstate will be facing it. The workers have a right to be
represented by a union if they wish it. The law will soon say so. The
Bronxville strikers should not be left out on the street because they stood
up for a just cause.

New York Times, March 5, 1965.

10.   TRUCE IN BRONXVILLE

The Bronxville hospital strike has ended with an honorable agreement. Most of the striking workers will be reinstated; the fate of the few who have been convicted of some offense will be submitted to arbitration. By October 1 the hospital will begin to negotiate with Local 1199 of the Hospital Employes Union in compliance with the statute soon to be enacted by the Legislature.

The union has accepted a limited victory; it has exhibited restraint and responsibility in doing so. The outcome is also a triumph for such Bronxville citizens as Mr. and Mrs. John Richardson and Mr. and Mrs. Harold Turner, who spoke out in behalf of justice in a bitterly hostile climate, and for Joseph T. Jackson, who led the Westchester civil rights forces in support of the strikers' cause.

The agreement averts the danger of new, tumultuous clashes such as the one that took place last Saturday when Bronxville resembled Selma. It is, we hope, the augury of a better day for both the underprivileged hospital employes and the whole community. It is also another bright chapter in the history of a union that has staunchly retained the idealism of organized labor's finest hours.

New York Post, March 14, 1965.

11.   BALLAD OF THE BRONXVILLE HOSPITAL STRIKE

Let me tell you the story
Of a union bound for glory--
Local 1199.
Amidst abundance and bounty
Up in Westchester County,
We collided with the color line.

Did we finally win?
Yes, we certainly did win--
And we know what the future's like:
When freedom's cause will ring out,
You'll hear hospital workers sing out
The Ballad of the Bronxville strike.

First the Board of Directors
Said, "How can you expect us
To overcome our grief and rage?
You're brutal and you're callous,
And you're full of spite and malice--
And besides you want a living wage."

Did we have to give in?
Yes, they finally gave in--
But listen well before you shed a tear:
Their average Board member
Made more last December
Than the workers earned the whole damned year.

Just when our hopes were fallin'
Two fine couples came a-callin'
And we made a tremendous find.
With the Richardsons and Turners
Operatin' on all burners,
They rekindled our faith in mankind.

Did we finally win?
Yes, we certainly did win--
We had the civil rights movement in our ranks.
With support behind our backs an'
With a guy like Joseph Jackson--
He's worth more than all the dough
    in Bronxville's banks.

We had what it took to save us
In two fellows named Davis--
I mean Ossie and Leon J.
Though they're differently shaded,
Otherwise, they're aptly mated:
They're both fighting for a better day.

Did we finally win?
Yes, we certainly did win
Because the strikers' morale was fine.
With Godoff, Nicholas and Black,
They turned the strikebreakers back
And they held fast to the picket line.

Then the gals from Sarah Lawrence
All expressed their abhorrence
At this medieval labor plan.
Lookin' spruced up and pretty,
They paraded through the city--
They were equal to any man.

Did we finally win?
Yes, we certainly did win--
We had both justice and femininity.
Then that bright press agent, Foner
Brought the boys up fron Iona,
And they marched hand in hand for liberty.

Well at last we were able
To get around the table
With the hospital hierarchy.
While the pickets did the walkin,'
Phil Sipser did the talkin'
Harry Weinstock kept the big wheels moving free.

Did we finally win?
Yes, we certainly did win
When we pledged a thousand marchers,
    white and black.
We made plans for assembly--
We got white-lipped and trembly,
And they took all our strikers back.

Now we've got our pressure steady
And the Legislature's ready
To fulfill our Bill of Rights throughout the state.
In our trade union jargon,
We'll collectively bargain,
And they're goin' to negotiate.

Are we goin' to win?
Yes, we certainly will win--
We'll set the hospital workers free.
From Albany to Yonkers,
We've a formula that conquers--
It's black and white unite for victory.

Like some great labor struggles of the past whose fighting memory is alive today in songs about them, the eight-week-long hospital strike of Bronxville will long be remembered in this song by Henry Foner. A brother of 1199 Exec. Sec. Moe Foner, Henry is president of the N.Y. Fur Joint Board of the Amalgamated Meat Cutters Union, AFL-CIO. The words are set to the tune of the The Ballad of the M.T.A., a song about the Boston transit strike of some years ago.

1199 Hospital News, 7 (March, 1965): 1.

12. FOR SAM SMITH, HOSPITAL ORDERLY: A BATTLE WHOSE TIME HAS COME

By John M. McClintock

We was making 40 cents an hour, working 12 hours at a stretch. And, man, I couldn't cut it. I couldn't make it with four kids."
The frail 58-year-old Negro was talking the other day about his job in a Baltimore nursing home in 1962. The workers had organized a strike, only to return to their jobs a few days later. Nobody had enough money to stay out.
"We had nothing. We got nothing. We was nothing," he said.
The worker's comment is typical of the plight of the nation's 2.5 million hospital and nursing home employees. And it partially explains the civil rights fervor that has characterized the recent union organizing drives at hospitals in the city. The workers are the dishwashers, nurses' aides, cooks, attendants and so-called "menials" whom one sees but never really recognizes.
The television soap operas do not thrill us with the exploits of Sam Smith, hospital orderly. The romance and fire is reserved for doctors and nurses.

Everyone knows

The orderlies and dishwashers are essentily only to the unromantic, unmentionable processes of health care: the dirty linen, the bed pans, the scraping of plates, the pushing of wheelchairs. These are the lowest jobs, jobs that attract workers from the lowest rung of the socio-economic ladder-- the Negroes, the Puerto Ricans, the Mexican-Americans.
When the Johns Hopkins Hospital talks about its workers as "employees whom we will continue to treat them with dignity and respect," everyone knows they are talking about Negroes. And when New York-based Local 1199E of the Hospital and Nursing Home Employees Union (AFL-CIO) began its Baltimore drive last April, everyone knew that its appeal was to Negroes.
The union was then in one of the greatest battles of the American labor movement.   It had confronted two public hospitals in Charleston, S.C., with a strike by Negro women hospital workers. The strike, which lasted 113 days, involved the Southern Christian Leadership Conference, and for months television screens in the nation were filled with pictures of Mrs. Martin Luther King, Jr., and the Rev. Ralph Abernathy marching in support of the workers.
It was not a labor battle in the traditional sense. The union was challenging racism in the home state of Strom Thurmond and Mendel Rivers.[141]
If the union could win there, it could win anywhere. The same conditions --perhaps to a lesser degree--prevailed in nearly every metropolitan hospital in the country. At stake were the allegiances of the nation's health-care workers who, for the most part, had never been unionized. These 2.5 million workers are greater in number than the workers in the country's basic steel industry.
The union victory in Charleston inextricably identified it with the civil rights movement of Martin Luther King, Jr. The union had won a series of tough strikes before in New York City, but this strike--with its curfews and National Guard troops-- the flavor of Selma, Ala., of the white establishment beating down on an oppressed minority.

The effect on the organizing drive in Baltimore has been spectacular.
In the past eight months, the union has achieved recognition at 5 major
hospitals, including the Hopkins, and 14 nursing homes. With 6,000 members,
it already has become one of the largest in the state; there are about 11,000
hospital workers in the Baltimore area. The union membership figure also includes nursing home employees whose total number is not known. The four other
hospitals that have recognized the union are Lutheran, Maryland General,
Franklin Square and Sinai. An election is to be held next week at the Greater
Baltimore Medical Center and at the John F. Kennedy Institute for retarded
children.

The victories at the hospitals were especially impressive since such
nonprofit institutions are exempted from federal collective bargaining laws
and they were not required to hold representative elections.

Flown in

But the Charleston message had been unmistakably clear. No one wanted
a Charleston in Baltimore. The union was granted its elections.

And in the key election at the Hopkins--the largest, most prestigious
hospital in the state--Mrs. King was flown to Baltimore to rally support. The
workers subsequently voted overwhelmingly for the union. The handwriting of
Martin Luther King, Jr., was on the wall. In only one case, that of tiny
North Charles General Hospital, was the union defeated in an election here.

Charleston had been the kickoff to a national organizing campaign that
went successively to Baltimore, Durham, N.C., Pittsburgh, Philadelphia-Harris-
burg and Dayton, Ohio. Only in Baltimore, however, has the union achieved
such open recognition. Two nursing homes have been signed in Philadelphia
and a Pittsburgh hospital has recognized the union. The other campaigns are
still in the organizing stages.

While much of the union appeal is oriented to minority groups, the union
demand for such things as a $100-a-week minimum, improved fringe benefits and
job mobility has an equally great appeal. A typical Baltimore hospital worker's starting wage is about $72 a week--or about $3,744 a year, which is barely
above the federal poverty line for a non-farm family of four.

The 22 metropolitan hospitals in the Baltimore area have estimated that
the union demands would push up labor costs by $37 million. Hospital officials,
though, are not worried so much by the $100 minimum as by the escalator effect
it will have in pushing up the wages of other employees.

As a result, for example, the Johns Hopkins Hospital has estimated the
rate for a semi-private room would be raised from $51 to $69 a day. The union
counters the cost argument with the statement that the workers "are not philanthropists." The union also says that higher wages insure against a hospital's
normal high rate of turnover among nonprofessional employees and thus reduce
training costs.

Implicit in much of the union actions is the threat of another Charleston. At the contract negotiations last week at the Hopkins, Elliott Godoff,
the union's national organizer, warned a state official: "We could make
Charleston look like a poker game."

The union's organizing drive is being made to expand its base in New York
city, New Jersey and Connecticut.

Local 1199 has enjoyed a spectacular growth since its beginning in 1958.
In 11 years its membership has increased from 5,500 to 42,500. The local is
actually a division of the Retail, Wholesale Drugstore Union which was founded
in 1932 by seven Jewish pharmacists in New York. The president of the union
is Leon J. Davis, one of the founders.

The drug union, started during the Depression, was instrumental in breaking the color-line for many Negro pharmacists in Harlem, where stores were
owned by whites.

The union also opened up to Negroes positions in drugstores that had
hitherto been for white only. Negroes were usually hired as porters.

The hospital division was formed in 1958 after the union's first victory
at Montefiore Hospital in the Bronx.

After two key 1199 strikes, in 1963 and 1965, the New York State Legislature smoothed the way when it granted unions the right to organize hospital
workers who were previously exempted from collective bargaining laws.

Baltimore Sun, December 7, 1969.

13. THE PLIGHT OF HOSPITAL WORKERS

The basic issue at stake in the lengthening struggle here between two
hospitals and Local 1199P is the right of working men and women to have union
representation and collective bargaining. The minimum hourly wage at Presbyterian-University and Mercy Hospitals is about $1.75 or $70 for a 40-hour
week, which is barely above the officially defined poverty level for a bread-
winner with a family of four.

The National Union of Hospital & Nursing Home Employes (the "P" in 1199P
stands for "Pittsburgh" and distinguishes the local here from the union's other
locals in the South and the East) is aiming for a $2.50-per-hour minimum. That
would come out to $100 a week for the approximately 600 service and maintenance
unit personnel at Presby and the 650 similar workers involved at Mercy.

The battle over the organization and bargaining rights of workers was,
ironically, fought and won largely in Pittsburgh in the first half of this
century. But in the ensuing national and state legislation which codified
these rights of labor, certain groups--such as hospital and farm workers--
were excluded from minimum wage and collective-bargaining guarantees because
they were then unorganized and not very vocal. The rationale for excluding
hospital workers was that they worked for non-profit institutions.

One result has been that hospital workers have, in general, been helping
to subsidize the community's health establishment by working for lower wages
than workers in private-profit enterprises. Hospital boards of directors,
often themselves captains of industry and banking who deal with unions in
their own fields as a matter of course, have generally been reluctant to grant
union recognition to hospital workers and have argued that making salaries
competitive with those of workers in private industry would boost the costs
of hospital care to patients. This is undoubtedly true. But it is unfair to
deny hospital workers--janitors, food preparers, plasterers, painters, etc.--
collective bargaining rights and expect them, just because they labor in a
non-profit institution, to subsidize indirectly the community's health care,
the costs for which are, after all, the responsibility of the whole community.

Both hospitals should adopt the position taken by the Jewish Home and
Hospital for the Aged here, which was that although it did not believe its
workers needed union representation it would not deny them the right to vote
on it. (The workers at the Jewish Home and Hospital did, and now Local 1199P
represents them). All unions which wish to represent the workers should be
welcome on the ballot.

As for the problem of increased costs--which admittedly will arise as a
result of the granting of bargaining rights to hospital employes--the hospitals
must be preparing now for this later eventuality. They must increase their
efforts to curb waste and to achieve greater efficiency. In the case of
Presbyterian-University Hospital, the University of Pittsburgh will have to
appeal to the state Legislature to help it to meet the higher costs of decent
wages for employes. Finally, patient fees must be raised if this is necessary
to avoid paying substandard wages. A real effort now to settle the hospital
worker dispute on an equitable basis could avoid the confrontations and the
suspension of health care services that have occurred in some other cities.

Pittsburgh Post-Gazette, January 8, 1970.

14. HOSPITAL WOES

If there is anyone who doesn't know that hospitals today are in need of
more money, he hasn't been reading the newspapers.

One of the reasons why the city of Pittsburgh's attempt to impose the
"sick tax" on hospitals was so obviously myopic was the fact that these institutions simply do not have excess funds. The tax, since struck down (but
being appealed), would have resulted in another hike in already soaring
hospital bills.

Another fact; Non-profit hospitals are legally exempt from recognizing
employe unions.

At this time in Pittsburgh, however, a strong effort is being made to organize hospital workers. If successful, it will undoubtedly result in wage increases. The hospitals are resisting.

What does one make of it all?

We submit that the right of workers to organize is a basic human right that every corporate entity, profit-making or non-profit, should recognize.

We say this with full sympathy for the economic plight of the hospitals. Wages and fringes may be negotiable, but the right to organize is not, with or without legal support.

To say that unionization would launch a wage-price spiral is not only beside the point; it is also to admit that low wages are, in effect, sub-sidizing the hospitals. If hospitals are in a bind, (and we believe they are), increased operating revenue should be devised from other sources, not clipped from the paychecks of hospital workers.

It is particularly distressing to see a Catholic hospital refuse to recognize the right of its workers to organize by falling back on the claim that the law does not compel this recognition.

Certainly any Catholic institution--particularly one so overtly concerned with suffering as a hospital--has a higher obligation. That obligation is to operate within the spirit of the social teaching of the Church, and one of the principles consistently articulated in that teaching is the right of workers to organize unions.

This is not just a hospital problem; it is also a community problem. However reluctant the hospitals may be, the right to organize will probably be recognized, wages will increase, and somebody will have to pay. Unless the sick are forced to carry the total burden or be refused care (unthinkable), monies from the public sector will have to be diverted into hospitals.

Perhaps partial relief could also come from a reorganization of prior-ities by agencies administering private contributions--churches, Community Chest, foundations, etc.

We suggest not only that the hospitals recognize workers' organizations, but that they also form a strong organization of their own to talk tough to the civic community. If the citizenry wants medical protection, it will have to pay for it--or at least that portion of the cost beyond the reach of the sick.

The economic salvation of hospitals lies in making demands on the com-munity and private charities, not in denying care to the sick or denying the right of workers to organize.

Pittsburgh Catholic, January 9, 1970.

15.
PITTSBURGH: HOSPITAL WORKERS FIGHT FOR UNION RIGHTS

The big labor story in Pittsburgh this winter has been the refusal of millionaire hospital trustees to extend the elementary right to vote for the union of their choice to $1.75-an-hour hospital workers.

It's a story that will get even bigger, because the 2,500 members of Local 1199P are determined to get the simple right to vote.

In Pittsburgh, a cradle of the labor movement where workers for almost 40 years have taken for granted the right to choose or reject a union at the ballot box, Presbyterian and Mercy Hospitals refused that right to 1199P last December. Presbyterian and Mercy are major Pittsburgh hospitals employing a total of almost 1,500 service and maintenance workers.

National Hospital Union Sec.-Treas. Henry Nicholas, who is leading the Pittsburgh organizing drive, made clear immediately after the refusals what caused them:

"The plain truth is that the vast majority of the workers are members of Local 1199P. They are sick and tired of working for poverty wages. They are fed up with being treated as second class citizens. They are determined to have a union, and they are prepared to take any and all steps necessary to win this basic right."

Pittsburgh hospital workers repeatedly have pointed out that, while the last thing they want is a hospital strike, they fear management's unyielding position may lead to one.

And, if one comes, the workers add, they will win it. One reason is their desire to win the $100 minimum attained by 1199 in New York, Baltimore and elsewhere.

Helen Lyles, waitress in the Presbyterian gift shop and chairman of the hospital's 1199P organizing committee, reflects this determination. "People here are really getting together even though there's been lots of intimidation. They're ready for anything," she said.

Mrs. Lyles knows about intimidation. After 20 Presbyterian gift shop workers were locked out January 5 for handing out leaflets, she was arrested the following day while leading a group demanding to see Administrator Edward Noroian. The charges were later dropped. The hospital also has harassed union members by suspending four dietary workers for wearing union buttons, obtaining an injunction against picketing and leafleting and trying to label the union as a bunch of outside agitators.

The outside agitator charge is put to rest by Presbyterian Co-chairman Labrone Epps, a plasterer. "1199 is a beautiful union because here the local people do their own thing," says Epps, who adds he became interested in the union when he saw plasterers working in private industry were earning twice as much as he was.

Presbyterian workers reacted to the hospital's injunction with an orderly evening march to the hospital January 7 by several hundred workers in weather that was two below. Despite an unusually bitter winter, 1199P organizers have criss-crossed the city, signing up large numbers of workers at over 20 institutions. Among them are St. Francis, Western Psychiatric, Allegheny General, Magee, Montefiore and Uniontown Hospitals.

When management granted an election at Jewish Home and Hospital, workers there voted in 1199P January 5 by a 157-40 margin.

Presbyterian and Mercy conducted a boycott of their hospital cafeterias January 15 that 99 percent effective. It honored the memory of Dr. Martin Luther King, Jr. by protesting the hospitals' refusal to grant such a basic freedom as the right to an election. Black and white workers cooperated in making the boycott a success. On the eve of Dr. King's birthday Presbyterian assistant housekeeping manager Archie Brooks resigned and joined the 1199P staff, commenting, "I can no longer be associated with an institution that denies the basic freedom for which Dr. King lived and died."

City-wide support for hospital workers' right to an election has mushroomed since the organizing drive began last October. Support has come from religious leaders like Pittsburgh's Roman Catholic Bishop Vincent M. Leonard and the city's Presbyterian clergymen; from many of the city's major unions; from a complete cross-section of civil rights and community groups; from major newspapers like the *Post-Gazette* and the *Pittsburgh Catholic;* and from students, professors, the American Civil Liberties Union and the Americans for Democratic Action.

Leading representatives from many of these groups joined to form the Committee for Justice for Pittsburgh Hospital Workers, chaired by University of Pittsburgh professor David Montgomery.

Over 100 1199ers lobbied at the state Capitol in Harrisburg January 26 for a bill that would require hospitals to hold union representation elections like other employers. The next day in Presbyterian Hospital, x-ray escort Mary Woodson, noticing the patient she was wheeling into x-ray was State Sen. Jack McGregor, went right on with the lobbying, getting Senator McGregor's assurance he would vote for the bill.

Chairman of the Mercy Hospital organizing committee is Woodrow Frasier, Jr., Mercy committee member, Thelma Lewis, a $1.75-an-hour housekeeper and mother of eight, says, "If it comes to a strike we'll go out and stay out. We need the union."

Mrs. Lewis recalls registering a complaint with a nun at the Catholic hospital and being told, "You have no rights here."

"I don't see any religion in that," says Mrs. Lewis. "That's why we're all pulling for the union here."

1199 Drug and Hospital News, 5 (February, 1970): 11-15.

16. BATTLE IN PITTSBURGH

By Dan North

A six-day strike at Presbyterian Hospital brought Local 1199P representation a step closer for Pittsburgh hospital workers March 26 when management agreed conditionally to an election.

"1199P is in Pittsburgh to stay," announced National Hospital Union Sec.-Treas. Henry Nicholas at a press conference at strike headquarters announcing the settlement.

The sole issue in the strike was the right of Presbyterian's 650 service and maintenance workers to an election to choose their own union.

A similar strike by 1199P for the right to an election was in progress at Uniontown (Pa.) Hospital as this magazine went to press.

A key part of the Pittsburgh settlement was management's promise to support pending state collective bargaining legislation for hospitals. The hospital agreed not to obstruct a speedy election once the bill is passed. It also returned striking workers to their jobs without reprisals, despite earlier threats that strikers out for five or more days would be fired. National Hospital Union Exec. Vice Pres. Eliott Godoff flew in from New York as strike tension mounted and led the negotiating efforts that brought about the settlement.

Jubilation by workers over the settlement was tempered by their realization that should the legislation not pass, Local 1199P will be forced into further action.

The Pittsburgh strike followed a pattern that led to the organization by Local 1199 of 40,000 hospital workers in the New York area. Strikes in New York City in 1952 and Bronxville, N.Y. in 1965 led to passage of state laws that made representation elections mandatory in hospitals.

The Pittsburgh strike, through focusing public attention on the plight of underpaid hospital workers and on the need for collective bargaining legislation covering them, paralleled the New York experience.

Important factors:

The dramatic appearance of Mrs. Coretta King, honorary chairman of the National Hospital Union, before a March 19 strike rally of 2,000 people. "It is depressing that in the year 1970, here in Pittsburgh, the cradle of the American labor movement, low paid hospital workers are being compelled to strike for the elementary right to have a union," said Mrs. King.

The willingness of 91 strikers and strike supporters to go to jail March 23 to concentrate public attention on the strike issue of the right to an election. The 91 arrests came during mass early morning picketing by 400 demonstrators protesting an anti-picketing injunction issued by Judge Gwilym Price, Jr., son of a Presbyterian Hospital trustee. Among those arrested were Father John O'Malley of St. Joseph's Roman Catholic Church. Rank and file strike leader Lynwood McBride, along with National Hospital Union Vice Pres. John Black, spent three days in Allegheny County Jail. The others arrested were released the same day with $15 fines.

A 26-hour sit-in by Org. Kay Tillow and eight workers in the office of Pittsburgh Plate Glass Corp. Director David Hill focused attention on just who the Presbyterian Hospital trustees are. Hill is one of 26 trustees whose corporate affiliations read like a Who's Who in industry—U.S. Steel, Mellon National Bank, Westinghouse and other big names in Pittsburgh business.

Vital support for the strike came from clergymen, professors, black community leaders, students, the Pennsylvania Nurses Assn., the Pittsburgh Federation of Teachers and other local unions, and from the editorial page of the *Pittsburgh Post-Gazette,* the city's only morning daily newspaper, which urged the hospital to grant an election.

Finally, the strike could not have been won without the dedication of strikers, most of them women making $1.75 per hour who braved picket duty through daily rain or snow. "We didn't come out here to lose," said striking nurses' aide Henrietta Goree on a wet and freezing 5:30 a.m. picketline on the steep Desoto St. entrance to Presbyterian.

In Uniontown, workers led by Black and volunteer organizer Walter Tillow struck February 26 in a soft coal mining community with a trade union tradition so strong one striking nurses' aide said. "The first good thing my mother-in-law said about me in 23 years was when she found I was out on strike."

Pickets from 1199P shut down the businesses run by four of the hospital's trustees. These included the long shaft of Robena Number 2 mine, the country's largest coal mine and a part of the U.S. Steel empire, where some 200 United Mine Workers refused to cross the 1199P line.

Striker Delbert Livengood, an elder in the local Christian Church and a hospital custodian for 12 years who now earns $302 per month, said: "This is actually a fight between rich and poor. The hospital trustees control this town and the men who work in the hospital need two jobs to stay alive."

It was, as Mrs. King said, "part and parcel of the struggle going on everywhere for dignity, justice and human rights."

And the meaning of the strike is that for hospital workers throughout Pennsylvania, 1199P is indeed here to stay.

1199 Drug and Hospital News, 5 (April, 1970): 14-15.

THE STRUGGLE IN CHARLESTON

17.   HUGH A. BRIMM, OFFICE OF CIVIL RIGHTS, TO
DR. WILLIAM M. McCORD, PRESIDENT OF MEDICAL
COLLEGE OF SOUTH CAROLINA, SEPTEMBER 19, 1968

Dear Dr. McCord:

Unforeseen circumstances prevented me from writing to you on the schedule I promised. I sincerely hope the delay has not been too inconvenient for you. I apologize for the length of this communication, but I am attempting to spell out all of our findings and recommendations as clearly and concisely as possible.

Our review was concentrated in three major areas. They were, a) Equal Educational Opportunities, b) Equal Health Opportunities, and c) Equal Employment Oppotrunities. I will list both our findings and recommendations for each of these areas of investigation.

Equal Educational Opportunities

Findings:

1.   The Medical College of South Carolina had not established an affirmative program designed to attract Negro students.

2.   There was no systematic or comprehensive recruitment program for predominantly Negro schools.

3.   The minority community had not been informed of loans or scholarships that were available to them.

4.   There were segregated housing advertisements on the college's bulletin boards.

5.   Students were placed with practicing physicians for the purpose of receiving on-the-job training. It appears from reports that some of these physicians practiced racial discrimination.

6.   The Medical College Hospital is owned and operated by the Medical College of Charleston. Physicians at the hospital

have faculty status--all are white. In order to practice
medicine in the hospital, physicians must be members of a
specialty board. No Negro physicians in Charleston County
are members of a specialty board. There are several Negro
physicians in Charleston.

7.   The School of Pharmacy places students for "apprenticeship"
     training with some pharmacies that engage in discriminatory
     practices.

8.   The fraternities in the School of Pharmacy discriminate
     racially in membership requirements.

9.   The School of Allied Sciences has affiliations with white
     schools only. This policy tends to limit the potential of
     the Negro students of the State of South Carolina.

Recommendations:

1.   That the Medical College catalogue, brochures and other
     printed promotional material and applications clearly
     indicate the nondiscrimatory policy of the college.

2.   That comparable action be taken to recruit Negro students
     to pursue a medical education at the Medical College. These
     steps should include:

     a.   Broad dissemination of information as to the avail-
          ability of a medical education, and the availability
          of financial assistance to undergradute colleges
          and high school counselors (especially to Negro
          colleges and high schools) in the state, and to Negro
          colleges throughout the eastern and southeastern states.

     b.   Due to the history of discrimination, special efforts
          should be directed toward the pre-med advisors at
          Negro undergraduate colleges and possibly high schools
          to help motivate more Negroes and minority group
          members toward a medical career.

     c.   The Medical College might consider developing a re-
          cruitment team from all of its related schools (e.g.,
          Pharmacy, Nursing, Allied Sciences, etc.) which could
          make concentrated recruitment efforts, some of which
          would be directed specifically toward minority students.
          Various techniques should be developed which would have
          considerable potential for recruitment of minority
          group students including:

          (1) Contact with Negro professional, civic, and
               social groups to elicit their help in
               recruitment, and in dispelling the image of
               the Medical College as a segregated institution.

          (2) Promotion of visits to the Medical College
               by Negro pre-med students over the state.

          (3) Visits to Negro college campuses, by Medical
               College staff.

          (4) Sponsorship of health-related career days,
               especially for Charleston County High Schools.

3.   That the College assure itself that no arrangements are
     made between the college and private physicians for the
     purpose of teaching students when the physician discriminates
     on the basis of race in his practice.

4. That the Medical College assure itself that no notices for
   rental or sale of living quarters are posted or lists kept by
   the College unless such housing is available to all students
   without regard to their race.

5. That the School of Pharmacy assure itself that every pharmacy
   to which they refer a student for work in an "apprenticeship"
   arrangement, will accept those who are referred without regard
   to race.

6. That the fraternities that have engaged in racially discriminatory policies and practices be informed of the College's
   posture on civil rights and asked to change. If they do not
   comply, that the organization should be banned from campus
   by the administration.

7. That the School of Allied Sciences establish affiliations
   with Negro colleges in the state immediately in order to give
   all students of South Carolina an equal educational opportunity.

Since the School of Nursing has not previously enrolled non-white
students, the following steps are recommended:

1. There are several non-white persons who have applied and have
   been admitted to study practical nursing. Persons in this
   category should be screened carefully as potentials for full
   professional training as graduate nurses.

2. That predominantly Negro schools be informed of the opportunities
   and policies in the School of Nursing.

3. That continuous attempts be made to identify students with
   potential at the high school level. Local Negro school
   counselors can be of great help in this endeavor.

Equal Health Opportunities

Findings:

1. There were no written nondiscriminatory policy statements.

2. It was alleged that the clerk at the admission office called
   the floor and gave the nurse the race of the patient, and
   asked what bed assignment should be made. This suggests that
   room assignments might follow a racial pattern.

3. We were informed in the community that patients were shifted
   around to achieve a bi-racial mix in anticipation of the
   H.E.W. visit. When white patients complained about rooming
   with Negroes, the Negroes were moved.

4. No comprehensive or systematic methods have been used to
   notify all of the people of Charleston (both Negro and white)
   of the hospital's nondiscriminatory policy..

5. Mr. Porter, who was assigned the responsibility for civil
   rights, has not developed any kind of affirmative action
   program. The subject of civil rights has not been a formal
   part of the staff meeting agenda.

6. It was alleged that courtesy titles are seldom used and staff
   members are often rude to Negro patients at the clinics.

7. Service (non-paying) patients and private patients are
   separated and are alleged to be treated differently.

8. It was alleged that senior medical students attend to private patients, while junior medical students attend service patients.

9. There is some degree of desegregation in the wards, but the separation of the service and private patients has created an apparent imbalance.

10. From interviews and observation, private patients appear to have received better nursing and other care than service patients. The majority of the private patients are white.

11. Private patients have three visiting periods per day; service patients have only one. It was alleged that on one floor, a white patient's sister was allowed to visit while the Negro patient's sister was not allowed to visit.

12. It was also alleged that husbands of Negro patients are not allowed in the labor room, while husbands of white patients are.

13. In many parts of the hospital, it was found that there are essentially "dual" restroom facilities, although "white" and "colored" signs have been removed. It is apparent that these signs have only recently been removed because outlines of the old signs are still visible. This suggests the possibility that old customs are still being practiced in the use of these facilities.

14. In the out-patient clinic, patients appear to be seen on a first-come, first-served basis, however Negro patients are told to wait in Room 18, while white patients are told to wait in Room 53. However, it was alleged that when an observer who appeared to be concerned with civil rights procedures was seen near the admitting station, patients were told to wait in either Room 18 or Room 53.

15. White staff members were observed acting in what appeared to be a rude manner to Negro out-patients. Courtesy titles were not being used.

Recommendations:

1. That policy statements regarding nondiscriminatory practices be written and widely distributed immediately.

2. That room assignments be made at the admitting desk without regard to the patient's race.

3. That a daily racial census be taken and forwarded to the Office for Civil Rights each week for one month, and thereafter upon request.

4. Since everyone will not read distributed material, and since it is the responsibility of the administration to see to it that everyone understands his/her responsibility, it is recommended that seminars be conducted which include the following topics: (a) specifics of the application of Title VI to hospitals; (b) Title 45; (c) H.E.W. guidelines; (d) equal opportunity in hospitals and all health programs; (e) the Federal dollar and nondiscrimination; (f) the Civil Rights Act of 1964; and (g) civil rights obligations of staff members at all levels. A schedule of when and where these meetings are held should be kept for your record.

5. That discussions of developments in civil rights accomplishments be placed regularly on the agenda at staff meetings.

6. That all staff be specifically instructed about the
   necessity for the use of courtesy titles. The breech of
   this policy should be dealt with severely by the administration.

7. That the quality of service be equalized immediately as
   between private and service patients.

8. That waiting rooms be truly integrated.

9. That staff restrooms be posted as such and all staff be
   advised accordingly.

Equal Employment Opportunities

Findings:

1. Bulletin boards did not have Equal Employment Opportunity
   (EEO) posters.

2. Personnel policy statements did not reflect contractor's
   equal opportunity posture.

3. There was no Equal Employment Opportunity Officer.

4. Advertisements for employment do not reflect that the
   facility is an equal opportunity employer.

5. Recruitment and employment sources were not informed of
   contractor's posture on EEO.   .

6. The old established personnel policies and procedures
   precluded affirmative action, which was needed to
   guarantee equal employment opportunity.

7. Interview reports are evaluated by a clerk who does not
   have personnel experience.

8. Applicants are given a written test that has not been
   validated. For some job categories, the test is irrelevant.

9. Some job descriptions require in-house experience for jobs
   that minorities have not had the opportunity to get. There
   is no training program to fill this gap.

10. Department heads and supervisory staff are not conversant
    with the contractor's position regarding equal employment
    opportunity.

11. Employment patterns clearly suggest a stratification of
    employees with regard to race, i.e., administrative
    and professional positions are occupied by whites; non-
    whites are concentrated in service and non-skilled categories.

12. The application for employment requires each applicant to sub-
    mit a photo.

13. The contractor (Medical College of Charleston) has not taken
    appropriate steps to insure the compliance under Executive
    Order 11246 by the company building the new addition to the
    Medical College.

Recommendations:

1. That there be a proper display of posters at key points such as main lobby, personnel office, and all employes bulletin boards.

2. That there be put in writing a firm equal employment opportunity policy statement to be disseminated to all department heads and supervisory personnel.

3. That an equal employment opportunity officer be appointed. This officer will assume the duties of, (a) disseminating information concerning equal employment opportunity; (b) keeping surveillance over the implementation of the equal employment opportunity policy; (c) planning equal employment opportunity actions and goals; and, (d) evaluating equal employment opportunity progress.

4. That all advertisements contain the tag line, "An Equal Opportunity Employer."

5. That all recruitment and employment sources be notified of the contractor's posture on equal employment opportunity. It will be desirable to receive an acknowledgment of this notification. This may be done by leaving a space at the bottom of the letter for endorsement, or in any other manner which the contractor chooses.

6. That purchase orders contain a reference to Executive Order 11246. This will serve to notify sub-contractors of their responsibility to the prime contractor in accordance with Executive Order 11246.

7. That all personnel procedures serve to support affirmative action as exacted by Executive Order 11246.

8. That all department heads and supervisory personnel be made fully conversant with the contractor's position with regard to equal employment opportunity.

9. That training programs support the total equal employment opportunity effort.

10. That persistent efforts be made to break the old patterns of stratified racial employment which have concentrated white employees in administrative and professional positions, while shunting non-white into the unskilled and service categories.

11. That the equal employment opportunity officer maintain a day-to-day file relating to the problems and progress of the implementation of the equal employment opportunity policy of the Charleston Medical School.

12. That anything that would identify the applicant, and which might cause him/her to be subjected to discriminatory acts, not be a part of the application form. Such information should not be a part of the employee's personnel folder.

13. That the contractor (Medical College of Charleston) take the necessary steps to ensure that the building contractors who are currently constructing the new physical plant for the school, comply fully with the requirements of Executive Order 11246 in all phases of phases of their employment.

In your response to the recommendations which are set forth above, it
will be helpful if you will structure your reply so as to address yourself
to each of the three areas separately. Upon receipt of your letter, this
office will evaluate your response and then advise you of our findings.

Please let me say once again, on behalf of our staff, that we appreciate your cooperation and that of your entire staff on whom we called.
Your personal concern and intentions to correct problem areas made our task
much easier than it would have otherwise been.

Sincerely yours,

Hugh A. Brimm
Chief, Contract Compliance Branch
Office for Civil Rights

District 1199 Archives.

18.   CAROLINA STRIKE UNITES RIGHTS, LABOR GROUPS

Efforts of Charleston Negroes to Form
Hospital Union Could Spread Across U. S.

By Murray Seeger

CHARLESTON, S.C. -- Two powerful forces, the civil rights movement and
organized labor, have formed an alliance in this unlikely location with the
potential of spreading through the rest of the South and much of the nation.

The specific issue in this old seaport is the desire of a group of
hospital workers to form a union to bargain with their employers, the county
and state governments, for higher pay and improved working conditions.

On March 20, more than 400 service and maintenance workers at State
Medical College Hospital walked off their jobs. An additional 100 workers
from Charleston County Hospital, a block away, followed March 28. The strikers
are nearly all women and all are Negroes.

Below U.S. Minimum

Most of them earn less than $1.60 an hour, the Federal minimum wage for
most workers. Hospitals have a special statutory minimum--$1.30 an hour, the
starting wage for many of the hospital workers here.

The scene in Charleston bears a remarkable resemblance to Memphis a year
ago, where a group of Negroes who worked for the city sanitation department
struck and won union recognition.

In that case civil rights groups allied themselves with the American
Federation of State, County and Municipal Workers, the union representing the
sanitation men. Dr. Martin Luther King had gone to Memphis to address a
rally in support of the strikers when he was assassinated April 4, 1968.

Now the organization Dr. King once called "my favorite union" is attempting to gain recognition as bargaining agent for hospital workers here.

State Won't Talk

State and county officials insist they cannot bargain with the union
representing the workers. They argue that wage scales and conditions are
set by law and they have refused to meet with the union committees.

Frustrated by this lack of communication, angered by what they consider
second-class treatment because they are black and determined to win union
recognition, the women have stepped up their battle.

Five persons were arrested and jailed Thursday, accused of interfering
with other workers entering the hospitals and of fighting with the police
who tried to enforce a court edict limiting the number of pickets at the
buildings.

Friday, 35 more were arrested when a mass picket line was established
in violation of the courts injunctions. The confrontation with the police
was peaceful--the women, augmented by male volunteer pickets, waved and
cheered as they climbed into three paddy wagons.

Talk to Governor

The escalated campaign was agreed to by the women at a union meeting
Wednesday after a committee returned from the state capitol in Columbia where
they talked for 45 minutes with Gov. Robert E. McNair.

Asked how many of them were ready to go to jail in support of their
campaign, dozens of the women stepped forward.

"It was one of the most dramatic things I ever saw," Elliott Godoff of
New York, a veteran organizer sent by his union to help the Charleston group,
said later.

The Rev. Ralph Abernathy, Dr. King's successor as head of the Southern
Christian Leadership Conference, is expected to return here for a second
visit to help generate more support in the large Negro community. Other
AFL-CIO unions in Charleston have given their backing to the walkout and will
be asked for more help.

More Money Needed

The strikers need to raise money since contributions received so far
total only about $5,000. The union has no money to post the bonds for the
arrested pickets.

The organizing effort started last fall at the state hospital, a training facility attached to the only publicly supported medical college in South
Carolina.

The Negroes were convinced that they were being paid too little, that
the few whites doing similar jobs such as nurses' aides, practical nurses,
orderlies and kitchen workers were paid more and that other grievances could
be settled only through representation. They also contended that Negroes
were barred from entering the better-paying jobs such as those of registered
nurses.

Grievance Offer

Dr. William M. McCord, president of the State Medical College, replied
that individuals could always enter a grievance through an established procedure. He would name grievance committees, he said. Anyone on the staff
who unfairly discriminates "will be gone today, not tomorrow," he pledged.

For help, the women turned to a local labor leader, Isiah Bennett,
business agent for a local of the Retail, Wholesale Department Store Union
which represents 1,000 workers at the American Tobacco Co. cigar factory
and three other companies here.

Bennett, after deciding a majority of the women wanted to affiliate
with the union, asked McCord for a meeting last October. He was rejected.

In a staff memo that month, McCord said: " have notified this union
that I am sure that a majority of you would not want to get mixed up in an
outfit such as this and I, of course, have no intention of meeting with this
tobacco workers' union."

"We don't want a union here at the Medical College," he continued. It
would mean "nothing worthwhile or constructive to any of you.

"This union is interested in only one thing and one thing only. That
is money, your money. This union is like a business--it is out to make a
profit. It is our intention to resist this union in its attempt to get in
here with every legal means at our disposal--make no mistake about that."

Attached to the memo were two antiunion cartoons, one showing a fat union
boss with a cigar in his mouth, a wine glass in his hand and a young girl
sitting on his lap. The characters were white.

The dispute came to a climax when some of the workers walked out of a grievance meeting, complaining that Dr. McCord had added antiunion workers to the group to outvote the militants.

12 Women Fired

Twelve women were fired. The union said it was for union activity and the hospital asserts it was because they had left their duties for more than an hour.

More than 400 other workers went on strike in sympathy for the 12. Eight days later the 100 county workers who had joined the union also walked out.

Earlier this year, Bennett called for help from local 1199 of his parent union because he knew it had been remarkably successful in organizing hospital workers in the New York area. Starting 10 years ago, the union has grown to 40,000 members, mostly Negroes. It recently negotiated a minimum starting wage of $100 a week for workers at private hospitals in New York.

Local 1199 has expanded its efforts nationwide by forming the National Organizing Committee of Hospital and Nursing Home Employes. Although aimed at private institutions, the group has taken on the Charleston campaign as its first among public employes.

"I'm hearing again all the arguments I first heard 10 years ago in New York," Godoff, the New York organizer, commented last week.

The 2 million nonprofessional hospital employes in the country represent one of the largest low-paid group of workers in the economy.

Several unions have shown interest in trying to organize them.

The handicaps to organizing here are many. This state is notoriously inhospitable to unions. There are only about 40,000 AFL-CIO members in the state, but about 25% of them are in the Charleston area including many who work for the huge U.S. naval base.

Public employes are not covered by the National Labor Relations Act which guarantees other workers the right to organize and provide machinery protecting those rights. In addition, South Carolina has a series of right-to-work laws designed to discourage organizing.

State officials are afraid that if the union wins at the hospitals it will open the way for organizing in other parts of the state and local governments.

They are aware that unions are scoring more success in organizing the vast field of public employes than any other segment of the work force.

When Gov. McNair met with the workers' committee headed by Miss Mary Moultrie, they talked about the other groups of workers, especially teachers, that have been agitating for higher pay.

While attention has been directed to the women strikers, 150 Negro men were fired from their jobs for staging a one-day strike at the State Port Authority docks. They had signed up with the International Longshoremens Assn., the union that represents stevedores employed by private companies operating on the same docks. These firings. Bennett feels, have created unrest in the Negro neighborhood.

The strike has made this city nervous since it comes at a time when tourists are flocking here to see the famous gardens in full spring bloom.

After his first bitter blast at the union, McCord has moderated his statement. He now emphasizes the legal limitations on changing working conditions.

"Wages are requested and appropriated annually by the Legislature," he said recently. "I cannot delegate authority of the Medical College to any other outside agent."

Some improvements have been made at the state hospital since the union started organizing. Annual leave policy was made more generous in mid-March and requirements for taking time off for holidays were loosened in January for the birthday of Gen. Robert E. Lee.

New Pay Minimum

Only in February, however, did the minimum wage of $1.30 go into effect.

In answer to a written question, McCord said he was aware that "some states have laws that permit public hospitals to negotiate with unions.

"However, this has no bearing on the question of South Carolina because the laws of South Carolina do not so provide."

Legal advisers to the union contend that while the state may not explicitly provide for granting union recognition, neither does the law bar
such recognition.

McCord will not answer reporters' questions directly. Before hospital
spokesmen will talk to reporters they are required to check with a recently
hired lawyer for authority.

U.S. Also Involved

"We are trying to handle this very carefully and delicately so we don't
inflame the community," one official said. Officials are also concerned
because representatives of the the Department of Health and Education and
Welfare are here checking on complaints of employment bias against Negroes.

In old Charleston, the portion of the city which is on a peninsula
between two rivers which contains the famous homes and other historic buildings, Negroes represent 70% of the population.

The city's six hospitals including one operated by the Veterans Administration are situated in the same immediate vicinity downtown. The city's
whites live mostly in the restored, older part of downtown and in recently
annexed neighborhoods across the Ashley River.

One of the workers' grievances that the VA hospital, organized by Service Employees Union, has a higher pay scale and more generous benefits than
the state and county hospitals.

Recognition Due

One of the other nearby hospitals, St. Francis Xavier, has indicated it
will recognize the union when it can show it represents the majority of the
workers.

A small citizen's committee representing clergymen, civil rights groups
and the Young Democrats has tried to open communications between the public
authorities and the union with no success. A settlement proposed by the group
of clergy was dismissed as "biased" by Dr. McCord.

The struck hospitals are operating on a "near normal" basis, according
to spokesmen, with the use of volunteers, nonstrikers and hired replacements.

Both sides appear determined to hold out indefinitely. South Carolina,
where the first shots of the Civil War were fired, has escaped the kind of
bitter civil rights confrontations seen in its sister states of the Deep South.
The hospital strike has the elements to end that record, however.

"I've told these people that they have to organize or they will be
20th-century slaves," Bennett said.

Los Angeles Times, April 14, 1969.

19. MRS. KING'S CRUSADE

It was a strike of exploited, miserably paid garbage workers for the
right of union recognition that led Martin Luther King to undertake his fate-
ful, final journey to Memphis last year. Now, in a fitting memorial to him,
the leaders of eight civil rights organizations--sharply divided on some
issues in recent times--have joined together under the leadership of Mrs.
Coretta King to speak up for 500 striking Negro hospital workers in Charleston,
S.C., who are engaged in a similar battle.

Most of them earn no more than $1.30 an hour; what is immediately at
stake--as it was in Memphis--is their quest for union representation. In
Memphis the city officialdom bitterly resisted unionization of the garbage
employes until Dr. King's murder suddenly changed things. Did Charleston
learn nothing from that horror story? Will state leaders and hospital trustees
hold out until the tensions explode in some ghastly collision? Mrs. King
and her associates are pleading for elementary justice and human dignity.
They should be heard.

New York Post, April 21, 1969.

20.   NATIONAL ORGANIZING COMMITTEE
HOSPITAL AND NURSING HOME EMPLOYEES

TEXT OF STATEMENT SIGNED BY NATIONAL CIVIL RIGHTS LEADERS
ON CHARLESTON, SOUTH CAROLINA HOSPITAL STRIKES ISSUED BY
MRS. CORETTA S. KING FOR RELEASE MONDAY A.M., APRIL 21, 1969

We wish to speak out in full support of the 600 black hospital workers
on strike for union and human rights at the Charleston Medical College and
Charleston County Hospitals in Charleston, South Carolina. The fact that
these workers earning as little as $1.30 an hour should be compelled to strike
for the simple right to have a union tells much about what is wrong with
America today.
        We view the struggle in Charleston as more than a fight for union rights.
It is part of the larger fight in our nation against discrimination and ex-
ploitation--against all forms of degradation that result from poverty and
human misery. It is a fight for human rights and human dignity.
        We, therefore, applaud the efforts of Local 1199B of the RWDSU/AFL-CIO's
National Organizing Committee of Hospital and Nursing Home Employees and the
Concerned Citizens Committee of Charleston for spearheading the campaign to
win justice for the terribly exploited hospital workers.
        Already, 180 workers have been arrested. And while there have been only
minor clashes to date, tensions are mounting. We cannot fail to recall that
the right of workers to be represented by a union is precisely the same issue
that led to tragedy in Memphis last year.
        We call on South Carolina's Governor, Robert E. McNair, and the hospital
officials to grant the workers this elementary right as a minimal gesture of
justice and humanity.

[SIGNED BY:]   NATIONAL CIVIL RIGHTS LEADERS[142]

[MRS.] CORRETTA SCOTT KING, honorary chairman, National Organizing
                            Committee of Hospital and Nursing Home Employees
RALPH D. ABERNATHY, president, Southern Christian Leadership Conference [SCLC]
ROY WILKINS, executive director, National Association for the Advancement of
                            Colored People [NAACP]
A. PHILIP RANDOLPH, national president, Negro American Labor Council
WHITNEY YOUNG, executive director, National Urban League
ROY INNIS, national director, Congress of Racial Equality [CORE]
BAYARD RUSTIN, executive director, A. Philip Randolph Institute
[MISS] DOROTHY I. HEIGHT, national president, National Council of Negro Women
GEORGE A. WILEY, executive director, National Welfare Rights Organization

OTHERS[143]

REPRESENTATIVE SHIRLEY CHISHOLM, member of Congress, Brooklyn, New York
REPRESENTATIVE JOHN M. CONYERS, member of Congress, Detroit, Michigan
MAYOR RICHARD G. HATCHER, Gary, Indiana
MAYOR CARL B. STOKES, Cleveland, Ohio
JULIAN BOND, member, House of Representatives, State of Georgia

District 1199 Archives.

21.   A GATHERING STORM IN CHARLESTON, S.C.

There are echoes of the strike of garbage workers in Memphis more than
a year ago reverberating in Charleston, S.C., where 400 non-professional Negro
hospital workers are striking for union recognition against a state and a county
hospital. The Memphis strike ended in the tragic assassination of Dr. Martin
Luther King, Jr., and eventual Federal intervention to settle the bitter dispute. Thus far, the only Federal presence in Charleston has been in an observer

capacity, but events appear to be moving rapidly toward a situation that only Federal intervention will be able to resolve. Prompt Federal intervention is indicated to prevent a tragic escalation into open violence.

Tensions have heightened with the arrest and jailing of the Rev. Ralph David Abernathy, Dr. King's successor as president of the Southern Christian Leadership Conference. Andrew Young, vice president of SCLC, has said SCLC will stay "until we win or die." Dr. King's widow yesterday was preparing to join the demonstrators and reportedly ready to be arrested and jailed herself. Many hundreds have been arrested including large numbers of school children and the Guard has been called to help State and local police enforce an injunction against mass picketing.

This response seems out of scale with the issue--recognition of a union sought by low paid black hospital workers, mainly women paid the legal $1.30 an hour minimum, who claim they are discriminated against because they are black. The authorities have refused to meet with the union, insisting that wages and working conditions of the public employes are set by law and there-fore not negotiable. Memphis held a similar hard-headed position before Dr. King's murder, but backed down afterward, spurred on by the tragedy and Federal intervention at the request of President Johnson.

Washington Post, April 30, 1969.

22. TEXT OF SPEECH BY MRS. CORETTA SCOTT KING
AT DINNER HONORING A. PHILIP RANDOLPH
TUESDAY, MAY 6, 1969

Governor Rockefeller, Mayor Lindsay, Mr. Rustin, distinguished members of the dais, I want to tell you how proud and happy I am to be at this dinner to pay tribute to A. Philip Randolph, a true giant in the struggle for justice and equal rights for all Americans, especially black Americans at the bottom of the economic ladder.

Just a week ago while I was enroute to Charleston, South Carolina to address a mass rally in that city, I mentioned to one of my campanions, Miss Doris Turner, a Vice-President of Local 1199, Drug and Hospital Union in this city, that I had been invited to speak here tonight.

Miss Turner, a former hospital worker, waxed eloquently over the role Phil Randolph had played in her union's great struggle to win union and human rights for voluntary hospital workers in this city.

She recalled that ten years ago--as a matter of fact, the 10th anniver-sary is this Thursday, May 8--that the hospital workers of this city, virtually all of them black and Puerto Rican workers and most of them women who earned as little as $30 and $32 a week, were compelled to strike for 46 days for the right to have a union.

The point I want to make is that the man who played a decisive role in this hospital organizing crusade is the man we honor tonight--Phil Randolph.

And now, exactly ten years later, a similar struggle is taking place in Charleston, South Carolina where 500 black workers, almost all of them women who earn as little as $1.30 an hour, are on strike for the same elementary right to have a union.

What began as a little known struggle by black hospital workers for elementary rights has captured the imagination and touched the conscience of decent-minded Americans everywhere. The Charleston strike is now a major national issue with tremendously important implications for the civil rights movement, for organized labor and for all Americans.

For as the New York Times noted in an editorial last week, this strike "involves values as fundamental as those in the original battles for school desegregation and equal employment opportunities."

You know, several months ago I was privileged to assume the position of honorary chairman of the National Organizing Committee of Hospital and Nursing Home employees of the RWDSU, AFL-CIO. You may have seen pictures of me wearing my Local 1199 hat in Charleston last week. I am interested in hospital workers because so many of them are women--black women, white women, Mexican-and Puerto Rican women. All of them are poor.

They work full-time jobs at part-time pay. Many of them are the sole
supporters of their families.

I know you will agree that $1.30 an hour is not a wage, it's an insult.

I spent two days in Charleston last week speaking at two overflow
rallies and participating in an inspiring march from the church to the hospital.
More than 7,500 people attended these rallies. When you consider that this
represents almost 30 percent of the entire black population of the inner city
of Charleston, you appreciate the tremendous unity that has been forded here.

The alliance that Mr. Randolph has devoted a lifetime to building--the
alliance of civil rights groups and organized labor--is a reality today in
Charleston.   The members of Local 1199B, the SCLC, the NAACP and all the
other rights groups working together with the clergy, the students, with old
people and young people, with Protestants, Catholics and Jews--are solidly
united in support of a clear cause--union and human rights for the Charleston
hospital workers.

I will not burden you with the facts of this strike. By now, they are
all well known. What is not too well known is the precise nature of the
opposition. For example, the president of the Charleston Medical College, Dr.
William M. McCord, expressed the management's point of view in an interview
with a reporter for a national magazine. He said, and I quote: "I am not
about to turn over a $25 million complex to people who never had a grammar
school education." This same gentleman attempted to head off the union organizing drive a few months ago. He offered some goodies to the workers. Dr.
McCord announced an additional paid holiday--the birthday of Robert E. Lee.

Listen to the columnist of the Charleston News and Courier, Ashley
Cooper, who wrote last week, and again I am quoting:

"It seems--at least to me--that the only way the illegal uprising can
be stopped is by force. That may have the ring of fascism--which I hate--
but honestly, what other conclusion is there?"

It is perfectly clear that we are dealing with a combination of stupidity,
arrogance and insults from a group of powerful people who refuse to join the
20th century.

Last week, when I arrived at the Charleston airport, I was greeted by
a reporter just back from covering the war in Southeast Asia. He came up to
me and said, "Mrs. King, welcome to Charleston, South Vietnam." The plain
truth is that the city of Charleston is an armed camp. More than 1,000
national guardsmen wearing gas masks and flashing bayonets encircle the black
community. Armored tanks rumble through the streets. Helmeted state troopers
surround Charleston's churches and hospitals. And hundreds of decent men and
women, young and old, black and white, have suffered jailings and mass
arrests. Why?

Simply because a courageous group of terribly exploited hospital workers
have dared to stand up and say to the people who run the city of Charleston
and the state of South Carolina that they are sick and tired of being sick
and tired.

And once you have seen these people. Once you have talked to them.
Once you have marched at their side--you know that they are determined to
continue this fight no matter what it takes. Because these people just ain't
gonna let anybody turn them around. And Charleston and the rest of the nation
had better believe it.

For the hospital strikers and their supporters have faced the tanks
and the bayonets with the unity of their souls. And with that spirit--the
spirit of non-violence, militantly conceived and massively organized, they
shall never give up until they win.

I wish I had time to tell you about the new breed of union leaders that
has emerged in this struggle. For one of the most remarkable aspects of this
most remarkable strike is that it has dramatized the emergence of black women
leaders like Miss Mary Ann Moultrie, Miss Rosetta Simmons, and many others.

When you talk with people like Mary Moultrie, the dynamic president of
Local 1199B, it is hard to escape the conclusion that the hospitals stubborn
resistance is doomed. The only question is how much blood and tears must be
shed before the victory is won. For these women are determined to achieve a
measure of dignity on this earth. And there comes a moment in their lives
when they decide to assert their humanity, no matter how large the risks, and
the prospect of defeat becomes unendurable, no matter how rough the road.

These women are following in the footsteps of Harriet Tubman and Sojourner Truth--of Rosa Parks and Daisy Bates and Fannie Lou Hamer. And they will be a source of great pride to the black people and to the entire labor movement.[144]

The hospital workers and the people of Charleston are making history. For Charleston, like Selma and Memphis, has now become a national test of conscience.

I believe with all my heart that what is now at stake in the state of Strom Thurmond and in the city of Mendel Rivers is more than just a battle for union and human rights for oppressed hospital workers. For Charleston now represents a tremendous challenge and a great opportunity.

These magnificent women, these courageous people are prepared to fight on, no matter how long it takes. The question before us now is whether we will understand the nature of this challenge and face up to this test. For if we win--and I know we can win--Charleston may become that moment in our history when the unity of black and white, of the civil rights movement with organized labor, may be recaptured. That unity was my husband's dream. That dream will never die. And I know that if my husband were alive today, he would tell you that this dream can be realized today in Charleston, South Carolina. All of which brings me back to our honored guest, Phil Randolph.

I believe that the best way we can honor Phil Randolph is by advancing the principles for which he has devoted his entire life. With that in mind, I say that at this moment in our history, the single most important issue before the forces of progress in this nation--the labor movement, the civil rights movement, our political leaders, the clergy--is the cause of the hospital workers in Charleston, South Carolina.

I want to appeal to you, and through you, to the organizations you represent, to demonstrate in whatever way you can your solidarity and support for these workers. I do not pretend to be an organizer of mass movements. But you are. The strikers and the people of Charleston are poor. They need funds desperately. I want to urge you to contribute as much money as you can to help these strikers. There are other ways in which you can personally identify with this struggle. There will be opportunities for to participate in marches and demonstrations in Charleston and elsewhere. I am confident that you will meet this challenge.

I learned last week that Charleston was the birthplace of the tune that now bears the title--"We Shall Overcome." Deep in my heart, I believe we will overcome in Charleston. That victory will be the best birthday gift that we can give to a true fighter for the rights of oppressed people everywhere--our good friend, Phil Randolph.

District 1199 Archives.

23. THE CHARLESTON COALITION

George Meany and Walter P. Reuther have parted company in organized labor, but they are standing together in support of striking Negro hospital workers in Charleston, S.C. A similar unity has been established by all the country's major civil rights groups, which rarely agree on tactics these days. They have put aside their differences to help a wretchedly underpaid work force win union recognition and a measure of human dignity.

The coalition that has been forged between the labor movement and the civil rights organizations in the Charleston struggle is as firm as the one that existed on Capitol Hill through the long fight to put across the Civil Rights Act of 1964. That coalition was re-formed during the Memphis sanitation strike before the assassination of the Rev. Dr. Martin Luther King, Jr. Its emergence now suggests that the coalition is no one-time thing and that, in easing the plight of the exploited black worker, both unions and civil rights groups have a role to play. Each can draw strength from the other in a period when both have seemed to flounder in many of their recent efforts.

Unions have been lagging in membership. Civil rights groups such as

Dr. King's Southern Christian Leadership Conference, now headed by the Rev.
Ralph David Abernathy, need fresh victories. They have a mutual interest in
the 500 striking Charleston hospital workers who are mostly women, mostly
blacks, employed as non-professional nurses' aides, orderlies, cooks, at wages
as little as $1.30 an hour or thirty cents below the Federal minimum wage
which establishes a floor for most jobs. Unions calculate that there are
2.5 million non-union black, Puerto Rican and Mexican hospital workers across
the country suffering similar wage injustices.

The best hope for ending the Charleston strike without a racial explosion or a tragedy of the type that struck down Dr. King lies in intervention by the Federal Government--precisely the kind of intervention that brought
labor peace after tragedy struck in Memphis a year ago. At a meeting in the
White House yesterday, Dr. King's successor, Mr. Abernathy, urged President
Nixon "to use his great and powerful office" to speed a settlement. "He said
nothing," was Mr. Abernathy's report after the session. That is not a good
enough answer; it cannot be the final one.

New York Times, May 14, 1969.

24. CHARLESTON'S RIGHTS BATTLEGROUND

By Ronald Sarro

CHARLESTON, S.C.--Mary Moultrie is a soft-spoken, almost shy black woman
who is trying to move a mountain of Southern tradition and economic power.

The 27-year-old nurses' aid, a native of this historic city where the
Civil War started 108 years ago, is the leader of workers who have been
striking two hospitals in this city of 80,000--half Negro, half white--since
late March.

"She has always been quiet," said a fellow worker at the South Carolina
Medical College Hospital. "But she was brave enough to take the leadership."

The 500 hospital workers, mostly Negro women, went on strike over union
recognition, discrimination and wages. Since Miss Moultrie took them out,
there have been these developments:

The Southern Christian Leadership Conference, which had other civil rights
plans for the spring, has committed itself to helping the Charleston strikers
indefinitely.

The AFL-CIO Executive Council last week established a Charleston Hospital
Strike Fund with $25,000, and urged all affiliates to support the strike.

United Auto Workers President Walter Reuther has given $10,000 to the
strikers as a "down payment," and is providing $500 a week to SCLC to aid
Charleston activities.

President Nixon has sent Justice Department representatives here to
apprise him of strike developments, and has called for the disputing parties
to "resolve their differences in a calm atmosphere of mutual good faith."

Seventeen U.S. senators have urged Nixon to send a federal mediator to
Charleston, emphasizing that the strike "is a test of the principle of non-
violence at a time when many in America are losing faith in that principle
as a strategy for social change." South Carolina's two senators objected.

A Mothers Day rally and march supporting the strikers was attended by
7,000 to 10,000 persons, including union and civil rights officials from
throughout the nation and five congressmen. SCLC officials said they were
surprised by the number of Charleston whites who hand-signaled the "V" for
victory during the march. "We've never had this in a Southern town," said
the Rev. Andrew Young, executive vice president.

What started out essentially as a labor dispute has developed into the
number one civil rights test of the year. It promises to equal Montgomery,
Selma, Birmingham, and Memphis as a milestone of the movement led by SCLC.

Although the workers have been seeking union recognition since last
August, the crisis didn't develop until March 17, when 12 of them, including
Miss Moultrie, were fired in a dispute with hospital officials.

As a result, about 400 janitors, kitchen workers, laundry workers, maids,

nurses' aides, orderlies and practical nurses walked out of the 550-bed
Medical College Hospital, largest of six in the city, on March 20. Another
100 struck Charleston County Hospital, which is the city's second largest with
150 beds, on March 28.

Both hospitals have been struggling along since with the aid of volunteers and extra duty by working employes. The College Hospital has cut back
its patients by 35 percent.

The conflict boils down to this: The workers want Hospital and Nursing
Home Workers Local 1199B or some other agreed-upon association to represent
them. The state's policy is that union recognition for any government employes is against the public interest.

Union officials say meetings with Gov. Robert E. McNair are fruitless,
and the latest attempt—on May 8—to get the workers and hospital trustees
together disintegrated in a dispute over the presence of national union
officials.

The prospect for another meeting? "We have met with Miss Moultrie
before," said William Hoff, vice president at the Medical College.

Meantime, Charleston's economy has been crippled by the effects of the
strike.

There has been sporadic violence, and about 300 state highway patrolmen
and 700 National Guardsmen have patrolled the city day and night since April
25, when they were sent in to curb the threat of further violence.

A curfew has been in effect since May 1.

More than 650 persons have been arrested on charges of violating the
curfew or a court injunction, which first prohibited strike activities, then
was modified to allow picketing.

Unionism at Issue

The stakes in South Carolina are considerably bigger than those sought
by the hospital workers alone. Only about 7 percent of the workers in the
state are unionized, despite its growing industrial development.

Textile magnates fear the labor movement could spread in a state where
cheap labor and a "right to work" law have helped attract industry. State and
local government officials fear all government employes from garbage workers
to teachers, would organize once the door was opened.

The union movement, with its support from civil rights and union officials,
have been severely attacked. Leaders have been accused of Communist connections, "using" poor people, and Nazi and Mafia tactics. Local newspapers
and politicians have emphasized what they see as divisions in the movement.

Racial slurs from the patrolling troops—most, if not all white, and
many from rural areas—are not uncommon.

But the strikers' supporters vow to stand by them to the end.

Dr. Martin Luther King's widow, Coretta, and 13 other civil rights
leaders issued a public statement saying, "We view the struggle in Charleston"
as "part of the larger fight in our nation . . . against all forms of degradation that result from poverty and misery."

The Rev. Ralph David Abernathy, SCLC president, told the strikers, 'As
long as there is life in my body, I will never desert you until you are recognized."

When asked the minimum the strikers would accept, Mary Moultrie says,
"We are going to have some kind of recognition" even if it is only some kind
of grievance committee.

WAGE RISE SOUGHT

On wages, the strikers seek an unspecified increase in their $1.30 an
hour minimum, which hospital officials say most exceed handsomely and which
is scheduled to rise to $1.45 on July 1.

Unless the dispute is settled soon, South Carolina, which has escaped
major civil rights confrontations could be in for greater economic losses and
mounting tensions as the summer gets hotter.

SCLC could get serious about a boycott of stores it now describes as
"half-hearted." And it is the kind of fight that could attract college
students who soon will be getting out of school for the summer.

In the battle, the county government, which has a similar policy against unionizing, sits back and lets the state government fight it out with the strikers. Most of the strikers' attacks are aimed at the governor, and the Medical College and its president, Dr. William M. McCord.

McCord is quoted as telling Business Week Magazine, "I am not about to turn a $25 million complex over to a bunch of people who don't have a grammar school education."

Union officials say McCord has upset scheduled meetings with them, and they point to a staff memo he sent out saying:

"I have notified this union that I am sure that a majority of you would not want to get mixed up in an outfit such as this and I, of course, have no intention of meeting with this tobacco workers' union."

The parent union also represents tobacco workers.

Gov. McNair, whose position is supported by 16 statewide business and industrial groups and was backed up by a state legislature resolution April 30, gave a major speech on the strike early this month.

"This is a test really of our whole government system as we have known it in South Carolina," he said.

Reuther Takes Stand

The UAW's Reuther told the Mothers Day rally: "Before we are finished, we are going to have the governor of this state catch up to the 20th century."

In addition to state policy, the governor's office also points to the scheduled increase in the hospital workers pay, saying the strikers' demand for bargaining would upset plans to equalize pay for similar jobs.

The scene of the dispute is a quiet Southern city which boasts the traditions of the Old South. It is noted for its magnolia, cypress and azalea gardens and old plantation mansions. The Cooper and Ashley Rivers flow by the city into Charleston Bay, where Fort Sumter, site of the start of the civil war, is located on an island.

Miss Moultrie went to Burke High School in Charleston and has lived in the same area all of her life except for five years in New York City. She has been a nurses' aide for three years at College Hospital.

Her movement to organize workers there started in January 1968, after three practical nurses and two nurses' aides were fired, then reinstated.

Workers started discussing a union and meeting weekly with organizers, Miss Moultrie said, and in August, a letter was sent Dr. McCord asking for an initial meeting to discuss a union. Other meetings—with the governor, citizens groups, "anyone who could help us"—followed.

A key session was the one set 10 a.m. on March 17 which led to the strike.

Union Foes at Talk

McCord brought eight workers all "definitely against the union," Miss Mouotrie said, and she and her committee of seven objected.

And, because she had informed her membership of the meeting, some 265 on-duty personnel also showed up. McCord called off the session, the workers staged a sit-in, police were called and they returned to work by noon.

At quitting time, Miss Moultrie and the 11 others who worked on the same floor with her were dismissed because of the incident—for abandoning patients on an entire floor.

Miss Moultrie said she then issued a call for help from the SCLC. "There was no other group we could think of, and then do it in a nonviolent way," she said.

But as strike activities increased, with marches and rallies scattered violence tension in the city rose, and Gov. McNair first sent in the patrolmen and Guard, then on May 1 put into effect a 9 p.m. to 5 a.m. curfew.

The parking lot of the Francis Marion Hotel on Calhoun Square looks like a used car lot for police cruisers. In the lobby, where there is a display of Civil War antiques including a rebel flag, police gather and trade stories and eat.

But "we wouldn't have any business at all if the highway patrol wasn't staying here," said the owner of the hotel, reflecting the bitter complaints of other hotelmen, cab drivers and bar owners about the way business has fallen off.

F. William Broome, executive director of the Charleston Chamber of Commerce, minimized the effect of the strike on the city's business in general and its $34-million-a-year tourist trade. "Only four or five conventions actually cancelled," he said, although he acknowledged a heavier impact on night-time business.

Pressure Discounted

He maintained that business in Charleston was not putting on pressure for a settlement.

Businessmen are more concerned with principle than economics, he said.

On May 12, Gov. McNair shortened the curfew hours to 11 p.m. to 5 a.m. Wayne Seal, his press secretary, said.

"Businessmen have been suffering pretty badly financially. We want to keep the economy moving."

SCLC officials say the situation ultimately is going to have to be settled by the businessmen.

"It is only when you create the same kind of a crisis in the life of the community as you have in the lives of the workers that the community will give in," Rev. Young said.

The official center for this community's business, the city hall, is, like many buildings here, historic. It was built in 1801 as a bank, with solid brick walls. The city council chambers doubles as a gallery for portraits of Southern heroes.

Presiding as mayor the past 10 years has been J. Palmer Gaillard, Jr. A Democrat, he supported Republican Richard M. Nixon for president last year. He is a longtime friend of the area's congressman, conservative Democrat L. Mendel Rivers.

On the strike--an issue between the state and its workers--Gaillard is a man in the middle in a racially split city where political futures could be decided by a man's stance during the dispute.

Asked where he stands, he said hospital officials and the state "made it abundantly clear they will not recognize the union." What will eventually happen, he said, is that the workers and administrators will get together and talk it out.

Gaillard set up a special committee, not to recommend a solution, but "to get the problem off the streets and onto the conference table." But it failed in its attempt to get the two sides to a meeting.

Streets Cleared

Despite the businesses losses, the curfew and troops "did the trick," he said. "It cleared the streets and got the troublemakers off the streets."

The chief of Charleston's police, John F. Conroy, agrees the troops have prevented violence from erupting.

"I don't question their sincerity in not wanting violence," he said of the SCLC. "I question their ability to prevent it."

Conroy, a native of New York State who was a Marine for 22 years and studied criminology at Florida State University, is in his rookie year as chief of the 150-man department which includes 22 blacks.

He and the SCLC have one big thing in common--they find each other easy to work with, as he puts the emphasis on restraint.

He has used plainsclothesmen to hold down vandalism and small fires, instead of more provocative uniformed men in cars with flashing lights. He did not make arrests when stragglers in the Mothers Day march technically violated the 9 p.m. curfew.

Overall, he said, "We are trying to avoid the racial aspect of the thing and keep in it the labor context--a dispute between the workers and the hospitals."

The labor headquarters for the strikers is the Retail, Wholesale and Department Store Union's hall at 655 East Bay St.

New York Minimum

The local, 1199B, is named after another arm of the RWDSU, Local 1199 in New York City, which was formed 18 months ago to represent hospital workers

ranging from janitors to research technicians. Last July it negotiated a
$100 a week minimum covering 30,000 workers in private New York City hospitals.

The rundown union hall here--a former VFW building which has several
bullet holes in the walls, apparently some of the livelier dances--is the
scene of constant activity and daily meetings.

Many of the strikers start coming in around 6 a.m. They help process
contributions and handle a growing number of union applications coming in from
other parts of the state.

The strikers are allowed two meals a day, plus snacks, and $15 a week in
benefits. Churches and members of the community help keep them in food.

There are outdoor rallies at churches and almost daily marches led by
SCLC officials along King Street, a main business street where the featured
attraction at the Lincoln Theater last week was "Uncle Tom's Cabin."

At one union meeting, in February, Mrs. King said, "My husband always
used to say that 1199 was his favorite union because 1199 is always out front,
always in the lead in our battle for justice . . . You see a nation in which
two million hospital and nursing home workers earn as little as $50 or $60 a
week and you want them to do better . . ."

Beyond Charleston, there is the prospect of organizing the more than two
million similar hospital workers throughout the nation--many of them blacks,
Puerto Ricans and poor whites--who constitute the largest block of unorganized
workers in the nation.

As one of the signs carried in Mother's Day march: "THE WORLD IS
WATCHING 1199B."

Washington Evening Star, May 21, 1969.

25. TEXT OF ADDRESS BY MRS. CORETTA SCOTT KING TO RALLY AT
CHARLESTON'S STONEY FIELD STADIUM, THURSDAY EVENING, MAY 29, 1969

I am happy to be back in Charleston.

On the plane this morning, I was reading a magazine article with the
title, "South Carolina Is Charming." It went on and on about Charleston's
"soft and pervasive charm, its lovely gardens and colonial homes," and so on.

You know, I just couldn't find one word about some of Charleston's other
attractions--the national guard, the tanks, the state police, the curfew and
those terribly awful people, those outside agitators and foreign agents. You
know who I mean. I'm referring to those remarkable women--the heroines of
1969--the hospital strikers.

I spent several hours with these women this afternoon over at the
headquarters on East Bay Street. And I can really understand why the city and
state officials are so worried about them. I was impressed by their determination and their dedication to continue this struggle no matter how long
it takes. One of the strikers put it this way. She said, "Mrs. King, you
know if this strike had never taken place I guess nobody would ever have
heard of us. We would have lived out our lives as nurses aides, dietary and
housekeeping workers. But now the whole world seems to know what we're trying
to do here. We never knew too much about demonstrations and picketing, about
going to jail and having to suffer for what's right. But we do now. And, we
also know a great deal more about ourselves."

"And Mrs. King, we're grateful to all the thousands of people from all
over America who are helping us. Please tell them tonight, because the
television people will be there. Tell them for us that we know how important
this fight is--not only for ourselves and our families--but for people everywhere. Please tell them for us that we are going to keep on marching and
we're going to keep on fighting until we win." So I want to say to you that
these remarkable women just ain't gonna let anybody turn them around. And
Charleston and the state of South Carolina had better believe it.

After talking to the strikers today I had a feeling that in addition
to such phrases as soul power, black power and green power, we're going to
have to add another one--and that's woman power. For these women and their
leaders are displaying the kind of quiet determination that can move mountains.

I guess that's why I was happy to become the honorary chairman of the National
Organizing Committee of Hospital and Nursing Home Employees of which Local
1199B is a part.

The hospitals of our nation are staffed by hundreds of thousands of
women—black women, white women, Mexican women and Puerto Rican women. They
have one thing in common. All of them are poor. Most of them earn as little
as $50 and $60 a week. They are sick and tired of working full-time jobs
at part-time pay. And as Mary Moultrie has put it, they are simply sick and
of being sick and tired.

You know, we always hear so much about menial labor. My husband used to
say that no labor is really menial unless you're not making adquate wages.
And if you're making four or five dollars an hour, that isn't menial labor.
What makes it menial is the income, the wages. And the time has come for
people of good will to understand the dignity of labor. The time has come to
see that a black person working in a hospital, even if she happens to be
scrubbing floors, is in the final analysis as important to that hospital as
the physician.

Very frankly, I am not impressed by complaints from the Charleston County
Medical Society that the union and the SCLC have raised the issues of race
and poverty in this strike. They say these issues are not what the strike is
all about.

Well, I should like to ask these distinguished physicians how many of
them would like to try to support their families on $1.30 an hour? And when
was the last time they took care of a patient and charged a fee of $1.30 an
hour? And since they have raised the issue of race, how is it that black
hospital workers earn less pay and get poorer treatment than white workers who
do the identical jobs? And when is the federal government going to do its
duty and expose this injustice? After all, the Medical College is receiving
federal funds and I don't know why they should be permitted to continue to
violate the federal law with federal funds.

Personally, I feel a bond of true friendship with the members of Local
1199B. I feel a bond of firm friendship with the wonderful students of
Charleston who have made so great a contribution to this struggle. I am proud
to be identified with the civil rights organizations of this city, with the
concerned clergy, with the organized labor movement all of whom have united
together behind 1199B and the Southern Christian Leadership Conference under
the inspiring leadership of my husband's close associate and friend, Rev.
Ralph David Abernathy.

For ours is a common struggle. A struggle to make it possible for all
of God's children to walk the earth in dignity and self-respect. Everywhere
I go people ask me about this strike. For what began as a little known
strike by black hospital workers has captured the imagination and touched the
conscience of millions of Americans.

The truth is that you are making history here in Charleston. You have
won the active support of every major civil rights organization in the nation.
You have won the full support of the organized labor movement. Just last
week, the AFL-CIO Executive Council set up a National AFL-CIO Charleston
Strike Fund with an initial contribution of $25,000. You have won the support
of all major religious groups. In Washington last week, 17 United States
Senators, including Senators Kennedy, Muskie, Brooke, Mondale, Javits, Harris,
Yarborough and others, endorsed your campaign and urged President Nixon to
intervene. Most of the major national newspapers have published editorials
backing you in your just fight. [145]

Every day, every week, more organizations add their voices to your
struggle. Mrs. Jackie Kennedy Onassis sent an unsolicited contribution to
express her support. And hardly a day goes by that I do not receive letters
or telegrams from young people in schools all over America informing me that
they are contributing their lunch monies, or organizing cake sales to help
the Charleston hospital strikers. School teachers write and ask how they may
obtain your beautiful blue 1199 hat for their students. Your 1199 hat has become a symbol of freedom and dignity wherever decent people gather. And it
has become the most fashionable hat of the spring season.

The fact is that millions of plain, ordinary, decent people want very
much to be able to identify with you, to extend their hands in friendship
and solidarity. They do so because your cause is so genuinely decent, so
inherently just and so supremely right. It is one of those clear causes
which united all decent-minded Americans.

That is why I say without any hesitation that at this moment in history your fight is the single most important social issue facing the forces of progress in America.

Unfortunately, those in positions of power in this state have failed completely to understand what is happening here in Charleston. They have already spent close to three-quarters of a million dollars to prevent black hospital workers from obtaining their inherent rights of first-class citizenship. They have failed to understand that the black people of Charleston will never give up this struggle for justice and dignity. And understand that fact, they will continue to send in troops and police against people who are determined to reply with the power of their souls. And no amount of force can overcome that determination.

Good people all over America have a right to ask some important questions. How many times must the terribly exploited hospital workers be compelled to go on strike and suffer jailings for the simple right to have a union? How many times must heroic men and women and children be compelled to place their lives on the line in daily confrontations with national guardsmen for this elementary right? And how long will it be before the leaders of this city, state and nation finally understand that the tensions now building up here in Charleston may explode into another horrible tragedy?

I expect that this will not be my final visit to Charleston. For I am determined to see this fight through to its final victory. There will be stormy days ahead. Freedom doesn't come easy. Freedom is never voluntarily handed down by the oppressor. It must be demanded. That is the lesson that history teaches us.

As I said at the beginning I am now supremely confident that the hospital strikers are going to carry on until they win this fight. Such leaders as Mary Moultrie and Rosetta Simmons are not going to stop fighting no matter how stormy the days ahead, no matter how great the sacrifice.

I thought about that as I read a report on this strike by the editor of the South Carolina Methodist Advocate. I recommend this article for careful study by the white citizens of this city and state. Here is what he wrote:

"Why has it happened? And to this everyone will have his own answer. Mine is simply to say that too many whites have not had the kind of experience which will enable them to understand the depth and strength of the black resolution to have a part in shaping his own destiny, even if it means that he chooses death."

Something deep inside of me tells me that this is an accurate statement of the problem now confronting many thoughtful and troubled white citizens of this city. And in this connection, I should like to read you a statement my husband wrote several years ago.

"If a man has not discovered something that he will die for, he isn't fit to live. And if a man happens to be 36 years old, as I happen to be, and he refuses to stand up because he wants to live a little longer, or he is afraid his home will get bombed, or he is afraid he will get shot, he may go on and live until he's 80. But a man dies when he refuses to stand up for that which is right. A man dies when he refuses to take a stand for that which is true. So we are going to stand up right here letting the world know that we are determined to be free."

I know that if my husband were alive today he would be at your side. He would be marching with Rev. Abernathy, with the hospital strikers, with the students, with the clergy, with the labor movement, demonstrating to this city and to the nation that Charleston can become that moment in our history when the unity of black and white, of the civil rights movement with organized labor may be recaptured. For that unity was my husband's dream. That dream will never die.

And if we will continue to work together, to march together and to fight together we will win this historic fight and help bring into being that day when America will no longer be two nations, but one nation, indivisible with liberty and justice for all.

District 1199 Archives.

26. CHARLESTON: OUR STRIKE FOR UNION AND HUMAN RIGHTS

A strike of 550 hospital workers in Charleston, S.C. has captured national attention as a test for the civil rights and labor movements.

The strike combines within it some of the most important issues facing Americans everywhere today. The black community of Charleston knows this, and has put its whole heart and soul into the struggle. Starting out as a fight for the simple right to have a union, the strike has become a nationally important struggle for the right of black people to live as first class citizens in the city where the first shot of the civil war was fired and where slaves first sang to the tune of what became "We Shall Overcome."

National television has brought Charleston's marching thousands with their blue and white 1199 hats into millions of American homes. Daily press coverage throughout the country has stressed the significance of the unity forged between labor and the civil rights movement. For their continued unity spells victory in Charleston and powerful inspiration to poor and black Americans everywhere to organize for a better life.

Charleston's black community is united as never before. When Mrs. Martin Luther King, Jr. came to address a rally April 29, two churches overflowed with a total of 7,500 people, nearly 30 percent of the city's ablebodied Negro population. Thousands of Charleston's people turn out regularly for marches along a route lined with local police, state troopers and national guardsmen brandishing fixed bayonets. Standing at the ready in side streets are more troops with tanks and other armored vehicles.

Heavily armed National Guardsmen patrol the streets. A curfew is in effect. Boycotts of stores and schools by black people have slowed Charleston's normal activity to a trickle. A dozen scheduled conventions have been canceled.

Members of the state legislature have criticized the unyielding anti-union position of Gov. Robert E. McNair, but state and county officials have refused to give an inch.

At first the opposition treated the movement with contempt. A sample was the offer by Dr. McCord, head of the Medical College Hospital, to give the workers an additional holiday--the birthday of Robert E. Lee.

When these actions backfired, contempt was replaced by force. The mood was expressed by Charleston and Courier columnist Ashley Cooper, who wrote, "It seems--at least to me--that the only way the illegal uprising can be stopped is by force. That may have the ring of fascism, which I hate, but honestly, what other conclusion is there?"

Close to 500 people have been arrested--mainly black women, whom Mrs. King called "these magnificent women"-- but the arrests have become another symbol of the people's readiness to sacrifice freedom temporarily in order to win it permanently.

The black churches of Charleston are at the heart of the strike there. Nightly rallies overflow churches such as the Rev. Z. L. Grady's Morris Brown A.M.E. Strikers and young people who march and picket all day return at night to sing, talk and listen at hand-clapping, cheer-filled church meetings. Speakers include dedicated local ministers, union leaders like Mary Moultrie and SCLC leaders like Coretta King and Rev. Ralph Abernathy. One black minister announced from the pulpit that scabs in the congregation had two choices: get out of the hospitals or get out of the church.

Local Catholic schools were closed so students, nuns and priests could participate in marches. Several priests were sentenced to jail, including Father Duffy, the prison chaplain.

Charleston's Catholic Bishop Ernest Unterkoefler affirmed the right of workers to decent pay and union membership, and urged hospitals to negotiate.

The interracial Concerned Clergy of Charleston continued strike support despite nonsense like an open letter from 59 right-wingers who accused clergymen of cooperating with "the forces of the anti-Christ."

Song propelled much of the strike, songs of freedom and of unions. Churches shook to "We Shall Not Be Moved" as well as "We're Gonna Roll the Union On." One thousand National Guardsmen turned Charleston into what the New York Times called an "armed camp."

Tanks, armored troop carriers, carbines and bayonets were used to seal off the black community from the rest of the city.

Gov. McNair declared a state of emergency May 1 and imposed a curfew from 9 p.m. to 5 a.m. The state which can't afford more than $1.30 for hospital workers admitted it was paying $10,000 a day to keep National Guardsmen in Charleston.

The military build-up was, as the Washington Post said in an April 30 editorial, "out of scale with the issue." A prominent State Senator from Charleston is reported to have denounced the show of force and told Gov. McNair "if anything happens the blood is on your hands."

Black students, who said the city was like a "concentration camp," were led by the SCLC in daily marches despite the attempted reign of terror. The marches were directed by Rev. Andrew Young of the SCLC.

In one confrontation the students ran full speed at rows of helmeted, masked, rifle-carrying Guardsmen. The startled Guardsmen lifted their bayonets to the ready. Inches from the extended bayonets the students stopped their rush and dropped to their knees in prayer.

"The jails of Charleston are jammed--not only with such prominent figures as the Rev. Ralph Abernathy and Local 1199 leader Leon Davis but with hundreds of anonymous strikers for whom this is the battle of a lifetime." New York Post editorial, May 2.

It was the battle of a lifetime, not just for Charleston's strikers but for the city's entire black community and its allies. Jails bulged with almost 500 strikers, students, white priests black ministers, longshoremen, white garment workers and housewives.

They sang spirituals, freedom songs and union songs. They slept among roaches on stinking mattresses and ate meals that at times were literally bread and water. But their courage and spirit of cooperation never wavered. After eight days in filthy cells, Davis said, "I feel cleansed." Cleansed, he explained, by "the friendliness, the unity, determination and understanding of people ready to make every sacrifice until victory is won."

People like those pictured here are the unsung heroes who win strikes. They are why Mary Moultrie could say with confidence: "We're not even thinking about going back without a union." For example:

Sadie Brown, with ladies like Ernestine Bryant and Luraline Terry, works 18-hour days at union headquarters. Asked what she did on a long-overdue day off, she said, "I marched."

Besides Miss Moultrie, other hard-working local leaders are Local 1199B Vice Pres. Jack Bradford, and Alma Hardin and Rosetta Simmons, co-chairman of the Charleston County Hospital unit.

"Hey, Mister," shouted a Charleston student to NOC Director Elliott Godoff, "I'm going to jail but I haven't got an 1199 hat. Can you get me one?" Black students boycotted schools and volunteered for jail. And blue and white 1199 hats have been everywhere in Charleston.

"We're so happy for the kind of people you've sent us," said Mary Moultrie about the New York 1199 staffers sent to help. Working efficiently with a minimum of fanfare were NOC Director Godoff and Ass't. Director Henry Nicholas, Guild Area Director Dave White, Exec. Sec. Moe Foner, Vice Pres. Doris Turner and press aide Dave Prosten.

From Dave White's strike diary: "The grass roots support is terrific. Donations come from the poorest people. Morale is excellent. . . ."

America took notice late in April when Coretta Scott King arrived in Charleston. A year earlier her husband was killed in a similar struggle in Memphis. Now she told 7,500 rapt listeners:

"I want to make it clear that I am in this historic struggle no matter what the consequences." Her audience, nearly 30% of Charleston's black population, overflowed a church that once served as an underground railway center for escaping slaves.

"I believe that Charleston, like Selma and Memphis, has now become a national test of purpose, with tremendously important implications for decent-minded Americans everywhere," she said.

"After we win here in Charleston," she added, "I would like to see our organizing crusade extend to other cities and states. The newly formed locals can be called Local 1199C, Local 1199D, until we run out of letters."

The New York Post said editorially May 1 that Mrs. King's very appearance in Charleston "dramatically underlined the national dimensions of this conflict."

Mrs. King led a march to Medical College Hospital April 30 through a cordon of heavily armed National Guardsmen, state troopers and local police.

She had been invited to Charleston by 1199B Pres. Mary Moultrie and 1199 Vice Pres. Doris Turner.

A key breakthrough in Charleston is the way the strike story has zoomed to national prominence through press, television and radio coverage.

National television networks have had several crews in Charleston. Their nightly newscasts brought marchers wearing the blue and white 1199 hat into millions of American living rooms.

Newspaper readers from New York to Los Angeles read thorough and often sympathetic stories written from Charleston by special correspondents as well as wire service reporters.Veteran newsmen repeatedly remarked in private that they were amazed and moved by the dedication and unity of the strikers.

Newsweek, Business Week and Time magazines gave the story major coverage. It also appeared in such diverse places as Stars and Stripes, radio reports in Jamaica, W.I. and a daily newspaper in Santo Domingo.

Editorials in the New York Times, New York Post, Washington Post, Atlanta Constitution and Charlotte (N.C.) Observer urged President Nixon to intervene in Charleston.

N.Y. Post columnist James Wechsler in his April 24 column summed up the role of publicity by observing that the Charleston story was escalated from a local to a national matter largely due to the work of Exec. Sec. Moe Foner, 1199's public relations director. Wechsler added that the publicity "mingled with the extraordinary solidarity of the strikers, is why there will be a hospital union in Charleston. They shall overcome."

The hospital strike in Charleston saw the first joint action by the nation's major civil rights groups since the assassination of Dr. Martin Luther King over a year ago.

"We cannot fail to recall that the right of workers to be represented by a union is precisely the same issue that led to the tragedy in Memphis last year," the rights leaders said in a statement that received national press coverage. The 14 leaders pictured at right signed the statement.

Other strike support actions:

AFL-CIO Pres. George Meany telegraphed Mary Moultrie: "The AFL-CIO fully supports your struggle for decent wages and a sense of dignity as first class citizens."

The South Carolina AFL-CIO and several predominantly white unions in Charleston have given money. An anonymous white plumber sends $10 every week. White motorists occasionally flash a V-for-victory signal while passing pickets.

In Washington, 21 Democratic Congressmen appealed to Pres. Nixon to intervene in the strikers' behalf.

Strike support was also expressed in a letter to the New York Times April 16 from first black Congresswoman Shirley Chisholm, Manhattan Borough President Percy Sutton and actor Ossie Davis.

Editorials in both the black press and the general press backed the strikers. Many called for intervention from Washington.

The outside of strike headquarters at 655 E. Bay St. is shabby, but the spirit inside is pure gold.

Busy strikers and their leaders labor up to 18 hours a day and often spend the rest of the night there on a tattered sofa. When someone suggested a party for a change of pace, he was told by the workers no party was necessary and there were more urgent uses for the money.

Meals at headquarters for strikers and their families consist of Kool-aid, rice, beans, turkey necks and bologna sandwiches. Sometimes there's real meat. But whatever there is, all say the cooks do a magnificent job. Some food is donated by local merchants.

Ladies who answer the phone at headquarters frequently use the greeting: "Union recognition."

Around-the-clock security is provided at headquarters by young men who have volunteered their services. Area Dir. Dave White's strike diary notes that "We are not permitted to stand in front of union headquarters at night for fear of being shot from a passing car. The local leaders sleep from place to place on different nights. It is not exactly fear, but precautions the local people feel must be observed."

1199ers in New York feel especially close to the Charleston strike for more reasons than you can shake a picket sign at.

Many fought a similar battle when 1199 was brought to New York hospitals in 1959 and 1962. Others have relatives in Charleston or places like it.

New York and Charleston 1199ers were brought closer when Vice-Pres. Doris Turner, veteran of the 1959 strike, introduced 1199B Pres. Mary Moultrie to last month's General Delegate Assembly. Recently released from 11 days in jail, Miss Moultrie moved many in the audience to tears. "We're asked to be treated equal and as human beings," she said. "And we are not going to let anybody turn us around, jail or no jail."

In a few weeks members in all divisions had collected more than $10,000 in badly needed cash support for the Charleston strikers.

Margaret Carter, a delegate from Mt. Sinai and a veteran of the '59 strike happens to be at home now recuperating from a heart ailment, but she said, "I wish I could go down there and help out." Bernest McRae of Brooklyn Jewish, another '59 veteran, said "we're raising money every payday for the strike. We remember what it was like before we had the union, and we know it's even worse in Charleston. We're proud our union is down there."

Marie Umstead, of Knickerbocker Hospital, who has relatives in Charleston, said, "Down there whites talk to blacks like they talk to dogs. Those workers aren't just fighting for better pay, but for self-respect as human beings."

1199 Drug and Hospital News, 4 (May, 1969):11-21.

27. 113-DAY HOSPITAL STRIKE IN CHARLESTON

"The strike enabled me to be enlightened about life itself. It helped me to realize how important I am as a person, which I'm afraid I didn't quite realize before . . . I further realized that the power structure isn't all-powerful, but that they are ready to do the bidding of the people and the people can make them do it."

The lady who wrote this is Mrs. Claire G. Brown, a worker at Charleston's Medical College Hospital, wife, and mother of five. She and several of her children were jailed for strike activity. "For anything else," she wrote, "I would never permit myself to be jailed. Looking back, I know if I had it to do again I would do the same thing."

Dozens of other strikers wrote similar letters to the union. They represent on the scale of the individual the changes that the 113-day strike brought about among Charleston's blacks as a community. As a result, Charleston, with its magnolia-scented memories of plantation days, will never be the same.

What happened in Charleston couldn't have happened in a more appropriate place. The city is full of history. The kind of history is suggested by the lovely old mansions and the gardens with moss-hung trees. It is plainly stated by the Old Slave Mart, a museum on the site where human beings used to be bought and sold. Recently, during the strike, the city dedicated as a historic site an island that used to be a prison for captured Union soldiers in the Civil War. Part of the ceremony was the raising of a Confederate flag.

But the strike, and the workers' victory brought the message to Charleston loud and clear: The times they are a-changin'.

Before the strike, Charleston whites considered that the black population was "happy." The fact is, the civil rights movement of the 1950's pretty much passed the city by. When desegregation became a legal fact in the early 1960's Charleston desegregated public facilities without too much pushing by blacks. Efforts to organize a civil rights movement in the city were never successful. It was said the people weren't interested in coming out to meetings, or marching on picket lines.

To say that Charleston was shocked by what it saw during the hospital strike is to put it mildly. 1199 Vice-Pres. Elliott Godoff, head of the National Organizing Committee of Hospital and Nursing Home Employees, said the first 100 days of the strike saw more than 100 rallies that brought out tens of thousands of people. "This was something that was considered impossible to accomplish--and this was the opinion of blacks as well as whites," he said.

A Fighting Community is Born

Not only the rallies and marches held day after day, but the numerous confrontations with police and National Guardsmen showed that the black community of Charleston was far from quiet and "happy." Any question about the people's willingness to put everything on the line for this struggle was answered by the hundreds who went to jail for its sake. Many were jailed several times in what finally totaled about 1,000 arrests.

How this was accomplished has been documented in virtually all of the countless news articles and editorials about the Charleston hospital strike that appeared all over the country. Local 1199B Pres. Mary Ann Moultrie calls it "The combination that loves the people and that the people love." It's 1199's ability to organize hospital workers and call public attention to their need for decent wages and union rights, plus the SCLC's ability to "turn a town around" by organizing all parts of the community -- students, poor people, middle class people, churchmen -- to come to the hospital workers' support.

This combination itself marks a sharp change in the way black people have organized before. In an analysis of the strike for the magazine *New South,* Charlotte (N.C.) *Observer* reporter Jack Bass wrote of the strike victory, ". . . it may have opened a new era in the struggle for economic improvement for poor people in the South.

Labor, Rights Movement Unite

The *New York Times* joined many other observers in pointing out that "The broader significance of the (Charleston) affair is that it successfully brought into cooperation the civil rights movement and organized labor, segments of American society that have too often viewed their interests as conflicting rather than common . . . They not only expect to win further economic gains in the South, but work together for voter registration and other goals."

As elsewhere in the South, Charleston politics has been the unchallenged activity of whites. Although they are a majority of Charleston proper, not counting suburbs, Negroes have no black representative on the County Council. The reason, say Asst. NOC Dir. Henry Nicholas and Area Dir. Dave White, who have been working on this problem, is that few are registered and fewer vote.

A registration campaign was started by the union, and since the College Hospital settlement July 1, more than 500 people have registered as voters. The campaign is community-wide, including everyone, not just 1199B members.

Lesson in Political Action

The idea of connecting politics with the strike came quite naturally, Godoff said. He told how the workers, trying to see state, county and city officials to explain their grievances before the strike, were repeatedly ignored by the politicians. "The fact that most of these officials got their jobs with the considerable help of the Negro vote meant nothing. The strike made the politicians sit up and take notice, and the workers began to realize that they had to form as solid a block in voting as they did in marching in order to get results in the future."

The strike also provided firsthand experience in organizing a movement to hundreds of people who never did anything of the kind before. The results of this on-the-job training were seen mainly among hospital workers, who helped organize the church rallies, marches, and shopping boycotts in Charleston. But the idea spread quickly and widely during those 113 days to other groups--in the city and elsewhere. Several strike rallies were held outside Charleston by citizens of Johns Island, James Island, Edisto Island and other communities, some as far away as 35 miles.

All of the strike activities, of course, were held under the banner that is becoming nationally if not world-famous -- 1199's blue and white hat. It became the height of fashion in Charleston to wear the hat as a badge of support not only for the strike but for the whole freedom movement around it. One group of women, not union members, organized a demonstration to protest cutbacks in the federal food stamp program. They delayed their action until they could get 1199 hats to wear for the occasion.

The courage and willingness to sacrifice that led to the victory in Charleston have been translated by the enormous press and TV coverage of the strike into inspiration for many thousands of hospital workers in other cities. As a result, requests for help in organizing have come to the NOC from a dozen cities in the Midwest and the South. Meanwhile, NOC continues to expand existing campaigns in Baltimore, Philadelphia and other cities. Godoff noted that the emphasis everywhere is on voluntary hospitals, unlike the situation in Charleston. There, he explained, NOC was thrust into the organization of workers in the State College and County Hospitals.

The outlook for widespread organization, Godoff said, is great. "There are about 2½ million unorganized hospital workers in this country, most of them members of minority groups, mostly women, and mostly victims of poverty wages," he said. "I think it's clear to everyone after the Charleston experience that these workers want to and can be organized. There's just no question that the combination of the NOC and SCLC, with support from the labor movement, churches and other groups of decent people have set the stage for a campaign to end poverty among hospital workers."

1199 Drug and Hospital News, 4 (September, 1969):7-10.

28. LETTERS FROM CHARLESTON STRIKERS

What the Strike Meant

Letter 1

I feel that the Charleston hospital strike was one of the most exciting, hardest and important period of my life.

I went places I had never been before in my life. There were times I even experienced how the other half lives. I met people from all walks of life which enable me to be enlightened about life itself. It help me to realize how important I am as a person, which I'm afraid I didn't quite realize before. I saw that when people are determined to do or get something accomplished, they can if they would just ban together and work hard for it. I further realized that the power structure isn't all powerful, but that they are to do the bidding of the people, and the people can make them do it.

It surprised me, and maybe it did because I never lived with anything like this before, that people like Reverend Abernathy, Mrs. King, our ministers, some of our teachers, a couple of whom was fired from their jobs, our precious students, and organizations like 1199 and SCLC would risk jail, time, money and their very lives to help poor people like me and hundreds of poor people like me, whom a lot of other people may think wasn't important enought even to consider. And all the thousands of people who came to aid us in our troubles. Our own people in Charleston and the wonderful people all across the country. God bless all of you.

It wasn't all exciting, however. There was some hard work involved. The walking, walking and more walking. The hours and efforts spent trying to get programs together for mass meetings. The sacrifice to my husband and children. Many times my husband performed many of the duties that were mine as a wife and mother, and at times became quite upset, but he beared with me. There were times my children didn't see me all day and sometimes not even at night because of the time I had to spend away from home. But I believe the sacrifice was well worth while because it has made me a better and stronger person due to the fact that I will now stand up and fight for their rights and mine if the need arises.

I have learned to accept criticisms and not worry about it. I have learned to disagree with anything, and say I don't agree, if I don't believe it's right and don't worry about it.

There were days I wanted to cry, I was so depressed, because it seemed that inspite of all the hard work and sweat, that we weren't accomplishing anything, but I knew within myself that I had to keep on working even harder because 1199 didn't lie to us, they laid it on the line and let us know just how hard it was going to be, and that it might have been harder than it was. I felt that I was prepared, maybe that's why I kept on pushing.

I had to go to jail a couple of times, for anything else, I know if I could help it, I would never permit myself to be jailed, looking back I know if I had it to do again I would do the same thing.

Working around and with people of all sorts have been most rewarding, especially with that bond binding us together.

Now if I didn't learn but one thing from this strike it was, if you are willing to help yourself, people will be more than willing to help you.

Mrs. Claire G. Brown
Obstetric Technician

in charge of program
in jail 6 times
5 kids, some of kids in jail

Letter 2

Having gone thru most of my young life, working as a slave for white power structure type people, being a member of 1199B, I feel that I am *reborn*.

I have learn from the hospital strike in Charleston that black people can be united together as one. And as brothers and sisters.

I have also learn that when united Black people mind is set upon an effort to better its way of living, it doesn't matter who is on the other side of the street, and it doesn't matter what's being said about them on the other side of the street. They just keep on doing their thing and bring *victory* their way. That's 1199B.

I've seen sometimes in 1199B meetings and picket-line *Satan* comes our way. But it appears to me that whenever Satan comes *1199B* has a prepared way to deal with him. That's the good part about being 1199B member.

SCLC, students of Charleston, our many friends here and abroad will always remain in my heart. Because their helping hands help the united Black people at the Medical College receive their *goal*.

Lottie Mae Glover
Aide
Medical College

Jail once

Letter 3

1. First of all to me the union is like a guidance counselor.
2. It's a lover.
3. It's a friend.

Now to explain the above statements.

The union guides its people to better their conditions, to stand behind them and with them in any struggle that might ensue and believe me they are many. The unionist are sincere people because they have lived your struggle long before now.

They were little people too. But the time came when they weren't going to be foot mats any longer so on thought came to mind. Get all the little people together and decide now or forget forever the hope of becoming a real *American Citizen* to say what you believe in and be what you want to be without having anyone push you around because you see no one dares to push a crowd. And being bonded together with your fellow man gives you a wonderful feeling of *strength*. And with the *union* a wonderful feeling of self respect, love for your fellow man and security. The union give us its complete aid and guidance 24 hours a day. When we are asleep the union was walking sentry doing our thing. I will never forget the people from *1199B* because they have truly been my *guidance counselor*.

To belong to the union is to *love the people*. There is always someone
to talk to. Someone who understands and after your little talk they make you
glad that you came.

To belong to the union is to have millions of friends. Friends that
will come to your aid and stand with you through trials and tribulation surrounding you with strength and love. *The union takes care of its own.* The
union is like an oak tree in a petrified forest and I am so happy to be a leaf
on it. May it stand forever and ever. 1199B and 1199. I love you both.

Mrs. D.P. Heyward

P.S. You will notice that I did not call names of any one of the union
leaders. Well that's because they are all so wonderful and I'm in love with
each and every one of them and I want to give you ladies and gents a chance
to express your love so my hopes are that wherever I go from here that I will
remain a member of 1199B and see them in every city in America doing their
thing. And when it's my turn to go and take my stand I have confidence that
was given to me free of charge by the union 1199B and my thoughts are elevated
to new heights. I am somebody now!!

Letter 4

To me, the strike was a means of letting the city of Charleston, the
state of South Carolina, as well as the nation, know that I, along with about
550 black hospital workers were standing up for justice and human dignity.

We were 550 black men and women committed to the well-being of the
sick men, women, and children of Charleston. As a reward, we only asked to
be paid decently so that we could invest in a better way of life for ourselves
and our families; we only asked for the justified right to unite and organize
ourselves into a stronger body of hard working people who could walk down the
hospital corridors, as well as our community with dignity and self-respect and
with the assurance of representation in a time of grievance.

The strike was also symbolic of the fact that the hospital workers at
the Medical University Hospital and the Charleston County Hospital would no
longer accept part-time wages for a full-time job and that they would no
longer stand quietly in a life of poverty, exploitation and discrimination.
Yes, this was the time to stand up and yell loudly for an end to these conditions, this was a time to stand up and be counted for what we know in our
heart was right.

As the strike continued with the expectations of a long, hard struggle,
I realized that this was not just a fight for union, dignity, self-respect and
higher wages for us, but it was a fight for union, dignity, self-respect and
higher wages for black and oppressed poor people.

A hidden slogan in the far corners of my mind during the strike was "if
Mr. Charlie can have union representation, Annie Lou can have hers too." With
this in mind, I continued in a fight for justice through a strike to better
my conditions, hospital workers' (present and future) condition, and most
important, my fellow brothers and sisters' condition with the vow to hold on,
keep my eyes on the price and let nobody turn me around.

I would like to take this time also to express my thanks to 1199 of New
York and the Southern Christian Leadership Conference for their undying spirit
and undying willingness to help in this struggle.

lots of arrests, in jail twice   Donna M. Whack
31 days - 11+9+11   Ward Clerk
photo (being dragged in street)   Charleston County Hospital
3rd sister, student, also in jail

Letter 5

The meaning of this strike to me, can be summarized in two incidents.
First: one of my church sisters, whom I have much respect for, didn't
understand why I saw fit to picket or join in a march. She said, "I would
walk out but picketing and marching are against my religion. You should pray
to God for what you want instead of picketing and marching."
Then one day as we demonstrated on King Street telling people not to
shop, a black woman came bursting through the crowd with a package under her
arms. Well, she was pretty mad but my soul Sister gave me some great advice.
She said "I don't know what you fussing for, you ought to be out working for
what you want." I think I got more out of that statement than all of the
beautiful expression ever said in our strike.
"You ought to be out working for what you want." It can't get any
plainer. Praying is not the only answer. You have to work for what you want.
Right there and then I felt a new meaning to the hospital strike which
in itself was a very delicate situation in which sick people were involved.
But it is plain that South Carolina is a sick society and maybe a strike like
ours was God's way of making his people realize that. It just wasn't a matter
of higher wage or love of a job. Discrimination against Black "non-professional workers," who were intrusted with the lives of sick people, became our
main target which really made us unite and love unity.
In church, the one thing I did learn was that salvation didn't come on
a silver platter. There would be suffering and sacrifice like what Jesus
spoke of and if wanted victory you had to work for it and hold out to the
perfect end; keep you eyes on the prize! And Soul Power!
During this strike my eyes were open to new strength I didn't know I
had. Now that it is over I pray that I never fall into the same old routine
but that I be as new born and tell black people everywhere that our strikers
stuck together. There was unity through love and respect for each other.
This is the only way to survive; through each other.

long terms in jail twice   Miss Virgie Lee Whack
                                                  Ward Clerk
                                                  Charleston County Hospital

Letter 6

The best thing happen to Charleston is when Medical College and County
Hospital walk out on strike. We were fighting for what we'll velieve in.
The strike was a hard struggle. We picket, day and night. We went to jail.
We did not have a fair fight, but we kept the faith in what we believed in,
but in this struggle we found out that the mayor of Charleston, S.C. and the
government is not our friend. Who we voted for, they proved to us that black
and poor white people belong in poverty, but 1199B and SCLC proved to them
that they are wrong. We have made it possible that we can walk in dignity
and respect. The strike have brought us together to love each other and try
to understand ourself as a person, to believe in our self that we are somebody. No matter how things may be with us, the strike have brought strength
to us to love each other as sisters and brothers. 1199B and SCLC made it
possible that the nation was looking at Charleston, the struggle had made it
possible that the salary was raised from $1.30 - $1.60 which is great. We
the 1199B and SCLC have brought a new day to Charleston through the strike so
that black and poor white people can walk in dignity and respect in 1969.
I would like to say to the organizer Mr. Nicholas May God Bless you for
trying to help others to live a better and happier life in places where
things look so hopeless.
Keep the faith.

                                                  Mrs. Georgetta Waye
Nurses' Aide at County   87 Line St.
                                                  Charleston, S.C.

Letter 7

I feel that the strike was a great experience for me. It gave me the opportunity of learning how unions are operated and mainly how to deal with people. It helped to motivate me to the point where I actually wanted to participate in all the activities involved in awakening the people of our community and acting as "strike leader."

It also eliminated any fear I might have had about speaking out in public, before large groups or being firm with the power structure.

During this struggle I was really shock by the support given by some of our local leaders who I heretofore had considered our leaders, only to find that some of these people were really Dr. Thomases and Miss and Mrs. Ann. There were really only a few real leaders. But I was very much elated of the interest and support shown by the grass-root people in our community.

The strike also made me conscious of other people around me. Although the majority of the people that were out on strike worked in the same hospital with me and attended membership meetings, I really didn't get to know them individually until the strike came about. I feel that walking the picket line, participating in the various demonstrations, mass rallies and sharing problems have really created a closer relationship between me and the other members.

It also made me aware of how important it is to make certain sacrifices, if one wants to accomplish his goal. When one is involved in a struggle it is not a crime to go to jail without bail, it's a pleasure. When one is in a struggle such as the one we were in, it is not to difficult to live on $15.00 a week, as we didn't earn much more than that anyway.

The fact that people all over the country made sacrifices and supported us financially and morally made me aware that there are still people that are concerned about poverty and the poor. It has injected in me the desire of wanting to make right that which is wrong. Whenever or wherever people are struggling to be treated with dignity and respect and the right to be free is where I want to be.

By working with the great Rev. Ralph D. Abernathy and the Southern Christian Leadership Conference my comprehension of their philosophy of non-violence have been made much clearer. I, too have adopted non-violence as a way of life and intend to work with this organization as close as I can.

But most of all, I have discovered that although we have already put in a lot of work, there is still a lot more to be done. I am not worried because I know that "only the strong survives."

Mary A. Moultrie

Letter 8

I was asked on several occasions why was I participating in the strike of non-professional workers against the Medical College and Charleston County Hospitals, by both relatives and friends . . . in my reply I was never hesitant, I answered them the same as I would answer you or any questioning agent, by saying, that it is true that I am not a non-professional worker, but neither were the LPN's who are affiliated with this union. These LPN's along with several of my co-strikers required as much training as I did for my secretarial position.

My sincere reason for becoming a part of Local 1199B is because I was tired doing professional work and receiving the wages of a non-professional.

I will say now and again that 1199B has been and will be the greatest organization that has ever come to Charleston, and I am immensely overwhelmed to be a part of such a terrific union.

In my conclusion I must not forget to say "Thanks" to the SCLC staff who worked so diligently to see that we as a union . . . seek and win this great battle. I must add that it took a long time coming, but Thank God it is here and not for only a month, but to stay.

A quote from our great Black leader, Dr. Martin L. King, Jr.

"Free at last, Free at last
Thank God we are free at last."

in jail 9 days   Brenda Brothers
                                                    Pediatric Secretary

Letter 9

This has been the most astonish struggle in the history for poor black
and poor white people in the world.
Let me start from the beginning. On September of 1968 I heard of about
the organizing of a union for all hospital workers. I went to the meetings
and took cards to let all interested persons working at Charleston County
Hospital Workers to join. The High Noon and sitting on the lawns at Medical
College Hospital was showing, but was not effective. The politicians was
changing one way or the other. This took place all because twelve (12)
members were fired from the Medical College Hospital. We took an oath "That
an injury to one - is an injury to all." Then we came out to support the
Medical College Hospital Strike. We had a lot of support from Local 15A for
letting us use their hall and really you wouldn't think it belong to Local
1199B.
The people in the community felt that the struggle was worth fighting
for.
At first I felt tense being with people that I didn't know. But after
being with them, I got to know and understand their problems; and try to
listen to them. I really went through a struggle. During the struggle I met
a lot of people of importance. I've seen interesting places.
I really enjoy the hit and run demonstrations. This was very offensive
to me, especially blocking the traffic on the historic Cooper River Bridge,
finding out where the Governor was having luncheon; which I think was very
funny.
The young girls and men with Civil War clothing on, you should have
seen them.
The strike have taught me to take criticism and take a lot of kidding
from other people. I have help other members from the medical establishment
sign cards and even visit them in their homes. One member was so afraid of
the boss it hurt very much to see how a person can be like that. Mr. Bradford
and I would keep going and talk with them but so far I haven't succeeded as
yet. We will keep on especially since we won our freedom from both County
and Medical College Hospitals.
One thing I enjoy, is that the community was with us and that no matter
what we have done - Charleston, S.C. will never be the same. The historic
sights will not be historic any more. The sacrificing Black people in
Charleston has been historic.
I thank everyone for their help. I will start from 1199, SCLC and the
community and the Concerned Clergy, we will remember that God takes care of
his own.

co-chairman,   Alma Harden
1199B chapter at County Hospital   aide
                                                    County Hospital

Letter 10

The way that I feel about the strike and surrounded events is I'm certain the views of many of the poor people of Charleston. I'm sorry that so
many innocent people had to suffer, but I'm also glad that it was experienced.
The strike brought a lot of things to light. And although the strike
involved whites as well as blacks, the press here made a special note of
"Striking Negro Workers." I was present on King Street when the State
troopers brutally beat Miss Richards in the open eye of the public, the press
failed to inform the public of this.

The strike maybe outwardly settled, but the scar which it left will always be evident. Civil rights had a great part to play in the strike, but the principles of integrity played a much stronger part. I believe that as long as people are subjugated the inevitable is protest.

I enjoy helping people, that's why I became a nurse. I didn't go on strike to hurt the patients, I feel I did what was necessary to make award conditions which were unfair. We live (supposedly) in a democratic society and that gives everybody the right to a fair share and opportunity, and we did no more than execute our rights.

Everyone pays taxes to pay for the protection of the police, and their job is to keep peace and quiet and enforce constituted laws. And when I see State troopers beating on women and the youth of the community (Black) I wonder who they are really protecting.

I feel that the curfew was mainly for the Blacks of Charleston, and the tensions were greatly focused on black and not white. I thought South Africa was the only place where blacks couldn't exercise the same rights as whites.

Everyone on earth wants their children to have, and be able to live like humans. I believe a sincere effort is being made to better the conditions, and I'm sure it will pay off for everybody all the way around.

The strike had a real meaning, and it's up to all involved to warrant its success.

Mrs. Beverly Kennedy
Nurses' Aide
Medical College

Letter 11

First of all it gives me the opportunity to meet new people with knowledge of unions, someone whom I can lean on where I have lack of understanding. It means hope for better living, recognition as a human being and my ability to serve humanity. I wish to say also that it had brought more community relationship, people who we had seen each and every day, were strangers until this union unite and brought us so close together, close enough for us to become sisters and brothers. It gives me a pride which I wish to show off proudly, with dignity and honor. I will never disregard or disrespect its concrete meaning, as long as I am a member.

One moment that instill within me a determination, and to fight whatever may come, "was" one afternoon in New York City, I went to make a speech there, in behalf of our President, "Miss Mary Moultrie," which I felt very honored! I met a group of people hard at work sorting and packing clothing to send to the striking hospital workers in Charleston, S.C. To see how faithful and untiring these people were at work, shock my mind to thinking and as I was being introduced to the other members of 1199 National Vice-President Mrs. Doris Turner they said to her she is our sister that is all that matters, one young lady in particular, "Isabelle," said to me, and I can hear her voice ringing in my ear, Mama, there are lots of work to do. Come over here and start folding and separating things in like manner because before time for the rally we want to have the most of these things packed in boxes and tied up. She was right because with the supervision of Mrs. Turner work was a pleasure when it was nearing the time for the Rally. I was invited upstairs to the "Office of the National 1199." Where we refreshed ourselves and got dress and on to the rally, which I thought was beautiful, the moral support given me, I couldn't but shed some tears of joy and happiness. People who were strangers, treated me as though I was one of them and as if they had known me all of their lives. People there were very generous financially as well as morally. I must mention Mr. Leon Davis, a great guy! I met him before, in Charleston, S.C. Also when he went to jail with Rev. Ralph Abernathy, but this night he was different, but still sincere. We said, we are going to dinner and have a good time. This night is ours to remember. After a very healthy meal, I went to Mrs. Turner's home for the night, here is where I really got to know her. Here is a woman with a family, a home, and every day problems, same as many of us, but finds time to share in the problem of

humanity and not just sharing but are doing much to deflate poverty.
    Another thing I will always remember and I learn this in Baltimore the
moment I step off the plane. I didn't know who was suppose to meet me, but
as I was walking across the ramp and into the airport building, this beautiful
well attractive young lady was standing inside holding a Local 1199 hat in
her hand, I went over to her, and she said to me, Are you the delegate from
Charleston, S.C.? No answer was necessary, we embraced with happiness, and I
think at that moment, we both found out that this is a good code. If you are
lost and you are a sister or a brother, Local 1199 hat will find you a guide.
Then Gwendolyn and another Associate drove me to the church where the rally
was held. The next day was when I really got to know Mr. Elliott Godoff.
Waiting for plane time, we had a chance to talk and get to know each other
better. I wanted to know that the advice given to me by him will go a long
way. I learn also that people variated, I found this out in Washington, D.C.
when I was a guest at the ALA Convention at the Washington Hilton Hotel, but
we are greatful for people like Mr. Myers; a delegate from New York City who
was very helpful. Also Iran Brown and Mr. Robinson from Detroit who made me
very comfortable, but the most exciting eventful period, was, when Mr. T.
presented a check for $25,000 to me for Local 1199B in support of the striking
workers. The person or persons who are responsible for me to enjoy this
wonderful experience are Mr. Henry Nicholas and Miss Mary Ann Moultrie, in
the past, few months I learn to rely on these two person's ability for
guidance. This union means togetherness. We have had good day, bad days very
trying day, days when some of our demonstrators were man handle, and thrown in
prison: But, as our president always say, "and I quote:", only the strong
survive. "Unquote". I find myself working with people, using their ideas
that were helpful, going to jail working with young people who were eager to
assist, what ever the outcome may be. I also know that it takes sacrifice,
loyalty, dedication, and money to build a union. And this is what it means to
me. Plus the determination of people who for sake themselves to help someone
who are not able to help themself but with the right help and guidance, can do
wonders. And in turn do the same for someone else.

photo appears on May 1969 cover   Mrs. Hermina Traeye
                                                   LPN
                                                   County Hospital

                              Letter 12

    The strike as a whole brought out a lot of changes in me. It has taught
me how to economize, how to go without things you really don't have. It has
taught me really to understand people and their well beings. Probably one
time or another if someone would've come to me with a problem I might've shun
them a little or never even considered their problems, but as the strike went
on I found myself being a little more consideration.
    It also made me look more at the political aspects of the situation in
Charleston and all over the country.
    Also with the help of the Southern Christian Leadership Conference and
with their great President Rev. Ralph David Abernathy, I've also learned the
concept of non-violence. Without their help the strike would've lasted
probably for a long time. Most of all I could never thanked the members from
Local 1199 in New York for their support and their moral support and their
financial support.
    I would like to thank everyone from 1199 for their help.
    Thank God. Bless you all!

                                                   Mrs. Ernestine Bryant
                                                   LPN
                                                   Medical College

Letter 13

I cannot express what the strike means to me as we progressed as best we
could during the 100 days I was not able to march or picket very much but I
was able to pray. This is some of the words that came to me.
O Lord God to whom vengeance belongeth show thyself. Lift up thyself,
thou Judge of the earth, how long shall the wicked triumph, how long shall
they utter and speak things, and all the workers of iniquity boast themselves.
Lord who will rise up for me against the evil doers, or workers of iniquity.
Who did rise up for me against these - 1199B and SCLC did. With God's guidance, and our prayers together, we won. Today I am glad for the small part I
had in breaking the states' right to work law.
I can now go forward with dignity and respect.
I am somebody. I am still praying that we can still go further.

Soul Sister
Mrs. Annie G. Fobbs, LPN
4-13 Felix Street
Charleston, S.C. 29403
July 4, 1969

Letter 14

To me, personally, the strike was an eye opener. During the strike I
was able to see how long the Black and poor people of Charleston and the
State of South Carolina were asleep.
I knew that, we as Black people were not getting our equal rights,
decent wages, nor were we able to enjoy the many privileges and opportunities
that were made possible for us but now that the strike has open our eyes to
the fact that if we as black and poor people do not stand up and fight and be
counted for, we will remain in slavery.
I also learned during the strike that the "Light of Freedom begin to
shine for the poor and black people of Charleston and South Carolina and if
we are to keep it shining we will have to unite and remain united. And when
we say that: "An injury to one, is an injury to all." We will have to show
it whenever the times come.
We will have to let the white men know that slavery is gone forever and
that the black men and women of America will stand united and will fight and
also be ready to pay any penalty that is required to maintain their freedom.

Forever Grateful,

Mrs. Rosabelle Deas (NA)

Letter 15

To me the strike show the way to fight for my dignity and freedom.   It
also gave me the strength to fight for my rights.
By going on strike, it unite the workers together, giving us security
and courage to stand up for what we believe in, and this something we don't
have before.
The strike has taught me that deep down, we had the ability and the
power we neede to fight slaveries.
These 100 days has taught me that the love of my Black brothers is
greater than all the money in this mix up world.
Now that we are united, we have the ability to change unjust laws.
I believe that with unity we have, we should not stop at Medical
College Hospital and County Hospital, but united all workers in South
Carolina.

We are organized now and with help of our brothers we will make it.

Mrs. Pearline R. Canty
July 31, 1969

District 1199 Archives.

BREAD AND ROSES

29. IS THIS ANY WAY TO RUN A UNION?

Results of Local 1199's Cultural Activities Say 'Yes'

In this organization, members seem to be going to one continual round of cultural happenings--dramatic presentations, concerts, recitals, poetry readings, forum discussions, exhibits, film festivals--all of them (except the last) live events sponsored and produced by the organization itself.

Is this a cultural society? An educational institution? A club for self-improvement? Yes and no. While it does have some elements of all of them within it, the organization in question is basically, and very functionally, a trade union.

In the labor community of New York City, it's not exactly a revelation that Local 1199, Drug and Hospital Employes Union (AFL-CIO) has been blending all of this cultural ferment with bread-and-butter trade unionism for many years.

But a bewildered outsider wonders: "Is this any way to run a union?"

And the answer given by Local 1199 President Leon J. Davis is: "You bet it is!"

"What our union and our members are doing," Mr. Davis explains, "merely is demonstrating again what most labor leaders know--that the fight for a living wage and decent working conditions is the start of the struggle for all the good things in life."

So pervasive throughout the organization are the cultural activities of Local 1199 that now they are part of its day-to-day operations. The union, which started out as a small group of retail drug store employes 35 years ago, has a current membership of almost 27,000 and is affiliated with the AFL-CIO Retail, Wholesale and Department Store Union.

The great growth of Local 1199 has taken place in the last eight years as it organized more than 20,000 workers employed in New York's hospitals as orderies, nurses' aides, porters, kitchen and housekeeping staff; plus a mounting number of their technical, professional and clerical employes.

It was during the early part of its hospital period -- marked by strikes in 1959 and 1972 -- that the cultural program underwent its first modern expansion. Since most of the non-medical hospital workers are Negroes and Puerto Ricans, the fights became intertwined with the escalating battle for civil rights, which in turn furnished its own impetus to the program.

Reporting on 1199's monthly live theater series featuring top stage and screen stars, *The New York Times* observed that "the members have dug the drama to a degree that could have the motivation research folks uncovering a whole new set of motives to research."

But 1199 Executive Secretary Moe Foner, who directs the program, thinks that organized labor folks do not have to dig too far back in their own experience to know what those motives are; and to know, too, that they've been there all the time.

"Long before our hospital organizing campaigns, we in 1199 had learned that speeches and reports at meetings alone are not enough," says Mr. Foner.

"And we developed some educational and cultural activities pretty early in our history. So part of the foundation of our present program lay there."

But, Mr. Foner emphasizes, the breadth and depth of the new needs could not be filled simply by more of the same things the union had been doing.

"What continues to be needed," he said, "are quality programs bringing to our members the best there is by way of information and inspiration. 'A good union doesn't have to be dull,' is the way we looked at it . . . So, in addition to stepping up and expanding the education and other programs already in operation, we developed two major new projects--Theater 1199 and the forum-discussion series."

Local 1199, whose headquarters are located in Manhattan's theater district, has had contacts with stage, screen and TV stars who have appeared at its social events over the years. Of this group, the now famous theater couple, actor-playwright Ossie Davis and actress Ruby Dee, have been devoted friends of the union for 15 years. They have participated in the union's happenings throughout that period--writing, directing and presenting dramatic material for the union's Negro History Week celebrations and other events.

Other early members of Local 1199 "repertory" group included Sidney Poitier, Godfrey Cambridge, Sam Levenson, Ricardo Montalban, Alan Alda, John Randolph, Morris Carnovsky and Will Geer.

"With this wonderful talent available to us and our union headquarters containing a 400-seat auditorium," Mr. Foner said, "we had the primary ingredients for a program of live theater."

Time: January 1965--Enter Theater 1199. A panarama of the two years of the series would show scenes from Sean O'Casey's plays performed by John Randolph and Sarah Cunningham, annotated by notes on Mr. O'Casey's life and work by Professor Frederick Ewen . . . scenes from works by Twain and Whitman performed by actor Will Geer . . . the Group Theater Workshop with Robert Hooks in scenes from "In White America" . . . readings from an 1199 organizer's poetry by Davis and Dee . . . scenes from Shakespeare by the Theater-in-Education . . . and a folk-song concert by The Mitchell Trio.

It has been an enriching experience for everyone involved in Theater 1199, Mr. Foner says, especially the patrons. Most of them, he pointed out, never had seen a live play and they found in these performances a remarkable rapport with "those who show us to ourselves."

That the actors have enjoyed these events "as much as the audience," he added, has been happily evident in the post-performance coffee klatches, when they mingle with the spectators.

Certainly no one has enjoyed it more than Mr. Foner, who in addition to being a talent scout, producer and impresario-at-large for Theater 1199, is editor of the union's award-winning magazine, *1199 Drug & Hospital News,* and producer of the union's two 30-minute organizing movies.

Program credits for the success of Theater 1199 would not be complete without a strong one for the rank-and-file Affairs Committee, Mr. Foner underlines. "This group," he says, "acts as a sounding board for project proposals and provides the brains, arms and legs for the many small but vital jobs."

Right now, there's a long intermission at Theater 1199. And this, paradoxically, is due to the union's organizing successes of the past few years. So much extra office space has been needed to take care of all the expanded administrative work for the union's increased membership, that much of the auditorium area in the headquarters had to be expropriated for this purpose.

However, a new home for Theater 1199 is on the way. It will be part of the union's new home, a 14-story building to be constructed just around the corner from its present building and scheduled for completion in 1969.

The other new segment of the union's cultural program is the series of Friday night forum-discussions. Designed mainly for 1199 delegates and active members, these events have presented talks on poverty by Michael Harrington, on the civil rights movement by Bayard Rustin, on peace by Norman Thomas, and on other key issues of the day by other prominent Americans. The floor is thrown open for comment and questions after each lecture and the lively exchanges that follow show that speakers and audience have definitely communicated.

A union publishing a book of poems? That may seem far-out even for such a heavily culture-oriented institution as Local 1199. But one finds that it's not really so distant when the volume's 60 poems deal with union life and experience, specifically the 1959 and 1962 strikes of hospital workers during the initial organizing drives.

The press acclaimed the event of publication, if not necessarily the contents of the book, "Talking With My Feet," in 1965. The former *New York Herald Tribune* did a long feature article on the volume and its author, Marshall Dubin of the 1199 organizing staff; *The New York Times* gave it a proper notice; and many union publications applauded, some with awe.

The Machinist, publication of the AFL-CIO International Association of Machinists, in an editorial on the book, said the poems "will warm the heart of anyone who has ever walked a union picket line." The editorial quoted several of the poems, ending with the lines:

> "Where is the union now,
>   friend,
> At the strike's end?
> Inside my heart, friend . . ."

and, added, "It's the only place where a labor union has ever lived. We're indebted to Marshall Dubin for saying it so well."

A favorite poem of Mr. Davis in "Talking With My Feet" is one that he thinks helps workers "to understand what they've won -- and, more important, what it means to be organized into a force whose very numbers bring a sense of dignity and self-respect unknown before." It reads:

> "I've been called 'boy' for
>   thirty years;
> Chained to the broom and
>   mop, my trade.
> No wonder 'Mr. Charlie' is
>   dismayed.
> To see a picket line led
>   by his porter.
> A cyclone has upset the
>   social order."

Incidentally, the 1962 hospital strikes led to historic legislation in whose enactment Governor Rockefeller was instrumental. Intervening to end the work stoppage, the Governor promised a State bill that would give hospital workers something that was not available to them at that time--collective bargaining rights. Such a law was enacted in 1963, giving those rights to employes of non-profit hospitals in cities of one million or more. In 1965 the law was extended to all voluntary nonprofit hospitals throughout the State.

One of the earliest expressions of the union's cultural aspirations was the annual celebration of Negro History Week in February. In recent years, the title of the event was changed to "Salute to Freedom"; but under either name, it has been an SRO highlight on the 1199 calendar for 17 years.

This year, the event broke all records. The doors of the 2,000-seat auditorium of the High School of Fashion Trades had to be closed an hour before curtain time with hundreds outside seeking admission. Reason: Miriam Makeba, Pete Seeger, the La Rocque Bey Dancers, and an address by Cleveland Robinson, national president of the Negro American Labor Council. Local 1199 contributed $2,650 to major civil rights organizations that night including three $500 NAACP life memberships awarded to George H. Fowler, chairman of the State Commission for Human Rights, Herman Badillo, Bronx Borough president, and Rev. Milton A. Galamison, pastor of Brooklyn's Siloam Presbyterian Church. Mr. Fowler is a former deputy industrial commissioner of the State Labor Department.

The most recent event on the 1199 cultural calendar is a photo exhibit. Under the title, "Never to Forget; Never to Forgive!" the photos dramatically depict the extermination of six million jews by Nazi Germany. With this event, Local 1199 commemorated the Warsaw Ghetto uprising 24 years ago.

Generally, management people at the hospitals organized by Local 1199 have come to acknowledge the union as a social agency dedicated to constructive social ends and serving the social and economic needs of low-income wage earners who largely are members of minority groups.

Industrial Bulletin of the New York State Department of Labor (May, 1967), copy in District 1199 Archives.

30. BREAD AND ROSES

By Moe Foner

Hearts starve as well as bodies;
Give us bread, but give us roses!

The lines are from a poem by James Oppenheim, commemorating the famous strike in 1912 by more than 20,000 multi-ethnic textile workers in Lawrence, Massachusetts. Young female workers carried picket signs reading, "We want bread, and roses too."

That bread and roses theme has become the focal point of the most ambitious project ever undertaken by a union in this country to bring culture directly to its rank-and-file members. The union is District 1199, National Union of Hospital and Health Care Employees.

Many of these union members represent a new audience for the arts and humanities in this country. They are workers who, because of their educational, economic, racial and ethnic backgrounds, have previously had severely limited access and exposure to these areas of our cultural life.

District 1199's project, aptly titled Bread and Roses, delivers the arts and humanities to workers in hospitals and nursing homes, where they are employed, at union headquarters (the Martin Luther King, Jr. Labor Center on West 43rd Street in New York City), and in their homes (1199 Plaza, the union-sponsored 1600 family housing development in East Harlem).

The project will cost about $1.3 million over its two-year period. About $550,000 is expected to be contributed in grants by the National Endowment for the Arts, National Endowment for the Humanities, New York State Council on the Arts and the Pennsylvania Council on the Arts. District 1199 will provide $350,000 in matching grants and services. Other funding has come from several private foundations, including: The Ford Foundation, the United Hospital Fund, United Church Board for Homeland Ministries, the Prudential Foundation, Boehm Enterprises, Carol and W. H. Ferry, Fund for Tomorrow, Inc., the J. J. Kaplan Fund, Inc., the Louise L. Ottinger Charitable Trust, the New York Times Foundation, the Shubert Foundation, Inc., the John Golden Fund, Inc., the Edna McConnell Clark Foundation, the Lila Acheson Wallace Fund, and the North Shore Unitarian Veatch Program. Other funding is being sought from similar private foundations.

So that all monies may be channeled directly into the various Bread and Roses programs, the project is administered by the smallest possible staff. Staff members include this writer, as project director; Mordecai Bauman, administrator; Nonnie Perry, coordinator, and Abigail Booth Gerdts, who is developing special projects for Gallery 1199, the only permanent art gallery at any labor union headquarters in the United States.

The staff is assisted by a group of distinguished performing artists and scholars who helped shape the original proposal. The staff also works with rank-and-file Bread and Roses committees, numbering 450. These committees were organized during the planning period and continue to meet regularly. Among them are an overall committee and special Hispanic, Retiree, and 1199 Plaza committees.

Bread and Roses began in January 1979 and will extend through 1980. It seeks to bring to members and their families a cultural diversity that will encourage them to reach beyond their daily tasks toward a fuller involvement in the arts and humanities.

The union has some 70,000 members in the New York metropolitan area, and about 30,000 in seventeen other states. More than 70 percent of the members are black and Hispanic, and almost 85 percent are women.

Artists and entertainers who have performed for Bread and Roses thus far emphasize the emotional experience they feel in bringing their art directly to the people. The fact that many in the audiences had never before witnessed a concert or a photography exhibition underscores the implications Bread and Roses holds for the future of the arts in the U.S. And despite the fact that many are being introduced to such events for the first time, Bread and Roses makes no move to "water down" the cultural content to make the programs more palatable. There is no pandering to so-called popular taste and, perhaps not surprisingly, the enthusiastic response by workers to Bread and Roses events is as high as the quality of those events.

Even with the concentration of members in the New York area, Bread and Roses has taken on national -- even international -- ramifications. The federal and state endowments regard the project as a prototype, one that might serve as a model for other U.S. unions. And a group of Swedish labor union members recently visited 1199 headquarters to determine if Bread and Roses is applicable to their country.

Cultural diversity is the goal of the Bread and Roses program. Included in the project are drama, music, poetry, art and photography exhibits; a celebration of the union's twentieth anniversary at New York's Lincoln Center, an original topical musical revue, a Labor Day Street Fair, conferences, seminars, films, and recordings.

Bread and Roses has also created a ripple effect, one that may affect hospital labor relations and health-care costs. Among the various project conferences is a series on the responsibility of hospital workers for patient care, which is sponsored by a grant from the United Hospital Fund.

Historically, the attempt to bring culture into the daily lives of union workers is not a new concept. Herbert G. Gutman, a historian and member of the Bread and Roses advisory board, has suggested that the deep cultural cohesiveness among workers helped the labor movement succeed during the long, difficult strikes of the late 1800s, a time when there were no strike benefits and most of our society was hostile to unions.

A *Business Week* article in January dealing with the Bread and Roses project noted that poetry readings, song festivals, and dramatic performances were an important part of community life for Welsh coal miners, German cigar makers, New England shoe workers, and Baltimore bricklayers. "But that tradition has long since died out -- and for a variety of reasons," said the *Business Week* writer.

That Bread and Roses has succeeded in involving its audiences in reviving that cultural cohesiveness among workers is illustrated by their enthusiastic response. A sellout crowd of 2,800, for example, attended a Bread and Roses anniversary concert by Harry Belafonte on Sunday evening, 18 March 1879 at Avery Fisher Hall in Lincoln Center. It is estimated that more than half of the audience had never been before been to Lincoln Center.

A major Bread and Roses program is Theater-in-the-Hospitals, for which a variety of music and drama groups perform free for workers, hospital staffs, and some patients during lunch hours. The first such group to perform was the Howard Roberts Chorale, and the reaction of its in-hospitals audiences proves the point.

A lab technician attending a performance at one hospital described District 1199 as "a little United Nations," and added: "This kind of fine performance brings us together to learn about each other's cultures and enrich ourselves during working hours."

A patient at another hospital called the Theater-in-Hospitals program "a wonderful idea." He said: "I've been bored silly staring at the four walls and watching T.V. This livened up the day. It was relaxing and I liked the togetherness." And a nurse's aide said the lunchtime performances "give us a good incentive to go back to work full of spirit."

That, in essence, is what Bread and Roses is all about.

District 1199 is proud of its record as a militant organizer and its alliance in social causes with liberal and civil rights organizations. This involvement has helped us enlist the aid of many professionals in planning Bread and Roses, such as Ossie Davis, the actor-director-writer; actress Ruby Dee; and Harry Belafonte.

Belafonte, for example, would accept no fee for his Bread and Roses concert, which marked his first New York appearance in eighteen years. "1199 means a great deal to me," he told the cheering crowd. "I come here with passion and sentiment. On every issue worth fighting for, your union has been there. I have to be involved with 1199 as long as there is an 1199."

Ossie Davis, allied with 1199 through two decades, serves as master of ceremonies for most Bread and Roses entertainment events. He is also playing an important role in one of the project's most ambitious programs, "Take Care," the oral history musical revue.

Raw material for the revue, which will have original songs, lyrics, and sketches, has been developed at workshop sessions by union members and retirees under the guidance of author and teacher Lewis Cole.

Davis, together with Eve Merriam and Micki Grant, all members of the Bread and Roses advisory board, are writing the revue based on materials obtained at the workshops. Davis will then direct a professional cast which will present the revue in 1980 at hospitals and nursing homes as part of the Theater-in-Hospitals program.

The Roberts Chorale performed before some 15,000 enthusiastic workers and patients in thirty-five hospitals and nursing homes in New York, on Long Island, and in New Jersey. The group also performed at 1199 headquarters for retired members and at the Brooklyn Museum for 1199 retirees and other groups.

The Labor Theater was next on the Theater-in-Hospitals tour with a production of "I Just Wanted Someone to Know," a 40-minute play with music about the role of women in the American labor movement. After visiting five hospitals and nursing homes in New York, the play traveled to Philadelphia and other Pennsylvania cities under the Bread and Roses banner before resuming its New York tour.

The other labor unions may launch similar programs is illustrated by the fact that three other unions have sponsored The Labor Theater production in seven other cities during the group's Pennsylvania travels.

On 27 April 1979 Odetta, the noted folk-singer, launched Theater 1199, a series of Friday evening Bread and Roses entertainments at union headquarters for members and guests. Following an Ossie Davis, Ruby Dee performance 18 May, this season's schedule concluded 15 June with an evening with humorist Sam Levenson.

Other Theater 1199 entertainers this year and in 1980 will include Judy Collins, the Billy Taylor Trio, Professor Irwin Corey, Pete Seeger, Elizabeth Swados and Friends, Eli Wallach and Anne Jackson, Arlo Guthrie, and others.

Another Bread and Roses series, presented in Spanish primarily for the benefit of Hispanic members, is staged on Sunday afternoons at union headquarters. Featuring well-known Hispanic entertainers, the series began in April with Mongo Santamaria and his band, followed in May by the Puerto Rican Traveling Theater, directed by Miriam Colon.

Bread and Roses programs at the union's Gallery 1199 opened in January with an exhibition of paintings by children from seventy-eight countries, arranged by the U.S. Committee for UNICEF to salute the International Year of the Child. Classes from seventy-nine elementary and private schools visited the exhibit, where an integrated program of story-telling, film, and active participation was conducted by a UNICEF-trained instructor.

The visits by school children were organized with the cooperation of the New York City Board of Education and the United Federation of Teachers, together with the Amalgamated Clothing & Textile Workers Union.

These same groups also arranged for high school and college classes and union groups to visit the second exhibition, entitled "Rise Gonna Rise: Portraits of Southern Textile Workers" by noted photographer Earl Dotter. Rank-and-file workers from J.P. Stevens plants, who were subjects of Dotter's photographs, came up from the South to discuss their work experiences. Pointing out the Bread and Roses ripple effect, the Dotter photographs have also widened their impact past 1199. Forty pages of his photos are included in a book published by Doubleday/Anchor, also entitled *Rise Gonna Rise,* with text by Mimi Conway. The United Church Board for Homeland Ministries is publishing a portfolio of the photographs for commercial distribution.

Beginning in October 1979, "The Working American" will occupy Gallery 1199. This is an exhibition of original paintings by American artists depicting the lives of American workers from 1850 to 1950, and will include works borrowed from the Metropolitan, Whitney, and Hirshhorn museums.

"The Working American" will also carry Bread and Roses beyond union confines. The exhibition is scheduled to visit a number of major museums in the U.S. under the auspices of the Smithsonian Institution's Traveling Exhibition Service (SITES).

Other Gallery 1199 exhibits for Bread and Roses will include a photo-essay of hospital workers by Georgeen Comerford and a series of paintings by Ralph Fasanella entitled "Bread and Roses: Lawrence 1912," in which the artist has rendered scenes of the workplace and the strike.

Also taking Bread and Roses nationwide is "The Legacy of Dr. Martin Luther King, Jr.," a series of four dialogues (two each year) dealing with Dr. King's contributions as they relate to current issues. The series is sponsored jointly by District 1199, the King Center for Social Change, and Columbia University.

The initial dialogue on Sunday, 1 April 1979 featured UN Ambassador Andrew J. Young, interviewed by Bill Moyers on "Dr. King: A Personal Memoir." The program was videotaped for presentation the following evening on *Bill Moyers Journal,* televised by more than 200 member stations on the Public Broadcasting Service across the country.

The exploration of Dr. King's philosophy as part of Bread and Roses is considered especially fitting. Dr. King appeared often before 1199 audiences and constantly referred to 1199 as "my favorite union."

Guest speakers in future King dialogues will include Coretta Scott King, Mayor Coleman Young of Detroit, and Douglas Fraser, President of the United Automobile Workers. They will be interviewed by Eleanor Holmes Norton, Chairperson of the U.S. Equal Employment Opportunities Commission; Roger Wilkins, urban affairs specialist for the *New York Times;* and author Studs Terkel.

A series of Bread and Roses conferences and seminars to investigate the ethical aspects of hospital work will directly involve rank-and-file members of 1199. A unionwide all-day conference scheduled for later this year and entitled "Patient Care: the Hospital Worker's Responsibility," will probe ethical, moral, and practical questions as they affect workers and patients. This is to be followed by a series of fifty mini-conferences at as many selected hospitals and nursing homes.

The conferences are being planned by a task force of 1199 members and hospital representatives, assisted by staffs of the United Hospital Fund, the Hastings Center Institute of Society, Ethics and the Life Sciences, and by the Baruch School of Hospital Administration.

A series of five lecture-discussions exploring "Health Care in the U.S. - What's Ahead?," is taking place at union headquarters this year sponsored by 1199's Professional and Health Care Committees. The first, attended by 125 members, heard Professor Uwe Reinhardt of Princeton University discuss the economics of health care. A second session, dealing with women in health care, was held in May.

Scheduled for 1980 is a two-day conference involving 1199 members, officers of other unions, and prominent figures in the arts and humanities. They will talk about "Labor and the Arts and Humanities."

One of the more ambitious Bread and Roses events, which will involve the entire community, is a Labor Day Street Fair, the first ever organized by a labor union. It's scheduled for Labor Day this year, and will take place on New York's West 42nd Street between Ninth and Eleventh Avenues.

Sharing sponsorship with 1199 will be Manhattan Plaza, located one block west of the Union, and the New York City Central Labor Council. Most of the 1800 tenants of Manhattan Plaza are members of the performing arts guilds.

The street fair will feature the casts of Broadway shows, the Big Apple Circus, the Bread and Puppet Theater, jazz bands, and folk singers. Workers will offer live demonstrations of their skills, using actual machines and tools.

Much of Bread and Roses will be preserved for union and other archives. Videotapes, for example, are being prepared on the following subjects:

. An overview of the entire Bread and Roses project, with special emphasis on the involvement, participation, and reaction of members.

. The patient care conference, from the planning and preparation stages to the union-wide all-day conference and the fifty mini-conferences.

. The Labor Day 1979 Street Fair.

. The 1199 Retirees. Besides oral history interviews, this tape will describe how retirees participate in an atmosphere where they may continue friendships developed during their working days, and discover how the learning process continues after retirement.

A documentary film is being produced, depicting how hospital workers of diverse skills, races, and backgrounds, work together to achieve common goals. The film, incorporating many Bread and Roses activities and programs, is being produced and directed by John Schultz.

Two LP recordings will help preserve Bread and Roses for the archives. One, based on the program of dramatic readings by Ossie Davis and Ruby Dee, will include poems about hospital workers by 1199's Marshall Dubin. A recording will be produced next year based on selections from literature, poetry, speeches, and oral history interviews describing the efforts of American workers to win "Bread and Roses." A cast of Broadway actors and actresses will participate.

Essays by artists and scholars about the arts and humanities as they relate to working people are appearing monthly in *1199 News*. The essays will be reprinted as a Bread and Roses history under the title, *A Primer for Labor in the Arts and Humanities*.

A theme Bread and Roses poster, designed by artist Paul Davis, was featured earlier this year in most New York City subway stations and in New York City public schools. Artist Milton Glaser is designing the Labor Day Street Fair poster.

Bread and Roses challenges the idea that culture must be elitist, alien to working people, and it does so not only with the support of governmental agencies but also with help from private organizations, including corporations. This project has established a pattern that leads the way for other labor unions to bring both bread and roses to their memberships.

It also opens up new horizons for artists by giving them the opportunity to practice their art in the area and among the people where it is most needed, and most appreciated. As one performer commented, quoting the lyricist Ira Gershwin, "Who could ask for anything more?"

Grants Magazine, 2 (June 1979):121-28.

31. BREAD AND ROSES UNION BRINGS
CULTURAL EVENTS TO MEMBERS

By Kay Bartlett

The union official interrupted his meeting to take this call. It was from Madeline Gilford, an old friend and wife of Jack Gilford, character actor and comic.

"I need a very good emcee. Got any good ideas?" asks Moe Foner, executive secretary of the union representing 110,000 health care workers.

"Sidney?" repeats Foner. "No, he's on the West Coast and he couldn't come back for this and I wouldn't ask him." That's Sidney Poitier, of course. "James Earl Jones? No, he's in Spain. Ossie? He's working in Flushing that night." That's Ossie Davis, actor and director. Names continue to drop -- Tony Randall, Lily Tomlin, Bella Abzug, Robert Klein.

Moe Foner sounds more like a theatrical agent than a man who must know about things like the Taft-Hartley law. Foner is certainly unusual in the annals of the labor movement, a man dedicated to the idea that culture belongs in the homes and workplaces of workers, especially those of District 1199, National Union of Hospital and Health Care Employees, his union.

Foner has staged so many productions -- musical revues, plays, concerts, art exhibits, street fairs, film documentaries -- that he has been called the "Sol Hurok of the labor movement."

"People often ask me why I do this. What good does it do, all this culture? I tell them it's like chicken soup. It won't cure you, but it won't hurt you."

The energetic Foner was holding a meeting about his newest project -- an art exhibit of original works designed to celebrate the contributions of the labor movement. But when his long-time pal Mrs. Gilford called, he quickly put on the other hat -- the one he wore as he organized a Lincoln

Center tribute to Rosa Parks, the woman who refused to go to the back of the bus in Montgomery, Ala., a quarter of a century ago.

He confides he's already lined up Marlo Thomas, Gregory Hines, star of Broadway's "Sophisticated Lady" and folksinger Leon Bibb, but it's an emcee he needs. No, he can't ask his pal Harry Belafonte to do it. Belafonte performed in concert at Lincoln Center for the last two years. He'll get an emcee, but for now, back to the art project, the most ambitious ever undertaken by a union, Foner announces unequivocally.

It's called "Images of Labor" and will feature original works by 32 prominent American artists. Foner, a lifelong collector of quotes about labor, called in some well-known historians just to make sure he had not missed a good one. They then chose 32 and one was given to each artist.

"There were no guidelines, no instructions," says Foner. "We simply said, 'Do with it as you will.'"

The quotes chosen ranged from the Bible to the words of an anonymous sitdown striker in Akron, Ohio, and included the thoughts of poets, presidents and union organizers in between. . . .

The artists commissioned to do the works include Milton Glaser, Ralph Fasanella, Judy Chicago, Paul Davis and Jacob Lawrence.

The first showing will be April 15 in Gallery 1199, organized labor's only permanent gallery. It's at the union's headquarters in the Times Square section of Manhattan. From there, the show will move to the National Museum of Natural History, in Washington, opening there on the Fourth of July.

Under the auspices of the Smithsonian Institution, the exhibit will travel to some 16 cities over the next two years, including Pasadena, Calif., Fort Dodge, Iowa, and Morgantown, W.Va.

At least 10 of the paintings will be turned into posters, which Foner says he hopes to see in schools, union offices and homes. Some of the works will also be reproduced as postcards.

"Images of Labor" is but one of the projects sponsored by 1199's "Bread and Roses" project, which has included concerts, big name entertainers, scholarships and summer camp for children.

Foner says this is an old union tradition, but one somewhat lost as other forms of entertainment, particularly television, became available. The old union halls served as forums for dances, songfests and skits as well as business.

"Unions had these things in the past," says Foner. "Samuel Gompers recalls union workers chipping in to pay a reader, a person who would read poetry, literature and even the newspaper as the workers rolled the cigar paper. There have always been people in the theater who wanted to identify with the working people, folk songs were about the working people."

In 1979, Foner was able to really bring culture to the workers. District 1199 was funded $1.3 million for a two-year Bread and Roses project. The project has since been refunded and has now acquired "on-going" status.

Besides grants from foundations and individuals, the project is funded by the National Endowment for the Humanities and the National Endowment for the Arts.

The name Bread and Roses comes from a historical textile workers strike in Lawrence, Mass., in 1912. Women carried placards saying, "We Want Bread and Roses, Too," a slogan later incorporated into a poem and often used as a labor theme.

The enormously successful program has brought 75,000 people to a gigantic street fair and introduced thousands to a new world. It has sponsored photography exhibits of the working man at union headquarters, appearances by the late comedian Sam Levenson at hospitals and nursing homes, books, including one on the Lawrence, Mass., strike, poetry programs at hospitals, folk singers during the lunch hours, plays at union headquarters on Friday nights and a musical revue called "Take Care," based on oral history sessions with 50 of the members.

Foner, who played tenor sax in the Borscht Belt as he worked his way through college, became friends with many of the entertainers working the Catskill Mountain circuit -- people like Zero Mostel, Levenson and Gilford.

His personal connections to these show business personalities has not hurt one bit.

"It's like a network. I know someone and he knows someone and so on," explains Foner, downplaying his role in making this project work.

He prefers to point to the union's reputation as an aggressive organizer and its strong alignment with liberal and civil rights organizations. That has provided access to many performers who identify with these causes. Jane Fonda, Davis and his wife Ruby Dee, Muhammad Ali, former U.N. Ambassador Andrew Young, and folksinger Odetta are among its many friends.

District 1199, whose membership is about 65 percent black and Hispanic and nearly 85 percent female, has a history of fighting for everything it has gained -- including the right for hospital workers to organize. Foner cites this as another big factor for the support these activities have received from the rank and file, many of whom had never been to Lincoln Center before 1199 brought them Harry Belafonte.

The union began in 1932 and was called the Pharmacists Union, representing only pharmacists and drug store clerks. In 1936, the fledgling organization with some 500 members joined the American Federation of Labor and acquired the name it keeps today -- Local 1199. It later broke with the AFL and joined the Congress of Industrial Organizations.

Today it is part of the Retail, Wholesale and Department Store Union, AFL-CIO.

It was not until 1959 when a handful of orderlies from Montefiore Hospital in the Bronx asked for help in organizing that 1199 moved into the health care field, now the bulk of its membership.

No other union wanted to get involved. A strike was inevitable, a strike any union could see would drain its funds and give it a black eye.

"We went in where angels feared to tread," Foner said at the time.

For bread.

Now it's the roses' turn.

Mansfield Ohio News-Journal, April 12, 1981.

32. IMAGES OF LABOR (GALLERY 1199)

By Cynthia Nadelman

When the executive secretary of District 1199 of the National Union of Hospital and Health Care Employees and a former art director of *The New York Times* op-ed page (the person who assigns the illustrations) get together to match 32 artists with that many labor-related phrases and quotations, the results are bound to be engrossing. This is what Moe Foner, also the director of District 1199's Bread and Roses cultural program, and Pamela Vassil have done. Given some strong and eloquent phrases, which are seen alongside the art, the artists have opted to be thoughtful and resourceful rather than shrill. The notion of working around a phrase has become a challenging exercise, directing the work and instilling a certain humility. We are once again able to accept work with a subject, a theme or a program-- and we are, not incidentally, also looking at 19th-century Realism, with its depictions of working classes and working conditions, without the acute embarrassment that this would have caused during the era of high modernism. While the 19th-century movement was something short of an active crusade, one might feel that anything produced now would have to be historical and definitely post-crusade. Sponsored by a union filled with women and minorities, though, the themes presented here are not passe and could currently use retelling.

While most of the work is two-dimensional, the sculptures stand out. Robert Arneson's ceramic mask of Samuel Gompers, first president of the American Federation of Labor, is a knockout, more serious than his customary work; Ed McGowin's mound of coal with a pickax at the top has as its "inscape" (an interior view through various openings) a shoe and a cone marked with the maps of states to accompany labor agitator Mother Jones' remark: "My address is like my shoes; it travels with me. I abide where there is a fight against wrong"; and Bill King shows a funny sculpture of Abraham Lincoln.

What would images of labor be without a strike? Sue Coe has scrawled the word across the bottom of a painting in which workers have just shut off their machines and stand with arms folded. This accompanies an Arkon, Ohio, sit-down striker's 1936 description of how it felt to shut down the machines in a rubber-tire plant. A statement by Eleanor Roosevelt expressing the need for women to find fulfillment is illustrated by Jacqueline Chwast in a paper cutout showing a weary black woman in silhouette dreaming of a liberated self who reaches for the stars. A handsome collage by Anita Siegel shows a black man's head brimming with ideas and the trappings of civilization in the machine age: this illustrates Socialist leader Eugene Debs' statement, "Intelligent discontent is the mainspring of civilization." Audrey Flack shows a striking black and white pseudo-photo realist painting of abolitionist and suffragette Sojourner Truth.

The one disappointing work is that of Ralph Fasanella, only because the smallish painting here does not live up to this folk artist's earlier exhaustive and triumphant versions of factory life, especially the Lawrence, Massachusetts, textile workers' strike of 1912. Works by, among others, Jack Beal, May Stevens, Mimi Gross, Barbara Nessim, Robert Grossman, Benny Andrews and Alice Neel also bear mentioning.

After closing in New York on June 5, the exhibition will be on view from July 16 to August 20 at the Smithsonian's National Museum of American History, under whose auspices it will travel for two more years to museums across the country. All of the images are presented in color in the book *Images of Labor* (Pilgrim Press, $29.95, cloth; $16.95, paper), with a preface by Joan Mondale, an introduction by author Irving Howe and background material on the quotations that are used.

For those who question the mutual significance of unions and artists, it is timely to consider the recent arrival in this country of a Polish poet. After trying unsuccessfully for three years to get to Harvard, where he had been invited to teach, Stanislaw Baranczak, finally here, was quoted in *The New York Times* as saying, "Only after Solidarity [the Polish independent labor union] was created was it possible for people like me to obtain passports." Unions do affect the overall quality of life and, as 1199 has been demonstrating, they don't live by bread alone.

Art News, 80 (June 1981).

33. STRONG 'IMAGES OF LABOR'

By Benjamin Forgey

"You can always measure the level of democracy in any country by the freedom its workers have to organize unions of their own choosing," writes Irving Howe in the catalog for the exhibition "Images of Labor," which opens today at the National Museum of American History.

An obvious parallel measurement is freedom of expression, which includes not only political advocacy but also the freedom of artists to treat subjects of their own choosing, and in styles and techniques they deem appropriate. The ugly history of totalitarian regimes in our century can be written in the violence done to creative, as well as economic and other freedoms.

Ironically, except for this fundamental parallel, perhaps even because of it, the history of the American labor movement and the history of American art have in large measure gone their separate directions. There was a time, in the 1930s, when the causes of economic justice and artistic expression did dovetail; but in the long run, the alliance foundered upon the built-in stresses between political advocacy and artistic individualism.

The decline of what was called social realism was part of the larger, complex story of the decline of figurative art, generally, in the minds of many of the best and most original artists in the land. But the labor movement played its part, too, either failing to give the issue much thought or demanding an art that conformed to stringent and explicit social goals.

The intrinsic worthiness of the goals is not the point. There is no more effective way to diminish or to kill creativity than to require it to adhere to a set of non-artistic standards, whatever they are. Again, the examples of Nazism and Soviet Communism write large the lessons that, in America, were written small.

The bedrock of artistic achievement is the freedom of the individual to choose. Artists can be as blindly conformist as any other social group, but left for long enough to their own devices, they will find new and wonderful ways to express ideas, including those of social justice and solidarity.

This is why the "Images of Labor" exhibition is refreshing. In a very healthy way, it reflects an important transformation in the visual arts that has taken place in the past 20 years or so, a period in which we have seen artists gradually cast away the self-set blinders that decreed the predominance of a given style -- abstract expressionism, say, or color field painting.

The fact is that artists today, especially when given a helpful nudge, have no difficulty in responding to the call for an imagery that richly, if sometimes ironically, expresses important social ideas. The nudge, in this case, was supplied by the Bread and Roses cultural project of District 1199, National Union of Hospital and Health Care employees, which commissioned works from 32 contemporary artists.

Wisely, the union established only one important condition: The images were to relate in some way to a specific quotation culled from the troubled and triumphant history of labor unions. Admittedly, in a few cases, the result is a somewhat bizarre friction between the verbal and visual messages, as when Ralph Fasanella paints a tribute to the cacophony of urban life alongside Phillip Murray's dire description: "Disease, sickness and poverty were rampant, and death stalked in the wake of every worker's family. . . ." Still, on its own, Fasanella's painting is a celebration of working-class life -- the flip side, in a way, of Murray's impassioned sympathy.

Most of the artists chose either to illustrate the quotation, more or less directly, or to invoke its spirit in an imaginative and stylistically freer way. A number of the social-protest illustrations are brilliant: Wedward Sorel's haunting, corrosive pen-and-ink drawing to go with a railroad mogul's cruel epigram, "They don't suffer; they can't even speak English," as well as works by Mimi Gross, Jack Beal, Milton Glaser and Benny Andrews. Gross' work is especially inventive, a tableau whose hominess heightens the terror of Walter Reuther's question, "What good is another $100 pension if the world goes up in atomic smoke?"

Ed McGowin's free-standing "inscape," a coal-black pyramid containing a tableau based upon the life of the itinerant labor activist Mother Jones -- "My address is wherever there is a fight against oppression" -- is the most forcefully original of the commissioned works (although, unfortunately, it will not go on view until some minor damage is repaired). Also outstanding are Miriam Wosk's wall construction and Anton van Dalen's hip and scary painting of a skeletal figure (based upon John L. Lewis' zinger, "The open shop is a harlot with a wig and artificial limbs, and her bones rattle").

Four of the artists chose simply to record the race of the person who supplied the words, and in each case produced a tremendously persuasive, if stylistically divergent, reading of a personality: Alice Neel's expressively blue portrait of Frances Perkins, Audrey Flack's photo-based painting of Sojourner Truth, May Stevens' lyrical and tough painting of Lucy E. Parsons and most mightily of all, Robert Arneson's ceramic version of Samuel Gompers, clearly one of the more important portrait busts created in our time.

Due to the enlightenment of its organizers and the talent of the artists they chose, the exhibition does indeed help us to recognize, as Howe puts it, "the centrality of the American working class . . . in our cultural arrangements and our cultural experience." Supported by a grant from the National Endowment for the Humanities, the exhibition is on a two-year tour organized by the Smithsonian Institution Traveling Exhibition Service. Its appearance in Washington through Aug. 21 will be accompanied by concerts and film programs.

Washington Star, July 17, 1981.

34. "TAKE CARE, TAKE CARE"

A New Musical Revue About Hospital Workers
Music, Lyrics and Sketches by
Lewis Cole, Ossie Davis, Micki Grant
Barbara Garson, Alan Menken and Michael Posnick

CAST
(In Alphabetical Order)

David Berman (yellow shirt)..............Ambulance Driver, Doctor, Lecturer
Ann Duquesnay (purple shirt)..............Nurse's Aide from Barbados, Delegate,
                                          Housekeeper
Jack Landron (blue shirt)................Pot Washer, Spanish Patient, Soap
                                         Opera Doctor
Barbara Niles (green shirt)..............Lab-technician from Kansas, Patient,
                                         Social Worker
Corliss Taylor-Dunn (orange shirt).......................Nurse, Burnout Nurse
With Billy McDaniel, Carline Ray and Ralph Dorsey

   The performance will consist of a selection from the following numbers

Opening: Take Care, Take Care Song by Alan Menken;
          Dialogue by Lewis Cole......................................The Company
Back Home Monologue: Pot Washer by Lewis Cole............................Jack
Soap Opera (skit) by Barbara Garson...............................The Company
          (song) by Alan Menken and Barbara Garson.............Corliss and Ann
Back Home Monologue: Lab-technician by Lewis Cole....................Barbara
Save the Race by Ossie Davis.................................Ann and Company
Back Home Monologue: Ambulance Driver by Lewis Cole....................David
Medical Abbreviations by Alan Menken.............................The Company
Back Home Monologue: Nurse's Aide by Lewis Cole.........................Ann
Back Home by Micki Grant.................................Corliss and Company
Reaganitis by Barbara Garson.....................................The Company
Hello! Florence Nightingale (Linda's Song) Music by Alan Menken;
          Lyrics by Lewis Cole.............................Barbara and Corliss
Burnout by Micki Grant; Dialogue by Lewis Cole....................The Company
Hands by Michael Posnick...The Company

PRODUCTION STAFF

Arranger and Orchestrator....................................Howard Roberts
Conductor/Pianist....................................William Foster McDaniel
Stage Manager..Stephen Howe
Assistant Stage Manager...Peter Brosius
Publicist...Matthew Alperin

   *Although Ossie Davis, Micki Grant, Lewis Cole, Alan Menken, Barbara
Garson and Michael Posnick are given credit for the lyrics and sketches, the
indispensable creators of "Take Care, Take Care" are a group of 17 hospital
workers including housekeepers, social workers, technicians, nurses, maintenance and dietary workers. These workers, members of District 1199, participated in a series of oral history workshops talking and writing about their
lives. Their discussions and writings are the foundation of "Take Care, Take
Care."*

District 1199 Archives.

35. UNITED WE LAUGH

By Barbara Garson

   Fifty dietitians, lab technicians, nurses aides and orderlies met weekly
last year to make notes on their lives; the results were turned over to

professional writers who created a popping musical revue for the hospital workers' union, District 1199. *Take Care,* now touring hospitals at lunch hours, is a series of skits and spiffy songs in soul, calypso, salsa, and plain white musical-comedy American (to match the union's membership). The response from unprepared hospital workers reminded me of myself, accidentally encountering the Mime Troupe in a San Francisco park--"My God! *Real* actors saying *our* words, right in the middle of the street!"

The revue includes some numbers you'd expect in any union show (if there were any other union shows). For instance, "Young People Today," a sarcastic song about the good old days before the union. It also includes things you'd never expect. At one quiet moment the black piano player becomes a hospital porter. He explains why he always seeks night shifts and overtime. "No, not for the money like everyone guesses," but because "I can't sleep." He had been a paramedic in Nam. He thought he'd grown "cold to it all." But suddenly, 10 years later, he can't close his eyes, at least not at night, not in the dark. So he spends those hours checking monitors, soothing patients, finding pillows. "I got a mind for little things."

Women's consciousness is expressed by talking together about getting out in the morning, not having the energy to smile at the kids' surprise rainbow cake, and finding no sympathy from women supervisors. "They get promoted and then it's like we're talking a different language." Feminist understanding here is far more subtle than you'd expect from most unions and far more substantial than you'd get from most feminists.

The skits and musical numbers are held together by five "characters," representative hospital workers embellished or streamlined from the original 50 workshop participants: Mildred, fiftyish West Indian dietitian; Gloria, black admitting clerk; Eileen, pretty Irish RN, twenties; Mac, Midwest lab technician; Rosita, Hispanic occupational therapist. Though the union and the writers are committed to the individuality of these workers, the five characterizations waver from skit to skit and their best speeches often get lost in the staging, which is uniformly fast-paced and concentrates on gimmicks rather than what's happening between people.

Only by listening hard the second time around (at each hospital the show is performed for both lunch hour shifts) did I glean that Gloria, 40, divorced and a union delegate, is supposed to be a no-nonsense character who makes the hospital run by standing up the bosses, while bouncy Rosita cajoles the doctors into doing their jobs. Implied in both their techniques, of course, is the idea that it's the union members who make the hospital function --when it does. Mac, the white lab technician is teased, as a ladies' man though he actually longs to be accepted in the girls' lives. These and other potentially interesting qualities are suggested fleetingly and with little consistency from scene to scene.

Some "individual" traits might be considered out and out racist slurs if we saw them on television, like Rosita's superstitious gambling--"Play your birthday, play your address, play your pension plan." And Mildred, the round, maternal, West Indian cafeteria worker, is really not too different from Beulah: She has the strength to feed the whole world, absorb its sorrow into her bulk, and still sing a rousing chorus of "Lookin' Good."

Clearly no one at 1199 was offended. Maybe the characters are stereotypes, but this isn't television. As people in the audience told me, "It's the union." "It's *us.*" "That makes it different." Personally I accept this double standard. "Us" does make it different. Writing for insiders, for people you really like, allows you to work through, above, around, and under the stereotypes until you come up with truer truths. Writing for people you like also inspires a healthy desire to entertain. That's the most obvious feature of *Take Care.*

Another product of writing for "us" is in-jokes. Critics generally consider in-jokes, at least the ones they don't get, to be unintelligent, illegitimate, cheap laughs. (The kind of cheap laughs Aristophanes went for with a Spartan walk-on). But good theatre is always written for a particular audience. People from groups that normally produce writers are used to finding their private jokes and insights in plays. Others almost never do. What a wave of shock, surprise, and finally wild joy sweeps over the 1199 audience when one of their own special words is heard on the stage for the first time! Whether you get it or not, who can deny the howls when anyone says, "Take it to the delegate"?

1199 cultural officials deserve extraordinary credit. *Take Care* contains not one single call to "build the union." Someone up there understood that laughing together automatically builds the union.

The Village Voice, February 18, 1980.

36. UNION MUSICAL TO PREMIERE AT BORO HOSPITAL

By Mark Liff

Brooklyn Jewish Hospital will be the site today of the premiere of "Take Care, Take Care," a musical based on hospital workers' lives and work experiences.

"Take Care, Take Care" is the first union-produced musical since the International Ladies Garment Workers Union produced "Pins and Needles" in the 1930s. "Take Care, Take Care" actually began in 1980 and the current production is a new, revised show.

The show is presented by District 1199 of the National Union of Hospital and Health Care Employes. It was culled from transcripts of 12-week workshops of aides, nurses, clerks, social workers and others who toil in hospitals.

Five professional actors--David Berman, Jack Landron, Corliss Taylor-Dunn, Barbara Niles and Ann Duquesnay--will perform in the 45-minute show. Music and sketches are by Micki Grant, Ossie Davis, Barbara Garson, Lewis Cole and others.

"Take Care, Take Care" will be presented free at lunchtime and again in the evening to hospital workers, patients and staffers at Brooklyn Jewish Hospital. The show later will be presented at Presbyterian, Montefiore, St. Luke's, Long Island Jewish and other hospitals.

Performances are also slated for hospitals in other states in a nationwide tour.

Stores of on-the-job life and home experiences will be spotlighted by the show. These include "Burnout," about a high-pressure job; "Save the Race," about racism at work, and "Soap Opera," which compares what you see on television to the real thing.

The program is funded by the National Endowment for the Arts, the New York State Council on the Arts and the city's Department of Cultural Affairs.

"Take Care, Take Care" is part of the Bread and Roses cultural project started by District 1199 nearly a decade ago. One of the program's most memorable projects is its annual street fair on Labor Day outside the union's W. 43d St. offices.

Last year, its "Images of Labor" paintings made its debut. The 32 originals were based on quotations about working life and are now on national tour.

All members of the National Football League Players Association, for example, received copies of a book containing the pictures and the quotations.

Daily News (N.Y.), March 1, 1982.

37. HOSPITAL REVUE HITS 'HOME' FOR EMPLOYEES

By Mark Finston

The musical isn't audience participation, but it's close to it.

It is called "Take Care, Take Care," and it is for, about -- and in a sense by -- hospital and nursing home employes.

At its New Jersey debut last week, at the Daughters of Miriam, a home for the aged in Clifton, a number of employes nodded their heads at the start when one actor referred to "not enough sheets."

When another performer spoke of the "supervisor callin' you so much you
hate the sound of your own name," several of the employes in the audience
became vocal: "That's it," "You got it," "Right on."

The show was conceived and produced by District 1199 of the National
Union of Health and Hospital Care Employes. It, and its predecessor, "Take
Care," are said to be the first labor union-produced musical since the International Ladies Garment Workers Union staged "Pins and Needles" in the early
1930s.

Local 1199 represents 65,000 health and hospital employes in New Jersey,
New York and Connecticut. The show is part of the union's "bread and roses"
program, now three years old, which includes art shows and other cultural
activities.

The name originated in a textile workers strike in 1912 in Lawrence,
Mass. This was known as the Bread and Roses strike -- bread for higher wages,
roses for better working conditions. Roses has since been expanded to include
culture, as in the term, "Man cannot live by bread alone."

The original musical was initiated as sort of an oral history project.
Hospital workers of all kinds were invited down to Local 1199's headquarters,
at 310 West 43rd Street, to discuss their lives: Social issues, labor-
management problems, racism, economic issues, family and friends.

Writers interested in the project formulated a play from the material,
named it "Take Care"; it played to 35,000 hospital workers in 11 states.

This show, "Take Care, Take Care," originated in the same manner, but
on a somewhat broader scale. Other hospital workers discussed their lives,
and writers such as Ossie Davis, famous actor and author of "Purlie Victorious,"
Micki Grant ("Don't Bother Me, I Can't Cope"; "Your Arms Too Short to Box with
God"), Barbara Garson and Alan Menken wrote music, lyrics and dialogue.

The play employs five actors -- three women, two men. They are all professionals, and are members of Actors Equity, all paid union scale. Also
touring are three union musicians.

The first performance was March 1, and each day, usually at lunchtime,
a different hospital or health care facility is scheduled. The Daughters of
Miriam last week was the first New Jersey date; others are on tap in April.

According to production coordinator Tony Gillotte, the show plays in
medical auditoriums, lecture halls, hospital cafeterias, as well as rooms
like the handsome Marcus Auditorium at Daughters of Miriam.

The most unusual setting was for the employes of Long Island Jewish
Hospital. The workers are on strike, but the production was presented on a
street platform for 1,000 picketers.

Gillotte says that the "majority" of hospital administrators are very
cooperative in allowing their facilities to be used for the show.

"They recognize it's in their best interests to have good morale for
their employes," said Gillotte.

A couple of administrators, however, refused to allow the show to go on,
believing that labor unions are still mortal enemies of management.

A few others throw up roadblocks. One nursing home said employes could
see the show -- but only if they gave up both their lunch period and morning
coffee break. Many employes watch the 50-minute performance on lunch breaks,
bringing food to much during the play. But this nursing home forbade that
too. Attendance at the performance was cut substantially.

One of the most amusing, and to the workers relevant, skits was the
contrast between the soap opera "General Hospital" and a real general hospital.

In the soap: "In between the sutures, you talk about your futures."

That's not true in lower case general hospital.

Or: "They always say 'please' and 'thank you',

"On soap operas doctors never outrank you . . .

"If you're depressed,

"They send you home to rest. . . ."

The show will play at hospitals in the metropolitan region till the
second week in May. (Members of the general public can watch a free performance at the headquarters of Local 1199 at 6:30 p.m. on April 12).

After that, "Take Care, Take Care" will tour health care facilities as
far away as the Pacific coast.

And Gillotte says the production might eventually become a cabaret
revue.

"It would have to be broadened to include doctors and administrators,"
says Gillotte.
    But that leaves most of us out . . .
    "And patients," concludes Gillotte.

The Sunday Star-Ledger, March 28, 1982.

38. A REVUE THAT'S GOOD MEDICINE

By Lucinda Fleeson

    Not in the gauze-filtered world of TV's "General Hospital" would the
starring roles be given to hospital housekeepers who moan about the drudgery
of their jobs or the inconsiderateness of doctors.
    But in the musical revue, *Take Care, Take Care,* produced by the national
hospital workers' union, it is those anonymous dietary aides and orderlies
who are on center stage, talking about the hard realities of hospital work,
and mixing it with a spectacular combination of humor, rock music, blues
singing and dancing.
    The revue, which is making an 11-week national tour, is part of the
union's highly praised Bread and Roses cultural project, and was created to
bring culture and the arts directly to union members. "This is for the
people who can't afford $50 to see a Broadway show. This is their history,"
said Corliss Taylor-Dunn, one of the five professional actors and actresses
in the cast.
    Although usually the revue is staged during lunch hours at hospitals
and nursing homes around the county, on Tuesday night it was performed for
more than 150 delegates and shop stewards of District 1199C, Hospital and
Nursing Home Employees Union, in Philadelphia headquarters at 1319 Locust St.
The show was so enthusiastically received that it was interrupted with
clapping and laughs of recognition as the play captured the joys and sometimes the boredom of health-care work.
    The dialogue is culled from taped autobiographical workshop sessions
with members of the National Union of Hospital and Health Care Employees.
Characters range from the pot scrubber who really wants to be a poet to the
lab technician who fled from Kansas to seek a career in the Big City and the
Vietnam veteran who thrills to his job as an ambulance driver. But the skits
also include biting commentary on racial prejudice and on the pathos of workers who try to deliver care to an endless stream of patients while hospital
budgets are shrinking.
    A Ronald Reagan figure appears in a coal-black rubber wig seeking
emergency room care because his hand is stuck in a jellybean jar. The President sheepishly explains, "The black ones are always at the bottom," to which
a nurse's aide snaps, "Don't you know it, sugar."
    With a nearly nonexistent set, and costumes that consist mostly of
hospital whites, the five-member cast and three musicians have taken hard-core
reality and made something of it that is not only entertaining, but also has
a strain of astute commentary on the politics of working-class America.
    Moe Foner, executive producer of the show (and also executive secretary
of the national union), says the revue -- which premiered two years ago in a
shorter version -- is the first musical produced by a labor union since the
famed *Pins and Needles* by the International Ladies' Garment Workers Union hit
Broadway in the 1930s.
    Using the technique that spawned *A Chorus Line,* the authors held work-
shops in New York with 17 health and hospital workers, who talked about their
frustrations, aspirations and the daily hassles of modern health-care work.
The result was a rich oral history that formed the lyrics and dialogue of the
songs and skits. "There's not a word in it that didn't come out of the mouths
of the workers themselves," said Foner.
    It is those 17 workers -- aides, dieticians, clerks, nurses and other
workers -- who are identified as the "indispensable creators" of the revue,

although the official credit for lyrics and sketches goes to some of the union's more famous friends in the theater -- Ossie Davis, Micki Grant, Alan Menken, Barbara Garson and Lewis Cole. Micki Grant, for instance, is author of *Your Arms Too Short to Box With God.*

Interspersed with the autobiographics and rousing union solidarity songs, there are other sketches, such as "Soap Opera," in which hospital aides and nurses fantasize about working at General Hospital, where the doctors thank the housekeepers for doing a good job and deliver flowers to the nurses.

In the song "Florence Nightingale," the nurses beseech their inspiration, "Did *your* back ever ache?" Actress Ann Duquesnay, as a nurse's aide, reminisces about being a child bride in Barbados. About her job, she says, "They used to call us maids, but we got them to drop the 'M'."

The five actors -- all Actor's Equity, naturally -- say they find the experience of playing to union members to be uplifting. Taylor-Dunn, formerly of *Bubbling Brown Sugar,* gives a particularly strong performance in one skit as a nurse suffering from "burnout," and says she based the character on her mother, a non-union nurse in Cleveland. "My mother died of burnout, so I can relate," she said just before Tuesday's show.

And the audience certainly relates. Emma Thomas, a dietary worker of the Philadelphia Geriatric Center, said, "I liked the part about the pot washer," referring to the worker who moaned, "I'm not going to be a pot washer all my life; I'm a man of sophistication."

Her co-worker, a housekeeper, seconded the appraisal. "It put it like it is, You take what you get until the right job comes along."

The show's one problem, Foner acknowledges, is that the audiences are primarily restricted to hospital patients, workers and union members. But that problem may be resolved, he says. Although he cautions that "nothing is definite," the union is discussing the possibility of opening Off-Broadway.

That's one possibility that Philadelphia should hope comes true, because, unfortunately, Tuesday night's performance was the city's one and only appearance of *Take Care, Take Care.*

Philadelphia Inquirer, April 15, 1982.

NOTES AND INDEX

1   Whitney M. Young, Jr. (1921–1971) was a graduate of Kentucky State College and earned a masters degree from the University of Minnesota in 1947. He spent his professional career with the National Urban League and served as executive director from 1961 to 1971.

2   Jacob K. Javits (b. 1904) received a law degree from New York University in 1927. From 1946 to 1954 he was a U.S. representative from New York, and from 1955 to 1957 attorney general of New York. He was elected to the U.S. Senate from New York in 1957, and served until 1980.
    Joseph S. Clark (b. 1901) graduated from Harvard University in 1923, and the University of Pennsylvania Law School in 1926. He commenced the practice of law in Philadelphia, and in 1952 was elected mayor of the city until 1956 when he became a Democratic senator from Pennsylvania. He held that position until 1969 when he was unsuccessful in his bid for re-election.

3   Lyndon B. Johnson (1908–1973) graduated from Southwest State Teachers College in 1930. After teaching in the public schools of Houston, Texas, he was elected to the U.S. House of Representatives (1937–1949), and then to the U.S. Senate (1953–61). He was elected vice president in 1961, and upon the assassination of President John F. Kennedy in 1963, Johnson became the thirty-sixth President. As president, Johnson secured passage of the 1964 Civil Rights Bill, and initiated the Great Society programs of the sixties. His term was marred by the unsuccessful war in Vietnam.

4   Title VII of the Civil Rights Act of 1964 prohibits discrimination in employment because of race, religion, sex, or national origin.

5   Executive Order 11246 requires government contractors to follow nondiscriminatory employment practices and to take "affirmative action" to ensure that job applicants and employees are not discriminated against on the basis of race, color, religion, sex, or national origin.

6   Vernon E. Jordan, Jr. (b. 1935) graduated from DePaul University and then Howard Law School in 1960. Jordan practiced law, and served in various civil rights capacities including director of the Voter Education Project of the Southern Regional Council (1964–1968), and executive director of the United Negro College Fund (1970–1971), before heading the National Urban League from 1972 to 1981. Following an attempted assassination by a deranged white supremist, Jordan resigned to practice law in Washington, D.C.

7   James D. Hodgson (b. 1915) graduated from the University of Minnesota in 1938, and did post-graduate work at the same institution and UCLA. He held several positions in industrial relations before being appointed undersecretary of labor in the cabinet of President Richard Nixon in 1969, and then secretary of labor in 1970.
    Maynard H. Jackson, Jr. (b. 1938) graduated from Morehouse College in 1956, and received a J.D. degree from North Carolina Central School of Law in 1959. He founded a law firm in Atlanta, Ga., and became vice mayor of the city, before being elected mayor of Atlanta, one of a growing number of Afro-American city mayors.
    Andrew Young (b. 1932) graduated from Howard University, and received a B.Div. from Hartford Theological Seminary and became a pastor in Alabama and Georgia. He became a close advisor of Martin Luther King in the civil rights movement, and became executive vice president of the Southern Christian Leadership Conference. Young was elected to the U.S. House of Representatives from Atlanta, Ga. from 1973 to 1977, and was appointed U.S. ambassador to the United Nations from 1977–1979. After leaving that post he was elected mayor of Atlanta.

Walter G. Davis (b. 1920), an Afro-American, graduated from Columbia University in 1956, and attended law school for two years. From 1952 to 1958 he served as president of Local 290, United Transportation Service Employees, C.I.O. He became a national organizer for the UTSE in 1958, but left that post to become assistant director of the AFL-CIO Civil Rights Department (1961-1965). In 1966 he became director of the AFL-CIO Department of Education, and served on the board of directors of the A. Philip Randolph Institute.

John R. Lewis (b. 1940) received a B.A. from the American Baptist Theological Seminary in 1961, and a B.A. from Fisk University in 1967. A leading figure in the civil rights movement, Lewis served as chairman of the Student Nonviolent Coordinating Committee (1963-1966), and has served in numerous public interest efforts. An Afro-American, he has been director of the Voter Education Project since 1970.

8   William Willard Wirtz (b. 1912) received a B.A. from Beloit College in 1933, and an LL.B. from Harvard University in 1937. He served as a professor of law from 1937 to 1942. In 1946 he became chairman of the National Wage Stabilization Board, but returned to the Northwestern University School of Law from 1946 to 1954. He advised Adlai Stevenson in his bid for the presidency in 1952, then joined his law firm. From 1962 to 1969 he served as secretary of labor under Presidents Kennedy and Johnson.

9   Eleanor Holmes Norton (b. 1938) graduated from Antioch College, and received a M.A. (1963) and a J.D. (1964) from Yale University. From 1970 to 1976 she was New York commissioner of Human Rights, and in 1977 was appointed chairperson of the U.S. Equal Employment Opportunity Commission.

10   William Brennan (b. 1906) received his law degree from Harvard Law School in 1931, and practiced law in Newark, N.J., until 1949 when he became a judge. He served as a justice of the New Jersey Supreme Court from 1952 to 1956 when he was appointed justice of the U.S. Supreme Court. He has consistently sided with liberals in cases involving civil rights.

11   Warren E. Burger (b. 1907) received his law degree from St. Paul College of Law in 1931, and practiced law in Minnesota until 1953. He served as assistant attorney general from 1953 to 1956 when he was appointed judge of the U.S. Court of Appeals in Washington, D.C. In 1969 President Nixon appointed him Chief Justice of the U.S. Supreme Court. Burger is an advocate of judicial restraint in social reform cases.

William H. Rehnquist (b. 1924) graduated from Stanford University, and then Stanford Law School in 1952. He practiced law in Phoenix, Arizona, until 1969 when he was appointed assistant attorney general. Rehnquist held that post until 1972 when he was appointed to the U.S. Supreme Court by President Richard Nixon. His nomination was opposed by civil rights groups because he holds a limited view of the equal rights clause.

Lewis F. Powell, Jr. (b. 1907) graduated from Washington and Lee University, and received his law degree there in 1931. A specialist in securities law, he practiced in Richmond, Virginia, served in numerous public and professional capacities, and was appointed justice of the U.S. Supreme Court in 1972. He has consistently favored judicial restraint in cases involving social reform.

John Paul Stevens (b. 1920) graduated from the University of Chicago, and received a law degree from Northwestern University Law School in 1947. An authority on anti-trust law, he was appointed judge of the U.S. Seventh Circuit Court of Appeals (1970-1975), and then justice of the U.S. Supreme Court in 1975. An independent, he has sided with both liberals and conservatives on various civil rights cases.

12   "Meany" refers to George Meany. See Vol. VII, note 229.

13   In the case of *University of California v. Bakke* (1978) the U.S. Supreme Court held that even though universities may consider race as a factor in evaluating candidates for admission, universities may not

establish fixed racial quotas. The case arose when the medical school
of the University of California at Davis rejected Allan Bakke's
application while admitting members of racial minorities who had lower
test scores.

14   For background on Emanuel Celler (D-N.Y.), see Vol. VI, note 52.

15   Hubert H. Humphrey, Jr. (1911-1978) graduated from the University of
Minnesota in 1939, and earned a Masters Degree from Louisiana State
University in 1940. From 1945 to 1948 he served as mayor of Minneapolis,
and was elected U.S. Senator from Minnesota from 1948 to 1964, and 1971
to 1978. He was elected to one term of vice president in 1964, and was
the unsuccessful presidential nominee of the Democratic Party in 1968.
Humphrey was considered a strong defender of civil rights, and a friend
of organized labor.

16   Thomas H. Kuchel (b. 1910), a graduate of the University of Southern
California, and U.S.C. law school in 1935, held several state offices in
California before his election as a Republican to the U.S. Senate from
1953 to 1969. Kuchel took a liberal position on civil rights.

17   Leverett Saltonstall (1892-1979), a graduate of Harvard University, and
Harvard Law School in 1917, served in several state posts prior to his
election as governor of Massachusetts on the Republican ticket (1938-
1944). From 1944 to 1967 he served as U.S. senator from Massachusetts
and voted as a moderate liberal on civil rights issues.

18   Ronald Reagan (b. 1911) graduated from Eureka College in 1932, and
became a sports announcer and actor. From 1947 to 1952 he was president
of the Screen Actors Guild. A Republican, he served as governor of
California from 1967 to 1974, and in 1980 was elected president of the
United States.

19   John F. Kennedy (1917-1963), a graduate of Harvard University, served
as a representative in the U.S. House from Massachusetts from 1947 to
1953. He was elected to the U.S. Senate and served from 1953 to 1960,
when he became a successful candidate for U.S. president. His
administration was committed to the disestablishment of racial
segregation.

20   For background on President Richard M. Nixon, see Vol. VII, note 227.
Gerald R. Ford, Jr. (b. 1913) graduated from the University of
Michigan, and received a law degree from Yale University in 1941. He
practiced law in Grand Rapids, Michigan, until 1949 when he was elected
to the U.S. House. He served in the House until 1973 when he became vice
president. Upon the resignation of Richard Nixon in 1974, Ford became
president of the United States, serving out the remainder of Nixon's
term. He failed to be elected to his own full term.

21   James Earl Carter, Jr. (b. 1924) graduated from the U.S. Naval Academy
in 1947. He was elected to the Georgia State Senate from 1963 to 1967,
and then governor of Georgia from 1971 to 1975. In 1977 he successfully
fought for the Democratic nomination for the presidency, and defeated
Gerald Ford for that office.

22   David Stockman, a one-time congressman from Michigan, became President
Ronald Reagan's director of the Office of Management and Budget. The
reference to "supply-siders" relates to the notion that the economy will
be better stimulated from the supply, rather than the demand, side.

23   For background on President Herbert Hoover, see Vol. VI, note 51.

24   For background on Frank R. Crosswaith, see Vol. VI, note 135.

25   For background on Roy Wilkins, see Vol. VII, note 5.

26   For background on President Dwight D. Eisenhower, see Vol. VII, note
205.

27   For background on the Ku Klux Klan, see Vol. II, pp. 183–239.

28   For background on Joseph E. Curran, see Vol. VII, note 63.

29   For background on James B. Carey, see Vol. VII, note 220. For Willard
        S. Townsend see Vol. VII, note 33. For A. Philip Randolph, see Vol. V,
        note 111.
            Thurgood Marshall (b. 1908) graduated from Lincoln University and
        Howard Law School in 1933. As chief counsel of the National Association
        for the Advancement of Colored People, Marshall argued numerous important
        civil rights cases before the U.S. Supreme Court. He was appointed judge
        of the U.S. Court of Appeals Second Circuit (1961–1965), and U.S.
        solicitor general (1965–1967) before taking a seat on the U.S. Supreme
        Court.

30   For background on President Harry S. Truman, see Vol. VII, note 181.
        Boris Shishkin was an economist and legislative consultant of the AFL,
        and then the AFL–CIO.

31   "Operation Dixie" was launched in 1946 by the CIO to organize southern
        industries.

32   George Leon-Paul Weaver (b. 1912), an Afro-American, attended Roosevelt
        University and Howard University Law School during World War II. He was
        a member of the CIO Relief Commission in 1941–1942, and was appointed
        assistant to the secretary-treasurer of the CIO from 1942 to 1955. From
        1955 to 1958 he served as executive secretary of the AFL–CIO. In 1961 he
        served as a special assistant to the U.S. secretary of labor, and as
        assistant secretary of labor for international affairs in 1969. That
        year he became special assistant to the director-general of the
        International Labor Organization, Geneva, Switzerland. See also, Vol.
        VII, pp. 374–75.

33   For background on Milton P. Webster, see Vol. VI, note 44.

34   For background on Chandler Owen, see Vol. V, note 110.

35   For the March on Washington Movement referred to here, see Vol. VII,
        pp. 251–62.

36   Anna Eleanor Roosevelt (1884–1962) married President Franklin Roosevelt
        in 1905, and was First Lady from 1933 to 1945. A champion of the
        underprivileged and minorities, she distinguished herself in their
        service, was a representative to the United Nations General Assembly in
        1945, 1949–1952, and 1961–62, and served as chairperson of the Commission
        on Human Rights.

37   For background on David J. McDonald, see Vol. VII, note 47.

38   For background on Charles S. Zimmerman, see Vol. VII, note 204.

39   For background on Walter P. Reuther, see Vol. VII, note 190.

40   For background on Samuel Gompers, see Vols. IV and V.
        For Jeremiah Grandison, see Vol. IV, p. 3.

41   For background on Arthur J. Goldberg, see Vol. VII, note 195.

42   Martin Luther King, Jr. (1929–1968) graduated from Morehouse College in
        1948, Crozier Theological Seminary in 1951, and received a Ph.D. from
        Boston University in 1955. As pastor of the Dexter Avenue Baptist Church
        in Montgomery, Alabama, he came to national prominence by leading the
        successful Montgomery Bus Boycott of 1955–1956. Founder of the Southern
        Christian Leadership Conference, King played the leading role in the
        struggle to desegregate southern institutions. In 1964 he was awarded
        the Nobel Peace Prize for his work, but was assassinated by a white
        racist in 1968.

43   NAM refers to the National Association of Manufacturers, a conservative
business organization.

44   Charles A. Hayes (b. 1918), a member of the Amalgamated Meat Cutters
and Butcher Workmen, became vice president of that organization in 1968.
An Afro-American, Hayes also served as director of District 12, MCBW, as
director of District 1, United Packinghouse, Food and Allied Workers of
America, from 1954 to 1968, and as vice president of Operation Push in
1972.

45   For background on George M. Harrison, see Vol. VII, note 184.

46   For background on the Marshall Plan, see Vol. VII, notes 181 and 219.

47   Frank W. Schnitzler (b. 1904) of Newark, N.J., a member of the Bakery
and Confectionery Workers International Union, became secretary-treasurer
of the AFL-CIO from 1953 to 1969, when he retired with emeritus status.

48   Eugene Frazier (b. 1905) moved from his birthplace of Birmingham,
Alabama, to Chicago, Illinois, and became vice president of the United
Transport Service Employees, CIO.
        Lee W. Minton (b. 1911), a member of the Glass Bottle Blowers
Association, was elected to its executive board in 1938, became union
treasurer in 1945, vice president in 1946, and from 1946 to 1971 he
served as president of the GBBA. In 1956 Minton became AFL-CIO vice
president and member of the executive council.
        Richard F. Walsh (b. 1900) of Brooklyn, New York, was elected president
of Local 4, International Alliance of Theatrical Stage Employees and
Moving Picture Operators from 1924 to 1937. In 1934 he became a vice
president of the union, and in 1941 was elected its president. Walsh
became an AFL-CIO vice president and executive council member in 1955.
        Albert J. Hayes (b. 1900) of Milwaukee, Wisconsin, rose through the
ranks of the International Association of Machinists to become president
in 1949, a position he held until 1965 when he retired. As president he
led the IAM back into the AFL, and served as AFL vice president and
executive council member.
        Ralph Helstein (b. 1908) graduated from the University of Minnesota Law
School in 1934, and served as general council for the United Packinghouse
Workers of America before becoming president in 1946. He also served as
an AFL-CIO vice president and executive council member. When the
Amalgamated Meat Cutters and Butcher Workmen absorbed the UPWA in 1968,
Helstein became president of the union for one term before he retired in
1969.
        Joseph D. Keenan (b. 1896) of Chicago, Illinois, was a member of the
International Brotherhood of Electrical Workers, and rose through the
ranks to become IBEW secretary in 1955. Considered a premier labor
politician, Keenan also served as secretary of the Chicago Federation of
Labor, director of Labor's League for Political Education (AFL), and was
elected secretary-treasurer of the AFL Building and Construction Trades
Department, 1951-1954.
        Emil Mazey (b. 1913), an international representative for the United
Automobile, Aircraft, and Agricultural Implement Workers, organized
Briggs Local 212 in 1937 and served as local president until 1941. He
transferred his loyalties to the United Automobile Workers, however, and
became a co-director of UAW Region I, a member of the UAW executive
board, UAW secretary-treasurer, and acting president in 1948.
        James A. Suffridge (b. 1909) was chief executive officer of an Oakland,
California, local of the Retail Clerks International Protective
Association, before becoming president of the state RCIA, and
international president in 1944. Suffridge also served as an AFL-CIO
vice president, and as vice president of the Union Label Department
before he retired in 1968.
        David Sullivan (1904-1976) immigrated to the United States from Ireland
in 1925, and settled in New York City. One of the founders of New York
Local 32B of the Building Service Employees International Union in 1934,

Sullivan served in various local posts, became international vice-president of the BSEIU in 1941, and international president from 1960 to 1971 when he retired. He also severd as an AFL-CIO vice president and executive council member.

49   Taft-Hartley Act was passed June 23, 1947. Also known as the Labor-Management Relations Act, it reflected the anti-labor sentiment of the post-war period. The Act passed over the veto of President Truman. It regulated the following labor activities: 1) banned the closed shop; 2) allowed employers to sue unions for broken contracts and damages during strikes; 3) established the Federal Mediation and Conciliation Service and required employers to submit a 60 day notice for termination of contract; 4) authorized the U.S. Government to obtain injunctions imposing a cooling off period of 80 days on any strike imperiling the national health or safety; 5) required unions to make public their financial statements; 6) forbade union contributions to political campaigns; 7) ended the check-off system for union dues; 8) required union leaders to take an oath that they were not communists.
        Landrum-Griffin Act was passed September 14, 1959. Also known as the Labor Management Reporting and Disclosure Act, it was designed to eliminate gangsterism, racketeering, and blackmail in labor organizations. In addition it included the following provisions: 1) contained a Bill of Rights for union members which provided for freedom of speech and assembly; 2) guaranteed union members the right to elect their officials; 3) revised the ban on secondary boycotts under the Taft-Hartley Act to prohibit unions from inducing an employer or employee to stop doing business with another firm or handling its goods and to extend the secondary boycott prohibitions to all unions.

50   Cleveland L. Robinson (b. 1914) was born in Jamaica, and after immigrating to the U.S., became secretary-treasurer of District 65, United Auto Workers of New York and New Jersey. He is one of the founders and a past president of the Distributive Workers of America, a founder and president of the National Negro Labor Council, and a founder and first vice president of the Coalition of Black Trade Unionists. He also served as a labor advisor to Martin Luther King, and was administrative chairman of the 1963 March on Washington.

51   For background on Matthew Woll, see Vol. VI, note 72. For David Dubinsky, see Vol. VI, note 136. For William Green, see Vol. VI, note 52.

52   C.O.R.E. is the acronym for Congress of Racial Equality, a civil rights organization founded in 1942 by James Farmer at the University of Chicago. Its tactics included sit-ins and freedom rides. In the late-1960s it changed from an integrationist organization to one of militant self-determination.

53   James C. Petrillo (b. 1892) of Chicago, Ilinois, learned to play the trumpet at Hull House, joined the American Musicians Union, and became its president from 1914 to 1917. Defeated for reelection, he joined the American Federation of Musicians and by 1932 had become a member of the AFM national executive board. In 1940 he was elected president of the AFM, and served as an AFL-CIO vice president from 1958 to 1962.

54   For background on Clarence M. Mitchell, see Vol. VI, note 186.

55   Jack T. Conway (b. 1917) graduated from the University of Chicago in 1940. A member of the American Federation of State, County, and Municipal Employees, he became executive director of the union in 1975. Conway also served as director of the Industrial Union Department, AFL-CIO, as president of Common Cause, and as deputy director of the Office of Equal Opportunity.

56   Andrew J. Biemiller (1906-1982) graduated from Cornell University in 1926, and served as an organizer for the Wisconsin State Federation of

Labor and the Milwaukee Federation of Trade Councils from 1932 to 1942.
In 1936 he was elected to the Wisconsin State Assembly as a Socialist-
Progressive, and then won a seat in the U.S. House in 1945-46, and again
in 1949-1950. He became the chief lobbyist for the AFL-CIO, the position
he held upon retirement in 1978.

Donald Slaiman (b. 1919) of New York graduated from the University of
Buffalo, was a member of the Newspaper Guild, and became deputy director
of Organizations and Field Service of the AFL-CIO in 1974. He also
served as assistant director of the Civil Rights Department from 1964 to
1974.

Jerry Wurf (1919-1981) was an organizer for the New York Hotel and
Restaurant Employees before becoming an organizer for the American
Federation of State, County, and Municipal Employees after World War II.
He became executive director of AFSCME District Council 37 in 1959, and
vice president of the AFL-CIO Industrial Union Department. Wurf served
as president of AFSCME from 1964 to 1981.

Wilbur Daniels (b. 1923) graduated from City College of New York, and
New York University Law School in 1950. He became executive vice
president of the International Ladies' Garment Workers Union in 1973, and
served as a member of the board of directors of the New York Urban
Coalition, and of the executive committee, New York City Manpower Board
from 1970 to 1973.

57   Murray H. Finley (b. 1922) graduated from the University of Michigan in
1946, and Northwestern Law School in 1949. A member of the Amalgamated
Clothing Workers, he became general president of the union in 1972, AFL-
CIO vice president in 1973, and served on the board of directors of the
A. Philip Randolph Institute.

58   Arthur F. Burns (b. 1904), an economist born in Austria, taught at
Rutgers and Columbia universities, and for many years was associated with
the National Bureau of Economic Research. He served as an economic
advisor to Presidents Eisenhower and Nixon, and as chairman of the Board
of Governors of the Federal Reserve System from 1970 to 1978.

59   Benjamin L. Hooks (b. 1925) graduated from Howard University in 1944,
and took his law degree from DePaul University in 1948. An Afro-
American, Hooks practiced law in Memphis, Tennessee, until 1966 when he
became county judge. Hooks also became a Baptist pastor in Memphis and
Detroit from 1956 to 1964, and 1964 to 1972 respectively. In 1972 he was
appointed a member of the Federal Communications Commission (1972-1978),
and in 1977 became the executive director of the National Associaton for
the Advancement of Colored People.

60   Proposition 13 was a ballot initiative approved by voters in California
in June, 1978 to reduce property taxes about 57%. The measure went into
effect July 1, 1978 but was immediately challenged by school districts,
educational groups, counties and cities. They argued that the
proposition was unconstitutional based on the equal protection clause
(inequitable treatment of property owners). The proposition was also
challenged on the grounds that it was not restricted to one topic. The
California Supreme Court upheld the constitutionality of the legislation
on September 22, 1978. It was estimated that local governments lost
approximately 7 billion dollars in property tax revenue. The proposition
was attacked by civil rights groups for its disasterous effect on social
welfare programs.

61   Joseph Lane Kirkland (b. 1922) graduated from the Merchant Marine
Academy and worked as a seaman before joining the AFL's research staff in
1948. In 1953 he became director of the AFL Social Security Department,
and served as executive assistant to George Meany, president of the AFL-
CIO. Kirkland became secretary-treasurer of the AFL-CIO in 1969, and
when Meany retired in 1979, became president of the federation.

62   Thomas R. Donahue graduated from Manhattan College in 1949, and took
his law degree from Fordham in 1956. A member of Local 32 B of the

Service Employees International Union, he was appointed assistant secretary for labor management relations, U.S. Department of Labor, from 1967 to 1969. From 1969 to 1973 he served as executive secretary and first vice president of the SEIU, then became executive assistant to the president of the AFL-CIO in 1973.

Frederick D. O'Neal (b. 1905), Afro-American actor and director, co-founder of American Negro Theater (New York 1940) was elected international president of the Associated Actors and Artists of America in 1970, and had served as president of the Actors Equity Association when he became president emeritus in 1973. O'Neal also was an AFL-CIO vice president, and chairman of the AFL-CIO Civil Rights Committee.

63   Eugene T. ("Bull") Connor was the police commissioner of Birmingham, Alabama, during the spring of 1963 when civil rights demonstrations led to the incarceration of Martin Luther King. A staunch segregationist, Connor turned loose K-9 dogs, fire hoses, and police clubs against the civil rights demonstrators in a fashion which shocked the nation.

64   For background on Michael J. Quill, see Vol. VII, note 14.

65   For background on John L. Lewis, see Vol. VI, note 68 and note 126.

66   Joseph L. Rauh, Jr. (b. 1911) graduated from Harvard University in 1932, and Harvard Law School in 1935. He served as vice chairperson of Americans for Democratic Action, and on the board of the National Association for the Advancement of Colored People, and as general counsel for the Leadership Conference on Civil Rights. From 1969 to 1972 Rauh acted as general counsel for Miners for Democracy, a reform group within the United Mine Workers of America.

67   John C. Stennis (b. 1901), a graduate of Mississippi State University, and the University of Virginia Law School in 1928, he immediately entered Mississippi politics. Stennis was elected to the state House of Representatives, became a judge, and was elected U.S. senator from Mississippi in 1947. A Democrat, he strenuously resisted the civil rights measures of the Kennedy and Johnson administrations.

Richard B. Russell (1897-1971) took his law degree from the University of Georgia in 1918 and entered politics. He was a state assemblyman from 1921 to 1930, governor of Georgia from 1930 to 1933, and Democratic U.S. senator from Georgia from 1933 to 1971. Russell was a major foe of civil rights reforms, and led numerous filabusters against such reforms.

68   The original document is incomplete.

69   Andrew F. Brimmer (b. 1926) graduated from the University of Washington, and received a Ph.D. from Harvard University in 1957. A member of the Board of Governors of the U.S. Federal Reserve System since 1966, Brimmer, an Afro-American, had served in various positions including a professorship at Harvard, and in Business Economic Research at DuPont Company.

70   For background on Marcus Garvey, see Vol. VI, note 32. For background on W. E. B. Du Bois, see Vol. IV, note 136.

71   For background on Executive Order 8802, see Vol. VII, p. 210.

72   John H. Rousselot (b. 1927), a graduate of Principia College, 1949, was a congressman from California from 1961 to 1963, and from 1970 to 1983. The owner of a public relations firm, Rousselot was an arch-conservative in politics, a member of the John Birch Society, and fought to have another California congressman, Thomas H. Kuchel, removed from office for being too liberal.

73   Ross R. Barnett (b. 1898) graduated from Mississippi College in 1922, and the University of Mississippi Law School in 1926. He practiced law

in Jackson, Mississippi, and made two unsuccessful bids for governor before winning the office in 1959. An adamant segregationist, he forcefully resisted desegregation, perhaps attracting the most attention in 1962 for his role in attempting to prevent James Meredith from becoming the first Afro-American to enroll in the University of Mississippi.

James O. Eastland (b. 1904) was educated at the University of Mississippi (1922-1924), Vanderbilt University (1925-1926), and the University of Alabama (1926-1927). He entered the practice of law in Mississippi, and was elected to the state House of Representatives from 1928 to 1932. In 1941 he was appointed to the U.S. Senate to fill an unexpired term, and subsequently won election to the Senate from 1943 to 1978. An arch-opponent of desegregation, Eastland opposed all civil rights reforms, including the acts of 1964, 1965, and 1968.

74   Paul Hall (1914-1980) was one of the founding members of the Seafarers International Union of North America in 1938, became its first vice president in 1948, and president in 1957. He also served as president of the AFL-CIO Maritime Trades Department, and an AFL-CIO vice president in 1962.

75   For background on Adam Clayton Powell, Jr., see Vol. VII, note 36.
Luigi Antonini (1883-1968) was born in Italy, immigrated to New York, and founded Local 89 International Ladies' Garment Workers Union in 1919. From 1934 to 1968 he served as vice president of the international. Antonini was active politically. He was a founder of the Liberal Party in New York, served as state chairperson of the American Labor Party, and was president of the Italian-American Labor Council.

76   Herbert Zelenko (b. 1906) graduated from Columbia College in 1926, and Columbia Law School in 1928. He was appointed assistant U.S. attorney in 1933-1934, and elected to the U.S. House of Representatives from New York from 1954 to 1962.

77   Louis D. Brandeis (1856-1941) received his law degree from Harvard University in 1878 and conducted private practice in Boston until 1916, when President Woodrow Wilson appointed him to the U.S. Supreme Court. As a justice from 1916 to 1939, Brandeis was aligned with Justices Holmes and Cardozo in supporting social reforms.

78   Douglas A. Fraser (b. 1916) immigrated to the United States from Scotland. In 1943 he was elected president of Local 227, United Automobile, Aerospace and Agricultural Implement Workers of America. He rose through the ranks of the union as administrative assistant to UAW president Walter Reuther, co-director of UAW Region 1-A in 1959, vice president in 1970, and UAW president from 1977 to 1983. As president of his union, Fraser was a member of the AFL executive council.

79   The John Birch Society is an ultraconservative organization founded in 1958 by Robert Welch, Jr., a retired businessman. The society has actively campaigned for U.S. withdrawal from the United Nations, repeal of social security and the income tax, and withdrawal of recognition of the Soviet Union, among other right-wing causes.

80   Rosa Parks (b. 1913) attended Alabama State College, and became active in the Montgomery NAACP. Her refusal to give up her seat on a Montgomery city bus to a white passenger triggered her arrest, and the Montgomery Bus Boycott which resulted in the desegregation of city buses in 1956. For her action she has come to be known as "the Mother of the Modern Civil Rights Movement."

81   For background on Joseph R. McCarthy, see Vol. VII, note 206.

82   SNCC is the acronym for Student Non-Violent Coordinating Committee, a civil rights organization founded in 1960. It was particularly effective

in desegregating lunch counters in the South. By 1966, under the leadership of Stokely Carmichael, SNCC changed its orientation from integration to militant self-determination. After 1969 it became virtually defunct.

83   Malcolm X (1925-1965), born Malcolm Little, served six years in prison from 1946 to 1952. In prison he became a Black Muslim, and, after his release, joined the New York Muslim Temple. He soon became the leading minister in the national organization, but resigned in 1964 because of personal and ideological differences between himself and Elijah Muhammad, the leader of the Muslims. Malcolm X adopted a black nationalist and confrontational approach, rather than withdrawal which characterized the Muslims, and Malcolm had great appeal among the black urban masses. He was assassinated on February 21, 1965.
        CPUSA refers to the Communist Party of the U.S.A.

84   The Black Panther Party was organized in October 1966 in Oakland, Ca., by Bobby Seale and Huey Newton. They spearheaded a revolutionary movement which departed from the nonviolent philosophy of the civil rights movement, and appealed to the poor black urban ghetto dweller. Self-defense and self-determination for the black community became their watchwords, and they often referred to themselves as "the children of Malcolm X." The Panthers were Marxists as well, and frequently quoted the works of Mao Tse-Tung, Lenin, and Marx. Numerous confrontations between police and Panthers in the big cities resulted in many of them being jailed or killed.

85   The Attica prison riot occurred Sept. 9-13, 1971 at New York State's maximum-security facility near Buffalo. The revolt involved 1,000 inmates who seized control of the prison taking 38 guards and employees. On Sept. 13 state troopers and prison guards took the prison by force, killing 29 prisoners and 10 hostages in the process. An investigation criticized the state's methods.

86   James Forman (b. 1929) graduated from Roosevelt University in 1951, taught school in Chicago, and became executive secretary of the Student Non-Violent Coordinating Committee from 1964 to 1968, and director of International Affairs in 1969. He was the author of the "Black Manifesto" calling for reparations to blacks for past wrongs, and wrote *The Making of Black Revolutionaries* (1972).

87   For background on Joseph V. Stalin, see Vol. VII, note 201.

88   Ho Chi Minh (Nguyen That Thanh, 1890-1969), organized the Indochinese Communist Party in 1930, and later the Vietminh. He led a guerrilla war against the Japanese during World War II, and assisted in the liberation of Hanoi in 1945. After the war he became president of the Independent Republic of Vietnam in 1945, but relinquished the title in 1955 when the country was split, and became the leader of North Vietnam. He led the nation through two wars with France and the United States for political reunification. He was regarded as the embodiment of an independent, unified Vietnam.

89   Henry A. Kissinger (b. 1923) received a Ph.D. from Harvard University in 1954. A naturalized U.S. citizen born in Germany, he became a professor of government at Harvard specializing in foreign relations until 1969. In that year he was appointed President Richard Nixon's director of the National Security Council (1969-1975). From 1973 to 1977 he served as Nixon's secretary of state, winning the Nobel Peace Prize in 1973 for his role in bringing an end to the Vietnam War.

90   George C. Wallace (b. 1919) received his law degree from the University of Alabama in 1942, and was appointed assistant attorney general of Alabama in 1946-1947. From 1947 to 1953 he served in the state legislature, and as a state judge from 1953 to 1958. Wallace was elected

to the Governor's Office for several terms: 1963–1966, and 1971–1979.
He was a candidate for president on the American Independent Party ticket
in 1968, and a candidate in the Democratic presidential primary in 1972,
and 1976.

91   Cyril Lionel Robert James (c. 1901), a prominent West Indian scholar
active in the Pan-African movement, and the struggle to decolonize the
West Indies and Africa, came to the U.S. in the 1960s and attracted a
following of young radical scholars. A marxist, James is the author of
numerous books, one of the best known of which is *The Black Jacobins,
Toussaint L'Ouverture and the San Domingo Revolution* (1938).

92   Frank E. Fitzsimmons (1908–1981), a member of the International
Brotherhood of Teamsters, Chauffeurs, Warehousemen, and Helpers of
America, rose through the ranks to become vice president and member of
the Executive Board in 1961. In 1967 he become president of the
Teamsters, and held that office until 1981 when he was forced to resign
under charges of fraud.
        William Anthony ("Tony") Boyle (b. 1904–1984)) attended schools in
Montana and Idaho and then became a coal miner. He was elected president
of United Mine Workers of America District 27 (Montana), and held that
position until 1948 when he became a regional director for the CIO and
UMWA District 50. From 1948 to 1960 he was John L. Lewis' assistant, and
UMWA vice-president, 1960–1963. He was acting president of the UMWA from
1962–1963, and elected international president in 1963. He was opposed
for the UMWA presidency in 1969 in a close, bitter election by Joseph
Yablonski who was murdered shortly thereafter, and Boyle was defeated by
Arnold Miller   in 1972. Subsequently, Boyle was convicted for ordering
the murder and sentenced to life in prison.
        Cornelius J. Haggerty (1894–1971) served as president of Local 42,
International Union of Wood, Wire, and Metal Lathers in California. From
1937 to 1943 he served as president of the California State Federation of
Labor, and then as secretary from 1943 to 1960. He became vice president
of the International, and president of the AFL–CIO Building and
Construction Trades Department in 1960.

93   Jesse M. Unruh (b. 1922) graduated from the University of Southern
California in 1948, and was elected to the California Assembly for 1954–
1970. He was Southern California manager of John F. Kennedy's
presidential campaign in 1960, and chairperson of Robert Kennedy's
California presidential campaign in 1968. In 1970 he was an unsuccessful
candidate for governor of California. Organized labor considered him an
unreliable supporter.
        For George Wallace, see note 90.
        Spiro T. Agnew (b. 1918), 39th vice president of the U.S. (1969–1973),
resigned from office when he was fined for income tax evasion. Born in
Baltimore, he received a law degree from the University of Baltimore in
1947, practiced law in that city, and became active in local politics. A
reform Republican, he was elected chief executive of predominantly
Democratic Baltimore County in 1962. Democrats also helped elect him
governor of Maryland in 1966. In 1968 Richard Nixon tapped him as his
running mate. While vice president he made numerous controversial
speeches denouncing the press, liberals, and college students and
faculty.
        For Joseph McCarthy, see note 81. For Ronald Reagan, see note 18.
        Richard J. Daley (1902–1976) took a law degree at DePaul University in
1933. He was elected as a Democrat to the Illinois House of
Representatives in 1936–1938, and the state Senate in 1939–1946. From
1950 to 1955 he served as clerk for Cook County, and was elected mayor of
Chicago from 1955 to 1976. He was one of the most powerful city bosses
in American history.

94   For background on *Plessy v. Ferguson* , see Vol. IV, p. 298.

95   This sentence is incomplete in the original.

96   Jesse Jackson (b. 1941) graduated from North Carolina A&T College in 1964, and received a D.D. from the Chicago Theological Seminary in 1966. Jackson was active in the civil rights movement, and in 1967 was appointed national director of SCLC's Operation Breadbasket by Dr. Martin Luther King. Later he became national president of Operation PUSH. In 1984 he became the first serious contender for the presidential nomination of the Democratic Party.
        James Farmer (b. 1920) graduated from Wiley College in Texas, and received a B.D. from Howard University in 1941. Farmer was the founder of the Congress of Racial Equality in 1941, and became National Chairman from 1941 to 1944, and national director from 1961 to 1966. He also served as race relations secretary of the Fellowship of Reconciliation from 1941 to 1945, and as program director of the NAACP from 1959 to 1961. He helped plan the Freedom Rides of 1961, and has served in numerous other public capacities.

97   "Mr. Hayes" refers to Charles Hayes. For Hayes see note 44.

98   Operation PUSH refers to the organization founded by Jesse Jackson in Chicago. The acronym stands for People United to Save Humanity, and is involved in various programs to assist poor blacks.

99   Ralph Metcalf (b. 1910), a graduate of Marquette University, and the University of Southern California, was a member of the 1931 and 1936 U.S. Olympic track teams. He was director of the Department of Civil Rights Commission on Human Relations in Chicago from 1945 to 1949, and alderman from 1955 to 1971. In 1970 he was elected to the U.S. House of Representatives, serving until 1979. He openly broke with Mayor Richard Daley over the issue of police brutality concerning the death of two members of the Black Panther Party in Chicago in 1969.

100   Operation Breadbasket was founded by the Southern Christian Leadership Conference in 1967 to assist in the distribution of care to poor, primarily black people in need of food.

101   Paul H. Douglas (1892–1976) received a Ph.D. from Columbia University in 1921. He was a professor of economics at several universities, and received the Sidney Hillman Award in 1957. From 1949 to 1966 he served as Democratic senator from Illinois.

102   George S. McGovern (b. 1922) received a Ph.D. from Northwestern University in 1953, and was a professor of history. After serving as a congressman from South Dakota, he became U.S. senator from 1963 to 1981. He was the unsuccessful Democratic candidate for president in 1972, and an unsuccessful candidate for the Democratic nomination for president in 1984.
        Sargent Shriver (Robert Sargent, Jr., b. 1915) received a law degree from Yale University in 1941, and was assistant editor of *Newsweek* in 1945–1946. A brother-in-law of President John Kennedy, Shriver was appointed director of the Peace Corps in 1961, and director of the Office of Economic Opportunity from 1964 to 1968. He was ambassador to France in 1968–1970, and Democratic candidate for vice president in 1972.

103   Edward Todd was appointed Midwest director of the Textile Workers Union of America in 1966, and served on the executive board of the Coalition of Black Trade Unionists.

104   Nelson Jack Edwards (1923?–1974) of Detroit, Michigan, was a member of the United Auto Workers for thirty-seven years, and the first black vice president of the UAW. He was murdered in a Detroit bar following an argument with another patron.

105   Hilton E. Hanna (b. 1907) was born in the West Indies, immigrated to the United States, and received degrees from Talladega College (1933),

and the University of Wisconsin (1949). A member of the Amalgamated Meat Cutters and Butcher Workmen, he became international vice president and executive assistant to the MCBW president, and international secretary-treasurer in 1972. Hanna also was president of the Eugene V. Debs Foundation, and president of the Madison, Wisconsin, Urban League, 1969–1972.

106   William L. Clay (b. 1931) graduated from St. Louis University in 1953, and entered city politics. He served as business agent for AFSME from 1961 to 1964, and as Democratic committeeman of the 26th Ward. He was active in the NAACP and CORE, and helped to open many unions to blacks before being elected to the U.S. House of Representatives.

107   Horace Julian Bond (b. 1940) of Atlanta, Georgia, graduated from Morehouse College in 1971. The son of the prominent black scholar, Horace Mann Bond, Julian has served in numerous public capacities, and was a founder of the Student Non-Violent Coordinating Committee (SNCC) in 1960. He is best known for having been elected to the Georgia House of Representatives in 1966 but barred, elected again and barred. After the third election in 1967 he was seated and still holds that post.

108   "Zieglers, Hartovans, Erlichmans, Schultzes, Kissingers, Klines" refers to President Richard Nixon's White House assistants some liberals characterized as "Nixon's Gestapos."

109   James McGregor Burns (b. 1918) graduated from Williams College in 1939, and received a Ph.D. from Harvard University in 1947. He joined the faculty of Williams College in 1941, and remained there throughout his professional career with several periods of public service. A prominent author, his books include *Roosevelt: The Lion and the Fox* (1956), *John Kennedy: A Political Profile* (1960), and *Roosevelt: The Soldier of Freedom* (1970). He won the 1971 Pulitzer Prize, and the National Book Award in History.

110   E. Franklin Frazier (1894–1962) received a Ph.D. from the University of Chicago in 1931. He was director of the Atlanta School of Social Work from 1922 to 1927, professor of Sociology at Fisk University (1927–1954), and chairperson of the Department of Sociology at Howard University from 1934 to 1959. His books include: *The Negro Family in Chicago* (1932); *The Free Negro Family* (1932); *The Negro Family in the United States* (1939); *Negro Youth at the Crossroads* (1940); *The Negro in the United States* (1949); *Race and Culture Contacts in the Modern World* (1957); *Black Bourgeoisie* (1957); *The Negro Church in America* (1964).

111   For background on Benjamin ("Pitchfork Ben") Tillman, see Vol. III, note 60.

112   Michael J. Mansfield (b. 1903–1972) graduated from the University of Montana in 1933, and received a M.A. from the same institution in 1934. After working as a mining engineer, and as a professor of history at U.M. (1933–1942), he was elected to the U.S. House of Representatives (1943–1953), and then to the U.S. Senate (1953–1976). A Democrat, Mansfield was majority leader of the Senate from 1961 to 1976. In 1977 he was appointed ambassador to Japan.
        Edward M. Kennedy (b. 1932) graduated from Harvard University in 1954, and received a law degree from the University of Virginia in 1959. The youngest brother of President John F. Kennedy, he entered politics, and in 1962 was elected U.S. senator from Massachusetts. He is one of the most liberal senators on civil rights issues.
        Rupert Vance Hartke (b. 1919) graduated from Evansville College, and received a law degree from Indiana University. He practiced law in Evansville, Indiana, from 1948 to 1958. He also was elected mayor of Evansville from 1956 to 1958 before his election to the U.S. Senate in 1958, where he served until 1976. In 1972 he was a candidate in the Democratic presidential primary. He was an opponent of the Vietnam war.

Philip Hart (1912-1976) graduated from Georgetown University, and received a law degree from the University of Michigan in 1937. He practiced law in Michigan until 1955 when he ws elected Lt. Governor, a post he held until he was elected to the U.S. Senate, 1959-1976. He was instrumental in shaping Democratic legislation on civil rights.

Howard M. Metzenbaum (b. 1917) graduated from Ohio State University, and OSU Law School in 1941. A native of Cleveland, he served in the Ohio House of Representatives 1943-1946, and in the Ohio State Senate 1947-1950. In 1974 he was elected as a Democrat to the U.S. Senate, where he is considered a strong supporter of civil rights, and a friend of organized labor.

Edmund Muskie (b. 1914) graduated from Bates College, and received a law degree from Cornell University in 1939. He practiced law in Waterville, Maine, until 1955 when he was elected governor. From 1959 to 1980 he served as U.S. senator from Maine, and was appointed secretary of state in 1980. He was the unsuccessful Democratic nominee for president in 1968.

113   For background on Philip Murray, see Vol. VII, note 34.

114   Peter Bommarito (b. 1915) of Detroit, Michigan, a member of the United Rubber, Cork, Linoleum and Plastic Workers of America, rose through the ranks to become international president of the URW in 1966. He has also served as vice president of the AFL-CIO, and as vice president of its Industrial Union Department.

115   Mahatma Gandhi (1869-1948) of India practiced law in Bombay, and in South Africa between 1893 and 1915. He gained international fame as the leader of protests against British colonial rule in India, and spent most of his adult life working for Indian independence through nonviolent acts of civil disobedience. One year after independence was achieved in 1947 he was assassinated.

116   Anatoly B. Scharansky (b. 1948) graduated from the Moscow Physical-Technical Institute in 1972, and was employed at the Oil and Gas Research Institute. A major figure in the struggle of Russian Jews to emigrate from the Soviet Union, he was denied a visa, and convicted of treason and espionage in 1978. He was sentenced to three years of prison and ten years of forced labor. Scharansky's case received wide publicity during President Carter's campaign to improve human rights in the world.

117   Iorwith W. Abel (b. 1908) of Magnolia, Ohio, helped to organize the first CIO local at Canton Timken Roller Bearing Co. in 1936, and participated in the "Little Steel" strike in 1937. In 1942 he became director of the Canton District of the United Steelworkers of America. He was elected secretary-treasurer of the United Steelworkers of America, and then president of the union in 1965. A vice president of the AFL-CIO, he became president of the Industrial Union Department in 1968.

118   William W. Scranton (b. 1917) received a B.A. from Yale University in 1939, and an LL.B. from Yale Law School in 1946. He was elected to the U.S. House of Representatives from Pennsylvania in 1961-1963, and as governor of Pennsylvania 1963-1967. He held numerous special appointments under Presidents Johnson and Nixon.

119   Wade H. McCree, Jr. (b. 1920) graduated from Fisk University in 1941, and received a law degree from Harvard Law School in 1948. He served as a commissioner on the Workmen's Compensation Commission from 1948-1954, and as judge on the Wayne County, Michigan, Circuit Court 1954-1961. From 1961 to 1966 he served as a justice on the U.S. District Court, and was appointed to the U.S. Circuit Court of Appeals in 1966.

Charles C. Diggs, Jr. (b. 1922) graduated from Wayne State University in 1946, and the Detroit College of Law in 1952. From 1951 to 1954 he was a state senator to the Michigan House from Detroit, and in 1955 he was elected to the U.S. House of Representatives. He is a founder and past chairman of the Congressional Black Caucus.

120   Rule 22 of the U.S. Senate required 2/3 of the total Senate body to limit and to close debate. After the merger of the AFL-CIO the federation supported a curb on filibustering by "strongly supporting" a change in Rule 22 to require 1/2 of the Senators to vote to close debate.

121   For background on Wayne L. Morse, see Vol. VII, note 119.

122   Ken Bannon (b. 1914) of Scranton, Pennsylvania, became vice president of the United Auto Workers in 1970. He had served as a member of the UAW International Executive Board, and as director of the UAW National Ford Department, and as an organizer in Detroit prior to this position.

123   Ronald V. Dellums (b. 1935) graduated from San Francisco State in 1960, and earned an M.A. from the University of California in 1962. An Afro-American, he entered politics and served on the Berkeley City Council, 1967-1971, before being elected to the U.S. House of Representatives from California's 8th District in 1971.

124   For background on Robert F. Wagner, see Vol. VII, note 136.

125   Richard J. Hughes (b. 1909) received a law degree from the New Jersey Law School in 1931. He served as assistant U.S. district attorney in New Jersey from 1939 to 1945, as Mercer County judge, 1948-952, and as New Jersey Superior Court judge, 1952-1959. He became governor of New Jersey in 1962, and held that post until 1970. In 1973 he became chief justice of the New Jersey Supreme Court, serving until 1979.

126   Peter J. Brennan (b. 1918) of New York, a member of the Brotherhood of Painters, Decorators and Paperhangers of America, became president of the Construction Trades Council of Greater New York in 1957, and vice president of the New York State AFL-CIO. He was criticized by civil rights leaders for discriminatory hiring practices in the New York Building Trades, and organized New York construction workers support for President Nixon's Vietnam war policies. Nixon appointed him U.S. Secretary of Labor in 1972.

127   Harry Van Arsdale, Jr. (b. 1905) of New York was a member of the International Brotherhood of Electrical Workers. From 1933 to 1968 he was business manager of Local 3, New York, and became president of the Greater New York Central Trades and Labor Council in 1957. After successfully organizing the New York City Taxi Drivers Union in 1965, he became president of Local 3036. He also served as treasurer of the IBEW, and was a member of the executive board of the Building and Construction Trades Council.

128   For background on Robert C. Weaver, see Vol. VI, note 25.

129   Gordon M. Freeman (b. 1896) was international vice president of the International Brotherhood of Electrical Workers.
       Peter T. Schoemann (b. 1893) was a member of the United Association of Journeymen and Apprentices of the Plumbing and Pipe Fitting Industry of the United States and Canada who rose through the ranks to become president of the union. From 1955 to 1972 he served as vice president of the AFL-CIO, and was a member of its Committee on Education.
       Edward J. Leonard (b. 1904), a member of the Operative Plasterers and Cement Masons' International Association of the United States and Canada, became president of the union from 1958 to 1970.
       John H. Lyons (b. 1919), a graduate of the Missouri School of Mines, and a member of the International Association of Bridge and Structural Iron Workers, became president of the union in 1961.
       Hunter P. Wharton (b. 1900), a member of the International Union of Operating Engineers, became its president in 1962, and served as an AFL-CIO vice president.
       Thomas F. Murphy (b. 1910), a member of the Bricklayers, Masons and Plasterers International Union of America, rose in the organization to the position of president in 1966. He also became vice president of the Union Label and Service Trades Department, AFL-CIO, in 1974.

Peter Fosco was president of the 60,000-member Laborers International Union of North America. He was a staunch supporter of the Nixon Administration, and President Nixon presented him with the Columbus Day Man of the Year Award in 1972.

Lawrence M. Raftery (b. 1895), a member of the International Brotherhood of Painters and Allied Trades of the United States and Canada, became its president between 1957 and 1965.

Wilbur D. Mills (b. 1909) attended Harvard Law School (1930–1933), and became a county and probate judge in Arkansas. From 1939 to 1977 he was elected U.S. Representative from Arkansas, and served as chairman of the powerful Ways and Means Committee from 1957 to 1974. Personal indiscretions and alcoholism prompted his party to strip him of power.

James Haughton (b. 1930) received a B.A. from City College of New York, and an M.A. from New York University. He helped organize the Negro-American Labor Council, and became identified as a militant champion of black construction workers, leading protests against builders, unions, and the government for more equal opportunity for blacks on construction sites in New York. Working out of his headquarters at the Harlem Unemployment Center, in 1969 he was involved in negotiations to hire more minorities at the building site of the World Trade Center in New York City.

130   Walter E. Williams (b. 1936) of Philadelphia, Pa., received a B.A. from California State University, and a Ph.D. in economics from UCLA in 1972. A professor of economics, Williams is one of the few black conservatives in that fraternity.

131   Leon J. Davis (b. 1912) was born in Russia and immigrated to New York where he attended Columbia School of Pharmacy (1927–1929), and became a pharmacist. He helped organize and became president of District 1199, National Union of Hospital and Health Care Employees, an affiliate of the Retail, Wholesale, and Department Store Union. He also served as international vice president of RWDSU. In 1981 he resigned as president of NUHHCE, and as president of 1199 in 1982.

132   For background on Herbert H. Lehman, see Vol. VII, note 143.

Moe Foner (b. 1915), executive secretary of Local 1199, National Union of Hospital and Health Care Employees, retired and was granted emeritus status in 1983. He is also deeply involved in the cultural program maintained by 1199.

133   James Baldwin (b. 1924), a prominent Afro-American novelist, was active in the civil rights movement during the 1960s. Among his numerous works are: Go Tell It on the Mountain (1953); Notes of a Native Son (1955); Giovanni's Room (1958); Nobody Knows My Name (1960); Another Country (1962); The Fire Next Time (1963); Going To Meet the Man (1966); Tell Me How Long the Train's Been Gone (1968); No Name in the Street (1972); One Day When I Lost (1973); If Beale Street Could Talk (1974); The Devil Finds Work (1976); Just Above My Head (1979); one play, Blues for Mr. Charlie (1964), and numerous articles.

134   For background on Norman Thomas, see Vol. VI, note 52.

William F. Ryan (1922–1972) received a law degree from Columbia University, and was assistant district attorney in Manhattan from 1950 to 1957. He was elected to the U.S. House of Representatives from New York in 1961 and served in that post until 1972. A liberal, he backed most of the civil rights bills which came before Congress. He was an early proponent of a permanent civil rights commission, and fought hard to end segregation in interstate travel.

135   For background on Frederick Douglass, see Vol. I, notes 8, 12, and 21.

136   Bella S. Abzug (b. 1920) of New York graduated from Hunter College in 1942, and took a law degree from Columbia University in 1945. She has practiced law since then, except for the period from 1971 to 1977 when she was elected to the U.S. House of Representatives from New York. She practiced labor law in the 1950s, became known as an outspoken opponent of the Vietnam war, and a flamboyant feminist.

137   Len Seelig was an organizer for 1199 in New York and Connecticut, and a
       vice president of the union. On October 3, 1971 he was killed in an
       automobile accident at age 41.

138   Robert E. McNair (b. 1923) graduated from the University of South
       Carolina in 1947, and received a law degree from U.S.C. in 1948. He
       entered politics as a Democrat, and was elected state representative
       1951-1962, lt. governor of South Carolina 1962-1965, and governor 1965-
       1971. After leaving office he continued to practice law, and sat on the
       board of directors of several corporations.

139   Ossie Davis (b. 1917) attended Howard University (1935-1938) and became
       an actor and writer. In 1948 he married actress Ruby Dee, and they have
       worked closely since then. He has acted on stage, film, television, and
       radio. He was writer, director, and actor in the film *Purlie Victorious,*
       and wrote the screenplay for *Cotton Comes to Harlem* (1969). He was
       closely associated with the civil rights movement and its leaders.
       Ruby Dee (b. 1923) graduated from Hunter College in 1945 and became an
       actress on stage, film, television, and radio. She won the Obie Award in
       1971, and the Drama Desk Award in 1974 among other honors. She also
       wrote *Glowchild* , and *Uptight.*

140   Ralph D. Abernathy (b. 1926) graduated from Alabama State College in
       1950, received an M.A. in sociology from Atlanta University in 1951, and
       was ordained a Baptist minister in 1948. He organized numerous civil
       rights demonstrations during the 1950s and 1960s, and initiated the
       Montgomery Bus Boycott of 1955. He was organizer, secretary-treasurer,
       vice president, and president of the Southern Christian Leadership
       Conference.

141   Strom Thurmond (b. 1902) was born in Edgefield, South Carolina, and
       received a B.S. from Clemson University in 1923. After teaching for
       several years during the twenties, he was admitted to the bar and
       practiced law during the thirties. He was elected to the South Carolina
       state senate from 1933 to 1938, and became a circuit judge from 1938 to
       1946, with several years break in his tenure while serving in the armed
       forces. From 1947 to 1951 he served as governor of South Carolina, and
       became a U.S. senator in 1954. A staunch states rights conservative, he
       became known for his resistance to the civil rights movement.
       L. Mendel Rivers (1905-1970) attended the College of Charleston, and
       law school at the University of South Carolina. He commenced to practice
       law in Charleston in 1932, and was elected to the state House of
       Representatives from 1933 to 1936. In 1936 he was elected to the U.S.
       Congress from South Carolina where he served until his death. He was a
       political ally of Strom Thurmond and resisted the civil rights movement.

142   Dorothy I. Height (b. 1913) of Richmond, Virginia, received the B.S.
       and the M.S. degrees from New York University. She began her career with
       the YWCA in 1937, and rose through the ranks to become director of the
       Center for Racial Justice (YWCA). In 1957 she became national president
       of the National Council of Negro Women.

143   Shirley Anita St. Hill Chisholm (b. 1924) graduated from Brooklyn
       College, and received an M.A. from Columbia University. She became a
       congresswoman from the 12th Cong. Dist. of New York, and in 1972 became
       the first woman to ever actively run for the presidency. She is the
       author of two books: *Unbought and Unbossed* (1970), and *The Good Fight*
       (1973).
       John Conyers (b. 1929) of Detroit, Michigan, graduated from Wayne State
       University in 1957, and received a law degree from that institution in
       1958. He has served in the U.S. House of Representatives since 1964. He
       clashed with the Nixon administration in 1969 over extending the 1965
       Voting Rights Act, and over Nixon's Vietnam war politics. Conyers also
       served as general counsel for the Trade Union Leadership Council.
       Carl B. Stokes (b. 1927) graduated from the University of Minnesota in
       1954, and received a law degree from Cleveland-Marshall Law School in
       1956. From 1958 to 1962 he was assistant prosecutor of Cleveland, and

served in the Ohio House of Representatives from 1962 to 1967. Stokes
was elected mayor of Cleveland in 1967 and served until 1971, the first
black mayor of a large American city.

144   For Harriet Tubman, see Vol. VII, note 70. For Sojourner Truth, see
Vol. II, note 86. For Rosa Parks, see note 80.
    Fannie Lou Hamer was forty-four when she learned about SNCC at a
meeting on voter registration in 1962. Born the youngest of twenty
children of black sharecroppers in Sunflower County, Mississippi, she
joined the organization and became a stalwart and able staff member. She
was arrested while attempting to register to vote in Indianola, and while
in jail she was beaten so severely that she never completely recovered
from her injuries.

145   Fred R. Harris (b. 1930) received a B.A. degree from the University of
Oklahoma, and an LL.B. in 1954 from the same institution. From 1956 to
1964 he served in the Oklahoma State Senate, and was elected to the U.S.
Senate from Oklahoma in 1964 serving until 1972. He is the author of two
books on politics, and is a professor of political science at the
University of New Mexico.
    Ralph W. Yarborough (b. 1903) received a law degree from the University
of Texas in 1927. He became assistant attorney general of Texas, 1931–
1934, and then a district judge, 1936–1941. In 1957 Texans elected him
to the U.S. Senate where he served until 1971. In 1975 he became a
professor of political science at the University of Texas.
    Edward W. Brooke (b. 1919) graduated from Howard University in 1941,
and received a law degree from Boston University in 1948. He served as
the attorney general of Massachusetts from 1963 to 1967, and was elected
to the U.S. Senate from 1967 to 1979, the first Afro-American to gain a
seat in that body in the 20th century.

Abdul-Jabbar, Kareem, 465
Abel, Iorwith W., 224, 232, 287, 392, 296, 399, n 117
Abernathy, Ralph David, 194, 405, 477, 487, 496, 509, 512, 513, 516, 517, 521, 522, 524, 528, 532, 534, 535, n 140
Abzug, Bella S., 475, 544, n 136
Afro-American League of the U.S., 340
Agnew, Spiro, 234, 269, 337, 351, 355, n 93
Ahlgren, Frank R., 409
Alcindor, Lew, 465
Alda, Alan, 538
Aldridge, Rev. John W., 419
Alexander, Kelly M., 134
Ali, Muhammad, 546
Allegheny County Labor Council, 391
Allen, Hazel, 308
Alliance for Labor Action, 278, 327
Allied Industrial Workers of America, 93, 364
Alperin, Matthew, 549
Alvarenga, Joyce, 490
Amalgamated Clothing and Textile Workers Union, 114, 287, 312, 364, 445, 542
Amalgamated Meat Cutters and Butcher Workmen (AMCBU), 70, 102, 192, 333, 347, 352, 361, 364, 366, 369, 370, 371
American Committee on Africa, 305
American Federation of Government Employees, 86, 364
AFL-CIO, 16, 33, 34, 35, 36, 49, 50, 51, 52, 53, 54, 55, 56, 57, 58, 59, 60, 61, 62, 63, 64, 65, 66, 67, 70, 71, 72, 73, 74, 75, 76, 77, 78, 79, 81, 82, 85, 92, 93, 94, 97, 98, 100, 102, 103, 105, 106, 107, 108, 109, 110, 111, 112, 113, 114, 115, 116, 117, 118, 119, 120, 121, 123, 124, 126, 127, 128, 131, 132, 133, 134, 135, 136, 137, 160, 161, 162, 163, 164, 166, 167, 168
American Federation of Labor (AFL) 290, 291
AFL-CIO Building and Construction Trades Department, 86, 87, 98, 103, 112, 401, 447, 451
AFL-CIO Central Labor Council, 418
AFL-CIO Civil Rights Committee, 181
AFL-CIO Civil Rights Department, 61, 62, 63, 77, 83, 98, 106, 107, 108, 110, 113, 116, 117, 118, 120, 127, 132, 133, 136, 137, 163, 169, 176, 181, 182
AFL-CIO Industrial Union Department, 75, 78, 92, 100, 114, 136, 152, 153
AFL-CIO Committee on Political Education, 197, 377, 418, 444, 449

AFL-CIO Maritime Trades Department, 449
AFL-CIO Metal Trades Council, 168
American Federation of Musicians, 109, 165, 364
American Federation of State, County, and Municipal Employees (AFSCME), 115, 192, 330, 339, 341, 347, 351, 355, 361, 364, 365, 366, 369, 370, 371, 404, 406, 408, 415, 417, 418, 445, 508
American Federation of Teachers, 192, 291, 361, 364, 369
American Jewish Committee, 127
American Jewish Congress, 127
American Medical Association, 94, 327
American Negro Labor Council, 539
American Newspaper Guild, 326
American Nurses Association, 480
American Postal Workers Union, 364
American Red Cross, 486
American Tobacco Company, 86, 509
American Civil Liberties Union, 500
Americans for Democratic Action, 500
Ancient and Accepted Scottish Rite Free Masons, 135
Anderson, Willard, 443
Andrews, Benny, 547, 548
Anti-War March on Washington, 487
Antonini, Luigi, 170, n 75
Apprenticeship, the U.S. Bureau of, 84
Arneson, Robert, 546, 548
Aronson, Arnold, 114
Ashlock, Ervin, 271
Assistant Printing Pressmen Union, 168
Associated Builders and Contractors, 468
Association of Fire Fighters, 167
Atlantic Coast Line Railroad, 165
Atomic Energy Commission, the U.S., 448
Attica Prison, 213, n 85
Austin, Dick, 353
Austin, Ollie, 305

Back to Africa Movement, 159, 161, 289
Badillo, Herman, 330, 539
Bailey, Pearl, 357
Bakery and Confectionary Workers' International Union of America, 364
Bakke, Allan, 35, n 13
Baldwin, James, 474, n 133
Ballard, Henry, 135
Balogh, James, 392
Balogh, Sigmund, 392
Baltimore Building Trades Council, 455
Banks, Richard, 305, 308, 310
Bannon, Ken, 439 n 122
Baranczak, Stanislaw, 547
Barnett, Ross R., 169, n 73
Barr, John U., 55

Bass, Jack, 527
Bates, Daisy, 515
Battle, 3rd, Robert, 257, 433, 434
Bauman, Mordecai, 540
Bayer, Pam, 31
Bazelon, David, 151
Beal, Jack, 547, 548
Becknell, Leotha, 490
Belafonte, Harry, 541, 545, 546
Bell, A. C., 308, 310, 311
Bell, Bobby, 274
Bell, Patricia, 311
Bennett, Isiah, 509, 510, 511
Berek, Judy, 481
Berg, Russell K., 449
Berking-Sutton Bill, 492
Berman, David, 549, 551
Betters, James, 392
Bibb, Leon, 545
Biemiller, Andrew J., 115, n 56
Bill of Rights, 49, 60, 64, 319, 495
Bimbo, Alonzo, 441
Black and White Get It Together
  Caucus, 443
Black capitalism, 278, 292, 289
Black, John, 478, 495, 501
Black Legislative Caucus, 334
Black Liberation Movement, 209, 211,
  212, 213, 220, 279, 281, 283, 288,
  289
Black Nationalism, 233, 239, 278
Black Panther Caucus (BPC), 267, 269
Black Panther Party, 208, 209, 210,
  211, 212, 278, n 84
Black Reconstruction, 312
Black Trade Unionists, 334, 335, 342,
  346, 347, 348, 355, 361, 364, 371,
  372
Black United Front, 255
Black Workers Congress, 207, 211, 212,
  213, 214, 215, 216, 217, 218, 219,
  220, 225, 228, 229, 233
Black Workers Congress Women's
  Commission, 228
Blackburn, Rev. Malcolm, 416, 419, 420
Blue, George, 348
Bluestone, Irving, 151
Boggs, Maywood, 451
Bommarito, Peter, 386, n 114
Bon, Anton, 392
Bonadio, Frank, 448
Bond, Horace Julian, 356, 512, n 107
Bonsal, Dudley, 465
Booth, William H., 446, 447
Boston State College Coalition, 456,
  457, 458
Boyd, Helen, 308, 309
Boykin, James, 481
Boyle, William A. ("Tony"), 225, 268,
  293, n 92
Braden, Henry, 455
Bradford, Jack, 524, 533
Brandeis, Louis D., 173, n 77
Bratcher, Neil, 338, 347, 352

Bread and Roses, 483, 537, 540, 541,
  542, 543, 544, 545, 546, 548, 551,
  552, 553
Brennan, Peter J., 152, 224, 366, 367,
  369, 371, 446, 447, 460, 463, 464, n
  126
Brennan, William, 35, 36, 38, 40 n 10
Brewster, Rev. W. Herbert, 420
Bricklayers, Masons, Plasterers'
  International Union of America, 125,
  163, 314, 364
Brimm, Hugh A., 502, 508
Brimmer, Andrew F., 157, n 69
Brooke, Edward W., 521, n 145
Brookins, Willie, 240
Brooks, Charles, 352
Broome, F. William, 519
Brooks, Thomas R., 383
Brosius, Peter, 549
Brotherhood of Locomotive Firemen and
  Enginemen, 166, 191
Brotherhood of Railroad Trainmen, 166
Brotherhood of Railway Clerks, 133,
  163, 164, 190
Brotherhood of Railway Carmen of
  America, 165
Brotherhood of Sleeping Car Porters,
  57, 58, 71, 79, 123, 125, 126, 128,
  129, 132, 133, 135, 159, 160, 161,
  306, 307, 317, 325, 371
Brothers, Brenda, 533
Brown, Bill, 455
Brown, Charles, 401
Brown, Charlotte, 25, 26
Brown, Claire G., 526, 529
Brown, Gloria, 441
Brown, H. Rap, 180, 263
Brown, Hank S., 94, 96, 97
Brown, Jerry, 478, 480
Brown, Iran, 535
Brown, Jim, 343, 354
Brown, Leo, 308
Brown, Sadie, 524
Brown v. Board of Education, 176, 180
Brulja, Matt, 392
Bryant, Baxter, 410, 412, 414
Bryant, Ernestine, 524, 535
Bryant, William Cullen, 188
Building and Construction Trades
  Council, 66, 110, 378
Building and Construction Trades
  Council of New York, 446, 460, 463
Bureau of Labor Statistics, the U.S.,
  371
Burger, Warren E., 35, 36, 37, n 11
Burke, Bob, 327
Burke, Joseph F., 450
Burke, Rufus, 265
Burke-Hartke Bill, 371
Burns, Arthur F., 118, n 58
Burns, Danny, 441
Burns, James McGregor, 374, n 109
Cafeteria Employees, 305, 307
Calderwood, Stan, 300
Callahan, Mary, 95

Cambridge, Godfrey, 538
Canty, Pearline, 537
capitalism, 221, 224, 227, 229, 224,
  233, 239, 244, 245, 252, 254, 260,
  262
capitalist, 232, 286, 289, 290, 291,
  296
capitalists, 230, 231, 248
Caplan, Marvin, 114
Carey, James B., 53, 58, 62, 64, 71,
  72, 75, 77, n 29
Carmichael, Stokely, 180, 404
Carnovsky, Morris, 538
Carter Administration, 444
Carter, Margaret, 526
Carter, Jimmy, 41, 44, 118, 160, 201,
  n 21
Carver Federal Savings and Loan
  Association, 135
Catholic Council on Human Relations,
  419
Catholic Interracial Council, 99, 121
Cavness, Charles, 400
Celler, Emanuel, 38, n 14
Center for Social Change, 118
Center for the Study of Democratic
  Institutions, 373
Central High School, 60
Chamberlain, Wilt, 354
Chandler, Dr. Cleveland A., 330
Chaney, James, 101, 135
Charleston Chamber of Commerce, 519
Charleston County Hospital, 476, 508,
  517, 524, 530, 531, 532, 533, 535,
  536
Charleston Medical College, 476, 507,
  512, 514
Chavez, Cesar, 113
Chicago, Judy, 545
Chicago Packinghouse Workers, 291
Chisholm, Shirley A., 512, 525, n 143
Chrysler Corporation, 210, 237, 238,
  247, 248, 249, 250, 251, 252, 256,
  257, 259, 266, 269, 270, 271, 275,
  425, 444
Church Ushers Association of Brooklyn
  and Long Island, 135
Churchill, Ray, 416
Churchill, Winston, 200
Chwast, Jacqueline, 547
Ciampa, P. J., 410, 412
Citizens Committee to Aid the Lawrence
  Hospital Strikers, 493
Civil Rights Act of 1957, 60
Civil Rights Act of 1964, 18, 35, 36,
  37, 38, 39, 100, 106, 111, 114, 115,
  117, 118, 135, 161, 192, 317, 328,
  386, 387, 421, 429, 451, 452, 459,
  505, 515
Civil Rights Act of 1965, 107, 176
Civil Rights Bill of 1966, 102, 151
Civil Rights Commission, the U.S., 60,
  111, 114, 125, 190, 191, 410, 464
Clark, Sondra, 480
Clarke, Oscar, 305

Clay, William L., 353, n 106
Cleveland Community Relations Board,
  191
Coalition for Labor Union Women, 120,
  181
Coalition of Black Trade Unionists,
  332, 361, 365, 366, 367, 368, 369,
  370, 371, 372, 44
Code on Fair Trade Union Racial
  Practices, 127
Coe, Sue, 547
Cole, Edward, 256
Cole, Lewis, 542, 549, 551, 554
Collins, Judy, 542
Colm, Gerhard, 374
Colon, Miriam, 542
Colorado Labor Council, 96
Committee for Justice for Pittsburgh
  Hospital Workers, 474, 500
Committee on Equal Opportunity in
  Apprenticeship and Training, 84
Committee on the Move for Equality
  (MOVE), 407
Communication Workers of America, 364,
  367
communism, 70, 89, 209, 226, 330, 425,
  548
Communist Party - U.S.A. (CPUSA), 207,
  208, 209, 211, 214, 218, 219, 220,
  225, 226. 227, 244, 268, 269
communistic, 73
communists, 65, 67, 70, 72, 125, 126,
  138, 159, 170, 188, 212, 215, 218,
  219, 220, 222, 226, 227, 280, 291,
  330, 348, 425, 517
Community Action Program (CAP), 444
Community Legal Services, Inc., 453
Community Progress, Inc., 87
Concerned Citizens Committee, 493
Concerned Clergy of Charleston, 523,
  533
Concerned Transit Workers, 224
Congress, the U.S., 78, 94, 100, 101,
  106, 107, 110, 115, 116, 127, 136,
  137, 158, 189, 319, 323, 338, 340,
  341, 343, 368, 375, 387, 425, 426,
  427, 428, 429, 451
Congress of Industrial Organizations
  Committee on Civil Rights, 53, 59,
  60, 62, 63, 91
Congress of Industrial Organizations
  Committee to Abolish Racial
  Discrimination, 53, 54
Congress of Racial Equality (CORE),
  103, 104, 127, 209, 315, 329, 493,
  474, 512, n 52
Congressional Black Caucus, 353, 354,
  357, 372
Connor, Eugene ("Bull") T., 121, 328,
  n 63
Cooper, Ashley, 514, 523
Copeland, Lehman, 433
Conroy, John F., 519
Constitution, the U.S., 49, 50, 51,
  52, 54, 56, 60, 67, 110, 319, 395,
  424

Construction Stabilization Board, 344
Conway, Jack T., 114, n 55
Conway, Mimi, 542
Conyers, John M., 512, n 143
Corbett, Ray, 460
Corey, Professor Irwin, 542
Cost of Living Council (COLC), 479
Cousy, Bob, 465
Cowan, Frank, 352
Creamer, J. Shane, 453
Crosswaith, Frank R., 50, 124, 305,
  306, 307, 308, 311, n 24
Cunningham, Sarah, 538
Curran, Joseph E., 53, 70, 76, n 28

Daley, Richard J., 269, n 93
Daniels, Floyd, 240
Daniels, Jonathan, 101, 135
Daniels, Wilbur, 115, n 56
Darnell, Emma, 16
Daughters of Israel, 490
Daughters of Jacob, 491
Daughters of Miriam, 551, 552
David, Aberdeen, 478
Davis, Angela, 263, 331
Davis, Fred, 409
Davis, Jim, 331, 400, 401
Davis, John F., 445
Davis, Leon J., 92, 472, 473, 474,
  475, 476, 477, 479, 482, 484, 487,
  489, 490, 491, 492, 495, 497, 524,
  534, 537, n 131
Davis, Ossie, 482, 485, 493, 495, 525,
  538, 539, 541, 542, 544, 546, 549,
  551, 552, n 139
Davis, Paul, 544, 545
Davis, Jr., Sammy, 343, 354, 356, 357
Davis, Walter, 16, 88, 108, n 7
Davis-Bacon Act, 468
Deas, Rosabelle, 536
Debs, Eugene, 547
Dee, Ruby, 482, 485, 538, 541, 542,
  544, 546, n 139
Dellums, C. L., 135
Dellums, Ronald V., 444, n 123
Democratic Party, 209, 244, 249, 252,
  333, 336, 337, 350, 356, 370, 371,
  445, 479
Democratic Republic of Vietnam, 233
Densmore, Henry, 166
Depression, the Great, 202, 203, 252,
  459, 497
diDonato, Pietro, 461
Diggs, Jr., Charles C., 424, n 119
Distillery, Rectifying, Wine and
  Allied Workers' International Union
  of America, 364
Distributive, Processing and Office
  Workers of America, 327, 329, 338,
  347, 352, 361, 364, 367, 369, 370,
  371
Dixiecrats, 51, 55, 81, 136, 186, 424,
  427
Dixon, Roy, 455
Dobbins, Anderson L., 190

Doctor, Bobby, 410
Dodge Main Plant, 236, 240, 241, 248,
  261, 264, 265, 266, 272
Dodge Revolutionary Union Movement
  (DRUM), 224, 235, 236, 237, 238,
  239, 240, 243, 244, 249, 264, 265,
  266
Donahue, Thomas R., 121, 177, n 62
Dorsey, Ralph, 549
Dotter, Earl, 542
Douglas, Paul H., 335, 336, n 101
Douglass, Frederick, 475, n 135
Downes, Kenneth, 472
Dress and Waist Pressers, 305
Dressmakers Union, 305
Drew, Cornelius J., 124
Drug and Hospital Employes Union, 287,
  482, 486, 513, 537
Drug Division Council, 484
Dubin, Marshall, 481, 539, 544
Dubinsky, David, 98, 169, 170, 171,
  173, 187, 294, n 51
Du Bois, W. E. B., 159, 161, n 70
Dubrow, Evelyn, 182
Duquesnay, Ann, 549, 551, 554

Eastland, James O., 89, 169, 358, 359,
  424, 425, 426, n 73
Economic Opportunity Act of 1964, 25
Edney, Steve, 182
Edwards, Nelson Jack, 330, 334, 339,
  341, 342, 347, 348, 351, 352, 361,
  366, 369, 371, n 104
Eisenhower, Dwight D., 51, 60, 61, 66,
  124, 125, 186, 337, n 26
Eldon Gear and Axle Plant, 237, 240,
  248, 261, 264, 265, 270, 271, 272
Eldon Avenue Revolutionary Movement
  (ELRUM), 235, 236, 237, 238, 249,
  270
Elliot, Joe, 237
Elliot, Walter, 353
Emancipation Proclamation, 92, 114,
  315
Emergency Summit Conference of Third
  World People, 215
Employment Act of 1946, 140, 144
Engels, Frederick, 221, 225
Epps, Jesse, 417
Epps, Labrone, 500
Equal Employment Opportunity
  Commission (EEOC), 13, 14, 15, 32,
  107, 108, 111, 114, 117, 118, 120,
  181, 190, 192, 397, 460, 506, 543
Equal Opportunity Employment Act of
  1972, 176
Equal Rights Amendment (ERA), 120, 176
Evans, Frank, 58, 93, 96, 97, 99
Evans, Fred Ahmed, 263
Evans, Sam, 409
Evers, Charles, 340
Evers, Medgar, 101, 135
Ewen, Frederick, 538
Executive Order 8802, 159, n 71
Executive Order 10925, 68, 69

Executive Order 11063, 78
Executive Order 11246, 15, 506, 507, n 5
Fair Employment Practices Commission (FEPC), 13, 58, 78, 84, 108, 127, 168, 183, 423, 427, 428
Fair Housing Act of 1968, 176
Fair Housing Act of 1979, 120
Fair, John, 401
Fair Labor Standards Act, 136, 375
Fair Union Practices Board, 63
Fagan, Edward, 308
Fanion, Gerald, 410, 416
Fanon, Frantz, 239
Farm Equipment-United Electrical Workers (FEUE), 435
Farm Workers Union, 287
Farmer, James, 326, 329, 474, n 96
Fasanella, Ralph, 542, 545, 547, 548
fascism, 67, 227, 268, 276, 279, 300, 330, 514
Featherstone, Ralph, 263
Federal Housing Authority (FHA), 78, 101, 309
Federal Reserve Board, 138
Federation for Constitutional Government, 55
Federation of Negro Civil Service Organizations, 305
Feinglass, Abe, 102, 104, 105
Fifteenth Amendment, 126, 175, 312
Fight Back, 224, 359, 371, 461, 465, 468
Finley, Murray H., 118, n 57
Fire Fighters Union, 372
Firestone Tire and Rubber Company, 86
First Amendment, 413
First National Trade Union Civil Rights Conference, 60
Fitzsimmons, Frank E., 268, n 92
Flack, Audrey, 547, 548
Fleary, George, 134
Floore, George, 17
Fobbs, Annie, 536
Fonda, Jane, 546
Foner, Henry, 495
Foner, Moe, 473, 476, 477, 482, 495, 496, 524, 525, 537, 538, 544, 545, 546, 553, 554, n 132
Food and Tobacco Workers, 327
Food Packers Association, 364
Food Trades Vocational High School, 485
Ford, Charles, 392
Ford, Father George B., 475
Ford, Gerald, 17, 43, 44, n 20
Ford Foundation, 209, 210, 540
Ford II, Henry, 256
Ford Motor Company, 236, 237, 240, 257, 259, 269, 270, 433, 439
Ford Revolutionary Union Movement (FRUM), 235, 236, 237, 238, 241, 242
Forge, Rushie, 272
Forman, James, 212, 214, 215, 216, 217, n 86

Forrester, Martin, 305
Fosco, Peter, 449, n 129
Foster, Stephen, 465
Four Freedoms, Inc., 392
Fourteenth Amendment, 126, 175, 312, 413
Fowler, George H., 445, 539
Fox, Art, 242
Fox, Joseph, 307
Frankel, Marvin E., 461, 467
Franklin, E. J., 531
Franklyn, Hardy, 134
Fraser, Douglas A., 179, 247, 251, 252, 253, 444, 445, 543, n 78
Frasier, Woodrow, 500
Frazier, Eugene, 88, n 48
Frazier, E. Franklin, 382, n 110
Freedom Budget, 139, 140, 141, 142, 143, 144, 145, 146, 147, 148, 149, 150, 151, 152, 153, 157, 158, 374, 376, 450
Freedom Rides, 134, 386
Freeman, Ellsworth, 431
Freeman, Gordon M., 449, n 129
Frost, Robert, 178
Fuller, Alex, 16
Fuller, Mabel, 305
Fund for Tomorrow, Inc., 540

Gaboury, Fred, 442, 443
Galamison, Rev. Milton A., 135, 539
Gandhi, Mahatma, 80, 386, n 115
Garrison, Lloyd, 124
Garson, Barbara, 549, 551, 552, 554
Garvey, Marcus, 159, 161, 233, n 70
Geer, Will, 538
General Building Contractors Association, 454
General Motors Corporation, 40, 66, 167, 210, 229, 256, 258, 259, 269, 270, 292, 425
Gerber, Martin, 444
Gerdts, Abigail Booth, 540
Giamboi, Joe, 459
Gianotti, Frank B., 412
Gibbons, Harold, 330
Gildea, James C., 16
Gilford, Jack, 544, 545
Gilford, Madeline, 544
Gillotte, Tony, 552, 553
Gilmore, Robert, 151, 152
Gittens, Winifred, 305, 307
Glaberman, Martin, 242, 243
Glaser, Milton, 544, 545, 548
Glover, Lottie Mae, 529
Godfrey, Bernice, 490
Godoff, Elliott, 472, 477, 480, 488, 490, 495, 497, 501, 509, 510, 524, 526, 527, 528, 535
Godwin, Lemond, 16
Goldberg, Arthur J., 66, 69, n 41
Goldberg, Moshe, 479
Golden Foundation, the John, 540
Goldman, Eric F., 385
Goldwater, Barry, 89, 201

Gompers, Samuel, 64, 118, 197, 222, 396, 545, 546, 548, n 40
Goodman, Andrew, 101, 135
Goodman, Howard, 453
Gootnick, Margery, 479
Goree, Henrietta, 501
Goudia, Kernell, 33
Grady, Rev. Z. L., 523
Grandison, Jeremiah, 64, n 40
Grant, Micki, 542, 549, 551, 552, 554
Great Society, 138, 141, 150, 153
Greathouse, Pat, 444
Greeley, Horace, 191
Green, Ernest, 462
Green, Richard, 135
Green, Sol, 311
Green, William, 98, 386, n 51
Griffin, Jim, 242, 243
Gross, Mimi, 547, 548
Grossman, Robert, 547
Guild of Professional, Technical and Clerical Employees, 475, 478
Guinan, Matthew, 96
Guthrie, Arlo, 542
Gutman, Herbert G., 541

Haggerty, Cornelius J., 268, 448, 449, n 92
Hague, Howard R., 392
Hall, Paul, 169, 448, 449, n 74
Hamer, Fannie Lou, 515, n 144
Hamilton, Edward, 464
Hamlin, Michael, 210, 228, 236, 237, 238, 239, 242, 243
Hampton, Fred, 263
Hanna, Hilton E., 347, n 105
Hardin, Alma, 524, 533
Harlem Labor Center, 305, 308
Harlem Trades Union, 124
Harris, Edward, 416
Harris, Fred R., 521, n 145
Harrington, Michael, 538
Harrison, George M., 71, 75, 76, 88, 131, 164, n 45
Harrison, Tony, 352
Hart, Philip, 384, n 112
Hart, William, 391
Hartford Plan, 455
Hartke, Rupert Vance, 384, n 112
Hartung, William, 59
Hastings Center Institute of Society, Ethics, and the Life Sciences, 543
Hatcher, Lillian, 338, 348, 352
Hatcher, Richard G., 358, 512
Haughton, James, 459, 460, 468, n 129
Hawkins-Humphrey Bill, 178
Hayes, Albert J., 88, n 48
Hayes, Charles, 67, 332, 333, 334, 338, 339, 342, 343, 346, 352, 361, 366, 369, 370, 371, n 44
Hayes, Vertis, 433
Health, Education and Welfare (HEW), the Department of, 100, 342, 504, 505, 511
Height, Dorothy I., 512, n 142

Heller, W. W., 15
Helstein, Ralph, 88, 151, n 48
Hemphill, Gwen, 338, 352
Henderson, Vivian, 16, 151, 153
Herberg, Will, 173
Heyward, Mrs. D. P., 530
Higgins, Msgr. George G., 467, 468
High School of Fashion Trades (N.Y.), 539
Hill, David, 501
Hill, Herbert, 170, 171, 172, 173, 445, 450, 460, 464, 466
Hill, Norman, 151
Hilbert, Paul, 391
Hines, Gregory, 545
Hinz, Gary L., 270, 272
Hitler, Adolph, 94, 200, 423, 424
Hod Carriers, Building and Common Laborers, 165
Hodgson, James D., 16, 232, n 7
Hoff, William, 517
Hoffman, Robert, 412, 413
Holland, James, 166
Hollie, Ronald, 478
Holloman, Frank, 416
Holman, M. Carl, 26
Holmes, Adolph, 16
Holmes, Robert, 444
Hometown Plan, 454, 455
Hooks, Benjamin L., 119, 175, 179, 195, 201, n 59
Hooks, Robert, 538
Hoover, President Herbert, 45
Horne, Gerald, 31
Horowitz, Rachelle, 151
Horston, Kenny, 269
Horton, Clarence, 271
Hosley, Fred, 265
Hospital and Nursing Home Workers, 517
Hospital Delegate Assembly, 492
Hotel and Allied Service Union, 305
Hotel and Restaurant Employees and Bartenders International Union, 132, 314, 364
House Judiciary Committee, 78
House Labor and Education Committee, 170
Housing Act of 1965, 158
Howe, Irving, 547, 548
Howe, Stephen, 549
Hughes, Randolph, 452, 453
Hughes, Richard J., 445, n 125
Hugo, Victor, 185
Human Resources Development Institute (HRDI), 116, 117
Humphrey, Hubert H., 38, 446, n 15
Humphrey-Hawkins Full Employment and Balanced Growth Act, 118, 119, 199
Hunton, George, 99
Hutcheson, M. A., 449
Hyde, Al, 352

Illinois Union of Social Services' Employees, 364

imperialism, 221, 224, 227, 228, 231,
  232, 233, 254, 260
imperialists, 231, 275, 277, 282
Industrial Workers of the World (IWW),
  290
Innis, Roy, 512
Interdenominational Ministers'
  Alliance, 414
Interdenominational Ministers'
  Alliance of Brooklyn and Long
  Island, 134
International Association of Bridge,
  Structural and Ornamental Iron
  Workers, 190
International Association of
  Machinists (IAM), 364, 372, 539
International Association of Marble,
  Slate and Stone Polishers, Rubbers,
  and Sawyers, Tile and Marble Setters
  Helpers and Terrazzo Helpers, 364
International Black Appeal (IBA), 264,
  265
International Brotherhood of
  Electrical Workers (IBEW), 62, 76,
  85, 87, 125, 163, 165, 166, 190,
  191, 448, 449, 462
International Brotherhood of Pulp,
  Sulphite and Paper Mill Workers of
  America and Canada, 67, 74, 86, 165
International Brotherhood of
  Teamsters, 325, 330, 331, 361, 364,
  371, 384, 444
International Chemical Workers Union,
  167
International Fire Fighters
  Association, 166
International Harvester Company, 87,
  434, 435, 436, 437, 438, 443
International Laborers Union of
  America, 16
International Ladies' Garment Workers
  Union, 95, 99, 115, 165, 169, 170,
  171, 172, 173, 187, 277, 293, 294,
  296, 306, 312, 364, 551, 552, 553
International Longshoremen's
  Association, 87, 364, 510
International Transport Workers Union
  of America, 64, 73, 96, 123, 124,
  176
International Union of Electrical
  Workers, 71, 72, 94, 95, 445
International Union of Operating
  Engineers, 168, 453, 464
International Woodworkers of America,
  364
Iron and Structural Steel Workers
  Union, 165, 314, 445
Italian American Labor Council, 369

Jackson, Allan, 305, 307, 308, 310
Jackson, Andrew, 200
Jackson, Anne, 542
Jackson, Jesse, 326, n 96
Jackson, Jimmy Lee, 101, 135
Jackson, Joseph T., 493, 494

Jackson, Maynard H., 16, 454, n 7
Jackson, Dr. Ralph, 415, 417, 418,
  419, 420
Jacobs, Jim, 241, 242
Jacobs, Sophi Yarnall, 124
James, C. L. R., 242, n 91
James, Stanley, 275
Javits, Senator Jacob, 13, 152, 521,
  n 2
Jefferson Avenue Revolutionary Union
  Movement (JARUM), 235, 238
Jennings, Colie, 406
Jernigan, Ike, 232, 269, 272
Jewish Labor Committee, 55
Jim Crow, 15, 57, 89, 105, 127, 132,
  133, 134, 170, 171, 173, 207, 288,
  382, 388, 423, 493
Job Development Program, 14
John Birch Society, 186, n 79
Johnson, Eddy, 465
Johnson, Edrena, 477
Johnson, James, 232, 263, 269, 270,
  271, 272
Johnson, President Lyndon Baines, 13,
  43, 66, 69, 100, 101, 107, 111, 115,
  135, 137, 153, 161, 198, 201, 202,
  429, 448, 513, n 3
Johnson II, Napoleon, 16
Johnson, Rae, 265
Johnson, Ray, 240
Jolly, A. C., 308
Jones, Hubert L., 17
Jones, Hugh M., 270, 272
Jones, James Earl, 544
Jones, Paul, 343
Jones, T. O., 404, 410, 412
Jordan, Jr., Vernon E., 16, 201, 392,
  n 6
Justice, U.S. Department of, 56, 60,
  61, 78, 100, 108, 111, 114, 166,
  181, 182, 190, 516

Kahn, Tom, 151
Kaiser Aluminum Company, 31, 32, 34,
  35, 36, 37, 38, 39, 177
Kaplan Fund, Inc., the J. J., 540
Keenen, Joseph D., 48, 88, 90, 91
Kempton, Murray, 385
Kennedy, Beverly, 534
Kennedy, Edward M., 384, 521, n 112
Kennedy, President John F., 43, 64,
  78, 94, 114, 125, 161, 186, 207,
  234, 338, 387, 497, n 19
Kennedy, Robert, 152, 277
Kerner Commission Report, 292, 325,
  430
Keyserling, Leon, 151, 152, 153, 450
Kheel, Theodore W., 124
Khomeini, Ayatollah, 203, 204
King, Bill, 546
King, Coretta Scott, 119, 194, 476,
  477, 478, 487, 496, 501, 502, 511,
  512, 513, 514, 517, 520, 523, 528,
  543
King, Jr., Martin Luther, 67, 68, 74,

104, 114, 118, 119, 126, 139, 180,
181, 184, 188 198, 201, 202, 243,
256, 277, 317, 326, 328, 329, 333,
350, 354, 383, 386, 404, 405, 406,
429 450, 472, 474, 477, 487, 493,
496, 500, 508, 511, 515, 516, 525,
532, 543, n 42
King Center for Social Change, 543
King, Rev. D. E., 332
Kircher, Bill, 193
Kirkland, Joseph Lane, 120, 159, 161,
176, 177, 178, 179, 180, 201, 202,
377, 386, n 61
Kissinger, Henry A., 210, 234, n 89
Klein, Robert, 544
Knight, Elizabeth, 305
Kosloski, Al, 471
Kowalski, Joseph, 270
Kuchel, Thomas H., 38, n 16
Ku Klux Klan, 52, 55, 101, 119, 135,
164, 177, 178, 181, 312, n 27
Kyles, Rev. S. B., 413, 416
Labor, the U.S. Department of, 14, 16,
84, 109, 112, 137, 168, 190, 191,
330, 450, 452
Labor Council for Latin-American
Advancement, 120, 181
Labor Education Advancement Program
(LEAP), 16, 17, 112, 116, 117, 454,
455
Labor Leadership Assembly for Peace,
476
Laborers International Union of North
America, 364
LaFrage Institute, the John, 152
Landron, Jack, 549, 551
Landrum-Griffin Act, 91, 96, 449, n 49
Laquer, Walter, 385
LaRocque Bey Dancers, 539
Lasley, Russell R., 74
Latin, Pete, 392
Laundry and Dry Cleaning International
Union, 364
Laurence, Jacob, 545
Lawson, Jr., Rev. James M., 404, 405,
407, 408, 413
Leadership Conference on Civil Rights
(LCCR), 107, 113, 114, 115, 120,
384, 430
League for Registered Nurses, 480
League of Revolutionary Black Workers,
210, 211, 235, 238, 241, 242, 245,
248, 249, 253, 254, 255, 257, 259,
287
League of Voluntary Hospitals, 479,
480
Lee, Curtis, 240
Lee, Rev. G. W., 183
Left-Center Coalition, 276, 279, 281,
384
Lehman, Herbert H., 473, n 132
Leonard, Eddie, 401
Leonard, Edward J., 449, n 129
Leonard, Vincent M., 500
Levenson, Sam, 538, 542, 545

Lewis, Anthony, 385
Lewis, Howard, 272
Lewis, John L., 123, 130, 197, 548,
n 65
Lewis, John R., 16, n 7
Lewis, Sid, 272
Lewis, Thelma, 500
Liberal Party, 172
Lincoln, Abraham, 89, 327, 546
Lincoln Center, 541, 545, 546
Lindsay, Mayor John, 459, 460, 462,
464, 465, 513
Little Rock High School, 462
Liuzzo, Viola, 101, 135, 429
Livengood, Delbert, 502
Livingston, David, 325, 326, 328, 475
Local 1199 (of the Drug and Hospital
Employees Union), 470-554 passim
Lockheed Aircraft Corporation, 272,
343, 356
Loeb, Henry, 404, 405, 406, 408, 409,
411, 412, 413, 415, 417, 420
Loeb, William, 411
Logan, Rose, 240
London, Jack, 185
Longstreth, W. Thatcher, 234, 450
Loughlin, James, 450
Lowell, Stanley, 445
Lucy, William, 330, 334, 338, 339,
341, 351, 355, 361, 365, 366, 367,
369, 370, 371
Lundstrom, Chet, 443
Lyerson, Frank T., 166
Lyles, Helen, 500
Lynch, Leon, 33, 35
Lynch, Matt, 414
Lyons, John H., 449, n 129

McCarthy, Joseph R., 207, n 81
McBride, Lynwood, 501
McCone Commission, 432
McCord, Dr. William M., 476, 477, 502
509, 510, 511, 514, 518, 523
McCormick Workers Reaper Division, 434
McCrae, Whit, 352
McCree, Jr., Wade H., 424, n 119
McDaniel, Billy, 549
McDaniel, William Foster, 549
McDonald, David J., 62, 64, 68, 79,
88, 123, 169, 170, 171, 187, 391,
392, 396, n 37
MacDonald, J. C., 416
McGovern, George, 337, 338, 340, 345,
350, 351, 356, 365, 370, 371, n 102
McGowin, Ed, 546, 548
McNair, Robert E., 509, 510, 512, 517,
518, 519, 523, 524, n 138
McNamara, James, 465
McRae, Bernest, 526
Madison Square Garden, 479
Magee, Henry, 335
Maimonides Medical Center, 472
Makeba, Miriam, 539
Malcolm X, 207, 475, n 83
Mallon, Edna, 482

Manning, Louis, 64, 73
Manpower Development and Training Act
  of 1962, 25
Mansfield, Michael J., 384, n 112
Mao Tse Tung, 213, 217, 219, 226
March, Ron, 237, 265
March on Washington Movement, 58, 81,
  82, 159, n 35
March on Washington, the 1963, 141,
  142, 160, 180, 326, 328, 329, 371,
  377
Marcuse, Herbert, 385
Marshall, Raymond, 107
Marshall, Thurgood, 171, 182, 194,
  341, 473, n 29
Marshall Plan, 81, 93, n 46
Marshall, William (Bill), 274, 444
Martin, Louie, 201
Marx, Karl, 217, 221, 225
Marxism, 209-42, 276-81 passim, 425
Maryland Freedom Union, 103
Mason-Dixon Line, 94
Mathias Amendment, 102
Matthews, Jr., John, 240, 241
May, Rev. Joseph H., 135
Mazey, Emil, 88, 96, 97, n 48
Meany, George, 34, 50-139 passim,
  170-202 passim, 222, 268, 306, 313-
  35 passim, 344, 349, 365-87 passim,
  428, 448, 461, 515, 525
Medal of Freedom, 161
Medical College of South Carolina,
  502, 503, 506, 509, 510, 520
Medical College Hospital (S.C.), 476,
  477, 503, 504, 508, 516, 517, 518,
  523, 524, 526, 529, 531, 533, 534,
  535, 536
Memphis City Council, 413, 414, 416,
  417, 420
Memphis Council on Human Rights, 419
Menapace, Jerry, 102, 104
Menken, Alan, 549, 552, 554
Metcalf, Ralph, 334, 338, 345, n 99
Metropolitan African Methodist-
  Episcopal Church, 159, 160
Metropolitan Ministry in Higher
  Education, 456
Metropolitan Transit Authority, 406
Metzenbaum, Howard M., 384, n 112
Michel, Robert, 173
Michelson, Bill, 491
Mid-Atlantic States Apprenticeship
  Conference, 110
Miller, Edward, 31, 32
Mills, Wilbur D., 449, n 129
Miners for Democracy, 225
Minh, Ho Chi, 223, n 88
Minkoff, Isaiah, 151, 153
Minton, Lee W., 88, n 48
Mitchell, Clarence, 114, 136, 199,
  201, 384, n 54
Mitchell, John, 455
Mitchell, Ted, 490
Mitchell, Theodore, 472
Model Cities, 264, 464
Molders International Union, 109

Mondale, Joan, 547
Mondale, Walter, 521
Monserrat, Joseph, 474
Montalban, Ricardo, 485, 538
Montgomery, David, 500
Montgomery Bus Boycott, 328
Montgomery Bus Company, 207
Moon, Prince, 352
Moore, Edith, 352
Moore, Ferman, 432
Moore, William L., 101, 135
Mooty, Rayfield, 399, 401, 402
Morse, Wayne L., 427, n 121
Mostel, Zero, 545
Motley, Constance, 309
Moultrie, Mary Ann, 193, 195, 477,
  510, 514, 516, 517, 518, 521, 522,
  523, 524, 525, 526, 527, 532, 534,
  535
Moyers, Bill, 543
Muehlenkamp, Bob, 480
Murphy, Hugh, 16
Murphy, John, 88
Murphy, Thomas F., 449, n 129
Murray, Philip, 386, 548, n 113
Murray-Green-Meany Award, 386
Muse, Benjamin, 416
Musicus, Milton, 463
Muskie, Edmund, 384, 521, n 112
Mussolini, Benito, 170
Myrdal, Gunnar, 80

Nagler, Isidore, 306
National Ad Hoc Committee of Concerned
  Negro UAW Members, 433
National Ad Hoc Committee of Concerned
  Steelworkers, 397, 398, 399, 402
National Advisory Commission on Civil
  Disorders, 414, 415
National Afro-American Labor Council,
  330, 331, 347, 350
National Association for the
  Advancement of Colored People
  (NAACP), 50, 54, 55, 62, 76, 77, 97,
  106, 114, 119, 126, 127, 133, 134,
  136, 152, 157, 162, 165, 167, 168-
  209 passim, 305, 306, 313, 314, 315,
  362, 371, 384, 406, 408, 422-28,
  439, 445, 446, 450, 460, 462, 464,
  466, 473, 474, 487, 493, 512, 514
National Association of Manufacturers
  (NAM), 67, 90, 189, 390, 468, n 43
National Catholic Council for
  Interracial Justice, 419
National Conference of Christians and
  Jews, 409
National Conference of Plans for
  Progress, 446
National Council of Churches, 419
National Council of Distributive
  Workers, 326
National Council of Negro Women, 512
National Council of Senior Citizens,
  181
National Defense Council, 91
National Education Association, 364,
  372, 445

National Endowment for the Arts, 540, 545, 551
National Endowment for the Humanities, 540, 545, 548
National Football League Players Association, 551
National Institute of Labor Education, 87
National Jewish Community Relations Advisory Council, 114
National Labor Relations Act, 446, 478, 510
National Labor Relations Board, 61, 65, 72, 75, 76, 163, 166, 173, 389, 446, 449, 478, 480
National League of Cities, 352
National Medical Association, 93
National Museum of American History, 547
National Negro Congress, 159
National Organizing Committee (NOC), 241, 242, 246, 247, 249, 250, 252, 253
National Organizing Committee of Hospital and Nursing Home Employes, 476, 510, 512, 513, 521, 526, 528
National Planning Association, 374
National Postal Office Mail Handlers Board, 372
National Sharecroppers Fund, 305
National Steelworkers Rank and File, 401
National Transport Association, 167
National Welfare Rights Organization, 512
National Youth Act, 331
National Union of Hospital and Health Care Employees, 478, 481 482, 540, 544, 546, 548, 551, 552, 553
National Union of Hospital and Nursing Home Employees (NUHNHE), 486, 487, 488, 496, 498
National Urban Coalition, 26, 120
National Urban League, 13, 14, 15, 16, 55, 152, 314, 315, 316, 512
Neel, Alice, 547, 548
Negro American Labor Council (NALC), 125, 127, 128, 133, 134, 311, 314, 315, 316, 317, 318, 320, 322, 324, 326, 328, 329, 330, 493, 512
Negro History Week, 538, 539
Negro Labor Assembly, 305, 308
Negro Labor Committee, 50, 305, 306, 307, 308, 309, 310, 311
Negro Steelworkers Leadership Committee, 402
Negro Trade Union Leadership Council, 110
Neibuhr, Reinhold, 483
Nelson, Chris, 352
Nessim, Barbara, 547
New Breed Democratic Trade Union Caucus, 434
New Detroit Committee, 239, 255
Newman, Winn, 108

Newport News (Va.) Shipbuilding and Dry Dock Company, 278
New York City Central Labor Council, 473, 543
New York City Commission on Human Rights, 326, 445, 446, 460, 539
New York Furriers Union Joint Council, 192
New York Plan, 459, 460, 463, 464, 465
New York State Building and Construction Trades Council 224, 369
New York Teachers Guild, 305
Nicholas, Henry, 476, 478, 487, 495, 499, 524, 527, 531, 535
Niles, Barbara, 549, 551
Nixon, Russell A., 461
Nixon, President Richard Milhous, 43, 44, 66, 111, 115, 118, 210, 215, 222, 223, 224, 228, 232, 234, 263, 269, 278, 293, 296, 330, 334, 336, 337, 340, 341, 342, 343, 349, 350, 351, 354, 356, 357, 358, 359, 362, 363, 365, 368, 380, 383, 385, 451, 464, 479, 516, 519, 521, 525, n 20
Normile, Paul, 392
Noroian, Edward, 500
Norton, Eleanor Holmes, 26, 151, 543, n 9
Norton, James, 462, 463
Nunez, Judge Emilio, 474

O'Casey, Sean, 538
Odetta, 542, 546
Office and Professional Employees International Union, 132, 364
Office of Civil Rights, the U.S., 502, 505, 508
Office of Economic Opportunity (OEO), the U.S., 148, 369
Office of Federal Contract Compliance, the U.S., 108, 181, 192, 369, 447, 448, 449, 450, 452, 454, 455, 460, 464
Office of Manpower Automation and Training, the U.S., 87
Oil, Chemical and Atomic Workers Union, 167, 372
Old Slave Mart, 526
Oliver, William, 176
Olson, Jesse, 475, 478
Olwell, William, 182
O'Malley, Father John, 501
O'Neal, Frederick D., 121, 182, n 62
Oneita Strike, 213
Operation Breadbasket, 335, n 100
Operation Dixie, 57, 421, n 31
Operation PUSH, 332, n 98
Operative Plasterers and Cement Masons Association, 166
Oppenheimer, James, 540
Ornamental and Structural Iron Workers, 168
Ottley, Peter, 305
Overton, L. Joseph, 308, 309, 310, 311, 314, 473

Owen, Chandler, 58, n 34

Palmer, Robert, 301
Palmieri, Victor, 373
Paper Box Makers, 305
Parker, Charlie Mack, 207
Parks, Rosa, 207, 515, 545, n 80
Parrish, Richard, 305, 306, 307, 308, 367
Parsons, Lucy E., 548
Patterson, J. O., 405, 416, 420
Payne, Larry, 405
Penn, Colonel Lemuel, 101
Pennsylvania Nurses Association, 501
Perkins, Frances, 548
Permanent Administrative Committee (PAC), 473, 484
Perry, Nonnie, 540
Petrillo, James C., 109, n 53
Philadelphia Building and Construction Trades Council, 450
Philadelphia Plan, 112, 113, 230, 369, 393, 451, 452, 453, 463
Pierce, Samuel, 307
Pipkin, Joe, 413
Pittman, Charles, 33
Pittsburgh Federation of Teachers, 501
Plastic and Novelty Workers, 305

Plumbers and Pipe Fitters Union, 125, 165, 168, 314, 461
Plumbers, Marine and Steamfitters Union, 454
Pocketbook Workers Union, 372
Poitier, Sidney, 485, 538, 544
Polaroid Revolutionary Workers Movement, 264, 299, 300, 301
Pollard, William E., 176, 198
Poor People's Campaign on Washington, 322, 329, 405, 450
Pope John XXIII, 391
Posnick, Michael, 549
Potofsky, Jacob S., 95, 131
Powell, Jr., Adam Clayton, 170, 171, 473, n 74
Powell, Don, 418
Powell, Jr., Lewis F., 35, n 11
Powell, Robert E., 16, 88, 136, n 48
Powell, Tom, 418
Pratt, Dr. Henry N., 472
President's Committee on Equal Employment Opportunity, 64, 66, 68, 72, 84, 85, 446
President's Committee on Fair Employment Practice, 129
President's Committee on Government Contracts, 51, 60, 61, 66, 166
President's Council of Economic Advisors, 15
President's Council on Wage and Price Stabilization, 479
Pressley, John, 307
Price, Jr., Judge Gwilym, 501
Price, Leontyne, 160
Progressive Labor Party, 275, 279, 280
Project Outreach, 439

Proposition 13, 119, 177, n 60
Prosten, Dave, 524
Pryon, Beverly, 331
Pryor, Downing, 410, 412, 414
Pullman Company, 128, 130, 132, 159
Punch, Fred, 487

Quill, Michael J., 122, 124, n 64
Quoc, Nguyen Ai, 233

Rabouine, Leo, 331
Radical Action Union, 456
Raftery, Lawrence M., 449, n 129
Rand School of Social Sciences, 58
Randall, Tony, 544
Randolph, A. Philip, 57, 58, 59, 62, 64, 71, 74, 79, 83, 85, 88, 93, 94, 95, 96, 97, 98, 99, 106, 114, 118, 123, 124, 127, 128, 129, 130, 131, 132, 133, 134, 135, 139, 142, 151, 152, 153, 159, 160, 161, 162, 180, 181, 306, 307, 314, 317, 318, 325, 326, 328, 329, 348, 349, 371, 386, 472, 475, 483, 512, 513, 514, 515, n 29
Randolph Education Fund, the A. Philip, 109, 112, 116, 380, 462
Randolph Institute, the A. Philip, 107, 114, 120, 136, 139, 150, 151, 152, 160, 162, 181, 362, 365, 371, 386, 450, 467, 512
Randolph, John, 538
Rangel, Charles, 330
Ransom, Edith, 305
Raskin, A. H., 385, 473
Rauh, Jr., Joseph L, 136, 424, n 66
Ray, Carline, 549
Reagan, President Ronald, 41, 42, 43, 44, 45, 179, 181, 182, 269, 553, n 18
Reddick, L. D., 151
Reeb, Rev. James, 101, 135, 429
Regional Federal Agencies Pools, 450
Rehnquist, William H. 35, 36, 37, 38, n 11
Reinhardt, Uwe, 543
Republican National Committee, 43
Republican Party, 81, 136, 337, 356, 423, 427
Retail Clerks and Workers Union of America, 364
Retail Drug Employees Union, 471
Retail, Wholesale and Department Store Union (RWDSU), 86, 91, 92, 192, 193, 195, 291, 317, 320, 325, 326, 364, 471, 482, 486, 497, 509, 512, 513, 519, 537, 546
Reuss, Henry, 122
Reuther, Walter P., 50, 57, 63, 65, 78, 82, 88, 90, 91, 92, 93, 94, 96, 98, 100, 114, 136, 169, 171, 173, 176, 187, 235, 254, 256, 257, 258, 259, 278, 279, 422, 425, 433, 434, 477, 515, 516, 518, 548, n 39
Rhoades, James, 272
Rice, Charles Owen, 391

Richardson, Elroy, 271
Right-to-Work Law, 94, 95, 187
Riley, Frank, 76, 77
Rivers, L. Mendel, 194, 496, 515, 519,
    n 141
Rizzo, Frank, 234
Roberts, Howard, 549
Robinson, Bill, 443
Robinson, Cleveland L., 91, 96, 317,
    320, 322, 323, 324, 325, 326, 327,
    328, 329, 331, 334, 338, 339, 342,
    346, 347, 348, 352, 361, 370, 371,
    539, n 50
Robinson, Howard, 353
Robinson, Remus, 424
Rockefeller, David, 222, 292
Rockefeller, Nelson, 92, 460, 464,
    474, 475, 492, 493, 513, 539
Rogers, Clyde, 74
Rogers, Donald, 463, 464
Rogers, Nathaniel, 135
Roper, Elmer, 125
Roosevelt, Eleanor, 59, 473, 547, n 36
Roosevelt, President Franklin D., 129,
    142, 159, 161, 344, 377, 435
Roosevelt, Theodore, 200
Ross, Arthur M., 191
Roth, Herrick S., 96, 97, 99
Roth, Norman, 443
Rourke, Joseph, 448, 449
Rousselot, John H., 162, n 72
Rowley, Ruby, 305
Roye, Wendell, 135
Rule 22, 426, n 120
Russell, Richard B., 138, n 67
Rustin, Bayard, 107, 114, 151, 152,
    153, 160, 161, 222, 326, 329, 330,
    365, 371, 372, 386, 387, 450, 467,
    468, 474, 475, 512, 513, 538
Ryan, William F., 475, n 134

Saltonstall, Leverett, 38, n 17
Samp, Nelson, 270
Sanders, Luevena, 490
Santamaria, Mongo, 542
Sawyer, Roland, 392
Schafer, Dr. Hugo H., 486
Scharansky, Anatoly, 386, n 116
Schnitzler, Frank William, 57, 83, 88,
    80, 91, 92, 95, 98, 110, n 47
Schoemann, Peter T., 449, n 129
Schulte, Maurice, 392
Schultz, George, 463
Schultz, John, 544
Schwerner, Michael, 101, 135
Scott, Bob, 465, 467
Scott, Christine, 308, 310
Scott, Ella, 490
Scott, John, 271
Scott, Howard, 305
Scottsboro Boys, 291
Scranton, William W., 392, n 118
Screvane, Paul, 309
Scumaci, Francis, 392
Seafarers International Union of North
    America, 163, 169, 355, 364, 365,
    448

Seal, Wayne, 519
Seale, Bobby, 263
Seeger, Pete, 539, 542
Seelig, Len, 476, n 137
Selma-to-Montgomery March, 135
Selpski, "Cannonball," 237
Senate, the U.S., 335, 426, 427
Senate Rule 22, 51, 52, 61, 426, 427
Service, Russell, 134
Service Employees Union, 511
Shafer, Mary, 480
Sharpeville Massacre, 438
Shea, William, 121
Sheet Metal Workers International
    Union, 165, 168, 314, 450, 454, 460
Sheffield, Horace, 352
Shelby County Community Relations
    Commission, 410
Shishkin, Boris, 54, 58, 62, 88, n 30
Shriver, Jr., Sargent (Robert), 338,
    n 102
Shubert Foundation, Inc., 540
Shulman, Dr. Donald, 448
Siegel, Anita, 547
Silverstein, Ted, 443
Simmons, Bill, 334, 361
Simmons, Mildred, 305
Simmons, Rosetta, 514, 522, 524
Simms, Leander, 399
Simon, Louis, 88
Simons, William, 366
Sinclair, John, 244
Siper, Phil, 495
Skills Bank Program, 14
Skirtmakers Union, 305
Slaiman, Donald, 88, 110, 115, 136,
    137, 151, 152, 365, 454, n 56
Smallwood, Kenneth, 460
Small, Horace, 490
Smith, Jethro, 166
Smith, Lamar, 183
Smith, Leo, 94
Smith, Sam, 496
Smith, Jr., Vascoe A., 410
Smithsonian Institution, 545
Social Security Bill, 189
Socialists, 58, 171, 172, 475, 547
Socialist Workers Party, 244
Soledad Brothers, 263, 331
Solidarity Caucus, 434, 435, 436, 437
Solidarity Day, 179
Solidarity House, 235, 237, 251, 346
Sorel, Wedward, 548
Sortre, Martin, 263
South Vietnamese Liberation Army, 233
Southern Christian Leadership
    Conference (SCLC), 126, 127, 139,
    184, 194, 195, 207, 209, 326, 328,
    405, 407, 429, 476, 478, 487, 496,
    509, 512, 513, 514, 516, 517, 518,
    520, 521, 523, 527, 528, 529, 530,
    531, 532, 533, 535, 536
Southern Regional Council, 320, 321
Southern Regional Council on Memphis,
    416

Southern States Apprenticeship
   Conference, 110
Sowell, Thomas, 41
Stalin, Joseph, 219, 225, n 87
Stallworth, Bennett O., 450
Stanton, Hugh, 413
Steelworkers, the Ad Hoc Committee of
   Black, 400, 401
Steel Workers Organizing Committee,
   402
Stennis, John C., 138, n 67
Stevens, May, 547, 548
Stevens, John Paul, 35, n 11
Stevens Co., the J. P., 178, 477, 542
Stockman, David, 44, n 22
Stokes, Carl B., 512, n 143
Stokes, Samuel, 401
Streator, Melvin D., 431
Strickland, Joe, 459
Student Non-Violent Coordinating
   Committee (SNCC), 207, 209, 210,
   211, 329, n 82
Students for a Democratic Society
   (SDS), 244, 250
Sturdivant, John, 182
Suffridge, James A., 88, n 48
Sullivan, David, 88, 136, n 48
Sullivan, Leon, 327
Supreme Court, the U.S., 50, 52, 54,
   60, 61, 100, 102, 105, 110, 111,
   116, 336, 337, 341, 357, 358, 389,
   390, 394, 426
Sutton, Percy, 330, 525
Sviridoff, Mike, 87
Sweeney, John, 182

Taft-Hartley Act, 91, 96, 135, 166,
   426, n 49
Talented Tenth, 159, 161
Talmadge, Senator Herman, 423, 426
Taylor, Ollie, 431
Taylor, William J., 480, 485
Taylor-Dunn, Corliss, 549, 551, 553,
   554
Tent City, 207
Terkel, Studs, 543
Terry, Amy, 330
Terry, Luraline, 524
Third World, 222, 223, 227, 228, 229,
   230, 232, 233
Thirteenth Amendment, 126, 312, 357
Thomas, Emma, 554
Thomas, Marlo, 545
Thomas, Norman, 475, 538, n 134
Thompson, Gary, 271
Thoreau, Henry David, 80
Thornton, John, 338
Thurmond, Strom, 194, 496, n 141
Till, Emmett, 183, 207
Tillman, Benjamin, 383, n 111
Tillow, Kay, 501
Tillow, Walter, 501
Timpson, Priscilla, 305
Title III, 60
Title IV, 102

Title VI, 505
Title VII of the Civil Rights Act of
   1964, 14, 35, 37, 38, 39, 107, 109,
   117, 137, 176, 192, n 4
Title 45, 505
Todd, Edward, 338, n 103
Tomlin, Lily, 544
Townsend, Lynn, 256
Townsend, Willard S., 56, 57, 59, 123,
   n 29
Toynbee, Arnold, 197
Trade Union Action and Democracy
   (TUAD), 442
Trade Union Leadership Council, 110
Trade Union Unity League (TUUL), 291
Traeye, Hermina, 535
Transport Workers of America, 364
Trotskyites, 212, 226, 244
Truman, President Harry S., 51, 54,
   114, 161, 186, 338, 450, n 30
Truth, Sojourner, 515, 547, 548, n 144
Tubman, Harriet, 213, 515, n 144
Turner, Doris, 471, 478, 479, 513,
   524, 525, 526, 534
Turner, Harold, 493, 494
Turner, Lionel, 33
Turner, Tom, 338
Tuskegee Institute, 76
Twain, Mark, 198
Tyler, Gus, 172

Ullman, Liv, 386
Umstead, Marie, 526
Undergarment and Negligee Workers, 305
United Association of Journeymen and
   Apprentices of the Plumbing and Pipe
   Fitting Industry of the United
   States and Canada, 166
United Automobile Workers (UAW), 58,
   67, 86, 167, 169, 173, 222, 223,
   235-96 passim, 307, 327, 330-39
   passim, 348, 352, 361-71 passim,
   422-45 passim, 516, 518, 543
United Black Brothers, 212, 224, 264
United Brotherhood of Carpenters and
   Joiners, 165
United Cement, Lime, and Gypsum
   Workers International Union, 364
United Church Board for Homeland
   Ministries, 540, 542
United Community Construction Workers,
   298, 456, 457, 458
United Farm Workers, 232
United Federation of Teachers, 277,
   278, 279, 542
United Foundation, 258
United Freedom Movement, 191
United Front, 213
United Front of Cairo, 212
United Hebrew Trades, 369
United Labor Coalition, 444
United Mine Workers of America, 260,
   293, 325, 502
United National Caucus, 225
United Nations, 94, 300, 343

United Office and Professional
  Workers, 327
United Packinghouse, Food and Allied
  Workers, 67, 74, 192
United Papermakers and Paperworkers
  Union, 165, 167
United Rubber Workers, 55
United States Phosphoric Company, 167
United States Steel Corporation, 34,
  192, 229, 232, 396, 425, 501, 502
United Steelworkers of America (USA),
  32, 16, 33, 34, 39, 68-70, 123, 167,
  169, 177, 192, 287, 325, 338, 347,
  361, 364, 369, 371, 387, 389, 390,
  391, 392, 396, 398, 399, 400, 401,
  402
United Steelworkers National Civil
  Rights Committee, 389, 390, 391
United Textile Workers of America, 364
United Transport Service Employes, 56,
  57, 59
Unity House, 313
Unruh, Jesse M., 269, n 93
Unterkoefler, Bishop Ernest, 523
Urban Coalition Conference, 106
Urban League, 76, 110, 124, 126, 127,
  135, 152, 201, 202, 203, 209, 354,
  362, 380, 445, 450, 454, 455, 474,
  493

Van Arsdale, Jr., Harry, 77, 152, 446,
  447, 473, 483, 491, n 127
Van Dalen, Anton, 548
Vaske, Stanley, 273
Vassil, Pamela, 546
Vauls, Travis, 455
Vietnam, 200, 208, 210, 229, 231, 234,
  249, 320, 323, 324, 370, 384, 475
Vietnam War, 215, 233, 288, 363, 464
Voting Bill of 1957, 114
Voting Rights Act of 1965, 100, 111,
  118, 135, 136, 179, 180, 182, 337,
  358, 362, 429
Wade, Lyndon, 454
Wage-Price Freeze, 231, 344, 400
Wagner Act, 173, 185
Wagner, Robert F., 445, n 124
Wakefield, Dan, 483
Walker, James, 305, 307
Walker, Willie, 441
Walker, Wyatt T., 493
Wallace, George C., 242, 269, 278,
  385, n 90
Wallach, Eli, 542
Walsh, Richard F., 88, 95, 131, n 48
War Labor Board, 54
Warren, Earl, 186
Washington, Jeff, 439
Washington, Joe, 455
Watkins, Ted, 430, 431, 432
Waters, Ethel, 357
Waters, Tom, 455
Watson, John, 228, 229, 233, 238, 239,
  243

Watts, Roosevelt, 176
Watts Labor Community Action
  Committee, 429-433
Waye, Georgetta, 531
Wayne, John, 359
Weaver, George L. P., 58, 123, n 32
Weaver, Robert C., 448, n 128
Weber, Brian, 31-40 passim, 177
Webster, Milton P., 58, 65, 88, 98,
  128, 131, n 33
Wechsler, James, 474, 525
Weihrauch, Milton, 71, 72
Weinstock, Harry, 495
Welfare Rights Organization, 296
Wellington, Al, 401
West, Duane, 433
West, Estella, 305, 308
Whack, Donna M., 530
Whack, Virgie Lee, 531
Whaley, Ruth Whitehead, 124
Wharton, Hunter P., 449, n 129
Whitaker, Willard, 18
White, Dave, 524, 525, 527
White, Walter, 207
White Citizens Councils, 52, 55, 67,
  99, 135, 163, 164, 171, 183
White Panthers, 244
Whitten Amendment, 111
Wickenden, Elizabeth, 376
Wilcox, William H., 453
Wiley, George A., 512
Wilkins, Roger, 543
Wilkins, Roy, 50, 104, 106, 107, 114,
  133, 180, 181, 189, 193, 197, 207,
  326, 377, 406, 422, 446, 474, 475,
  512, n 25
Wilks, John L., 464
Willis, A. W., 406, 408
Williams, George, 431
Williams, Harrison, 369
Williams, Joe, 274
Williams, Ken, 299
Williams, Mamie, 271, 272
Williams, Robert, 207
Williams, Walter, 41
Williams, Walter E., 468, n 130
Wilmore, Jacques, 410
Wilson, Charles, 331
Wilson, Charles E., 40
Wiltz, Clinton, 32
Wirtz, W. Willard, 26, 448, n 8
Woll, Matthew, 98, n 51
Wood, Wire and Metal Lathers Union,
  461, 463, 467
Woodcock, Leonard, 222, 268, 269, 442
Woodson, Mary, 500
Wooten, Chuck, 240, 243, 244, 272
Workers Defense League, 109, 112, 116,
  127, 152, 380, 462, 465
World Trade Center, 458, 462, 465, 467
World War II, 138, 150, 200, 231
Wosk, Mariam, 548
Wright, Norm, 455
Wurf, Jerry, 115, 369, 412, 413, 415,
  418, 419, n 56
Wyatt, Addie, 334, 352

Wyatt, Rev. Claude, 352

Yarborough, Ralph W., 521, n 145
Young, the Rev. Andrew J., 16, 114,
    476, 516, 519, 524, 543, 546, n 7
Young, Coleman, 444, 543
Young, Jr., Whitney M., 13, 107, 114,
    151, 153, 181, 314, 326, 446, 450,
    454, 474, 512, n 1
Young, William, 272
Young Democrats, 511
Young People's Socialist League, 172
Young Workers Liberation League, 331
Youngstown Steel Workers Group, 225

Zappa, Joe, 274
Zelenko, Herbert, 171, n 76
Zimmerman, Charles, 62, 77, 88, 136,
    170, 172, n 38
Zupko, Dr. Arthur G., 485